TORT AND INJURY LAW

TORT AND INJURY LAW

THIRD EDITION

Marshall S. Shapo
FREDERIC P. VOSE PROFESSOR OF LAW
NORTHWESTERN UNIVERSITY SCHOOL OF LAW

Richard J. Peltz
PROFESSOR OF LAW
WILLIAM H. BOWEN SCHOOL OF LAW
UNIVERSITY OF ARKANSAS AT LITTLE ROCK

CAROLINA ACADEMIC PRESS
Durham, North Carolina

ISBN 0-89089-205-9
LCCN 2006929442
Paperback ISBN 978-1-5310-0883-3

CAROLINA ACADEMIC PRESS
700 Kent Street
Durham, NC 27701
Telephone (919) 489-7486
Fax (919) 493-5668
www.cap-press.com

Printed in the United States of America

For Helene

For Nat and Robin   *For Ben and Jackie*

For Noah   *For Gabrielle, Aaron and Joshua*

To the memory of my parents

Mitchell Shapo   *Norma S. Shapo*

—M.S.S.

In memory of my grandparents
John & Tonina Rocchi
Sam & Althea Peltz

My godmother
Renée Peri Shank

And my torts professor
Jerome Culp

—R.J.P.

CONTENTS

PREFACE

Torts is, I think, the best subject to initiate learning about the law. It features human conflict, often at a raw level. It is chock full of interesting stories, but it also requires students to look underneath the stories to do the form of analysis that distinguishes lawyers.

This book presents the fundamentals of torts—theories of liability and duty and of defenses based on the plaintiff's conduct, theories of duty and causation, and damages. It offers those materials, which are rooted in ordinary tort litigation, against the broad fabric of society's many responses to the problems caused by injuries. These include compensation systems like workers compensation and regulatory systems.

Besides introducing material on those subjects, the book explores what are now basic tort law issues that arise from the application of health and safety statutes and regulations to personal injury actions. The next to last chapter poses the ultimate question of whether we should have a tort system at all. Throughout, the overarching question is the first one in the book: what should society do when A injures B?

The book also introduces the role of tort law as a response to imbalances in power and illustrates how law and science interact, uneasily, at the dawn of a new millennium.

In this twenty-first century, torts teachers are taking quite diverse approaches to their subject. This book offers points of departures for several of those approaches, including law and economics and feminism. At base, however, it is a book about the law. Its audience is students who seek to earn a law degree, mindful that there is a wide variety of professions and businesses in which they ultimately may live their working lives. In focusing on the law, as well as on various modes of thinking about the law, these materials are designed to instruct students in diverse ways of analyzing legal problems. Believing that legal education is generally a good and versatile education, I hope this approach will help to give students perspectives and tools that will enable them to work successfully in a variety of occupations.

* * *   * * *

After forty-one years in law teaching, I cannot hardly list all my debts to people who have helped me to understand the law, and to produce this book. I can mention just a few.

It was my great good fortune to begin my teaching career at the University of Texas School of Law in the mid-nineteen sixties. It was a clinic for a young teacher to be with two certified giants of torts teaching: Page Keeton, an incomparable dean who found time to be a formidable scholar, and Leon Green, a transcendent legal mind. Russell Weintraub was a vital mentor. The late Charles Alan Wright also gave me welcome support. Roy Mersky, still a leader in librarianship, provided a beacon for service that still holds up in an electronic world.

I have had the immeasurable benefit of continuing seminars in the law, both the law of tort and the law generally, with many other colleagues at each of my institutions—at Texas, at Virginia and now at Northwestern. I want to mention, in particular, two Northwestern colleagues: David Ruder, who provided me great encouragement to expand my horizons in mid-career; and the late Victor Rosenblum, truly a man for all seasons, for his sage comments on torts and a world of other issues, and for his friendship.

Students at all my schools—now thousands of them—have provided continuing stimulation in the quest for the elusive and provisional truths that challenge Torts students and teachers. Generations of student assistants have helped me, directly and indirectly, with the development of materials for this book. Among my most recent assistants, I particularly thank Cris Carmody.

Librarians at Northwestern, under the directorship of Chris Simoni, have been equal to every task I have assigned them. I especially appreciate the help of a splendid reference librarian, Marcia Lehr, whose good cheer and patience matches her ability and industry. I also thank Northwestern librarians Kathryn H. Amato, Pegeen Bassett, Irene Berkey, David Daskal, Heidi F. Kuehl, and Jim McMasters.

I appreciate all the aid I have received from the Northwestern University School of Law, under Deans David Ruder, Bob Bennett, and David Van Zandt. Many Northwestern grantors have provided financial support for the work that has gone into this book, with the most recent support coming from the Clemens and Jane Werner Faculty Enrichment Fund.

My secretary, Derek Gundersen, has been invaluable in his work on this book. Threading his way through the mysteries of various softwares, and enduring many revisions, he has earned my great thanks.

My parents, Mitchell Shapo and Norma S. Shapo, were my first teachers. I have often quoted to my classes from a letter I received from them in 1959. In particular, I quoted a sentence written by my father, who, studying law at night in the depths of the Depression while working full time, was able to produce the Note, Recent Trends in Housing Legislation, 8 TEMPLE L.Q. 99 (1933). He wrote to me, "When I studied law, it was my ambition to fight injustice." These words I do not forget. My brother, Ronald A. Shapo, has been a constant source of wisdom concerning the current practice of law on the front lines.

My sons, Ben and Nat, have proved that you can be exposed to Torts hypotheticals from the time you are a toddler and still grow up to become productive citizens. Whenever I finish a book, however much I have labored to make it seamless, I am humbled by a definition that Ben, now a research engineer, offered of "files" when he was five years old: "Files are something you put papers in, and then you staple them together and put a cover on them, and you have a book." Ben, a humanist who is a scientist, has helped to convince me that computers, properly handled, are an author's friend. And I carry forward into this edition research on sports torts that Nat, a lawyer and formerly Director of Insurance for the State of Illinois, provided at age 11.

Finally, I most gratefully thank Helene S. Shapo, who read and criticized the manuscript, and who as a spouse and as a standard setter for law and for writing is a nonpareil.

MARSHALL S. SHAPO
Chicago and Evanston
April 2006

PREFACE TO THE THIRD EDITION

The teacher familiar with this book in its preceding editions will note modest but important changes. Naturally, references to the *Third Restatement of Torts*, as its development continues, have been added where appropriate. A number of cases and some secondary materials have been cut as duplicative or outdated, replaced where needed by concise and updated notes. Developments have been recorded in areas including product liability litigation, punitive damages limitations, and compensation for terrorist acts. Overall, though, the book retains its familiar organization, format, and tone.

* * * * * *

I am grateful to Professor Shapo for bringing me on board to contribute to this third edition of his *Tort and Injury Law*. I selected this book in its second edition for my first Torts class, and never have I regretted it. Professor Shapo has a singular talent for winnowing the most salient and instructive passages from the vast body of primary and secondary materials on torts. He adds notes that are pointed and provocative, ample fodder for class discussion. The naturally colorful material that makes up our body of tort law demands a textbook writer who, like a landscape artist, can render boundless shades and tints for the secondhand observer, and Professor Shapo teaches through his texts with that capacity. Whether or not I have contributed with the same vision and zeal, it has been my privilege to make the endeavor.

My torts professor was Jerome M. Culp., Jr., at Duke Law School in 1993 and 1994. Professor Culp died in 2004, at age 53, after a long and courageous battle with kidney disease. He is widely well regarded and remembered for his prolific scholarship in areas such as critical race theory and law and economics. But to me as a timid first-year, Professor Culp was first and foremost a torts professor, and sometimes a scary one. Armed with a seating chart of cut-out faces, he was unhesitant to call on students. He once had the class wait in agonizing silence while an unprepared student silently read a case. He mystified us—well, me, at least—with graphs on the economic impact of different models of tort law. It seemed at times that he delighted in torturing students.

But if it was his design to make a Kingsfield-ian impression, he did not have the heart to finish the job. For Professor Culp outside of class was ever jovial, ever concerned over his students' tribulations, and ever proud of his students' accomplishments. He eagerly talked basketball, literature, and popular culture, all with acumen. He brought fruit for students during exams because he worried they were not eating healthily. If Professor Culp seemed stubborn and mystifying in class, it was because he had the highest expectations and refused to settle for less.

I am grateful to the many persons who supported me in the preparation of this work. In Little Rock, at the University of Arkansas, I am grateful for the friendship and professional support of my dean, Chuck Goldner, and of many colleagues, especially, but not exclusively, Coleen Barger, Mike Beaird, Terri Beiner, Jessie Burchfield, John DiPippa, Michael Flannery, Ken Gallant, Kelly Olson, Rob Steinbuch, and Tom Sullivan; for the kind support of our professional staff, including Laura Austin, Cheryl Bigelow, Gail Harris, and Glennis Jackson; for the aid of my capable research assistants, Elizabeth Dulong and Joi Leonard; and for the guidance of Andrew McClurg, now at Florida International University, and Glenn Pasvogel, retired.

I had the privilege while working on this project of visiting at The Catholic University of America, in Washington, D.C., where I was welcomed with the greatest warmth and kindness. I especially thank at CUA Deans Veryl Miles, Bill Fox, and Bill Wagner; librarian Greg Stack; faculty Sylvia Bacon, Sarah Duggin, Lisa Lerman, Rett Ludwikowski, the Rev. Ray O'Brien, Nerissa Skillman, Leah Wortham, and Harvey Zuckman; professional staff Stephanie Michael, Laurie Fraser, and Katie Aaron; and my teaching assistant, Elizabeth Cox. I thank as well my many students at UALR and CUA who have made this job the reward that it is.

Finally, and above all, I thank my family for their support of my education and career, especially my parents, Yvonne and Jack Serio, and Rich and Patricia Peltz, and my brothers and sisters, whether by law, blood, or heart, Andrea Serio, Nick and Spencer Peltz, and Chris and Sallie Crenshaw.

RICHARD J. PELTZ
Little Rock and Washington
April 2006

Tort and Injury Law

Chapter 1

INTRODUCTION

A MAXIM

Lawyering is the art of convincing someone that a client's interest is in the interest of the commonwealth.

NOTE

Criticize this proposition now. Then think about it as you progress through your first year, deciding whether you think it is accurate as a description of reality, and whether you find its implications agreeable as a matter of philosophy.

A PROBLEM

A injures B and could have avoided it. What should society do about it?

INTRODUCTION TO THE *NADER* CASE

Typically, law students confronting their first assignment will complain that the instructor finds considerably more in the opinion than can reasonably be expected. Among the questions you should ask yourself in trying to wring as much from the Nader case as can humanly be accomplished are the following:

(1) What is a "cause of action"?

(2) What is the "common law"?

(3) What happened in the lower court? What is the question before this appellate court?

(4) What technical problems of classification of giving a proper legal label to the case did Nader's lawyers face in bringing this action to court?

(5) What "rules of law" do the competing opinions announce? Which ones seem most directly to govern this case? Why does the majority opinion regard legal doctrine as so important?

(6) Why does New York's highest court seek out precedents from the District of Columbia? Which opinion uses them more persuasively?

(7) What social policies appear to be fostered by this decision?

(8) What qualities does the decision appear to reflect in the mechanics of the administration of justice?

NADER v. GENERAL MOTORS CORP.

New York Court of Appeals
25 N.Y.2d 560, 307 N.Y.S.2d 647, 255 N.E.2d 765 (1970)

FULD, CHIEF JUDGE.

On this appeal, taken by permission of the Appellate Division on a certified question, we are called upon to determine the reach of the tort of invasion of privacy as it exists under the law of the District of Columbia.

The complaint, in this action by Ralph Nader, pleads four causes of action against the appellant, General Motors Corporation, and three other defendants allegedly acting as its agents. The first two causes of action charge an invasion of privacy, the third is predicated on the intentional infliction of severe emotional distress and the fourth on interference with the plaintiff's economic advantage. This appeal concerns only the legal sufficiency of the first two causes of action, which were upheld in the courts below as against the appellant's motion to dismiss (CPLR 3211, subd. (a), par. 7).

The plaintiff, an author and lecturer on automotive safety, has, for some years, been an articulate and severe critic of General Motors' products from the standpoint of safety and design. According to the complaint which—for present purposes, we must assume to be true—the appellant, having learned of the imminent publication of the plaintiff's book "Unsafe at any Speed," decided to conduct a campaign of intimidation against him in order to "suppress plaintiff's criticism of and prevent his disclosure of information" about its products. To that end, the appellant authorized and directed the other defendants to engage in a series of activities which, the plaintiff claims in his first two causes of action, violated his right to privacy.[1]

Specifically, the plaintiff alleges that the appellant's agents (1) conducted a series of interviews with acquaintances of the plaintiff, "questioning them about, and casting aspersions upon (his) political, social ... racial and religious views ... ; his integrity; his sexual proclivities and inclinations; and his personal habits" (Complaint, par. 9(b)); (2) kept him under surveillance in public places for an unreasonable length of time (par. 9(c)); (3) caused him to be accosted by girls for the purpose of entrapping him into illicit relationships (par. 9(d)); (4) made threatening, harassing and obnoxious telephone calls to him (par. 9(e)); (5) tapped his telephone and eavesdropped, by means of mechanical and electronic equipment, on his private conversations with others (par. 9(f)); and (6) conducted a "continuing" and harassing investigation of him (par. 9(g)). These charges are amplified in the plaintiff's bill of particulars, and those particulars are, of course, to be taken into account in considering the sufficiency of the challenged causes of action.

The threshold choice of law question requires no extended discussion. In point of fact, the parties have agreed at least—for purposes of this motion—that the sufficiency of these allegations is to be determined under the law of the District of Columbia. The District is the jurisdiction in which most of the acts are alleged to have occurred, and it was there, too, that the plaintiff lived and suffered the impact of those acts. It is, in

---

1. The first cause of action contains allegations of several types of activity which took place, for the most part, in the District of Columbia, while the second charges the appellant with engaging in similar activity in New York. It appears that, at least to some extent, both counts are premised on the same conduct and should be treated as stating alternative rather than cumulative claims for damages. In any event, however, the substantive nature of the two counts is the same.

short, the place which has the most significant relationship with the subject matter of the tort charged.

···

Turning, then, to the law of the District of Columbia, it appears that its courts have not only recognized a common-law action for invasion of privacy but have broadened the scope of that tort beyond its traditional limits. [I]n the most recent of its cases on the subject, Pearson v. Dodd (133 U.S.App.D.C. 279, 410 F.2d 701 ...), the Federal Court of Appeals for the District of Columbia declared (p. 704):

We approve the extension of the tort of invasion of privacy to instances of *intrusion*, whether by physical trespass or not, into spheres from which an ordinary man in a plaintiffs position could reasonably expect that the particular defendant should be excluded. (Italics supplied.)

It is this form of invasion of privacy-initially termed "intrusion" by Dean Prosser in 1960 (Privacy, 48 Cal.L.Rev. 383, 389 et seq.; Torts, § 112)—on which the two challenged causes of action are predicated.

Quite obviously, some intrusions into one's private sphere are inevitable concomitants of life in an industrial and densely populated society, which the law does not seek to proscribe even if it were possible to do so. "The law does not provide a remedy for every annoyance that occurs in everyday life." (Kelley v. Post Pub. Co., 327 Mass. 275, 278, 98 N.E.2d 286, 287.) However, the District of Columbia courts have held that the law should and does protect against certain types of intrusive conduct, and we must, therefore, determine whether the plaintiff's allegations are actionable as violations of the right to privacy under the law of that jurisdiction. To do so, we must, in effect, predict what the judges of that jurisdiction's highest court would hold if this case were presented to them. In other words, what would the Court of Appeals for the District of Columbia say is the character of the "privacy" sought to be protected? More specifically, would that court accord an individual a right, as the plaintiff before us insists, to be protected against any interference whatsoever with his personal seclusion and solitude? Or would it adopt a more restrictive view of the right, as the appellant urges, merely protecting the individual from intrusion into "something secret," from snooping and [prying] into his private affairs?

The classic article by Warren and Brandeis (The Right to Privacy, 4 Harv.L.Rev. 193)—to which the court in the Pearson case referred as the source of the District's common-law action for invasion of privacy (410 F.2d, at p. 703)—was premised, to a large extent, on principles originally developed in the field of copyright law. The authors thus based their thesis on a right granted by the common law to "each individual ... of determining, ordinarily, to what extent his thoughts, sentiments and emotions shall be communicated to others" (4 Harv.L.Rev., at p. 198). Their principal concern appeared to be not with a broad "right to be let alone" (Cooley, Torts [2d ed.], p. 29) but, rather, with the right to protect oneself from having one's private affairs known to others and to keep secret or intimate facts about oneself from the prying eyes or ears of others.

In recognizing the existence of a common-law cause of action for invasion of privacy in the District of Columbia, the Court of Appeals has expressly adopted this latter formulation of the nature of the right. (See, e.g., Afro-American Pub. Co. v. Jaffe, 125 U.S.App.D.C. 70, 366 F.2d 649, 653, supra.) Quoting from the Restatement, Torts (§ 867), the court in the Jaffe case (366 F.2d, at p. 653) has declared that "[l]iability attaches to a person 'who unreasonably and seriously interferes with another's interest in *not having his affairs known to others.'*" (Emphasis supplied.) And, in *Pearson*, where the court extended the tort of invasion of privacy to instances of "intrusion," it again indicated, contrary to the plaintiff's submission, that the interest protected was one's right to keep knowledge about oneself from exposure to others, the right to prevent "*the obtaining of the information* by improperly intrusive means*" (410 F.2d, at p. 704; emphasis supplied). In other jurisdictions, too, the cases which have recognized a remedy for invasion of privacy founded upon intrusive conduct have generally involved the gathering of private facts or information through improper means....

It should be emphasized that the mere gathering of information about a particular individual does not give rise to a cause of action under this theory. Privacy is invaded only if the information sought is of a confidential nature and the defendant's conduct was unreasonably intrusive. Just as a common-law copyright is lost when material is published, so, too, there can be no invasion of privacy where the information sought is open to public view or has been voluntarily revealed to others.... In order to sustain a cause of action for invasion of privacy, therefore, the plaintiff must show that the appellant's conduct was truly "intrusive" and that it was designed to elicit information which would not be available through normal inquiry or observation.

The majority of the Appellate Division in the present case stated that all of "[t]he activities complained of" in the first two counts constituted actionable invasions of privacy under the law of the District of Columbia. We do not agree with that sweeping determination. At most, only two of the activities charged to the appellant are, in our view, actionable as invasions of privacy under the law of the District of Columbia.[2]

However, since the first two counts include allegations which are sufficient to state a cause of action, we could — as the concurring opinion notes ... — merely affirm the order before us without further elaboration. To do so, though, would be a disservice both to the judge who will be called upon to try this case and to the litigants themselves. In other words, we deem it desirable, nay essential, that we go further and, for the guidance of the trial court and counsel, indicate the extent to which the plaintiff is entitled to rely on the various allegations in support of his privacy claim.

In following such a course, we are prompted not only by a desire to avoid any misconceptions that might stem from the opinion below but also by recognition of the fact that we are dealing with a new and developing area of the law. Indeed, we would fail to meet our responsibility if we were to withhold determination particularly since the parties have fully briefed and argued the points involved and thereby thrust upon the trial judge the initial burden of appraising the impact of a doctrine still in the process of growth and of predicting its reach in another jurisdiction.

Turning, then, to the particular acts charged in the complaint, we cannot find any basis for a claim of invasion of privacy, under District of Columbia law, in the allegations that the appellant, through its agents or employees, interviewed many persons who knew the plaintiff, asking questions about him and casting aspersions on his character. Although those inquiries may have uncovered information of a personal nature, it is difficult to see how they may be said to have invaded the plaintiff's privacy. Information about the plaintiff which was already known to others could hardly be regarded as private to the plaintiff. Presumably, the plaintiff had previously revealed the informa-

---

2. "The activities complained of:" wrote the Appellate Division majority, "the shadowing, the indiscriminate interviewing of third persons about features of his intimate life, the wiretapping and eavesdropping, the prying into his bank accounts, taxes, the alleged accosting by young women and the receipt of threatening phone calls, all are within the purview of these cases."...

tion to such other persons, and he would necessarily assume the risk that a friend or acquaintance in whom he had confided might breach the confidence. If, as alleged, the questions tended to disparage the plaintiff's character, his remedy would seem to be by way of an action for defamation, not for breach of his right to privacy. (Cf. Morrison v. National Broadcasting Co., 19 N.Y.2d 453, 458 459, 280 N.Y.S.2d 641, 643–644, 227 N.E.2d 572, 573–574.)

Nor can we find any actionable invasion of privacy in the allegations that the appellant caused the plaintiff to be accosted by girls with illicit proposals, or that it was responsible for the making of a large number of threatening and harassing telephone calls to the plaintiff's home at odd hours. Neither of these activities, howsoever offensive and disturbing, involved intrusion for the purpose of gathering information of a private and confidential nature.

As already indicated, it is manifestly neither practical nor desirable for the law to provide a remedy against any and all activity which an individual might find annoying. On the other hand, where severe mental pain or anguish is inflicted through a deliberate and malicious campaign of harassment or intimidation, a remedy is available in the form of an action for the intentional infliction of emotional distress—the theory underlying the plaintiff's third cause of action. But the elements of such an action are decidedly different from those governing the tort of invasion of privacy, and ... we should be wary of any attempt to rely on the tort of invasion of privacy as a means of avoiding the more stringent pleading and proof requirements for an action for infliction of emotional distress. (See, e.g., Clark v. Associated Retail Credit Men, 70 App.D.C. 183, 105 F.2d 62, 65).

Apart, however, from the foregoing allegations which we find inadequate to spell out a cause of action for invasion of privacy under District of Columbia law, the complaint contains allegations concerning other activities by the appellant or its agents which do satisfy the requirements for such a cause of action. The one which most clearly meets those requirements is the charge that the appellant and its codefendants engaged in unauthorized wiretapping and eavesdropping by mechanical and electronic means. The Court of Appeals in the Pearson case expressly recognized that such conduct constitutes a tortious intrusion (133 U.S.App.D.C. 279, 410 F.2d 701, 704, supra), and other jurisdictions have reached a similar conclusion.... [3] In point of fact, the appellant does not dispute this, acknowledging that, to the extent the two challenged counts charge it with wiretapping and eavesdropping, an actionable invasion of privacy has been stated.

There are additional allegations that the appellant hired people to shadow the plaintiff and keep him under surveillance. In particular, he claims that, on one occasion, one of its agents followed him into a bank, getting sufficiently close to him to see the denomination of the bills he was withdrawing from his account. From what we have already said, it is manifest that the mere observation of the plaintiff in a public place does not amount to an invasion of his privacy. But, under certain circumstances, surveillance may be so "overzealous" as to render it actionable. (See Pearson v. Dodd, ..., supra; ....) Whether or not the surveillance in the present case falls into this latter category will depend on the nature of the proof. A person does not automatically make public everything he does merely by being in a public place, and the

---

3. Indeed, although the question whether wiretapping affords a predicate for an invasion of privacy action has not yet arisen in our own jurisdiction, we note that our Penal Law—in an article entitled "Offenses Against the Right to Privacy"—makes eavesdropping by such means a felony (Penal Law, art. 250, § 250.05).

mere fact that Nader was in a bank did not give anyone the right to try to discover the amount of money he was withdrawing. On the other hand, if the plaintiff acted in such a way as to reveal that fact to any casual observer, then, it may not be said that the appellant intruded into his private sphere. In any event, though, it is enough for present purposes to say that the surveillance allegation is not insufficient as a matter of law.

Since, then, the first two causes of action do contain allegations which are adequate to state a cause of action for invasion of privacy under District of Columbia law, the courts below properly denied the appellant's motion to dismiss those causes of action. It is settled that, so long as a pleading sets forth allegations which suffice to spell out a claim for relief, it is not subject to dismissal by reason of the inclusion therein of additional nonactionable allegations.

We would but add that the allegations concerning the interviewing of third persons, the accosting by girls and the annoying and threatening telephone calls, though insufficient to support a cause of action for invasion of privacy, are pertinent to the plaintiffs third cause of action—in which those allegations are reiterated-charging the intentional infliction of emotional distress. However, as already noted, it will be necessary for the plaintiff to meet the additional requirements prescribed by the law of the District of Columbia for the maintenance of a cause of action under that theory.

The order appealed from should be affirmed, with costs, and the question certified answered in the affirmative.

BREITEL, JUDGE (concurring in result). There is no doubt that the first and second causes of action are sufficient in alleging an invasion of privacy under what appears to be the applicable law in the District of Columbia (Pearson v. Dodd ... ; Afro-American Pub. Co. v. Jaffe; ...). This should be the end of this court's proper concern with the pleadings, the only matter before the court being a motion to dismiss specified causes of action for insufficiency.

Thus it is not proper, it is submitted, for the court directly or indirectly to analyze particular allegations in the pleadings, once the causes of action are found sufficient, in order to determine whether they would alternatively sustain one cause of action or another, or whether evidence offered in support of the allegations is relevant only as to one rather than to another cause of action. Particularly, it is inappropriate to decide that several of the allegations as they now appear are referable only to the more restricted tort of intentional infliction of mental distress rather than to the common-law right of privacy upon which the first and second causes of action depend. The third cause of action is quite restricted. Thus many of the quite offensive acts charged will not be actionable unless plaintiff succeeds in the very difficult, if not impossible, task of showing that defendants' activities were designed, actually or virtually, to make plaintiff unhappy and not to uncover disgraceful information about him. The real issue in the volatile and developing law of privacy is whether a private person is entitled to be free of certain grave offensive intrusions unsupported by palpable social or economic excuse or justification.

True, scholars, in trying to define the elusive concept of the right of privacy, have, as of the present, subdivided the common law right into separate classifications, most significantly distinguishing between unreasonable intrusion and unreasonable publicity (Restatement, 2d, Torts, Tent. Draft No. 13 [April 27, 1967], §652A, 652B, 652D; Prosser, Torts [3d ed.], pp. 832–837). This does not mean, however, that the classifications are either frozen or exhausted, or that several of the classifications may not overlap.

Concretely applied to this case, it is suggested, for example, that it is premature to hold that the attempted entrapment of plaintiff in a public place by seemingly promiscuous ladies is no invasion of any of the categories of the right to privacy and is restricted to a much more limited cause of action for intentional infliction of mental distress. Moreover, it does not strain credulity or imagination to conceive of the systematic "public" surveillance of another as being the implementation of a plan to intrude on the privacy of another. Although acts performed in "public", especially if taken singly or in small numbers, may not be confidential, at least arguably a right to privacy may nevertheless be invaded through extensive or exhaustive monitoring and cataloguing of acts normally disconnected and anonymous.

These are but illustrations of the problems raised in attempting to determine issues of relevancy and allocability of evidence in advance of a trial record. The other allegations so treated involve harassing telephone calls, and investigatory interviews. It is just as important that while allegations treated singly may not constitute a cause of action, they may do so in combination, or serve to enhance other violations of the right to privacy.

It is not unimportant that plaintiff contends that a giant corporation had allegedly sought by surreptitious and unusual methods to silence an unusually effective critic. If there was such a plan, and only a trial would show that, it is unduly restrictive of the future trial to allocate the evidence beforehand based only on a pleader's specification of overt acts on the bold assumption that they are not connected causally or do not bear on intent and motive.

It should be observed, too, that the right to privacy, even as thus far developed, does not always refer to that which is not known to the public or is confidential. Indeed, the statutory right of privacy in this State and perhaps the most traditional right of privacy in the "common law sense" relates to the commercialized publicity of one's face or name, perhaps the two most public aspects of an individual (see Civil Rights, Law, §§ 50, 51; Restatement, 2d, Torts, Tent. Draft No. 13 [April 27, 1967], § 625C).

There is still further difficulty. In this State thus far there has been no recognition of a common law right of privacy, but only that which derives from a statute of rather limited scope (Civil Rights Law, §§ 50, 51; . . .). Consequently, this court must undertake the hazardous task of applying what is at present the quite different law of the District of Columbia. True, this may be the court's burden eventually, if the case were to return to it for review after trial, especially if the plaintiff were to prevail upon such a trial. However, there is no occasion to advance, now, into a complicated, subtle and still-changing field of law of another jurisdiction, solely to determine before trial the relevancy and allocability among pleaded causes of action or projected but not yet offered items of evidence. It is not overstatement to say that in the District of Columbia the law of the right of privacy is still inchoate in its development, perhaps more so than in many other jurisdictions that accept this newly coined common-law cause of action, despite unequivocal acceptance as a doctrine and extension by dictum to cases of intrusion (Pearson v. Dodd, supra, 410 F.2d, at p. 704).* In the absence of a trial record, the

---

* This is what the latest pronouncement from the Court of Appeals in the District of Columbia has to say about this "new" tort, as applied to intrusion:

"Unlike other types of invasion of privacy, intrusion does not involve as one of its essential elements the publication of the information obtained. The tort is completed with the obtaining of the information by improperly intrusive means. 'Intrusion' has not been either recognized or rejected as a tort in the District of Columbia. It has been recognized by a number of state courts, most recently by the New Hampshire Supreme Court in *Hamberger v. Eastman*, 106 N.H. 107 (206 A.2d 239). *Hamberger* found liable a defendant who eavesdropped upon the marital bedroom of plaintiffs by

court should avoid any unnecessary extrapolation of what the District of Columbia Court of Appeals has characterized as "an untried and developing area of tort law" (Pearson v. Dodd, supra, p. 705).

· · ·

The plaintiff, naturally enough, is trying to broaden his warrant, and defendant-appellant is correspondingly trying to narrow that warrant. But the eagerness of the parties in briefing hypothetical problems does not require an advisory opinion or a declaratory judgment by the highest court of the State without the benefit of a trial judge's rulings on relevancy, and an Appellate Division's review of those rulings on a trial record. There is no justification, on the present record, for giving an illiberal and restrictive scope to a cause of action based on the right of privacy as that right is likely to be defined under the applicable law of another jurisdiction.

The broad statements in the opinion of the Appellate Division can be met, as this court has done so often, by declaring that they are not necessarily adopted in concluding that a cause or causes of action have been stated. Accordingly, because of the prematurity of ruling on any other question but the sufficiency of the causes of action, I concur in result only.

SCILEPPI, BERGAN and GIBSON, JJ., concur with FULD, C.J.

BREITEL, J., concurs in result in an opinion in which BURKE and JASEN, JJ., concur.

Order affirmed, etc.

EPILOGUE: A SETTLEMENT

Nader settled his suit for $425,000 in August 1970, saying in a statement issued by his lawyer that he would use the money for a "continuous legal monitoring of General Motors activity in the safety, pollution and consumer relations area."

Nader's statement indicated that his decision to settle involved a calculation of the problems involved in drawn-out litigation. "There is every likelihood," he said, "that General Motors could have delayed this case into the 1980s, when all the culpable officials would have retired." With this prospect, he said, "it was deemed wiser to settle the case and devote the proceeds, after deduction of legal fees and expenses, to the cause of consumer protection and corporate responsibility, especially in the latter area General Motors' responsibility."

Perhaps the nub of the matter from Nader's perspective was his statement that the defendants "are going to be financing their own ombudsman."[1]

Under Nader's fee arrangement with his lawyer, Stuart Speiser, he would have netted $277,500 from the settlement, with lawyers' fees coming to $137,000 plus $10,000 out-of-pocket expenses. Speiser's firm agreed to reduce their fee so that Nader would net

---

electronic means, holding that 'the invasion of the plaintiffs' solitude or seclusion ... was a violation of their right of privacy.'

"We approve the extension of the tort of invasion of privacy to instances of intrusion, whether by physical trespass or not, into spheres from which an ordinary man in a plaintiff's position could reasonably expect that the particular defendant should be excluded. Just as the Fourth Amendment has expanded to protect citizens from government intrusions where intrusion is not reasonably expected, so should tort law protect citizens from other citizens. The protection should not turn exclusively on the question of whether the intrusion involves a technical trespass under the law of property. The common law, like the Fourth Amendment, should 'protect people, not places.'" (footnotes omitted).

1. *G.M. Settles Nader Suit on Privacy for $425,000*, N.Y. Times, August 14, 1970, at 1, 62.

$300,000, and, at Nader's request, contributed $10,000 to help start an aviation consumer organization. Saying that "we loved every minute of it," Speiser nevertheless pointed out that had the case been billed at an hourly rate, his firm's lawyers would have worked "for less than $30 an hour, a rate charged by young attorneys to fill out the simplest legal forms."[2]

The defendant commented that it considered the settlement "desirable from the point of view of General Motors to avoid the very substantial additional expense and demand upon the time of corporation personnel which would be incident to a trial and subsequent appeal of the case."[3]

Speiser's "balance sheet" on the case found that "[i]t helped to speed up diffusion of litigation power ... furnished a winning model for David-Goliath confrontations," and gave Nader the opportunity to use "the settlement proceeds to build the world's first effective consumer movement, saving thousands of lives and changing American government, business, and society as no private individual had ever done before."[4]

Roscoe Pound, *Interests of Personality*
28 HARV. L. REV. 343, 356–357 (1915)*

Injuries to the body are the first wrongs dealt with in the history of law. But they are not thought of at first as infringements of an individual interest. Rather they are thought of as involving infringement of an interest of a group or kindred or of a social interest in peace and good order. They are taken to involve affront to the kindred whose kinsman is assailed, or it is taken that a desire for revenge will be awakened, and hence that they involve danger of private vengeance and private war. It is not an individual interest which is regarded, but a group interest. Hence the remedy (composition) is imposed to secure the social interest in peace and order, not to vindicate an individual private right. Often in primitive law a composition is payable to the kindred as well as to the person injured. Likewise in case of killing, the *wer* is payable to the kindred, not to dependents; it is exacted to satisfy vengeance for an insult to the kindred, not to compensate those who are deprived of support. At first, then, the ideas are (1) a group interest against insult and (2) a social interest against disorder, rather than an individual interest in the physical person. Out of these evolves slowly the idea of an individual interest secured by an individual right.

Again, when the individual interest is recognized, it is regarded at first as an interest in one's honor, in one's standing among brave men regardful of their honor, rather than as an interest in the integrity of the physical person. In Greek law every infringement of the personality of another is ... (contumelia); the injury to honor, the insult, being the essential point, not the injury to the body. In Roman law, injury to the person is called iniuria, meaning originally insult, but coming to mean any willful disregard of another's personality. In consequence the beginnings of law measure composition not by the extent of the injury to the body, but by the extent of the injury to honor and the extent of the desire for vengeance thus aroused, since the interest secured is really the social interest in preserving the peace.

---

2. Stuart Speiser, Lawsuit 102 (1980).
3. N.Y. Times, supra note 1, at 62.
4. Speiser, supra note 2, at 110.
* Copyright © 1915 by the Harvard Law School Association. Reprinted by permission.

While the law secures the interest of the individual in his honor at least as soon as his interest in his physical person, when presently it distinguishes between injuries to the person and injuries to honor or reputation, it moves very slowly in protecting feelings in any respect other than against insult or dishonor. Three steps may be noted. At first only physical injury is considered. Later overcoming the will is held a legal wrong; in other words, an individual interest in free exercise of the will is recognized and secured. Finally the law begins to take account of purely subjective mental injuries to a certain extent and even to regard infringement of another's sensibilities.

NOTES

(1) What interest of Nader's is the court protecting? Can you do better in defining it than by using the highly abstract concept of dignity? Why should society, through the court, intervene in this matter? Is the reason at base utilitarian? For example, is the court concerned about adverse effects on productivity if people constantly must worry about staving off inquiries into personal matters about which they would not wish others to know? Or is the principal reason for decision something else, more connected with fundamental notions of justice?

(2) Why does the majority insist on such separated analysis of each allegation? Would you call this "thinking like a lawyer"?

(3) How do you react to the controversy between the Nader opinions concerning the tort classifications emphasized by the majority as guideposts for decision? What is the reason to require that allegations of personal injury must fit such discrete categories in order to invoke a legal remedy? Specifically, what difference should it make that harassing phone calls are charged up under the heading of "privacy," or "intentional infliction of mental distress"?

(4) Had the case gone to the jury, through what mental process could jurors have placed an appropriate price tag on Nader's claim, if they had been sympathetic to it?

(5) Suppose that a reporter had made the inquiries that GM's agents made in *Nader*. Or suppose a journalist had engaged in the allegedly overzealous shadowing. Or, if General Motors' investigation had turned up derogatory information, suppose a news medium had published it. How would any of these factual profiles affect the decision in a case otherwise like *Nader*? (It may be noted that the Court of Appeals had held in *Pearson v. Dodd* that Pearson and Anderson had not themselves intruded when they received copies of documents stolen from the plaintiff Senator by his aides, and then used excerpts in their newspaper column. See *Pearson*, 410 F.2d at 705. Therefore, the ringing statements of that court quoted in Judge Breitel's starred footnote were, as he points out, dicta, rather than representing the holding of the case).

(6) Should General Motors be able to insure against liability of this kind?

(7) Given the Epilogue on the settlement, does justice seem to have been administered efficiently in this controversy?

(8) The most famous American baby doctor survived a motion to dismiss in a suit against the director and unknown agents of the National Security Agency for "alleged interception of ... oral, wire, telephone and telegraph communications." The court saw this result as being "foreshadow[ed]" by *Nader*, noting that in that case the New York court "had no hesitancy in deciding that allegations of illegal wiretapping and eaves-

dropping were sufficient to sustain the complaint under the law of the District of Columbia." *Spock v. United States*, 464 F. Supp. 510, 515–16 (S.D.N.Y. 1978).

(9) Security guards at a fashion show made videotapes of models in a makeshift dressing area. Was this a tortious invasion of privacy? Does it make a difference whether some of the plaintiffs did not allege that they were undressed when they were taped?

(10) The simple proposition that wiretapping and electronic eavesdropping are actionable invasions of individual rights will doubtless govern more and more litigation as American law moves into a century that features even more sophisticated electronic devices. For a description of an "elaborate wiretapping connection" that provided the basis for a damage award, in a case in which the "bugging" was designed to acquire information that would help parties to litigation anticipate their opponents' trial strategies, see *Scutieri v. Paige*, 808 F.2d 785, 787–88 (11th Cir. 1987).

(11) Is use of a listening device to monitor an employee's telephone conversations during work time actionable? At least one court has found that this conduct is sufficient to deny summary judgment to an employer with respect to the monitoring of personal calls, under a theory of intrusion on seclusion. However, the court stresses that employees "cannot reasonably claim any offensive intrusion by the monitoring or recording of their business calls at the work place," saying that those calls "were made for the benefit and in the interest of their employer." *Ali v. Douglas Cable Communications*, 929 F. Supp. 1362, 1382 (D. Kan. 1996).

Judge Rovner's dissent in *Harriston v. Chicago Tribune Co.*, 992 F.2d 697, 706 (7th Cir. 1993), poses the question as to whether wiretapping of phone conversations at work is "sufficiently extreme" to support a cause of action for intentional infliction of emotional distress, a tort mentioned in the Nader opinions that is examined later in this text, infra §2.04. Judge Rovner notes that an Illinois constitutional provision "recognizes a right to be secure from 'invasions of privacy or interceptions of communications by eavesdropping devices or other means.'"

(12) Probably the most famous covert recordings of telephone conversations were Linda Tripp's taping of phone conversations with Monica Lewinsky, a principal trigger of events leading to the impeachment of President Clinton. Could Lewinsky have successfully sued Tripp for recording her without her knowledge or consent? What legal analysis would a court apply to that case?*

PROBLEM
JONES v. CLINTON
United States District Court, E.D. Arkansas, Western Division
990 F. Supp. 657 (1998)

I.

This lawsuit is based on an incident that is said to have taken place on the afternoon of May 8, 1991, in a suite at the Excelsior Hotel in Little Rock, Arkansas. President Clinton was Governor of the State of Arkansas at the time, and plaintiff was a State employee with the Arkansas Industrial Development Commission ("AIDC"), having begun

---

* The authors are grateful to Helene Shapo for suggesting this question.

her State employment on March 11, 1991. Ferguson was an Arkansas State Police officer assigned to the Governor's security detail.

According to the record, then-Governor Clinton was at the Excelsior Hotel on the day in question delivering a speech at an official conference being sponsored by the AIDC.... Plaintiff states that she and another AIDC employee, Pamela Blackard, were working at a registration desk for the AIDC when a man approached the desk and informed her and Blackard that he was Trooper Danny Ferguson, the Governor's bodyguard.... She states that Ferguson made small talk with her and Blackard and that they asked him if he had a gun as he was in street clothes and they "wanted to know."... Ferguson acknowledged that he did and, after being asked to show the gun to them, left the registration desk to return to the Governor.... The conversation between plaintiff, Blackard, and Ferguson lasted approximately five minutes and consisted of light, friendly banter; there was nothing intimidating, threatening, or coercive about it....

... Upon leaving the registration desk, Ferguson apparently had a conversation with the Governor about the possibility of meeting with plaintiff, during which Ferguson states the Governor remarked that plaintiff had "that come-hither look," i.e. "a sort of [sexually] suggestive appearance from the look or dress."... He states that "some time later" the Governor asked him to "get him a room, that he was expecting a call from the White House and ... had several phone calls that he needed to make," and asked him to go to the car and get his briefcase containing the phone messages.... Ferguson states that upon obtaining the room, the Governor told him that if plaintiff wanted to meet him, she could "come up."... Plaintiff states that Ferguson later reappeared at the registration desk, delivered a piece of paper to her with a four-digit number written on it, and said that the Governor would like to meet with her in this suite number.... She states that she, Blackard, and Ferguson talked about what the Governor could want and that Ferguson stated, among other things, "We do this all the time."... Thinking that it was an honor to be asked to meet the Governor and that it might lead to an enhanced employment opportunity, plaintiff states that she agreed to the meeting and that Ferguson escorted her to the floor of the hotel upon which the Governor's suite was located.

Plaintiff states that upon arriving at the suite and announcing herself, the Governor shook her hand, invited her in, and closed the door.... She states that a few minutes of small talk ensued, which included the Governor asking her about her job and him mentioning that Dave Harrington, plaintiff's ultimate superior within the AIDC and a Clinton appointee, was his "good friend."... Plaintiff states that the Governor then "unexpectedly reached over to [her], took her hand, and pulled her toward him, so that their bodies were close to each other."... She states she removed her hand from his and retreated several feet, but that the Governor approached her again and, while saying, "I love the way your hair flows down your back" and "I love your curves," put his hand on her leg, started sliding it toward her pelvic area, and bent down to attempt to kiss her on the neck, all without her consent.... Plaintiff states that she exclaimed, "What are you doing?," told the Governor that she was "not that kind of girl," and "escaped" from the Governor's reach "by walking away from him."... She states she was extremely upset and confused and, not knowing what to do, attempted to distract the Governor by chatting about his wife.... Plaintiff states that she sat down at the end of the sofa nearest the door, but that the Governor approached the sofa where she had taken a seat and, as he sat down, "lowered his trousers and underwear, exposed his penis (which was erect) and told [her] to 'kiss it.'"... She states that she was "horrified" by this and that she "jumped up from the couch" and told the Governor that she had to go, saying something to the effect that she had to get back to the registration desk.... Plaintiff states that the Governor, "while fondling his penis," said, "Well, I don't want to make you do anything you don't want to do," and then pulled up his pants and said, "If you get in trouble for leaving work, have Dave call me immediately and I'll take care of it." ... She states that as she left the room (the door of which was not locked), the Governor "detained" her momentarily, "looked sternly" at her, and said, "You are smart. Let's keep this between ourselves.".....

Plaintiff states that the Governor's advances to her were unwelcome, that she never said or did anything to suggest to the Governor that she was willing to have sex with him, and that during the time they were together in the hotel suite, she resisted his advances although she was "stunned by them and intimidated by who he was." ... She states that when the Governor referred to Dave Harrington, she "understood that he was telling her that he had control over Mr. Harrington and over her job, and that he was willing to use that power." ... She states that from that point on, she was "very fearful" that her refusal to submit to the Governor's advances could damage her career and even jeopardize her employment....

Plaintiff states that when she left the hotel suite, she was in shock and upset but tried to maintain her composure.... She states she saw Ferguson waiting outside the suite but that he did not escort her back to the registration desk and nothing was said between them.... Ferguson states that five or ten minutes after plaintiff exited the suite he joined the Governor for their return to the Governor's Mansion and that the Governor, who was working on some papers that he had spread out on the desk, said, "She came up here, and nothing happened." ...

Plaintiff states she returned to the registration desk and told Blackard some of what had happened.... Blackard states that plaintiff was shaking and embarrassed.... Following the Conference, plaintiff states she went to the workplace of a friend, Debra Ballentine, and told her of the incident as well ... Ballentine states that plaintiff was upset and crying.... Later that same day, plaintiff states she told her sister, Charlotte Corbin Brown, what had happened and, within the next two days, also told her other sister, Lydia Corbin Cathey, of the incident.... Brown's observations of plaintiff's demeanor apparently are not included in the record. Cathey, however, states that plaintiff was "bawling" and "squalling," and that she appeared scared, embarrassed, and ashamed.

Ballentine states that she encouraged plaintiff to report the incident to her boss or to the police, but that plaintiff declined, pointing out that her boss was friends with the Governor and that the police were the ones who took her to the hotel suite.... Ballentine further states that plaintiff stated she did not want her fiance to know of the incident and that she "just want[ed] this thing to go away." ... Plaintiff states that what the Governor and Ferguson had said and done made her "afraid" to file charges.

QUESTIONS

Without reference to the rest of the opinion, or to what you may have otherwise read about this case, how would you formulate the issue—the legal question—that the case presents?

In formulating this issue, you should identify the factual elements of Jones's grievance against Clinton. You should also ask yourself the following questions:

- What interests of Jones were infringed?

- What legal "rights" allegedly were violated?
- What is a legal "injury"?
- What is the "justice" of the case?

NOTE

A state court summarized the facts of a case this way:

The evidence shows that, when after a brief extra-marital affair Downey told Kramer he did not want to see her anymore, she did not yield to his wishes but instead began a pattern of conduct to thrust herself into his presence and otherwise to disrupt his domestic and professional life. Several days a week, for several years, Kramer would be at Downey's home when he left for work or at his office when he left for lunch or for dinner and would follow him to his destination, always on a motor scooter or bicycle. She followed him as well on trips he made with his wife and children to school during the day and to restaurants in the evening. Often Kramer was observed waiting in the park across the street from the Downey residence or outside the office entrance to the hospital where Downey worked. At many of these times, she was attired in a fashion so unusual as to attract the attention of Downey's acquaintances. Downey's wife, daughter, neighbors and co-workers witnessed these activities, and some overheard Kramer on occasion make sexually vulgar remarks to Downey. In addition, by devious means, Kramer caused to be delivered to Downey numerous unwanted letters, cards and gifts. Downey testified that Kramer's incessant behavior increasingly caused him to be upset agitated, depressed and fearful for the safety of himself and his family. He became unable to sleep at night and unable to concentrate at work; finally, he sought psychological counseling.

Should Downey be able to get legal relief against Kramer? Why, or why not? If so, what kind of relief?

Chapter 2

INTENTIONAL INTERFERENCE WITH THE PERSON

PRELIMINARY NOTE

The problems that you confront in this book arise principally from lawsuits by one private party against either a person, or a corporation or governmental unit, seeking a remedy for the physical or emotional consequences of some act or omission. In most of these cases, the relief sought by the injured person will be monetary compensation, and in that connection it is always helpful to ask yourself the question of whether it is socially desirable to transfer wealth between the parties to the litigation. In some cases, the answer will appear principally to be an economic one, deriving from a judicial attempt to assign liability in a way that best reflects the social cost of various kinds of activity. Other decisions appear to focus on reduction of the frequency of accidents, or the severity of their consequences, sometimes regardless of whether that outcome is "efficient" in technical economic terms. You will also see judges seeking to achieve practically "just" or "fair" results with respect to the particular misfortune at issue.

These are only some of the major policy goals to which courts refer when they deal with efforts by injured persons to secure compensation from those whose conduct is arguably responsible for their injuries. Other interesting questions that recur include these:

To what kind of law does the plaintiff look for his or her remedy? Is it basically judge-made law, or law made by legislatures or administrative agencies? How directly does it command the result for which the plaintiff contends?

What remedies alternative to the payment of money might be appropriate, including remedies involving judicial orders that the defendant do something—for example, take measures to make a particular activity safer—or stop doing something, for example, discontinue a dangerous course of conduct?

Are there criminal sanctions available to vindicate society's interest in preventing or punishing conduct that presents a danger to its members?

As you study these materials, keep these questions in mind, and formulate what seem to you to be the other basic questions that are crucial to the resolution of particular cases.

§ 2.01 Assault

READ v. COKER
138 Eng. Rep. 1437 (1853)

....

Plea, not guilty "by statute," upon which issue was joined.

The cause was tried before Talfourd, J., at the first sitting in London in Easter Term last. The facts which appeared in evidence were as follows:—The plaintiff was a paper-stainer, carrying on business in the City Road, upon premises which he rented of one Molineux, at a rent of 8s. per week. In January, 1852, the rent being sixteen weeks in arrear, the landlord employed one Holliwell to distrain for it. Holliwell accordingly seized certain presses, lathes, and other trade fixtures, and, at the plaintiff's request, advanced him 16l. upon the security of the goods, for the purpose of paying off the rent. The plaintiff, being unable to redeem his goods, on the 23rd of February applied to the defendant for assistance. The goods were thereupon sold to the defendant by Holliwell, on the part of Read, for 25l. 11s. 6d.; and it was agreed between the plaintiff and the defendant, that the business should be carried on for their mutual benefit, the defendant paying the rent of the premises and other ... outgoings, and allowing the plaintiff a certain sum weekly.

The defendant becoming dissatisfied with the speculation, dismissed the plaintiff on the 22nd of March. On the 24th, the plaintiff came to the premises, and refusing to leave when ordered by the defendant, the latter collected together some of his workmen, who mustered round the plaintiff, tucking up their sleeves and aprons, and threatened to break his neck if he did not go out; and, fearing that the men would strike him if he did not do so, the plaintiff went out. This was the assault complained of in the first count. Upon this evidence, the learned judge left it to the jury to say, whether there was an intention on the part of the defendant to assault the plaintiff, and whether the plaintiff was apprehensive of personal violence if he did not retire. The jury found for the plaintiff on this count, damages one farthing....

Byles, Serjt., on a former day in this term, in pursuance of leave reserved to him at the trial, moved for a rule nisi to enter the verdict for the defendant upon the first, third, and four issues, or for a new trial on the ground of misdirection, and that the verdict was not warranted by the evidence. That which was proved as to the first count, clearly did not amount to an assault. [Jervis, C.J. It was as much an assault as a sheriff's officer being in a room with a man against whom he has a writ, and saying to him "You are my prisoner," is an arrest.] To constitute an assault, there must be something more than a threat of violence. An assault is thus defined in Buller's Nisi Prius, p. 15,—"An assault is an attempt or offer, by force or violence, to do a corporal hurt to another, as, by pointing a pitchfork at him, when standing within reach; presenting a gun at him [within shooting distance]; drawing a sword, and waving it in a menacing manner, The Queen v. Ingram, ... But no words can amount to an assault, though perhaps they may in some cases serve to explain a doubtful action,— ... ; as, if a man were to lay his hand upon his sword, and say, If it were not assize time, he would not take such language:" the words would prevent the action from being construed to be an assault, because they shew he had no intent to do him any corporal hurt at that time: Tuberville v. Savage,....." So, in Selwyn's Nisi Prius, 11th edit. 26, it is said,—"An assault is an attempt, with force or violence, to do a corporal injury to another, as, by holding up a fist in a menacing manner; striking at another with a cane or stick, though the party striking may miss his aim; drawing a sword or bayonet; throwing a bottle or glass with intent to wound or strike; presenting a gun at a person who is within the distance to which the gun will carry; pointing a pitchfork at a person who is within reach,—Genner v. Sparks,...,—or by any other similar act, accompanied with such circumstances as denote at the time an intention (coupled with a present ability,—see Stephens v. Myers, ... —of using actual violence, against the person of another." So, in 3 Bl.Comm. 120, an assault is said to be "an attempt or offer to beat another, without touching him; as, if one lifts up his cane or his fist, in a threatening manner, at another; or strikes at him but misses him; this is an assault, insultus, which Finch ... describes to be "an unlawful setting upon one's person." [Jervis, C.J. If a man comes into a room, and lays his cane on the table, and says to another, "If you don't go out, I will knock you on the head," would not that be an assault?] Clearly not: it is a mere threat, unaccompanied by any gesture or action towards carrying it into effect. The direction of the learned judge as to this point was erroneous. He should have told the jury, that, to constitute an assault, there must be an attempt, coupled with a present ability to do personal violence to the party; instead of leaving it to them, as he did, to say what the plaintiff thought, and not what they (the jury) thought was the defendant's intention. There must be some act done denoting a present ability and an intention to assault.

                                              ...

A rule nisi having been granted,

Allen, Serjt., and Charnock, now shewed cause. The first question is, whether the evidence was sufficient, as to the first count, to justify the learned judge in putting it to the jury whether or not the defendant had been guilty of an assault. The evidence was, that the plaintiff was surrounded by the defendant and his men, who, with their sleeves and aprons tucked up, threatened to break his neck if he did not quit the workshop. [Maule, J. If there can be such a thing as an assault, without an actual beating, this is an assault.] ...

JERVIS, C. J. I am of opinion that this rule cannot be made absolute to its full extent; but that, so far as regards the first count of the declaration, it must be discharged. If anything short of actual striking will in law constitute an assault, the facts here clearly shewed that the defendant was guilty of an assault. There was a threat of violence exhibiting an intention to assault, and a present ability to carry the threat into execution....

[The other judges concurred, and the rule was discharged as to the first count.]

NOTES

(1) What is a "rule nisi"? What does it mean in *Read* that the rule was "discharged" as to the first count?

(2) Does the court procedure in *Read* seem designed efficiently to lay bare the facts and to derive the applicable legal principle? What is that principle? For which legal rule did Byles, Serjt., argue?

(3) The Restatement of Torts is a project that attempts to summarize the principles of the common law of torts. It is part of a much larger enterprise, including Restatements of many other subjects, under the sponsorship of the American Law Institute, a private organization comprised of judges, practicing lawyers and scholars. The first *Re-*

statement of Torts was published in four volumes beginning in 1934. Publication of the *Restatement (Second)* began in 1965 and continued in four volumes published over a period of a dozen years.

A *Restatement (Third)* is now underway, progressing in segments. The first published volume deals with a functionally defined area of the law, that is, products liability. RE-STATEMENT (THIRD) OF TORTS: PRODUCTS LIABILITY (1998). Work has now been completed on a Torts Restatement project that focuses on the apportionment of liability between plaintiffs and defendants, as well as among defendants. RESTATEMENT (THIRD) OF TORTS: APPORTIONMENT OF LIABILITY (2000).

The style of the *Restatement* is to present, literally in "blackletter" boldfaced type, as crisp as possible a statement of law on a particular question, and then, in commentary, to explain the rule and its implications. The *Second Restatement's* definition of "Assault," which appears in section 21, includes the following language:

(1) An actor is subject to liability to another for assault if

(a) he acts intending to cause a harmful or offensive contact with the person of the other or a third person, or an imminent apprehension of such a contact, and

(b) the other is thereby put in such imminent apprehension.

Does this definition help you to solve the legal problem in *Read v. Coker*? What parts of it are most helpful?

(4) Why did the jury find for the plaintiff and then award only one farthing?

(5) What would have been the reaction of Jervis, C.J., to a case based only on menacing glares from the defendant's workmen, who had gathered around the plaintiff but took no physical action such as rolling up their sleeves? Suppose a single workman had glared in an especially savage way from atop a ladder five feet away?

(6) How much difference does it make that the menacing look or the menacing look plus the preliminary act emanates from a middle linebacker or from a midget?

Is the standard in *Read* an objective or a subjective one in terms of the perception of the plaintiff? From the viewpoint of the defendant?

(7) What interests of the plaintiff were being protected by the decision in *Read*? Suppose that the plaintiff in *Read* was unable to cope with stressful situations and had an emotional breakdown as a result of the incident:

(a) Should this subjective reaction influence the determination of whether or not there has been an assault?

(b) Should the plaintiff be awarded damages equal to his psychiatric bills and lost wages?

(c) Should the jury be allowed to grant punitive damages—that is, a sum awarded expressly as a punishment that is added on to the plaintiff's wage losses, medical bills, and pain and suffering?

What is the main reason that we are prepared to make the defendant pay anything in *Read*?

(8) The manager of a Shoney's restaurant conducted a search of employees, with the aid of police officers, after the discovery that $600 was missing from a cash register. After the search was concluded, one employee said, the manager told her that "there would be some 'ass whippings' if a lawsuit was filed." Did the manager assault the employee?

(9) A high school student, vexed with a guidance counselor who would not make a requested schedule change, allegedly told the counselor, "I'm so angry, I could just shoot someone." Was that an assault? The school district suspended the student for three days. Was that a violation of the student's constitutional right to free speech?

SPECIAL NOTE ON STREET HARASSMENT

Is it an assault for a man to give a woman a lustful look as she walks through a parking lot? How about a lustful look accompanied by the words "Let's go home and go to bed, baby"? Cf. *Taylor v. Centennial Bowl, Inc.*, 65 Cal.2d 114, 52 Cal. Rptr. 561, 416 P.2d 793 (1966); *Samms v. Eccles*, 11 Utah 2d 289, 358 P.2d 344 (1961).

The problem of sexually oriented street harassment has proved resistant to tort remedies. Explaining this barrier in traditional law, Professor Bowman borrows the definition of street harassment of the anthropologist Micaela di Leonardo as an occurrence

> when one or more strange men accost one or more women ... in a public place which is not the woman's/women's worksite. Through looks, words or gestures the man asserts his right to intrude on the woman's attention, defining her as a sexual object, and forcing her to interact with him.[1]

Reviewing the traditional intentional torts, Bowman points out that the assault tort will not usually give a remedy for street harassment "because it requires a finding both of intent on the part of the harasser and an 'objective' reasonableness of the woman's apprehension," as well as, in many states, a "present capacity to inflict injury" and the use of "more than mere words."[2] Inter alia, Bowman points out that the intrusion branch of tort privacy has not aided plaintiffs "because such harassment takes place in public and because the 'man of ordinary sensibilities' does not regard such conduct as highly offensive."[3] Because of the difficulty in fitting this conduct within the definitions of traditional tort categories, Bowman suggests the passage of statutes or ordinances on the subject.[4]

SPECIAL NOTE ON STALKING

Legislatures have now begun to deal with a group of serious matters that may be likened to the fact situation in *Read v. Coker*. The growing concern with "stalking" crimes, which often result in serious bodily injury or death, has inspired the passage of statutes to deal with that sort of conduct. An Illinois law seeks to capture the gist of this "assault-plus" offense:

§ 12-7.3 Stalking

(a) A person commits stalking when he or she, knowingly and without lawful justification, on at least 2 separate occasions follows another person or places the person under surveillance or any combination thereof and:

---

1. Cynthia Bowman, *Street Harassment and the Informal Ghettoization of Women*, 106 Harv. L. Rev. 517, 524 (1993), quoting Micaela di Leonardo, *Political Economy of Street Harassment*, Aegis, Summer 1981, at 51–52.
2. *Id.* at 555.
3. *Id.* at 569.
4. Bowman offers and comments on a draft statute, *id.* at 575–77.

(1) at any time transmits a threat to that person of immediate or future bodily harm, sexual assault, confinement or restraint; or

(2) places that person in reasonable apprehension of immediate or future bodily harm, sexual assault, confinement or restraint.

(b) Sentence. Stalking is a class 4 felony. A second or subsequent conviction for stalking is a Class 3 felony.

(c) Exemption. This Section does not apply to picketing occurring at the workplace that is otherwise lawful and arises out of a bona fide labor dispute, or any exercise of the right of free speech or assembly that is otherwise lawful.

(d) For the purpose of this Section, a defendant "places a person under surveillance" by remaining present outside the person's school, place of employment, vehicle, other place occupied by the person, or residence other than the residence of the defendant.

(e) For the purpose of this Section, "follows another person" means (i) to move in relative proximity to a person as that person moves from place to place or (ii) to remain in relative proximity to a person who is stationary or whose movements are confined to a small area. "Follows another person" does not include a following within the residence of the defendant.

Il. St. ch. 720 § 5/12-7.3.

NAVRATIL v. PARKER

United States District Court, Colorado
726 F. Supp. 800 (1989)

MATSCH, DISTRICT JUDGE.

This is an action under 42 U.S.C. § 1983 with state law claims brought under diversity jurisdiction. The suit arises from a traffic stop. On the evening of January 25, 1986, Eagle County Sheriff's Lieutenant Randy Parker (Parker), on patrol in a police vehicle, heard on his radio that a large dark car was heading west on I-70 at a high rate of speed. About 20 to 30 minutes later, Parker saw an automobile of that description. That vehicle was occupied by three persons: the plaintiff, Boris F. Navratil (Navratil); his son, John Navratil, who was driving; and John Navratil's fiancee. Parker radioed to nearby Eagle Police officer David Pierson (Pierson), who was parked farther west on I-70, requesting him to take a radar speed check. Pierson radioed to Parker that the car was traveling in excess of the speed limit.... John Navratil disputes that his speed was checked by radar because his radar detector did not go off, and because the occupants did not see any cars on the ramp where Pierson claims to have been parked. John Navratil also denies that he was speeding. Navratil states that he did not look at the speedometer of the car so he does not know if the car was speeding. However, the plaintiff does not dispute that Pierson reported back to Parker that the Navratil car was traveling in excess of the speed limit.

After hearing the report, Parker followed the car and shined his spotlight on it to get the driver to pull over. Parker claims that he had his roof lights on, but that is disputed. While Parker was following the car, he saw an object being passed from the front to the back seat. John Navratil acknowledged that he passed a radar detector to the plaintiff in the back seat.

John Navratil stopped the car and got out. The plaintiff also got out of the car. Parker told him to get back in. Navratil says that Parker was rude. Navratil asked why the car had been stopped. Parker repeatedly told Navratil to return to his car, and Navratil repeatedly asked why they had been stopped. Finally, Navratil got back in the car. Parker took John Navratil's driver's license and returned to his police car.

Several minutes later, after Parker came back to the Navratil car, Navratil got out, and walked towards Parker and John Navratil in order to give a coat to John. Navratil admits that he was agitated and waved his arms for emphasis. Navratil Dep. at 60. More police officers arrived on the scene. John Navratil said to his father "Dad, why don't you get back in the car and let me finish up." ... Parker's police dog came out from Parker's car and stood next to Parker, who restrained him. The plaintiff claims that Parker let the dog out of the car, while Parker claims that the dog was following his training to jump out of the open window of the back seat of the police car when he sensed danger. After his son's suggestion, and further orders from Parker, Navratil returned to his car.

Navratil came out of the car a third time, "To tell Parker to buzz off and let us go on our way." ... He was agitated and "may have chopped the air ... for emphasis." ... John Navratil stated that his father "slapped the trunk of the car ... two or three times," ... although Navratil denies this. Parker told him to get back into his car or he would be arrested.... At this point, the car had been stopped for ten to fifteen minutes. Navratil then said "Look if you're going to arrest me, let's do it and let's get it over with and let's be on our way." ... Navratil was arrested and handcuffed. Parker searched the interior of the car. Navratil was taken to jail, and John Navratil followed in his car. Navratil posted bond and was released, and John Navratil was issued a warning ticket.

Navratil was first charged for violating Colo.Rev.Stat. § 42-4-105, which at that time provided: "No person shall willfully fail or refuse to comply with any lawful order or direction of any police officer invested by law with authority to direct, control, or regulate traffic. Any person who violates any provisions of this section commits a class 2 traffic offense." The county court dismissed that charge, ruling that the prohibition applied only to a police officer who was actually directing motorists or pedestrians.

Navratil was then charged with a violation of Colo.Rev.Stat. § 18-8-104, which provides: "a person commits obstructing a peace officer or fireman when, by using or threatening to use violence, force, or physical interference, or obstacle, he knowingly obstructs, impairs, or hinders the enforcement of the penal law or the preservation of the peace by a peace officer, acting under color of his official authority...." Navratil moved to suppress evidence based on allegations that the stop and arrest were without probable cause. That motion was denied.... Navratil was convicted after a jury trial in county court on June 26, 1987. That conviction was reversed by the district court's conclusion that the issuance of a warning ticket was not the enforcement of a penal law.

Parker has moved for summary judgment under Fed.R.Civ.P. 56 on all the plaintiff's claims.

...

II. The State Law Claims

As the parties agree, Colorado law applies to the remaining claims. Navratil alleges that he was the victim of an assault. The only acts alleged that could conceivably constitute assault are the presence of the police dog and of the other officers who appeared at the scene. According to Navratil and his son, the dog never touched either of them, and was restrained by Parker. John Navratil stated that he did not recall the dog ever growling or showing its teeth.... He also testified that "the mishandling of the dog was getting the dog out of the car." ... At the criminal trial, John Navratil was asked if the dog was threatening, and he replied "It—You know, no one was going to argue with that dog." "Did the dog drool or snarl or anything like that?" "No. The dog did not. The dog was being appropriately handled." ... Parker is no more liable for having a trained attack dog with him when it was arguably not necessary than any other police officer would be liable for assault for possessing a revolver or nightstick under circumstances when no weapons of any kind were necessary. The public policy of the state of Colorado is to permit its peace officers to be armed. See Colo.Rev.Stat. § 18-12-101(2); Colo.Rev.Stat. § 18-12-102(5); Colo.Rev.Stat. § 18-12-105(2)(d) & (e) (provisions allowing peace officers to possess weapons). Where, as here, the weapons are not used in what objectively could be considered a threatening or intimidating manner, there is no assault.

For the same reason, Parker's decision to call for additional officers was not an assault. People may be intimidated by a police show of force, but it is inconceivable that a police officer's judgment as to how much assistance he needs can be second-guessed by a court in the absence of some threatening behavior. There is no evidence that the other officers were doing anything but standing nearby. Boris Navratil's individual sensitivity is not the measure for determining the defendant's liability.

Navratil claims invasion of privacy. In Rugg v. McCarty, 476 P.2d 753, 755 (Colo.1970) the court allowed a claim for invasion of privacy to proceed where "*unreasonable action* ... is taken which foreseeably will probably result in extreme mental anguish, embarrassment, humiliation or mental suffering and injury to a person possessed of *ordinary sensibilities*, under the same or similar circumstances...." (emphasis in original) (citations omitted). See also Otten v. Birdseye, 527 P.2d 925, 927 (Colo.App.1974) (affirming dismissal of invasion of privacy claim where actions "would not foreseeably result in extreme mental anguish, embarrassment, humiliation, or mental suffering"). The only allegation in the complaint that could possibly implicate this interest is that "Parker directed a high intensity searchlight into plaintiff's car." A car on the highway is not a cloister. Automobiles are equipped with powerful headlights that can shine through the window of another car, illuminating its interior. Further, as the Supreme Court noted in Texas v. Brown, 460 U.S. 730, 740, 103 S.Ct. 1535, 1542, 75 L.Ed.2d 502 (1983) (plurality opinion), cars have windows, which permit persons nearby to see inside. The plaintiff's allegations evidence no hope of meeting the Rugg standard, because the average person would not suffer extreme mental humiliation from the shining of a light into the automobile in which he was a passenger.

...

... Navratil alleges false arrest and false imprisonment, and related torts. The injury that must have been willfully and wantonly caused is being subjected to an unlawful arrest, for being lawfully arrested is not a cognizable harm. Evidence that Parker knew the arrest was illegal would be the most direct evidence of willful and wanton conduct, but there is no evidence of subjective knowledge.

The circumstances of an incident often constitute the only available evidence on the issue of the state of mind of the actor. The circumstances of this case do not support an inference that the defendant acted willfully and wantonly. Navratil was arrested for violation of Colo.Rev.Stat. § 42-4-105, prohibiting disobedience to police officers. When Parker made the arrest, no reported opinion had limited § 42-4-105 to disobedience to actual traffic directions, as opposed to instructions incident to controlling traffic. Accordingly, Navratil was arrested based on an objectively reasonable interpretation of the statute. Although Parker's view was not adopted by the county court, to date no reported Colorado appellate court decision has limited the statute in that way.

Further, an officer in Parker's position could have thought that Colo.Rev.Stat. § 18-8-105 justified making an arrest for interference with writing a warning ticket. In People v. Shockley, 591 P.2d 589, 591 (Colo.App.1978), the court concluded that "the term 'enforcement' as used in the statute encompasses those activities which a peace officer is under a duty to perform in order to give effect to a penal law." It is by no means obvious that the issuance of a warning ticket does not contribute to giving effect to the law prohibiting speeding. While the district court concluded that interference with the warning ticket was not a violation of the statute, the county court denied a motion to suppress based in part on a lack of probable cause for the arrest.... The county court permitted the prosecution to go forward, and the jury convicted, all on the theory that interference with a warning ticket was an interference with enforcement of the penal law. These facts suggest that Parker's view of the statute was not unreasonable. Assuming that the Colorado Supreme Court would conclude that the statutes at issue do not apply to Navratil's conduct, it would do so based on sophisticated legal reasoning. That Parker failed to anticipate such analysis does not suggest that his actions constituted willful and wanton misconduct.

Navratil's allegations of fact do not otherwise suggest that Parker willfully and wantonly arrested Navratil illegally. Under Navratil's version of the facts Parker was rude, but nothing in Navratil's allegations suggests that Parker had an invidious motive for arresting Navratil, or that Parker was searching for an excuse to arrest Navratil. There is no evidence contradicting Parker's testimony at the trial that his purpose in ordering Navratil to return to the car was to protect himself from possible harm. Moreover, it was Navratil who initiated the exchanges with Parker that resulted in the arrest. It was only after warning Navratil that he would be arrested if he failed to stay in the car, and after Navratil asked to be arrested, that Parker took the plaintiff into custody.

The facts as alleged by Navratil are entirely consistent with Parker's good faith, and none suggest an improper purpose. If the facts were susceptible to either of two interpretations, the existence of willful and wanton conduct would be a jury question. But here, any finding of willful and wanton misconduct in this case would be based on speculation, rather than fair inference from the evidence. Accordingly, the false imprisonment claim against Parker is barred by immunity.

Navratil alleges that Parker committed a battery against him, claiming that Parker used excessive and unreasonable force during and after the arrest. At his deposition, Navratil was asked "[w]as there any physical contact between you and Officer Parker other than when he touched you to put the handcuffs on?" The answer: "No." ... From the plaintiff's briefs, it is clear that the force complained of is the presence of the dog and backup officers, and the loudness of Parker's voice. These things do not constitute battery because they do not involve any physical contact. Accordingly, the battery claim fails to state a claim.

The only force mentioned in the briefs and deposition testimony is the use of handcuffs, which is neither pleaded in the complaint nor raised in the pre-trial order. Navratil said in a deposition that his wrists became numb from the handcuffs, but he did not seek medical attention after his release, and he did not tell any officers that they were too tight.... There is no evidence upon which a jury could find that Navratil was handcuffed in spite of Parker's knowledge that there was no probable cause for arrest, and thus that there was no privilege to handcuff Navratil. Therefore, even if this allegation were in the pleadings, Parker would be immune from liability.

The final substantive claim is outrageous conduct. To state a claim, the plaintiff must allege "conduct … so outrageous in character, and so extreme in degree, as to go beyond all possible bounds of decency, and to be regarded as atrocious, and utterly intolerable in a civilized community." Rugg v. McCarty, 173 Colo. 170, 476 P.2d 753, 756 (Colo.1970) (quoting Restatement (Second) of Torts § 46, comment d at 73). The distress must be caused intentionally or recklessly. See Rubenstein v. South Denver Nat. Bank, 762 P.2d 755, 757 (Colo.App.1988). Presumably, the outrageous conduct is the result of an aggregation of all the other torts alleged. On the facts alleged here this claim must be dismissed because there is no genuine issue of material fact that Parker went beyond the bounds of reasonable police procedure in making an arrest, or that the arrest or any of the associated acts were willful and wanton.

…

Upon the foregoing, it is ORDERED that the defendant's motion for summary judgment is granted.

NOTES

(1) If "no one was going to argue with that dog," why wasn't the use of the dog an assault? If it was not, by itself, isn't there an assault within the entire cluster of police actions, including the appearance of the backup officers?

(2) Consider the other claims that the court dismisses—invasion of privacy, false arrest, willful and wanton misconduct, battery, and outrageous conduct. This is a substantial part of the array of the category of torts called "intentional torts," many of which are analyzed in detail later in this Part. If the trial judge was unwilling to find that there was any tort in this case, what do you think was his general perspective on this incident?

(3) *Navratil* began as an action under 42 U.S.C. § 1983, a federal civil rights statute often used in suits against police officers. This edited version of the case deals principally with claims under state law that were attached to those under section 1983. Material later in the book focuses more closely on the federal statute.

§ 2.02 Battery

[A] Generally

PROBLEM

The following episode is described in a case in which both plaintiff and defendant were employees of the same firm. The incident took place at a lunch hour during which several employees, including the plaintiff and the defendant, were seated at a work table in the company's plant:

> Respondent, in an effort to tease petitioner, whom he knew to be shy, intentionally put his arm around petitioner and pulled her head toward him. Immediately after this "friendly unsolicited hug," petitioner suffered a sharp pain in the back of her neck and ear, and sharp pains into the base of her skull. As a result, petitioner was paralyzed on the left side of her face and mouth.

Is it likely that the plaintiff can successfully maintain an action for damages? If a battery is an intended, nonconsensual, and unprivileged touching, what would the defendant have to have intended in this case for the plaintiff to succeed?

VOSBURG v. PUTNEY

Wisconsin Supreme Court
80 Wis. 523, 50 N.W. 403 (1891)

The action was brought to recover damages for an assault and battery, alleged to have been committed by the defendant upon the plaintiff on February 20, 1889. The answer is a general denial. At the date of the alleged assault the plaintiff was a little more than 14 years of age, and the defendant a little less than 12 years of age. The injury complained of was caused by a kick inflicted by defendant upon the leg of the plaintiff, a little below the knee. The transaction occurred in a school-room in Waukesha, during school hours, both parties being pupils in the school. A former trial of the cause resulted in a verdict and judgment for the plaintiff for $2,800. The defendant appealed from such judgment to this court, and the same was reversed for error, and a new trial awarded. 78 Wis. 84, 47 N.W.Rep. 99. The case has been again tried in the circuit court, and the trial resulted in a verdict for plaintiff for $2,500. The facts of the case, as they appeared on both trials, are sufficiently stated in the opinion by Mr. Justice Orton on the former appeal, and require no repetition. On the last trial the jury found a special verdict, as follows: "(1) Had the plaintiff during the month of January, 1889, received an injury just above the knee, which became inflamed, and produced pus? Answer. Yes. (2) Had such injury on the 20th day of February, 1889, nearly healed at the point of the injury? A. Yes. (3) Was the plaintiff, before said 20th of February, lame, as the result of such injury? A. No. (4) Had the tibia in the plaintiff's right leg become inflamed or diseased to some extent before he received the blow or kick from the defendant? A. No. (5) What was the exciting cause of the injury to the plaintiff's leg? A. Kick. (6) Did the defendant, in touching the plaintiff with his foot, intend to do him any harm? A. No. (7) At what sum do you assess the damages of the plaintiff? A. Twenty-five hundred dollars." The defendant moved for judgment in his favor on the verdict, and also for a new trial. The plaintiff moved for judgment on the verdict in his favor. The motions of defendant were overruled, and that of the plaintiff granted. Thereupon judgment for plaintiff, for $2,500 damages and costs of suit, was duly entered. The defendant appeals from the judgment....

LYON, J., (after stating the facts.) Several errors are assigned, only three of which will be considered.

I. The jury having found that the defendant, in touching the plaintiff with his foot, did not intend to do him any harm, counsel for defendant maintain that the plaintiff has no cause of action, and that defendant's motion for judgment on the special verdict should have been granted. In support of this proposition counsel quote from 2 Greenl.Ev. § 83, the rule that "the intention to do harm is of the essence of an assault." Such is the rule, no doubt, in actions or prosecutions for mere assaults. But this is an action to recover damages for an alleged assault and battery. In such case the rule is correctly stated, in many of the authorities cited by counsel, that plaintiff must show either that the intention was unlawful, or that the defendant is in fault. If the intended act is unlawful, the intention to commit it must necessarily be unlawful. Hence, as applied to this case, if the kicking of the plaintiff by the defendant was an unlawful act, the intention of defendant to kick him was also unlawful. Had the parties been upon the play-grounds of the school, engaged in the usual boyish sports, the defendant being free from malice, wantonness, or negligence, and intending no harm to plaintiff in what he did, we should hesitate to hold the act of the defendant unlawful, or that he could be held liable in this action. Some consideration is due to the implied license of the play-grounds. But it appears that the injury was inflicted in the school, after it had been called to order by the teacher, and after the regular exercises of the school had com-menced. Under these circumstances, no implied license to do the act complained of ex-isted, and such act was a violation of the order and decorum of the school, and neces-sarily unlawful. Hence we are of the opinion that, under the evidence and verdict, the action may be sustained.

...

III. Certain questions proposed on behalf of defendant to be submitted to the jury, founded upon the theory that only such damages could be recovered as the defendant might reasonably be supposed to have contemplated as likely to result from his kicking the plaintiff. The court refused to submit such questions to the jury. The ruling was cor-rect. The rule of damages in actions for torts was held in Brown v. Railway Co., 54 Wis. 342, 11 N.W.Rep. 356, 911, to be that the wrongdoer is liable for all injuries resulting directly from the wrongful act, whether they could or could not have been foreseen by him.

[The case was remanded for a new trial, however, because the trial court erroneously failed to sustain an objection to a hypothetical question based on a witness' testimony that left out some facts concerning the January wound-facts which had already been proved by that witness.]

Mark Twain, *Adventures of Tom Sawyer*
33 (Mo. 1875, Harper & Bros., 1920)

He entered the church, now, with a swarm of clean and noisy boys and girls, pro-ceeded to his seat and started a quarrel with the first boy that came handy. The teacher, a grave, elderly man, interfered; then turned his back a moment and Tom pulled a boy's hair in the next bench, and was absorbed in his book when the boy turned around; stuck a pin in another boy, presently, in order to hear him say, 'Ouch!' and got a new repri-mand from his teacher. Tom's whole class were a pattern restless, noisy, and trouble-some.

HISTORIC FUNCTIONS OF TORT-LIKE LAW
A.B.A. Special Committee on The Tort Liability System,
Towards a Jurisprudence of Injury 3–17
(ABA 1984, M. Shapo Rptr.)[*]

... The researches of Dean Pound ... revealed how ancient tort-like rules served as grievance mechanisms for the protection of group interests. Other scholarship has recorded the role of compensation for personal injury and death as a mediator of con-

---

flict since the time of Alfred the Great. In Professor Malone's summary of the literature, "[t]he earliest exactions of payment were made in a single proceeding which served the dual purpose both of buying off the vengeful anger of the clan and of placating the king or lord for the disturbance of his peace."

The development of modern liability on the foundations of the *bot*, the payment for appeasement of the family, and the *wite*, the payment to the king, has called forth a variety of explanations. Holmes thought the historical evidence showed "that the various forms of liability known to modern law spring from the common ground of revenge."

Perhaps at least as appealing to intuition is Dean Green's argument that the purpose of the old rules was "to require the one who has hurt another, however innocently, to make atonement, expiation or reparation for the hurt." If these forms of "retribution" seem crude to the modern eye, he wrote, "they can also be conceived as the highest expressions of morality." We simply add that such an appeal to morality was consistent with a perceived need to preserve the peace of the community.

NOTES

(1) Be sure that you have mastered the procedural steps in *Vosburg*. What is the issue in the case? How does the court implicitly formulate an abstract question that pins the facts of this case to more general considerations?

(2) Would the "implied license of the play-grounds" extend to a classroom before it is called to order? Suppose a school regulation, posted in every corridor and classroom, said, "When the class is called to order, each pupil shall sit quietly at his or her desk and shall not arise unless the teacher tells him to. No pupil shall push, pull, strike or throw missiles at any other pupil." What effect, if any, would this regulation have in a suit for injuries caused by a Vosburg-type incident?

(3) Suppose that a school is run on the basis of "open classroom" principles, and that it is so "open" that students are allowed to leave their seats at any time, and to blow off steam by romping in the corridor or on the playground when they feel like it. Would a Vosburg-type defendant be held for exciting an old wound by a kick in rough corridor play? Assume that kicks, though not the norm in this classroom, generally were endured by all and were by no means unique.

(4) A remarkable monograph exhaustively analyzes *Vosburg*, employing primary sources like newspapers in Waukesha, where the incident took place: Zigurds Zile, *Vosburg v. Putney: A Centennial Story*, 1992 WIS. L. REV. 877. Zile's history of the case, which runs to more than 100 pages, sets the Wisconsin Supreme Court's several decisions concerning the incident in the context of social history, the tactics of the lawyers, and journalistic critiques of the litigation.

(5) A review of Jerome Bruner's book ACTUAL MINDS, POSSIBLE WORLDS characterizes the author's position this way: "[T]he center of human worlds is not the soul, but intention. To understand people is to understand what they intend to do." Ian Hacking, *The Other Side of the Mind* (Book Review), NEW REPUBLIC, June 9, 1986, 30 at 32. Is this concept helpful in analyzing *Vosburg*? Compare this observation by Sharon Lamb, in a book focused in large part on sexual abuse, "If we rely on intentionality as our guide for moral culpability we will be in deep water. First, a man can be cruel without this being his primary aim.... Second, the prepetrator can dissociate his character from the acts in many ways," for example by showing that he has a sterling reputation generally. THE TROUBLE WITH BLAME 83 (Harv. Univ. Press 1996). Does the battery tort require moral culpability?

(6) HIV poses a serious modern problem relating to the liability for unusual consequences imposed for battery. Consider, for example, a suit against American Airlines by a passenger who quarreled with an airline employee about whether he should give her a boarding pass. The plaintiff's lawyer said that when the employee refused to tell the plaintiff his name, the plaintiff grabbed the employee's arm and he retaliated by biting her hand. A test requested by the plaintiff allegedly showed that the employee was positive for HIV. *American Airlines is Sued for Alleged Biting Incident*, WALL ST. J., c. Sept. 1986. If the plaintiff does not show that she herself tests positive for the disease, what are her damages for battery?

(7) Suppose that the wound in *Vosburg* had been caused when the defendant, rushing to his seat when the teacher called the class to order, stumbled against the plaintiff's leg. Should the applicable principle be different?

(8) In his book *On Aggression*, Konrad Lorenz argued that there is "no legitimate outlet for aggressive behavior" in modern communities. He referred to studies by Sydney Margolin of Ute Indians, who were said to "suffer more frequently from neurosis than any other human group," characterizing Margolin's conclusions as that the "cause of the trouble [is] undischarged aggression." Lorenz viewed it as especially significant that Utes are "particularly susceptible to accidents"—specifically, vehicle accidents. He said that "even the expression 'death wish' seems apt" when one considers the "strong inclination ... to self-destructive behavior" familiar to "[a]nybody who has ever driven a fast car when really angry." K. LORENZ, ON AGGRESSION 244–45, 253 (Harcourt Brace & World ed. 1966).

How do you view the *Vosburg* rule in light of Lorenz's conclusions? Ought it to make a difference in the applicable rule as to what constitutes a battery, if the children attend an unpleasant, overcrowded school in a disadvantaged neighborhood? Would it matter if the occurrence had taken place in Tom Sawyer's classroom? In a present-day high school in which physical attacks result in injuries requiring medical attention nearly every day? Suppose the parties were Utes. Would this alter your formulation of the rule?

(9) Would it call for a different rule if the plaintiff in *Vosburg* had been a hemophiliac and the kick caused near-fatal bleeding?

Assume that after the second kick, the plaintiff fell victim to improper medical treatment; would the defendant be responsible for the consequences of that malpractice?

(10) Suppose child A stumbles into child B and bumps against B's raw wound, causing B to jump up screaming, upsetting his desk into a nearby student, C, and injuring C. Or suppose that the impact caused child B to have a temporary tantrum during which he struck out at everyone in the vicinity, and broke the glasses of C. Can C recover in either case? If so, from whom?

(11) It should be noted that the technical requirements for battery do not necessarily include an intended "harmful" contact; an "offensive" one will do. See RESTATEMENT (SECOND) OF TORTS § 13 (1965). But an everyday touching, such as a tap on the shoulder to attract attention, is not usually a battery.[1]

---

1. This is the lesson of *Coward v. Baddeley*, 4 H. & N. 478, 157 Eng. Rep. 927 (Excheq. 1859), in which the plaintiff sued for a beating and imprisonment that he attributed to the defendant firefighter, who apparently took offense when the plaintiff touched him on the shoulder in an effort to get the defendant to change the direction of his hose with the goal of fighting the fire more effectively. Given a jury finding that "the plaintiff did lay hands on the defendant, intending to attract his attention," Pollock, C.B., refused to set aside a plaintiff's verdict, saying that the plaintiff had not acted "with violence to justify giving the plaintiff into custody for an assault."

Yet what if B's casual acquaintance A, rather tipsy at a cocktail party, claps him solidly on the back in hearty greeting and thereby aggravates a wound beneath his shirt?

(12) It is well established that it may be a battery for the defendant to touch an object closely connected with the plaintiff. Recently illustrative, in the context of a case involving a "hostile and abusive working environment," is the action of a company supervisor who pulled open the plaintiff's pants, "exposing her underwear to coworkers." Chavez v. Thomas & Betts Corp., 396 F.3d 1088, 1094, 1100–01 (10th Cir. 2005).

[B] The Culpability Standard in the "Intentional Torts"

PROBLEM*

On September 16, 1975 there was a professional baseball game at Fenway Park in Boston between the defendant, the Baltimore Baseball Club, Inc., playing under the name the Baltimore Orioles, and the Boston Red Sox. The defendant, Ross Grimsley, was a pitcher employed by the defendant Baltimore Club. Some spectators, including the plaintiff, were seated, behind a wire mesh fence, in bleachers located in right field. In order to be ready to pitch in the game, Grimsley, during the first three innings of play, had been warming up by throwing a ball from a pitcher's mound to a plate in the bullpen located near those right field bleachers. The spectators in the bleachers continuously heckled him. On several occasions immediately following heckling Grimsley looked directly at the hecklers, not just into the stands. At the end of the third inning of the game, Grimsley, after his catcher had left his catching position and was walking over to the bench, faced the bleachers and wound up or stretched as though to pitch in the direction of the plate toward which he had been throwing but the ball traveled from Grimsley's hand at more than 80 miles an hour at an angle of 90 degrees to the path from the pitcher's mound to the plate and directly toward the hecklers in the bleachers. The ball passed through the wire mesh fence and hit the plaintiff.

Has Grimsley committed a battery on the plaintiff? What reasoning process would you use to decide the case?

GARRATT v. DAILEY
Washington Supreme Court
46 Wash.2d 197, 279 P.2d 1091 (1955)

HILL, JUSTICE.

The liability of an infant for an alleged battery is presented to this court for the first time. Brian Dailey (age five years, nine months) was visiting with Naomi Garratt, an adult and a sister of the plaintiff, Ruth Garratt, likewise an adult, in the back yard of the plaintiff's home, on July 16, 1951. It is plaintiff's contention that she came out into the back yard to talk with Naomi and that, as she started to sit down in a wood and canvas lawn chair, Brian deliberately pulled it out from under her. The only one of the

* Taken from the statement of facts in a reported case.

three persons present so testifying was Naomi Garratt. (Ruth Garratt, the plaintiff, did not testify as to how or why she fell.) The trial court, unwilling to accept this testimony, adopted instead Brian Dailey's version of what happened, and made the following findings:

III.... that while Naomi Garratt and Brian Dailey were in the back yard the plaintiff, Ruth Garratt, came out of her house into the back yard. Some time subsequent thereto defendant, Brian Dailey, picked up a lightly built wood and canvas lawn chair which was then and there located in the back yard of the above described premises, moved it sideways a few feet and seated himself therein, at which time he discovered the plaintiff, Ruth Garratt, about to sit down at the place where the lawn chair had formerly been, at which time he hurriedly got up from the chair and attempted to move it toward Ruth Garratt to aid her in sitting down in the chair; that due to the defendant's small size and lack of dexterity he was unable to get the lawn chair under the plaintiff in time to prevent her from falling to the ground. That plaintiff fell to the ground and sustained a fracture of her hip, and other injuries and damages as hereinafter set forth.

IV. That the preponderance of the evidence in this case establishes that when the defendant, Brian Dailey, moved the chair in question *he did not have any wilful or unlawful purpose* in doing so; that *he did not have any intent to injure the plaintiff, or any intent to bring about any unauthorized or offensive contact with her person* or any objects appurtenant thereto; that the circumstances which immediately preceded the fall of the plaintiff established that the defendant, *Brian Dailey, did not have purpose, intent or design to perform a prank or to effect an assault and battery upon the person of the plaintiff.*" (Italics ours, for a purpose hereinafter indicated.)

It is conceded that Ruth Garratt's fall resulted in a fractured hip and other painful and serious injuries. To obviate the necessity of a retrial in the event this court determines that she was entitled to a judgment against Brian Dailey, the amount of her damage was found to be $11,000. Plaintiff appeals from a judgment dismissing the action and asks for the entry of a judgment in that amount or a new trial.

. . .

It is urged that Brian's action in moving the chair constituted a battery. A definition (not all-inclusive but sufficient for [our] purpose) of a battery is the intentional infliction of a harmful bodily contact upon another. The rule that determines liability for battery is given in 1 Restatement, Torts, 29, § 13, as:

"An act which, directly or indirectly, is the legal cause of a harmful contact with another's person makes the actor liable to the other, if

"(a) the act is done with the intention of bringing about a harmful or offensive contact or an apprehension thereof to the other or a third person, and

"(b) the contact is not consented to by the other or the other's consent thereto is procured by fraud or duress, and

"(c) the contact is not otherwise privileged."

We have in this case no question of consent or privilege. We therefore proceed to an immediate consideration of intent and its place in the law of battery. In the comment on clause (a), the Restatement says:

"Character of actor's intention. In order that an act may be done with the intention of bringing about a harmful or offensive contact or an apprehension thereof to a particular person, either the other or a third person, the act must be done for the purpose of causing the contact or apprehension or with knowledge on the part of the actor that such contact or apprehension is substantially certain to be produced." See, also, Prosser on Torts 41, § 8.

We have here the conceded volitional act of Brian, i.e., the moving of a chair. Had the plaintiff proved to the satisfaction of the trial court that Brian moved the chair while she was in the act of sitting down, Brian's action would patently have been for the purpose or with the intent of causing the plaintiff's bodily contact with the ground, and she would be entitled to a judgment against him for the resulting damages. Vosburg v. Putney, 1891, 80 Wis. 523, 50 N.W. 403, 14 L.R.A. 226; Briese v. Maechtle,....

The plaintiff based her case on that theory, and the trial court held that she failed in her proof and accepted Brian's version of the facts rather than that given by the eyewitness who testified for the plaintiff. After the trial court determined that the plaintiff had not established her theory of a battery (i.e., that Brian had pulled the chair out from under the plaintiff while she was in the act of sitting down), it then became concerned with whether a battery was established under the facts as it found them to be.

In this connection, we quote another portion of the comment on the "Character of actor's intention," relating to clause (a) of the rule from the Restatement heretofore set forth:

> It is not enough that the act itself is intentionally done and this, even though the actor realizes or should realize that it contains a very grave risk of bringing about the contact or apprehension. Such realization may make the actor's conduct negligent or even reckless but unless he realizes that to a substantial certainty, the contact or apprehension will result, the actor has not that intention which is necessary to make him liable under the rule stated in this section.

A battery would be established if, in addition to plaintiff's fall, it was proved that, when Brian moved the chair, he knew with substantial certainty that the plaintiff would attempt to sit down where the chair had been. If Brian had any of the intents which the trial court found, in the italicized portions of the findings of fact quoted above, that he did not have, he would of course have had the knowledge to which we have referred. The mere absence of any intent to injure the plaintiff or to play a prank on her or to embarrass her, or to commit an assault and battery on her would not absolve him from liability if in fact he had such knowledge. Mercer v. Corbin, 1889, 117 Ind. 450, 20 N.E. 132, 3 L.R.A. 221. Without such knowledge, there would be nothing wrongful about Brian's act in moving the chair and, there being no wrongful act, there would be no liability.

While a finding that Brian had no such knowledge can be inferred from the findings made, we believe that before the plaintiff's action in such a case should be dismissed there should be no question but that the trial court had passed upon that issue; hence, the case should be remanded for clarification of the findings to specifically cover the question of Brian's knowledge, because intent could be inferred therefrom. If the court finds that he had such knowledge the necessary intent will be established and the plaintiff will be entitled to recover, even though there was no purpose to injure or embarrass the plaintiff. Vosburg v. Putney, supra. If Brian did not have such knowledge, there was no wrongful act by him and the basic premise of liability on the theory of a battery was not established.

Holdings

It will be noted that the law of battery as we have discussed it is the law applicable to adults, and no significance has been attached to the fact that Brian was a child less than six years of age when the alleged battery occurred. The only circumstance where Brian's age is of any consequence is in determining what he knew, and there his experience, capacity, and understanding are of course material....

The cause is remanded for clarification, with instructions to make definite findings on the issue of whether Brian Dailey knew with substantial certainty that the plaintiff would attempt to sit down where the chair which he moved had been, and to change the judgment if the findings warrant it....

A TRANSCRIPT

[Cross-examination of Brian Dailey by Mr. Healy, plaintiff's counsel.]

There isn't any question but what at the time that Ruth fell, that you had your hands on the chair and were moving it, is there?

A: Yes. I was moving it over to put it under her, so that she would sit down in it.

Q: Did you pick it up off the ground, or were you just pushing it along the ground?

A: I had picked it up.

Q: You picked it up.

A: Yes.

Q: And you say you were about a head shorter than you are now?

A: Yes.

Q: I wonder if you would stand up, Brian for just a moment. (The witness complied with the request.)

Q: Do you know how tall you are?

A: About four foot four.

Q: About four foot four?

A: Yes.

Q: And if you were a head shorter you would be about six inches shorter than that, wouldn't you?

A: I think so.

Q: I'll put this yardstick alongside of you and I think we can come pretty close to — you are just about right. You are just about four foot four, and your head is just about eight inches long.

Q: Do you think that if you were that much smaller you were able to pick that chair up, instead of pushing it, do you?

A: I might have.

Q: You are not sure whether you picked it up, or whether you were pulling it or pushing it, is that true?

A: Yes.

Q: You might have been pulling it at the time?

A: I might have.

MR. HEALY: You may be seated, Brian.

Q: You don't mean that Ruth started to sit down there was nothing under her, do you?

A: That's right.

Q: What's that?

A: That's right.

Q: That's right?

A: She started to sit down and there was nothing under her.

Q: Well, when you testified here, that when she fell that she was about a foot and a half away, do you mean that she was about a foot and a half away from the chair?

A: Oh, what do you call it? I'll just call it the hole in the ground.

Q: Well, how far away from the chair was she?

A: Oh, I would say about—

Q: Four feet?

A: No. About three and a half feet.

Q: About three and a half feet. And you were in the process of carrying a chair toward her at that time? Is that your testimony?

A: Well, sliding or carrying it.

Q: What's that?

A: Sliding or carrying it.

Q: Sliding or carrying it?

A: Yes.

Q: The chair didn't ever collapse, did it?

A: Well, no.

Q: And it was still standing upright when she fell, wasn't it?

A: Yes.

Q: And if you had been sliding it, it would have collapsed, wouldn't it?

A: Yes.

Q: In order to slide this chair, if there is any grass, or any or any depression at all, it just goes right down, doesn't it?

A: Yes.

Q: The only way in which it stays up is to have it be pulled backwards, so it can't collapse, isn't that true?

A: Yes.

Q: Brian, have you gone home crying because people had talked about you pulling this chair out from under Ruth?

MR. ORTH: Well now, just a minute. I don't think that is pertinent to the issues in this case.

THE COURT: Objection sustained.

Q: You did feel responsible for Ruth's falling, didn't you?

A: Yes.

Q: And—

MR. ORTH: (Interrupting) I'll object to the form of that question. I think this

THE COURT: Well maybe, I can clear it up. Brian, what do you mean when you say you think that you felt responsible? What does that mean to you?

THE WITNESS: I just felt responsible.

THE COURT: Well, do you mean that you felt badly, because this lady was hurt?

THE WITNESS: Yes.

THE COURT: Is that what you mean by responsible?

THE WITNESS: Yes.

THE COURT: Or do you think that you felt that you caused her to be hurt? Which do you mean? Do you think felt bad, because she was hurt, or do you feel that you were the one that caused it?

THE WITNESS: I felt badly that she was hurt.

THE COURT: That's what you mean, when you say that you say that you felt responsible?

THE WITNESS: Yes.

THE COURT: All right. You may proceed.

Q: Brian do you think you had caused her to fall?

A: No.

Q: How far away from Ruth were you when you first picked up the chair?

A: Oh, I would say just about a foot.

Q: You were about a foot away from her, when you first picked up the chair and you were about three and a half feet away from her, when she fell, is that right?

A: Yes.

Q: Then you were further away from her when she fell, than you were when you first picked up the chair?

A: Yes.

Q: Now, you understand what I mean when I say "further away from her", don't you?

A: Yes.

Q: Well, what did I mean?

A: It means a longer ways.

Q: Are you sure you didn't tell your mother some different story than you have told Judge Hale here now, right after the accident?

A: No.

Q: What?

A: No.

Q: Are you sure?

A: Yes.

Q: Did you tell me any different story?

A: I don't recall.

NOTES

(1) How would you put into words the difference between the views of the trial court and the appellate court in *Garratt* about the meaning of the intent requirement of the battery tort?

(2) What social policies would be served by holding Brian Dailey liable for pulling the chair out from under Ms. Garratt? On what empirical assumptions rests the law of battery as the court applies it to Brian Dailey?

What difference should it make in terms of social response to an occurrence like that in *Garratt* or *Vosburg* that it is characterized as a "battery," as "negligence," or as an "accident"?

(3) We have noted that the Federal Tort Claims Act's imposition of liability on the federal government for the torts of employees excludes a group of "intentional" torts including "assault and battery" except, it should be noted, that a 1974 amendment requires the government to compensate for intentional torts by law enforcement officers. Indicative of the technicality of analysis under the statute, paralleling the common law, is a case in which an employee at a receiving dock jumped upon a fellow worker, screaming "boo," pulled the other worker's wool stocking hat over his eyes and began to ride him piggyback. As a result of what was generally viewed as "one-sided horseplay" with no intent to injure, the plaintiff fell forward and struck his face on some meat hooks on the dock. Rejecting an argument that the complaint sounded in negligence, the court emphasized the hornbook rule that the intent necessary for battery was intent to make contact and not to injure. A concurrence, although suggesting that legislative draftsmen might opt otherwise on a clean slate, found that the weight of precedent compelled this interpretation in the "usual, legalistic sense." *Lambertson v. United States*, 528 F.2d 441 (2d Cir.), cert. denied, 426 U.S. 921 (1976).

(4) There is law that a four-year-old may be held for a battery, though not for "negligence." Can you reason why? See *Ellis v. D'Angelo*, 116 Cal. App. 2d 310, 253 P.2d 675 (1953).

Is a four-year-old liable for firing a pistol that he finds behind an unmanned restaurant counter, if he wounds a patron? Compare *Sagnibene v. State Wholesalers, Inc.*, 117 Ga. App. 239, 160 S.E.2d 274 (1968) with *Davis v. Cooper*, 1968 Negl. Cas. 2862 (Tenn. App.1968).

(5) Can a dog commit a battery? A press story reported that a German shepherd caused a gunshot wound to its owner when it picked up a loaded .22-caliber pistol in its teeth and dropped it, whereupon the weapon went off. The owner had been outside his home, training the animal to attack and disarm intruders. He said that he then came back into the house, cleaned the gun and loaded it, and "threw it on a couch." His father then told the dog, "Get it," and the dog picked up the weapon in a holster. However, "the holster wasn't snapped and the gun fell out." *Dog Shoots Owner Who Was Training It*, WASH. POST, Mar. 10, 1981, at A7.

Even if a dog cannot commit a battery, could the owner's father have had to pay a tort judgment for his son's wound?

(6) Can a battery be committed without an assault?

(7) Generally speaking, contributory fault is not a valid defense to an intentional tort. Illustrative of this point is a Maine case in which a job training counselor em-

ployed by the defendant told the plaintiff that he could get him into the Marine Corps—for which the plaintiff had failed to pass the written entrance exam—if he would undergo certain physical tests. These tests turned out to include "bizarre physical activities" that entailed "substantial pain and humiliation." After the plaintiff again failed the Marines' written exam, to which the "tests" devised, by the counselor were obviously irrelevant, he quit the defendant's program, and the defendant fired the counselor. The plaintiff sued for negligence and assault and battery, and the jury brought back a unitary verdict in his favor, without apportioning his injuries between the different liability theories. Although the trial judge refused to give a comparative fault instruction with respect to the intentional tort theories, the jury reduced its verdict by what was described as a "just and equitable sum" to represent the plaintiff's "fault." The trial judge refused to allow this reduction of the judgment, and the supreme court affirmed the full judgment, specifically ratifying the trial judge's refusal to instruct on comparative fault with respect to the assault and battery counts. Effectively viewing the total amount of damages as allocable to the assault and battery claims under the unitary verdict, the supreme court based its decision on the common law principle that contributory negligence is not a defense to intentional torts. *McLain v. Training & Development Corp.*, 572 A.2d 494 (Me. 1990).

(8) What assessment as to the value of Ms. Garratt's claim would you have made as her attorney, considering the facts as they appeared before trial and the possible uncertainty in the law of battery? How would you have viewed the case as a matter of dollars and cents as lawyer for the Daileys? How would the valuations of the respective attorneys likely have changed after the remand? Before the decision in *Vosburg v. Putney, supra* at page 27, what value would you have placed on the plaintiff's claim in that case?

(9) The *Restatement* defines a battery as involving acts "intending to cause a harmful or offensive contact" or "an imminent apprehension of such a contact." RESTATEMENT (SECOND) OF TORTS § 13 (1965). The *Restatement Second*'s definition of intent, adopted after *Garratt v. Dailey*, declares that the term denotes "that the actor desires to cause consequences of his act, or that he believes that the consequences are substantially certain to result from it." *Id.* § 8A. A comment to that section says that "If the actor knows that the consequences are certain, or substantially certain, to result from his act, and still goes ahead, he is treated by the law as if he had in fact desired to produce the result." Would the outcome in *Garratt* be different under this group of definitions?

A draft of the *Third Restatement* varies the language still further. It says that "[a] person acts with the intent to produce a consequence if (a) The person acts with the purpose of producing that consequence; or (b) The person acts knowing that the consequence is substantially certain to result." Restatement (Third) of Torts: Liability for Physical Harm § 1 (Proposed Final Draft No. 1, Apr. 6, 2005).

(10) Tim, who was eight or nine, put a firecracker in the sneaker of Maurice, a seven-year-old playmate, and then lit the firecracker, causing burns to Maurice. Tim "had been lighting firecrackers for about ten minutes before the incident, not holding them, but tossing them on the ground and watching them ignite, jump and spin." Can Maurice successfully sue Tim?

(11) Should a court accept an application for political asylum from a six-year-old child? What is the difference between that issue and the issue of whether a child of almost six can be liable for a battery?

[C] Battered-Woman's Syndrome: A Modern Battery-Related Tort

CUSSEAUX v. PICKETT

Superior Court of New Jersey, Law Division, Bergen County
279 N.J. Super. 335, 652 A.2d 789 (1994)

NAPOLITANO, J.S.C.

I. INTRODUCTION

This matter is before the court on defendant's motion to dismiss the first count of plaintiff's complaint for failure to state a cause of action pursuant to R. 4:6-2(e). The defendant argues that the "battered-woman's syndrome" is not recognized as an affirmative cause of action by the courts of this State. This court denies the motion to dismiss and holds that the "battered-woman's syndrome" is now a cognizable cause of action under the laws of New Jersey.

II. FACTS

Plaintiff, Jean Marie Cusseaux, lived with the defendant, Wilson Pickett, Jr., for a period of about ten years, from 1982 to 1992. Plaintiff alleges that, during this time period, defendant severely mistreated her, jeopardized her health and well-being, and caused her physical injuries on numerous occasions. Plaintiff further alleges that defendant's actions were part of a continuous course of conduct and constituted a pattern of violent behavior, frequently associated with his being intoxicated. Plaintiff alleges that the acts of abuse and violence are too numerous to detail with specificity; however, on a number of occasions, she was required to seek medical attention.[1] As a result of the defendant's behavior, plaintiff alleges that she was caused to suffer the condition of the battered-woman's syndrome, which includes serious personal and emotional injuries that will require medical and other attention. On April 15, 1992, defendant's final assault allegedly caused plaintiff finally to end the relationship.

… [T]he New Jersey Supreme Court has expressly held that trial courts must accord any plaintiff's complaint a "meticulous" and "indulgent" examination. Printing Mart v. Sharp Electronics, 116 N.J. 739, 771, 563 A.2d 31 (1989). In Printing Mart, the Supreme Court held that a reviewing court must [search] the complaint in depth and with liberality [] ascertain whether the fundament of a cause of action may be gleaned even from an obscure statement of a claim, opportunity being given to amend if necessary.

. . .

… [I]t is in keeping with this clear signal from the Supreme Court to seek to preserve a plaintiff's cause of action that this trial court will consider the present application.

---

1. In plaintiff's motion papers, plaintiff alleges several of the acts of violence. Plaintiff was physically assaulted by defendant's fists on April 14, 1986 and July 7, 1990, in December 1990, on April 5, 1992, and on May 15, 1992. On at least one of those dates, her nose was broken and on three of those occasions she was forced to seek treatment at three separate hospital emergency rooms. On other occasions, defendant threw objects at the plaintiff. Specifically, in November of 1988, the defendant struck the plaintiff with a heavy kitchen pot; in March of 1989, plaintiff was struck with an unidentified object; in February 1990, plaintiff was struck with a large corningware dish; and in March of 1990, plaintiff was struck by a gallon container of Chlorox [sic] bleach. The defendant denies these allegations.

B. Battered-Woman's Syndrome

The battered-woman's syndrome was first recognized by the courts in New Jersey in State v. Kelly, 97 N.J. 178, 478 A.2d 364 (1984), where the Court acknowledged it as an element of self-defense....

The Kelly Court relied heavily on the then recently enacted Prevention of Domestic Violence Act, N.J.S.A. 2C:25-1 to 2C:25-16.

[The court quotes from a later reenactment of the statute]:

> The Legislature finds and declares that domestic violence is a serious crime against society; that there are thousands of persons in this State who are regularly beaten, tortured and in some cases even killed by their spouses or cohabitant; that a significant number of women who are assaulted are pregnant; that victims of domestic violence come from all social and economic backgrounds and ethnic groups; that there is a positive correlation between spousal abuse and child abuse; and that children, even when they are not themselves physically assaulted, suffer deep and lasting emotional effects from exposure to domestic violence. It is therefore, the intent of the Legislature to assure the victims of domestic violence the maximum protection from abuse the law can provide.

> * * *

> ... Further, <u>it is the responsibility of the courts to protect victims of violence that occurs in a family or family-like setting by providing access to both emergent and long-term civil and criminal remedies and sanctions</u>, and by ordering those remedies and sanctions that are available to assure the safety of the victims and the public. To that end, the Legislature encourages ... the broad application of the remedies available under this act in the civil and criminal courts of this state....

[N.J.S.A. 2C:25-18 (emphases added).]

The Court stated that there is a high incidence of unreported abuse because there exists a stigma against battered women that is institutionalized in the attitudes of law enforcement agencies, not to mention the stereotypes and myths concerning the characteristics of battered women and their reasons for staying in battering relationships.... [4] However, as the problem began receiving more attention, the focus turned to the effects a sustained pattern of physical and psychological abuse can have on a woman.

The Kelly Court stated that the battered-woman's syndrome is

> a series of common characteristics that appear in women who are abused physically and psychologically over an extended period of time by the dominant male figure in their lives. [Kelly, supra, 97 N.J. at 193, 478 A.2d 364.]

The abuse is cyclical. The first stage is characterized by minor battering incidents and verbal abuse while the woman, beset by fear and tension, attempts to be as placating and passive as possible in order to stave off more serious violence ... The second phase is characterized by acute battering, which is triggered when the tension between the woman and the batterer becomes intolerable ... The third phase is characterized by extreme contrition and loving behavior on the part of the battering male.

---

4. Some of the popular misconceptions are that battered women actually enjoy being beaten and that they purposely provoke their mates into beating them and that they are free to leave those relationships at any time. *Kelly, supra* 97 N.J. at 192, 478 A.2d 364....

During this period the man will often mix his pleas for forgiveness and protestations of devotion with promises to seek professional help, to stop drinking, and to refrain from further violence ...

It is this third phase that explains why more women simply do not leave their abusers.

Different women have different reactions to this cycle. Some perceive it as normal, some may not wish to acknowledge the reality of the situation and still others become so demoralized and degraded by the fact that they cannot predict or control the violence that they sink into a state of psychological paralysis and become unable to take any action at all to improve or alter the situation. There is a tendency in battered women to believe in the omnipotence or strength of their battering husbands and thus to feel that any attempt to resist is hopeless ... Further, external social and economic factors often make it difficult for some women to extricate themselves from battering relationships.... Women typically earn less money and are more responsible for child care than men.

> Thus, in a violent confrontation where the first reaction might be to flee, women realize soon that there may be no place to go. Moreover, the stigma that attaches to a woman who leaves the family unit without her children undoubtedly acts as a further deterrent to moving out ... In addition, these women are frequently unwilling to confide in others because of the shame, humiliation, and fear of reprisal by their husbands. Thus, they literally become trapped by their own fear....

The Kelly Court stated that

> [t]he combination of all of these symptoms—resulting from sustained psychological and physical trauma compounded by aggravating social and economic factors—constitutes the battered-woman's syndrome. Only by understanding these unique pressures that force battered women to remain with their mates, despite their long-standing and reasonable fear of severe bodily harm and the isolation that being a battered woman creates, can a battered woman's state of mind be accurately and fairly understood....

Notwithstanding, there has yet to be a civil case in New Jersey that has recognized the battered-woman's syndrome. Thus, it is this case of first impression which now addresses whether the battered-woman's syndrome is a cognizable cause of action under the laws of New Jersey.

IV. ANALYSIS

It is well established in this State that an injured party may sustain a cause of action for serious personal and emotional injuries that are directly and causally related to the actions of another person.... As discussed above, the Legislature has specifically found domestic violence to be a serious crime against society.... More importantly, in enacting the Prevention of Domestic Violence Act, the Legislature recognized that our judicial and law enforcement system was insufficient to address the problem. If this Act had never become law, the ubiquitous deficiency of our legal system would continue in spite of the fact that the acts listed among those classified as "domestic violence" under the statute were already criminal offenses.[5]

---

5. N.J.S.A. 2C:25-19 states that "Domestic Violence" means the occurrence of one or more of the following acts inflicted upon a person protected under this act by an adult or an emancipated minor:

(1) Homicide	N.J.S. 2C:11-1 et seq.
(2) Assault	N.J.S. 2C:12-1
(3) Terroristic threats	N.J.S. 2C:12-3

The efforts of the Legislature to this end should be applauded. However, they are but steps in the right direction. As is the case with the domestic violence statute where existing criminal statutes were inadequate, so too are the civil laws of assault and battery insufficient to redress the harms suffered as a result of domestic violence. Domestic violence is a plague on our social structure and a frontal assault on the institution of the family. The battered-woman's syndrome is but one of the pernicious symptoms of that plague. Though the courts would be hard-pressed to prescribe a panacea for all domestic violence, they are entrusted with the power to fashion a palliative when necessary. The underpinning of our common law and public policy demand that, where the Legislature has not gone far enough, the courts must fill the interstices. As the Legislature stated,

> it is the responsibility of the courts to protect victims of violence that occurs in a family or family-like setting by providing access to both emergent and long-term civil and criminal remedies and sanctions....

[N.J.S.A. 2C:25-18....]

Thus, this court will recognize the battered-woman's syndrome as an affirmative cause of action under the laws of New Jersey.

In order to state a cause of action for the battered-woman's syndrome, the plaintiff must allege the following elements. The plaintiff must show 1) involvement in a marital or marital-like intimate relationship; and 2) physical or psychological abuse perpetrated by the dominant partner to the relationship over an extended period of time[6] and 3) the aforestated abuse has caused recurring physical or psychological injury over the course of the relationship; and 4) a past or present inability to take any action to improve or alter the situation unilaterally.[7]

In Laughlin v. Breaux, 515 So.2d 480 (La.App. 1 Cir.1987), the court was faced with a similar application by a woman seeking affirmative damages based upon the battered-woman's syndrome. The Louisiana court rejected the argument that the battered-woman's syndrome constituted a continuing tort.... Rather, the court stated that each incident of battery and assault was a separate cause of action. Thus, the plaintiff was precluded from recovering damages for incidents that occurred beyond the effective

---

(4) Kidnapping	N.J.S. 2C:13-1
(5) Criminal restraint	N.J.S. 2C:13-2
(6) False imprisonment	N.J.S. 2C:13-3
(7) Sexual assault	N.J.S. 2C:14-2
(8) Criminal sexual conduct	N.J.S. 2C:14-3
(9) Lewdness	N.J.S. 2C:14-4
(10) Criminal mischief	N.J.S. 2C:17-3
(11) Burglary	N.J.S. 2C:18-2
(12) Criminal trespass	N.J.S. 2C:18-3
(13) Harassment	N.J.S. 2C:33-4

6. In order to be classified as a battered woman, the victim must go through the battering cycle at least twice. Any woman may find herself in an abusive relationship with a man once. If it occurs a second time, and she remains in the situation, she may be a battered woman. *Kelly*, supra, 97 N.J. at 193, 478 A.2d 364....

7. Nothing in this opinion should be construed to limit the application of these principles only to women in traditional marital or marital-like relationships. Indeed, in any domestic intimate partnership, the victim, whether female or male, whether the union is heterosexual or homosexual, may plead a battered-person syndrome so long as the aforementioned requirements are met. It is the unhappy history of domestic violence against women in traditional marital relationships which has given this tort its name.

statute of limitations period. This Court totally rejects the Laughlin holding to the extent that it asserts that the incidents of assault and battery were individual causes of action rather than a continuing tort. Because the battered-woman's syndrome is the result of a continuing pattern of abuse and violent behavior that causes continuing damage, it must be treated in the same way as a continuing tort. It would be contrary to the public policy of this State, not to mention cruel, to limit recovery to only those individual incidents of assault and battery for which the applicable statute of limitations has not yet run. The mate who is responsible for creating the condition suffered by the battered victim must be made to account for his actions—all of his actions. Failure to allow affirmative recovery under these circumstances would be tantamount to the courts condoning the continued abusive treatment of women in the domestic sphere. This the courts cannot and will never do.

...

Douglas D. Scherer, *Tort Remedies for Victims of Domestic Abuse*
43 S.C. L. Rev. 543 (1992)*

More than three million American women suffer severe beatings from their husbands each year.[1]

...

In light of this, why have trial lawyers not been more active in bringing civil actions for money damages based upon domestic violence? Why have they not furthered the public interest by combatting this morally repugnant conduct? The assumption of the author is that trial lawyers simply are unaware of the potential for significant monetary damages in these actions.

...

Follingstad and others evaluated the interrelationship between physical and emotional abuse through interviews with 234 abused women. They identified different types of emotional abuse and analyzed the frequency of occurrence and impact on the victim. They discussed the forms of emotional abuse identified by other researchers, including "ridicule, verbal harassment, and name-calling"; "isolation (either social or financial)"; "jealousy/possessiveness"; "verbal threats of abuse, harm, or torture"; "threats to divorce or abandon ... or to have an affair"; and "damage to or destruction of the personal property of the woman." The Follingstad study revealed that 229 of the 234 abused women (98%) had "experienced at least one incident of emotional abuse" and that "[t]he vast majority of the women (72%) reported experiencing four or more types of emotional abuse." ...

According to Sonkin, Martin, and Walker, "[p]erception of loss of control, which is inherent in battering relationships, is one of the critical factors causing psychological injury to the battered woman." This combines with feelings of betrayal, fear of another beating, lack of justice, and "fear that men will make good their threats to take away

---

1. HANDBOOK OF FAMILY VIOLENCE 3 (VINCENT B. VAN HASSELT et al. eds., 1988).

their children" and creates a condition of "learned helplessness." In many women psychological injury "forms a constellation of symptoms named Battered Women's Syndrome." Symptoms "include anxiety, fear, depression, shock, anger, compassion, guilt, humiliation, confused thinking, intrusive memories, uncontrolled reexperiencing of traumatic events, rigidity, lack of trust, suspiciousness, hypervigilance, and increased startle response to cues of possible violence."

. . .

Civil actions for battery, assault, and intentional infliction of emotional distress are effective, victim-controlled means for obtaining remedy and discouraging future abusive conduct, especially if there is no existing marital relationship. Research for this Article revealed, however, an astonishing underutilization of these civil causes of action. Among approximately 2600 reported state cases of battery, assault, or both, from 1981 through 1990, only fifty-three involved adult parties in domestic relationships. Similarly, during the same time frame, only four reported federal cases involved a claim or counterclaim between adult parties in a domestic relationship. From 1958 through 1990 slightly more than 6000 intentional infliction of emotional distress cases were reported from all state and federal courts. Evaluation of these cases revealed a total of eighteen in which courts have applied the tort action to a domestic abuse fact pattern. The infrequent use of tort actions reflects surprising reluctance by lawyers to use civil actions for damages in domestic abuse cases, even though the judicial response to such cases has been overwhelmingly favorable.

. . .

NOTE

How do you account for the statistics indicating that there are so relatively few suits by abused spouses against their abusers? Is the main reason the lack of knowledge by lawyers about the legal potential of such litigation?

[D] Constitutional Dimensions of Intentional Violations of Individual Rights

GRAHAM v. CONNOR
United States Supreme Court
490 U.S. 386, 109 S.Ct. 1865 (1989)

Chief Justice REHNQUIST delivered the opinion of the Court.

This case requires us to decide what constitutional standard governs a free citizen's claim that law enforcement officials used excessive force in the course of making an arrest, investigatory stop, or other "seizure" of his person. We hold that such claims are properly analyzed under the Fourth Amendment's "objective reasonableness" standard, rather than under a substantive due process standard.

In this action under 42 U.S.C. § 1983, petitioner Dethorne Graham seeks to recover damages for injuries allegedly sustained when law enforcement officers used physical force against him during the course of an investigatory stop. Because the case comes to us from a decision of the Court of Appeals affirming the entry of a directed verdict for respondents, we take the evidence hereafter noted in the light most favorable to petitioner. On November 12, 1984, Graham, a diabetic, felt the onset of an insulin reaction. He asked a friend, William Berry, to drive him to a nearby convenience store so he could purchase some orange juice to counteract the reaction. Berry agreed, but when Graham entered the store, he saw a number of people ahead of him in the checkout line. Concerned about the delay, he hurried out of the store and asked Berry to drive him to a friend's house instead.

Respondent Connor, an officer of the Charlotte, North Carolina, Police Department, saw Graham hastily enter and leave the store. The officer became suspicious that something was amiss and followed Berry's car. About one-half mile from the store, he made an investigative stop. Although Berry told Connor that Graham was simply suffering from a "sugar reaction," the officer ordered Berry and Graham to wait while he found out what, if anything, had happened at the convenience store. When Officer Connor returned to his patrol car to call for backup assistance, Graham got out of the car, ran around it twice, and finally sat down on the curb, where he passed out briefly.

In the ensuing confusion, a number of other Charlotte police officers arrived on the scene in response to Officer Connor's request for backup. One of the officers rolled Graham over on the sidewalk and cuffed his hands tightly behind his back, ignoring Berry's pleas to get him some sugar. Another officer said: "I've seen a lot of people with sugar diabetes that never acted like this. Ain't nothing wrong with the M.F. but drunk. Lock the S.B. up." ... Several officers then lifted Graham up from behind, carried him over to Berry's car, and placed him face down on its hood. Regaining consciousness, Graham asked the officers to check in his wallet for a diabetic decal that he carried. In response, one of the officers told him to "shut up" and shoved his face down against the hood of the car. Four officers grabbed Graham and threw him headfirst into the police car. A friend of Graham's brought some orange juice to the car, but the officers refused to let him have it. Finally, Officer O'Connor received a report that Graham had done nothing wrong at the convenience store, and the officers drove him home and released him.

At some point during his encounter with the police, Graham sustained a broken foot, cuts on his wrists, a bruised forehead, and an injured shoulder; he also claims to have developed a loud ringing in his right ear that continues to this day. He commenced this action under 42 U.S.C. § 1983 against the individual officers involved in the incident, all of whom are respondents here, alleging that they had used excessive force in making the investigatory stop, in violation of "rights secured to him under the Fourteenth Amendment to the United States Constitution and 42 U.S.C. § 1983." ... [2] The case was tried before a jury. At the close of petitioner's evidence, respondents moved for a directed verdict. In ruling on that motion, the District Court considered the following four factors, which it identified as "[t]he factors to be considered in determining when the excessive use of force gives rise to a cause of action under § 1983: (1) the need for the application of force; (2) the relationship between that need and the amount of force that was used; (3) the extent of the injury inflicted; and (4) [w]hether the force was applied in a good faith effort to maintain and restore discipline or maliciously and sadistically for the very purpose of causing harm." ... Finding that the amount of force used by the officers was "appropriate under the circumstances," that "[t]here was no discernable injury inflicted," and that the force used "was not applied maliciously or sadistically for the very purpose of causing harm," but in "a good faith effort to maintain or restore

---

2. Petitioner also asserted pendent state-law claims of assault, false imprisonment, and intentional infliction of emotional distress. Those claims have been dismissed from the case and are not before this Court.

order in the face of a potentially explosive situation," ... the District Court granted respondents' motion for a directed verdict.

A divided panel of the Court of Appeals for the Fourth Circuit affirmed.... The majority ruled first that the District Court had applied the correct legal standard in assessing petitioner's excessive force claim.... Without attempting to identify the specific constitutional provision under which that claim arose, the majority endorsed the four-factor test applied by the District Court as generally applicable to all claims of "constitutionally excessive force" brought against governmental officials.... The majority rejected petitioner's argument, based on Circuit precedent, that it was error to require him to prove that the allegedly excessive force used against him was applied "maliciously and sadistically for the very purpose of causing harm." Ibid. Finally, the majority held that a reasonable jury applying the four-part test it had just endorsed to petitioner's evidence "could not find that the force applied was constitutionally excessive." ... We granted certiorari ... and now reverse.

Fifteen years ago, in Johnson v. Glick, 481 F.2d 1028, ... the Court of Appeals for the Second Circuit addressed a § 1983 damages claim filed by a pretrial detainee who claimed that a guard had assaulted him without justification. In evaluating the detainee's claim, Judge Friendly applied neither the Fourth Amendment nor the Eighth, the two most textually obvious sources of constitutional protection against physically abusive governmental conduct. Instead, he looked to "substantive due process," holding that "quite apart from any 'specific' of the Bill of Rights, application of undue force by law enforcement officers deprives a suspect of liberty without due process of law." ... As support for this proposition, he relied upon our decision in Rochin v. California ... which used the Due Process Clause to avoid a criminal conviction based on evidence obtained by pumping the defendant's stomach.... If a police officer's use of force which "shocks the conscience" could justify setting aside a criminal conviction, Judge Friendly reasoned, a correctional officer's use of similarly excessive force must give rise to a due process violation actionable under § 1983. Ibid. Judge Friendly went on to set forth four factors to guide courts in determining "whether the constitutional line has been crossed" by a particular use of force—the same four factors relied upon by the courts below in this case....

In the years following Johnson v. Glick, the vast majority of federal courts have applied its four-part "substantive due process" test indiscriminately to all excessive force claims lodged against law enforcement and prison officials under § 1983, without considering whether the particular application of force might implicate a more specific constitutional right governed by a different standard. Indeed, many courts have seemed to assume, as did the courts below in this case, that there is a generic "right" to be free from excessive force, grounded not in any particular constitutional provision but rather in "basic principles of § 1983 jurisprudence."

We reject this notion that all excessive force claims brought under § 1983 are governed by a single generic standard. As we have said many times, § 1983 "is not itself a source of substantive rights," but merely provides "a method for vindicating federal rights elsewhere conferred." Baker v. McCollan.... In addressing an excessive force claim brought under § 1983, analysis begins by identifying the specific constitutional right allegedly infringed by the challenged application of force.... In most instances, that will be either the Fourth Amendment's prohibition against unreasonable seizures of the person, or the Eighth Amendment's ban on cruel and unusual punishments, which are the two primary sources of constitutional protection against physically abusive governmental conduct. The validity of the claim must then be judged by reference to the specific constitutional standard which governs that right, rather than to some generalized "excessive force" standard....

Where, as here, the excessive force claim arises in the context of an arrest or investigatory stop of a free citizen, it is most properly characterized as one invoking the protections of the Fourth Amendment, which guarantees citizens the right "to be secure in their persons ... against unreasonable ... seizures" of the person. This much is clear from our decision in Tennessee v. Garner.... In Garner, we addressed a claim that the use of deadly force to apprehend a fleeing suspect who did not appear to be armed or otherwise dangerous violated the suspect's constitutional rights, notwithstanding the existence of probable cause to arrest. Though the complaint alleged violations of both the Fourth Amendment and the Due Process Clause, ... we analyzed the constitutionality of the challenged application of force solely by reference to the Fourth Amendment's prohibition against unreasonable seizures of the person, holding that the "reasonableness" of a particular seizure depends not only on when it is made, but also on how it is carried out.... Today we make explicit what was implicit in Garner's analysis, and hold that all claims that law enforcement officers have used excessive force—deadly or not—in the course of an arrest, investigatory stop, or other "seizure" of a free citizen should be analyzed under the Fourth Amendment and its "reasonableness" standard, rather than under a "substantive due process" approach. Because the Fourth Amendment provides an explicit textual source of constitutional protection against this sort of physically intrusive governmental conduct, that Amendment, not the more generalized notion of "substantive due process," must be the guide for analyzing these claims.

Determining whether the force used to effect a particular seizure is "reasonable" under the Fourth Amendment requires a careful balancing of "'the nature and quality of the intrusion on the individual's Fourth Amendment interests'" against the countervailing governmental interests at stake.... Our Fourth Amendment jurisprudence has long recognized that the right to make an arrest or investigatory stop necessarily carries with it the right to use some degree of physical coercion or threat thereof to effect it.... Because "[t]he test of reasonableness under the Fourth Amendment is not capable of precise definition or mechanical application," ... however, its proper application requires careful attention to the facts and circumstances of each particular case, including the severity of the crime at issue, whether the suspect poses an immediate threat to the safety of the officers or others, and whether he is actively resisting arrest or attempting to evade arrest by flight....

The "reasonableness" of a particular use of force must be judged from the perspective of a reasonable officer on the scene, rather than with the 20/20 vision of hindsight.... With respect to a claim of excessive force, the same standard of reasonableness at the moment applies:

"Not every push or shove, even if it may later seem unnecessary in the peace of a judge's chambers," ... violates the Fourth Amendment. The calculus of reasonableness must embody allowance for the fact that police officers are often forced to make split-second judgments—in circumstances that are tense, uncertain, and rapidly evolving—about the amount of force that is necessary in a particular situation.

As in other Fourth Amendment contexts, however, the "reasonableness" inquiry in an excessive force case is an objective one: the question is whether the officers' actions are "objectively reasonable" in light of the facts and circumstances confronting them, without regard to their underlying intent or motivation.... An officer's evil intentions will not make a Fourth Amendment violation out of an objectively reasonable use of force; nor will an officer's good intentions make an objectively unreasonable use of force constitutional....

Because petitioner's excessive force claim is one arising under the Fourth Amendment, the Court of Appeals erred in analyzing it under the four-part Johnson v. Glick test. That test, which requires consideration of whether the individual officers acted in "good faith" or "maliciously and sadistically for the very purpose of causing harm," is incompatible with a proper Fourth Amendment analysis. We do not agree with the Court of Appeals' suggestion ... that the "malicious and sadistic" inquiry is merely another way of describing conduct that is objectively unreasonable under the circumstances. Whatever the empirical correlations between "malicious and sadistic" behavior and objective unreasonableness may be, the fact remains that the "malicious and sadistic" factor puts in issue the subjective motivations of the individual officers, which our prior cases make clear has no bearing on whether a particular seizure is "unreasonable" under the Fourth Amendment. Nor do we agree with the Court of Appeals' conclusion ... that because the subjective motivations of the individual officers are of central importance in deciding whether force used against a convicted prisoner violates the Eighth Amendment, ... it cannot be reversible error to inquire into them in deciding whether force used against a suspect or arrestee violates the Fourth Amendment. Differing standards under the Fourth and Eighth Amendments are hardly surprising: the terms "cruel" and "punishments" clearly suggest some inquiry into subjective state of mind, whereas the term "unreasonable" does not. Moreover, the less protective Eighth Amendment standard applies "only after the State has complied with the constitutional guarantees traditionally associated with criminal prosecutions." ... The Fourth Amendment inquiry is one of "objective reasonableness" under the circumstances, and subjective concepts like "malice" and "sadism" have no proper place in that inquiry.

Because the Court of Appeals reviewed the District Court's ruling on the motion for directed verdict under an erroneous view of the governing substantive law, its judgment must be vacated and the case remanded to that court for reconsideration of that issue under the proper Fourth Amendment standard.

. . .

[The concurring opinion of Justice Blackmun is omitted.]

NOTES

(1) The governing law in *Graham*, 42 U.S.C. § 1983, is a civil rights statute from the Reconstruction era that has been expanded, by interpretation by the Supreme Court, to cover a multitude of citizens' claims against government officers and, in some cases, against governments themselves. The very last material in this book deals with the development of the section 1983 cause of action in more detail.

(2) What are the sources of law, both constitutional and statutory, that are at issue in *Graham*? Which source of constitutional law prevails?

(3) How does the standard for constitutionally excessive force adopted by the Court compare with the *Restatement*'s definition of the intentionality requirement for battery?

(4) The Court points out, in footnote 2, that the plaintiff had also asserted state law tort claims. Was this an assault or battery at common law? If those remedies were available, why would Congress have intended at all that a federal statutory remedy, based on the Constitution, should apply to situations of this sort?

(5) How do the following legal standards compare with one another?

 (a) The intentionality requirement for battery

 (b) The standard employed by the district court in *Graham*

    (c) A test that asks whether the defendant "used greater force than was reasonably necessary"[1]

    (d) The majority's test in *Graham*

What is the relationship between these standards governing the conduct of police defendants and the legal privileges of police officers in arrest situations? Is there a parallel between the legal standard applicable to a policeman in an arrest situation and that applicable to battery claims like those of the plaintiffs in *Vosburg* and *Garratt*?

NOTE ON POLICE BRUTALITY

Although section 1983 has applications across a wide range of government activity, one of its most frequent appearances in court concerns police brutality. That sort of conduct may also be the subject of ordinary tort suits in state court, under such headings as assault, battery, false arrest, and false imprisonment.

The problem is perennial, stemming from the very existence of crime and the need to control it, as well as the emotions that, often understandably, accompany police behavior in highly charged and sometimes dangerous circumstances. Indicative of the quantitative importance of the problem are 1997 New York City data, indicating that personal injury claims against the police department increased by 80 per cent in a decade and that payouts for such claims rose from $19.5 million to $27.5 million in the year ending June 1997.[1]

As is the case with tort suits generally, the overwhelming number of police misconduct suits are settled. New York City lawyers took only 24 of 527 cases to court in 1996, winning 16. A news report summarizes the "pragmatic reasons" for settlement as including the sympathetic nature of some plaintiffs and the fact that officers may be "defensive, inarticulate or sloppy in procedural work."[2]

A byproduct of lawsuits for police misconduct is information about that kind of behavior. The Los Angeles Sheriff's Department reportedly uses data on those suits "to help identify troublesome police officers and patterns of misconduct," and this may have contributed to a substantial drop in lawsuits and payouts.[3]

§ 2.03 False Imprisonment

THE RESTATEMENT ON FALSE IMPRISONMENT[1]

§ 35. False Imprisonment

(1) An actor is subject to liability to another for false imprisonment if

(a) he acts intending to confine the other or a third person within boundaries fixed by the actor, and

(b) his act directly or indirectly results in such a confinement of the other, and

---

1. This was the test used in jury instructions in a Fourth Circuit case contemporaneous with *Graham*, *Justice v. Dennis*, 834 F.2d 380 (4th Cir. 1987).

1. Deborah Sontag & Dan Barry, *The Price of Brutality*, N.Y. Times, Sept. 17, 1997, page A-1 & jump.

2. *Id.*

3. *Id.*

1. Restatement (Second) of Torts §§ 35–37, 40–42, © 1965 by The American Law Institute. Reproduced with permission.

(c) the other is conscious of the confinement or is harmed by it.

(2) An act which is not done with the intention stated in Subsection (1, a) does not make the actor liable to the other for a merely transitory or otherwise harmless confinement, although the act involves an unreasonable risk of imposing it and therefore would be negligent or reckless if the risk threatened bodily harm.

§36. What Constitutes Confinement

(1) To make the actor liable for false imprisonment, the other's confinement within the boundaries fixed by the actor must be complete.

(2) The confinement is complete although there is a reasonable means of escape, unless the other knows of it.

(3) The actor does not become liable for false imprisonment by intentionally preventing another from going in a particular direction in which he has a right or privilege to go.

§37. Confinement: How Caused

If an act is done with the intent to confine another, and such act is the legal cause of confinement to another, it is immaterial whether the act directly or indirectly causes the confinement.

§40. Confinement by Threats of Physical Force

The confinement may be by submission to a threat to apply physical force to the other's person immediately upon the other's going or attempting to go beyond the area in which the actor intends to confine him.

§40A. Confinement by Other Duress

The confinement may be by submission to duress other than threats of physical force, where such duress is sufficient to make the consent given ineffective to bar the action.

§41. Confinement by Asserted Legal Authority

(1) The confinement may be by taking a person into custody under an asserted legal authority.

(2) The custody is complete if the person against whom and in whose presence the authority is asserted believes it to be valid, or is in doubt as to its validity, and submits to it.

§42. Knowledge of Confinement

Under the rule stated in §35, there is no liability for intentionally confining another unless the person physically restrained knows of the confinement or is harmed by it.

Donald S. Cohen, *False Imprisonment: A Re-Examination of the Necessity for Awareness of Confinement*
43 Tenn. L. Rev. 109, 117–119 (1975)[*]

. . .

Elimination of this antiquated element is consistent with the continuing trend of extending liability for false imprisonment and infusing increased flexibility into judi-

---

* The full text of this article appeared at 43 Tenn. L. Rev. 109 (1975) and this excerpt appears here by permission of the Tennessee Law Review Association, Inc.

cial analysis of the traditional prerequisites for recovery. For instance, recovery does not depend on confinement for a particular period of time. Any unlawful incarceration without consent, however short, is compensable. It may even be momentary. If even momentary detention is redressable, it appears anomalous to deny recovery for what may be a lengthy intentional confinement merely because the damage to personal security and dignity resulting from it occurs after it has ended. The consequences may be as serious then as they would have been with earlier recognition of the confinement.

....

A recent case dealing with awareness of restraint is Tufte v. City of Tacoma,[52] in which the city was held liable for imprisoning a diabetic suffering from an insulin reaction. Although the initial arrest was held proper because the red-eyed plaintiff was found slumped over the steering wheel of his automobile and exhibited slurred speech and unsteady gait when aroused, the court said this evidence of apparent intoxication would not prevent recovery for the period of incarceration beginning after the city received such knowledge as would negative the belief of intoxication. During most of his detention in the drunk tank, Tufte was totally oblivious to his surroundings, and the court found that the wrongful confinement began after the initial privilege elapsed but apparently while Tufte was still unaware of his surroundings. Although the court did discuss the possible physical brain damage that might have resulted from the restraint, it did not rely on that physical injury as a necessary element.

> [A]ppellant was under a duty to release respondent from confinement, more particularly because of the extreme danger to respondent's health attendant upon lack of immediate care.[53]

The Tufte case, therefore, provides more current support for the conclusion that wrongful confinement of an unaware plaintiff is compensable, and it does not rely entirely on the presence of physical harm.

NOTES

(1) If you were drafting a false imprisonment section for the *Restatement Third*, would you make reasonableness a test of the defendant's conduct?

(2) What is the principal interest protected by the tort of false imprisonment? Is it an interest in the physical freedom of the body, an interest in not having the psychological feeling of restraint, or something else?

(3) What policy bases are predominant for the tort of false imprisonment? Would a court be concerned primarily with deterring behavior of that sort in the future? With compensating the plaintiff for dignitary or other losses? With preventing the plaintiff from taking revenge on the defendant? With some other goal?

(4) Suppose an airplane passenger concludes, after boarding the craft that it will be dangerous to fly. After a three-hour delay in leaving the runway, he thrice asks the captain to let him off the plane, but the captain refuses. Has the captain falsely imprisoned him? The case from which this question was taken involved a flight from Washington, D.C. to New York City. Would it make a difference if the destination were Hong Kong?

---

52. 71 Wash. 2d 866, 431 P.2d 183 (1967).
53. *Id.* at 872, 431 P.2d 186–87 (emphasis added).

§ 2.04 Intentional Infliction of Emotional Distress

PROBLEM

Suit Hits Broadcast Citing Boy's Cancer

CHICAGO SUN-TIMES, Aug. 9, 1978, at 100
By Lillian Williams

The parents of a 12-year-old boy, who learned while watching a televised baseball game that he was dying of bone cancer, filed suit Tuesday for $1 million against the American Broadcasting Co. and the Chicago Cubs.

Scott Crull died last Aug. 22, two weeks after it was announced during the game that the boy had terminal cancer.

The Circuit Court suit charged the network, the Cubs and other defendants with ... causing Scott and his parent, Mr. and Mrs. Dwight L. Crull, "extreme emotional distress."

Because of "reckless acts and outrageous conduct" the Crulls have suffered emotionally and are taking sedatives and other medication, the suit said.

The complaint recounted as background for the claim:

Scott was bedridden with incurable bone cancer but was unaware of the terminal nature of his illness. He was a baseball fan and idolized Cubs outfielder Bobby Murcer.

A friend of the Crull family telephoned the public relations department of the Cubs and asked if Murcer would call the boy to cheer him up and create a "happy diversion" for him.

In the call, the Cubs employee was specifically told that the family wanted no mention made of Scott's terminal condition because the youngster did not know it.

During the broadcast, exactly a year ago Tuesday, ABC Monday Night Baseball announcer Keith Jackson said in substance "that Murcer had hit his home run for Scott, and that Scott was dying of bone cancer," the suit related.

Should the court deny a motion to dismiss?

RUSSELL v. SALVE REGINA COLLEGE

United States District Court, Rhode Island
649 F. Supp. 391 (1986)

SELYA, DISTRICT JUDGE.

This case, brought under diversity jurisdiction, 28 U.S.C. § 1332(a), raises a host of intriguing federal and state law questions in an exotic factual context. Briefly put, the plaintiff, Sharon Russell, a citizen and resident of East Hartford, Connecticut, was expelled from Salve Regina College ("Salve" or "College") because of her unwillingness and/or inability to control an extreme chronic weight problem. She now sues for damages....

I. BACKGROUND

Salve is a religiously affiliated college located in Newport, Rhode Island, administered by the Sisters of Mercy of the Roman Catholic Church. Russell was admitted to the College by early decision in the winter of 1981–82. She began her studies in September 1982. Russell's interest in a nursing career antedated her matriculation: she had applied only to colleges with nursing programs and had expressed her intention to pursue such a course of study both in her original application to Salve and in her admissions interview. She commenced her academic endeavors at the College with the avowed intention of gaining admittance to Salve's program of nursing education.

During her inaugural year at the College, there is rather fragile evidence that Russell sought some treatment for obesity. At various times during that school year, her 5' 6" frame recorded weights between 306 and 315 pounds according to data on file at the College's health services unit. It is plain that, although she achieved no meaningful weight loss during her freshman year, Russell was considerably more successful as a student. Her work in liberal arts courses was adequate and her grades were respectable. Consequently, Russell was admitted to the nursing program, effective at the start of her sophomore year. She was given a copy of the "Nursing Handbook" (Handbook) issued by the College, and clearly understood that the Handbook set out the requirements for successful completion of the degree in nursing.

The fabric of Russell's aspirations began to unravel in the fall of 1983, when she entered her sophomore year (her first as a nursing student per se). The parties have presented an intricate (and sometimes conflicting) history of the interaction between the plaintiff and her sundry academic supervisors. It would serve no useful purpose at this juncture fully to recapitulate those events, or to attempt to reconcile every conflict. After all, the mechanism of Rule 56 does not require that there be no unresolved questions of fact; it is sufficient if there are no genuine issues remaining as to any material facts.

It suffices for the moment to say that there were myriad problems along the way: the agonizing search for uniforms and scrub gowns that would fit a woman of Russell's girth; a tendency on the part of faculty members to employ Russell in order to model hospital procedures incident to the care of obese patients; prolonged lectures and discussions about the desirability of weight loss; and so on and so forth. Indeed, the record reveals a veritable smorgasbord of verbal exchanges characterized by one side as "torment" or "humiliation" and by the other as "expressions of concern" or "forthright statements of school policy." (It takes little imagination to decipher which litigants are wont to apply which epithets to which actions.)

The court recognizes, of course, that sadism and benevolence—like beauty—often reside principally in the eye of the beholder. And, the court has neither the need nor the means to attempt to discern the subjective motives of myriad actors on the cold, fleshless record of a Rule 56 motion. For the purposes at hand, it is enough to acknowledge that an array of such incidents occurred and that, by the end of her sophomore year, Russell's size had become a matter of concern for all of the parties.

In her junior year, the plaintiff executed a contract (Contract) purporting to make her further participation in the College's nursing curriculum contingent upon an average weight loss of two pounds per week. The Contract was a singular sort of agreement.... Notwithstanding the signing of the Contract, Russell proved unable to meet the commitment, or even closely to approach it. Her body weight never fell appreciably below 300 pounds. Though the circumstances are complex, she seems to have made—and invariably to have broken—a series of promises in this regard. Predictably, an escalating level of tension began to characterize dealings between Russell and certain of the individual defendants.

The climax occurred on or about August 23, 1985. The plaintiff received a letter from the coordinator of the nursing program, defendant Chapdelaine, advising that she had been dismissed from the nursing department and from the College. Russell's education was concededly interrupted at that point (though, after a year's hiatus, she resumed her studies in nursing at another institution).

....

[The plaintiff's Count III invoked the theory of intentional infliction of emotional distress.]

...

... In attempting to invoke the standard of the Restatement (Second) Torts § 46, Count III tracks a path which is theoretically viable. Indeed, the state supreme court has heretofore recognized the existence of a cause of action patterned after § 46. See Champlin [v. Washington Trust Co., 478 A.2d 985], at 988 [R.I. 1984].

The basic requisites of an intentional infliction claim are easily stated:

> One who by extreme and outrageous conduct intentionally or recklessly causes severe emotional distress to another is subject to liability for such emotional distress, and if bodily harm to the other results from it, for such body harms.

Restatement (Second) of Torts § 46 (1965).

Before addressing any questions related to the conduct alleged and its supposed effects, the court must first determine whether the university/student relationship comprises the kind of soil in which the seeds of a § 46 claim for emotional harm may sprout. We start, again, with Champlin, which recognized a cause of action for intentional infliction of emotional distress in the debtor-creditor context. Id. at 989. Any belief that Champlin might be limited to its own facts, or to the collection milieu, has been dispelled by the ensuing decision in Elias v. Youngken, 493 A.2d 158 (R.I.1985). Elias held that some rather unpleasant communications between an employee and his supervisor could, in theory, furnish the basis for a cause of action for intentional infliction of emotional distress (though the particular conduct alleged in Elias did not meet the rigorous standard of § 46). Id. at 163–64. The state supreme court again assumed the existence of this particular cause of action without inquiry into its jurisprudential antecedents or conceptual underpinnings, and considered only the "threshold of conduct," 493 A.2d at 164, at which liability might be imposed. Id. at 163–64. Though Elias is sparse of phrase, both its language and tenor buttress a broad reading and application of Champlin. By extending the potential reach of the tort to the supervisor/employee relationship, Elias enhances the (already bright) prospect of construing the scope of § 46 so as to embrace other (kindred) pairings.

The caselaw from other jurisdictions does not suggest any basis for insulating the university/student setting from the operation of the general rule. See Note, 38 A.L.R.4th 998, 1003–1030 (1985) (reviewing cases). Without reaching the question of whether Rhode Island would limit the bounds of this tort to some particular sets of relationships, this court is persuaded that the uniquely vulnerable nature of the student's standing in the world of the university places that pairing squarely within the category of relationships which, on any reasonable taxonomy, would give rise to a duty to avoid the intentional infliction of emotional harm.

Such a conclusion marks only the beginning of the odyssey. While Elias and Champlin together imply a cause of action for intentional infliction of emotional distress, generally applicable in the circumstances of this case, there are high hurdles along the road to success on such claims. First, the concept of what might be termed "intentionality" is required to do double duty in these precincts. The interdicted conduct itself must be "intentional," that is, purposeful, wilful, or wanton. What is more, the harm that results must also be "intentional," that is, it must have been intended or least recklessly caused.

The face side of the coin is undoubtedly legible in this case. The conduct which the defendants undertook was volitional; what was done, was done purposefully. Whether or not the defendants intended the consequences that ensued, the acts that they committed vis-a-vis Russell were, without exception, the products of forethought and the conscious exercise of free will.

The flip side of the § 46 coin is much harder to read. In the Champlin phrase, the challenged conduct "must be intentional or in reckless disregard of the probability of causing emotional distress." 478 A.2d at 989. The plaintiff does not argue that these defendants desired to cause her to suffer, or even that they knew such suffering was substantially certain to follow from their course of conduct. Rather, Russell contends that the concept of recklessness is subsumed within the concept of intentionality for these purposes. Prosser and Keeton weigh in on plaintiff's side of this issue:

> [L]iability for extreme outrage is broader [than a literal interpretation of intentionality would allow] and extends to situations in which there is no certainty, but merely a high degree of probability that the mental distress will follow, and the defendant goes ahead in conscious disregard of it. This is the type of conduct which commonly is called wilful or wanton, or reckless.

Prosser and Keeton, The Law of Torts (5th ed. 1984) § 12 at 64 (discussing the requirement of extreme outrage).

There are four elements which must coincide under Rhode Island law to impose liability on such a theory:

> (1) the conduct must be intentional or in reckless disregard of the probability of causing emotional distress, (2) the conduct must be extreme and outrageous, (3) there must be a causal connection between the wrongful conduct and the emotional distress, and (4) the emotional distress in question must be severe.

Champlin, 478 A.2d at 989.

Points (3) and (4) are of only passing interest at this juncture. The plaintiff has testified that she suffered nightmares, sleeplessness, nausea, vomiting, diarrhea, gastric upset, and hypoglycemic attacks in the wake of the defendants' conduct. There is ample evidence in the record to withstand Rule 56 scrutiny on the last two prongs of the Champlin test. And, the first two prongs can, for the purposes at hand, be viewed as susceptible to measurement by a merged yardstick: reckless disregard cum outrageousness. The question becomes whether or not Russell has proffered enough in the way of proof to create a genuine issue of material fact as to this criterion.

The combined standard is a stringent one. The oft-cited comment (d) to § 46 of the Restatement (Second) of Torts (1965) provides:

> It has not been enough that the defendant has acted with an intent which is tortious or even criminal, or that he has intended to inflict emotional distress,

or even that his conduct has been characterized by "malice," or a degree of aggravation which would entitle the plaintiff to punitive damages for another tort. Liability has been found only where the conduct has been so outrageous in character, and so extreme in degree, as to go beyond all possible bounds of decency, and to be regarded as atrocious, and utterly intolerable in a civilized community. Generally, the case is one in which the recitation of the facts to an average member of the community would arouse his resentment against the actor, and lead him to exclaim, "Outrageous!"

Whether the conduct of a given defendant surpasses the bounds of decency is a function of three factors: (i) the conduct itself, (ii) in light of the particular relationship of the parties, (iii) having in mind the known (or knowable) susceptibility of the aggrieved party to emotional injury. These can best be assayed, in this case, in the inverse order of their appearance. Russell was a known quantity. Despite her evident sensitivity to weight-related emotional trauma, and her documented history of precarious emotional balance and tenuous self-esteem, the individual defendants—well-educated professionals all—plowed ahead. Given the full panoply of the circumstances, the proposition that they acted in reckless disregard of the probability that an obese youngster's psychic equilibrium could easily be knocked askew seems fairly debatable. This conclusion is fortified by a glimpse of the middle factor. The student stands in a particularly vulnerable relationship vis-a-vis the university, the administration, and the faculty. She is away from home, subject to the authority and discipline of the institution, and under enormous pressure to succeed. The relationship of these parties was such that the defendants could fairly be expected to have acted maturely—and even with some tenderness and solicitude—toward the plaintiff.

Seen in this context, the defendants' conduct, as the plaintiff has portrayed it, cannot be said as a matter of law to stumble on the threshold of outrageousness. To be sure, the law does not shield a person from words or deeds which are merely inconsiderate, insulting, unflattering, or unkind. The courts possess no roving writ, which warrants intervention whenever someone's feelings are hurt or someone has been subjected to a series of petty indignities. And, there must be room for some lack of courtesy and finesse in interpersonal relations. In Champlin, for example, the state court ultimately declined to impose liability because of the need to afford a creditor "reasonable latitude in the manner in which it seeks to collect overdue notes, even though there may be times when these methods might cause some inconvenience or embarrassment to the debtor." Champlin, 478 A.2d at 989–90.

Yet, the behavior challenged here, viewed in the light most favorable to the plaintiff's case, seems to be shaped of sterner stuff. Although a private college must be afforded wide discretion in enforcing its scholastic standards and in disciplining its students, there is no justification for debasement, harassment, or humiliation. The academic mise en scene, in any reasoned view, is considerably more civilized than the debtor-creditor environment, and there is correspondingly less play for roughness.[8]

Given the trust implicit in the student's selection of a college, and the peculiar vulnerability of undergraduates, the facts set forth by the plaintiff, if ultimately proven,

---

8. The relationship among students—as opposed to that between the institution and the student body—is a different kettle of fish, not on today's menu.

comprise a scenario which is far more conscience-provoking than the Champlin counterpart. The indignities which Russell asserts have been practiced on her are arguably offensive in the extreme, perhaps repugnant to the norms which one would expect to flourish in the academic world. Taken from the plaintiff's coign of vantage, the behavior in question, if it is shown to be as obnoxious as the plaintiff in her Rule 56 opposition suggests, might well be thought by a properly-instructed jury to be so atrocious as to be actionable. As a general matter, the plaintiff appears to have raised sufficient doubt as to the quality of the defendants' actions to blunt the summary judgment ax. See Cortes Quinones v. Jimenez Nettleship, 773 F.2d 10, 15 (1st Cir.1985) (per curiam) (summary judgment inappropriate where the parties "have raised sufficient unanswered questions to require [the] case to go forward with more complete development of the facts.")....

[The court denied the defendants' motion for summary judgment on Count III.]

NOTE

Russell and the College fought the case to close quarters for more than five years. The trial of the case passed to a new district judge, who gave a directed verdict for the college on the intentional infliction count as well as a claim for invasion of privacy. However, he let a breach of contract claim go to the jury, which found for the plaintiff on that count. In affirming on all counts, the court of appeals gave short shrift to the intentional infliction count. Conceding that in context, the comments of the school officials were "doubly hurtful," the court of appeals noted that the "extreme and outrageous" standard was "amorphous." On the facts of *Russell*, it concluded, "[t]he College's conduct may have been unprofessional, but we cannot say it was so far removed from the bounds of civilization as not to comply with the test set forth in § 46." Having noted that Russell had transferred to another school where she completed her degree and that she went on to become a registered nurse, the court said that her "commendable resiliency lends support to our conclusion." *Russell v. Salve Regina College*, 890 F.2d 484, 488 (1st Cir. 1989). The Supreme Court reversed on other grounds, related to the scope of the district court's review of the state law on the breach of contract claim. 111 S. Ct. 1217 (1991).

SHAFFER v. NATIONAL CAN CORPORATION

United States District Court, Eastern District of Pennsylvania
565 F. Supp. 909 (1983)

GILES, DISTRICT JUDGE

Nancy Shaffer ("Shaffer") charges her former employer, National Can Corporation ("National"), with employment discrimination in the form of sexual harassment. National moves to dismiss the Title VII claim, contending that the complaint was not filed timely before the Equal Employment Opportunity Commission ("EEOC"). National also alleges that the pendent state causes of action for wrongful discharge and intentional infliction of emotional distress have been supplanted by the remedies provided in the Pennsylvania Human Relations Act ("PHRA"). Finally, National argues that the complaint fails to state a claim for intentional infliction of emotional distress. For the reasons outlined below, National's motion will be granted in part and denied in part.

I. FACTS

Taking as true all of plaintiff's well-plead allegations, as I must on a motion to dismiss, the salient facts follow. Shaffer was employed at National's Morrisville plant from March 13, 1975 until March 27, 1981, first as a secretary-receptionist and then as a billing clerk. In June of 1977, Pat Dettorre ("Dettorre") was hired as the plant manager of the Morrisville facility. From that point until Shaffer left National's employ, Dettorre allegedly engaged in a continuing course of sexual harassment. Dettorre, who was married, attempted to induce plaintiff to go out with him socially and was very insistent despite her refusals. After plaintiff did not accept his publicly made invitation to the company Christmas celebration, Dettorre told her that "if she did not change her tune he would turn the conversation around and it would not be to her benefit." ... He then loudly asked her where she lived and what time he should pick her up, refusing to take "no" for an answer. He made subtle threats, alluding to his power at the plant by calling himself the "king-pin" and noting that "things could get better or worse, depending on whether she decided to 'play ball' with him." ... Dettorre made verbal sexual advances, discussed the relative sizes of female employees' chests, suggested she would be better attired in skirts with slits and generally endeavored to engage her in sexually related conversation.... When Shaffer repeatedly refused to succumb to his dubious charm, Dettorre began to retaliate by alternately mistreating and ignoring her. For example, it is claimed that he excluded her from certain luncheons and ignored her, at the same time being overly friendly towards other female employees. His conduct allegedly made it impossible for Shaffer to carry out her responsibilities caused her severe mental anguish and ultimately lead to her resignation on March 27, 1981. Plaintiff characterizes this resignation as a constructive discharge.

... [D]efendant challenges Shaffer's claim of intentional infliction of emotional distress, alleging that she has failed to state a cause of action. According to National, the behavior at issue does not rise to the level of "extreme and outrageous." Taking as true all of plaintiff's well-plead allegations, I conclude that her claim for emotional distress is sufficient to survive a motion to dismiss.

... Although Pennsylvania has apparently adopted the Restatement [(Second) §46] formulation sub silentio, see D'Ambrosio v. Pennsylvania National Mutual Casualty Insurance Co., 494 Pa. 501, 511 n. 8, 431 A.2d 966, 971–72 n. 8 (1981); Papieves v. Lawrence, 437 Pa. 373, 379, 263 A.2d 118, 121 (1970); Jones v. Nissenbaum, Rudolph & Seidner, 244 Pa.Super. 377, 382, 368 A.2d 770, 772 (1976), there is a paucity of caselaw on this topic. Generally, Pennsylvania has accorded this tort a narrow scope, finding a cause of action in only very egregious cases. See, e.g., Chuy v. Philadelphia Eagles Football Club, 595 F.2d 1265, 1274 (3d Cir.1979) (team physician tells sports writer that famous football player suffering from fatal disease, knowing it is not true); Papieves v. Lawrence, 437 Pa. 373, 375, 263 A.2d 118, 121 (1970) (concealing child's death and withholding body from parents). See also, Hume v. Bayer, 178 N.J.Super. 310, 428 A.2d 966, 970–71 (1981) (intentionally tells parents that child's medical condition much worse than it was). But cf.: D'Ambrosio, 494 Pa. at 511 n. 8, 431 A.2d at 971–72 n. 8 (insurance company's alleged "bad faith" failure to honor a claim does not rise to level of extreme or outrageous conduct); Forster v. Manchester, 410 Pa. 192, 199–200, 189 A.2d 147, 151–52 (not outrageous to follow an accident victim, conducting surveillance to determine the extent of the injury); Mullen v. Suchko, 279 Pa.Super. 499, 505, 421 A.2d 310, 313 (1980) (broken promise of financial support from lover not extreme and outrageous); Jones v. Nissenbaum, Rudolph & Seidner, 244 Pa.Super. 377, 383–85, 368 A.2d 770, 774 (1976) (threatening and insulting debt collection not actionable). See also Cautilli v. GAF Corp., 531 F.Supp. 71, 74–75 (E.D.Pa.1982) (employer's plans to sell business after attempting to induce plaintiff to commit to long term employment not extreme and outrageous); Mazzula v. Monarch Life Insurance Co., 487 F.Supp. 1299, 1302 (E.D.Pa.1980) (not outrageous to refuse to continue to pay disability insurance).

The above cited cases appear to fall into categories at each extreme. The behavior involved was either intensely egregious, as in Papieves, or mildly disturbing or annoying, as in D'Ambrosio.[11]

Since the factual situation here does not fall neatly into either category, the cases decided in Pennsylvania lend little guidance. However, a recent case in this district, predicting how the courts of Pennsylvania would resolve the issue, held that a complaint similar to Shaffer's stated a cause of action for intentional infliction of emotional distress. See Vegh v. General Electric Co., et al., No. 83-744 slip op. at 3 (E.D.Pa. May 18, 1983). In Vegh, plaintiff's supervisor subjected her to sexual advances, harassment and unequal treatment.... Sexual harassment cases decided in other jurisdictions also shed some light on this issue.

In Rogers v. Loews L'Enfant Plaza Hotel, 526 F.Supp. 523 (D.D.C.1981), plaintiff's immediate supervisor made sexual advances toward her, verbally and in writing, telephoned her and used crude and abusive language. He tried to convince her to date him, despite the fact that he was married, and upon occasion pulled at her hair and touched her. Rogers repeatedly refused his advances. As here, the supervisor in Rogers reacted to the plaintiff's refusals by making working conditions intolerable. 526 F.Supp. at 525–26. The court noted that "plaintiff has clearly alleged conditions and circumstances which are beyond mere insults, indignities and petty oppressions and which, if proved, could be construed as outrageous." Id. at 531. Similarly, in Stewart v. Thomas, 538 F.Supp. 891 (D.D.C.1982) an employee was subjected to sexual advances, verbal pressure, abuse and touching from her employer. Again refusal lead to retaliation. Citing Rogers, the court held the complaint to have stated a claim for intentional infliction of emotional distress. Id. at 894.

Rogers and Stewart are almost factually identical to Shaffer's plight. The only major distinction between them lies in Shaffer's failure to claim that Dettorre attempted any physical contact. However, all three cases contain a common thread—a continued course of sexual advances, followed by refusals and ultimately, retaliation. All three plaintiffs alleged that the work place atmosphere became oppressive, causing severe emotional distress.[12] I agree with the analyses in Rogers and Stewart and hold Shaffer's complaint sufficient to state a cause of action for intentional infliction of emotional distress.

National relies on Doyle v. Continental Airlines, Inc., No. 75-C2407 (N.D.Ill. Oct. 29, 1979) in support of its motion. Continental launched an advertising campaign using the slogan "we really move our tails for you." Plaintiffs, six female flight attendants purporting to represent a class, alleged that the slogan subjected them to harassment and ridicule. For example, passengers would request flight attendants to "move

---

11. *Fair v. Negley*, 257 Pa. Super. 50, 390 A. 2d 240 (1978) and *Beasley v. Freedman*, 256 Pa. Super. 208, 389 A. 2d 1087 (1978) arguably reflect exceptions to this conclusion. In both cases, breach of the implied warranty of habitability and "slumlordism" were held to state a cause of action for intentional infliction.... However, *Fair* and *Beasley* may well be limited to the landlord-tenant genre.... Alternatively, the conditions in the living quarters involved might have been "outrageous."

12. ... In *Rogers*, plaintiff went and spoke to hotel management and the hotel attempted to resolve the problem, albeit by means unsatisfactory to Ms. Rogers.... Shaffer brought the problem to the plant controller and Personnel Manager, both of whom told her to "roll with it," advising her that "there was nothing she could do...."

their tails" and other variations on that theme. The court granted Continental's motion for summary judgment, holding these demeaning remarks insufficient for a claim of emotional distress. Doyle is instructive to the extent that it points up that "liability 'clearly does not extend to mere insults, indignities, threats, annoyances, petty oppressions, or other trivialities.'" Stewart, 538 F.Supp. at 894 (citing Restatement (Second) of Torts § 46 Comment d). However, Doyle is clearly distinguishable from Rogers, Stewart and the instant case. Sexual advances were not focused at any one plaintiff in Doyle and the future success of plaintiff's employment did not hinge upon their performance of sexual favors. Perhaps the point was made best by the court in Seritis v. Lane, 30 FEP 423 (Cal.Super.1980). In Seritis, a local union official premised job opportunities on sexual favors. With respect to emotional distress the court candidly observed:

> verbal "propositioning" does not create such a tort [intentional infliction of emotional distress] and though deplored by those who would prefer return to the more discreet courtship of the past, open and direct solicitation of sexual intimacy is, like unchecked inflation, a sign of our times. Even solicitation for prostitution, though a crime, has not been held to be civilly actionable wrong. However, where, as here, <u>a person in a position to grant or withhold employment opportunities uses that authority to attempt to induce workers and job seekers to submit to sexual advances, prostitution and pornographic entertainment, and boasts of an ability to intimidate those who displease him, the tort of willful infliction of emotional distress is committed if harm shown.</u> 30 FEP at 425. (emphasis added).

Dettorre allegedly endeavored to use his authority to gain Shaffer's sexual favors and employed subtle threats, boasting of his power at the plant. Further, retaliatory behavior takes this case far beyond the ambit of insults or demeaning jingles. Therefore, I conclude that Shaffer has stated a cause of action for intentional infliction of emotional distress and National's motion shall be denied.

NOTES

(1) If you were constructing a rule to define, and limit, a tort action for one individual's serious emotional reactions to the actions or words of another, what would be the principal concerns you would have in mind:

(a) From the standpoint of making sure that there was some sort of remedy of that sort

(b) Ensuring that the tort had sensible limits.

(2) A deliberate attempt by one party to intimidate another provides natural soil for the intentional infliction tort. A good example is a case in which a group of tenants provided proof that their landlord tried to force them out of their apartments to clear the building for re-conversion to a condominium. In addition to proof that the defendants had allowed conditions in the building to deteriorate dangerously, the evidence included a showing that the management of the apartments sent a man to the tenants who kept "accidentally" dropping a gun when he tried to get them to vacate. There was also evidence that a person called a "resident manager" engaged in drug use and brandished a pistol, and that management personnel handed out liquor to so-called "workmen" who moved into the building. In holding that there was sufficient evidence to support a finding of outrageous conduct, the court focused on management's "position of authority over the tenants by virtue of their status as owner and manager, their access to resources, and their ultimate control over the building." *Jonathan Woodner Co. v. Breeden,* 665 A.2d 929, 933–36 (D.C. Ct. App. 1995).

(3) What is the role of the judge in intentional infliction cases as to the determination of outrageousness? Is it:

(a) To decide what ordinary citizens do think about such acts?

(b) What they should think about such acts?

(c) What the ordinary citizen would think about such acts if he or she were informed and not swayed by undue sympathy? (If you accept this formulation, do you read it as meaning people who are informed as ordinary citizens as distinguished from those who are informed as judges learned in the law?)

(4) A remarkable criminal analog to the intentional infliction tort appears in a press report concerning a man who escaped a murder conviction for killing his wife, when the jury deadlocked. The man was subsequently convicted for "'mentally assaulting' his son by allowing him to find his mother's body," under a new Ohio criminal statute that was described as being "intended to protect people who develop a mental illness as the result of a crime." Associated Press, *Guilty in a Murder, But Not of a Murder*, N.Y. TIMES, Aug. 2, 1994, at A15.

(5) Vermont adopted the intentional infliction tort on the bare pleading that the "Defendant willfully, maliciously, intentionally, and outrageously inflicted extreme mental suffering and acute mental distress on the Plaintiff, by willfully, maliciously, and outrageously rendering it impossible for any personal contact or other communication to take place between the Plaintiff and her daughter Monica Smith." Although the court viewed the complaint as "unadvisedly cursory," it said that the plaintiff has alleged the elements of the tort necessary to establish the prima facie case. *Sheltra v. Smith*, 136 Vt. 472, 392 A.2d 431 (1978).

Would it make a difference whether such allegations were directed to a family member of the plaintiff or to a non-relative?

(6) Persons who are present when someone inflicts severe emotional distress on family members may recover for their own severe emotional distress resulting from the incident. See RESTATEMENT § 46(2). The West Virginia court applied this rule to determine that a child could recover for severe emotional distress caused by witnessing verbal abuse and physical assaults on his mother. Since the defendant in this litigation was the child's father, the court also decided that the child's action was not barred by the doctrine of intra-family immunity. *Courtney v. Courtney*, 413 S.E.2d 418 (W. Va. 1991).

(7) How specifically must a defendant's conduct target a particular plaintiff to constitute intentional infliction of emotional distress?

In *Potter v. Firestone Tire & Rubber Co.*, 863 P.2d 795 (Cal. 1993), the defendant knowingly deposited toxic materials, including carcinogens, at a landfill adjacent to the homes of the four plaintiffs. The supreme court concluded that the plaintiffs did not meet the standard of showing requisite knowledge on the part of the defendant, and remanded to the court of appeal in an order that permitted that court to remand for a retrial on that issue. The supreme court focused on the declaration in *Christensen v. Superior Court*, 820 P.2d 181 (Cal. 1991) that "[t]he requirement that the defendant's conduct be directed primarily at the plaintiff is a factor which distinguishes intentional infliction of emotional distress from the negligent infliction of such injury." The supreme court's analysis wove in references to factual uncertainties in the record before it:

> ... [I]t is ambiguous whether the lower courts determined that Firestone's conduct was directed at these particular plaintiffs in the sense intended by Christensen.... Although the Court of Appeal correctly rejected Firestone's con-

tention that Firestone was not liable because it did not know the particular names of any individual whose groundwater was contaminated by the hazardous waste, it is unclear whether it believed that Firestone was actually aware of the presence of these particular plaintiffs and their consumption and use of the water.

Furthermore, it is questionable whether the trial court made a finding that Firestone possessed the requisite knowledge, and if so, whether such a finding would be supported by substantial evidence. Although the trial court concluded that Firestone "had to realize" that the eventual discovery of the toxic contamination "by those drinking the contaminated water would almost certainly result in their suffering severe emotional distress," this may be interpreted in one of two ways. First, this may have been a finding that Firestone actually knew of these particular plaintiffs and their consumption of the water, and nevertheless sent prohibited wastes to Crazy Horse despite a realization that plaintiffs would almost certainly suffer severe emotional distress upon their discovery of the facts. Alternatively, this may have been a finding that Firestone had to have realized that its misconduct was almost certain to cause severe emotional distress to any person who might foreseeably consume the water and subsequently discover the facts. Although the knowledge requirement is met under the first interpretation of the court's ruling, it is not satisfied under the second because knowledge of these particular plaintiffs is lacking.

This conclusion is consistent with the result reached in *Christensen....* There we held that, even though it was alleged that defendants' conduct in mishandling the remains of deceased persons was intentional and outrageous and was substantially certain to cause extreme emotional distress to relatives and close friends of the deceased, the plaintiffs' cause of action for intentional infliction of emotional distress was not sufficiently supported where there was no allegation that the defendants' misconduct was directed primarily at plaintiffs, or that it was calculated to cause them severe emotional distress, or that it was done with knowledge of their presence and with a substantial certainty that they would suffer severe emotional injury....

(8) One of the historic roots of the section 46 tort, which was defined as a separate action only in the 1940's, was the problem of abusive bill collection. One may compare two cases. In *Medlin v. Allied Investment Co.*, 217 Tenn. 469, 398 S.W.2d 270 (1966), the action arose from a controversy over payments on a house. The court summarized the allegations this way:

During the months of November and December of 1963, Mrs. Medlin made telephone calls to the defendant's office in an attempt to convince defendant that the disputed October payment had been made. It is alleged that in the course of these conversations that the defendant's agent was abusive and insulting. The plaintiffs' daughter had recently died and the defendant knew this fact at the time of these telephone conversations and the dispute over the house payments.

It is alleged that these telephone conversations and the defendant's erroneous sending of default notices to the Federal Housing Administration which caused two warnings of foreclosure to be sent to the plaintiffs resulted in an aggravation of plaintiff Mrs. Medlin's already nervous condition; Mrs. Medlin having recently lost her daughter. It is further alleged that this aggravation was to such an extent that Mrs. Medlin's nervous condition became manifest in the form of headaches.

While the court employed the occasion to indicate its acceptance of section 46 for Tennessee, it did not think the facts of the particular case justified application of the tort. It said that the declaration could be taken to show that the defendant was negligent in record keeping and that he was abusive to the plaintiff, but that since "the substance and severity of the abuse is not set out in the declaration we cannot ascribe the term 'outrageous' to this alleged abuse."

The case for comparison is a bill collector decision upholding a section 46 cause of action, *George v. Jordan Marsh Co.*, 359 Mass. 244, 268 N.E.2d 915 (1971). In that case, which involved a debt incurred by the plaintiff's emancipated son, the plaintiff alleged that the defendant "badgered and harassed her" with late night phone calls, and repeatedly mailed bills marked "account referred to law and collection department." She also claimed that the defendants sent letters "saying that her credit was revoked, that the debt was charged to her personal account, and that late charges were being added to the debt," and that the defendants had asserted that she had guaranteed her son's debt in writing when they knew that was not true. After the plaintiff's health deteriorated and she had a heart attack, her lawyer tried to stop the harassing tactics but the defendants persisted and she suffered a second heart attack.

What appear to be the principal grounds on which one might distinguish these two collection cases?

(9) Can a vicious published parody constitute an intentional infliction of emotional distress or is that material protected by the First Amendment? The Supreme Court had to take a stand on this issue in a case involving a parody advertisement, labeled as a parody in small print, in which Hustler Magazine portrayed by cartoon a "drunken incestuous rendezvous" of the plaintiff, the Reverend Jerry Falwell, "with his mother in an outhouse." Although the Court pronounced the ad "doubtless gross and repugnant in the eyes of most," it held unanimously for the magazine on First Amendment grounds. Writing the principal opinion, Chief Justice Rehnquist declared that "public figures and public officials" could not succeed on an "intentional infliction" claim "by reason of publications such as the one here at issue without showing in addition that the publication contains a false statement of fact which was made with 'actual malice.'" The court had defined that term in an earlier case dealing with defamation of public officials to mean "knowledge that the statement was false or with reckless disregard as to whether or not it was true." *Hustler Magazine v. Falwell*, 485 U.S. 46, 56 (1988), rev'g *Falwell v. Flynt*, 797 F.2d 1270 (4th Cir. 1986).

———

There appears below the section of the district judge's decision on the plaintiff's claim for intentional infliction of emotional distress in *Jones v. Clinton*, for which the allegations are detailed in the excerpts from the decision in Chapter 1, supra. It will be useful to reread that portion of the opinion together with the part of the opinion that follows:

JONES v. CLINTON

United States District Court, Eastern District of Arkansas
990 F. Supp. 657 (1998)

Susan Webber Wright, District Judge.

... [T]he Court addresses plaintiff's state law claim of intentional infliction of emotional distress or outrage. Arkansas recognizes a claim of intentional infliction of emo-

tional distress based on sexual harassment.... To establish a claim of intentional infliction of emotional distress, a plaintiff must prove that: (1) the defendant intended to inflict emotional distress or knew or should have known that emotional distress was the
likely result of his conduct; (2) the conduct was extreme and outrageous and utterly intolerable in a civilized community; (3) the defendant's conduct was the cause of the
plaintiff's distress; and (4) the plaintiff's emotional distress was so severe in nature that
no reasonable person could be expected to endure it....

The President argues that the alleged conduct of which plaintiff complains was
brief and isolated; did not result in any physical harm or objective symptoms of the
requisite severe distress; did not result in distress so severe that no reasonable person
could be expected to endure it; and he had no knowledge of any special condition of
plaintiff that would render her particularly susceptible to distress. He argues that
plaintiff has failed to identify the kind of clear cut proof that Arkansas courts require
for a claim of outrage and that he is therefore entitled to summary judgment. The
Court agrees.

One is subject to liability for the tort of outrage or intentional infliction of emotional distress if he or she wilfully or wantonly causes severe emotional distress to another by extreme and outrageous conduct.... In M.B.M. Co. v. Counce, 268 Ark.
269, 278–80, 596 S.W.2d 681, 687 (1980), the Arkansas Supreme Court stated that
"[b]y extreme and outrageous conduct, we mean conduct that is so outrageous in
character, and so extreme in degree, as to go beyond all possible bounds of decency,
and to be regarded as atrocious, and utterly intolerable in civilized society." Whether
conduct is "extreme and outrageous" is determined by looking at "the conduct at
issue; the period of time over which the conduct took place; the relation between
plaintiff and defendant; and defendant's knowledge that plaintiff is particularly susceptible to emotional distress by reason of some physical or mental peculiarity." Doe
v. Wright, 82 F.3d 265, 269 (8th Cir. 1996) (citing Hamaker [v. Ivy], 51 F.3d [108] at
111) [8th Cir. 1995]. The tort is clearly not intended to provide legal redress for every
slight insult or indignity that one must endure. Manning, 127 F.3d at 690 (citing
Hamaker, 51 F.3d at 110). The Arkansas courts take a strict approach and give a narrow view to claims of outrage, see id., and merely describing conduct as outrageous
does not make it so....

Plaintiff seems to base her claim of outrage on her erroneous belief that the allegations she has presented are sufficient to constitute criminal sexual assault. She states
that "Mr. Clinton's outrageous conduct includes offensive language, an offensive proposition, offensive touching (constituting sexual assault under both federal and state definitions), and actual exposure of an intimate private body part," and that "[t]here are
few more outrageous acts than a criminal sexual assault followed by unwanted exposure, coupled with a demand for oral sex by the most powerful man in the state against
a very young, low-level employee." ...

While the Court will certainly agree that plaintiffs allegations describe offensive conduct, the Court, as previously noted, has found that the Governor's alleged conduct
does not constitute sexual assault. Rather, the conduct as alleged by plaintiff describes a
mere sexual proposition or encounter, albeit an odious one, that was relatively brief in
duration, did not involve any coercion or threats of reprisal, and was abandoned as
soon as plaintiff made clear that the advance was not welcome. The Court is not aware
of any authority holding that such a sexual encounter or proposition of the type alleged
in this case, without more, gives rise to a claim of outrage. Cf. Croom [v. Younts], 913
S.W.2d [283] at 287, [Ark. 1996] (use of wine and medication by a vastly older relative

to foist sex on a minor cousin went "beyond a mere sexual encounter" and offended all sense of decency).

Moreover, notwithstanding the offensive nature of the Governor's alleged conduct, plaintiff admits that she never missed a day of work following the alleged incident, she continued to work at AIDC another nineteen months (leaving only because of her husband's job transfer), she continued to go on a daily basis to the Governor's Office to deliver items and never asked to be relieved of that duty, she never filed a formal complaint or told her supervisors of the incident while at AIDC, she never consulted a psychiatrist, psychologist, or incurred medical bills as a result of the alleged incident, and she acknowledges that her two subsequent contacts with the Governor involved comments made "in a light vein" and nonsexual contact that was done in a "friendly fashion." Further, despite earlier claiming that she suffered marital discord and humiliation, plaintiff stated in her deposition that she was not claiming damages to her marriage as a result of the Governor's alleged conduct,..., and she acknowledged the request to drop her claim of injury to reputation by stating, "I didn't really care if it was dropped or not personally." ... Plaintiff's actions and statements in this case do not portray someone who experienced emotional distress so severe in nature that no reasonable person could be expected to endure it. Cf. Hamaker, 51 F.3d 108 (no claim of outrage where plaintiff, who had a speech impediment and an I.Q. of between 75 and 100, was "red-faced and angry," had an "increased heart rate and blood pressure," and had trouble sleeping four days after incident involving "rather nasty" practical joke).

Nevertheless, plaintiff submits a declaration from a purported expert with a Ph.D. in education and counseling, Patrick J. Carnes, who, after a 3.5 hour meeting with plaintiff and her husband a mere four days prior to the filing of President Clinton's motion for summary judgment, opines that her alleged encounter with Governor Clinton in 1991, "and the ensuing events," have caused plaintiff to suffer severe emotional distress and "consequent sexual aversion." The Court does not credit this declaration.

In Angle v. Alexander, 328 Ark. 714, 945 S.W.2d 933 (1997), the Arkansas Supreme Court noted that absent physical harm, courts look for more in the way of extreme outrage as an assurance that the mental disturbance claimed is not fictitious. Id. at 936–37. In that case, the plaintiffs offered their own testimony that they had experienced emotional distress, thoughts of death, fear, anger, and worry, but little else. Id. In concluding that there was no evidence of extreme emotional distress required to prevail on an outrage claim, the Court found it significant that none had seen a physician or mental health professional for these concerns. Id. The Court did not allow the fact that one plaintiff "on the advice of her attorney, spoke to a psychologist," to overcome her failure of proof on this point. Id. at 937 n. 3.

Aside from other deficiencies with the Carnes' declaration (including the fact that the substance of this declaration apparently was not disclosed in accordance with rules governing pre-trial discovery), the opinions stated therein are vague and conclusory and, as in Angle, do not suffice to overcome plaintiff's failure of proof on her claim of outrage. Cf. Crenshaw v. Georgia-Pacific Corp., 915 F.Supp. 93, 99 (W.D.Ark.1995) (affidavit prepared after opposing motion for summary judgment filed detailing symptoms of weight loss, lack of sleep, headache, worry, and nausea, failed to present sufficient evidence of emotional distress).

In sum, plaintiff's allegations fall far short of the rigorous standards for establishing a claim of outrage under Arkansas law and the Court therefore grants the President's motion for summary judgment on this claim....

NOTES

(1) What were the strongest allegations in the plaintiff's pleading in *Jones*? Why weren't they "odious" enough to be "outrageous"? If one compares *Jones* to *Shaffer*, what elements of *Shaffer* are stronger for the plaintiff? Are there elements of Jones's pleading that make a case that is much stronger than *Shaffer*, even if Jones's complaint did not mention retaliation?

(2) An interesting contrast to the requirements of the section 46 tort appears in the Supreme Court's interpretation of the concept of an "abusive work environment," itself an interpretation of the provision of Title VII of the Civil Rights Act of 1964 that makes it unlawful "to discriminate against any individual with respect to his compensation, terms, conditions, or privileges of employment, because of such individual's race, color, religion, sex, or national origin." The case at issue arose from a company president's insults to a female employee "because of her gender" as well as "unwanted sexual innuendoes." These included the remark that she was "a dumb ass woman," and the suggestion, in front of others, that the president and the plaintiff "go to the Holiday Inn to negotiate [the plaintiff's] raise." Although the district court found that some of these remarks "offended [the plaintiff] and would offend the reasonable woman," it denied recovery. It reasoned that the remarks were "not so severe as to be expected to seriously injure [the plaintiff's] well-being" and said it did not believe that she "was subjectively so offended that she suffered injury."

Reversing, the Supreme Court sought "a middle path between making actionable any conduct that is merely offensive and requiring the conduct to cause a tangible psychological injury." Justice O'Connor's opinion for the Court set as the standard a showing that the "environment would reasonably be perceived, and is perceived, as hostile and abusive," without necessarily requiring that the environment "also ... be psychologically injurious." The question of "whether an environment is 'hostile' or 'abusive'" would depend on "all the circumstances," including such factors as "the frequency of the discriminatory conduct; its severity; whether it is physically threatening or humiliating, or a mere offensive utterance; and whether it unreasonably interferes with an employee's work performance." Psychological harm would be a relevant factor, but "no single factor is required." *Harris v. Forklift Sys.*, 510 U.S. 17, 23 (1993).

(3) At least one court has declared that "an employer owes his or her employee a greater degree of respect because of the employment relationship." From that premise, the Ninth Circuit reasoned that there might be grounds for the intentional infliction tort in the "public humiliation of an employee by her employer, accomplished through rude, crude sexually explicit remarks and actions." *Steiner v. Showboat Operating Co.*, 25 F.3d 1459, 1466–67 (9th Cir. 1994), drawing on *Dias v. Sky Chefs, Inc.*, 919 F.2d 1370, 1374 (9th Cir. 1990).

(4) In the federal trial court cases printed above—*Russell, Shaffer*, and *Jones*—what are the factors that appear most strongly to have influenced the district judges? Why should two cases go to the jury and the other case be declared lacking in legal merit? How much legal weight would you assign to the kinds of relationships involved in such cases? To the personal vulnerability of plaintiffs? What are the values made explicit, or apparently held implicitly by these judges, concerning the need for people to develop thick skins in dealing with the world, and the contrasting need for solicitude for those with tender emotional fabrics?

(5) Maryland adopted section 46 in a case by an employee who alleged that a foreman and supervisor for General Motors, over a period of several months, would come by him and imitate his stuttering. Although the Maryland Court of Special Appeals found that a directed verdict motion for the foreman was sustainable on the grounds that the emotional distress caused by this harassment was not "severe," it did say that the evidence was sufficient to establish that the conduct "was outrageous and intolerable in form." The court epitomized the foreman's conduct by an incident related by a co-worker, who told of the plaintiff approaching the defendant to ask for a transfer to a different department. In this version, the defendant "just smiled at [the plaintiff] and he said, you can't have the job, he said, because you always call the mmitteeman [i.e., the committeeman who handled grievances]. When he said mmitteeman he was mimicking Bill about his speech, shaking his head up and down. Like, he don't bring the word out, and then he told him to get the hell away from there." *Jones v. Harris*, 35 Md. App. 556, 371 A.2d 1104 (1977). In affirming the defendant's judgment on the basis that the plaintiff had not proved the severity element of the tort, the Maryland Court of Appeals said it was "crystal clear" that the defendant's "conduct was intentional" but did not reach the issue of whether the conduct was "extreme or outrageous." 281 Md. 560, 380 A.2d 611 (1977).

(6) In his analysis of the section 46 tort, Professor Givelber finds confirmation of "the essential fact about the tort: its focus is the outrageousness of defendant's conduct," and indeed contends that the various elements of the tort effectively are "collapse[d]" into the outrageousness element. Givelber, *The Right to Minimum Social Decency and the Limits of Evenhandedness: Intentional Infliction of Emotional Distress by Outrageous Conduct*, 82 Colum. L. Rev. 42, 46–49 (1982). In cases involving parties to a pre-existing legal relationship, Givelber declares, "the tort functions as an instrument of legal change ... add[ing] to the bundle of rights of those who occupy the typically weaker bargaining position." *Id.* at 63–69. Focusing on cases between strangers, the author generally concludes that "courts have used the tort to achieve just results in egregious cases but they have not articulated principled bases for decisionmaking." *Id.* at 74. Indeed, he discerns "little evidence that this tort will ever provide the basis for principled adjudication," but that "it has provided and probably will continue to provide the basis for achieving situational justice." *Id.* at 75.

Givelber does emphasize the need to limit the tort: "Incivility is so pervasive in our society that it is inappropriate for the law to attempt to provide a remedy for it in every instance.... [T]here is concern for personal liberty both for its own sake and for its purported capability to enhance mental health and reduce aggression. This liberty interest includes much more than the freedom to get mad or be impolite." *Id.* at 56–57. Citing cases, Givelber says that the liberty interest "includes the freedom to exercise privacy rights even in the face of certain knowledge that it will severely distress another; extramarital affairs, divorce, and abortion are prime examples." Moreover,

> there is the perceived social utility of mild (or not so mild) oppression. There are simply a large number of situations in which intentional making others uncomfortable, unhappy, and upset is viewed as justified either in pursuit of one's legal rights (e.g., debt collection) or in service of a greater social good (e.g., cross-examination at trial) or for the person's "own good" (e.g., basic training)(citing cases and Restatement comment).

(7) Does fairness in judicial decisionmaking require a judge who is neutral? Cardozo wrote, "Deep below consciousness are other forces, the likes and dislikes, the predilections and the prejudices, the complex of instincts and emotions and habits and convictions, which make the man, whether he be litigant or judge." The Nature of the Judicial Process 167 (Yale Univ. Press 1921, rpt. 1949).

How can a judge be neutral about cases like *Jones* and *Shaffer*, not to mention *Russell*? How can she keep herself from being influenced by her own attitude toward the nature of the activities alleged, in the context of cultural attitudes? How would you advise a new judge about her duties concerning fairness in the sense of not pre-judging cases?

§ 2.05 Fraud*

Misrepresentation is the general tort category that embraces traditional actions for deprivation of property or loss of economic value, attributable to statements by the defendant that turn out to be false. Some courts have also employed classifications of innocent misrepresentation and "negligent misrepresentation." However, the bulk of the legal action in the area falls under the rubrics of "fraud" or "deceit," labels that imply "scienter"—a knowing or at least reckless disregard by the representer of the truth or falsity of his statements.

Verbal formulas for fraud or deceit vary in both their language and their classification of the elements necessary to present a prima facie case. However, there is a general agreement on the basic elements, which Harper, James and Gray define as "(1) false representations (2) fraudulently made (3) with the intention of inducing another to rely thereon. If such misrepresentations (4) induce reliance (5) and the reliance is justified and (6) causes damage, the defendant is liable."[2] Generally, the fraudulent statement must be material to the plaintiff's reliance, as explained below.

. . .

Scienter

The issue of culpability standards is one of the principal battlegrounds of fraud law. In many jurisdictions, a fraud case demands proof of scienter, which, in its most extreme formulation, is a standard requiring "actual moral guilt." A slightly less demanding standard, but still a rigorous one for plaintiffs to meet, requires that the defendant have "knowledge" of the falsity of the representation. In a prescription drug case, this standard yielded a holding that while a pharmaceutical firm had knowledge of the "possible teratogenicity" of a product, a failure to produce evidence that the firm "had knowledge" that the product "was a teratogen" was fatal to claims based on birth defects. The plaintiffs' proof did not measure up to the standard of "clear and convincing evidence that the necessary elements of knowledge of false representation exist."[6]

A more common scienter test is that associated with the 1889 English decision of *Derry v. Peek*.[7] In that case, Lord Herschell said that to make out a fraud claim, one must show a false representation made "(1) knowingly, or (2) without belief in its truth,

---

* Much of the material in this section is taken or adapted from Marshall S. Shapo, The Law of Products Liability ¶ 2.02 (3d ed. 1994).

2. F. Harper, F. James & O. Gray, The Law of Torts 381 (2d ed. 1986).

6. *Raynor v. Richardson-Merrell, Inc.*, 643 F. Supp. 238, 243–244 (D.D.C. 1986).

7. 14 App. Cas. 337 (H.L. 1889).

8. *Id.* at 374. The Second Restatement calls a misrepresentation "fraudulent" if the maker:
(a) knows or believes that the matter is not as he represents it be
(b) does not have the confidence in the accuracy of his representation that he states or implies, or

or (3) recklessly, careless whether it be true or false."[8] This standard has been held to insulate sellers who had a sincere belief in a statement that later proved false, especially when they reasonably held the belief on the basis of the statements of others. However, this rule is strong enough to impose liability when an individual makes statements as if they were based on his or her own knowledge even if the statements concern "unverified subsidiary facts.... which [are] susceptible of verification." The bare pleading requirement is that the defendant has made "false statements with knowledge of their falsity."

...

Materiality and Causation

Materiality is a very important element of fraud law. It often blends into the causation issue to the point of practical equivalence. The verbal formulas defining materiality vary. For some courts, the key question is whether the defendant's misrepresentation or failure to disclose had a probable influence on purchase at a particular price. It should be noted that, in this connection, the quality and price of goods are dependent variables. Beyond the criterion of probable effect, there is authority that presents a somewhat broader pasture to plaintiffs litigating the materiality issue. Associated with the field of securities regulation, these precedents refuse to require that the seller's conduct have a decisive effect on the buyer's choice: rather, they emphasize the general likelihood of such an effect, the propensity of the representation to influence conduct, or the fact that it "might have been considered important."

This sort of reasoning may apply both to materiality requirements and to the rules on specificity of causation. As a matter of strict logic, it might be argued that when A claims injury from B's product on the basis of B's representations, A must be able to relate his or her conduct rather precisely to the alleged misstatements. However, the difficulties of proving exact reliance on specific representations tend to militate against rigorous causation requirements and to foster a standard that requires some probability of influence rather than a clearly proved linkage.[30]

Rationales of Fraud Law

Although there is general agreement that the kind of conduct that deserves the scienter label is socially undesirable, the rationales for imposing liability vary. A strong component of equity frequently underlies fraud holdings. In particular, the use of the terminology of "right to rely" reflects a notion that those with superior information owe a special obligation to those who lack knowledge, in situations in which the knowledgeable party tries to take advantage of the other's impression that the former knows the quality of goods. Parallel to this appears an often implicit judicial concern with efficiency, for example, in the sense of optimizing the cost of searching for information. If consumers do not feel that they can trust their sellers, they will waste resources trying to find out the truth for themselves. The law of fraud aims to prevent conduct that has these inefficient consequences and to deter misrepresentations or failures to disclose

---

(c) knows that he does not have the basis for his representation that he states or implies." RESTATEMENT (SECOND) OF TORTS § 526 (1977).

30. Cf. *Wright v. Carter Prod., Inc.*, 244 F.2d 53, 62–63 (2d Cir. 1957) (on claims for breach of duty to warn or false advertising in violation of statute, court rejected contention that plaintiff must prove reliance on single advertisement; sufficient to "establish that the defendant's repeated assertions of safety came to [the plaintiff's] attention and that she relied upon them").

that have the effect of reducing trust in routine transactions and increasing consumer costs in acquiring information. These rationales also generally support other doctrines that impose liability for product disappointment.

It should be noted that in the case of fraud and conduct bordering on fraud, many courts are inclined to preserve some flexibility in doctrine, with an eye to achieving marginally extra deterrence of conduct that may be borderline in both economic and ethical terms. An often cited paragraph in a 1913 case captures the reason for keeping potential fraud defendants guessing:

> Messieurs, the fraud-feasors, would like nothing half so well as for courts to say they would go thus far and no further in its pursuit.... Accordingly definitions of fraud are of set purpose left general and flexible, and thereto courts match their astuteness against the versatile inventions of fraud-doers.[33]

From an economic point of view, in theory, this judicial philosophy might require transacting parties to disgorge too much information if judges apply it under strict forms of liability. Moreover, it is true that if fraud law were employed too stringently, especially in applications that entail the use of punitive damages, it might curtail creativity in selling techniques. However, the demands of the scienter test tend to ensure that this will not happen. It seems clear that the scienter-based fraud doctrine, at least, generates better information at less cost to consumers than would a legal world without it. Another benefit is the reduction of the social frustrations associated with the deliberate or reckless commission of deceitful practices. In this area of culpability doctrine, reputable sellers can generally have little quarrel with the law as it is articulated and applied.

§ 2.06 Developing Concepts of Tort

MORRISON v. NATIONAL BROADCASTING CO.
New York Supreme Court, Appellate Division
24 A.D.2d 284, 266 N.Y.S.2d 406 (1965)

BREITEL, J....

Two questions are raised. The first is whether plaintiff's complaint states a cause of action, and the second is, if a claim is stated, whether it is barred by an applicable statute of limitations....

The conduct concerning which plaintiff complains and with which he was involved occurred in 1958, although it had its genesis earlier. The public exposure to which the complaint refers occurred in 1959. This action was begun in 1961.

The gist of the claim is that defendants, associated in various ways in television, acting in concert, falsely represented to plaintiff, a young university academic, that they were conducting an authentic and honest contest on television, a "quiz" show, when in fact it was rigged. They made these misrepresentations in order to induce his participation as a contestant. As a result of his innocent participation and the public scandals thereafter occurring, plaintiff sustained harm to his good reputation and in particular was deprived of scholastic fellowships for which he had applied. For purposes of this

---

33. *Stonemets v. Head*, 248 Mo. 243, 263, 154 S.W. 108, 114 (1913).

appeal the description of the promotion and sponsorship of the program must be assumed to be true. As for the harm to plaintiff's reputation and prospects, and his innocent participation in the contest, for the present this too must be assumed to be true. The claim then charges defendants with corrupt purposes, lying to plaintiff to induce his innocent participation in a corrupt enterprise, as a result of which, on public exposure of the enterprise, plaintiff sustained harm to his reputation and academic prospects. In referring to corrupt purposes or enterprises it is not intended to suggest essential illegality but to import necessarily a violation of strong and prevalent moral standards with respect to competitive contests for material awards. The point is that everything that is not illegal is not therefore legitimate or sanctioned conduct.

Notably, each of the ultimate elements of the claim is a recognized element in the law of remedies for one sustaining harms. Nevertheless, defendants contend that there is a failure to state a claim or cause of action because the separate elements do not all fall into any one classic category of tort but are found only in a combination of such categories. If this be right, then once again our jurisprudence would suffer a hardening of its categories making neither for sense nor justice and mark a return to a specious procedural formalism. (See, generally, Halpern: Intentional Torts and the Restatement, 7 Buffalo L.Rev. 7, esp. 7–17.)

In the first place, misplaced speculation about the applicability of "prima facie tort" doctrine to this case should be eliminated. That open-ended, non-category, class or sub-class of tort covers "disinterested malevolence,[2] that is, the intentional malicious injury to another by otherwise lawful means without economic or social justification, but solely to harm the other (Prosser on Torts [3rd ed.], p. 978). The elements in this case are distinguishable and stronger. The means used were not lawful or privileged, in the sense of affirmatively sanctioned conduct, but were intentional falsehood without benevolent purpose uttered to induce action by another to his detriment. The ultimate purpose and the scheme were corrupt, in the sense that no socially useful purpose but only gain by deceit was intended, although perhaps not "illegal." Defendants were engaged in operating a dishonest contest. Innocent contestants were being cheated of the chances for rewards they thought they had. The public was being deceived as to the kind of spectacle it was viewing. Defendants lied to plaintiff to induce his innocent participation. They were engaged in the pursuit of economic gain for themselves. Hence, this is no instance of otherwise lawfully privileged means being made actionable, because without economic or social justification, and because of the exclusive purpose to injure plaintiff, which are the identifying qualities of so-called "prima facie" tort.

Secondly, the claim is not for defamation, as defendants correctly argue, because defendants did not publish in any form anything derogatory to or concerning plaintiff. Instead, they put him in an unduly hazardous position where his reputation might be injured, not because this was their purpose, but because they did not care what happened to him in the pursuit of their purposes for selfish gain. Yet the harm sustained is exactly like that from defamation, albeit induced neither by slander nor libel. Thus, the causative acts are different from those in defamation, but the effect, that is, harm to reputation, is the same.

Thirdly, the acts of defendants are not in deceit although they fit precisely all but one of the several elements of deceit. They fall short with respect to the nature of the harm

---

2. *Aikens v. State of Wisconsin*, 195 U.S. 194, 206, 25 S.Ct. 3, 49 L.Ed. 154 (per Holmes, J.). See, also, *American Bank & Trust Co. v. Federal Bank*, 256 U.S. 350, 358, 41 S.Ct. 499, 65 L.Ed. 983 (per Holmes, J.).

sustained by plaintiff. There is knowing misrepresentation of fact, for the purpose of
inducing plaintiff to act, upon which he relies. But the resulting harm is not the obtaining of plaintiff's property, or even his services; instead, it is the putting him into a hazardous false position, that is, of a cheater or corrupt contestant, to which he would not
have consented if he had known the truth. While the harm to plaintiff was never intended, for defendants were gambling that there would be no exposure, the risk of
harm to plaintiff's reputation was known or should have been known and therefore
completely foreseeable to defendants. In this last respect there is a touch of an element
in the law of negligence. But the claim is not for negligence, because while the harm
may not have been intended, the act and effect of putting plaintiff into the false position of appearing to be a cheater was. It is not necessary that the intent in tort law be
hostile....

In short, and in repetition, every element in plaintiff's claim descriptive of defendants' acts, his reliance, and the harm sustained, are identifiable in the most ancient of
the tort categories and in the law of negligence. What is more important, the elements
of defendants' conduct and the harm to plaintiff fall neatly within general principles of
law, even if not within any of the numbered forms of a form book[]. The intentional
use of wrongful means and the intentional exposure of another to the known, unreasonable risk of harm, which results in such harm, provides classic basis for remedy. The
harm must, of course, have been intended, foreseeable, or the "nature [sic] consequence" of the wrong. Even in intentional tort there is no liability for "remote"
harms.... What troubled the lawyers in another day was not the intentional infliction of
harm by wrongful means or for wrongful purpose, but harms inflicted without intention or by otherwise lawfully privileged conduct.

The root of the present trouble is that every kind of wrongful conduct, like lying, is not
actionable per se. The analysis should not stop short, however, but must continue by examination of the purpose for which one lies, the harm produced by the lie, and whether
the harm was foreseeable or the natural consequence of the wrong. The problem may also
be looked at conversely. If there be no remedy, then the law would be saying in effect that
one is free to lie to another as distinguished from lying about another (which is defamation), for one's private gain, so long as the consequence of the lie is not to take the victim's
property (which is deceit), but rather to expose him and his reputation to likely injury.

In passing it should be observed that criminal statutes which must be explicitly directed to conduct forbidden are not involved. Rather this case explores the common law
reach in providing a remedy for foreseeable harms resulting from intentional conduct.

In the late nineteenth and early twentieth centuries a great controversy raged over
whether there was a law of tort based on general principles or only a law of torts based
on specific remedies which could not be rationally correlated but only historically explained. Pollock in England was the chief exponent for the view of a general theory of
tort and Salmond was the chief exponent for the contrary view (see Pollock on Torts
[15th ed.], pp. 16–17 and Salmond on Torts [12th ed.], pp. 17–19, 20–31; see, also,
Advance Music Corp. v. American Tobacco Co., 296 N.Y. 79, 83–84, 70 N.E.2d 401–
403). It is significant that the later editors of Salmond retreat from his hard position
that "every plaintiff must bring his case under one of the recognized heads of tort."
(Salmond, op. cit., supra, at pp. 17–19.) And there is no doubt that the generality of
Pollock's position must be a bit restrained, if history is not to be ignored....

But there is no need to join in the overseas controversy. The Court of Appeals in the Advance Music case, supra, resolved the dispute for this State. After discussing the Pollock-Salmond controversy, Chief Judge Loughran had this to say ... :

> This difference over the general principles of liability in tort was composed for us in Opera on Tour, Inc., v. Weber, 285 N.Y. 348, 34 N.E.2d 349, 136 A.L.R. 267. We there adopted from Aikens v. State of Wisconsin ... the declaration that "prima facie, the intentional infliction of temporal damage is a cause of action, which requires a justification if the defendant is to escape."

Then, dropping the commas around the words "prima facie," a new name was created in this State for not such a new tort, the Chief Judge saying: "The above second cause of action alleges such a prima facie tort and, therefore, is sufficient in law on its face."

It is not important to the present analysis that the so-called "prima facie" tort was thus rationalized. It is important that the Court aligned itself with the Holmes-Pollack view that tort concepts of liability did not depend solely upon procedural categories, important as they were, and that intentional harm, without excuse or justification, was actionable, simpliciter. The extension of these principles is well beyond what has been since dubbed the "prima facie" tort. Indeed, the subclassification of "prima facie" tort has perhaps caused more trouble in understanding than what it was supposed to clarify. (See, e.g., Ruza v. Ruza, 286 App.Div. 767, 1 A.D.2d 669, cf. Brandt v. Winchell, 286 App.Div. 249, 250, 141 N.Y.S.2d 674, 675 suggesting that "prima facie" tort is concerned only with loss to plaintiff's occupation or business; but see Brandt v. Winchell, 283 App.Div. 338, 342, 127 N.Y.S.2d 865, 869, where the generalization was limited to "ordinarily."... What should be clear enough is that "prima facie" tort does not embrace all intentional tort outside the classic categories of intentional torts....

There has been some discussion whether plaintiff's reputation could have been harmed, turning on whether it was reasonable, and therefore credible, for the public to generalize that the corruption exposed applied to all rather than only to some of the contestants in the rigged contest. That is a question of fact. The pleading alleges that it happened. The proof of the pleading may well be another matter. Then it will be time enough to speak of what plaintiff has shown. At this stage he succeeds merely by alleging, so long as he alleges enough.

Sufficient has already been said to suggest the answer to the limitations problem. Only if plaintiff were suing in defamation would the one-year statute for libel or slander apply (Civ.Prac.Act, § 51, subd. 3). The acts charged here are neither libel nor slander; only the harm which resulted was the same as that in the law of defamation. Consequently, the applicable statute of limitation is the six-year statute covering personal injuries other than those covered elsewhere in the limitation statutes under the Civil Practice Act, which controlled when this action was started in 1961.... The injury was a personal one because a harm to reputation accomplished by intentional falsehood (General Construction Law, § 37-a).

It has been assumed by most in the discussion of this case that plaintiff has the burden of alleging special damages. If he does, the allegations are somewhat deficient but only in a very technical sense; and if so, these could and should be easily cured by allowing him to amend.[4]

---

4. Plaintiff's allegations of special damage do not allege that he would have received either of two fellowships for which he had applied, except for the scandal, but only that he had reason to believe that he would receive one of them....

But plaintiff's claim should not depend upon the allegation and proof of special damages. The reason is that the harm to reputation alleged here is exactly of the kind for which in the law of defamation recovery is allowed in the way of general damages. In short, on plaintiff's allegations he was in effect exposed to the charge of being a cheat, that is, a corrupt conniver in a scheme to divert rewards in a contest from those entitled to them to those who cheated. Put another way: defendants never said of plaintiff that he was a cheater, they only caused him to appear to be one. It hardly requires additional proof that this is destructive of plaintiff's standing or prospects as a university teacher of the young.

The situation should not be confused with that kind of action on the case addressed to specific economic harms or the "prima facie tort" doctrine, where other nonintentional conduct is involved or where otherwise lawfully privileged means are used. Then the policy of the law is very strong in not hobbling privileged or morally innocent conduct unless it results in specifically established economic harm. On the other hand, where the conduct is purposively corrupt by conventional standards, intentional as to consequences, or utilizes vicious means (again by conventional standards), the law will allow general recovery for foreseeable harm to established protected interests, such as reputation in trade or occupation, reputation for chastity or honesty, consortium, and, at one time, the love and affection of another.

If it be true, as he alleges, that plaintiff, a young academic at the beginning of his professional university career, was tarred as a corrupt conniver with others in a rigged television contest, as a result of defendants' misrepresentations to him, the harm to his professional reputation would be great indeed. Paradoxically, the greater the harm, the less likely would he be able to show future prospects that never materialized because of the scandal associated with his name. Thus the principles implicit in this case associate, as to damages, with those found in the law of defamation, just as in other respects the applicable principles are found in the law of deceit, in the law of injurious falsehood, and in one respect, in the law of negligence. The justification for allowing general damages is the practical recognition that harm normally occurs from a type of conduct even if specific damages are not provable, while general damages are not justified where there is no likelihood or practical presumption that the wrong will result in harm.... A bad reason for requiring allegation and proof of special damages is to discourage "new" causes of action. So too, because only "older" forms of action allowed recovery for general damages.

It is especially interesting that Ratcliffe v. Evans ([1892] 2 Q.B. 524, ...) upon which this Court relied in [a precedent to which reference is herein omitted] contains a fine analysis of the applicable rules in determining whether or not general damages will be allowed or whether the victim of a tort will be confined to the damages he can allege and prove specifically. The English Court, per the distinguished Bowen, L. J., after discussing the fluctuating use of the terms "general" and "special damages," observed that general damages will be allowed wherever in the course of experience the loss is a direct and natural consequence of the wrongdoing. More important, however, is that, in discussing recovery for the non-category tort of injurious falsehood, the Court made it clear that general damages might be allowed. In this connection it analogized the rule of damages in defamation, not because injurious falsehood was like defamation but because the harm sustained is like that resulting from defamation....

In conclusion, it should be observed that the classical categories of tort were merely classifications, and incomplete ones at that. Omitted were all the law of negligence, the intentional tort committed by lawful means but solely out of malevolence (the "prima facie" tort), and innumerable other remediable wrongs wrought in the later common law years from the formless mold of "action on the case," out of which even the action on assumpsit had to arise because the "contract" categories had hardened into debt, covenant, and the like. This history should create no problems for a modern court but, instead, provides modes of solution, especially so where the claim rests on elements each of which, considered separately, has been recognized as an operative fact in the law of torts. Nor should a slavish formalism apply to the rule of damages any more than to the statement of a substantive claim. In either case, a rule should stand or fall because of its reason or lack of it. . . .

[JUSTICE EAGER, dissenting in part, would have required special damages.]

[The dissenting opinion of Justice Steuer is omitted.]

[**The Court of Appeals reversed, 19 N.Y.2d 453, 227 N.E.2d 572, 280 N.Y.S.2d 641 (1967), applying the statute of limitations for defamation: "[T]he Legislature should be understood to have established the policy that any action to recover damages for injury to reputation must be begun within that period." — Ed.**]

NOTES

(1) We have seen that in the traditional way that lawyers are educated, some of the "intentional torts," such as assault and battery, may be defined by "elements." Can you, in an analogous way, spell out the "elements" of the *Morrison* tort? Doesn't Judge Breitel seem to give two, or even three, separate definitions of the cause of action he is exploring? How do you collate those definitions?

(2) In reversing the Appellate Division, the Court of Appeals in *Morrison* concluded that "[U]nlike most torts, defamation is defined in terms of the injury, damage to reputation, and not in terms of the manner in which the injury is accomplished." 19 N.Y.2d at 458, 227 N.E.2d at 574, 280 N.Y.S.2d at 644. Does Judge Breitel persuade you that it was respectable for him to characterize facts that so closely fit this formulation as something else?

(3) Are rigged quiz shows socially valueless? Given the majority's summary of the prima facie tort doctrine, would it appear that a claimant under that theory must show that the defendant's conduct produces no social benefit?

(4) In *Nader v. General Motors*, supra Chapter 1, could some of Nader's causes of action, not cognizable in privacy, properly have been slotted in the Morrison category?

(5) Is there a common thread that connects *Morrison* to *Vosburg*? Is *Morrison* based on an intentional tort?

(6) A "frontier" tort claim with a flavor of international conspiracy founders on the ultimate decision of the New York Court of Appeals in the Morrison case in *Korry v. International Tel. & Tel. Corp.*, 444 F. Supp. 193 (S.D.N.Y. 1978). The plaintiff, at one time the American ambassador to Chile, alleged that the defendant's employees had made false statements to the effect that he had known of, and had responsibility for, efforts by the corporation to undermine the Chilean government. He claimed that the firm was trying vindictively to harm him, and that its activities had destroyed his ability to pursue a career in international relations or journalism. The district court, "look[ing] to the essence of plaintiff's claim, not the label he chooses to tag onto it," applied the short defamation statute of limitations. Moreover, given that there were some allegations that the corporation had undertaken some of the sued-upon activities in an effort to protect itself, for example from possible civil and criminal liability, the court refused to uphold a claim for

"prima facie tort." The court said that cause of action "does not lie where the defendants' action has any motive other than a desire to injure a plaintiff."

(7) The tort of injurious falsehood, or disparagement, requires publication of "matter derogatory to the plaintiff's title to his property, or its quality, or to his business in general, or even to some element of his personal affairs, of a kind calculated to prevent others from dealing with him, or otherwise to interfere with his relations with others to his disadvantage." See W. PROSSER AND W.P. KEETON ON TORTS 967 (5th ed. 1984). Although the tort resembles defamation, there is no presumption, as in defamation actions, that the statement is false; moreover, the plaintiff must always prove special damages. *Id.* Special damage in this sense means a pecuniary loss generally, a loss of prospective contracts with customers. *Id.* at 972–73.

(8) What is the essential utility of the tort "categories" anyway?

PROBLEM*

How should the New York Court of Appeals have ruled on the controversy described below?

* * *

This appeal arises in the context of an apparently bitter dispute between a school district and a teachers' association. The school district contends that the association and its attorney are liable for abusing legal process by subpoenaing, with the intent to harass and to injure, 87 teachers and refusing to stagger their appearances. As a result the school district was compelled to hire substitutes in order to avert a total shutdown.

The controversy began in March, 1972 when a number of teachers employed by the district were absent from their classes on two successive days. The school district considered this illegal and a state agency charged the teachers' association with violating a law prohibiting strikes by public employees. The association vehemently denied having engaged in or condoned a strike and the matter was scheduled for a hearing to be held on October 5, 6, 10 and 11.

The complaint contains the following version of the ensuing events. Sometime between September 5, 1972 and October 5, 1972, the attorney for the association prepared and issued judicial subpoenas duces tecum to 87 teachers in order to compel their attendance as witnesses on October 5. The school district learned of these subpoenas on or about October 3, 1972 when the individual teachers requested approved absences from teaching duties in accordance with the collective bargaining agreement. The complaint further alleges that the district's prompt oral request that the majority of teachers be excused from attendance at the initial hearing date was refused by the defendant. Indeed, the defendant refused even to grant the request to stagger the appearances. Consequently, all 87 teachers attended the hearing and 77 substitute teachers were hired to replace them.

The school district alleges that the defendants wrongfully and maliciously and with intent to injure and harass the plaintiff issued 87 subpoenas with knowledge that all the teachers could not have possibly testified on the initial hearing date. As damages for this

---

* Adapted from a summary of facts in a state case.

cause of action plaintiff seeks the amount expended to engage substitute teachers and an amount representing the aggregate salary of the subpoenaed teachers. Defendants moved to dismiss primarily for failure to state a cause of action.

BURNS JACKSON MILLER SUMMIT & SPITZER v. LINDNER
New York Court of Appeals
59 N.Y.2d 314, 451 N.E.2d 459, 464 N.Y.S.2d 712 (1983)

OPINION OF THE COURT

MEYER, JUDGE.

The Taylor Law proscription against strikes by public employees neither preempts the right of persons injured by an unlawful strike to sue for damages nor provides a private right to sue for violation of its provisions. The causes of action pleaded by plaintiffs are, however, either not recognized under New York law or as pleaded do not sufficiently state a cause of action. The order of the Appellate Division, 88 A.D.2d 50, 452 N.Y.S.2d 80, should, therefore, be affirmed, with costs.

I

This appeal involves separate action by two New York City law firms to recover damages resulting from the April, 1980 transit strike. The first, begun in Queens County by Burns Jackson Miller Summit & Spitzer ("Burns Jackson"), is a class action against the Transport Workers Union of America, AFL-CIO (TWU), the Amalgamated Transit Union, AFL-CIO (ATU), Local 100 of TWU, Locals 726 and 1056 of ATU and their respective officers. It alleges that the strike was intentional and in violation of both section 210 of the Civil Service Law and of a preliminary injunction issued March 31, 1980 by the Supreme Court and seeks damages of $50,000,000 per day for each day of the strike. The complaint sets forth two causes of action: prima facie tort and public nuisance.

The second action, begun in New York County by Jackson, Lewis, Schnitzler and Krupman ("Jackson, Lewis"), likewise alleges an intentional strike in violation of the statute and preliminary injunction. It was, however, brought only against the TWU and its Local 100, and officers of both, sought but $25,000 in damages, and did not ask class action status. It declared on six causes of action: for violation of the Taylor Law, prima facie tort, intentional interference with plaintiff's business, willful injury, conspiracy and breach of plaintiff's rights as third-party beneficiary of the contract between defendant unions and the New York City Transit Authority (NYCTA) and the Manhattan and Bronx Surface Transit Operating Authority (MABSTOA).

By stipulation the New York County action was removed to Queens and joined with the Queens action for trial. Thereafter defendants moved pursuant to CPLR 3211 (subd. [a], par. 7) to dismiss both actions for failure to state a cause of action. Special Term denied the motions, except as to the Jackson, Lewis contract cause of action (108 Misc.2d 458, 437 N.Y.S.2d 895). On cross appeals to the Appellate Division, that court, in an extensive opinion, modified the order appealed from to dismiss both complaints in their entirety (88 A.D.2d 50, 452 N.Y.S.2d 80). Both plaintiffs appeal to us as of right (CPLR 5601, subd. [a]). We conclude ... that the complaints fail to state a cause of action for (a) prima facie tort, (b) public nuisance, (c) intentional interference with business, or (d) breach of plaintiffs' rights as third-party beneficiary of defendants' contracts with NYCTA or MABSTOA. We, therefore, affirm.

[Omitted is a discussion of the claim based on the Taylor Law.]

The cause of action common to the two complaints is that in prima facie tort. The elements of such a cause of action as stated in prior New York cases are (1) intentional infliction of harm, (2) resulting in special damages, (3) without excuse or justification, and (4) by an act or series of acts that would otherwise be lawful.... Plaintiff suggests, however, that it is anomalous to deny a cause of action on the ground that the injury-causing act was unlawful and the balancing analysis espoused in Comment e of section 870 of the Restatement of Torts, Second, lends some credence to that argument.

It can be argued that unlawful acts are not covered by prima facie tort because they will normally be compensable in traditional tort forms of action, unless the policy underlying the traditional tort excludes such an act. But it can also be argued that the reference to "lawful" acts was a result of the genesis of prima facie tort, which was conceived as a means of avoiding a "hardening of ... categories" (Morrison v. National Broadcasting Co., 24 A.D.2d 284, 287, 266 N.Y.S.2d 406 [Breitel, J.], revd. on other grounds 19 N.Y.2d 453, 280 N.Y.S.2d 641, 227 N.E.2d 572), by providing redress for an act, even though otherwise lawful and not encompassed by a traditional tort, done solely for an improper or evil motive.

As it has evolved prima facie tort is neither a "'catch-all' alternative for every cause of action which cannot stand on its legs" (Belsky v. Lowenthal, 62 A.D.2d 319, 323, 405 N.Y.S.2d 62, affd. 47 N.Y.2d 820, 418 N.Y.S.2d 573, 392 N.E.2d 560), nor will the existence of a traditional tort foreclose alternative pleading of prima facie tort, though, of course, double recoveries will not be allowed.... The "categories" argument, therefore, need not exclude an unlawful act, as, indeed, the Restatement of Torts, Second, has recognized (§ 870, Comment h).

We need not now decide whether an unlawful act can be the predicate for prima facie tort, for there is no recovery in prima facie tort unless malevolence is the sole motive for defendant's otherwise lawful act or, in Justice Holmes' characteristically colorful language, unless defendant acts from "disinterested malevolence"..., by which is meant "that the genesis which will make a lawful act unlawful must be a malicious one unmixed with any other and exclusively directed to injury and damage of another" (Beardsley v. Kilmer, 236 N.Y. 80, 90, 140 N.E. 203).

Here the prima facie tort causes of action cannot stand because, although they allege intentional and malicious action, they do not allege that defendants' sole motivation was "disinterested malevolence."

[Omitted are discussions of the other theories pleaded by the plaintiffs.]

[Affirmed.]

RESTATEMENT (SECOND) OF TORTS § 870 (1979)
Liability for Intended Consequences — General Principle*

One who intentionally causes injury to another is subject to liability to the other for that injury, if his conduct is generally culpable and not justifiable under the circum-

---

stances. This liability may be imposed although the actor's conduct does not come within a traditional category of tort liability.

Comment:

a. Nature of Section. This Section is intended to supply a generalization for tortious conduct involving harm intentionally inflicted. Generalizations have long existed for negligence liability, involving conduct producing unreasonable risk of harm to others ... and for strict liability, involving the carrying on of an activity that is abnormally dangerous.... As for conduct intentionally causing harm, however, it has traditionally been assumed that the several established intentional torts developed separately and independently and not in accordance with any unifying principle. This Section purports to supply that unifying principle and to explain the basis for the development of the more recently created intentional torts. More than that, it is intended to serve as a guide for determining when liability should be imposed for harm that was intentionally inflicted, even though the conduct does not come within the requirements of one of the well established and named intentional torts.

NOTES

(1) Does section 870 satisfactorily solve the problem presented by the *Morrison* case, and by the *Burns Jackson Miller* case?

(2) Could you make a more precise statement of the general residual principles of tort that would enable judges to deal with such cases more coherently?

(3) There are two tort actions that relate to the actual bringing of lawsuits.

The elements of the first, malicious prosecution, are initiation or procurement "of criminal proceedings against an innocent person for any improper purpose and without probable cause..., if the proceedings terminate favorably for the person thus prosecuted." 1 F. HARPER, F. JAMES & O. GRAY, LAW OF TORTS § 4.1, at 4:1 (Gray, 3d ed. 1996). For these purposes "probable cause" requires "reasonable belief that the plaintiff was guilty," and malice or actual ill will do not, by themselves, show a lack of probable cause. *Id.* § 4.5, at 4:21–22. There is a parallel tort of malicious civil litigation. This tort is quite similar to malicious criminal prosecution, but it differs with respect to the motivation of the accuser. In a criminal proceeding, the accuser "must believe that the accused is guilty," but in malicious civil prosecution, it is enough that he has a "reasonable belief in the possibility that the claim may be held valid." *Id.* § 4.8, at 4-66.

The separate action for abuse of process is different, focusing on the misuse of the process itself—that is, the defendant must invoke the process "'primarily' to accomplish the ulterior end." The principal contrast with malicious prosecution is that the plaintiff in an abuse of process case does not have to show that the defendant complained without probable cause or that the plaintiff was successful in defending against the claim. *Id.* § 4.9, at 4-84–85. Frequently, the factual focus of an abuse of process case is the use of the legal system to extort money from the plaintiff. See *id.* at 4-87. Spite

Chapter 3

DEFENSES TO CLAIMS OF INTENTIONAL TORT

§ 3.01 Self-Defense

PROBLEM

A 68-year-old man, Mr. Walters, often takes an evening walk to the corner grocery to buy milk or pipe tobacco. He has taken to carrying a gun, because one of his neighbors was murdered a few weeks ago by people he describes as "young toughs."

One snowy night, as he is returning from his walk with a packet of tobacco, he meets four teenagers walking toward him on the sidewalk. As they come to a point about 50 feet away, they begin taunting him and throwing snowballs at him. Later explaining that the youths "frightened" him and "made me fear for my safety," he pulls out the gun and shoots one through the heart.

What are the chances that the youth's family will be able to bring a claim for his death against Mr. Walters based on a battery theory?

Would it make a difference if the youths were 25 feet away when Mr. Walters shot?

What if two had moved in back of him, and two were advancing to within 10 feet in front of him, and one said, "Let's see if the old bastard would like to eat snow"?

What if Mr. Walters had stabbed one of the youths with an ice pick, fatally wounding him? Inflicting a wound that was not fatal, but required surgery and several weeks of hospitalization?

RESTATEMENT (SECOND) OF TORTS § 65 (1965)*

§ 65. Self-Defense by Force Threatening Death or Serious Bodily Harm

(1) Subject to the statement in Subsection (3), an actor is privileged to defend himself against another by force intended or likely to cause death or serious bodily harm, when he reasonably believes that

(a) the other is about to inflict upon him an intentional contact or other bodily harm, and that

(b) he is thereby put in peril of death or serious bodily harm or ravishment, which can safely be prevented only by the immediate use of such force.

---

(2) The privilege stated in Subsection (1) exists although the actor correctly or reasonably believes that he can safely avoid the necessity of so defending himself by

(a) retreating if he is attacked within his dwelling place, which is not also the dwelling place of the other, or

(b) permitting the other to intrude upon or dispossess him of his dwelling place, or

(c) abandoning an attempt to effect a lawful arrest.

(3) The privilege stated in Subsection (1) does not exist if the actor correctly or reasonably believes that he can with complete safety avoid the necessity of so defending himself by

(a) retreating if attacked in any place other than his dwelling place, or in a place which is also the dwelling of the other, or

(b) relinquishing the exercise of any right or privilege other than his privilege to prevent intrusion upon or dispossession of his dwelling place or to effect a lawful arrest.

FORMER TEXAS PENAL CODE § 220

Homicide is justifiable when committed by the husband upon one taken in the act of adultery with the wife, provided the killing take place before the parties to the act have separated. Such circumstance cannot justify a homicide where it appears that there has been, on the part of the husband, any connivance in or assent to the adulterous connection. [Repealed 1973.]

NOTES

(1) Reconsider the basic profile of the Problem involving Mr. Walters. Now suppose that Mr. Walters had been beaten twice by the same group of four youths, one of whom was obviously the ringleader, and that on another of Mr. Walters' walks, that youth had come up to him and said, "One of these nights, we're going to get you, once and for all." Suppose further that Mr. Walters knew that the group frequently "hung out" around a particular lamppost. If on his walk one night he walked up to the ringleader and shot him, is there any chance that he could plead self-defense successfully?

Consider, in this regard, the following news story:

Alexander Innis, the 16-year-old son of CORE [Congress of Racial Equality] director Roy Innis, got caught up in the law of the blackboard jungle last week.

It all started on Tuesday afternoon when young Innis was beaten by some fellow students at James Monroe High School in the Bronx. He appealed to CORE for protection from further harassment. The next day, according to police, four men from CORE entered his classroom and, taking him along as guide, searched 12 other rooms until they found his assailants.

Two of the youths, police say, were taken back to CORE headquarters in Harlem, forced to strip and then beaten with coat hangers and rubber hoses. The police quickly arrested two CORE officials on charges of kidnapping, coercion and felonious assault. A day later, Bronx District Attorney Burton Roberts ordered the arrest of young Innis himself on juvenile delinquency charges for fingering his attackers.

—News of Week in Review, N.Y. Times, c. 1971.

Should the following statement by Roy Innis be considered as evidence of the reasonableness of the force? "I have had one son shot in the back and killed and it's not going to happen again. I grew up in Harlem and I know that a lot of people get shot, stabbed and maimed."

(2) Police behavior naturally provides a font of self-defense issues. Illustrative of judicial sympathy for split-second judgments is a section 1983 case in which police answered a call from a woman whose anniversary celebration turned ugly, with her husband striking her in the face. A uniformed officer approached the husband, who was swinging a baseball bat and yelling, "I'll kill you, mother f*****." After two commands to the husband to drop the bat, punctuated with another threat by the husband to kill the officer, the officer closed to within three or four feet. The husband kept waving the bat, and the officer fired a single shot, which proved fatal. The decedent's blood alcohol level was 0.245, after two blood transfusions that were said to have lowered the blood alcohol significantly. The court granted summary judgment, saying that the officer had "probable cause to believe that [the decedent] posed a significant threat of serious bodily injury" and concluding that "[t]he use of deadly force under such circumstances was reasonable." *James v. City of Chester*, 852 F. Supp. 1288, 1295 (D.S.C. 1994).

(3) Should a police officer be permitted to sue the victim of an illegal arrest for the latter's battery committed during his resistance to that arrest? The common law rule on the criminal side suggests that no action would lie, for that rule holds that citizens may resist illegal arrests. The position of the Uniform Arrest Act and the Model Penal Code is to the contrary, as is evident in a criminal case holding against the citizen's right to resist. *State v. Koonce*, 89 N.J. Super. 169, 214 A.2d 428 (1965). The rationale for the rule prohibiting resistance emphasizes the deadly consequences of resistance in a day of heavy firepower. However, it also suggests that there is no longer a problem of falsely arrested persons languishing in hideous jails. The court in *Koonce*, supra, cites a commentary on the Uniform Act to the effect that "the fate of today's arrestee is usually a few hours in a reasonably clean place of detention rather than the probable consequences awaiting the arrestee of yore." *Id.* at 182, 214 A.2d at 434. But the question of the conditions of detention is one that demands empirical evidence, and that evidence is not favorable to the new, supposedly more civilized rule. See, e.g., *The Arrests That Can Lead to Terror and Humiliation*, Washington Post, Sept. 27, 1982, at A-1 & A-8, reporting that "[v]iolent gang rapes and sexual assaults occur in the Prince George's County jail about a dozen times a week," and that "the jail routinely places those most likely to rape with those particularly vulnerable." Does this convince you that the architects of the common law rule still have the better of the argument, at least with respect to an officer's civil suit for a battery committed on the officer by a person he has illegally arrested?

(4) The *Restatement* says that one may defend himself against a battery or "other bodily harm which he reasonably believes that another is about to inflict intentionally upon him" by the use of "reasonable force, not intended or likely to cause death or serious bodily harm." This privilege applies even though the self-defender correctly or reasonably believes that he can avoid the necessity to defend himself, for example by retreating. Restatement (Second) of Torts § 63 (1965).

(5) American jurisdictions have mostly moved toward a law of comparative responsibility for negligence—a contrast with the old rule that made a plaintiff's contributory negligence a complete bar to recovery. Material on comparative fault with respect to negligence and strict liability appears infra at § 5.05. But what do you think about a rule

that allows an intentional tortfeasor to use a victim's conduct to mitigate liability—for example, reducing or eliminating the liability of a self-defender when the person he kills or injures initiated violence between the two parties?

(6) Suppose a public school teacher perceives that an angry student is about to grab him or her in an unfriendly way. Should he or she be liable for using a device that sprays out a chemical which causes temporary numbness to any areas of the body it hits, assuming it produces no long-term effects? What about spraying from a can of insecticide that happens to be on his or her desk, which makes the student quite sick for a day or two but causes no provable lingering illness? Should the case of a classroom teacher liberalize the self-defense rules beyond those available to ordinary citizens? Cf. *Owens v. Commonwealth*, 473 S.W.2d 827 (Ky. 1971) ("sneeze gun," causing "temporary eye irritation"; teacher's conviction reversed).

(7) Consider the following statement of North African Islamic law:

§ 2038.... [P]ecuniary responsibility rests on:

(c) him who, by quickly pulling away his hand, pulls out the teeth of another who was biting him.

F. H. Ruxton, Maliki Law: Being A Summary from French Translations of the Mukhtasar of Sidi Khalil 348 (London: Luzac & Co. 1916).*

From your acquaintance with the culture of the United States, and a little bit of its law, can you provide a rationalization for this rule? What might be the rationale provided by a judge in Morocco?

§ 3.02 Defense of Property

PROBLEM
Man Held In Electrocution of Intruder
Miami Herald, Oct. 6, 1986**
By Herbert Buchsbaum and Richard Wallace

Miami detectives charged a shop owner with manslaughter Tuesday after a suspected burglar was found entangled and electrocuted in a booby trap rigged under the store's ceiling.

"It was just like an animal caught in a trap," Detective Jon Spear said.

Store proprietor Prentice Rasheed, 43, was in custody Tuesday, charged with manslaughter and setting a man-trap.

"It's a sad situation," Spear said. "The man was obviously upset about the burglaries in the area. He was a legitimate businessman and just took extreme measures."

---

* The authors are grateful to Larry Rosen for pointing out this rule. Professor Rosen describes Khalil as "one of the most important commentators of the school of Islamic law applied across the whole of North Africa from Morocco to Egypt."

** Copyright © 1986 by The Miami Herald. Reprinted by permission.

Rasheed had bolted a grate above the front door of his store, where thieves had entered through the ceiling several times before. The grate was wired with an extension cord to a 110-volt outlet.

Odell Hicks of 746 NW 61st St. had broken a hole in the ceiling of Rasheed's Amcop Station & Trading Post, also called the Central City Flea Market, at 6040 NW Seventh Ave.

Hicks climbed through the hole, his sneakers protecting him from the electric current in the grate below.

Police said Hicks removed several loads of discount clothing and was killed when he touched the metal mesh on his way out.

Rasheed told police he thought the voltage would shock an intruder, not kill him.

The store's manager, John El-Amin, discovered the body lying across the mesh when he opened the store at 9:30 a.m. Piles of merchandise—discount clothes, costume jewelry, dollar watches and $5 shoes—had been shoved through the store's iron-bar back gate and were found in the alley behind the store.

"We've been broken into eight times," El-Amin said as he swept up the crumbled plaster under the hole in the ceiling. Police said the shop had been burglarized four times in the past two weeks.

Amcop, which stands for American Muslim Committee to Purchase 100,000 Commodities Plus, occupies the former Carver movie theater building in what is now a largely Jamaican neighborhood. The surrounding blocks of mom-and-pop storefronts, most bearing matching burglar bars, have been plagued in the past two weeks by what the police call "roof jobs."

Police are investigating whether Hicks may have been involved in the other cases. Area merchants said Tuesday that Hicks not only committed previous burglaries, but bragged about them.

"He would boast and tell what he does," said Willie Williams, owner of the Dupont Wash Center car wash at 60th Street and Northwest Seventh Avenue. "He would sit up in this tree and drink beer and tell everybody what he does."

Williams sympathized with Rasheed. "I guess he was tired of being vandalized," Williams said. "He's an honest man. We don't want to do evil for evil, but how'd you like it if you had a business that kept getting robbed? We call the police and don't get results."

Next door at Just Coool, a Jamaican bakery, manager Al Wallace said that he suspected Hicks of stealing paintings from his shop. After that burglary, Wallace said, some of his customers purchased the paintings from a street peddler. "And they said it's the same guy," Wallace said.

Assistant State Attorney Rafael Rodriguez said the case was considered manslaughter because of the owner's "disregard for human life."

Rasheed, he said, "was using deadly force for defense of property, which is not acceptable."

———————

If Hicks's family sued Rasheed for this death, what defense would Rasheed offer? What would be his likely chances of success?

[A] The Spring Gun as a Symbol of Rights in Conflict

KATKO v. BRINEY
Iowa Supreme Court
183 N.W.2d 657 (1971)

MOORE, CHIEF JUSTICE.

The primary issue presented here is whether an owner may protect personal property in an unoccupied boarded-up farm house against trespassers and thieves by a spring gun capable of inflicting death or serious injury.

We are not here concerned with a man's right to protect his home and members of his family. Defendants' home was several miles from the scene of the incident to which we refer infra.

Plaintiff's action is for damages resulting from serious injury caused by a shot from a 20-gauge spring shotgun set by defendants in a bedroom of an old farm house which had been uninhabited for several years. Plaintiff and his companion, Marvin McDonough, had broken and entered the house to find and steal old bottles and dated fruit jars which they considered antiques.

At defendants' request plaintiff's action was tried to a jury consisting of residents of the community where defendants' property was located. The jury returned a verdict for plaintiff and against defendants for $20,000 actual and $10,000 punitive damages.

After careful consideration of defendants' motions for judgment notwithstanding the verdict and for new trial, the experienced and capable trial judge overruled them and entered judgment on the verdict. Thus we have this appeal by defendants.

. . .

II. Most of the facts are not disputed. In 1957 defendant Bertha L. Briney inherited her parents' farm land in Mahaska and Monroe Counties. Included was an 80-acre tract in southwest Mahaska County where her grandparents and parents had lived. No one occupied the house thereafter. Her husband, Edward, attempted to care for the land. He kept no farm machinery thereon. The outbuildings became dilapidated.

For about 10 years, 1957 to 1967, there occurred a series of trespassing and housebreaking events with loss of some household items, the breaking of windows and "messing up of the property in general". The latest occurred June 8, 1967, prior to the event on July 16, 1967 herein involved.

Defendants through the years boarded up the windows and doors in an attempt to stop the intrusions. They had posted "no trespass" signs on the land several years before 1967. The nearest one was 35 feet from the house. On June 11, 1967 defendants set "a shotgun trap" in the north bedroom. After Mr. Briney cleaned and oiled his 20-gauge shotgun, the power of which he was well aware, defendants took it to the old house where they secured it to an iron bed with the barrel pointed at the bedroom door. It was rigged with wire from the doorknob to the gun's trigger so it would fire when the door was opened. Briney first pointed the gun so an intruder would be hit in the stomach but at Mrs. Briney's suggestion it was lowered to hit the legs. He admitted he did so "because I was mad and tired of being tormented" but "he did not intend to injure anyone". He gave no explanation of why he used a loaded shell and set it to hit a person already in the house. Tin was nailed over the bedroom window. The spring gun could not be seen from the outside. No warning of its presence was posted.

Plaintiff lived with his wife and worked regularly as a gasoline station attendant in Eddyville, seven miles from the old house. He had observed it for several years while hunting in the area and considered it as being abandoned. He knew it had long been uninhabited. In 1967 the area around the house was covered with high weeds. Prior to July 16, 1967 plaintiff and McDonough had been to the premises and found several old bottles and fruit jars which they took and added to their collection of antiques. On the latter date about 9:30 p.m. they made a second trip to the Briney property. They entered the old house by removing a board from a porch window which was without glass. While McDonough was looking around the kitchen area plaintiff went to another part of the house. As he started to open the north bedroom door the shotgun went off striking him in the right leg above the ankle bone. Much of his leg, including part of the tibia, was blown away. Only by McDonough's assistance was plaintiff able to get out of the house and after crawling some distance was put in his vehicle and rushed to a doctor and then to a hospital. He remained in the hospital 40 days....

IV. The main thrust of defendants' defense in the trial court and on this appeal is that "the law permits use of a spring gun in a dwelling or warehouse for the purpose of preventing the unlawful entry of a burglar or thief". They repeated this contention in their exceptions to the trial court's instructions 2, 5 and 6. They took no exception to the trial court's statement of the issues or to other instructions.

In the statement of issues the trial court stated plaintiff and his companion committed a felony when they broke and entered defendants' house. In instruction 2 the court referred to the early case history of the use of spring guns and stated under the law their use was prohibited except to prevent the commission of felonies of violence and where human life is in anger. The instruction included a statement breaking and entering is not a felony of violence.

Instruction 5 stated: "You are hereby instructed that one may use reasonable force in the protection of his property, but such right is subject to the qualification that one may not use such means of force as will take human life or inflict great bodily injury. Such is the rule even though the injured party is a trespasser and is in violation of the law himself."

Instruction 6 stated: "An owner of premises is prohibited from willfully or intentionally injuring a trespasser by means of force that either takes life or inflicts great bodily injury; and therefore a person owning a premise is prohibited from setting out spring guns' and like dangerous devices which will likely take life or inflict great bodily injury, for the purpose of harming trespassers. The fact that the trespasser may be acting in violation of the law does not change the rule. The only time when such conduct of setting a spring gun' or a like dangerous device is justified would be when the trespasser was committing a felony of violence or a felony punishable by death, or where the trespasser was endangering human life by his act."

Instruction 7, to which defendants made no objection or exception, stated: "To entitle the plaintiff to recover for compensatory damages, the burden of proof is upon him to establish by a preponderance of the evidence each and all of the following propositions:

1. That defendants erected a shotgun trap in a vacant house on land owned by defendant, Bertha L. Briney, on or about June 11, 1967, which fact was known only by them, to protect household goods from trespassers and thieves.

2. That the force used by defendants was in excess of that force reasonably necessary and which persons are entitled to use in the protection of their property.

3. That plaintiff was injured and damaged and the amount thereof.

4. That plaintiff's injuries and damages resulted directly from the discharge of the shotgun trap which was set and used by defendants."

The overwhelming weight of authority, both textbook and case law, supports the trial court's statement of the applicable principles of law.

Prosser on Torts, Third Edition, pages 116–118, states:

> " … the law has always placed a higher value upon human safety than upon mere rights in property, it is the accepted rule that there is no privilege to use any force calculated to cause death or serious bodily injury to repel the threat to land or chattels, unless there is also such a threat to the defendant's personal safety as to justify a self-defense.… spring guns and other mankilling devices are not justifiable against a mere trespasser, or even a petty thief. They are privileged only against those upon whom the landowner, if he were present in person would be free to inflict injury of the same kind."

Restatement of Torts, section 85, page 180, states: "The value of human life and limb, not only to the individual concerned but also to society, so outweighs the interest of a possessor of land in excluding from it those whom he is not willing to admit thereto that a possessor of land has, as is stated in §79, no privilege to use force intended or likely to cause death or serious harm against another whom the possessor sees about to enter his premises or meddle with his chattel, unless the intrusion threatens death or serious bodily harm to the occupiers or users of the premises.… A possessor of land cannot do indirectly and by a mechanical device that which, were he present, he could not do immediately and in person. Therefore, he cannot gain a privilege to install, for the purpose of protecting his land from intrusions harmless to the lives and limbs of the occupiers or users of it, a mechanical device whose only purpose is to inflict death or serious harm upon such as may intrude, by giving notice of his intention to inflict, by mechanical means and indirectly, harm which he could not, even after request, inflict directly were he present."

[After citation of numerous primary and secondary sources that support these authorities, the court concludes that the trial judge's instructions 2, 5 and 6 correctly stated the law and that the defendant's objections and exceptions were without merit.]

All Justices concur except LARSON, J., who dissents.

LARSON, JUSTICE. I respectfully dissent, first, because the majority wrongfully assumes that by installing a spring gun in the bedroom of their unoccupied house the defendants intended to shoot any intruder who attempted to enter the room. Under the record presented here, that was a fact question. Unless it is held that … property owners are liable for any injury to a intruder from such a device regardless of the intent with which it is installed, liability under these pleadings must rest upon two definite issues of fact, i.e., did the defendants intend to shoot the invader, and if so, did they employ unnecessary and unreasonable force against him?

· · ·

… I would hold there is no absolute liability for injury to a criminal intruder by setting up such a device on his property, and unless done with an intent to kill or seriously injure the intruder, I would absolve the owner from liability other than for negligence.…

The Mahaska County Grand Jury issued a true bill charging plaintiff with breaking and entering in the nighttime, but the county attorney accepted a plea of guilty to the lesser offense of larceny in the nighttime of property of a value of less than $20 and did not press the greater charge....

I have been unable to find a case exactly like the case at bar, although there have been many cases which consider liability to a mere trespasser for injuries incurred by a spring gun or other dangerous instruments set to protect against intrusion and theft. True, some of these cases seem to turn on the negligence of the party setting the trap and an absence of adequate warning thereof, but most of them involve an alleged intentional tort. It is also true some hold as a matter of public policy there is liability for any injury following the setting of a device which is intended to kill or inflict great bodily injury on one coming on the owner's property without permission, unless the invader poses a threat to human life, and this is so even though there is no statutory prohibition against the setting of spring guns in the jurisdiction.

Since our decision in Hooker v. Miller [37 Iowa 613 (1873)], we have recognized in this state the doctrine that the owner of a premise is liable in damages to a mere trespasser coming upon his property for any injury occasioned by the unsafe condition of the property which the owner has intentionally permitted to exist, such as installed spring guns, unless adequate warning is given thereof. In Hooker, which involved stealing grapes from a vineyard, we held a property owner had no right to resist such a trespass by means which may kill or inflict great bodily injury to the trespasser. But it does appear therein that we recognized some distinction between a mere trespass against property and a trespass involving a serious crime or involving a dwelling. Except when the trespass involves a serious crime, a crime posing a threat to human life, it may be argued that the law in this jurisdiction should limit the right of one to protect his property, that he does not have a privilege to resist a mere trespass by using a spring gun or other device which poses a threat to life.

However, left unsettled by this and other court pronouncements is the means which may be used to repel, prevent, or apprehend a trespasser engaged in a more serious criminal offense. True, there is a line of cases which seem to apply the same rule to all criminal trespasses except those involving arson, rape, assault, or other acts of violence against persons residing on the property invaded.... There are others which at least infer that any serious law violation by the trespasser might permit the reasonable use of dangerous instrumentalities to repel the intruder and prevent loss or damage to one's valuable property....

Most ... discussions center around what should be public policy regarding a property owner's right to use a dangerous weapon or instrumentality to protect his premises from intruders or trespassers, and his duty to protect the trespasser from serious injury while upon his premises.

Some states, including Wisconsin, have statutes which announce the jurisdiction's public policy. Often they prohibit the use of spring guns or such devices to protect real and personal property, and of course in those instances a property owner, regardless of his intent or purpose, has no right to make use of them and is liable to anyone injured thereby. Since there has been no such statutory prohibition or direct judicial pronouncement to that effect prior to this time in this state, it could not be said as a matter of law that the mere placing of a spring gun in a building on one's premises is unlawful. Much depends upon its placement and purpose. Whether an owner exceeds his privilege to reasonably defend his property by such an installation, and whether liability is incurred in a given case, should therefore depend upon the circumstances revealed, the intent of the property owner, and his care in setting the device. In any event, I question whether it should be determined solely by the results of his act or its effect upon the intruder.

It appears there are cases and some authority which would relieve one setting a spring gun on his premises of any liability if adequate warning had been given an intruder and he ignores the warning. In all of these cases there is a question as to the intent of the property owner in setting the device. Intent, of course, may be determined from both direct and indirect evidence, and it is true the physical facts may be and often are sufficient to present a jury issue. I think they were here, but no clear instruction was given in this regard.

If, after proper instructions, the finder of fact determines that the gun was set with an intent and purpose to kill or inflict great bodily injury on an intruder, then and only then may it be said liability is established unless the property so protected is shown to be an occupied dwelling house. Of course, under this concept, if the finder of fact determines the gun set in an unoccupied house was intended to do no more than to frighten the intruder or sting him a bit, no liability would be incurred under such pleadings as are now presented. If such a concept of the law were adopted in Iowa, we would have here a question for the fact-finder or jury as to whether the gun was willfully and intentionally set so as to seriously injure the thief or merely scare him away.

I feel the better rule is that an owner of buildings housing valuable property may employ the use of spring guns or other devices intended to repel but not seriously injure an intruder who enters his secured premises with or without a criminal intent, but I do not advocate its general use, for there may also be liability for negligent installation of such a device. What I mean to say is that under such circumstances as we have here the issue as to whether the set was with an intent to seriously injure or kill an intruder is a question of fact that should be left to the jury under proper instructions, that the mere setting of such a device with a resultant serious injury should not as a matter of law establish liability.

In the case of a mere trespass able authorities have reasoned that absolute liability may rightfully be fixed on the landowner for injuries to the trespasser because very little damage could be inflicted upon the property owner and the danger is great that a child or other innocent trespasser might be seriously injured by the device. In such matters they say no privilege to set up the device should be recognized by the courts regardless of the owner's intent. I agree.

On the other hand, where the intruder may pose a danger to the inhabitants of a dwelling, the privilege of using such a device to repel has been recognized by most authorities, and the mere setting thereof in the dwelling has not been held to create liability for an injury as a matter of law. In such cases intent and the reasonableness of the force would seem relevant to liability.

Although I am aware of the often-repeated statement that personal rights are more important than property rights, where the owner has stored his valuables representing his life's accumulations, his livelihood business, his tools and implements, and his treasured antiques as appears in the case at bar, and where the evidence is sufficient to sustain a finding that the installation was intended only as a warning to ward off thieves and criminals, I can see no compelling reason why the use of such a device alone would create liability as a matter of law.

[Justice Larson's summary of the decisional law includes the following quotations, full case citations of which are earlier omitted:]

In Allison v. Fiscus, ... at page 241 of 100 N.E.2d, it is said: "Assuredly, ... the court had no right to hold as a matter of law that defendant was liable to plaintiff, as the *defendant's good faith* in using the force which he did to protect his building and the good faith of his belief as to the nature of the force he was using were questions for the jury to determine under proper instructions." (Emphasis supplied.)

. . .

Also see State v. Metcalfe, 203 Iowa 155, 212 N.W. 382, where this court discussed the force that a property owner may use to oppose an unlawful effort to carry away his goods, and held the essential issue in such matters which must be explained to the jury is not the nature of the weapon employed but whether the defendant employed only that degree of force to accomplish such purpose which a reasonable person would deem reasonably necessary under the circumstances as they appeared in good faith to the defendant.

Like the Ohio Supreme Court in Allison v. Fiscus, supra, I believe that the basis of liability, if any, in such a case should be either the intentional, reckless, or grossly negligent conduct of the owner in setting the device.

If this is not a desirable expression of policy in this jurisdiction, I suggest the body selected and best fitted to establish a different public policy would be the State Legislature.

The next question presented is, which view of the law set out above did the trial court take, the view that the mere setting of a spring gun or like device in defendants' building created liability for the resulting injury, or the view that there must be a setting of the device with an intent to shoot, kill, or seriously injure one engaged in breaking and entering this house? Appellants argue this was not made clear in the court's instructions to the jury and, being material, is error. I agree....

Appellants argue from these instructions [2, 5 & 6] the jury could conclude it must find any setting of a spring gun or such other device to protect his property from a burglar or other criminal invader made the owner absolutely liable for injuries suffered by the intruder, unless the building being so protected was a dwelling, regardless of the owner's intent and purpose in setting the device in his building. On the other hand, in Instruction No. 6 the court refers to such a setting with the intent and purpose of killing or seriously injuring the intruder in order to make the owner liable for damages.

I too find these instructions are confusing. If the court was telling the jury, as appellants contend, that an owner of a premise may not set a spring gun to protect his property unless the trespasser's act amounts to a felony of violence and endangers human life, the phrase used, "for the purpose of harming trespassers", introduces the element of intent and would tend to confuse the jury as to the law on that issue. If the issue here was that such an intent was necessary to establish liability, the instruction was erroneous and confusing; otherwise the error was without prejudice.

I would, therefore, conclude there is merit in appellants' contention that the law was not made clear to the jury as to whether the act of placing a spring gun on this premise was prohibited by law, or whether the act of placing such a device requires a finding of intention to shoot the intruder or cause him great bodily injury to establish liability. I cannot tell whether the jury found liability on the mere act of placing the gun as Mr. Briney did in this house or on the fact that he did so with the intent to seriously harm a trespasser.

In the case at bar, as I have pointed out, there is a sharp conflict in the evidence. The physical facts and certain admissions as to how the gun was aimed would tend to support a finding of intent to injure, while the direct testimony of both defendants was that the gun was placed so it would "hit the floor eventually" and that it was set "low so it couldn't kill anybody." Mr. Briney testified, "My purpose in setting up the gun was not to injure somebody. I thought more or less that the gun would be at a distance of where anyone would grab the door, it would scare them", and in setting the angle of the gun to hit the lower part of the door, he said, "I didn't think it would go through quite that hard."

If the law in this jurisdiction permits, which I think it does, an explanation of the setting of a spring gun to repel invaders of certain private property, then the intent with which the set is made is a vital element in the liability issue.

In view of the failure to distinguish and clearly give the jury the basis upon which it should determine that liability issue, I would reverse and remand the entire case for a new trial....

NOTES

(1) For conflicting commentary on the *Katko* problem, compare Posner, *Killing or Wounding to Protect a Property Interest*, 14 J.L. & ECON. 201 (1971) with Palmer, *The Iowa Spring Gun Case: A Study in American Gothic*, 56 IOWA L. REV. 1219 (1971).

(2) A Georgia court of appeals imposed liability on the owner of a cigarette vending machine for the death of a youth killed by a dynamite charge with which the defendant had booby-trapped the machine. The defendant's purpose, he said, was to scare vandals; the machine had been burglarized several times. The court noted that the owner made no tests to determine how severe the explosion would be and it also observed that the dynamite had the potential for harming not only trespassers or wrongdoers but also innocent bystanders. Viewing the defendant's conduct as "conscious indifference to consequences," the court concluded that one could "characterize his negligence as willful and wanton conduct." *McKinsey v. Wade*, 136 Ga. App. 109, 220 S.E.2d 30 (1975).

(3) After the *Katko* lawsuit, Briney was quoted as saying, "[I]t seems to me that a boarded up house ought to be like a bank. It shouldn't make any difference if you live there or not—a man's got to have a right to protect his property." *A Town Puzzles Over Farmer Briney's Bizarre Lawsuit*, PEOPLE, Nov. 24. 1975, at 35. How would you explain to Briney why it "make[s] a difference"?

(4) Is it clear from *Katko* whether the court thought that the Brineys had committed an "intentional tort"? Does the dissent offer clarification on this conceptual problem?

(5) The pages of the *Oskaloosa* (Iowa) *Daily Herald* reflected poignantly the plight of the Brineys. On Jan. 27, 1970, the paper featured a picture of a sheriff's sale of 80 acres of the Brineys' farmland to satisfy the judgment. A photograph showed part of a crowd of several hundred who showed up for the sale, at which a bid of $10,001 entered by the chairman of the "Briney Defense Fund" topped by $1 a bid by Katko's attorney. Another picture shows a dour, fur-capped Mr. Briney and a shawled Mrs. Briney, handkerchief under her glasses to her eye. A *National Observer* article (c. Feb. 1971) quoted Mrs. Briney's restrained comment: "My stars ... I still think a person should have the right to protect his property." The UPI reported that inmates at a state reformatory had raised about $100 to help the Brineys. WASHINGTON POST, Feb. 10, 1970. Later the Brineys sued Katko for trespass.[1]

---

1. Probably too late. See Palmer, *supra* note 1, at 1225, saying that this would be a compulsory counterclaim under Iowa law, and thus barred if not brought in conjunction with Katko's damage action.

On another front, a bill was introduced in the Iowa Senate that would have allowed trespassers to file criminal charges against property owners but that would have prohibited the filing of damage suits. Oskaloosa Daily Herald, Jan. 18, 1972, at 1.

(6) Why would it not be appropriate to have a reasonableness test for the defense of property? That way someone using a spring gun would have to take his chances on positioning the weapon, given the value of the property he had to defend, in a way that he would not be found at least negligent. For a list of reasonableness factors, see Posner, *supra* note 1, at 214–16.

(7) The focus in this course is on litigation occurring after an injury has happened. But an important purpose of the course is to stimulate you to think about the consultative function of lawyers who are asked to try to avoid trouble before it occurs.

Consider, for example, the case of Rasheed, the storeowner in the Problem case at the start of this section, who told reporters, "I've been broke into several times in 10 days." Lee, *Merchant Sought Police Aid Before Setting Trap*, Miami Herald, Oct. 4, 1984.

How would you advise the owner of a small business in a high-crime area who asks whether he may use in his store a gadget which he can control from his loft to swing great weights at intruders, causing a probability of substantial physical harm but only a small possibility of death? How about the use of an electrified storefront? German Shepherds? (A number of big department stores have used Shepherds to catch people who secrete themselves at closing so they can shoplift after hours.)

Should it make a difference if the entrepreneur who uses any of these measures posts a very conspicuous sign reading, "DEATH TO ROBBERS; THIS STORE IS PROTECTED BY DEADLY WEAPONS"?

(8) Colorado and Oklahoma statutes grant citizens "a right to expect absolute safety within their own homes." Colo. Rev. Stat. Ann. § 18-1-704.5; 21 Okl. Stat. Ann. § 1289.25. While the Oklahoma law authorizes deadly force to resist intrusion upon "reasonable belief that [the intruder] might use any physical force, no matter how slight, against any occupant of the dwelling," the Colorado law authorizes deadly force when the intruder "has committed . . . or intends to commit a crime against a person *or property* in addition to the uninvited entry" (emphasis added). In 2003, Richard Hammock broke a glass pane in his neighbor's window with a club amid a dispute over Hammock's barking dog, Mojo. The neighbor, Eric Griffin, shot and killed Hammock with a shotgun. Citing Colorado's "Make My Day Law," the district attorney reluctantly declined to prosecute Griffin. Garner, *Ault Struggles with Shooting*, Rocky Mountain News, Nov. 28, 2003, at 61A. Should Griffin have been required to summon police before firing? Should it have mattered that Hammock outweighed Griffin by more than 100 pounds? Is the scope of either the Oklahoma or the Colorado law adequately circumscribed?

(9) Ought there to be a difference between the law applicable in rural and urban settings? Between situations in which potential robbers are or are not likely to have weapons themselves? One news story recorded the tale of James Hawkins, a prosperous 72-year-old businessman whose enterprises included a "tiny grocery" in the Watts section of Los Angeles. Refusing to move to the more affluent neighborhood he could afford, Hawkins kept a loaded revolver near the grocery's cash register and frequently used it, not only against robbers but also people stealing purses or bicycles in the vicinity.

The story described the store as being "under siege," and chronicled a situation in which police raided the homes of the store owner's gang enemies, and in which "city politicians who usually favor laws to limit handguns [come by] to congratulate him."

The reporter recorded that when elderly neighbors would visit Hawkins to thank him for his activities, "[he] has the same message for each: 'I want to let the hoodlums know that they can't push a citizen around.'" Mathews, *In Los Angeles 'War Zone,' Merchant Fends Off Gangs*, WASHINGTON POST, Nov. 25, 1983, at A16.

[B] The Merchant's Privilege

The Merchant, The Shoplifter and The Law
55 MINN. L. REV. 825 (1971)*

[At common law, the privilege of merchants to detain for shoplifting was practically limited to cases in which the defendant actually had taken goods.]

[The traditional] limitations reflected the common law view that no innocent person should have to suffer the indignity of being involuntarily restrained without there being a remedy against the person detaining him....

In 1936, in Collyer v. Kress, the Supreme Court of California significantly modified the common law privilege....

[The *Collyer* decision established] the principle that in certain circumstances a merchant was privileged to detain a suspect even though that suspect was later found innocent. This ruling instituted a wave of similar decisions in California and other states, broken only by occasional decisions which persistently continued to uphold the original common law privilege.

... [M]any states during the past 20 years have codified this expanded privilege originally adopted by their courts, and many others whose courts had previously followed the original common law doctrine have enacted legislation modifying that doctrine to include the enlarged defense. Today, of the 38 states which provide by statute for the detention of suspected shoplifters, 33 definitely protect the merchant from liability for false imprisonment if there is "probable cause," "reasonable cause" or "reasonable grounds" for believing an offense had been committed even though, in fact, there had been no theft....

Even though a majority of states have expanded the common law privilege either judicially or by statute, the privilege remains subject to several limitations. In most states it is effective only when: 1) the agent detaining the suspect has a certain degree of belief in his guilt; 2) the detention is for specified purpose; 3) the restraint occurs in a limited area; 4) the detention is exercised in a reasonable manner; 5) the suspect is held for a limited time, and 6) the detention has occurred within a reasonable time after the alleged theft has been committed. Other detentions will not be privileged, and the merchant exceeding the narrow statutory boundaries will therefore be liable for false imprisonment.

[Selected portions of the discussion of these elements appear below.]

1. Belief in Suspect's Guilt

... Eighteen statutes adopt the Collyer rule which states that "probable cause" to believe that the suspect has committed or is committing a crime is sufficient. Six statutes require that there must be "reasonable cause" to believe the suspect guilty of the theft;

---

* Copyright © 1971, *Minnesota Law Review*. Reprinted by permission.

six say there must be "reasonable grounds"; one requires "reasonable grounds or probable cause" to exist; two state that there must be "good faith and probable cause based on reasonable grounds"; one declares that if a "man of reasonable prudence" would believe the plaintiff was shoplifting, the detention is privileged, and one requires "reasonable and probable grounds." Although some courts have held that these various incantations have somewhat different meanings when referring to the right of policemen to make arrests, they have generally been regarded as equivalent in determining the right of merchants to detain shoplifters.

Since only five state statutes attempt to specify in any manner the situations where probable cause or reasonable grounds exist, the courts are generally free to determine the applicability of these statutes to specific cases. Judges have consistently been reluctant to admit the existence of reasonable grounds or probable cause because of the concern that the expanded privilege will seriously impair the personal rights of both the innocent and the guilty customer. They have therefore held that a "reasonable belief" is more than an "honest belief" based upon mere suspicion that a suspect is guilty.... While there are some situations then in which a merchant may detail an innocent customer without subjecting himself to liability, the stringent interpretation of the "reasonable grounds" standard by the courts has prevented the legal balance between personal rights and property interests from shifting drastically in favor of the merchant's right to recover his goods.

2. Purpose of Detention

. . .

Thirteen statutes allow merchants to detain in order to effect a recovery of their property. Such language apparently authorizes a search of the suspects and permits merchants to question customers concerning their possession of merchandize.

. . .

Eight states authorize the merchant to detain only to investigate ownership or to question and investigate ownership. This includes questioning the plaintiff concerning whether he possess the goods, where he got them and whether he paid for them. Whether it permits the retailer to request the suspect to identify himself, however, is uncertain. Moreover, it is difficult to ascertain whether under such statutes, the store manager or owner can search the suspect without exceeding his privilege.

. . .

Six states provide that the merchant may detain to interrogate or to question concerning guilt or ownership....

In Delaware, Minnesota, South Dakota and Wisconsin, a merchant may detain for the sole purpose of delivering the suspect to a law enforcement officer. This apparently indicates that he may not question the suspect under any circumstances, that he may not search the suspect and that he may not use any other means of self-help to recover his goods. The rationale behind the law is sound. It is easy for a merchant to overstep his statutory authority and to abuse suspects physically or mentally, and therefore, that authority should be narrowly defined.

. . .

3. Area of Detention

The Restatement (Second) of Torts, after stating that a person who reasonably believes that another has stolen his chattel may detain the suspect, adds:

Thus far the cases which have recognized the privilege stated in this Section have been concerned with a detention on the premises of the actor. In the absence of sufficient authority, the Caveat is intended to leave open the question whether the privilege extends to the detention of one who has left the premises but is still in their immediate vicinity, as, for example, where the person suspected has gone out of the door of a shop, and is half-way across the sidewalk on the way to his car.

...

[C]ases decided both prior and subsequent to the publication of the Restatement (Second) of Torts indicate that detention will be permitted not only upon the premises of the merchant but also in the immediate vicinity thereof.

...

5. Period of Detention

It is evident that the statutes and courts adopting the expanded privilege require that the suspect only be detained for a limited time, even though five statutes do not explicitly list that restriction. The question then is to determine what constitutes a permissible period of detention....

[The Note writer then summarizes the law on this question, citing principally the case of Cooke v. J. J. Newberry & Co., 96 N.J.Super. 9, 232 A.2d 425 (1967). In that case the court held that the 27-minute detention of a woman with a large, easily opened handbag, who had engaged in actions that aroused suspicions of a security officer, did not exceed the statutory permission to detain "for not more than a reasonable time."]

NOTE ON MERCHANTS' RESPONSES TO RULES ON SHOPLIFTING

For a summary of how merchants react to their perceptions of the law related to apprehension of shoplifting suspects, see Note, *Merchants' Response to Shoplifting: An Empirical Study,* 28 Stan. L. Rev. 589 (1976). The student investigators conclude, among other things, that "[t]he apprehension of suspects was severely limited by many stores' strict interpretation of what was required to trigger a legal apprehension," and that "[t]he procedures of the stores were often substantially more cautious than required by California law." The investigators conclude that "[t]he main cause of this conservatism seems to have been a misunderstanding of the probable cause requirement," specifically, that "[m]any store representatives did not realize that honest mistakes, if based on probable cause, do not expose the employee or store to civil liability."

NOTES

(1) Can you describe the general economic and ethical premises that underlie both the *Katko* decision and the body of law concerning merchants' privileges described in the two Notes above? Is the balance struck too far in favor of thieves?

(2) Which standard currently in the judicial or case law is the most desirable one with respect to striking the appropriate balance? Can you write a blackletter rule that is better than that standard?

(3) What would be the most practical set of suggestions that you could make to the proprietor of a neighborhood convenience store for the prevention of shoplifting?

§ 3.03 The Privilege to Arrest

McINTOSH v. ARKANSAS REPUBLICAN PARTY-FRANK WHITE ELECTION COMMITTEE

United States Court of Appeals, Eighth Circuit
766 F.2d 337 (1985)

FAGG, CIRCUIT JUDGE.

Robert McIntosh appeals the dismissal of his civil lawsuit....

McIntosh, a black citizen of Little Rock, Arkansas, is a local political activist. On February 25, 1982, McIntosh purchased a ticket to the Frank White Appreciation Luncheon which was scheduled to take place the next day. Frank White was at that time the Governor of Arkansas and this luncheon was intended to raise funds for his re-election bid. Two private organizations, the Frank White Election Committee and the Arkansas Republican Party, sponsored the luncheon. Vice President George Bush was scheduled to be the luncheon's guest speaker.

After purchasing his ticket, McIntosh sent a letter to Governor White's office in which he unequivocally stated that he would speak at the luncheon. McIntosh's letter specifically requested that Governor White confirm his demand and further requested that he be told whether he would be scheduled to make his remarks before or after the Vice President's speech. When Curtis Finch, Jr., a private businessman and the individual in charge of the event, learned of this letter, he was understandably concerned, since McIntosh had not been invited to speak. His concern, however, stemmed not only from the fact that McIntosh intended to make an unsolicited speech but also from the fact that McIntosh was one of Governor White's most active and vocal opponents and had previously sent a number of harassing articles to Governor White. Further, Finch had no reason to question McIntosh's sincerity of purpose because McIntosh had, in the past, disrupted other events with unsolicited and often unwelcome speeches. Given these factors, Finch decided that McIntosh could not be allowed to disrupt and possibly ruin Governor White's luncheon. As a result, Finch determined that rather than allow McIntosh to attend, he would refund McIntosh the full purchase price of his ticket.

The luncheon was scheduled to be held in a banquet hall located in the Little Rock Convention Center. The convention center is owned and operated by the City of Little Rock and the banquet hall in question is regularly and nondiscriminately made available to private groups seeking to use the hall for their private gatherings. On the day of the luncheon, McIntosh was on hand at the convention center. Prior to entering the banquet hall, McIntosh was approached by Finch. Finch informed McIntosh that he would not be allowed to attend and offered McIntosh a full refund. McIntosh refused and insisted that he had the right to attend. Finch repeatedly told McIntosh that he could not enter the banquet hall and McIntosh repeatedly refused any refund. Further, McIntosh did nothing to disclaim his intent to intrude upon the program and make an unsolicited speech.

As the exchange between Finch and McIntosh became more heated, two Arkansas state troopers who were assigned to provide security for the luncheon, and who had been warned that McIntosh might attempt to disrupt the event, identified themselves, informed McIntosh that he would not be allowed to attend the luncheon, and requested that he leave. The officers further told McIntosh that if he insisted on entering the luncheon he would be arrested. In response to this statement, McIntosh replied, "Well, take me to jail." The officers, taking McIntosh at his word, arrested McIntosh and took him to the North Little Rock jail where he was charged with disorderly conduct. After processing, which took approximately one hour and forty-five minutes, McIntosh was released on his own recognizance.

. . .

We turn to McIntosh's section 1983 claim based upon false arrest. While this claim was pleaded and tried below, the district court did not make a ruling on this claim. Instead, the district court addressed McIntosh's claim of false arrest only in the context of his pendent state-law claims of false arrest and false imprisonment. While McIntosh has not specifically challenged the district court's failure to rule on this claim, certain passages in his brief convince us that he has not abandoned this claim. Given our disposition of McIntosh's pendent state-law claims of false arrest and false imprisonment, we conclude that this claim should be remanded to the district court for a new trial and a ruling on the merits.

We turn finally to McIntosh's pendent state-law claims of false arrest and false imprisonment. At trial, the district court, relying on its prior opinion in Perkins v. Cross, 562 F.Supp. 85 (E.D.Ark.1983) (a federal civil rights case), determined that to recover on his state-law claims McIntosh was "required to show that the police officers who effected the arrest were not acting ... upon probable cause." McIntosh, 582 F.Supp. at 1251 (citing Perkins, 562 F.Supp. at 87). Under this standard, the burden of proving lack of probable cause was placed on McIntosh.

On appeal, McIntosh, although inartfully, challenges the legal standard of recovery applied by the district court. After carefully reviewing the record, the district court's opinion, and the applicable state law, we conclude that the district court incorrectly placed the burden of proving lack of probable cause on McIntosh. As a result, we reverse the district court's dismissal of McIntosh's state-law claims.

McIntosh's claims of false arrest and false imprisonment are state-law claims governed solely by Arkansas state law. Under Arkansas law, "[a]n essential element of the tort of false arrest, which is basically the same wrong as false imprisonment, is the unlawful detention of the plaintiff against his will." Faulkinbury v. United States Fire Insurance Co., 247 Ark. 70, 444 S.W.2d 254, 255 (1969). Further, once the plaintiff establishes that he or she was restrained, "the burden [is] upon the defendant to show that [the detention] was by authority of law" or as here was made upon probable cause....

If the defendant is unable to carry this burden, plaintiff's claim has been established and recovery of compensatory damages is appropriate.

Here, the district court improperly placed the burden of proving the absence of probable cause on McIntosh. This error requires reversal since the issue of probable cause is, as the district court recognized, a close one. Because of the closeness of this question, the allocation of the burden of proof takes on particular importance. As such, we reverse the district court's disposition of McIntosh's state-law claims and remand these claims to the district court for reconsideration in light of this opinion. We do so, however, with the proviso that the district court may, in its discretion, hear further testimony if necessary.

. . .

Affirmed in part, reversed in part, and remanded with instructions.

LAY, CHIEF JUDGE, concurring.

In my judgment it is factually clear the state police officers lacked probable cause to arrest McIntosh for disorderly conduct. I would so hold that there existed no probable cause to arrest McIntosh as a matter of law. At the time of his arrest, McIntosh was standing in a public access area of a public building. The uncontradicted testimony at trial revealed that McIntosh was neither loud nor disruptive prior to his arrest, and that he did not use abusive or profane language when requesting entrance to the luncheon. The district court conceded that the probable cause issue was a "close question," but stated it was convinced by the officers' "forthright testimony, their courteous treatment of Mr. McIntosh and the fact that Mr. McIntosh did refuse their lawful order to leave the premises." I cannot accept the court's reasoning. McIntosh had every right to be in the public hallway, and therefore the officers' order to leave the premises was not "lawful." In fact, McIntosh had paid $125.00 for a ticket to attend the luncheon. The officers' conduct in arresting, handcuffing, and hauling McIntosh to the North Little Rock Police Station (although he was arrested in Little Rock) where he was jailed, interrogated, and detained for over two hours until the luncheon was over, can hardly be termed "courteous." Finally, although the officers' testimony may indeed have been forthright, I fail to see how an officers' testimony that McIntosh "was not loud or disruptive at any time prior to his arrest" lends support to the district court's erroneous finding that probable cause existed to arrest McIntosh for disorderly conduct. Under these circumstances, I would also hold that the officers' conduct violated "clearly established statutory or constitutional rights of which a reasonable person would have known," thus depriving the officers of the defense of qualified immunity. Harlow v. Fitzgerald, 457 U.S. 800, 818, 102 S.Ct. 2727, 2738, 73 L.Ed.2d 396 (1982).

JOHN R. GIBSON, CIRCUIT JUDGE, concurring.

I concur in the court's opinion today but I write separately only because Chief Judge Lay has expressed his view that it is factually clear that the police officers lacked probable cause to arrest McIntosh for disorderly conduct. I read the record to demonstrate probable cause. Probable cause for an arrest simply requires that an officer have enough facts or circumstances to justify a prudent person in believing that an offense is about to be committed. Michigan v. DeFillippo, 443 U.S. 31, 37, 99 S.Ct. 2627, 2632, 61 L.Ed.2d 343, 349 (1979). Disorderly conduct is defined as disrupting or disturbing any lawful assembly or meeting of persons with the purpose to cause public inconvenience, annoyance or alarm or recklessly creating a risk thereof. Ark.Stat.Ann. § 41-2908 (Repl.1977).

The officers knew that McIntosh had established a pattern of disrupting previous meetings. When he came to the luncheon he was dressed in an uncharacteristic manner, and they had been informed that McIntosh had written a letter to the Governor stating that he intended to speak at the luncheon. When the chairman of the luncheon, Finch, approached McIntosh and told him that his ticket was purchased illegally and that he would not be permitted to enter and that his money would be refunded, McIntosh answered "I've got my ticket. I am going to enter." He repeated the statement in response to Finch two or three times. At this time Sergeant Reinold identified himself and told McIntosh that he was not being allowed into the private function and had been asked to leave and McIntosh told him "I've got my ticket. I'm going in." McIntosh refused a second and third request by Reinold to leave. Reinold stated that McIntosh became agitated and his voice was rising, although it did not get to the point of loud shouting. He stated that in his opinion the situation was approaching a point where it could get out of hand. He stated that McIntosh's speech was that of not normal demeanor. McIntosh became very anxious and began speaking quickly. His voice rose from a normal conversation but it did not get to the point of loud shouting. Reinold felt that McIntosh was going to lose control or could possibly lose control and told him that they were going to place him under arrest. He left with the officers in an orderly manner and the officers thanked him for doing so.

In my view this evidence is sufficient to satisfy the officers' burden that they had probable cause for believing that an offense of disorderly conduct was about to be committed.

NOTES

(1) "The tort of false arrest arises out of an unlawful assertion of police authority over a person resulting in a restraint on his liberty." Satter and Kalom, *False Arrest: Compensation and Deterrence*, 43 CONN. B.J. 598, 600 (1969). In litigation over arrests, a frequent issue will be whether the arrest was a lawful one—in tort terms, whether the arresting officer was privileged. One way for a police officer to claim that an arrest was privileged is to show that it was made with probable cause.

Technically the action for false arrest differs from false imprisonment, inter alia, in that a private individual—e.g., a store owner—can falsely imprison one without making an arrest. Moreover, one legally arrested may be falsely imprisoned if there is "an unreasonable delay in taking him before a magistrate" or if he is detained when he has a right to be released.

(2) What would be the likely effect of the decision in *McIntosh* on the lectures that the Little Rock Police Department gives its officers on "street law"? Will the Department have to provide officers with a short course in the constitutional law of the first amendment? Is it possible to instruct in the "tort" law of "false arrest" with respect to cases of this sort without going into constitutional detail?

(3) *McIntosh* did not raise the specter of violence, but the reader can easily imagine situations in which the situation is more explosive. What are the social stakes at issue in arrest cases where the arrestee's conduct threatens personal injury to others?

(4) What would you expect to be the effect of the *McIntosh* decision on the future behavior of political activists? Of policemen in the vicinity of political luncheons? Do you think that this combination of tort law and "section 1983" law has achieved a good social balance? Will the decision promote law and order? What is the main policy argument in favor of giving McIntosh a cause of action for false arrest? Would you write a fourth opinion if you were another judge on the court? What position would you take?

(5) In a later episode of a complicated history, in which the district court had to deal with an intervening Supreme Court decision on qualified immunity, the trial judge held that the defendant officers had "sustained their burden of proof" on the question of probable cause to arrest for disorderly conduct. The district judge cited "Mr. McIntosh's expressed intent to disrupt, plus his continuous refusal to leave the immediate proximity of the private luncheon, plus his increased agitation and rising voice, in addition to his letter of intention."

(6) Frank White, the Governor of Arkansas at the time of the incident that led to the *McIntosh* litigation, had succeeded the 34-year-old Governor Bill Clinton. One of the things that led to White's election was Clinton's failure to push a bill that would have allowed higher truck weights on Arkansas highways. This angered Don Tyson, the head of Tyson Foods, a strong supporter of the proposed legislation. As one report summarized it, "[w]hen Clinton ran again for Governor in 1980, against a little known Republican businessman named Frank White, Tyson took revenge: "I said, 'Hell, I'll support Frank

White.'" Michael Kelly, *The President's Past*, N.Y. TIMES MAGAZINE, July 31, 1994, at 20, 22. Clinton's 1980 defeat "threatened to end his political career. But in 1982, after a brutal campaign against White, he won back the Governor's seat." *Id.*

PROBLEM

A woman is jogging shortly after dark on a late spring evening. A man pursues her, catches up with her, knocks her down and tries to rape her. She escapes, and runs to the village police station. She describes her assailant to the desk sergeant as a blond man, five foot ten, in a green jogging suit, and says that the attack took place along K Street, which runs east and west, four blocks west of First Avenue, which runs north and south. Fifteen minutes later, police given this description arrest a man walking along First Avenue in a flourescent yellow jogging suit. He is six feet tall and has reddish-brown hair. After questioning, the man is let go. Other officers later pick up a man who more closely fits the woman's description, and he confesses to the crime.

Does the first man arrested have a tort claim against the village?

TENNESSEE v. GARNER
United States Supreme Court
471 U.S. 1 (1985)

JUSTICE WHITE delivered the opinion of the Court.

This case requires us to determine the constitutionality of the use of deadly force to prevent the escape of an apparently unarmed suspected felon. We conclude that such force may not be used unless it is necessary to prevent the escape and the officer has probable cause to believe that the suspect poses a significant threat of death or serious physical injury to the officer or others.

I

At about 10:45 p.m. on October 3, 1974, Memphis Police Officers Elton Hymon and Leslie Wright were dispatched to answer a "prowler inside call." Upon arriving at the scene they saw a woman standing on her porch and gesturing toward the adjacent house.[1]

She told them she had heard glass breaking and that "they" or "someone" was breaking in next door. While Wright radioed the dispatcher to say that they were on the scene, Hymon went behind the house. He heard a door slam and saw someone run across the back yard. The fleeing suspect, who was appellee-respondent's decedent, Edward Garner, stopped at a 6-feet-high chain link fence at the edge of the yard. With the aid of a flashlight, Hymon was able to see Garner's face and hands. He saw no sign of a weapon, and, though not certain, was "reasonably sure" and "figured" that Garner was unarmed. App. 41, 56; Record 219. He thought Garner was 17 or 18 years old and about 5' 5" or 5' 7" tall.[2]

While Garner was crouched at the base of the fence, Hymon called out "police, halt" and took a few steps toward him. Garner then began to climb over the fence. Convinced

---

1. The owner of the house testified that no lights were on in the house, but that a back door light was on. Record 160. Officer Hymon, though uncertain, stated in his deposition that there were lights on in the house. Record 209.

2. In fact, Garner, an eighth-grader, was 15. He was 5'4" and weighed somewhere around 100 or 110 pounds....

that if Garner made it over the fence he would elude capture,[3] Hymon shot him. The bullet hit Garner in the back of the head. Garner was taken by ambulance to a hospital, where he died on the operating table. Ten dollars and a purse taken from the house were found on his body.[4]

In using deadly force to prevent the escape, Hymon was acting under the authority of a Tennessee statute and pursuant to Police Department policy. The statute provides that "[i]f, after notice of the intention to arrest the defendant, he either flee or forcibly resist, the officer may use all the necessary means to effect the arrest." Tenn.Code Ann. § 40-7-108 (1982).[5]

The Department policy was slightly more restrictive than the statute, but still allowed the use of deadly force in cases of burglary.... The incident was reviewed by the Memphis Police Firearm's Review Board and presented to a grand jury. Neither took any action. App. 57.

Garner's father then brought this action in the Federal District Court for the Western District of Tennessee, seeking damages under 42 U.S.C. § 1983 for asserted violations of Garner's constitutional rights. The complaint alleged that the shooting violated the Fourth, Fifth, Sixth, Eighth, and Fourteenth Amendments of the United States Constitution. It named as defendants Officer Hymon, the Police Department, its Director, and the Mayor and city of Memphis. After a 3-day bench trial, the District Court entered judgment for all defendants. It dismissed the claims against the Mayor and the Director for lack of evidence. It then concluded that Hymon's actions were authorized by the Tennessee statute, which in turn was constitutional. Hymon had employed the only reasonable and practicable means of preventing Garner's escape. Garner had "recklessly and heedlessly attempted to vault over the fence to escape, thereby assuming the risk of being fired upon." ...

[Omitted is a description of a procedural history, the effect of which is that this appeal is from a reversal by the Court of Appeals with respect to the city's liability. The district court decision that was reversed "found that the statute, and Hymon's actions, were constitutional."]

[The Court of Appeals, in 710 F.2d 240 (6th Cir. 1983)] reasoned that the killing of a fleeing suspect is a "seizure" under the Fourth Amendment,[6] and is therefore constitu-

---

3. When asked at trial why he fired, Hymon stated:

> Well, first of all it was apparent to me from the little bit that I knew about the area at the time that he was going to get away because, number 1, I couldn't get to him. My partner then couldn't find where he was because, you know, he was late coming around. He didn't know where I was talking about. I couldn't get to him because of the fence here, I couldn't have jumped this fence and come up, consequently jumped this fence and caught him before he got away because he was already up on the fence, just one leap and he was already over the fence, and so there is no way that I could have caught him.

App. 52.

He also stated that the area beyond the fence was dark, that he could not have gotten over the fence easily because he was carrying a lot of equipment and wearing heavy boots, and that Garner, being younger and more energetic, could have outrun him. *Id.*, at 53–54.

4. Garner had rummaged through one room in the house, in which, in the words of the owner, "[a]ll the stuff was out on the floors, all the drawers was pulled out, and stuff was scattered all over." App. 34. The owner testified that his valuables were untouched but that, in addition to the purse and the 10 dollars, one of his wife's rings was missing. The ring was not recovered. App. 34–35.

5. Although the statute does not say so explicitly, Tennessee law forbids the use of deadly force in the arrest of a misdemeanant. See *Johnson v. State*, 173 Tenn. 134, 114 S.W.2d 819 (1938).

6. The right of the people to be secure in their persons ... against unreasonable searches and seizures, shall not be violated.... U.S. Const., Amdt. 4.

tional only if "reasonable." The Tennessee statute failed as applied to this case because it did not adequately limit the use of deadly force by distinguishing between felonies of different magnitudes—"the facts, as found, did not justify the use of deadly force under the Fourth Amendment." Id., at 246. Officers cannot resort to deadly force unless they "have probable cause ... to believe that the suspect [has committed a felony and] poses a threat to the safety of the officers or a danger to the community if left at large." Ibid.[7]

...

II

Whenever an officer restrains the freedom of a person to walk away, he has seized that person.... While it is not always clear just when minimal police interference becomes a seizure, ... there can be no question that apprehension by the use of deadly force is a seizure subject to the reasonableness requirement of the Fourth Amendment.

...

A police officer may arrest a person if he has probable cause to believe that person committed a crime.... Petitioners and appellant argue that if this requirement is satisfied the Fourth Amendment has nothing to say about how that seizure is made. This submission ignores the many cases in which this Court, by balancing the extent of the intrusion against the need for it, has examined the reasonableness of the manner in which a search or seizure is conducted....

The same balancing process ... demonstrates that, notwithstanding probable cause to seize a suspect, an officer may not always do so by killing him. The intrusiveness of a seizure by means of deadly force is unmatched. The suspect's fundamental interest in his own life need not be elaborated upon. The use of deadly force also frustrates the interest of the individual, and of society, in judicial determination of guilt and punishment. Against these interests are ranged governmental interests in effective law enforcement. It is argued that overall violence will be reduced by encouraging the peaceful submission of suspects who know that they may be shot if they flee. Effectiveness in making arrests requires the resort to deadly force, or at least the meaningful threat thereof. "Being able to arrest such individuals is a condition precedent to the state's entire system of law enforcement." ...

Without in any way disparaging the importance of these goals, we are not convinced that the use of deadly force is a sufficiently productive means of accomplishing

---

7. The Court of Appeals concluded that the rule set out in the Model Penal Code "accurately states Fourth Amendment limitations on the use of deadly force against fleeing felons." 710 F.2d, at 247. The relevant portion of the Model Penal Code provides: The use of deadly force is not justifiable ... unless (i) the arrest is for a felony; and (ii) the person effecting the arrest is authorized to act as a peace officer; or is assisting a person whom he believes to be authorized to act as a peace officer, and (iii) the actor believes that the force employed creates no substantial risk of injury to innocent persons; and (iv) the actor believes that (1) the crime for which the arrest is made involved conduct including the use or threatened use of deadly force; or (2) there is a substantial risk that the person to be arrested will cause death or serious bodily harm if his apprehension is delayed. American Law Institute, Model Penal Code § 3.07(2)(b) (Proposed Official Draft 1962).

The court also found that "[a]n analysis of the facts of this case under the Due Process Clause" required the same result, because the statute was not narrowly drawn to further a compelling state interest. 710 F.2d, at 246–247. The court considered the generalized interest in effective law enforcement sufficiently compelling only when the suspect is dangerous. Finally, the court held, relying on *Owen v. City of Independence*, 445 U.S. 622, 100 S.Ct. 1398, 63 L.Ed.2d 673 (1980), that the city was not immune.

them to justify the killing of nonviolent suspects.... The use of deadly force is a self-defeating way of apprehending a suspect and so setting the criminal justice mechanism in motion. If successful, it guarantees that that mechanism will not be set in motion. And while the meaningful threat of deadly force might be thought to lead to the arrest of more live suspects by discouraging escape attempts,[9] the presently available evidence does not support this thesis. The fact is that a majority of police departments in this country have forbidden the use of deadly force against nonviolent suspects.... If those charged with the enforcement of the criminal law have abjured the use of deadly force in arresting nondangerous felons, there is a substantial basis for doubting that the use of such force is an essential attribute of the arrest power in all felony cases.... Petitioners and appellant have not persuaded us that shooting nondangerous fleeing suspects is so vital as to outweigh the suspect's interest in his own life.

The use of deadly force to prevent the escape of all felony suspects, whatever the circumstances, is constitutionally unreasonable. It is not better that all felony suspects die than that they escape. Where the suspect poses no immediate threat to the officer and no threat to others, the harm resulting from failing to apprehend him does not justify the use of deadly force to do so. It is no doubt unfortunate when a suspect who is in sight escapes, but the fact that the police arrive a little late or are a little slower afoot does not always justify killing the suspect. A police officer may not seize an unarmed, nondangerous suspect by shooting him dead. The Tennessee statute is unconstitutional insofar as it authorizes the use of deadly force against such fleeing suspects.

It is not, however, unconstitutional on its face. Where the officer has probable cause to believe that the suspect poses a threat of serious physical harm, either to the officer or to others, it is not constitutionally unreasonable to prevent escape by using deadly force. Thus, if the suspect threatens the officer with a weapon or there is probable cause to believe that he has committed a crime involving the infliction or threatened infliction of serious physical harm, deadly force may be used if necessary to prevent escape, and if, where feasible, some warning has been given. As applied in such circumstances, the Tennessee statute would pass constitutional muster.

III

A

It is insisted that the Fourth Amendment must be construed in light of the common-law rule, which allowed the use of whatever force was necessary to effect the arrest of a fleeing felon, though not a misdemeanant....

...

---

9. We note that the usual manner of deterring illegal conduct—through punishment—has been largely ignored in connection with flight from arrest. Arkansas, for example, specifically excepts flight from arrest from the offense of "obstruction of governmental operations." The commentary notes that this "reflects the basic policy judgment that, absent the use of force or violence, a mere attempt to avoid apprehension by a law enforcement officer does not give rise to an independent offense." Ark.Stat.Ann. §41-2802(3)(a) (1977) and commentary. In the few States that do outlaw flight from an arresting officer, the crime is only a misdemeanor....

This lenient approach does avoid the anomaly of automatically transforming every fleeing misdemeanant into a fleeing felon—subject, under the common-law rule, to apprehension by deadly force—solely by virtue of his flight. However, it is in real tension with the harsh consequences of flight in cases where deadly force is employed. For example, Tennessee does not outlaw fleeing from arrest....

B

It has been pointed out many times that the common-law rule is best understood in light of the fact that it arose at a time when virtually all felonies were punishable by death. "Though effected without the protections and formalities of an orderly trial and conviction, the killing of a resisting or fleeing felon resulted in no greater consequences than those authorized for punishment of the felony of which the individual was charged or suspected." American Law Institute, Model Penal Code § 3.07, Comment 3, p. 56 (Tentative Draft No. 8, 1958) (hereinafter Model Penal Code Comment). Courts have also justified the common-law rule by emphasizing the relative dangerousness of felons....

Neither of these justifications makes sense today. Almost all crimes formerly punishable by death no longer are or can be.... Many crimes classified as misdemeanors, or nonexistent, at common law are now felonies....

There is an additional reason why the common-law rule cannot be directly translated to the present day. The common-law rule developed at a time when weapons were rudimentary. Deadly force could be inflicted almost solely in a hand-to-hand struggle during which, necessarily, the safety of the arresting officer was at risk. Handguns were not carried by police officers until the latter half of the last century. L. Kennett & J. Anderson, The Gun in America 150–151 (1975). Only then did it become possible to use deadly force from a distance as a means of apprehension. As a practical matter, the use of deadly force under the standard articulation of the common-law rule has an altogether different meaning—and harsher consequences—now than in past centuries. See Wechsler & Michael, A Rationale for the Law of Homicide: I, 37 Colum.L.Rev. 701, 741 (1937).[13]

One other aspect of the common-law rule bears emphasis. It forbids the use of deadly force to apprehend a misdemeanant, condemning such action as disproportionately severe....

In short, though the common law pedigree of Tennessee's rule is pure on its face, changes in the legal and technological context mean the rule is distorted almost beyond recognition when literally applied.

C

In evaluating the reasonableness of police procedures under the Fourth Amendment, we have also looked to prevailing rules in individual jurisdictions.... Some 19 States have codified the common-law rule, though in two of these the courts have significantly limited the statute. Four States, though without a relevant statute, apparently retain the common-law rule. Two States have adopted the Model Penal Code's provision verbatim. Eighteen others allow, in slightly varying language, the use of deadly force only if the suspect has committed a felony involving the use or threat of physical or deadly force, or

---

13. It has been argued that sophisticated techniques of apprehension and increased communication between the police in different jurisdictions have made it more likely that an escapee will be caught than was once the case, and that this change has also reduced the "reasonableness" of the use of deadly force to prevent escape. E.g., Sherman, *Execution Without Trial: Police Homicide and the Constitution*, 33 Vand.L.Rev. 71, 76 (1980). We are unaware of any data that would permit sensible evaluation of this claim. Current arrest rates are sufficiently low, however, that we have some doubt whether in past centuries the failure to arrest at the scene meant that the police had missed their only chance in a way that is not presently the case. In 1983, 21% of the offenses in the FBI crime index were cleared by arrest. Federal Bureau of Investigation, Uniform Crime Reports, Crime in the United States 159 (1984). The clearance rate for burglary was 15%. Ibid.

is escaping with a deadly weapon, or is likely to endanger life or inflict serious physical injury if not arrested. Louisiana and Vermont, though without statutes or case law on point, do forbid the use of deadly force to prevent any but violent felonies. The remaining States either have no relevant statute or case-law, or have positions that are unclear.

It cannot be said that there is a constant or overwhelming trend away from the common-law rule. In recent years, some States have reviewed their laws and expressly rejected abandonment of the common-law rule. Nonetheless, the long-term movement has been away from the rule that deadly force may be used against any fleeing felon, and that remains the rule in less than half the States.

This trend is more evident and impressive when viewed in light of the policies adopted by the police departments themselves. Overwhelmingly, these are more restrictive than the common-law rule....

For accreditation by the Commission on Accreditation for Law Enforcement Agencies, a department must restrict the use of deadly force to situations where "the officer reasonably believes that the action is in defense of human life ... or in defense of any person in immediate danger of serious physical injury." Commission on Accreditation for Law Enforcement Agencies, Inc., Standards for Law Enforcement Agencies 1–2 (1983) (italics deleted). A 1974 study reported that the police department regulations in a majority of the large cities of the United States allowed the firing of a weapon only when a felon presented a threat of death or serious bodily harm. Boston Police Department, Planning & Research Division, The Use of Deadly Force by Boston Police Personnel (1974), cited in Mattis v. Schnarr, 547 F.2d 1007, 1016, n. 19 (CA8 1976).... Overall, only 7.5% of departmental and municipal policies explicitly permit the use of deadly force against any felon; 86.8% explicitly do not....

D

Actual departmental policies are important for an additional reason. We would hesitate to declare a police practice of long standing "unreasonable" if doing so would severely hamper effective law enforcement. But the indications are to the contrary. There has been no suggestion that crime has worsened in any way in jurisdictions that have adopted, by legislation or departmental policy, rules similar to that announced today....

Nor do we agree with petitioners and appellant that the rule we have adopted requires the police to make impossible, split-second evaluations of unknowable facts.... We do not deny the practical difficulties of attempting to assess the suspect's dangerousness. However, similarly difficult judgments must be made by the police in equally uncertain circumstances.... Nor is there any indication that in States that allow the use of deadly force only against dangerous suspects, ... the standard has been difficult to apply or has led to a rash of litigation involving inappropriate second-guessing of police officers' split-second decisions. Moreover, the highly technical felony/misdemeanor distinction is equally, if not more, difficult to apply in the field. An officer is in no position to know, for example, the precise value of property stolen, or whether the crime was a first or second offense. Finally, as noted above, this claim must be viewed with suspicion in light of the similar self-imposed limitations of so many police departments.

IV

The District Court concluded that Hymon was justified in shooting Garner because state law allows, and the Federal Constitution does not forbid, the use of deadly force to prevent the escape of a fleeing felony suspect if no alternative means of apprehension is available.... This conclusion made a determination of Garner's apparent dangerousness unnecessary. The court did find, however, that Garner appeared to be unarmed, though Hymon could not be certain that was the case.... [S]tated in Fourth Amendment terms, this means Hymon had no articulable basis to think Garner was armed.

In reversing, the Court of Appeals accepted the District Court's factual conclusions and held that "the facts, as found, did not justify the use of deadly force." 710 F.2d, at 246. We agree. Officer Hymon could not reasonably have believed that Garner—young, slight, and unarmed—posed any threat. Indeed, Hymon never attempted to justify his actions on any basis other than the need to prevent an escape. The District Court stated in passing that "[t]he facts of this case did not indicate to Officer Hymon that Garner was 'non-dangerous.'" App. to Pet. for Cert. A34. This conclusion is not explained, and seems to be based solely on the fact that Garner had broken into a house at night. However, the fact that Garner was a suspected burglar could not, without regard to the other circumstances, automatically justify the use of deadly force. Hymon did not have probable cause to believe that Garner, whom he correctly believed to be unarmed, posed any physical danger to himself or others.

The dissent argues that the shooting was justified by the fact that Officer Hymon had probable cause to believe that Garner had committed a nighttime burglary.... While we agree that burglary is a serious crime, we cannot agree that it is so dangerous as automatically to justify the use of deadly force. The FBI classifies burglary as a "property" rather than a "violent" crime. See Federal Bureau of Investigation, Uniform Crime Reports, Crime in the United States 1 (1984).[22]

Although the armed burglar would present a different situation, the fact that an unarmed suspect has broken into a dwelling at night does not automatically mean he is physically dangerous. This case demonstrates as much.... In fact, the available statistics demonstrate that burglaries only rarely involve physical violence. During the 10-year period from 1973–1982, only 3.8% of all burglaries involved violent crime. Bureau of Justice Statistics, Household Burglary, p. 4 (1985)....[23]

V

We wish to make clear what our holding means in the context of this case. The complaint has been dismissed as to all the individual defendants.... We hold that the statute is invalid insofar as it purported to give Hymon the authority to act as he did. As for the policy of the Police Department, the absence of any discussion of this issue by the courts below, and the uncertain state of the record, preclude any consideration of its validity.

The judgment of the Court of Appeals is affirmed, and the case is remanded for further proceedings consistent with this opinion....

---

22. In a recent report, the Department of Corrections of the District of Columbia also noted that "there is nothing inherently dangerous or violent about the offense," which is a crime against property. D.C. Department of Corrections, Prisoner Screening Project 2 (1985).

23. The dissent points out that three-fifths of all rapes in the home, three-fifths of all home robberies, and about a third of home assaults are committed by burglars.... These figures mean only that if one knows that a suspect committed a rape in the home, there is a good chance that the suspect is also a burglar. That has nothing to do with the question here, which is whether the fact that someone has committed a burglary indicates that he has committed, or might commit, a violent crime.

JUSTICE O'CONNOR, with whom THE CHIEF JUSTICE and JUSTICE REHN-QUIST join, dissenting.

The Court today holds that the Fourth Amendment prohibits a police officer from using deadly force as a last resort to apprehend a criminal suspect who refuses to halt when fleeing the scene of a nighttime burglary. This conclusion rests on the majority's balancing of the interests of the suspect and the public interest in effective law enforcement.... Notwithstanding the venerable common-law rule authorizing the use of deadly force if necessary to apprehend a fleeing felon, and continued acceptance of this rule by nearly half the States, ... the majority concludes that Tennessee's statute is unconstitutional inasmuch as it allows the use of such force to apprehend a burglary suspect who is not obviously armed or otherwise dangerous. Although the circumstances of this case are unquestionably tragic and unfortunate, our constitutional holdings must be sensitive both to the history of the Fourth Amendment and to the general implications of the Court's reasoning. By disregarding the serious and dangerous nature of residential burglaries and the longstanding practice of many States, the Court effectively creates a Fourth Amendment right allowing a burglary suspect to flee unimpeded from a police officer who has probable cause to arrest, who has ordered the suspect to halt, and who has no means short of firing his weapon to prevent escape. I do not believe that the Fourth Amendment supports such a right, and I accordingly dissent.

I

The facts below warrant brief review because they highlight the difficult, split-second decisions police officers must make in these circumstances. Memphis Police Officers Elton Hymon and Leslie Wright responded to a late-night call that a burglary was in progress at a private residence. When the officers arrived at the scene, the caller said that "they" were breaking into the house next door.... The officers found the residence had been forcibly entered through a window and saw lights on inside the house. Officer Hymon testified that when he saw the broken window he realized "that something was wrong inside," ... but that he could not determine whether anyone — either a burglar or a member of the household — was within the residence.... As Officer Hymon walked behind the house, he heard a door slam. He saw Edward Eugene Garner run away from the house through the dark and cluttered backyard. Garner crouched next to a 6-foot-high fence. Officer Hymon thought Garner was an adult and was unsure whether Garner was armed because Hymon "had no idea what was in the hand [that he could not see] or what he might have had on his person." ... In fact, Garner was 15-years old and unarmed. Hymon also did not know whether accomplices remained inside the house.... The officer identified himself as a police officer and ordered Garner to halt. Garner paused briefly and then sprang to the top of the fence. Believing that Garner would escape if he climbed over the fence, Hymon fired his revolver and mortally wounded the suspected burglar....

...

II

For purposes of Fourth Amendment analysis, I agree with the Court that Officer Hymon "seized" Garner by shooting him. Whether that seizure was reasonable and therefore permitted by the Fourth Amendment requires a careful balancing of the important public interest in crime prevention and detection and the nature and quality of the intrusion upon legitimate interests of the individual ... In striking this balance here, it is crucial to acknowledge that police use of deadly force to apprehend a fleeing criminal suspect falls within the "rubric of police conduct ... necessarily [involving] swift action predicated upon the on-the-spot observations of the officer on the beat." Terry v. Ohio, 392 U.S. 1, 20, 88 S.Ct. 1868, 1879, 20 L.Ed.2d 889 (1968). The clarity of hindsight cannot provide the standard for judging the reasonableness of police decisions made in uncertain and often dangerous circumstances....

The public interest involved in the use of deadly force as a last resort to apprehend a fleeing burglary suspect relates primarily to the serious nature of the crime. Household burglaries represent not only the illegal entry into a person's home, but also "pos[e] real risk of serious harm to others." Solem v. Helm, 463 U.S. 277, 315–316, 103 S.Ct. 3001, 3023, 77 L.Ed.2d 637 (1983) (BURGER, C.J., dissenting). According to recent Department of Justice statistics, "[t]hree-fifths of all rapes in the home, three-fifths of all home robberies, and about a third of home aggravated and simple assaults are committed by burglars." Bureau of Justice Statistics Bulletin, Household Burglary 1 (January 1985). During the period 1973–1982, 2.8 million such violent crimes were committed in the course of burglaries. Ibid. Victims of a forcible intrusion into their home by a nighttime prowler will find little consolation in the majority's confident assertion that "burglaries only rarely involve physical violence." ... Moreover, even if a particular burglary, when viewed in retrospect, does not involve physical harm to others, the "harsh potentialities for violence" inherent in the forced entry into a home preclude characterization of the crime as "innocuous, inconsequential, minor, or 'nonviolent.'" Solem v. Helm, supra, at 316, 103 S.Ct., at 3023 (BURGER, C.J., dissenting). See also Restatement of Torts § 131, Comment g (1934) (burglary is among felonies that normally cause or threaten death or serious bodily harm); R. Perkins & R. Boyce, Criminal Law 1110 (3d ed. 1982) (burglary is a dangerous felony that creates unreasonable risk of great personal harm).

Because burglary is a serious and dangerous felony, the public interest in the prevention and detection of the crime is of compelling importance. Where a police officer has probable cause to arrest a suspected burglar, the use of deadly force as a last resort might well be the only means of apprehending the suspect. With respect to a particular burglary, subsequent investigation simply cannot represent a substitute for immediate apprehension of the criminal suspect at the scene. See Report of President's Commission on Law Enforcement and Administration of Justice, The Challenge of Crime in a Free Society 97 (1967). Indeed, the Captain of the Memphis Police Department testified that in his city, if apprehension is not immediate, it is likely that the suspect will not be caught.... Although some law enforcement agencies may choose to assume the risk that a criminal will remain at large, the Tennessee statute reflects a legislative determination that the use of deadly force in prescribed circumstances will serve generally to protect the public. Such statutes assist the police in apprehending suspected perpetrators of serious crimes and provide notice that a lawful police order to stop and submit to arrest may not be ignored with impunity....

The Court unconvincingly dismisses the general deterrence effects by stating that "the presently available evidence does not support [the] thesis" that the threat of force discourages escape and that "there is a substantial basis for doubting that the use of such force is an essential attribute to the arrest power in all felony cases." Ante, at 1700–1701. There is no question that the effectiveness of police use of deadly force is arguable and that many States or individual police departments have decided not to authorize it in circumstances similar to those presented here. But it should go without saying that the effectiveness or popularity of a particular police practice does not determine its constitutionality.... Moreover, the fact that police conduct pursuant to a state statute is challenged on constitutional grounds does not impose a burden on the State to produce social science statistics or to dispel any possible doubts about the necessity of the conduct. This observation, I believe, has particular force where the challenged practice both predates enactment of the Bill of Rights and continues to be accepted by a substantial number of the States.

Against the strong public interests justifying the conduct at issue here must be weighed the individual interests implicated in the use of deadly force by police officers. The majority declares that "[t]he suspect's fundamental interest in his own life need not be elaborated upon." ... This blithe assertion hardly provides an adequate substitute for the majority's failure to acknowledge the distinctive manner in which the suspect's interest in his life is even exposed to risk. For purposes of this case, we must recall that the police officer, in the course of investigating a nighttime burglary, had reasonable cause to arrest the suspect and ordered him to halt. The officer's use of force resulted because the suspected burglar refused to heed this command and the officer reasonably believed that there was no means short of firing his weapon to apprehend the suspect. Without questioning the importance of a person's interest in his life, I do not think this interest encompasses a right to flee unimpeded from the scene of a burglary.... The legitimate interests of the suspect in these circumstances are adequately accommodated by the Tennessee statute: to avoid the use of deadly force and the consequent risk to his life, the suspect need merely obey the valid order to halt.

A proper balancing of the interests involved suggests that use of deadly force as a last resort to apprehend a criminal suspect fleeing from the scene of a nighttime burglary is not unreasonable within the meaning of the Fourth Amendment. Admittedly, the events giving rise to this case are in retrospect deeply regrettable. No one can view the death of an unarmed and apparently nonviolent 15-year old without sorrow, much less disapproval. Nonetheless, the reasonableness of Officer Hymon's conduct for purposes of the Fourth Amendment cannot be evaluated by what later appears to have been a preferable course of police action. The officer pursued a suspect in the darkened backyard of a house that from all indications had just been burglarized. The police officer was not certain whether the suspect was alone or unarmed; nor did he know what had transpired inside the house. He ordered the suspect to halt, and when the suspect refused to obey and attempted to flee into the night, the officer fired his weapon to prevent escape. The reasonableness of this action for purposes of the Fourth Amendment is not determined by the unfortunate nature of this particular case; instead, the question is whether it is constitutionally impermissible for police officers, as a last resort, to shoot a burglary suspect fleeing the scene of the crime.

. . .

The Court's silence on critical factors in the decision to use deadly force simply invites second-guessing of difficult police decisions that must be made quickly in the most trying of circumstances ... Police are given no guidance for determining which objects, among an array of potentially lethal weapons ranging from guns to knives to baseball bats to rope, will justify the use of deadly force. The Court also declines to outline the additional factors necessary to provide "probable cause" for believing that a suspect "poses a significant threat of death or serious physical injury," ante, at 1697, when the officer has probable cause to arrest and the suspect refuses to obey an order to halt. But even if it were appropriate in this case to limit the use of deadly force to that ambiguous class of suspects, I believe the class should include nighttime residential burglars who resist arrest by attempting to flee the scene of the crime. We can expect an escalating volume of litigation as the lower courts struggle to determine if a police officer's split-second decision to shoot was justified by the danger posed by a particular object and other facts related to the crime. Thus, the majority opinion portends a burgeoning area of Fourth Amendment doctrine concerning the circumstances in which police officers can reasonably employ deadly force.

...

NOTES

(1) Considering *Garner* as a straight "tort" case, how would you state the legal issue?

(2) Do the opinions in *Garner* agree on what the principal empirical question is? Will this decision likely be associated with an upward trend in burglaries?

(3) Where is the majority's opinion factually the most vulnerable? What are the principal differences of emphasis in the recitations of the facts by each opinion?

(4) What are the principal divergences of the two opinions in their reading of the relevant social facts?

(5) Is the majority making a per se determination of unreasonableness in the particular sort of factual profile it describes?

Is *Garner* analogous to *Katko*?

(6) In a case in which there were "sharp factual issues" concerning the shooting of the plaintiff by a police officer, one opinion described the testimony this way:

> ... Plaintiff testified that when he was shot he had fled down a flight of stairs and was already some distance away from the scene of the attempted robbery and from Officer Rodriguez who was at the top of the stairs. Plaintiff stated that he was running away from Officer Rodriguez when Officer Rodriguez fired and hit him twice in the back. Officer Rodriguez, on the other hand, testified that the shooting occurred at the top of the stairs. Plaintiff and his companion, according to Rodriguez, were lunging toward him and only four feet away when he fired. Corroborating plaintiff's testimony are the following items of proof: plaintiff was shot in the back; blood was found only on the platform at the bottom of the stairs where plaintiff was lying; according to expert testimony plaintiff could not have run down the stairs after the bullet severed his spinal cord; both the victim and the officer accompanying Rodriguez testified that plaintiff did not lunge at Rodriguez. The victim himself testified that he was standing against the wall when the officers approached, and plaintiff fled down the stairs before shots were fired.

This fact situation evoked citations to *Garner* from both sides of a divided appellate court, on appeal from a $4.3 million jury award for the plaintiff. Should the court have affirmed? How would each side have used *Garner* to support its position?

(7) Is it tortious for a policeman to arrest a man who is walking down a street in a low-income urban neighborhood late at night, carrying an apparently new color television set, if the officer knows no other facts?

———————

§ 3.04 Consent

[A] Generally

We have noted that "fraud" or "deceit" is a separate tort, typically associated with the deprivation of property or the loss of economic value in commercial or consumer settings. See supra § 2.05. The case law presented below often speaks the language of "fraud," but the context tends to be different than that of the traditional marketplace.

PROBLEM
Suit Claims Hudson Concealed Illness from Lover
72 A.B.A. J. 40 (1986)*

Even in death, AIDS continues to haunt Rock Hudson. A man claiming to be the actor's former lover has filed a $14 million suit against Hudson's estate. Marc Christ-ian..., who said he lived with Hudson for the last two and a half years of the actor's life, claims that Hudson continued to have sex with Christian for several months after Hudson learned that he was stricken with AIDS.

Christian included Hudson's secretary, Mark Miller, his executor, Wallace Sheft, and unnamed physicians in his suit. The complaint demands $10 million from the estate, and $1 million each from Miller, Sheft and two doctors. Christian, 31, claims that the defendants and Hudson conspired to conceal their knowledge of Hudson's illness from him.

According to the lawsuit, Hudson learned that he was afflicted with AIDS in June 1984, but had sex with Christian through February 1985. Hudson died of complications from AIDS on Oct. 2, 1985.

Christian has not been diagnosed as having the AIDS virus yet, but his suit claims, "It is probable that claimant has contracted AIDS from Hudson."

———————

What are the potential tort issues?

KATHLEEN K. v. ROBERT B.
California Court of Appeal
Cal. App. 3d 992, 198 Cal. Rptr. 273 (1984)

HASTINGS, ASSOCIATE JUSTICE.

In this action, plaintiff and appellant Kathleen K. seeks damages because she contracted genital herpes, allegedly by way of sexual intercourse with defendant and respondent Robert B. The trial court granted respondent's motion for judgment on the pleadings based upon failure to state a cause of action. We reverse the judgment.

. . .

The complaint sets forth four causes of action: (1) negligence (alleging that respondent inflicted injury upon appellant by having sexual intercourse with her at a time when he knew, or in the exercise of reasonable care should have known, that he was a carrier of venereal disease); (2) battery; (3) intentional infliction of emotional distress; and (4) fraud (alleging that respondent deliberately misrepresented to appellant that he was free from venereal disease, and that appellant, relying on such representations, had sexual intercourse with respondent, which she would not have done had she known the true state of affairs).

———————

In granting respondent's motion for judgment on the pleadings, the trial court relied upon the case of Stephen K. v. Roni L., 105 Cal.App.3d 640, 164 Cal.Rptr. 618. In Stephen K., the father of a child filed a cross-complaint against the child's mother who had brought a paternity action, claiming that the mother had falsely represented to him that she was taking birth control pills. The father alleged that in reliance upon that misrepresentation, he engaged in sexual intercourse with the mother, resulting in the birth of a child which he did not want. He further alleged that as a proximate result of the misrepresentation, he had become obligated to support the child financially and had suffered emotional distress.

In affirming dismissal of the cross-complaint, the court held that the misrepresentation was not actionable: "The claim of Stephen is phrased in the language of the tort of misrepresentation. Despite its legalism, it is nothing more than asking the court to supervise the promises made between two consenting adults as to the circumstances of their private sexual conduct. To do so would encourage unwarranted governmental intrusion into matters affecting the individual's right to privacy ... We reject Stephen's contention that tortious liability should be imposed against Roni, and conclude that as a matter of public policy the practice of birth control, if any, engaged in by two partners in a consensual sexual relationship is best left to the individuals involved, free from any governmental interference." (Stephen K. v. Roni L., supra, 105 Cal.App.3d 640, 644–645, 164 Cal.Rptr. 618.)[1]

After the trial court entered its judgment, the First District Court of Appeal decided the case of Barbara A. v. John G., 145 Cal.App.3d 369, 193 Cal.Rptr. 422 (hrg. den. September 29, 1983). In Barbara A., a woman who suffered an ectopic pregnancy and was forced to undergo surgery to save her life, which rendered her sterile, brought an action against the man who impregnated her (her former attorney), alleging that she consented to sexual intercourse in reliance on the man's knowingly false representation that he was sterile. The court reversed a judgment on the pleadings in favor of the defendant and held that the complaint stated causes of action for battery and for deceit.

The court distinguished Stephen K., noting that: "In essence, Stephen was seeking damages for the 'wrongful birth' of his child resulting in support obligations and alleged damages for mental suffering. Here, no child is involved; appellant is seeking damages for severe injury to her own body." (145 Cal.App.3d at pp. 378–379, 193 Cal.Rptr. 422.) We conclude that these same factors distinguish this case from Stephen K., and accordingly hold that Barbara A. is controlling here.

Respondent, urging us to follow Stephen K., criticizes Barbara A. in several respects. First, he argues that the viability of appellant's cause of action should not depend upon whether the injury alleged is mental or physical. However, the Barbara A. court did not focus solely on the type of injury involved in Stephen K., but upon the fact that Stephen was alleging an injury which had significant public policy overtones:

> To assess damages against the mother for false representations about birth control would have the practical effect of reducing or eliminating support from the father by way of offset. Erasing much or all of the father's financial support, to the detriment of the child, is clearly against public policy and the statutory mandate.[2]

---

1. The court also commented: "As to Stephen's claim that he was tricked into fathering a child he did not want, no good reason appears why he himself could not have taken any precautionary measures." (Id., at p. 645, 164 Cal.Rptr. 618.)

2. The court was referring to Civil Code section 196a, which imposes upon both the natural father and natural mother of a child the obligation to give the child support and education suitable to his or her circumstances.

> Further, we think it is not sound social policy to allow one parent to sue the other over the wrongful birth of their child. Using the child as the damage element in a tortious claim of one parent against the other could seldom, if ever, result in benefit to a child.

(145 Cal.App.3d at p. 379, 193 Cal.Rptr. 422.)

In the present case, as in Barbara A., there is no child involved, and the public policy considerations with respect to parental obligations are absent.

Respondent also argues that it is not the business of courts to "supervise the promises made between two consenting adults as to the circumstances of their private sexual conduct." (Stephen K. v. Roni L., supra, 105 Cal.App.3d at pp. 644–645, 164 Cal.Rptr. 618.)

Respondent correctly focuses on the constitutional right of privacy as the crux of this case. Courts have long recognized the right of privacy in matters relating to marriage, family and sex (Griswold v. Connecticut, 381 U.S. 479, 85 S.Ct. 1678, 14 L.Ed.2d 510; Eisenstadt v. Baird, 405 U.S. 438, 92 S.Ct. 1029, 31 L.Ed.2d 349), and accordingly have frowned upon unwarranted governmental intrusion into matters affecting the individual's right of privacy. (Stanley v. Georgia, 394 U.S. 557, 89 S.Ct. 1243, 22 L.Ed.2d 542.) The key word here, however, is unwarranted. The right of privacy is not absolute, and in some cases is subordinate to the state's fundamental right to enact laws which promote public health, welfare and safety, even though such laws may invade the offender's right of privacy. (Barbara A. v. John G., supra, 145 Cal.App.3d at p. 380, 193 Cal.Rptr. 422.) Examples cited by the Barbara A. court were the penal statutes covering both forcible and consensual sexual acts, registration of convicted sex offenders, the recently enacted criminal statute prohibiting spousal rape (Pen.Code, § 262), and the various laws relating to the paternity of children. In each of these cases, the right of privacy is outweighed by the right of the state to protect the health, welfare and safety of its citizens. The Barbara A. court concluded that the right of privacy "does not insulate a person from all judicial inquiry into his or her sexual relations," and expanded the exceptions to the right of privacy to impose liability upon "one sexual partner who by intentionally tortious conduct causes physical injury to the other." (145 Cal.App.3d at p. 381, 193 Cal.Rptr. 422.)

This is precisely the type of conduct alleged in appellant's complaint. Appellant has alleged that she sustained physical injury due to respondent's tortious conduct in either negligently or deliberately failing to inform her that he was infected with venereal disease. The disease which appellant contracted is serious and (thus far) incurable. The tortious nature of respondent's conduct, coupled with the interest of this state in the prevention and control of contagious and dangerous diseases,[3] brings appellant's injury within the type of physical injury contemplated by the court in Barbara A. The constitutional right of privacy does not protect respondent here.

It should be noted that several out-of-state cases, cited by the court in Barbara A., have held that a woman's consent to sexual intercourse was vitiated by the man's fraud-

---

3. Respondent's argument that genital herpes is not a venereal disease is unpersuasive. Although herpes is not listed among the "venereal diseases" covered by the Health & Safety Code (specifically section 3001), that section was enacted in 1957, long before herpes achieved its present notoriety. We are not inclined to bar appellant's cause of action on the basis that genital herpes is not a venereal disease. It is a disease that can be propagated by sexual contact. Like AIDS it is now known by the public to be a contagious and dreadful disease. At the core of this action is the misrepresentation of defendant that he did not have a contagious disease that could be passed to his partner. If a person knowingly has genital herpes, AIDS or some other contagious and serious disease, a limited representation that he or she does not have a venereal disease is no defense to this type of action.

ulent concealment of the risk of infection with venereal disease. (De Vall v. Strunk (Tex.Civ.App.1936) 96 S.W.2d 245; Crowell v. Crowell (1920) 180 N.C. 516, 105 S.E. 206; State v. Lankford (1917) 29 Del. 594, 102 A. 63.) Respondent contends that these cases are old and, if decided today, would be dismissed under the public policy considerations outlined in Stephen K., supra. He distinguishes Crowell and Lankford (involving suits by a wife against her husband for damages resulting from contraction of venereal disease) on the basis that a husband and wife occupy a confidential relationship of trust and confidence in one another which does not exist between non-married persons. However, a certain amount of trust and confidence exists in any intimate relationship, at least to the extent that one sexual partner represents to the other that he or she is free from venereal or other dangerous contagious disease. The basic premise underlying these old cases — consent to sexual intercourse vitiated by one partner's fraudulent concealment of the risk of infection with venereal disease — is equally applicable today, whether or not the partners involved are married to each other.

We are also unpersuaded by respondent's argument that this is really an action for seduction (which he calls "the use of deception to effect intercourse"), and is therefore barred by Civil Code section 43.5.[4]

"'Seduction imports the idea of illicit intercourse accomplished by the use of arts, persuasions, or wiles to overcome the resistance of a female who is not disposed of her own volition to step aside from the paths of virtue.'" (Barbara A. v. John G., supra, 145 Cal.App.3d at p. 377, 193 Cal.Rptr. 422, citing Davis v. Stroud, 52 Cal.App.2d 308, 317, 126 P.2d 409.) Appellant is not complaining that respondent induced her to "step aside from the paths of virtue," and in fact she willingly engaged in sexual intercourse with him. This is an action for damages based upon severe injury to appellant's body, which allegedly occurred because of respondent's misrepresentation that he was disease-free. Such an action is not barred by Civil Code section 43.5.

In summary, we conclude that Stephen K. v. Roni L., on which the trial court relied, is inapplicable here, and that the reasoning of Barbara A. v. John G., in which a hearing was denied by our Supreme Court, is controlling.

The judgment is reversed.

FEINERMAN, P.J., and ASHBY, J., concur.

NOTES

(1) A "Medical Intelligence" report in a 1986 issue of the New England Journal of Medicine begins with the laconic statement, "The incidence of genital herpes simplex infection is increasing in the United States." The essay goes on to document the transmission of the disease by one patient, who had acquired it from another, to a third person. Disturbingly, "The only sexual contact between Patients 2 and 3 during the two weeks before infection was reported to have occurred on [a day when] Patient 2 was reported to be asymptomatic." Rooney, et al., *Acquisition of Genital Herpes from an Asymptomatic Sexual Partner*, 314 N. ENG. J. MED. 1561 (1986).

In the particular case at issue, Patient 2 had positive cultures before as well as after the day in question. But suppose someone is sued for transmitting herpes at a time when he or she has had no signs of the disease, with the symptoms appearing only after

---

4. Civil Code section 43.5, part of the "Anti-Heart Balm" Statute, provides that no cause of action arises for "seduction of a person over the age of legal consent."

the incident of intercourse that allegedly transmitted the virus? What is the appropriate tort doctrine, if any, on which to base suit? What would be the defense, and would it be successful?

(2) What was the most appropriate doctrine on which to plead Kathleen K's case? How would you describe the appellate court's response to the trial court's characterization of the case as involving "two consenting adults"?

(3) The court in *Kathleen K* refers to "trust and confidence" in "intimate relationship[s]" as part of the basis for its decision. Do those elements of human relations have a proper basis in "tort" decisions?

(4) If "[t]he incidence of genital herpes ... is increasing in the United States," is tort law likely to provide any significant help in controlling it? If not, what is the best rationale for the decision in *Kathleen K*?

(5) A decision similar to *Kathleen K* in spirit is *Long v. Adams*, 175 Ga. App. 538, 333 S.E.2d 852 (1985), in which the court reversed a defendant's summary judgment on a claim for transmission of genital herpes by a woman who allegedly knew that she was infected. Concentrating on a negligence count, although the plaintiff also had claimed for battery, the court emphasized that it was not holding "that herpes victims have a specific duty to warn any person of their condition," but said that such persons, "like all citizens, are to be guided by those considerations which ordinarily regulate the conduct of human affairs, and they may be sued in this state for negligence in the omission to do something which a reasonable person would do."

A different doctrinal angle, yielding the same result, appears in *Stopera v. DiMarco*, 218 Mich. App. 565, 554 N.W.2d 379 (1996), leave denied, 567 N.W.2d 242 (Mich. 1997)(table), in which the plaintiff, an unmarried woman, sued for her contraction of human papillomavirus (HPV) from the defendant, a married man. The court was unpersuaded by the plaintiff's argument that a statute that made adultery a felony was "never enforced, regularly ignored," and was subordinate to "public policy concerns regarding the spread of venereal diseases." Noting that the statute not been repealed, despite arguments that it was archaic, the court said that the legislature might believe that it "still exerts a moral authority on people's behavior for the common good." 554 N.W.2d at 381.

However, the court reversed a dismissal on the grounds of a "culpability exception," applied in cases in which both parties have "engaged in illegal conduct, but one is more culpable than the other." It said that it is "one thing to engage in illegal adultery" but "quite another to do so knowing that a likely result will be infecting a sexual partner with a serious disease without making that fact known." It declared that in those circumstances, "the blame for plaintiff's contracting HPV rests largely with [the defendant] because he is almost entirely responsible for that injury." The consent-based root of the case is evident in the court's comment that since the plaintiff did not have the knowledge that the defendant had, she "could not adjust her conduct accordingly." *Id.* at 381–82.

(6) In terms of quantitative significance, the disease Acquired Immune Deficiency Syndrome (AIDS) has become a matter of much greater concern than genital herpes simplex. Symbolizing a criminal side to the AIDS problem is the Army's effort to court-martial a private for sexual activity with his fiancee, who he told he had a fatal contagious disease and who he eventually told he had AIDS; with another woman, who said that the soldier had told her only that he had an "incurable blood disease"; and with a male friend, who said he did not know that the private had tested positive for the HIV

virus that causes AIDS. *HIV-Positive Private Charged with Assault*, AMERICAN MEDICAL NEWS, May 22/29, 1987, at l. What would be the theories of liability and defense in tort actions against the private by each of his three sexual partners? What would be the likely result in each case?

(7) Another form of potential sexual tort in which consent is a key issue is "date rape." One news story quotes the director of health education in Brown University's health services department as saying that "[a] woman does not necessarily have to be on a formal 'date' for this to happen.... We have had cases where students come in and say that their boyfriends, whom they had known for months or even years, had forced them to have sexual intercourse." Sherman, *A New Recognition of the Realities of Date Rape*, N.Y. TIMES, Oct. 23, 1985, at C1, C14.

If you were trying to draft a tort rule that would give both parties "justice" in cases of "date rape," how would you phrase it?

SPECIAL NOTE ON CONSENT AND TORT DOCTRINE IN MEDICAL MALPRACTICE

Adapted from Shapo, *Some Legal Perspectives toward Personal Injury Compensation*, in Compensating for Research Injuries: The Ethical and Legal Implications of Programs to Redress Injuries Caused by Biomedical and Behavioral Research, in Vol. 2 (Appendices) 205, at 208–09 (President's Commission for the Study of Ethical Problems in Medicine and Biomedical and Behavioral Research 1982)

With specific reference to the medical area, one must keep in mind the basic definition of a battery as being an intended, unprivileged and unconsented contact. Syllogistically, it would appear that any time a physician probes more widely in a patient's body than the patient would have desired, a prima facie case of battery has occurred. Because of the delicacy of the judgment that may be involved, and the pressure of time, the courts have begun to establish principles to guide physicians through this legal minefield. An important rule in this area declares that a surgeon may be guided by the standard of sound surgical procedure in the area of the original incision. Thus, a surgeon who punctures ovarian cysts while performing what was originally billed only as an appendectomy is safe from liability, if he or she acts carefully. On the other hand, it should be noted that the physician who does act carefully but goes beyond the scope of his or her consent may be liable for a battery.

The courts are now developing a special doctrine, familiar at least in terminology to any newspaper reader, as a response to medical cases in which the patient complains that he or she has not been properly put on notice of the implications of a medical procedure. This is the doctrine of "informed consent," which applies to both batteries and negligence actions. This body of law gets full treatment infra § 5.01[B].

NOTES

(1) An interesting twist on the problem of lack of consent to a medical procedure appears in a suit by a couple against a physician who performed an abortion on their minor daughter, without a notarized form bearing the signatures of the parents.

The parents sued the doctor, claiming that his failure to secure the notarized parental consent form had deprived their daughter "of the ability to carry a child to normal delivery [and of] the joys of motherhood," as well as depriving her parents of "the joys of grandparenting." Would you grant a motion to dismiss?

(2) An especially agonizing variation concerns a patient in a rehabilitation hospital, who is there because of paralyzing injuries that resulted in a "locked-in" state, the effect of which is that he can only move his eyes and, with great difficulty, his head. He cannot speak or swallow. He pleads with his doctors to discontinue medication, nutrition and hydration that is being provided through a tube through his nose. The doctors refuse to discontinue the use of the tube and the patient's representative sues them to make them stop feeding the patient. Both sides move for summary judgment. Would you grant either motion?

[B] The Special Case of Sports

PROBLEM

A judicial opinion summarized the facts this way in litigation between college students:

While waiting in a dormitory lobby for friends, plaintiff, defendant and two other students spontaneously began kicking a crushed aluminum soda can. The four students divided into two teams with two persons on each team, and set up informal goals against the walls of the dormitory lobby. Each team attempted to kick the crushed can into the opposing team's goal. Plaintiff allegedly pushed defendant toward a wall in an attempt to gain control of the can. Defendant responded by allegedly pushing plaintiff, causing plaintiff to fall. While attempting to break his fall, plaintiff put his left hand and forearm through the glass door of a fire extinguisher case on the wall of the dormitory. Plaintiff sustained injuries to his left hand and forearm ...

* * *

What theory of recovery will the plaintiff offer, what will be the defendant's theory of defense, and who will win?

HACKBART v. CINCINNATI BENGALS, INC.

United States District Court, District of Colorado
435 F. Supp. 352 (1977)

MATSCH, JUDGE.

...

... The case arises as a result of an incident which occurred in the course of a professional football game played between the Denver Broncos and the Cincinnati Bengals, in Denver, Colorado, on September 16, 1973.

The Parties

The plaintiff, Dale Hackbart, is a citizen of Colorado who was a 35 year old contract player for the Denver Broncos Football Club in the National Football League at the time of the incident. He was then 6 feet 3 inches tall and weighed 210 pounds. Mr. Hackbart had 13 years' experience as a professional football player after competing in college and high school football, making a total of 21 years of experience in organized football.

The Denver game was the first regular season professional football game for the defendant, Charles Clark, who was then 23 years old with a weight of 240 pounds and a height of 6 feet 1-3/4 inches. Mr. Clark was a contract player for the Cincinnati Bengals Football Club, Inc., defendant herein, which was also a member of the National Football League. Both defendants are citizens of states other than Colorado.

The Incident

The incident which gave rise to this lawsuit occurred near the end of the first half of the game at a time when the Denver team was leading by a score of 21 to 3. Dale Hackbart was playing a free safety position on the Broncos' defensive team and Charles Clark was playing fullback on the Bengals' offensive team. The Cincinnati team attempted a forward pass play during which Charles Clark ran into a corner of the north end zone as a prospective receiver. That took him into an area which was the defensive responsibility of Mr. Hackbart. The thrown pass was intercepted near the goal line by a Denver linebacker who then began to run the ball upfield. The interception reversed the offensive and defensive roles of the two teams. As a result of an attempt to block Charles Clark in the end zone, Dale Hackbart fell to the ground. He then turned and, with one knee on the ground and the other leg extended, watched the play continue upfield. Acting out of anger and frustration, but without a specific intent to injure, Charles Clark stepped forward and struck a blow with his right forearm to the back of the kneeling plaintiff's head with sufficient force to cause both players to fall forward to the ground. Both players arose and, without comment, went to their respective teams along the sidelines. They both returned to play during the second half of the game.

Because no official observed it, no foul was called on the disputed play and Dale Hackbart made no report of this incident to his coaches or to anyone else during the game. Mr. Hackbart experienced pain and soreness to the extent that he was unable to play golf as he had planned on the day after the game, he did not seek any medical attention and, although he continued to feel pain, he played on specialty team assignments for the Denver Broncos in games against the Chicago Bears and the San Francisco Forty-Niners on successive Sundays. The Denver Broncos then released Mr. Hackbart on waivers and he was not claimed by any other team. After losing his employment, Mr. Hackbart sought medical assistance, at which time it was discovered that he had a neck injury. When that information was given to the Denver Broncos Football Club, Mr. Hackbart received his full payment for the 1973 season pursuant to an injury clause in his contract.

The Professional Football Industry

The claim of the plaintiff in this case must be considered in the context of football as a commercial enterprise....

The National Football League Players' Association is an unincorporated association which is the sole and exclusive bargaining representative of all professional football players in the NFL as a labor organization under the National Labor Relations Act. A collective bargaining contract between that association and the National Football League Player Relations Association, as bargaining agent for the member clubs, was in effect during 1973.... There is no provision for disputes between players of different teams.

Football is a contest for territory. The objective of the offensive team is to move the ball through the defending team's area and across the vertical plane of the goal line. The defensive players seek to prevent that movement with their bodies. Each attempted movement involves collisions between the bodies of offensive and defensive players with considerable force and with differing areas of contact. The most obvious characteristic of the game is that all of the players engage in violent physical behavior.

The rules of play which govern the method and style by which the NFL teams compete include limitations on the manner in which players may strike or otherwise physically contact opposing players. During 1973, the rules were enforced by six officials on the playing field. The primary sanction for a violation was territorial with the amounts of yardage lost being dependent upon the particular infraction. Players were also subject to expulsion from the game and to monetary penalties imposed by the league commissioner.

The written rules are difficult to understand and, because of the speed and violence of the game, their application is often a matter of subjective evaluation of the circumstances. Officials differ with each other in their rulings. The players are not specifically instructed in the interpretation of the rules, and they acquire their working knowledge of them only from the actual experience of enforcement by the game officials during contests.

Many violations of the rules do occur during each game. Ordinarily each team receives several yardage penalties, but many fouls go undetected or undeclared by the officials.

Disabling injuries are also common occurrences in each contest. Hospitalization and surgery are frequently required for repairs. Protective clothing is worn by all players, but it is often inadequate to prevent bodily damage. Professional football players are conditioned to "play with pain" and they are expected to perform even though they are hurt. The standard player contract imposes an obligation to play when the club physician determines that an injured player has the requisite physical ability.

The violence of professional football is carefully orchestrated. Both offensive and defensive players must be extremely aggressive in their actions and they must play with a reckless abandonment of self-protective instincts. The coaches make studied and deliberate efforts to build the emotional levels of their players to what some call a "controlled rage."

John Ralston, the 1973 Broncos coach, testified that the pre-game psychological preparation should be designed to generate an emotion equivalent to that which would be experienced by a father whose family had been endangered by another driver who had attempted to force the family car off the edge of a mountain road. The precise pitch of motivation for the players at the beginning of the game should be the feeling of that father when, after overtaking and stopping the offending vehicle, he is about to open the door to take revenge upon the person of the other driver.

The large and noisy crowds in attendance at the games contribute to the emotional levels of the players. Quick changes in the fortunes of the teams, the shock of violent collisions and the intensity of the competition make behavioral control extremely difficult, and it is not uncommon for players to "flare up" and begin fighting. The record made at this trial indicates that such incidents as that which gave rise to this action are not so unusual as to be unexpected in any NFL game.

The end product of all of the organization and effort involved in the professional football industry is an exhibition of highly developed individual skills in coordinated team competition for the benefit of large numbers of paying spectators, together with radio and television audiences. It is appropriate to infer that while some of those persons are attracted by the individual skills and precision performances of the teams, the appeal to others is the spectacle of savagery.

Plaintiff's Theories of Liability

This case is controlled by the law of Colorado. While a theory of intentional misconduct is barred by the applicable statute of limitations, the plaintiff contends that

Charles Clark's foul was so far outside of the rules of play and accepted practices of professional football that it should be characterized as reckless misconduct within the principles of Section 500 of the Restatement of Torts, 2d.

... Alternatively, the plaintiff claims that his injury was at least the result of a negligent act by the defendant....

Two coaches testified at the trial of this case. Paul Brown has had 40 years of experience at all levels of organized football, with 20 years of coaching professional football. Both Mr. Brown and Mr. Ralston emphasized that the coaching and instructing of professional football players did not include any training with respect to a responsibility or even any regard for the safety of opposing players. They both said that aggressiveness was the primary attribute which they sought in the selection of players. Both emphasized the importance of emotional preparation of the teams. Mr. Brown said that flare-up fighting often occurred, even in practice sessions of his teams.

It is wholly incongruous to talk about a professional football player's duty of care for the safety of opposing players when he has been trained and motivated to be heedless of injury to himself. The character of NFL competition negates any notion that the playing conduct can be circumscribed by any standard of reasonableness.

Both theories of liability are also subject to the recognized defenses of consent and assumption of the risk. Here the question is what would a professional football player in the plaintiff's circumstances reasonably expect to encounter in a professional contest?

All of the witnesses with playing or coaching experience in the NFL agreed that players are urged to avoid penalties. The emphasis, however, is on the unfavorable effects of the loss of yardage, not the safety of the players. It is undisputed that no game is without penalties and that players frequently lose control in surges of emotion.

The conflict in the testimony is the difference in the witnesses' opinions as to whether Mr. Clark's act of striking the plaintiff on the back of the head in reaction to anger and frustration can be considered as "a part of the game." Several former players denounced this incident and said that Mr. Clark's conduct could not be considered customary or acceptable.

It is noteworthy that while this incident was clearly shown on the Denver Broncos' defensive game films, which were routinely reviewed by the defensive players and coaching staff, none of them made it a matter of special attention or concern.

Upon all of the evidence, my finding is that the level of violence and the frequency of emotional outbursts in NFL football games are such that Dale Hackbart must have recognized and accepted the risk that he would be injured by such an act as that committed by the defendant Clark on September 16, 1973. Accordingly, the plaintiff must be held to have assumed the risk of such an occurrence. Therefore, even if the defendant breached a duty which he owed to the plaintiff, there can be no recovery because of assumption of the risk.

...

The Application of Tort Principles to Professional Football — A Question of Social Policy

> The business of the law of torts is to fix the dividing line between those cases in which a man is liable for harm which he has done, and those in which he is not. Justice O. W. Holmes, The Common Law (1881).

While the foregoing findings of fact and conclusions of law are determinative of the claim made by Dale Hackbart against Charles Clark and his employer, this case raises the larger question of whether playing field action in the business of professional football should become a subject for the business of the courts.

To compensate the injured at the expense of the wrongdoer, the courts have been compelled to construct principles of social policy. Through the processes of trial and error the judicial branch of government has historically evolved the common law principles which necessarily affect behavior in many contexts. The potential threat of liability for damages can have a significant deterrent effect and private civil actions are an important mechanism for societal control of human conduct. In recent years the pace of technical progress has accelerated and human conflicts have intensified. The resulting need to expand the body of governing law with greater rapidity and certainty than can be achieved through the litigation process has been met by legislation and administrative regulation. That is particularly true of industrial injuries. The coal mines became subject to the Federal Coal Mine Safety Act. The railroads have long been governed by the Federal Employers Liability Act and the Safety Appliance Act. The Occupational Health and Safety Act has broad application.

To this time professional football has been a self-regulated industry. The only protection which NFL contract players have beyond self-defense and real or threatened retaliation is that which is provided by the league rules and sanctions. It may well be true that what has been provided is inadequate and that these young athletes have been exploited and subjected to risks which should be unacceptable in our social order. In this respect, it is interesting to compare football with boxing. Because of the essential brutality of the contest, prize fighting has been held to be unlawful unless conducted under the sanction and authority of a governmental commission. Antlers Athletic Association v. Hartung, 85 Colo. 125, 129, 274 P. 831 (1929). See C.R.S. (1973) §§ 12-10-101 et seq.*

Football has been presumed to be lawful and, indeed, professional football has received the implicit approval of government because these contests take place in arenas owned by local governments and the revenues are subject to taxation. Like coal mining and railroading, professional football is hazardous to the health and welfare of those who are employed as players.

What is the interest of the larger community in limiting the violence of professional football? That question concerns not only the protection of the participants, but also the effects of such violence on those who observe it. Can the courts answer this question? I think not. An ordinary citizen is entitled to protection according to the usages of the society in which he lives, and in the context of common community standards there can be no question but that Mr. Clark's blow here would generate civil liability. It would involve a criminal sanction if the requisite intent were present. The difference here is that this blow was delivered on the field of play during the course of action in a regularly scheduled professional football game. The Illinois court was concerned with the safety of high school athletes in Nabozny v. Barnhill, 31 Ill.App.3d at 215, 334 N.E.2d at 260 and said:

> This court believes that the law should not place unreasonable burdens on the free and vigorous participation in sports by our youth. However, we also believe that organized, athletic competition does not exist in a vacuum. Rather, some of the restraints of civilization must accompany every athlete onto the playing field. One of the educational benefits of organized athletic competition to our youth is the development of discipline and self control.

* Professional boxing was apparently legalized, without regulation, by a repeal of the cited statute by Senate Bill No. 418, effective July 1, 1977.

The difficulty with that view as applied to professional football is that to decide which restraints should be made applicable is a task for which the courts are not well suited. There is no discernible code of conduct for NFL players. The dictionary definition of a sportsman is one who abides by the rules of a contest and accepts victory or defeat graciously. Webster's Third New International Dictionary, p. 2206 (1971). That is not the prevalent attitude in professional football. There are no Athenian virtues in this form of athletics. The NFL has substituted the morality of the battlefield for that of the playing field, and the "restraints of civilization" have been left on the sidelines.

Mr. Justice Holmes' simple statement of the function of tort law and the evidentiary record now before me clearly reveal the density of the thicket in which the courts would become entangled if they undertook the task of allocation of fault in professional football games. The NFL rules of play are so legalistic in their statement and so difficult of application because of the speed and violence of the play that the differences between violations which could fairly be called deliberate, reckless or outrageous and those which are "fair play" would be so small and subjective as to be incapable of articulation. The question of causation would be extremely difficult in view of the frequency of forceful collisions. The volume of such litigation would be enormous and it is reasonable to expect that the court systems of the many states in which NFL games are played would develop differing and conflicting principles of law. It is highly unlikely that the NFL could continue to produce anything like the present games under such multiple systems of overview by judges and juries. If there is to be any governmental involvement in this industry, it is a matter which can be best considered by the legislative branch.

My conclusion that the civil courts cannot be expected to control the violence in professional football is limited by the facts of the case before me. I have considered only a claim for an injury resulting from a blow, without weaponry, delivered emotionally without a specific intent to injure, in the course of regular play in a league-approved game involving adult, contract players. Football as a commercial enterprise is something quite different from athletics as an extension of the academic experience and what I have said here may have no applicability in other areas of physical competition.

Upon the foregoing findings of fact and conclusions of law, it is

ORDERED that judgment shall enter for the defendants....

HACKBART v. CINCINNATI BENGALS, INC.

United States Court of Appeals, Tenth Circuit
601 F.2d 516, cert. denied, 444 U.S. 931 (1979)

WILLIAM E. DOYLE, CIRCUIT JUDGE.

...

We are forced to conclude that the result reached is not supported by evidence.

WHETHER INTENTIONAL INJURY IS ALLOWED BY EITHER WRITTEN RULE OR CUSTOM

Plaintiff, of course, maintains that tort law applicable to the injury in this case applies on the football field as well as in other places. On the other hand, plaintiff does not rely on the theory of negligence being applicable. This is in recognition of the fact that subjecting another to unreasonable risk of harm, the essence of negligence, is inherent in the game of football, for admittedly it is violent. Plaintiff maintains that in the area of contributory fault, a vacuum exists in relationship to intentional infliction of injury. Since negligence does not apply, contributory negligence is inapplicable. Intentional or reckless contributory fault could theoretically at least apply to infliction of injuries in reckless disregard of the rights of others. This has some similarity to contributory negligence and undoubtedly it would apply if the evidence would justify it. But it is highly questionable whether a professional football player consents or submits to injuries caused by conduct not within the rules, and there is no evidence which we have seen which shows this. However, the trial court did not consider this question and we are not deciding it.

Contrary to the position of the court then, there are no principles of law which allow a court to rule out certain tortious conduct by reason of general roughness of the game or difficulty of administering it.

Indeed, the evidence shows that there are rules of the game which prohibit the intentional striking of blows. Thus, Article 1, Item 1, Subsection C, provides that:

> All players are prohibited from striking on the head, face or neck with the heel, back or side of the hand, wrist, forearm, elbow or clasped hands.

Thus the very conduct which was present here is expressly prohibited by the rule which is quoted above.

The general customs of football do not approve the intentional punching or striking of others. That this is prohibited was supported by the testimony of all of the witnesses. They testified that the intentional striking of a player in the face or from the rear is prohibited by the playing rules as well as the general customs of the game. Punching or hitting with the arms is prohibited. Undoubtedly these restraints are intended to establish reasonable boundaries so that one football player cannot intentionally inflict a serious injury on another. Therefore, the notion is not correct that all reason has been abandoned, whereby the only possible remedy for the person who has been the victim of an unlawful blow is retaliation.

. . .

IS THE STANDARD OF RECKLESS DISREGARD OF THE RIGHTS OF OTHERS APPLICABLE TO THE PRESENT SITUATION?

The Restatement of Torts Second, § 500, distinguishes between reckless and negligent misconduct. Reckless misconduct differs from negligence, according to the authors, in that negligence consists of mere inadvertence, lack of skillfulness or failure to take precautions; reckless misconduct, on the other hand, involves a choice or adoption of a course of action either with knowledge of the danger or with knowledge of facts which would disclose this danger to a reasonable man. Recklessness also differs in that it consists of intentionally doing an act with knowledge not only that it contains a risk of harm to others as does negligence, but that it actually involves a risk substantially greater in magnitude than is necessary in the case of negligence. The authors explain the difference, therefore, in the degree of risk by saying that the difference is so significant as to amount to a difference in kind.

Subsection (f) also distinguishes between reckless misconduct and intentional wrongdoing. To be reckless the Act must have been intended by the actor. At the same time, the actor does not intend to cause the harm which results from it. It is enough that he realized, or from the facts should have realized, that there was a strong probability that harm would result even though he may hope or expect that this conduct will prove harmless. Nevertheless, existence of probability is different from substantial certainty which is an ingredient of intent to cause the harm which results from the act.

Therefore, recklessness exists where a person knows that the act is harmful but fails to realize that it will produce the extreme harm which it did produce. It is in this respect that recklessness and intentional conduct differ in degree.

In the case at bar the defendant Clark admittedly acted impulsively and in the heat of anger, and even though it could be said from the admitted facts that he intended the act, it could also be said that he did not intend to inflict serious injury which resulted from the blow which he struck.

In ruling that recklessness is the appropriate standard and that assault and battery is not the exclusive one, we are saying that these two liability concepts are not necessarily opposed one to the other. Rather, recklessness under § 500 of the Restatement might be regarded, for the purpose of analysis at least, a lesser included act.

Assault and battery, having originated in a common law writ, is narrower than recklessness in its scope. In essence, two definitions enter into it. The assault is an attempt coupled with the present ability to commit a violent harm against another. Battery is the unprivileged or unlawful touching of another. Assault and battery then call for an intent, as does recklessness. But in recklessness the intent is to do the act, but without an intent to cause the particular harm. It is enough if the actor knows that there is a strong probability that harm will result. Thus, the definition fits perfectly the fact situation here. Surely, then, no reason exists to compel appellant to employ the assault and battery standard which does not comfortably apply fully in preference to the standard which meets this fact situation.

. . .

[Reversed and remanded.]

NOTES

(1) If Clark committed a tort, what is the most appropriate legal category to describe that tort?

(2) Did either the district court or the court of appeals properly conceptualize the defense of Clark and the Bengals? Does it ring true to say that there is a defense of "assumption of risk" to an "intentional tort," or even the tort of "reckless misconduct"? If "assumption of risk" is properly a defense reserved to "negligent" acts, then what is the best way to describe the defense that the district judge employed on behalf of Clark and the Bengals? Would "consent" be an appropriate description of Hackbart's state of mind, or of his actions in playing in an NFL game?

(3) What is your reaction to the proposition that the NFL has adopted "the morality of the battlefield"? Are there any professional sports or games about which that statement can convincingly be made with respect to tort claims by injured athletes?

Consider the following quotations concerning two other rough sports:

"Hockey has to be the only body contact sport in the world that allows fighting and in fact, in my view, actively encourages it." (Reed, *Week of Disgrace on the Ice*, Sports Illustrated, April 26, 1976, 22 at 24) (reporting remark of a Canadian attorney general).

"Enforcers are vital. They are part of the game by whatever name you call them. Basketball is not a non-contact sport." (Papanek, *Nobody, But Nobody, is Going to Hurt my Teammates*, Sports Illustrated, Oct. 31, 1977, at 43) (quoting a pro basketball scout). This report, which appeared little more than a month before a much-publicized attack by Kermit Washington on Rudy Tomjanovich, quoted an observer of a "skirmish" between Washington and John Shumate as saying, "Shumate came apart in sections."*

Does an athlete who plays in the environments described by these two quotations "consent" to, say, being hit in the head with a hockey stick? Being punched in the mouth by a fellow basketball player?

(4) Do you see a sharp line between "law" and "morality"? What are the major elements of each that are likely to come into conflict in cases of this sort?

(5) An interesting way station along the consent spectrum, analogous to sports, is the case of injuries associated with fraternity hazing. In a 1967 incident, a 19-year-old pledge in a Baylor service club died after being commanded to run in place after ingesting various items and potions, including five different kind of laxatives and garlic and a "large dose of mineral oil." *Baylor Student Dies at Initiation*, Austin American, Oct. 11, 1967; *Chamber Members Silent, But Schedule Tells Story*, Waco News-Tribune, Oct. 11, 1967, at 2A. In just one later demonstration that college boys will be college boys, a Western Illinois student was found dead in his room after a lacrosse club initiation that featured "rookie juice," a mixture of, "among other things, beer, schnapps, tuna, tomato paste, and Tabasco sauce," allegedly followed by a "drinking relay that involved various alcoholic beverages." Reportedly, 20 students faced expulsion for their participation. *Lacrosse Player Dies After Initiation Rite*, Chronicle of Higher Education, Oct. 31, 1990, at A2.

Although there are only isolated reported appellate cases on such incidents, one account refers to "an insurance analysis of more than 900 claims against fraternities in a six-year period," including "claims for sexual assaults, fights and falls from the roofs of fraternity houses." Nina Bernstein, *Behind Some Fraternity Walls, Brothers in Crime*, N.Y. Times, May 6, 1996, at A-1, A14. One reason that there would be reluctance by injured persons to litigate such claims, at least in hazing cases, is evident in an episode in which a pledge was made to drink a fifth of whisky in 45 minutes and had to be put on a resuscitator to save his life. Although the University of Georgia suspended his fraternity for five years, there was no criminal prosecution or tort suit. The student reportedly "blamed himself at first and still hoped to join the fraternity." He asked his mother not to say anything about it. After they had decided to bring out the facts, they both came to "believe that ... public attention made the sanction stick" against the fraternity. *Id.*

What would be the theories of liability and defense in a suit against a fraternity for injuries attributed to hazing?

---

* The authors are grateful to Nathaniel S. Shapo, then age 11, for research that produced these quotations.

Chapter 4

NEGLIGENCE

§ 4.01 Introduction

[A] Negligence in the Courts

PROBLEM

A motorist was driving along a flat stretch of state highway at 50 miles per hour. Noticing a pickup truck in the ditch to his left, he then saw "something lying near the center of the road." He could not swerve in time to avoid that object, which was a human body, and he ran over it. There were no skid marks indicating that the driver had tried to take evasive action. The person lying in the road died. An autopsy indicated that he had been drunk, having a blood alcohol level of .37 grams percent.

What are the chances that the personal representatives of the man lying in the road will recover from the driver? How would you frame the principal legal issues?

Consider, in this regard, the definition of negligence in *Restatement (Second) of Torts* section 282 as "conduct which falls below the standard established by law for the protection of others against unreasonable risk of harm," and in a late draft of section 3 of the *Restatement (Third) of Torts*, which says that "[a] person acts negligently if the person does not exercise reasonable care under the circumstances." Restatement (Third) of Torts: Liability for Physical Harm § 3 (Proposed Final Draft Apr. 6, 2005). Was the motorist negligent?

Keep this definition in mind as you read the case below. How does the court decide what the "standard established by law" is? How does the court fit the facts into the procedural framework of the case, and how does it view the roles of judge and jury in deciding what negligence is?

LaPLANTE v. RADISSON HOTEL CO.

United States District Court, District of Minnesota
292 F. Supp. 705 (1968)

NEVILLE, DISTRICT JUDGE.

This case involves what appears to be a novel question concerning which there is a paucity of authority. It is presently before the court on the defendant's motion for judgment notwithstanding the jury verdict for plaintiff or, in the alternative, for a new trial. Simply stated, the question is whether a jury may find a hotel negligent and an injured plaintiff free from contributory negligence where the hotel in hiring itself out to stage a banquet for 1,200 paying guests in one of its banquet rooms allegedly set the banquet

127

tables so close to each other as to leave inadequate aisles and room between seated guests, causing plaintiff to trip over a chair when attempting to leave the room and thereby injuring herself.

On this motion, the evidence must be viewed in the light most favorable to the verdict. The jury could find that the plaintiff, a semi-retired school teacher from Kalamazoo, Michigan, 67 years of age, was a guest at defendant's hotel for the purpose of attending the national convention of a professional education sorority of which she was a member. The convention meetings and related banquets were all held at the defendant hotel.

On August 10, 1967, the convention staged its final banquet and plaintiff was in attendance. The banquet arrangements had been made some months earlier, with the accession and prior approval of a seating sketch or chart by at least some of the sorority's national officers, though not seen by plaintiff. The room in which the banquet was held is claimed by defendant to have a maximum seating capacity of 2,000 though only 1,200 were in attendance that evening.

Long tables, seating 12 to 18 persons each, were placed at pre-set distances apart which defendant claims was 42 inches though the jury could find from evidence plaintiff introduced that the actual distance between tables was somewhat less. Further there was evidence that at least at some of the tables, the chairs were back to back to those at the next table. The testimony of at least one witness other than the plaintiff indicated a crowded condition.

There was testimony that near the entrance to the banquet hall there was ten feet of vacant space, more or less, from which the inference could be drawn that if used such would have permitted the spacing of all the tables farther apart. Also in a certain area were a number of circular tables, seating a lesser number of persons per square foot than the long banquet tables and which if replaced by long banquet tables the jury could find would have allowed more space for all tables. The room was set up with a series of three head tables in stages and nearby a large simulated birthday cake commemorating an anniversary of the sorority.

There was testimony that waitresses were unable to move down the aisles between the long tables and at the table at which plaintiff was seated, the plates of food were passed down by the waitresses from person to person from the end of the table. The hotel manager testified this was not a good practice and he did not permit it, if discovered. Plaintiff testified she had determined by later experimentation that seated at a table in normal manner there were 18 inches between the edge of the table and the back of her chair; that on this night her chair touched that of the person at the next table backing into her; that if his or her similar distance was no more than 18 inches, this left but six inches between the backs of chairs even if, as the hotel manager stated, the edges of the tables were placed 42 inches apart.

The banquet began at 8:00 P.M. and plaintiff came to the hall and selected a seat about in the middle of one of the long tables.

Several hours later at approximately 11:15 P.M. before the banquet program was over and while the lights were dimmed, with a spotlight on the head table and/or the birthday cake, plaintiff decided to leave the banquet hall to meet her son-in-law as prearranged. Moving sideways she negotiated a path between chairs as the various people moved in toward the table to accommodate her. The jury could find that not realizing the position of the final chair and believing she had negotiated herself to the main aisle, plaintiff caught her foot on the leg of that last chair and tripped and fell injuring herself. Based on this evidence and the medical testimony as to the extent of her injuries, the jury awarded plaintiff the sum of $3,500.

Defendant's first challenge is that the evidence as a matter of law is insufficient to allow a finding of negligence on the part of defendant to stand. The court believes to the contrary and that the evidence above recited is sufficient to permit the jury to come to the factual conclusion that they did, that plaintiff's injuries were the proximate result of the defendant's negligence in crowding the tables too closely.

Defendant contends that since there was no violation of any statute or ordinance pleaded nor proved, the burden was on the plaintiff to show by expert testimony or otherwise the standard of care to which defendant's conduct should have conformed. Put another way, defendant claims that there was insufficient proof of a violation of any duty since there was no evidence of what reasonably prudent hotel management would do under the same or similar circumstances and thus it was error to permit the jury to speculate as to the standard of care against which defendant's conduct should be measured.

The issue becomes one of whether a jury should be permitted without expert testimony to draw upon their own knowledge, background and common experience to determine what the standard of care should be and hence whether any departure therefrom occurred.

Certainly the nature of the case is not scientifically complicated nor technical. While some training and experience in catering and hotel management may be a necessary prerequisite to the handling of a banquet for 1,200 people, the court is of the view that such training or background is not a sine qua non to the ability to determine what is unreasonable crowding and what is not. The lay juror knowing no more than the next man about catering procedures could determine from the evidence in this case whether or not the tables were too close for safety. Though the evidence on the point is not conclusive one way or the other, the court is of the opinion that this was a fair question for the jury and not insufficient as a matter of law. The rule of evidence applied in determining the appropriateness of opinion "expert testimony" is whether the subject involved is so distinctively related to some science, profession, business or occupation as to be beyond the ken of the average layman.... Further the trial court has great discretion in determining the need for such testimony.... Here the court is not convinced that expert testimony was required or would necessarily have been helpful to the jury.

Defendant refers the court to the case of Hemmen v. Clark's Restaurant Enterprises, 434 P.2d 729 (Wash.1967), for the proposition that it is not a jury question under these circumstances as to the degree of care required. In the court's opinion that case is inapposite. In Hemmen, the chair upon which plaintiff had tripped inadvertently had been placed in her way by another patron of the restaurant and there was not enough time for the defendant to remedy the hazardous situation before the accident happened. Further in Hemmen the aisle between the back of the last row of chairs and the adjoining wall was two to two and one-half feet wide while here there was believable testimony that the chairs were at some points back to back. That issues such as appear in the case at bar can and should be decided by the trier of fact is recognized in Hemmen. 434 P.2d at 733.

Plaintiff argues, perhaps with some merit, that if a standard is required to be established by evidence from a caterer or other expert person engaged in the industry, defendant's catering manager himself testified 42 inches to be the standard and there was evidence from plaintiff herself and from another witness that the tables were less than that distance apart and perhaps no more than 36 inches. The court, while retaining some doubt as to the accuracy of the measurement observations of these witnesses, cannot say as a matter of law that the jury could not believe and be convinced by their testimony.

Defendant's next claim is that the court erred in refusing to direct a verdict in defendant's favor on the issue of plaintiff's contributory negligence and assumption of risk. While there is evidence to support a favorable jury finding on either or both of those theories and the court did instruct liberally on both of them, in no way can it be said that reasonable minds could not differ on these issues. Hence a directed verdict would have been inappropriate. At the time of plaintiff's fall, the room was nearly dark, though plaintiff did testify she could see her feet. The spot-light was on the headtable and the birthday cake. The jury could find that the hotel reasonably could foresee that during a banquet commencing at 8:00 P.M. and lasting until after 11:00 P.M., a number of people would leave the hall to go to the rest rooms or for other purposes; that with a program in progress the lights might well be dimmed and vision made more difficult; and that with the crowded or overcrowded conditions such a fall as occurred might be anticipated. The question of plaintiff's contributory negligence was a fair fact question for the jury and this court does not feel it can substitute its judgment for the jury's where there is substantial evidence upon which a finding could be based.

. . .

TOLBERT v. DUCKWORTH

Supreme Court of Georgia
423 S.E.2d 229 (1992)

FLETCHER, Justice.

We granted the writ of certiorari to determine whether the jury instruction on accident should be eliminated as a defense in civil cases. We conclude that the accident charge should not be given in future civil cases and affirm.

Larry Duckworth was driving on a rain slick road when he turned a corner, hit a drainage area from a car wash, lost control of his car, and crashed into Bruce Tolbert's car. The investigating police officer gave Duckworth a ticket for driving too fast for conditions, but testified at the trial that Duckworth could not have anticipated that water would be in the road as he drove around the corner. In the second personal injury action, Brenda Smith was driving under the speed limit in the rain when she hydroplaned into the next lane, hitting the car of William O. Shelton, III. Tolbert and Shelton sued for negligence. In both cases, the trial court gave a jury instruction on the law of accident, the juries returned a verdict in favor of the defendant, and the Court of Appeals affirmed....

1. The pattern jury charge on accident in Georgia states: If you should find from the evidence in this case that neither plaintiff nor defendant were guilty of negligence, then any injuries or damages would be the result of an accident. The word "accident" has a specific and distinct meaning, as it is used in connection with this case. Accident is strictly defined as an occurrence which takes place in the absence of negligence and for which [no] one would be liable. 1 Council of Superior Court Judges, Suggested Pattern Jury Instructions: Civil Cases 237 (3d ed. 1991). This instruction, which was based partly on the Court of Appeals' decision in Chadwick v. Miller, 169 Ga.App. 338, 344, 312 S.E.2d 835 (1983), creates two problems. The first paragraph is misleading in that it implies an accident occurs when the negligence of someone other than the plaintiff or

defendant causes the plaintiff's injuries. The second paragraph's reference to the word "accident" creates confusion because of the difference between the legal definition of "accident" and the commonly understood meaning of the word as an unintended act.

We choose to follow the jurisdictions that have repudiated the use of the accident instruction in all civil cases as unnecessary, misleading, and confusing. See 57A Am.Jur.2d 104, Negligence § 48 n. 58 (1989) (listing cases); Annotation, Instructions on Unavoidable Accident, or the Like, in Motor Vehicle Cases, 65 A.L.R.2d 12, § 4 (1959) (listing cases).[1] The defense of inevitable accident "is nothing more than a denial by the defendant of negligence, or a contention that his negligence, if any, was not the proximate cause of the injury." Butigan v. Yellow Cab Co., 49 Cal.2d 652, 320 P.2d 500, 505 (1959); see Alabama Great So. R. Co. v. Brown, 138 Ga. 328, 332, 75 S.E. 330 (1912) (accident instruction merely elaborates that the defendant is not liable if without fault). The standard instructions on negligence, proximate cause, and burden of proof are sufficient to instruct the jury that the plaintiff may not recover when an injury occurs without the defendant's fault. Therefore, the instruction on accident should no longer be given in civil cases in Georgia after January 21, 1993, the date this opinion is published in the advance sheets of the Georgia Reports....

2. In each of these actions, the trial court properly charged the jury on accident under existing case law. There is no evidence of a third party's negligence in either action, but there is evidence that the defendants could not have foreseen the collisions or prevented them by the exercise of ordinary diligence. After reviewing the records, we find the accident instruction was not prejudicial under the circumstances of these cases and affirm the judgments.

Judgment affirmed.

NOTES

(1) In the case of *Heaven v. Pender* [1883], 11 Q.B.D. 503, Brett, M.R., provided this classic definition of negligence:

> When one person is by circumstances placed in such a position with regard to another ... that every one of ordinary sense who did think would at once recognize that if he did not use ordinary care and skill in his own conduct with regard to those circumstances he would cause danger or injury to the person or property of the other, a duty arises to use ordinary care and skill to avoid such danger.

We noted at the outset that section 282 of the *Restatement (Second)* simply defines negligence as "conduct which falls below the standard established by law for the protection of others against unreasonable risk of harm." Is this a more helpful formula than that in the passage quoted above from *Heaven v. Pender*?

(2) Could not the court rationally have granted a motion for judgment n.o.v. on the negligence issue in *LaPlante*? If not on the question of the defendant's negligence, then why not on the contributory negligence issue—that is, whether the plaintiff behaved with reasonable care for her own safety? Who was in a position to avoid this accident at the least cost? Would the court have granted judgment n. o. v. if the plaintiff were a 25-year-old physical education instructor, rather than a semiretired teacher?

---

1. Besides the judicial abolition of the charge, committees from several states recommend that no charge be given on "unavoidable accident".... Other states do not refer to the unavoidable accident instruction in their pattern jury instructions....

(3) In *Dunnaway v. Duquesne Light Co.*, 423 F.2d 66 (3d Cir. 1970), the court refused to impose liability on the defendant electric company for the electrocution of a construction firm's workman. The death was caused by the operation of a one hundred foot boom beneath the utility's wires, which were located sixteen feet above the minimum height required by safety regulations. The court characterized the use of the crane as "a very unusual occurrence," and took note of the fact that the contractor's decision to use it, rather than another kind of machine, was made only about a week before the accident. Evidently the crane had been used on the project for only one day prior to the accident, and on that occasion on the other side of a stream. The court declared that to hold the electric company liable in these circumstances would be like demanding that it keep the land under its line under "constant surveillance."

How does the standard of care by which the defendant is judged in *LaPlante* differ from that apparently employed in *Dunnaway*? In *Dunnaway*, the court granted a motion for dismissal of the complaint despite a jury verdict of $75,000 for the plaintiff, rendered against both the electric company and the decedent's employer on a third party complaint. Why should the court have overruled the jury in a case like that? Suppose the hotel management in *LaPlante* could have shown that the tables were further apart when the room was set up, but that in the course of the evening they had been moved about, causing congestion in some areas. Would the court have been more likely to overrule the jury verdict, citing the impossibility of "constant surveillance"?

(4) Even assuming that a lay juror could determine what "unreasonable crowding" is, why couldn't a professionally trained judge decide that as a policy matter the cost of Ms. LaPlante's injury was best left with her? What basis in social policy do you see as underlying the *LaPlante* decision? Is there an alternative solution that would have been more just? What schemes might be created to take the burden of this litigation off the legal system?

(5) Why shouldn't the fact that there was no violation of a statute or ordinance be conclusive for the Radisson Hotel? In determining what was "unreasonable crowding," was the jury assuming the role of legislature? Viewed in that perspective, does the decision bother you? Would a legislative determination be more or less flexible on the question of crowding? Would a statute distinguish between the elderly pensioner and the young athlete? Should it?

[B] Negligence in History

Holmes, *The Common Law*
94–95, 102–106, 109–110 (1881)

The general principle of our law is that loss from accident must lie where it falls, and this principle is not affected by the fact that a human being is the instrument of misfortune. But relatively to a given human being anything is accident which he could not fairly have been expected to contemplate as possible, and therefore to avoid. In the language of the late Chief Justice Nelson of New York: "No case or principle can be found, or if found can be maintained, subjecting an individual to liability for an act done without fault on his part.... All the cases concede that an injury arising from inevitable accident, or which in law or reason is the same thing, from an act that ordinary human care and foresight are unable to guard against, is but the misfortune of the suffered, and lays no foundation for legal responsibility." If this were not so, any act would be sufficient, however remote, which set in motion or opened the door for a series of physical sequences ending in damage; such as riding the horse, in the case of the runaway, or even coming to a place where one is seized with a fit and strikes the plaintiff in an unconscious spasm. Nay, why need the defendant have acted at all, and why is it not enough that his existence has been at the expense of the plaintiff? The requirement of an act is the requirement that the defendant should have made a choice. But the only possible purpose of introducing this moral element is to make the power of avoiding the evil complained on a condition of liability. There is no such power where the evil cannot be foreseen....

[T]he question in the Year Books* is not a loose or general inquiry of the jury whether they think the alleged trespasser was negligent on such facts as they may find, but a well-defined issue of law, to be determined by the court, whether certain acts set forth upon the record are a ground of liability. It is possible that the judges may have dealt pretty strictly with defendants, and it is quite easy to pass from the premise that defendants have been held trespassers for a variety of acts, without mention of neglect, to the conclusion that any act by which another was damaged will make the actor chargeable. But a more exact scrutiny of the early books will show that liability in general, then as later, was founded on the opinion of the tribunal that the defendant ought to have acted otherwise, or, in other words, that he was to blame.

Returning first to the case of the thorns in the Year Book, it will be seen that the falling of the thorns into the plaintiff's close, although a result not wished by the defendant, was in no other sense against his will. When he cut the thorns, he did an act which obviously and necessarily would have that consequence, and he must be taken to have foreseen and not to have perceived it. Choke, C.J. says, "As to what was said about their falling in, ipso invito, that is no plea, but he ought to show that he could not do it any other way, or that he did all in his power to keep them out"; and both judges put the unlawfulness of the entry upon the plaintiff's land as a consequence of the unlawfulness of dropping the thorns there. Choke admits that, if the thorns or a tree had been blown over upon the plaintiff's land, the defendant might have entered to get them. Chief Justice Crew says of this case, in Millen v. Fawdry, that the opinion was that "trespass lies, because he did not plead that he did his best endeavor to hinder their falling there; yet this was a hard case." ...

The principal authorities are the shooting cases, and, as shooting is an extra-hazardous act, it would not be surprising if it should be held that men do it at their peril in public places. The liability has been put on the general ground of fault, however, wherever the line of necessary precaution may be drawn. In Weaver v. Ward, the defendant set up that the plaintiff and he were skirmishing in a train and, that when discharging his piece he wounded the plaintiff by accident and misfortune, and against his own will. On demurrer, the court says that "no man shall be excused of a trespass, ... except it may be judged utterly without his fault. As if a man by force take my hand and strike you, or if here the defendant had said, that the plaintiff ran across his piece when it was discharging, or had set forth the case with the circumstances so as it had appeared to the county that it had been inevitable, and that the defendant had committed no negligence to give occasion to the hurt." The later cases simply follow Weaver v. Ward....

---

* Year Books were books of case reports that were published from the time of Edward I in the late thirteenth century through the reign of Henry VIII in the first part of the sixteenth century.—Ed.

In Brown v. Kendall, Chief Justice Shaw settled the question for Massachusetts. That was trespass for assault and battery, and it appeared that the defendant, while trying to separate two fighting dogs, had raised his stick over his shoulder in the act of striking, and had accidentally hit the plaintiff in the eye, inflicting upon him a severe injury. The case was stronger for the plaintiff than if the defendant had been acting in self-defense; but the court held that although the defendant was bound by no duty to separate the dogs, yet, if he was doing a lawful act, he was not liable unless he was wanting in the care which men of ordinary prudence would use under the circumstances, and that the burden was on the plaintiff to prove the want of such care.

In such a matter no authority is more deserving of respect than that of Chief Justice Shaw, for the strength of that great judge lay in an accurate appreciation of the requirements of the community whose officer he was. Some, indeed many, English judges could be named who have surpassed him in accurate technical knowledge, but few have lived who were his equals in their understanding of the grounds of public policy to which all laws must ultimately be referred....

[Holmes next addresses the nature of the "fault or blameworthiness" to which liability should attach, and sets up a general objective standard of ordinary intelligence and prudence, with exceptions for the "distinct defect of such a nature that all can recognize it as making certain precautions impossible." He continues:]

[I]t will now be assumed that, on the one hand, the law presumes or requires a man to possess ordinary capacity to avoid harming his neighbors, unless a clear and manifest incapacity be shown; but that, on the other, it does not in general hold him liable for unintentional injury, unless, possessing such capacity, he might and ought to have foreseen the danger, or, in other words, unless a man of ordinary intelligence and forethought would have been to blame for acting as he did....

Notwithstanding the fact that the grounds of legal liability are moral to the extent above explained, it must be borne in mind that law only works within the sphere of the senses. If the external phenomena, the manifest acts and omissions, are such as it requires, it is wholly indifferent to the internal phenomena on conscience. A man may have as bad a heart as he chooses, if his conduct is within the rules. In other words, the standards of the law are external standards, and, however much it may take moral considerations into account, it does so only for the purpose of drawing a line between such bodily motions and rests as it permits, and such as it does not. What the law really forbids, and the only thing it forbids, is the act on the wrong side of the line, be that act blameworthy or otherwise.

Morris S. Arnold, *Accident, Mistake, and Rules of Liability in the Fourteenth-Century Law of Torts*
128 U. Pa. L. Rev. 361, 368, 374–375, 377–378 (1979)**

II. ACTIONS IN WHICH THE DEFENDANT ATTEMPTED TO PLEAD IN BAR A LACK OF FAULT

If a defendant had ever pleaded a lack of negligence when a plaintiff had made no mention of negligence, that would be some evidence that fault was thought of as part of the plaintiff's case. Defendants apparently never did so, however.

....

[T]he fact that defendants never attempted to take issue on their lack of fault is a relevant datum, even though reading appropriate conclusions from it concerning current notions of liability appears, at first, somewhat perilous.

The most telling difficulty is that the absence of pleas of this sort may simply be attributable not to any abstract liability rule but rather to a pleading rule that barred the defendant from asserting such facts purely as a technical matter. To simplify somewhat, a defendant in a writ of trespass was obligated to choose between two kinds of answer: He either had to deny the physical acts he was alleged to have done, or he had to admit them and assign a cause for them. In the case of an assault and battery, for instance, an acceptable "cause" would have been self-defense. Now if a defendant wanted to say that he had hit the plaintiff accidentally (that is, nonnegligently), his story would not technically have fit either of the two modes of responding to complaints. He had, in fact, hit the plaintiff, so a denial was obviously of no use; moreover, he had had no cause, no justification, for hitting him because "cause," as we have seen, was thought of in motivational terms. Here, the defendant's case was that he had had no motive at all in hitting the plaintiff, for the act of hitting him had been unintentional. If his facts were usable at all, therefore, they were appropriately shown only at trial as evidence. If, however, a rule of materiality was enforced at trial, there is a question whether these facts were receivable as evidence. If they were, it is odd that no trace of an attempt to plead them is to be found in the Year Books in light of the fact that serjeants expended so much energy in attempting to plead evidence in so many other kinds of cases. The absence of such an effort seems, therefore, to argue for the immateriality of the facts and thus for a rule of strict liability....

[T]he inference to be drawn from all the available evidence is that in fourteenth-century trespass actions civil liability was strict. It would be for a later age to invent the proposition that some showing of fault was ordinarily necessary in order to impose on an actor the duty to compensate.

NOTES

(1) Are you persuaded more by Holmes's view of history, or by Arnold's?

(2) A judicial focus on fault as the primary basis of tort liability appears in a case involving highway design in which the court says that "[t]he original concept of justice as established in the early English law, required anyone who caused harm to another to make good the loss regardless of any fault or intent to injure.... But, as civilization advanced, the law advanced with it by adopting the modern view that it is unjust to require a person to pay losses resulting from harm caused innocently or accidentally without fault. Fault therefore becomes the basis of liability except in a limited class of cases." *Sweet v. State*, 195 Misc. 494, 89 N.Y.S.2d 506 (Ct. Cl. 1949).

(3) The predictability of a hazard obviously will be an important element in the decision of whether someone was "negligent" in failing to guard against it. A classic defense employs the argument that an injurious occurrence was an "Act of God." But here the development of technology may supply data that makes even natural disasters predictable to a point that prudence dictates the use of safeguards. See Comment, *Earthquake Damage: Need for a Viable Cause of Action*, 1972 Law & Soc. Order 450.

[C] The Role of Insurance

Tort litigation in modern life takes place almost entirely against a background of liability insurance, carried by persons who engage in risky activities to protect themselves against the financial consequences of judgments rendered against them under tort law. The excerpts below provide an introduction to principles and concepts that apply to all kinds of insurance, including liability insurance. As you proceed through the law-oriented materials in this coursebook, you should keep in mind that when a lawyer for an injury claimant decides to take a case, and as litigation progresses, the insurance coverage of the defendant is typically assumed by both sides to provide a pool of money that will pay for all, or a significant part, of any judgment. Indeed, if the potential defendant has no liability insurance, and no independent wealth, it is not likely that there will be a suit at all.

Mehr, Cammack & Rose, *Principles of Insurance*
19, 32–35 (8th ed. 1985)*

Definition of Risk

Risk is a concept with several meanings depending on the context and the scientific discipline in which it is used. For people who use the term loosely, the concept of risk means exposure to adversity or danger....

... The definition of risk that both facilitates communication and analysis of risk as it affects insurance is a simple one: *risk is uncertainty concerning loss.* This definition contains two concepts: uncertainty and loss. While both concepts are important to insurance, risk represents the uncertainty and not the loss, the cause of loss, or the chance of loss. The basic function of insurance is to handle risk, and this definition of risk considers effectively the question of how insurance deals with risk. It limits attention to pure risk rather than speculative risk, and therefore confines attention to risk from the viewpoint of the insured rather than the insurer. Pure risk can produce loss only, whereas speculative risk can result in either gain or loss. To illustrate: If lightning strikes and damages a house, the result is loss, but if the lightning bypasses the house, the homeowner does not gain; that is, his or her financial position is not improved....

Insurance as a Device for Handling Risk

The real nature of insurance is often confused. The word "insurance" sometimes is applied to a fund accumulated to meet uncertain losses. For example, a specialty shop dealing in seasonal goods must charge more early in the season to build up funds to cover the possibility of loss at the end of the season, when the price must be reduced below cost to sell the product. This method of meeting a risk is not insurance. An accumulation of funds for meeting uncertain losses is not sufficient to qualify as insurance.

A transfer of risk often is called insurance. A store selling television sets promises to service the set one year without additional charge and to replace the picture tube should the glories of televised spring football prove too much for its delicate wiring. This agreement, loosely referred to as an "insurance policy," is simply one that transfers risk,

---

* © 1985 by Richard D. Irwin, Inc. Reproduced with permission of The McGraw-Hill Companies.

and risk transfer in itself is insufficient for an economic or legal definition of insurance. If it were, then insurance regulation would extend to a host of commercial promises for which the insurance regulating system was not designed.

Definition of insurance

An adequate definition of insurance must include either the accumulation of a fund or the transference of risk, but not necessarily both. In addition, it must include a combination of a large number of separate, independent exposure units having the same common risk characteristics into an interrelated group.

Insurance may be defined as a device for reducing risk by combining a sufficient number of exposure units to make their individual losses collectively predictable. The predictable loss is then shared proportionately by all units in the combination.

These exposure units include both an entity (for example, one automobile, one house, or one business) and a time unit (for example, one year). Commonly, insurance involves spreading losses over more than one entity within one unit of time. However, insurance also can involve spreading losses of one entity over a long enough time period to increase the predictability of the losses. This technique of spreading losses for a single entity over a long time span is known as self-insurance. The question of whether that technique should be called insurance has caused considerable controversy within academic circles, the accounting profession, and in Internal Revenue Service rulings. That issue is tangential to the discussion at this point. The important characteristics of the concept of insurance as used in this text is that *uncertainty is reduced* and that *losses are shared or distributed* among the exposure units.

Insurance allows the individual insured to substitute a small, definite cost (the premium) for a large but uncertain loss (not to exceed the amount of insurance) under an arrangement whereby the fortunate many who escape loss will help compensate the unfortunate few who suffer loss. Even if no loss materializes, insurance helps to eliminate any anxiety the insured have about potential loss. Insurance, therefore, provides the insured not only postloss but also preloss utility.

Indemnity

With some notable exceptions ... the purpose of an insurance contract is to provide indemnity. Webster defines indemnity as "security against hurt, loss, or damage." Thus insurance policies limit payments for loss to the amount of that loss subject to policy limits. For example, if an insured has a $75,000 fire policy covering a $50,000 house and later sells it during the policy term, nothing will be paid if the house is destroyed by fire, for no loss is suffered by the insured. If the house is destroyed before it is sold, the insured can collect only $50,000, for that is the extent of the loss. Indemnity is the only legitimate use for insurance, for otherwise insurance would be a gambling instrument and therefore contrary to public policy.

Insurance may be distinguished from gambling. In gambling, the risk is created by the transaction; in insurance, the risk is reduced by the transaction. For example, no chance of loss exists at the racetrack until a bet has been placed; but the risk of loss of property by fire or windstorm is present until reduced or eliminated by insurance. Therefore, gambling and insurance are opposites: one creates risk, the other reduces it.

The law of large numbers

At first glance, it may seem strange that a combination of individual risks would result in the reduction of total risk. The principle that explains this phenomenon is called the "law of large numbers."[5] It is sometimes loosely termed the "law of averages," or the "law of probability." However, it is but one portion of the subject of probability. The latter is not a law but an entire branch of mathematics.

In the 17th century, European mathematicians were constructing crude mortality tables. From these investigations they discovered the percentage of male and female deaths among each year's births tended toward a constant if sufficient numbers of births were tabulated. In the 19th century, Simeon Denis Poisson named this principle the "law of large numbers." This law is based on the regularity of events. What seems a random occurrence in the individual happening appears so because of insufficient or incomplete knowledge of what is expected. For practical purposes, the law of large numbers may be stated as follows: The greater the number of exposures, the more nearly will the actual results obtained approach the probable result expected with an infinite number of exposures. Thus if a coin is flipped a sufficiently large number of times, the results of the trials will approach half heads and half tails — the theoretical probability if the coin is flipped an infinite number of times.

Events that seem the result of chance occur with surprising regularity as the number of observations increase. A car races around a corner one July 4th. A tire blows, and the car crashes, killing the driver. If the car had been moving slowly and its tires were in good condition, the accident might not have happened. It seems impossible to have predicted this particular accident, yet the National Safety Council predicts within a small margin of error how many motorists will die in accidents over the July 4th holiday. Even more accurate is the Safety Council's estimates of yearly accidental deaths, as the greater the number of exposures to loss, the closer are the results to the underlying probability.

Similarly, insurers with statistics on millions of lives can make a close forecast of the number of deaths in a given period; the longer the period, the greater accuracy. The prediction of the number of persons in a college class who will die during the year probably would be far from accurate. The prediction on the basis of enrollment in a large university would show a moderate degree of accuracy; and the prediction of deaths in all U.S. colleges and universities would have a high degree of accuracy.

The law of large numbers is the basis of insurance. Under this law, the impossibility of predicting a happening in an individual case is replaced by the demonstrable ability to forecast collective losses when considering a large number of cases. Applying these conclusions to insurance, one observes that every year a given number of dwellings burn or a particular number of deaths occur. If a small group of cases were isolated, a wide variation between actual loss experienced and average loss expected might be found. Insurers within their financial limits use the benefits of the law of large numbers by insuring the greatest possible number of acceptable exposure units to facilitate loss forecasting. In addition, the insurers want the units spread widely to minimize deviation from underlying probabilities occurring when the units are concentrated in one location.

Insurance does not completely eliminate risk because achieving an infinite number of exposure units is impossible. Thus some deviation of actual from expected results can be anticipated. Furthermore, statistics on which predictions are based are not perfect. Even if they were, no reason exists to believe that tomorrow's losses will conform to yesterday's because so many dynamic elements are involved. The possibility of the presence of moral hazards also may interfere with loss prediction.

---

5. Called the "law of great numbers" by our British cousins. Economist John Maynard Keynes suggests a more accurate term would be the "stability of statistical frequencies."

Criteria of an insurable exposure

Considering that insurance seems such a logical method of handling risk, why not combine all uncertainties in one big pool and rid the world of most risk? The limiting factor is that several broad criteria need to be considered before attempting to operate a successful insurance plan: (1) a large group of homogeneous exposure units must be involved, (2) the loss produced by the peril must be definite, (3) the occurrence of the loss in the individual cases must be accidental or fortuitous, (4) the potential loss in the individual cases must be large enough to cause hardship, (5) the cost of the insurance must be economically feasible, (6) the chance of loss must be calculable, and (7) the peril must be unlikely to produce loss to a great many insured units at one time.

SPECIAL NOTE ON LOSS SPREADING

One of the rationales that courts sometimes advance for imposing liability is that of "loss spreading." The theory is that in the case of an injury that causes a significant, even tremendous, financial loss to one person, the most socially desirable way to deal with that loss is to cushion it among all the people who benefit, without injury, from the activity or product at issue. Thus, for example, if one person suffers a $10,000 injury from an activity that benefits a million other people, it is just to "spread" the cost of the injury by charging an extra penny to each of the million persons who benefit from the activity.

Is this, in general, an appealing rationale? More specifically, are you favorably inclined toward the spreading of loss through the mechanism of insurance? What would be your principal concerns about a legal regime in which most of the cost of most injuries was spread through the liability insurance of those whose conduct principally caused the injuries?

Should it make a difference that spreading is achieved by "third party" liability insurance held by the injurer, or "first party" loss insurance held by the injured person? In this connection, it is important to understand the difference between a person insuring herself against the peril that she will be hurt (accident insurance or "first party" insurance) and someone insuring herself against the risk that she will be held liable for an injury she inflicts on someone else (liability insurance or "third party" insurance).

NOTES

(1) Would you think that insurance would be easily obtainable by the Radisson Hotel for injuries like those in *LaPlante*, supra § 4.01[A]?

(2) Would it be easier for Ms. LaPlante to secure insurance on herself for the injury she suffered?

(3) From a social point of view, which would be the party who you would prefer to get insurance for this sort of accident? Should insurance be compulsory, whether it is "first party" (i.e., accident insurance held by Ms. LaPlante) or "third party" (i.e., liability insurance held by the hotel)?

---

§ 4.02 Specific Features of Negligence Doctrine

[A] Foreseeability

The negligence standard relies significantly on the concept of foreseeability. A failure to take precautions against the extraordinary event is not negligence. A quintessential example of the unforeseeable event — at least one so statistically unusual that the law would deem it unforeseeable — is what has been called "The Perfect Storm." Assessing a book by that name, a reviewer describes a situation that arose in 1991, in which "[a] violent nor'easter out of Canada merges with the remnants of Hurricane Grace and is squeezed by high pressure from the north back toward the New England coast." This "once-in-a-hundred years event" entails winds over 100 miles per hour and "waves 70 to 100 feet high for about 17 hours." Anthony Bailey, reviewing SEBASTIAN JUNGER, THE PERFECT STORM, in *N.Y. Times Book Review*, June 22, 1997, at 8.

The most time-honored torts case on the point is *Blyth v. Company of Proprietors of Birmingham Waterworks*, 11 Ex. 781, 156 Eng. Rep. 1047 (Exchequer 1856). The court there turned down a claim by plaintiffs for flooding attributed to freezing that left "[a]n incrustation of ice and snow" around components of the defendant's water system. This resulted from "[o]ne of the severest [frosts] ever known," which "penetrated to a greater depth than any which ordinarily occurs south of the polar regions." One of the judges who rejected the action, Bramwell, B., opined that it would be "monstrous to hold the defendants responsible because they did not foresee and prevent an accident, the cause of which was so obscure, that it was not discovered until many months after the accident had happened." *Id.* at 785, 156 Eng. Rep. at 1049.

In the very different context of the modern employment relationship, inadequate precautions throughout a working environment can cost an employer substantial amounts when many workers suffer injuries from recognizable hazards. Cryptic official reports provide an umbrella for a firefighter's allegations that New York City did not provide him with adequate protective gear. A trade press summary of the case indicated that the fireman's coat and his boots only shielded him when he stood upright, leaving him exposed to scalding water when he would have to crawl, squat or lie prone — common enough postures when fighting fires. The plaintiff's lawyer said that in investigating the case, he found the problem to be a "commonplace" one, recognized as such by "every officer on the line." *New York Court Upholds $400,000 Award to Firefighter Not Adequately Equipped*, 26 BNA O.S.H. REP. 694 (Nov. 6, 1996). The Appellate Division's brief opinion, finding that a jury verdict for the plaintiff was supported by sufficient evidence, appears in *Lyall v. City of New York*, 228 A.D.2d 566, 645 N.Y.S.2d 34 (1996), aff'd without opinion, 674 N.E.2d 336 (N.Y. 1996). Although the city later issued neck-to-toe apparel to protect firefighters, the plaintiff's lawyer said that the court's ruling could aid 40 to 50 other firefighters with suits at various stages of the judicial process.

[B] Industry Custom; Expert Testimony; Safer Alternatives

The question often arises in negligence cases whether the defendant may exonerate itself by showing that it adopted and lived up to the standard existing in the industry.

Judge Learned Hand wrote the most cited chapter on this subject in a case involving the failure of a tug owner to provide radio sets for the vessel:

> [I]n most cases reasonable prudence is in fact common prudence; but strictly it is never its measure; a whole calling may have unduly lagged in the adoption of new and available devices. It never may set its own tests, however persuasive be its usages. Courts must in the end say what is required; there are precautions so imperative that even their universal disregard will not excuse their omission.

The T.J. Hooper, 60 F.2d 737, 740 (2d Cir.), cert. denied, 287 U.S. 662 (1932).

The industry custom issue can become entwined with the questions of how much expert evidence is necessary to establish a case for the jury on whether the defendant was negligent, and of how the plaintiff must go about proving feasible alternatives. An interesting confrontation on such a question appears in a Seventh Circuit case in which the plaintiff sued for injuries that she alleged occurred because the door latch system of her auto was designed so that a side impact collision would release the latch. The plaintiff was hurt after her car was hit broadside by another vehicle; she was ejected from the car and thrown to the ground 65 feet away from the point of impact. Judge Flaum spoke for the majority of a divided panel. He took note of the defendants' argument that, with respect to collisions in which an auto body stretches and pulls the latch apart, the plaintiff's expert "faulted almost every car he was asked to consider," and indeed criticized alternate latch designs that he said were safer than the design in the plaintiff's vehicle. However, the accident before the court did not involve "stretching," but rather activation of the door latch by direct force. And although the plaintiff's expert "again faulted many cars," Judge Flaum emphasized that the expert "also clearly testified that other, safer designs were available at the time that would not have given way in a side impact collision and that a reasonable design engineer should have foreseen such an accident." When "[t]his testimony was not substantially shaken during cross-examination," and the plaintiffs' evidence was not refuted by testimony that this kind of collision "was not foreseeable or that alternate designs would not have been safer," the court reversed a defendants' judgment and remanded the case for a new trial. *Chaulk v. Volkswagen of America, Inc.*, 808 F.2d 639, 642–43 (7th Cir. 1986).

Judge Posner, dissenting, stressed that "[o]urs is not a system of people's justice, where six laymen are allowed to condemn an entire industry on the basis of absurd testimony by a professional witness." Judge Posner conceded that "[c]ompliance with industry custom is not a defense in a tort suit," but stressed that "something more than a professional witness's conclusion, offered without substantiation, that a whole industry is lagging behind the standard of due care is necessary to create a jury issue." *Id.* at 645.

[C] Higher Standards of Care for Highly Dangerous Activities and Things

The two most highly litigated liability categories in modern tort are those of negligence and strict liability—that is, liability without fault, imposed even when the defendant has observed the standard of care of a reasonable person in the activity at issue. There is a lot of litigation at the border between these categories, with defendants often arguing that what is pleaded as a negligence action is really one for strict liability, and plaintiffs who allege negligence trying to show that the defendant truly did behave in a way that fulfills the "fault" requirement.

An intermediate position between alleging simple negligence and suing on a strict liability theory is to advance a negligence claim that the defendant's activity was exceptionally dangerous, and therefore required an especially high degree of care. When the plaintiff makes this argument, the defendant may be expected to respond that the plaintiff essentially is contending for strict liability under a negligence mask. This sort of warfare underlies a suit involving asbestos-caused injuries, *Krull v. Keene Corp.*, 601 F. Supp. 547 (N.D. Ill. 1985), in which Judge Shadur makes the following distinctions:

> Complaint Count I sounds in strict liability. Count II alleges negligence and invokes the duty of ordinary care. Count III—which is styled "Negligence-Ultrahazardous Product"—also alleges negligence, but it asserts asbestos is an "ultrahazardous product" such that ... :
>
> > The defendants owed the plaintiff a duty greater than that of ordinary care.
>
> > ...
>
> Krull's counsel appears simply to misunderstand the duty of ordinary care...."Ordinary care" is by definition a reasonableness standard whose application varies with the circumstances.
>
> As Prosser and Keeton on the Law of Torts § 34, at 209 (5th ed. 1984) put it:
>
> > What is required is merely the conduct of the reasonable person of ordinary prudence under the circumstances, and the greater danger, or the greater responsibility, is merely one of the circumstances, demanding only an increased amount of care.
>
> That statement of hornbook law (literally) necessarily carries with it a requirement of different conduct in differing circumstances (id. at 208, footnotes omitted and emphasis added):
>
> > The amount of care demanded by the standard of reasonable conduct must be in proportion to the apparent risk. As the danger becomes greater, the actor is required to exercise caution commensurate with it.
>
> Thus the duty is always one of ordinary care, but ordinary care requires a greater exercise of caution where there are greater risks of injury....
>
> All this may seem a matter of mere semantics, but it nevertheless mandates dismissal of Count III. Krull has failed to show a legal basis for applying a standard to defendants greater than the duty of ordinary care asserted in Count II. Consistent with the standard, of course, he may attempt to show ... asbestos is an "inherently dangerous" product requiring manufacturers to take "special precautions" and otherwise exercise a high degree of care.

Some courts continue to insist that there is an especially high standard for certain kinds of activities—notably, the provision of electricity, innkeeping, and the operation of common carriers. Even here, though, there are limits to how high the standard should be set. An example is a case in which the plaintiff argued that a transit authority should have bought a safety device for an escalator when the device had been developed after the defendant purchased the escalator. The Georgia Supreme Court accepted the traditional premise that "[a] carrier of passenger ... must use extraordinary diligence to protect the lives and persons of its passengers," and as a general matter, the premise that a carrier, "exercising extraordinary care, must stay informed of safety advances in product design." But it drew the line against "a *per se* rule that requires ... carriers to buy and incorporate those safety advances into previously-purchased, non-defective products." Metrop. Atlanta Rapid Transit Auth. v. Rouse, 612 S.E.2d 308, 308, 310–11 (Ga. 2005).

§ 4.03 Quantifying Tort Standards

[A] The *Restatement* on Risk/Utility

RESTATEMENT (SECOND) OF TORTS
§§ 291, 292 (1965)*

§ 291. Unreasonableness; How Determined; Magnitude of Risk and Utility of Conduct

Where an act is one which a reasonable man would recognize as involving a risk of harm to another, the risk is unreasonable and the act is negligent if the risk is of such magnitude as to outweigh what the law regards as the utility of the act or of the particular manner in which it is done.

§ 292. Factors Considered in Determining Utility of Actor's Conduct

In determining what the law regards as the utility of the actor's conduct for the purpose of determining whether the actor is negligent, the following factors are important:

(a) The social value which the law attaches to the interest which is to be advanced or protected by the conduct;

(b) the extent of the chance that this interest will be advanced or protected by the particular course of conduct;

(c) the extent of the chance that such interest can be adequately advanced or protected by another and less dangerous course of conduct.

[B] Economic Analysis of Tort Law

How much of a role would you think that economics—in the sense of comparing accident costs and accident avoidance costs—plays in judicial decisions in the landowner liability cases? Is it clear that if the possessor's avoidance cost is greater than the plaintiff's damages, the possessor should not have to pay for the injuries? If there were a case in which it could be shown that the possessor would have to spend a million dollars to avoid a $500,000 injury, would that settle the issue in favor of the defendant? If not, then what factors would militate in favor of imposing liability on the defendant?

* * *

A modern statement of the negligence formula that many courts cite and that forms a basis for much scholarly discussion was devised by Judge Learned Hand, and is represented by the following passage from his opinion in *United States v. Carroll Towing Co.*, 159 F.2d 169, 173 (2d Cir. 1947):

---

* 1965 by THE AMERICAN LAW INSTITUTE. Reproduced with permission.

It appears ... that there is no general rule to determine when the absence of a bargee or other attendant will make the owner of the barge liable for injuries to other vessel, if she breaks away from her moorings. However, in any cases where he would be so liable for injuries to others, obviously he must reduce his damages proportionately, if the injury is to his own barge. It becomes apparent why there can be no such general rule, when we consider the grounds for such a liability. Since there are occasions when every vessel will break from her moorings, and since, if she does, she becomes a menace to those about her; the owner's duty, as in other similar situations, to provide against resulting injuries is a function of three variables: (1) The probability that she will break away; (2) the gravity of the resulting injury, if she does; (3) the burden of adequate precautions. Possibly it serves to bring this motion into relief to state it in algebraic terms: if the probability be called P; the injury, L; and the burden B; liability depends upon whether B is less than L multiplied by P: i.e, whether $B<PL$....

A later, highly influential economic analysis carries important implications for tort law. This is Ronald Coase's article *The Problem of Social Cost*.[1]

In this famous essay, Coase demonstrated arithmetically that in simple interactions in which parties compete for use of the same resource, it will make no difference to the allocation of resources which way courts impose liability. He gave as an example a situation in which increases in the size of a cattle rancher's herd result in an increased tendency of the cattle to move onto the neighboring farmer's land and eat the corn that grows there. Coase showed that in the absence of "transaction costs," such as the costs of bargaining and negotiation and rounding up multiple parties with the same economic interests, it will make no difference to "resource allocation" which way the courts impose liability. Thus, he hypothesized, if the court makes the rancher pay the farmer for the damage caused by maintaining a three-steer herd, the rancher will forego having the third steer in his herd. And if the court says that the rancher is not liable, the farmer will bribe the rancher to keep the third steer out of his herd. The result is that the mix of cattle and corn—"resource allocation"—will be the same under either legal rule.

You should consider two things in particular when reflecting on this analysis:

(a) It speaks only of situations in which "transaction costs" are zero. The implication is that in "real world transactions," where there are often substantial transaction costs, the court that wishes to achieve the efficient result should look for the "least cost avoider." The practical import of this point frequently is that in many situations, it may be possible for the plaintiff to take accident-avoiding precautions more cheaply than the defendant.

For example, Coase hypothesizes a factory which emits smoke, causing $100 worth of damage a year. He assumes that a tax would impose a levy of $100 a year so long as the factory emits the smoke but that an effective smoke-prevention device would cost $90 a year to operate. Thus, "[d]amage of $100 would have been avoided at an expenditure of $90 and the factory-owner would be better off by $10 per annum." However, this may not be the optimal solution since, for example, those suffering smoke damage might move or take other precautions on their own which would cost them only $40 a year. In that case, "there would be a gain in the value of production of $50 if the factory continues to emit its smoke and those now in the district moved elsewhere or made

---

1. 3 J. L. & Econ. 1 (1960).

other adjustments to avoid the damage." See 3 J.L. & ECON. at 41 (1960). Is it clear who is in the best position to lower social cost in those cases?

(b) The analysis concerns itself only with considerations of resource allocation and economic efficiency. This means that the student, and the judge, are free to make choices among legal rules based on normative considerations, including notions of ethics, morality and "fairness," or, probably covertly, even on the basis of sentiment. What is important, at this stage of your legal education, is that you force yourself to identify what part of your thoughts are oriented toward facilitating the free working of an efficient market, and how much of your concern is with non-economic factors.

NOTES

(1) An important contribution to the literature of economic analysis of tort law, a quarter century after the decision that set out the "Learned Hand test" in the *Carroll Towing* case, supra, and more than a decade after the publication of the "Coase Theorem," was a study by then Professor (now Judge) Posner. Analyzing appellate cases from several American jurisdictions over a thirty-year period beginning in 1875, Posner concluded that liability rules in negligence cases reflect a judicial search for "the efficient (cost-justified) level of accidents and safety, or more likely, an approximation thereto." See Posner, *A Theory of Negligence*, 1 J. LEGAL STUDIES 29, e.g., at 73 (1972).

(2) In *Bammerlin v. Navistar Int'l Transp. Corp.*, 30 F.3d 898 (7th Cir. 1994), a case arising from an accident involving a tractor-trailer driven by the plaintiff, Judge Easterbrook summarized the allegations this way:

> Bammerlin contends that Navistar, which built the tractor, designed the seat belt assembly improperly by anchoring one end to a door pillar and the other to the engine housing. When the cab broke apart, the engine housing and seat belt anchor separated from the portion of the cab containing the driver's seat, releasing tension on the belt. Bammerlin adds that even if this placement of the anchorage was not negligent, the assembly did not comply with federal safety standards.

Judge Easterbrook's analysis included this passage:

> Suppose the probability of the latch opening in a crash is 0.0001 if both anchors hold and 0.0002 if one anchor fails. Neither probability can be reduced by a redesign of the latch, which therefore cannot be called "defective." Suppose further that the loss if the latch opens in an accident is $500,000. Then the expected costs per vehicle attributable to belt opening are $50 if both anchors hold and $100 if only one anchor holds. If it costs, say, an extra $10 to ensure that an anchor holds (as by securing it to the cab's floor rather than its engine tunnel), then a prudent designer will incur the cost—and the vehicle is defective if an anchor fails. This is nothing but an application of Learned Hand's formula for negligence.... Our court has applied Judge Hand's approach in many kinds of negligence actions, ... and as the definition of a product defect in Indiana depends on general principles of negligence,..., we have no reason to think that state would see things otherwise. Thus the fact that the probability of a particular failure is low is no defense if the costs of protecting against it are even lower.

(3) A draft of the *Restatement (Third) of Torts* employs a Learned Hand type formula with an emphasis on foreseeability:

> A person acts negligently if the person does not exercise reasonable care under the circumstances. Primary factors to consider in ascertaining whether the per-

son's conduct lacks reasonable care are the foreseeable likelihood that the person's conduct will result in harm, the foreseeable severity of any harm that may ensue, and the burden of precautions to eliminate or reduce the risk of harm.

—Restatement (Third) of Torts: Liability for Physical Harm § 3 (Proposed Final Draft No. 1, Apr. 6, 2005).

A comment to this draft section indicates that its definition of negligence "suggest[s] a 'risk-benefit' test..., where the 'risk' is the overall level of the foreseeable risk created by the actor's conduct and the 'benefit' is the advantages that the actor or others gain if the actor refrains from taking precautions." The draft comment says that "[t]his benefit is the same as the burdens that the precautions, if adopted, would entail." It notes that the risk-benefit test "can also be called a 'cost-benefit test,' where 'cost' signifies the cost of precautions and the 'benefit' is the reduction in risk those precautions would achieve." *Id*. cmt. e.

§ 4.04 The Standard of Care for Owners and Possessors of Land

[A] An Introduction to Legal Competition Between Landowners

PROBLEM[1]

A New Jersey village had a bout of anguish over a problem involving a little boy with a heart condition and a fire siren. The child, a three-year-old, had what was described as a "dime-sized hole in his heart." The siren, owned by the village, was designed to call volunteer firefighters to action. The child's parents had moved into their five-room house, built on a plot that had been in his father's family, in hearing distance of the siren. The village tested the siren each evening, and when it went off, it threw the boy into cardiac spasms.

Even without the spasms, the boy's life expectancy was estimated at no more than twelve years, but there was a strong probability that he would suffer a fatal seizure on any evening when the siren sounded. There was a dispute about whether the village had assured the father that it would move the siren when the family occupied their new home.

Whatever the facts were about the alleged assurances given by the village, it would cost $570 to move the siren, and moving it would place it out of hearing distance of eight of the volunteer firefighters. The village would be able to contact those eight people with two-way radios, but those devices would cost $150 per radio.

There was quite a controversy in the village about the matter, which received national publicity. Finally, the village decided to move the siren and purchase the two-way radios. A press report quoted the president of the village fire company as calling this a "sensible solution," saying that "we're tired of being called 'baby killers.'" As to the cost

---

1. The basis for this Problem is "Firemen to Move Siren in Effort to Save Boy," Austin American-Statesman, Sept. 24, 1967, at 1.

of moving the siren and buying the radios, the village mayor reportedly said that the child's life "should not be contingent on 'dollars and cents.'"

ARISTOTLE ON CORRECTIVE JUSTICE
2 JONATHAN BARNES, THE COMPLETE WORKS OF ARISTOTLE
1786–87 (1984)*

This, then, is what the just is—the proportional; the unjust is what violates the proportion. Hence one term becomes too great, the other too small, as indeed happens in practice; for the man who acts unjustly has too much, and the man who is unjustly treated too little, of what is good. In the case of evil the reverse is true; for the lesser evil is reckoned a good in comparison with the greater evil, since the lesser evil is rather to be chosen than the greater, and what is worthy of choice is good, and what is worthier of choice a greater good.

This, then, is one species of the just.

The remaining one is the rectificatory, which arises in connexion with transaction both voluntary and involuntary. This form of the just has a different specific character from the former. For the justice which distributes common possessions is always in accordance with the kind of proportion mentioned above (for in the case also in which the distribution is made from common funds it will be according to the same ratio which the funds put into the business bear to one another); and the injustice opposed to this kind of justice is that which violates the proportion. But the justice in transactions is a sort of equality indeed, and the injustice a sort of inequality; not according to that kind of proportion, however, but according to arithmetical proportion. For it makes no difference whether a good man has defrauded a bad man or a bad man a good one, nor whether it is a good or a bad man that has committed adultery; the law looks only the distinctive character of the injury, and treats the parties as equals, if one is in the wrong and the other is being wronged, and if one inflicted injury and the other has received it. Therefore, this kind of injustice being an inequality, the judge tries to equalize it; for in the case also in which one has received and the other has inflicted a wound, or one has slain and the other been slain, the suffering and the action have been unequally distributed; but the judge tries to equalize things by means of the penalty, taking away from the gain of the assailant. For the term 'gain' is applied generally to such cases, even if it be not a term appropriate to certain cases, e.g., to the person who inflicts a wound—and 'loss' to the sufferer; at all events when the suffering has been estimated, the one is called loss and the other gain. Therefore the equal is intermediate between the greater and the less, but the gain and the loss are respectively greater and less in contrary ways; more of the good and less of the evil are gain, and the contrary is loss; intermediate between them is, as we saw, the equal, which we say is just; therefore corrective justice will be the intermediate between loss and gain. This is why, when people dispute, they take refuge in the judge; and to go to the judge is to go to justice; for the nature of the judge is to be a sort of animate justice; and they seek the judge as an intermediate, and in some states they call judges mediators, on the assumption that if they get what is intermediate they will get what is just. The just, then, is an intermediate, since the judge is so. Now the judge restores equality; it is as though there were a line divided into unequal parts, and he took away that by which the greater segment exceeds the half, and added it to the smaller segment. And when the whole has been equally divided, then they say they have their own—i.e. when they have got what is equal.... These names, both loss and gain, have come from voluntary exchange; for to have more than one's own is called gaining, and to have less than one's original share is called losing, e.g. in buying and selling and in all other matters in which the law has left people free to make their terms; but when they get neither more nor less but just what belongs to themselves, they say that they have their own and that they neither lose nor gain.

Therefore the just is intermediate between a sort of gain and a sort of loss, viz. those which are involuntary; it consists in having an equal amount before and after the transaction.

NOTE

Professor Richard Wright launches a fierce attack on the idea that the proper test for negligence is an "aggregate-risk-utility" test, which he defines, citing Jeremy Bentham, as "maximizing the total utility for the citizenry in the aggregate." *Justice and Reasonable Care in Negligence Law*, 47 AM. J. JURISPRUDENCE 143, 167 (2002). Under this test, Wright stresses, "each individual's freedom and interests are subordinated to the maximization of the total happiness or preference-satisfaction of the citizenry of the aggregate." *Id.* Wright says that scholars have improperly tried to base the negligence test on John Stuart Mill's "impartiality" principle, expressed by Mill as saying that utilitarianism requires a person "to be as strictly impartial as a disinterested and benevolent spectator." *Id.* at 168.

Wright argues, by contrast, that the negligence standard should be based on "principles of justice." Specifically, he refers to a concept of "interactive justice" that "requires that others who interact with you in ways that may affect your person or property do so in a way that is consistent with your right to equal negative freedom, and vice versa." This does not mean, he notes, that people cannot expose others to risk. Rather, they may do so "if and only if the allowance of such conduct by everyone in similar circumstances will increase everyone's equal freedom, rather than increasing some persons' external freedom at the expense of others' external freedom." *Id.* at 166. Wright's attack is not only on the philosophical correctness of the "aggregate-risk-utility test" but on the idea that it represents case law. He pointed out that "only a small minority of courts even mention the Hand formula [see supra § 4.03[B]] or risk-utility balancing." *Id.* at 189.

QUESTIONS

(1) If a court had compelled the firemen in the New Jersey story to move their siren, what would have been the net social cost of that decision? Would there have been any non-pecuniary advantages that accrued to society from such a decision? Who was in the best position to avoid fatal injury to the child?

(2) Would it make a difference to you if the plaintiffs had built their home at the same time the siren was installed with each party unmindful of what the other was doing?

(3) If the child had died as a result of a siren blast, what would it have taken to provide "corrective justice" to his parents?

[B] The Status of the Visitor

PROBLEM*

Deseret owns the Skull Valley Ranch located approximately 40 miles from Salt Lake City, Utah. A state highway (also referred to as the Skull Valley Road) traverses most of the ranch property running from north to south. In 1960, Deseret constructed power lines to supply electricity to irrigation pumping stations on its ranch. Deseret owns the power line, poles and attendant electrical equipment which caused the injury to Mr. Madison.

Rains fell in the area of the Skull Valley Ranch from October 29 through November 1, 1974. Plaintiffs submitted expert testimony that contamination had previously occurred to the insulation and weathered cross-arm of the second pole west of the Skull Valley Road supporting the line. The pole is clearly visible from the road. There was expert opinion that with the application of rain the contamination caused leakage of current and a fire commenced; the cross-arm of this pole burned through and fell during the rains; and the north and south energized lines sagged to within four or five feet from the ground and remained in this position until Mr. Madison came in contact with them.

The two outside primary lines fell to a position where they sagged from the pole next to the west side of the highway approximately four or five feet from the ground for an overall distance of approximately 1000 feet. The burned pole, crossarm and sagging wires could be seen from the highway.

The foreman of Deseret's ranch, Donald Taylor, stated in his deposition that on any given day he would travel up and down this highway under this power line an average of "probably five times, four or five times." However, Taylor also said that "on the morning of November 7, prior to the time the accident occurred, I drove between the south and north ranch and looked and did not observe any conductors on the Deseret Livestock line going to the west pump sagging at the point where the conductors crossed the highway approximately 500 feet east of where the accident occurred."

On November 7, 1974, plaintiff Gray F. Madison went to the Skull Valley Ranch at Deseret's invitation to hunt pheasants. Included in the hunting party were three officers and directors of Deseret and the sons of two of those men. The hunting party started from the north ranch, divided into two groups, and generally worked south with the intention to regroup in the vicinity of the accident scene. Taylor stated that he knew the party was to be hunting that day, but said he did not know where they would be hunting. There was evidence, however, that Taylor knew that the hunting party was going to hunt in the field where the line was located.

Madison testified that he had no recollection of seeing the fallen line before the accident. He was an experienced hunter and approached a wire fence encountered just before the accident and looked at it "well." The last thing Madison remembers is crawling under the fence and standing up.

None of the hunting party observed how Madison came in contact with the wire, but they did see him later with the wire across his chest. Madison received severe multiple electrical burns throughout his body, requiring some amputation and loss of function and use of extremities such as his hands and feet.

---

* From the statement of facts in a federal case.

The district court granted summary judgment to Deseret. Would you uphold that judgment on appeal? What standard of care should the court apply to Deseret with reference to its obligation to discover hazards or to warn of them?

YOUNCE v. FERGUSON

Washington Supreme Court
106 Wash.2d 658, 724 P.2d 991 (1986)

GOODLOE, JUSTICE.

In this case, we determine whether the common law classifications of entrants as invitees, licensees, or trespassers should continue to be determinative of the standard of care owed by an owner or occupier of land and whether the status of the entrant in this case was correctly determined. We answer both questions affirmatively and affirm the trial court.

Appellant Lisa Younce appeals the dismissal of respondents Charles, Thelma, and Dean Strunk from the suit. Lisa was injured when a car driven by Tamera Ferguson ran into her on a parcel of Strunk property, where a high school graduation "kegger" party was being held.

Dean Strunk, the son of Charles and Thelma Strunk, was a member of the 1977 Evergreen High School graduating class. Class members planned a graduation party to follow commencement exercises on June 7, 1977. Tickets to the party were sold for $4.00 to purchase beer, food, and music. Dean made arrangements to and did buy 15 kegs of beer from a local tavern for the party with ticket proceeds. The party was originally scheduled to be held on another class member's property, but during the commencement exercises it was generally agreed that the party would be moved to the Strunk property on 109th Avenue.

The 109th Avenue property was the largest of eight parcels of land that Charles and Thelma Strunk had under lease for farming purposes. The property was located 6 miles or 8–9 minutes driving time from the Strunk residence. Dean and his younger brother, Brad, took care of family duties at the property.

Following commencement exercises, Dean went home, changed clothes, and transported the kegs to the 109th Avenue property. Charles and Thelma returned home from the commencement exercises around 10:20 p.m. to 10:30 p.m. From about 11 p.m. to 11:10 p.m., four or five carloads of people arrived at the Strunk residence asking the location of the party. The Strunks also received a phone call from someone looking for the site. More than one inquirer advised the Strunks that the party was on Strunk property. Charles Strunk drove to 4 parcels within 1 mile of the family residence to see if there was a party, testifying he would have run the kids off the property if he had found them. He did not, however, check the 109th Avenue property.

When Dean arrived at the 109th Avenue property around 11 p.m. with the kegs, 100–400 minors were present, including graduating seniors, school mates, students from other schools, and other minors not attending school. Brad was collecting tickets, directing cars to parking areas, and advising cars' occupants of the kegs' location.

Tamera Ferguson, a minor, paid for attendance when she arrived. Lisa Younce, a minor, arrived around 11:30 p.m. with Judy Bock, who had previously bought two tickets for their admission. Lisa and Judy had had one mixed drink before arriving. They mixed another after arriving but Lisa did not drink it.

When the accident occurred, at approximately 12:15 a.m., drinking had been going on at the site for at least an hour, but the party attendees were well behaved. There had been no excessive drinking except for Dean and Tamera, who both admitted they were intoxicated from alcohol consumed at the party site. No automobile had been driven through the area where party attendees were standing. Lisa was standing in a dimly lit grassy and gravel area near the main barn and approximately 150 feet away from the kegs. Lisa was hit from behind by a Volkswagen driven by Tamera. The car hit her in the right knee and knocked her to the ground. Lisa was not under the influence of or affected by alcohol at the time she was hit. Tamera left or was taken from the scene. Lisa was taken to the hospital. Charles and Thelma Strunk were notified of the accident. They went to the 109th Avenue property with cooking utensils and prepared hamburgers from 1:30 a.m. to 5:30 a.m. when the kegs were emptied and the last attendees left.

Dean and Lisa both knew that when minors drink they become intoxicated, and when they become intoxicated they will drive. Charles and Thelma Strunk knew that minors drink at parties.

Lisa sued Tamera. The trial court found that Tamera had negligently injured Lisa and entered judgment for $69,543.31. Tamera did not appear at trial and has not appealed.

Lisa also sued the Strunks.... Lisa's ... theory which is the basis of the entire appeal relates to the common law classifications between invitee, licensee, and trespasser and the duty of care owed by the owner or occupier of land.

The trial court found that liability on the part of the Strunks depended upon Lisa's status on the property. The court found Lisa was a social guest, and therefore only a licensee. Applying the duty of care applicable to licensees and articulated in Restatement (Second) of Torts § 332 (1965), the trial court found the duty had not been breached. The Strunks were dismissed with prejudice. The court explained in its memorandum opinion, however, that if Lisa had been an invitee and the duty of care therefore had been one of reasonable care under all the circumstances, the court would have concluded that the Strunks had breached their duty to Lisa. The court also noted, however, that this was a case where Lisa could appreciate the dangers or conditions of the premises. Lisa appealed. The case is before this court on an administrative transfer from the Court of Appeals, Division Two.

Two issues must be addressed. First, we must decide whether in a claim for injury against an owner or occupier of land, the standard of care owed should continue to turn upon the common law distinctions between invitee, licensee, and trespasser, or whether such distinctions should be replaced by a negligence standard of reasonable care under all the circumstances. Because we retain the common law classifications, we must also decide whether Lisa Younce was properly characterized as a licensee or whether she should have been characterized as an invitee.

Lisa argues that the common law distinctions of invitee, licensee, and trespasser should no longer determine the applicable standard of care owed by an owner or occupier of land in Washington. She urges they be abandoned and replaced by a standard of reasonable care under all the circumstances. See 16 Gonz.L.Rev. 479 (1981). Washington relies upon and has adopted many of the definitions and corresponding duties outlined in Restatement (Second) of Torts (1965). Egede-Nissen v. Crystal Mt., Inc., 93 Wash.2d 127, 131–32, 606 P.2d 1214 (1980).

In Egede-Nissen we acknowledged past questioning of the common law classification scheme, see Ward v. Thompson, 57 Wash.2d 655, 660, 359 P.2d 143 (1961) ("timeworn distinctions"); Mills v. Orcas Power & Light Co., 56 Wash.2d 807, 820, 355 P.2d 781 (1960) ("ancient categories"), but decided that we were not ready then to totally abandon the traditional categories and adopt a unified standard. Egede-Nissen, 93 Wash.2d at 131, 606 P.2d 1214. We still are not ready and reaffirm use of common law classifications to determine the duty of care owed by an owner or occupier of land.

... Retention of the common law classifications continues to be the majority position.

Nine jurisdictions have abolished use of the common law classifications of invitees, licensees, and trespassers as determinative of the landowner's or land occupier's duty of care....

The typical analysis in these cases includes noting that England, where the distinctions originated, has abolished them by statute. Occupiers' Liability Act, 1957, 5 and 6 Eliz. 2, ch. 31. The cases also note that the United States Supreme Court refused to adopt the rules relating to the liability of a possessor of land for the law of admiralty. Kermarec v. Compagnie Generale Transalantique, 358 U.S. 625, 630–31, 79 S.Ct. 406, 409–10, 3 L.Ed.2d 550 (1959).

The cases rejecting the classifications list the subtleties and subclassifications created in their respective jurisdictions. The opinions explain that it is difficult to justify a system with so many exceptions and that while the distinctions were justified in feudal times, they are not justified in modern society. As explained in Rowland, 69 Cal.2d at page 118, 443 P.2d 561, 70 Cal.Rptr. 97, the first case to reject the classifications:

> A man's life or limb does not become less worthy of protection by the law nor a loss less worthy of compensation under the law because he has come upon the land of another without permission or with permission but without a business purpose. Reasonable people do not ordinarily vary their conduct depending upon such matters, and to focus upon the status of the injured party as a trespasser, licensee, or invitee in order to determine the question whether the landowner has a duty of care, is contrary to our modern social mores and humanitarian values. The common law rules obscure rather than illuminate the proper considerations which should govern determination of the question of duty.

Rowland then announced the standard for determining the liability of the possessor of land would be "whether in the management of his property he has acted as a reasonable man in view of the probability of injury to others, and, although the plaintiff's status as a trespasser, licensee, or invitee may in the light of the facts giving rise to such status have some bearing on the question of liability, the status is not determinative." ... The principle is generally referred to as the reasonable care under all of the circumstances standard.

Six jurisdictions have abolished the distinction between licensee and invitee....

The rationales for abandoning the distinction between invitee and licensee are the same as the rationales given by the cases abolishing the distinction between all three classifications. The reason given for not extending the standard of reasonable care to trespassers is that even in modern society it is significant that a trespasser does not come upon property under a color of right or that a trespasser was not involved in the case where the distinction between licensee and invitee was abolished.

However, the majority of jurisdictions have not rejected the classifications.... Some have directly confronted the issue of whether to abandon the distinctions and have declined to do so....

The reasons proffered for continuing the distinctions include that the distinctions have been applied and developed over the years, offering a degree of stability and predictability and that a unitary standard would not lessen the confusion. Furthermore, a slow, piecemeal development rather than a wholesale change has been advocated. Some courts fear a wholesale change will delegate social policy decisions to the jury with minimal guidance from the court.... Also, it is feared that the landowner could be subjected to unlimited liability.

We find these reasons to be compelling. As noted by the Kansas court in Gerchberg, 223 Kan. at pages 450–51, 576 P.2d 593: "The traditional classifications were worked out and the exceptions were spelled out with much thought, sweat and even tears". We are not ready to abandon them for a standard with no contours. It has been argued that jury instructions can provide adequate guidance. In fact, amicus has suggested and other courts have found that the following factors should be considered by the jury: (1) the circumstances under which the entrant was on the property; (2) the foreseeability of the injury or damage given the type of condition involved; (3) the nature of the property and its uses; (4) the feasibility of either correcting the condition on the property or issuing appropriate warnings; and (5) such other factors as may be relevant in the particular case. These factors are similar to the concerns being addressed by the current Restatement rules and caselaw. We do not choose to erase our developed jurisprudence for a blank slate. Common law classifications continue to determine the duty owed by an owner or occupier of land in Washington.

Lisa argues alternatively that, if the common law classifications are retained, she was incorrectly characterized as a licensee at trial. Lisa argues that she should have been characterized as an invitee under the facts of this case. Lisa's status on the property determines the standard of care owed her by the Strunks.

In McKinnon v. Washington Fed. Sav. & Loan Ass'n, 68 Wash.2d 644, 650, 414 P.2d 773 (1966), this court adopted the Restatement (Second) of Torts § 332 (1965) definition of invitee. An invitee is owed a duty of ordinary care.

Section 332 defines an invitee as follows:

(1) An invitee is either a public invitee or a business visitor.

(2) A public invitee is a person who is invited to enter or remain on land as a member of the public for a purpose for which the land is held open to the public.

(3) A business visitor is a person who is invited to enter or remain on land for a purpose directly or indirectly connected with business dealings with the possessor of the land.

A licensee is defined as "a person who is privileged to enter or remain on land only by virtue of the possessor's consent." Restatement, § 330. A licensee includes a social guest, that is, a person who has been invited but does not meet the legal definition of invitee. In Memel v. Reimer, 85 Wash.2d 685, 689, 538 P.2d 517 (1975), this court replaced the willful and wanton misconduct standard of care toward licensees with a duty to exercise reasonable care toward licensees where there is a known dangerous condition on the property which the possessor can reasonably anticipate the licensee will not discover or will fail to realize the risks involved. Memel specifically adopted the standard of care for licensees outlined in Restatement, § 342:

A possessor of land is subject to liability for physical harm caused to licensees by a condition on the land *if*, but *only if*,

(a) the possessor knows or has reason to know of the condition and should realize that it involves an *unreasonable risk of harm* to such licensees, and should expect that they will not discover or realize the danger, *and*

(b) he fails to exercise reasonable care to make the condition safe, or to warn the licensees of the condition and the risk involved, *and*

(c) *the licensees do not know or have reason to know of the condition and the risk involved.*

(Italics ours.) Memel, at 689, 691, 538 P.2d 517. The possessor fulfills his duty by making the condition safe or warning of its existence.

Lisa contends that she was a member of the public on the land for a purpose for which the land is held open and therefore is an invitee. We disagree. The facts of this case do not parallel the facts of other cases where the plaintiff was found to be a public invitee. In McKinnon, a federal savings and loan association posted a sign saying it had meeting rooms available for public use. The plaintiff in McKinnon was part of a Girl Scout group using the room for Scout meetings. In Fosbre v. State, 70 Wash.2d 578, 424 P.2d 901 (1967), the plaintiff was injured at a recreational area on a National Guard fort. The area had been improved and maintained for use by National Guard families of which plaintiff was a member. In these "invitee" cases, "the occupier, *by his arrangement of the premises or other conduct,* has led the entrant to believe that the premises were intended to be used by visitors, as members of the public, for the purpose which the entrant was pursuing, and *that reasonable care was taken to make the place safe for those who enter for that purpose.*" (Italics ours.) McKinnon, 68 Wash.2d at 649, 414 P.2d 773. See W. Prosser, Torts § 61, at 388–89 (4th ed. 1971); Restatement, § 332, comment d.

This implied assurance helps to distinguish between invitees and social guests, who are considered licensees. As explained in comment h(3) to Restatement, § 330:

> The explanation usually given by the courts for the classification of social guests as licensees is that there is a common understanding that the guest is expected to take the premises as the possessor himself uses them, and does not expect and is not entitled to expect that they will be prepared for his reception, or that precautions will be taken for his safety, in any manner in which the possessor does not prepare or take precautions for his own safety, or that of the members of his family.

Under the facts of this case, it is hard to imagine how the Strunks could have prepared or could have been expected to prepare a dairy farm for a kegger.

We are not persuaded by Lisa's argument that payment of a $4.00 admission price made her an invitee. Analysis in cases where an admission was paid and the plaintiff was characterized as an invitee did not focus on the money as indicative of the plaintiff's status as an invitee. Hooser v. Loyal Order of Moose, Inc., 69 Wash.2d 1, 416 P.2d 462, 15 A.L.R.3d 1008 (1966) ($1.00 for New Year's Eve Party held at Moose Lodge); Dickinson v. Tesia, 2 Wash.App. 262, 467 P.2d 356 (1970) ($2.00 for picnic in recreational area).

The trial court correctly identified Lisa as a licensee. She was privileged to enter or remain on the land only by virtue of the owner's consent. We question whether Charles and Thelma did consent to her presence on the property, but recognize that Dean did consent. In any event, we find the duty owed licensees was not breached because no known dangerous condition existed of which Lisa was not aware, or of which she did not realize the risks involved. Lisa had knowledge of the risks involved by staying on the property. We affirm the trial court.

. . . .

NOTES

(1) *Restatement (Second)* § 343 imposes liability on a possessor of land to his invitee if, but only if, he

(a) knows or by the exercise of reasonable care would discover the condition, and should realize that it involves an unreasonable risk of harm to such invitees, and

(b) should expect that they will not discover or realize the danger, or will fail to protect themselves against it, and

(c) fails to exercise reasonable care to protect them against the danger.

Can you justify the difference between this standard and the lesser standard that the *Younce* court quoted from *Memel v. Reimer*? Or do you think that the standard should be the same for invitees and licensees?

(2) If you accept the distinction between these two categories, do you think that the Washington court properly slotted Lisa Younce as a licensee? What social policies support the court's classification of Lisa that way?

(3) Is economic analysis helpful to the decision of cases involving injuries to visitors to land? Consider the Problem case at the start of this section. What if someone with Madison's status dived into a lake on the Skull Valley Ranch property to cool off on a hot day? Would it be conclusive on the negligence question that the injuries were crippling — for example, quadriplegia from striking a shallow bottom — and that it would have cost just a few dollars to put up a warning sign? How can one quantify the landowner's cost of learning about how shallow the water is and the likelihood of diving by licensees — even trespassers — on hot summer days?

(4) The *Restatement* sets out a number of rules concerning the liability of possessors of land to trespassers — who, whatever the distinctions drawn or not drawn between invitees and licensees, get rather short shift from the law. The "general rule," in section 333, is that a possessor is not liable to trespassers for physical harm caused by his failure to exercise reasonable care

(a) to put the land in a condition reasonably safe for their reception, or

(b) to carry on his activities so as not to endanger them.

The rules in sections 334–339 qualify this general rule. They refer to such circumstances as the extreme danger of the activity, the limited area in which the trespasser roams, and the possessor's knowledge of the presence of trespassers.

Can you justify this relatively low level of protection? Why shouldn't the duty of a landowner to anyone on her land be one of reasonable care, determined by all the circumstances — one of the circumstances being the trespassory nature of the plaintiff's conduct?

(5) A special rule concerning the duties of landowners appears in "recreational use" statutes. One statute of this kind, the Connecticut legislation, declares that there is no duty to keep land safe, or to warn about dangerous conditions, when an owner "makes all or any part of the land available to the public without charge, rent, fee or other commercial service for recreational purposes." Conn. Gen. Stat. § 52-557g(a). The statute specifically says that owners who make their land available on this basis do not confer

upon visitors "the legal status of an invitee or licensee to whom a duty of care is owed." *Id.* §52-557g(b)(2). However, the owner cannot avoid liability that would "otherwise exist[]" in the case of "wilful or malicious failure to guard or warn against a dangerous condition, use, structure or activity." *Id.* §52-557h.

An illustrative case spelling out the application of the statute and refusing to find "wilful or malicious conduct" is *Kurisoo v. Providence & Worcester R. Co.*, 68 F.3d 591 (2d Cir. 1995). The railroad permitted fishermen to use a riverbank adjoining its right of way, and the area became a popular fishing spot. There were no "No Trespassing" signs near the pathway that fishermen took to the fishing area, and indeed local newspaper articles had publicized the availability of fishing there. Some anglers would prop their poles against the rail tracks, and use a rock to lodge their poles against the rail. The plaintiff suffered injuries, resulting in an amputation, when a train hit a rock, propelling it so that it hit the plaintiff. Using a "substantially certain" definition for "wilful or malicious," the court rejected the argument that the railroad's conduct fit that definition. It noted that there had been no previous accidents of that kind and pointed out that the railroad had "frequently removed rocks from the tracks, told fishermen not to put rocks against the tracks, and regularly warned fishermen about approaching trains." *Id.* at 596.

(6) A special category of trespassers is child trespassers. A separate section treats the rules for this group, infra §6.01.

---

§4.05 Standard of Conduct Concerning the Activities of Third Parties

The negligence formula is broad in its generality, imposing liability for conduct that is unreasonable, falling below the standard of prudent persons in the circumstances. Because of the multitude of activities in which people may behave carelessly, a useful way to make the general formula more precise is to relate it to specific clusters of activities or fact situations.

The material below presents a recurrent set of negligence issues in a functional context. The specific functional problem concerns the responsibility of one who is in a position to control other persons or groups of persons, in situations when it is a third party who directly inflicts the injury suffered by the plaintiff. Given the increasing number of cases that present this problem, the subject is worth study for itself. It is also a particularly interesting example of a specific application of the general negligence formula.

BUTLER v. DISTRICT OF COLUMBIA

United States Court of Appeals, District of Columbia Circuit
135 U.S. App. D.C. 203, 417 F.2d 1150 (1969)

PRETTYMAN, SENIOR CIRCUIT JUDGE:

Our appellants were plaintiffs in a civil action in the District Court against the District of Columbia. At the close of their case the trial judge directed a verdict for the defendant-appellee. This verdict was on alternative grounds.... [T]he judge held that the evidence adduced showed that the alleged negligent act was "a clearly discretionary matter" that had been determined by the school authorities and, therefore, suit against the District of Columbia was barred by governmental immunity. Alternatively the judge held that the plaintiffs failed to present adequate evidence upon which a jury "could reasonably determine that the allocation of the available teachers was a negligent act." We affirm on the latter, alternate ground and do not reach the other contention.

The facts are very simple. On the day of the alleged negligent act, Ronald T. Butler, the minor appellant, was a seventh grade student at the Woodson Junior High School. En route to his printing class, following lunch, he encountered a classmate who warned him that the boys already in the classroom intended to scare him as he entered. He was no more than three steps inside the classroom when an object that "was pointed and ... sharp and ... felt like a piece of metal" struck him in the left eye, causing pain and resulting in permanent loss of sight in the eye. It was shown that small metallic type was a part of the equipment used in the classroom, and one witness testified that he noticed a few pieces of such type lying on the floor in the general area where Ronald had fallen.

A teacher from another classroom came into the printing class and, apparently not realizing the seriousness of the injury, nudged Ronald with his foot and told him to get up. Several minutes later (no more than ten and possibly as few as five), Mr. Weir, the printing class teacher, came into the room. Ronald was taken to the nurse's office, his parents were summoned, and in due course he was taken to D.C. General Hospital for treatment.

Dr. John O'Neill, a pediatric ophthalmologist, the only expert witness called by the plaintiffs, testified that, although neither he nor the other doctors who treated Ronald could determine what the object was that had caused the damage, generally speaking the sharper the object the less force was required to cause such an injury.

The plaintiffs' case rested on their contention that the school authorities were negligent in their supervision of this classroom and that this negligence was the proximate cause of Ronald's injury. This argument rested on two bits of evidence: (1) that the printing teacher was not physically present to supervise the students when the class convened and (2) testimony tending to show that both Mr. Weir and the principal had prior knowledge that "horseplay" and throwing occurred in this classroom when the teacher was not present.[3]

The evidence showed that the teacher was not present at the start of this particular class, because he had been assigned to duty as a hall or cafeteria supervisor. Under a plan established by the principal, who was the general supervisor of internal school functions, each teacher had been designated duties during the lunch period. This plan was designed to place teachers in positions where supervision was most needed. There were some twelve hundred students in the school, and, in an effort to provide for maximum safety and order, the teachers were deployed in various places outside their own classrooms during certain periods when the students generally were outside the classrooms. One of these periods was the lunch break.

---

3. Now, for the first time, on appeal appellant makes reference to the teacher's failure to lock up these dangerous metallic pieces of type as further evidence of negligence. This theory, or the alternative theory that the students should not have been allowed in the room in the absence of their teacher were not raised at trial. No evidence appears on any theory except the teacher's failure to be present when class convened.

Plaintiffs offered no evidence that Mr. Weir was not performing his assigned duty on the day in question but, to carry their burden of showing negligence on this point,[4] rely on the fact that the teacher was not present in the classroom. In essence they contend that it was negligent for the school authorities not to have a teacher assigned to a particular classroom containing fourteen pupils while this same teacher, in the exercise of the principal's discretion, was supervising part of an area that may have contained a thousand pupils.

Appellants stress the trial judge's assumption that "there had been complaints of previous horseplay by students in the absence of the classroom teacher."[5]

This factor does not support the argument based upon it. It is common knowledge susceptible of judicial notice that small boys may indulge in horseplay—shoot a paperclip, snap a rubberband, or throw a pencil—when a teacher is tardy or turns his or her back. The possibility of such an occurrence had been anticipated by the school authorities here involved. Knowing that if a teacher was assigned cafeteria duty, or that if, in patrol of a corridor not near his own classroom during the lunch break, he might not be physically present in that classroom at the start of the following class period, various rules had been established. The principal had given the students instructions on the first day of school that were designed to govern their conduct in the absence of a teacher. These were buttressed by fourteen specific rules established by Mr. Weir to apply specifically to the conduct of his printing class students. These were printed and distributed to each class member. They directed the students, upon entering the room in the absence of the teacher, to sit down, work on their projects, not throw type, and await further instructions. Thus, faced with the knowledge that children, and especially thirteen-year-old boys, will throw at, kick, hit or push a fellow pupil if a teacher is not immediately present, and using the available supervisory personnel, the authorities balanced the need for a teacher to supervise several hundred students milling about the corridors and the cafeteria against the need to supervise fourteen students in a certain classroom for a short period of time.

The problem is not unlike that relating to other governmental operations involving the safety or well-being of numbers of people; such are streets, sidewalks, sewers, snow removal, playgrounds, and many others.... In the case now before us the plaintiffs do not say there was no plan, or that the plan was defective, or that the plan was not being followed. They say simply that the teacher was absent from the classroom at the critical moment in this affair, and they say that was negligence. Liability for negligence is not established by such allegations or evidence.

Affirmed.

LEVENTHAL, CIRCUIT JUDGE (dissenting):

In my opinion the ruling of the court reflects a narrow view of scope of liability of the District of Columbia in tort that is contrary to sound doctrine....

The majority opinion, which assertedly rests not on governmental immunity, but on the ground that there was no evidence of negligence, concludes that the problem is essentially that of "governmental operations involving the safety or well-being of numbers of people"....

---

4. The plaintiffs did not call Mr. Weir. No explanation for this is present in the papers before us. Nor was any attempt made to show that Mr. Weir was unnecessarily late for his class.

5. This assumption was based on testimony by Ronald's father, who, along with his wife, visited the principal of the school on the day following the injury to their son. The elder Butler testified that the principal told them that he had had complaints of students throwing type while Mr. Weir was not present in the room. This was denied by the principal at trial.

Plaintiff's case, as I see it once the immunity question is ignored, may stand firmly on the point that if this were an action against a private school his evidence suffices to go to the jury. Taking it, as we must, most favorably to plaintiff, it showed that he was in a vocational instruction room where he was required to be, his teacher was not present at the start of the class, and he was struck by a piece of movable type thrown by another boy. The teacher and school were on notice that in their rough-housing the boys do throw type and had done so in the past. One student testified when Mr. Weir arrived after Ronald's injury he tried to find out if anybody was throwing type. Indeed the principal's own testimony reflected this notice, by reference to the regulation that instructed the boys not to throw type. It is a jury question whether this kind of formal instruction is enough to show due care and negative liability.

It seems to me the absence of teacher at the start of class, with a room involving this hazard, made a prima facie case, subject to explanation by the principal or other officer of the school that its agent was unavailable at that time due to overriding school needs.

The majority opinion says the teacher was absent because he had been assigned to hall duty or cafeteria duty. This was a permissible but not a necessary inference. The school did not meet the burden of showing where its agent was. The principal, on questioning by counsel for the District, was unable to say what duty he had assigned in the preceding period to the teacher.

One student testified the teacher had hall duty that day. On that premise there is evidence that would uphold a finding of negligence in the teacher's failure to fulfill this duty on the day of the injury. The principal testified that the school wanted each teacher in close touch with his room, and hence he was required to be in his class, or if on hall duty, to be "by his class, or on duty outside of his class by the time the class arrived."

Furthermore, even if the school had showed the teacher was on cafeteria duty, that factor, though certainly relevant as to liability, would not in my view suffice to take the case from the jury. For the question would remain why the teacher was not on time at the start of the class, following the lunch period. There was evidence that he arrived 10 minutes after Ronald was hit, and hence 12 minutes after the class began. If there was a good reason in school business, involving an exercise of discretion by policy officials, why the teacher was elsewhere, it was the school's burden to show where its agent was and what he had been doing.

Finally, even if the teacher was assigned to a duty that would require him to be late for his shop class, I must say that I do not see why such a confession-and-avoidance would take away from the jury the possibility of finding negligence in the absence of an explanation why attractive printing type could not have been closed up in some way. This was not an ordinary classroom, but a shop of sorts with mobile paraphernalia and attractive and throwable material. Taking into account the notice that the obviously dangerous type throwing had occurred before, a juror, exercising his common sense experience with school situations and limitations, could find that a reasonably prudent teacher or administrator would lock up the type, the classroom, or at least provide substitute supervision such as an upperclass student, to lessen the degree of a known danger when the teacher was unable to be present.

Though the decision is cast in terms of insufficiency of evidence of negligence, I feel that it essentially reflects a special protection accorded the defendant because it is a government agency whose employees were on public business. I respectfully dissent from the opinion of the court.

FRANCES T. v. VILLAGE GREEN OWNERS ASSOCIATION

California Supreme Court, In Bank
42 Cal. 3d 490, 723 P.2d 573, 229 Cal. Rptr. 456 (1986)

BROUSSARD, JUSTICE.

The question presented is whether a condominium owners association and the individual members of its board of directors may be held liable for injuries to a unit owner caused by third-party criminal conduct. Plaintiff, Frances T., brought suit against the Village Green Owners Association (the Association) and individual members of its board of directors for injuries sustained when she was attacked in her condominium unit, a part of the Village Green Condominium Project (Project). Her complaint stated three causes of action: negligence, breach of contract and breach of fiduciary duty. The trial court sustained defendants' general demurrers to plaintiff's three causes of action without leave to amend and entered a judgment of dismissal. Plaintiff appealed.

I.

On the night of October 8, 1980, an unidentified person entered plaintiff's condominium unit under cover of darkness and molested, raped and robbed her. At the time of the incident, plaintiff's unit had no exterior lighting. The manner in which her unit came to be without exterior lighting on this particular evening forms the basis of her lawsuit against the defendants.

The Association, of which plaintiff was a member, is a nonprofit corporation composed of owners of individual condominium units. The Association was formed and exists for the purposes set forth in the Project's declaration of covenants, conditions and restrictions (CC&Rs). The board of directors (board) exercises the powers of the Association and conducts, manages and controls the affairs of the Project and the Association. Among other things the Association, through its board, is authorized to enforce the regulations set forth in the CC&Rs. The Association, through the board, is also responsible for the management of the Project and for the maintenance of the Project's common areas.

At the time of the incident, the Project consisted of 92 buildings, each containing several individual condominium units, situated in grassy golf course and park-like areas known as "courts." Plaintiff's unit faced the largest court. She alleges that "the lighting in [the] park-like area was exceedingly poor, and after sunset, aside from the miniscule park light of plaintiff's, the area was in virtual ... darkness. Of all the condominium units in [plaintiff's court] ... plaintiff's unit was in the darkest place."

Throughout 1980, the Project was subject to what plaintiff terms an "exceptional crimewave" that included car thefts, purse snatchings, dwelling burglaries and robberies. All of the Project's residents, including the board, were aware of and concerned about this "crimewave." From January through July 1980, articles about the crimewave and possible protective measures were published in the Association's newsletter and distributed to the residents of the Project, including the directors. The newsletters show that residents, including the directors, were aware of some of the residents' complaints regarding lighting.[3]

---

3. Many of the Association's newsletters were attached to the complaint as exhibits. The newsletters included such items as: "LIGHTS! LIGHTS! LIGHTS! You are doing a disservice to your neighbors as well as yourself if you keep your front and back doors in darkness. Many who live upstairs are able to gaze out on the Green at night and see perfectly the presence or absence of a prowler where there is a lighted doorway. But where porches are shrouded in darkness, NOTHING is visible. AS A CIVIC DUTY—WON'T YOU KEEP THOSE LIGHTS ON? If you would like to try out a Sen-

In early 1980 the board began to investigate what could be done to improve the lighting in the Project. The investigation was conducted by the Project's architectural guidelines committee.

Plaintiff's unit was first burglarized in April 1980. Believing the incident would not have occurred if there had been adequate lighting at the end of her court, plaintiff caused the following item to be printed in the Association's newsletter: "With reference to other lighting, Fran [T.] of Ct. 4, whose home was entered, feels certain (and asked that this be mentioned) that the break-in would not have occurred if there had been adequate lighting at the end of her Court. This has since been corrected. We hope other areas which need improvement will soon be taken care of ..."[4]

In May 1980 plaintiff and other residents of her court had a meeting. As court representative plaintiff transmitted a formal request to the Project's manager with a copy to the board that more lighting be installed in their court as soon as possible.[5]

Plaintiff submitted another memorandum in August 1980 because the board had taken no action on the previous requests. The memorandum stated that none of the lighting requests from plaintiff's court had been responded to. Plaintiff also requested that a copy of the memorandum be placed in the board's correspondence file.

By late August, the board had still taken no action. Plaintiff then installed additional exterior lighting at her unit, believing that this would protect her from crime. In a letter dated August 29, 1980, however, the site manager told plaintiff that she would have to remove the lighting because it violated the CC & Rs. Plaintiff refused to comply with this request. After appearing at a board meeting, where she requested permission to maintain her lighting until the board improved the general lighting that she believed to be a hazard, she received a communication from the board stating in part:

> The Board has indicated their appreciation for your appearance on October 1, and for the information you presented to them. After deliberation, however, the Board resolved as follows: [&] You are requested to remove the exterior lighting you added to your front door and in your patio and to restore the Association Property to its original condition on or before October 6. If this is not done on or before that date, the Association will have the work done and bill you for the costs incurred.

The site manager subsequently instructed plaintiff that pending their removal, she could not use the additional exterior lighting. The security lights had been installed using the same circuitry used for the original exterior lighting and were operated by the same switches. In order not to use her additional lighting, plaintiff was required to forego the use of all of her exterior lights. In spite of this, however, plaintiff complied with the board's order and cut off the electric power on the circuitry controlling the exterior lighting during the daylight hours of October 8, 1980. As a result, her unit was in total darkness on October 8, 1980, the night she was raped and robbed.

---

sor Light on a 30-day trial basis to see how efficient and economical it is, we are sure it can be arranged through the Court Council and Court Reps."

4. Plaintiff, of course, alleges that nothing was done to correct the lighting problem.

5. The letter stated:

June 12, 1980. REPORT FROM YOUR COURT REP.... It was requested that the following items be relayed to the on-site mgr. for consideration and action if possible.

1. Lights be installed on the northeast corner of bldg. 18 promptly.

．．．

... Item No. 1 above was put into the form of a motion with the request that action be taken on this item particularly by the site manager....

II.

Negligence

In her first cause of action plaintiff alleged that the Association and the board negligently failed to complete the investigation of lighting alternatives within a reasonable time, failed to present proposals regarding lighting alternatives to members of the Association, negligently failed to respond to the requests for additional lighting and wrongfully ordered her to remove the lighting that she had installed. She contends that these negligent acts and omissions were the proximate cause of her injuries.

The fundamental issue here is whether petitioners, the condominium Association and its individual directors, owed plaintiff the same duty of care as would a landlord in the traditional landlord-tenant relationship. We conclude that plaintiff has pleaded facts sufficient to state a cause of action for negligence against both the Association and the individual directors.

A. The Association's Duty of Care.

The scope of a condominium association's duty to a unit owner in a situation such as this is a question of first impression. Plaintiff contends, and we agree, that under the circumstances of this case the Association should be held to the same standard of care as a landlord.

Defendants based their demurrer to the negligence cause of action on the theory that the Association owed no duty to plaintiff to improve the lighting outside her unit. The Association argues that it would be unfair to impose upon it a duty to provide "expensive security measures" when it is not a landlord in the traditional sense, but a nonprofit association of homeowners. The Association contends that under its own CC & Rs, it cannot permit residents to improve the security of the common areas without prior written permission, nor can it substantially increase its limited budget for common-area improvements without the approval of a majority of the members.

But regardless of these self-imposed constraints, the Association is, for all practical purposes, the Project's "landlord." And traditional tort principles impose on landlords, no less than on homeowner associations that function as a landlord in maintaining the common areas of a large condominium complex, a duty to exercise due care for the residents' safety in those areas under their control. (See, e.g., Kwaitkowski v. Superior Trading Co. (1981) 123 Cal.App.3d 324, 328, 176 Cal.Rptr. 494; O'Hara v. Western Seven Trees Corp., 75 Cal.App.3d 798, 802–803, 142 Cal.Rptr. 487; Kline v. 1500 Massachusetts Avenue Apartment Corp. (D.C. Cir.1970) 439 F.2d 477, 480–481; Scott v. Watson (1976) 278 Md. 160, 359 A.2d 548, 552.)

Two previous California decisions support our conclusion that a condominium association may properly be held to a landlord's standard of care as to the common areas under its control. In White v. Cox, 17 Cal.App.3d 824, 95 Cal.Rptr. 259, the court held that a condominium owner could sue the unincorporated association for negligently maintaining a sprinkler in a common area of the complex. In so holding, the court recognized that the plaintiff, a member of the unincorporated association, had no "effective control over the operation of the common areas ... for in fact he had no more control over operations than he would have had as a stockholder in a corporation which owned and operated the project." (Id., at p. 830, 95 Cal.Rptr. 259.)[7]

---

7. The court's analogy is particularly apt because the case before us involves a plaintiff who is a member of a nonprofit incorporated association. It has been observed that "[U]nder the new non-

Since the condominium association was a management body over which the individual owner had no effective control, the court held that the association could be sued for negligence by an individual member.

In O'Connor v. Village Green Owners Assn., 33 Cal.3d 790, 191 Cal.Rptr. 320, 662 P.2d 427, this court held that the Association's restriction limiting residency in the project to persons over 18 years of age was a violation of the Unruh Civil Rights Act (Civ.Code, § 51).[8]

In so doing, we were mindful of the Association's role in the day-to-day functioning of the project: "Contrary to the association's attempt to characterize itself as but an organization that 'mows lawns' for owners, the association in reality has a far broader and more businesslike purpose. The association, through a board of directors, is charged with employing a professional property management firm, with obtaining insurance for the benefit of all owners and with maintaining and repairing all common areas and facilities of the 629-unit project.... *In brief, the association performs all the customary business functions which in the traditional landlord-tenant relationship rest on the landlord's shoulders.*" (O'Connor v. Village Green Owners Assn., supra, 33 Cal.3d 790, 796, 191 Cal.Rptr. 320, 662 P.2d 427, italics added.)[9]

[The court turns to landlord-tenant cases as analogies.]

O'Hara v. Western Seven Trees Corp., ... established that in some instances a landlord has a duty to take reasonable steps to protect a tenant from the criminal acts of third parties and may be held liable for failing to do so. In O'Hara plaintiff alleged that the defendant landlords were aware that a man had raped several tenants and additionally "were aware of the conditions indicating a likelihood that the rapist would repeat his attacks." ... In addressing the question of the landlords' liability the court observed: "Traditionally, a landlord had no duty to protect his tenants from the criminal acts of others, but an innkeeper was under a duty to protect his guests. [Citations.] But in recent years, the landlord-tenant relationship, at least in the urban, residential context, has given rise to liability under circumstances where landlords have failed to take reasonable steps to protect tenants from criminal activity. [Citations.] ... [S]ince only the landlord is in the position to secure common areas, he has a duty to protect against types of crimes of which he has notice and which are likely to recur if the common areas are not secure.... [Citations.]" ...

---

profit mutual benefit corporation law, members are like shareholders in a business corporation." (Hanna, Cal. Condominium Handbook (1975) p. 77.)

8. Section 51 provides in relevant part: "All persons within the jurisdiction of this state are free and equal, and no matter what their sex, race, color, religion, ancestry, or national origin are entitled to the full and equal accommodations, advantages, facilities, privileges, or services in all business establishments of every kind whatsoever."

9. We also take judicial notice of the fact that a rapidly growing share of California's population reside in condominiums, cooperatives and other types of common-interest housing projects. Homeowner associations manage the housing for an estimated 15 percent of the American population and, for example, as much as 70 percent of the new housing built in Los Angeles and San Diego Counties. (See Bowler & McKenzie, Invisible Kingdoms (Dec. 1985) Cal.Law., at p. 55.) Nationally, "[t]hey are growing at a rate of 5,000 a year and represent more than 50 percent of new construction sales in the urban areas. Projects average about 100 units each, so the associations affect some 10 million owners," according to C. James Dowden, executive vice president of the Community Association Institute in Alexandria, Virginia. (Ibid.) According to Bowler & McKenzie, supra, housing experts estimate that there already are 15,000 common-interest housing associations in California. While in some projects the maintenance of common areas is truly cooperative, in most of the larger projects control of the common area is delegated or controlled by ruling bodies that do not exercise the members' collective will on a one-person, one-vote basis. (Ibid.)

The court concluded that, as in the case before us, plaintiff had alleged the most important factor pointing to the landlord's liability: foreseeability. "[The landlords] allegedly knew of the past assaults and of conditions making future attacks likely. By not acting affirmatively to protect [the plaintiff], they increased the likelihood that she would also be a victim." ... [10] Moreover, "evidence of prior similar incidents is not the sine qua non of a finding of foreseeability." (Isaacs v. Huntington Memorial Hospital (1985) 38 Cal.3d 112, 127, 211 Cal.Rptr. 356, 695 P.2d 653.) "[F]oreseeability is determined in light of all the circumstances and not by a rigid application of a mechanical 'prior similars' rule." ...

Similarly, in Kwaitkowski v. Superior Trading Co., ... the court held that the plaintiff had stated a cause of action against the landlords for negligence in failing to protect her from assault, battery, rape and robbery by a person who had accosted her in the dimly lit lobby of an apartment building. The facts, as alleged, indicated that complaints by tenants and a prior assault on a tenant provided the landlords with notice of the injuries that might result from the level of crime in the area. The landlords also had notice that a defective lock on the lobby entrance door was allowing strangers access to the building. Relying primarily on O'Hara, the court concluded that the plaintiff had alleged facts sufficient to show that her injuries were the foreseeable result of the landlord's negligence in maintaining the entrance door....

As in O'Hara and Kwaitkowski, it is beyond dispute here that the Association, rather than the unit owners, controlled the maintenance of the common areas. This is clearly illustrated by the fact that when plaintiff attempted to improve security by installing additional exterior lighting, the board ordered her to remove them because they were placed in an area over which the Association exercised exclusive authority.

...

The facts alleged here, if proven, demonstrate defendant's awareness of the need for additional lighting and of the fact that lighting could aid in deterring criminal conduct, especially break-ins. As in O'Hara and Kwaitkowski, the Association was on notice that crimes were being committed against the Project's residents. Correspondence from plaintiff and other residents of her court, along with the articles in the Project's newsletter, demonstrate affirmatively that defendant was aware of the link between the lack of lighting and crime.

Plaintiff's unit had, in fact, been recently burglarized and defendant knew this. It is not necessary, as defendant appears to imply, that the prior crimes be identical to the

---

10. The court also concluded that several sections of the Restatement Second of Torts suggest that landlords can be held liable under certain circumstances for injuries inflicted during criminal assaults on tenants. Section 302B provides: "An act or an omission may be negligent if the actor realizes or should realize that it involves an unreasonable risk of harm to another through the conduct of the other or a third person which is intended to cause harm, *even though such conduct is criminal.*" (Italics added.)

Section 448 provides: "The act of a third person in committing an intentional tort or crime is a superseding cause of harm to another resulting therefrom, although the actor's negligent conduct created a situation which afforded an opportunity to the third person to commit such a tort or crime, *unless the actor* at the time of his negligent conduct *realized or should have realized the likelihood* that such a situation might be created, and *that a third person might* avail himself of the opportunity to *commit such a tort or crime.*" (Italics added.)

Section 449 provides: "If the likelihood that a third person may act in a particular manner is the hazard or one of the hazards which makes the actor negligent, such an act whether innocent, negligent, intentionally tortious, *or criminal* does not prevent the actor from being liable for harm caused thereby." (Italics added.)

ones perpetrated against the plaintiff.... Defendant need not have foreseen the precise injury to plaintiff so long as the possibility of this type of harm was foreseeable....

Thus, plaintiff has alleged facts sufficient to show the existence of a duty, that defendant may have breached that duty of care by failing to respond in a timely manner to the need for additional lighting and by ordering her to disconnect her additional lights, and that this negligence—if established—was the legal cause of her injuries.

[Omitted, inter alia, is the court's discussion of the duty of care of the Association's director.]

V.

Conclusion

We conclude that the trial court erred in sustaining the Association's and directors' demurrer to the negligence cause of action. We affirm dismissal of plaintiff's other causes of action. The judgment is therefore reversed and remanded to the trial court for further proceedings consistent with this opinion.

BIRD, C.J., and REYNOSO and GRODIN, JJ., concur.

[Omitted is Chief Justice Bird's concurrence, discussing the liability of the directors.]

MOSK, JUSTICE, concurring and dissenting.

I concur in the judgment insofar as it affirms the judgment of the trial court dismissing plaintiff's causes of action for breach of contract and breach of fiduciary duty. I dissent, however, from the judgment insofar as it reverses the judgment of the trial court dismissing plaintiff's negligence cause of action.

Once again the majority make condominium ownership which, as they themselves impliedly recognize, is a preferred form of home ownership available to many Californians—much more difficult and risky than it reasonably need be. In Griffin Development Co. v. City of Oxnard, (1985) 39 Cal.3d 256, 217 Cal.Rptr. 1, 703 P.2d 339, they approved a local ordinance that made conversion of rental apartments to condominiums a practical impossibility in an entire city. Now, contrary to the common law principles applicable here, they impose on a voluntary nonprofit association of condominium owners the affirmative duty to protect the individual unit owner against the criminal acts of third parties committed outside common areas and within that person's own unit, and thereby expose the association to unwarranted and potentially substantial civil liability....

Even though understandable sympathy is aroused for this plaintiff, the analysis employed by the majority does not withstand close scrutiny.

On the question of the Association's potential liability, the analysis is unpersuasive because the claimed similarity between the relationship of condominium association to unit owner and that of landlord and tenant is not adequately probed. This is a crucial weakness since the potential liability of the Association to plaintiff is premised on the alleged similarity of these two relationships. Specifically, the majority's reliance on O'-Connor v. Village Green Owners Assn., ... Kwaitowski v. Superior Trading Co., ... and O'Hara v. Western Seven Trees Corp., ... is ill founded.

O'Connor, on which the majority rely in holding condominium associations relevantly similar to landlords, has been subjected to strong criticism on its own terms.... In any event it is plainly inapposite: whether a condominium association is similar to a landlord for the purposes of an antidiscrimination statute that covers "'all business establishments of every kind whatsoever'" ... is irrelevant to the issue whether such an association is similar to a landlord for the purposes of the general common law of torts. Kwaitowski and O'Hara, which discuss the basis and scope of the landlord's potential liability, constitute too slender a reed to support the majority's extension of such potential liability to a condominium association.

On the question of the directors' potential liability, a major weakness appears: Corporations Code section 7231, as I shall show, is misconstrued.

Contrary to the majority's implied holding, the Association is not under a duty to protect unit owners against the criminal acts of third parties that result from its nonfeasance, or failure to act: such a duty arises generally from a "special relationship," and the condominium association-unit owner is not such a relationship.

It is well settled that a private person has no duty to protect another against the criminal acts of third parties absent a special relationship between the person on whom the duty is sought to be imposed and either the victim or the criminal actor....

As a result, the traditional rule has been that the landlord is not subject to a duty "to protect the tenant from criminal acts of third parties absent a contract or a statute imposing the duty." ...

Since the landmark case of Kline v. 1500 Massachusetts Avenue Apartment Corp., however, the rule has been undermined, ... and today several jurisdictions impose a limited duty on landlords to protect their tenants against the criminal acts of third parties....

Nevertheless, the emerging view that landlords may be under a limited duty to protect their tenants against the criminal acts of third parties—on which the majority here rely—does not appear to support excepting the Association from the traditional common law "no duty" rule: the five basic theories that support the landlord-tenant exception are largely inapplicable to the condominium association-unit owner relationship.

First, landlords have been subjected to a duty to protect on the theory that when, for consideration, a landlord undertakes to provide protection against the known hazard of criminal activity, he assumes a duty to protect.... Condominium associations, however, do not generally enter into such undertakings, and indeed the Association here is not alleged to have done so.

Second, landlords have been subjected to a duty to protect on the theory that the lease impliedly guarantees such protection: "the value of the lease to the modern apartment dweller is that it gives him 'a well known package of goods and services—a package which includes not merely walls and ceilings, but also adequate heat, light and ventilation, serviceable plumbing facilities, secure windows and doors, proper sanitation, and proper maintenance.'" ... There is no lease, of course, between condominium association and unit owner. Nor apparently do the unit owner and the condominium association between whom no consideration passes—impliedly agree on such a package of goods and services. No such agreement, moreover, is alleged here.

Third, landlords have been subjected to a duty to protect on the theory that the landlord-tenant relationship is similar to the special relationship of innkeeper and guest...."In [special] relationships the plaintiff is typically in some respect particularly vulnerable and dependent upon the defendant who, correspondingly, holds considerable power over the plaintiff's welfare. In addition, such relations have often involved some existing or potential economic advantage to the defendant." (Prosser & Keeton, ...) Whatever the force of the analogy in the landlord-tenant context, it fails when applied to the condominium association-unit owner relationship. First, although the unit owner is dependent on the association for the general management of the complex, he is nevertheless a member of the association and can participate in its activities. Indeed, in the case at bar, as the allegations of the complaint show, plaintiff participated quite actively and successfully. Second, the condominium association-unit owner relationship involves no existing or potential economic advantage to the association. To be sure, no such advantage is alleged here.

Fourth, landlords have been subjected to a duty to protect on the theory that "traditional tort principles ... [impose on] the landlord ... a duty to exercise reasonable care for the tenant's safety in common areas under his control...." (Haines, ... 2 Cardozo L.Rev. at p. 333....) Because the similarity of the landlord-tenant and condominium association-unit owner relationships is the issue here in question, to conclude that the condominium association should be subjected to such a duty under traditional tort principles governing the landlord-tenant relationship is, in effect, to beg the question. In any event, the existence of such a limited duty would be immaterial on the facts pleaded in the complaint: the criminal acts plaintiff alleges she suffered were committed not in common areas subject to the Association's control, but within her own unit.

Finally, landlords have been subjected to a duty to protect on the theory that the criminal activity in question was foreseeable.... It is not at all clear, however, that the criminal activity alleged here falls within even the broad definition of foreseeability articulated in Kwaitowski, i.e., knowledge on the part of the defendant of prior criminal activity of the same general type in the same general area.... Rather, the criminal acts plaintiff alleges she suffered were rape and robbery; the prior criminal activity she alleges defendants had knowledge of included such offenses as automobile theft, purse snatching, and burglary.

In any event, foreseeability as the basis of the landlord's duty is problematic. "[I]t is generally understood that foreseeability alone does not justify the imposition of a duty...." (Haines, ... 2 Cardozo L.Rev. at p. 339; ... Landlord's Duty, ... 59 Geo.L.J. at p. 1178....) Hence, to reason from the foreseeability of harm to the existence of a duty to prevent such harm again begs the question. It follows that if foreseeability cannot support the imposition of a duty on landlords, it cannot support the imposition of a duty on condominium associations.

Thus, insofar as the criminal acts of third parties in this case are alleged to result from the Association's nonfeasance—in the majority's words, the failure "to complete the investigation of lighting alternatives[,] ... to present proposals regarding lighting alternatives to members of the Association, ... [and] to respond to the requests for additional lighting"—they are not within the scope of any duty that the Association may have owed to plaintiff.

It is at least arguable that the Association may be under a duty to protect unit owners against the criminal acts of third parties that result from its misfeasance. (Cf. Haines, ... 2 Cardozo L.Rev. at p. 311, fn. 55 ["Despite the general 'no duty' rule, a landlord at common law was nevertheless liable for third party criminal acts against his tenants if his direct act of negligence precipitated the injury"].) Nevertheless, the Association is not under such a duty on the facts pleaded in the complaint: the allegations fail effectively to state that the Association's request that plaintiff remove the additional lighting she had installed—the only conduct alleged that rises above the level of nonfeasance—constituted misfeasance, or active misconduct.

"Misfeasance" evidently denotes conduct that is blameworthy in itself, apart from its alleged causal connection to the plaintiff's injury. (See, e.g., Gidwani v. Wasserman,

(1977) 373 Mass. 162, 166–167, 365 N.E.2d 827, 830–831 [landlord liable for loss arising from burglary after he disconnected tenant's burglar alarm during an unlawful entry to repossess premises for nonpayment of rent]; De Lorena v. Slud (N.Y.City Ct.1949), 95 N.Y.S.2d 163, 164–165 [landlord liable for loss of property stolen by person who had obtained the key to the premises from landlord without tenant's authorization].) The misconduct alleged here does not rise to such a level of blameworthiness—especially in view of plaintiff's implied concession that the Association made the request on the ground that she had installed the additional lighting in violation of the declaration of covenants, conditions and restrictions (CC & R's).

[Justice Mosk's discussion of the liability of the directors is omitted.]

LUCAS, J., concurs.

GARRETT v. UNITED STATES
United States District Court, Northern District of Georgia
501 F. Supp. 337 (1980)

ORINDA DALE EVANS, DISTRICT JUDGE.

This suit for damages under the Federal Tort Claims Act, in which an ex-inmate of the Atlanta Federal Penitentiary sues for injuries inflicted upon him while he was incarcerated, is now before the Court for findings of fact and conclusions of law upon completion of a non-jury trial. Having considered the evidence and arguments of counsel, the Court hereby finds and concludes as follows:

On August 30, 1976, Plaintiff was stabbed twice in the back by Steve Rollins, a fellow inmate at the Atlanta Penitentiary. One of Plaintiff's lungs was punctured and partially collapsed as a result.

Steven Rollins was originally transferred to the U. S. Penitentiary in Atlanta on March 22, 1976 from a state prison in Rhode Island, where he had been serving time for second degree murder.[1]

When Rollins arrived in Atlanta his prison file came with him. It disclosed the fact that during the period of his incarceration in Rhode Island he had committed the following offenses: assault upon a correctional officer (three separate incidents), assault upon another inmate, murder of an inmate, attempted escape, threatening correctional officers, fighting, possession of a dangerous weapon, and contraband. The file contained no psychological evaluations of the prisoner.

Rollins was placed in administrative detention (a form of segregation) when he arrived at Atlanta. He remained there for nine days. Rollins' file ... reflects an entry on March 22, "Referred to caseworker." The Court assumes and finds that Rollins did see a caseworker, as the Government's evidence indicated this was customary procedure. However, no evidence was presented as to the substance of the caseworker's findings. On March 31, 1976, Rollins was released from administrative segregation.

Rollins was placed in "A" cellhouse, which is a large area housing 500 to 600 prisoners in multi-tiered cells. It is manned by two or three guards, depending upon the time of

---

1. The transfer was pursuant to a program whereby a state prisoner may be incarcerated in a federal facility on a contract basis. The program is used frequently where state facilities are not adequate to deal with an incorrigible prisoner.

day. Individual cells in "A" cellhouse are occupied by two or more inmates. Except during specified times, inmates are free to mix with each other in the common areas and in individual cells in "A" cellhouse.

Plaintiff was also housed in "A" cellhouse. He was a slight acquaintance of Rollins. The incident in question occurred around dinnertime one afternoon when Plaintiff and Rollins had a brief conversational exchange. Rollins made an overture to Plaintiff which Plaintiff interpreted as an offer to share a joint of marijuana with him. Plaintiff indicated he was not interested and Rollins stabbed him in the back with a steel building rod.

The duty of care owed by the Government to federal prisoners is set forth in 18 U.S.C. § 4042, which provides in pertinent part that the government shall provide for the "safe keeping" and "protection" of prisoners.... The standard is one of ordinary diligence.... A prisoner who seeks to recover damages must show, as in any negligence case, that such damages were proximately caused by the asserted negligence. The legal standard for proximate cause requires the injuries to have been a foreseeable result of the alleged negligence. "Foreseeability" does not require the anticipation of a particular injury to a particular person, however, but only the anticipation of a general type or category of harm which in ordinary experience might be expected to flow from a particular type of negligence....

On the negligence issue, the Government contends that when compared with other prisoners at the Atlanta Penitentiary, Rollins was not so unusual so as to require special housing arrangements.[3]

It also points to Rollins' segregation for observation when he first arrived in Atlanta, which apparently resulted in the decision that it was all right to release him to the general population. On the proximate cause question, the Government contends it could not have reasonably anticipated Rollins' attack on a fellow inmate, arguing that human behavior is not susceptible of such prediction.

The Court concludes the Government was negligent in failing to provide closer supervision for Rollins than that provided in "A" cellhouse. Rollins' prior institutional record was good reason to think he might act violently toward another inmate. The mere fact that his file was referred to a caseworker and that he was held in segregation for nine days before release to the general prison population does not, standing alone, alter the Court's view. Neither does the Court find persuasive the Government's argument that Rollins was not substantially different from other prisoners at the penitentiary, because it merely compares prisoners according to category of offense for which they are serving time. While category of offense is relevant to determination of appropriate institutional handling, so is prior institutional behavior.

The evidence persuades the Court that the Government should have reasonably anticipated that Rollins would harm another inmate if housed in an environment such as "A" cellhouse. This conclusion is not based primarily upon the nature of the crime for which Rollins was serving time, but rather on his prior institutional record which includes as stated above the murder of another inmate and assaults on correctional officers and an inmate. In the Court's view, prior institutional behavior has predictive value for future institutional behavior. Also relevant is the absence of evidence that the incidents at the Rhode Island facility were provoked by someone other than Rollins.

---

3. At the time of the stabbing incident, Atlanta was a "Level Five" or maximum security institution for long term prisoners. In 1976, the average length of sentence was at least ten years and approximately 40% of the inmate population were serving time for violent offenses including robbery, kidnapping, assault, homicide, and sex offenses.

The Court concludes that the Government's negligence was the direct and proximate cause of the injuries sustained by Plaintiff.

...

NOTES

(1) Can you articulate a rule more specific than the *Restatement*'s general negligence formula, quoted in the introductory Problem in §4.01[A], that rationalizes all of the three preceding decisions?

Are there any general conclusions that you now are able to reach concerning the responsibility of those who have general control over groups of persons, with regard to injuries inflicted by some members of a group on others?

· (2) How would you describe the "rule" of each of the three cases above in terms of the procedural setting of each case? Was the court in *Butler* deciding a question of "law"?

(3) Compare with *Butler* the case of *Edwards v. Hollywood Canteen*, 27 Cal. 2d 802, 167 P.2d 729 (1946), in which a volunteer hostess at an armed forces canteen recovered against the canteen for injuries inflicted by her dance partner, a marine, when he spun her around in a series of "wild jitterbug antics." The court said that "the trier of fact could reasonably conclude that those in charge of the dance, in the exercise of due care, should have observed the marine's conduct, realized that it was likely to result in injury, and stopped it."

SPECIAL NOTE ON EMPLOYER LIABILITY FOR EMPLOYEE MISCONDUCT

A specialized example of one party's responsibility to another for the acts of third persons occurs in the employment relationship. An employer may be liable for the torts of its servant committed within the course of employment either because of the employment relationship itself or because the employer was independently negligent:

Respondeat superior: A nonfault liability. In some cases, this liability may be the nonfault vicarious liability imposed under the agency doctrine of "respondeat superior." In those cases, the liability exists just because of the employment relationship and the fact that the tort was committed within the scope of employment.

Negligent hiring or retention. In other cases, the court imposes liability because of the negligence of the defendant in hiring or retaining the employee. A particularly tragic example of this sort of event is a Texas case, involving a suit against a cab company whose driver raped and sodomized a passenger in the presence of her two young children. The Texas Supreme Court affirmed a finding that the cab company was negligent in hiring a driver with a record of several arrests that included an indictment for attempted murder for assaulting a woman with a hammer. The indictment, which had been handed down a few months before the driver was employed, was still pending at the time he was hired.* It is worth emphasis that this decision imposes liability on an employer for its negligence in relation to an intentional tort of its employee.

---

* *Salinas v. Fort Worth Cab & Baggage Co.*, 725 S.W.2d 701 (Tex. 1987). The cab company did not object to a trial court instruction holding it to a "high degree of care," and thus waived its argument that it should have been held only to a standard of ordinary care.

---

§ 4.06 Sources of Standards: Legislative Rules

INTRODUCTION TO THE ROLE OF STATUTES AND OTHER ENACTMENTS IN TORT LAW

Tort law has basically been common law. But with the rise of legislative concern with both safety and compensation, statutes now have considerable impact on judicial decisions in tort cases. These statutes are as diverse as the federal Occupational Safety and Health Act, the Flammable Fabrics Act, and the National Motor Vehicle Traffic Safety Act, and include state legislation on occupational health and safety as well as a variety of criminal and quasi-criminal statutes for the regulation of traffic.

The impact of a statutory violation in litigation may occur in several ways:

(1) A statute may provide a tort standard outright. That is, the legislature may create a tort, or may modify a tort action that already has been created. Illustratively, many state legislatures recently have changed tort rules in the fields of products liability and medical malpractice—for example, attempting to redefine the theory of liability in products cases and placing dollar limits on the amount of damages recoverable for malpractice.

(2) A court may "imply" a tort cause of action from a statute that regulates certain kinds of conduct. In this sort of situation, the statute will not specifically speak to the existence of a tort cause of action on the subject, but the court will infer from the statute a legislative purpose to permit a claimant to sue on the statute. In such cases, the court in effect views the statute as creating the cause of action.

A key case on this question is *Cort v. Ash*, 422 U.S. 66 (1975), in which the Supreme Court rejected an attempt to employ a criminal statute that prohibited corporations from contributing to campaigns to imply a private action for damages for corporate stockholders against a firm's directors. The court found that the plaintiff's claim did not fulfill a four-part test that it fashioned for the implication from statutes of private rights of action. That test inquired (1) whether the plaintiff was "one of the class for whose especial benefit the statute was enacted"; (2) whether there was "any indication of legislative intent, explicit or implicit, either to create such a remedy or to deny one"; (3) whether it was "consistent with the underlying purposes of the legislative scheme to imply such a remedy for the plaintiff"; and (4) whether "the cause of action [is] one traditionally relegated to state law, in an area basically the concern of the States, so that it would be inappropriate to infer a cause of action based solely on federal law[.]" *Id.* at 78.*

Each of these elements, save the last one, presumably would be applicable in actions based on state statutes, with the decision being based on state law.

---

* The Court later emphasized that it "did not decide that each of these facts is entitled to equal weight," and that "[t]he central inquiry remains whether Congress intended to create, either expressly or by implication, a private cause of action." *Touche Ross & Co. v. Redington*, 442 U.S. 560, 575 (1979). The Court continued to invoke the *Cort* factors in *Thompson v. Thompson*, 484 U.S. 174, 178 (1988), although Justice Scalia asserted that *Cort* had been "effectively overruled by our later opinions," *id.* at 188–189.

A decision applying the *Cort v. Ash* elements in a safety context involved an effort by a New Jersey municipality to prohibit a railroad from storing butane on a siding. The claim was that the railroad's practice violated the Hazardous Materials Transportation Act, which gave the Secretary of Transportation the authority to make regulations for the transportation of hazardous materials. In dismissing the action, the Third Circuit said, inter alia, that neither the statute nor its legislative history "reveal any intent especially to protect a class that includes the plaintiffs, municipalities, among its members"; rather, "[a]ll residents of the United States are the HMTA's intended beneficiaries." *Borough of Ridgefield v. New York S. & W. R.R.*, 810 F.2d 57, 59 (3d Cir. 1987).

(3) A third group of issues in this area concerns the question of whether conduct that technically violates a statute is actionable when the plaintiff's injury arguably is not of a sort that the drafters of the statute contemplated. The materials at §12.01, infra, treat this question.

(4) The other major category involving the use of statutes in injury cases may generally be classified as dealing with the effect of statutes in proving the standard of care. The *TMI* case that follows the Problem just below presents this sort of legal issue. As you read the case, keep in mind the possible effects that a court might give to a statutory violation—for example, making the violation conclusive that the defendant fell below the applicable standard of care, viewing the violation as creating a presumption that the defendant was negligent, or simply viewing it as providing evidence of negligence.

PROBLEM

Suppose that a city ordinance prohibits the use of slingshots, imposing criminal penalties for its violation. A boy who is on the streets at 2 a.m. uses his slingshot to fire a rock at a bat that is disappearing around the corner of a building. The missile misses the bat but hits a man who is just coming around the corner, and puts out his eye. Will the man, bringing a tort action against the boy, be able successfully to use the statute to support his case? If he can, what effect will the court give the statute? If the court will not allow use of the statute, what would be its reasons for that holding?

IN RE TMI

United States Court of Appeals, Third Circuit
67 F.3d 1103 (1995)

SCIRICA, Circuit Judge.

In 1979, an accident occurred at a nuclear power facility near Harrisburg, Pennsylvania, releasing radiation into the atmosphere and catapulting the name, "Three Mile Island," into the national consciousness. Sixteen years later, we are called on once again to consider the Three Mile Island accident as we determine the appropriate standard of care for the operators of the facility.

I. Procedural History

The accident at the Three Mile Island ("TMI") nuclear power facility occurred on March 28, 1979. As a result, thousands of area residents and businesses filed suit against the owners and operators of the facility, alleging various injuries. This case involves the consolidated claims of more than 2000 plaintiffs for personal injuries allegedly caused by exposure to radiation released during the TMI accident.

These cases began more than a decade ago, when plaintiffs filed damage actions in the Pennsylvania state courts and the Mississippi federal and state courts. After defendants removed the state cases to federal court, asserting federal jurisdiction under the Price-Anderson Act, we held that the Act created no federal cause of action and was not intended to confer jurisdiction on the federal courts.... The actions were remanded to the appropriate state courts.

Subsequently, Congress enacted the Price-Anderson Amendments Act of 1988 ("1988 Amendments" or "Amendments Act"), Pub.L. No. 100-408, 102 Stat. 1066, which expressly created a federal cause of action for "public liability actions"[2] and provided that such suits arose under the Price-Anderson Act. 42 U.S.C. §2014(hh) (1988). The Amendments Act also provided for consolidation of such actions, including those already filed, in one federal district court.... Accordingly, these personal injury actions were removed to federal court and consolidated in the Middle District of Pennsylvania. We upheld the constitutionality of the retroactive application of the federal jurisdiction provisions of the Amendments Act and remanded the actions back to the district court....

Contending they had not breached the duty of care, defendants then moved for summary judgment, which the district court denied.... After holding that federal law determines the standard of care and preempts state tort law, id. at 23, the district court found the standard of care was set by the federal regulations: 1) prescribing the maximum permissible levels of human exposure to radiation and 2) requiring radiation releases to be "as low as is reasonably achievable," which is known as the "ALARA" principle[6].... The court held that each plaintiff must prove individual exposure to radiation in order to establish causation, but not to establish a breach of the duty of care....

Upon defendants' motion, the district court certified for interlocutory appeal the duty of care and causation issues: 1) Whether 10 C.F.R. §§ 20.105 and 20.106, and not ALARA, constitute the standard of care to be applied in these actions; 2) Whether a particular Plaintiff's level of exposure to radiation or radioactive effluents relates solely to causation or also to the duty owed by Defendants.... We granted the petition for interlocutory appeal.

. . .

III. Statutory and Regulatory History

Although it is clear that federal law governs the standard of care for tort claims arising from nuclear accidents, it is more difficult to discern the precise contours of that federal duty. The question appears to be one of first impression for a federal appellate court. Accordingly, we will examine the language of the relevant statutes and regulations, and the underlying history and policies.

A. Statutes

Nearly a half century ago, Congress initiated its regulation of nuclear power through the enactment of the Atomic Energy Act of 1946, Pub.L. No. 79-585, 60 Stat. 755. The

---

2. The Amendments Act defined a "public liability action" as "any suit asserting public liability." 42 U.S.C. §2014(hh) (1988). "[P]ublic liability" was defined as "any legal liability arising out of or resulting from a nuclear incident or precautionary evacuation," except for certain claims covered by workers' compensation, incurred in wartime, or that involve the licensed property where the nuclear incident occurs. Id. §2014(w).

6. "ALARA" is defined to mean "as low as is reasonably achievable taking into account the state of technology, and the economics of improvements in relation to benefits to the public health and safety, and other societal and socioeconomic considerations, and in relation to the utilization of atomic energy in the public interest." ...

Act was designed to establish an industry to generate inexpensive electrical power, transforming "atomic power into a source of energy" and turning "swords into plowshares." ...

Although the 1946 Act designated the nuclear industry a government monopoly, Congress later decided to permit private sector involvement.... The 1954 Act "grew out of Congress' determination that the national interest would be best served if the Government encouraged the private sector to become involved in the development of atomic energy for peaceful purposes under a program of federal regulation and licensing." ...

Nevertheless, because of the unique nature of this form of energy production, the fledgling nuclear industry faced many problems, particularly: the risk of potentially vast liability in the event of a nuclear accident of a sizable magnitude.... [W]hile repeatedly stressing that the risk of a major nuclear accident was extremely remote, spokesmen for the private sector informed Congress that they would be forced to withdraw from the field if their liability were not limited by appropriate legislation....

In response, Congress enacted the Price-Anderson Act "to protect the public and to encourage the development of the atomic energy industry." ... The Act limited the potential civil liability of nuclear plant operators and provided federal funds to help pay damages caused by nuclear accidents. Id. Congress has amended the Price-Anderson Act three times, most recently in 1988, "provid[ing] a mechanism whereby the federal government can continue to encourage private sector participation in the beneficial uses of nuclear materials." ...

Throughout this period, Congress repeatedly sought to encourage the development of the nuclear power industry. Yet, Congress has continued the "dual regulation of nuclear-powered electricity generation: the Federal Government maintains complete control of the safety and 'nuclear' aspects of energy generation; the States exercise their traditional authority over the need for additional generating capacity, the type of generating facilities to be licensed, land use, ratemaking, and the like." ...

B. Regulations

Volume 10 of the Code of Federal Regulations (1979) governs energy matters, and its first chapter regulates the Nuclear Regulatory Commission ("NRC"). Parts 20 and 50 of Chapter 1 are the relevant sections.

1. 10 C.F.R. Part 20

Part 20 of 10 C.F.R. ch. 1 outlines "Standards for Protection Against Radiation." Under the "General Provisions" of Part 20, § 20.1(c) provides a statement of the ALARA principle: In accordance with recommendations of the Federal Radiation Council, approved by the President, persons engaged in activities under licenses issued by the Nuclear Regulatory Commission ... should, in addition to complying with the requirements set forth in this part, make every reasonable effort to maintain radiation exposures, and releases of radioactive materials in effluents to unrestricted areas, *as low as is reasonably achievable*. The term "as low as is reasonably achievable" means as low as is reasonably achievable taking into account the state of technology, and the economics of improvements in relation to benefits to the public health and safety, and other societal and socioeconomic considerations, and in relation to the utilization of atomic energy in the public interest. (emphasis added).

Immediately following the "General Provisions" of Part 20 is a subpart covering "Permissible Doses, Levels, and Concentrations," which regulates exposures of radiation to persons on the property of a nuclear facility, see 10 C.F.R. §§ 20.101-.104,[12] as well as those off premises, see id. § 20.105–.106. The latter regulations, governing "unrestricted areas,"[13] are relevant here because plaintiffs were outside the TMI premises when the alleged radiation exposures occurred.

Section 20.105 sets the "[p]ermissible levels of radiation in unrestricted areas," i.e., outside the TMI facility's boundaries. It mandates that the NRC approve license applications if the applicant shows its plan is not likely to cause anyone to receive radiation in excess of 0.5 rem[14] per year. § 20.105(a). In subsection (b), the regulation provides that except as authorized by the NRC, no licensee shall cause "[r]adiation levels which, if an individual were continually present in the area, could result in his receiving a dose in excess of" two millirems in any hour or 100 millirems in any week. The parties dispute whether the § 20.105 standard governing off-site exposure was violated during or after the TMI accident.

While § 20.105 defines the levels of radiation permitted in unrestricted areas, § 20.106 defines the levels of radioactivity permitted in liquid or airborne effluents released off premises. It provides that licensees "shall not possess, use, or transfer licensed material so as to release to an unrestricted area radioactive material in concentrations which exceed the limits specified in Appendix 'B', Table II of this part, except as authorized...." Appendix B then lists more than 100 isotopes of almost 100 radioactive elements and provides the maximum permissible level of releases. Defendants admit that the radiation levels at the boundary of the TMI facility exceeded the § 20.106 standards after the 1979 accident.[15] Nevertheless, they claim that no plaintiff was in an area exposed to the impermissible levels.

[The court summarizes arguments in favor of both the ALARA standard and sections 20.105 and 20.106 as setting the standard of care. It concludes:]

After reviewing the regulations, the reasons behind their promulgation, and the relevant case law, we hold that §§ 20.105 and 20.106 constitute the federal standard of care.[24] These regulations represent the considered judgment of the relevant regulatory

---

12. These regulations apply to persons in "restricted areas," which are defined as "any area access to which is controlled by the licensee for purposes of protection of individuals from exposure to radiation and radioactive materials." 10 C.F.R. § 20.3(a)(14).

13. An "unrestricted area" is "any area access to which is not controlled by the licensee for purposes of protection of individuals from exposure to radiation and radioactive materials, and any area used for residential quarters." Id. § 20.1(a)(17).

14. Doses of radiation of different ionizations are expressed in "rems," a unit of measurement that "embodies both the magnitude of the dose and its biological effectiveness." U.S. Dep't of Commerce, Permissible Dose From External Sources of Ionizing Radiation: National Bureau of Standards Handbook 59 30–31 (1954); see also 10 C.F.R. § 20.4(c) (defining rem as "a measure of the dose of any ionizing radiation to body tissues in terms of its estimated biological effect relative to a dose of one roentgen (r) of X-rays").

15. See Appellants' Brf. at 6 ("[T]he concentrations of radioactivity at the site boundary exceeded the permissible levels set by 10 C.F.R. § 20.106 (1979)"); id. at 33 ("[D]efendants would concede" that "the amount of radiation at the edge of Three Mile Island exceeded the federal permissible dose levels"). Nevertheless, defendants contend "that no excess releases reached any inhabited areas, much less those inhabited by Plaintiffs. For example, Defendants' evidence indicates that the only regions where the effluents and the dose exceeded the federal levels were Three Mile Island itself, some of the Susquehanna River, and some other uninhabited islands in the river." ...

24. The Restatement (Second) of Torts expressly provides that, in certain situations, a "court may adopt as the standard of conduct of a reasonable man the requirements of a legislative enactment or an administrative regulation." Restatement (Second) of Torts § 286 (1965); see also W. Page Keeton et al., Prosser and Keeton on the Law of Torts § 36, at 220 (5th ed. 1984) (citing numerous cases) ("When a statute provides that under certain circumstances particular acts shall be done or not done, it may be interpreted as fixing a standard for all members of the community, from which

bodies—the Federal Radiation Council, EPA, AEC, and NRC—on the appropriate levels of radiation to which the general public may be exposed.[25] See, e.g., 25 Fed.Reg. 8595, 8595 (1960) (Sections 20.105 and 20.106 "provide an appropriate regulatory basis for protection of the health and safety of employees and the public without imposing undue burdens upon licensed users of radioactive material."). In fact, the heading for this category of regulations is "Permissible Doses, Levels, and Concentrations," and the relevant regulations are phrased in terms of the maximum levels of radiation that may be released....

Although plaintiffs assert that § 20.105 applies exclusively to nuclear plant employees, we disagree. Part 20 of 10 C.F.R. ch. 1 is divided into separate sections governing permissible dose limits for individuals in "restricted areas," see §§ 20.101, 20.103, and "unrestricted areas," see §§ 20.105, 20.106. The definitions of "restricted" and "unrestricted areas"[26] demonstrate that the C.F.R. sections governing persons in "unrestricted areas" were intended to cover persons outside a nuclear plant's boundaries, i.e., the general public. The case law, while differing over the use of the ALARA standard, appears to have uniformly accepted this meaning. See, e.g., Akins, 8 Cal.Rptr.2d at 794; Crawford, 784 F.Supp. at 447.

Plaintiffs also contend that the Part 20 dose standards govern only during normal operating conditions, not during accidents. But neither the language of the regulations nor its history suggests this interpretation. Instead, we believe the Part 20 dose limits were intended as the maximum permitted under all conditions, accident and normal operations alike. The NRC itself has adopted this interpretation, stating it "believes that the dose limits for normal operation should remain the primary guidelines in emergencies," 56 Fed.Reg. 23360, 23365 (1991), and we believe this agency interpretation is entitled to some deference. See Chevron, U.S.A. Inc. v. Natural Resources Defense Council, Inc., ...

For many of the same reasons that we adopt §§ 20.105 and 20.106 as the applicable standard of care, we reject the ALARA regulations as part of that standard....

· · ·

Adoption of a standard as vague as ALARA would give no real guidance to operators and would allow juries to fix the standard case by case and plant by plant. An operator

---

it is negligence to deviate. The same may be true of ... regulations of administrative bodies."). We believe it appropriate to adopt §§ 20.105 and 20.106 as the standard of conduct in this situation. As one commentator noted:

> The element of breach of duty is a critical issue in the adjudication of radiation cases and one that presents significant problems. The problems arise out of the necessity to create or adopt a legally sufficient standard by which to measure breach. The answer to the problem in this highly regulated area should be straightforward: compliance or noncompliance with applicable government safety standards provides an excellent measure of breach.

David S. Gooden, Radiation Injury and the Law, 1989 B.Y.U.L.Rev. 1155, 1167–68 (1989); see also John C. Berghoff, Jr., NRC Regulations as a Standard for Legal Actions: Has the Public Shield Been Forged Into a Private Sword?, in Nuclear Litigation 1984, at 57, 66 (PLI Litig. & Admin. Practice Course Handbook Series No. 272, 1984) ("It can be argued that the nuclear industry is appropriate for considering compliance to be conclusive proof of 'non-negligence' because Congress and the NRC have retained such close control over radiological hazards. The nation's leading experts on radiation danger were involved in establishing the federal standards, and a reasonably prudent person should be able to rely on them as a standard of conduct.")....

25. As we have noted, these agencies have promulgated different standards regarding radiation levels for workers at nuclear power plants....

acting in the utmost good faith and diligence could still find itself liable for failing to meet such an elusive and undeterminable standard. Our holding protects the public and provides owners and operators of nuclear power plants with a definitive standard by which their conduct will be measured.[30]

. . .

[Affirmed in part and reversed in part.]

NOTES

(1) What is the procedural effect of the court's decision concerning sections 20.105 and 20.106? Of what burdens does the decision free the plaintiffs? What burdens remain on them?

(2) It is rather unusual for a court to view an administrative regulation, as contrasted with violation of a statute, as setting the standard of care. Why did this court give such a strong effect to a regulatory violation?

(3) Would it have been better to decide that the violation of sections 20.105 and 20.106 was only evidence of negligence? What would be the competing arguments?

(4) Compare the following formulations concerning the effect of statutory violations:

(a) They should create a per se form of liability—that is, the violation should be conclusive on the negligence issue, and the court should permit no defense based on the plaintiff's conduct.

(b) Statutory violation is "negligence per se," the effect of which is that the violation is conclusive on the question of whether the defendant used due care, but the defendant may offer a defense based on the plaintiff's conduct. (Should the defendant be allowed to offer an excuse to, or justification of, his conduct that otherwise would be considered "negligence per se"?)

(c) Violations create a "presumption" of negligence. The technical definition of a presumption views it as a rule of law that one must draw certain conclusions from certain facts. In this view, which is not always followed, a "presumption" is not "evidence," and if it is rebutted, it is destroyed.

(i) Is there a practical difference between a rebuttable presumption and "negligence per se"?

(ii) Is there a practical difference between an irrebuttable presumption and "liability per se"?

(d) Violation of a statute is simply evidence of negligence, to be weighed by the jury along with other evidence on that issue, both pro and con.

(5) Should there be a difference between the effect that courts will give, in tort-type damage actions, to:

---

30. As one court noted, in adopting parallel regulations applicable to nuclear plant workers as the standard of care:

In a highly technical field such as this, although a plaintiff should be provided a very high level [of] protection from excessive exposure to radiation, a defendant public utility should also be provided with some clear statement regarding how it may limit a worker's dose without exposing the worker to injury or itself to liability. O'Conner v. Commonwealth Edison Co., 748 F.Supp. 672, 678 (C.D.Ill.1990), aff'd, 13 F.3d 1090, 1103–05 (7th Cir.)....

(a) the violation of the regulations in the TMI case;

(b) the violation of this road safety rule: "The driver of a vehicle overtaking another vehicle proceeding in the same direction shall pass to the left thereof at a safe distance and shall not again drive to the right side of the roadway until safely clear of the overtaken vehicle";

(c) the violation of a regulation concerning construction excavations, which requires those making such excavations to shore them up or cut vertical walls back to a safe angle of repose; and

(d) the violation of a building code section that requires that the paving on top of the sidewalk vaults must be "flush with the pavement," in a case where there was a one-inch projection of the hinge of a vault covering, on which the plaintiff stumbled?

(6) It should be pointed out, in this connection, that a threshold question in cases involving the effect of statutes in injury cases is whether the legislation applies at all to the event at issue. Illustrative is a highly particularized statute, the Federal Safety Appliance Act, which has generated litigation concerning the requirement that rail cars be equipped with "couplers coupling automatically by impact, and capable of being uncoupled, without the necessity of individuals going between the ends of the vehicles." As explained in a Supreme Court opinion, "[a] coupler consists of a knuckle joined to the end of a drawbar, which itself is fastened to a housing mechanism on the car." In the normal course of railroading, drawbars have a tendency to become misaligned, and railroad employees have to realign them by hand "to ensure proper coupling." In the case at issue, the plaintiff injured his back when he went between cars to adjust a misaligned drawbar. Although the Court agreed with him that the duty imposed that the statute imposed on the railroad was an "absolute" one, requiring neither a showing of negligence or of a defect, it rejected his claim that the misaligned drawbar constituted a violation of the statute for the purposes of this civil litigation. The Court distinguished what it labeled "failure-to-perform cases" as involving "malfunctioning equipment," but it refused to find "that a misaligned drawbar is, as a matter of law, a malfunctioning drawbar." Given that the misalignment of drawbars was such a common event—an "inevitable byproduct" of stresses on them created by the curving of track—the court expressed itself "hesitant to adopt a reading of [the statute] that would suggest that almost every railroad car in service for nearly a century has been in violation of the SAA." *Norfolk & W. Ry. Co. v. Hiles*, 516 U.S. 400, 412 (1996).

One may compare a decision on the question of whether in-line skates are a "vehicle," regulated by the safety rules applicable to highways. In a case involving a fatal accident to a 19-year-old skater who was skating at night in a dark area, the court concluded that in-line skates were a "vehicle." The defendant claimed, inter alia, that the decedent should have taken greater safety precautions, for example, using lights or reflectors, as required by the state highway traffic regulation statute. Saying that in-line skaters "[i]deally" should not use the highway, the court declared that if they do, "they must comply with pertinent statutory provisions—particularly in regard to appropriate equipment—that are in place for their safety and the safety of other travellers." It thus affirmed a judgment for the defendants based on a jury finding that the plaintiff's decedent was 85 per cent causally negligent. *Boschee v. Duevel*, 530 N.W.2d 834, 840 (Minn. Ct. App. 1995).

(7) Morris reviews the general problem in his essay, *The Role of Criminal Statutes in Negligence Actions*, 49 COLUM. L. REV. 21 (1949).

(8) Consider the following documents and testimony, offered to define a medical standard of care:

(a) Standards of the Department of Health and Human Services, set up to govern the administration of federal medical grant programs

(b) Hospital rules and regulations

(c) The testimony of a doctor

(d) The testimony of a nurse

(e) Recommendations for improvements in medical practice, made in a study done by private researchers under funding from the National Institutes of Health

(f) A statement of opinion by a first-year medical student.

Would violations of standards articulated in any of these documents or statements appropriately be held "negligence as a matter of law"? Would any of them be held not to constitute even evidence of negligence? What suppositions do your answers embody about the ability of the judicial process to find medical "facts"? To make social determinations of medical policy?

§ 4.07 Sources of Standards: Professional Communities

MEDICAL MALPRACTICE: THEORIES OF LIABILITY

Medical malpractice is one of the most controversial areas of tort liability. It pits two of the learned professions against each other in struggles that often involve grievous loss to the claimant and serious potential professional risk to the physician. There is particular irony in the fact that the same medical sophistication that has enhanced the doctor's opportunity to alleviate pain and to save lives has created more possibilities of medical error.

As you read these materials, keep in mind that the legal doctrine that applies to medical malpractice is varied and plastic. The theories of liability range from battery to negligence and include a category simply called "medical malpractice." The cases focus on the standard of care for negligence claims in malpractice cases, but also refer to such concepts as informed consent, and the methods of proving breach of the standard of care.

PROBLEM

A study of men and women with symptoms of coronary artery disease found that physicians recommended men for bypass surgery from seven to ten times more than women. A press story quoted an author of the report as saying that this data indicated "an enormous, disturbing difference that cannot be explained by the distribution of heart disease in the population." The study reported that doctors would dismiss symptoms like chest pain and shortness of breath as being something other than heart disease in twice as many cases involving women as men. However, some authorities stressed that men are often considered better candidates for coronary surgery because they tend to have larger coronary arteries than women.[1]

---

1. Michael Specter, *Heart Bypass Surgery Recommended for Comparatively Few Women*, WASH. POST, July 22, 1987, at A3.

Do you think that this evidence, or testimony by the author of the study that embodied these findings, could be used on behalf of a woman who sued a cardiologist for not recommending her for bypass surgery, if another cardiologist would testify that the claimant had clinical symptoms indicating that a bypass operation was the optimum medical strategy? What subconscious biases against admitting such evidence would the claimant's attorney have to combat? How would the attorney do that?

OUELLETTE v. SUBAK
Minnesota Supreme Court
391 N.W.2d 810 (1986)

KELLEY, JUSTICE.

The father of a child born with brain damage brought this negligence action on behalf of the child and himself against two medical general practitioners. The trial court refused to give the doctors' requested jury instructions that physicians are not responsible for an honest error in judgment. A Hennepin County jury by special verdict found the doctors negligent and awarded $1 million in damages. Following denial of their post-trial motions and entry of judgment on the verdict, the doctors appealed. Holding that the trial court erred when it refused to give the so-called "honest error in judgment" instruction, the court of appeals reversed and remanded for a new trial on all issues....

For the purpose of this opinion, the Ouellettes will be denominated appellants and the physicians, respondents. Appellants here challenge the court of appeals' reversal, claiming the trial court correctly refused to give the "honest error in judgment" instruction. Respondents allege error in admission of an alleged expert's testimony on causation, and claim insufficiency of the evidence to support the findings of negligence and causation. We affirm the court of appeals.

Kristian Ouellette is a brain-impaired child with profound physical and mental retardation. Six and one-half years after his birth he was functioning developmentally between the age of 6 and 13 months. He can sit and crawl, but cannot stand without braces nor walk without help. He can drink from a cup and hold a spoon but is unable to feed himself. He can neither talk nor communicate basic needs. His problems are permanent. Doctors expect no significant development in his higher intellectual function nor in his self help skills. His parents contend his problems were caused by the negligence of respondents, two family practitioners—Dr. Barbara H. Subak and Dr. Maxine O. Nelson. The negligence claimed is failure to intervene in a prolonged pregnancy.

Julie Ouellette, then 20, suspected she was pregnant with her first child in February 1977. She and her husband had regularly practiced birth control but had a single act of unprotected intercourse on January 23, 1977. On March 11, she first saw Dr. Subak, a board certified family practitioner. Approximately 15 percent of Dr. Subak's practice was obstetrics. She told the doctor that the onset of her last menstrual period was January 5, 1977. A pregnancy test was positive. After taking a history and making a physical examination, Dr. Subak calculated the "estimated date of confinement" (EDC), or due date, as October 12, 1977.

At a May 12 prenatal visit, Dr. Maxine Nelson, Dr. Subak's associate, detected no fetal heart tones, usually heard at 18 to 19 weeks. These heart tones were detected by Dr. Subak for the first time on June 11.

As the pregnancy progressed, Dr. Subak began to entertain doubts about the validity of the EDC. A September 8 examination revealed that the fetus was still floating rather than "engaging" in the pelvis. Normally, the fetus descends into the mother's pelvis approximately one month before delivery. On a September 28 examination, the fetus was still floating, a fact Dr. Subak considered unusual at 38 weeks, two weeks before the calculated due date.[4]

More doubts as to the EDC were raised in Dr. Subak's mind when at an October 7 examination, only five days from the EDC, the fetus was still floating and the cervix was still closed. On a pelvimetry, an x-ray of the pelvis, taken that day, the femoral epiphysis of the fetus—the growth plate at the end of the femur—was not visible. The femoral epiphysis, which ossifies separately from the femur, is normally visible by x-ray on a male fetus at 36 weeks.

Five days after the EDC, on October 17, Dr. Subak found the cervix was beginning to soften, but the head of the fetus was barely into the pelvis. A week later Dr. Nelson noted a soft but closed cervix and that the baby's head was at the same station in the birth canal as the previous week. Similar findings were made on November 2.

On November 9 Dr. Subak admitted Mrs. Ouellette to Metropolitan Medical Center to induce labor and conduct an oxytocin challenge test (OCT).[5]

Dr. Subak consulted with Dr. John N. Maunder, a board-certified obstetrician. Although Mrs. Ouellette was at 43 weeks, or three weeks overdue by medical history, Dr. Subak felt from her clinical observation the pregnancy was at 39 weeks. Dr. Maunder examined Mrs. Ouellette and found her cervix thick and closed and her membranes intact. He saw no immediate need to terminate the pregnancy. Dr. Maunder noted the baby was very active, making it difficult to get heart tracings. He considered the EDC off and advised Dr. Subak to stimulate labor cautiously and conduct a prolonged OCT.

Results of the OCT were normal on November 9 and 10. Mrs. Ouellette did not go into labor and was discharged from the Center. She returned November 17 for another OCT which was again negative and failed to lead to real labor. When Dr. Nelson saw Mrs. Ouellette on November 25, she observed the cervix was softening but the fetus' head was still floating. On November 30, Dr. Subak admitted Mrs. Ouellette for another OCT and induction of labor. The OCT was again normal but Mrs. Ouellette still did not progress into labor. Dr. Nelson visited the patient in the hospital that evening and consulted with Dr. John T. Moehn, an obstetrician. On examination, he found the fetus was large but still floating. He recommended terminating the pregnancy by Caesarean section. The situation was not considered an emergency because the fetal monitoring strips were normal, indicating the baby was not in jeopardy.

The following morning, Dr. Mitchell Pincus performed a Caesarean section and delivered a baby weighing 9 pounds, 13 ounces. The Caesarean section was performed be-

---

4. Only four percent of babies are born on the actual "due date," calculated as 40 weeks after the onset of the last menstrual period. Delivery anytime between 38 and 42 weeks is considered a term pregnancy. Approximately 10 percent of births occur after the 42nd week and are considered higher risk. After 44 weeks, risks of fetal death or injury increase significantly. This occurs principally because the placenta, the organ that transfers nutrients and oxygen from the mother to the fetus, deteriorates. This deterioration is called placental insufficiency.

5. The oxytocin challenge test is designed to measure fetal well-being by seeing how the fetus responds to the stress of induced labor contractions. This is done by monitoring fetal heart tones while stimulating contractions. A negative or normal result means the baby is not in distress and can remain in the uterus another week.

cause the baby was considered large and post-mature. Dr. Pincus, however, observed no classic signs of "post-mature syndrome," such as shriveled skin. He found no gross abnormalities in the placenta, so it was not sent to a pathologist for microscopic evaluation. Dr. Pincus also recalled no meconium in the amniotic fluid, an indicator of fetal distress.

The evidence is conflicting on the state of Kristian's health at birth and during his hospital stay. Generally, the appellants assert he displayed signs indicative of previous fetal distress. To the contrary, the medical evidence, photographs, and recognized tests such as the Apgar scores,[6] respondents contend, show the absence of the alleged fetal distress blamed for Kristian's admittedly severe developmental impairments.

The complaint charged the two physicians with negligence in permitting a prolonged pregnancy, failing to timely induce labor or recognize increased risks of injury to the fetus, and ignoring signs of fetal distress. In defense, the physicians alleged: (1) they neither erred in their diagnosis nor treatment of the pregnancy; (2) if they did err, it was not negligence, but an honest error in professional judgment, and (3) any alleged negligence was not the cause of Kristian's condition.

1. The trial court refused to give the "honest error in judgment" instruction found in the last sentence of 4 Minn.Dist. Judges Ass'n, Minnesota Practice, JIG II, 425 G-S (2d ed.1974).[7] This was done notwithstanding one of respondents' defenses was that even had they erred in handling Mrs. Ouellette's pregnancy, the error was not negligence but an honest error in judgment. The portion of the JIG II, 425 G-S instruction omitted reads:

> A [physician] is not a guarantor of a cure or a good result from his treatment and he is not responsible for an honest error in judgment in choosing between accepted methods of treatment.

The court of appeals ruled that elimination of the "honest error in judgment" instruction rendered the trial court's instruction insufficient to state the standard of care applicable to a physician. In doing so, it noted and relied upon the fact the "honest error in judgment" rule has been recognized in Minnesota since at least 1907 and followed in a long line of medical negligence cases up until recent times. Ouellette, 379 N.W.2d at 128, 130. That observation and reliance was well placed. See, e.g., Staloch v. Holm, 100 Minn. 276, 111 N.W. 264 (1907)....

In Staloch, the court first outlined reasons for applying the rule in medical negligence cases:

> In an ordinary action for negligence, that a man has acted according to his best judgment is no defense. The standard of careful conduct is not the opinion of the individual, but is the conduct of an ordinarily prudent man under the circumstances.... With respect to matters resting upon pure theory, judgment,

---

6. Apgar scores are given on a 10 point scale with 2 points assigned to each of 5 areas: heart rate, respiration, muscle tone, reflex irritation and skin color.

7. The full instruction given by the trial court is as follows:

In performing professional services for a patient, a physician must use that degree of skill and learning which is normally possessed and used by physicians in good standing in a similar practice and under like circumstances.

In the application of this skill and learning, the physician must also use reasonable care.

The fact standing alone that a good result may not have followed from the treatment by a physician is not evidence of negligence or unskilled treatment.

and opinion, however, there is a generally recognized variation from this sound general principle....

Cases of malpractice may be within the exception. A physician entitled to practice his profession, possessing the requisite qualifications, and applying his skill and judgment with due care, is not ordinarily liable for damages consequent upon an honest mistake or an error of judgment in making a diagnosis, in prescribing treatment, or in determining upon an operation, where there is reasonable doubt as to the nature of the physical conditions involved or as to what should have been done, in accordance with recognized authority and good current practice....

. . . .

... Most professional men are retained or employed in order that they may give the benefit of their peculiar and individual judgment and skill. A lawyer, for example, does not contract to win a lawsuit, but to give his best opinion and ability. He has never been held to liability in damages for a failure to determine disputed questions of law in accordance with their final decision by courts of appeal. It would be just as unreasonable to hold a physician responsible for an honest error of judgment on so uncertain problems as are presented in surgery and medicine.[8]

100 Minn. at 280–283, 111 N.W. at 266–67.

Moreover, in protecting a physician from liability for mere errors in judgment in choosing between alternate diagnoses or treatments, this court has followed a rule recognized by at least 29 other jurisdictions....

Appellants would have us rule: (a) that even if the "honest error in judgment" instruction correctly states the law applicable in certain circumstances, it was inapplicable here and, therefore, the trial court's instruction was sufficient to convey a clear and correct understanding of the law to the jury ... and (b) that this court should follow a so-called "modern trend" of authorities excluding the "honest error" language from the physician liability instruction.

(a) We agree with the majority of the court of appeals that if the respondents were entitled to the "honest error in judgment" instruction, the trial court's refusal to give it in this case was prejudicial error. Here the standard of care was crucial. The respondent physicians were receiving conflicting information. Their physical observations and tests, made periodically during the course of the pregnancy, conflicted with the presumed date of conception, and therefore the EDC. Determination of whether to allow the pregnancy to continue or terminate depended upon an exercise of their judgment at a time when a reasonable doubt existed as to the stage of the pregnancy and what should be done. Failure to give the requested instructions deprived the physician of the right to have the conduct evaluated in that light, and likewise deprived their counsel of the right to argue the issue before the jury.

(b) Moreover, we reject, in part at least, appellants' invitation to follow a few courts that have rejected the "honest error" rule claiming it to be potentially misleading ... or claiming it presumably conflicts with ordinary care language suggesting a disjunctive

---

8. Indeed, this court has recently applied the honest error rule in attorney malpractice cases. See, e.g., *Cook v. Connolly*, 366 N.W.2d 287, 292 (Minn.1985) (no liability for error within bounds of an honest exercise of professional judgment); *Glenna v. Sullivan*, 310 Minn. 162, 169, 245 N.W.2d 869, 872–73 (1976) (good faith judgment, even if error, not deemed malpractice).

standard of care for a physician; or claiming the language "confuses" the jury by implying only bad faith errors are actionable....

Nevertheless, appellants' contention, joined by at least two dissenting judges of the court of appeals, that the words "honest error" are inherently subjective and inject into a negligence action irrelevancies of good or bad faith, is not completely meritless. Elimination of subjective words such as "honest" or "good faith" while retaining a jury instruction on the limitations of professional liability seems to us to strike a medium that will meet most of the objections raised about the "honest error in judgment" rule, but yet serve to caution the jury that liability should not be imposed merely because of a bad result or the "wrong" choice of an accepted method of professional care.

Professionals are hired for their judgment and skill. If there is a lack of skill (the knife slips for a doctor or a statute of limitations is missed by a lawyer), we have a straight-forward enough malpractice claim. But if the claim involves a question of professional judgment, a choice of strategies or treatment, there may be a need, as we explained in Staloch v. Holm, 100 Minn. 276, 111 N.W. 264 (1907), to caution the trier of fact in applying the standard of care to the professional's conduct. The instruction that a doctor "is not responsible for an honest error in judgment in choosing between accepted methods of treatment," is an attempt to meet this problem, but the instruction, because it tries to set out the Staloch rationale in shorthand fashion, tends to be subjective and, perhaps on occasion, misleading.

If there are two methods of treatment for a particular medical condition, both accepted by the medical profession, then it is a matter of professional opinion or judgment which is best, and the doctor's choice of either is, ordinarily, not negligence. But what if the two methods of treatment depend on different factual bases, i.e., if one method is acceptable if the facts are one way and the other method is acceptable if the facts are another way, and neither method is acceptable for both sets of facts? Then the doctor who fails to use reasonable care to ascertain the facts may be negligent if he or she does not choose the accepted method of treatment for the factual condition a reasonably prudent doctor would have ascertained.

But what if, at the time a decision must be made, all the requisite facts, even with the exercise of reasonable care, cannot be ascertained and either of two methods of treatment reasonably appears acceptable? At times a doctor may have to make a decision on the basis of incomplete, unclear, or tentative data, a situation which leaves a doctor vulnerable to hindsight and second guessing if the result is bad. Because of this problem, particularly characteristic of a professional practice, this court in Staloch said a doctor should not ordinarily be liable for an honest error of judgment *where there is reasonable doubt* as to the nature of the physical conditions involved or as to what should have been done." Id., 100 Minn. at 281, 111 N.W. at 266 (emphasis added).

Upon reflection we now conclude the time has come to hold that in professional malpractice cases the mostly subjective "honest error in judgment" language is inappropriate in defining the scope of the professional's duty toward those the professional serves. In our view, henceforth, in a medical negligence case, preferably the jury should be instructed as follows: A doctor is not negligent simply because his or her efforts prove unsuccessful. The fact a doctor may have chosen a method of treatment that later proves to be unsuccessful is not negligence if the treatment chosen was an accepted treatment on the basis of the information available to the doctor at the time a choice had to be made; a doctor must, however, use reasonable care to obtain the information needed to exercise his or her professional judgment, and an unsuccessful method of treatment chosen because of a failure to use such reasonable care would be negligence.

Notwithstanding that conclusion, it does not follow that the court of appeals erred in remanding this case for a new trial. An extremely close issue existed whether the respondents' prenatal judgment not to terminate the pregnancy was due to failure to exercise reasonable care. In the light of the facts of this case, had the jury been given even the modified instruction that we today propose eliminating the "honest error" language, the verdict might well have been different. This is particularly true because of the existence of controverted causation issues. Therefore, we agree with the court of appeals that failure to sufficiently inform the jury on professional liability rules was prejudicial, requiring a new trial.

2. Respondents on appeal contend that Dr. Stephen Smith, a pediatric neurologist who testified as an expert witness for the plaintiffs, was incompetent to testify on the obstetric cause of Kristian's condition. Respondents assert that Dr. Smith was utterly inexperienced and unqualified in the field of obstetrics. He had never managed a pregnancy nor had he delivered a baby in the ten years preceding the trial. His sole experience in delivering babies occurred while he was an intern during his first year out of medical school. He had no expertise in the use and analysis of oxytocin challenge tests. He admitted he was unqualified to read OCT fetal monitoring strips. He did not regularly read obstetrical/gynecological journals. All those facts were educed on cross-examination and therefore were known to the jury. In claiming Dr. Smith's testimonial incompetency to testify on the issue of causation, respondents rely on Lundgren v. Eustermann, 370 N.W.2d 877 (Minn.1985) where we did emphasize that a witness testifying as an expert must have some practical knowledge or experience. Here the trial judge could have found, unlike the witness in Lundgren, that Dr. Smith did have at least a minimal practical experience.

Determination of witness competency is a question of fact within the discretionary province of the trial judge. Unless the judge's ruling is based on an erroneous view of the law or is clearly not justified by the evidence, it will not be set aside by an appellate court.... Notwithstanding its existence, that discretion is not without bounds. We have held certain witnesses incompetent in medical negligence cases....

In this case, the resolution of the challenge to the competency of Dr. Smith is extremely close. Had we been in the position of the trial judge, we might well have found Dr. Smith incompetent to testify as an expert on the issue of obstetrical causation. However, we cannot conclude the admission of his testimony was reversible error. It was not clearly erroneous. Additionally, the admission of the causation opinion of Dr. Smith was not prejudicial. By cross-examination, respondents were able to point out not only the inherent weakness of his opinion, given the absence of clinical evidence, but also his minimal training and experience in the field of obstetrics. Finally, we note that respondents elicited an opinion on causation from a defense expert who was also, like Dr. Smith, a pediatric neurologist.

3. Lastly, respondents contend the evidence is insufficient as a matter of law to sustain the jury verdict finding them causally negligent and responsible for Kristian's damages. If respondents are correct, of course, the judgments of the trial court should be reversed, and a remand for a new trial would be unnecessary.

We commence our consideration with reiterating the fundamental rule that jury verdicts are to be set aside only if manifestly contrary to the evidence viewed in a light most favorable to the verdict.... A verdict will not be set aside unless the evidence against it is practically conclusive....

A reading of this record demonstrates that the issues of negligence and obstetrical causation were not only contraverted, but extremely close. Had proper instructions been given to the jury, the jury's verdict could well have been different. However, without reciting the often conflicting evidence in detail, we are convinced resolution of those issues was for the jury. If properly instructed, the jury could find the existence or lack of negligence and causation. Accordingly, since we cannot concur with the respondents' contention that the evidence against the verdict was "practically conclusive" we decline to set aside the verdict and order entry of judgment notwithstanding the verdict. Accordingly, we affirm the court of appeals and remand for new trial on all issues.

...

NOTES

(1) Do you think the opinion in *Ouellette* clarifies the law? If you were lecturing to a group of new pediatric residents, how would you describe the law embodied in the *Ouellette* case to them, in a few paragraphs?

Do you think the standard announced in the opinion represents an advance in terms of the jury's ability to understand instructions on the law?

(2) Are there broader social stakes at issue than whether a million dollars passes from Drs. Subak and Nelson to the Ouellettes?

(3) A threshold question with respect to proof of malpractice is whether the plaintiff must present any expert testimony in order to get to the jury. We deal with this problem infra § 10.04. Sometimes the existence of some other authoritative pronouncement will substitute for expert testimony. An example is a case in which the Louisiana Supreme Court employed hospital bylaws to establish the standard of care of a hospital and physician with reference to the duty of an emergency room doctor to notify the chief of the hospital's service when a doctor refuses a call. In this case, after determining that an emergency patient did not have insurance, the thoracic surgeon who was on call asked that the patient be transferred. The hospital's bylaws specifically commanded that emergency room personnel "should ... call the chief of the service who is responsible for getting someone there or taking care of it himself," but no such report was made. The court observed that the bylaws defined the standard of care. *Hastings v. Baton Rouge Gen. Hosp.*, 498 So.2d 713, 722 (La. 1986).

(4) We have seen that one of Learned Hand's great pronouncements on negligence standards was that one could not rely on industry custom to set the standard of care. See supra § 4.02[B]. A striking example of a possible application of the principle appears in the astonishing report that two-thirds of psychiatrists in a survey said that they had treated patients "who had been sexually involved with previous therapists." *Mandatory Reporting of Psychiatrist Sex Sought*, AMERICAN MEDICAL NEWS, May 1, 1987, at 3. If these statistics are reliable, but if standard psychiatric treatises indicate that it is a breach of professional ethics to have sexual relations with patients, would it be a per se violation of the standard of psychiatric care to have sexual relations with a patient, even if the psychiatrist claims that he or she was employing that method toward a therapeutic goal? Note also that of the two-thirds of psychiatrists who confided their patients' prior involvements with other therapists, only eight percent had made reports about those involvements. Would the failure to make that report necessarily be negligent?

(5) In a Minnesota case, a man told an attorney about an episode in a hospital, in which a surgeon placed a clamp on his carotid artery to relieve problems associated with

an aneurysm. Within a couple of days after the clamp was implanted on the artery, the man suffered unexpected paralysis and loss of speech. In this case, according to the plaintiff's testimony, the defendant said that he did not think there was "a legal case" but that he would discuss the matter with his partner. The plaintiff asserted that she understood that if the defendant changed his mind he would call her, and when he did not, she assumed that meant "that there wasn't a case." The state supreme court held it sufficient in a legal malpractice action to present expert testimony that the "minimum" an attorney should do in deciding on the merits of a possible medical malpractice claim is to review hospital records and consult with an expert on that area of the law. In a case with those facts, the court affirmed a plaintiff's judgment based on testimony of his expert to that effect, as well as testimony of a defendant's expert who distinguished the obligation of a lawyer who decides not to take a case—which is simply to inform the potential client of his refusal—and the duty of a lawyer who is asked to render an opinion on the potential merits of a case. *Togstad v. Vesely, Otto, Miller & Keefe*, 291 N.W.2d 686 (Minn. 1980).

(6) The standard of care for physicians presumably is the same for all patients, rich and poor. Is this realistic, given that patients are spread out along a long economic spectrum?

Could you visualize the development of a flexible medical standard of care that set a minimum for care rendered to all patients, with the understanding that the standard became higher for care given to patients who were able to pay more for especially highly qualified physicians and for frontier technology?

PROBLEM

A fifty-five-year-old man, a resident of a small Michigan town, complained to his general practitioner of erectile dysfunction. After an examination, the physician attributed the patient's problems to high blood pressure. The patient later learned that he had a prostate problem that would have been correctible at the time by surgery, but that deteriorated irreversibly during the time it could have been corrected. He sued his physician for negligence, offering as an expert a board-certified urologist from Toledo, who was prepared to testify that a Michigan general practitioner should have given a prostate examination to a patient with the symptoms the plaintiff had presented, or should have referred him to a specialist. Should the court allow the Toledo doctor to testify?

VERGARA v. DOAN

Supreme Court of Indiana
593 N.E.2d 185 (1992)

SHEPARD, Chief Justice.

Javier Vergara was born on May 31, 1979, at the Adams Memorial Hospital in Decatur, Indiana. His parents, Jose and Concepcion, claimed that negligence on the part of Dr. John Doan during Javier's delivery caused him severe and permanent injuries. A jury returned a verdict for Dr. Doan and the plaintiffs appealed. The Court of Appeals affirmed.... Plaintiffs seek transfer, asking us to abandon Indiana's modified locality rule. We grant transfer to examine the standard of care appropriate for medical malpractice cases.

In most negligence cases, the defendant's conduct is tested against the hypothetical reasonable and prudent person acting under the same or similar circumstances.... In medical malpractice cases, however, Indiana has applied a more specific articulation of this standard. It has become known as the modified locality rule: "The standard of care ... is that degree of care, skill, and proficiency which is commonly exercised by ordinarily careful, skillful, and prudent [physicians], at the time of the operation and in similar localities." Burke v. Capello (1988), Ind., 520 N.E.2d 439, 441 ... Appellants have urged us to abandon this standard, arguing that the reasons for the modified locality rule are no longer applicable in today's society. We agree.

The modified locality rule is a less stringent version of the strict locality rule, which measured the defendant's conduct against that of other doctors in the same community. When the strict locality rule originated in the late 19th century, there was great disparity between the medical opportunities, equipment, facilities, and training in rural and urban communities. Travel and communication between rural and urban communities were difficult. The locality rule was intended to prevent the inequity that would result from holding rural doctors to the same standards as doctors in large cities....

With advances in communication, travel, and medical education, the disparity between rural and urban health care diminished and justification for the locality rule waned. The strict locality rule also had two major drawbacks, especially as applied to smaller communities. First, there was a scarcity of local doctors to serve as expert witnesses against other local doctors. Second, there was the possibility that practices among a small group of doctors would establish a local standard of care below that which the law required. Pederson v. Dumouchel, 72 Wash.2d 73, 431 P.2d 973, 977 (1967). In response to these changes and criticisms, many courts adopted a modified locality rule, expanding the area of comparison to similar localities. This is the standard applied in Indiana....

Use of a modified locality rule has not quelled the criticism. See Jon R. Waltz, The Rise and Gradual Fall of the Locality Rule in Medical Malpractice Litigation, 18 DePaul L.Rev. 408 (1969) (predicting eventual disappearance of locality rule); Brent R. Cohen, The Locality Rule in Colorado: Updating the Standard of Care, 51 U.Colo.L.Rev. 587 (1980) (urging a standard based on medical resources available to the doctor under the circumstances in which patient was treated). Many of the common criticisms seem valid. The modified locality rule still permits a lower standard of care to be exercised in smaller communities because other similar communities are likely to have the same care.... We also spend time and money on the difficulty of defining what is a similar community.... The rule also seems inconsistent with the reality of modern medical practice. The disparity between small town and urban medicine continues to lessen with advances in communication, transportation, and education. In addition, widespread insurance coverage has provided patients with more choice of doctors and hospitals by reducing the financial constraints on the consumer in selecting caregivers....

Many states describe the care a physician owes without emphasizing the locality of practice. Today we join these states and adopt the following: a physician must exercise that degree of care, skill, and proficiency exercised by reasonably careful, skillful, and prudent practitioners in the same class to which he belongs, acting under the same or similar circumstances. Rather than focusing on different standards for different communities, this standard uses locality as but one of the factors to be considered in determining whether the doctor acted reasonably. Other relevant considerations would include advances in the profession, availability of facilities, and whether the doctor is a specialist or general practitioner....

We now turn to whether the instruction given at trial, legally correct at the time, requires a reversal in light of our decision today. Appellant urges us to remand for a new trial, claiming that the jury instructions overemphasized the same or similar locality. We analyze this contention by reference to the appellate standard for erroneous instructions. We assume that the erroneous instruction influenced the verdict and will reverse for such error, unless it appears from the evidence that the verdict could not have differed even with a proper instruction....

The court gave the following instructions regarding the standard of care:

Court's additional instruction 23:

"I instruct you that the degree of skill and care required of a general practice physician who is employed prior to and during May, 1979 is that degree of skill and knowledge which ordinarily was possessed by general practice physicians who devote attention to obstetrics and its treatment in Decatur and similar localities of similar size in 1979.

Therefore, in determining whether or not John Doan, M.D. exercised due care in treating and delivering the child of Concepcion Vergara during the period in question, you may consider his background, training and the care and skill required of general practice physicians rendering similar care under similar circumstances in areas similar in size to the area of Decatur, Indiana or similar localities in 1979." ...

Court's additional instruction 26:

"If you find from the testimony of the experts, by a preponderance of the evidence, that certain minimum standards of care, uniform throughout the country, existed for a particular practice then you may judge the doctor's conduct by that minimum standard of care for the particular practice." ...

Although our holding that the modified locality rule no longer applies makes instruction 23 erroneous, the standard we have adopted today hardly prohibits consideration of the locality of practice. Locality of practice remains a proper subject for evidence and argument because it may be relevant to the circumstances in which the doctor acted.

Moreover, although instruction 23 mentions Decatur or similar localities, instruction 26 refers to a national standard of care. Plaintiff was permitted to present his expert witness, Dr. Harlan Giles, even though he was from Pittsburgh, Pennsylvania (not Decatur or a similar locality). Dr. Giles testified regarding his experience and knowledge of the standard of care in communities similar to Decatur and in hospitals similar in size to Adams County Memorial Hospital. He testified that in his opinion, considering all the factors incident to the pregnancy and birth of Javier Vergara, the standard of care required Dr. Doan to have delivered the baby by cesarean section. He stated that this opinion was based on the standard of care as it existed in 1979 in Decatur or similar communities. He also testified that the failure to have either an anesthesiologist or a qualified nurse anesthetist present at the delivery was a breach of the national standard of care for hospitals the size of Adams County Memorial and smaller. Evidently the jury disagreed with Dr. Giles and found Dr. Doan's conduct reasonable under the circumstances.

We regard our new formulation of a doctor's duty as a relatively modest alteration of existing law. It is unlikely to have changed the way this case was tried. We are satisfied that an instruction without the locality language would not lead a new jury to a different conclusion.

Therefore, we hold that giving instruction 23 was harmless and does not require reversal. In a different factual situation, however, an erroneous instruction with the locality language present might well constitute reversible error. The standard that we set out today, without the locality language, should be used from today forward.

We affirm the judgment of the trial court.

. . .

GIVAN, Justice, concurring in result.

Although the majority opinion states that it is abandoning the modified locality rule, they claim the rule now to be that the physician must exercise the care and skill of practitioners in the same class to which he belongs and "acting in the same or similar circumstances." They go on to state that "[o]ther relevant considerations would include advances in the profession, availability of facilities, and whether the doctor is a specialist or general practitioner."

I do not perceive this "new standard" to differ materially from the modified locality rule. The ability of a physician to perform may well be vastly different in a small rural community hospital than that same physician might be able to perform in a large well-equipped metropolitan hospital.

I believe the majority has articulated a distinction without a difference. I would not confuse the issue by purporting to do away with the modified locality rule.

KELLOS v. SAWILOWSKY

Georgia Supreme Court
254 Ga. 4, 325 S.E.2d 757 (1985)

MARSHALL, PRESIDING JUSTICE.

In this legal-malpractice action, defendant Sawilowsky supported his motion for summary judgment by his own affidavit that he exercised "that degree of skill, prudence and diligence as lawyers of ordinary skill and capacity commonly possess and exercise *in the State of Georgia* ..." (Emphasis supplied.) Plaintiffs Kellos opposed the motion with the affidavit of an attorney, averring that, in his opinion, Sawilowsky "failed to exercise that degree of skill, prudence and diligence as lawyers of ordinary skill and capacity ... possess and exercise *in the State of Georgia*." (Emphasis supplied.) The trial court granted summary judgment to the defendant-attorney without stating any reason. The Court of Appeals, in a split decision, affirmed. Kellos v. Sawilowsky, 172 Ga.App. 263, 322 S.E.2d 897 (1984). The majority opinion held, on p. 264, that "[t]he appellant's expert evidence did not create an issue of fact according to the above requirements," and that the affidavit had used the standard of the practice "in the State of Georgia," rather than "in the profession generally." We granted certiorari to determine whether, in a legal-malpractice action in Georgia, the applicable standard of skill, prudence and diligence of attorneys practicing in Georgia is that of the "locality" (i.e., the State of Georgia) or of the legal profession generally, *if these standards differ....*

In the final analysis, the local standard versus the standard of the legal profession generally may be a distinction without a difference. Our courts have held that an attorney's duty is "'to use such skill, prudence, and diligence as lawyers of ordinary skill and capacity commonly possess and exercise in the performance of the tasks which they undertake[,]'" and that "'[a]n attorney is not bound to extraordinary diligence. He is bound to *reasonable* skill and diligence, and the *skill* has reference to the character of the business he undertakes to do.' [Emphasis in original.] Cox v. Sullivan, 7 Ga. 144, 148 (50 AD [Am.Dec.] 386). Thus, *while the standard of care required of an attorney remains constant, its application may vary.* O'Barr v. Alexander, 37 Ga. 195 [Emphasis supplied.]. Two important considerations in particularizing this rather general standard in a given case are the number of options available to the attorney and the amount of time which he has to consider them." Berman v. Rubin, 138 Ga.App. 849, 851, 227 S.E.2d 802 (1976). "The effectiveness of representation may also be judged by the familiarity of counsel with the case, including counsel's opportunity to investigate and diligence in doing so, in order meaningfully to advise the client of his options." Hughes v. Malone, 146 Ga.App. 341, ... p. 346, 247 S.E.2d 107. Our conclusion from the above is that the standard of care required of an attorney remains constant — whether he is considered as a practitioner of a given State or as a practitioner of "the legal profession generally" — and that only the applications of care vary from jurisdiction to jurisdiction and from situation to situation. Hence, there is no particular value in using the standard in the individual State, but on the other hand there is nothing inaccurate or wrong with it either. In other words, in the case at bar, the fact that the standard used was that of the State of Georgia did not adversely affect the sufficiency of the showing on the motion for summary judgment.

For purposes of practicality in pleading, however, we hold that the applicable standard in Georgia is that of the practitioners in Georgia, there being no ascertainable standard of "the legal ... profession generally."

Since the plaintiffs' affidavit did not "establish the parameters of acceptable professional conduct, a significant deviation from which would constitute malpractice," as the majority of the Court of Appeals held, the unjustified insistence upon the standard of care in the legal profession generally does not mandate a reversal of the grant of summary judgment in favor of the defendant.

Judgment affirmed.

Hal R. Arkes & Cindy A. Schipani, *Medical Malpractice v. The Business Judgment Rule: Differences in Hindsight Bias*
73 ORE. L. REV. 587, 588–91, 621–22*

When retrospectively considering the occurrence of a past event, people tend to exaggerate the extent to which it could have been correctly predicted beforehand. This tendency is known in the psychological literature as the hindsight bias.[2] More colloquially it is known as "Monday morning quarterbacking." People with knowledge of an outcome often falsely believe that they would have predicted the reported outcome of an event.[3]

Yet, notwithstanding the potential for hindsight bias, jurors deciding cases of alleged negligence are routinely required to determine whether at the time of the original decision or procedure the defendant performed in a reasonable manner. The determination is necessarily made from a perspective of hindsight. The alleged wrongdoing has taken

---

  * © 1994 University of Oregon; Hal R. Arkes, Cindy A. Schipani. Reprinted by permission of the *Oregon Law Review.*
  2. Baruch Fischoff, *Hindsight≠Foresight: The Effect of Outcome Knowledge on Judgment Under Uncertainty*, 1 J. Experimental Psychol. Hum. Perception & Performance 288, 297 (1975).
  3. Scott A. Hawkins & Reid Hastie, *Hindsight Biased Judgments of Past Events After the Outcomes Are Known*, 107 Psychol. Bull. 311, 311 (1990).

place sometime in the past. There is a presumption that the jurors can somehow erase their knowledge of the negative outcome and return to the perspective of the defendant who could not know for certain the future outcome of any course of action. Substantial evidence suggests, however, that this presumption is not warranted. Instead, people cannot ignore their knowledge of the negative outcome.

In the context of medical malpractice actions, research studies support the contention that plaintiffs often receive payments for alleged malpractice even if the physician's performance was defensible. For example, Frederick W. Cheney, Karen L. Posner, Robert A. Caplan, and Richard J. Ward asked a panel of practicing anesthesiologists to review 1004 closed lawsuits.[6] The panel members were asked to judge whether the care received by the patient met the appropriate standard of care. Based on the panel members' evaluations, Cheney, Posner, Caplan and Ward determined that payment was made in forty percent of the cases when the anesthetic care was judged to be defensible. Mark I. Taragin, Laura R. Willett, Adam P. Wilczek, Richard Trout, and Jeffrey L. Carson[7] similarly report that payment was made in twenty-one percent of cases in which physician care was deemed defensible. Insurance companies may settle many of these cases for fear that, in hindsight, the physician will appear to be negligent, even though in foresight no such determination would be warranted. Awards may be granted in jury trials for the same reason. Unfortunately, the law provides no protection for the physician against the effects of the hindsight bias. This is especially problematic when considering that from pre-1981 to 1985 alone, the percentage of all physicians having malpractice claims filed against them tripled.

In contrast, business persons are insulated from the hindsight bias. In deciding whether to hold a business person liable for a faulty outcome, the courts provide the corporate official with the benefit of a presumption that the decision was made in good faith and in the best interests of the corporation. The courts generally refuse to substitute their judgment for the business acumen of corporate officials. Consequently, it is quite rare for a court to hold a corporate director liable for a negligent business decision. Moreover, most states have explicitly passed legislation permitting corporations to limit or eliminate director liability for negligence. Thus, in evaluating business decisions, the courts and legislatures have devised rules that effectively limit the impact of the hindsight bias in negligence actions against corporate officials.

· · ·

Unlike courts analyzing cases of medical negligence, courts considering corporate officials' liability for bad business decisions seem to have explicitly acknowledged the potential for hindsight bias. Rationales given to justify the business judgment rule include concerns that "courts are not competent to make, much less to second-guess, business decisions." It has been asserted that courts do not possess the requisite experience and expertise to make complex business decisions and are poorly equipped to evaluate the

---

6. Frederick W. Cheney et al., *Standard of Care and Anesthesia Liability*, 261 JAMA 1599 (1989). A lawsuit is considered closed when resolution occurs. Less than 10 percent of the cases in the sample went to the jury. Id.

7. Mark I. Taragin et al., *The Influence of Standard of Care and Severity of Injury on the Resolution of Medical Malpractice Claims*, 117 Annals Internal Med. 780 (1992). Note that although malpractice claim frequency varies drastically with specialty, there is no evidence that incompetent people gravitate to particular specialty areas. Peter D. Jacobson, *Medical Malpractice and the Tort System*, 262 JAMA 3320, 3321 (1989) ("In all likelihood, this occurs because certain procedures have a higher probability of producing adverse outcomes in the absence of error.") Of course, absence of error is an occasion for inappropriate payments for adverse outcomes.

quality of informed business decisions which, with hindsight, turn out poorly. Courts will only consider whether due care was exercised in making the decision, and will not substitute their own judgment exercised by the corporate official. As discussed above, courts will even presume that business persons have exercised due care absent evidence to the contrary. In contrast, no similar presumptions are available in actions against physicians. It is curious that courts do not similarly hesitate to substitute their judgment for the judgment of physicians.

There are, however, a number of possible explanations for the differences in legal treatment of liability for the corporate director and the physician. These explanations include differences in the role of risk-taking and failure, fear of liability, lack of an accepted methodology with respect to business decision-making, the aura of science, differences in the threshold requirements to enter the business and health professions, differences in the ability to rely on market efficiency and differences in whether plaintiffs have voluntarily exposed themselves to risk.

NOTES

(1) In *Hall v. Hilbun*, 466 So.2d 856 (Miss. 1985), a case involving the death of a surgical patient, the court said that "[a] a pulse rate of 140 per minute provides a danger signal in Pascagoula, Miss, the same as it does in Cleveland, Ohio. Bacteria, physiology and the life process itself know little of geography and nothing of political boundaries." In spelling out a "competence-based national standard of care," the court announced the following standards and qualifications:

> Each physician may with reason and fairness be expected to possess or have reasonable access to such medical knowledge as is commonly possessed or reasonably available to minimally competent physicians in the same specialty or general field of practice throughout the United States, to have a realistic understanding of the limitations on his or her knowledge or competence, and, in general, to exercise minimally adequate medical judgment. Beyond that, each physician has a duty to have a practical working knowledge of the facilities, equipment, resources (including personnel in health related fields and their general level of knowledge and competence), and options (including what specialized services or facilities may be available in larger communities, e.g., Memphis, Birmingham, Jackson, New Orleans, etc.) reasonably available to him or her as well as the practical limitations on same.

The court then provided a "resources-based caveat to the national standard of care":

> For reasons well known to all, the facilities, equipment, health care personnel, and other such resources reasonably available to Mississippi's physicians vary from community to community. Major differences exist between the tools the physician has to work within rural Mississippi as contrasted with our more urban areas. Generally speaking, the most comprehensive availability of sophisticated medical facilities and equipment in this state may be found in Jackson.

> Because of these differences in facilities, equipment, etc., what a physician may reasonably be expected to do in the treatment of a patient in rural Humphreys County or Greene County may vary from what a physician in Jackson may be able to do. A physician practicing in Noxubee County, for example, may hardly be faulted for failure to perform a CAT scan when the necessary facilities and equipment are not reasonably available. In contradistinction, objectively reasonable expectations regarding the physician's knowledge, skill, capacity for

sound medical judgment and general competence are, consistent with his field of practice and the facts and circumstances in which the patient may be found, the same everywhere.

...

As a result of its resources-based component, the physician's non-delegable duty of care is this: given the circumstances of each patient, each physician has a duty to use his or her knowledge and therewith treat through maximum reasonable medical recovery, each patient, with such reasonable diligence, skill, competence, and prudence as are practiced by minimally competent physicians in the same specialty or general field of practice throughout the United States, who have available to them the same general facilities, services, equipment and options.

(2) A divided Arkansas Supreme Court established a version of a modified locality rule in *Gambill v. Stroud*, 258 Ark. 766, 531 S.W.2d 945 (1976). The case involved a surgical operation for the removal of a thyroid cyst, in which after being put under anesthesia, the patient suffered a cardiac arrest and subsequent respiratory arrest that caused irreversible brain damage. The defendant Stroud, who was characterized at one point as a general practitioner and impliedly at another as a surgeon, stopped the operation immediately after his incision when he found the plaintiff's blood "very dark," indicative of an inadequate oxygen supply. The supreme court affirmed a jury verdict for the defendant, rendered on the basis of instructions grounded on a "same or similar locality" rule. The court emphasized that this rule was not a "strict locality rule," but "incorporate[d] the similar community into the picture," and that it was a standard of "persons engaged in a similar practice in similar localities, giving consideration to geographical location, size and character of the community."

The court declared it still to be "an ideal" to posit a paradigm of medical practice in which doctors in small communities have the same opportunities and resources to keep up with medical advances as doctors in big cities. However, the court was not convinced "that we have reached the time when the same postgraduate medical education, research and experience is equally available to all physicians, regardless of the community in which they practice." It commented that "[t]he opportunities for doctors in small towns, of which we have many, to leave a demanding practice to attend seminars and regional medical meetings cannot be the same as those for doctors practicing in clinics in larger centers." Moreover, the court noted that these small town doctors did not "have the clinical and hospital facilities available in the larger cities where there are large, modern hospitals," or the "advantage of observing others who have been trained, or have developed expertise, in the use of new skills, facilities and procedures." Conceding that the appropriate community standard might require that small town doctors send patients to larger centers, the court said that "when this is not practicable, the small town doctor should not be penalized for not utilizing means or facilities not reasonably available to him."

One of the dissenting justices noted that given the instructions on the "same or similar locality" rule, defense counsel was able to make a "devastating jury argument" with respect to the testimony of the plaintiff's expert, who had taught in medical schools, and who could not give "an altogether satisfactory answer" to the question, "If you do not know what the standard of care in Jonesboro, Arkansas, is, then what is your point of reference, how do you compare it to another locality?"

(3) Physicians are subject to liability both for acting—performing a surgical procedure, for example—and failures to act, for example, to institute a course of therapeutic

treatment. How much agreement is there among doctors concerning the right course of action? Lay persons might be disturbed to learn how often there is disagreement.

Studies of two kinds of procedures, using three panels of experts, are illustrative. The investigators used an "appropriateness method" developed by researchers at the Rand Corporation and the University of California at Los Angeles, which "combines a systematic review of the scientific literature with expert opinion and yields specific criteria of appropriateness," employing a risk-benefit scale. In a sample of 2352 randomly selected patients who underwent coronary revascularization, one panel would have classified 160 procedures as inappropriate, with the other two panels respectively rating 186 and 97 procedures as inappropriate.

Another study focused on a sample of 636 women, patients in seven managed care organizations, who underwent hysterectomies. The three expert panels who reviewed these files rated as inappropriate 200, 153, and an astonishing 331 operations, respectively.

The authors of the report concerning these studies noted that "[t]he degree of agreement among panels about care identified as inappropriate was only moderate" and that "the number of cases categorized as inappropriate varied by a factor of two for both procedures." The investigators did note, however, that with respect to identifying underuse of procedures, "[a]greement among panels was nearly perfect," and that "the number of cases classified as necessary varied by only 20 percent among panels."

An important practical comment on these statistics was that "[u]nder no circumstances should the care of individual patients be guided solely by the results of the appropriateness method without additional clinical information." Paul G. Shekelle et al., *The Reproducibility of a Method to Identify the Overuse and Underuse of Medical Procedures*, 338 N. Eng. J. Med. 1888, 1894 (1998).

Is it clear what the message is from these figures with respect to the justice and efficacy of tort law as a control on medical malpractice? Note that the authors of this report point out that "several" other studies had "estimate[d] that only 15 to 20 percent of medical practices can be justified on the basis of rigorous scientific data establishing their effectiveness." *Id.* at 1888, citing sources.

(4) Some states have tilted toward a locality rule by requiring that expert witnesses in medical malpractice cases must be licensed to practice in that state. A Tennessee statute of that sort has two qualifications: it permits the proffer of a witness from a "contiguous bordering state," and it allows the trial court to waive the requirement "when it determines that the appropriate witnesses otherwise would not be available." At least with a statute so qualified, the Tennessee Supreme Court rejected a constitutional challenge offered on the basis that the statute was arbitrary and irrational. Given that the legislation provided a "'safety valve' for those situations in which a party is unable to locate a qualified expert within this state or one of our bordering states," the court thought the statute had a "rational basis." *Sutphin v. Platt*, 720 S.W.2d 455 (Tenn. 1986). Would you uphold a statute that did not have the "safety valve"? A statute that required witnesses to be from only that state?

(5) An interesting set of legal issues appears in a suit joining medical malpractice and constitutional tort claims against a number of prison officials, physicians and hospital employees in connection with the death of a prisoner. One aspect of this complicated litigation concerned a physician's discontinuance of antipsychotic medications after the prisoner and her family had complained about the administration of those drugs. The court thought that a jury reasonably could have found that the physician's contact with the prisoner decreased after she and her parents opposed the drug treatment, and that the deterioration in the prisoner's condition, ending in her death, coincided with the

decrease in medical attention. The doctor argued, in effect, that the opposition of the prisoner and her family put the physician in a position where she could not prescribe proper medication, but the court said that if the doctor wanted to prescribe "egregiously inappropriate" medicine, she could not, on summary judgment, "rebut an allegation that she failed to tender medical care." Indeed, the court said that if the doctor "reacted to being prevented from providing inappropriate care by discontinuing efforts to provide medically defensible care," she "may well have been 'deliberately indifferent'" under the standard of a "constitutional tort" precedent. *Rogers v. Evans*, 792 F.2d 1052, 1060–61 (11th Cir. 1986).

(6) *Littleton v. Good Samaritan Hosp.*, 39 Ohio St.3d 86, 529 N.E.2d 449 (1988), dealt with a suit for the death of an infant by an overdose of aspirin administered by her mother, a psychiatric patient. The plaintiff argued that the patient's psychiatrist had violated his duty to protect the child from the mother's violent propensities. The Ohio Supreme Court formulated this test:

> ... [We] hold that a psychiatrist will not be held liable for the violent acts of a voluntarily hospitalized mental patient subsequent to the patient's discharge if (1) the patient did not manifest violent propensities while being hospitalized and there was no reason to suspect the patient would become violent after discharge, or (2) a thorough evaluation of the patient's propensity for violence was conducted, taking into account all relevant factors, and a good faith decision was made by the psychiatrist that the patient had no violent propensity, or (3) the patient was diagnosed as having violent propensities and, after a thorough evaluation of the severity of the propensities and a balancing of the patient's interests and the interests of potential victims, a treatment plan was formulated in good faith which included discharge of the patient.

(7) Which of these rules, or what combination of them, do you find preferable as the standard of care for physicians?

(a) A general standard for physicians in the same specialty, employing

(1) A national standard of care

(2) A "same class" rule like that in *Vergara*, supra at page 199.

(3) A modified locality rule

(4) A straight locality rule

(b) An honest error in judgment rule

(c) A "business judgment" rule of the sort discussed by Arkes and Schipani, supra at page 202.

(d) A rule allowing presentation of the existence of "two schools of thought"

(e) A "good faith" rule of the sort set out in the quotation from *Littleton*, *supra* note 6.

§ 4.08 The Culpability Spectrum Beyond Negligence

There are various gradations of culpability along a spectrum that extends from negligence to intentional torts. The labels that appear along this spectrum include gross negligence, recklessness, and "wanton, willful and reckless conduct," often employed as an inseparable triad.

Frequently these labels—especially gross negligence—may be no more than adjectives that add little, if anything, to the analysis. One jurist of the nineteenth century described gross negligence as negligence "with the addition of a vituperative epithet."[1] Yet there are instances in which the question of whether to classify conduct under such labels may involve high financial stakes. One situation where the label placed on conduct may be crucial is litigation under the Financial Institutions, Reform, Recovery and Enforcement Act (FIRREA), 12 U.S.C. § 1821(k), which sets as the standard for suits against directors or officers of savings institutions a showing of "gross negligence, including similar conduct or conduct that demonstrates a greater disregard of a duty of care (than gross negligence) including intentional tortious conduct, as those terms are defined under State law."

Another standard subject to litigation appears in the Warsaw Convention, which limits air carrier liability for damage to checked bags and cargo. According to Article 25 of the Convention, liability limits do not apply when the carrier acts with "willful misconduct." One federal district court awarded damages to a shipper of carpets that Air France agents had left in the rain without adequate cover. The district court reasoned that "a combination of factors can, taken together, amount to willful misconduct, and … merely the act itself needs to be intended, not the resulting injury or the wrongfulness of the act." *Saba v. Compagnie Nationale Air France*, 866 F. Supp. 588 (D.D.C. 1994).

The Court of Appeals for the D.C. Circuit reversed. Ruling that "willful misconduct" equates to "reckless disregard," the appellate court concluded that the defendant not only must "intend[] the act that ultimately causes harm," but must be "subjectively aware of the consequences of his act—not necessarily that it would cause the exact injury, but at least that it was certainly likely to cause an injury to plaintiff." At the same time, the court suggested that the requisite subjective awareness may be inferred. Dissenting Circuit Judge Patricia Wald accused the court of confusing the question by allowing "objective evidence" to meet a subjective test. In her formulation, absent direct proof of intent, the question is invariably one of degree. The issue involves an inquiry, using a scale from negligence to gross negligence to reckless disregard, about how far from the norm the defendant's conduct deviated. *Saba v. Compagnie Nationale Air France*, 78 F.3d 664 (D.C. Cir. 1996).

Which side has the better argument? Is there a principled distinction between subjective reckless disregard proved by inference from "objective evidence," on the one hand, and reckless disregard as a more serious deviation than gross negligence from an objective standard, on the other hand?

SPECIAL NOTE ON SPOLIATION OF EVIDENCE

Negligence is a very general tort doctrine that covers a large spectrum of activities and harms. On occasion, courts find it useful to fashion a specific category for particular type of occurrences. "Spoliation of evidence," which may not be limited to negligent conduct, is such a tort. One jurisdiction has defined the elements of the tort as

---

1. *Wilson v. Brett*, 11 M. & W. 113, 152 Eng. Rep. 737 (1843) (Rolfe, B.)

(1) the existence of a potential civil action, (2) a legal or contractual duty to preserve evidence which is relevant to the potential civil action, (3) destruction of that evidence, (4) a significant impairment in the ability to prove the lawsuit, (5) a causal relationship between the evidence destruction and inability to prove the lawsuit, and (6) damages.... *Continental Ins. Co. v. Herman*, 576 So.2d 313, 315 (Fla. Dist. Ct. App. 1990).

An Illinois decision takes the position that there is no reason to call spoliation a separate tort, rather than simply defining it as a sub-branch of negligence. In that case, *Boyd v. Travelers Ins. Co.*, 652 N.E.2d 267 (Ill. 1995), the plaintiff suffered injuries from an explosion attributed to the escape of propane gas from a heater made by one defendant, whose insurer was another defendant. The insurer's representatives took possession of the heater from the plaintiff's wife, saying that it was needed to investigate a workers compensation claim by her husband. The heater disappeared. The plaintiffs alleged that the loss of the heater "irrevocably prejudiced and adversely affected their products liability action against" the manufacturer. The court concluded that "[a]n action for negligent spoliation can be stated under existing negligence law without creating a new tort." *Id.* at 270. It noted that a couple of other courts had "recognized negligent spoliation of evidence as an independent tort," that others had "recognized intentional spoliation ... as a new tort," and that several courts had declined to recognize "a new tort of spoliation." *Id.* at n.1.

In fleshing out spoliation as a negligence cause of action, the court specifically rejected the defendant's contention that in order for the plaintiffs to prove "actual injury from the loss of the heater," they would have to "first pursue and lose the underlying claim." Rather, the court said that "in a negligence action invoking the loss or destruction of evidence, a plaintiff must allege sufficient facts to support a claim that the loss or destruction of the evidence caused the plaintiff to be unable to prove an underlying lawsuit." *Id.* at 271.

The court stressed that it would be "too difficult a burden" for the plaintiff to have to show that, "but for the loss or destruction of the evidence, the plaintiff would have prevailed in the underlying action." Instead, the court said that the plaintiff would have to show that he "had a reasonable probability of succeeding in the underlying suit." The court also encouraged joinder of the claim for negligent spoliation with the underlying action, reasoning that "[a] single trier of fact who heard the case would be in the best position to resolve all the claims fairly and consistently." *Id.* at 272.

Chapter 5

DEFENSES IN NEGLIGENCE LAW

§ 5.01 Express Assumption of Risk

[A] Generally

HENRIOULLE v. MARIN VENTURES, INC.
California Supreme Court, In Bank
20 Cal. 3d 512, 573 P.2d 465, 143 Cal. Rptr. 247 (1978)

BIRD, CHIEF JUSTICE.

Appellant, John Henrioulle, seeks to set aside orders of the superior court granting his landlord, respondent Marin Ventures, Inc., a judgment notwithstanding the jury's verdict and a new trial. Appellant contends that the exculpatory clause in his lease could not relieve the landlord of liability for the personal injuries appellant sustained in a fall on a common stairway in the apartment building. This court agrees.

. . .

… From the record, it appears that on April 3, 1974, appellant entered into a lease agreement with respondent for an apartment in San Rafael, California. At that time, appellant was an unemployed widower with two children who received public assistance in the form of a rent subsidy from the Marin County Department of Social Services. There was also evidence of a shortage of housing accommodations for persons of low income in Marin County.[1]

The printed form lease agreement which appellant signed contained the following exculpatory clause: "INDEMNIFICATION: Owner shall not be liable for any damage or injury to Tenant, or any other person, or to any property, occurring on the premises, or any part thereof, or in the common areas thereof, and Tenant agrees to hold Owner harmless from any claims for damages no matter how caused."

On May 22, 1974, appellant fractured his wrist when he tripped over a rock on a common stairway in the apartment building. At the time of the accident the landlord had been having difficulty keeping the common areas of the apartment building clean. An on-site manager, whose duties included keeping these areas clean, had proven unsatisfactory and had been terminated in the month prior to the accident. The landlord

---

1. The Marin County Planning Department in its 1973 countywide plan report documents the relative decline in the amount of low-cost housing available in that county. That report indicates that between 1960 and 1970 the proportion of the county's housing in the low-price category decreased from 41.8 percent to 19.4 percent. (The Marin Countywide Plan, 1973, Marin County Planning Dept.)

had also employed an additional person to do maintenance work, but he had worked only a few hours at the apartment building in the month preceding the accident.

... After a three-day trial, the jury rendered a special verdict under Code of Civil Procedure section 624, consisting of four findings of fact: (1) appellant had been injured as a proximate result of respondent's negligence; (2) appellant was damaged in the sum of $5,000; (3) appellant had been contributorily negligent; and (4) relative fault was to be apportioned at 30 percent for appellant and 70 percent for respondent.

[Omitted is a discussion of matters related to the jury vote.]

... The court then stated a verdict had been reached and judgment would be entered for appellant in the sum of $3,500. At this point, the jury was discharged.

Thereafter, respondent moved for judgment notwithstanding the verdict, contending that the exculpatory clause in the rental agreement relieved it of liability. This motion was granted. Respondent's additional motion for a new trial under Code of Civil Procedure section 629 was granted on the ground that the same nine jurors had not assented to each and every question set forth in the special verdict and, therefore, no verdict had been reached. This appeal followed.

II

In Tunkl v. Regents of the University of California (1963), 60 Cal.2d 92, 32 Cal.Rptr. 33, 383 P.2d 441, this court held invalid a clause in a hospital admission form which released the hospital from liability for future negligence.[5]

This court noted that although courts have made "diverse" interpretations of Civil Code section 1668,[6] which invalidates contracts which exempt one from responsibility for certain wilful or negligent acts, all the decisions were in accord that exculpatory clauses affecting the public interest are invalid....

In Tunkl, six criteria are used to identify the kind of agreement in which an exculpatory clause is invalid as contrary to public policy: "(1) It concerns a business of a type generally thought suitable for public regulation. (2) The party seeking exculpation is engaged in performing a service of great importance to the public, which is often a matter of practical necessity for some members of the public. (3) The party holds himself out as willing to perform this service for any member of the public who seeks it, or at least any member coming within certain established standards. (4) As a result of the essential nature of the service, in the economic setting of the transaction, the party invoking exculpation possesses a decisive advantage of bargaining strength against any member of the public who seeks his services. (5) In exercising a superior bargaining power the party confronts the public with a standardized adhesion contract of exculpation, and makes no provision whereby a purchaser may pay additional fees and obtain protection against negligence. (6) Finally, as a result of the transaction, the person or prop-

---

5. The pertinent provision in the hospital admission form read as follows: "RELEASE: The hospital is a nonprofit, charitable institution. In consideration of the hospital and allied services to be rendered and the rates charged therefor, the patient or his legal representative agrees to and hereby releases The Regents of the University of California, and the hospital from any and all liability for the negligent or wrongful acts or omissions of its employees ..." (*Tunkl v. Regents of the University of California, supra,* 60 Cal.2d at p. 94, 32 Cal.Rptr. at p. 34, 383 P.2d at p. 442.)

6. Civil Code section 1668 provides: "All contracts which have for their object, directly or indirectly, to exempt anyone from responsibility for his own fraud, or willful injury to the person or property of another, or violation of law, whether willful or negligent, are against the policy of the law."

erty of the purchaser is placed under the control of the seller, subject to the risk of carelessness by the seller or his agents." ...

The transaction before this court, a residential rental agreement, meets the Tunkl criteria. Housing in general, and residential leases in particular, are increasingly the subject of governmental regulation, the first of the Tunkl criteria. In Green v. Superior Court (1974) 10 Cal.3d 616, 627, 111 Cal.Rptr. 704, 711, 517 P.2d 1168, 1175, this court noted: "The past half century has brought the widespread enactment of comprehensive housing codes throughout the nation; in California, the Department of Housing and Community Development has established detailed, statewide housing regulations (see Health & Saf.Code, § 17921; Cal.Admin.Code, tit. 25, §§ 1000–1090), and the Legislature has expressly authorized local entities to impose even more stringent regulations.... These comprehensive housing codes affirm that, under contemporary conditions, public policy compels landlords to bear the primary responsibility for maintaining safe, clean and habitable housing in our state." Moreover, the Legislature in 1970 enacted stricter standards of "tenantability" (see Civ.Code, § 1941.1) and has limited landlords' ability to impose waivers of tenants' rights in leases....

A lessor of residential property provides shelter, a basic necessity of life, the second Tunkl criterion. Moreover, the landlord in this case offered to rent his units to all members of the public, the third Tunkl criterion.

Unequal bargaining strength, the fourth Tunkl criterion, is also present. In a state and local market characterized by a severe shortage of low-cost housing,[7] tenants are likely to be in a poor position to bargain with landlords. As this court observed in Green, "the severe shortage of low and moderate cost housing has left tenants with little bargaining power through which they might gain express warranties of habitability from landlords ..." ...

Finally, the fifth and sixth Tunkl criteria are also present. Thus, it does not appear that respondent made any "provision whereby a purchaser may pay additional fees and obtain protection against negligence," (Tunkl ... supra, ...) and appellant was exposed to the risk of injury through respondent's carelessness.

However, respondent asserts that the principles discussed in Tunkl do not apply to private residential leases. It is true that Tunkl cites language in Barkett v. Brucato, (1953) 122 Cal.App.2d 264, 276, 264 P.2d 978, 987 to the effect that "the relationship of landlord and tenant does not affect the public interest...." In Tunkl, this court cited Barkett and other cases as examples of the uniform inquiry by courts into whether or not an exculpatory clause involved the public interest. Although this court held that an exculpatory clause could stand only if it did not involve the public interest, it did not endorse the result reached in applying that rule in each of those cases.

Furthermore, even if at the time of Barkett and the earlier decisions cited therein, a residential lease may have been correctly characterized as not involving the public interest, for the reasons stated above this court is convinced this is not true today. Since the residential lease transaction entered into by the parties exhibits all of the characteristics of a relationship that "affects the public interest" under Tunkl, the exculpatory clause cannot operate to relieve the landlord of liability in this case.

---

7. The statewide shortage of such housing was documented by the Legislature in 1970: "(The Legislature) finds and declares that there continues to exist throughout the state a seriously inadequate supply of safe and sanitary dwelling accommodations for persons and families of low income. This condition is contrary to the public interest and threatens the health, safety, welfare, comfort and security of the people of this state." (HEALTH & SAF. CODE, § 33250....)

In holding that exculpatory clauses in residential leases violate public policy, this court joins an increasing number of jurisdictions.... Indeed, in 1975 the California Legislature enacted Civil Code section 1953, which declared invalid exculpatory clauses in residential leases executed on or after January 1, 1976. (Civ.Code, § 1953, Stats. 1975, ch. 302, § 1, p. 749.)[8]

. . .

The orders of the superior court granting respondent's motions for judgment notwithstanding the jury's verdict and a new trial are reversed, and the cause is remanded with direction to enter judgment for appellant on the verdict.

HULSEY v. ELSINORE PARACHUTE CENTER

California Court of Appeal
168 Cal. App. 3d 333, 214 Cal. Rptr. 194 (1985)

OPINION

MCDANIEL, ASSOCIATE JUSTICE.

In this appeal, we are called upon to review the propriety of a summary judgment entered for defendant in a sports risk case. The action in the trial court was to recover for personal injuries suffered by plaintiff at the time of his first parachute jump, one attempted under the auspices of defendant. At the hearing of the motion for summary judgment, no disputed issues of fact were raised in connection either with the count based on negligence or the count based on strict liability. As a consequence, the trial court was concerned generally with only two issues of law. One is whether the Agreement & Release of Liability signed by plaintiff at the time of the instructional preparation for his first parachute jump is enforceable against him. The other is whether sport parachuting is an extra-hazardous activity such as precludes the effectiveness of the release. In our view, the trial court correctly ruled that the release is enforceable and that parachute jumping is not the kind of activity which precludes the valid use of the release procedure followed here by defendant.

... As established by plaintiff's deposition, he went to defendant's place of business, the Elsinore Parachute Center (EPC), in the company of three friends, two of whom had had previous experience in sport parachuting. Upon arriving at EPC, plaintiff enrolled in the "First Jump Course" offered by defendant. Although plaintiff stated he had no recollection of filling out or signing the "Parachute Center Adult Registration Form," he did admit that the written inscriptions, the initials and the signature on the form were his.

Continuing, plaintiff also disclaimed any recollection of reading or signing the "Agreement & Release of Liability," but he did admit once again that the signature and the initials on the agreement were his. Plaintiff admitted that he voluntarily enrolled in the first-jump course and was not coerced in any way during the registration process.

After enrolling in the course and signing the items noted, plaintiff received a complete U.S. Parachute Association approved course of instruction in sport parachuting

---

8. Civil Code section 1953 provides in pertinent part:

(a) Any provision of a lease or rental agreement of a dwelling by which the lessee agrees to modify or waive any of the following rights shall be void as contrary to public policy:

. . .

(5) His right to have the landlord exercise a duty of care to prevent personal injury or personal property damage where that duty is imposed by law....

taught by an instructor certified by that association. This instruction consisted of about three hours of classroom training plus an additional hour of practical, clinical training.

During the classroom training, the instructor advised the class that students occasionally break their legs while jumping. In addition, canopy control was discussed and plaintiff received instruction on the proper procedure to be followed in maneuvering the parachute for landing. Plaintiff admitted that he understood the information provided and felt he was one of the better students in the class.

After the instructional phase of the course had been completed, plaintiff was issued a jumpsuit, boots, goggles, a harness with main and reserve parachutes, a helmet and a life vest. Plaintiff admitted that he had no problems with his equipment.

Plaintiff's actual jump was postponed several hours because of wind. At approximately 6:30 p.m., plaintiff boarded the aircraft for his first jump. Plaintiff recalled that the wind was "still" or "very calm" when he boarded the aircraft.

Plaintiff's exit from the aircraft was normal. Plaintiff testified that he attempted to steer toward the target area but was unable to reach it. Plaintiff attempted to land in a vacant lot but collided with electric power lines as he neared the ground. As he drifted into the wires, plaintiff saw a bright flash. Plaintiff's next recollection was of regaining consciousness on the ground. Despite the extreme risk to which he was thereby exposed, plaintiff sustained only a broken wrist.

...

... The trial court was faced with having to decide only issues of law. These issues were resolved in favor of defendant, and the motion was granted. A judgment reflecting this ruling was then entered, and this appeal followed.

...

... It is well established, in the absence of fraud, overreaching or excusable neglect, that one who signs an instrument may not avoid the impact of its terms on the ground that he failed to read the instrument before signing it. (Madden v. Kaiser Foundation Hospitals, 17 Cal.3d 699, 710, 131 Cal.Rptr. 882, 552 P.2d 1178....) On the record here, there is no indication whatsoever of fraud or other behavior by defendant which would otherwise have made the Madden rule inapplicable.

Another aspect of this preliminary inquiry into the circumstances surrounding plaintiff's filling out the registration card and signing the release involves the size of the type used in printing the release. In the case of Conservatorship of Link, 158 Cal.App.3d 138, 205 Cal.Rptr. 513, the court held the purported exculpatory documents unenforceable for several reasons, including the fact that they were printed in five-and-one-half point type and thus could not easily be read by persons of ordinary vision. (Id., at pp. 141–142, 205 Cal.Rptr. 513.) Actually, as observed in Link, "The five-and-one-half point print is so small that one would conclude defendants never intended it to be read ... the lengthy fine print seems calculated to conceal and not to warn the unwary." ...

The type size contained in Link is not present here. As appears from the actual size reproduction in the Appendix, the release is in 10 point type, both caps and lower case letters. This size comports with a number of minimums prescribed by statute.[1]

---

1. "Examples: Civil Code sections 1630 [eight to ten-point: parking lots]; 1677 [eight-point bold red or ten-point bold: liquidated damages provision in realty purchase contract]; 1803.1 and 1803.2 [eight to fourteen-point: retail installment sales]; 1812.85 [ten-point bold: health studio services]; 1812.205 and 1812.209 [ten to sixteen-point bold: seller assisted marketing plan]; 1812.302 and 1812.303 [ten-point bold: membership camping]; 1812.402 [ten-point: disability insurance];

As appears from a copy of the agreement reproduced in actual size and attached as an Appendix, the second paragraph recites in bold-faced type:

I AM AWARE THAT PARACHUTE INSTRUCTION AND JUMPING ARE HAZ-ARDOUS ACTIVITIES, AND I AM VOLUNTARILY PARTICIPATING IN THESE AC-TIVITIES WITH KNOWLEDGE OF THE DANGER INVOLVED AND HEREBY AGREE TO ACCEPT ANY AND ALL RISKS OF INJURY OR DEATH. PLEASE INI-TIAL. Plaintiff affixed his initials.

The third paragraph recites that the subscriber will not sue EPC or its employees "for injury or damage resulting from the negligence or other acts, howsoever caused, by any employee, agent or contractor of [EPC] or its affiliates, as a result of my participation in parachuting activities." That paragraph goes on to recite that the subscriber will "release and discharge" EPC and its employees "from all actions, claims or demands ... for in-jury or damage resulting from [the subscriber's] participation in parachuting activities."

The fourth paragraph, also in bold-faced type, recites that:

I HAVE CAREFULLY READ THIS AGREEMENT AND FULLY UNDERSTAND ITS CONTENTS. I AM AWARE THAT THIS IS A RELEASE OF LIABILITY AND A CON-TRACT BETWEEN MYSELF AND ELSINORE PARACHUTE CENTER AND/OR ITS AFFILIATED ORGANIZATIONS AND SIGN IT OF MY OWN FREE WILL. Plaintiff's signature was thereto subscribed.

I

Plaintiff's first contention involves an inquiry into whether plaintiff could reasonably have been expected to understand its legal consequences for him....

...

... We have already quoted the pertinent provision, and it would be hard to imagine language more clearly designed to put a layperson on notice of the significance and legal effect of subscribing it....

II

Turning to plaintiff's second contention, namely that releases of the type here used are against public policy, we note first that such agreements as this are arguably contem-plated by section 1668 of the Civil Code. That section provides:

All contracts which have for their object, directly or indirectly, to exempt anyone from the responsibility for his own fraud, or willful injury to the person or property of an-other, or violation of law, whether willful or negligent, are against the policy of the law.

Whatever it proscribes, this section does not invalidate contracts which seek to ex-cept one from liability for simple negligence or strict liability. (Mills v. Ruppert, 167 Cal.App.2d 58, 62–63, 333 P.2d 818.)

Civil Code section 1668 refers to limitations which are described as against the policy of the law. Such policy is the aggregate of judicial pronouncements on a given issue, and in this context deal with the concept characterized as "the public interest." This concept calls up for discussion Tunkl v. Regents of University of California....

1861.8 [ten-point bold: innkeepers]; 1916.5 and 1916.7 [ten-point bold: loan of money]; 2924c [twelve to fourteen-point bold: mortgage default notice]; 2982.5 and 2983.2 [eight to ten-point bold: automobile sales finance]; 2985.8, 2986.2 and 2986.4 [six to ten-point bold: vehicle leasing act]; 3052.5 [ten-point bold: service dealer lien]." (*Conservatorship of Link, supra,* 158 Cal.App.3d 138, 141, 205 Cal.Rptr. 513.)

. . .

Applying the Tunkl factors to the facts here, several distinctions are readily apparent. First, parachute jumping is not subject to the same level of public regulation as is the delivery of medical and hospital services. Second, the Tunkl agreement was executed in connection with services of great importance to the public and of practical necessity to anyone suffering from a physical infirmity or illness. Parachute jumping, on the other hand, is not an activity of great importance to the public and is a matter of necessity to no one.

Finally, because of the essential nature of medical treatment, the consuming party in Tunkl had little or no choice but to accept the terms offered by the hospital. Defendant had no decisive advantage in bargaining power over plaintiff by virtue of any "essential services" offered by defendant. When referring to "essential services" the court in Tunkl clearly had in mind medical, legal, housing, transportation or similar services which must necessarily be utilized by the general public. Purely recreational activities such as sport parachuting can hardly be considered "essential."

In sum, measuring the transaction here against the Tunkl factors, we can see no logical reason for extending the "public interest" limitation on the freedom to contract to the exculpatory agreement here relied on by defendant.

There are no California cases directly on point dealing with exculpatory contracts in the context of high risk sports activities, but there are an ample number on the books in other states. Jones v. Dressel, 623 P.2d 370, a Colorado case, was decided on very similar facts by means of a summary judgment. The case is especially persuasive because the Colorado court relied extensively on Tunkl in arriving at its holding that the exculpatory agreement there relied upon by an operator of business furnishing sky diving facilities did not fall within the ambit of agreements proscribed as against the public interest. . . .

. . .

Accordingly, following both logic and the persuasive holdings cited from other jurisdictions, we hold that the exculpatory agreement here under discussion is not against the "public interest" so as to bring it within the prohibitions of section 1688 of the Civil Code because contrary to "the policy of the law."

III

We come now to the narrower issue of whether the exculpatory contract here relied upon as an affirmative defense by defendant should not be enforced because, as to plaintiff, it would be "unconscionable." This inquiry necessarily imports the more precise question of whether this contract was one of adhesion as a further ground to reject its enforcement.

Going back several decades, we can pick up a thread on this point which can be followed in the decisions. In Neal v. State Farm Ins. Cos., 188 Cal.App.2d 690, 10 Cal.Rptr. 781, the court said, "[A contract of adhesion] signifies a standardized contract, which, imposed and drafted by the party of superior bargaining strength, relegates to the subscribing party only the opportunity to adhere to the contract or reject it." (Id., at p. 694, 10 Cal.Rptr. 781.) About 16 years later Justice Tamura of this court discoursed in depth on the subject in Wheeler v. St. Joseph Hospital, 63 Cal.App.3d 345, 133 Cal.Rptr. 775, carrying the issue of enforceability beyond a matter of rote definition. He said, "However, a determination that a contract is adhesive is merely the beginning and not the end of the analysis insofar as enforceability of its terms is concerned. Enforceability depends upon whether the terms of which the adherent was unaware are beyond the reasonable expectations of an ordinary person or are oppressive or unconscionable ... [Citing cases.] A provision which limits the duties or liability of the stronger party will not be enforced against the forced adherent absent 'plain and clear notification' of the terms and an 'understanding consent' thereto....

The marshalling of authorities on this point calls in Graham v. Scissor-Tail, Inc., ... 28 Cal.3d 807, 171 Cal.Rptr. 604, 623 P.2d 165. Scissor-Tail restated the rule as enforceable unless to do so would defeat judicial or legislative limitations on the right to contract freely. Such limitations, as noted, are: (1) that the agreement must not defeat the weaker party's reasonable expectations; and (2) the agreement must not be unconscionable....

Applying the rule, the court in Scissor-Tail determined that a performing group's union contract with its promoter was adhesive, because the contract was a standard American Federation of Musicians' contract, and the promoter "was required by the realities of his business as a concert promoter to sign A.F. of M. form contracts with any concert artist with whom he wished to do business ..." ...

Although the foregoing rule is now well established, its application to a contract used in the kind of activity here in issue is untried in California. As an a priori matter, however, it presents no difficulty. Plaintiff has made the picturesque if not ludicrous contention that he "was led to believe" that the urgent thing confronting him at the time he signed and initialed the agreement was to sign up to purchase a photograph, and that as a consequence he did not realize the significance of the agreement when he signed it. He makes this contention despite the fact that his initials appear immediately adjacent to the capitalized words in bold-faced type, "AGREEMENT & RELEASE OF LIABILITY." It is hard to imagine that plaintiff, after having initialed the agreement in three places and signed it in one could have harbored any reasonable expectations other than what was unambiguously recited in the title and text of the agreement.

Because the agreement, in both its language and format, was not one which could even remotely operate to defeat the reasonable expectations of plaintiff and hence be unconscionable if enforced, we hold that it did not so operate and hence that its enforcement against him was not unconscionable.

...

The judgment is affirmed.

APPENDIX
Exhibit "C" to McBreen Declaration

AGREEMENT & RELEASE OF LIABILITY

I, [handwritten name of Anthony Hulsey] , HEREBY ACKNOWLEDGE that I have voluntarily applied to participate in parachuting instruction and training, culminating in a parachute jump at the premises of Elsinore Parachute Center.

I AM AWARE THAT THE PARACHUTE INSTRUCTION AND JUMPING ARE HAZARDOUS ACTIVITIES, AND I AM VOLUNTARILY PARTICIPATING IN THESE ACTIVITIES WITH KNOWLEDGE OF THE DANGER INVOLVED AND HEREBY AGREE TO ACCEPT AN AND ALL RISKS OF INJURY OR DEATH. PLEASE INITIAL. [handwritten ajh]

AS LAWFUL CONSIDERATION for being permitted by Elsinore Parachute Center or one of its affiliated organizations to participate in these activities and use their facilities, I hereby agree that I, my heirs, distributees, guardians, legal represenatives and assigns will not make a claim against, sue, attach the property of, or prosecute Elsinore Parachute Center, Inc., and Elsinore Sport Parachuting Center, Inc., and Lakewood Sport Parachuting Center, Inc. for injury or damage resulting from the negligence or other acts, howsoever caused, by an employee, agent or contractor of Elsinore Parachute Center or its affiliates, as a result of my participating in parachuting activities. In addition, I hereby release and discharge Elsinore Parachute Center, Parachutes, Inc., Skydive, Skydive II, and its affiliated organizations, and Aurora Leasing Company, and Orange Sport Parachutes, Inc., and Elsinore Sport Parachuting Center, Inc., and Lakewood Sport Parachuting Center, Inc. from all actions, claims or demands I, my heirs, distributees, guardians, legal representatives, or assigns now have or may hereafter have for injury or damage resulting from my participation in parachuting activities.

I HAVE CAREFULLY READ THIS AGREEMENT AND FULLY UNDERSTAND ITS CONTENTS. I AM AWARE THAT THIS IS A RELEASE OF LIABILITY AND A CONTRACT BETWEEN MYSELF AND ELSINORE PARACHUTE CENTER AND/OR ITS AFFILIATED ORGANIZATIONS AND SIGN IT OF MY OWN FREE WILL.

DATED: 5/22/

WITNESS [signature of Rebecca Avila]

SIGNATURE [signature of Anthony James Hulsey]

DATE 5/22/82

NOTES

(1) What precisely is the "public policy" that the clause in *Henrioulle* violates?

(2) Would it have made a difference if the landlord had sat down with Henrioulle and spoken with him specifically about the clause, making sure that he understood it, and that only after that had Henrioulle signed the lease?

(3) The question presented in *Henrioulle* is a quantitatively important one. The Washington Supreme Court emphasized this feature of the problem in *McCutcheon v. United Homes Corp.*, 79 Wash. 2d 443, 486 P.2d 1093 (1971), in holding that an exculpatory clause "contravenes long established common law rules of tort liability that exist in the landlord-tenant relationship":

> We no longer live in an era of the occasional rental of rooms in a private home or over the corner grocery. In the relatively short span of 30 years the public's use of rental units in this state has expanded dramatically. In the past 10 years alone, in the state of Washington, there has been an increase of over 77,000 rental units. It takes no imagination to see that a business which once had a minor impact upon the living habits of the citizenry has developed into a major commercial enterprise directly touching the lives of hundreds of thousands of people who depend upon it for shelter.

> Thus, we are not faced merely with the theoretical duty of construing a provision in an isolated contract specifically bargained for by one landlord and one tenant as a purely private affair. Considered realistically, we are asked to construe an exculpatory clause, the generalized use of which may have an impact upon thousands of potential tenants.

> Under these circumstances it cannot be said that such exculpatory clauses are "purely a private affair" or that they are "not a matter of public interest."

The real question is whether we should sanction a technique of immunizing lessors of residential units within a multi-family dwelling complex, from liability for personal injuries sustained by a tenant, which injuries result from the lessor's own negligence in maintaining the "common areas"; particularly when the technique employed destroys the concept of negligence and the standard of affirmative duty imposed upon the landlord for protection of the tenant.

... It makes little sense for us to insist, on the one hand, that a workman have a safe place in which to work, but, on the other hand, to deny him a reasonably safe place in which to live.

For other authority holding that exculpatory clauses are void as against public policy when applied to common areas on leased premises, see *Cappaert v. Junker*, 413 So.2d 378 (Miss. 1982) (common stairway).

(4) Is it clear that the rule in *Henrioulle* would apply to a public housing project? Does the rule make economic sense in that setting? What would your view be if it could be shown that to enforce the *Henrioulle* rule in a public housing project would boost the cost of housing there and reduce the number of apartments available?

Assume that a family that lives in public housing has signed a lease with an exculpatory clause. Would you permit a suit against the public housing authority for a case of frostbite, suffered by a child in a rundown apartment unit that was all the family could afford, in which the heat was consistently inadequate?

(5) How much difference should it make if the defendant pleading an exclusionary clause is the landlord of a fancy private apartment complex? Consider a claim for negligent maintenance of a swimming pool, brought by a tenant who has signed a lease that absolves the landlord of liability for accidents at the pool as a pre-condition for use of it. Assume that the operating cost of the pool is included in the rentals. See *Tenants Council of Tiber Island-Carrollsburg Square v. DeFranceaux*, 305 F. Supp. 560 (D.D.C. 1969). If an exclusionary clause is as broad as the one in *Henrioulle*, should it make a difference whether injury is caused by negligent maintenance of a swimming pool or by the failure to remove all ice and snow from a sidewalk in front of a high-rent apartment building?

(6) Do you think the results in *Henrioulle* and *Hulsey* are consistent? What is the most important distinction between the cases?

Paul M. Jakus and W. Douglass Shaw, *An Empirical Analysis of Rock Climbers' Response to Hazard Warnings*

16 Risk Analysis, No. 4, at 581–86 (1996)*

1. INTRODUCTION

In this paper, we examine the responses of rock climbers to hazard warnings using measures of climbers' actual behavior. To our knowledge, this is the first study of hazard response by climbers; it also represents one of the few field tests of a hazard warning system. We first review the literature with respect to the technical elements of a hazard warning, its contribution to hazard perception, and hazard response measurement. Second, the sport of rock climbing, communication of hazards, and climbers' exposure

---

* Reprinted by permission of the Society for Risk Analysis.

to hazard are analyzed. Data collection issues are then discussed, followed by empirical models of climbers' responses to hazard warnings. Conclusions finish the paper.

2. HAZARD WARNING, HAZARD PERCEPTION, AND RESPONSE MEASUREMENT

Wolgalter et al, found that effective hazard warnings consist of a *signal word* (such as CAUTION, DANGER, WARNING), a *hazard statement* (stating the source of hazard), *consequences* (what will happen), and *instructions* on how to avoid the hazard. In experimental settings, warnings with all elements were found to be more effective in eliciting precautionary behavior than warnings in which some elements were missing. If elements missing from the warning were obvious or implied, however, effectiveness was not diminished.

Hazard warnings inform an individual of a hazard and how to avoid it. Slovic et al. have argued that hazard perception is the key factor affecting behavior. Hazard perception is a function of both the severity of injury (the consequences) and the likelihood of injury, so that low probability events with dire outcomes may be judged more hazardous than events with minor injuries but relatively high probabilities.[4] Thus, response analysis should focus on factors determining the likelihood of an injury as well as injury severity. Walker notes that people often reject "expert" opinions of injury likelihood, instead using "personal" probability estimates. Factors used to generate personal probability estimates are called "individuating factors."

Both individuating factors and a measure of hazard severity are needed to estimate a hazard response model. In evaluating such models, Weinstein and Sandman note there must be consistency between responses and hazards: people facing greater hazards must show greater responsiveness than those facing lesser hazards. Unfortunately, field tests of response to hazard warnings are difficult to implement because precautionary behavior may be biased by the simple act of trying to measure it. In the next section we will see that rock climbers provide excellent subjects for a field test of a hazard warning system.

3. ROCK CLIMBING

3.1 Rock Climbers: A Day in the Life

Technical rock climbing on smaller cliffs or "crags" refers to climbing a route up a rockface using ropes and other gear for protection.[6] The "leader" advances using the features of the rock alone, threading the rope through metal devices placed in rock crevices. Each device ("nut" or "camming unit") acts as a potential pivot point in the event of a fall. Should the leader fall, the "second" holds (belays) the rope from the below, stopping the fall. The equipment is used only to protect against the consequences of a fall. The second climbs after having belayed the leader, but is protected by the rope from above and is not often exposed to hazard.

Climbing routes follow distinct lines up the cliff and are rated according to technical difficulty and potential for injury (hazard). These ratings are subjective, but consensus ratings are achieved as many people climb the route. Ratings are published in guidebooks (for popular areas) or spread by word of mouth (for less popular areas). The technical

---

4. Wolgalter et al. find hazard perception is primarily formed by injury severity. Injury probability is a minor but significant contributing factor to hazard perception.

6. Some climbers climb unroped. A fall from a reasonable distance above the ground will almost certainly result in death or serious injury.

difficulty scale used throughout North America is the Yosemite Decimal Scale (YDS). The easiest technical climbs are rated 5.0 while the most difficult are rated 5.14....

The technical difficulty scale communicates no hazard information. On some climbs, however, the opportunities to place protective devices are few, so that a climber may fall relatively far, generally meaning a greater chance for injury. The climbing hazard scale infers "exposure" to injury, borrowing the "G" through "X" motion picture rating scale. A "G" rating implies little exposure to injury while an "X" ratings implies full exposure. Table I defines the scale used in the study area.

Climbers rarely choose to climb a route in an information void. The technical and hazard ratings of a particular route are generally well-known from published guidebooks or word-of-mouth. A team of climbers will negotiate with one another about which routes to attempt, who will lead what sections, etc. For R- or X-rated routes, the location of the hazardous section is usually known beforehand and the leader for that section can be selected. In general, only the leader is subject to the hazard. Climbers thus may choose from a variety of potential experiences, ranging from very hazardous (leading an X-rated route close to one's maximum technical ability) to the not-so-hazardous (always climbing with a rope from above).

3.2 Evaluating the Hazard Rating

Using the Wolgalter et al. taxonomy for hazard warnings, the letters G, PG, R, and X serve as signal words. The source of hazard (a fall) is implied by the activity and the consequences of a fall are clearly articulated. The instruction for avoiding the hazard is implied—don't do the route. The system also embodies desirable characteristics of a hazard warning system outlined by Magat and Viscusi: it succinctly conveys the hazards of a given route; it differentiates between hazards of different magnitude; and the hazard information scale has been adopted throughout North America, establishing a widespread "warnings vocabulary." Another attractive property of the information system is that it is consistent with the choices that climbers have historically made. Climbers have always voluntarily assumed some degree of hazard, and the hazard warning scale corresponds to the caveat emptor system of Johnson and Luken. The hazard warning tells only of the consequences of a fall and leaves to the individual his or her own assessment of the likelihood of a fall. The scale makes no attempt to assess "expert" probabilities of hazard; rather, it allows for individuating factors to determine the likelihood of injury.

...

... If climbers respond to warnings of injury and or death, we should observe climbers adjusting the difficulty of the hazardous climbs they attempt.

5. THE SAMPLE AND INDICATIONS OF RISK-TAKING BEHAVIOR

Data were collected using a mail survey of members of the Mohonk Preserve in New York state. Located 65 miles from the New York metropolitan area, visitors can become Preserve members by paying an annual fee entitling them to free entry for the year. About 2500 members received a mail questionnaire in Fall 1993, with 892 usable surveys returned. Of the 892 respondents, 220 reported using the Preserve "primarily" to climb. These "climbers" were asked to describe their climbing, but answers were not necessary limited to experiences at the Preserve. While all respondents are Preserve members, we have no reason to believe they are any different from nonmembers.

One hundred and ninety-five climbers completed the detailed questions on rock climbing, and about 75% of these reported they always or usually led climbs, thus placing themselves at risk. These "leaders" were asked to use the technical grade scale to indicate the level at which they usually led climbs. This response was transformed to a monotonic "technical ability" scale....

Climbers were also asked whether they led climbs that were rated "R" or "X" and, if so, at what level of technical difficulty. Of those who led climbs, 46% said they led R climbs and 27% said they led X climbs or climbed without a rope. Climbers who said they led R-rated routes had a mean technical ability about 5.10, yet the R-rated routes they reported climbing had a mean difficulty of 5.8. The same phenomenon occurred with X-rated routes, providing initial support for the hypothesis that climbers respond to hazard warning.

6. EMPIRICAL HAZARD RESPONSE MODELS

Discrete choice analysis was used to estimate two kinds of models. The first examines the decision to assume hazard: does the climber choose to lead R or X routes? This model isolates the role of individuating factors in the choice to lead hazardous routes. The second model estimates the response to a hazard warning. The response measure is discussed in more detail below.

6.1 The Decision to Assume Hazard

It is hypothesized that the more highly skilled the climber, the more likely an injury free ascent of a hazardous route can be made. Thus, the individuating factor *Technical Ability* should identify climbers voluntarily subjecting themselves to hazardous climbs. Probit analysis using the full sample of leaders supports this hypothesis, where *Technical Ability* is positive and significant at the 0.01 level.... About 70% of the responses are correctly predicted by the model, with climbers above technical ability 11 (5.10a) choosing to lead R routes and climbers above 14 (5.10d) choosing to lead X routes. Looking only at the sample of those who choose to lead R-rated climbs, those with greater Technical Ability are more likely to lead the even more hazardous X routes.

6.2 Hazard Response Functions

... [C]limbers of greater ability respond to a lesser degree than those with lesser ability, e.g., a 16 (5.11) climber lowers technical difficulty by 41%, while a 12 (5.10) climber lowers technical difficulty by 61%. The sign for *Injury Severity* indicates that all else being equal, a greater response is observed for greater hazards.

...

7. CONCLUSIONS

This study represents a true field test of a hazard warning system. It is also the first study that we know of which has estimated climbers' response to hazard warnings. Response models include an individuating factor influencing the likelihood of injury as well as the warning about the severity of injury. Empirical models correspond with the theoretical framework. Climbers of greater technical ability are more likely to climb routes that are physically hazardous, suggesting that technical ability is an important individuating factor influencing the likelihood of injury. However, climbers mitigate the likelihood of the hazardous outcome by reducing the technical difficulty of the hazardous route chosen. Further, hazard response models show that when the severity of injury increases from "broken bones" to "death" as the hazardous outcome, climbers mitigate to an even greater degree.

NOTES

1. Should any owner of a rated rockface ever be liable to someone injured when she falls? If you think there never should be liability in such a case, does this mean that you believe that the standard of risk acceptance for potential tort plaintiffs is a completely objective one? Is there any other way for the law to work effectively in this area? How would you react to the case of the plaintiff who correctly reads the rating, but overrates her own ability and slips on a crag?

2. If a business has a risk history, should it ever be able to exculpate itself from liability completely without notifying consumers about risks with some degree of particularity?

3. When businesses seek to exculpate themselves from liability to consumers, should the requirement of specificity of warning be different as among

(a) consumer products used in the workplace—e.g., industrial presses and computer keyboards (b) consumer products used for mixed commercial and recreational purposes—e.g., automobiles, and (c) entirely recreational products—e.g., diving equipment and rockfaces?

[B] In Medicine: The Doctrine of Informed Consent

RIZZO v. SCHILLER

Supreme Court of Virginia
248 Va. 155, 445 S.E.2d 153 (1994)

HASSELL, JUSTICE.

In this appeal, we consider whether the plaintiffs presented sufficient evidence to establish a prima facie case of medical malpractice against a physician who allegedly failed to obtain the mother's informed consent to use obstetrical forceps to deliver her baby.

Michael Sean Rizzo, Jr., by Pamela Rizzo, his mother and next friend, Pamela Rizzo, individually, and Michael Sean Rizzo, Sr., filed this action against Maurice Schiller, M.D. The plaintiffs alleged that Dr. Schiller, an obstetrician and gynecologist, breached the standard of care owed to them when he assisted Ms. Rizzo with the delivery of Michael. Specifically, the plaintiffs alleged that Dr. Schiller was negligent in the use of obstetrical forceps during the delivery and that he failed to obtain Ms. Rizzo's informed consent to use the forceps.

The case was tried before a jury. The trial court granted Dr. Schiller's motion to strike the plaintiffs' informed consent claim. The case proceeded to the jury on the theory that Dr. Schiller was negligent in the use of the obstetrical forceps. The jury returned a verdict in favor of Dr. Schiller, and we awarded the plaintiffs an appeal on issues related to their informed consent claim.

In reviewing the trial court's decision to strike the plaintiffs' evidence, we must consider the evidence and all reasonable inferences deducible therefrom in the light most favorable to the plaintiffs. Furthermore, any reasonable doubt as to the sufficiency of the evidence must be resolved in favor of the plaintiffs....

Pamela Rizzo was admitted to Fairfax Hospital on November 7, 1989, about 9:00 a.m. She was in active labor, and Dr. Schiller was notified of her admission. Upon admission to the hospital, Ms. Rizzo signed the following form:

Authorization for Medical and Surgical Procedures
Patient History No. /P/9456

I hereby authorize Dr. Schiller, and/or other members of the Medical Staff of The Fairfax Hospital of his choice, to perform diagnostic or therapeutic medical and surgical procedures on and to administer anesthetics to Pamela Rizzo. I further authorize The Fairfax Hospital to dispose of any removed tissue or amputated parts.

 11/07/89   [Signed] Pamela S. Rizzo

(Date)   (Signature)

 [Signed] Vera Thomas   _____

(Witness)   (Relationship)

About 12 hours later, Ms. Rizzo's fetal membranes were artificially ruptured at 8:50 p.m., and about 10:00 p.m., she was "pushing with contractions." At 10:15 p.m., Dr. Schiller ordered that Ms. Rizzo be taken to the delivery room. While in the delivery room, Ms. Rizzo made a few, but unsuccessful, attempts to "push" the baby through the birth canal with her abdominal muscles. When Ms. Rizzo's attempts to "push" were unsuccessful, Dr. Schiller told her that he was going to use forceps to deliver the baby. Ms. Rizzo testified that "before I could even get my composure together, ask what they were for, why, [the forceps] were inside me. And my son's head was out, just the head."

Michael was born about 10:30 p.m. About one and one-half hours later, he began to look pale. He was transferred to the intensive care nursery for evaluation. The following morning, Dr. Kathleen B. French, a neurosurgeon, performed a surgical procedure on Michael, and she determined that he had a subdural hematoma. Dr. French testified that a subdural hematoma, which is caused by a trauma to the head, can be described as a collection of blood between the brain tissue and the covering to the brain that is called the dura.

Dr. French, as well as Dr. Mark C. Arner, a physician who practices obstetrics and gynecology, testified that Michael's subdural hematoma was caused by trauma associated with the use of the forceps. Dr. Lawrence T. Taft, who qualified as an expert witness on the subjects of rehabilitative medicine, pediatrics, and neurology, testified that Michael has cerebral palsy and is permanently disabled as a result of this injury.

Dr. Arner qualified as an expert witness on the subjects of obstetrics and gynecology and gave the following testimony. Even though Ms. Rizzo had been given certain medication, she was capable of making medical decisions. Ms. Rizzo would have been able to deliver Michael spontaneously, without the use of forceps, had Dr. Schiller simply waited. If forceps are used in "non-emergent situations," the patient should be informed about the use of the forceps and should be given the opportunity to participate in the decision regarding whether the forceps will be used. Dr. Arner opined that Dr. Schiller breached the standard of care owed to Ms. Rizzo because he failed to allow her to participate in the decision to use forceps.

The plaintiffs contend that the trial court erred by striking their evidence because they established a prima facie case that Dr. Schiller failed to obtain Ms. Rizzo's informed consent for the use of obstetrical forceps during Michael's delivery. Dr. Schiller, however, argues that the plaintiffs' evidence fails to establish a prima facie case and that the plaintiffs failed to present evidence of proximate causation. Furthermore, Dr. Schiller asserts that Ms. Rizzo was allowed to participate in the decision to use forceps because she signed the authorization form. We disagree with Dr. Schiller.

In Hunter v. Burroughs, 123 Va. 113, 133, 96 S.E. 360, 366–67 (1918), we held that "it is the duty of a physician in the exercise of ordinary care to warn a patient of the danger of possible bad consequences of using a remedy," but that the physician's failure to warn "is not per se an act of negligence." Rather, the physician owes a duty to make a reasonable disclosure to the patient of all significant facts under the circumstances. This duty is limited to those disclosures that a reasonable medical practitioner would provide under the same or similar circumstances.... In most cases, expert testimony is necessary to establish those instances where the duty to disclose arises and what disclosures a reasonable medical practitioner would have made under the same or similar circumstances. Id.

We are of opinion that the plaintiffs presented sufficient evidence to establish a prima facie case that Dr. Schiller failed to obtain Ms. Rizzo's informed consent to use the obstetrical forceps. As we have already mentioned, Dr. Arner testified that the appropriate standard of care required that Dr. Schiller inform Ms. Rizzo about the use of the forceps and that she be given an opportunity to participate in the decision whether to use forceps. Ms. Rizzo testified that Dr. Schiller did not disclose any information to her about the use of the forceps and that he used the forceps without her consent.

It is true that Ms. Rizzo signed a document that purportedly is a consent form. However, this form did not inform her of any specific procedures that Dr. Schiller intended to perform; nor did it inform her of foreseeable risks associated with any procedures or risks in failing to perform any procedures. As Dr. Arner observed, the form is so general in nature that "you could also justify amputating her foot." We hold that the duty imposed upon a physician to obtain a patient's informed consent requires more than simply securing the patient's signature on a generalized consent form, similar to the form present here. The law requires informed consent, not mere consent, and the failure to obtain informed consent is tantamount to no consent.

. . .

Accordingly we will remand this case for a trial of the plaintiff's claims of lack of consent.

Reversed and remanded.

A JUDICIAL NOTE ON THE DEVELOPMENT OF INFORMED CONSENT

The court summarized the development of the informed consent doctrine this way in *Logan v. Greenwich Hosp. Ass'n*, 191 Conn. 282, 465 A.2d 294 (1983):

> The incongruity of making the medical profession the sole arbiter of what information was necessary for an informed decision to be made by a patient concerning his own physical well-being has led to various judicial and legislative attempts within the last decade to define a standard tailored to the needs of the patient but not unreasonably burdensome upon the physician or wholly dispensing with the notion that "doctor knows best" in some situations. While the essential ambivalence between the right of the patient to make a knowledgeable choice and the duty of the doctor to prescribe the treatment his pro-

fessional judgment deems best for the patient has not been fully resolved, the outline has begun to emerge.

In a trilogy of cases decided in 1972 the traditional standard of customary medical practice in the community was abandoned by three jurisdictions as the criterion for informed consent in favor of a judicially imposed standard designed to provide a patient with information material to his decision upon a course of therapy. Canterbury v. Spence, 464 F.2d 772 (D.C.Cir.), cert. denied, 409 U.S. 1064, 93 S.Ct. 560, 34 L.Ed.2d 518 (1972); Cobbs v. Grant, [8 Cal.3d 229, 502 P.2d 1, 104 Cal. Rptr. 505 (1972)]; Wilkinson v. Vesey, [110 R.I. 606, 295 A.2d 676 (1972)]. The formulations of the disclosure standard in these cases vary. "Thus the test for determining whether a particular peril must be divulged is its materiality to the patient's decision: all risks potentially affecting the decision must be unmasked." Canterbury v. Spence, supra, 786–87. "The scope of the physician's communications to the patient, then, must be measured by the patient's need, and that need is whatever information is material to the decision." Cobbs v. Grant, supra, 8 Cal.3d at 245, 104 Cal.Rptr. 505, 502 P.2d 1. "It is our belief that, in due deference to the patient's right to self determination, a physician is bound to disclose all the known material risks peculiar to the proposed procedure." Wilkinson v. Vesey, supra, 110 R.I. at 627, 295 A.2d 676. These decisions require something less than a full disclosure of all information which may have some bearing, however remote, upon the patient's decision. Canterbury v. Spence, supra, 786. Although the test is phrased in terms of the "patient's need," rather than impose on the physician an obligation to disclose at his peril whatever the particular patient might deem material to his choice, most courts have attempted to frame a less subjective measure of the physician's duty. "[N]o less than any other aspect of negligence, the issue on nondisclosure must be approached from the viewpoint of the reasonableness of the physician's divulgence in terms of what he knows or should know to be the patient's informational needs." Canterbury v. Spence, supra, 787. "Materiality may be said to be the significance a reasonable person, in what the physician knows or should know is his patient's position, would attach to the disclosed risk or risks in deciding whether to submit or not to submit to surgery or treatment." Wilkinson v. Vesey, supra, 627, 295 A.2d 676; Waltz & Scheuneman, Informed Consent to Therapy, 64 Nw.U.L.Rev. 628, 640 (1970). In states which have legislated this so-called "lay" standard of disclosure vis-a-vis the orthodox professional standard, the statutes typically impose a duty to disclose such information as a "reasonable patient would consider material to the decision whether or not to undergo treatment or diagnosis." See Pa.Stat.Ann. tit. 40, § 1301.103 (Purdon Cum.Sup. 1983)....

The standard has been further delineated by specifying various elements which the physician's disclosure should include: "(1) the 'nature' of the procedure, (2) the 'risks' and 'hazards' of the procedure, (3) the 'alternatives' to the procedure, and (4) the anticipated 'benefits' of the procedure." Meisel & Kabnick, Informed Consent to Medical Treatment: An Analysis of Recent Legislation, 41 U.Pitt.L.Rev. 407, 427 (1980); Canterbury v. Spence, supra, 787–88. "Obviously there is no need to disclose risks that are likely to be known by the average patient or that are in fact known to the patient usually because of a past experience with the procedure in question." Wilkinson v. Vesey, supra, 627, 295 A.2d 676.... Some limited recognition has been given also to the therapeutic privilege of a physician to withhold information where disclosure might jeopardize a course of therapy....

The leading case of Canterbury v. Spence ... was given a generally favorable reception by the judiciary, and soon the lay standard of disclosure had been adopted in eight states, obligating the physician to provide the patient with that information which a reasonable patient would have found material for making a decision whether to embark upon a contemplated course of therapy. Meisel & Kabnick, supra, 423. Three of these states subsequently have abandoned this standard by statutes which expressly or implicitly adopt the professional standard of disclosure in accordance with the practice of a reasonable medical practitioner under similar circumstances....

NOTES

(1) Apart from the factor of possible emotional consequences attendant on full disclosure, what other qualifications likely will have to attach to the "informed consent" approach in practice? What difficulties will arise for physicians under this standard?

Consider the premises of legal philosophy on which the general notion of informed consent rests. In *Canterbury v. Spence*, 464 F.2d 772 (D.C. Cir. 1972), cert. denied, 409 U.S. 1064 (1972), the court set out a basic postulate with its quotation of Cardozo's declaration in a 1914 case that "[E]very human being of adult years and sound mind has a right to determine what shall be done with his own body." Working from that premise, the *Canterbury* court declared that "[t]rue consent to what happens to one's self is the informed exercise of a choice, and that entails an opportunity to evaluate knowledgeably the options available and the risks attendant upon each." Does *Rizzo* apply these principles in a fair and sensible way?

(2) Is the idea of participatory decisionmaking that the *Rizzo* court uses a realistic one?

Is there a way that the hospital could have worded the consent form in *Rizzo* to make Ms. Rizzo's consent an "informed" one? What would Dr. Schiller himself have had to do in order to elicit informed consent at the time that the baby's head appeared during the birth process?

(3) In another forceps/birth case, a majority of the Pennsylvania court employed a rather technical definition of informed consent in upholding a nonsuit. The following passages summarize the court's reasoning:

> [The doctrine as interpreted in Pennsylvania] protects the patient's right to make an informed choice as to whether to proceed with a *surgical* or *operative procedure*.
>
> ...
>
> The Superior Court correctly determined that the use of forceps is not an operative procedure. Under the circumstances of this case, the physician's use of forceps involved the application of a tool to assist in the natural delivery process, and as such, was merely an extension of the physician's hands. We agree with the Superior Court's conclusion that the physician's use of forceps in this case is indistinguishable from a physician's use of an otoscope to examine the ear canal or a physician's insertion of a speculum into a woman's vagina in order to perform a vaginal examination.... [3] Moreover, we find that the

---

3. Appellants submit that this Court should consider the use of forceps an operative or surgical procedure because the medical community does. However, because we find that the use of forceps is indistinguishable from the use of tools such as an otoscope or speculum, we reject this argument.

physician's attempt to use forceps is part of one event: the natural delivery process. Thus, the physician's use of forceps to facilitate natural delivery is not a distinct surgical or operative procedure and, as a result, does not require additional consent to use the forceps.

Appellants also assert that, even if this Court finds that the use of forceps during the natural delivery process does not constitute an operative or surgical procedure, the informed consent doctrine should nevertheless apply to this case because the Appellants were not apprised of the risks associated with the forceps delivery. Restated, Appellants argue that regardless of whether a forceps delivery is a surgical or operative procedure, they were not informed of all material facts, risks, complications and alternatives of the delivery process. Appellants submit that, while there are limits to informed consent, nonetheless, any touching of the patient which involves risks of serious injury requires that the physician inform the patient of said risks and then receive the patient's consent in order to perform the procedure. Under the circumstances of this case, we disagree.

The goal of the informed consent doctrine is to provide the patient with material information necessary to determine whether to proceed with the surgical or operative procedure or to remain in the present condition.... The doctrine presupposes that the patient has a choice to exercise. Instantly, however, Mrs. Sinclair had no decision to make. Having carried her child to term, she could not elect to remain in her present condition. Regardless of any decision that she might attempt to make, the natural delivery process was inevitable. During the course of natural delivery, as opposed to an operative or surgical procedure, the physician is present to assist nature. The physician intervenes if complications arise during the natural delivery process. At that point, the physician might have to conduct an operative or surgical procedure such as a Caesarian section which, except in an emergency situation, would require the patient's informed consent. Thus, because labor is inevitable and there is no choice to make, the informed consent doctrine does not apply to the natural delivery process.

By reason of the fact that the woman does not make the decision to proceed with an operative or surgical procedure or to remain in the present condition and that the natural delivery process does not require an incision, or the excision of tissue, bone, etc., we hold that the natural delivery process does not require that the patient give specific informed consent for the procedure; rather, general consent is appropriate.... [6]

Sinclair By Sinclair v. Block, 534 Pa. 563, 633 A.2d 1137, 1140–41 (1993).

Does this reasoning persuade you? Is this a discriminatorily sexist resolution of the issue?

(4) Should the standard for eliciting informed consent be a local one, or should it be more broadly defined? In *Logan v. Greenwich Hosp. Ass'n.*, 191 Conn. 282, 465 A.2d 294

---

6. We note that this case is distinguishable from cases where the physician exceeded the scope of the consent.... Mrs. Sinclair authorized Appellees to perform any procedure which was necessary to accomplish the delivery of her baby. Thus, Appellants cannot argue that Appellee went beyond the scope of the general consent in this case when he attempted to facilitate the natural delivery process by using forceps. The forceps were merely a tool Appellee used to facilitate the natural delivery process, and thus, it falls within the general consent to the natural delivery process.

(1983), excerpted above at pages 214–216 on the development of informed consent doctrine, the court said that the medical standard generally, including the informed consent standard, is one that "include[s] the entire nation." The court observed that it was "not aware of any differences in the educational background and training of physicians practicing in Connecticut compared with those in other states," and noted that "[m]edical literature of significance is normally disseminated throughout this country and not confined to a particular state." 191 Conn. at 301–02, 465 A.2d at 304–05.

(5) While most "informed consent" decisions tend to treat the question under a "negligence" or "malpractice" label, the theory of battery has continued viability. An Arizona federal court emphasized this in holding unconstitutional a state statute that abrogated the right to sue doctors on "assault and battery" theories. In a case in which a doctor excised a vaccination mark without his patient's consent, the court distinguished the societal interests served by the different theories of liability: "The battery theory sustains a patient's right of self-determination; the negligence theory recognizes a physician's obligation to provide reasonable disclosure of the available choices with respect to the proposed procedures and the dangers inherently and potentially involved in each." The court emphasized that "A patient's right of self-determination may be violated, even though his health is significantly improved." *Rubino v. de Fretias*, 638 F. Supp. 182 (D. Ariz. 1986).

(6) It is pretty well established that a doctor or dentist may not employ an exculpatory clause to relieve himself of the duty to be reasonably careful. See, e.g., *Emory Univ. v. Porubiansky*, 248 Ga. 391, 282 S.E.2d 903 (1981)(dentist). But why should this be so as a matter of theory? Why shouldn't a patient be able to contract away her liability rights against a physician in exchange for an agreement by the doctor to render services for a fee lower than a price that does not include an exculpatory arrangement? In the case just cited, the Georgia Supreme Court said it was "against the public policy of this state" to allow a dentist to contract out of liability for negligence. What public policy is that?

(7) Professor Sugarman emphasizes the "social role" of the physician with respect to the doctor's role to communicate information: "[D]octors are understood in today's society to be fiduciaries and ... as such, they should disclose to their patients not only the risk of treatment they propose, but also the risks of nontreatment, as well as a range of risks and benefits associated with the reasonably plausible alternative treatments that might be tried, if any. This is because a fiduciary is someone we turn to in order to obtain the full range of information that is needed to make a sound decision." Stephen D. Sugarman, *Rethinking Tort Doctrine: Visions of a Restatement (Fourth) of Torts*, 50 U.C.L.A. L. Rev. 585, 598 (2002).

NOTE ON INFORMED CONSENT IN ATTORNEY MALPRACTICE

Should courts apply an informed consent requirement to the giving of professional advice by lawyers? In *Conklin v. Weisman*, 145 N.J. 395, 414–15, 678 A.2d 1060, 1069–70 (1996), the court concluded that the theory did not fit very well in the attorney-client situation. The occasion was a case in which the plaintiffs, owners of a farm that they listed for sale, sued their law firm for, inter alia, failing "adequately and accurately to explain ... the meaning and risks" of the concept of subordination in mortgage law. The case involved the subordination of a purchase-money mortgage held by the plaintiffs to another mortgage. That other mortgage secured a loan that the buyer of the farm was to get to raise any balance of cash it had to pay at the closing on the property.

The result of the subordination was that the plaintiffs would have to take a back seat to other lenders. In rejecting the application of informed consent to lawyers' advice, the court said:

> The objective theory of informed consent, under which the jury would be asked to consider whether a reasonably prudent client would have entered into a business transaction if adequately informed of its attendant risks, fails to reflect the many highly subjective, personal, financial and strategic concerns that underlay most legal decisions and that are not present in the majority of medical decisions. A majority of medical patients are sick and consult a doctor for a single purpose — to get well. The patients usually bring little or no personal knowledge to the evaluation of the risks associated with their recovery.
>
> Without any insight into the make-up and needs of the legal malpractice plaintiff, expert testimony regarding what a reasonably prudent client would have done under similar circumstances in weighing the risks and complications of complex commercial business transactions appears of dubious value to the trier of fact. (Would a client wish not to be presented as a prudent person?) Clients such as Donald Trump or Harry Helmsley might view such matters differently than family farmers or business people or real estate developers. Defendants' expert acknowledged that the measure of the attorney's advice "depends on the expertise of the individual [client] involved."
>
> In short, some clients may sufficiently understand aspects of a financial transaction, such as the priority of mortgages, so as not to impose a duty on their lawyer to explain the transaction in detail. For them, what a prudent client might do is largely irrelevant. On the other hand, each would probably approach by-pass surgery with a single purpose — to get well.

The court declared that instead of "importing the doctrine of informed consent into attorney malpractice," it would hold "that the usual principles of negligence apply to legal malpractice."

PROBLEM

A surgeon told a patient who was contemplating a complicated operation on his neck that he had done sixty operations of that kind every year over an eleven-year period. In fact, he had only done twenty such operations during his career. The plaintiff emerged from the operation a quadriplegic. What are his chances in a tort suit?

HARTKE v. McKELWAY

United States Court of Appeals, District of Columbia
707 F.2d 1544, cert. denied, 464 U.S. 983 (1983)

MCGOWAN, SENIOR CIRCUIT JUDGE:

... We are ... called upon to decide whether, in the light of certain language in our opinion in Henderson v. Milobsky, 595 F.2d 654, 657–58 (D.C.Cir.1978), patients in informed-consent cases must testify that they would not have undergone the procedure had they known of all the material risks involved. Finally, we must decide whether the risk of subsequent pregnancy in this case could reasonably have been considered material to a decision whether to undergo the treatment.

[The district court held for the plaintiff on her claim for medical expenses, pain and suffering and mental anguish connected with pregnancy and childbirth, but denied her claim for childrearing expenses.]

I

In the winter of 1978, Sandra J. Hartke, the plaintiff in this action, discovered she was pregnant and elected to have an abortion. For reasons that are crucial to the disposition of this appeal, and that are discussed at length below, she also sought to have herself sterilized. Her usual doctor recommended a hysterectomy, the complete removal of the uterus. Hartke, then 33, thought this a rather drastic procedure, so she approached the defendant, Dr. William McKelway, for a second opinion. Dr. McKelway recommended a procedure known as laparoscopic tubal cauterization, which involves blocking the Fallopian tubes by burning them with instruments inserted through one or two small incisions in the abdomen. Hartke consented to the procedure, and on March 14, 1978, an abortion and tubal cauterization were performed on her. Dr. McKelway subsequently examined Hartke and termed the operation successful.

There was testimony from which the jury could infer that prior to the operation Dr. McKelway failed to disclose to Hartke that there was a risk of recanalization—where a Fallopian tube spontaneously reopens—of one to three out of one thousand. Hartke and her boyfriend, with whom she had lived for four years and whom she later married, also testified that the boyfriend offered to undergo a vasectomy if there was any risk of subsequent pregnancy, but that McKelway told them that the procedure was "a 100 percent sure operation," and that Hartke would not have to worry about becoming pregnant again....

Despite the surgery, Hartke again became pregnant in September 1979. After an examination confirmed that the pregnancy was normal—she had had a tubal or ectopic pregnancy in 1968—she elected to carry it to term and in June 1980 gave birth by Caesarean section to a baby girl. At the same time, Hartke had herself resterilized by a tubal ligation, which involves actually cutting the Fallopian tubes. The record suggests that this method of sterilization involves about the same risk of subsequent pregnancy as cauterization....

... The jury returned a special verdict, finding that McKelway negligently failed to cauterize Hartke's Fallopian tubes and that he failed to inform her of a material risk of the procedure. It awarded Hartke $10,000 in medical expenses, $100,000 for pain, suffering, and mental anguish, and $200,000 for the "[a]nticipated costs of raising this child until age 18 less any benefit [Hartke] received or in the future will receive by reason of the love, joy, happiness, etc. she experienced in raising a healthy, happy child."...

...

II

We deal first with the judgment that Dr. McKelway failed to disclose material risks to Hartke.

A. Materiality of the Risk

McKelway first argues that he had no duty to disclose the risks of pregnancy in this case since no "reasonable person in what the physician [knew] or should [have known] to be the patient's position would be likely to attach significance to the risks in deciding whether to accept or forego the proposed treatment," Crain v. Allison, 443 A.2d 558, 562 (D.C.App.1982). The risk of pregnancy after laparoscopic cauterization was testified to be one to three out of one thousand.

For present purposes, the crucial language in the above formulation is "what the physician [knew] or should [have known] to be the patient's position." The "patient's position" must include the patient's medical history and other factors that might make knowledge of certain risks particularly important to a certain patient, acting reasonably. Here, there were two factors that would make even a small risk of pregnancy unusually dangerous for a patient in Hartke's position. First, Dr. McKelway knew that Hartke had a history of gynecological and pregnancy-related problems. She had contracted peritonitis after the birth by Caesarean section of her first child in 1964, resulting in a lengthy and traumatic hospital stay. She had had an ectopic pregnancy in 1968, apparently begun while using an IUD. She had been hospitalized numerous times for minor gynecological procedures. Hartke testified she informed Dr. McKelway that other doctors had advised her she "would not make it through [another] pregnancy." ... Second, Dr. McKelway had before him conclusive evidence of the psychological effect of pregnancy on his patient. He testified that she was "extremely upset" and "very agitated" about the pregnancy.... She testified that she told him she thought she was going to die from the pregnancy....

In sum, the jury could conclude that a subsequent pregnancy would be a very serious consequence for this particular patient, which would result possibly in physical and certainly in psychological trauma. This was underscored by the testimony that Hartke's boyfriend told the doctor he would undergo a vasectomy instead if the sterilization was not sure to be successful.

Moreover, less risky paths than relying on the cauterization were open to Hartke. Had she been able to compare the relative risks of failure, she might reasonably have changed her mind and decided to undergo a hysterectomy if, as the evidence suggested,[5] the latter procedure would have reduced the risk. Perhaps more likely given her ultimate course of conduct, even if Hartke had agreed to the cauterization, she might reasonably have decided to have her boyfriend undergo a vasectomy, abstained from intercourse, or taken other precautions that would reduce the risk.

In Canterbury v. Spence, 464 F.2d 772 (D.C.Cir.), cert. denied, 409 U.S. 1064, 93 S.Ct. 560, 34 L.Ed.2d 518 (1972), this court noted in this connection, "Whenever nondisclosure of particular risk information is open to debate by reasonable-minded men, the issue is for the finder of the facts." Id. at 788 (footnote deleted). There we held that the jury could have found a one percent risk of a very serious harm—permanent urinary incontinence and paralysis of the bowels—to be material to a decision whether to undergo an operation for back pain. Id. at 794. In Henderson v. Milobsky, 595 F.2d 654, 659 (D.C.Cir.1978), we held that a .001% risk of permanent loss of sensation in a small section of the face could not reasonably be deemed material to a decision whether to have impacted wisdom teeth removed. In this case, the undisclosed risk was a .1% to .3% chance of subsequent pregnancy. For most people, this risk would be considered very small, but this patient was in a particularly unusual position. In view of the very serious expected consequences of pregnancy for her—possibly including death—as well as the ready availability of ways to reduce the risk, we agree with the District Court that a jury could conclude that a reasonable person in what Dr. McKelway knew to be plaintiff's position would be likely to attach significance to the risk here.

---

5. Compare Transcript of July 23, 1981, at 237 (Dr. Marlow) ("*surprisingly* ... there have been a number of pregnancies" after hysterectomies) (emphasis added) and id. at 151 (Dr. Falk) (25 abdominal pregnancies have been reported in the literature) with id. at 148 (Falk) (risk of pregnancy after laparoscopic sterilization is one to three or four per thousand) and id. at 236 (Marlow) ("I know of no series in the world where there have not be[en] failures following laparoscopic sterilization.").

B. Proximate Cause

In order for there to be liability in tort, there must be both breach of duty—here, the failure to divulge a material risk—and proximate causation. McKelway argues that the issue of whether the failure to disclose the risk of subsequent pregnancy here proximately caused the harm should not have gone to the jury because Hartke had not testified that she would not have undergone the treatment had she known of the risks. The source of McKelway's argument is certain language in our opinion in Henderson v. Milobsky, 595 F.2d 654 (D.C.Cir.1978). Discussing the earlier case of Haven v. Randolph, 494 F.2d 1069 (D.C.Cir.1974), the Henderson court wrote:

> *Haven* did not, however, add anything really novel to our jurisprudence on risk-disclosure. In result, it merely reemphasized the claimant's burden of showing that the alleged breach of duty to disclose led to the injury for which compensation is sought. In *Canterbury* we had held that when damages are sought for a condition attributed to a medical procedure, causation by breach of duty cannot be demonstrated simply by the claimant's unadorned hindsight-statement that had he known of the risk he would not have consented to the procedure. *Haven merely stands for the cognate proposition that when the claimant has not even made such an assertion, the issue of causation cannot possibly go to the jury.*

595 F.2d at 657–58 (emphasis added, footnote deleted).

The District Court rejected McKelway's argument, finding that *Henderson* should not be read to require in haec verba testimony from the plaintiff "as long as there is sufficient evidence from which the jury could infer that she would have refused." 526 F.Supp. at 103. The court held that to require such testimony in such a case "would only set a trap for the unwary." Id. Citing Hartke's husband's offer to undergo a vasectomy, the court found that there was evidence in this case "from which the jury could find that plaintiff would have declined the procedure had she been informed of the risks." Id.

In its ruling the District Court appears to have applied a standard of causation based on what Hartke herself would have done. This is inconsistent with the standard of causation adopted by this court in Canterbury v. Spence, 464 F.2d at 790–91. In that case the court held that the issue of causation should be resolved on an objective basis, "in terms of what a prudent person in the patient's position would have decided if suitably informed of all perils bearing significance." Id. at 791 (footnote deleted). The rule was based on a distrust of the patient's hindsight testimony that he or she would have foregone the treatment. Id. at 790 (The patient's testimony "hardly represents more than a guess, perhaps tinged by the circumstance that the uncommunicated hazard has in fact materialized.") (footnote deleted). Such testimony was believed to be the primary, if not only, evidence on the question of causation in the usual case.

The District Court's confusion in this case—it charged the jury under a reasonable-person standard, Transcript of July 29, 1981, at 431—is understandable, because in both *Henderson* and *Haven*, issued after the Canterbury decision, this court appears to have applied a causation-in-fact rather than a reasonable-person standard....

Since the trial court's ruling in this case, however, the District of Columbia Court of Appeals has unequivocally adopted, albeit in dictum, the objective, prudent-person standard. Citing the Canterbury case, the court in Crain v. Allison, 443 A.2d 558, 563 n. 14 (D.C.App.1982), wrote, "[T]he test of causation is objective. The test is what would a prudent person in the patient's position have decided if informed of all relevant factors...."

Under this standard, it is no longer possible to argue that a patient's testimony is necessary for the issue of causation to get to the jury. The entire motivation for jettisoning the subjective standard of causation was distrust of precisely this testimony. As the Canterbury court pointed out, under the objective standard "[t]he plaintiff's testimony is relevant ... but it would not threaten to dominate the findings." 464 F.2d at 791; accord Crain, 443 A.2d at 563 n. 14 ("Although the patient's testimony is relevant on the issue of causation, the test of causation is objective."); Sard v. Hardy, 281 Md. 432, 450, 379 A.2d 1014, 1025 (1977) ("Under this rule, the patient's hindsight testimony as to what he would have hypothetically done, though relevant, is not determinative of the issue."). While it might be helpful, the jury certainly does not need the patient's testimony to decide what a reasonable person in that position would have done.

...

[Affirmed.]

Donald A. Redelmeier, Paul Rozin and Daniel Kahneman, *Understanding Patients' Decisions: Cognitive and Emotional Perspectives*
270 J.A.M.A. No. 1, at 72 (1993)*

Helping patients reach reasonable decisions is an important part of the art of medicine. The patient's perspective can be decisive in choosing when to seek help, the degree of compliance with treatment, and whether to change one's life-style. In a break from some traditional views, active patient participation is now considered desirable because of the ethical principle of patient autonomy and the legal requirement of informed consent. A patient who takes responsibility for a decision may also be less likely to blame the physician if things go wrong. Yet it is not always easy to elicit reasonable and informed decisions from patients. Their beliefs are susceptible to biases and their preferences sometimes appear irrational. This article reviews recent findings from research on judgment and decision making that help explain some of the difficulties that arise when patients are called on to make decisions about their care.

The ideal decision maker would gather all available information about the situation, calculate the costs and benefits of every feasible option, and then decide on the optimal choice. In contrast to the ideal, people reach judgments based on simplifying heuristic rules and search until they find an acceptable solution, not necessarily the best. These strategies are often effective because they economize on time and usually lead to sensible decisions. However, the departures from strict rationality can also lead to mistakes. Errors in reasoning arise from many sources, such as misinformation, denial, overconfidence, distrust, and confusion. In this article we present examples of research on the common biases in peoples' perceptions of risk and describe some new lines of investigation that focus on the role of emotion in decision making.

PERCEPTIONS OF RISK
Categorical Safety and Danger

One feature of human judgment is the tendency to categorize an entity as either "dangerous" or "safe" without recognizing that low and high levels of exposure can have different or even opposite effects. For example, many respondents in a recent survey believed that a teaspoon of ice cream has more calories than a pint of cottage cheese.... Presumably, ice cream is considered as inherently high in calories and cottage cheese low, regardless of the amount consumed. The same type of thinking that brands an activity as healthy or dangerous independent of dose can lead individuals to believe that a person cannot ingest too many vitamins, that infinitesimal amounts of salt or sugar are harmful, or that even the most trivial contact with anyone having the acquired immunodeficiency syndrome (AIDS) is dangerous.

Insensitivity to dosage and to the frequency of exposure also appear in situations that are coded as safe. For example, automobile travel entails only a one in 1 million risk of dying during an average trip, yet a one in 50 risk over a lifetime of driving. Fear diminishes as the anticipated danger fails to materialize over multiple occasions, even though individuals make many trips so that the cumulative risk is substantial. One method for lessening peoples' tendency to categorize an entity as either dangerous or safe is to explicitly discuss dose-response relationships; for example, emphasize that ingesting large quantities of vitamin C can cause kidney stones, that taking higher doses of antibiotics will not lead to faster recovery, or that years of uneventful cigarette smoking do not indicate invulnerability to the adverse effects of future cigarettes.

The Enchanting Appeal of Zero Risk

People often discriminate more sharply than is appropriate between interventions that eliminate a risk and interventions that merely reduce it. Imagine a container of pesticide priced at $10 that produces a harmful toxic reaction 15 times for every 10,000 containers used. How much is an equally effective product worth if it reduces the risk to 10, 5, or 0 incidents per 10,000 containers? The results of a survey showed that people were willing to pay $1.04 extra for the reduction from 15 to 10 reactions, whereas they would pay $2.41 extra for the reduction from five to zero events per 10,000 containers. Apparently, the absolute elimination of a risk is more attractive than a mere reduction of the probability of harm. However, the special premium that people are willing to pay to avoid worry cannot be justified as a purchase of improved safety. Indeed, the hope of eliminating risk is usually illusory given the many similar hazards that remain. In this particular scenario, for example, there are multiple sources of toxic reactions in any home so that complete protection against one possibility provides only partial protection against the overall risk of poisoning.

Lessening the odds is the realistic aim in most cases, yet it has far less appeal than the illusion of perfect safety. One explanation is that small probabilities all seem similar. "One chance in 20,000" is, for most people, an abstract notion: no living organism can accumulate sufficient personal experience to encompass such a low frequency. Thus, it is not surprising that, biologically, we have little intuitive understanding of the difference between a risk of one in 20,000 and a risk of one in 200,000. Helping patients to understand such small probabilities requires listing concrete events that have similar likelihoods; for example, one in 20,000 corresponds to the chance that a person will live more than 100 years and one in 200,000 to the chance that an airline flight will be hijacked. Additionally, epidemiologic analyses can help explain the importance of competing risks; for example, estimates suggest that a perfect cure for cancer would yield less than a 4-year increase in average life expectancy in North America. Finally, medical outcomes data can illustrate that even well-accepted treatments are imperfect; for example, in symptomatic patients with high-grade carotid stenosis, endarterectomy performed by expert surgeons reduces the annual risk of stroke from about 14% to 6%—not to 0%.

Framing and Presentation

Peoples' interpretation of most events depends on both the nature of the experience and the manner in which the situation is presented or "framed." For example, a foul odor near a sewer may be disgusting, whereas the same aroma emanating from a cheese counter can be enticing. Psychological research has shown that people are often sensitive to the presentation of problems and that they fail to realize the extent to which their preferences can be altered by an inconsequential change in formulation.

Consider how patients interpret data from medical research. Based on published reports, the outcome statistics for 100 middle-aged men undergoing surgery for lung cancer can be described as "90 live through the postoperative period ... and 34 are alive at the end of 5 years." Now consider an alternative way of expressing the same results: "10 die during the postoperative period ... and 66 die by the end of 5 years." Is one of these formulations more frightening than the other, relative to the minimal risk of early mortality found with radiation therapy for lung cancer? Using these data an experiment showed that surgery appeared much less attractive than radiation therapy when described using mortality rather than survival statistics. The explanation is that the difference between 10% mortality and 0% mortality is more impressive than the difference between 90% survival and 100% survival. The framing effect was just as large with physicians as with lay people.

Framing effects are difficult to avoid because there is no one optimal method for presenting statistics. However, it is disturbing that the preferences of both physicians and patients can be swayed by the accidental choice of one formulation of results rather than another. Equally troubling is the possibility of deliberately exploiting framing effects, as often occurs in the marketing of drugs and surgical supplies. Two useful defenses against framing effects are to consider the data from multiple perspectives and to discuss the issue with a person whose opinion on the same problem is different. When different formulations yield identical choices, one gains confidence in the final assessment. In situations where framing effects cannot be avoided, they sometimes may be redirected; for example, presenting data as the negative consequences of nonadherence, rather than the positive outcomes of adherence, might allow clinicians to be more persuasive when recommending health-promoting behaviors.

Hindsight Bias

Peer review organizations often presume that a detailed review of a patient's medical chart provides an unbiased assessment of quality of care. In contrast, psychologists have shown that such retrospective judgments can be distorted by knowledge of the ultimate outcome. For example, expert reviewers were asked to judge the appropriateness of care in surgical cases that involved an adverse anaesthetic outcome. Each case was formulated in one of two versions, describing the patient's outcome as either permanent or temporary. The two versions otherwise contained identical information and were assigned randomly to reviewers. However, the reviewers were more likely to rate the quality of care as "less than appropriate" if the outcome was permanent rather than temporary. Furthermore, knowledge of the outcome influenced both the harshness of the rating and the willingness to offer a judgment.

Hindsight bias occurs when people examine past decisions because they tend to highlight data that were consistent with the final outcome and de-emphasize data that were contradictory or ambiguous. Estimates of probability and risk are particularly prone to this bias; for example, people are more likely to indicate that a given outcome was inevitable if they later learn that it occurred. Individuals are more likely to classify a decision as a mistake if it was followed by a significant adverse consequence. Even the clinical dictum of Sutton's law ("to go where the money is") can be deceptive because the most rewarding strategy is often only apparent after the fact. Physicians can lessen the illusory confidence that arises from retrospective second-guessing by providing explicit statements of probabilities prior to obtaining informed consent. Doing so might promote a more proactive attitude about untoward medical events, lessen the chances of subsequent distortions, and prevent unduly negative evaluations of the wisdom of choices that were made prospectively.

EMOTIONS, FEELINGS, AND DECISION MAKING

In science there is a strong tendency to neglect variables that cannot be measured accurately. Mortality risk is much easier to measure and quantify than is emotion, so that medical research tends to focus on mortality rather than on quality of life. However, many medical interventions provide benefits primarily to a patient's sense of well-being, so that a lack of objective measures can lead to misleading conclusions about a lack of therapeutic efficacy. Patients often seek medical care for the sympathy, reassurance, and validation provided; thus, these outcomes should be included when measuring the effectiveness of a clinical intervention. We cannot afford to ignore feelings just because they present difficult scientific problems. To be sure, quality of life measures are gaining popularity in medical studies, yet standard instruments primarily focus on physical disabilities, mental impairments, and functional status, rather than comfort, satisfaction, and peace of mind.

...

Loss Aversion and Preference for Status Quo

A fully rational agent would not distinguish between an action that leads to a loss (of money, health, or time) and a missed opportunity to realize the equivalent gain. An actual loss and a foregone gain are similar because both represent the same failure to achieve the best possible outcome. However, people take actual losses far more seriously than foregone gains and are therefore reluctant to accept a loss in one dimension of life to achieve an improvement in another dimension. Recall the pesticide example where respondents were willing to pay only about $1.04 to purchase extra safety (decreasing the risk from 15 to 10 incidents per 10,000 containers). When asked whether they would be willing to sell safety (increasing the risk from 15 to 16 incidents per 10,000 containers) most respondents refused altogether, and the mean price the others demanded was $2.86. Apparently, the trade-off between money and safety is different when people evaluate deteriorations rather than improvements.

Losses loom larger than corresponding gains in many clinical situations. Patients are often hesitant to take chloramphenicol due to its one in 25,000 risk of producing a fatal reaction but remain unenthusiastic about hepatitis vaccinations, which offer a one in 10,000 chance of preventing death. A similar pattern occurs in peoples' preferences for the status quo; for example, scientific evidence suggests that dipyridamole is ineffective at preventing strokes, yet many patients with cerebrovascular disease who have been receiving this drug are unwilling to accept its discontinuation. More generally, peoples' reluctance to relinquish current routines helps explain the difficulties in encouraging patients to change their diet, drive carefully, and exercise regularly. One method for lessening peoples' differential attitudes toward losses and gains is to confront them with different reference points, such as highlighting that if the individual were newly diagnosed with cerebrovascular disease the medical management would not entail initiation of dipyridamole therapy.

What factors determine the patient's reference point? In most cases the reference point corresponds to the status quo, the customary outcome, or some other value that is considered normal. However, reference points can also be designated or suggested almost arbitrarily. For example, people are willing to sit for 5 hours in an airplane during a transcontinental flight but can become annoyed if their baggage is returned 5 minutes late. In medical contexts, the sequence in which options are presented, the designation of some outcomes as normal, and the description of costs and benefits relative to the norm all can influence patients' choice and satisfaction. The physician has considerable power to define the dominant reference point from which patients will judge outcomes, and this power should be used with care.

Predicting Future Feelings

To understand the role of feelings and emotions as costs or benefits in decision making requires examining how these intangibles are represented in the mind. Typically, a person chooses between alternatives by trying to imagine what it will feel like to experience the available choices. As a consequence, medicolegal doctrine contends that providing patients with informed consent entails describing the possible outcomes of a given treatment and their relative probabilities. Yet psychologists have shown that people are prone to err when making decisions about long-term consequences because they fail to anticipate how their preferences will change over time. An informed decision about whether to undergo surgery for rectal cancer, for example, requires having patients understand both how their lives are likely to change with a colostomy as well as how their own attitudes toward a colostomy are likely to change.

. . .

Medical outcomes can be much more difficult for patients to envision because of their unfamiliar character and the uncertain nature of human adaptation. Most individuals are surprised that 1 year after one group of people won a large lottery, and another group became paraplegic, the quality-of-life ratings of both groups were fairly similar. Likewise, people may gauge their reaction to colostomy by how they would feel about it immediately after the operation, rather than considering whether these concerns will fade over time. To the extent that physicians anticipate their patients' adapting to different health states, true informed consent would require highlighting these future preferences when discussing current therapeutic alternatives. This might include both statistics and interviews of people who underwent each therapeutic alternative months or years previously.

Memories of Past Experiences

When people make a medical decision between alternatives that they have already experienced (eg, a second round of radiation therapy), they compare their mental representations of each of the alternatives and, presumably, choose the alternative that they remember as less unpleasant. But memories are inaccurate and subject to error. One major distortion is that duration may not be as well represented as peak intensity. Thus, a few days of intense acute pain may be remembered as more unpleasant than many weeks of moderate chronic pain, in the same way that a brief media soundbite may be more memorable than a longer detailed report. When choosing between two unpleasant medical procedures, a patient might reasonably select the procedure that is shorter but more intense because it entails a smaller loss in quality of life, productivity, and well-being. However, the patient and the physician need to realize, especially if subsequent choices of the same sort are to be made, that the memory for the shorter procedure may be more potent and more aversive.

The difference between a patient's experience of an unpleasant medical procedure and the patient's memory of the experience also poses ethical problems for clinicians. For example, dressing changes on burn patients can be extremely painful. Should patients be prescribed amnesia-producing medications to deliberately lessen their memories of the experience? Doing so may not change the essential characteristics of the procedure but might increase compliance with subsequent treatments. Similarly, when choosing between equally effective treatments, should one recommend a treatment that is more unpleasant as it is experienced but may be remembered more favorably? Physicians who wish to respect patient autonomy will face conflicting priorities in situations where prospective and retrospective evaluations lead to different treatment recommendations.

Irrational Concerns

Emotional responses can be intense; in such cases, people may "realize" that their reactions are not "rational," yet they remain unable to reconcile priorities. Consider the case of disgust. Almost all college students claim that they would not drink a glass of their favorite juice if a cockroach had been briefly dipped into the beverage and then removed. The typical account from respondents for this aversion involves the possibility of bodily harm from dangerous microorganisms on the cockroach. However, almost everyone continues to claim reluctance to drink another glass of their favorite juice into which a dead, sterilized cockroach has been dipped and removed. Under these circumstances, people change the account of their rejection by ultimately concluding that there must be something inherently bad about cockroaches. Yet, one third of these subjects are also reluctant to drink a third glass of their favorite juice after it has been stirred by a brand new fly swatter.(38) Apparently, just the association of fly swatters with an offensive entity, such as a cockroach, accounts for the negative response. Hence, disgust can influence decisions in situations where people may recognize that they have no rational account for their reaction.

A similar pattern of response can occur in peoples' reactions to other aversive situations. Many college students are reluctant to put on a sweater after it has been worn by a person with AIDS, justifying this decision in terms of health risk.... However, a sweater that was sterilized after being worn by a person with AIDS is almost as aversive as the original sweater. Furthermore, this same type of reluctance occurs in reactions to wearing sterilized sweaters of people who have tuberculosis, an amputated foot, or who have committed moral offenses.... The reaction to contact, therefore, is only weakly related to the risk of infection; instead, disgust may be under the control of cognitions that are not immediately acknowledged and that cannot be classified as rational. In accord with what has been described as the "law of contagion" (once in contact, always in contact), people may believe that temporary contact has permanently transferred the properties of AIDS into the sweater. Physicians need to realize that such beliefs are often not volunteered by the patient unless directly questioned, may be influenced by thoughts that the patient is unable to fully articulate, and can persist despite a discussion of valid scientific counterarguments.

. . .

How Informed Must Consent Be?

AMERICAN MEDICAL NEWS, Feb. 3, 1969*

Informed consent by the patient being prepared for surgery can be carried to an extreme. Paul Huffington, MD, Easton, Md., told the Maryland State Bar Assn. a typical extreme session with a patient might go like this:

"Good evening, Mrs. X. I am Dr. Y, your anesthesiologist. The nurse tells me that you are somewhat apprehensive about having anesthesia...

"I'll tell you exactly what we are going to do so that there will be no difficulty. I will give you several pills in the morning to take the edge off your nerves. You will then be brought to the operating room where I will see you. We will put a blood pressure cuff on your arm and a needle in your vein.

"I will put you to sleep with pentothal, administered in your vein. After you are asleep, I will paralyze you with a curare and place a tube in your windpipe. I will use cyclopropane, a general anesthetic, to keep you anesthetized throughout the operation.

"As you know, you are having your stomach removed, so I will breathe for you throughout this operation, which usually lasts for about 3 1/2 hours. General anesthetic will depress your heart appreciably, affect your liver adversely from three to five days, halve your blood facilities to your vital abdominal organs, and the chance of your lung collapsing, or part of it, is about 10 to 40%, depending upon the literature you read.

"During the operation, I will have to decide how much blood and fluid to give you, but usually two pints of blood and three quarts of solution are required. At the end of the operation I will give you some potent medicine that temporarily poisons your enzymes, so that the curare will no longer be effective.

"After getting you breathing on your own, I will remove the tube and make sure you don't stop ... because of airway obstructions.

"I then will move you into the recovery room and give you potent pain killing drugs and drugs to prevent your vomiting. I hope that by explaining my responsibilities, I have set your mind at ease, and you will sleep well tonight."

Dr. Huffington added, "I have not told her of the risk of each drug, the danger of air embolism from the needle stick, the possibility of death from vomiting and aspiration, the danger from explosion from the anesthesia that I am using (there were about 254 deaths from anesthesia last year in this country).

"So I have not really informed her," he said. "Literally, I could go on for hours without [explaining] all the possible complications she may have."

NOTES

(1) Consider the following formulation of an informed consent standard:

A physician is under an obligation (1) to make a full disclosure of all known material risks in a proposed operation or course of treatment except for those risks of which the patient is likely to know or (2) to prove the reasonableness of any lesser disclosure or the immateriality of the undisclosed risk.

---

* Copyright © 1969 American Medical Association. Reprinted by permission.

Comment, *Informed Consent in Medical Malpractice*, 55 Calif. L. Rev. 1396, 1407 (1967). The comment writer defines materiality as being "a function of the incidence and severity of [the] risk," and says that "[t]he ultimate question of materiality is whether knowledge of the risk before the patient gave his consent would have altered the patient's decision." *Id.* at 1407 n.68.

Can you improve on this formula?

(2) A significant aspect of "informed consent" concerns the question of when a physician must tell a patient about alternative therapies.

Judicial inclination to require maximum patient information extends to some fairly complicated choices. See, e.g., *Marino v. Ballestas*, 749 F.2d 162 (3d Cir. 1984), in which an orthopedic surgeon recommended immediate open reduction of a fractured humerus in order to reduce the risk of permanent nerve damage. While the appeals court opined that a doctor "may, and indeed should, express his opinion regarding preferable methods of treatment," it said that he should have fairly presented the fact that "one school of medical thought favors immobilizing the arm and delaying surgery indefinitely in order to facilitate spontaneous regeneration of the damaged nerve." *Id.* at 168.

Often, this issue reduces itself to a question of materiality. For example, in *Smith v. Karen S. Reisig, M.D., Inc.*, 686 P.2d 285 (Okla. 1984), a patient "testified unequivocally" that she would not have consented to a hysterectomy if the doctor had told her that hormonal therapy was a viable alternative for her condition. Although the trial court sustained a demurrer, in part on the ground that "reasonable minds could not differ that the plaintiff would have consented even if adequately informed," the Oklahoma Supreme Court said the question was for the jury on the plaintiff's credibility.

(3) Treatment for an overactive thyroid gland involves three possibilities:

(1) Surgery, which produces successful results in 83.5% of cases but involves a risk of damage to the laryngeal nerves, which may cause paralysis of the vocal cords.

(a) The so-called "standard technique" for surgery is to remove a major part of the thyroid by dissection, leaving a small residue of tissue as a buffer against the dissection. Using this procedure, the surgeon makes no attempt to see, identify and separate the laryngeal nerves from the thyroid.

(b) The second, or Lahey method, requires the surgeon to see the nerves and to put them aside from the area of dissection.

[When a case involving use of one of these methods was decided in 1961, medical literature showed an incidence of permanent damage to the laryngeal nerves of about 2 percent no matter which of the two techniques was used, and even if the surgeon was extremely careful in the operation. See *DiFilippo v. Preston*, 53 Del. 539, 173 A.2d 333 (1961). — Ed.]

(2) Radioiodine therapy, which carries an 80 per cent success rate. However, there are difficulties in calculating the proper dosage, and if there is an overdose it will cause hypothyroidism.

(3) Antithyroid drugs, which avoid the possibility of damage to the laryngeal nerves or to the parathyroid gland (also a risk of surgery), but this method proves successful in only 52 per cent of cases and permanent cures take up to two years.

See Comment, 55 Calif. L. Rev. at 1396–97, n.1.

What does "informed consent" require if a doctor advises surgery as the initial treatment for hyperthyroidism?

Suppose the doctor has already used surgery once on that patient with no ill effects, but the incidence of laryngeal nerve damage in a second operation is 14 percent.

(4) What assumptions do courts probably make concerning the nature of an effective "consent"? Would it be your behavioral guess that once a doctor selects a treatment, consent is practically a formality for most patients?

(5) *Hartke,* supra, introduces the disagreement over whether the patient standard for informed consent should be subjective or objective. The landmark precedent of *Canterbury v. Spence* opted for an objective standard for causation of harm to the plaintiff by the defendant's failure to disclose the risks of a treatment—a standard based on "what a prudent person would have decided if suitably informed of all perils bearing significance." 464 F.2d 772, 791 (D.C. Cir. 1972).[1] The court rationalized this standard on the basis of concern about incentives for patients, in hindsight, to testify that had they known of the risks at issue, they would not have gone through with a treatment. Yet there is medical opinion that, especially with more cost consciousness in medical malpractice, "it will be essential to identify decisions in which it is especially important to consider patients' values and to protect such decisions from intrusive external decision making." A catalog of circumstances that ought to alert physicians that they "may be dealing with a utility-sensitive situation" includes situations in which "there are major differences in the kinds of possible outcomes," for example, death or disability; situations where "there are major differences between treatments in the likelihood and impact of complications"; choices that "involve trade-offs between near-term and long-term outcomes"; and patients who are particularly risk-averse or who "attach[] unusual importance to certain possible outcomes." Joseph Kassirer, *Editorial, Incorporating Patients' Preferences into Medical Decisions,* 330 New Eng. J. Med. 1895, 1896 (1994).

(6) What is communicated to patients in "informed consent" recitations, and how much do they understand? As indicated in the article by Redelmeier and his colleagues, supra, research indicates that the way questions are put may significantly affect the answers. As to how much patients understand generally, it is sobering to consider that within a day of signing consent forms for major medical procedures, "[o]nly 60 per cent of all patients correctly described what their treatment would involve, 59 per cent could describe the essential purpose of the treatment, only 55 per cent were able to list even a single major risk or complication, and only 27 per cent could name one alternative treatment." Barrie R. Cassileth, et al., *Informed Consent—Why Are its Goals Imperfectly Realized?,* 302 New Eng. J. Med. 896, 897 (1980).

What percentage of lay persons do you think can ever be adequately informed about the risks of treatment for a life-threatening disease?

(7) "Hypothetical: 'Dr. D diagnosed P as having a serious abdominal problem which required rather serious and risky surgery. Dr. D began to explain the problem to P but P stated "I do not want to hear about it. You just do what you think is necessary." Dr. D tried to inform P later, but got the same reaction from P. P signed a consent form.'

---

1. One decision in accord is *Aronson v. Harriman,* 321 Ark. 359, 901 S.W.2d 832, 840 (1995) (rejecting surgeon's argument that plaintiff's "failure to state that he absolutely would not have undergone" an operation if he had been "informed of the risk of paralysis" should have kept the jury from considering the informed consent issue; "[t]he objective approach ... permits the jury to take into account [the plaintiff's] testimony" about whether he would have consented "but would not predicate the outcome ... solely on that testimony").

"Question: 'Can Dr. D proceed with the operation?'"

Hagman, *The Medical Patient's Right to Know: Report on a Medical-Legal-Ethical, Empirical Study*, 17 U.C.L.A. L. REV. 758, 785 nn. 109 & 110 (1970).

BOYLE v. REVICI
United States Court of Appeals, Second Circuit
961 F.2d 1060 (1992)

Before: MESKILL, WINTER and WALKER, Circuit Judges.

MESKILL, Circuit Judge:

This diversity case involves claims for pain and suffering and wrongful death arising from the alleged medical malpractice of Emanuel Revici, M.D., a ninety-six year old New York citizen who is a practitioner of nonconventional cancer therapy, and his Institute of Applied Biology, Inc., a center incorporated and located in New York. The suit was filed by Cecelia Zyjewski, a citizen of Connecticut, who has since died, and is carried on by Arthur Boyle, the administrator of her estate.

Before the trial below was complete, we decided another case involving Dr. Revici, Schneider v. Revici, 817 F.2d 987, 995 (2d Cir.1987), which held that under New York law a jury charge on express assumption of risk is proper in medical malpractice cases where a patient knowingly forwent conventional medical treatment and instead accepted the risks that caused the injuries. Despite our decision in Schneider, the United States District Court for the Southern District of New York, Lowe, J., denied the defendants' request for an instruction on express assumption of risk. Ultimately, the jury found in favor of the plaintiff and awarded $1,353,277.50 in damages.

The appellants claim that the district court erred by failing to instruct the jury to decide whether the decedent expressly assumed the risks that caused her injuries....

We reverse the judgment of the district court and remand for further proceedings....

BACKGROUND

Cecelia Zyjewski was sixty-five years old and unmarried when a doctor diagnosed her as having cancer in March 1982. She initially sought the advice of conventional cancer specialists, each of whom advised her to undergo surgery to resect her tumor. Although, as doctors testified, early surgery would have given her a very good chance at recovery, she did not heed the doctors' advice, instead seeking first to explore noninvasive alternatives.

On March 25, 1982, Zyjewski, accompanied by her niece and her niece's husband, Carol and Dominic Palumbo, first consulted with Dr. Emanuel Revici at the Institute of Applied Biology. Dr. Revici's treatments consist of urine monitoring, urinalyses and the ingestion of various mineral compounds that Dr. Revici claims retard and reduce the size of cancerous tumors.

According to the testimony of Dr. Revici and the Palumbos, Dr. Revici told Zyjewski at this meeting that he thought she would respond to his treatment and that he thought that he could cure her. Dr. Revici allegedly alerted her, however, that his medications were not FDA approved and that he could offer no guarantees. Despite being so informed, Zyjewski entered Revici's care. Within a year, Zyjewski's condition had deteriorated greatly and in November 1983 she died.

At trial, the parties stipulated that Dr. Revici's method of treating cancer was legally negligent in that it did not conform to accepted medical standards in the New York area. The jury was asked to decide whether Dr. Revici's negligence as stipulated caused the decedent's injuries.

The defendants asked the district court to instruct the jury on express assumption of risk, which, if found, would be a total bar to recovery. They argued that Zyjewski knowingly forwent conventional treatment and instead chose to accept the risks that accompanied Dr. Revici's treatment. The district court refused this request and instead instructed the jury to reduce any award for the plaintiff by an amount representing Zyjewski's own negligence.

The jury rendered a verdict for the plaintiff on wrongful death for $3,450 and on pain and suffering for $1,500,000. The jury found the decedent five percent liable for her death, reducing that award to $3,277.50, and ten percent liable for her pain and suffering, reducing that award to $1,350,000, for the total award of $1,353,277.50.

. . .

A. Express Assumption of Risk

The defendants presented evidence at trial that Zyjewski consciously decided not to accept conventional cancer treatment and instead sought Dr. Revici's care, despite known risks of which she was aware. Accordingly, the defendants argue that the jury should have been asked not only whether Dr. Revici's negligence caused Zyjewski's injuries but whether she expressly assumed the risks that caused those injuries. We agree.

Under New York law, "[e]xpress assumption [of risk], which ... preclude [s] any recovery, result[s] from agreement in advance that defendant need not use reasonable care for the benefit of plaintiff and would not be liable for the consequence of conduct that would otherwise be negligent." ... Express assumption of risk is a total bar to recovery....

In Schneider, we stated that "[w]hile a patient should be encouraged to exercise care for his own safety, we believe that an informed decision to avoid surgery and conventional chemotherapy is within the patient's right 'to determine what shall be done with his own body.'" 817 F.2d at 995 (citations omitted). This conclusion led us to hold that a patient may expressly assume the risk of malpractice and dissolve the physician's duty to treat a patient according to the medical community's accepted standards. Id.

Boyle emphasizes in his papers that Dr. Revici was unable to produce a consent form signed by Zyjewski. He points out that such a form existed in Schneider and suggests that in a case concerning unorthodox medical treatment an express assumption of risk charge is inappropriate where the defendant cannot produce such a form. We disagree.

Absent a statutory requirement that express assumption of risk requires a writing, we believe that a jury should decide whether a plaintiff has knowingly accepted all of the risks of a defendant's negligence. A defendant's failure to introduce a consent form goes to the weight of the evidence in support of the defendant's argument that an express assumption of risk has occurred. However, it does not justify keeping the express assumption of risk issue from the jury.

In this case, Dr. Revici presented evidence that Zyjewski had expressly assumed a risk in opting for the unconventional cancer treatment.[2] The credibility of that evidence

---

2. We note that the jury was not asked whether Dr. Revici had acted negligently by failing to inform or misinforming the decedent as to her deteriorating condition. Therefore, we need not decide whether sufficient evidence existed to support an express assumption of risk instruction on this question.

should have been an issue for the jury. Accordingly, we reverse the judgment of the district court and remand for a new trial.

...

NOTES

(1) The court notes that the parties stipulated that the defendant's methods were "legally negligent." Can a physician using nonconventional treatment be negligent to a patient who specifically accedes to that treatment?

(2) Do you suppose that Cecelia Zyjewski was exercising "free will" when she agreed to have Dr. Revici treat her? Given the data and conclusions presented by Redelmeier and his colleagues, supra, what assumptions will courts be likely to make in practice about the degree of choice that patients have when "informed consent" is at issue?

(3) Why should a court allow a lay person's consent to a doctor's employment of procedures for which there is no scientific confirmation of effectiveness?

(4) If consent of the sort that Dr. Revici relied on can be effective, should product manufacturers be able to protect themselves completely against liability for products that turn out to be defective by having consumers sign forms that contain blanket disclaimers?

(5) As the technology of medical science progresses, the literature of informed consent inevitably will feature more issues concerning experimental procedures. An interesting resolution of this type of problem appears in a North Carolina case in which surgeons employed on a gunshot victim a procedure called a "percutaneous steel coil embolization," which in the court's description required insertion of a small steel coil into an artery, presumably weakened by a bullet, in order to cut off the flow of blood and prevent a rupture. Responding to the plaintiff's complaint that the surgeons had not told him about the "highly experimental" nature of the procedure, the appellate court said,

> where the health care provider offers an experimental procedure or treatment
> to a patient, the health care provider has a duty, in exercising reasonable care
> under the circumstances, to inform the patient of the experimental nature of
> the proposed procedure.

The court reasoned that "[i]f the health care provider has a duty to inform of *known* risks for *established* procedures, common sense and the purposes of the statute equally require that the health care provider inform the patient of any *uncertainty* regarding the risks associated with *experimental* procedures." This obligation, the court said, "includes the experimental nature of the procedure and the *known or projected most likely risks.*" *Estrada v. Jaques*, 70 N.C. App. 627, 321 S.E.2d 240 (1984).

(6) The fierce legal and medical infighting over the particular experimental vehicle of the artificial heart is multidimensional, involving public regulation as well as private law. A case with high legal, and human, drama, is *Karp v. Cooley*, 493 F.2d 408 (5th Cir. 1974), in which the appellate court affirmed a directed verdict for Dr. Denton Cooley, in a litigation concerning his implantation of the "first totally mechanical heart" in the plaintiff's decedent. A dozen years after Dr. Cooley performed this procedure, the FDA criticized him for using such a device without the agency's authorization. *MD's Unauthorized Use Of Artificial Heart Criticized By FDA*, AMERICAN MEDICAL NEWS, Oct. 16, 1981, at 17. Should there be legal barriers to a patient who wishes to bargain with a doctor for the use of an experimental surgical device that has not been approved by a government agency that has statutory authorization to pass on such devices? What

about an experimental drug? Would it change your opinion if the drug was one that showed promise for a widespread and life-threatening disease?

---

§ 5.02   "Implied Assumption of the Risk"

[A]   In Everyday Life

GULFWAY GENERAL HOSP., INC. v. PURSLEY
Texas Court of Civil Appeals
397 S.W.2d 93 (1965)

WILSON, JUSTICE. Plaintiff recovered judgment for personal injuries resulting from falling on the icy entrance of a private hospital which she was entering to obtain emergency treatment.

Plaintiff severed the tip of her finger in her kitchen. She walked over her own iced-over sidewalk and driveway to her car, and drove slowly two miles over ice-covered streets to the nearest hospital, that of defendant. Ice covered the ground. Plaintiff and her daughter walked to the emergency entrance on grass, because it was not so slick as the sidewalk. She had cautioned her daughter, "Now, we are going to have to be awfully careful," as they began the trip. "It was still misting rain and still had ice on the streets." She had not been to the hospital before, but she parked and followed signs reading, "emergency room," again cautioning her daughter "to be very careful." As plaintiff stepped on the porch and walked toward the emergency entrance door, she slipped and fell on the ice, sustaining injuries.

Plaintiff testified she saw the ice on the porch before she stepped on it; "the porch was open, and it was light there, where you could see the ice"; there was no doubt in her mind that there was ice on the porch and "it was slippery". On her counsel's examination she testified: "Q. If you knew that there was ice everywhere, ice was on the porch, and you knew there was a risk, why did you walk on the porch? A. That was the only way you could get into the hospital. You had to go through some door."

Jury findings were to the effect that defendant's negligence in allowing ice to remain on the porch proximately caused plaintiff's injuries; that plaintiff knew of the icy condition of the porch before she went on it; that she appreciated the danger of walking on it; and the occurrence was not the result of an unavoidable accident.

We sustain defendant hospital's contention that plaintiff was not entitled to recover because plaintiff failed to establish that defendant owed her a duty to warn or protect her from the dangerous condition. Plaintiff concedes: "Frankly, this is a case where the invitee, Mrs. Pursley, had knowledge of the condition and appreciated the danger," and ordinarily defendant would owe her no duty. She urges, nevertheless, that this case presents an exceptional situation because she did not encounter the risk as a result of an intelligent choice; she was under the compulsion of obtaining emergency medical treatment. She also insists that an extraordinary, or "very high" standard of care should be imposed in the maintenance of a hospital emergency entrance.

Did plaintiff's conduct, motive or justification affect defendant's duty? In Halepeska v. Callihan Interests, Inc., Tex., 1963, 371 S.W.2d 368, 379, the Supreme Court said: "A basic difference between contributory negligence on the one hand, and 'no duty' and volenti on the other,* is the question of justification. Whether the plaintiff's conduct was justified may be an evidentiary consideration in deciding that a person of ordinary prudence should, or should not have so acted, but it is not a separate ultimate inquiry or issue." After thus relating "justification" to contributory negligence, and the volenti cases, the court emphasized, "The question of plaintiff's justification is not ordinarily involved in the 'no duty' concept." To this general rule the opinion did not foreclose possible exceptions: "as where the plaintiff is motivated by humanitarian or rescue impulses."

The reason plaintiff assumed the risk, and whether he voluntarily exposed himself to an open and obvious danger in an occupier-invitee situation ordinarily "becomes immaterial and passes out of the case" in determining whether defendant owes a duty to plaintiff. It is, by this, distinguished from the "volenti defense" under which voluntary exposure to risk is a material and necessary inquiry.

Plaintiff's exigency does not impose a duty on defendant in the present case. In our opinion, under the Halepeska decision, since the danger encountered was open and obvious, and the risk was known and appreciated by plaintiff, recovery is barred without regard to plaintiff's claimed justification.

We do not reach appellant's other points. The judgment is reversed, and judgment is here rendered that plaintiff take nothing.

NOTES

(1) Did Ms. Pursley act unreasonably?

(2) Does the court persuasively classify *Pursley* as a "no duty" case? How do the plaintiff's knowledge and appreciation of the risk figure in the court's conclusion?

(3) What ethical premises are implicit in the court's application of the law in *Pursley*? What would a court taking the *Pursley* position be concerned about in making a decision in favor of Ms. Pursley?

What policy justification is there for *Pursley*? Would it likely have made a difference to the court if the hospital had been a public one?

(4) Assume that the court had decided *Pursley* the other way and that an official of the hospital sought your advice about how to avoid liability in similar cases in the future, on days when it is icy. Is there a way that could be done, if it would be inconvenient for the hospital to clear the ice?

PROBLEM

Does the concept that a risk is "open and obvious" add anything to the analysis of cases involving the alleged negligence of possessors of land? Consider the following deposition testimony of a woman, suffering from a form of muscular dystrophy, who sued Sears Roebuck for injuries occurring when her wheelchair tipped backwards on a ramp that she claimed was too steep:

> Q: And once your mother had pushed you to approximately five feet from the ramp, what happened?

---

* The court in *Halepeska* described the Texas "volenti" doctrine as an affirmative defense, meaning that a person "may not recover for an injury received when he voluntarily exposes himself to a known and appreciated danger," where the "decision to incur the risk" was "deliberate," "so that it may be said that the person acted as a result of an intelligent choice." 371 S.W.2d at 379.—Ed.

A: She was looking at one of the chairs and I saw a chair that I wanted to look at so I was pushing myself towards the ramp and assessing to see if it was something I could accomplish.

...

Q: So you decided to attempt to go up the ramp and look at that recliner, correct?

A: Correct.

Q: And you said you were assessing the ramp?

A: Yes.

Q: What do you mean by that?

A: If I felt it was too steep to go up, I would have waited for my mother to help me go up and take a look at the chair I was looking at.

... Schollenberger also testified about how she determined that the ramp was not too steep for her to ascend:

Q: And I assume that after you assessed the ramp, you made a determination that it did not appear too steep?

A: Correct.

Q: And that you believed that you could wheel yourself up that ramp?

A: Correct.

...

Q: Did you believe that the ramp was adequately lit when you used it?

A: No.

Q: Did you believe that prior to trying to go up the ramp?

A: That to me, in my way of thinking it didn't—as long as I felt I was able to go up that ramp for the amount of lighting that was there, I still could have done it.

Q: You had enough lighting to make the assessment?

A: Correct.

... Finally, Schollenberger testified....

Q: Did you consider yourself to be experienced in wheelchair use?

A: Yes.

Q: You understood that if a ramp was too steep, it could pose a danger to you if you tried to negotiate it on your own?

A: Correct.

Q: You understood that there would potentially be a danger of the chair tipping backwards?

A: Correct.

Q: Did you also know that it was safer for someone to assist you when you were negotiating a ramp as opposed to trying to do that yourself?

A: The possibility was there, yes.

...

Given this testimony, should Sears get summary judgment?

[B] At Play and in Sport

PROBLEM

A news dispatch reported that a Detroit area man named Jerry Pasciak sued for injuries that occurred when he was served a drink called an Upside Down Kamikaze. The procedure for serving the drink, at Cagney's bar in suburban Westland, Michigan, involved seating the customer in a barber chair and pouring the drink down his throat while the chair was "tilted backward and then propelled forward." Pasciak sued the bar for cuts around his eyes and nose that he attributed to being knocked unconscious "after being served the drink in the prescribed manner."*

What are his chances of recovery?

TURCOTTE v. FELL

New York Court of Appeals
68 N.Y.2d 432, 502 N.E.2d 964, 510 N.Y.S.2d 49 (1986)

SIMONS, JUDGE.

The issue raised in this appeal is the scope of the duty of care owed to a professional athlete injured during a sporting event. The defendants are a coparticipant and his employer and the owner and operator of the sports facility in which the event took place.

Plaintiff Ronald J. Turcotte is a former jockey. Before his injury he had ridden over 22,000 races in his 17-year career and achieved international fame as the jockey aboard "Secretariat" when that horse won the "Triple Crown" races in 1973. On July 13, 1978 plaintiff was injured while riding in the eighth race at Belmont Park, a racetrack owned and operated by defendant New York Racing Association (NYRA). Plaintiff had been assigned the third pole position for the race on a horse named "Flag of Leyte Gulf". Defendant jockey Jeffrey Fell was in the second pole position riding "Small Raja", a horse owned by defendant David P. Reynolds. On the other side of plaintiff, in the fourth position, was the horse "Walter Malone". Seconds after the race began, Turcotte's horse clipped the heels of "Walter Malone" and then tripped and fell, propelling plaintiff to the ground and causing him severe personal injuries which left him a paraplegic.

Plaintiffs, husband and wife, commenced this action against Jeffrey Fell, David P. Reynolds, NYRA and others no longer before the court. In their supplemental complaint, they charge that Fell is liable to them because guilty of common-law negligence and of violating the rules of the New York Racing and Wagering Board regulating "foul riding", that Reynolds is liable for Fell's negligence under the doctrine of respondent superior, and that defendant NYRA is liable because it "negligently failed to water and groom that portion of the racetrack near the starting gate or watered and groomed the same in an improper and careless manner" causing it to be unsafe.

Special Term granted the motions of Fell and Reynolds for summary judgment, holding that Turcotte, by engaging in the sport of horseracing, relieved other partici-

---

* *Drink Packed Too Much of a Wallop, Patron Says*, WASHINGTON POST, Copyright © 1986, undated.

pants of any duty of reasonable care with respect to known dangers or risks which in-
here in that activity. Finding no allegations of Fell's wanton, reckless, or intentional
conduct, it dismissed the complaint as to Fell and Reynolds with leave to replead.
NYRA subsequently moved for summary judgment and Special Term denied its motion
because it found there were questions of fact concerning NYRA's negligent maintenance
of the track. On separate appeals, the Appellate Division affirmed, with one Justice dissenting from the order denying NYRA's motion for summary judgment, and the matters are before us as cross appeals by its leave. The order should be affirmed as to defendants Fell and Reynolds and reversed as to defendant NYRA, and NYRA's motion for
summary judgment should be granted. The complaint should be dismissed as to all defendants because by participating in the race, plaintiff consented that the duty of care
owed him by defendants was no more than a duty to avoid reckless or intentionally
harmful conduct. Although a sport's safety rules are an important consideration in determining the scope of plaintiff's consent, the alleged violation of the rule in this case
did not constitute reckless or intentional conduct and the complaint against defendants
Fell and Reynolds was properly dismissed. NYRA's duty is similarly measured by plaintiff's consent to accept the risk of injuries that are known, apparent or reasonably foreseeable consequences of his participation in the race. Inasmuch as there are no factual
issues concerning its liability, its motion for summary judgment should have been
granted also.

I

It is fundamental that to recover in a negligence action a plaintiff must establish that
the defendant owed him a duty to use reasonable care, and that it breached that duty....
The statement that there is or is not a duty, however, "begs the essential question —
whether the plaintiff's interests are entitled to legal protection against the defendant's
conduct".... Thus, while the determination of the existence of a duty and the concomitant scope of that duty involve a consideration not only of the wrongfulness of the defendant's action or inaction, they also necessitate an examination of plaintiff's reasonable expectations of the care owed him by others. This is particularly true in
professional sporting contests, which by their nature involve an elevated degree of danger. If a participant makes an informed estimate of the risks involved in the activity and
willingly undertakes them, then there can be no liability if he is injured as a result of
those risks.

Traditionally, the participant's conduct was conveniently analyzed in terms of the defensive doctrine of assumption of risk. With the enactment of the comparative negligence statute, however, assumption of risk is no longer an absolute defense (see, CPLR
1411, eff. Sept. 1, 1975). Thus, it has become necessary, and quite proper, when measuring a defendant's duty to a plaintiff to consider the risks assumed by the plaintiff ...
The shift in analysis is proper because the "doctrine [of assumption of risk] deserves no
separate existence (except for express assumption of risk) and is simply a confusing way
of stating certain no-duty rules" (James, Assumption of Risk: Unhappy Reincarnation,
78 Yale L.J. 185, 187–188). Accordingly, the analysis of care owed to plaintiff in the professional sporting event by a coparticipant and by the proprietor of the facility in which
it takes place must be evaluated by considering the risks plaintiff assumed when he
elected to participate in the event and how those assumed risks qualified defendants'
duty to him.

The risk assumed has been defined a number of ways but in its most basic sense it
"means that the plaintiff, in advance, has given his ... consent to relieve the defendant
of an obligation of conduct toward him, and to take his chances of injury from a

known risk arising from what the defendant is to do or leave undone. The situation is then the same as where the plaintiff consents to the infliction of what would otherwise be an intentional tort, except that the consent is to run the risk of unintended injury ... The result is that the defendant is relieved of legal duty to the plaintiff; and being under no duty, he cannot be charged with negligence" (Prosser and Keeton, Torts § 68, at 480–481 [5th ed.]; 4 Harper, James & Gray, Torts § 21.0 et seq. [2d ed.]; Restatement [Second] of Torts § 496A comments b, c; see also, Bohlen, Voluntary Assumption of Risk, 20 Harv.L.Rev. 14 [assumption of risk is another way of finding no duty of care]....

The doctrine has been divided into several categories but as the term applies to sporting events it involves what commentators call "primary" assumption of risk. Risks in this category are incidental to a relationship of free association between the defendant and the plaintiff in the sense that either party is perfectly free to engage in the activity or not as he wishes. Defendant's duty under such circumstances is a duty to exercise care to make the conditions as safe as they appear to be. If the risks of the activity are fully comprehended or perfectly obvious, plaintiff has consented to them and defendant has performed its duty.... Plaintiff's "consent" is not constructive consent; it is actual consent implied from the act of the electing to participate in the activity (see, Restatement [Second] of Torts § 892[2]). When thus analyzed and applied, assumption of risk is not an absolute defense but a measure of the defendant's duty of care and thus survives the enactment of the comparative fault statute....

II

We turn then to an analysis of these two requirements—the nature and scope of plaintiff's consent. It would be a rare thing, indeed, if the election of a professional athlete to participate in a sport at which he makes his living could be said to be involuntary. Plaintiff's participation certainly was not involuntary in this case and thus we are concerned only with the scope of his consent.

As a general rule, participants properly may be held to have consented, by their participation, to those injury-causing events which are known, apparent or reasonably foreseeable consequences of the participation.... But while the courts have traditionally exercised great restraint in the belief that "the law should not place unreasonable burdens on the free and vigorous participation in sports", they have recognized that organized, athletic competition does not exist in a vacuum. Some "of the restraints of civilization must accompany every athlete onto the playing field" (Nabozny v. Barnhill, 31 Ill.App.3d 212, 214–215, 334 N.E.2d 258, 260). Thus, the rule is qualified to the extent that participants do not consent to acts which are reckless or intentional....

Whether a professional athlete should be held under this standard to have consented to the act or omission of a coparticipant which caused his injury involves consideration of a variety of factors including but not limited to: the ultimate purpose of the game and the method or methods of winning it; the relationship of defendant's conduct to the game's ultimate purpose, especially his conduct with respect to rules and customs whose purpose is to enhance the safety of the participants; and the equipment or animals involved in the playing of the game. The question of whether the consent was an informed one includes consideration of the participant's knowledge and experience in the activity generally. Manifestly a professional athlete is more aware of the dangers of the activity, and presumably more willing to accept them in exchange for a salary, than is an amateur.

In this case plaintiff testified before trial to facts establishing that horse racing is a dangerous activity. A thoroughbred race horse is the result of years of breeding and that breeding, and all the horse's training, are directed to building speed. A thoroughbred horse weighs about one-half ton and, during the course of the race, will reach speeds of 40 miles per hour or more. Jockeys weighing between 100 and 120 pounds, attempt to control these animals, all the while trying to prevail in a race whose very rules require them to exert a maximum effort to win. Plaintiff testified that every professional jockey had experiences when he was not able to keep a horse running on a straight line, or a horse would veer, or jump up on its hind legs, or go faster or slower than the jockey indicated. He further acknowledged that horses in a race do not run in prescribed lanes and it is lawful, under the rules of racing, for horses to move out of their starting lane to other parts of the track provided that the horse does not interfere with other horses when doing so. Indeed, during the course of a race, speeding horses lawfully and properly come within inches of other horses and frequently bump each other. Turcotte conceded that there is a fine line between what is lawful and unlawful in the movement of a horse on the track during a race and that when and where a horse can lawfully change its position is a matter of judgment. Such dangers are inherent in the sport. Because they are recognized as such by plaintiff, the courts below properly held that he consented to relieve defendant Jeffrey Fell of the legal duty to use reasonable care to avoid crossing into his lane of travel.

Plaintiffs nonetheless contend that Fell's alleged violation of 9 NYCRR 4035.2 [a rule of the New York Racing and Wagering Board—Ed.], which prohibits foul riding, is sufficient to sustain their complaint. They assert that the rule is a safety rule and that a participant does not accept or consent to the violation of the rules of a game even though the violation is foreseeable. They rely principally on Hackbart v. Cincinnati Bengals, 601 F.2d 516, supra in which the plaintiff was injured when intentionally struck in the neck from behind by an opposing football player after the play was over and Nabozny v. Barnhill, ... supra, in which the plaintiff, playing goal tender in a high school soccer match, was injured after picking up the ball in a free kick zone when kicked in the head by player on an opposing team (see also, Restatement [Second] of Torts § 50 comment b).

The rules of the sport, however, do not necessarily limit the scope of the professional's consent. Although the foul riding rule is a safety measure, it is not by its terms absolute for it establishes a spectrum of conduct and penalties, depending on whether the violation is careless or willful and whether the contact was the result of mutual fault. As the rule recognizes, bumping and jostling are normal incidents of the sport. They are not, as were the blows in Nabozny and Hackbart, flagrant infractions unrelated to the normal method of playing the game and done without any competitive purpose. Plaintiff does not claim that Fell intentionally or recklessly bumped him, he claims only that as a result of carelessness, Fell failed to control his mount as the horses raced for the lead and a preferred position on the track. While a participant's "consent" to join in a sporting activity is not a waiver of all rules infractions, nonetheless a professional clearly understands the usual incidents of competition resulting from carelessness, particularly those which result from the customarily accepted method of playing the sport, and accepts them. They are within the known, apparent and foreseeable dangers of the sport and not actionable and thus plaintiffs' complaint against defendant Fell was properly dismissed.

. . .

IV

The complaint against NYRA should also be dismissed. . . .

NYRA's duty to plaintiff is similarly measured by his position and purpose for being on the track on July 13 and the risks he accepted by being there. In deciding whether plaintiff consented to the conditions which existed at the time, the court should consider the nature of professional horseracing and the facilities used for it, the playing conditions under which horseracing is carried out, the frequency of the track's use and the correlative ability of the owner to repair or refurbish the track, and the standards maintained by other similarly used facilities.

Plaintiffs charge that NYRA was negligent in failing to water the "chute", which leads to the main track, and "overwatering" the main track. Thus, they claim the horses had to run from the dry surface of the chute onto the overly watered, unsafe "cuppy" surface of the main track.[2]

Plaintiff testified, however, that "cupping" conditions are common on racetracks and that he had experienced them before at Belmont Park and also at many other tracks. Indeed, he testified that he had never ridden on a track where he had not observed a cupping condition at one time or another. Thus, Turcotte's participation in three prior races at this same track on the day of his injury, his ability to observe the condition of the track before the eighth race and his general knowledge and experience with cupping conditions and their prevalence establish that he was well aware of these conditions and the possible dangers from them and that he accepted the risk....

... Although the circumstances in the present case are similar to those in Maddox v. City of New York, 66 N.Y.2d 270, 496 N.Y.S.2d 726, 487 N.E.2d 553, supra, Maddox was decided under the law as it existed before enactment of the comparative negligence statute. The case involved a professional baseball player voluntarily playing on a field he knew was wet and soft. His claim for damages for injuries resulting when he stepped on a soft spot in the outfield was denied because the city was allowed to assert assumption of risk as a complete defense. Had that cause of action arisen under the present law, it could appropriately have been decided on the basis of duty under the same rules formulated here and with the same result.

...

On the appeal by plaintiffs, order affirmed, etc.

On the appeal by defendant NYRA, order reversed, etc.

NOTES

(1) An interesting conflict on the definition—and the concept—of assumption of risk appeared in a case involving a jockey who suffered serious injuries when he was thrown from a young horse that he was qualifying for its first race track appearance. As the horse left the starting gate, it "spooked and attempted to duck or turn and run the wrong way around the race track." As the jockey tried to restrain the animal, it "saddled sideways and struck the inside rail," throwing the rider into the rail. The plaintiff claimed that the "design of the track caused a hazardous traffic pattern near the starting gate," citing various aspects of the configuration of the gate that created "a great potential for horses entering or exiting the track to 'spook' horses coming out of the starting gate." He also asserted that the track operators had been negligent in not installing a special type of safety rail. The trial judge gave an instruction on "assumption of risk," which included a statement that to assume the risk

---

2. "Cuppiness" is the tendency of wet track surface to stick to the underside of a horse's hoof within the shoe.

[The plaintiff] must have known of these specific hazards and resolved that the defendant owed him no duty of due care with respect to them. In other words, to assume the risk of another's negligence, a person must consent to it and not merely acquiesce in it.

Thus instructed, over objection from the plaintiff that "implied assumption of risk" could not be used as a defense because of Arkansas' adoption of the doctrine of comparative fault, the jury found for the race track and the trial judge denied a judgment n.o.v. *Rini v. Oaklawn Jockey Club*, 662 F. Supp. 569 (W.D. Ark. 1987).

The Eighth Circuit disagreed, in *Rini v. Oaklawn Jockey Club*, 861 F.2d 502 (8th Cir. 1988). In presenting a typology of different kinds of "assumption of risk," it referred to "Implied Secondary Reasonable Assumption of Risk," which occurs "where the plaintiff is aware of a risk created by the negligence of the defendant and proceeds or continues voluntarily to encounter it and the plaintiff's conduct in doing so is entirely reasonable in that the risk is small or the plaintiff proceeds with all due caution." *Id.* at 506. The court of appeals also defined an "Implied Secondary Unreasonable Assumption of Risk—where the plaintiff voluntarily encounters a known risk created by the defendant but the plaintiff's conduct in doing so is unreasonable." *Id.* Neither of these types of "assumption of risk," the court of appeals concluded, could be a complete bar to recovery under comparative fault.

With specific reference to "Implied Secondary Reasonable Assumption of Risk"— "Type 3" in its classification system—the court mentioned two reasons that sort of conduct should not be a defense after Arkansas adopted comparative fault:

> The first of these reasons is the anomaly that would result if reasonable assumption of risk were to continue as a defense while conduct amounting to unreasonable assumption of risk is factored in as only a partial defense under comparative fault. The anomaly, simply put, is that the plaintiff who has acted unreasonably would be allowed a partial recovery (as long as the plaintiff's negligence is less than that of the defendant) while the plaintiff who has acted reasonably would be completely barred from recovery....

> The second reason for concluding that Type 3 assumption of risk is no longer a defense in Arkansas is that it inequitably punishes reasonable conduct....

> The district court was of the opinion that the conduct of the parties in this case presented assumption of risk in its primary sense; it reached this conclusion, however, by defining primary assumption of risk as implied consent to a risk, whether that risk was inherent in the activity or created by the defendant's negligence. We believe this analysis erroneously blurred the line between primary and secondary assumption of risk; if all implied consent to known risks were primary assumption of risk it would completely swallow up the secondary types of assumption of risk. We believe ... that primary assumption of risk is limited to implied consent to risks that are inherent in the activity; implied assumption of non-inherent risks of the defendant's creation is assumption of risk in its secondary form.

> Properly understood, this case does not involve assumption of risk in its primary form. Rini alleges that he was injured due to Oaklawn's negligence in maintaining a defectively designed gate area and in failing to install a proper safety rail. Neither of these risks is inherent in the activity of horse racing....

Id. at 509–10.

(2) The New York Court of Appeals stated the facts in a case this way:

> Plaintiff, a 14-year-old girl, was watching a professional baseball game at Shea
> Stadium from a box seat behind first base, separated from the playing field
> only by a three-foot fence. At a moment when her attention was diverted from
> the game, she was struck by a sharply hit foul ball and sustained serious in-
> juries including the loss of vision in one eye. Plaintiff brought this negligence
> action against the City of New York (owner of Shea Stadium) and the Metro-
> politan Baseball Club, Inc. (its lessee). The Appellate Division, in reversing
> Special Term, granted defendants' motions for summary judgment and dis-
> missed the complaint.

The court of appeals was divided in its response to the plaintiff's appeal. What are
the most persuasive arguments that the disagreeing opinions could have made, and
which side would you think would have the better argument?

SMITH v. SEVEN SPRINGS FARM, INC.

United States Court of Appeals, Third Circuit
716 F.2d 1002 (1983)

ALDISERT, CIRCUIT JUDGE.

This diversity case, governed by Pennsylvania law, asks us to interpret the Pennsylvania Skier's Responsibility Act, 42 Pa.Cons.Stat.Ann. §7102 (Purdon Supp.1982), to decide whether appellant Peter Smith assumed the risk of skiing injuries sustained at Seven
Springs Ski Resort so as to discharge the resort from its duty of care and preclude a finding that it was negligent. The district court found that Smith assumed the risk as a matter of law and granted summary judgment in favor of Seven Springs. We affirm.

I.

Appellant Peter Smith is no novice to the sport of downhill skiing. He has skied for
over thirteen years and characterizes himself as an advanced intermediate skier.

On February 2, 1980, Smith skied at Seven Springs for the first time. He went to the
top of the mountain to ski the North Face, a trail that consists of two short, gentle
slopes, one at the top of the mountain and one at the bottom with a steep headwall in
between. A sign is posted at the beginning of the trail displaying the international skiing
symbol of a black diamond below which are printed the words "MOST DIFFICULT."
Heeding the sign and deciding not to take a less difficult trail that branches off to the
side at the top of the mountain, Smith began his descent down North Face. As he approached the headwall, he stated that he was aware that the headwall was icy and that
skiers ahead of him were having trouble negotiating its steep slope. He also stated that
he was aware that a series of unprotected telephone-like poles, part of the resort's snowmaking apparatus, lined the center of the headwall.

These conditions, however, did not prompt Smith to change course. Although he
had the option to stop, turn around, and side-step back uphill to a gentler slope, he instead proceeded to traverse the headwall. Seconds later, he encountered the icy conditions and attempted to move to the center of the slope, toward the snowmaking apparatus, in search of less icy terrain. The maneuver was unsuccessful. He fell, lost his skis,
and slid into one of the telephone-like poles and two nearby snowmaking pipes. As a
result, he sustained serious and permanent injuries to his right knee.

Smith brought the present negligence action seeking to recover for his injuries. The district court, relying in part on the Pennsylvania Skier's Responsibility Act, 42 Pa.Cons.Stat.Ann. § 7102(c) (Purdon Supp.1982), ruled against him in summary judgment, concluding that, as a matter of law, he had assumed the risk of injury so as to discharge Seven Springs from its duty of care....

II.

The law of assumption of risk, generally, is not free from confusion. Pennsylvania law is no exception. The complexity of the doctrine and the consequent difficulty of its application are well illustrated by three disparate meanings given the term by the courts:

> In its simplest form, assumption of risk means that the plaintiff has given his express consent to relieve the defendant of an obligation to exercise care for his protection, and agrees to take his chances as to injury from a known or possible risk....

> A second, and closely related, meaning is that the plaintiff has entered voluntarily into some relation with the defendant which he knows to involve the risk....

> In a third type of situation the plaintiff, aware of a risk created by the negligence of the defendant, proceeds or continues voluntarily to encounter it.

...

Restatement (Second) of Torts § 496A comment c (1965).

For our purposes, however, we believe these three situations give rise to two types of assumption of risk defenses. It may be that plaintiff's conduct in voluntarily encountering a known risk was reasonable. If so, the defense of assumption of risk in its primary sense operates to deny the defendant's negligence by denying the duty of care element of that offense; plaintiff does not recover because defendant's conduct is not a legal wrong as to him. See Pritchard v. Liggett & Myers Tobacco Co., 350 F.2d 479, 484 (3d Cir.1965) (smoking cigarettes).... But if plaintiff's conduct was unreasonable, the defense of assumption of risk in its secondary sense operates to bar his recovery for two reasons—because he implicitly consented to accept the risk, and on the policy grounds that it would be inappropriate to impose on the defendant a loss for which plaintiff's own negligence was in part responsible. See Pritchard, 350 F.2d at 484; ... Restatement (Second) of Torts § 496A comment c(4) (1965).

In its secondary sense, therefore, the defense of assumption of risk overlaps with the defense of contributory negligence....

> Where [these defenses] have been distinguished, the traditional basis has been that assumption of risk is a matter of knowledge of the danger and intelligent acquiescence in it, while contributory negligence is a matter of some fault or departure from the standard of conduct of the reasonable man, however unaware, unwilling, or even protesting the plaintiff may be. Obviously the two may co-exist, when the plaintiff makes an unreasonable choice to incur the risk; but either may exist without the other. The significant difference, when there is one, is likely to be one between risks which were *in fact* known to the plaintiff and risks which he *merely might have discovered* by the exercise of ordinary care.

Prosser, Law of Torts, § 68, at 441 (4th ed. 1971) (emphasis added); see also Koshorek v. Pennsylvania Railroad Co., 318 F.2d 364, 367 (3d Cir.1963).

Thus, if a distinction must be made, it is that assumption of risk involves the meeting of a subjectively known risk, whereas contributory negligence may involve the plaintiff exposing himself to a danger of which he was subjectively unaware but which would have been apparent had he used due care. With the former, plaintiff's conduct may be quite reasonable because its advantages outweigh its risks; but regardless, if plaintiff is injured, defendant is not liable. With the latter, plaintiff's conduct may be considered in itself unreasonable; if plaintiff is injured, he is barred from recovering because of his failure to exercise due care.

[Judge Aldisert quotes the Pennsylvania comparative negligence statute, which includes a section known as the Skier's Responsibility Act, which he characterizes as "preserv[ing] assumption of risk as a defense to negligence suits stemming from downhill skiing injuries." He finds that part of the statute "preserve[s] only the defense of assumption of risk in its primary sense in downhill skiing cases."]

Our interpretation of § 7102(c) is meaningless, however, unless we find that the defense of assumption of risk in its primary sense is still available under Pennsylvania common law. This is a question we have discussed before.

In Rutter v. Northeastern Beaver County School District, 496 Pa. 590, 612, 437 A.2d 1198, 1209 (1981), a plurality of the Pennsylvania Supreme Court purported, in dicta, to abolish the doctrine of assumption of risk altogether, reasoning that it was duplicative of the more widely understood concepts of negligence and contributory negligence. We rejected this view in Vargus v. Pitman Manufacturing Co., 675 F.2d 73 (3d Cir.1982), noting that Rutter could not be authority for the abolition of the doctrine of assumption of risk without the support of a majority of the court.

Even if we had viewed Rutter as abolishing the common law doctrine of assumption of risk in Pennsylvania, however, this case would not come within the terms of that abolition. The Rutter plurality sought to abolish the doctrine "except where specifically preserved by statute." 496 Pa. at 613, 437 A.2d at 1209. As § 7102(c) specifically preserves assumption of risk as a defense to negligence in downhill skiing cases, the defense survives, even in the eyes of the Rutter plurality.

In addition, the district court in Vargus v. Pitman Manufacturing Co., 510 F.Supp. 116 (E.D.Pa.1981), aff'd on reh'g, 675 F.2d 73 (3d Cir.1982), ruled that Pennsylvania's Comparative Negligence Act does not preclude the survival of the defense of assumption of risk in its primary sense. It reasoned that because the Pennsylvania courts had already merged the defense of assumption of risk in its secondary sense with the defense of contributory negligence, the legislature's abolition of the latter defense through the enactment of § 7102(a) and (b) implicitly abolished the former defense. Id. at 118. It further reasoned that this abolition did not encompass the defense of assumption of risk in its primary sense because that defense does not concern fault-based liability. Id. at 118–20. We implicitly adopted this reasoning when we affirmed the district court's decision. See Vargus v. Pitman Manufacturing Co., 675 F.2d 73 (3d Cir.1982), ... cf. Keegan v. Anchor Inns, Inc., 606 F.2d 35 (3d Cir.1979) (reaching same conclusion as court in Vargus under Virgin Islands comparative negligence statute). Thus, in our view, the defense of assumption of risk, at least in its primary sense, is still alive in Pennsylvania.

...

Smith contends that Seven Springs owed him the duty of care that a business invitor owes a business invitee: "not only the duty not to injure him by unreasonably dangerous conduct while he is upon the premises, but also the affirmative duty to use reasonable care to discover unreasonably dangerous conditions of the premises and either put the premises in a reasonably safe condition for use in a manner consistent with the purpose of the invitation or warn him of the danger." Andrasko v. Chamberlain Manufacturing Corp., 608 F.2d 944, 945 (3d Cir.1979); Crotty v. Reading Industries, Inc., 237 Pa.Super. 1, 8, 345 A.2d 259, 263 (1975). Specifically, Smith argues that Seven Springs had a two-fold duty: (1) to warn him of the hazardous conditions on North Face; and (2) to place protective padding around the snowmaking apparatus to guard him against collision injuries.

Smith's own deposition, however, provided the district court with all the information it needed to conclude that, as a matter of law, Smith assumed the risk of injury and thereby discharged Seven Springs from any duty of care to him. Smith's testimony shows that he subjectively appreciated the risks of skiing North Face and voluntarily chose to confront them. Before descending the headwall, he knew that North Face was marked with the international symbol designating it one of the most difficult slopes at Seven Springs, that people ahead of him were having trouble negotiating its steep icy slope, and that unprotected telephone-like poles that were part of the resort's snowmaking apparatus lined the center of the headwall. Nevertheless, he voluntarily made the descent. Rather than stop, side-step back uphill to a gentler slope that branched off from North Face, or side-step down the slope to safety, he took his chances. Such action, although confronting a known risk, was probably quite reasonable in light of his extensive skiing experience and ability. But in electing to pursue that course, Smith absolved defendant of any obligation to exercise care for his protection.

. . .

V.

The judgment of the district court will be affirmed.

NOTES

(1) The rigor with which some courts will interpret skiers' responsibility legislation is evident in *Collins v. Schweitzer, Inc.*, 21 F.3d 1491 (9th Cir. 1994). The Idaho skiers' statute in that case provided that "[e]ach skier expressly assumes the risk" of injury from a variety of conditions, fixtures and machines, including "lift towers and components thereof." It also declared that ski area operators had "no duty to eliminate, alter, control or lessen the risks inherent in the sport of skiing, which risks include but are not limited to" the catalog of risks specified in the statute. The plaintiff, an experienced amateur ski racer, suffered injuries that made him a quadriplegic when he was racing on a slalom course that the defendant had set up, on which the finish line was 123 feet above and 48 feet to the right of a chairlift tower. The defendant had put nylon net fencing in front of the tower, around which it had padding that was two to four inches thick. As the plaintiff turned to avoid his competitor, he fell, slid through the netting and hit the tower. Pointing out that the statute specifically identified lift towers among the risks assumed by skiers, the court rejected the plaintiff's argument that the risks of racing sponsored by the corporate organizer of the race were not "inherent in the sport of skiing." *Id.* at 1494.

(2) An eleven-year-old girl suffered serious injuries when she was riding a "razor" scooter on the sidewalk near her home, where she encountered a part of the sidewalk that was raised more than three inches above the rest of the walk. She sued the city,

which countered that the doctrine of primary assumption of risk barred recovery, arguing that the "risk of coming upon uneven surfaces and falling from a scooter is inherent in the activity of riding a scooter." What result?

...

[C] At Work

PROBLEM

There follows a summary of facts in a federal case:

Plaintiff Arnold was injured in an explosion and fire on a drilling platform off the Louisiana coast. Union Oil hired Arnold's employer, Hydraulic Workover, Inc., to clean out a clogged well. As part of the job, natural gas under pressure was brought in by hose from another well close by and its pressure used to force liquid out of the formerly clogged well, a technique known as "gas lifting." Arnold had been employed by Hydraulic Workover for approximately two months. He was a class "C" worker, the lowest experience rating for a Hydraulic Workover employee. He had never before participated in a gas lift operation.

The rubber hose used to carry the pressurized gas from one well to the other burst, the escaping gas caught fire, and Arnold was injured....

While pressurized gas was moving from one well to the other through the hose, Arnold observed bubbles or blisters forming on the hose. Broussard, Union's production supervisor for the oil field (including this particular platform), was on the platform and exercised some degree of supervision over the gas lifting operation. It is undisputed that the following events happened. Arnold was apprehensive or even frightened by the bubbles, fearing that the hose might rupture and bring about a fire or an explosion. He and his co-worker, Lee, shut off the flow of pressurized gas and set about to get a larger and stronger hose to replace the one in use. Broussard heard a popping noise "like you would slap your hands together real loud," went to the well-head of one of the wells, saw bubbles on the hose, and observed that at least one bubble had burst and caused a split in the outside layer of the hose. Arnold and Lee told Broussard they were concerned about the hose. Broussard told them that it was normal for bubbles to form on a hose and for the bubbles to burst, that they should not be concerned, that he saw no need to change the hose, and that the bubbles did not affect the integrity of the hose. He instructed them to go ahead and use the hose and to resume the gas lifting operation using the same hose. They complied.

Broussard made no inquiry about the experience of the Hydraulic Workover crew in gas lift operations. He asked no questions concerning the capacity of the rubber hose.

A few minutes after Arnold and Lee turned the pressure on again pursuant to Broussard's instructions, Broussard left the platform. Soon thereafter the hose burst and the explosion and fire ensued.

* * *

What defenses will Union Oil offer to Arnold's action for his injuries, and with what likely results?

DiSALVATORE v. UNITED STATES

United States District Court, Eastern District of Pennsylvania
499 F. Supp. 338 (1980)

OPINION

JOSEPH S. LORD, III, CHIEF JUDGE.

I. PRELIMINARY STATEMENT

This case is in a somewhat anomalous posture. It was tried before me without a jury. I made findings of fact to which I applied certain conclusions of law, resulting in a verdict for defendant. Plaintiff moved for a new trial. Following oral argument on the motion, I was persuaded that I had applied an incorrect standard of law. In effect, I had given an erroneous charge to the factfinder and I therefore granted the plaintiffs' motion. I have now reconsidered the testimony presented in both trials and have reached the conclusions which follow.

Preliminarily, I adopt and reaffirm the findings of fact and conclusions of law previously filed, except as hereinafter noted, and as may be augmented by any additional findings of fact or conclusions of law appearing in this opinion....

Finding of Fact No. 8A is added following Finding of Fact No. 8 as follows: Defendant's failure to provide or require a safety net in the open shaft was negligence....

Finding of Fact No. 12 is amended to read as follows: it is impossible to determine from the evidence (a) whether, at the time of the accident, there was one plank remaining ... or three ... ; (b) whether decedent was caused to fall because he attempted to remove a plank alone ... or because of the warped and rough condition of the plank he was standing on ... ; (c) whether it was unsafe or improper for one man to continue to remove planking alone....

Finding of Fact No. 14 is amended to read as follows: The absence of a required safety device, i.e., a net hung in the shaft, was the cause of DiSalvatore's death, although not the precipitating cause of his fall.

Finding of Fact No. 15 is amended to read as follows: Ordinarily the removal of planking for an elevator shaft is a two-man job. However, there is an unwritten rule of construction work that an employee found standing idly, even if awaiting the return of his "buddy" to continue a two-man job, is subject to immediate dismissal.... The following findings are added following Finding of Fact No. 15.

Finding of Fact 15A—In continuing to remove the planking alone, plaintiff acted under the economic duress of the possible loss of his job if he stood idle and in working alone decedent did not act voluntarily or unreasonably.

...

III. CONTRIBUTORY NEGLIGENCE

In my original adjudication I found plaintiff guilty of contributory negligence. I am now convinced I was in error because I failed to accord proper weight to the burden of proof.

Two propositions are too well settled to require citation of authority. First, a decedent is presumed to have exercised reasonable care for his own safety; second, the burden of proving contributory negligence is on the defendant. I am not convinced that the defendant has sustained that burden.

The evidence presented by defendant on the issue of contributory negligence was so conflicting that I find myself as a factfinder left to speculation and conjecture. William Simpson testified that originally there had been five planks covering the elevator shaft. Two had been removed by DiSalvatore and his co-worker, Harry Rolf. According to Simpson, decedent was standing in the middle of the fourth plank attempting to remove the third plank when he fell. According to Rolf, however, they had started with six or seven planks and had removed all but one. It would defy the laws of nature to conclude that decedent was standing on one plank removing another, as Simpson testified, if there was only one plank remaining, as Rolf testified.

Simpson was the only eyewitness to the accident and his testimony in itself was conflicting and uncertain as to the cause of the decedent's fall. He testified:

> Well, I observed that he tried to pick it up and lift it and remove it and he had—I believe that the one that he was standing on was a little warped and he had lost his balance trying to pick this other one up, and he fell forward with it.

* * *

Again:

> Well, in other words, he had leaned over, but I guess the plank was too heavy to pick up for himself, and then when he tried to pick it up he had lost his balance, and the plank that he was standing on I guess was warped a little, and he had lost his balance and had fell forward with it, and then went over in between where he had picked up 1 and 2 planks.

…

On the other hand, the testimony was consistent on one critical point. Both Simpson and Rolf testified that the planking was uneven, difficult to walk on, easy to slip on or to turn one's ankle on, and if that happened, the worker would be likely to fall into the open shaft. From this testimony, the factfinder could legitimately infer that the condition of the planking caused decedent's fall.

All this evidence makes a finding as to whether the fall was caused by the warped planking, by the decedent's trying to do his job alone, or by the rough, uneven surface of the planking would be nothing but a guess.

…

Since I would have to guess at the cause of decedent's fall, I cannot say that any negligence on his part was a causative factor in his death.

Finally, even if the testimony pointed unequivocally to decedent's unassisted continuance of his work as the cause of his fall, I would still hold that plaintiffs are not barred from recovery. Defendant has pleaded contributory negligence and assumption of risk, but has only argued contributory negligence. However, in this case the difference is not significant. "The great majority of the cases involving assumption of risk have been of this type, where the defense overlaps that of contributory negligence. The same kind of conduct frequently is given either name, or both. Ordinarily it makes no difference which the defense is called." Restatement of Torts (Second) §496A, Comment d....

Here, the defendant can only and does only point to a simple act as a basis for finding contributory negligence, decedent's working alone. There is no evidence and no claim that decedent mishandled the plank or that his feet were placed wrongly or that he stood too near to the edge of the plank or that he was not looking at what he was doing. There is only the fact that he worked alone.

"The question of contributory negligence is usually one of fact for determination by the jury." Walsh v. Miehle-Goss-Dexter, Inc., 378 F.2d 409, 414 (3d Cir. 1967)...."In passing on the question of negligence, courts and juries must consider the realities of the situation." Mogren v. Gadinas, 358 Pa. 507, 512, 58 A.2d 150, 152 (1948). The reality here was that if DiSalvatore had stood idle in his teammate's absence, his job would have been in jeopardy. The law is not so cruel as to demand a choice between economic devastation and a potential danger inherent in his job. Prosser states:

> Even where the plaintiff does not protest, the risk is not assumed where the conduct of the defendant has left him no reasonable alternative. Where the defendant puts him to a choice of evils, there is a species of duress, which destroys all idea of freedom of election.

Prosser, Law of Torts 452.

There is a clear indication of how Pennsylvania courts would react to the situation of economic duress. In Houston v. Tri-State Machinery, 2 Pa.D. & C.3d 796 (C.P. Beaver County 1977), plaintiff was injured while using a defectively guarded saw. Plaintiff did not deny that he was aware of the danger. In sustaining a jury verdict for plaintiff, the court referred to "the form of contributory negligence which consists in voluntarily and unreasonably proceeding to encounter a known danger ..." Id. at 798, quoting Restatement of Torts (Second) § 402A, Comment n.

> One hired as a laborer on a construction site is simply not free to choose which equipment he will operate and which he will not. His use of dangerous machinery is dictated by the terms of his employment, and it would be absurd for this court to hold that he unreasonably and voluntarily used a product he was directed by his superiors to use....
>
> ... There is an obvious distinction to be drawn between the employe-employer situation and the consumer-seller situation. The routine consumer who purchases an obviously defective product can and should refuse to use it in light of the obvious danger presented. While the consumer has alternatives to using the product, the employe simply does not, and his "consent" is in reality predicated upon his maintaining his status as an employe.

Id. at 799. In view of the recent liberalization in Pennsylvania tort law, see supra, I predict that its Supreme Court would adopt similar reasoning and would not consider decedent's conduct negligent as a matter of law.

For the same reasons, which I need embroider no more, I find as a fact that decedent was neither contributorily negligent nor voluntarily or unreasonably assumed the risk.

. . .

NOTES

(1) The problems which this section addresses concern large numbers. Whenever a court considers a tort case that deals with the mangling of an arm in a punch press, in which the defense is that the worker assumed the risk—or a worker's compensation case on that type of facts—it does so against a grim statistical background. Data assembled in a comprehensive study of occupational injuries in 1992, published in 1997, indicated that there were 6,500 deaths from injury in American workplaces annually, and 60,000 deaths from disease. Researchers estimated annual totals of 13.2 million nonfatal injuries and 862,000 occupationally related illnesses. The economic toll of occupational illnesses and injuries was estimated at $171 billion. BNA EMPLOYMENT POLICY AND

LAW DAILY (July 30, 1997), reporting results of J. Paul Leigh, et al., *Occupational Injury and Illness in the United States: Estimates of Costs, Morbidity and Mortality*, 157 ARCH. INTERNAL MED. 1557 (1997).

One hopeful sign by the mid-1990s was the fact that injury and illness rates had declined over a 20-year period. However, time lost from work was on the rise over the period 1972–1993. An official for the Bureau of Labor Statistics said that a principal factor in this increase was "growth in reported cases of repeated trauma," including such injuries as carpal tunnel syndrome and hearing loss caused by exposure to noise. BLS statistics indicated that "[t]he greatest number of repeated trauma cases were in the motor vehicle and equipment manufacturing and meat products industries." A particularly sobering statistic from one area— New York-Northern New Jersey-Long Island—was that assaults or violent acts accounted for more than half of the fatal injuries in the region in one year. Serious workplace injuries increasing as general rate falls, BLS study reports, 24 O.S.H. REP. (BNA) 1834 (Feb. 15, 1995).

(2) Courts are often stringent about the requirement, under the assumption of risk doctrine, that the plaintiff have specific knowledge of a hazard. Illustrative is a case in which a worker knew, from past experience, of pipes sliding off a ramp. However, "at the time of the accident he had no knowledge that the hook of the air hoist line, which secured the pipe, had come loose, and that the pipe was no longer being held in place by the air hoist, and was free to roll off of the ramp." In this situation, his prior knowledge of pipes falling off the ramp "establish[ed] only general knowledge." *Hobbs v. Armco, Inc.*, 413 So.2d 118, 121 (Fla. Dist. Ct. App. 1982).

(3) The area of workers' "assumption of risk" is one in which judicial notions of ethics rather directly confront economic theory. Consider the following declaration by the Florida court that decided the case just summarized, involving the pipe that rolled off the ramp:

> We are not persuaded that the requirements of assumption of risk are satisfied merely because Hobbs continued to work on the oil rig. To so hold would virtually eliminate actions for personal injury suffered by workers engaged in potentially hazardous occupations.

413 So.2d at 121.

Why aren't "the requirements of assumption of risk" satisfied in this situation? Wouldn't economic theory suggest that the worker has made a bargain to work, at a given wage rate, in conditions of risk including the hazard that caused his injury? How can there be a better example of "assumption of risk"? But it is clear, isn't it, that the court is not inclined to "virtually eliminate" tort actions for injuries that occur in dangerous work? If this is a fairly general judicial attitude, is that because judges are not good economists?

(4) A defensive doctrine that is dying out in workers' tort cases is the "fellow servant rule," which immunizes employers from suits by their employees for injuries caused by the negligence of fellow employees. In "inter[ring]" the "remains" of this rule, the New York Court of Appeals reviewed the rationales that had been advanced for it, of which it found the "most convincing" argument to be that it "promotes the safety of the public and of the workers by encouraging each employee to be watchful of the conduct of others for his own protection." Yet the court thought that the rule did not deserve further life:

> Logically, there appears to be little reason for denying an employee the right which a third party possesses to recover from the employer in respondeat supe-

rior, since for one thing, in both instances the employer might have avoided the injury by selection of more careful employees. Moreover, the class of persons most frequently endangered by the negligence of an employee—his fellow workers—should not, without compelling reason, be denied a remedy accorded to the general public.

Buckley v. City of New York, 56 N.Y.2d 300, 437 N.E.2d 331, 452 N.Y.S.2d 331 (1982).

§ 5.03 Contributory Negligence

GARCIA v. BYNUM

United States District Court, District of Columbia
635 F. Supp. 745 (1986), aff'd without opinion, 816 F.2d 791 (D.C. Cir. 1987)

JOYCE HENS GREEN, DISTRICT JUDGE.

Before the Court is defendant John H. Bynum's motion for judgment notwithstanding the verdict, or for a new trial. This personal injury action was tried to a jury in January, 1986, which returned a verdict in favor of plaintiff Jose Garcia in the amount of $80,000. Defendant moves to have this decision set aside on the grounds that the verdict is contrary to the law and evidence presented, that no reasonable person could have found for plaintiff based on the evidence adduced at the trial, and that the verdict is based on sympathy, passion or prejudice. For the reasons set forth below, the Court grants defendant's motion.

On April 17, 1983, plaintiff was struck by a car driven by defendant while crossing in the vicinity of Fessenden Street, in northwest Washington, D.C. As a result of the accident, plaintiff suffered, among other injuries, a fractured leg....

The Court is well aware that motions for judgment notwithstanding the verdict are much disfavored, and should not be granted "unless the evidence, together with all inferences that can reasonably be drawn therefrom is so one-sided that reasonable men could not disagree on the result." ... The Court must weigh the evidence in the light most favorable to the plaintiff, and give him the advantage of every fair and reasonable inference.... The Court is not to substitute its judgment for that of the jury, nor weigh the credibility of witnesses.... Given this standard, it is the rare case in which a court is justified in granting judgment notwithstanding the verdict. Nevertheless, this is such a case.

Under the standards discussed above, the Court must accept plaintiff's version of the accident, notwithstanding the contrary testimony of two non-party witnesses and plaintiff's own prior inconsistent statements. According to plaintiff, he saw defendant's car five car lengths north of the Fessenden Street intersection, stepped out from between two parked cars into Wisconsin Avenue one-third of a block south of that intersection, and strolled across the street to just short of the median line, where he was struck by defendant. This version of events is far more favorable to plaintiff than that offered by defendant and the two witnesses, who stated that plaintiff walked out from between two parked cars in the middle of the block and stepped immediately into the path of defendant's oncoming car. Even so plaintiff's account of the accident demonstrates that he was contributorily negligent as a matter of law. By his own testimony, plaintiff crossed Wisconsin Avenue in an area which was neither a cross-walk nor an intersection, emerging from between parked cars at night wearing dark clothing, fully aware that a car was approaching. He then walked at a leisurely pace across three lanes without once looking to see whether he was correct in assuming that defendant would stop at the yellow light. It may be that a pedestrian crossing in a cross-walk, with a traffic light indicating that it is proper to cross, can reasonably assume that all traffic will stop and that he or she can cross without looking to the left or right. Plaintiff, however, crossed the street in an unmarked area at night, in a relatively darkened area, in violation of governing laws, see 18 D.C.M.R. §§ 2303 and 2304, knowing that a car was approaching a yellow light not far from him. Under these circumstances, plaintiff had a responsibility to exercise due care for his own safety, since he most certainly should have appreciated the danger in crossing when and where he did. It was wholly unreasonable, therefore, for plaintiff to walk in an unhurried fashion without looking to see whether defendant's car had actually stopped.

The fact that several people crossed the street safely shortly before him is entirely irrelevant. No reasonable juror could conclude that a pedestrian crossing in the middle of the street at night, fully aware that a car was approaching, was acting reasonably simply because others had crossed before him. It may be perfectly reasonable to cross a street at one moment, and suicidally dangerous the next; the reasonableness of a pedestrian's crossing of a street can only be judged at the moment he or she crosses it, and not at some time shortly before or after, when others cross. Moreover, it may be that the other pedestrians acted unreasonably too in crossing the street when they did, or that they crossed it much more rapidly than plaintiff. In any event, the mere fact that others had crossed the street before him in no way excuses plaintiff's failure to look to see if defendant's car had stopped. It was simply unreasonable for plaintiff to cross as he did in the middle of the block, with knowledge that a car was approaching, without looking around; that others crossed ahead of him in no way negates his inattentiveness or makes it reasonable.

So too, the fact that plaintiff believed a sign opposite him on Wisconsin Avenue indicated that it was appropriate to cross the street at that point[1] in no way excuses his heedlessness. The sign certainly did not guarantee his safety such that he could reasonably cross the street without paying any attention to defendant's car or any other traffic. The mere fact that plaintiff believed it was legal to cross the street in the middle of the block simply has no bearing on whether or not he exercised due care when he crossed; it clearly is not evidence from which a jury could find that his failure to watch for oncoming traffic was reasonable.

In sum, then, plaintiff crossed Wisconsin Avenue somewhere in the middle of the block at two in the morning wearing dark clothing in a dark area. He saw defendant's car approaching the Fessenden Street intersection about one-third of a city block to his north, but proceeded to cross anyway, in an unhurried, casual manner without looking around to see if defendant had stopped. Under the circumstances, plaintiff's inattentiveness was so unreasonable that no jury could properly conclude that he was not contributorily negligent. Nor could a jury reasonably infer that plaintiff acted in a reasonable manner based on his testimony concerning the yellow light on Wisconsin Avenue, the pedestrians who crossed before him, or the sign on the opposite side of the street:

---

1. The sign in question pictures a pedestrian and faces motorists on Wisconsin Avenue, presumably to warn drivers that they are approaching a pedestrian crossing. For purposes of deciding this motion, of course, the Court accepts plaintiff's testimony that he understood the sign to mean it was proper to cross in the street at that point.

these facts in no way excuse his failure to exercise even the slightest caution when crossing a street at night in the middle of the block. In crossing when and where he did, plaintiff failed to exercise due care for his own safety. No reasonable jury could find otherwise.

For all the foregoing reasons, the Court will grant defendant's motion and enter judgment, notwithstanding the verdict, in favor of defendant.

VOSS v. UNITED STATES

United States District Court, Eastern District of Missouri
423 F. Supp. 751 (1976)

MEMORANDUM

NANGLE, DISTRICT JUDGE.

Plaintiffs, Rene LaRaine Voss and Scott David Ross, both minors, brought suit, by their mother and next friend, Eileen Voss, pursuant to the Federal Tort Claims Act, 28 U.S.C. §§ 1346, 2671 et seq., seeking damages for the wrongful death of their father, William Voss.

This case was tried to the Court without a jury....

3. William Giles, a veteran of the United States Army, was admitted to the Veterans Administration Hospital at Jefferson Barracks on April 13, 1974 following a threat to blow up a VFW Hall. He was brought to the hospital by the St. Louis County Police. Giles, however, was a voluntary patient, and it was his first visit to the hospital.

4. Upon admission, Giles was interviewed by Dr. Johanna Fetmer. Dr. Fetmer, who was serving a medical residency at the hospital under the supervision of Dr. Thomas Moran, made a tentative diagnosis of "anxiety reaction?", "Paranoid personality?". Giles was placed in an open ward, in which doors were normally left unlocked.

5. It was the overwhelming consensus of the doctors who testified herein that an open ward is more conducive to the establishment of a therapeutic atmosphere in which the patient comes to trust the doctors, than is a locked ward situation.

6. Shortly after his admission, on April 15, 1974, Giles was given a battery of tests. The results of these tests were discussed informally with Dr. Fetmer and were later incorporated in a written report. The tests indicated presence of paranoid schizophrenia but did not conclusively establish that Giles was dangerous either to himself or others.

7. Giles' case was discussed frequently at team meetings and during informal staff discussions.

8. On April 19, 1974, Giles left the hospital. Since he was a voluntary patient, he did not escape from the hospital. This leaving is called an "elopement".

9. Giles returned on April 21, 1974 voluntarily. At a staff meeting on April 22, 1974, Giles' case was discussed and it was decided that Giles would be left in the open ward but watched more closely. This decision was reached in part because it was felt that Giles was not dangerous to himself or others.

10. On April 22, 1974, Giles again left the hospital.

11. The Court finds that the hospital was not negligent in its diagnosis of Giles. The Court further finds that the hospital was not negligent in failing to restrain Giles or in failing to seek judicial commitment.

12. On April 24, 1974, William Voss, deceased, was driving on Ashby Road. Mary O'Brien was a passenger in his car. Voss stopped his car on Ashby and observed Giles, who was crossing in front of their car, carrying a .22 caliber rifle. Giles stopped in front of the car and pointed the rifle towards the windshield of the car. Giles then continued walking. Voss continued driving but decided to return to Giles because of the danger Giles presented to a neighborhood in which there were children. Accordingly, he drove his car around several blocks in order to circle back to Giles. During this return drive, Ms. O'Brien pointed out to Voss that there was a police car a few cars ahead of them and suggested that Voss inform the police. Instead, Voss continued driving. Voss observed Giles walking on Driver Avenue and brought his car to a stop somewhat ahead of where Giles was walking. Voss left the car and shouted to Giles "Hey, jackoff, what are you doing pointing a fucking gun at people?". Moments later, Giles shot Voss with the rifle. Voss died as a result of this shooting.

. . .

Assuming arguendo that the hospital was negligent, the Court must conclude that plaintiffs' decedent was contributorily negligent as a matter of fact, thus precluding recovery. . . .

Plaintiffs argue that decedent was unaware that Giles had eloped from the hospital and was therefore unaware of the danger. Thus, plaintiffs argue, decedent could not have been contributorily negligent. . . . The Court, however, must conclude that the facts known to decedent at the time he approached Giles were sufficient to apprise him of the danger and risk of injury. Decedent approached a man armed with a rifle. This man had previously stopped in the middle of crossing a street and pointed the rifle at decedent for no apparent reason. Decedent had the opportunity to inform the police of the situation but chose not to. The language decedent used in confronting Giles was, at the very least, extremely inflammatory language to use to a man holding a rifle. The Court must conclude that decedent was contributorily negligent.

Accordingly, judgment will be entered for defendant.

NOTES

(1) What legal wisdom did Judge Green think she had that the *Garcia* jury did not have? Why could a "reasonable jury" not "find otherwise"? Why would this jury have reacted unreasonably to Garcia's case? What principles of judicial administration are vindicated by the judgment n.o.v.?

(2) The suit for Voss's death was brought under the Federal Tort Claims Act, for the negligence of the United States. Suppose that Giles had enough money to make it economically worthwhile for Voss's survivors to sue Giles. Should contributory negligence be permitted as a defense in such a suit?

(3) The contributory negligence defense occasionally generates interesting legal issues in cases of alleged medical malpractice. Consider, for example, whether you would permit the defense in the following cases:

(a) A patient claims that his physician was negligent in permitting him to return to work, despite a heart condition and associated ailments. The trial judge

refers to possible contributory negligence residing in the patient's refusal to refrain from smoking and drinking and his failure to lose weight.

(b) A psychiatric patient sues for injuries that occurred when she jumped from
a second floor hospital where she was in intensive care. The defendants claim
that the plaintiff's conduct was contributory negligence.

(4) The application of contributory negligence can be harsh, for example, in cases
where an everyday hazardous condition does not call attention to itself and even in
cases of momentary forgetfulness. In one case, the 79-year-old plaintiff went into the
cashier's booth at a gas station, which was located on a raised platform five or six inches
above the pavement, to pay for a fillup. The paint on the raised platform of the island
was not visible to people who were coming out of the booth to go back to their cars,
and there was "[n]o special marking or paint … on the traveled surface of the island" or
any warning signs. The plaintiff fell, suffering serious injuries. Although the court concluded that there was negligence in the defendant's failure to mark the step down or to
warn about it, it found the plaintiff contributorily negligent as a matter of law and
barred her recovery. It observed that the "completely candid" plaintiff had "admitted
that she remembered the step down" but "proceeded even though she could not see it."
The court pointed out that state precedents had barred even plaintiffs who were familiar
with hazards but momentarily forgot about them. *Arthur v. Crown Central Petroleum
Corp.*, 866 F. Supp. 951, 954–55 (E.D. Va. 1994).

Is this a just result? What is the meaning of contributory negligence in such cases?
Does it involve a moral judgment? Should not a plaintiff who temporarily forgets a
hazard be entitled to at least some recovery, when the defendant is shown to have been
negligent?

(5) Two opinions by Judge Posner in the same year provide interesting comparisons
on the issue of contributory negligence in diverse contexts.

In one case, the plaintiff sued a resort hotel for injuries suffered in a criminal assault by an intruder, who entered a guest room through a sliding glass door that was
unlocked but on which the plaintiff had connected the safety chain. On the one
hand, Judge Posner conceded that the hotel was not an urban one and that "it might
not occur to a guest that a safety chain on a sliding door to the outside was an inadequate protection against nocturnal marauders." Yet, the plaintiff "was an experienced
business traveler, so maybe she should have known better; and most people don't
consider a safety chain an adequate substitute for a lock." In any event, "even if there
was no evidence of contributory negligence, there was no prejudicial error in giving
an instruction on it" in a comparative negligence jurisdiction where contributory
fault would only reduce the amount of recovery against a negligent defendant. *Mc-
Carty v. Pheasant Run*, 826 F.2d 1554, 1559 (7th Cir. 1987). Are you persuaded by
this argument?

The other case centered on a lawyer's representation that he had "conducted a
U.C.C., tax, and judgment search" on farm machinery that was being offered as security
for a loan, a representation alleged to have been false and at least negligent. The plaintiff lent money to the farm owner based on this representation, and sued the lawyer for
damages related to the fact that most of the farm machinery had previously been
pledged to other lenders, leaving the plaintiff without effective collateral. Judge Posner
wrote for a Seventh Circuit panel that it was not careless of the lender "not to conduct
its own UCC search": "The law normally does not require duplicative precautions unless one is likely to fail or the consequences of failure (slight though the likelihood may

be) would be catastrophic." On such facts, "one UCC search is enough to disclose prior liens, and [the lender] acted reasonably in relying on [the lawyer] to conduct it." *Greycas, Inc. v. Proud*, 826 F.2d 1560 (7th Cir. 1987), *cert. denied*, 108 S. Ct. 775 (1988).

Can you extract the seed of a general contributory negligence rule from these two decisions?

(6) Consider the following classification scheme:

(a) Cases in which the defendant does not fall below the standard of care;

(b) Cases in which the defendant falls below the standard of care and the plaintiff acts unreasonably in subjecting himself to dangerous conditions;

(c) Cases in which the defendant falls below the standard of care and the plaintiff subjectively knows of the danger or can be charged with knowledge, yet acts reasonably in the circumstances.

In light of your study of this section, what do you think are the proper results for cases in each of these categories? Are there any other basic classifications? Specifically, is it appropriate to classify separately the case in which the defendant falls below the standard of care he owes to the public but arguably behaves reasonably in his relation to the plaintiff? Consider a hypothetical offered by Laurence Eldredge in Restatement (Second) of Torts, Tent. Draft No. 9, at 73–74 (1963). Eldredge pictures a "plaintiff who receives a phone call informing him that his house a quarter of a mile down the road is on fire and that his pregnant wife is trapped in a third-floor room. He rushes out to the highway and sees a very drunk man about to drive down the road in an automobile and realizes his condition. At the plaintiff's solicitation the drunk agrees to accept plaintiff as a passenger." Eldredge contends that "[i]n operating his car incompetently the drunk is not a tortfeasor to the plaintiff who has voluntarily assumed the risk," although "[t]he drunk would be operating the car negligently with respect to other persons on the highway."

The question of whether there is a separate defense of "'implied' assumption of risk" is the subject of heated debate in "the Battle of the Wilderness," a struggle over *Restatement* drafting in which engagements are fought by several distinguished law teachers and judges. See Restatement (Second) of Torts, Tent. Draft No. 9 at 70ff.

SPECIAL NOTE: DOES GENDER AFFECT THE CARE THAT IS DUE?

Consider the situation of the pregnant woman in the nineteenth century who has to board a train in an unsheltered setting in winter, using only a little stool provided by the railroad, and constricted by a floor length skirt. When she falls in the attempt, an event followed by the birth of stillborn twins, could the railroad succeed with a defense of contributory negligence? Useful information and ideas appear in Barbara Welke's summary of the trial and appellate results in such a case, incorporating some relevant facts, and her commentary:

> Hannah Eichorn's lawyer asked the court to tell the jurors that the words "carelessly," "negligently," and "negligence" both as to the trainmen and Mrs. Eichorn's actions meant "the lack of such care and caution as reasonable and prudent men would exercise under like circumstances." The railroad's lawyer objected to this instruction and asked the court to instruct the jury that if Hannah Eichorn's injury resulted in whole or in part through her "failure or neglect

to exercise such care, caution and foresight as a woman of ordinary care, caution and foresight would have exercised under the circumstances surrounding the plaintiff at the time," then they should find for the defendant. The judge gave both instructions. The jury returned a verdict for Hannah Eichorn for $3,000.[49]

In appealing the judgment, the defendant objected that the court had defined negligence in terms of the care of a reasonable "man" rather than "woman." The Missouri Supreme Court rejected the defendant's argument: "the jury would have been utterly unfit to try any case if they did not understand that 'men' in this instruction was generic and embraced women." In any event, noted the court, assuming there was a defect, the defendant's own instruction had cured it. But having suggested that gender was "generic," the court went on to explain the jury's verdict in distinctly gendered terms. As the court explained, "[t]he jury might well have deemed" the delay in rebuilding the depot and the lack of any suitable waiting area "most unreasonable," compelling this pregnant woman to remain as long as possible in her house rather than exposing herself on a "cold February day in an open field." Moreover, "carriers of passengers should anticipate that both old and young women, feeble and delicate people, as well as strong and robust, will seek passage on their cars and provide suitable platforms or steps for that purpose."[50]

Hannah Eichorn's case was about the most common of acts—boarding a train. Yet her dilemma and her accident were quintessentially female. While, without doubt, it was no great harm to leave men standing in the elements, was it an equally reasonable act to force women, pregnant women, to stand exposed? While, without doubt, it would have been reasonable for a man to leap on a train unaided, was it reasonable for a woman, a pregnant woman, to do so when help was at hand?

. . .

Not surprisingly, ... the law ... reinforced gender norms of conduct for women and men. For example, in the context of women accompanied by a man, the law specifically encouraged women to remain properly submissive by excusing them from not taking care for their own safety.[89] In such cases, courts admitted that they essentially were excusing women from exercising any care for their own safety. These cases, though, were exceptional. In most cases, the standard of care required of women was not absolutely lower (or higher) than that required of men. Courts required women and men alike to take account of women's physical disabilities, whether resulting from nature, experience, or clothing. The resulting standard was a balance: Men had to consider women's situation, but women themselves were also required to consider it. In this way, courts refused to impose solely on women the risk of what would have been ordinary acts for a man and seemed inclined to "understand" women's fail-

---

49. Record in *Eichorn v. Missouri, Kansas & Texas Ry. Co.* (Missouri State Archives, Jefferson City). Many of the facts are restated in the Missouri Supreme Court's opinion in *Eichorn v. Missouri, Kansas & Texas Ry.*, 130 Mo. 575 (1895).

50. 130 Mo. 588–89.

89. *Minard v. Boston & M.R.*, 184 F.211 (C.C.A. 1st Cir. 1910); *Colorado Springs & I. Ry. v. Cohun*, 66 Colo. 149 (1919). *See also Wicker v. North States Constr. Co.*, 183 Minn. 79 (1931); *Graves v. Mickel*, 176 Wash. 329 (1934).

ings.[90] For example, a pregnant woman was not contributorily negligent in boarding or alighting from a train without assistance, and she most certainly was not required to notify the defendant's employees (all male) of her condition.[91] On the courts' terms, the law acted like a scoring handicap in a round of golf: the unequal were made equal.

But this handicapping system of law, as I have described it, was not absolute. In matters requiring judgment, where it was unlikely that the defendant would have what amounted to a "last clear chance" to avoid injury, at least some courts strongly argued that the care of a reasonable man should bind even women and defendants should be able to assume that all would act as reasonable men. The classic example, of course, is crossing accidents. In such cases, some courts firmly believed that gender mattered: They rejected a standard of care based on a woman's inferior capacity to reach reasoned judgments. Yet, even here, the assumption of women's incapacity to reason was offset by the equally powerful assumption that women were naturally timid and, in contrast to men, assiduously avoided danger. The fact that every gender assumption for women could be stated negatively and positively in terms of how women encountered risk was what made the facts in cases involving women absolutely essential. When considered collectively, cases involving injury to women suggest that courts constrained women to act within the acceptable bounds of ladylike conduct, as defined by men. In this way, courts incorporated into law the general social norms governing gender relations.

No doubt, many judges saw themselves as protecting women.[94] And they were. A rule holding women to the same standard of care as men would have left women, in many situations, in an unequal position before the law. The effect would have been to require women to exercise greater diligence than men to guard against injury. Women, after all, encumbered by long, heavy skirts, constrained by corsets and shirts with small armholes, did not enjoy the same freedom of movement as men in making their way through congested urban thoroughfares and on and off trains and streetcars. Most women, too, did not have the variety of experience of most men in negotiating the perils of an industrialized world. But for women who were accustomed to travel, the image itself became an additional constraint on their movements.[95]

---

90. *See, e.g., Poulin v. Broadway & Seventh Ave. R.R.*, 61 N.Y. 621 (1874) (trial court properly refused to instruct jury that a woman wearing a hoop-skirt was bound to use extra caution to avoid accidents in attempting to alight from a streetcar); *Foss v. Boston & Me. R.R.*, 66 N.H. 256, 259–60 (if the female plaintiff failed to look ahead as she was alighting because she was in a flustered state of ... mind caused by the train passing the station before stopping, it was appropriate for the jury to find no contributory negligence); *Bass v. Concord St. Ry.*, 70 N.H. 170 (1899) (alighting female passenger preoccupied by her wraps and bundles not contributorily negligent).

91. See, e.g., *Missouri Pac. Ry. v. Watson*, 72 Tex. 631 (1889).

94. Melvin Urofsky and Aviam Soifer have both explored the paternalistic rationales that underlay laws limiting working hours and regulating working conditions for women. See Melvin I. Urofsky, *State Courts and Protective Legislation during the Progressive Era: A Reevaluation*, 73 J. Am. Hist. 63, 71–75 (1985); Aviam Soifer, *The Paradox of Paternalism and Laissez-Faire Constitutionalism: United States Supreme Court, 1888–1921*, 5 Law & Hist. Rev. 249 (1987).

95. For example, in *Chenery v. Fitchburg R.R.*, among other facts, the evidence showed that Mary Chenery, a 40-year old woman, had been accustomed to driving for many years, that her horse was gentle, that travelers on business and pleasure regularly had used the private way which crossed over the railroads tracks for more than 25 years with the railroads knowledge, and that though it was past the time for the scheduled train, Mary Chenery stopped the buggy she was dri-

—Barbara Welke, *Unreasonable Women: Gender and the Law of Accidental Injury*, 19 LAW & SOC. INQUIRY 369, 385–86, 397–99 (1994).*

NOTES

(1) Do the nineteenth century decisions summarized by Welke appear to have been based on a "sexist" view of society held by the judges? Or did they simply respond to the consequences of sexism in society?

(2) Can you think of any twenty-first century situations in which the defense of contributory negligence would be ruled out of order on the grounds that the plaintiff is female?

BALTIMORE & O. R. CO. v. GOODMAN
275 U.S. 66 (1927)

Mr. Justice HOLMES delivered the opinion of the Court.

This is a suit brought by the widow and administratrix of Nathan Goodman against the petitioner for causing his death by running him down at a grade crossing. The defence is that Goodman's own negligence caused the death. At the trial the defendant asked the Court to direct a verdict for it, but the request and others looking to the same direction were refused, and the plaintiff got a verdict and a judgment which was affirmed by the Circuit Court of Appeals. 10 F.(2d) 58.

Goodman was driving an automobile truck in an easterly direction and was killed by a train running southwesterly across the road at a rate of not less than 60 miles an hour. The line was straight but it is said by the respondent that Goodman 'had no practical view' beyond a section house 243 feet north of the crossing until he was about 20 feet from the first rail, or, as the respondent argues, 12 feet from danger, and that then the engine was still obscured by the section house. He had been driving at the rate of 10 or 12 miles an hour but had cut down his rate to 5 or 6 miles at about 40 feet from the crossing. It is thought that there was an emergency in which, so far as appears, Goodman did all that he could.

We do not go into further details as to Goodman's precise situation, beyond mentioning that it was daylight and that he was familiar with the crossing, for it appears to us plain that nothing is suggested by the evidence to relieve Goodman from responsibility for his own death. When a man goes upon a railroad track he knows that he goes to a place where he will be killed if a train comes upon him before he is clear of the track. He knows that he must stop for the train not the train stop for him. In such circumstances it seems to us that if a driver cannot be sure otherwise whether a train is dangerously near he must stop and get out of his vehicle, although obviously he will not often

---

ving twice along the private way to listen for the sound of the train. Nonetheless, the court strongly suggested to the jury that she had been negligent, saying that the jurors should not consider whether a woman would think she was entitled to treat this road as a public way, but must consider whether a reasonably intelligent and prudent man would have thought it a public way. Moreover, the court said the defendant should only have to consider what such a prudent man would have done. Record in *Chenery v. Fitchburg R.R. Co.* (Social Law Library, Boston, Mass.). The Massachusetts high court affirmed the verdict for the defendant railroad in 160 Mass. 211 (1893)....

* © 1998 American Bar Foundation, originally published by the University of Chicago, now published by Blackwell Publishing. Reprinted by permission.

be required to do more than to stop and look. It seems to us that if he relies upon not hearing the train or any signal and takes no further precaution he does so at his own risk. If at the last moment Goodman found himself in an emergency it was his own fault that he did not reduce his speed earlier or come to a stop. It is true as said in Flannelly v. Delaware & Hudson Co., 225 U. S. 597, 603, 32 S. Ct. 783, 56 L. Ed. 1221, 44 L. R. A. (N. S.) 154, that the question of due care very generally is left to the jury. But we are dealing with a standard of conduct, and when the standard is clear it should be laid down once for all by the Courts....

Judgment reversed.

Mr. Justice SUTHERLAND was absent.

POKORA v. WABASH RY. CO.
292 U.S. 98 (1934)

Mr. Justice CARDOZO delivered the opinion of the Court.

John Pokora, driving his truck across a railway grade crossing in the city of Springfield, Ill., was struck by a train and injured. Upon the trial of his suit for damages, the District Court held that he had been guilty of contributory negligence, and directed a verdict for the defendant. The Circuit Court of Appeals (one judge dissenting) affirmed (66 F.(2d) 166), resting its judgment on the opinion of this court in B. & O.R. Co. v. Goodman, 275 U.S. 66, 48 S.Ct. 24, 25, 72 L.Ed. 167, 56 A.L.R. 645. A writ of certiorari brings the case here.

Pokora was an ice dealer, and had come to the crossing to load his truck with ice. The tracks of the Wabash Railway are laid along Tenth street, which runs north and south. There is a crossing at Edwards street running east and west. Two ice depots are on opposite corners of Tenth and Edward streets; one at the northeast corner, the other at the southwest. Pokora, driving west along Edwards street, stopped at the first of these corners to get his load of ice, but found so many trucks ahead of him that he decided to try the depot on the other side of the way. In this crossing of the railway, the accident occurred.

The defendant has four tracks on Tenth street; a switch track on the east, then the main track, and then two switches. Pokora, as he left the northeast corner where his truck had been stopped, looked to the north for approaching trains. He did this at a point about ten or fifteen feet east of the switch ahead of him. A string of box cars standing on the switch, about five to ten feet from the north line of Edwards street, cut off his view of the tracks beyond him to the north. At the same time he listened. There was neither bell nor whistle. Still listening, he crossed the switch, and reaching the main track was struck by a passenger train coming from the north at a speed of twenty-five to thirty miles an hour.

The burden of proof was on the defendant to make out the defense of contributory negligence.... The record does not show in any conclusive way that the train was visible to Pokora while there was still time to stop. A space of eight feet lay between the west rail of the switch and the east rail of the main track, but there was an overhang of the locomotive (perhaps two and a half or three feet), as well as an overhang of the box cars, which brought the zone of danger even nearer. When the front of the truck had come within this zone, Pokora was on his seat, and so was farther back (perhaps five feet or even more), just how far we do not know, for the defendant has omitted to make proof of the dimensions. Nice calculations are submitted in an effort to make out that there was a glimpse of the main track before the switch was fully cleared. Two feet farther back the track was visible, it is said, for about 130 or 140 feet. But the view from that position does not tell us anything of significance unless we know also the position of the train. Pokora was not protected by his glimpse of 130 feet if the train at the same moment was 150 feet away or farther. For all that appears he had no view of the main track northward, or none for a substantial distance, till the train was so near that escape had been cut off. . . .

In such circumstances the question, we think, was for the jury whether reasonable caution forbade his going forward in reliance on the sense of hearing, unaided by that of sight. No doubt it was his duty to look along the track from his seat, if looking would avail to warn him of the danger. This does not mean, however, that if vision was cut off by obstacles, there was negligence in going on, any more than there would have been in trusting to his ears if vision had been cut off by the darkness of the night. . . . Pokora made his crossing in the daytime, but like the traveler by night he used the faculties available to one in his position. . . . A jury, but not the court, might say that with faculties thus limited he should have found some other means of assuring himself of safety before venturing to cross. The crossing was a frequented highway in a populous city. Behind him was a line of other cars, making ready to follow him. To some extent, at least, there was assurance in the thought that the defendant would not run its train at such a time and place without sounding bell or whistle. . . . Illinois Revised Statutes (1933 Ed.), c. 114, par. 84.[1] Indeed, the statutory signals did not exhaust the defendant's duty when to its knowledge there was special danger to the traveler through obstructions on the roadbed narrowing the field of vision. . . . All this the plaintiff, like any other reasonable traveler, might fairly take into account. All this must be taken into account by us in comparing what he did with the conduct reasonably to be expected of reasonable men. . . .

The argument is made, however, that our decision in B. & O.R. Co. v. Goodman, supra, is a barrier in the plaintiff's path, irrespective of the conclusion that might commend itself if the question were at large. There is no doubt that the opinion in that case is correct in its result. Goodman, the driver, traveling only five or six miles an hour, had, before reaching the track, a clear space of eighteen feet within which the train was plainly visible. With that opportunity, he fell short of the legal standard of duty established for a traveler when he failed to look and see. This was decisive of the case. But the court did not stop there. It added a remark, unnecessary upon the facts before it, which has been a fertile source of controversy. 'In such circumstances it seems to us that if a driver cannot be sure otherwise whether a train is dangerously near he must stop and get out of his vehicle, although obviously he will not often be required to do more than to stop and look.'

There is need at this stage to clear the ground of brushwood that may obscure the point at issue. We do not now inquire into the existence of a duty to stop, disconnected from a duty to get out and reconnoitre. The inquiry, if pursued, would lead us into the thickets of conflicting judgments. Some courts apply what is often spoken of as the

---

1. The Illinois Act provides: 'Every railroad corporation shall cause a bell of at least thirty pounds weight, and a steam whistle placed and kept on each locomotive engine, and shall cause the same to be rung or whistled by the engineer or fireman, at the distance of at least eighty rods from the place where the railroad crosses or intersects any public highway, and shall be kept ringing or whistling until such highway is reached.'

Pennsylvania rule, and impose an unyielding duty to stop, as well as to look and listen, no matter how clear the crossing or the tracks on either side.... Other courts, the majority, adopt the rule that the traveler must look and listen, but that the existence of a duty to stop depends upon the circumstances, and hence generally, even if not invariably, upon the judgment of the jury.... The subject has been less considered in this court, but in none of its opinions is there a suggestion that at any and every crossing the duty to stop is absolute, irrespective of the danger. Not even in B. & O.R. Co. v. Goodman, supra, which goes farther than the earlier cases, is there support for such a rule. To the contrary, the opinion makes it clear that the duty is conditioned upon the presence of impediments whereby sight and hearing become inadequate for the traveler's protection....

Choice between these diversities of doctrine is unnecessary for the decision of the case at hand. Here the fact is not disputed that the plaintiff did stop before he started to cross the tracks. If we assume that by reason of the box cars, there was a duty to stop again when the obstructions had been cleared, that duty did not arise unless a stop could be made safely after the point of clearance had been reached.... For reasons already stated, the testimony permits the inference that the truck was in the zone of danger by the time the field of vision was enlarged. No stop would then have helped the plaintiff if he remained seated on his truck, or so the triers of the facts might find. His case was for the jury, unless as a matter of law he was subject to a duty to get out of the vehicle before it crossed the switch, walk forward to the front, and then, afoot, survey the scene. We must say whether his failure to do this was negligence so obvious and certain that one conclusion and one only is permissible for rational and candid minds....

Standards of prudent conduct are declared at times by courts, but they are taken over from the facts of life. To get out of a vehicle and reconnoitre is an uncommon precaution, as everyday experience informs us. Besides being uncommon, it is very likely to be futile, and sometimes even dangerous. If the driver leaves his vehicle when he nears a cut or curve, he will learn nothing by getting out about the perils that lurk beyond. By the time he regains his seat and sets his car in motion, the hidden train may be upon him.... Where was Pokora to leave his truck after getting out to reconnoitre? If he was to leave it on the switch, there was the possibility that the box cars would be shunted down upon him before he could regain his seat. The defendant did not show whether there was a locomotive at the forward end, or whether the cars were so few that a locomotive could be seen. If he was to leave his vehicle near the curb, there was even stronger reason to believe that the space to be covered in going back and forth would make his observations worthless. One must remember that while the traveler turns his eyes in one direction, a train or a loose engine may be approaching from the other.

Illustrations such as these bear witness to the need for caution in framing standards of behavior that amount to rules of law. The need is the more urgent when there is no background of experience out of which the standards have emerged. They are then, not the natural flowerings of behavior in its customary forms, but rules artificially developed, and imposed from without. Extraordinary situations may not wisely or fairly be subjected to tests or regulations that are fitting for the commonplace or normal. In default of the guide of customary conduct, what is suitable for the traveler caught in a mesh where the ordinary safeguards fail him is for the judgment of a jury.... The opinion in Goodman's Case has been a source of confusion in the federal courts to the extent that it imposes a standard for application by the judge, and has had only wavering support in the courts of the states. We limit it accordingly.

The judgment should be reversed, and the cause remanded for further proceedings in accordance with this opinion.

...

NOTES

(1) Holmes left the Supreme Court in 1932, at the age of 91. Was Cardozo in *Pokora* simply being kind to a revered, recently retired Justice in saying that *Goodman* was correctly decided? Was *Goodman*, indeed, still good law after *Pokora*?

(2) How did each of these distinguished judges view the issues in their cases with respect to questions of fact and questions of law? How did they define the roles of judge and jury?

(3) Cardozo says that judges should exercise "caution in framing standards of behavior that amount to rules of law." Did Holmes exercise enough caution in that respect in *Goodman*? What about the judges in *Garcia*, supra at page 294, and *Voss*, supra at page 296? Give an example of a case, other than *Pokora*, where the court was appropriately wary about not turning a fact pattern into a rule.

(4) What effects would either decision be likely to have on the conduct of companies that run trains or drivers who must negotiate train tracks?

§ 5.04 "The Last Clear Chance"

In those jurisdictions where contributory negligence remains a complete defense to a negligence action, one of the principal antidotes to the defense is the doctrine of "last clear chance." This theory, the principal application of which is in vehicle cases, posits a series of consecutive culpabilities. Simplified, the notion is that (1) a defendant is negligent, (2) a plaintiff is contributorily negligent, (3) the defendant has the "last clear chance" to avoid the accident.

There is general agreement that the "last clear chance" effectively cancels the doctrine of contributory negligence and permits the plaintiff to recover if he was in a position of helpless peril, if the defendant discovered him when there was time to avoid the accident, and if the defendant failed to take reasonable care to avoid the injury. A variation is the case in which the plaintiff is helpless and the defendant should have discovered his peril but did not; in this case, a majority of courts will impose liability on the defendant. A third category is the case in which both parties are careless by way of inattentiveness that continues up to the moment of the accident, but the defendant would have discovered the plaintiff's peril in the exercise of proper care. Only Missouri, employing its unique "humanitarian doctrine," has been inclined to allow recovery to plaintiffs in this category. Another case in which plaintiffs lose in almost all jurisdictions is the episode of "antecedent negligence." In that situation, the plaintiff claims that the defendant's original negligence—for example, in not fixing defective brakes—prevented him from avoiding the accident when the situation later became critical.*

---

* This discussion synthesizes the syntheses in 4 HARPER, JAMES & GRAY, LAW OF TORTS 22.13 (1986), and PROSSER & KEETON ON TORTS 66 (5th ed. 1984).

With respect to the last category, ask yourself why most courts would deny recovery when a defendant speeds while driving with what he knows to be bad brakes, if he tries vainly to stop and would have stopped successfully before impact if his brakes were good. Can you explain why there should be a difference in result between that kind of case and the one in which the defendant discovers the plaintiff's peril but is slow to react?

§ 5.05 Comparative Fault Doctrines

ALVIS v. RIBAR
Illinois Supreme Court
85 Ill. 2d 1, 421 N.E.2d 886, 52 Ill. Dec. 23 (1981)

MORAN, JUSTICE:

. . .

Plaintiffs ask this court to abolish the doctrine of contributory negligence and to adopt in its place the doctrine of comparative negligence as the law in Illinois.

In Alvis v. Ribar, a motor vehicle operated by defendant Ribar skidded out of control and collided with a metal barrel which anchored an official intersection stop sign. The sign had been temporarily placed at the intersection while construction work on the intersecting road was being done by the defendant contractor, Milburn Brothers, Inc., under the supervision of defendant Cook County. Plaintiff Alvis, who was a passenger in defendant Ribar's vehicle, sustained injuries as a result of the collision....

In Krohn v. Abbott Laboratories, Inc., a tractor trailer operated by defendant Sweetwood and owned by defendant Abbott Laboratories, Inc., was traveling west when it collided with an eastbound vehicle operated by decedent, Klaus D. Krohn. The collision occurred in the eastbound lane. As a result of the collision, Klaus D. Krohn sustained fatal injuries....

I

THE HISTORY OF CONTRIBUTORY NEGLIGENCE

Generally, under the doctrine of contributory negligence, a plaintiff is barred from recovering compensation for his injuries if his negligence contributed to the accident. The origin of the doctrine can be traced to the case of Butterfield v. Forrester (1809), 11 East 60, 103 Eng.Rep. 926. There defendant had placed a pole across part of a public road. Plaintiff, riding his horse too fast to see the obstruction, rode into the pole and was injured. The concept of contributory negligence was created by the words of Chief Justice Lord Ellenborough:

> Two things must concur to support this action, an obstruction in the road by
> the fault of the defendant, and no want of ordinary care to avoid it on the part
> of the plaintiff.

Butterfield v. Forrester (1809), 11 East 60, 61, 103 Eng.Rep. 926, 927.

The doctrine was swiftly adopted in American jurisprudence, commencing with the case of Smith v. Smith (1824), 19 Mass. (2 Pick.) 621, 13 Am.Dec. 464.... Legal scholars attribute the swift and universal acceptance of the doctrine to newly formed industry's need for protection "against the ravages which might have been wrought by over-sympathetic juries." (Turk, Comparative Negligence on the March, 28 Chi.-Kent L.Rev. 189, 201 (1950); H. Woods, The Negligence Case: Comparative Fault 8 (1978) ... Judicial concern was particularly evident in the area of personal injury suits brought by railroad employees against the railroads. The courts realized that, in the pervading public view that saw railroads as "harmful entities with deep pockets" (H. Woods, The Negligence Case: Comparative Fault 9 (1978)), juries' sympathies toward plaintiffs could wreak financial disaster upon that burgeoning industry.

Case law developed the doctrine of contributory negligence in Illinois....

...

Comparative negligence made its first permanent entry into American law in 1908 in the form of the Federal Employers' Liability Act (45 U.S.C. sec. 53)....

Today, a total of 36 States have adopted comparative negligence....

CONTRIBUTORY NEGLIGENCE v. COMPARATIVE NEGLIGENCE

The contributory negligence defense has been subject to attack because of its failure to apportion damages according to the fault of the parties. Under a comparative negligence standard, the parties are allowed to recover the proportion of damages not attributable to their own fault. The basic logic and fairness of such apportionment is difficult to dispute....

... Certainly, the concern which prompted the adoption of the rule can no longer support its retention. There is no longer any justification for providing the protective barrier of the contributory negligence rule for industries of the nation at the expense of deserving litigants.... It must be pointed out that today most cases against industrial defendants are brought under the Worker's Compensation Act, under which plaintiff's negligence is not an issue.... The United States Supreme Court recognized the obsolescence of the rule in relation to present-day needs in one sphere of the law:

> The harsh rule of the common law under which contributory negligence wholly barred an injured person from recovery is completely incompatible with modern admiralty policy and practice.

(Pope & Talbot v. Hawn (1953), 346 U.S. 406, 408–09, 74 S.Ct. 202, 204, 98 L.Ed. 143, 150.)

We believe that the concept of comparative negligence which produces a more just and socially desirable distribution of loss is demanded by today's society.

Defendants contend that the apportionment of relative fault by a jury cannot be scientifically done, as such precise measurement is impossible. The simple and obvious answer to this contention is that in 36 jurisdictions of the United States such apportionment is being accomplished by juries. The Supreme Court of California, in responding to a similar contention, stated:

> These inherent difficulties are not, however, insurmountable. Guidelines might be provided the jury which will assist it in keeping focussed upon the true inquiry (citation), and the utilization of special verdicts or jury interrogatories can be of invaluable assistance in assuring that the jury has approached its sensitive and often complex task with proper standards and appropriate reverence.

(Li v. Yellow Cab Co. (1975), 13 Cal.3d 804, 824, 119 Cal.Rptr. 858, 872, 532 P.2d 1226, 1240.)

We agree that such guidelines can assist a jury in making apportionment decisions and view the necessary subtle calculations no more difficult or sophisticated for jury determination than others in a jury's purview, such as compensation for pain and suffering. Although it is admitted that percentage allocations of fault are only approximations, the results are far superior to the "all or nothing" results of the contributory negligence rule. "Small imperfections can be disregarded, small inequities tolerated, if the final result is generally satisfactory." Turk, Comparative Negligence on the March, 28 Chi.-Kent L.Rev. 189, 341–42 (1950).

Defendants assert that the contributory negligence rule should be retained in that the comparative negligence doctrine rewards carelessness and ignores the value of requiring prudent behavior. The fallacy of this premise was underscored by Dean Prosser:

> [T]he assumption that the speeding motorist is, or should be meditating on the possible failure of a lawsuit for his possible injuries lacks all reality, and it is quite as reasonable to say that the rule promotes accidents by encouraging the negligent defendant.

(Prosser, Comparative Negligence, 41 Cal.L.Rev. 1, 4 (1953).) ...

... Contrary to defendants' assertion, we believe that the need to deter negligent parties supports the adoption of the comparative negligence doctrine in which each party would be liable for damages in direct proportion to his degree of carelessness.

Defendants claim that the change to comparative negligence will cause administrative difficulties due to an increase in claims, a decrease in settlements, and a resulting overcrowded docket. An Arkansas study showed that, there, the adoption of comparative negligence prompted no drastic change in court burden; that the change increased potential litigation but promoted more pretrial settlements. The report concluded that concern over court congestion should not be a factor in a State's decision to adopt comparative negligence. Rosenberg, Comparative Negligence in Arkansas; A "Before and After" Survey, 13 Ark.L.Rev. 89, 108 (1959). See also Note, Comparative Negligence: A Survey of the Arkansas Experience, 22 Ark.L.Rev. 692 (1969).

In United States v. Reliable Transfer Co. (1975), 421 U.S. 397, 95 S.Ct. 1708, 44 L.Ed.2d 251, wherein the court adopted apportionment of damages over the previous rule of divided damages in admiralty, the court addressed an argument similar to that posited by defendants herein.

> [Defendants ask] us to continue the operation of an archaic rule because its facile application out of court yields quick, though inequitable, settlements, and relieves the courts of some litigation. Congestion in the courts cannot justify a legal rule that produces unjust results in litigation simply to encourage speedy out-of-court accommodations....

We believe that the defendants' fears concerning the judicial administrative problems attendant upon the adoption of comparative negligence are exaggerated.... But were defendants' fears well founded, we could nevertheless not allow the contributory negligence rule to remain the law of this State in the face of overwhelming evidence of its harsh and unjust results.

Defendants' claim that the adoption of comparative negligence would escalate insurance rates to an unbearable level. This has not been found to be the case. Effects, in fact, have been found to be minimal. Rosenberg, Comparative Negligence in Arkansas: A "Before and After" Survey, 13 Ark.L.Rev. 89, 108 (1959)....

The amicus curiae brief submitted by the Illinois Defense Counsel suggests that, under the contributory negligence rule, the jury has sufficient flexibility to do substantial justice and that this flexibility negates the necessity for the adoption of comparative

negligence. In essence, the Illinois Defense Counsel alludes to the oft-observed phenomenon that, once inside the jury room, juries often ignore the harshness of the contributory negligence rule and, instead, dole out justice by a common sense approach according to the relative culpability of the litigants. We agree that such may be the case
and, in fact, find the proclivity of juries to ignore the law to be a compelling reason for
the abolition of that law. The Supreme Court of Florida addressed this concern.

> [T]here is something basically wrong with a rule of law that is so contrary to
> the settled convictions of the lay community that laymen will almost always
> refuse to enforce it, even when solemnly told to do so by a judge whose in-
> structions they have sworn to follow.

> …

> The disrespect for law engendered by putting our citizens in a position in
> which they feel it is necessary to deliberately violate the law is not something to
> be lightly brushed aside; and it comes ill from the mouths of lawyers, who as
> officers of the courts have sworn to uphold the law, to defend the present sys-
> tem by arguing that it works because jurors can be trusted to disregard that
> very law.

(Hoffman v. Jones (Fla.1973), 280 So.2d 431, 437.)

There is something inherently wrong with a rule of law so repulsive to a jury's common
sense of justice that veniremen feel compelled to ignore the law.…

JUDICIAL v. LEGISLATIVE CHANGE

It is urged by defendants that the decision to replace the doctrine of contributory
negligence with the doctrine of comparative negligence must be made by the legislature,
not by this court. In each of the States that have judicially adopted comparative negligence, the court addressed the propriety of judicial versus legislative adoption. In each,
the court found that contributory negligence is a judicially created doctrine which can
be altered or totally replaced by the court which created it.…

We believe that the proper relationship between the legislature and the court is one
of cooperation and assistance in examining and changing the common law to conform
with the ever-changing demands of the community. There are, however, times when
there exists a mutual state of inaction in which the court awaits action by the legislature
and the legislature awaits guidance from the court. Such a stalemate is a manifest injustice to the public. When such a stalemate exists and the legislature has, for whatever
reason, failed to act to remedy a gap in the common law that results in injustice, it is the
imperative duty of the court to repair that injustice and reform the law to be responsive
to the demands of society.

…

THE "PURE" VERSUS THE "MODIFIED" FORM OF COMPARATIVE NEGLIGENCE

There remains the question of the form of comparative negligence to be adopted.
Under a "pure" form, the plaintiff's damages are simply reduced by the percentage of
fault attributable to him. Under a "modified" form, a negligent plaintiff may recover so
long as the percentage of his fault does not exceed 50% of the total.

Defendants argue that should this court decide to adopt comparative negligence, the
modified approach should be selected. They point to the basic unfairness of the "pure"
system by example: A plaintiff who is 90% negligent has suffered $100,000 in damages.
A defendant who is only 10% negligent has suffered only $10,000 in damages. Defen-

dants here point out the basic unfairness of requiring the 10% negligent defendant to pay $10,000 to a plaintiff who was 90% at fault. The United States Supreme Court answered a similar claim concerning liability under admiralty law.

> That a vessel is primarily negligent does not justify its shouldering all responsibility, nor excuse the slightly negligent vessel from bearing any liability at all.

(United States v. Reliable Transfer Co. (1975), 421 U.S. 397, 406.) ...

The liability of a defendant should not depend upon what damages he sustained but should be determined by the relationship of his fault to the ultimate damages. In a suit under a "pure" form of comparative negligence in which the defendant counterclaims for his own damages, each party must bear the burden of the percentage of damages of all parties in direct proportion to his fault. In the example above, the 90% negligent plaintiff will bear 90% of his own damages as well as 90% of defendant's. On the other hand, the 10% negligent defendant will be made to bear 10% of his own damages as well as 10% of plaintiff's. Neither party is unjustly enriched. Neither party escapes liability resulting from his negligent acts or omissions. It is difficult to see unfairness in such a distribution of liability ...

Opponents of the "pure" form of comparative negligence claim that the "modified" form is superior in that it will increase the likelihood of settlement and will keep down insurance costs. However, studies done comparing the effects of the "pure" versus the "modified" forms show the differences in insurance rates to be inconsequential. (V. Schwartz, Comparative Negligence, 346 (1974).) Fears as to the likelihood of settlement are not supported in fact or logic. It is argued that the negligent plaintiff will refuse to settle knowing that, under the "pure" system he will be able to recover "something" in court. The converse can as easily apply: the defendant may be encouraged to settle knowing that he cannot rely on the "modified" 50% cut-off point to relieve him of liability. A comparison of results under both the "pure" and "modified" forms showed that in Arkansas there was only a slight decrease in number of settlements when the State changed from "pure" to "modified." Rosenberg, Comparative Negligence in Arkansas: A "Before and After" Survey, 13 Ark.L.Rev. 89 (1959).

Wisconsin's "modified" system has been criticized because a large number of cases appealed focused on the narrow question of whether plaintiff's negligence amounted to 50% or less of the aggregate.... This, in fact, caused the Wisconsin Supreme Court to examine the question of whether the "modified" system should be replaced with the "pure" form of comparative negligence. (Vincent v. Pabst Brewing Co. (1970), 47 Wis.2d 120, 177 N.W.2d 513.) There, as in Maki v. Frelk (1968), 40 Ill.2d 193, 239 N.E. 445, the merits of the case were not addressed, for the majority of the court ruled that the determination should be left to the legislature, which had originally adopted the "modified" form by statute. One dissenting and three concurring justices, however, expressed their intent to judicially adopt the "pure" form if the legislature failed to do so....

The "pure" form of comparative negligence is the only system which truly apportions damages according to the relative fault of the parties and, thus, achieves total justice. We agree with the Li court that "the '50 percent' system simply shifts the lottery aspect of the contributory negligence rule to a different ground." (Li v. Yellow Cab Co. (1975), 13 Cal.3d 804, 827 ...) There is no better justification for allowing a defendant who is 49% at fault to completely escape liability than there is to allow a defendant who is 99% at fault under the old rule to escape liability.

Mindful of the facts stated and that the vast majority of legal scholars who have studied the area recommend the "pure" approach, we are persuaded that the "pure" form of comparative negligence is preferable, and we therefore adopt it as the law of Illinois....

...

[The dissenting opinion of Justice Underwood is omitted.]

RYAN, JUSTICE, dissenting:

... I am bothered by the idea that no more than four individuals, four members of this court (five members have joined in the majority in this case), can radically change the fabric of the law that will hereafter govern the conduct of the 11 million residents of this State. I am bothered by the fact that this court has snatched the problem from the hands of the 236 elected representatives of those 11 million people and has decreed that it, not the elected representatives, shall determine whether this State will follow comparative negligence and whether it will be the "pure" or "modified" form....

Contributory negligence is, of course, based upon the fault concept of tort law. Comparative negligence, while ostensibly involving the fault concept, is, in reality, a product of that school of tort law which has held that it was unjust for one who is injured not to be compensated for his loss. This is particularly true of "pure," as compared with "modified," comparative negligence. Thus the focus of pure comparative negligence is on compensation and the distribution of the loss and retains only a semblance of the fault basis as a means of accomplishing its main purpose. In other words, in my opinion, pure comparative negligence is another fiction in the law which those who refuse to accept the no-fault theory of recovery have promoted to accomplish essentially no-fault recovery.

The history of the popularity of comparative negligence indicates that between 1908 and 1941 various statutory modifications of contributory negligence were passed by Congress and by a few State legislatures. Also during that period a few States enacted general comparative negligence statutes. From 1941 to 1970 there was little activity by either the courts or legislative bodies promoting comparative negligence. During this period the writers on the subject, while supporting the principles of comparative negligence, acknowledged the problems attendant to its implementation. (See W. Prosser, Comparative Negligence, 51 Mich.L.Rev. 465 (1953).) It was not until the early 1970's that interest was again evidenced in comparative negligence, when 13 States adopted the doctrine by legislation between 1971 and 1973. Coincidentally, at about this same time, academicians had mounted an attack against the negligence theory of recovery and had suggested alternatives to the common law fault standard of tort liability. (See O'Connell, Expanding No Fault Beyond Auto Insurance: Some Proposals, 59 Va.L.Rev. 749 (1973).) It has been suggested that the rush to embrace comparative negligence in the early 1970's may be seen as an effort to preserve the negligence theory against the prospective competition of no-fault theories. See G. P. White, Tort Law in America, 164–68 (1980).

I have heretofore ... deplored the use of legal fictions to enable injured persons to recover under a negligence theory when in fact the fiction employed permits recovery on a no-fault basis....

Statutory remedies permitting recovery without fault traditionally have required a quid pro quo for the right to recover free from defenses available to a defendant under the common law. The quid pro quo in many statutes, such as the Worker's Compensation Act (Ill.Rev.Stat.1979, ch. 48, par. 138.1 et seq.), is a limitation on the amount that may be recovered.... Under pure comparative negligence, as adopted by the majority, the injured plaintiff will have the best of both worlds. He will be able to recover for his injuries without fault and at the same time not be limited in the amount he may recover.

To say that a jury will discount a plaintiff's recovery by his degree of negligence is not realistic. Just as sympathetic juries operating under limitations of contributory negligence apply a form of comparative negligence, juries operating under pure comparative negligence will, in effect, compensate a plaintiff for his injuries, regardless of the degree of his fault.

Again I urge the legislature ... to review the entire negligence tort field and either out and out adopt a no-fault theory or retain the fault concept and adopt a modified no-fault theory for those who are injured as a result of their own negligence or who cannot recover because of some defense available under the common law. To me, there is something basically false about devising fictions to permit recovery under a negligence theory when, in fact, recovery is had under the principle of no fault. I am sure that these fictions will in the future be viewed with the same degree of derision with which we now view the fictions developed in the Middle Ages to circumvent the strictures of the law, both civil and criminal, of that time....

Gary Schwartz, *Contributory and Comparative Negligence: A Reappraisal*
87 Yale L. J. 697, 721–26 (1978)*

... Can an adequate rationale for a contributory negligence rule be found somewhere outside economics? A few commentators believe that efficiency should be the sole determinant of liability rules. Most disagree with this view and insist that appeals to other norms be given their due. Even among most economics-oriented scholars, there is an understanding that "justice" or "fairness" is such a norm. For me, at least, the language of justice is well suited to larger questions of societal organization, while the language of fairness may relate to the kinds of issues that typically arise in ordinary private litigation; accordingly, it is fairness language that will primarily be employed below.

In fairness terms, contributory negligence starts out with a clear intuitive appeal. If the defendant is being held liable because of his "faulty," "unreasonable," or "wrongful" behavior, the fact that the plaintiff himself has likewise been guilty of "faulty" conduct seems clearly something that the law should take into account, either by reducing the plaintiff's damages[112] or by entirely denying the plaintiff's right to sue on the theory that a faulty plaintiff should not be heard to complain about a defendant's fault. For the law to fail totally to take the plaintiff's conduct into account would seem unfair because it would involve an uneven application of the fault standard.

---

* Reprinted by permission of The Yale Law Journal Company and William S. Hein Company from *The Yale Law Journal*, Vol. 87, pages 697–727.

112. "Liability in proportion to fault" is the slogan of sorts for comparative negligence. See *Li v. Yellow Cab Co.*, 13 Cal. 3d 804, 810, 532 P.2d 1226, 119 Cal. Rptr. 858, 862 (1975).

What this obvious argument in defense of a contributory negligence rule rests on is the moral equivalency of the plaintiff's and defendant's "fault." But the appearance of this equivalency is quite misleading. The objectively egotistical or antisocial character of the defendant's negligence has been described above. With contributory negligence, however, the conduct in question is conduct that runs an unjustified risk to the actor himself, rather than to others. Given this difference, the conduct that establishes contributory negligence cannot be regarded as egoistical or antisocial; instead it is behavior that, from the actor's or others' perspective, is merely foolish or stupid. This assessment undermines the supposed moral parity between the "fault" of negligence and the "fault" of contributory negligence.[117] Foolish behavior is of course disadvantageous to the actor, but it is difficult to identify any clear moral principle that it contravenes;[118] the language of "wrongfulness" seems largely out of place in the contributory negligence context. To state the matter in the formal legal parlance of Lord Denning, "negligence depends on a breach of duty, whereas contributory negligence does not."

Thus the standard fairness argument adduced in support of a contributory negligence rule, depending as it does on the supposed equivalence of the plaintiff's and defendant's fault, does not deserve to be accepted. There are, however, two other fairness considerations that may support some contributory negligence rule.

The first of these builds on the fact that contributory negligence though defined in terms of an unreasonable risk to self, involves conduct that in an individual case may also run an unreasonable risk to others. If so, such conduct involves elements of negligence as well as contributory negligence. Although such an overlap between negligence and contributory negligence is technically fortuitous, in the real world it can occur, and it does occur regularly in one major class of accidents: those involving motor vehicles. The motorist who drives at night without lights creates an unreasonable risk to himself and to others at the same time. When the plaintiff is suing a negligent defendant and when the plaintiff's conduct was itself negligent in the sense of running an unreasonable risk to others, it could be argued that a fair application of the fault principle requires the recognition of an affirmative defense. The defense in question would be one that asserts the plaintiff's negligence, rather than his contributory negligence, as a limit on the plaintiff's own negligence claim.

Although the somewhat novel idea of a negligence defense[122] is not without some initial appeal, when examined more carefully the idea is not persuasive. Assume a person

---

117. Existing law, in various limited ways, is responsive to the view of contributory negligence put forward here. The law is rather gentle, for example, in dealing with plaintiffs who have been merely "momentarily inadvertent" or "momentarily inattentive" as they approach a known or visible hazard.... In comparative negligence jurisdictions, plaintiffs tend to fare quite well in the reduction of damages when their unreasonable conduct is merely foolish in the sense described.... In particular, pedestrians typically suffer only a small reduction in damages in their suits against negligent motorists.... One can even cast an eye at workers' compensation: the carelessness of the worker, which the law ignores, is generally misbehavior threatening the worker alone. It is true that in a number of jurisdictions, the worker's recovery is either reduced or eliminated if he has willfully failed to observe a safety rule.... In such cases, however, the worker's conduct is morally improper in the special sense that it implicates him in the disobedience of authority.

118. Some religions find acts of intentional self-destruction morally objectionable on grounds that they violate God's rights in the individual — a belief not applied to accidental harms. One can also imagine a moral complaint about foolish acts of contributory negligence as impugning the high moral value that all persons should place upon human welfare, even their own. In my view, such a moral objection is too uncertain and slender to serve as the predicate for an official liability rule.

122. *Butterfield v. Forrester*, 103 Eng. Rep. 926 (K.B. 1809), the origin of the contributory negligence defense, was itself a highway case, in which the plaintiff, riding his horse "violently," clearly

whose conduct involves both negligence and contributory negligence. The most direct and appropriate way to respond to the negligence in his conduct is to render him liable in tort for any injury to another that his negligence produces. And this, of course, is a liability that tort law does firmly impose. Given this unquestioned negligence liability, it would entail an inappropriate form of double-counting for the law to go farther by relying on the negligent aspect of the person's conduct as a reason for disparaging his recovery for an injury that he has suffered as a result of some other person's negligence. Putting the matter in causal terms, even if the victim's conduct has contained a negligent aspect, it is not this aspect of his conduct that has caused his own injury.

The second fairness consideration in favor of a contributory negligence defense begins with a distinction between our evaluation of the plaintiff's original conduct and our evaluation of the issues in his eventual lawsuit. With respect to a tort defendant, it is now widely agreed that even if the defendant's conduct has not been morally improper, there may be sufficient reasons of fairness to hold him liable for the harm that his conduct has occasioned. This basic, correct distinction between the moral aspects of original conduct and the fairness aspects of the consequent lawsuit applies on the plaintiff's side as well. The plaintiff's original act of contributory negligence may not have been morally improper, since it created risk only to the plaintiff himself. When that risk eventuates in an injury to the plaintiff, however, and when the plaintiff then seeks to collect in tort for that injury against a negligent defendant, at the time of this lawsuit the harm involved in the plaintiff's original conduct "reaches" the defendant, another person. The defendant, concededly, has engaged in negligent conduct that has contributed to the plaintiff's accident. Nevertheless, that accident would never have occurred had the plaintiff himself not behaved in a foolish way. In these circumstances, it would be basically unfair[125] for the law to ignore entirely the plaintiff's conduct by imposing full liability on the negligent defendant.[126]

If this idea of fairness thus calls on tort law to take some account of the plaintiff's contributory negligence in ascertaining the liability of a negligent defendant, the question arises of what appropriate form the legal doctrine should assume. As presented, the fairness idea is entirely satisfied by a liability-dividing rule like comparative negligence. Should the idea be carried further, however, so as to disqualify the foolish plaintiff from receiving any recovery from a negligent defendant? The contributory negligence idea does not seem to be one of those that presses itself to its logical extremes; when stated as above, in a moderate form, the idea is both intelligible and stable. There is nothing in its logic that would be impaired or compromised were it deployed in support of a liability-reducing rule rather than a liability-denying rule. Moreover, as we have seen, the rule of

---

created a risk to others as well as to himself. But in explaining the contributory negligence defense, the court dealt exclusively with the risk to self.

125. *Cf.* E. Cahn, The Sense of Injustice (1949) (arguing that it is easier to recognize instances of "injustice" than to prescribe general, affirmative rules of "justice").

126. This finding of unfairness arises from a commonsense judgement, rather than being deduced from any comprehensive fairness principle. When such principles are ventured, they are typically expressed in general terms that are quite without relevance to particular tort issues like contributory negligence. *See, e.g.*, J. Rawls, A Theory of Justice 114–17 (1971) ("duty not to harm or injure others" is fundamental to principle of justice). Most people rely on commonsense moral judgments most of the time; even the notion that economic efficiency is in the public interest can be justified only in a commonsense way. *See also*, Thayer, *Public Wrong and Private Action*, 27 Harv. L. Rev. 317, 318 (1914) (insisting that all doctrines within negligence system "respond to the test of common sense"). Since, however, commonsense judgments do not carry the power of deductive proof, the article's analysis can be understood as proposing and recommending to its readers a certain justification for a contributory negligence defense....

negligence liability itself has a satisfactory moral basis, one that is based on our disapproval of antisocial or egoistical conduct. To negate altogether a plaintiff's lawsuit against a negligent defendant would be to allow the fairness idea associated with the contributory negligence defense to extinguish the moral idea that predicates negligence liability.

The law frequently encounters tension between alternative principles. Occasionally, the law concludes that one of the principles simply is much more important than the other, or that since the tension between the principles entails an outright conflict, one of them should be vindicated even at the other's total expense. When possible, however, the law's preferred course is to seek an accommodating rule or result that is able to reduce, or if possible to resolve, the original tension. In the contributory negligence context, a liability-dividing rule like comparative negligence is one obvious form of accommodation or reconciliation. The fairness idea behind contributory negligence is not clearly superior to the moral idea supporting negligence liability, and, as indicated, those ideas can quite properly be stated in terms that avoid any element of necessary conflict. That American juries, instructed on the traditional rule, have so clearly striven in a liability-dividing direction[130] and that virtually every other common law and civil law jurisdiction has adopted some form of comparative negligence are elements that can be taken at least somewhat into account in reassuring ourselves of the fairness of a liability-dividing rule.

There is, however, another factor. The earlier discussion of tort law's safety objective concluded that, while it was not clear that any contributory negligence rule is an effective technique for accident prevention, there are important psychological considerations indicating that the traditional contributory negligence rule is peculiarly likely to be counterproductive. By now, the appropriateness of some contributory negligence rule has been affirmed on fairness grounds, and considerations of fairness have been seen to suggest a preference for a liability-dividing rule over the traditional rule. At this stage, the earlier accident-prevention conclusion can be introduced for purposes of reinforcing this suggested preference. Lurking in the background is the vexing question of whether the accident-prevention goal can ever justify a legal rule that would otherwise be regarded as unfair. That question can remain quite in the background, since accident-prevention considerations are here being employed to support a liability-dividing result that is independently supported by fairness values.

. . .

Robert D. Cooter & Thomas S. Ulen, *An Economic Case for Comparative Negligence*
61 N.Y.U. L. Rev. 1067, 1090–92 (1986)*

A decisionmaker's incentive to exceed the legal standard of care will vary ... depending on which negligence rule is in effect. To explain these differences in terms of incentives, it is useful to introduce the concept of discounting. The term discounting is used here to express the relationship between the total accident costs and the costs that a decisionmaker bears. To illustrate, consider the case where the defendant, A, is forty per-

---

130. See Keeton, *Creative Continuity in the Law of Torts*, 75 Harv. L. Rev. 463, 506 (1962).

cent negligent and the victim, B, is sixty percent negligent. Under the rule of negligence with a defense of contributory negligence A will not be liable even though he was at fault. Thus, his liability will be discounted under the rule by one hundred percent. By contrast, under comparative negligence, the defendant's liability will be discounted by the victim's relative fault; in this example, the court will discount A's damages by sixty percent. Finally, under the rule of simple negligence, a victim's conduct will not be considered at all; the court will discount A's liability by zero percent.

This illustration shows that an injurer's potential liability is discounted the most under the rule of negligence with a defense of contributory negligence, somewhat less under comparative negligence, and least under the simple negligence rule. His incentives for taking precaution are inversely related to the discount. Therefore, the greater the discount—for example under the contributory negligence rule—the weaker the potential injurer's incentive to take precaution.

A decisionmaker's incentive also varies with the different forms of the comparative negligence rule. To illustrate, consider our example in which the injurer, A, is forty percent responsible for an accident and the victim, B, is sixty percent at fault. The pure form of comparative negligence allows the damages owed by A to be reduced by sixty percent. In contrast the modified form of comparative negligence allows one hundred percent discounting under these circumstances. Consequently, the expected discount of the injurer's liability is greater under the modified form of comparative negligence than under the pure form. Therefore, the injurer's incentives for precaution are greater under the pure form than under the modified form.

In summary, it is possible to rank the forms of negligence rules according to the strength of the incentives they create for injurer's precaution:

injurer's incentives for precaution

strong   weak

simple negligence	pure comparative negligence	modified comparative negligence	slight/gross comparative negligence	contributory negligence

Turning to the victim, his incentive to take precaution is strongest when the injurer's incentive to take precaution is smallest, because the victim bears the residual cost of any uncompensated harm. Conversely, the victim's incentive is weakest where the defendant's incentive is greatest. Therefore, his incentive ranking is the mirror image of the injurer's:

victim's incentives for precaution

strong   weak

contributory negligence	slight/gross comparative negligence	modified comparative negligence	pure comparative negligence	simple negligence

These variations in the incentive effects determine the conditions under which a particular rule is preferable over its alternatives. Evidentiary uncertainty distorts incentives for precaution and prompts rational decisionmakers to exceed the legal standard of care. Although evidentiary uncertainty distorts incentives for precaution under any form of the negligence rule, the amount of distortion varies under the different forms. The rule of comparative negligence gives moderate incentives for precaution to both injurers and victims, while its alternatives give strong incentives to one party and weak incentives to the other. For this reason, comparative negligence minimizes the total amount of excessive precaution when the parties are "symmetrically situated"—i.e., when efficiency requires both parties to take similar amounts of precaution. Therefore, comparative negligence is the preferable rule in such situations.

Conversely, when the parties are asymmetrically situated, so that it is better to give strong incentives to one party and weak incentives to the other, comparative negligence is inferior to other forms of the negligence rule. For example, if injurers are better situated to take precaution than victims, the simple negligence rule provides better incentives than the rule of comparative negligence or the rule of contributory negligence. But if victims are better situated to take precaution than injurers, the contributory negligence rule provides better incentives than the other two forms of the negligence rule.

NOTES

(1) Which of the following kinds of comparative negligence arrangements would you prefer?

(a) A law under which the plaintiff's damages are diminished in proportion to his negligence, no matter how much it is.

(b) A law that allows the plaintiff proportional recovery so long as his negligence is not greater than the defendant's.

(c) A rule that allows proportional recovery only if the plaintiff's negligence is not as great as the defendant's.

(d) A system under which contributory negligence is not a complete bar only when it is "slight" and the defendant's negligence is "gross by comparison," with contributory negligence to be considered in mitigation of damages.

Would you expect any of these arrangements to have significantly different economic effects?

Are economic incentives the key to the comparative negligence question, or do you agree with Schwartz that the principal question is one of fairness?

(2) *Alvis v. Ribar*, the Illinois decision that begins this section, involved two motoring accident cases. Would you think the automotive context, with its need for quick decision and corresponding penalties in injury for inadvertent error, is an especially good place for the adoption of comparative fault, as compared with other areas of risky activity? How does it compare with slip and fall cases? Products liability cases involving injuries sustained on industrial or farm machinery?

(3) The Arkansas study mentioned by Justice Moran in *Alvis* focused on the operation of a comparative negligence statute which diminished the amount of the plaintiff's recovery in accordance with the degree of culpability, with no 50 percent or 49 percent cut-off. The findings were that the rule "did not appreciably affect the length of trials; increased potential litigation; promoted before-trial settlements; and made damages harder to determine." Although judges said generally that the rule was helpful to their work, "when pinned down to specifics their consensus disappeared." Although plaintiffs "won a higher proportion of the verdicts," they did not win larger ones. On the other hand again, "injury claims were valued higher for compromise purposes." The author comments that "these findings refute the commonly-expressed view that a shift to comparative negligence does not alter the value of personal injury cases because (so it is alleged) juries apply a rough comparative negligence rule anyway, and lawyers expect them to do so." Rosenberg, *Comparative Negligence in Arkansas: A "Before and After" Survey*, 13 Ark. L. Rev. 89, 108 (1959).

KNIGHT v. JEWETT

Supreme Court of California, In Bank.
834 P.2d 696, 3 Cal. 4th 296, 11 Cal. Rptr. 2d 2 (1992)

GEORGE, Justice.

In this case ... we face the question of the proper application of the "assumption of risk" doctrine in light of this court's adoption of comparative fault principles in Li v. Yellow Cab Co. (1975) 13 Cal.3d 804, 119 Cal. Rptr. 858, 532 P.2d 1226....

...

On January 25, 1987, the day of the 1987 Super Bowl football game, plaintiff Kendra Knight and defendant Michael Jewett, together with a number of other social acquaintances, attended a Super Bowl party at the home of a mutual friend. During half time of the Super Bowl, several guests decided to play an informal game of touch football on an adjoining dirt lot, using a "peewee" football. Each team had four or five players and included both women and men; plaintiff and defendant were on opposing teams. No rules were explicitly discussed before the game.

Five to ten minutes into the game, defendant ran into plaintiff during a play. According to plaintiff, at that point she told defendant "not to play so rough or I was going to have to stop playing." Her declaration stated that "[defendant] seemed to acknowledge my statement and left me with the impression that he would play less rough prospectively." In his deposition, defendant recalled that plaintiff had asked him to "be careful," but did not remember plaintiff saying that she would stop playing.

On the very next play, plaintiff sustained the injuries that gave rise to the present lawsuit. As defendant recalled the incident, his team was on defense on that play, and he jumped up in an attempt to intercept a pass. He touched the ball but did not catch it, and in coming down he collided with plaintiff, knocking her over. When he landed, he stepped backward onto plaintiff's right hand, injuring her hand and little finger.

Both plaintiff and Andrea Starr, another participant in the game who was on the same team as plaintiff, recalled the incident differently from defendant. According to their declarations, at the time plaintiff was injured, Starr already had caught the pass. Defendant was running toward Starr, when he ran into plaintiff from behind, knocked her down, and stepped on her hand. Starr also stated that, after knocking plaintiff down, defendant continued running until he tagged Starr, "which tag was hard enough to cause me to lose my balance, resulting in a twisting or spraining of my ankle."

The game ended with plaintiff's injury, and plaintiff sought treatment shortly thereafter. After three operations failed to restore the movement in her little finger or to relieve the ongoing pain of the injury, plaintiff's finger was amputated....

...

... [T]he Li decision ... clearly contemplated that the assumption of risk doctrine was to be partially merged or subsumed into the comparative negligence scheme.... Subsequent Court of Appeal decisions have disagreed, however, in interpreting Li, as to what category of assumption of risk cases would be merged into the comparative negligence scheme.

...

[Precedents] ... have misinterpreted Li by suggesting that our decision contemplated less favorable legal treatment for a plaintiff who reasonably encounters a known risk than for a plaintiff who unreasonably encounters such a risk. Although the relevant passage in Li indicates that the assumption of risk doctrine would be merged into the comparative fault scheme in instances in which a plaintiff "'unreasonably undertakes to encounter a specific known risk imposed by a defendant's negligence'" (13 Cal.3d at p. 824, 119 Cal.Rptr. 858, 532 P.2d 1226), nothing in this passage suggests that the assumption of risk doctrine should survive as a total bar to the plaintiff's recovery whenever a plaintiff acts reasonably in encountering such a risk. Instead, this portion of our opinion expressly contrasts the category of assumption of risk cases which "'involve contributory negligence'" (and which therefore should be merged into the comparative fault scheme) with those assumption of risk cases which involve "'a reduction of defendant's duty of care.'" (Id. at p. 825, 119 Cal.Rptr. 858, 532 P.2d 1226.)

Indeed, particularly when the relevant passage in Li, supra, 13 Cal.3d at pp. 824–825, 119 Cal.Rptr. 858, 532 P.2d 1226, is read as a whole and in conjunction with the authorities it cites, we believe it becomes clear that the distinction in assumption of risk cases to which the Li court referred in this passage was not a distinction between instances in which a plaintiff unreasonably encounters a known risk imposed by a defendant's negligence and instances in which a plaintiff reasonably encounters such a risk. Rather, the distinction to which the Li court referred was between (1) those instances in which the assumption of risk doctrine embodies a legal conclusion that there is "no duty" on the part of the defendant to protect the plaintiff from a particular risk—the category of assumption of risk that the legal commentators generally refer to as "primary assumption of risk"—and (2) those instances in which the defendant does owe a duty of care to the plaintiff but the plaintiff knowingly encounters a risk of injury caused by the defendant's breach of that duty—what most commentators have termed "secondary assumption of risk." Properly interpreted, the relevant passage in Li provides that the category of assumption of risk cases that is not merged into the comparative negligence system and in which the plaintiff's recovery continues to be completely barred involves those cases in which the defendant's conduct did not breach a legal duty of care to the plaintiff, i.e., "primary assumption of risk" cases, whereas cases involving "secondary assumption of risk" properly are merged into the comprehensive comparative fault system adopted in Li.

...

... [W]e believe that under California's comparative fault doctrine, a jury in a "secondary assumption of risk" case would be entitled to take into consideration a plaintiff's voluntary action in choosing to engage in an unusually risky sport, whether or not the plaintiff's decision to encounter the risk should be characterized as unreasonable, in determining whether the plaintiff properly should bear some share of responsibility for the injuries he or she suffered.... Thus, in a case in which an injury has been caused by both a defendant's breach of a legal duty to the plaintiff and the plaintiff's voluntary decision to engage in an unusually risky sport, application of comparative fault principles will not operate to relieve either individual of responsibility for his or her actions, but rather will ensure that neither party will escape such responsibility.

It may be helpful at this point to summarize our general conclusions as to the current state of the doctrine of assumption of risk in light of the adoption of comparative fault principles in Li, supra, 13 Cal.3d 804, 119 Cal.Rptr. 858, 532 P.2d 1226, general conclusions that reflect the view of a majority of the justices of the court (i.e., the three justices who have signed this opinion and Justice Mosk (see conc. and dis. opn. by Mosk, J., ante, p. 18 of 11 Cal.Rptr.2d, p. 712 of 834 P.2d)). In cases involving "primary assumption of risk"—where, by virtue of the nature of the activity and the parties' relationship to the activity, the defendant owes no legal duty to protect the plaintiff from the particular risk of harm that caused the injury—the doctrine continues to operate as a complete bar to the plaintiff's recovery. In cases involving "secondary assumption of risk"—where the defendant does owe a duty of care to the plaintiff, but the plaintiff proceeds to encounter a known risk imposed by the defendant's breach of duty—the doctrine is merged into the comparative fault scheme, and the trier of fact, in apportioning the loss resulting from the injury, may consider the relative responsibility of the parties.

Accordingly, in determining the propriety of the trial court's grant of summary judgment in favor of the defendant in this case, our inquiry does not turn on the reasonableness or unreasonableness of plaintiff's conduct in choosing to subject herself to the risks of touch football or in continuing to participate in the game after she became aware of defendant's allegedly rough play. Nor do we focus upon whether there is a factual dispute with regard to whether plaintiff subjectively knew of, and voluntarily chose to encounter, the risk of defendant's conduct, or impliedly consented to relieve or excuse defendant from any duty of care to her. Instead, our resolution of this issue turns on whether, in light of the nature of the sporting activity in which defendant and plaintiff were engaged, defendant's conduct breached a legal duty of care to plaintiff. We now turn to that question.

. . .

In the present case, defendant was a participant in the touch football game in which plaintiff was engaged at the time of her injury, and thus the question before us involves the circumstances under which a participant in such a sport may be held liable for an injury sustained by another participant.

The overwhelming majority of the cases, both within and outside California, that have addressed the issue of coparticipant liability in such a sport, have concluded that it is improper to hold a sports participant liable to a coparticipant for ordinary careless conduct committed during the sport—for example, for an injury resulting from a carelessly thrown ball or bat during a baseball game—and that liability properly may be imposed on a participant only when he or she intentionally injures another player or engages in reckless conduct that is totally outside the range of the ordinary activity involved in the sport. (See, e.g., Gauvin v. Clark (1989) 404 Mass. 450, 537 N.E.2d 94, 96–97 and cases cited.)

In reaching the conclusion that a coparticipant's duty of care should be limited in this fashion, the cases have explained that, in the heat of an active sporting event like baseball or football, a participant's normal energetic conduct often includes accidentally careless behavior. The courts have concluded that vigorous participation in such sporting events likely would be chilled if legal liability were to be imposed on a participant on the basis of his or her ordinary careless conduct. The cases have recognized that, in such a sport, even when a participant's conduct violates a rule of the game and may subject the violator to internal sanctions prescribed by the sport itself, imposition of legal liability for such conduct might well alter fundamentally the nature of the sport by deterring participants from vigorously engaging in activity that falls close to, but on the permissible side of, a prescribed rule.

. . .

As applied to the present case, the foregoing legal principle clearly supports the trial court's entry of summary judgment in favor of defendant. The declarations filed in support of and in opposition to the summary judgment motion establish that defendant was, at most, careless or negligent in knocking over plaintiff, stepping on her hand, and injuring her finger. Although plaintiff maintains that defendant's rough play as described in her declaration and the declaration of Andrea Starr properly can be characterized as "reckless," the conduct alleged in those declarations is not even closely comparable to the kind of conduct—conduct so reckless as to be totally outside the range of the ordinary activity involved in the sport—that is a prerequisite to the imposition of legal liability upon a participant in such a sport.

Therefore, we conclude that defendant's conduct in the course of the touch football game did not breach any legal duty of care owed to plaintiff. Accordingly, this case falls within the primary assumption of risk doctrine, and thus the trial court properly granted summary judgment in favor of defendant. Because plaintiff's action is barred under the primary assumption of risk doctrine, comparative fault principles do not come into play.

The judgment of the Court of Appeal, upholding the summary judgment entered by the trial court, is affirmed.

. . .

[Several separate opinions are omitted.]

NOTES

(1) Is the structure of law set out in *Knight* a logical one? What are the legal premises of the logical structure with respect to duty and the level of care?

(2) Does *Knight* allocate the risk of injury in casual athletic activity justly? Does it comport with common sense notions of morality? Will it be likely to promote desirable incentives?

(3) Should comparative fault apply to a case in which a plaintiff rides with a driver he knows to be intoxicated, and there is a collision?

Should it apply in a case in which a worker's hand is mangled on an industrial machine that does not have a guard, where there is evidence that the worker was well aware that if she put her hand among sharp machine teeth, she would be injured?

———————

SPECIAL NOTE ON STATUTES OF LIMITATIONS

Every jurisdiction has statutes of limitations—legislation that sets limits on the period of time in which people may bring lawsuits. These limits vary with the subject, even varying within general areas of the law like tort law. For example, a general tort statute of limitations might be two years, whereas the statute of limitations for defamation actions might be only one year. Typically, these statutes would run from the time of "injury." Ordinarily, that will be a straightforward inquiry. If someone slips on a banana peel and breaks a limb, there will be no ambiguity about either the time of injury or her knowledge that she was hurt.

However, in certain kinds of cases, a plaintiff may not reasonably have discovered the injury at the time that it occurred. A frequently litigated case of this type occurs when the harm at issue is an illness attributable to exposure to some kind of toxic substance— fibers or chemicals—or an illness or injury caused by a drug or medical device. Some courts, and a few legislatures, have responded to this problem by developing a "discovery rule," the effect of which is to extend the running of the statute of limitations to a time when the plaintiff reasonably could have been expected to learn about an injury.

Implicit in the idea of reasonable discovery is the notion that the plaintiff must have exercised "due diligence" in discovering the injury. A case involving several so-called "DES daughters"—women claiming illness caused by a hormone that their mothers took while pregnant—drew a comprehensive examination of the due diligence issue under a New York statute instituting a discovery rule for toxic products.[1]

Judge Weinstein's far-ranging opinion developed the principle that "if a person has a medical problem, unless she has good reason to conclude that, contrary to the usual course of events, a human-made product led to the difficulty, she has not 'discovered' that it was 'caused.'[2] Judge Weinstein observed that "[a] plaintiff who is aware that she has a medical problem, but who does not know that it resulted from a human cause, is, as a practical matter, in no better position to file suit than a plaintiff who does not know that she has a medical problem."[3] He suggested that "[a] plaintiff may only discover aspects of her claim in pieces: (1) the fact that she has a medical problem; (2) the fact that the problem has a human cause; (3) the nature of the injurious agent (e.g., drug, gas, etc.); (4) the specific identity of the injurious agent (e.g., DES, asbestos); and (5) the fact that someone or some entity was liable, in some way, in connection with marketing, producing or distributing the causative agent."[4]

Within this framework, Judge Weinstein declared that ordinarily laypersons do "not think of 'diseases' or their manifestations as 'injuries' but rather as acts of nature." He declared that "[w]hile paranoia is widespread, the law does not build upon it to demand that ill people assume that every medical problem that they suffer resulted from the intervention of a malefactor." Instead, he opined that "[t]he public may reasonably assume the best rather than the worst about the pharmaceutical industry." In a situation "[w]here a plaintiff's belief that her medical problems are based on some organic process is reasonable," Judge Weinstein said, "it would subvert the statute's purpose to automatically cut off her claims on the ground that the manifestations of a particular toxicological hazard might be discoverable."[5]

Judge Weinstein also drew on critical and feminist perspectives for the premise that "[t]he law must take into account the reasonable intellectual and emotional states of people and plaintiffs' particular positions." He referred, in this respect, both to matters of sophistication and gender. For example, he said that "[a] plaintiff who is illiterate, non-English speaking, legally and medically unsophisticated, living in an isolated location or lacking in intelligence cannot be treated as if she were a sophisticated, well-read, English-speaking medical professional living in Manhattan and married to a malpractice lawyer." Moreover, he declared that "[i]n a society in which many women's self-worth remains tied to their ability to produce healthy children, every woman who has been told that she will forever be childless cannot be expected as a matter of law to begin immediately a wide ranging, dispassionate study and analysis of the basis for her condition."[6]

Judge Weinstein declared that "[i]n a sometimes male-dominated legal and scientific world, we impose a requirement of absolute rationality, as viewed in hindsight, only at great risk to a just society." In a remarkable statement of particularization, he said that "[t]he legal principle remains the same and applies to all people, but in different situations it is reasonable for reasonable people to know and react differently to that principle."[7]

---

1. *Braune v. Abbott Labs.*, 895 F. Supp. 530 (E.D.N.Y. 1995).
2. *Id.* at 545.
3. *Id.* at 551.
4. *Id.* at 545.
5. *Id.* at 551–52.
6. *Id.* at 555.
7. *Id.*

Chapter 6

SUBJECTIVE STANDARDS FOR INJURED PERSONS AND INJURERS

§ 6.01 Child Trespassers

EDWARDS v. CONSOLIDATED RAIL CORP.

United States District Court, District of Columbia
567 F. Supp. 1087 (1983), aff'd without opinion,
733 F.2d 966, cert. denied, 469 U.S. 883 (1984)

OBERDORFER, DISTRICT JUDGE....

FACTS

On the afternoon of July 7, 1979, the 11-year-old minor plaintiff and three friends of the same general age rode on their bicycles to the railroad tracks which lay between RFK Stadium and the Anacostia River, east of the Sousa Bridge, in the District of Columbia. They rode to the stadium, through the stadium parking lot, and onto a path or road.... They passed a sign at the entrance to that road that bore the words "No Unauthorized Vehicles." One of the plaintiff's friends saw the sign; plaintiff did not.... They followed the road for about ... one-half mile past the D.C. Jail, behind the D.C. General Hospital, behind a fenced cemetery and down toward defendant's railroad tracks. They then came to a grassy area. Beyond this grassy area lay the railroad tracks; on the far side of the tracks was another grassy area and then the Anacostia River.

A train was stopped on the tracks, extending beneath the bridge and awaiting clearance for passage through the Virginia Avenue tunnel. Plaintiff and two of his friends rode their bicycles off the road and over the grass next to the tracks and dismounted.[1] Accepting plaintiff's testimony as true, this train had been stopped there when the boys arrived; the train was stopped there for about twenty minutes prior to the accident.[2] All

---

1. Plaintiff's friend Tyrone Brown refused to ride closer to the train, because "something told me to stay up there [on the road]" and "maybe the police would see us getting on the train ... and try to lock them up." Brown Deposition at 14–15. Brown proceeded to ride his bicycle under the bridge and did not see the injury to plaintiff occur. *Id.* at 28–29.

2. Plaintiffs have never proffered evidence as to how long, specifically, the train was stopped. Defendant's records indicate that the train was stopped for seven minutes before the accident; a fisherman witness, Charles Riddick, who was deposed by defendant, said that the train was stopped "for 20 minutes or better" and that was the longest period of time he had seen a train stop there in 10 years....

three boys climbed up ladders on the sides of the railroad cars. Wayne Childress and Andre Stukes climbed up the ladders but not onto the top of the railroad cars; Childress put his head above the roof level of a car, and Stukes climbed up the ladder only "halfway." ... Stukes stopped "[b]ecause I was scared, I was afraid it was too high up there. I was afraid I was going to fall."

. . .

Plaintiff was still climbing a car when the other two boys had finished climbing. Unlike the other two boys, plaintiff climbed all the way onto the top of a car, and stood up. He walked around a little, became "a little dizzy," and started to leave.... Plaintiff remembers that Stukes said to him "Come on. Let's go." ... Both Childress and Stukes told plaintiff not to climb onto the last car; Stukes stated that he was afraid of falling and said to plaintiff "Get down, man, before you fall." ... All three boys stated in deposition that they neither thought about nor realized the danger in the wires.

As plaintiff decided to leave the top of the railroad car, he either grabbed or came quite close to the catenary wires, which were near his head or shoulder level.[8] In any case, "[s]omething went 'Pow,' there was a red flash and ... [plaintiff] was laying across the train, injured." ... He then apparently rolled or fell from the top of the railroad car to the ground next to the tracks, landing on top of one of the bicycles.... He was severely burned and injured, and has received extensive medical treatment for his injuries. The boys stated that only a few minutes elapsed from when they began to climb the cars until plaintiff was injured.[9]

This was the sixth time that plaintiff had bicycled through this area. His friends had also visited there before on different occasions. They had seen other boys on bicycles there, as well as fishermen along the river and cars on the road from the stadium. Clarence Riddick, who had fished at the site intermittently for over a decade, had also seen children and adults in the area on numerous occasions.... The area itself, however, appears to be isolated as far as residential housing located directly at the site is concerned. For purposes of summary judgment, this record indicates that the adults and children trespassed in the area not infrequently for recreational purposes.[10]

---

8. Plaintiff has stated that he "grabbed" the wire for no particular reason, although he was "a little dizzy." Brown stated that he had been told by Childress that plaintiff "looked like he was going to fall or something and he caught onto one of [the wires]." Childress stated that he did not actually see how plaintiff came into contact with the electricity. At a discovery conference, plaintiffs' counsel indicated to that Court that his expert medical testimony would suggest that plaintiff did not actually come into contact with the wire, but that he came close and the electric current "arced" into his body.

9. Clarence Riddick, the fisherman who witnessed the accident stated an account of the incident in deposition that differed in some respects from the version in the text, which has been developed in large part from the depositions of the four boys. Riddick stated that the train had been stopped for about 20 minutes, and that the boys had been climbing on, in, and through the cars for about 15 minutes, although none of the boys climbed on top of a car until plaintiff did and was injured. Riddick and his fishing companion Laura Watkins both stated that they yelled at the boys two or three times to "get off the train," and that they specifically yelled at plaintiff to get off the car on which he was injured. Although they believed that the boys heard them because the boys looked at them when they yelled, the boys did not heed the warnings or say anything in response. The boys stated in deposition that they did not hear anyone yell at them or tell them to get off the train before plaintiff was injured.

10. Defendant proffers that its witnesses would testify otherwise at trial. Defendant's former Special Police Officer McCabe stated in deposition that he patrolled this area as part of his regular duties, that he did not recall ever finding trespassing children within one-half mile of the spot where plaintiff was injured, and that he considered it to be "one of the most isolated" areas he "had on the

Plaintiff and his friends stated that they had never seen a standing train on the tracks in their previous visits to this area. Thus they had never before climbed on a train there (or anywhere else by their testimony). They all stated in deposition that they did not consider trains dangerous, and that they were not aware of the electrical danger contained in the catenary wires above the tracks, although they had seen the wires.

The tracks at the point of the incident are "mainline" or "through" tracks. Twenty to twenty-eight through trains pass there every day. Trains are not stored, loaded or switched in the area nor are there side tracks there for such purposes. Trains stop there only en route when required by signals for operational purposes of the railroad.

The high-voltage catenary wires supply defendant's trains with electric power through devices mounted atop the electric locomotives. Of necessity, the wires are not insulated. This catenary system has been in place above railroad tracks in Washington, D.C., since the mid-1930s. At the site where plaintiff was injured, the wires are suspended 18-1/2 feet above the ground, and are "ordinarily inaccessible." ... At bridges or ground-level storage areas and other places where catenary wires would be accessible to pedestrians, defendant has either erected fences or cement walls, or "de-energized" the wires (i.e., turned off the current). Otherwise, the wires are suspended out of normal reach.... On the poles from which the catenary lines are suspended the words "No Trespassing" have been stencilled; these words were faded or rusted so as to be obscured in some places.

· · ·

It is ... undisputed that the District of Columbia has not enacted any fencing requirements or other safety regulations for railroad rights-of-way or catenary wires within the District, despite the fact that the [Railroad Safety] Act expressly preserves the power of state authorities to regulate local railroad safety problems....

Moreover, it is also undisputed that despite the absence of statutory or regulatory requirements, defendant has voluntarily instituted an active safety protection program in areas where trains are stored or where catenary wires come into normal reach. Defendant's voluntary actions in this regard have included construction of fences and walls, posting of "high-voltage" warning signs, and de-energizing of the catenary wires. Thus it is undisputed that defendant was in compliance with all existing federal and local safety requirements at the site and on the date of plaintiff's accident, and that throughout its railroad system defendant has gone beyond statutory requirements in the area of catenary safety.

· · ·

... In Holland [v. B & O R.R., 431 A.2d 597 (D.C. Ct. App. 1981)], a nine-year-old boy was injured by a moving train while trespassing on the unfenced tracks of two railroads.... Because the case involved a minor, the court authoritatively stated that the "narrow exception" of the "attractive nuisance" doctrine, as spelled out in § 339 of the Restatement (Second) of Torts, could be invoked. That section, however, was to be "strictly applied, and [permits liability] only when all five elements of the section [§ 339] are satisfied." Id. at 602. Applying § 339 to the facts in Holland the court held that "a moving train is a danger so obvious that any nine-year-old child allowed at large would readily discover it and realize the risk involved." Id. at 603. Therefore, the court ruled that as a matter of law under § 339(c), no trespassing minor can recover for in-

railroad." ... Other of defendant's officials testified similarly that the area where plaintiff was injured was not known for having child trespassers....

juries caused by a moving train in the District of Columbia. The grant of summary judgment for the railroad was consequently affirmed. Id.

Having decided that requirement (c) of Restatement § 339 was not satisfied, the Holland court stated that it was "unnecessary to consider whether other elements of" § 339 were also satisfied. Id. at 603 n. 11. The court noted, however, that

> courts have consistently held that in the absence of statutory requirements[,] railroads are generally under no duty to erect fences or maintain other safeguards and that, therefore, allegations [in a child-trespasser case seeking recovery on the basis of a failure to safeguard railroad tracks] do not satisfy the requirements of the Restatement rule.

> . . .

… [T]his case must be governed by the principles of Restatement (Second) of Torts § 339 (1965). Because of that section's importance to this case, it will be set out in full:

> *§ 339 Artificial Conditions Highly Dangerous to Trespassing Children:*

> A possessor of land is subject to liability for physical harm to children trespassing thereon caused by an artificial condition upon the land if

> (a) the place where the condition exists is one upon which the possessor knows or has reason to know that children are likely to trespass, and

> (b) the condition is one of which the possessor knows or has reason to know and which he realizes or should realize will involve an unreasonable risk of death or serious bodily harm to such children, and

> (c) the children because of their youth do not discover the condition or realize the risk involved in intermeddling with it or in coming within the area made dangerous by it, and

> (d) the utility to the possessor of maintaining the condition and the burden of eliminating the danger are slight as compared with the risk to children involved, and

> (e) the possessor fails to exercise reasonable care to eliminate the danger or otherwise to protect the children.

Section 339 is stated in the conjunctive, and the D.C. Court of Appeals in Holland noted that it permits a finding of liability "only when all five elements of the section are satisfied." 431 A.2d at 602 (emphasis supplied). After careful consideration of all the undisputed facts and circumstances of this case, viewed most favorably to plaintiffs, only one possible conclusion could be drawn by a reasonable trier of fact: defendant cannot be held liable under § 339 as a matter of law. Plaintiffs' case fails to satisfy, at the very least, elements (b), (d) and (e) of § 339. Detailed explanation follows, after an initial discussion of plaintiffs' evidence under elements (a) and (c).

A. Possessor's Knowledge of Trespassers and Child's Knowledge of Danger.

Plaintiffs have proffered sufficient evidence on elements (a) and (c) of § 339 to present a disputed issue for a jury on those factors. The dangerous condition at issue here is the high-voltage catenary wires suspended 18-1/2 feet above defendant's railroad tracks. In the District of Columbia high-voltage electric wires are considered to be inherently dangerous. Brown v. Potomac Electric Power Co., 236 F.Supp. 815, 817 (D.D.C.1964); cf. Holland, supra, 431 A.2d at 603 (referring to the "silent, deadly danger of high-power electricity"). Defendant knows that its catenary wires are dangerous;

it maintains a rule that its own employees must never come within three feet of a catenary wire unless they are certain it has been "de-energized."

If "the place where the condition exists" in §339(a) is considered to be the track and surrounding area where plaintiff and his friends rode their bicycles and climbed on railroad cars, then the most favorable inferences drawn from plaintiffs' facts suggest that defendant knew or had reason to know that child trespassers visited the area with some frequency.[24] The plaintiff, his friends, and the fishermen witnesses all state that they have visited the area next to the Sousa Bridge many times without obstruction. They have often seen other persons there. The fisherman had seen children there, and had even seen them climb onto (but not on top of) trains.... Various witnesses have stated that there was a worn path leading to the area where the incident occurred. All these facts, taken together with defendant's evidence that from 20 to 28 trains per day pass through this area, could permit a jury to draw the inference that defendant had reason to know about juvenile trespassers there. Conrail personnel on the trains passing by daily may well have observed children in the area and reported it, and a jury could so find even on this bare record.

Defendant argues for a different interpretation of the language of §339(a), however. Conrail contends that, in this case, the "place where the condition exists" was located 18-1/2 feet in the air where the wires were suspended, and that defendant had no reason to know that minors were obtaining access to that place. This argument holds some attraction. Plaintiff has proffered no evidence that would support a finding that Conrail had reason to know that children were "likely" to gain access to the catenary wires by climbing on top of through trains which only occasionally and briefly stopped in that area. Clarence Riddick stated that in 10 years he had never before seen a child climb on top of a train, and the four boys here testified that they had never done so before. Even if evidence of [two prior] incidents were admissible at trial (and it is not ...), two arguably similar incidents in the previous 11 years cannot reasonably support a finding that such access is "likely," as §339(a) requires.

The Court need not decide which interpretation of the language of §339(a) is correct, in light of the dispositive effect that other subsections discussed below have on these facts. The likelihood of minors coming into contact with defendant's suspended wires involves some consideration of foreseeability, an inquiry which merges to some extent with the inquiry as to realization of whether the condition "will involve an unreasonable risk" under subsection (b) of §339, discussed below.

As for subsection (c), plaintiffs' evidence would show that Eldee Edwards, Jr., did not "realize the risk" of coming close to the catenary wire. Plaintiff stated in deposition that he did not realize that the wires were dangerous. This alone creates a triable issue, and it would be for the jury to evaluate the testimony. The Court must take plaintiff's statement as a fact at this summary judgment stage. See also Prosser, supra, at 374 (high school-age boys "may reasonably be expected not to appreciate" dangers of high-voltage wires).

---

24. Comment (g) to §339 and the Reporter's Notes make it clear that "[t]he possessor is under no duty to make any investigation or inquiry as to whether children are trespassing, or are likely to trespass, until he is notified, or otherwise receives information, which would lead a reasonable man to that conclusion." Restatement, Ch. 13, at 201. Plaintiffs' allegation that Conrail "should have known" of child trespassers in the area ... employs the exact phraseology that was rejected by the Restatement (Second) authors in favor of the "has reason to know" language. See RESTATEMENT (SECOND) OF TORTS §339, Appendix at 130 (Reporter's Notes, # 3). Nevertheless, if a jury were to hear the undisputed evidence and draw favorable inferences for the plaintiff, the "has reason to know" standard could arguably be met here, despite plaintiffs' failure to appreciate its meaning.

B. The Risk, the Balance of Burdens, and Reasonable Care.

Although there are triable disputes with regard to § 339(a) & (c), these disputes are not "material" issues if any one of the other elements of § 339 is not satisfied. And the undisputed facts leave no room for rational doubt that plaintiffs' case fails to satisfy the remaining elements. These elements are interrelated to some extent, and build on much of the same evidence. They will be treated seriatim here, however, in an attempt to present plaintiffs' best case in the clearest manner possible.

1. Section 339(b)

The second subsection of § 339 embodies an element of reasonable foreseeability: the dangerous condition must also be one "which [the possessor] realizes or should realize will involve an unreasonable risk of death or serious bodily harm to" children. The comments to § 339 make it clear that the dangerous condition must be realized to be "one with which [children] are *likely* to meddle." § 339, comment (e) at 200 (emphasis supplied).

Plaintiffs concede that the wire that injured plaintiff was suspended 18-1/2 feet in the air and was "ordinarily inaccessible." … In Brown v. Potomac Electric Power Co., … then-District Judge Spottswood Robinson stated the general rule that there is no "duty to insulate properly suspended overhead wires so located that no one could reasonably be expected to come into contact with them." 236 F.Supp. at 819. The area where plaintiff was injured was not a side track or storage yard where trains normally stand for long periods of time; the uncontroverted evidence is that the tracks there are through tracks with at least 20 trains per day passing over them. Plaintiff made no contention and proffered no evidence that trees or other tall structures were close enough to the wires to permit access by climbing or the catenary poles themselves have steps or rungs. Photographs of the site show that there were no such means of access close to the wires. See Defendant's Memorandum, Exs. B, C, & D (photographs of the area). It is undisputed that standing trains are the only means of access to the wires available to children at the site.

Further, it is also uncontroverted that through trains were stopped at the site only occasionally and briefly, awaiting signals; the most favorable evidence to plaintiffs is that the train on which plaintiff was injured was stopped for twenty minutes. As the D.C. Court of Appeals stated in Holland, supra, "'the possessor [of railroad tracks] is *free to rely upon the assumption* that any child of sufficient age to be allowed at large by his parents, and so to be at all likely to trespass, will appreciate the danger [of moving trains] and avoid it.'" 431 A.2d at 603 (quoting Prosser, supra, at 371) (emphasis supplied). Defendant was therefore entitled to assume as a matter of D.C. law that, if any children were in the area where plaintiff was injured, they would not climb onto the moving through trains there.

The usual absence of stationary means of access and the normal presence only of moving through trains are thus undisputed. These facts preclude a reasonable trier of facts from finding that catenary wires suspended 18-1/2 feet in the air posed a danger that Conrail "realize[d] or should [have] realize[d] will involve an unreasonable risk" to children under § 339(b). The risk was not "unreasonable" but, rather, was unlikely, and no facts in the record suggest that defendants should have "realized" otherwise.

· · ·

… [T]here are many venerable precedents finding as a matter of law that, under the "attractive nuisance" doctrine, injuries to child trespassers from electrical wires suspended high above the ground cannot normally provide a basis for tort liability.

Plaintiff has not cited a single case holding to the contrary and the Court has discovered only one, which is clearly distinguishable both on the law and its facts.

...

2. Section 339(d)

Subsection (d) of § 339 requires that, for liability to attach in a child trespasser case, both the "utility" of the dangerous condition and the "burden of eliminating the danger" must be "slight" when compared to the "risk to children involved." The utility of the catenary wires to defendant is clear and considerable; the wires are necessary to provide power to enable defendant to run its interstate trains. The physical and financial burden on defendant of "eliminating" the wires and changing completely to another system of power obviously would be prohibitive, and plaintiffs have not even suggested such a wholesale change. As to the risk involved, the analysis of the evidence under § 339(b) made above ... indicates that the risk of harm posed by the catenary system to child trespassers at the site where plaintiff was injured is "slight" by any standard.[34] The very low risk that accidents such as this one will occur is evidenced by the uncontroverted testimony of defendant's Assistant Vice-President that, generally, "catenary accidents comprise approximately 0.01% of all [railroad] accidents." ...

Even if the risk of harm in this case is not considered to be prohibitively low, the analysis under subsection (d) requires a balancing of the burden to defendant of taking steps to eliminate accidents such as plaintiff suffered, against the risk of such accidents actually occurring.[35]

Plaintiffs' only proffered evidence under § 339(d) is a factually unsupported statement that defendant could have "purchased" enough warning signs to post one on each side of the track every 25 feet along its 17.7 miles of electrified track in Washington, D.C., at a cost of $30,000. ... The cost of installing and maintaining such signs is not estimated by plaintiffs; no witness or other factual basis is proffered as support for the estimate. It is again clear that plaintiffs have generally failed to meet the minimal requirements of Rule 56(e), ... by their failure to support this alleged cost estimate either in their opposition to the summary judgment or in their pretrial brief. One incomplete and unsupported estimate (which is the only specific cost estimate of any kind proffered by plaintiffs) is totally insufficient to put at issue a material fact for trial.

Even assuming that plaintiffs' signing cost estimate included the cost of installation and maintenance and were competent under Rule 56(e), it simply does not create a jury issue under § 339(d). The facts are undisputed that there was already a "No Unauthorized Vehicles" sign posted along the road that plaintiff traveled to the site, and there were "No Trespassing" warnings stenciled on the catenary poles at the site. The undisputed evidence supplied by plaintiff and plaintiffs' proffered expert witnesses, however, is that signs by themselves do not deter children in general, and did not deter this plaintiff in particular, from proceeding past them. Plaintiffs themselves adduced expert testimony as to the general point. ... As to this particular case, plaintiff's companion Tryone Brown

---

34. Subsection (d) of § 339 does not mandate that if injury is certain when the wires are touched then the risk must be calculated as great, as plaintiffs appear to suggest in their pretrial brief at 195. This argument omits from the equation the factor of the possibility and likelihood of access to the wires. The question is not whether the harm itself is great, but whether the risk of that harm actually occurring is great. Although the harm to plaintiff in this case was undeniably great, one catenary accident in six years (1973–79) indicates that the risk of that harm occurring to children is slight.

35. No evidence at all on this issue is cited in plaintiffs' opposition to summary judgment; their only statement is that "[p]laintiffs ... contend that the burden ... as compared to the danger to children is slight," with reference to "plaintiffs' engineer, sign company representative, fencing company representative, and others." ...

saw the "No Unauthorized Vehicles" sign but paid it no attention and did not even call it to his companions' attention. "No trespassing" signs already were posted at this site; they did not stop the plaintiff.[36] The undisputed material evidence therefore establishes that signs alone would not "*eliminat[e]* the danger" within the meaning of subsection (d) (emphasis supplied), and plaintiffs' proffer as to the burden of putting up such signs is therefore irrelevant as well as insufficient.

Moreover, the burden on this defendant to protect against a particular danger must be considered on a system-wide level, and not just with regard to a particular location or a particular city or state. Given that the site of plaintiff's accident was not a storage yard or side track, there was no way for defendant to pinpoint it as a site more "likely" to have such an accident occur than many other urban rights-of-way. Therefore, as the Pennsylvania Supreme Court has noted,

> It is, of course, obvious that if there were imposed upon the defendant the requirement of fencing the place where this accident occurred, it would likewise be subject to the duty of fencing the innumerable places along its many miles of tracks frequented by trespassing children.

Dugan v. Pennsylvania RR, 387 Pa. 25, 127 A.2d 343, 348 (Pa.1956), cert. den., 353 U.S. 946, 77 S.Ct. 825, 1 L.Ed.2d 856 (1957). The cost of such protective measures is arguably prohibitive, and at the very least not "slight" as a matter of law under § 339(d). For example, defendant proffers without dispute from plaintiffs that it would cost over $2.5 billion to fence Conrail's 33,529 miles of track. Memorandum in Support at 30 n. 23. Plaintiffs' $30,000 cost estimate for signs is restricted to the District of Columbia tracks alone, and is on this ground as well deficient under § 339(d). Moreover, even fencing, like signing, is not "child-proof," ... ; in fact, fencing can create other problems or dangers of its own....

...

Defendant must select priorities for protecting against accidents, and cannot protect against them all without an unbearable burden to itself, and thereby to a rail system which is a vital public necessity. As noted above, ... the Federal Railroad Administration has not imposed an obligation on railroads to fence their urban rights-of-way, noting the high cost that such a requirement would involve. The Secretary's stance and the adoption of Dugan by the authors of the Restatement and of the Holland decision, taken together with all the other factors discussed above under § 339(d), establish as a matter of law that neither the utility of the catenary system nor the burden of eliminating its dangers is "slight" when compared to the risk of an injury such as was regrettably incurred by this plaintiff. On the undisputed material facts in this record, no rational dispute is presented for a jury as to this conclusion.

3. Section 339(e)

Even if all the other conditions of § 339 were satisfied by plaintiffs' case, "there is liability only if the possessor fails to take the steps which a reasonable man would take under such circumstances. If the possessor has exercised all reasonable care..., and still

---

36. Plaintiffs argue here that defendant should have posted signs that warn specifically against the danger of the high-voltage catenary wires. But as defendant points out, there are many dangers associated with railroad tracks, and catenary accidents are not the most common. Rather than put up a specific sign warning against each particular danger at a site, defendant posts "No Trespassing" warnings which, if obeyed, protect against all the myriad dangers. Plaintiffs suggested signs would be no more effective than defendant's, and perhaps less so, if children chose to ignore them.

has not succeeded, there is no liability." Restatement (Second) of Torts § 339, comment (o). Professor Prosser has commented in this regard that "[s]uch things as standing freight cars ... are undeniably attractive to children, but are socially useful and very difficult to safeguard, and so may call for very little in the way of care."

...

... It is uncontested that Conrail was in compliance with all applicable statutes and safety regulations with regard to its Washington, D.C., tracks on the date of plaintiff's accident, and that there was no statutory requirement that it fence the tracks or post signs where plaintiff was injured. Thus the dictum in Holland indicates that as a matter of District of Columbia law, defendant exercised reasonable care under § 339 with regard to the location at issue here.

Moreover, the considered decision of Congress and the FRA not to require fencing or signs at urban rights-of-way is further persuasive and uncontested evidence that defendant was exercising reasonable care at the site at issue. As Justice Holmes noted long ago, "what is usually done may be evidence of what ought to be done." Texas & P. Ry. Co. v. Behymer, 189 U.S. 468, 470.... At the point where plaintiff was injured the wires could not be de-energized, if the 20–28 through trains that pass by each day were to have power to operate. Defendant was in compliance with all statutes and regulations at that point, and had no reason to suspect that that particular location was any more likely to have a catenary accident occur than any other used by through trains along its lines. Finally, at different sites on the Conrail line where trains stand for long periods or where the catenary wires are not beyond normal reach (such as at bridges or where cables may go underground), thereby making injurious contact more likely and foreseeable, it is undisputed that defendant has a policy of either fencing the surrounding area or of de-energizing the wires.... It is therefore, in effect, conceded that defendant has taken reasonable precautions to protect against the risk of harm from catenary wires where it is reasonably foreseeable that such harm might occur. In light of all these uncontested facts, defendant did as a matter of law exercise all reasonable care with regard to the site of plaintiff's accident, and no rational jury could find to the contrary.

...

Plaintiffs have totally ignored defendant's comprehensive proffers of evidence and arguments directed at subsection (e) of § 339, as they have on other points. They assert, without citing specific facts and without further argument, that the issues "are properly for resolution by the trier of fact, the jury." ... In many cases, it is true that reasonableness is an issue of fact. However, when all the material facts are undisputed and before the Court on summary judgment, reasonableness may be "a question of law where only one inference is possible from the evidence.":....

...

... As a matter of law, defendant cannot be held liable in this case under a number of factors under 339, and the failure to fulfill any one of those factors requires summary judgment. While summary judgment normally should be granted only reluctantly, it is warranted in exceptional cases where only one result or inference is possible under any view of the undisputed evidence.... The Court feels sympathy for the minor plaintiff's injuries, but as a matter of law he cannot recover on this record.

...

[Dismissed.]

NOTES

(1) Why should child trespassers be treated differently from other trespassers?

Compare with *Edwards* the case of Cargill v. Zimmer, 374 F.2d 924 (8th Cir. 1967), affirming a jury verdict in favor of the survivors of a 12-year-old boy who fell to his death from a 72-foot-high grain silo. The boy had climbed there, apparently, to chase pigeons. The silo was unfenced, but in order to begin climbing it the decedent had to get a boost from a friend onto a ladder that began about seven feet from the ground. There was evidence that an official of the corporate owner of the silo had told the property custodian to make the area as pigeon tight as possible because "we knew there was a problem with pigeons and problems with young boys and the pigeons."

On its way to affirmance of the plaintiffs' verdict, which was for $15,482, the Eighth Circuit characterized "modern decisions in this area" as "increasingly acknowledg[ing] the humanitarian viewpoint that the life of a child is to be balanced as a heavy interest when weighed against the utility of simple precautions to guard against danger." 374 F.2d at 930.

What are the social or philosophical premises for that "humanitarian viewpoint"? If one starts on that slope, how can one define the principle that stops a slide that would include *Edwards* on the liability side of the line?

(2) Suppose that in *Edwards*, there was testimony that railroad officials "knew there was a problem" with boys climbing on railroad cars and touching catenary wires (in a part of the opinion here omitted, the court holds inadmissible evidence of prior catenary accidents involving trespassing boys). Holding constant the cost figures mentioned in the case, would that have made a difference?

(3) After this exposure to the child trespasser doctrine, what is your evaluation of the comparative importance in tort law of achieving economic efficiency and of enforcing "moral" notions of "justice" in personal injury cases?

Should courts ever dispense compassion in cases involving private litigants? Should they ever take into account the risk-bearing capacity of defendants?

(4) Does the child trespasser doctrine introduce an element of subjectivity into the determination of what otherwise would be a simple issue of contributory negligence? On this point, see the material in the next section, raising the question of when, if ever, it is appropriate to use a subjective test for the conduct of tort plaintiffs as well as defendants.

§ 6.02 The Legal Effect of Mental and Emotional Limitations

PROBLEM

In a tragic case involving drunk driving, the court summarized the mental capacity of the plaintiff's decedent, Leslie Wright, this way:

> Plaintiff's decedent, who was 22 years old at the time of his death, was single, resided with and supported his parents. His sister, Vieda Wright, testified that plaintiff's decedent dropped out of school about the fifth or sixth grade and worked as a farm laborer; that he could "read and write to an extent, and some

things he could learn"; that he "never could learn like other children" and was called "Dummy"; that he was able to do the chores that are normally required on a farm, and that he lacked initiative.

. . .

At the time of his death, Leslie Wright was employed as a general farm worker by Rex Morehead. Morehead stated that Leslie Wright could not be trusted "very far on his own"; that "[h]e wasn't capable of thinking for himself, or he would complete some small job, and he just couldn't go on to anything else. He would be digging postholes on a few occasions, and if you weren't there to tell him to go to the next post hole he would just keep digging. He couldn't understand where to quit."

. . .

There was no showing that he was insane or that a guardian had ever been appointed to care for either his person or property. There was no medical testimony with regard to his mental status. Moreover, plaintiff's decedent was regularly employed as a farm worker and supported the family. His sister testified that he could "read and write to an extent, and some things he could learn." He was able to cash his pay checks and to purchase provisions for the family. According to his brother-in-law, "[h]e was strong and . . . proud to work."

Wright was one of several passengers in a car piloted by an inebriated driver. One of the other passengers, Gussler, requested that he be allowed to drive, but the driver refused. After the driver rejected Gussler's offer, Gussler suggested that the passengers get out and hitchhike. No one got out, although Wright commented that he thought Gussler "ought to drive back." On a return trip from a restaurant where the group stopped for beer, the driver stopped to put water in the car radiator. Gussler "renewed his invitation to 'hitchhike,'" but the plaintiff stayed in the car. The trip proceeded to a fatal conclusion when the driver hit a tree.

The trial judge overruled a defendant's motion to strike the plaintiff's evidence on his decedent's mental capacity, saying that the plaintiff had "sought to show the decedent Wright was of low mentality and not able to recognize danger as it existed, which I think poses a jury question." Was this ruling correct?

ROBINSON v. LINDSAY

Washington Supreme Court, En Banc
92 Wash. 2d 410, 598 P.2d 392 (1979)

UTTER, CHIEF JUSTICE.

An action seeking damages for personal injuries was brought on behalf of Kelly Robinson who lost full use of a thumb in a snowmobile accident when she was 11 years of age. The petitioner, Billy Anderson, 13 years of age at the time of the accident, was the driver of the snowmobile. After a jury verdict in favor of Anderson, the trial court ordered a new trial.

The single issue on appeal is whether a minor operating a snowmobile is to be held to an adult standard of care. The trial court failed to instruct the jury as to that standard and ordered a new trial because it believed the jury should have been so instructed. We agree and affirm the order granting a new trial.

The trial court instructed the jury under WPI 10.05 that:

> In considering the claimed negligence of a child, you are instructed that it is
> the duty of a child to exercise the same care that a reasonably careful child of
> the same age, intelligence, maturity, training and experience would exercise
> under the same or similar circumstances.

Respondent properly excepted to the giving of this instruction and to the court's failure
to give an adult standard of care.

The question of what standard of care should apply to acts of children has a long historical background. Traditionally, a flexible standard of care has been used to determine
if children's actions were negligent. Under some circumstances, however, courts have
developed a rationale for applying an adult standard.

In the courts' search for a uniform standard of behavior to use in determining
whether or not a person's conduct has fallen below minimal acceptable standards, the
law has developed a fictitious person, the "reasonable man of ordinary prudence." That
term was first used in Vaughan v. Menlove, 132 Eng.Rep. 490 (1837).

Exceptions to the reasonable person standard developed when the individual whose
conduct was alleged to have been negligent suffered from some physical impairment,
such as blindness, deafness, or lameness. Courts also found it necessary, as a practical
matter, to depart considerably from the objective standard when dealing with children's
behavior. Children are traditionally encouraged to pursue childhood activities without
the same burdens and responsibilities with which adults must contend. See Bahr, Tort
Law and the Games Kids Play, 23 S.D.L.Rev. 275 (1978). As a result, courts evolved a
special standard of care to measure a child's negligence in a particular situation.

In Roth v. Union Depot Co., 13 Wash. 525, 43 P. 641 (1896), Washington joined "the
overwhelming weight of authority" in distinguishing between the capacity of a child
and that of an adult. As the court then stated, at page 544, 43 P. at page 647:

> [I]t would be a monstrous doctrine to hold that a child of inexperience and ex-
> perience can come only with years should be held to the same degree of care in
> avoiding danger as a person of mature years and accumulated experience.

The court went on to hold, at page 545, 43 P. at page 647:

> The care or caution required is according to the capacity of the child, and this
> is to be determined, ordinarily, by the age of the child.
>
> "... a child is held ... only to the exercise of such degree of care and discretion
> as is reasonably to be expected from children of his age."

The current law in this state is fairly reflected in WPI 10.05, given in this case. In the
past we have always compared a child's conduct to that expected of a reasonably careful
child of the same age, intelligence, maturity, training and experience. This case is the
first to consider the question of a child's liability for injuries sustained as a result of his or
her operation of a motorized vehicle or participation in an inherently dangerous activity.

Courts in other jurisdictions have created an exception to the special child standard
because of the apparent injustice that would occur if a child who caused injury while
engaged in certain dangerous activities were permitted to defend himself by saying that
other children similarly situated would not have exercised a degree of care higher than
his, and he is, therefore, not liable for his tort. Some courts have couched the exception
in terms of children engaging in an activity which is normally one for adults only.... We
believe a better rationale is that when the activity a child engages in is inherently dan-

gerous, as is the operation of powerful mechanized vehicles, the child should be held to an adult standard of care.

Such a rule protects the need of children to be children but at the same time discourages immature individuals from engaging in inherently dangerous activities. Children will still be free to enjoy traditional childhood activities without being held to an adult standard of care. Although accidents sometimes occur as the result of such activities, they are not activities generally considered capable of resulting in "grave danger to others and to the minor himself if the care used in the course of the activity drops below that care which the reasonable and prudent adult would use ..." Daniels v. Evans, 107 N.H. 407, 408, 224 A.2d 63, 64 (1966).

Other courts adopting the adult standard of care for children engaged in adult activities have emphasized the hazards to the public if the rule is otherwise. We agree with the Minnesota Supreme Court's language in its decision in Dellwo v. Pearson, supra, 259 Minn. at 457–58, 107 N.W.2d at 863:

> Certainly in the circumstances of modern life, where vehicles moved by powerful motors are readily available and frequently operated by immature individuals, we should be skeptical of a rule that would allow motor vehicles to be operated to the hazard of the public with less than the normal minimum degree of care and competence.

Dellwo applied the adult standard to a 12-year-old defendant operating a motor boat. Other jurisdictions have applied the adult standard to minors engaged in analogous activities.... The holding of minors to an adult standard of care when they operate motorized vehicles is gaining approval from an increasing number of courts and commentators....

The operation of a snowmobile likewise requires adult care and competence. Currently 2.2 million snowmobiles are in operation in the United States.... Studies show that collisions and other snowmobile accidents claim hundreds of casualties each year and that the incidence of accidents is particularly high among inexperienced operators....

At the time of the accident, the 13-year-old petitioner had operated snowmobiles for about 2 years. When the injury occurred, petitioner was operating a 30-horsepower snowmobile at speeds of 10–20 miles per hour. The record indicates that the machine itself was capable of 65 miles per hour. Because petitioner was operating a powerful motorized vehicle, he should be held to the standard of care and conduct expected of an adult.

The order granting a new trial is affirmed.

MARTIN v. LOUISIANA POWER & LIGHT CO.

United States District Court, Eastern District of Louisiana
546 F. Supp. 780 (1982), aff'd without opinion, 719 F.2d 403
(5th Cir. 1983)

WICKER, DISTRICT JUDGE.

On or about March 17, 1978, plaintiff, Billie J. Martin had been drinking alcohol for a substantial period of time at the Sassy B. Lounge. After becoming intoxicated, he entered into a bet that he could climb a certain utility pole located across the street from the lounge. He managed to climb the pole, and upon reaching the top, came into contact with an electrical line carrying approximately 8,000 volts, sustaining a severe electrical shock. As a result of this accident, plaintiff lost his right arm slightly below the elbow and his right leg slightly below the knee. . . .

. . . [T]he only remaining defendant is Louisiana Power and Light Company (LP&L) who now moves for summary judgment, contending that plaintiff was guilty of contributory negligence and his conduct bars his recovery as a matter of law.

For purposes of this motion, counsel have stipulated that on the night in question, plaintiff was intoxicated; plaintiff was an alcoholic; plaintiff climbed the utility pole and came in contact with an overhead energized wire owned by LP&L and that the first step on the utility pole was 6' 4-1/2" from the ground.

After considering the record, the stipulations, the briefs and arguments of counsel, and the law applicable to this case, motion of defendant LP&L for summary judgment dismissing plaintiff's claim is granted for the following reasons, to wit:

. . .

Contributory negligence is determined by an objective standard. The test is whether or not the plaintiff was exercising ordinary care at the time of the accident. . . . In other words, it is a question of whether plaintiff was acting reasonably under the circumstances. . . . This objective standard is applicable to plaintiffs regardless of whether they are careless or inattentive, intoxicated, or even insane.

Plaintiff's argument that he was not guilty of contributory negligence because he lacked "volition" due to his alcoholism is not the law of this jurisdiction. Plaintiff cites no Louisiana cases that support the proposition that an alcoholic is not responsible for his own negligent conduct while intoxicated.[5]

Plaintiff submitted a report and affidavit by a psychiatrist that plaintiff is an alcoholic, suffering from organic brain disease. Although I agree that alcoholism is a bona fide disease, see, Martin v. New York Life Ins. Co., 621 F.2d 159, 160 (5th Cir. 1980), I do not agree that plaintiff is being penalized for his status as an alcoholic; rather, the focus here is on his conduct. Thus, even accepting plaintiff's mental debilities as a fact, I apply the "reasonable man" test and find plaintiff to be guilty of contributory negligence as a matter of law.[6]

[Omitted is a discussion of other issues of duty and negligence.]

---

5. *Driver v. Hinnant*, 356 F.2d 761 (4th Cir. 1966) and *Easter v. District of Columbia*, 361 F.2d 50 (D.C.1966) cited by plaintiff, both involve habeas corpus proceedings attacking a conviction, under criminal law, prohibiting public intoxication. These cases held that since alcoholism is a disease, incarceration of an alcoholic on the grounds of public drunkenness would violate the prohibition of cruel and unusual punishment of the eighth amendment to the United States Constitution. Bazley v. Tortorich, 397 So.2d 475 (La.1981) also cited by plaintiff, involved the issue of what constitutes intentional acts, which are held to be outside the protections afforded to employers by the Louisiana Workmen's Compensation Act. The considerations involved in imposing criminal liability on an alcoholic or other person suffering from diminished mental capacity, or in determining whether or not a tort committed by one suffering from an impairment of judgment is intentional, are entirely different from the considerations involved in the determination of whether a plaintiff in a civil action is guilty of contributory negligence.

6. The "reasonable man" test was applied by the Fifth Circuit to an alcoholic who negligently smoked in bed and started a fire, which led to his death in *Guss v. Jack Tar Management*, 407 F.2d 859 (5th Cir. 1969).

Note, *Tort Liability of the Mentally Ill in Negligence Actions*
93 Yale L.J. 153, 156–160, 163–164, 166–170 (1983)*

···

Courts have traditionally given four rationales for holding the mentally ill to an objective standard of tort liability. The most common is that the mentally ill should be required to compensate the victims of any damage they cause. A second frequently cited rationale is that a defense of mental illness raises evidentiary problems because of the difficulty of determining the existence and degree of mental illness and because of the possibility of a person's feigning mental illness. The two remaining rationales are less persuasive and have been given decreasing attention by the courts. One, cited mostly in early cases, is that holding the mentally ill liable will encourage their caretakers to exercise greater diligence in preventing them from committing torts. The other is that the difficulty of distinguishing between mental illness and other variations in emotional, intellectual, or physical make-up would ultimately result in a complete erosion of the objective standard.

B. Contributory Negligence

In contrast to the use of the objective standard in primary negligence cases, the overwhelming majority of courts have held that a completely insane person is incapable of contributory negligence and that lesser degrees of mental impairment, not amounting to complete insanity, may be considered by the jury in determining whether the plaintiff is guilty of contributory negligence. A minority of courts have held that although completely insane persons cannot be held contributorily negligent, no lesser degrees of mental impairment may be considered.

No policy reasons for this distinction between primary and contributory negligence standards have ever been clearly articulated. Several factors, however, have been suggested. First, there is a vague supposition that the policy rationales supporting an objective standard in primary negligence cases have less force in cases of contributory negligence. Second, there seems to be less equitable discomfort in allowing mentally ill plaintiffs to recover since the mentally ill victim appears less threatening and more deserving of sympathy than a mentally ill tortfeasor who causes an injury. Third, the doctrine of contributory negligence is widely considered to be too harsh; this approach thus provides a means of avoiding some harsh results.

No court appears to have formulated a new standard of care for mentally ill plaintiffs in states which have abandoned the doctrine of contributory negligence in favor of comparative negligence. In comparative fault states, the courts have been willing merely to carry over their approach under contributory negligence.

C. Criticisms of the Law

Legal commentators have criticized the common law doctrine of holding the mentally ill liable for their torts since its inception. The first criticisms appeared in the early 1900's, apparently in response to the case of Williams v. Hays and to various commentators who declared the doctrine a settled principle of law. These early critics claimed that it was inconsistent with justice and reason to hold the mentally ill liable for their

---

* Reprinted by permission of The Yale Law Journal Company and William S. Hein Company from *The Yale Law Journal*, Vol. 93, pages 153–170.

torts. Such liability purportedly violated the fault principle since the mentally ill could not control their actions and thus were morally blameless.

As society's views of the mentally ill changed, calls for reform of the common law tort doctrine became more squarely grounded in social policy arguments. Critics assert that, given psychiatric and legal advances, it is no longer justifiable for society to hold the mentally ill to a tort standard impossible for them to meet. Since the mentally ill are in this view incapable of conforming to a "reasonable person" standard, these commentators argue that holding the mentally ill liable for their torts violates the fault principle and imposes strict liability upon them without sound justification.

Critics have faulted each of the traditional rationales for the objective standard. They contend that psychiatry and psychology can now provide reasonably reliable diagnoses, thus minimizing evidentiary problems. Critics attack the law's denying a defense of mental illness simply because a few "normal" persons may attempt to feign mental illness as unnecessarily harsh toward the mentally ill, especially since "normal persons" would be unlikely to feign such a defense because of the stigma associated with mental illness. Moreover, critics respond to the potential erosion of the objective standard by noting that exceptions to the objective standard of liability have already been created with respect to children and the physically disabled. Finally, a few courts have considered or rejected the common law doctrine.

II. AN OBJECTIVE STANDARD IS CONSISTENT WITH CURRENT MENTAL HEALTH TREATMENT POLICY

Commentators have argued that recent changes in the medical and legal treatment of the mentally ill indicate that a subjective standard should be adopted. The shift from institutionalization to community treatment, however, suggests the appropriateness of the objective standard.

. . .

As a result of deinstitutionalization and community treatment, most mentally ill persons in the United States spend the majority of their time in the community. The substantial increase in the number of mentally ill persons now living in the community increases the importance of holding them to an appropriate standard of care....

1. An Objective Standard is Appropriate in Determining Primary Negligence

The mentally ill must be held to a uniform objective standard of tort liability in order to meet the present requirements and aims of community treatment. The objective standard helps minimize the burden on the community from deinstitutionalization, helps foster community acceptance of the mentally ill, and encourages the mentally ill to become self-sufficient, responsible members of the community.

. . .

An important consideration in minimizing the community burden of deinstitutionalization is the impact of the law on the total number of torts committed. Since deinstitutionalization has significantly increased the number of mentally ill persons in the community, it will also probably increase the number of torts they, as a class, commit. One of the purposes of tort law is to encourage people to prevent accidents from occurring. Just as holding average persons liable for their torts may make them behave more conscientiously, holding the mentally ill liable may have a similar effect. If the mentally ill are not held responsible for their torts, the community might become concerned that such immunity would result in an increased number of torts.

Correspondingly, if the mentally ill were allowed to escape tort liability, there is a risk that the public might become outraged by the perceived injustice of denying compensation to innocent victims. This is the compensation rationale most often cited by the courts. And although many mentally ill defendants are likely to be judgment proof, victims should not be denied compensation in those cases where there is insurance to cover the judgment or where the defendant has the means to pay.

Ultimately, the important point is not the mentally ill person's liability to pay, but the symbolic act of holding the person liable regardless of his or her ability to pay. Otherwise society will be treating the mentally ill as a special sub-class of inept citizens who cannot be blamed or held accountable for socially undesirable conduct.

. . .

. . . [T]he law should not adopt a tort standard which tells both the returning mental patient and society that the mentally ill are considered incapable of behaving in a reasonable, responsible manner.

Critics of the common law tort doctrine contend that the objective standard unjustly imposes a form of strict liability upon the mentally ill. This argument, however, makes the untenable assumption that the mentally ill have no capacity to conform to the law or to control their behavior. The introduction of psychotropic medications has greatly facilitated the control of psychotic behavior. Two-thirds of deinstitutionalized patients never become severely symptomatic. Although severe mental illness does exist, the gravely mentally ill are the most likely to be institutionalized, and the least likely to be in the community committing torts. With psychotropic medications and outpatient therapy, most mentally ill persons in the community can conduct themselves in accord with minimally acceptable behavioral standards.

Holding the mentally ill to an objective standard does not work an "extraordinary injustice" upon them, as critics claim. The mentally ill are not by definition incapable of conforming to a reasonable person standard. Moreover, the whole aim of community treatment is to foster and encourage the mentally ill to behave "reasonably" and "normally" in the community. The objective standard is no more unjust to the mentally ill than it is to numerous other persons whose individual capacities do not quite match up to the capacities of the "ideal prudent person."

A final practical consideration should be noted. A defense of mental illness to a tort action could have undesirable, collateral effects for the released mental patient. If a person's mental illness were considered sufficient to excuse him or her from tort liability, then society might consider it sufficient to warrant commitment to a mental institution. Even if commitment were not deemed warranted, the person might still be vulnerable to having a guardian or conservator, thus hampering the development of personal independence and self-reliance.

2. An Objective Standard is Appropriate in Determining Contributory Negligence

The arguments favoring an objective standard for the mentally ill in primary negligence cases equally support an objective standard in determining contributory negligence. There are no clearly articulated policy rationales for using a subjective standard in cases involving mentally ill plaintiffs, although one rationale is that mentally ill plaintiffs are less threatening to the public and evoke more sympathy than mentally ill defendants. The validity of this assertion is open to serious doubt. The increase in the number of mentally ill in the community is likely to lead to an increase in the number of mentally ill persons involved in accidents. The public is likely to be dismayed if it becomes apparent through tort cases that they are expected to keep a "special eye" out for the safety of the mentally ill. If mentally ill persons, who have contributed significantly to causing their own injuries, are allowed to recover total damages, then the public is in effect being charged for not exercising greater care for their safety for the average person. This could result in especially negative consequences in such areas as housing or employment. Employers would have an added justification not to hire discharged mental patients, and landlords not to rent to them, if the mentally ill could contribute to causing their own injuries and then recover complete damages.

It has also been suggested that allowing a subjective standard for mentally ill plaintiffs provides a means of mitigating the generally harsh results of the contributory negligence doctrine. Such a standard, however, singles out the mentally ill as a distinct class of incompetents requiring heightened protection. The mentally ill living in the community are expected to take care of their own basic needs including the need to look out for their own safety. It is no more unfair or inequitable to require them to exercise due care for their own safety than it is for the average person.

...

NOTES

(1) Is negligence an "objective" or "subjective" concept?

Should the law ever make allowances in personal injury actions for the fact that either party possesses less than normal intelligence? At least with respect to the defendant of limited capacity, but some competence, venerable authority establishes that the standard is that of a person of "ordinary prudence," with the court declaring that otherwise "liability for negligence should be co-extensive with the judgment of each individual, which would be as variable as the length of the foot of each individual." *Vaughan v. Menlove*, 3 Bing., N.C. 468 (C.P. 1837). But should this rule be applied without qualification? If the general rule in the case of children is that they should be judged only with reference to those of similar age, intelligence and experience—see, e.g., *Robinson* for a statement of that rule—why should not a similarly subjective standard apply to an adult with the mind of a child, even in the posture of a defendant?

(2) With respect to the legal capacity to be either negligent or contributorily negligent, how would you judge the following classes of persons:

(a) Those of significantly below average intelligence

(b) Those suffering from mental illness that requires "intermittent or continual medication, psychotherapy, or brief hospitalization," the category covered by the *Yale Law Journal* Note, *supra*, 93 YALE L.J. 153, at 154 n.5.

(c) Alcoholics

(d) Physically handicapped persons, for example, visually impaired or hearing impaired individuals.

(3) Consider the case of an elderly patient in a convalescent hospital, who suffers from Alzheimer's disease, who is occasionally "very combative," and is rated a "[h]igh risk for injury." Nurses in the hospital receive training in how to approach, handle and restrain such patients. The patient in question becomes "combative" when a nurse's aide tries to move her from a chair to bed. The plaintiff, also a nurse's aide, comes into the room to help out, fearing that the patient will fall. As she assists the other aide in moving the patient to the bed, the patient strikes her several times on the jaw. A state statute

provides that "[a] person of unsound mind, of whatever degree, is civilly liable for a wrong done by the person." What are the issues, and how should they be resolved?

(4) Should the fact of momentary distraction excuse temporary inadvertence? Should distinctions be drawn among causes for distraction on the basis of merit, for example, between worry about a personal problem and looking at a billboard?

Chapter 7

STRICT LIABILITIES

§ 7.01 Landowners' Activities

PROBLEM

At least one officially reported torts case has arisen from facts that were the subject of a movie: *Silkwood* (1983), with Meryl Streep as the doomed heroine. The passage below, from a Tenth Circuit opinion, recites the facts of *Silkwood v. Kerr-McGee Corp.*, various versions of which occupied federal district and appellate courts and the United States Supreme Court over a period of seven years. As you read the passage, consider whether Silkwood's survivors should be able to recover against Kerr-McGee even if they could not show that the company was negligent, that is, whether the company should be strictly liable.

*   *   *   *   *   *

Karen Silkwood was a laboratory analyst at the Cimmaron plant of Kerr-McGee located near Crescent, Oklahoma. The plant fabricated fuel pins containing plutonium for use as reactor fuel. Silkwood was contaminated by plutonium on November 5, 6, and 7, 1974, and the parties have stipulated that this plutonium came from the Kerr-McGee plant. Precisely how and when the contamination occurred is not stipulated and there is little evidence to fill this void.

Plutonium is an artificially produced radioactive chemical element which has been instrumental in the development of nuclear weapons and nuclear power. It emits alpha particles, beta particles, neutrons, gamma rays, and x-rays. The extent of radiation damage to human cells exposed to plutonium is dependent upon the amount of energy in the radiation. Alpha particles have the largest mass, carry the greatest amount of energy, and are the most hazardous. Damage can occur when alpha particles strike a cell. Damage to an individual cell is not, however, invariably harmful to the human body; a cell is capable of repairing itself and the body normally sheds and replaces millions of cells on a continuous basis. It is acknowledged, however, that plutonium is one of the most carcinogenic and dangerous substances known.

There is no real dispute in the evidence concerning Silkwood's contamination. She reported to work at the Cimmaron plant on November 5, 1974, at 1:20 p.m. At 2:45 p.m. and at 3:15 p.m., before and after taking a break, Silkwood monitored herself with plutonium detecting devices provided by Kerr-McGee in accordance with the company policies and AEC license requirements. No plutonium was detected on her person. At about 3:45 p.m. Silkwood began to work in two glove boxes containing plutonium. A glove box is a supposedly impervious box surrounding the plutonium processing equipment which has glove holes permitting the operator to work on the equipment or with the plutonium from outside the box. Silkwood again monitored herself before and after her break at 5:30 p.m. and at 5:45 p.m., and at those times detected no contamination. She continued to work in the glove boxes and, upon withdrawing her hands from one of the boxes at about 6:30 p.m., she found contamination. Further checks were made in the laboratory and other contaminations were found, particularly inside the gloves in the glove box in which Silkwood had been polishing and cleaning plutonium.

Contamination was found on Silkwood's left hand, right wrist, upper arm, neck, face, hair, and in her nostrils. Pursuant to regulations, Silkwood was immediately decontaminated and placed on a five-day voiding collection program, and furnished urine and fecal kits to take home for the purpose of obtaining samples which would be sent to the United States testing laboratory for analysis. Later that day Silkwood returned to work, but not to the glove boxes; she monitored herself when she left work at about 1:10 a.m. and found no contamination. The glove box was later tested by the AEC investigators, and no leaks were found. Further, the investigators found no significant airborne contamination in the laboratory.

The next day, November 6, 1974, Silkwood arrived at work at 7:50 a.m., and did some paper work in the lab until 8:50 a.m., at which time she left to attend a union meeting. At that time she tested herself and found contamination on her hands; tests showed fixed contamination on her right forearm, face, and neck. Her hands were decontaminated; since the other spots appeared to be fixed contamination she was allowed to attend the union meeting. She returned to the health office at 4:30 p.m., where slight contamination was found on her right forearm, neck and face, and in her nostrils. She was again decontaminated and, at her request, her locker and auto were tested and found to be free of contamination.

On November 7, 1974, when she reported to work Silkwood went directly to the plant's health physics office. She was found to be contaminated in her nostrils and on her hands, arms, chest, back, neck and right ear. Four urine and one fecal sample collected on November 5th, 6th and 7th were found to be contaminated, although the exterior of the kits showed no contamination. The parties stipulated that urine samples brought to the plant had been spiked with plutonium; that is, they contained insoluble, not naturally excreted, plutonium. Also, Silkwood's apartment was found to have been contaminated, with highest concentrations of plutonium found in the bathroom and on a package of bologna and cheese in the refrigerator.

Silkwood's roommate, Sherri Ellis, was also a laboratory analyst at Kerr-McGee, and was found not to be contaminated when she left work at 8:00 a.m. on November 7th after working a midnight shift. After returning to the apartment, Ellis used the bathroom and retired to her bedroom. Subsequent checks revealed contamination of Ellis' buttocks and hands. Ellis' auto and the refrigerator where her lunch had been placed in the plant lunchroom were free of contamination. Silkwood's boyfriend, who spent the night of November 6th in Silkwood's apartment, had left the apartment at about 7:00 a.m. on November 7th after using the bathroom. Neither he, his car, nor his residence were contaminated.

Silkwood's possessions were destroyed and Silkwood was sent to the Los Alamos Scientific Laboratory in New Mexico to undergo further tests concerning her contamination. She reported back to work on November 13th at which time she was reassigned. She participated in a union negotiating session that day, met with AEC inspectors concerning her contamination, and attended a union strategy session. On her way to meet a New York Times reporter and an OCAW leader, Silkwood was killed in an automobile accident. A subsequent autopsy revealed that the amount of plutonium within Silkwood's body at the time of her death was between 25% and 50% of the permissible lifetime body burden allowed by the AEC for plutonium workers.

Silkwood made statements that she had spilled her urine sample in her bathroom between 7:00 and 7:50 a.m. on November 7th, after her boyfriend left and before her roommate returned to the apartment from work. Silkwood stated that at the time she spilled the urine sample, a package of bologna was on top of the commode, where she had placed it in anticipation of preparing a sandwich to take to work. Following the spilling of the sample, Silkwood stated that she wiped off the bathroom floor with a tissue and placed the bologna back in the refrigerator. That evidence was admitted only to show Silkwood's state of mind, motivation, or intention relevant to the issue whether she intentionally removed the plutonium from the plant; it was not admitted to show the truth of the statements.

The only other evidence supporting inferences relevant to where and how Silkwood was contaminated is as follows. Except for the fact that Silkwood was in a radiation zone for an hour on November 6 before discovering contamination on her person, and Silkwood's statement that she thought she was inadequately decontaminated on November 5, there is no evidence of where, when or how she became contaminated on November 6th. She did not work the glove boxes that day and no other contamination was observed. Apparently employees were not monitored for radiation upon arriving at work, although they were subject to self and other monitoring each time they removed their hands from glove boxes and when exiting rooms and air locks. Evidence showed Silkwood was sloppy in her safety habits, failing to monitor herself or tuck her hair into the cap she was required to wear in the laboratory.

The insoluble plutonium used to spike the urine samples was not of the same batch Silkwood was working with in the glove boxes at the time of her exposures. The material could have come, however, from a slot box in the laboratory area to which Silkwood and other Kerr-McGee employees had access. The Kerr-McGee inspection system would not detect amounts of plutonium of less than about 1/2 gram taken from the plant in a nonmetallic container. (The amount in Silkwood's apartment was estimated at less than .0003 gram.)

There was evidence that Kerr-McGee's supervisory employees knew Silkwood was attempting to gather evidence of Kerr-McGee's negligent and improper practices in the operation of the plant and that some disapproved of her and these activities. There was also evidence that Silkwood was unhappy with a reprimand she had received shortly before her November 5 contamination and that she wanted to embarrass Kerr-McGee.

... [T]he complaint asserted that all exposures originated in Silkwood's apartment.

* * *

RYLANDS v. FLETCHER
L.R. 3 H.L. 330 (1868)

THE LORD CHANCELLOR (Lord Cairns):

My Lords, in this case the Plaintiff is the occupier of a mine and works under a close of land. The Defendants are the owners of a mill in his neighbourhood, and they proposed to make a reservoir for the purpose of keeping and storing water to be used about their mill upon another close of land, which, for the purposes of this case, may be taken as being adjoining to the close of the Plaintiff although in point of fact, some intervening land lay between the two. Underneath the close of land of the Defendants on which they proposed to construct their reservoir there were certain old and disused mining passages and works. There were five vertical shafts, and some horizontal shafts communicating with them. The vertical shafts had been filled up with soil and rubbish, and it does not appear that any person was aware of the existence either of the vertical shafts or of the horizontal works communicating with them. In the course of the working by the Plaintiff of his mine, he had gradually worked through the seams of coal underneath the close, and had come into contact with the old and disused works underneath the close of the Defendants.

In that state of things the reservoir of the Defendants was constructed. It was constructed by them through the agency and inspection of an engineer and contractor. Personally, the Defendants appear to have taken no part in the works, or to have been aware of any want of security connected with them. As regards to the engineer and the contractor, we must take it from the case that they did not exercise, as far as they were concerned, that reasonable care and caution which they might have exercised, taking notice, as they appear to have taken notice, of the vertical shafts filed up in the manner which I have mentioned. However, my Lords, when the reservoir was constructed, and filled, with water, the weight of the water bearing upon the disused and imperfectly filled-up vertical shafts, broke through those shafts. The water passed down them and into the horizontal workings, and from the horizontal workings under the close of the Defendant's it passed on into the workings under the close of the Plaintiff, and flooded his mine, causing considerable damage, for which this action was brought.

. . .

My Lords, the principles on which this case must be determined appear to me to be extremely simple. The Defendants, treating them as the owners or occupiers of the close on which the reservoir was constructed, might lawfully have used that close for any purpose for which it might in the ordinary course of the enjoyment of land be used; and if, in what I may term the natural user of that land, there had been any accumulation of water, either on the surface or underground, and if, by the operation of the laws of nature, that accumulation of water had passed off into the close occupied by the Plaintiff, the Plaintiff could not have complained that that result had taken place. If he had desired to guard himself against it, it would have lain upon him to have done so, by leaving, or by interposing, some barrier between his close and the close of the Defendants in order to have prevented that operation of the laws of nature.

. . .

On the other hand if the Defendants, not stopping at the natural use of their close, had desired to use it for any purpose which I may term a non-natural use, for the purpose of introducing into the close that which in its natural condition was not in or upon it, for the purpose of introducing water either above or below ground in quantities and in a manner not the result of any work or operation on or under the land, and if in consequence of their doing so, or in consequence of any imperfection in the mode of their doing so, the water came to escape and to pass off into the close of the Plaintiff, then it appears to me that that which the Defendants were doing they were doing at their own peril; and, if in the course of their doing it, the evil arose to which I have referred, the evil, namely, of the escape of the water and its passing away to the close of the Plaintiff and injuring the Plaintiff, then for the consequence of that, in my opinion, the Defendants would be liable. . . .

The same result is arrived at on the principles referred to by Mr. Justice Blackburn in his judgment, in the Court of Exchequer Chamber, where he states the opinion of that Court as to the law in these words: "We think that the true rule of law is, that the person who, for his own purposes, brings on his land and collects and keeps there anything likely to do mischief if it escapes, must keep it in at his peril; and if he does not do so, is prima facie answerable for all the damage which is the natural consequence of its escape. He can excuse himself by shewing that the escape was owing to the Plaintiff's default; or, perhaps, that the escape was the consequence of vis major, or the act of God; but as nothing of this sort exists here, it is unnecessary to inquire what excuse would be sufficient. The General rule, as above stated, seems on principle just. The person whose grass or corn is eaten down by the escaping cattle of his neighbour, or whose mine is flooded by the water from his neighbours' reservoir, or whose cellar is invaded by the filth of his neighbour's privy, or whose habitation is made unhealthy by the fumes and noisome vapours of his neighbour's alkali works, is damnified without any fault of his own; and it seems but reasonable and just that the neighbour who has brought something on his won property (which was not naturally there), harmless to others so long as it is confined to his own property, but which he knows will be mischievous if it gets on his neighbour's, should be obligated to make good the damage which ensues if he does not succeed in confining it to his own property. But for his act in bringing it there no mischief could have accrued, and it seems but just that he should at his peril keep it there, so that no mischief may accrue, or answer for the natural and anticipated consequence. And upon authority this we think is established to be the law, whether the things so brought be beasts, or water, or filth, or stenches."

. . .

LORD CRANWORTH:

My Lords, I concur with my noble and learned friend in thinking that the rule of law was correctly stated by Mr. Justice Blackburn in delivering the opinion of the Exchequer Chamber. If a person brings, or accumulates, on his land anything which, if it should escape, may cause damage to his neighbour, he does so at his peril. If it does escape, and cause damage, he is responsible, however careful he may have been, and whatever precautions he may have taken to prevent the damage.

. . .

. . . The Plaintiff had a right to work his coal through the lands of Mr. Whitehead, and up to the old workings. If water naturally rising in the Defendants' land (we may treat the land as the land of the Defendants for the purpose of this case) had by percolation found its way down to the Plaintiff's mine through the old workings, and so had impeded his operations, that would not have afforded him any ground of complaint. Even if all the old workings had been made by the Plaintiff, he would have done no more than he was entitled to do; for, according to the principle acted on in *Smith v. Kenrick*, the person working the mine, under the close in which the reservoir was made, had a right to win and carry away all the coal without leaving any wall or barrier against Whitehead's land. But that is not the real state of the case. The Defendants, in order to effect an object of their own, brought on to their land, or on the land which for this purpose may be treated as being theirs, a large accumulated mass of water, and stored it up in a reservoir. The consequence of this was damage to the Plaintiff, and for that damage, however skilfully and carefully accumulation was made, the Defendants, according to the principles and authorities to which I have adverted, were certainly responsible.

...

INDIANA HARBOR BELT RAILROAD COMPANY v. AMERICAN CYANAMID COMPANY

United States Court of Appeals, Seventh Circuit
916 F.2d 1174 (1990)

POSNER, Circuit Judge.

American Cyanamid Company, the defendant in this diversity tort suit governed by Illinois law, is a major manufacturer of chemicals, including acrylonitrile, a chemical used in large quantities in making acrylic fibers, plastics, dyes, pharmaceutical chemicals, and other intermediate and final goods. On January 2, 1979, at its manufacturing plant in Louisiana, Cyanamid loaded 20,000 gallons of liquid acrylonitrile into a railroad tank car that it had leased from the North American Car Corporation. The next day, a train of the Missouri Pacific Railroad picked up the car at Cyanamid's siding. The car's ultimate destination was a Cyanamid plant in New Jersey served by Conrail rather than by Missouri Pacific. The Missouri Pacific train carried the car north to the Blue Island railroad yard of Indiana Harbor Belt Railroad, the plaintiff in this case, a small switching line that has a contract with Conrail to switch cars from other lines to Conrail, in this case for travel east. The Blue Island yard is in the Village of Riverdale, which is just south of Chicago and part of the Chicago metropolitan area.

The car arrived in the Blue Island yard on the morning of January 9, 1979. Several hours after it arrived, employees of the switching line noticed fluid gushing from the bottom outlet of the car. The lid on the outlet was broken. After two hours, the line's supervisor of equipment was able to stop the leak by closing a shut-off valve controlled from the top of the car. No one was sure at the time just how much of the contents of the car had leaked, but it was feared that all 20,000 gallons had, and since acrylonitrile is flammable at a temperature of 30 degrees Fahrenheit or above, highly toxic, and possibly carcinogenic (Acrylonitrile, 9 International Toxicity Update, no. 3, May–June 1989, at 2, 4), the local authorities ordered the homes near the yard evacuated. The evacuation lasted only a few hours, until the car was moved to a remote part of the yard and it was discovered that only about a quarter of the acrylonitrile had leaked. Concerned nevertheless that there had been some contamination of soil and water, the Illinois Department of Environmental Protection ordered the switching line to take decontamination measures that cost the line $981,022.75, which it sought to recover by this suit.

One count of the two-count complaint charges Cyanamid with having maintained the leased tank car negligently. The other count asserts that the transportation of acrylonitrile in bulk through the Chicago metropolitan area is an abnormally dangerous activity, for the consequences of which the shipper (Cyanamid) is strictly liable to the switching line, which bore the financial brunt of those consequences because of the decontamination measures that it was forced to take. After the district judge denied Cyanamid's motion to dismiss the strict liability count, 517 F.Supp. 314 (N.D.Ill.1981), the switching line moved for summary judgment on that count—and won. 662 F.Supp. 635 (N.D.Ill.1987). The judge directed the entry of judgment for $981,022.75 under Fed.R.Civ.P. 54(b).... [Cyanamid appealed the judgment against it on strict liability.] ... The switching line has cross-appealed, challenging the dismissal of the negligence count.

The question whether the shipper of a hazardous chemical by rail should be strictly liable for the consequences of a spill or other accident to the shipment en route is a novel one in Illinois....

The parties agree that the question whether placing acrylonitrile in a rail shipment that will pass through a metropolitan area subjects the shipper to strict liability is, as recommended in Restatement (Second) of Torts § 520, comment l (1977), a question of law, so that we owe no particular deference to the conclusion of the district court. They also agree ... that the Supreme Court of Illinois would treat as authoritative the provisions of the Restatement governing abnormally dangerous activities. The key provision is section 520, which sets forth six factors to be considered in deciding whether an activity is abnormally dangerous and the actor therefore strictly liable.

The roots of section 520 are in nineteenth-century cases. The most famous one is Rylands v. Fletcher, 1 Ex. 265, aff'd, L.R. 3 H.L. 300 (1868), but a more illuminating one in the present context is Guille v. Swan, 19 Johns. (N.Y.) 381 (1822). A man took off in a hot-air balloon and landed, without intending to, in a vegetable garden in New York City. A crowd that had been anxiously watching his involuntary descent trampled the vegetables in their endeavor to rescue him when he landed. The owner of the garden sued the balloonist for the resulting damage, and won. Yet the balloonist had not been careless. In the then state of ballooning it was impossible to make a pinpoint landing.

Guille is a paradigmatic case for strict liability. (a) The risk (probability) of harm was great, and (b) the harm that would ensue if the risk materialized could be, although luckily was not, great (the balloonist could have crashed into the crowd rather than into the vegetables). The confluence of these two factors established the urgency of seeking to prevent such accidents. (c) Yet such accidents could not be prevented by the exercise of due care; the technology of care in ballooning was insufficiently developed. (d) The activity was not a matter of common usage, so there was no presumption that it was a highly valuable activity despite its unavoidable riskiness. (e) The activity was inappropriate to the place in which it took place—densely populated New York City. The risk of serious harm to others (other than the balloonist himself, that is) could have been reduced by shifting the activity to the sparsely inhabited areas that surrounded the city in those days. (f) Reinforcing (d), the value to the community of the activity of recreational ballooning did not appear to be great enough to offset its unavoidable risks.

These are, of course, the six factors in section 520. They are related to each other in that each is a different facet of a common quest for a proper legal regime to govern accidents that negligence liability cannot adequately control. The interrelations might be more perspicuous if the six factors were reordered. One might for example start with (c), inability to eliminate the risk of accident by the exercise of due care.... The baseline common law regime of tort liability is negligence. When it is a workable regime, because the hazards of an activity can be avoided by being careful (which is to say, nonnegligent), there is no need to switch to strict liability. Sometimes, however, a particular type of accident cannot be prevented by taking care but can be avoided, or its consequences minimized, by shifting the activity in which the accident occurs to another locale, where the risk or harm of an accident will be less ((e)), or by reducing the scale of the activity in order to minimize the number of accidents caused by it ((f)).... By making the actor strictly liable—by denying him in other words an excuse based on his inability to avoid accidents by being more careful—we give him an incentive, missing in a negligence regime, to experiment with methods of preventing accidents that involve not greater exertions of care, assumed to be futile, but instead relocating, changing, or reducing (perhaps to the vanishing point) the activity giving rise to the accident.... The greater the risk of an accident ((a)) and the costs of an accident if one occurs ((b)), the more we want the actor to consider the possibility of making accident-reducing activity changes; the stronger, therefore, is the case for strict liability. Finally, if an activity is extremely common ((d)), like driving an automobile, it is unlikely either that its hazards are perceived as great or that there is no technology of care available to minimize them; so the case for strict liability is weakened.

The largest class of cases in which strict liability has been imposed under the standard codified in the Second Restatement of Torts involves the use of dynamite and other explosives for demolition in residential or urban areas....

... Acrylonitrile is one of a large number of chemicals that are hazardous in the sense of being flammable, toxic, or both; acrylonitrile is both, as are many others. A table in the record ... contains a list of the 125 hazardous materials that are shipped in highest volume on the nation's railroads. Acrylonitrile is the fifty-third most hazardous on the list. Number 1 is phosphorus (white or yellow), and among the other materials that rank higher than acrylonitrile on the hazard scale are anhydrous ammonia, liquified petroleum gas, vinyl chloride, gasoline, crude petroleum, motor fuel antiknock compound, methyl and ethyl chloride, sulphuric acid, sodium metal, and chloroform. The plaintiff's lawyer acknowledged at argument that the logic of the district court's opinion dictated strict liability for all 52 materials that rank higher than acrylonitrile on the list, and quite possibly for the 72 that rank lower as well, since all are hazardous if spilled in quantity while being shipped by rail. Every shipper of any of these materials would therefore be strictly liable for the consequences of a spill or other accident that occurred while the material was being shipped through a metropolitan area. The plaintiff's lawyer further acknowledged the irrelevance, on her view of the case, of the fact that Cyanamid had leased and filled the car that spilled the acrylonitrile; all she thought important is that Cyanamid introduced the product into the stream of commerce that happened to pass through the Chicago metropolitan area. Her concession may have been incautious. One might want to distinguish between the shipper who merely places his goods on his loading dock to be picked up by the carrier and the shipper who, as in this case, participates actively in the transportation. But the concession is illustrative of the potential scope of the district court's decision.

No cases recognize so sweeping a liability....

Siegler v. Kuhlman, 81 Wash.2d 448, 502 P.2d 1181 (1972) ... imposed strict liability on a transporter of hazardous materials, but the circumstances were ... rather special. A gasoline truck blew up, obliterating the plaintiff's decedent and her car. The court emphasized that the explosion had destroyed the evidence necessary to establish whether the accident had been due to negligence; so, unless liability was strict, there would be no liability—and this as the very consequence of the defendant's hazardous activity.... But when the Supreme Court of Washington came to decide the New Meadows case, [New Meadows Holding Co. v. Washington Power Co., 102 Wash. 2d 495, 687 P.2d 212 (1984)], it did not distinguish Siegler on this ground, perhaps realizing that the plaintiff in Siegler could have overcome the destruction of the evidence by basing a negligence claim on the doctrine of res ipsa loquitur. Instead it stressed that the transmission of natural gas through underground pipes, the activity in New Meadows, is less dangerous than the transportation of gasoline by highway, where the risk of an accident is omnipresent. 102 Wash.2d at 502–03, 687 P.2d at 216–17. We shall see that a further distinction of great importance between the present case and Siegler is that the defendant there was the transporter, and here it is the shipper.

...

... [W]e can get little help from precedent, and might as well apply section 520 to the acrylonitrile problem from the ground up. To begin with, we have been given no reason, whether the reason in Siegler or any other, for believing that a negligence regime is not perfectly adequate to remedy and deter, at reasonable cost, the accidental spillage of acrylonitrile from rail cars.... Acrylonitrile could explode and destroy evidence, but of course did not here, making imposition of strict liability on the theory of the Siegler decision premature. More important, although acrylonitrile is flammable even at relatively low temperatures, and toxic, it is not so corrosive or otherwise destructive that it will eat through or otherwise damage or weaken a tank car's valves although they are maintained with due (which essentially means, with average) care. No one suggests, therefore, that the leak in this case was caused by the inherent properties of acrylonitrile. It was caused by carelessness—whether that of the North American Car Corporation in failing to maintain or inspect the car properly, or that of Cyanamid in failing to maintain or inspect it, or that of the Missouri Pacific when it had custody of the car, or that of the switching line itself in failing to notice the ruptured lid, or some combination of these possible failures of care. Accidents that are due to a lack of care can be prevented by taking care; and when a lack of care can (unlike Siegler) be shown in court, such accidents are adequately deterred by the threat of liability for negligence.

It is true that the district court purported to find as a fact that there is an inevitable risk of derailment or other calamity in transporting "large quantities of anything." 662 F.Supp. at 642. This is not a finding of fact, but a truism: anything can happen. The question is, how likely is this type of accident if the actor uses due care? For all that appears from the record of the case or any other sources of information that we have found, if a tank car is carefully maintained the danger of a spill of acrylonitrile is negligible. If this is right, there is no compelling reason to move to a regime of strict liability, especially one that might embrace all other hazardous materials shipped by rail as well. This also means, however, that the amici curiae who have filed briefs in support of Cyanamid cry wolf in predicting "devastating" effects on the chemical industry if the district court's decision is affirmed. If the vast majority of chemical spills by railroads are preventable by due care, the imposition of strict liability should cause only a slight, not as they argue a substantial, rise in liability insurance rates, because the incremental liability should be slight. The amici have momentarily lost sight of the fact that the feasibility of avoiding accidents simply by being careful is an argument against strict liability.

This discussion helps to show why Siegler is indeed distinguishable even as interpreted in New Meadows. There are so many highway hazards that the transportation of gasoline by truck is, or at least might plausibly be thought, inherently dangerous in the sense that a serious danger of accident would remain even if the truckdriver used all due care.... Which in turn means, contrary to our earlier suggestion, that the plaintiff really might have difficulty invoking res ipsa loquitur, because a gasoline truck might well blow up without negligence on the part of the driver. The plaintiff in this case has not shown that the danger of a comparable disaster to a tank car filled with acrylonitrile is as great and might have similar consequences for proof of negligence. And to repeat a previous point, if the reason for strict liability is fear that an accident might destroy the critical evidence of negligence we should wait to impose such liability until such a case appears.

The district judge and the plaintiff's lawyer make much of the fact that the spill occurred in a densely inhabited metropolitan area. Only 4,000 gallons spilled; what if all 20,000 had done so? Isn't the risk that this might happen even if everybody were careful sufficient to warrant giving the shipper an incentive to explore alternative routes? Strict liability would supply that incentive. But this argument overlooks the fact that, like other transportation networks, the railroad network is a hub-and-spoke system. And the hubs are in metropolitan areas. Chicago is one of the nation's largest railroad hubs. In 1983, the latest year for which we have figures, Chicago's railroad yards handled the third highest volume of hazardous-material shipments in the nation. East St. Louis, which is also in Illinois, handled the second highest volume. Office of Technology Assessment, Transportation of Hazardous Materials 53 (1986). With most hazardous chemicals (by volume of shipments) being at least as hazardous as acrylonitrile, it is unlikely—and certainly not demonstrated by the plaintiff—that they can be rerouted around all the metropolitan areas in the country, except at prohibitive cost. Even if it were feasible to reroute them one would hardly expect shippers, as distinct from carriers, to be the firms best situated to do the rerouting. Granted, the usual view is that common carriers are not subject to strict liability for the carriage of materials that make the transportation of them abnormally dangerous, because a common carrier cannot refuse service to a shipper of a lawful commodity. Restatement, supra, §521. Two courts, however, have rejected the common carrier exception. National Steel Service Center, Inc. v. Gibbons, 319 N.W.2d 269 (Ia.1982); Chavez v. Southern Pacific Transportation Co., 413 F.Supp. 1203, 1213–14 (E.D.Cal.1976). If it were rejected in Illinois, this would weaken still further the case for imposing strict liability on shippers whose goods pass through the densely inhabited portions of the state.

The difference between shipper and carrier points to a deep flaw in the plaintiff's case. Unlike Guille, and unlike Siegler, and unlike the storage cases, beginning with Rylands itself, here it is not the actors—that is, the transporters of acrylonitrile and other chemicals—but the manufacturers, who are sought to be held strictly liable.... A shipper can in the bill of lading designate the route of his shipment if he likes, 49 U.S.C. §11710(a)(1), but is it realistic to suppose that shippers will become students of railroading in order to lay out the safest route by which to ship their goods? Anyway, rerouting is no panacea. Often it will increase the length of the journey, or compel the use of poorer track, or both. When this happens, the probability of an accident is increased, even if the consequences of an accident if one occurs are reduced; so the expected accident cost, being the product of the probability of an accident and the harm if the accident occurs, may rise.... It is easy to see how the accident in this case might have been prevented at reasonable cost by greater care on the part of those who handled the tank car of acrylonitrile. It is difficult to see how it might have been prevented at reasonable cost by a change in the activity of transporting the chemical. This is therefore not an apt case for strict liability.

We said earlier that Cyanamid, because of the role it played in the transportation of the acrylonitrile—leasing, and especially loading, and also it appears undertaking by contract with North American Car Corporation to maintain, the tank car in which the railroad carried Cyanamid's acrylonitrile to Riverdale—might be viewed as a special type of shipper (call it a "shipper-transporter"), rather than as a passive shipper. But neither the district judge nor the plaintiff's counsel has attempted to distinguish Cyanamid from an ordinary manufacturer of chemicals on this ground, and we consider it waived. Which is not to say that had it not been waived it would have changed the outcome of the case. The very fact that Cyanamid participated actively in the transportation of the acrylonitrile imposed upon it a duty of due care and by doing so brought into play a threat of negligence liability that, for all we know, may provide an adequate regime of accident control in the transportation of this particular chemical.

In emphasizing the flammability and toxicity of acrylonitrile rather than the hazards of transporting it, as in failing to distinguish between the active and the passive shipper, the plaintiff overlooks the fact that ultrahazardousness or abnormal dangerousness is, in the contemplation of the law at least, a property not of substances, but of activities: not of acrylonitrile, but of the transportation of acrylonitrile by rail through populated areas.... Natural gas is both flammable and poisonous, but the operation of a natural gas well is not an ultrahazardous activity.... Whatever the situation under products liability law (section 402A of the Restatement), the manufacturer of a product is not considered to be engaged in an abnormally dangerous activity merely because the product becomes dangerous when it is handled or used in some way after it leaves his premises, even if the danger is foreseeable.... The plaintiff does not suggest that Cyanamid should switch to making some less hazardous chemical that would substitute for acrylonitrile in the textiles and other goods in which acrylonitrile is used. Were this a feasible method of accident avoidance, there would be an argument for making manufacturers strictly liable for accidents that occur during the shipment of their products (how strong an argument we need not decide). Apparently it is not a feasible method.

The relevant activity is transportation, not manufacturing and shipping. This essential distinction the plaintiff ignores. But even if the plaintiff is treated as a transporter and not merely a shipper, it has not shown that the transportation of acrylonitrile in bulk by rail through populated areas is so hazardous an activity, even when due care is exercised, that the law should seek to create—perhaps quixotically—incentives to relocate the activity to nonpopulated areas, or to reduce the scale of the activity, or to switch to transporting acrylonitrile by road rather than by rail, perhaps to set the stage for a replay of Siegler v. Kuhlman. It is no more realistic to propose to reroute the shipment of all hazardous materials around Chicago than it is to propose the relocation of homes adjacent to the Blue Island switching yard to more distant suburbs. It may be less realistic. Brutal though it may seem to say it, the inappropriate use to which land is being put in the Blue Island yard and neighborhood may be, not the transportation of hazardous chemicals, but residential living. The analogy is to building your home between the runways at O'Hare.

The briefs hew closely to the Restatement, whose approach to the issue of strict liability is mainly allocative rather than distributive. By this we mean that the emphasis is on picking a liability regime (negligence or strict liability) that will control the particular class of accidents in question most effectively, rather than on finding the deepest pocket and placing liability there. At argument, however, the plaintiff's lawyer invoked distributive considerations by pointing out that Cyanamid is a huge firm and the Indiana Harbor Belt Railroad a fifty-mile-long switching line that almost went broke in the winter of 1979, when the accident occurred. Well, so what? A corporation is not a living person but a set of contracts the terms of which determine who will bear the brunt of liability. Tracing the incidence of a cost is a complex undertaking which the plaintiff sensibly has made no effort to assume, since its legal relevance would be dubious. We add only that however small the plaintiff may be, it has mighty parents: it is a jointly owned subsidiary of Conrail and the Soo line.

The case for strict liability has not been made. Not in this suit in any event. We need not speculate on the possibility of imposing strict liability on shippers of more hazardous materials, such as the bombs carried in Chavez v. Southern Pacific Transportation Co., supra, any more than we need differentiate (given how the plaintiff has shaped its case) between active and passive shippers. We noted earlier that acrylonitrile is far from being the most hazardous among hazardous materials shipped by rail in highest volume. Or among materials shipped, period. The Department of Transportation has classified transported materials into sixteen separate classes by the degree to which transporting them is hazardous. Class number 1 is radioactive material. Class number 2 is poisons. Class 3 is flammable gas and 4 is nonflammable gas. Acrylonitrile is in Class 5....

...

The judgment is reversed (with no award of costs in this court) and the case remanded for further proceedings, consistent with this opinion, on the plaintiff's claim for negligence.

...

George C. Christie, *An Essay on Discretion*
1986 Duke L.J. 747, 767–770*

This statement of the test [of Restatement (Second) § 520] leaves two overriding questions: Who is to make the determination of what is an abnormally dangerous activity, and how is the required factor analysis and interest balancing to be done? As to the first question, the commentary to the Second Restatement declares that the judge, not the jury, is to decide whether an activity is abnormally dangerous. Although the commentary concedes that in a negligence case a jury might have to make a host of subject determinations in deciding the reasonableness of an activity, it concludes that the decision whether an activity is abnormally dangerous is of a different type. The principal difference asserted is that, unlike a jury's decision in a negligence case, the classification of an activity as abnormally dangerous could destroy an entire industry. But of course a ruling that a product, say an airliner, is negligently designed could also destroy an industrial enterprise. Moreover, it seems to be generally accepted that, in actions brought on a theory of strict liability for defective products, the issue of product defect is submitted to the jury. Why should strict liability under an abnormally dangerous activity theory be treated differently than strict liability for a defective product?

The second question raised by section 520 of the Second Restatement, and the one that most immediately concerns this discussion, is how the court should weight the six factors that are to guide the determination whether an activity is abnormally dangerous. The commentary declares that the determination is to be made by the court, "upon consideration of all the factors listed in this Section, and weight given to each that it merits upon the facts in evidence."[97]

I submit that this is no weighting method at all. If taken literally, the commentary seems to suggest that each case is sui generis and that one need have no fear that an individual decision, whether made by a judge or by a jury, might ruin an entire industry. Thus, in any case involving an activity not covered four-square by a precedent, one would have to litigate up to the highest court of the jurisdiction before knowing how the activity would be classified. The value of precedents covering other activities would be minimal. Whether or not one liked the old test, it was certainly easier to administer, since it asked only whether the activity involved "a risk of serious harm" to others that

---

97. Restatement (Second) of Torts § 520 comment 1 (1977).

"[could not] be eliminated by the exercise of the utmost care," and whether the activity was "a matter of common usage."[98]

Some may object that the Second Restatement merely made explicit the factors courts already considered. This is not so. Of course, in any close case, a court is likely to consider individual equities like the comparative wealth of the parties and the social importance of the activity, and these factors will likely influence the decision. A court should never be expected to ignore individual equities. But to recognize that a court will be *influenced* by individual equities in deciding some legal issue is not the same as saying that these individual features themselves *are* the legal issue.

An enormous range of legal decisions could all be plausibly justified under section 520 of the Second Restatement. For example, it was held in Maryland that operating a neighborhood gas station, whose leaking storage tanks fouled the well of an adjoining landowner, was an abnormally dangerous activity.[99] An Oregon court disagreed.[100] In a Florida court, a mine operator seriously urged, again on the basis of the new version of section 520, that a mine producing phosphatic wastes was not an abnormally dangerous activity because of the location of the mine and its social importance.[101] But the court ruled against the mine operator because of the size of the activity and the possibility of enormous damage if the activity miscarried.

Section 520 of the Second Restatement is not an isolated instance of the urge to inject factor analysis into judicial decisionmaking. For example, under the original Restatement, an intentional invasion of another's interest in the use and enjoyment of land was unreasonable (and hence a nuisance) "unless the utility of the actor's conduct outweigh[ed] the gravity of the harm."[103] The Second Restatement has now added a provision declaring that the invasion may also be unreasonable if "the harm caused by the conduct is serious and the financial burden of compensating for this and similar harm to others would not make the continuation of the conduct not feasible."[104] Admittedly, under the original Restatement, which tracked the traditional common law, courts were obliged to make the potentially open-ended decision about the utility of the defendant's conduct. Courts must still make that determination under the Second Restatement, but now, even if courts decide that the utility outweighs the harm, they must make the additional problematic decision as to whether it was nevertheless "feasible" for the defendant to compensate the plaintiff.

---

98. RESTATEMENT OF TORTS § 520 (1938).

99. *See Yommer v. McKenzie*, 255 Md. 220, 222–27, 257 A.2d 138, 139–41 (1969). The court specifically held that section 520 of the SECOND RESTATEMENT (considered in draft form) had the effect of enlarging the circumstances under which the rule of strict liability will apply. *Id.* at 223–25, 257 A.2d at 139–40.

100. See *Hudson v. Peavey Oil Co.*, 279 Or. 3, 8, 566 P.2d 175, 178 (1977). The court held that the operation of a gas station was not so exceptional a circumstance nor was the danger from seepage so grave as to warrant classifying the activity as "abnormally dangerous." *Id.*

101. See *Cities Serv. Co. v. State*, 312 So.2d 799, 801–03 (Fla. Dist. Ct. App. 1975).

103. RESTATEMENT OF TORTS § 826 (1939).

104. RESTATEMENT (SECOND) OF TORTS § 826(b) (1977). The substance of the original section 826 is now contained in RESTATEMENT (SECOND) OF TORTS § 826(a). The Second Restatement has added a new section, section 829A, to flesh out section 826. Section 829A provides that "[a]n intentional invasion of another's interest in the use and enjoyment of land is unreasonable if the harm resulting from the invasion is severe and greater than the other should be required to bear without compensation."

George P. Fletcher, *Fairness and Utility in Tort Theory*
85 Harv. L. Rev. 537, 541–42, 550–51 (1972)*

[In this article, Fletcher counterposes two "paradigms of liability." One is the "paradigm of reasonableness," under which the question of whether a risk is unreasonable is "determined by a straightforward balancing of costs and benefits." The other is the "paradigm of reciprocity," for which he argues in these terms:]

... I shall propose a specific standard of risk that makes sense of the Restatement's emphasis on uncommon, extra-hazardous risks, but which shows that the Restatement's theory is part of a larger rationale of liability that cuts across negligence, intentional torts, and numerous pockets of strict liability. The general principle expressed in all of these situations governed by diverse doctrinal standards is that a victim has a right to recover for injuries caused by a risk greater in degree and different in order from those created by the victim and imposed on the defendant—in short, for injuries resulting from nonreciprocal risks. Cases of liability are those in which the defendant generates a disproportionate, excessive risk of harm, relative to the victim's risk-creating activity. For example, a pilot or an airplane owner subjects those beneath the path of flight to nonreciprocal risks of harm. Conversely cases of nonliability are those of reciprocal risks, namely those in which the victim and the defendant subject each other to roughly the same degree of risk. For example, two airplanes flying in the same vicinity subject each other to reciprocal risks of a mid-air collision. Of course, there are significant problems in determining when risks are nonreciprocal, and we shall turn to these difficulties later. For now, it is sufficient to note that the paradigm of reciprocity represents (1) a bifurcation of the questions of who is entitled to compensation and who ought to pay, (2) a commitment to resolving both of those issues by looking only to the activity of the victim and the risk-creator, and (3) a specific criterion for determining who is entitled to recover for loss, namely all those injured by nonreciprocal risks.

[Fletcher presents applications of his paradigm of reciprocity to several areas of tort doctrine. They include cases like *Rylands*, as well as *Vincent v. Lake Erie Transportation Co.*, reprinted *infra* in these materials in Chapter 8. He also refers to a "negligent risk, an 'unreasonable' risk," as "but one that unduly exceeds the bounds of reciprocity," and he deals with assault and battery on the basis that "the nonreciprocity of risk, and the deprivation of security it represents render irrelevant the attitudes of the risk creator."]

All of these manifestations of the paradigm of reciprocity—strict liability, negligence and intentional battery—express the same principle of fairness: All individuals in society have the right to roughly the same degree of security from risk. By analogy to John Rawls' first principle of justice,[50] the principle might read: We all have the right to the maximum amount of security compatible with a like security for everyone else. This means that we are subject to harm, without compensation, from background risks, but that no one may suffer harm from additional risks without recourse for damages against the risk-creator. Compensation is a surrogate for the individual's

---

* Reprinted by permission of the Harvard Law Review Association and William S. Hein Company from *The Harvard Law Review*, Vol. 85, pages 537–551.

50. Rawls, *Justice as Fairness*, 67 Philosophical Rev. 164, 165 (1958) ("[E]ach person participating in a practice, or affected by it, has an equal right to the most extensive liberty compatible with a like liberty for all."). The ideas expressed in *Justice as Fairness* are elaborated in J. Rawls, A Theory of Justice (1971).

right to the same security as enjoyed by others. But the violation of the right to equal security does not mean that one should be able to enjoin the risk-creating activity or impose criminal penalties against the risk-creator. The interests of society may often require a disproportionate distribution of risk. Yet, according to the paradigm of reciprocity, the interests of the individual require us to grant compensation whenever this disproportionate distribution of risk injures someone subject to more than his fair share of risk.

————————

Gerry Spence,[*] *How to Make a Complex Case Come Alive for a Jury*
72 A.B.A. J. 62, 65–66 (1986)[**]

The case could consume months of trial, but it also could be a story. Let me tell you the story.

Once upon a time there was a courageous young woman who discovered that her fellow workers were being contaminated with a terrible poison, an insidious substance called plutonium, that, when even the tiniest amounts were breathed into the lungs, could cause one of the most dreaded and deadly diseases of all—lung cancer. They were ordinary folks, trusting folks—red-faced farm boys and housewives, people who worked hard and tried to get ahead and who took their children to church, and who wanted to be good citizens and to live decent and honest lives.

But some of this young woman's fellow workers were already dying and others soon would be stricken and, worse, they didn't know it. They went home at night and watched television and played with their children. But this young woman knew, and she decided to tell her fellow workers the truth. Then something happened to her.

Ants and lions

If you were seated on the jury perhaps you would hear more. Perhaps I would tell you a story about how truly evil the poison was this young woman had discovered.

It put me in mind of a government scientist I once knew who was trying to rid Wyoming of the harvester ant, those indefatigable creatures whose ant hills took up thousands of acres of range and who ate away at the prairie grasses the ranchers wished to save for their cattle.

First this scientist fixed up a delectable but poisonous ant food, which some of the ants immediately ate. But as soon as they began to die the other ants spurned it. Then the scientist invented a lethal substance that, when walked upon by the ants, was absorbed into their bodies through their feet. He put the vile stuff around the entire ant hill, but the ants soon discovered what was causing their fellows to die and so they built bridges over the poison.

Finally, in desperation, the scientist invented a hideous formula. It was a food the ants ate. After they ate it they seemed healthy enough and they went on with their lives—they went home at night, and tended their offspring, and they did all of the other things that good ants do. Then one terrible day after all of the ants had eaten the

————————

[*] Gerry Spence, a Wyoming trial lawyer, represented the plaintiffs in the *Silkwood* litigation.
[**] Reprinted by permission of Gerry Spence.

poison they began to die, but by then, children, it was too late—much too late, and the whole ant village was annihilated, one hapless, pitiful, dying ant at a time.

If you were in the jury box you also could hear about the law pertaining to inherently dangerous substances, but perhaps if you were a juror you would rather hear a story about a man who had captured a vicious lion, and who brought it to his own private property and there, very carefully, he put it in a cage. To make sure the lion didn't get away he put another cage around the cage, and he locked all the doors, and then to make sure that the locks held he put on more locks, and locks on the locks.

But one night while the lion's owner was sleeping the lion escaped—no one knows just how—and he went charging through the village injuring and killing innocent people. When the townspeople came to the owner and demanded their damages he said, "Can't you see—it was not my fault the lion escaped. See here! See the cage! It was very secure. See the locks! They were very strong. I am not to be blamed!"

"And so, ladies and gentlemen of the jury"—and one could, of course, walk to the blackboard and write down the law of the case—"'if the lion gets away, the defendant here must pay.' And so, that is the law of the case, and that, my children, would also be justice, would it not?"

———————

NOTES

(1) What is the principal difference between the rule of liability announced in *Rylands* and the conventional "negligence" standard?

(2) Does *Rylands* provide an efficient solution? How would the allocation of resources between extraction and agriculture have been affected if the *Rylands* court had gone the other way?

(3) Whatever the allocational consequences of decisions either way in *Rylands*, should the principal concern in such a case be with weighing economic costs and benefits? Or does the mode of analysis represented by Fletcher's "paradigm of reciprocity" provide a more compelling basis for the assignment of liability?

(4) Do you think that the factors identified in *Restatement (Second)* section 520, as summarized in *the Indiana Harbor Belt* case, supra, adequately capture the reasons for imposing strict liability for activities?

(5) A draft of the *Restatement (Third)* eliminates the six-factor analysis in section 520 of the *Second Restatement*, summarized by Judge Posner in *Indiana Harbor Belt*, supra, in favor of the following compressed definition of an "abnormally dangerous activity" as one that

> (1) ... creates a foreseeable and highly significant risk of physical harm even when reasonable care is exercised by all actors; and

> (2) the activity is not one of common usage.

Restatement (Third) of Torts: Liability for Physical Harm §20 (Proposed Final Draft No. 1, Apr. 6, 2005).

Do you prefer this definition or the six-factor test?

(6) Would you impose strict liability on the *railroad* for mischief done by acrylonitrile that escapes? There is a disagreement on the issue of common carrier liability for the escape of hazardous substances in *National Steel Service Center, Inc. v. Gibbons*, 319

N.W.2d 269 (Iowa 1982). This case involved a derailment of tank cars, followed by an explosion that caused "extensive damage" to the plaintiff's warehouse. In replying to the Eighth Circuit on a certified question that the theory of "strict liability for abnormally dangerous activities" applied to the case, a majority of the state court emphasized that "[t]he carrier was part of the dangerous enterprise, and the victim was not." Moreover, "[t]he carrier was in a better position to investigate and identify the cause of the accident," and was "also in a better position than the ordinary victim to evaluate and guard against the risk financially." *Id.* at 272. A dissenter relied on section 521 of the *Second Restatement*, which articulates an exception for common carriers, to the extent they are "required to carry such explosives as are offered" to them.

(7) The frightening span of the spectrum of hazardousness of toxic chemicals is evident in the reported effect of acrylonitrile, which, as Judge Posner notes in *Indiana Harbor Belt*, is ranked only fifty-third on the list of hazardousness of chemicals carried by rail. Acrylonitrile is also known as vinyl cyanide, and its "biological effects ... may be associated with cyanide." Workers who have handled the chemical "for 20 to 45 minutes have developed headache, chest fullness, mucous membrane irritation, apprehension, and irritability." There is "conflicting evidence" on the carcinogenicity of the product, with one study reporting an increase in respiratory cancer in workers exposed to acrylonitrile and a followup study that "revealed no increase in respiratory tract cancers, yet a noticeable increase in prostate cancer."[1]

(8) Is it a case for strict liability on the *Rylands* model when fire from a magician's "fire-eating" act "escapes" into the audience and injures a watcher?

(9) Should a strict liability rule be applied to injuries caused in the following situations?

(a) Dynamiting for construction

(b) Use of poison gas for fumigation

(c) Keeping of wild animals

(d) Testing of powerful rocket motors in rural areas

(e) Use by a research institute of AIDS-family viruses that escape into the surrounding community

(f) The filling of an empty cylinder with propane gas, when the cylinder is located next to a water cooler that emits a spark as it switches on to chill more water, creating an explosion in the gas

(g) Aerial spraying of pesticides to control corn pests, with fatal effects on bees in hives near the corn fields

(h) Use of a sprinkler system on a residential lawn, from which the overflow of water makes the adjoining street slippery, causing a collision (*North Little Rock Transp. Co. v. Finkbeiner*, 243 Ark. 596, 420 S.W.2d 874 (1967)) ("By no stretch of the imagination could the use of a lawn sprinkler be called 'non-natural use' of the land" under Lord Cairns' test in *Rylands*)

(i) Parking an automobile at the top of a hill on private property, when the parking brake fails and unleashes the vehicle on pedestrians traversing adjoining land below

---

1. HAMILTON & HARDY'S INDUSTRIAL TOXICOLOGY 384 (1998). The authors are grateful to Hilary Black, Northwestern Law School 2000, for calling this material to our attention.

(10) How should the determination of "abnormal dangerousness" under the *Restatement* test be allocated between judge and jury?

(11) With the advent of an era of toxic chemicals, legislatures have begun setting up regulatory schemes to control the escape of these substances. See, e.g., the New Jersey Toxic Catastrophe Prevention Act, 13 N.J. Stat. 1: K-19-32 (1991), requiring firms that make "extraordinarily hazardous substances"—defined initially by a list in the statute and afterwards by state agencies—to submit risk management plans for agency approval.

Should the existence of such a regulatory mechanism affect the application of strict tort liability to toxic chemicals?

(12) After a prolonged court battle over numerous issues, including federal preemption and punitive damages, Kerr-McGee settled with Karen Silkwood's estate for $1.38 million. This money was divided in the following way: $501,000 for Silkwood's three children, $70,000 for her father, $576,000 for attorneys' fees, and $235,000 for legal expenses. 29 ATLA L. REP. 473.

§ 7.02 Product Manufacture and Sale: The Basic Theory of Strict Products Liability

OGLE v. CATERPILLAR TRACTOR CO.

Wyoming Supreme Court
716 P.2d 334 (1986)

CARDINE, JUSTICE.

In this products liability action, the district court granted summary judgment in favor of appellee Caterpillar Tractor Company, the manufacturer, and appellee Wyoming Machinery Company, the dealer. The court held that the applicable statutes of limitation barred the claims of appellant, Timothy Ogle, for negligence and breach of warranty, and that the suit could not be sustained because the caterpillar scraper which allegedly caused the accident had been altered after it left the hands of the manufacturer and dealer.

. . .

We affirm in part and reverse in part.

On January 9, 1980, appellant was injured when he fell from the hood of a caterpillar scraper he was operating at a uranium mine in Carbon County. Appellant's employer, Utah International, had purchased the scraper in 1976 from appellee Wyoming Machinery Company. It had been manufactured by appellee Caterpillar Tractor Company.

[The plaintiff alleged defects that included a "lack of proper hand grips and toeholds" on the machine as well as a "lack of adequate non-skid surface material."—Dissenting opinion of Brown, J., 716 P.2d at 346.—Ed.]

On January 9, 1984, exactly four years after his accident, appellant brought suit in the district court against Wyoming Machinery and Caterpillar Tractor stating three claims for relief. The first claim sounded in negligence and the second in breach of warranty. The third, although it did not use the words "strict liability," was intended by appellant to allege strict liability in tort. In it, appellant states that appellees put the scraper on the market representing that "it could be safely operated while doing the job for which it was intended," even though it was "unsafe for its intended use." He also alleged that he "was injured as a direct result of the defects herein alleged."

. . .

[Omitted are discussions of two issues involving statutes of limitations. The court holds that the trial court erred in ruling the plaintiff's negligence claim barred under the statute of limitations. As to the other issue, it concludes:]

In summary, we hold that a plaintiff must bring a breach of warranty action for personal injury within four years after the warrantied goods have been tendered. Here appellant failed to commence his action for breach of warranty within that time, and the summary judgment on the second cause of action is affirmed.

STRICT LIABILITY

In its order, the district court outlined its reasons for granting summary judgment on appellant's negligence and breach of warranty claims. But the court did not state the reasons for granting summary judgment as to the strict liability claim. In their briefs, appellees have attempted to fill the gap by offering several rationales. First, they argue that strict liability in tort is not available as a cause of action in Wyoming since this court has declined to adopt the doctrine on several occasions. *See, e.g., Buckley v. Bell,* Wyo., 703 P.2d 1089 (1985). Second, they contend that appellant's third claim was merely a redundant breach of warranty claim which was filed after the warranty statute of limitations expired....

... [B]efore we can begin our analysis of the pleadings, the statute of limitations, and defenses raised, we must first determine whether the doctrine of strict liability is available to state a claim in Wyoming. We hold that it is. Today we join the overwhelming majority of American jurisdictions and hold that strict liability in tort is a valid cause of action in Wyoming. It is truly an independent cause of action that can be successfully pled and proven without regard to a manufacturer's or seller's negligence and without regard to the UCC's restrictions on breach of warranty actions.

While we recognize that some jurisdictions have departed from the parameters of the strict liability action that are set forth in § 402A, Restatement, Second, Torts, we believe that the restatement definition forms the best starting place from which the cause of action can evolve in Wyoming. The definition is reasonably complete and will allow the district courts and Wyoming lawyers to litigate these cases with some measure of confidence. In addition, many of the finer points that are not explicitly covered in § 402A or its official comments have been considered and resolved elsewhere. The district courts will enter well-charted territory on most strict liability issues that arise. We adopt Restatement, Second, Torts § 402A (1965) which provides:

402A. *Special Liability of Seller of Product for Physical Harm to User or Consumer*

(1) One who sells any product in a defective condition unreasonably dangerous to the user or consumer or to his property is subject to liability for physical harm thereby caused to the ultimate user or consumer, or to his property, if

(a) the seller is engaged in the business of selling such a product, and

(b) it is expected to and does reach the user or consumer without substantial change in the condition in which it is sold.

(2) The rule stated in Subsection (1) applies although

(a) the seller has exercised all possible care in the preparation and sale of his product, and

(b) the user or consumer has not bought the product from or entered into any contractual relation with the seller.

REASONS FOR STRICT LIABILITY

As the Vermont Supreme Court noted when it adopted strict liability in tort, "[a]n extensive review of the history and development of the doctrine embodied in the Restatement would serve little purpose." *Zaleskie v. Joyce*, 133 Vt. 150, 333 A.2d 110, 113 (1975). The history of the doctrine is well known and readily discoverable in basic torts treatises. *See, e.g.*, W. Keeton, Prosser and Keeton on Torts §§ 96–97, at 681–692 (1984). On the other hand, although the policies supporting the adoption of § 402A have been discussed elsewhere, we think it worth noting some of the policies that we find persuasive. While these policy rationales are not exclusive, they should help guide the district courts and litigants who will inevitably grapple with strict liability law.

When a defective article enters the stream of commerce and an innocent person is hurt, it is better that the loss fall on the manufacturer, distributor or seller than on the innocent victim. This is true even if the entities in the chain of production and distribution exercise due care in the defective product's manufacture and delivery. They are simply in the best position to either insure against the loss or spread the loss among all the consumers of the product. W. Prosser, The Assault upon the Citadel, 69 Yale L.J. 1099, 1120 (1960); W. Keeton, *supra*, at 692–693; Restatement, Second, Torts § 402A, comment c (1965).

There are many products liability cases in which the plaintiff must essentially show negligence in order to prove that a product is defective. And there are cases where the doctrine of res ipsa loquitur can provide the missing link to an otherwise solid negligence case. Under these circumstances, the strict liability action is unnecessary to ensure that the deserving plaintiff is made whole. There are cases, however, in which the negligence action proves inadequate. For instance, when a person is injured by a defect that causes the wheel of a car to come apart, it may be practically impossible to establish that the manufacturer's negligence caused the failure. Let us assume that 5,000,000 wheels for automobiles were manufactured and one was defective. The manufacturing, inspection, and testing procedures may have exceeded engineering standards. Due care was exercised and yet there was one defective wheel. Thus, there may have been an entire absence of negligence in the total manufacturing and sale of the product, yet a totally innocent person was injured when the defective wheel came apart. On these facts, that person justly ought to have a claim. But he can recover only if strict liability has been adopted and the fault requirement discarded. Manufacturers and distributors can easily and efficiently apportion the injured person's loss among themselves and ultimately among their customers, and that is better than affording no relief to the person injured. W. Prosser, The Assault upon the Citadel, *supra*, at 1116–1117.

The problems with the negligence cause of action when applied to products have been recognized for many years and courts and legislatures long ago responded by creating a cause of action in breach of warranty. E.g., §§ 34-21-230 through 34-21-235, W.S.1977. Whenever strict liability in tort is suggested, those opposing the doctrine argue that the warranty action is adequate in products cases. This argument has consistently failed, however, because most courts have recognized

> that strict liability on "warranty" concepts based on implied misrepresentation or promise involving an objective manifestation of an intent to guarantee carries far too much luggage in the way of undesirable complications, and is more trouble than it is worth.

W. Keeton, *supra*, at 692; *see also* Annot., 13 A.L.R.3d 1057, 1074 (1967).

Earlier in this opinion we discussed the commercial connotations of the warranty action which interfere with its usefulness to those suffering personal injury. We pointed out that the UCC's breach of warranty action carries a statute of limitations which begins to run on the date of tender and can bar an injured user from recovery before he suffers an injury. Because the statute is explicit and has some justification in a commercial setting, we declined to give it a strained interpretation that could have altered its impact in personal injury cases. We concluded that it was far better to recognize an independent strict liability action based on tort principles, which carries a tort statute of limitations, than it was to compromise the commercial code with unsound statutory construction.[9]

The notice requirement of § 34-21-270(c)(i), W.S.1977 (U.C.C. § 2-607) is another requirement which causes difficulty in warranty actions for personal injury. The statute provides:

> (c) Where a tender has been accepted:
>
> > (i) The buyer must within a reasonable time after he discovers or should have discovered any breach notify the seller of breach or be barred from any remedy.

In *Western Equipment Company, Inc. v. Sheridan Iron Works, Inc.*, Wyo., 605 P.2d 806, 810 (1980), we held that this statute means what it says in cases involving commercial damages. Perhaps we could interpret the section so that it does not apply in personal injury cases. But such a construction might diminish the effectiveness of the notice requirement in the commercial context where it serves a useful purpose. Again, the best solution to this statutory dilemma is to recognize strict liability in tort as an independent cause of action to which the statute does not apply. *See Greenman v. Yuba Power Products, Inc.*, 59 Cal.2d 57, 27 Cal.Rptr. 697, 377 P.2d 897, 13 A.L.R.3d 1049 (1962).

A third piece of excess baggage carried by the UCC warranty action is the doctrine of disclaimer of warranties. An injured person's warranty action may be barred if the seller has properly disclaimed all express and implied warranties. The drafters of the U.C.C. have attempted to solve this problem by providing in § 2-719 that "[l]imitation of consequential damages for injury to the person in the case of consumer goods is prima facie unconscionable but limitation of damages where the loss is commercial is not." Section 34-21-298(c), W.S.1977. Unfortunately, § 34-21-298(c) (U.C.C. § 2-719) is only a partial remedy because it applies only in cases of consumer goods. In the case at bar, where the scraper was not a consumer good, appellant's cause of action in warranty could have been barred by a disclaimer of warranty even though he did not personally bargain with the manufacturer and accept the disclaimer. We have explicitly held that a remote buyer cannot prevent the manufacturer from disclaiming warranties in his original contract with the original buyer. *Western Equipment Company, Inc. v. Sheridan Iron Works, Inc.*, *supra*, 605 P.2d at 810. Strict liability in tort, however, is not hampered by the disclaimer problem because it is not based on express or implied warranties created by the U.C.C.

---

9. Several states that have adopted strict liability by statute have done so by explicitly amending their commercial codes. They have essentially stripped the commercial trappings—such as the statute of limitations, the notice requirement, and privity—from the warranty cause of action in personal injury cases. "The result is to provide a remedy as comprehensive as that provided by § 402A of the Restatement...." *Swartz v. General Motors Corporation*, 375 Mass. 628, 378 N.E.2d 61, 63 (1978); *see generally* Annot., 15 A.L.R.4th 791 (1982).

In summary, the cause of action for strict liability in tort is necessary because of the inadequacies of breach of warranty actions when applied to claims in tort for personal injury.

. . .

In **POLIUS v. CLARK EQUIP. CO.**, 802 F.2d 75, 81–82 (3d Cir. 1986), the court primarily discussed the technical question of whether a corporate successor to a firm that made an allegedly defective product ought to be liable to an injured person. The following observations by the court deal more generally with the strict liability theory:

* * *   * * *

. . . [S]ome of the difficulty stems from § 402A itself. Although theoretically enticing, it has demonstrated significant economic weakness in practice. That a corporation the size of General Motors may be able to spread the cost of § 402A among its millions of customers does not mean that a machine shop employing five or ten individuals has similar capabilities. And General Motors' ability to self-insure if no liability policies are available does not aid the machine shop when its premium for a policy (assuming it can get one) rises to confiscatory heights. The problem of compensating injured individuals for their losses is indeed serious; it extends across a broad spectrum not limited to products liability, and whether the costs of piecemeal measures like § 402A exceed the societal benefits remains questionable.

. . .

As Professor Calabresi noted, "[a] system that compensates for accidents perfectly once they have occurred but does nothing to prevent them in the first place is obviously not desirable." G. Calabresi, *The Cost of Accidents*, 64 (1975). *See generally*, Note, 58 Ind.L.J. at 696–98.

As another justification for strict liability, comment c to the Restatement also cites the premise that the expense of claims may become a production cost against which liability insurance can be obtained. The validity of that underlying assumption, however, is highly questionable. Insuring their own operations, even without protection against possible claims set in motion by their predecessor's conduct, has proven difficult for many manufacturers. This potential derivative liability, described as a time bomb that can be ticking for as many as fifty years, does not present an easily calculable risk with readily available insurance.

In the mid-1970's, an insurance availability "crisis" occurred. Many businesses experienced skyrocketing premiums for product liability policies, and others were unable to secure coverage at any cost. . . .

The tightening of the products liability insurance market was one of the influential forces behind the passage of the Product Liability Risk Retention Act of 1981. That legislation permits the formation of risk retention groups within an industry to insure and disperse the products liability of its members. 15 U.S.C. §§ 3901, 3092.

Although some risk retention groups have been formed, the problem has proved to be a tenacious one. A Department of Commerce report, submitted when the 1981 legislation was pending, noted that even though the availability problems of the 1970's had eased in some industries, "[t]his situation cannot be expected to continue." The product-related losses continue to increase, and declining interest rates will produce "a very difficult market for product liability insurance." H.Rep. No. 190, 97th Cong., 1st Sess. 24, *reprinted* in 1981 U.S.Code Cong. & Ad.News 1432, 1453.

The accuracy of that prediction is borne out by a later report of the Attorney General's Tort Policy Working Group, submitted to Congress in support of proposed revisions in tort law. The report, which addresses the liability insurance industry generally, identifies three problems currently facing businesses: "availability of insurance, affordability of insurance coverage and adequacy of coverage." *Report of the Tort Policy Working Group on the Causes, Extent and Policy Implications of the Current Crisis in Insurance Availability and Affordability*, 6 (1986).

That insurance coverage, one of the underlying premises of § 402A, has proved to be a source of considerable difficulty also counsels against the extension of liability to entities that have no actual causal connection with the loss.

. . .

NOTES

(1) Does the *Ogle* court cite convincing reasons for its approval of strict liability for products?

(2) An extended catalog of the "public policy considerations" that support strict liability for products appears in a concurring opinion by Jacobson, J., in *Lechuga, Inc. v. Montgomery*, 12 Ariz. App. 32, 37–38, 467 P.2d 256, 261–62 (1970):

> (1) The manufacturer can anticipate some hazards and guard against their recurrence, which the consumer cannot do. RESTATEMENT, *supra*, comment c.

> (2) The cost of injury may be overwhelming to the person injured while the risk of injury can be insured by the manufacturer and be distributed among the public as a cost of doing business. *Greenman v. Yuba Power Products, Inc.* (59 Cal.2d 57), 27 Cal.Rptr. 697, 377 P.2d 897 (1962).

> (3) It is in the public interest to discourage the marketing of defective products. *Escola v. Coca Cola Bottling Co. of Fresno*, [24 Cal. 2d 453, 150 P.2d 436 (1944)].

> (4) It is in the public interest to place responsibility for injury upon the manufacturer who was responsible for its reaching the market. *Greenman v. Yuba Power Products, Inc., supra.*

> (5) That this responsibility should also be placed upon the retailer and wholesaler of the defective product in order that they may act as the conduit through which liability may flow to reach the manufacturer, where ultimate responsibility lies. *Vandermark v. Ford Motor Co.* (61 Cal.2d 256), 37 Cal.Rptr. 896, 391 P.2d 168 (1964).

> (6) That because of the complexity of present day manufacturing processes and their secretiveness, the ability to prove negligent conduct by the injured plaintiff is almost impossible. *Escola v. Coca Cola Bottling Co. of Fresno, supra.*

> (7) That the consumer does not have the ability to investigate for himself the soundness of the product. *Santor v. A and M Karagheusian, Inc.*, 44 N.J. 52, 207 A.2d 305 (1965).

> (8) That this consumer's vigilance has been lulled by advertising, marketing devices and trademarks. Concurring opinion, Lockwood, J., *Nalbandian v. Byron Jackson Pumps, Inc.*, 97 Ariz. 280, 399 P.2d 681 (1965).

Which of these ideas or assertions provide the most persuasive rationalizations of strict liability? Which of them are unconvincing?

(3) In addition to strict liability, courts use a number of other theories in products cases. Basic negligence doctrine is a mainstay. Theories of "implied warranty," both of "fitness" and "merchantability," have also been used extensively. There is much judicial argument about the compatibility of warranty doctrine with strict liability in tort. Indeed, there is considerable controversy about the nature of warranty theory itself— whether it is basically a "contract" doctrine, a "hybrid" of "tort" and "contract," or "sui generis." Various aspects of this controversy stud other parts of these materials.

Courts usually apply strict liability, negligence and implied warranty theories in cases in which the plaintiff has not specifically relied on representations made by the defendant. There also are a number of doctrines used to rationalize liability for product disappointment on the basis of explicit representations. Among these are various theories of misrepresentation, including deceit—an intentional tort—and negligent misrepresentation. Moreover, there exist non-fault theories based directly on misstatements of fact. In this category are a theory of innocent tortious misrepresentation, of which there has been a codification in section 402B of the *Second Torts Restatement*, and the basically commercial law doctrine of express warranty, a modern version of which appears in section 2-313 of the Uniform Commercial Code.

(4) What similarities, and what differences, do you perceive between the rule of liability announced in *Rylands*, and that defined in *Ogle*?

§ 7.03 The Concept of Defect

INTRODUCTORY NOTE ON DEFECT[1]

I. OVERVIEW

The concept of defect is central to products liability law. It is crucial to the definition of strict liability, and, in one form or another, it is vital to cases based on implied warranty and negligence. Courts require a showing that a product is defective—that is, has fallen below some standard of safety—for a variety of reasons. These include the belief that if there were no defect requirement, then sellers would be held to be "insurers" of their products. An allied fairness argument stresses that if the law does not articulate a standard of product safety to which sellers must adhere, then decisions to hold them liable would be arbitrary.

There are two principal categories of liability based on the idea that the physical or chemical characteristics of a product place it below the legal standard. One of these, on which there is general agreement that strict liability should apply, is the <u>manufacturing defect</u>. This designation applies to products that have a flaw—something in the product that the seller itself would concede takes the product outside of its design specifications. A classic example, from the time when almost all soda was marketed in glass bottles, was a hairline crack in a bottle that caused it to explode. In an automotive age, a metallurgical imperfection in a connecting rod on a vehicle would be such a flaw.

---

1. Parts of this note are adapted from Marshall Shapo, Principles of Tort Law ch. 39 (2d ed. 2003).

The other major category of defect based on a characteristic of the product itself is that of the <u>design defect</u>. There is much controversy on the question of what an actionable design defect is, and the material infra § 7.04 focuses on this controversy. We introduce this subject here by stressing that a claim of design defect attacks the model of product that the manufacturer actually intended to sell. This is by contrast with the manufacturing defect, which is something in the product that the manufacturer did not wish to be there.

A third major category of product suit embraces allegations that the defendant <u>failed to warn adequately</u> of the dangers of a product. Many commentators and courts refer to this kind of case as involving a "warning defect." The material infra § 7.05 treats this type of case.

II. TESTS FOR DEFECT

Courts and commentators have developed several verbal tests in their efforts to formulate a standard for defect. This section discusses a number of these competing and complementary formulas.

A. The stark definition

The starkest definition of defect is one that defines the concept by reference to itself, requiring only that the court and jury find that a product was "defective."[2] The generality of this spare definition is superficially attractive, because of its broad applicability to the vast number of situations in which the defect concept is at issue. However, that generality is also a vice, for in its self-referential character, the definition lacks an explanation of what a defect is. For that reason, practically all courts have insisted on putting more flesh on the bare bones of the concept.

B. Unreasonably dangerous

The definition that has attracted most courts is the one presented in section 402A of the *Restatement (Second)*, which requires the plaintiff to show that a product was in "a defective condition unreasonably dangerous."[3] This definition parallels the requirement of the basic negligence formula that the defendant's conduct be unreasonable. However, a principal theoretical distinction between strict liability and negligence is that the concept of defect in strict liability focuses on the product, rather than on the behavior of the seller. In any event, courts have found it desirable to elaborate the "unreasonably dangerous" concept beyond the general language of section 402A.

C. Dean Wade's catalog

Many courts have drawn on a list of factors, devised by Dean John Wade, that "seem ... of significance in applying the [unreasonably dangerous] standard." Dean Wade's catalog of factors included:

(1) the usefulness and desirability of the product—its utility to the user and to the public as a whole.

(2) The safety aspects of the product—the likelihood that it will cause injury, and the probable seriousness of the injury.

(3) The availability of a substitute product which would meet the same need and not be as unsafe.

---

2. See, e.g., *Cronin v. J.B.E. Olson Corp.*, 501 P.2d 1153, 1155 (Cal. 1972).
3. RESTATEMENT (SECOND) OF TORTS § 402A(1) (1965).

(4) The manufacturer's ability to eliminate the unsafe character of the product without impairing its usefulness or making it too expensive to maintain its utility.

(5) The user's ability to avoid danger by the exercise of care in the use of the product.

(6) The user's anticipated awareness of the dangers inherent in the product and their avoidability, because of general public knowledge of the obvious condition of the product, or of the existence of suitable warnings or instructions.

(7) The feasibility, on the part of the manufacturer, of spreading the loss by setting the price of the product or carrying liability insurance.[4]

Many courts have quoted and paraphrased this diverse catalog as the basis for their analysis of the defect question. Others have drawn on one or more of these factors, plus others, in formulating their own standards.

D. The *Barker* test

A much discussed test for defect appears in the California Supreme Court's decision in *Barker v. Lull Engineering Co.*[5] The *Barker* test included two principal factors, each of which provided the plaintiff an independent opportunity to prove a defect. The first "prong" of the *Barker* formula was a consumer expectations test, under which the plaintiff could demonstrate that the product failed to perform "as safely as an ordinary consumer would expect when used in an intended or reasonably foreseeable manner."[6] Alternatively, if the consumer could show that the "product's design proximately caused his injury," the product could be found defective if the defendant did not "establish, in light of the relevant factors, that, on balance, the benefits of the challenged design outweigh the risk of danger inherent in such design."[7] These factors, singularly and in combination, have commended themselves to other courts.

E. The *Restatement of Products Liability*

A recent subject of commentary has been the defect definitions of the *Restatement of Products Liability*, section 2, particularly the definition of design defect. See infra § 7.04.

[A] Strict Liability for Unknowable Defects

HALPHEN v. JOHNS-MANVILLE SALES CORPORATION
United States Court of Appeals, Fifth Circuit
788 F.2d 274 (1986)

POLITZ, Circuit Judge:

A divided panel affirmed the judgment in favor of Jean Halphen, entered upon a jury verdict, awarding damages against Johns-Manville Sales Corporation for the wrongful

---

4. John Wade, *On the Nature of Strict Tort Liability for Products*, 44 Miss. L. J. 825, 837–38 (1973).
5. 573 P.2d 443 (Cal. 1978).
6. *Id.* at 454.
7. *Id.* at 456.

death of her husband.... Acting en banc, the court vacated the panel opinion, 752 F.2d 124 (5th Cir. 1985), and certified this question to the Supreme Court of Louisiana: "In a strict products liability case, may a manufacturer be held liable for injuries caused by an unreasonably dangerous product if the manufacturer establishes that it did not know and reasonably could not have known of the inherent danger posed by its product?" 755 F.2d 393, 394 (5th Cir. 1985). The Supreme Court of Louisiana accepted our certification ... and has now rendered its opinion in response to our inquiry. Halphen v. Johns-Manville Sales Corporation, 484 So.2d 110 (La.1986).

The Louisiana Supreme Court answered our certified question as follows:

> In a strict products liability case, if the plaintiff proves that the product was unreasonably dangerous per se (whether because of defective design or another kind of defect) or unreasonably dangerous in construction or composition, a manufacturer may be held liable for injuries caused by an unreasonably dangerous product, although the manufacturer did not know and reasonably could not have known of the danger. 484 So.2d at 115.

In answering the question certified, Louisiana's highest court noted two distinct classes of unreasonably dangerous products that strict liability would govern: those products which are unreasonably dangerous per se and those products which are merely unreasonably dangerous. The court advised that the knowledge of the manufacturer is material to the latter category but has no relevance in an action involving the former.

The unreasonably dangerous per se category received this definition: "A product is unreasonably dangerous per se if a reasonable person would conclude that the danger-in-fact of the product, whether foreseeable or not, outweighs the utility of the product." Id. at 114. The court followed this definition with citations to several cases, including two which involved asbestos fibers. In Elmore v. Owens-Illinois, Inc., 673 S.W.2d 434 (Mo.1984), the Supreme Court of Missouri rejected the state-of-the-art defense and imposed strict liability on the manufacturer of an asbestos product without regard to what the manufacturer knew or could have known about the product's danger. In Carter v. Johns-Manville Sales Corp., 557 F.Supp. 1317 (E.D.Tex.1983), the court, applying Texas strict products liability precepts, held that knowledge was not relevant in a case involving a product which was unreasonably dangerous as designed.

We claim no prescience as to the universe of products which ultimately will be given the cognomen "unreasonably dangerous per se," but we find it apparent from the citations and discussion in the certification response that the Supreme Court of Louisiana places asbestos in that category. Accordingly, what the manufacturer knew or could have known about the inherent danger of asbestos was irrelevant to the question of its liability for proximately-caused injury.

Guided by the opinion of the Louisiana Supreme Court as to applicable Louisiana law, we again conclude that the district court correctly disposed of the proffered state-of-the-art defense in the instant case. Accordingly, the judgment of the district court is AFFIRMED.

NOTES

1. Asbestos is a fiber with excellent insulating properties that made it a staple item in American industry for many years, but exposure to it caused cancer and other serious diseases in a large number of persons; several hundred thousand people have filed claims for asbestos-caused illness. Given the established utility of the product—it was

widely used, for example, in the building of naval vessels in World War II—how could a court decide that asbestos was "unreasonably dangerous per se"?

2. Is it ever reasonable to conclude that a product is unreasonably dangerous if the seller could not possibly have known of its hazards at the time of marketing—that is, that its hazards were both unforeseeable and unknowable? What is the justice of holding a firm for selling a product that no one could have forecast would cause harm, and that had the exact characteristics that the firm wanted it to have?

It should be noted that substantial evidence developed over a period of a half century about the dangers of asbestos, and that, as this evidence surfaced, claimants had the opportunity to pursue negligence claims. However, asbestos plaintiffs sometimes have found it tactically useful to plead strict liability, and this is why several courts were presented with the question of whether an asbestos seller could be held liable for an unknowable risk.

3. What would be the social benefits of a decision that asbestos sellers are liable even for unknowable risks? Would such a decision create significant disincentives to the production and sale of useful products?

[B] Vehicle Crashworthiness

LARSEN v. GENERAL MOTORS CORPORATION

United States Court of Appeals, Eighth Circuit
391 F.2d 495 (1968)

FLOYD R. GIBSON, Circuit Judge.

The driver of an automobile claims injury as a result of an alleged negligent design of the steering assembly of the automobile. The alleged defect in design did not cause the accident, and the manufacturer asserts the law imposes no duty of care in the design of an automobile to make it more safe to occupy in the event of a collision. The trial court agreed, rendering summary judgment in favor of the manufacturer, reported at 274 F.Supp. 461 (D.C.Minn.1967). We reverse and remand.

The plaintiff-appellant, Erling David Larsen, received severe bodily injuries while driving, with the consent of the owner, a 1963 Chevrolet Corvair on February 18, 1964 in the state of Michigan. A head-on collision, with the impact occurring on the left front corner of the Corvair, caused a severe rearward thrust of the steering mechanism into the plaintiff's head. The Corvair was manufactured by General Motors Corporation and liability is asserted against General Motors on an alleged design defect in the steering assembly and the placement or attachment of the component parts of the steering assembly to the structure of the Corvair.[2]

The plaintiff does not contend that the design caused the accident but that because of the design he received injuries he would not have otherwise received or, in the alter-

---

2. The plaintiff alleges that the design and placement of the solid steering shaft, which extends without interruption from a point 2.7 inches in front of the leading surface of the front tires to a position directly in front of the driver, exposes the driver to an unreasonable risk of injury from the rearward displacement of that shaft in the event of a left-of-center head-on collision. So positioned it receives the initial impact of forces generated by a left-of-center head-on collision. The unabsorbed forces of the collision in this area are transmitted directly toward the driver's head, the shaft acting as a spear aimed at a vital part of the driver's anatomy.

native, his injuries would not have been as severe. The rearward displacement of the steering shaft on the left frontal impact was much greater on the Corvair than it would be in other cars that were designed to protect against such a rearward displacement. The plaintiff's complaint alleges (1) negligence in design of the steering assembly; (2) negligent failure to warn of the alleged latent or inherently dangerous condition to the user of the steering assembly placement; and (3) breach of express and implied warranties of merchantability of the vehicle's intended use.

General Motors contends it "has no duty whatsoever to design and manufacture a vehicle * * * which is otherwise 'safe' or 'safer' to occupy during collision impacts," and since there is no duty there can be no actionable negligence on its part to either design a safe or more safe car or to warn of any inherent or latent defects in design that might make its cars less safe than some other cars manufactured either by it or other manufacturers.

The District Court for the District of Minnesota rendered summary judgment in favor of General Motors on the basis that there was no common law duty on the manufacturer "to make a vehicle which would protect the plaintiff from injury in the event of a head-on collision" and dismissed the complaint....

...

The District Court found this case to be closely related to the factual situation of Evans v. General Motors Corporation, 359 F.2d 822 (7 Cir. 1966), cert. denied 385 U.S. 836, 87 S.Ct. 83, 17 L.Ed.2d 70 (1966), which held in a divided decision that a manufacturer is under no duty to make its automobile "accident-proof" or "fool-proof" nor to render its vehicle "more" safe where the danger to be avoided is obvious to all. The District Court discussed other cases, which will be set forth in this opinion, and concluded as follows:

"All of these factors when considered together lead to but one conclusion: The defendant G.M.'s duty toward the public is to design an automobile which is reasonably safe when driven and which contains no latent or hidden defects which could cause an accident and subsequent injury * * *. No contention is here made * * * that any design defect caused the accident which allegedly resulted in the plaintiff's injuries. In view of this fact and because this Court believes that any standards in this area must be left to the Legislature, this court has no alternative but to find that the defendant was not negligent in its design and construction of the 1963 Corvair automobile in that it was under no duty to make a vehicle which would protect the plaintiff from injury in the event of a head-on collision." 274 F.Supp. at p. 464.

The District Court also held that there was no duty to warn since the law only requires a warning when the defects would render the product unsafe for its intended use and that its intended purpose was transportation.

Both parties agree that the question of a manufacturer's duty in the design of an automobile or of any chattel is a question of law for the court....

General Motors contends that it has no duty to produce a vehicle in which it is safe to collide or which is accident-proof or incapable of injurious misuse. It views its duty as extending only to producing a vehicle that is reasonably fit for its intended use or for the purpose for which it was made and that is free from hidden defects; and that the intended use of a vehicle and the purpose for which it is manufactured do not include its participation in head-on collisions or any other type of impact, regardless of the manufacturer's ability to foresee that such collisions may occur....

The plaintiff maintains that General Motors' view of its duty is too narrow and restrictive and that an automobile manufacturer is under a duty to use reasonable care in the design of the automobile to make it safe to the user for its foreseeable use and that its intended use or purpose is for travel on the streets and highways, including the possibility of impact or collision with other vehicles or stationary objects....

There is a line of cases directly supporting General Motors' contention that negligent design of an automobile is not actionable, where the alleged defective design is not a causative factor in the accident. The latest leading case on this point is Evans v. General Motors Corporation, 359 F.2d 822 (7 Cir. 1966), cert. denied, 385 U.S. 836, 87 S.Ct. 83, 17 L.Ed.2d 70 (1966). A divided court there held that General Motors in designing an "X" body frame without perimeter support, instead of an allegedly more safe perimeter body frame, was not liable for the death of a user allegedly caused by the designed defect because the defendant's design could not have functioned to avoid the collision. The Court reasoned at pp. 824 and 825 of 359 F.2d:

"A manufacturer is not under a duty to make his automobile accident-proof or foolproof; nor must he render the vehicle 'more' safe where the danger to be avoided is obvious to all. Campo v. Scofield, 1950, 301 N.Y. 468, 95 N.E.2d 802, 804. Perhaps it would be desirable to require manufacturers to construct automobiles in which it would be safe to collide, but that would be a legislative function, not an aspect of judicial interpretation of existing law....

"The intended purpose of an automobile does not include its participation in collisions with other objects, despite the manufacturer's ability to foresee the possibility that such collisions may occur."

. . .

A strong dissent was written by Judge Kiley in which he contended that General Motors had a duty in designing its automobile to use such care that reasonable protection would be given a user against death or injuries from foreseeable yet unavoidable accidents.

. . .

Since General Motors concedes on the negligence count that its duty of care extends to designing and constructing an automobile that is reasonably safe for its intended use of being driven on the roads and highways and that contains no latent or hidden defects which could cause an accident and subsequent injuries, it would be superfluous to review the decisions holding manufacturers liable for negligent construction or design that were the proximate cause of an accident and subsequent injuries. Since MacPherson v. Buick Motor Co., 217 N.Y. 382, 111 N.E. 1050, L.R.A. 1916F, 696 (1916), the courts have consistently held a manufacturer liable for negligent construction of an automobile....

The Courts, however have been somewhat reluctant to impose liability upon a manufacturer for negligent product design in the automotive field. In Gossett v. Chrysler Corporation, 359 F.2d 84 (6 Cir. 1966) the Court reversed a judgment based on an alleged defectively designed truck hood latch that allowed the hood to spring open while the vehicle was in motion causing an accident, but did recognize a duty in connection with design, stating:

"The general rule may be stated as follows: It is the duty of a manufacturer to use reasonable care under the circumstances to so design his product as to make it not accident or foolproof, but safe for the use for which it is intended. This duty includes a *duty to design the product* so that it will *fairly meet any emergency of use* which can *reasonably be anticipated*. The manufacturer is not an insurer that his product is, from a design viewpoint, incapable of producing injury." (Emphasis supplied.)

...

A pertinent case recognizing a duty of reasonable care in design is Carpini v. Pittsburgh and Weirton Bus Company, 216 F.2d 404 (3 Cir. 1954) where the Court permitted recovery for a defectively designed and placed pet cock in the undercarriage of a bus where the design and placement left the pet cock unprotected from debris on the road. The heavily overloaded bus in proceeding on a highway filled with rocks and debris, occasioned by a severe storm the night before, suffered a brake failure, causing an accident. The pet cock became disengaged by the debris, allowing the brakes to drain. In this case the defective design might be said to have caused the accident, though there was the questioned intervening cause of the improper use of the bus by overloading it. In any event this does not reach the plaintiff's factual situation of where the alleged negligent design was not a causative factor in the accident, but is contended to have severely enhanced plaintiff's injuries....

A case closely bearing on this precise point is Ford Motor Company v. Zahn, 265 F.2d 729 (8 Cir. 1959) where the plaintiff lost sight of one eye on being thrown against a defectively designed ash tray having a jagged edge. The ash tray had nothing to do in a causative way of setting up an emergency braking situation, which in turn projected the plaintiff into the ash tray, but the Court recognized a duty to use reasonable care in design, recognized the foreseeability of injury resulting from a defective ash tray so placed, and also recognized the duty resting on the manufacturer to make reasonable inspections or tests to discover defects. Judge Matthes stated the rule at p. 731:

"By force of law there is imposed upon the manufacturer of an article for sale or use the duty to exercise reasonable care to prevent defective conditions caused by a miscarriage in the manufacturing process. This duty requires reasonable skill and care in the process of manufacture and for reasonable inspection or tests to discover defects."

Generally, as noted in 76 A.L.R.2d 93, Anno.: Products Liability — Duty As To Design, the manufacturer has a duty to use reasonable care under the circumstances in the design of a product but is not an insurer that his product is incapable of producing injury, and this duty of design is met when the article is safe for its intended use and when it will fairly meet any "emergency of use" which is foreseeable. Davlin v. Henry Ford & Son, 20 F.2d 317 (6 Cir. 1927). This doctrine has even been extended to cover an unintended use where the injury resulting from that unintended use was foreseeable or should have been anticipated. Simpson Timber Co. v. Parks (9 Cir. 1965). [Lengthy case history omitted. — Ed.]

Accepting, therefore, the principle that a manufacturer's duty of design and construction extends to producing a product that is reasonably fit for its intended use and free of hidden defects that could render it unsafe for such use, the issue narrows on the proper interpretation of "intended use." Automobiles are made for use on the roads and highways in transporting persons and cargo to and from various points. This intended use cannot be carried out without encountering in varying degrees the statistically proved hazard of injury-producing impacts of various types. The manufacturer should not be heard to say that it does not intend its product to be involved in any accident when it can easily foresee and when it knows that the probability over the life of its product is high, that it will be involved in some type of injury-producing accident. O'-Connell in his article "Taming the Automobile," 58 Nw.U.L.Rev. 299, 348 (1963) cites that between one-fourth to two-thirds of all automobiles during their use at some time are involved in an accident producing injury or death. Other statistics are available showing the frequency and certainty of fatal and injury-producing accidents.... It should be recognized that the environment in which a product is used must be taken into consideration by the manufacturer. Spruill v. Boyle-Midway, Inc., 308 F.2d 79 (4 Cir. 1962).

We think the "intended use" construction urged by General Motors is much too narrow and unrealistic. Where the manufacturer's negligence in design causes an unreasonable risk to be imposed upon the user of its products, the manufacturer should be liable for the injury caused by its failure to exercise reasonable care in the design. These injuries are readily foreseeable an an incident to the normal and expected use of an automobile. While automobiles are not made for the purpose of colliding with each other, a frequent and inevitable contingency of normal automobile use will result in collisions and injury-producing impacts. No rational basis exists for limiting recovery to situations where the defect in design or manufacture was the causative factor of the accident, as the accident and the resulting injury, usually caused by the so-called 'second collision' of the passenger with the interior part of the automobile, all are foreseeable. Where the injuries or enhanced injuries are due to the manufacturer's failure to use reasonable care to avoid subjecting the user of its products to an unreasonable risk of injury, general negligence principles should be applicable.[3] The sole function of an automobile is not just to provide a means of transportation, it is to provide a means of safe transportation or as safe as is reasonably possible under the present state of the art.

We do agree that under the present state of the art an automobile manufacturer is under no duty to design an accident-proof or fool-proof vehicle or even one that floats on water, but such manufacturer is under a duty to use reasonable care in the design of its vehicle to avoid subjecting the user to an unreasonable risk of injury in the event of a collision. Collisions with or without fault of the user are clearly foreseeable by the manufacturer and are statistically inevitable.[4]

The intended use and purpose of an automobile is to travel on the streets and highways, which travel more often than not is in close proximity to other vehicles and at speeds that carry the possibility, probability, and potential of injury-producing impacts. The realities of the intended and actual use are well known to the manufacturer and to the public and these realities should be squarely faced by the manufacturer and the courts. We perceive of no sound reason, either in logic or experience, nor any command in precedent, why the manufacturer should not be held to a reasonable duty of care in the design of its vehicle consonant with the state of the art to minimize the effect of accidents. The manufacturers are not insurers but should be held to a standard of reasonable care in design to provide a reasonably safe vehicle in which to travel.... Our streets and highways are increasingly hazardous for the intended normal use of travel and transportation. While advances in highway engineering and non-access, dual highways have considerably increased the safety factor on a miles traveled ratio to accidents,

___

3. As aptly and concisely phrased by Noel, *Manufacturer's Negligence of Design or Directions for Use of a Product*, 71 YALE L.J. 816, 818 (1962); "The manufacturer does not have to make a product which is 'accident-proof' or 'fool-proof'. Liability is imposed only when an unreasonable danger is created. Whether or not this has occurred should be determined by general negligence principles, which involve a balancing of the likelihood of harm, and the gravity of harm if it happens against the burden of the precautions which would be effective to avoid the harm."

4. NATIONAL SAFETY COUNCIL, ACCIDENT FACTS 40 (1966 ed.) reports: In 1965 motor vehicle accidents caused 49,000 deaths, 1.8 million disabling injuries. In automobile accidents since the advent of the horseless carriage up to the end of 1965, 1.5 million people have been killed in the United States. In 1966 the annual toll of those killed in automobile accidents rose to 52,500 and 1.9 million suffered disabling injuries.

the constant increasing number of vehicles gives impetus to the need of designing and constructing a vehicle that is reasonably safe for the purpose of such travel. At least, the unreasonable risk should be eliminated and reasonable steps in design taken to minimize the injury-producing effect of impacts.

This duty of reasonable care in design rests on common law negligence that a manufacturer of an article should use reasonable care in the design and manufacture of his product to eliminate any unreasonable risk of foreseeable injury. The duty of reasonable care in design should be viewed in light of the risk. While all risks cannot be eliminated nor can a crash-proof vehicle be designed under the present state of the art, there are many common-sense factors in design, which are or should be well known to the manufacturer that will minimize or lessen the injurious effects of a collision. The standard of reasonable care is applied in many other negligence situations and should be applied here.

The courts since MacPherson v. Buick Motor Co.... have held that a manufacturer of automobiles is under a duty to construct a vehicle that is free of latent and hidden defects. We can perceive of no significant difference in imposing a common law duty of a reasonable standard of care in design the same as in construction. A defect in either can cause severe injury or death and a negligent design defect should be actionable. Any design defect not causing the accident would not subject the manufacturer to liability for the entire damage, but the manufacturer should be liable for that portion of the damage or injury caused by the defective design over and above the damage or injury that probably would have occurred as a result of the impact or collision absent the defective design. The manufacturer argues that this is difficult to assess. This is no persuasive answer and, even if difficult, there is no reason to abandon the injured party to his dismal fate as a traffic statistic, when the manufacturer owed, at least, a common law duty of reasonable care in the design and construction of its product. The obstacles of apportionment are not insurmountable....

General Motors in arguing against what it views as an expanded duty of a care in design makes the statement that this duty "must be considered in its application to all products. Automobile manufacturers cannot be made a special class." With this we quite agree. We think the duty of the use of reasonable care in design to protect against foreseeable injury to the user of a product and perhaps others injured as an incident of that use should be and is equally applicable to all manufacturers with the customary limitations now applied to protect the manufacturer in case of an unintended and unforeseeable use. The courts have imposed this duty, perhaps more readily against other manufacturers than against the automotive industry.

We, therefore, do not think the automotive industry is being singled out for any special adverse treatment by applying to it general negligence principles in (1) imposing a duty on the manufacturer to use reasonable care in the design of its products to protect against an unreasonable risk of injury or enhancement of injury to a user of the product, and (2) holding that the intended use of an automotive product contemplates its travel on crowded and high speed roads and highways that inevitably subject it to the foreseeable hazards of collisions and impacts. Neither reason, logic, nor controlling precedents compel the courts to make a distinction between negligent design and negligent construction.

The manufacturer's duty to use reasonable care in the design and manufacture of a product to minimize injuries to its users and not to subject its users to an unreasonable risk of injury in the event of a collision or impact should be recognized by the courts.

The manufacturers themselves have, in various public utterances in discussing automotive safety, expressed their concern for making safer vehicles.[7] And General Motors admits the foreseeability of accidents which are matters of public and common knowledge over a long period of time.[8] Legal acceptance or imposition of this duty would go far in protecting the user from unreasonable risks. The normal risk of driving must be accepted by the user but there is no need to further penalize the user by subjecting him to an unreasonable risk of injury due to negligence in design.

On the second count of plaintiff's petition alleging negligence in failure to warn of an alleged dangerous condition in vehicle design the same principles would apply. We think a cause of action is alleged and that under the law the manufacturer has a duty to inspect and to test for designs that would cause an unreasonable risk of foreseeable injury.... The failure to use reasonable care in design or knowledge of a defective design gives rise to the reasonable duty on the manufacturer to warn of this condition.

. . .

If, because of the alleged undisclosed defect in design of the 1963 Corvair steering assembly, an extra hazard is created over and above the normal hazard, General Motors should be liable for this unreasonable hazard. Admittedly, it would not sell many cars of this particular model if its sale's 'pitch' included the cautionary statement that the user is subjected to an extra hazard or unreasonable risk in the event of a head-on collision. But the duty of reasonable care should command a warning of this latent defect that could under certain circumstances accentuate the possibility of severe injury....

On the issue of strict liability or implied warranty of merchantability for intended use, we make no comment as our holding of sufficiency of counts one and two are dispositive....

General Motors contends that any safety standards in design and equipment should be imposed as envisioned by the National Traffic and Motor Vehicle Safety Act of 1966 (Pub.L. 89-563), 80 Stat. 718, 15 U.S.C.A. § 1381 et seq. Recognizing the need to reduce traffic accidents and deaths and injuries resulting therefrom, Congress found it neces-

---

7. C. A. Chayne, then vice-president in charge of the engineering staff of defendant General Motors, made a statement before the Subcommittee on Interstate and Foreign Commerce, House of Representatives, 84th Cong., 2nd Sess., on Investigation of Highway Traffic Accidents, Traffic Safety (1956), pp. 325–327:
"* * * it is always relatively easy to come up with a new design of an old part, or the design of a new feature or part, but until we are able to adequately test this part and have a pretty clear picture of what it will do under the circumstances to which it is subjected, we are exposing ourselves, the users of our products, and frequently others on the highways to risks."
K. A. Stonex, Automobile Safety Engineer for General Motors in an article 'Vehicle Aspects of the Highway Safety Problem,' appearing in TRAFFIC SAFETY, National Safety Council, Chicago, Illinois, June 1962, at p. 22, said: "The two-car collision * * * is so important statistically that car structure has to be evaluated under these conditions."
The president of General Motors in Hearings on the Federal Role in Traffic Safety Before the Subcommittee on Executive Reorganization of the Senate Committee on Government Operations, 89th Cong., 1st Sess. pt. 2 at 667 (1965), stated: "We recognize that the increasing movement of people and goods by motor vehicles contributes naturally to a higher possibility of accidents. This imposes new responsibilities on all of us. Automobile manufacturers must continue to seek all possible ways in which the built-in protection for car occupants can be improved."
8. Goddard & Haddon in their article "Passenger Car Design in Highway Safety" published by Consumers Union of U.S., Inc. make the statement that: "Between one-fourth and two-thirds of all vehicles manufactured are at sometime during their subsequent use involved in the tragedy of human injury and death. Consequently the anticipation of this result by both designer and manufacturer is mandatory."

sary to establish motor vehicle safety standards, and by this Act set up the machinery and administrative process to establish minimum safety standards. The purpose of this Act is manifest and the Congress recognizes in § 1391(1) that the public should be protected against unreasonable risks of accidents occurring as a result of the design, construction or performance of motor vehicles and also be protected against unreasonable risk of death or injury in the event accidents do occur. Section 108(c) of the Act, 15 U.S.C. § 1397(c), expressly negatives any intention of Congress to acquire exclusive jurisdiction in this field and leaves the common law liability intact. Subsection (c) reads: "(c) Compliance with any Federal motor vehicle safety standard issued under this subchapter does not exempt any person from any liability under common law."

It is apparent that the National Traffic Safety Act is intended to be supplementary of and in addition to the common law of negligence and product liability. The common law is not sterile or rigid and serves the best interests of society by adapting standards of conduct and responsibility that fairly meet the emerging and developing needs of our time. The common law standard of a duty to use reasonable care in light of all the circumstances can at least serve the needs of our society until the legislature imposes higher standards or the courts expand the doctrine of strict liability for tort. The Act is a salutary step in this direction and not an exemption from common law liability.

For the reasons set forth, we reverse and remand. . . .

NOTES

(1) At the time *Larsen* was decided, the issue of whether courts would allow a cause of action for alleged uncrashworthiness of a vehicle was very much an open question. *Evans v. General Motors*, quoted in *Larsen*, strongly argued the case against such liability. But *Larsen* has prevailed. Why? Surely, the intended use of automobiles, as the court said in *Evans*, is not to come into collision with other objects.

(2) Does *Larsen* take judicial lawmaking too far into the province of legislation? As the *Larsen* court indicates, its decision followed closely on Congress' passage of the National Motor Vehicle & Traffic Safety Act. Why should courts not defer entirely to the level of regulation the National Highway Traffic Safety Administration chooses to promulgate under the Act, and refuse to permit causes of action for failures to provide crash protection that are not the subject of specific regulation?

(3) What should be the plaintiff's burden of proof in a crashworthiness case? There are two strong competing points of view. One requires the plaintiff to show how much the defendant's design enhanced her injuries beyond those that would have occurred if there had been a safer alternative design. *Huddell v. Levin*, 537 F.2d 726 (3d Cir. 1976). At the other pole is a rule that has been stated in different ways. One version of a rule that tends to favor plaintiffs allows a plaintiff who suffers indivisible injuries in a so-called second collision that are beyond "those that otherwise would have occurred in the first collision" to shift the burden "to the defendant to show that the damages that arose from the enhanced injury are apportionable." *Czarnecki v. Volkswagen of Am.*, 172 Ariz. 408, 837 P.2d 1143, 1148 (App. 1991). The *Restatement of Products Liability* also leans toward a claimant-oriented position, saying that if the evidence does not support a finding of harm "that would have resulted from other causes in the absence of the product defect," then "the product seller is liable for all of the plaintiff's harm attributable to the defect and other causes." RESTATEMENT (THIRD) OF TORTS: PRODUCT LIABILITY § 16 (b), (c) (1998). This rule, the drafters observe, "does not formally shift any burden of proof to the defendant." Reporters' Note to § 16, at 244.

(4) Six years after *Larsen*, the Fourth Circuit considered a claim against Volkswagen after a passenger was injured when a microbus hit a telephone pole. The court observed that the microbus design was popular with consumers, even though it maximized interior cargo room at the expense of "crush space" that would insulate passengers in case of collision. Taking its lead from Congress, the court decided that a vehicle's "special type" bears on the question of whether a design is "reasonable, practicable, and appropriate." A convertible, the court pointed out, does not provide "the exact kind of protection in a roll-over accident" as "the standard American passenger car." *Dreisonstok v. Volkswagenwerk, A.G.*, 489 F.2d 1066 (4th Cir. 1974). Do you suppose that most purchasers of the Volkswagen microbus were conscious of a lack of front-end collision protection in those vehicles? Does *Dreisonstok* leave any room to find design defect with respect to a risky feature of a motor vehicle about which a consumer is generally aware?

(5) What percentage of consumers do you think would choose, for a price reduction, a car that lacked a collapsible steering column when one was available as an option?

[C] Prescription Drugs and Vaccines

BROWN v. SUPERIOR COURT

Supreme Court of California
44 Cal. 3d 1049, 751 P.2d 470, 245 Cal. Rptr. 412 (1988)

MOSK, Justice.

In current litigation several significant issues have arisen relating to the liability of manufacturers of prescription drugs for injuries caused by their products. Our first and broadest inquiry is whether such a manufacturer may be held strictly liable for a product that is defective in design....

A number of plaintiffs filed actions in the San Francisco Superior Court against numerous drug manufacturers which allegedly produced DES, a substance plaintiffs claimed was used by their mothers to prevent miscarriage. They alleged that the drug was defective and they were injured in utero when their mothers ingested it....

A typical complaint in the complex litigation names 170 or more drug companies as defendants. It is alleged that they manufactured DES from the same formula, and that the drug was unsafe for use in preventing miscarriage and resulted in severe injury to plaintiff. Defendants knew that the drug contained a cancer-causing substance, yet they failed to warn users or their physicians of these dangerous characteristics....

The trial court made pretrial rulings in favor of defendants on the issues stated above. That is, it determined that defendants could not be held strictly liable for the alleged defect in DES but only for their failure to warn of known or knowable side effects of the drug....

Plaintiff sought a writ of mandate or prohibition in the Court of Appeal to review the foregoing rulings. That court issued an alternative writ and, after considering the issues, upheld the trial court's determination and denied a peremptory writ. We granted review to examine the conclusions of the Court of Appeal and its potential conflict with Kearl v. Lederle Laboratories (1985) 172 Cal.App.3d 812, 218 Cal.Rptr. 453, on the issue of strict liability of a drug manufacturer for a defect in the design of a prescription drug.

...

The doctrine of strict liability had its genesis in a concurring opinion by Justice Roger Traynor in Escola v. Coca Cola Bottling Co. (1944) 24 Cal.2d 453, 461, 150 P.2d 436. He suggested that a manufacturer should be absolutely liable if, in placing a product on the market, it knew the product was to be used without inspection, and it proved to have a defect that caused injury. The policy considerations underlying this suggestion were that the manufacturer, unlike the public, can anticipate or guard against the recurrence of hazards, that the cost of injury may be an overwhelming misfortune to the person injured whereas the manufacturer can insure against the risk and distribute the cost among the consuming public, and that it is in the public interest to discourage the marketing of defective products. This court unanimously adopted Justice Traynor's concept in Greenman v. Yuba Power Products, Inc. (1963) 59 Cal.2d 57, 62, 27 Cal.Rptr. 697, 377 P.2d 897, holding a manufacturer strictly liable in tort and using the formulation of the doctrine set forth in Escola.

Strict liability differs from negligence in that it eliminates the necessity for the injured party to prove that the manufacturer of the product which caused injury was negligent. It focusses not on the conduct of the manufacturer but on the product itself, and holds the manufacturer liable if the product was defective.

In 1965, soon after our decision in Greenman, the Restatement Second of Torts published section 402A, which set forth the strict liability doctrine (hereinafter section 402A)....

B. Strict Liability and Prescription Drugs

Even before Greenman was decided, the members of the American Law Institute, in considering whether to adopt a rule of strict liability, pondered whether the manufacturer of a prescription drug should be subject to the doctrine.... (38 ALI Proc. 19, 90–92, 98 (1961).) During a rather confusing discussion of a draft of what was to become section 402A, a member of the institute proposed that drugs should be exempted from strict liability on the ground that it would be "against the public interest" to apply the doctrine to such products because of "the very serious tendency to stifle medical research and testing." Dean Prosser, who was the reporter for the Restatement Second of Torts, responded that the problem was a real one, and that he had it in mind in drafting section 402A. A motion to exempt prescription drugs from the section was defeated on the suggestion of Dean Prosser that the problem could be dealt with in the comments to the section. However, a motion to state the exemption in a comment was also defeated. (38 ALI Proc. 19, 90–98, supra.) At the next meeting of the institute in 1962, section 402A was approved together with comment k thereto. (41 ALI Proc. 227, 244 (1962).)

The comment provides that the producer of a properly manufactured prescription drug may be held liable for injuries caused by the product only if it was not accompanied by a warning of dangers that the manufacturer knew or should have known about. It declares: "k. Unavoidably unsafe products. There are some products which, in the present state of human knowledge, are quite incapable of being made safe for their intended and ordinary use. These are especially common in the field of drugs. An outstanding example is the vaccine for the Pasteur treatment of rabies, which not uncommonly leads to very serious and damaging consequences when it is injected. Since the disease itself invariably leads to a dreadful death, both the marketing and use of the vaccine are fully justified, notwithstanding the unavoidable high degree of risk which they involve. Such a product, properly prepared, and accompanied by proper directions and warning, is not defective, nor is it unreasonably dangerous. The same is true of many other drugs, vaccines, and the like, many of which for this very reason cannot legally be sold except to physicians, or under the prescription of a physician. It is also true in particular of many new or experimental drugs as to which, because of lack of time and opportunity for sufficient medical experience, there can be no assurance of safety, or perhaps even of purity of ingredients, but such experience as there is justifies the marketing and use of the drug notwithstanding a medically recognizable risk. The seller of such products, again with the qualification that they are properly prepared and marketed, and proper warning is given, where the situation calls for it, is not to be held to strict liability for unfortunate consequences attending their use, merely because he has undertaken to supply the public with an apparently useful and desirable product, attended with a known but apparently reasonable risk."

Comment k has been analyzed and criticized by numerous commentators. While there is some disagreement as to its scope and meaning, there is a general consensus that, although it purports to explain the strict liability doctrine, in fact the principle it states is based on negligence.... That is, comment k would impose liability on a drug manufacturer only if it failed to warn of a defect of which it either knew or should have known. This concept focuses not on a deficiency in the product—the hallmark of strict liability—but on the fault of the producer in failing to warn of dangers inherent in the use of its product that were either known or knowable—an idea which "rings of negligence," ... [4]

Comment k has been adopted in the overwhelming majority of jurisdictions that have considered the matter.

We are aware of only one decision that has applied the doctrine of strict liability to prescription drugs. (Brochu v. Ortho Pharmaceutical Corp. (1st Cir.1981) 642 F.2d 652, 654–657.) Most cases have embraced the rule of comment k without detailed analysis of its language. A few, notably Kearl v. Lederle Laboratories, supra, 172 Cal.App.3d 812, 218 Cal.Rptr. 453 (hereafter Kearl), have conditioned application of the exemption stated therein on a finding that the drug involved is in fact "unavoidably dangerous," reasoning that the comment was intended to exempt only such drugs from strict liability. (Accord, Toner v. Lederle Laboratories (1987) 112 Idaho 328, 732 P.2d 297, 303–309; see also Feldman v. Lederle Laboratories (1984) 97 N.J. 429, 479 A.2d 374, 382–383 [involving allegations of a failure to warn, but stating that "whether a drug is unavoidably unsafe should be decided on a case-by-case basis."].) ...

We appear ... to have three distinct choices: (1) to hold that the manufacturer of a prescription drug is strictly liable for a defect in its product because it was defectively designed, as that term is defined in Barker [v. Lull Eng'g Co., 20 Cal. 3d 413, 573 P.2d 443, 143 Cal. Rptr. 225 (1978)], or because of a failure to warn of its dangerous propensities even though such dangers were neither known nor scientifically knowable at the time of distribution; (2) to determine that liability attaches only if a manufacturer fails to warn of dangerous propensities of which it was or should have been aware, in conformity with

---

4. The test stated in comment k is to be distinguished from strict liability for failure to warn. Although both concepts identify failure to warn as the basis of liability, comment k imposes liability only if the manufacturer knew or should have known of the defect at the time the product was sold or distributed. Under strict liability, the reason why the warning was not issued is irrelevant, and the manufacturer is liable even if it neither knew nor could have known of the defect about which the warning was required. Thus, comment k, by focussing on the blameworthiness of the manufacturer, sets forth a test which sounds in negligence, while imposition of liability for failure to warn without regard to the reason for such failure is consistent with strict liability since it asks only whether the product that caused injury contained a defect. (See *Little v. PPG Industries, Inc.* (1978), 19 Wash.App. 812, 579 P.2d 940, 946.)

comment k; or (3) to decide, like Kearl and Toner v. Lederle Laboratories, ... that strict liability for design defects should apply to prescription drugs unless the particular drug which caused the injury is found to be "unavoidably dangerous."

We shall conclude that (1) a drug manufacturer's liability for a defectively designed drug should not be measured by the standards of strict liability; (2) because of the public interest in the development, availability, and reasonable price of drugs, the appropriate test for determining responsibility is the test stated in comment k; and (3) for these same reasons of policy, we disapprove the holding of Kearl that only those prescription drugs found to be "unavoidably dangerous" should be measured by the comment k standard and that strict liability should apply to drugs that do not meet that description.

1. Design defect

Barker ... set forth two alternative tests to measure a design defect: first, whether the product performed as safely as the ordinary consumer would expect when used in an intended and reasonably foreseeable manner, and second, whether, on balance, the benefits of the challenged design outweighed the risk of danger inherent in the design. In making the latter determination, the jury may consider these factors: "the gravity of the danger posed by the challenged design, the likelihood that such danger would occur, the mechanical feasibility of a safer alternative design, the financial cost of an improved design, and the adverse consequences to the product and to the consumer that would result from an alternative design." (20 Cal.3d at p. 431, 143 Cal.Rptr. 225, 573 P.2d 443.)

Defendants assert that neither of these tests is applicable to a prescription drug like DES. As to the "consumer expectation" standard, they claim, the "consumer" is not the plaintiff but the physician who prescribes the drug, and it is to him that the manufacturer's warnings are directed. A physician appreciates the fact that all prescription drugs involve inherent risks, known and unknown, and he does not expect that the drug is without such risks. We agree that the "consumer expectation" aspect of the Barker test is inappropriate to prescription drugs. While the "ordinary consumer" may have a reasonable expectation that a product such as a machine he purchases will operate safely when used as intended, a patient's expectations regarding the effects of such a drug are those related to him by his physician, to whom the manufacturer directs the warnings regarding the drug's properties.[9] The manufacturer cannot be held liable if it has provided appropriate warnings and the doctor fails in his duty to transmit these warnings to the patient or if the patient relies on inaccurate information from others regarding side effects of the drug.

The second test, which calls for the balancing of risks and benefits, is inapposite to prescription drugs, according to defendants, because it contemplates that a safer alternative design is feasible. While the defective equipment in Barker and other cases involving mechanical devices might be "redesigned" by the addition of safety devices, there is no possibility for an alternative design for a drug like DES, which is a scientific constant compounded in accordance with a required formula....

We agree with defendants that Barker contemplates a safer alternative design is possible, but we seriously doubt their claim that a drug like DES cannot be "redesigned" to make it safer. For example, plaintiff might be able to demonstrate at trial that a particular component of DES rendered it unsafe as a miscarriage preventative and that removal

---

9. It is well established that a manufacturer fulfills its duty to warn if it provides adequate warning to the physician....

of that component would not have affected the efficacy of the drug. Even if the resulting product, without the damaging component, would bear a name other than DES, it would do no violence to semantics to view it as a "redesign" of DES.

Or plaintiff might be able to prove that other, less harmful drugs were available to prevent miscarriage; the benefit of such alternate drugs could be weighed against the advantages of DES in making the risk/benefit analysis of Barker. As the Court of Appeal observed, defendants' attempt to confine the issue to whether there is an "alternative design" for DES poses the problem in an "unreasonably narrow" fashion. (See Comment, The Failure to Warn Defect (1983) 17 U.S.F.L.Rev. 743, 755–762.)

Of course, the fact that a drug with dangerous side effects may be characterized as containing a defect in design does not necessarily mean that its producer is to be held strictly liable for the defect. The determination of that issue depends on whether the public interest would be served by the imposition of such liability. As we have seen, the fundamental reasons underlying the imposition of strict liability are to deter manufacturers from marketing products that are unsafe, and to spread the cost of injury from the plaintiff to the consuming public, which will pay a higher price for the product to reflect the increased expense of insurance to the manufacturer resulting from its greater exposure to liability.

These reasons could justify application of the doctrine to the manufacturers of prescription drugs. It is indisputable, as plaintiff contends, that the risk of injury from such drugs is unavoidable, that a consumer may be helpless to protect himself from serious harm caused by them, and that, like other products, the cost of insuring against strict liability can be passed on by the producer to the consumer who buys the item. Moreover, as we observe below, in some cases additional testing of drugs before they are marketed might reveal dangerous side effects, resulting in a safer product.

But there is an important distinction between prescription drugs and other products such as construction machinery..., a lawnmower..., or perfume (Moran v. Faberge, Inc. (1975) 273 Md. 538, 332 A.2d 11), the producers of which were held strictly liable. In the latter cases, the product is used to make work easier or to provide pleasure, while in the former it may be necessary to alleviate pain and suffering or to sustain life. Moreover, unlike other important medical products (wheelchairs, for example), harm to some users from prescription drugs is unavoidable. Because of these distinctions, the broader public interest in the availability of drugs at an affordable price must be considered in deciding the appropriate standard of liability for injuries resulting from their use.

Perhaps a drug might be made safer if it was withheld from the market until scientific skill and knowledge advanced to the point at which additional dangerous side effects would be revealed. But in most cases such a delay in marketing new drugs—added to the delay required to obtain approval for release of the product from the Food and Drug Administration—would not serve the public welfare. Public policy favors the development and marketing of beneficial new drugs, even though some risks, perhaps serious ones, might accompany their introduction, because drugs can save lives and reduce pain and suffering.

If drug manufacturers were subject to strict liability, they might be reluctant to undertake research programs to develop some pharmaceuticals that would prove beneficial or to distribute others that are available to be marketed, because of the fear of large adverse monetary judgments. Further, the additional expense of insuring against such liability—assuming insurance would be available—and of research programs to reveal possible dangers not detectable by available scientific methods could place the cost of medication beyond the reach of those who need it most.

Dean Prosser summed up the justification for exempting prescription drugs from strict liability as follows: "The argument that industries producing potentially dangerous products should make good the harm, distribute it by liability insurance, and add the cost to the price of the product, encounters reason for pause, when we consider that two of the greatest medical boons to the human race, penicillin and cortisone, both have their dangerous side effects, and that drug companies might well have been deterred from producing and selling them.

"Thus far the courts have tended to hold the manufacturer to a high standard of care in preparing and testing drugs of unknown potentiality and in giving warning; but in the absence of evidence that this standard has not been met, they have refused to hold the maker liable for unforeseeable harm." (Prosser, Torts (4th ed. 1971) § 99, at p. 661, fns. omitted.)

The possibility that the cost of insurance and of defending against lawsuits will diminish the availability and increase the price of pharmaceuticals is far from theoretical. Defendants cite a host of examples of products which have greatly increased in price or have been withdrawn or withheld from the market because of the fear that their producers would be held liable for large judgments.

For example, according to defendant E.R. Squibb & Sons, Inc., Benedictin [sic], the only antinauseant drug available for pregnant women, was withdrawn from sale in 1983 because the cost of insurance almost equalled the entire income from sale of the drug. Before it was withdrawn, the price of Benedictin [sic] increased by over 300 percent. (132 Chemical Week (June 12, 1983) p. 14.)

Drug manufacturers refused to supply a newly discovered vaccine for influenza on the ground that mass inoculation would subject them to enormous liability. The government therefore assumed the risk of lawsuits resulting from injuries caused by the vaccine.... One producer of diphtheria-tetanus-pertussis vaccine withdrew from the market, giving as its reason "extreme liability exposure, cost of litigation and the difficulty of continuing to obtain adequate insurance." ... There are only two manufacturers of the vaccine remaining in the market, and the cost of each dose rose a hundredfold from 11 cents in 1982 to $11.40 in 1986, $8 of which was for an insurance reserve. The price increase roughly paralleled an increase in the number of lawsuits from one in 1978 to 219 in 1985.... Finally, a manufacturer was unable to market a new drug for the treatment of vision problems because it could not obtain adequate liability insurance at a reasonable cost....

There is no doubt that, from the public's standpoint, these are unfortunate consequences. And they occurred even though almost all jurisdictions follow the negligence standard of comment k. It is not unreasonable to conclude in these circumstances that the imposition of a harsher test for liability would not further the public interest in the development and availability of these important products.

We decline to hold, therefore, that a drug manufacturer's liability for injuries caused by the defective design of a prescription drug should be measured by the standard set forth in Barker.

2. Failure to warn

For these same reasons of policy, we reject plaintiff's assertion that a drug manufacturer should be held strictly liable for failure to warn of risks inherent in a drug even though it neither knew nor could have known by the application of scientific knowledge available at the time of distribution that the drug could produce the undesirable side effects suffered by the plaintiff.

Numerous cases have recognized that a product may be defective because of the absence of a warning that was necessary to allow its safe use.... While some decisions apply strict liability principles to such a defect by holding that it is irrelevant whether the manufacturer knew of the danger or should have known of it..., most jurisdictions hold to the contrary. That is, liability is conditioned on the actual or constructive knowledge of the risk by the manufacturer as of the time the product was sold or distributed.... This rule is consistent with comment j to section 402A, which confines the duty to warn to a situation in which the seller "has knowledge, or by the application of reasonable, developed human skill and foresight should have knowledge of ... the danger."

It has been said that to "hold the manufacturer liable for failure to warn of a danger of which it would be impossible to know based on the present state of human knowledge would make the manufacturer the virtual insurer of the product...." ... The likelihood of the producer's liability would increase with significant advances in scientific knowledge, discouraging the development of new and improved drugs to combat disease. Thus, we disagree with plaintiff's assertion that defendants should be held liable for failing to warn the physician who prescribed DES to plaintiff's mother of alleged defects in the drug that were neither known by defendants nor scientifically knowable at the time the drug was distributed.

3. The Kearl test

One further question remains in this aspect of the case. Comment k, as we have seen, provides that the maker of an "unavoidably unsafe" product is not liable for injuries resulting from its use if the product is "properly prepared, and accompanied by proper directions and warning." With the few exceptions noted above, the courts which have adopted comment k have viewed all prescription drugs as coming within its scope.

Kearl suggested that not all drugs are "unavoidably dangerous" so as to merit the protection of the negligence standard of comment k, and it devised a test to separate those which meet that description from those which do not. It held that the question whether a drug should be exempt from strict liability as "unavoidably dangerous" presents a mixed question of law and fact which should be decided on the basis of evidence to be taken by the trial judge out of the presence of the jury. The judge should determine, after hearing the evidence, "(1) whether, when distributed, the product was intended to confer an exceptionally important benefit that made its availability highly desirable; (2) whether the then-existing risk posed by the product was both 'substantial' and 'unavoidable'; and (3) whether the interest in availability (again measured as of the time of distribution) outweighs the interest in promoting enhanced accountability through strict liability design defect review." ... If these questions are answered in the affirmative the liability of the manufacturer is tested by the standards of comment k; otherwise, strict liability is the applicable test.

...

We acknowledge that there is some appeal in the basic premise of Kearl. It seems unjust to grant the same protection from liability to those who gave us thalidomide as to the producers of penicillin. If some method could be devised to confine the benefit of the comment k negligence standard to those drugs that have proved useful to mankind while denying the privilege to those that are clearly harmful, it would deserve serious consideration. But we know of no means by which this can be accomplished without substantially impairing the public interest in the development and marketing of new drugs, because the harm to this interest arises in the very process of attempting to make the distinction.

Under the "mini-trial" directed by Kearl, a drug manufacturer has no assurance that a product he places on the market will be measured by the liability standard of comment k because a trial judge could decide that the benefit of the drug was not "exceptionally important" so as to make its availability "highly desirable," or that the interest in its availability did not outweigh the public's interest in subjecting the producer to strict liability. In determining whether the injury was "unavoidable" under the second prong of the test, Kearl requires that the trial court must consider "any alternative product that would have as effectively accomplished the full intended purpose of the ... product." (172 Cal.App.3d at p. 830, 218 Cal.Rptr. 453.) A manufacturer's incentive to develop what it might consider a superior product would be diminished if it might be held strictly liable for harmful side effects because a trial court could decide, perhaps many years later, that in fact another product which was available on the market would have accomplished the same result. Further, the question of the superiority of one drug over another would have to be decided not in the abstract but in reference to the plaintiff, since the advantages of a drug cannot be isolated from the condition of a particular patient. Thus, in one case the drug that injured the plaintiff might be the better choice, while this would not be true as to another user.

An additional matter that militates against adoption of the Kearl approach is that, as the Court of Appeal observed, different trial judges might reach different conclusions as to whether the same drug should be measured by strict liability principles, because the determination in each case depends on the evidence as well as the subjective determination of the judge regarding such matters as what constitutes an "exceptionally important benefit" of a drug....

In addition, there is a danger of inconsistency between the findings of the judge and the jury in the same case....

... [W]e disapprove the portion of Kearl which holds that comment k should not be applied to a prescription drug unless the trial court first determines that the drug is "unavoidably dangerous."

In conclusion, and in accord with almost all our sister states that have considered the issue, we hold that a manufacturer is not strictly liable for injuries caused by a prescription drug so long as the drug was properly prepared and accompanied by warnings of its dangerous propensities that were either known or reasonably scientifically knowable at the time of distribution.[12]

...

[Affirmed.]

---

12. Our conclusion does not mean, of course, that drug manufacturers are free of all liability for defective drugs. They are subject to liability for manufacturing defects, as well as under general principles of negligence, and for failure to warn of known or reasonably knowable side effects.

It should also be noted that the consumers of prescription drugs are afforded greater protection against defects than consumers of other products, since "the drug industry is closely regulated by the Food and Drug Administration, which actively controls the testing and manufacture of drugs and the method by which they are marketed, including the contents of warning labels." ...

ALLISON v. MERCK AND COMPANY

Supreme Court of Nevada
110 Nev. 762, 878 P.2d 948 (1994)

SPRINGER, Justice:

The trial court entered summary judgment against appellant Jo Ann Allison and her son Thomas, who are suing the Merck pharmaceutical company ("Merck") and the Clark County Health District ("Health District") because they claim that a Merck-manufactured measles, mumps and rubella vaccine (the MMR II) administered by the Health District caused then seventeen-month-old Thomas to contract encephalitis and to suffer from consequent blindness, deafness, mental retardation and spastic contractures. We conclude that Merck may be liable to Thomas Allison by reason of its strict liability as manufacturer if Thomas can prove that the vaccine in question is the cause of his disabilities. In addition, we conclude that Merck may be liable to Thomas and Ms. Allison for failing to provide a proper warning regarding the vaccine. Accordingly, we reverse the summary judgment in favor of Merck and remand to the trial court for a trial on Thomas' strict liability claim and on Thomas' and Ms. Allison's failure-to-warn claims.

STRICT LIABILITY

To establish liability under a strict tort liability theory, Thomas must establish that his injury "was caused by a defect in the product, and that such defect existed when the product left the hands of the defendant." Shoshone Coca-Cola Co. v. Dolinski, 82 Nev. 439, 443, 420 P.2d 855, 858 (1966)....

We have already considered the meaning of the word "defect" in connection with strict products liability. In Ginnis v. Mapes Hotel Corp., we adopted a definition of "defect" that is still useful and applicable to the case at hand: "'Although the definitions of the term "defect" in the context of products liability law use varying language, all of them rest upon the common premise that those products are defective which are dangerous because they fail to perform in the manner reasonably to be expected in light of their nature and intended function.'" 86 Nev. 408, 413, 470 P.2d 135, 138 (1970) (quoting Dunham v. Vaughn & Bushnell Mfg. Co., 42 Ill.2d 339, 247 N.E.2d 401, 403 (1969)). If Thomas can establish that the vaccine caused him to suffer permanent brain damage, then surely the vaccine failed to perform in the manner reasonably to be expected "in light of [its] nature and intended function." The nature and intended function of this vaccine, of course, is to create an immunity to measles, mumps and rubella without attendant blindness, deafness, mental retardation and permanent brain damage.[4]

Under the law of strict liability in this state, responsibility for injuries caused by defective products is properly fixed wherever it will most effectively reduce the hazards to life and health inherent in defective products that reach the market. Although manufacturers are not insurers of their products, where injury is caused by a defective product, responsibility is placed upon the manufacturer and the distributor of the defective product rather than on the injured consumer....

...

---

4. Indeed, Merck seems to concede that the vaccine was defective, albeit "unavoidably" so....

"UNAVOIDABLY UNSAFE"?

Merck claims that it is free from strict manufacturer's liability by virtue of the dictum stated in comment k to section 402A of the Restatement (Second) of Torts.[7] This comment suggests that a drug manufacturer should not be held liable for "the unfortunate consequences attending" the use of its drugs if: (1) the manufacturer supplies "the public with an apparently useful and desirable product, attended by a known but apparently reasonable risk," (2) the drug is "properly prepared and marketed," and (3) "proper warning is given."

It is not easy to divine just why the framers of the comment thought that a drug manufacturer should be excused in cases in which it manufactured a drug that was "known" to be dangerous. The whole idea behind strict tort liability is that the manufacturer, not the consumer, should bear the responsibility for injuries, even when the product is ostensibly properly prepared and marketed and when the plaintiff is not in a position to prove the origin of the defect.[8] See Stackiewicz, 100 Nev. at 443, 686 P.2d at 925.

What the question in this case really gets down to is whether an exception should be made in a case in which a drug manufacturer injures a consumer with a drug that it knows is dangerous, but not too ("unreasonably") dangerous. That is to say, should a drug manufacturer be allowed to profit with impunity from the distribution of a drug that it knows is capable of resulting in physical injury, so long as the drug can somehow be certified as not being unreasonably dangerous? We answer that question in the negative and say that a drug manufacturer should, under the strict liability jurisprudence of this state, be held liable in tort even when the drug is "properly prepared and marketed" (that is to say, non-negligently) and even when the known danger inherent in the drug may be what the comment calls "reasonable."

The apparent rationale of comment k in relieving drug manufacturers from liability is that where the manufacturer is free from fault, that is to say it produces a product that is unsafe because of a claim by the manufacturer that it is "incapable of being made safe," the manufacturer should not be responsible for injuries resulting from use of the drug. The comment itself gives as an example of such an "unavoidably unsafe" drug the Pasteur treatment of rabies "which not uncommonly leads to very serious and damaging consequences when it is injected." We would note, however, that the reason why serious and damaging consequences of the Pasteur rabies treatment do not result in tort liability is not because of the "unreasonably dangerous" doctrine proposed by comment k, but, rather, because the victim chooses to be injected with a drug having known "damaging consequences" rather than to die from rabies. It is the voluntary choice to take the antirabies serum that eliminates tort liability and not the serum's being said to be unavoidably or reasonably dangerous. There is no need to make an exception to the rules of strict liability such as that suggested by comment k in the rabies example because the rabies victim waives tort claims by accepting what the victim knows to be the necessary risk involved in the treatment.[9]

---

7. [The court quotes comment k, quoted in *Brown*, supra.]

8. "Properly prepared and marketed" means to me simply that the injured consumer is unable to prove that the manufacturer was guilty of negligence. This should not be able to defeat a strict liability action. "Proper warning" is a subject apart and is akin to informed consent. If a consumer uses a dangerous product after having been fairly and properly warned of its dangers, we are really not talking about strict liability at all. See discussion of comment k and voluntary use of dangerous drugs below.

9. Obviously, the situation in mass immunization projects is quite different from the emergency, voluntarily accepted treatment of rabies cases. Ms. Allison never had any real choice as to whether her son was to receive the vaccine in question. Not only was she, let us say, "strongly encouraged" to make the decision to go ahead with her child's vaccination, she was faced with the Hobson's choice

Speaking of "unavoidable" danger or fault-free infliction of harm, or speaking of reasonable (and therefore acceptable) risk of harm, is very much alien to strict liability theory and should have no place in the Restatement provisions relating to strict liability. Mixing concepts of fault-free ("unavoidable") manufacture and "reasonable risk" into the context of non-negligent, strict liability is entirely inconsistent with our products liability cases and with the law established in this state for almost thirty years. The well-accepted principle supporting our products liability cases is expressed in comment c of section 402 A of the Restatement:

> [P]ublic policy demands that the burden of accidental injuries caused by products intended for consumption be placed upon those who market them, and be treated as a cost of production against which liability insurance can be obtained; and that the consumer of such products is entitled to the maximum of protection at the hands of someone, and the proper persons to afford it are those who market the products.

It could not be said any more clearly than this. Merck, not Thomas Allison, must, if the Merck product did in fact cause Thomas' overwhelming misfortune, bear the "burden of the accidental [intended] injuries caused by products intended for consumption." Restatement (Second) of Torts, § 402 A, cmt. c (1965).

The Dissent and Merck urge that the imposition of liability on Merck for Thomas' injuries in this case would act as a deterrent to necessary and beneficial research and development of new drugs. The Dissent and Merck appear to be arguing that if Merck were to be held liable for statistically infrequent injuries such as the one at bar, society would be the worse because Merck and other drug manufacturers would be fearful and retarded in the development of new and greatly needed immunological products. If Merck were to have to pay for what its vaccine has done to Thomas, this would, Merck says, necessarily inhibit the development and marketing of immunological products which are helpful to many and "unfortunately" devastating to others.

Although, on policy grounds, Merck might talk some legislative body into immunizing it from liability, it would be certainly inappropriate for the court to make such a radical change in our well-established products liability law. Further, one would think that if a legislature were going to give such special benefits to drug manufacturers, most certainly the resultant legislation, to be just, would have to afford some kind of compensation or relief to the victims of "unavoidably unsafe" drugs. If, for example, a legislature provided that automobile manufacturers would be held to a standard of strict liability for manufacturing defects, even if injuries caused by a given defect are statistically infrequent and perhaps "unavoidable," and at the same time immunized drug manufacturers from liability for injuries caused by their vaccines, the legislature would, as mentioned, very probably and properly include in such discriminatory legislation some kind of no-fault victim compensation plan to set off the advantage given to drug manufacturers over other kinds of manufacturers.[10]

---

of either having the vaccine administered or not having the privilege of sending her son to private or public school. See NRS 392.435; NRS 394.192. Choosing not to have her son attend school, of course, would have subjected her to criminal penalties unless she had the means to have her son educated at home. NRS 392.200–.210. Even if the Allisons could be seen to have been properly warned of the risk inherent in this vaccine, it is hard to conclude that they freely accepted the risk of the horrible injuries resulting in this case.

10. In fact, four years after Thomas suffered his injuries, the United States Congress enacted the "National Childhood Vaccine Injury Act of 1986." This Act provides for compensation by the federal government to individuals who have sustained vaccine-related injuries after the effective date of the

In summary, this court cannot, under our law, read comment k as giving immunity to liability in cases such as the present one. It would be in harmony with our cases if comment k were read to mean that when drug consumers know of a danger and decide to accept the risk because of hoped-for benefits, strict tort liability cannot fairly attach to the dispenser of such a drug; however, insofar as comment k might be read as justifying release from liability of manufacturers and distributors of "reasonably dangerous" vaccines that are administered throughout our population and read as placing the burden of loss on the consumer, we must reject any such interpretation. It must be remembered that these inoculation programs are nationwide and that those who are required to take the vaccines have little or no choice as to whether to take them or not. We see no public policy need for changing our law or for shifting from the drug manufacturers to the consumer/victim the responsibility for all of the "unfortunate consequences" suffered by the Allisons of the world. If this kind of reallocation of resources is to be made, it is properly a legislative rather than a judicial function to do so. Considerable research and legislative committee activity would be necessary before an intelligent and informed judgment could be made as to whether we should leave "unfortunate" victims of drug injury to their own resources and free drug manufacturers from tort liability, on the unsubstantiated pretext that such a drastic measure is necessary in order to encourage drug research and development.

STRICT TORT LIABILITY MAY BE IMPOSED EVEN IF MERCK'S INTERPRETA-
TION OF COMMENT K WERE ACCEPTED

This court rejects the idea of freeing drug manufacturers from liability for defective drugs simply because they claim that the drugs are reasonably or unavoidably dangerous. However, even if, like the dissenting justice, we were to accept Merck's interpretation of comment k in this case, Thomas and his mother would still be entitled to a trial. A factfinder could find in this case that the product here, if not defective or dangerous "per se," was "unreasonably dangerous as marketed." ...

. . .

It would appear that a factfinder in this case could reasonably conclude that the vaccine given to Thomas Allison was not accompanied by a proper warning. Although Merck does not admit that this vaccine can cause disastrous central nervous system disorders, it announces in its MMR II package circular (which is not distributed to vaccinees) that "significant central nervous system reactions such as encephalitis and encephalopathy occurring within 30 days after vaccination, have been *temporally associated* with measles vaccine approximately once for every million doses." (Emphasis added.) In dealing with the mass consumers of the vaccine, the Health District revised this information when it issued its "Important Information" (not a "Warning") flyer prepared by the Center for Disease Control ("CDC"). The "Important Information" flyer is a revision of Merck's package circular, and it contains a much less dissuading statement, namely, that, "[a]lthough experts are not sure," there might be a very remote possibility—a chance in a million—that takers of the vaccine "may have a more seri-

---

Act, and limits vaccine manufacturers' liability for vaccine-related injuries sustained after the effective date of the Act.... The Act also provides for somewhat more limited compensation for injured vaccinees who had civil actions pending at the time the Act was passed, if the injured vaccinees elect to dismiss their pending civil actions.... The Act does not apply to this case as the Allisons did not elect to dismiss their civil action and proceed under the Act, as was their right. In the absence of federal law preemption or state legislative exculpation of drug manufacturers, there is no reason to depart from our existing strict liability jurisprudence....

ous reaction, such as inflammation of the brain (encephalitis)." The gist of the faulty warning aspect of liability in this case is that none of the prospective vacinees was warned of the actual possibility of permanent brain damage. Rashes, yes; sore throats, yes; "inflammation of the brain," yes; but permanent blindness, deafness, and mental retardation, no.

Viewing the facts in the light most favorable to the Allisons, Thomas is entitled under Nevada law to pursue an action against Merck under a strict tort liability theory. Also, it appears that the Allisons did not receive fair warning as to the vaccine's true danger and that they never had any real choice as to whether Thomas Allison was to be vaccinated. Comment k cannot be invoked to exculpate Merck from strict tort liability, and this case can be distinguished from the kinds of cases represented in the rabies example relied upon in comment k. It is one thing to proffer a medicine to a prospective user, saying: "You have a pernicious disease. We have a medicine that has serious side effects, even, possibly, blindness and deafness. You make the choice." It is quite another thing to say: "You must have your son vaccinated or he cannot go to school. Your son might get a rash or, on 'one out of a million' odds, might get a 'brain inflammation.'" In the first case, the user's knowing acceptance of the risks frees the purveyor of liability. In the second case, the traditional public policy behind strict product liability comes into play. Ms. Allison did not and could not have bargained for this misfortune. She had no real choice. "[T]he burden of accidental injuries caused by products intended for consumption [must] be placed upon those who market them." Restatement (Second) of Torts, § 402 A, cmt. c (1965).

In summary, if we apply the principles of product liability law that have been in effect in this state…, Thomas Allison is entitled to try to prove to a factfinder that the vaccine caused his disabilities and that the vaccine was defective and unsafe, because … the vaccine failed to perform in the manner reasonably to be expected of a vaccine. Further, even if we were, as some courts apparently have done, to accept the exculpatory, "unavoidably unsafe" interpretation of comment k, it is quite clear that there is a jury issue in this case as to whether the vaccine was "safe as marketed," that is to say whether it was marketed with an adequate warning.

· · ·

[A concurring opinion by Rose, C.J., is omitted.]

YOUNG, Justice, with whom STEFFEN, J., agrees, concurring in part and dissenting in part:

… I respectfully dissent from [Justice Springer's] opinion as to Merck. This court's decisions must be guided not by emotion but by the law, no matter how troubling the facts. And yet, today's decision seems to be directed by something other than our current law.

· · ·

COMMENT k

Justice Springer expresses great disapproval of comment k of Section 402A of the Restatement (Second) of Torts (1965), holding that in this state a drug manufacturer will be held strictly liable for any injuries caused by the drug even if the drug is "'properly prepared and marketed' and even when the known danger inherent in the drug may be what the comment calls 'reasonable.'" I fear that the result of this holding will be that this state will never allow a drug company to benefit from the protections of this comment. While I agree that comment k should not provide blanket protection to all drug manufacturers of any FDA approved drugs,[2] I am of the opinion that those manufacturers of drugs that are clearly useful and desirable should be afforded such protection. Accordingly, I believe that a better way is to apply a balancing test weighing the benefits of the particular drug against the risks inherent in the use of the drug. See Toner v. Lederle Laboratories, 112 Idaho 328, 732 P.2d 297, 308 (1987) ("The products comment k shields cannot be designed to be more safe at the time of distribution, but bestow benefits which clearly appear at the time of distribution to outweigh their concomitant risks.").... It is clear that the benefits of the MMR II vaccine far outweigh the risks.

According to Health and Human Services Secretary Donna Shalala, more turkeys, chickens and household pets are immunized in this country than preschool children. Donna E. Shalala, Secretary of Health and Human Services, Make Each Week Immunization Week, Chi. Trib., April 26, 1994, at 20. Due to this recent decrease in immunization, outbreaks of diseases long thought to be eradicated, such as measles, polio and whooping cough, are increasing at an alarming rate. Between 1989 and 1991, a measles epidemic left 132 people dead and 11,000 hospitalized, many of them under the age of two. Id. The only method of protection from these highly contagious and sometimes fatal childhood diseases is the widespread use of vaccines. And yet, few pharmaceutical manufacturers are willing to produce vaccines due to the increasing risk of litigation. I fear a decision such as the court is making today will only serve to further inhibit the development and production of such life-saving vaccines.

The record includes a recommendation of the CDC's Immunization Practices Advisory Committee regarding measles prevention. Recommendation of the Immunization Practices Advisory Committee (ACIP), Measles Prevention, Morbidity and Mortality Weekly Report, May 7, 1982, at 217-31. The article states that encephalitis occurred in approximately 1 out of every 2,000 cases of natural measles, often resulting in permanent brain damage and mental retardation, and death is said to have resulted in 1 out of every 3,000 measles cases. The article further states that prior to the introduction of the measles vaccine, 400,000 measles cases were reported every year. Since licensure of the vaccine in 1963, there has been a ninety-nine percent reduction in the reported incidence of measles. The article also states that with 131 million doses of measles vaccine distributed throughout the United States through 1981, encephalitis and encephalopathy were reported approximately once per million doses. Finally the article claims that "[t]he incidence rate of encephalitis or encephalopathy following measles vaccine is lower than the observed incidence of encephalitis of unknown etiology, suggesting that some or most of the reported severe neurological disorders may be only temporally related to measles vaccination rather than due to vaccination." Id. at 221.

Given the figures derived by the CDC as of May 1982, there is little question that the vaccine at issue has produced a major benefit for the majority of this country's population. At the same time, the incidence of adverse reactions resulting in serious injuries is very rare. Such information illustrates that this is an unavoidably unsafe and yet not unreasonably dangerous drug. Accordingly, the MMR II vaccine is extremely beneficial and thus its manufacturer deserves comment k protection from strict liability.

The purpose of comment k is to provide protection for manufacturers of products that are unavoidably unsafe. As the comment mentions, vaccines which can be made no safer are the best examples of such products whose benefits outweigh their risks. Companies whose vaccines are recognized to be highly beneficial but which can be made no

---

2. Some courts have chosen to provide blanket protection for drug manufacturers for any drug which has received FDA approval. See, e.g., *Grundberg v. Upjohn Co.*, 813 P.2d 89 (Utah 1991).

safer should be given the protection provided by comment k. To do so would not be such an affront to our system of products liability law as Justice Springer opines, but rather a wise and logical extension of that law.

· · ·

CONCLUSION

This is a tragic case. A young boy has been left in a grievous condition while his mother has been left to suffer her child's pain on a daily basis. Though Thomas and Mrs. Allison are receiving Social Security, Medicaid and Aid to Dependent Children benefits, their lives surely cannot be easy.

And yet, however heartbreaking the facts, we cannot forget the law. Our job is to interpret the law as it applies to each case. However tragic the case may be, we cannot bend or change the law simply to achieve results.

As Cardozo once wrote, we should strive for certainty in our law that will keep it "consistent with verities and principles as broad as the common law itself, and as deep and fundamental as the postulates of justice." Benjamin N. Cardozo, The Growth of the Law 17 (1924). I fear that the court's decision today strays from the certainty of our law to an inconsistent end.

NOTES

(1) If a court would otherwise conclude that the imposition of strict liability would provide incentives to make safer products, or would achieve desirable risk spreading, or both, then why should the fact that a product is medically useful immunize its manufacturer?

(2) What policy considerations appear to drive the *Brown* court, on the one hand, and the majority in *Allison*, on the other? Is the principal key to either decision:

(a) An attempt to make the market for drugs and vaccines efficient, taking into account the risks and benefits of particular pharmaceutical products

(b) A concern for spreading the losses of seriously injured persons

(c) The vindication of consumer expectations

(d) Providing manufacturers "technology-forcing" incentives to make drugs and vaccines safer.

How much does the majority's decision in *Allison* depend on risk spreading? Aren't the ultimate bearers of the risk consumers of vaccines?

(3) Is there a legally significant difference between prescription products like drugs and vaccines and other products that justifies separate treatment for prescription products? Does viewing prescription products as requiring a liability rule more generous to producers than the rules applicable to other products start a slide on a slippery slope to government control of the market for such products?

(4) Are the decisions in *Brown* and *Allison* unavoidably "legislative"? What legislative aspects of the decisions are unavoidable for a court faced with these types of cases?

(5) What presuppositions are crucial to these decisions about how manufacturers, and legislatures, will behave if strict liability were imposed? For example, if *Allison* were to drive manufacturers further out of the vaccine market, would the legislature pass a statute immunizing vaccine manufacturers on a comment k basis? Or would it be more

likely to take over the process of making vaccines entirely, and/or to set up a legislative compensation scheme for vaccine injuries?

(6) Does it appear that the risks of the vaccine that so seriously injured Thomas Allison outweighed its utility? If they did not, why shouldn't the net gain to society from the vaccine be conclusive against liability?

(7) The edited version of *Allison* omits much of the discussion on warnings. Suppose that Ms. Allison had been given a detailed warning about the very small chance that the vaccine would cause catastrophic injuries to her son. Should that be conclusive against strict liability?

(8) What role, if any, should there be for juries to determine the liability question in cases of this sort? Would it be appropriate to ask jurors whether they would favor compensation for people injured by prescription products, without knowing whether they or their children would be the unlucky recipients of a drug — or would benefit from it, like most people who used the product? Is that inquiry a legally relevant one? If so, is it entirely for the judge?

(9) Could you fashion a better formulation of the defect concept applicable to prescription drugs and vaccines than comment k — one that would take into account the concern that strict liability would sometimes create disincentives to the development of useful products, but would more closely align the law's treatment of prescription products with its treatment of products in general?

(10) More than 40 states have now legislated to prohibit the imposition of liability without fault for blood transfusions. Do the rationales for strict liability announced in *Ogle*, § 7.02, and elaborated in the quotation in note 2 following *Ogle* apply persuasively in the case of virus-contaminated blood? What effects on conduct would you expect to result from the imposition of strict liability on blood suppliers in cases of hepatitis, or AIDS, caused by a transfusion?

(11) A virtual industry of litigation sprang up in the wake of revelations about risks of heart attacks and strokes associated with so-called "Cox-2" drugs, mainly Vioxx and Celebrex. Key arguments in lawsuits involving Vioxx, in particular, centered on the alleged withholding of information that had accumulated about the possible side effects of the product, and on the admissibility of scientific evidence. A press story reported that a "senior scientist" of Merck, the maker of Vioxx, had pressured one of the company's researchers to "change his views" about the drug being the probable cause of a fatal heart attack. See Alex Berenson, *Evidence in Vioxx Suits Shows Intervention by Merck Officials*, N.Y. TIMES, Apr. 25, 2005, at A1. Moreover, there was evidence that the company had "abruptly" canceled a planned "major cardiovascular study" of Vioxx "just before it was set to start." Barry Meier, *Merck Canceled an Early Study of Vioxx*, N.Y. TIMES, Feb. 8, 2005, at C1. After Merck withdrew Vioxx from the market, at least 6500 people filed lawsuits ascribing deaths and injuries to the drug. At this writing, the early test cases had taken on the character of a big league sports playoff. Summarizing the background of a trial slated to begin in Houston, one reporter said that Merck had "hopes of taking the lead in its Vioxx-related litigation series, now tied 1–1" on the basis of verdicts in other courts. Heather Won Tesoriero, *Judge's Ruling Tempers Merck's Hopes for Trial No. 3*, WALL ST. J., Nov. 25, 2005, at B1. A crucial issue in the case involved the admissibility of scientific evidence, *see infra* § 10.05. A pre-trial ruling by the trial judge in the third case indicated that he would allow the plaintiffs to present their evidence. "In essence," he wrote, "both the Plaintiff and Merck rely on the same material. They simply interpret it differently and reach contrary conclusions." *Id.*

[D] Tobacco

BURTON v. R.J. REYNOLDS TOBACCO CO.
United States District Court, District of Kansas
884 F. Supp. 1515 (1995)

LUNGSTRUM, District Judge.

...

Plaintiffs David Burton and Ora Burton filed this lawsuit on May 25, 1994, and later filed an amended complaint against defendants R.J. Reynolds Tobacco Company and The American Tobacco Company. Plaintiff alleges numerous claims, including fraud and misrepresentation, negligence, strict liability, breach of express warranty, conspiracy and violation of consumer protection statutes.

... The defendants advance a number of theories, chief among these that a majority of plaintiff's claims are pre-empted by the Federal Cigarette Labeling and Advertising Act and that plaintiff's strict liability claims fail to state a claim under the Restatement (Second) of Torts Section 402A....

For the reasons set forth below, the court finds that defendants' joint motion to dismiss and for judgment on the pleadings should be granted in part and denied in part....

From approximately 1950 to 1993, plaintiff David Burton purchased and smoked Camel cigarettes, manufactured and sold by defendant RJR, and Lucky Strike cigarettes, manufactured and sold by defendant American Tobacco. Plaintiff contends that as a direct and proximate result of the use of defendants' products, he developed peripheral vascular disease. As a result of the disease, plaintiff underwent a series of operations in 1993 and 1994 which resulted in the amputation of both of his legs.

[Omitted are parts of the opinion that include rulings on preemption questions.]

Defendants ... contend that Counts 1 and 5 of plaintiff's amended complaint,[3] which are based on strict liability in tort for manufacture of a defective product, should be dismissed because they are barred by Section 402A of the Restatement (Second) of Torts, Comment i. The Kansas Supreme Court has expressly adopted Section 402A and Comment i thereto. See Lester v. Magic Chef, Inc., 230 Kan. 643, 641 P.2d 353, 361 (1982). Section 402A creates liability for physical injury caused by a product "in a defective condition unreasonably dangerous to the user." Kansas law is clear that the product must be both "defective" and "unreasonably dangerous." ... Under Comment i, a product is not unreasonably dangerous unless it is "dangerous to an extent beyond that which would be contemplated by the ordinary consumer who purchases it, with the ordinary knowledge common to the community as to its characteristics." Comment i expressly limits liability with respect to certain categories of products, including "good whiskey," "good tobacco," and "good butter." The comment illustrates with the example that "[g]ood tobacco is not unreasonably dangerous merely because the effects of smoking may be harmful: but tobacco containing something like marijuana may be unrea-

---

3. Count 1 is a strict liability claim in which plaintiffs contend that the cigarettes placed in the stream of commerce by the defendants were dangerous to an extent beyond what would be contemplated by ordinary consumers and were in an unsafe and defective condition. Count 5 is a strict liability claim in which plaintiffs contend that the cigarettes were defective as a result of the cigarettes causing addiction and dependency, therefore rendering any warning meaningless.

sonably dangerous." Defendants contend that plaintiff has not alleged that defendants' cigarettes were anything but "good tobacco" under Comment i, and, accordingly, defendants' cigarettes are neither "defective" nor "unreasonably dangerous" under Section 402A as a matter of law.

The court does not find the preclusionary effect of Comment i to be as broad as defendants contend. The court finds that the reference in Comment i to tobacco to illustrate the operation of the consumer expectations principle does not, as a matter of law, remove all claims of defective tobacco products from the operation of Section 402A. Although "good tobacco," without any additives or foreign substances, may not be unreasonably dangerous, that does not automatically mean that all tobacco-containing products are not unreasonably dangerous. The cigarettes sold by defendants are manufactured products and, as such, the court finds that they are subject to design, packaging, and manufacturing variations which may render them defective even if the tobacco used in their manufacture was initially unadulterated. Accord, Grinnell v. American Tobacco Co., Inc., 883 S.W.2d 791, 799 (Tex.App.—Beaumont 1994); Rogers v. R.J. Reynolds Tobacco Co., 557 N.E.2d 1045, 1053 (Ind.App. 2 Dist.1990). Accordingly, the court finds that plaintiff's strict liability claims are not necessarily barred under Section 402A and defendants' motion to dismiss as to those claims is therefore denied.

Defendants make an additional argument that plaintiff's strict liability claims should be dismissed because plaintiff merely attacks cigarettes generically and fails to allege a specific defect. The court agrees that under Kansas law, as to plaintiff's claim of design defect, it will be necessary for plaintiff to specifically identify what aspect of defendants' products was defectively designed. See Jenkins v. Amchem Products, Inc., 256 Kan. 602, 886 P.2d 869, 890 (1994). However, because the plaintiff has not yet been allowed to conduct discovery to flesh out the specifics of his design defect claim, the court believes that it would be premature to dismiss plaintiff's strict liability design defect claims at this point in the litigation.

. . .

AMERICAN TOBACCO COMPANY v. GRINNELL

Supreme Court of Texas
951 S.W.2d 420 (1997)

CORNYN, Justice, delivered the opinion of the Court, in which PHILLIPS, Chief Justice, and GONZALEZ, SPECTOR, BAKER and ABBOTT, Justices, join.

In this wrongful death case, we confront an issue with profound health and public policy consequences: whether "common knowledge" of the health risks of cigarette smoking relieves tobacco companies of any duty to warn smokers of those risks. Applying our usual summary judgment standard, we conclude that the defendant has conclusively established the defense of common knowledge with regard to the general health risks of smoking. We also conclude, however, that the defendant has not conclusively established the common knowledge defense with regard to the addictive nature of cigarettes. Accordingly, we conclude that the defendant is entitled to summary judgment on most, but not all of the plaintiffs' claims, and remand the surviving claims to the trial court for further proceedings.

In 1952, nineteen-year-old Wiley Grinnell began smoking Lucky Strikes, cigarettes manufactured by the American Tobacco Company. Almost a year later, Grinnell changed to Pall Malls, also manufactured by American. After smoking for approximately thirty-three years, Grinnell was diagnosed with lung cancer in July 1985. Shortly thereafter, he filed this lawsuit. He died less than a year later. Grinnell's family continued this suit after his death, adding wrongful death and survival claims. The family alleges that American failed to warn of, and actively concealed, facts that it knew or should have known, including the facts that Grinnell could quickly become addicted to cigarettes and that his smoking could result in injury or death from the cancer-causing ingredients if he used the cigarettes as American intended. They also allege that, even though American knew or should have known that its cigarettes were dangerous and could not be used safely, American represented to consumers that cigarettes were not harmful, dangerous, or capable of causing injury.

. . .

I. Common-Law Duties

A. Strict Liability

The Grinnells allege that cigarettes are both defective and unreasonably dangerous under section 402A of the Restatement (Second) of Torts. Specifically, they assert that American's cigarettes are (1) defectively designed because ingredients found in cigarettes cause cancer, addiction, and disease, (2) defectively marketed, because the cigarette packages contain inadequate warnings, and (3) defectively manufactured because cigarettes contain pesticide residue. In his deposition taken one month before his death, Grinnell testified that had he known of the dangers inherent in cigarettes he would never have started smoking in the first place.

In Texas, section 402A of the Restatement (Second) of Torts governs claims for strict liability in tort....

1. Marketing Defect

A defendant's failure to warn of a product's potential dangers when warnings are required is a type of marketing defect. Caterpillar, Inc., 911 S.W.2d at 382; Lucas v. Texas Indus., Inc., 696 S.W.2d 372, 377 (Tex.1984). The existence of a duty to warn of dangers or instruct as to the proper use of a product is a question of law. Firestone Steel, 927 S.W.2d at 613; General Motors Corp. v. Saenz, 873 S.W.2d 353, 356 (Tex.1993). Generally, a manufacturer has a duty to warn if it knows or should know of the potential harm to a user because of the nature of its product.... Nevertheless, this Court has recognized that there is no duty to warn when the risks associated with a particular product are matters "within the ordinary knowledge common to the community." Joseph E. Seagram & Sons, Inc. v. McGuire, 814 S.W.2d 385, 388 (Tex.1991) (holding that no legal duty exists to warn of the health risks of alcohol consumption because such risks are common knowledge). American argues that it had no duty to warn Grinnell of the risks associated with smoking its cigarettes because the dangers of smoking were common knowledge when Grinnell began smoking in 1952.

Comments i and j to Restatement section 402A incorporate common knowledge into the analysis of whether a product is "unreasonably dangerous" under that section. Comment i, which defines "unreasonably dangerous," forecloses liability against manufacturers unless a product is dangerous to an extent beyond that which would be contemplated by the ordinary consumer with knowledge common to the community:

> Many products cannot possibly be made entirely safe for all consumption, and
> any food or drug necessarily involves some risk of harm, if only from over-
> consumption.... That is not what is meant by "unreasonably dangerous" in

this Section. *The article sold must be dangerous to an extent beyond that which would be contemplated by the ordinary consumer who purchases it, with the ordinary knowledge common to the community as to its characteristics.... Good tobacco is not unreasonably dangerous* merely because the effects of smoking may be harmful; but tobacco containing something like marijuana may be unreasonably dangerous.

RESTATEMENT (SECOND) OF TORTS § 402A cmt. i (1965)(emphasis added). Comment j excuses a seller from the duty to warn about dangers that are generally known and recognized:

In order to prevent the product from being unreasonably dangerous, the seller may be required to give directions or warning, on the container, as to its use.... But a seller is not required to warn with respect to products, or ingredients in them, which are only dangerous, or potentially so, when consumed in excess quantity, or over a long period of time, *when the danger, or potentiality of danger, is generally known and recognized....* [T]he dangers of alcoholic beverages are an example....

Id. § 402A cmt. j (1965)(emphasis added).

Common knowledge, in the context of comments i and j, connotes a general societal understanding of the risks inherent in a specific product or class of products. Seagram, 814 S.W.2d at 388. In Seagram we also emphasized that the standard for finding common knowledge as a matter of law is a strict one. First holding that the term "common knowledge" encompasses "those facts that are so well known to the community as to be beyond dispute," id., we then noted:

Because Seagram is asking this court to determine common knowledge as a matter of law, we find the judicial notice rule helpful in providing a standard. Compare 33 S. Goode, O. Wellborn, III & M. Sharlot, Guide to Texas Rules of Evidence § 201.2 (Tex.Prac.1988)(requiring "high degree of indisputability" as prerequisite to judicial notice) with Brune v. Brown Forman Corp....

Thus, common knowledge is an extraordinary defense that applies only in limited circumstances. As the court in Brune noted, common knowledge encompasses only those things "so patently obvious and so well known to the community generally, that there can be no question or dispute concerning their existence." ... We will find common knowledge as a matter of law only when the standard set out in Seagram is met. It is not met in all respects here.

For example, we do not find the dangers of alcohol and cigarettes, or the public's awareness of those respective dangers, to be commensurate. Unlike Seagram & Sons, which did not dispute the health dangers of prolonged alcohol use, Seagram, 814 S.W.2d at 387, the tobacco industry, including American, actively disputed that cigarettes posed any health risk at the time Grinnell began smoking in 1952. Indeed, the industry continues to dispute the health risks of smoking and the addictive nature of cigarettes, before Congress, in the national press,[4] and even at oral argument before the

---

4. See *Castano v. American Tobacco Co.*, 870 F.Supp. 1425, 1433 (E.D.La.1994)(noting that in hearing before Congress on April 14, 1994, the chief executive officers of the major tobacco manufacturers testified that nicotine is not addictive, and that Phillip Morris purchased full-page newspaper ads following that testimony, which read in part: "Phillip Morris does not believe cigarette smoking is addictive"); but see *Tobacco Executives Still Claim Smoking not Killer, Paper Says*, Hous. Chron., April 21, 1997, at 3 ("On March 20, Liggett, maker of L & Ms and Chesterfields, settled 22

Court in this case.[5] Despite this ongoing "dispute," we are bound to apply the rule that whether knowledge has become common to the community is an objective determination....

The party asserting the common-knowledge defense must establish that the dangers attributable to alcohol, tobacco, or other products were a matter of common knowledge when the consumer began using the product. Based on the summary judgment record, we hold American established that the general ill-effects of smoking were commonly known when Grinnell started smoking in 1952. However, we also hold that American did not establish that the addictive quality of cigarettes was commonly known when Grinnell began smoking in 1952.

Regarding the general health risks associated with smoking, the Tennessee Supreme Court held as early as 1898 that these risks were "generally known." Austin v. State, 101 Tenn. 563, 48 S.W. 305, 306 (1898), aff'd as modified sub nom. Austin v. Tennessee, 179 U.S. 343, 21 S.Ct. 132, 45 L.Ed. 224 (1900). On certiorari, the United States Supreme Court observed:

> [W]e should be shutting our eyes to what is constantly passing before them were we to affect an ignorance of the fact that a belief in [cigarettes'] deleterious effects, particularly upon young people, *has become very general*, and that communications are constantly finding their way into the public press denouncing their use as fraught with great danger....

179 U.S. at 348, 21 S.Ct. at 134 (emphasis added). Other early courts also recognized the harmful effects of smoking cigarettes.... More recently, courts have similarly acknowledged that the inherent dangers of smoking cigarettes are within the community's common knowledge....

Moreover, by 1962, when the Surgeon General's advisory committee began examining the health risks associated with smoking, there were already more than seven thousand publications of professional and general circulation examining the relationship between smoking and health. PUBLIC HEALTH SERVICE, U.S. DEP'T OF HEALTH AND HUMAN SERVS., PUB. NO. 89-8411, REDUCING THE HEALTH CONSEQUENCES OF SMOKING: 25 YEARS OF PROGRESS: A REPORT OF THE SURGEON GENERAL 2 (1989). Of these publications, articles published in nationally circulated magazines dating back to the early 1900s informed readers about the deleterious effects of smoking....

During this same period, many books examined the health risks associated with smoking and argued against the use of cigarettes....

Not only does historical evidence illustrate the public's pre-1952 awareness of smoking's dangerous effects, but the Grinnells' experts also confirmed that the health hazards of smoking were common knowledge when Grinnell began smoking. Dr. Ravenholt, an expert on cancer and its causes, testified that the dangers of smoking were well known

---

state lawsuits by agreeing to label its cigarettes addictive and admitting cigarettes are targeted to teen-agers and cause cancer.").

5. The following colloquy occurring between the Court and American's counsel at the oral argument of this case:

COURT: Does your client agree or disagree that cigarette smoking is dangerous to one's health?

COUNSEL: Our client agrees that there is a risk factor in smoking cigarettes.

COURT: Rendering it dangerous to one's health?

COUNSEL: There is a risk factor from a statistical standpoint. We do not agree that smoking causes lung cancer because we don't know.

by the 1950s: "I think the majority [of people] would have been aware, you know, an adult, reasonably intelligent." He also testified that, in 1950, "evidence emerged of the lung cancer producing capability of smoking" and that the dangers attributable to smoking were extensively published and frequently front-page news stories in the 1950s. Dr. Greenberg likewise testified that the decision to smoke or refrain from smoking cigarettes is a matter of "individual personal responsibility" in light of the health risks.

We conclude that the general health dangers attributable to cigarettes were commonly known as a matter of law by the community when Grinnell began smoking. See Caterpillar, Inc. v. Shears, 911 S.W.2d at 383 (common knowledge is usually determined as a matter of law). We cannot conclude, however, that the specific danger of nicotine addiction was common knowledge when Grinnell began smoking. Addiction is a danger apart from the direct physical dangers of smoking because the addictive nature of cigarettes multiplies the likelihood of and contributes to the smoker's ultimate injury, in Grinnell's case, lung cancer. See Garner, Cigarette Dependency and Civil Liability: A Modest Proposal, 53 S. Cal. L.Rev. 1423, 1430 (1980) ("[D]ependency adds a new dimension to smoking, for it greatly increases the likelihood of high volume, long term use which leads to disease, disability, and early death."). This Court has also recognized the seriousness of addiction and the need for manufacturers to warn of this danger in the context of prescription drugs. Crocker v. Winthrop Labs., 514 S.W.2d 429, 432–33 (Tex.1974) (holding drug manufacturer liable under Restatement (Second) of Torts § 402B for misrepresenting that drug "was free and safe from all dangers of addiction"); see also Carlisle v. Philip Morris, Inc., 805 S.W.2d 498, 516 (Tex.App.—Austin 1991, writ denied) ("Indeed, the failure to warn of cigarettes' addictive nature could be the essence of a plaintiff's complaint."). We acknowledge that some authorities support the proposition that some members of the community associated addiction with smoking cigarettes earlier in this century. Ploch v. City of St. Louis, 345 Mo. 1069, 138 S.W.2d 1020, 1023 (1940) (cigarettes have "harmful properties" and it is common knowledge that nicotine produces "tobacco addicts"); Wiley, The Little White Slaver, GOOD HOUSEKEEPING, Jan. 1916, at 91 (people can become "slaves" to the cigarette habit and cigarette smoking can "shorten their lives").

The Surgeon General spoke to the addictive nature of tobacco in the most recent and comprehensive report on the subject in 1988. . . .

But we cannot simply assume that common knowledge of the general health risks of tobacco use naturally includes common knowledge of tobacco's addictive quality. Indeed, as David Kessler, former head of the FDA, has pointed out:

> Before 1980, when FDA last considered its jurisdiction over tobacco products, no major public health organization had determined that nicotine was an addictive drug. Today, however, *all* major public health organizations in the United States and abroad with expertise in tobacco or drug addiction recognize that the nicotine delivered by cigarettes and smokeless tobacco is addictive.

Kessler et al., The Legal and Scientific Basis for FDA's Assertion of Jurisdiction over Cigarettes and Smokeless Tobacco, 277 JAMA 405, 406 (1997) (emphasis added). The FDA based its 1996 assertion of jurisdiction on "a wealth of epidemiologic and laboratory data establishing that tobacco users display the clinical symptoms of addiction and that nicotine has the characteristics of other addictive drugs." Id. Thus, unlike the general dangers associated with smoking, as late as 1988 and certainly in 1952, the danger of addiction from smoking cigarettes was not widely known and recognized in the community in general, or, particularly, by children or adolescents. NICOTINE ADDIC-

TION at vi. The FDA has explained that because of tobacco's addictive effects, the only way to prevent the ensuing disease and death is to prevent children and adolescents from starting to use tobacco: "Most people who suffer the adverse health consequences of using cigarettes and smokeless tobacco begin their use before they reach the age of 18, an age when they are not prepared for, or equipped to, make a decision that, for many, will have lifelong consequences." Regulations, 61 FED. REG. at 44398.

Because the community's knowledge concerning the danger of nicotine addiction associated with cigarettes was not beyond dispute in 1952, the Seagram standard for finding common knowledge as a matter of law has not been met. We agree with the court in Rogers v. R.J. Reynolds Tobacco Co.:

> There is no basis for our judicially noticing what the ordinary consumer's knowledge concerning the addictive qualities of cigarettes may have been when [the plaintiff] began smoking in 1940. The state of knowledge attributable to the community of individuals consuming cigarettes has changed over time and will continue to do so. It was not until 1988 that the Surgeon General published a report informing of the addictive nature of cigarettes.

557 N.E.2d 1045, 1054 (Ind.Ct.App.1990). Accordingly, we hold that American did not establish as a matter of law that the danger of addiction associated with cigarettes was commonly known in 1952.

Because we conclude that American did not conclusively establish that the danger of addiction to nicotine was common knowledge, the Grinnells may maintain their strict liability marketing defect claims to the extent they are based on the addictive qualities of cigarettes, if no other defenses defeat those claims.

The Grinnells assert that American breached its duty to warn users about its product's addictive nature because before January 1, 1966, the product's packages contained no warnings. A manufacturer is required to give an adequate warning if it knows or should know that potential harm may result from use of the product. Bristol-Myers Co. v. Gonzales, 561 S.W.2d 801, 804 (Tex.1978). In the absence of a warning, a rebuttable presumption arises that the "user would have read and heeded such warnings and instructions." ... A manufacturer may rebut the presumption with evidence that the plaintiff did not heed whatever warnings were given, or would not have heeded any proposed warnings....

The Grinnells assert that when Grinnell started smoking in 1952 he did not know and had heard nothing about any risk of addiction associated with smoking. The Grinnells further assert that American's failure to warn of the addictive nature of cigarettes caused Grinnell's eventual death because Grinnell testified that had he known what he later learned, he would never have started smoking. In rebuttal, American cites testimony that in the late 1950s and the 1960s, Grinnell continued smoking despite warnings from his father, coaches, and friends.

At most, the evidence relied on by American establishes that some people warned Grinnell about the general dangers of smoking. It does not conclusively establish that had Grinnell been warned that cigarettes were addictive before he began smoking he would have refused to follow the warnings. Grinnell testified at his deposition that if he had known of the dangers associated with smoking, including addiction, he never would have started smoking. At the very least, this testimony creates a fact issue regarding whether Grinnell would have heeded warnings had they been given to him before he began smoking. Dr. Grabowski, an expert on addiction, testified that Grinnell was addicted to cigarettes by the late 1950s and early 1960s and could not have stopped smoking without "intensive intervention." In short, American's summary judgment evidence does not conclusively establish that adequate warnings would not have been followed and thus would not have "made a difference in the outcome." ... Summary judgment on the Grinnells' marketing defect theory related to the addictive nature of cigarettes was therefore improper.

Thus, to the extent we hold that the general health risks of smoking were within the knowledge common to the community even before Grinnell began smoking in 1952, American has established that its cigarettes were not unreasonably dangerous. Summary judgment was, therefore, proper to the extent the Grinnells' strict liability claims relate to the general health risks associated with smoking. However, we also hold that American did not establish as a matter of law that the specific danger of addiction from smoking was knowledge common to the community. Therefore, we hold that the Grinnells' marketing defect claim survives to the extent it is based on the allegation that the addictive nature of cigarettes rendered American's products unreasonably dangerous, and to the extent it is not preempted by federal law.

2. Design Defect

The duty to design a safe product is "an obligation imposed by law." McKisson v. Sales Affiliates, Inc., 416 S.W.2d 787, 789 (Tex.1967). Whether a seller has breached this duty, that is, whether a product is unreasonably dangerous, is a question of fact for the jury.... In determining whether a product is defectively designed, the jury must conclude that the product is unreasonably dangerous as designed, taking into consideration the utility of the product and the risk involved in its use.

...

American argues that the common-knowledge defense bars the Grinnells' design defect claims as a matter of law. But, as we stated in Turner [v. General Motors Corp., 584 S.W. 2d 844 (Tex. 1979)], "the user's anticipated awareness of the dangers inherent in the product and their avoidability because of general public knowledge of the obvious condition of the product," and "the expectations of the ordinary consumer," are but two factors for the jury to consider when determining whether a product was defectively designed. American's attempt to invoke the common-knowledge defense is actually an attempt to invoke the "open and obvious defense" or "patent danger rule," which this Court has rejected in design defect cases....

Alternatively, American argues that it is entitled to summary judgment because no safer alternative cigarette design exists. In Turner we held that "the availability of a substitute product which would meet the same need and not be unsafe or unreasonably expensive," was one factor for juries to consider when determining whether a product was defectively designed. We reaffirmed this holding in Caterpillar, Inc. v. Shears by stating that "if there are no safer alternatives, a product is not unreasonably dangerous as a matter of law." 911 S.W.2d at 384.[9] Accordingly, if there is no safer alternative to the cigarette manufactured by American, then its cigarettes are not unreasonably dangerous as a matter of law.

---

9. Although not applicable to the present case, the Texas Legislature has codified the "safer alternative" requirement. Tex. Civ. Prac. & Rem.Code § 82.005 (safer alternative design must be shown by preponderance of the evidence in design defect case).

The Grinnells assert that American's cigarettes could have been made reasonably safer by filtration, and by reducing the amount of tobacco, tar, nicotine, and toxins in them. In making its argument that no reasonably safer alternative design exists, American relies on the testimony of the Grinnells' experts, Drs. Greenberg, Stevens, and Ginzel. These experts testified that Grinnell would have developed cancer and died regardless of whether filters, lower tar, or less tobacco had been used. Specifically, Dr. Greenberg testified:

Q: It didn't matter to you and your opinion would not have changed as to the cause of the lung cancer, regardless of the brand, whether it was filtered or nonfiltered, short or long cigarette. Is that right?

A: That's correct.

Dr. Ginzel testified similarly:

Q: Doctor, is there any safe cigarette with respect to lung cancer?

A: Not that I know of.

Q: Is there any design for a cigarette that Mr. Grinnell could have smoked that would have avoided his claimed lung cancer?

A: Not during his lifetime, no.

Ultimately, the Grinnells essentially concede that no reasonably safer alternatives exist, but argue that all cigarettes are defective and unreasonably dangerous nonetheless. Because American conclusively proved that no reasonably safer alternative design exists for its cigarettes, we hold that summary judgment was proper on all of the Grinnells' design defect claims, including those based on the addictive quality of cigarettes.

...

[Reversed in part and affirmed in part.]

[The separate opinion of Justice Hecht is omitted.]

ENOCH, Justice, joined by HECHT, Justice, concurring and dissenting.

Wiley Grinnell, Jr. died of lung cancer, a risk that this Court holds as a matter of law he knowingly and willingly undertook when he began smoking American's cigarettes in 1952. Despite this conclusion, and despite the fact that Grinnell knowingly and willingly began smoking three packs a day, the Court holds that American Tobacco may be liable for Grinnell's death because some thirty-three years later Grinnell did in fact develop the disease the risk of which he freely accepted at age nineteen.

The Court hinges its decision today on the premise that while the "general health risks" of smoking were commonly known in 1952, the specific risk of addiction was not commonly known when Grinnell started smoking. However, the Court fails to explain what it means by the phrase "general health risks," giving no guidance to the parties or to the public about which cigarette-related dangers may have given rise to a duty to warn in 1952 and which did not. This shortcoming illustrates the fundamental problem with the Court's analysis—the "general health risk" of cigarettes, found by the Court to be commonly known in 1952, is that when used as intended, they can kill you.... I would hold that summary judgment was proper on all of the Grinnells' claims.

...

Given the Court's decision today, the common knowledge doctrine retains little if any relevance in our products liability jurisprudence because the specific trumps the general. We can now say "I knew smoking was bad for me and could even kill me, but I didn't know I could become addicted." There are limits to what the law can and should require in warnings. The Court's retreat from McGuire may sap the common knowledge doctrine of any vitality it has in the law.

...

NOTES

(1) Is there such a thing as "good tobacco"? If all tobacco is "bad," does that necessarily make it a defective product? Comment i to section 402A, besides referring to "good tobacco" as not being "unreasonably dangerous merely because the effects of smoking may be harmful," opines that "[g]ood whiskey is not unreasonably dangerous merely because it will make some people drunk, and is especially dangerous to alcoholics" and that "[g]ood butter is not unreasonably dangerous merely because, if such be the case, it deposits cholesterol in the arteries and leads to heart attacks."

Are tobacco, liquor, and butter fairly analogous?

(2) What are the primary policy considerations that bear on the decision of whether to apply strict liability to claims for cigarette-caused illness?

(3) Does the majority of the *Grinnell* court split hairs with its approach? What are the various "rules" it announces under the heading of "marketing defect" and "design defect"? Can they be harmonized?

(4) What is the strongest argument that cigarette makers have that tobacco is nondefective? Is the argument focused on the qualities of tobacco, or on the information available to consumers? If the latter, why is that not chalked up as a defense, rather than under the defect question?

(5) Compensation for, and prevention of, cigarette-caused illness has been the subject of major legislative initiatives, including a proposal for comprehensive federal legislation. Should the subject of compensation for illness caused by smoking be left entirely to the legislature?

(6) Is the argument that a product is "common and widely distributed" the equivalent of a cultural defense? For about two decades beginning in the 1880s, there was a great vogue for cocaine in the United States. The drug was "so readily available in a Philadelphia drugstore in 1903 that regular customers would hold up one finger for 'a "five-cent powder"; two fingers ten cents worth; fifteen cents, and so on.'" Marshall S. Shapo, *Freud, Cocaine & Products Liability*, 77 B.U. L. Rev. 421, 424 (1997), quoting Richard Ashley, Cocaine: Its History, Uses and Effects 65 (1975). Was cocaine an "unreasonably dangerous product" then? If it was not, and it is now, what has changed?

(7) What legal distinctions should be drawn with respect to the following cases:

(1) A product is made in the same way each time, but it harmfully affects a few individuals unpredictably (as in the case of cosmetics that cause dermatitis in a few users).

(2) A product is made in the same way each time, but statistically it will cause serious harmful effects to a significant percentage of users (cigarettes).

(3) A product is made according to the best standards of the industry, but statistically it is known that a few units will always be unreasonably dangerous to any user, and these units cannot be identified in advance:

(a) When the few units are contaminated by disease-causing organisms (blood-borne viruses)

(b) When the few units have physical flaws that are undetectable in practice (auto assemblies that collapse).

(4) A product is made in the same way as are all goods of that line, but it does not protect users from statistically predictable trauma caused by the carelessness of other parties (automobile crashworthiness).

(8) In 1998, lawsuits by forty-six states against tobacco manufacturers ended in a structured Master Settlement Agreement (MSA) that called for a payout of more than $200 billion.

(9) Plaintiffs' success against "Big Tobacco" emboldened attorneys—in many cases the same attorneys—to pursue manufacturers of other products thought to be shielded by comment i to section 402A. Despite the failure of earlier suits such as *Joseph E. Seagram & Sons, Inc. v. McGuire*, cited in *Grinnell*, brewers and distillers since 2003 faced a spate of new liability theories. See Myron Levin, *Lawsuits Take Aim at Ads for Alcohol*, L.A. TIMES, Jan. 27, 2005, at C1; Richard Willing, *Lawsuits target alcohol industry*, USA TODAY, May 14, 2004, at A3. Patterned after the tobacco complaints, these latest lawsuits focused on alcohol advertising, typically alleging under statutory consumer protection law that ads improperly target underage consumers and gloss over the risks of drinking.

(10) Plaintiff-attorney veterans of the tobacco litigation are also eyeing "Big Food," or "Big Fat," Sarah Avery, *Is Big Fat the Next Big Tobacco?*, NEWS & OBSERVER (Raleigh, N.C.), Aug. 18, 2002, at A25. See also John Alan Cohan, *Obesity, Public Policy, and Tort Claims Against Fast Food Companies*, 12 WIDENER L.J. 103 (2003). District Judge Sweet rejected one "overly vague" product liability claim that did not clearly allege addiction or another theory to go beyond "what is normally known about fast food." *Pelman v. McDonald's Corp.*, 237 F. Supp. 512 (S.D.N.Y. 2003), *vacated in part*, 396 F. 3d 508 (2d Cir. 2005). The Circuit Court vacated dismissal of plaintiffs' statutory consumer protection claims and remanded on those counts. Considering McDonald's Chicken McNuggets, which even Judge Sweet described as "a McFrankenstein creation of various elements not utilized by the home cook," would you consider processed fast food "good butter"?

(11) Gun manufacturers have been another target of tobacco-style litigation. Beset by gun violence and eager for a recovery like that which the states won in tobacco litigation, municipalities around the country have sued on theories of product liability, negligence, and nuisance. Some of these suits—for examples, suits in New Orleans, Philadelphia, and St. Louis—ran into procedural problems related to cities' capacity to litigate. Of note in this area is legislative action to prohibit or enable such suits. A suit by the City of Atlanta was held preempted by a statute that reserved to the state itself the regulation of the manufacture and sale of firearms. *Sturm, Ruger & Co. v. Atlanta*, 560 S.E.2d 525 (Ga. Ct. App. 2002) (applying GA. CODE ANN. § 16-11-184, as amended in 1999). The New York City Council meanwhile passed a law to enhance gun manufacturer liability for gun crime when the manufacturer fails to follow city sales regulations. Gun Industry Responsibility Act, N.Y. City Council Intro. 365-A (passed Jan. 5, 2005).

[E] Product Spectrums

LINEGAR v. ARMOUR OF AMERICA, INC.
United States Court of Appeals, Eighth Circuit
909 F.2d 1150 (1990)

BOWMAN, Circuit Judge.

This action was brought as a products liability case and heard under the District Court's diversity jurisdiction. Armour of America, Inc. (Armour) appeals a judgment based on a jury verdict in favor of the widow and children of Jimmy Linegar, a Missouri State Highway Patrol trooper who was killed in the line of duty. The jury found that the bullet-resistant vest manufactured by Armour and worn by Linegar at the time of the murder was defectively designed, and it awarded his family $1.5 million in damages. We reverse.

On April 15, 1985, as part of a routine traffic check, Linegar stopped a van with Nevada license plates near Branson, Missouri. The van's driver produced an Oregon operator's license bearing the name Matthew Mark Samuels. Linegar ascertained from the Patrol dispatcher that the name was an alias for David Tate, for whom there was an outstanding warrant on a weapons charge. Linegar did not believe the driver matched the description the dispatcher gave him for Tate, so he decided to investigate further.

A fellow trooper, Allen Hines, who was working the spot check with Linegar, then approached the passenger's side of the van while Linegar approached the driver's side. After a moment of questioning, Linegar asked the driver to step out of the van. The driver, who was in fact David Tate, brandished an automatic weapon and fired at the troopers first from inside and then from outside the van. By the time Tate stopped firing, Hines had been wounded by three shots and Linegar, whose body had been penetrated by six bullets, lay dead or dying. None of the shots that hit the contour-style, concealable protective vest Linegar was wearing—there were five such shots—penetrated the vest or caused injury. The wounds Linegar suffered all were caused by shots that struck parts of his body not protected by the vest.

The Missouri State Highway Patrol issued the vest to Linegar when he joined the Patrol in 1981. The vest was one of a lot of various sizes of the same style vest the Patrol purchased in 1979 directly from Armour. The contour style was one of several different styles then on the market. It provided more protection to the sides of the body than the style featuring rectangular panels in front and back, but not as much protection as a wrap-around style. The front and back panels of the contour vest, held together with Velcro closures under the arms, did not meet at the sides of the wearer's body, leaving an area along the sides of the body under the arms exposed when the vest was worn. This feature of the vest was obvious to the Patrol when it selected this vest as standard issue for its troopers and could only have been obvious to any trooper who chose to wear it. The bullet that proved fatal to Linegar entered between his seventh and eighth ribs, approximately three-and-one-fourth inches down from his armpit, and pierced his heart.

The theory upon which Linegar's widow and children sought and won recovery from Armour was strict liability in tort based on a design defect in the vest....

...

... We conclude that, as a matter of law, the contour vest Trooper Linegar was wearing when he was murdered was not defective and unreasonably dangerous.

Under the Missouri law of strict liability in tort for defective design, before a plaintiff can recover from the seller or manufacturer he must show that "the design renders the product unreasonably dangerous." Nesselrode v. Executive Beechcraft, Inc., 707 S.W.2d 371, 377 (Mo.1986) (en banc). Ordinarily, that will be a jury question, and "the concept of unreasonable danger, which is determinative of whether a product is defective in a design case, is presented to the jury as an ultimate issue without further definition," id. at 378, as it was here. In this case, however, there was simply no evidence that the vest's design made it unreasonably dangerous, and the District Court should have declared that, as a matter of law, the vest was not defective, and directed a verdict or granted judgment for Armour notwithstanding the verdict....

The Missouri cases leave the meaning of the phrase "unreasonably dangerous" largely a matter of common sense, the court's or the jury's. The Missouri Supreme Court has stated, however, that a product is defectively designed if it "creates an unreasonable risk of danger to the consumer or user when put to normal use." Nesselrode, 707 S.W.2d at 375. Among the factors to be considered are "the conditions and circumstances that will foreseeably attend the use of the product." Jarrell v. Fort Worth Steel & Mfg. Co., 666 S.W.2d 828, 836 (Mo.Ct.App.1984). The conditions under which a bullet-resistant vest will be called upon to perform its intended function most assuredly will be dangerous, indeed life-threatening, and Armour surely knew that. It defies logic, however, to suggest that Armour reasonably should have anticipated that anyone would wear its vest for protection of areas of the body that the vest obviously did not cover.

Courts applying Missouri law also have applied what has become known as the "consumer expectation" test for unreasonable dangerousness: "The article sold must be dangerous to an extent beyond that which would be contemplated by the ordinary consumer who purchases it, with the ordinary knowledge common to the community as to its characteristics." Restatement (Second) of Torts § 402A comment i (1965); accord id. comment g....

The consumer expectation test focuses attention on the vest's wearer rather than on its manufacturer. The inherent limitations in the amount of coverage offered by Armour's contour vest were obvious to this Court, observing a demonstration from the bench during oral argument, as they would be to anyone with ordinary knowledge, most especially the vest's wearer. A person wearing the vest would no more expect to be shielded from a shot taken under the arm than he would expect the vest to deflect bullets aimed at his head or neck or lower abdomen or any other area not covered by the vest.

Plaintiff insists that the user's expectations should not be considered by us, since doing so would effectively afford Armour the benefit of the "open and obvious" defense, inappropriate, they say, in a defective design strict products liability action. We disagree. Although not conclusive, "[t]he obviousness of a defect or danger is material to the issue whether a product is 'unreasonably dangerous.'" ... Here, the vest's purported dangerous defect — its lack of closure at the sides — could not have been more open and obvious. An otherwise completely effective protective vest cannot be regarded as dangerous, much less unreasonably so, simply because it leaves some parts of the body obviously exposed.[6] See Richardson v. Holland, 741 S.W.2d 751, 754 (Mo.Ct.App.1987)

---

6. The wrap-around vest style advocated by appellees as preferable still must have an armhole that will be open some distance below the armpit to allow freedom of movement. See, e.g., Transcript Vol. II at 334 (testimony of Missouri Highway Patrol Trooper Don Phillips that his wrap-around-style vest left a four-inch opening beneath his armpit).

(no recovery in strict liability in tort against manufacturer of handgun because product was not defective and dangerousness was obvious); Aronson's Men's Stores, Inc., 632 S.W.2d at 474 (no recovery in strict liability in tort against manufacturer of burglar alarm because, although arguably defective, it was not unreasonably dangerous).

We have no difficulty in concluding as a matter of law that the product at issue here was neither defective nor unreasonably dangerous. Trooper Linegar's protective vest performed precisely as expected and stopped all of the bullets that hit it. No part of the vest nor any malfunction of the vest caused Linegar's injuries. See Richardson, 741 S.W.2d at 754 ("The cases uniformly hold that the doctrine of strict liability under the doctrine of 402A is not applicable unless there is some malfunction due to an improper or inadequate design or defect in manufacturing."). The vest was designed to prevent the penetration of bullets where there was coverage, and it did so; the amount of coverage was the buyer's choice. The Missouri Highway Patrol could have chosen to buy, and Armour could have sold the Patrol, a vest with more coverage; no one contests that. But it is not the place of courts or juries to set specifications as to the parts of the body a bullet-resistant garment must cover. A manufacturer is not obliged to market only one version of a product, that being the very safest design possible. If that were so, automobile manufacturers could not offer consumers sports cars, convertibles, jeeps, or compact cars. All boaters would have to buy full life vests instead of choosing a ski belt or even a flotation cushion. Personal safety devices, in particular, require personal choices, and it is beyond the province of courts and juries to act as legislators and preordain those choices.

In this case, there obviously were trade-offs to be made. A contour vest like the one here in question permits the wearer more flexibility and mobility and allows better heat dissipation and sweat evaporation, and thus is more likely to be worn than a more confining vest. It is less expensive than styles of vests providing more complete coverage. If manufacturers like Armour are threatened with economically devastating litigation if they market any vest style except that offering maximum coverage, they may decide, since one can always argue that more coverage is possible, to get out of the business altogether. Or they may continue to market the vest style that, according to the latest lawsuit, affords the "best" coverage. Officers who find the "safest" style confining or uncomfortable will either wear it at risk to their mobility or opt not to wear it at all. See Transcript Vol. II at 333 (testimony of Missouri Highway Patrol Trooper Don Phillips that he continued to wear the Armour contour-style vest with his summer uniform, even though the Patrol had issued him a wrap-around vest). Law enforcement agencies trying to work within the confines of a budget may be forced to purchase fewer vests or none at all. How "safe" are those possibilities? "The core concern in strict tort liability law is safety." Nesselrode, 707 S.W.2d at 375. We are firmly convinced that to allow this verdict to stand would run counter to the law's purpose of promoting the development of safe and useful products, and would have an especially pernicious effect on the development and marketing of equipment designed to make the always-dangerous work of law enforcement officers a little safer.

The death of Jimmy Linegar by the hand of a depraved killer was a tragic event. We keenly feel the loss that this young trooper's family has suffered, and our sympathies go out to them. But we cannot allow recovery from a blameless defendant on the basis of sympathy for the plaintiffs. To hold Armour liable for Linegar's death would cast it in the role of insurer for anyone shot while wearing an Armour vest, regardless of whether any shots penetrated the vest. That a manufacturer may be cast in such a role has been soundly rejected by courts applying Missouri law....

The judgment of the District Court is reversed. The District Court shall enter a final judgment in favor of Armour.

NOTES

(1) Is the decision in *Linegar* a "common sense" one?

(2) How elastic, or inelastic, is the definition of a product category for products liability purposes? Is the relevant category in this case that of bullet-resistant vests? Or "contour-style bullet resistant vests"? What about a case involving an industrial machine? For example, would the relevant category be that of "hydraulic press" or "unguarded hydraulic press"?

(3) Accepting the court's analysis on the particular facts as plausible, how slippery is the slope from *Linegar* to cases in other product categories? Could it be extended, for example, to argue that there should be no crashworthiness doctrine for motor vehicles? Could not a manufacturer of a flimsy automobile contend that riding in its car is still safer than riding on a motorcycle, and that therefore consumer choice has been vindicated?

Does *Linegar* promote maximum consumer choice? Is there any answer to the court's suggestion that it does? Should consumers ever be able to sue on the dangers of one model of product if others models had optional, safer features that would have prevented an injury? Consider, for example:

(a) An industrial vehicle that lacks a rollover protective structure, which could be acquired at an extra price

(b) An automobile without seat belts, which are optional for more money

(c) A workplace machine that lacks a guard, which is optional equipment at a higher price.

(4) Does the *Linegar* decision simply enforce an implicit bargain between the defendant and Linegar, or at least between the defendant and Linegar's employer?

(5) Should obviousness of danger be conclusive against a finding of defect?

(6) Why shouldn't a jury have had an opportunity to decide whether the design of Linegar's vest was defective?

§ 7.04 The *Products Restatement*'s Defect Definitions

RESTATEMENT (THIRD) OF TORTS: PRODUCTS LIABILITY*
Section 1, Section 2 & comments (1998)

§ 1. Liability of Commercial Seller or Distributor for Harm Caused by Defective Products

One engaged in the business of selling or otherwise distributing products who sells or distributes a defective product is subject to liability for harm to persons or property caused by the defect.

---

§ 2. Categories of Product Defect

A product is defective when, at the time of sale or distribution, it contains a manufacturing defect, is defective in design, or is defective because of inadequate instructions or warnings. A product:

(a) contains a manufacturing defect when the product departs from its intended design even though all possible care was exercised in the preparation and marketing of the product;

(b) is defective in design when the foreseeable risks of harm posed by the product could have been reduced or avoided by the adoption of a reasonable alternative design by the seller or other distributor, or a predecessor in the commercial chain of distribution, and the omission of the alternative design renders the product not reasonably safe;

(c) is defective because of inadequate instructions or warnings when the foreseeable risks of harm posed by the product could have been reduced or avoided by the provision of reasonable instructions or warnings by the seller or other distributor, or a predecessor in the commercial chain of distribution, and the omission of the instructions or warnings renders the product not reasonably safe.

[Comments to Section 2]

...

(d) *Design defect: general considerations.* Whereas a manufacturing defect consists of a product unit's failure to meet the manufacturer's design specifications, a product asserted to have a defective design meets the manufacturer's design specifications but raises the question whether the specifications themselves create unreasonable risks. Answering that question requires reference to a standard outside the specifications. Subsection (b) adopts a reasonableness ("risk-utility" balancing) test as the standard for judging the defectiveness of product designs. More specifically, the test is whether a reasonable alternative design would, at reasonable cost, have reduced the foreseeable risks of harm posed by the product and, if so, whether the omission of the alternative design by the seller or a predecessor in the distributive chain rendered the product not reasonably safe. Under prevailing rules concerning allocation of burden of proof, the plaintiff must prove that such a reasonable alternative was, or reasonably could have been, available at time of sale or distribution....

Assessment of a product design in most instances requires a comparison between an alternative design and the product design that caused the injury, undertaken from the viewpoint of a reasonable person. That standard is also used in administering the traditional reasonableness standard in negligence.... The policy reasons that support use of a reasonable person perspective in connection with the general negligence standard also support its use in the products liability context.

How the defendant's design compares with other, competing designs in actual use is relevant to the issue of whether the defendant's design is defective. Defendants often seek to defend their product designs on the ground that the designs conform to the "state of the art." The term "state of the art" has been variously defined to mean that the product design conforms to industry custom, that it reflects the safest and most advanced technology developed and in commercial use, or that it reflects technology at the cutting edge of scientific knowledge. The confusion brought about by these various definitions is unfortunate. This Section states that a design is defective if the product could have been made safer by the adoption of a reasonable alternative design. If such a design could have been practically adopted, the plaintiff establishes defect under Subsection (b)....

...

The requirement in Subsection (b) that the plaintiff show a reasonable alternative design applies in most instances even though the plaintiff alleges that the category of product sold by the defendant is so dangerous that it should not have been marketed at all.... Common and widely distributed products such as alcoholic beverages, firearms, and above-ground swimming pools may be found to be defective only upon proof of the requisite conditions in Subsection (a), (b), or (c). If such products are defectively manufactured or sold without reasonable warnings as to their danger when such warnings are appropriate, or if reasonable alternative designs could have been adopted, then liability under §§ 1 and 2 may attach. Absent proof of defect under those Sections, however, courts have not imposed liability for categories of products that are generally available and widely used and consumed, even if they pose substantial risks of harm. Instead, courts have concluded that legislatures and administrative agencies can, more appropriately than courts, consider the desirability of commercial distribution of some categories of widely used and consumed, but nevertheless dangerous products.

· · ·

(e) *Design defects: possibility of manifestly unreasonable design.* Several courts have suggested that the designs of some products are so manifestly unreasonable, in that they have low social utility and high degree of danger, that liability should attach even absent proof of a reasonable alternative design. In large part the problem is one of how the range of relevant alternative designs is described. For example, a toy gun that shoots hard rubber pellets with sufficient velocity to cause injury to children could be found to be defectively designed within the rule of Subsection (b). Toy guns unlikely to cause injury would constitute reasonable alternatives to the dangerous toy. Thus, toy guns that project ping pong balls, soft gelatin pellets, or water might be found to be reasonable alternative designs to a toy gun that shoots hard pellets. However, if the realism of the hard-pellet gun, and thus its capacity to cause injury, is sufficiently important to those who purchase and use such product to justify the court's limiting consideration to toy guns that achieve realism by shooting hard pellets, then no reasonable alternative will, by hypothesis, be available. In that instance, the design feature that defines which alternatives are relevant—the realism of the hard-pellet gun and thus its capacity to injure—is precisely the feature on which the user places value and of which the plaintiff complains. If a court were to adopt this characterization of the product, and deem the capacity to cause injury an egregiously unacceptable quality in a toy for use by children, it could conclude that liability should attach without proof of a reasonable alternative design. The court would declare the product design to be defective and not reasonably safe because the extremely high degree of danger posed by its use or consumption so substantially outweighs its negligible social utility that no rational, reasonable person, fully aware of the relevant facts, would choose to use, or to allow children to use, the product.

· · ·

(f) *Design defects: factors relevant in determining whether the omission of a reasonable alternative renders a product not reasonably safe.* Subsection (b) states that a product is defective in design if the omission of a reasonable alternative design renders the product not reasonably safe. A broad range of factors may be considered in determining whether an alternative design is reasonable and whether its omission renders a product not reasonably safe. The factors include, among others, the magnitude and probability of the foreseeable risks of harm, the instructions and warnings accompanying the product, and the nature and strength of consumer expectations regarding the product, including expectations arising from product portrayal and marketing.... The relative advantages and disadvantages of the product as designed and as it alternatively could have been designed may also be considered. Thus, the likely effects of the alternative design on production costs; the effects of the alternative design on product longevity, maintenance, repair, and esthetics; and the range of consumer choice among products are factors that may be taken into account. A plaintiff is not necessarily required to introduce proof on all of these factors; their relevance, and the relevance of other factors, will vary from case to case....

When evaluating the reasonableness of a design alternative, the overall safety of the product must be considered. It is not sufficient that the alternative design would have reduced or prevented the harm suffered by the plaintiff if it would also have introduced into the product other dangers of equal or greater magnitude.

. . .

(g) *Consumer expectations: general considerations.* Under Subsection (b), consumer expectations do not constitute an independent standard for judging the defectiveness of product designs. Courts frequently rely, in part, on consumer expectations when discussing liability based on other theories of liability. Some courts, for example, use the term "reasonable consumer expectations" as an equivalent of "proof of a reasonable, safer design alternative," since reasonable consumers have a right to expect product designs that conform to the reasonableness standard in Subsection (b). Other courts, allowing an inference of defect to be drawn when the incident is of a kind that ordinarily would occur as a result of product defect, observe that products that fail when put to their manifestly intended use disappoint reasonable consumer expectations.... However, consumer expectations do not play a determinative role in determining defectiveness.... Consumer expectations, standing alone, do not take into account whether the proposed alternative design could be implemented at reasonable cost, or whether an alternative design would provide greater overall safety. Nevertheless, consumer expectations about product performance and the dangers attendant to product use affect how risks are perceived and relate to foreseeability and frequency of the risks of harm, both of which are relevant under Subsection (b).... Such expectations are often influenced by how products are portrayed and marketed and can have a significant impact on consumer behavior. Thus, although consumer expectations do not constitute an independent standard for judging the defectiveness of product designs, they may substantially influence or even be ultimately determinative on risk-utility balancing in judging whether the omission of a proposed alternative design renders the product not reasonably safe.

Subsection (b) likewise rejects conformance to consumer expectations as a defense. The mere fact that a risk presented by a product design is open and obvious, or generally known, and that the product thus satisfies expectations, does not prevent a finding that the design is defective. But the fact that a product design meets consumer expectations may substantially influence or even be ultimately determinative on risk-utility balancing in judging whether the omission of a proposed alternative design renders the product not reasonably safe....

(h) *Consumer expectations: food products and used products.* With regard to two special product categories consumer expectations play a special role in determining product defect. See § 7 (food products) and § 8 (used products)....

NOTES

(1) What are the principal differences between section 2 of the *Restatement of Products Liability* and section 402A of the *Restatement (Second) of Torts*? Which verbal for-

mula do you think provides the preferable test for determining whether a product is defective?

(2) Why should a plaintiff have to show a reasonable alternative design to prove that a product is "not reasonably safe," except in cases of "manifestly unreasonable design"?

(3) Does a risk-utility test necessarily require a showing of a reasonable alternative design? Why should a plaintiff not be able to plead simply that a product is unreasonably dangerous?

(4) Is a risk-utility test significantly easier to administer than a consumer expectations test?

(5) An exhaustive compendium of research that suggests that the *Products Restatement* does not represent the main body of American case law is John Vargo's massive article, *The Emperor's New Clothes: the American Law Institute Adorns a "New Cloth" for Section 402A Products Liability Design Defects — A Survey of the States Reveals a Different Weave*, 26 U. Memphis L. Rev. 493 (1996). Vargo's state-by-state analysis includes the following conclusions:

> • At most nine states impose an "absolute requirement" that the plaintiff show a reasonable alternative design, see *id.* at 536–38.

> • Although 32 states "use some form of risk/utility examination in the test for design liability, id. at 550, only "[s]even states apply a pure risk-utility test," *id.* at 545, ten states apply an "ordinary consumer expectation test," *id.* at 539, and "25 states apply some form of a consumer expectation test to design defect cases," including six states that use "a modified consumer expectation test which involves the use of risk/utility factors," *id.* at 556.

(6) A broad argument against the *Restatement*'s adoption of a risk-utility test, and its general requirement of proof of a reasonable alternative design, appears in Marshall S. Shapo, *In Search of the Law of Products Liability: The ALI Restatement Project*, 48 Vand. L. Rev. 631 (1995). Criticizing both of these elements of the *Restatement*, the article points out that "a plaintiff could show that the risks of a product outweigh its utility and still not prevail if the plaintiff is unable to show a reasonable alternative design." *Id.* at 669. The article also:

> • Criticizes the *Restatement* for "downgrading ... consumer expectations as a factor in judging design defect issues," and stresses the "centrality of product promotion in consumer choice." See *id.* at 665–66.

> • Suggests that the general requirement of a reasonable alternative design tends "to allow defendants to create litigation-proof categories of product" by permitting them to argue that their products are so special in function that there can be no reasonable design alternative and that therefore their designs are not defective. See *id.* at 670.

> • Points out that the alternative design requirement poses an "apparent bar to the argument that a product is unreasonably dangerous because of its high degree of risk," thus "exclud[ing]" from the defect category some products with the greatest harmful potential for large numbers of consumers," for example, asbestos. See *id.* at 671–75.

(7) In a dramatic moment at the very end of several hours of debate on section 2 of the *Restatement of Products Liability*, a member of the American Law Institute made a motion to eliminate tobacco from the comment d list of "[c]ommon and widely distrib-

uted products" that could be held to have design defects only on a showing of a reasonable alternative design. The full Institute accepted the proposed amendment, and tobacco does not appear in the list of products that have this categorical protection. See Restatement (Third) of Torts: Products Liability § 2, cmt. d, at 20 (1998), reprinted above.

(8) Can you distinguish among these various categories as candidates for categorical immunity?

    (a) Cigarettes

    (b) Alcoholic beverages

    (c) Handguns

What are the considerations that influence your analysis—both with respect to whether these products are distinguishable from one another and whether they should be treated separately from other products generally? With respect to cigarettes in particular, is there a viable middle ground between declaring them the subject of categorical immunity or of categorical liability?

§ 7.05 The Duty to Warn in Products Cases

BAUGHN v. HONDA MOTOR COMPANY
Washington Supreme Court, En Banc
727 P.2d 655 (1986)

ANDERSEN, JUSTICE.

. . .

On August 14, 1972, Douglas Bratz and Bradley Lester Baughn were injured while riding a Honda Z50AK3 mini-trail bike. Douglas, whose birthdate is October 21, 1963, was driving the mini-trail bike on a public road in Pierce County. Bradley, born October 15, 1963, was riding behind Douglas as a passenger. The boys were being chased by Donna Tillman and Rory Baughn on Donna's minibike. Douglas drove through three stop signs without stopping before colliding with a truck. Just before the collision, Douglas was looking at Donna instead of the road ahead of him. Bradley was not wearing a helmet; Douglas apparently wore one that flew off on impact because it was unfastened.

The mini-trail bike had been purchased a few days before the accident by Vernon Bratz for his three children. Bratz had bought his children another minibike in 1969, which all three of them rode. Bratz bought two motorcycles for himself in 1967. He told his children several times not to ride either minibike in the street. Before the accident occurred, Douglas and Bradley were riding the Honda in the street outside the Bratz home. Douglas' mother, June, knew where they were but did nothing to stop them.

Bradley Baughn's father Jack bought two minibikes for his children before the accident, and had his own motorcycle as well. He had instructed his children that the two minibikes were not meant for road use. Two weeks before the accident, he had punished Bradley for riding his minibike in the street. He spanked him and took the bike away. He had also told his children not to ride on the Bratz bikes as passengers because they could get hurt.

The mini-trail bike contained its own instructions regarding road use. A decal on the mini-trail bike stated that the bike was manufactured for off-the-road use only, and added "Always Wear a Helmet". The first page of the owner's manual stated in bold print that the bike was for off-the-road use only....

ISSUE

Is a manufacturer liable when children are injured while riding one of its mini-trail bikes on a public road in violation of manufacturer and parental warnings?

DECISION

CONCLUSION. Where there are no design or manufacturing defects in the product, and where the warnings concerning its use are adequate, a manufacturer is not liable for an accident and resulting injuries. The mini-trail bike was, as its name implied, a "trail" bike. It was not designed or equipped for on-the-road use. The accident in this case occurred because the boys who were injured ignored Honda's and their parents' warnings not to ride the mini-trail bike on streets and roadways, and because they ignored stop signs on the roadway and collided with a truck they had not seen because they were looking elsewhere. Honda is not legally responsible for the boys' injuries.

[Omitted is the court's discussion of the basic test for strict liability, in which it rejects the plaintiff's argument that the standard should be exclusively a risk/utility test, and describes the Washington rule as "combin[ing] the consideration of consumer expectations with an analysis of the risk and utility inherent in a product's use."]

A comment to §402A of the Restatement (Second) of Torts is dispositive of the plaintiffs'... contention that Honda should be held strictly liable for manufacturing an unreasonably unsafe or dangerous product. Comment *j* states that to prevent a product from being unreasonably dangerous, a seller may be required to give directions or warnings as to its use. The comment adds:

> Where warning is given, the seller may reasonably assume that it will be read and heeded; and a product bearing such a warning, which is safe for use if it is followed, is not in defective condition, nor is it unreasonably dangerous.

Restatement (Second) of Torts §402A, comment j (1965).

While our application of this comment effectively denies the parties' other strict liability claims, we will briefly discuss those claims in conjunction with similar issues raised under the theory of negligence. The warnings provided by Honda will be outlined in discussing the first such issue: whether Honda fulfilled its duty to warn of the mini-trail bike's potential dangers.

Duty to warn. Under the law of negligence, a defendant's duty is to exercise ordinary care. A manufacturer's duty of ordinary care includes a duty to warn of hazards involved in the use of a product which are or should be known to the manufacturer.

Under principles of strict liability, the manufacturer has a duty to design a product which is reasonably safe for its intended use. Strict liability may be established if a product, though faultlessly manufactured, is unreasonably dangerous when placed in the hands of the ultimate user by a manufacturer without giving adequate warnings concerning the manner in which to use it safely.

Honda placed warnings against using its mini-trail bike on public streets in a prominent place on the bike itself as well as in the owner's manual. The following warning appears in the owner's manual on the inside cover, set off by a bright red back drop and encircled with dark ink for emphasis:

READ OWNER'S MANUAL CAREFULLY:

THIS VEHICLE WAS MANUFACTURED

FOR OFF-THE-ROAD USE ONLY.

DO NOT OPERATE ON PUBLIC STREETS, ROADS, OR HIGHWAYS.

A second warning and an explanation appears on the first inside page of the owner's manual:

> Most Honda Mini-Trails will be operated by junior riders. In many instances, this is their initial introduction to the sport of motorcycling. Before your sons or daughters start to ride, it is important that you review the contents of this manual with them. A preliminary understanding of proper operation and maintenance will facilitate training and will contribute to their safety and the service life of the machine.
>
> The Honda Z50A is designed and equipped for off-the-road use only and should not be operated on public streets. A mini-bike is less visible to traffic than larger machines. If the rider must cross a street to reach his riding area, then for safety and to comply with laws in many states, he should shut off the engine and walk the mini-bike across. When training your son or daughter, select a safe practice area with an even surface, free of obstacles.

The first page of the manual shows a drawing of a youthful rider, who is wearing a safety helmet and gloves, walking a mini-trail bike across a public street.

The mini-trail bike also had a warning label prominently displayed on top of the gas tank immediately in front of the operator. It read:

READ OWNER'S MANUAL CAREFULLY

THIS VEHICLE WAS MANUFACTURED FOR OFF-THE-ROAD USE ONLY. DO NOT OPERATE ON PUBLIC STREETS, ROADS OR HIGHWAYS.

Directly below the warning set forth above was another warning label, printed in even larger bold type. It read:

> **REMEMBER**
> **PRESERVE NATURE**
> **ALWAYS WEAR A HELMET**
> **THINK SAFETY**

Baughn and Bratz argue that these warnings were inadequate because they did not describe what might happen if a child did ride a mini-trail bike on a public street. They also criticize Honda for failing to advise parents how to determine if their child was ready to ride a mini-trail bike.

It is established law that a warning need not be given at all in instances where a danger is obvious or known. Although public policy favors holding liable those who produce products causing injury, strict liability is not absolute liability. "A manufacturer is not an insurer, and need not warn against hazards known to everyone."

Baughn and Bratz contend, however, that a special duty to warn is owed when a manufacturer markets an item for children. They point to our recent decision in *Bauman v. Crawford*, 104 Wash.2d 241, 704 P.2d 1181 (1985) as signalling a new sensitivity to the special needs of children. In *Bauman*, we declined to apply a negligence per se standard to children, and instead adopted a special child's standard of care. Bratz and Baughn also point to § 390 of the Restatement (Second) of Torts in support of their claim that Honda should have addressed its warnings to children:

§ 390. Chattel for Use by Person Known to be Incompetent

One who supplies directly or through a third person a chattel for the use of another whom the supplier knows or has reason to know to be likely because of his youth, inexperience, or otherwise, to use it in a manner involving unreasonable risk of physical harm to himself and others whom the supplier should expect to share in or be endangered by its use, is subject to liability for physical harm resulting to them.

We have phrased the question to be asked regarding a warning's sufficiency and the user's expectations in the following way: "Was the warning sufficient to catch the attention of persons who could be expected to use the product; to apprise them of its dangers and to advise them of the measures to take to avoid those dangers?" Under such a standard, the persons who will use the product — adults or children — should be able to understand a manufacturer's warnings of potential dangers and the ways to avoid them.

In *Novak v. Piggly Wiggly Puget Sound Co.*, 22 Wash.App. 407, 412, 591 P.2d 791 (1979), in which plaintiff argued liability both in negligence and strict liability, the Court of Appeals concluded that warnings on a BB gun sufficiently informed an 11-year-old of the dangers involved in its use. In that case, the minor plaintiff was struck in the eye by a ricocheting BB while watching a friend shoot his BB gun. The court pointed to several statements regarding the danger of ricochet in the gun's operator's manual, and observed that they were related to the precise danger encountered but were simply disregarded by the user. "Whether under a strict liability or negligence theory, Daisy's warnings were sufficient to preclude liability."

In another BB gun case argued solely in terms of strict liability, the court held that there was no duty to warn even a 7-year-old of obvious dangers:

A warning by the defendant Daisy that a BB gun, if fired at a person, could injure an eye, is nothing that even a seven-year-old child does not already know.

Menard v. Newhall, 135 Vt. 53, 56, 373 A.2d 505, 94 A.L.R.3d 287 (1977).

Finally, in the context of negligence, the First Circuit has observed that a failure to warn amounts to negligence only where the supplier of a dangerous good has no reason to believe that those for whom the good is supplied will realize its dangerous condition. "'If this were not true, a manufacturer could not design and sell a pocket knife, axe, planer or gun.'" Indeed, if the law required suppliers to warn of all obvious dangers inherent in a product, "'[t]he list of foolish practices warned against would be so long, it would fill a volume.'"

Honda did not warn of every conceivable danger that could be encountered if children rode its mini-trail bikes on public streets and roadways. It did, however, specifically instruct that they were intended for off-the-road use only and that riders should wear helmets. There was no contention that Douglas or Bradley could not read the sticker prominently displayed on the mini-trail bike. There is no evidence that they read the owner's manual; Vernon Bratz said he only checked it to see how to adjust the mini-trail bike.

Honda did not inform parents how to determine if their child was ready to ride a mini-trail bike. In this case, however, both fathers owned motorcycles and had previously bought mini-trail bikes for their children which their children could ride. We cannot perceive that they did not think their children were ready to ride them.

While Honda did not warn Bradley and Douglas of the precise danger they eventually encountered, their parents did and did so repeatedly. The two boys were almost 9 years old. They were apparently normal children and undoubtedly knew that riding their mini-trail bikes on public roads and ignoring stop signs could cause them injury. Despite Honda's warnings and their parents' warnings, they rode into the street through several stop signs, did not watch where they were going and were injured when they collided with a truck they had not seen. The trial court did not err when it ruled that Honda satisfied its duty to warn under the law of negligence and strict liability.

. . .

[Affirmed.]

NOTES

(1) Did Honda have a duty to communicate information to anyone about the hazards of riding its minibikes? Is this a case that deals primarily with whether there was a duty, or whether Honda gave adequate warnings about dangers about which it should have warned?

(2) Can you articulate the relationship among "duty to warn," "consumer expectations," the defense that a danger was obvious, and the defense that a consumer did not act reasonably with respect to his own safety?

(3) What room, if any, should an injured employee have to argue that a product manufacturer had reason to know that the employer was not adequately communicating the hazards of the product to employees? Section 388 of the *Restatement (Second) of Torts* permits failure-to-warn liability against the supplier of a product such as a toxic chemical that is known to be dangerous to anticipated end-users of the product, such as a company's employees. But comment n to the section relieves the supplier of a duty to warn the employee if the supplier informs the employer of the danger, and the employer—a "sophisticated user"—can be reasonably relied upon to communicate that warning to employees.

(4) Without the opportunity to sue third parties for injuries caused by products used in the workplace, an employee generally is remitted to recovery under the no-fault scheme of workers' compensation, which is usually more certain than tort recoveries but also frequently less lucrative than many tort judgments. When an employee sues a manufacturer of a product used in the workplace, he or she is usually seeking to augment workers' compensation benefits with a tort award. If you were fashioning a system aimed at fair apportionment of the costs of injuries caused by toxic substances or machines used in the workplace, how would you construct that system with respect to the responsibility of employers and of the suppliers of machines and dangerous substances? What role, if any, would a fault requirement play in your scheme?

(5) What is the difference between a claim of "failure to warn" under negligence and a claim with that designation under strict liability? Would a strict liability failure to warn claim be essentially a retrospective imposition of liability on the grounds of the dangerousness of a product in a situation in which a seller could not reasonably have known of the hazards of that product? Consider, for example, the controversial decision in the asbestos case of *Beshada v. Johns-Manville Prods. Corp.*, 90 N.J. 191, 447 A.2d 539 (1984), holding that it was appropriate to impose strict liability "for failure to warn of dangers undiscoverable at the time of manufacture," see *id.* at 205, 447 A.2d at 547. Is it appropriate, linguistically or conceptually, to refer to this kind of liability as one for "failure to warn"?

§ 7.06 Defenses Based on the Plaintiff's Conduct

AUSTIN v. LINCOLN EQUIPMENT ASSOCIATES
United States Court of Appeals, First Circuit
888 F.2d 934 (1st Cir. 1989)

BOWNES, Circuit Judge.

In this strict product liability diversity action, defendant-appellant Garlock Equipment Company appeals from an order of the District Court of Rhode Island denying the company's motions for a directed verdict, judgment notwithstanding the verdict, or a new trial.

I. BACKGROUND

Plaintiff-appellee Otis Austin, a roofer, suffered injuries when he fell off a roof while using a power roof sweeper manufactured by Garlock. The accident occurred as Austin was sweeping a flat roof on a building in Providence, Rhode Island. He had made two laps around the perimeter of the roof when he stopped the machine approximately two to five feet from the roof's edge to add fuel. When Austin restarted the sweeper it bucked backwards against him and he lost his balance and fell off the roof. He severely injured his back, left ankle and right wrist.

Austin sued Garlock Equipment Company as manufacturer and Lincoln Equipment Associates, Inc. as seller of the sweeper. Plaintiff alleged that the sweeper was defective because its brush and wheel clutches failed to engage simultaneously due to a poorly designed interlock mechanism. After the evidence closed, the court submitted six questions to the jury, including the following:

1. Do you find Garlock Equipment Company strictly liable?

Yes _____

No _____.

2. Do you find Lincoln Equipment Associates, Inc. strictly liable?

Yes _____

No _____.

The jury found Garlock strictly liable and Lincoln not liable. It also found that plaintiff had not assumed the risk of his injuries in operating the sweeper but that he was 60% negligent. No general verdict was given. The jury calculated Austin's damages as $400,000. Reducing the figure to take account of plaintiff's own negligence, the court awarded him $160,000.

. . .

... [W]e find that Austin produced evidence from which it could be found that the sweeper was unreasonably dangerous when it left Garlock's hands. Austin's expert witness testified that the use of a spring pin in the interlock mechanism between the brush and wheel clutches was a poor design. The purpose of the interlock mechanism was to ensure that the two clutches engaged simultaneously, thereby preventing the machine from moving backward, as it would do if only the brush were engaged. Since a sudden backward motion by the sweeper could upset a roofer's balance whether he was near the edge of a roof or not, the design and subsequent failure of the clutch interlock mechanism could reasonably be found to be a defect under Section 402A of the Restatement.

The next element of proof is causation. A plaintiff must prove that the defect in the product was a proximate cause of his or her injury. Thomas, 488 A.2d at 722. The record shows that Austin was standing on a flat roof parallel to the roof's edge at a distance of two to five feet from the edge when he restarted the machine. He testified that the sweeper jumped back a foot and caught him off guard so that he fell over the roof's edge. It could reasonably be found that the proximate cause of Austin's accident was the bucking motion of the Garlock sweeper due to a failure of the brush and wheel clutches to engage simultaneously.

III. MOTIONS FOR DIRECTED VERDICT AND JUDGMENT NOTWITHSTANDING THE VERDICT

Garlock contends that any liability on its part for a defective product is defeated by plaintiff's assumption of the risk and misuse of the sweeper, and that the judge should have directed a verdict in its favor as a matter of law.

...

A. Assumption of the Risk

Garlock argues that Austin assumed the risk by using a machine that he knew to be "awkward" at a precipitous location when the availability of hand brooms and shovels provided a safer alternative. To warrant a directed verdict or judgment notwithstanding the verdict premised on plaintiff's assumption of the risk, Garlock must prove conclusively that Austin knew about the existence of a danger, appreciated its unreasonable character, and then voluntarily exposed himself to it. Drew v. Wall, 495 A.2d 229, 231 (R.I.1985). It is not Austin's exercise of care but his voluntary acceptance of the risk which is at issue. "The standard for determining whether a plaintiff voluntarily encountered a risk is subjective; therefore, we must look to the record to ascertain what this particular individual in fact saw, knew, understood, and appreciated." Id.

There is no doubt that Austin understood the danger inherent in working on a roof. A roofer inevitably takes chances by working atop buildings. Austin had seen two co-workers fall to their deaths from rooftops. The deaths were not related to the use of a sweeper. What would have to be proven in order for defendant to prevail on its motions is that Austin appreciated the specific danger of the power sweeper knocking him off balance, and proceeded in the face of that danger. Cf. Iadevaia v. Aetna Bridge Co., 120 R.I. 610, 389 A.2d 1246, 1250 (1978) (plaintiff did not assume specific risk of serious back injury by continuing to operate backhoe to break up cement).

As an employee of a roofing company, Austin's job was to sweep gravel into rows so that other workers could remove it with hand brooms and shovels. Austin testified that he had used the Garlock sweeper many times and found that each time he started it the machine exerted some backward pressure, but that he did not know the machine could jump back a foot, as it did when he started it the second time. Although there was a warning label on the sweeper which cautioned against using the machine within ten feet of the edge of a roof, Austin stated that he had never read the label nor received any instructions on operating safety.

Viewing the record in the light most favorable to the plaintiff, there is at least a reasonable inference that Austin did not appreciate the risk involved in starting the sweeper. Therefore, we find that the trial judge properly submitted the question of plaintiff's assumption of the risk to the jury.

B. Misuse of the Product

Defendant also contends that Austin's act of starting the sweeper two to five feet from the roof's edge was a misuse of the product because the machine bore a label which read:

!CAUTION!
DO NOT OPERATE WITHIN TEN FEET OF EDGE OF ROOF.

Garlock argues that the use of a product in a manner contrary to warnings given by the manufacturer is "misuse" which breaks the chain of causation between any defect and the injury. When a plaintiff's injuries result from his misuse of a product, strict liability does not attach because a product is not regarded as defective. Restatement (Second) Torts, § 402A, comment h at 351.[1] Misuse is use of a product for a purpose neither intended nor foreseeable by the manufacturer or supplier. Williams v. Brown Mfg. Co., 45 Ill.2d 418, 261 N.E.2d 305, 309 (1970) (subsequently overruled as to effect but not definition of misuse, see Coney v. J.L.G. Indus., Inc., 97 Ill.2d 104, 73 Ill.Dec. 337, 454 N.E.2d 197 (1983)); accord Ritter, 283 A.2d 255; Turcotte v. Ford Motor Co., 494 F.2d 173 (1st Cir.1974) (under Rhode Island law "intended use" encompasses foreseeable consequences of normal use of a product).

It is undisputed that Austin was attempting to use the sweeper for its intended purpose of sweeping gravel. Therefore Austin did not misuse the product. Rather, the question is whether the plaintiff's use of a product for a normal purpose, but in a careless manner, has the same effect on the defendant's liability as does misuse. Defendant argues that it does where a warning is provided as to a particular manner of using a product. Garlock relies on comment j to section 402A of the Restatement (Second) Torts which states in pertinent part:

> Where warning is given, the seller may reasonably assume that it will be read and heeded; and a product bearing such a warning, which is safe for use if it is followed, is not in defective condition, nor is it unreasonably dangerous.

Id. at 353. Defendant cites two cases in which a plaintiff's use of a product in a manner contrary to instructions and warnings given by the manufacturer was held to be "misuse" freeing the manufacturer from strict liability. In Procter & Gamble Manufacturing Co. v. Langley, 422 S.W.2d 773 (Tex.Civ.App.1967) the plaintiff used a home permanent solution to wave her hair, but failed to follow instructions for making a test curl and disregarded a warning to stop if hair showed signs of damage. In Kay v. Cessna Aircraft Co., 548 F.2d 1370 (9th Cir.1977), an airplane crashed when the pilot attempted to take off without making routine safety checks which were spelled out in detail in the owner's manual.

Neither comment j nor these cases supports defendant's argument. In the present action, there was evidence from which it could be found that the sweeper was not safe for use even if the warning was followed. Following the warning would not have protected Austin from the erratic motion of the sweeper due to the defective clutch interlock mechanism; the warning mentioned nothing about the machine's propensity to buck. There was nothing magic about the ten-foot zone. Austin could just as easily have been knocked off balance and hurt himself while using the sweeper in the middle of the roof. He could have fallen on a sharp object or into hot roofing tar. Austin's proximity to the roof's edge compounded the danger posed by the machine, but his conduct does not relieve defendant from strict liability for a defect in the sweeper. A warning only relieves

---

1. Comment h reads in part: "A product is not in a defective condition when it is safe for normal handling and consumption. If the injury results from abnormal handling ... the seller is not liable."

a manufacturer or supplier from strict liability if the product bearing such warning "is safe for use if it is followed." Restatement (Second) Torts, § 402A, comment j at 353. If a product is unsafe regardless of whether the user has followed a manufacturer's warning, the user's careless failure to do so is simply contributory negligence....

As discussed above, there was evidence that defendant's product was defective and that the defect caused Austin's injuries. There was no evidence of misuse, that is, use of the sweeper for a purpose neither intended nor foreseeable. The district court did not err in denying Garlock's motions based on misuse.

. . .

[Affirmed.]

EGELHOFF v. HOLT
Supreme Court of Missouri, En Banc
875 S.W.2d 543 (1994)

Anita Egelhoff brought an action for personal injuries against Linda Jo Holt and Kero Metal Products. Egelhoff's claim against Holt was submitted on negligence, and her claims against Kero were submitted on MAI 25.04, Strict Liability—Defective Product, and MAI 25.05, Strict Liability—Failure to Warn. The jury awarded Egelhoff $250,000 and found her to be eighty percent at fault, Kero fifteen percent at fault, and Holt five percent at fault. Egelhoff appealed the trial court's denial of her motion for new trial. Kero cross-appealed the trial court's denial of its motion for a judgment notwithstanding the verdict. The Court of Appeals, Eastern District, (1) affirmed the trial court's denial of Egelhoff's motion for new trial and (2) reversed the trial court's denial of Kero's motion for judgment notwithstanding the verdict. Both parties now appeal to this Court. We affirm the judgment of the trial court.

FACTS

Linda Holt had an aboveground swimming pool in her backyard. The swimming pool, which was manufactured by Kero Metal Products, came with several insertable plastic caps that were designed to cover the top of the pool deck railing support posts. On July 9, 1988, upon entering her yard, Holt noticed that several of these plastic caps were on the ground. She testified that this happened often. Holt picked up these caps and placed them on a table in her backyard. She did not insert the caps back into the railing supports.

After cleaning the pool, Holt invited her tenant, Anita Egelhoff, to go swimming. Egelhoff was in the pool when Holt asked her to help set up a volleyball net. Egelhoff climbed out of the pool onto a narrow deck and tied the volleyball net to one of the swimming pool's support posts. After securing the net, Egelhoff turned around and lowered herself toward the deck. To assist her in getting back into the pool, Egelhoff reached back and grabbed one of the support posts, which cut her thumb. The pain caused Egelhoff to twist away from the post and fall into the pool. As a result of the twisting fall, Egelhoff claims she injured her back. She has since had therapy and numerous surgeries to treat her back problem.

... Egelhoff cites to Lippard v. Houdaille Industries, Inc., 715 S.W.2d 491 (Mo. banc 1986), in arguing that it is improper to submit a comparative fault instruction in products cases alleging strict liability. Lippard was decided, however, prior to the enactment of section 537.765, RSMo Supp.1993, which specifically authorizes fault apportionment in product liability cases. Section 537.765 became effective on July 1, 1987. The alleged injury in this case occurred on July 9, 1988. Thus, section 537.765 is controlling, and it authorized the submission of a comparative fault instruction in this case.

... Egelhoff argues that the comparative fault instruction that was submitted failed to track MAI 32.28. Instruction 10 proffered by Kero stated:

> In your verdict you must assess a percentage of fault to plaintiff whether or not defendants were partly at fault if you believe:

> First, plaintiff knew or by using ordinary care should have known that the plastic cap was missing from the top of the pool deck railing support post and as a result the pool deck railing support post was not reasonably safe, and

> Second, plaintiff unreasonably failed to appreciate the danger involved [sic] the use of the pool or the consequences thereof and unreasonably exposed herself to said danger, or plaintiff failed to undertake the precautions a reasonably careful user of the pool would take to protect herself against dangers which a reasonably careful user would reasonably appreciate under the same or similar circumstances, and

> Third, such failure directly caused or directly contributed to cause any damage plaintiff may have sustained.

This instruction submits two of the six types of comparative fault specified in section 537.765, which states:

> 537.765 Contributory fault as complete bar to plaintiff's recovery abolished— doctrine of comparative fault to apply—fault of plaintiff an affirmative defense to diminish damages—fault defined.—1. Contributory fault, as a complete bar to plaintiff's recovery in a products liability claim, is abolished. The doctrine of pure comparative fault shall apply to products liability claims as provided in this section.

> 2. Defendant may plead and prove the fault of the plaintiff as an affirmative defense. Any fault chargeable to the plaintiff shall diminish proportionately the amount awarded as compensatory damages but shall not bar recovery.

> 3. For purposes of this section, "fault" is limited to:

> (1) The failure to use the product as reasonably anticipated by the manufacturer;

> (2) Use of the product for a purpose not intended by the manufacturer;

> (3) Use of the product with knowledge of a danger involved in such use with reasonable appreciation of the consequences and the voluntary and unreasonable exposure to said danger;

> (4) Unreasonable failure to appreciate the danger involved in use of the product or the consequences thereof and the unreasonable exposure to said danger;

> (5) The failure to undertake the precautions a reasonably careful user of the product would take to protect himself against dangers which he would reasonably appreciate under the same or similar circumstances; or

> (6) The failure to mitigate damages.

The subdivisions of subsection 3 of this statute generally constitute the following defenses: (1) unforeseeable misuse; (2) foreseeable misuse; (3) assumption of the risk; (4) negligent assumption of the risk; (5) contributory negligence; and, (6) failure to mitigate damages. Kero submitted an instruction that included (4) negligent assumption of the risk and (5) contributory negligence. Kero could not submit these defenses solely in their statutory form because such a submission likely would constitute a "roving commission." It was necessary to specify the conduct by Egelhoff that was claimed to constitute the fault; the instruction does so in paragraph second.

...

THE SUBMISSIBILITY OF THE COMPARATIVE FAULT INSTRUCTION

Here, there was substantial evidence from which the jury could find that Egelhoff negligently assumed the risk (unreasonable failure to appreciate the danger involved in use of the product or the consequences thereof and the unreasonable exposure to said danger) or that Egelhoff was contributorily negligent (the failure to undertake the precautions a reasonably careful user of the product would take to protect herself against dangers that she would reasonably appreciate under the same or similar circumstances). Egelhoff testified that she was not looking where she put her hand when she cut it on the post and that if she had been looking she would have never put her hand on top of the post because "it was very sharp." This evidence is particularly important in establishing that the sharp edge upon which Egelhoff sustained her cut was in plain view when the caps were removed from the posts. Moreover, Egelhoff testified she frequently swam in Holt's swimming pool. Since Holt testified that she had problems almost daily with the caps coming off, it could be inferred that Egelhoff had constructive knowledge of the danger from the exposed posts. This constitutes sufficient evidence to submit on negligent assumption of the risk and contributory negligence.

Egelhoff also claims there was insufficient evidence to submit Instruction 10 because Kero failed to prove she possessed "knowledge respecting the latent defect in [Kero's] handrail." Section 537.765 does not require actual knowledge to submit negligent assumption of the risk or contributory negligence. Negligent assumption of the risk requires only that Egelhoff "knew or by using ordinary care should have known" of the defect. Contributory negligence requires only that Egelhoff fail to act as a "reasonably careful user of the product would" in that situation. Constructive knowledge is sufficient for a submissible case under either theory; there is no requirement that Egelhoff have actual knowledge of the allegedly defective post.

Instruction 10 was submissible under the evidence in this case.

...

[Inter alia, the court rejects Kero's argument that there was no defect in the pool when it left Kero's possession, based on the idea that the pool was modified because the caps on the support posts were cut.]

Egelhoff made a submissible case on strict liability—defective product. It is clear from the evidence that the modification relied upon by Kero was separate and distinct from the defect relied upon by Egelhoff. Therefore, the trial court correctly overruled Kero's motion for judgment notwithstanding the verdict.

...

The judgment of the trial court is affirmed.

...

NOTES

(1) Which of these types of these situations should be used to bar, or reduce, recovery in a products liability case?

"Ordinary" contributory negligence

"Assumption of risk" type contributory negligence

A voluntary, but reasonable, confrontation with a known risk

"Foreseeable misuse"

"Unforeseeable misuse"

Obvious product danger

(2) Comment n to section 402A of the *Restatement (Second)* said that contributory negligence would not be a defense to a strict liability products claim "when such negligence consists merely in a failure to discover the defect in the product, or to guard against the possibility of its existence." The comment distinguished "the form of contributory negligence which consists in voluntarily and unreasonably proceeding to encounter a known danger, and commonly passes under the name of assumption of risk." It said that if a user or consumer does discover a defect and becomes aware of the danger and then "proceeds unreasonably to make use of the product and is injured..., he is barred." By contrast, the *Restatement of Products Liability* says that "[c]ourts today do not limit the relevance of plaintiff's fault as did the Restatement, Second ... to conduct characterized as voluntary assumption of risk." RESTATEMENT (THIRD) OF TORTS: PRODUCTS LIABILITY, § 17, cmt. a (1998). However, the *Products Restatement* also reports that "[a] number of courts take the position that when the plaintiff's negligence consists solely in the failure to discover the defect in the product, no reduction of damages is warranted." *Id.* at 262, Reporters' Note to cmt. d.

Is there something about products cases, as compared with other types of tort cases, that makes it a better rule to require, as did comment n of the *Restatement (Second)*, that a defendant show assumption of risk to bar a negligent plaintiff or even to reduce his or her judgment? In Austin's case, should it have barred recovery if the defendant had shown that Austin "should have known" of the danger that caused his injuries, but could not prove that he actually knew of the specific risk?

(3) What effect should comparative fault doctrines have on the allocation of loss between product sellers and consumers? Should the adoption of comparative doctrines wipe out all distinctions among defenses based on consumer conduct in products cases? Does the milieu of dangerous products make as good a case for application of comparative doctrines as that of auto accidents?

(4) How can one "compare" a plaintiff's negligence with the unreasonable dangerousness of a product? Are you troubled, to the point that you would reject the application of comparative doctrines to strict liability, by the conceptual inconsistency of comparative fault with strict liability?

(5) When courts employ comparative doctrines in products cases, what is it that they really are comparing? Culpability? Causation? Something else? What should they be comparing?

(6) On the facts of *Austin*, page 378, and *Egelhoff*, page 381, what would be the most just allocation of loss between the parties? The most efficient allocation of loss?

(7) Should a products manufacturer be able to escape liability when it has good reason to know that firms that purchase its products will put pressure on their workers to use those goods in ways that run counter to their knowledge of the risk and their best judgment?

Chapter 8

NECESSITY

VINCENT v. LAKE ERIE TRANSP. CO.
Minnesota Supreme Court
109 Minn. 456, 124 N.W. 221 (1910)

O'BRIEN, J.

The steamship Reynolds, owned by the defendant, was for the purpose of discharging her cargo on November 27, 1905, moored to plaintiff's dock in Duluth. While the unloading of the boat was taking place a storm from the northeast developed, which at about 10 o'clock p.m., when the unloading was completed, had so grown in violence that the wind was then moving at 50 miles per hour and continued to increase during the night. There is some evidence that one, and perhaps two, boats were able to enter the harbor that night, but it is plain that navigation was practically suspended from the hour mentioned until the morning of the 29th, when the storm abated, and during that time no master would have been justified in attempting to navigate his vessel, if he could avoid doing so. After the discharge of the cargo the Reynolds signaled for a tug to tow her from the dock, but none could be obtained because of the severity of the storm. If the lines holding the ship to the dock had been cast off, she would doubtless have drifted away; but, instead, the lines were kept fast, and as soon as one parted or chafed it was replaced, sometimes with a larger one. The vessel lay upon the outside of the dock, her bow to the east, the wind and waves striking her starboard quarter with such force that she was constantly being lifted and thrown against the dock, resulting in its damage, as found by the jury, to the amount of $500.

We are satisfied that the character of the storm was such that it would have been highly imprudent for the master of the Reynolds to have attempted to leave the dock or to have permitted his vessel to drift a way from it. One witness testified upon the trial that the vessel could have been warped into a slip, and that, if the attempt to bring the ship into the slip had failed, the worst that could have happened would be that the vessel would have been blown ashore upon a soft and muddy bank. The witness was not present in Duluth at the time of the storm, and, while he may have been right in his conclusions, those in charge of the dock and the vessel at the time of the storm were not required to use the highest human intelligence, nor were they required to resort to every possible experiment which could be suggested for the preservation of their property. Nothing more was demanded of them than ordinary prudence and care, and the record in this case fully sustains the contention of the appellant that, in holding the vessel fast to the dock, those in charge of her exercised good judgment and prudent seamanship.

It is claimed by the respondent that it was negligence to moor the boat at an exposed part of the wharf, and to continue in that position after it became apparent that the storm was to be more than usually severe. We do not agree with this position. The part of the wharf where the vessel was moored appears to have been commonly used for that purpose. It was situated within the harbor at Duluth, and must, we think, be considered a proper and safe place, and would undoubtedly have been such during what would be considered a very severe storm. The storm which made it unsafe was one which surpassed in violence any which might have reasonably been anticipated.

The appellant contends by ample assignments of error that, because its conduct during the storm was rendered necessary by prudence and good seamanship under conditions over which it had no control, it cannot be held liable for any injury resulting to the property of others, and claims that the jury should have been so instructed. An analysis of the charge given by the trial court is not necessary, as in our opinion the only question for the jury was the amount of damages which the plaintiffs were entitled to recover, and no complaint is made upon that score.

The situation was one in which the ordinary rules regulating property rights were suspended by forces beyond human control, and if, without the direct intervention of some act by the one sought to be held liable, the property of another was injured, such injury must be attributed to the act of God, and not to the wrongful act of the person sought to be charged. If during the storm the Reynolds had entered the harbor, and while there had become disabled and been thrown against the plaintiffs' dock, the plaintiffs could not have recovered. Again, if while attempting to hold fast to the dock the lines had parted, without any negligence, and the vessel carried against some other boat or dock in the harbor, there would be no liability upon her owner. But here those in charge of the vessel deliberately and by their direct efforts held her in such a position that the damage to the dock resulted, and, having thus preserved the ship at the expense of the dock, it seems to us that her owners are responsible to the dock owners to the extent of the injury inflicted.

In *Depue v. Flatau*, 100 Minn. 299, 111 N. W. 1, 8 L. R. A. (N. S.) 485, this court held that where the plaintiff, while lawfully in the defendants' house, became so ill that he was incapable of traveling with safety, the defendants were responsible to him in damages for compelling him to leave the premises. If, however, the owner of the premises had furnished the traveler with proper accommodations and medical attendance, would he have been able to defeat an action brought against him for their reasonable worth?

In *Ploof v. Putnam*, 71 Atl. 188, 20 L. R. A. (N. S.) 152, the Supreme Court of Vermont held that where, under stress of weather, a vessel was without permission moored to a private dock at an island in Lake Champlain owned by the defendant, the plaintiff was not guilty of trespass, and that the defendant was responsible in damages because his representative upon the island unmoored the vessel, permitting it to drift upon the shore, with resultant injuries to it. If, in that case, the vessel had been permitted to remain, and the dock had suffered an injury, we believe the shipowner would have been held liable for the injury done.

Theologians hold that a starving man may, without moral guilt, take what is necessary to sustain life; but it could hardly be said that the obligation would not be upon such person to pay the value of the property so taken when he became able to do so. And so public necessity, in times of war or peace, may require the taking of private property for public purposes; but under our system of jurisprudence compensation must be made.

Let us imagine in this case that for the better mooring of the vessel those in charge of her had appropriated a valuable cable lying upon the dock. No matter how justifiable such appropriation might have been, it would not be claimed that, because of the overwhelming necessity of the situation, the owner of the cable could not recover its value.

This is not a case where life or property was menaced by any object or thing belonging to the plaintiff, the destruction of which became necessary to prevent the threatened disaster. Nor is it a case where, because of the act of God, or unavoidable accident, the infliction of the injury was beyond the control of the defendant, but is one where the defendant prudently and advisedly availed itself of the plaintiffs' property for the purpose of preserving its own more valuable property, and the plaintiffs are entitled to compensation for the injury done.

Order affirmed.

LEWIS, J. I dissent. It was assumed on the trial before the lower court that appellant's liability depended on whether the master of the ship might, in the exercise of reasonable care, have sought a place of safety before the storm made it impossible to leave the dock. The majority opinion assumes that the evidence is conclusive that appellant moored its boat at respondent's dock pursuant to contract, and that the vessel was lawfully in position at the time the additional cables were fastened to the dock, and the reasoning of the opinion is that, because appellant made use of the stronger cables to hold the boat in position, it became liable under the rule that it had voluntarily made use of the property of another for the purpose of saving its own.

In my judgment, if the boat was lawfully in position at the time the storm broke, and the master could not, in the exercise of due care, have left that position without subjecting his vessel to the hazards of the storm, then the damage to the dock, caused by the pounding of the boat, was the result of an inevitable accident. If the master was in the exercise of due care, he was not at fault. The reasoning of the opinion admits that if the ropes, or cables, first attached to the dock had not parted, or if, in the first instance, the master had used the stronger cables, there would be no liability. If the master could not, in the exercise of reasonable care, have anticipated the severity of the storm and sought a place of safety before it became impossible, why should he be required to anticipate the severity of the storm, and, in the first instance, use the stronger cables?

I am of the opinion that one who constructs a dock to the navigable line of waters, and enters into contractual relations with the owner of a vessel to moor at the same, takes the risk of damage to his dock by a boat caught there by a storm, which event could not have been avoided in the exercise of due care, and further, that the legal status of the parties in such a case is not changed by renewal of cables to keep the boat from being cast adrift at the mercy of the tempest.

...

Robert E. Keeton, *Conditional Fault in the Law of Torts*
72 Harv. L. Rev. 401, 418, 427–436, 438–441 (1959)*

... Cases such as *Vincent*, on the one hand, and on the other hand cases of strict liability, as for ultrahazardous activities, have been regarded generally as independent di-

* Reprinted by permission of the Harvard Law Review Association and William S. Hein Company from *The Harvard Law Review*, Vol. 72, pages 401–441.

versions from the main theme of fault. But it is useful to view them as closely related aspects of a single concept which, though different from fault as we use it in tort law generally, bears some important similarities. Though there is no magic in the term, "conditional fault" is a convenient way to designate this concept....

[After discussing a variety of hypothetical cases dealing with personal injury and property damages, Keeton continues:]

E. Blameworthiness — Three Classes of Conduct

Though it appears that the community sense of morality finds blameworthiness in the nonnegligent, risky conduct as to which courts have imposed liability, yet this is distinctly different from the blameworthiness found in most cases of negligence or intentional tort. The sanctions which the courts impose are sometimes different. In view of these differences, it may be helpful to identify three types of conduct with which tort law must be concerned. This is a classification from the point of view of blameworthiness and does not coincide with the three-fold classification of tort liability as intentional torts, negligence, and strict liability.

Type one: It is the moral sense of the community that one should not engage in this type of conduct, even though he makes provision for compensation of resulting losses.

Type two: It is the moral sense of the community that one should not engage in this type of conduct, because of risk or certainty of losses to others, without making reasonable provision for compensation of losses. But if he makes such a provision, his conduct is permissible.

Type three: It is the moral sense of the community that this type of conduct is permissible, and there is no moral obligation to provide for resulting losses, unless the conduct violates some legal standard not concerned with blameworthiness. When such a legal standard exists, it is a true deviation from the principle that liability in tort is based on blameworthiness. Of course the legal standard when promulgated invokes moral support for law, but the standard itself is based on some policy other than the principle of liability for blameworthy conduct.

Type one is fault. The legal result usually reached in cases involving this type of conduct is liability or, from another point of view, absence of privilege. Type three is absence of fault. The legal result usually reached in cases involving this type of conduct is nonliability or, from another point of view, privilege. Type two is conditional fault. From another point of view, this type of conduct supports the legal conclusion of conditional privilege. In this type fall the cases of privilege to use the property of another in circumstances of private necessity, the privilege being subject to a duty to compensate for any harm done. *Vincent* is such a case of conditional privilege. Cases of so-called strict liability for nonnegligent risky conduct, such as blasting, are also of this type. The blaster is privileged to engage in the reasonable use of explosives, despite the fact that his conduct imposes risks upon others, but his privilege is subject to a duty to compensate for harm done.

The analogy between conditional privilege to use the property of another because of private necessity and conditional privilege to make reasonable use of explosives is very close. It might be argued that they should be treated exactly alike. Probably a difference is justified, however, in favor of a broader privilege, i.e., a less restrictive condition upon the privilege, in the case of private necessity, at least when preservation of life is involved. This point may be seen if we assume, first, the case of a blaster who is judgment-proof and has no liability insurance. I submit that his blasting could be enjoined. Though blasting under given circumstances may be reasonable conduct for one who is able to compensate the victims of foreseeable injuries, it is unreasonable conduct under circumstances which are identical except for the fact that the blaster is judgment-proof and without bond or insurance. The conduct in the latter situation should be enjoined as an unreasonable interference with the use and enjoyment of lands within the area of risk— as a nuisance. The conduct of blasting is of such a nature that it is the moral sense of the community that it should not occur without an advance provision for compensation.

On the other hand, it may well be that in the cases of private necessity involving the preservation of one's own life, the condition would not be an advance provision for compensation, but rather only an obligation to compensate after loss has occurred. A reason for the distinction lies in the absence of opportunity to make advance provisions in the emergency situation. Another arguable ground for the distinction lies is that the interest in preservation of life deserves greater weight than interests concerned with property. But this ground has the weakness that, though one does not ordinarily think of blasting as being closely associated with the preservation of life, such an association can be clearly seen in cases of blasting to construct a hospital, and it is often present in other cases as well.

If, assuming still another variation of the facts, the case of private necessity is one involving prudent conduct of the actor for the preservation of the lives of others and not his own life, it is less likely that his conduct, including failure to pay for resulting harm, would be considered blameworthy. Arguably, at least, this type of case involves no more blameworthiness and should be treated in law as a case of absolute privilege or no fault, rather than a case of conditional privilege or conditional fault.

. . .

F. The Moral Element in Conditional Fault

. . .

The moral element in the legal rules based on conditional fault involves more than the mere fact that they do not offend the community's sense of fairness. These types of cases do not present situations of moral indifference to the choice of one or another method of social engineering. Moreover, the moral element is not adequately explained by the suggestion that the conduct of the individual employer or blaster has been anti-social but not blameworthy when no provision has been made for compensation of the expectable injuries from nonnegligent operations. Social morality is an important influence of law, but there is in these cases a sense of blame against the individual as well. Of course the assertion that the individual blameworthiness is sensed in these cases is not demonstrable by logic. Rather its validity is dependent upon an observation of the moral views of the community. The appeal for the reader's agreement with this assertion is an appeal for confirmation from his own observations. . . .

The references in this article to moral standards generally accepted in the community as appropriate for judging the moral quality of an individual's conduct are not intended to suggest that there is a community moral sense which is an existing datum awaiting our discovery and application. Rather, this community moral sense is something in the process of articulation. . . .

G. Risk-Spreading Capacity as an Element in Conditional Fault

The theme of placing legal responsibility upon the superior risk bearer, if carried to its ultimate implications, would stand in opposition to the shifting of losses through tort law. Were people not inspired to obstruction or co-operation depending on their moral judgments, a plan of accident insurance carried by each person to cover injuries to himself would be more efficient than either a plan of liability insurance or a plan of accident insurance carried by each person to cover injuries his activities cause to others. The plan of insurance covering one's own injuries would avoid many difficult problems of legal cause inherent in any plan fixing responsibility for injuries to others. If each person were carrying insurance for injuries to others rather than to himself, hearings would sometimes be required to determined whether an injury arose out of motoring, and if so, whose motoring, just as hearings have been required in workmen's compensation cases to determine whether injury arose out of employment, and if so, for whom. For example, cases of successive impacts separated by seconds, days, or years would require hearings for the determination of responsibility for the end result of disability; there might be doubts as to what impacts contributed to the disability, and in what degrees, and doubts as to what motorists contributed to each impact. Of course, a plan of accident insurance for one's own protection as a possible victim would have to be compulsory to be effective. The average man probably would gamble that the accidents would happen only to somebody else, and would save the insurance premium to buy a fancier car for himself. But the necessity of compulsion is also true of any plan requiring provision for injuries to others. If the system of insurance for one's own protection seems less feasible than the system of insurance for the protection of others harmed by one's activities, perhaps the reason lies more in what persons affected consider to be fair than in the efficiency of one system over the other apart from such moral attitudes.

Even more efficient, but for the possible effect of moral attitudes, would be a plan under which all injuries, of whatever nature and from whatever cause, were compensated out of a single fund, to which all contributed—either a government fund supported by taxes, or an insurance fund supported by compulsory contributions from all. Yet it is plain that we are nowhere near to acceptance of that form of loss distribution in our law. The sacrifice of other interests which it would entail is one we are not prepared to make. Two such interests are noted here.

Responsibility for injuries caused to others serves as a selector of socially useful activities and methods. Without such responsibility, some governmental authority would be needed to decide, for example, whether one who is under contract to remove a ledge may use one form of explosive or another, or must not blast at all, and whether manufacturers of apricot-puff cookies must incur the expense of electronic devices to catch and remove each cookie which contains wire. Though economic incentive is only one factor among many in the complex motivation for accident prevention, it can be an important one. In the absence of responsibility for injuries caused, it tends to work against safety. If all injuries from whatever cause were compensated out of a general fund, the cost to blasters and cookie manufacturers in the form of their respective shares of the increased assessment on all contributors to the fund would be less than the cost of them making ledge removals and cookies safe.

On the other hand, if liability is imposed upon one whose activities cause injury to another, a control factor is present in the form of an increase in price of the product to recoup the cost of compensating for the injuries. This factor is present when liability is based either on negligence or on conditional fault. For the individual, this control factor serves as an incentive to avoid hazards to others—an incentive which, however, is somewhat diluted by liability insurance. For society, this control factor serves as a selector separating from socially useful activities, which can pay their way even with this added cost, the socially undesirable activities which cause more harm than they are worth. It serves to improve the opportunity for free and rational choice, both for the individual and for the group, in matters concerning the worth of products and activities....

A second important interest which would be sacrificed by the adoption of a plan of compensating all losses from a single fund is that of fairness. Under currently prevailing views, equal payments per capita would be regarded as grossly unfair to careful persons who cause relatively few of the losses and risks. Few would argue that one is morally obligated to carry accident insurance covering harms to himself. Such sense of obligation as has developed with respect to life insurance is no exception; the risk of harm against which it protects is not harm to oneself, but rather to one's dependents. The moral obligation is one between a person and his dependents, not between him and others whose activities might cause his death.

There are sensible reasons for placing upon the blaster, rather than upon everyone as a potential blasting victim, the moral and legal responsibility for making advance provision against the hazard of nonnegligence blasting accidents. One reason for preferring this method is that it serves aims of deterrence of undesirably risky conduct and encourages safety precautions. A second and perhaps more important reason is that it better spreads the loss in proportion to benefits realized. That is, it effects distribution, according to the principle of unjust enrichment, among those who realize benefits from the blasting. It would be difficult and perhaps impossible to find a basis for a class definition which would include the victim and would also commend itself to one's sense of fairness and reason as a definition of a group which ought to bear the loss. On the other hand, one aspect of such a class definition which includes the blaster can be found readily in the unjust enrichment notion—the notion that those who benefit by receiving the products of blasting activities ought to bear the losses if they can be distributed at a reasonable cost. They should pay, as part of the price of construction, the equivalent of an insurance premium or contribution to a fund to cover risks from blasting accidents. The accent is not upon efficiency but upon fairness of distribution.

The influence of risk-spreading capacity in tort decisions is primarily on the role of what might be called an enabling or rebuttal factor. It removes a barrier which might have prevented the imposition of liability based primarily on other grounds. [Omitted is Keeton's discussion of examples including charitable immunity and retailer liability for canned goods.]

···

Richard A. Epstein, *A Theory of Strict Liability*
2 J. Legal Stud. 151, 158–59, 168–69, 186–88 (1973)*

···

The result in *Vincent* seems inconsistent with either of the customary explanations, moral or economic, of negligence in the law of tort. There is no argument that the conduct of the defendant was "blameworthy" in any sense. The coercion on him was great, even though not imposed by some human agency. Any person in the position of the defendant's captain would have made the same choice under the circumstances. It is true that he knew that his conduct could damage the dock, but nonetheless the necessity of the situation would serve as an adequate defense against any charge of intentional wrongdoing. Similarly, if the economic conception of negligence is adopted, the same result must be reached once it is admitted that the conduct of the defendant served to minimize the total amount of damage suffered; the expected benefits of further precautions were outweighed by their costs.

Had the Lake Erie Transportation Company owned both the dock and the ship, there could have been no lawsuit as a result of the incident. The Transportation Company, now the sole party involved, would, when faced with the storm, apply some form of cost-benefit analysis in order to decide whether to sacrifice its ship or its dock to the elements. Regardless of the choice made, it would bear the consequences and would have no recourse against anyone else. There is no reason why the company as a defendant in a lawsuit should be able to shift the loss in question because the dock belonged to someone else. The action in tort in effect enables the injured party to require the defendant to treat the loss he has inflicted on another as though it were his own. If the Transportation Company must bear all the costs in those cases in which it damages its own property, then it should bear those costs when it damages the property of another. The necessity may justify the decision to cause the damage, but it cannot justify a refusal to make compensation for the damage so caused.

The argument is not limited to the case where the defendant acts with the certain knowledge that his conduct will cause harm to others. It applies with equal force to cases where the defendant acts when he knows that there is only a *risk* that he will cause harm to others. In *Morris v. Platt*, the plaintiff requested a jury instruction that the defendant should be found liable where he accidentally shot the plaintiff in an attempt to defend himself against an attack by third persons, even if he acted prudently under the circumstances. The court rejected that request and held instead that the plaintiff, even if an innocent bystander, could not recover for his injuries; the accident had been "inevitable." [Epstein here argues that "*Morris* is not distinguishable from *Vincent* on any principled ground...."]

. . .

[Epstein proceeds to consider "four distinct paradigm cases covered by the proposition 'A caused B harm.'" The first three are the situation involving "the application of force to a person or thing," the case in which the defendant frightens the plaintiff, and the case in which one person injures another under the compulsion of a third person. The essence of his argument with respect to each is symbolized in the following passage concerning the simplest case, involving the application of physical force:]

... Briefly put, the argument is that proof of the proposition *A hit B* should be sufficient to establish a prima facie case of liability.[48]

I do not argue that proof of causation is equivalent to a conclusive demonstration of responsibility. Both the modern and classical systems of law are based upon the development of prima facie cases and defenses thereto. They differ not in their use of presumptions but in the elements needed to create the initial presumption in favor of the plaintiff. The doctrine of strict liability holds that proof that the defendant caused harm creates that presumption because proof of the non-reciprocal source of the harm is sufficient to upset the balance where one person must win and the other must lose. There

---

48. The argument depends upon "a deep sense of common law morality that one who hurts another should compensate him." Leon Green, [61 COLUM. L. REV. 1401], at 1412.

is no room to consider, as part of the prima facie case, allegations that the defendant intended to harm the plaintiff, or could have avoided the harm he caused by the use of reasonable care. The choice is plaintiff or defendant, and the analysis of causation is the tool which, prima facie, fastens responsibility upon the defendant. Indeed for most persons, the difficult question is often not whether these causal assertions create the presumption, but whether there are in fact any means to distinguish between causation and responsibility, so close is the connection between what a man does and what he is answerable for....

[The fourth paradigm which Epstein addresses is that "involving creation of dangerous conditions that result in harm to either person or property." In this category, he discussed three principal cases: (1) "[T]hings that are 'inherently' dangerous ... because they retain their *potential* energy in full, even if they are stored or handled with the highest possible care," [e.g., explosives]; (2) Situations in which "a person places a thing—not dangerous in itself—in a dangerous position" ["*Vincent v. Lake Erie*, taken in its own terms, is a case of this sort"]; (3) "Products or other things dangerous because defective" [principally referring to products liability cases].

[After analyzing these categories of "dangerous conditions" and noting similarities and distinctions in the applicable causation rules, Epstein concludes:]

The rules of liability thus far developed have not relied upon any form of cost-benefit analysis. But even though they have not sought to take into account any economic principles, it does not follow that they must offend them. Consider the two most difficult cases—simple accident and necessity—that could arise under any of these causal paradigms. In both these cases the rules imposing liability upon the defendant should not in principle create any new incentives, once it is settled that the plaintiff's conduct is not in issue. For example, in *Bolton v. Stone* [a case in which a cricket batsman hit an unusually long ball that struck the plaintiff while she stood on an adjoining highway] the defendant will not take any precautions, because it is cheaper to satisfy the judgment if the accident should occur. There is no question of resource allocation. There is only the question whether the courts will compel the transfer of wealth from one person to another, and on that issue it seems appropriate that the decision should be made on grounds of fairness.

The same analysis applies to the case of necessity. Defendants in cases like *Vincent* will be required to make compensation for avoidable damages, regardless of the theory invoked. The theories of strict liability diverge from those of negligence only with regard to that portion of the damages against which no prudent precautions could have been taken. As to these the economic situation is exactly what it was in *Bolton v. Stone*; it will be cheaper for the defendant to pay the damages than to take the precautions, so the precautions will not be taken. There is still no question of resource allocation, and as before, it is appropriate to rely upon fairness grounds in order to decide whether the transfer payment will be required.

Finally, it can be argued that rules of strict liability are in the end preferable on economic grounds because they reduce the administrative costs of decision. The point is clear in cases like *Vincent* because rules of strict liability eliminate the need to allocate between recoverable and nonrecoverable damages. But more importantly, the rules or strict liability tell the courts that they need not take into account any form of economic analysis in order to decide the concrete case. There is no need to ask the hard question of which branch of government is best able to make cost-benefit determinations, because the matter is left in private hands where it belongs. It is true that the rules of strict liability may in the aggregate lead to some small increase in the number of cases to be decided by the courts, but even that is doubtful since it is so simple for plaintiffs to include some allegation of negligence in their complaint in order to state a prima facie case....

NOTES

(1) Must not analysis of *Vincent* begin with the fact that the defendant did not act negligently? What elements must a plaintiff prove to succeed in a case in which he relies on *Vincent*?

(2) As a corollary to *Vincent*, it should be noted that courts will fix the standard of care for emergencies in light of the circumstances—which principally include the emergency. This rule holds with respect to the actions of vessel masters in storms, see *Hart v. Blakemore*, 410 F.2d 218 (5th Cir. 1969), as well as vehicular emergencies, see *Wendelken v. McMurray*, 388 F.2d 553 (5th Cir. 1967), cert. denied, 391 U.S. 952 (1968). It also applies in more unusual situations, e.g., to the actions of a person whose employee has an epileptic seizure, see *Newman v. Redstone*, 354 Mass. 379, 237 N.E.2d 666 (1968).

An approach of this kind also rationalized a victory for a quick-thinking cabbie who sacrificed the safety of others for his own in *Cordas v. Peerless Transportation Co.*, 27 N.Y.S.2d 198 (N.Y. City Ct. 1941). In that case a thief commandeered the defendant's cab, threatening to blow out his brains if he did not obey. A pursuing posse gained in a chase through lower Manhattan. The cabbie threw his car out of gear, pulled on the emergency brake, jammed on his brakes, swung open the door and jumped out. The driverless cab proceeded onto the sidewalk, where it struck and slightly injured the plaintiff mother and her two children. Emphasizing the split-second nature of the defendant's reaction in an "emergency," the court dismissed the case.

Does the opportunity to deliberate possessed by the defendant master in *Vincent* adequately distinguish that case from decisions exonerating actors on the basis of the emergency doctrine?

(3) Can you distinguish the following situation from the cab driver's case summarized in note 2?:

X works for Y, a millionaire. Z comes into Y's office, where X is present, and hands Y a note, demanding a million dollars as ransom against his dropping a dynamite-filled bag. Y shakes his head, and as Z drops the bag, Y ducks behind X, whose body shields him from the ensuing explosion. Does X have a cause of action against Y for injuries sustained from the blast? Cf. *Laidlaw v. Sage*, 158 N.Y. 73, 52 N.E. 679 (1899).

(4) Would the result have been different in *Vincent* if the first cable had held?

(5) Is there a clear-cut efficiency justification for *Vincent*? Could a decision the other way be convincingly justified by the argument that dock owners could adjust their rate structures to take account of this kind of occurrence? How would decisions either way on *Vincent* facts affect the conduct of ship captains and dock owners?

Had the decision gone the other way, what would its significance be, beyond a limited determination about wealth distribution between these two parties?

(6) As a matter of equity, which placement of the loss is preferable in *Vincent*?

(7) Compare Keeton's "conditional fault" theory with Epstein's causation analysis and with Fletcher's "paradigm of reciprocity," excerpted supra §7.01. Which provides

the most consistently persuasive explanation for the results you think proper in cases like *Rylands*, supra § 7.01, and *Vincent*, as well as *LaPlante*, supra § 4.01?

(8) Calabresi and Hirschoff elaborate a legal and economic analysis of accident costs in *Toward a Test for Strict Liability in Torts*, 81 Yale L.J. 155 (1972), proposing an approach under which the principal question is which party "is in the best position to make the cost-benefit analysis between accident costs and accident avoidance costs and to act on that decision once it [is] made." For further exegesis, see Calabresi, *Optimal Deterrence and Accidents*, 84 Yale L.J. 656 (1975).

For criticism of the strict liability analyses of Fletcher, Epstein, Calabresi and Hirschoff and others, see Posner, *Strict Liability: A Comment*, 2 J. Legal Stud. 25 (1973).

Epstein extends his thesis in *Defenses and Subsequent Pleas in a System of Strict Liability*, 3 J. Legal Stud. 165 (1974).

(9) Consider a case involving a nuclear power plant, shut down for repairs and refueling, that is besieged by demonstrators with the goal of preventing workers from entering the plant and restoring it to the business of generating power.

If the owner of the plant sues demonstrators for damages for trespass, should they be able to defend on the basis that they are trying to shield local citizens from the dangers of low-level radiation or nuclear waste? Do you find more, or less, persuasive the argument that the demonstrators are trying to reduce the harm to the nation, and other nations, posed by the risk of a large-scale nuclear accident that would release large quantities of radioactive material into the atmosphere?

(10) Suppose that a mass transportation accident overstrains the facilities of a hospital emergency room. One victim, Mr. A, is lying on the ground on a stretcher outside the emergency room, having been pronounced a lower priority patient than several others who are being treated. However, he is losing blood at what seems an alarming rate in the view of a friend at the scene, a former medical corpsman. The friend knows that Mr. A has a particular rare blood type. He slips into the emergency room, where in the confusion he secures devices from which he puts together a makeshift transfusion unit. He somehow discovers where the blood supply is kept, takes a container of the needed blood type and administers it to Mr. A. Has the hospital any action against Mr. A or his friend? If so, for what should it be able to recover?

(11) Why is *Vincent* a torts case, rather than a property or contracts case? Consider the following suggestions:

> Perhaps the answer lies in the realization that *Vincent* is a social contract tort. In using this term I refer to the way that tort law bridges the gap between judicial enforcement of the contractual intentions of litigants and the expression of legislative will on matters of distributive justice. The notion of individualized justice applied in *Vincent* permits judges confronting cases of injury, occurring in the absence of prior arrangements, to focus on various elements of factual situations that commend themselves to a community sense of fairness. In *Vincent* the central element of justice appears to lie in the ability of the defendant, in pursuance of its own advantage, to do a legal act that damaged the plaintiff's property in a situation in which he had no practical opportunity to avoid the harm.
>
> · · ·
>
> Justice O'Brien's opinion in *Vincent* conforms to a power-centered view of tort law. Courts had already laid down the law restricting the dock owner's use

of his power to cut the ship loose, recognizing that this would have been tortious conduct.[64] Yet, power having been restrained on the part of the dock owner, the legal power to cause injury remained in the ship's master. It was to check this power that the *Vincent* court fashioned a social connecting rod among doctrines that absolved the shipowner of intentional tort liability, recognized the prudence of the master's conduct, and yet required compensation.

—Marshall Shapo, *A Social Contract Tort*, 75 Tex. L. Rev. 1835, 1841, 1845 (1997).

(12) Is the real problem in *Vincent* simply a subset of what is often characterized as "the poverty problem"?

---

64. *See, e.g., Ploof v. Putnam*, 71 A. 188 (Vt. 1908).

Chapter 9

DAMAGES

§ 9.01   General Considerations

DePASS v. UNITED STATES
United States Court of Appeals, Seventh Circuit
721 F.2d 203 (1983)

FLAUM, CIRCUIT JUDGE.

This appeal arises out of the denial of damages to plaintiff James DePass for alleged increased risk of cardiovascular disease and loss of life expectancy. The district court, in a bench trial, found that DePass had not proved the injury by a preponderance of the evidence. This appeal requires us to determine whether the district court was "clearly erroneous" in its finding. Fed.R.Civ.P. 52(a). For the reasons set out below, we affirm the district court.

I

On December 9, 1978, DePass was struck by a car driven by an employee of the defendant United States. DePass sustained severe injuries, including a traumatic amputation of his left leg below the knee. DePass brought suit under the Federal Tort Claims Act, 28 U.S.C. §§ 2671–2680. The United States admitted liability, and the case was tried as to damages only.

At trial, DePass introduced evidence as to the nature and extent of his injuries, and as to past and future pain and suffering. DePass's witnesses included Dr. Jerome D. Cohen, a medical doctor.[1] Dr. Cohen testified that he had examined DePass and found that DePass had had a traumatic amputation of the left leg just below the knee. Dr. Cohen then testified that he had read an article, *Traumatic Limb Amputation and the Subsequent Mortality from Cardiovascular Disease and Other Causes*, published in volume 33 of the Journal of Chronic Diseases, by Zdenek Hrubec and Richard Ryder ("the Hrubec and Ryder study") (Pl.Ex. 10). This article involved a study of 3,890 Americans who had suffered traumatic limb amputations during World War II. The study established a statistical connection between traumatic limb amputations and future cardiovascular problems and decreased life expectancy.

---

1. The record reveals that Dr. Cohen is board certified in internal medicine. Dr. Cohen's testimony at trial, and his curriculum vitae (Pl.Ex. 9), fail to establish whether he is certified in cardiology or in the subspecialty of cardiovascular diseases.

Dr. Cohen testified that DePass fits within the class of persons who had sustained a traumatic amputation of a limb. He testified that, based on his own experience, his examination of DePass, and his analysis of the Hrubec and Ryder study, because DePass is a traumatic amputee he has a greater risk of cardiovascular problems and decreased life expectancy. At the conclusion of Dr. Cohen's testimony, the trial court questioned him as follows:

The Court: Is it your testimony that based on your examination of this plaintiff, Mr. DePass, plus your knowledge in the field of cardiovascular disease and including your analysis and a reading of the article which is Exhibit 10, is your opinion that he, because he is the amputee that he is on the left leg below the knee, that he has a greater risk for developing cardiovascular disease in the future and also a greater risk for shorter mortality, shorter longevity? Is that what you're saying, that he is a risk for that?

[**Dr. Cohen**]: Yes, that's correct.

The Court: And you're not saying that he will develop it or that he will live shorter, but he is a greater risk for both of those?

[**Dr. Cohen**]: That's correct.

(Tr. at 289–90).

On cross-examination, Dr. Cohen testified to the existence of several other studies on the relationship between traumatic limb amputation and decreased life expectancy. In particular, he testified as to a 1954 English study of 27,000 amputees that showed no statistical connection between amputation and decreased life expectancy. Several studies conducted on a smaller scale also failed to show a connection. One study, done in Finland, found a statistical connection. He testified that he had not personally reviewed any of the other studies. Dr. Cohen testified that no one knows if in fact the Hrubec and Ryder study is correct. Dr. Cohen then read from the study, "The reasons for the statistically significant relationship demonstrated between limb amputation and cardiovascular disorders are not obvious. Stringent deadlines set by Congress for the completion of this work made impossible detailed studies of individuals." (Tr. at 285).[2]

The district court, in its order, awarded DePass $800,000 for the nature and extent of his injuries and for his past and future pain and suffering. In its findings of fact, the court found no evidence demonstrating by a preponderance that DePass had suffered a loss of life expectancy. The court found that Dr. Cohen's testimony dealt with "possibilities and speculation."[3]

---

2. The study goes on to state:
Pilot surveys indicated that for few of those in our sample could one determine from existing hard-copy records the epidemiologic variables of possible importance. A definitive clarification of the mechanisms which relate traumatic amputation to later cardiovascular disease will require detailed investigation of the particular circumstances of individual subjects.
Pl.Ex. 10 at 247–48. The study outlines several possible causes of the increased risk of decreased life expectancy. It then states, "The study was not designed to test specific hypotheses about the causes of the increased risk." *Id.* at 249.
3. The court's Finding of Fact No. 14 reads as follows:
The Court finds that there is no evidence demonstrating by a preponderance a loss of life expectancy due to the traumatic limb amputation. The Court heard the testimony of Dr. Jerome D. Cohen of St. Louis, Missouri, who testified to an American study of 3,600 traumatic single limb amputations, in which the researchers found a thirty percent higher than normal incidence of cardiovascular disease in the amputees. However, the doctor admitted to the existence of an English study of 27,000 traumatic limb amputations in the earlier part of the century which reached an opposite conclusion. More fundamentally, the doctor never established that this individual plaintiff

On appeal, DePass argues that the district court was clearly erroneous in its findings of fact. He argues that his evidence was clear, convincing, and uncontradicted. He also argues that the United States is bound by the Hrubec and Ryder study as an admission by the government. The United States argues that the district court could reject Dr. Cohen's testimony and the Hrubec and Ryder study. The United States also argues that the evidence at best establishes only that DePass is, on the average, at an increased risk of injury, and that this increased risk is not compensable under Illinois law.

· · ·

Based on the record before us, we cannot say that the district court was clearly erroneous. The findings of fact demonstrate that the district court considered the Hrubec and Ryder study and Dr. Cohen's testimony. The court, however, declined to accept the study and the testimony as establishing the fact of injury by a preponderance. There is substantial evidence in the record to support this. Dr. Cohen testified that he based certain of his conclusions on the Hrubec and Ryder study. The study itself states, and Dr. Cohen testified, that other studies exist that reach a different conclusion. Dr. Cohen stated that no one knows if the Hrubec and Ryder study is correct. The study does not establish a reason for the statistical relationship between amputation and decreased life expectancy.

There was conflicting evidence in the record as to the conclusiveness of the Hrubec and Ryder study. It was for the district court to weigh the evidence; the court did not find the evidence strong enough to be a preponderance.

Moreover, even if there were no contradictory evidence on this point, the district court could still reject the conclusions of the Hrubec and Ryder study. The plaintiff had the burden of proving injury. The court could reject the evidence even when the defendant introduces no contradictory evidence....

Because we find that the district court could reject the Hrubec and Ryder study as inconclusive, we do not reach the issue of whether merely placing plaintiff in a class of persons subject, on the average, to an increased risk of injury is sufficient to establish a compensable injury under Illinois law. We note, however, that Illinois law is not settled as to whether increased risk of future injury is compensable. *Compare Lindsay v. Appleby*, 91 Ill.App.3d 705, 46 Ill.Dec. 832, 414 N.E.2d 885 (1980) *with Morrissy v. Eli Lilly and Co.*, 76 Ill.App.3d 753, 32 Ill.Dec. 30, 394 N.E.2d 1369 (1979).

We have considered appellant's other arguments and determine them to be without merit.

Affirmed.

POSNER, CIRCUIT JUDGE, dissenting.

Although this may seem like a routine personal-injury case, it raises important questions relating to the use of scientific evidence in federal trials. The plaintiff, a 37-year-old man named DePass, was hit by a car owned and operated by the government. He was seriously injured—one of his legs had to be amputated just below the knee, the other was crippled, and one eye was badly injured. He brought suit under the Federal Tort Claims Act and the district court held the government liable and awarded DePass $800,000 in damages. The entire award is for "pain and suffering," since DePass in-

---

would suffer a loss of life expectancy, or even that it was more likely than not that he would suffer the loss. At best, his testimony dealt with possibilities and speculation and failed to establish the existence of such a loss in plaintiff.

curred no medical expenses (he received all medical treatment free of charge from the Veterans Administration) and proved no loss of earnings from the accident. This is a generous award, maybe too generous, even though "pain and suffering" does not mean just physical pain and suffering but includes the unhappiness caused by disfiguring and crippling injuries.... In any event, the judge's failure to explain the basis of the award seems inconsistent with the requirements of Rule 52(a) of the Federal Rules of Civil Procedure....

But the government has not appealed, so for purposes of this appeal we must accept that $800,000 is a reasonable estimate of DePass's damages, assuming as the judge found that DePass's life was not shortened by the accident. This appeal challenges that finding. Although the additional loss inflicted by shortening what is now likely to be a rather miserable life may be slight in pecuniary terms, especially after being discounted to present value, if DePass proved that the accident probably shortened his life he was entitled to some additional damages and it should be no concern of ours whether the addition would be small or large or whether as an original matter we might think $800,000 adequate or even excessive to compensate him for all of his losses.

If the finding that the accident will not shorten DePass's life had been based in whole or part on the judge's opinion of the believability of a witness I would agree that we should affirm. But there are no "credibility" issues in this case. The government acknowledged at oral argument that DePass's medical expert witness, Dr. Cohen, a cardiovascular epidemiologist, was a candid and truthful witness. I do not understand the district judge to have disbelieved Cohen. I do not even think the judge rejected the finding in the National Institutes of Health study on which Cohen relied (Hrubec & Ryder, *Traumatic Limb Amputations and Subsequent Mortality from Cardiovascular Disease and Other Causes*, 33 J. Chronic Diseases 239 (1980)) that a person who has had a major amputation—knee or above, or elbow or above—is more likely to develop heart disease and therefore likely to die younger than a person who has not had a major amputation. The judge did remark that a British study apparently had found no association between amputation and longevity. (I say "apparently" because no one connected with this case has ever read the study, which was not published in a medical journal and may not even be available in the United States. All remarks about it are based on a couple of sentences in the NIH study.) Dr. Cohen explained why he thought the British study was probably less pertinent than the NIH study to estimating DePass's life expectancy. The British study was older (1954 versus 1979); and it was of a foreign population in a much earlier period (British veterans of World War I versus American veterans of World War II in the NIH study), a population moreover that has different health characteristics from ours (heart disease is less common in Britain than in the United States). Cohen's testimony was not shaken by cross-examination and the government did not introduce any medical testimony, live or documentary, of its own.... It did not even place the British study in evidence. The district judge could have had no basis for rejecting Dr. Cohen's assessment of the relative weight of the two studies.

But as I have said, I do not think the judge rejected DePass's medical evidence because he thought it false (how could he have?) or outweighed by other evidence (there was no contrary evidence). He appears to have rejected the entire class of evidence— statistical evidence—illustrated by the medical evidence in this case. This is suggested by his finding that "the doctor never established that this individual plaintiff would suffer a loss of life expectancy, or even that it was more likely than not that he would suffer the loss. At best, his testimony dealt with possibilities and speculation and failed to establish the existence of such a loss in plaintiff." Another clue is found at the close of Dr.

Cohen's testimony when the judge asked him: "Is it your testimony … that because [De-Pass] is the amputee that he is … he has a greater risk for developing cardiovascular disease in the future and also a greater risk for shorter mortality, shorter longevity? Is that what you're saying, that he is a risk for that?" When Dr. Cohen answered, "That's correct," the judge said: "And you're not saying that he will develop [cardiovascular disease] or that he will live shorter, but he is a greater risk for both of those?" When Dr. Cohen again said, "That's correct," the judge remarked: "I won't get into any statistics. I'll just drop it at that."

Maybe the judge just misunderstood the term "life expectancy." When he said that Dr. Cohen had "never established that this individual plaintiff would suffer a loss of life expectancy," he was stating a truism rather than, as he thought, throwing doubt on the cogency of the plaintiff's medical evidence. A man's life expectancy is not his actual life span, which cannot be known till he dies; it is a prediction founded on the average experience of many people having the same characteristics as he. When we say that a heavy smoker has a shorter life expectancy than a nonsmoker we do not mean that Jones who smokes heavily will in fact predecease Smith who does not smoke or that Jones will die sooner than he would have if he did not smoke; we just mean that, on the average, nonsmokers outlive smokers.

But it seems more likely from his remarks that the district judge thought that all probabilities are too uncertain to provide a basis for awarding damages. Yet most knowledge, and almost all legal evidence, is probabilistic. Even the proposition that De-Pass will die some day is merely empirical. It is of course highly probable that he will die but it is not certain in the way it is certain that 10^3 is 1000 or that I am my wife's husband—propositions that are true as a matter of definition rather than of observation. If Dr. Cohen had testified that DePass had heart disease and was therefore likely to die younger than most men in his age group, he would have been making a probabilistic statement; and the probabilities that are derived from statistical studies are no less reliable in general than the probabilities that are derived from direct observation, from intuition, or from case studies of a single person or event—all familiar sources of legal evidence.

All this has long been recognized in personal-injury cases, as it is throughout the law. If a tort victim is seriously injured and will require medical attention for the rest of his life, the court in deciding how much to award him for future medical expenses will have to estimate how long he can be expected to live and it will make this estimate by consulting a mortality table, which is to say by looking at a statistical summation of the experience of thousands or millions of people none of whom is a party or a witness in the case, rather than by studying the lifelines on the victim's palms. And if a study has been made of the mortality of people with the same kind of injury as the plaintiff, the court will consult that study in addition to or instead of standard mortality tables. That is what DePass asked the district judge to do here.

It makes no logical or even legal difference whether the question is how long a permanently injured person will require medical attention or how soon a delayed consequence of the accident (death in this case) will occur. The factual question is the same: when will he die? The Illinois courts (Illinois law governs the substantive questions in this Federal Tort Claims Act suit) recognize that the risk of a future consequence of an accident, even though not certain to materialize, is compensable. *See Lindsay v. Appleby*, 91 Ill.App.3d 705, 712, 46 Ill.Dec. 832, 837, 414 N.E.2d 885, 890 (1980) ("evidence tending to show an increased risk of further injury caused by defendant's conduct was admissible as tending to show plaintiff's future damages"). Although *Morrissy v. Eli Lilly*

& Co., 76 Ill.App.3d 753, 761, 32 Ill.Dec. 30, 37, 394 N.E.2d 1369, 1376 (1979), cited by the majority opinion in the present case, recites the formula, "possible future damages in a personal injury action are not compensable unless reasonably certain to occur," *Morrissy* is distinguishable from this case. The plaintiff had not yet suffered any ascertainable injury as a result of her mother's having taken DES while pregnant; the complaint was that she might some day develop an illness as a delayed consequence of the DES. DePass was seriously injured; the only issue is the extent of his injury, an issue on which courts traditionally do not impose a heavy burden of proof on plaintiffs.... Thus in *Harp v. Illinois Central Gulf R.R.*, 55 Ill.App.3d 822, 827, 12 Ill.Dec. 915, 918–19, 370 N.E.2d 826, 829–30 (1977), a case where, as in this case but not in *Morrissy*, the issue was extent of injury, the "reasonable certainty" formula was invoked but then liberally interpreted to allow an accident victim to recover damages for the possible future rupture of a disc injured in the accident.

Although few reported cases (none from Illinois) deal with the specific question whether a reduction in life expectancy is compensable, the trend is toward allowing recovery in such cases. *See, e.g., Downie v. United States Lines Co.*, 359 F.2d 344, 347–48 (3d Cir.1966); *McNeill v. United States*, 519 F.Supp. 283, 289 (D.S.C.1981); *James v. United States*, 483 F.Supp. 581, 586–87 (N.D.Cal.1980); Schultheis & Rheingold, *Making Up for Lost Time: Recovering for Shortened Life Expectancy*, 19 Trial 44 (Feb. 1983). As it should be. A tortfeasor should not get off scot-free because instead of killing his victim outright he inflicts an injury that is likely though not certain to shorten the victim's life.

In any event, the government conceded at oral argument that a reduction in life expectancy is compensable under Illinois tort law. So the only question is the reliability of the study on which Dr. Cohen relied. The study is of the 30-year medical history of 12,000 Americans injured in combat in World War II of whom almost 4,000 had major amputations as a result of their injuries. (The British study was larger, but we do not know how many of the persons studied were major amputees, or even whether the study distinguished between major and minor—though no one seriously believes that losing your pinky will significantly increase the risk of dying prematurely from heart disease.) Although the NIH study does not establish the exact causal linkage between major amputation and early death from heart disease, it suggests a linkage. Emotional stress and (more important) lack of exercise are believed to be among the causes of heart disease, and a major amputation is a source of stress (reflected for example in higher suicide and alcoholism rates among amputees) and makes exercise more difficult. Consistently with this hypothesis, the study found that the increased incidence of heart disease was greater for men who had lost two legs than for men who had lost one (functionally, DePass is closer to the former than to the latter category), and greater for those who had lost one leg than for those who had lost just an arm.

The NIH study does not pretend to be conclusive and its results are presented with appropriate scientific caution. Subsequent studies may overthrow them. But as I have already noted a tort plaintiff's burden of proving the extent of his injury is not a heavy one. Doubts are resolved against the tortfeasor. All of the medical evidence introduced in this case (the government, it will be recalled, presented none) points in one direction—that DePass will probably die younger because of the accident. On the basis of the study Dr. Cohen testified that DePass had a 44–58 percent higher than normal risk of dying from heart disease, resulting in a 30 percent reduction in DePass's life expectancy—from 37 to 26 years, a difference of 11 years. This reduction in life expectancy is just a convenient summation of the probabilistic results of the NIH study applied to a man of DePass's age. To illustrate very simply what is involved, imagine that before the accident DePass had a 10 percent chance of dying at age 60, a 50 percent chance of dying at age 65, and a 40 percent chance of dying at age 70. Multiply each age by the corresponding percentage, sum up the results, and you have his expected age at death: 66.5 years. Assume the accident changed these percentages as follows: he now has a 40 percent chance of dying at age 60 and a 60 percent chance of dying at age 65. His expected age of death is now 63, so the accident reduced his life expectancy by 3-1/2 years. From the way I have set up this highly stylized example we know for a fact that DePass will not die at the age of 63. All we know is that he is likelier, by given percentages, to die at either 60 or 65 than he was before the accident. But if we want to summarize all of our information in a single figure, we can do so by means of the concept of life expectancy. It provides a perfectly objective basis for awarding damages.

If any corroboration of the applicability of the NIH study to DePass's personal situation was needed, it was supplied by Dr. Cohen's finding, in an examination of DePass, that DePass's cardiovascular function had fallen below normal for men of his age. This is not evidence of heart disease but it shows that DePass is, as one would expect given the nature of his injuries, perforce leading an extremely sedentary life—which according to the NIH study is probably the main cause of the much greater incidence of heart disease among major amputees.

It is of course unlikely that DePass will die exactly 11 years earlier because of the accident. He may never get heart disease. Or he may be cut down by it long before he is within 11 years of the expected end of his life. It was unlikely that the accident victim in *Abernathy v. Superior Hardwoods, Inc.*, 704 F.2d 963, 972–74 (7th Cir.1983), to pick a recent personal-injury case almost at random, would die 40 years after the accident—a number plucked from a mortality table, reflecting as the NIH study reflects statistical experience. And yet Abernathy was awarded damages as if he would die in 40 years. That is how damages are calculated in personal-injury cases; and a judge is not free to say, in my court we do not allow statistical inference. Knowledge increasingly is statistical, and judges must not let themselves lag too far behind the progress of knowledge. As a matter of fact they have not lagged. The kind of evidence that the district judge rejected in this case, evidence of probability of survival, invariably based on studies of a group of people rather than of just the individual plaintiff, is an increasingly common basis for awarding damages. *See, e.g.*, Wolfstone & Wolfstone, *Recovery of Damages for the Loss of a Chance*, 1978 Personal Injury Annual 744.

The district judge's rejection of such evidence, if widely followed, would lead to systematically undercompensating the victims of serious accidents and thus to systematically underdeterring such accidents. Accidents that require the amputation of a limb, particularly a leg, are apparently even more catastrophic than one had thought. They do not just cause a lifetime of disfigurement and reduced mobility; they create a high risk of premature death from heart disease. The goal of awarding damages in tort law is to put the tort victim as nearly as possible in the position he would have occupied if the tort had not been committed. This goal cannot be attained or even approached if judges shut their eyes to consequences that scientists have found are likely to follow from particular types of accident, merely because the scientists' evidence is statistical. But unless I have mistaken the true grounds of the district judge's decision in this case that is what he did.

The finding that DePass failed to prove a reduction in life expectancy as a result of the accident should be vacated as clearly erroneous and the case should be remanded to the district court for a determination of the amount of damages necessary to compensate DePass for an 11-year reduction in his life expectancy.

Fleming James, Jr., *Damages in Accident Cases*
41 CORNELL L. Q. 582, 582–585 (1956)*

. . .

The cardinal principle of damages in Anglo-American law is that of compensation of the injury caused to plaintiff by defendant's breach of duty. . . .

The principle of compensation is a natural enough corollary of the fault principle. If defendant is a wrongdoer and he is to pay damages to an innocent plaintiff, it seems eminently fair that these damages should (at least) put plaintiff, as nearly as may be, in the same position he would have been in if defendant's wrong had not injured him. So deeply does this correspond to our natural feelings that the basic principle has been taken pretty much for granted. Its validity in a system of liability based on the personal moral shortcoming of him who pays the judgment may well be conceded. Today, however, the trend in accident law is running heavily towards diluting the requirement of fault for liability and the defense of the victim's fault. Increasingly the personal participants in the accident—even where their fault is clear—do not pay the judgments awarded. These are paid by absentee employers or by large insurance companies and through them distributed widely over a large segment of society. Accident law is approaching—perhaps by faltering steps[15]—an enterprise liability without fault. If such a system is to be justified, it cannot be in terms of the personal ethical evaluation which gave rise to the compensatory theory of damages. Justification must come, rather, from the kind of considerations of social morality which led to workman's compensation. In this view the ethical evaluation of the conduct of participants in an ordinary accident situation is overshadowed in importance by these outstanding facts: some classes of accidents are the inevitable by-product of enterprises which can distribute such accident losses efficiently and broadly among the beneficiaries of the enterprises. These accident losses fall initially on those who are ill-equipped to meet them; and if the losses are not shifted from the initial victims, ruin and dislocation with widely unfortunate social repercussions will result. Social morality and expediency therefore demand that these losses be met and distributed by the enterprises which caused the hazards that brought on the losses, *but only to the extent that this is necessary to obviate the evils that call for the system of strict liability.* After all, the payment and distribution of losses are burdens to all concerned in the process, and these burdens should not be imposed on persons or classes of persons without some reason, nor to an extent beyond that which the reason calls for. The reason for strict liability here is to provide assurance that accident victims will be rehabilitated, and that they and their dependents will be cared for during the period of disability without imposing on the victims or their families a crushing burden. The amount of damages measured by this functional standard may be less than the compensatory damages provided by the common law, especially since compensation is presently attempted for many speculative nonpecuniary items. Even when we consider the victim's pecuniary loss, we must remember that accidents bring a net pecuniary loss to society as a whole—the social wealth and income is thereby diminished—so that if the victim is made entirely whole, he will fare better than society and will not himself

---

   15. The most complete integration of this thesis (with considerable emphasis on the faltering nature of the steps) appears in EHRENZWEIG, NEGLIGENCE WITHOUT FAULT (1951). *See also* EHRENZWEIG, FULL AID INSURANCE (1954).

share the economic burden he is asking society to distribute. If social need is invoked to justify strict liability without regard to moral fault, then the demands of that need should measure the extent of the liability. In that context, what is fair is only what is needed, though here as elsewhere in life too stingy a view of the need might frustrate the meeting of it.[16]

SPECIAL NOTE: BASIC RATIONALES OF TORT DAMAGES

Towards a Jurisprudence of Injury 5-164 to 5-175
(ABA 1984, M. Shapo, Reporter)*

Rationales: Uncertain. Beyond the problem of deciding whether particular awards are too high or too low, the analyst of damages rules encounters difficulty in determining just why damages are awarded. One commentator remarks generally on the "absence of coherent principle in the law on damages for personal injuries."[14] In the course of an examination of the Canadian rules on collateral benefits, that writer declares that the "unsatisfactory state of the law" is "directly attributable to the fact that the courts have not settled the problem of what they are seeking to accomplish with damage awards."[15]

The problem arises partly from the tension between compensation and deterrence goals. This tension is evident in a recent case in which the evidence clearly did not warrant the submission of a punitive damages issue. The court in that case holds that it was improper for the plaintiff's attorney, while arguing on compensatory damages, to invite the jury to punish the defendant and to deter others from conduct of the sort that cause the injury. The court effectively rejects the argument that counsel's statements were "mere reminders that jury verdicts—whether punitive or compensatory—affect behavior," and approves a quotation from a precedent to the effect that juries should not be told directly or indirectly that they may consider punishment or deterrence in figuring compensatory damages.[16]

A contrasting view appears in a decision refusing to deduct from a widow's damages the value of support that she would receive by her subsequent remarriage.[17] Saying that "[c]ourts do not award 'punitive' damages when they refuse to reduce damages by taking these kinds of considerations into account," the court declares that "the purpose of ordinary tort damages, as distinguished from 'punitive' damages, is both to compensate and to deter." Underlining the point, it says that "[t]ort law mixes these two purposes, compensation and deterrence, when it awards ordinary damages."[18]

Economic Analysis. Economists have propounded several models for calculating the worth of life and limb. Under one line of analysis, the inquiry is how much of a de-

---

16. See Jaffe, *Damages for Personal Injury: The Impact of Insurance*, 18 LAW & CONTEMP. PROB. 219 (1953) (an analysis to which the present author is heavily indebted)....

   * Adapted. Copyright © 1984, The American Bar Association. Reprinted by permission.

14. McLachlin, *What Price Disability? A Perspective on the Law of Damages for Personal Injury*, 59 CAN. B. REV. 1, 1 (1981).

15. *Id.* at 45.

16. *Vanskike v. ACF Industries, Inc.*, 665 F.2d 188, 209–10 (8th Cir. 1981), cert. denied *sub nom. St. L.-S.F. Ry. v. Vanskike*, 455 U.S. 1000 (1982).

17. *Kalavity v. United States*, 584 F.2d 809 (6th Cir. 1978).

18. *Id.* at 811.

crease in pay a worker would take to reduce to zero the extra probability of death connected with his or her job. On this basis, writing in 1976, Thaler and Rosen calculated from wage rates in a variety of occupations that the value of a life saved was $176,000.[26] Viscusi, noting in a 1978 article that Thaler and Rosen "focuse[d] on a group who have shown themselves to be less averse to severe death risks than the rest of the population,"[27] found that "most of the death risk equations in which other job risk variables are included indicate a value of life in the range of $1 to $1.5 million in 1969 dollars."

An interesting parallel appears in the differences among regulatory agencies with respect to the effective cost per life saved of the safety choices those agencies have made in their respective ranges of policy options. The figures vary from $50,000 for the Consumer Product Safety Commission and $64,000 for one estimate of the National Highway Traffic Safety Administration to $2.6 million for the Environmental Protection Agency and $12.1 million for the Occupational Safety and Health Administration. At the same time that it has tried to develop a precise calculus of the cost of lifesaving, one of these agencies has emphasized that it does not consider a cost-benefit analysis as the sole criterion for decision making.[30]

Quite another perspective on the subject appears in the clash between those who see injury damages as "rent" against those who view them as "capital." Professor Fleming has noted that at a high level of abstraction, the "capital" notion symbolizes "free enterprise and individualism" while the concept of "rent" represents "a social philosophy of paternalism." Rather less abstractly, the "rent" thesis posits that "the function of damages [is] to restore the plaintiff's former position as far as practically possible," so that "prospective earnings are accordingly compensable by corresponding periodic payments." The correlative argument for the "capital" concept is "wholly pragmatic," with "[t]he most accredited theory" simply "explaining that the purpose of the award is to compensate the plaintiff for a present loss of earning capacity, a capital asset, rather than for future loss of earnings."[31]

. . .

In the present state of the law of tort damages, which typically involves the payment of lump sums unless negotiation has produced a structured periodic award, litigation has come to draw heavily on economic appraisals. The use of professional economists has become commonplace in tort cases, to the point that one economist finds it necessary to caution that members of his profession "should base judgments of economic loss on economic theory rather than legal issues."[33]

Illustrative of the number and complexity of the economic issues is Speiser's thick volume, *Recovery For Wrongful Death*, which is subtitled "Economic Handbook." In setting out "principles of appraisal well established in government, business and academic inquiries,"[34]4 Speiser emphasizes the "*dynamic* character of appraisal," pointing to the changes over the last several decades in hourly earnings, price levels, and rates of interest[35]5 He posits that there are "striking similarities between the factors underlying eval-

26. Thaler and Rosen, *The Value of Saving a Life: Evidence from the Labor Market*, in 40 STUDIES IN INCOME & WEALTH: HOUSEHOLD PRODUCT & CONSUMPTION 265, 292 (N. Terleckj ed. 1976).
27. Viscusi, *Labor Market Evaluations of Life and Limb: Empirical Evidence and Policy Implications*, 26 PUBLIC POLICY 359, 373 (1978).
30. *NHTSA Says It Opposes Conversion of Life and Limb into Dollar Figures*, 9 PROD. SAFETY & LIAB. REP. (BNA) 884 (1981).
31. Fleming, *Damages: Capital or Rent?*, 19 U. TORONTO L. J. 295, 299 (1969).
33. Ward, *The Economist in Personal Injury and Death Litigation*, 15 TRIAL No. 11, at 60, 60 (Nov. 1979).
34. SPEISER, RECOVERY FOR WRONGFUL DEATH: ECONOMIC HANDBOOK 4 (2d ed. 1979).
35. *Id.* at 7 (emphasis in original).

uation of the assets of a business, and those involved in determination of pecuniary loss arising from the death of a human being." Beginning with this analogy, Speiser proceeds to argue that there is "no reason why economic data and economists' forecasts should be used for determining the value of a business or a machine over the next forty years, and then be ignored when trying to determine the value of a man's earning power over the same period in the same economy.[36]

From this perspective, competent analysis of a damages case requires not only an assessment of earning capacity but a discount of future values to present worth—a subject on which there is often conflicting economic testimony. It will also involve calculations of fringe benefits. In appropriate cases, it will bring to the jury evaluations of lost earnings of professionals, or of the economic contributions of stay at-home spouses, including those with primary child-care responsibilities, or of the potential earnings of children.[37]

With respect to lost earning capacity, we take particular note of a ... contribution by Saul Levmore, a lawyer-economist, proposing a "self-assessment" mechanism for determining tort damages.[38] The pivot of Levmore's proposal is a designation of "the *first-party insurance coverage of the injured party* as the self-assessed amount," on the theory that potential tort victims guarantee their "valuation of damages in the event of a nontortious accident."[39] In order to avoid injustice to individuals who remain ignorant of "self-assessment" possibilities or are too poor to afford first-party accident insurance, Levmore suggests the use of a schedule of damages akin to those used under workers' compensation.[40] The theoretical appeal of Levmore's analysis lies in the way it avoids the necessity to choose among models associated with "institutional" valuations—in the case of tort actions, valuations by courts—of injury damages.

Use of experts. So long as courts make independent calculations of tort damages, however, litigation on these questions frequently will produce controversy on the proper role of experts. In a decision illustrating the sorts of issues that may arise, a federal appeals court explains that it does not favor expert testimony which directly discusses future inflation because this sort of testimony "may require exploration of the expert's views of world finance or digressions on the validity of a particular economic theory" which will tend to "waste time and confuse the issues.[41] By comparison, the same court opines that expert testimony on future wage increases is "not as likely to confuse the issues," especially when it is limited to "future trends in earnings of a particular group of employees." By thus narrowing the issue, the court says, one may avoid the distortions produced by testimony that is "overly specific as to a particular future earnings figure or excessively general as to the overall national inflation rate."[42]

NOTES

(1) What underlying premises about the purpose of tort damages appear to inform the views of the majority judges and the dissent in *DePass*?

---

36. *Id.* at v (preface to first edition).
37. *See id., passim.*
38. Levmore, *Self-Assessed Valuation Systems for Tort and Other Law*, 68 Va. L. Rev. 771 (1982).
39. *Id.* at 811 (emphasis in original).
40. *Id.* at 815.
41. *Taenzler v. Burlington Northern*, 608 F.2d 796, 801 (8th Cir. 1979).
42. *Id.*

(2) What were the principal questions of "fact" in *DePass*? Of "law"?

(3) Are you able to divine a "coherent principle" underlying damages for personal injuries? Is it, in fact, "compensation," as Professor James argued? How would that principle relate to other goals of tort law, such as affecting the conduct of risky activities?

(4) A recurrent problem in the estimation of future damages arises from uncertainty about what will happen in the future. Tort law, as Judge Posner observes in *DePass*, takes care of this probabilistically. An interesting presentation of the problem appears in a case in which the 25-year-old plaintiff suffered "permanent cognitive defects" from a vehicle collision. The defendant argued that state-sponsored programs would provide the plaintiff "all of the professional care and treatment he needs, medical, educational, and vocational, in the present and in the future at 'no cost.'" But the appellate court said that even if it assumed that the state "can and will offer all of these professional services to [the plaintiff] in the present, there is no way of knowing whether these so-called cost-free services will continue to be available for the duration of [the plaintiff's] needs in the future." The court therefore reversed a damages award based on the assumption of future benefits and sent the damages issue back for retrial. *Thompson v. Lee County Sch. Dist.*, 925 So. 2d 121 (Miss. Ct. App. 2005). The Mississippi Supreme Court reversed the appellate court's finding that the amount of damages was inadequate. However, the supreme court did not specifically refer to the issue concerning the assumption of future benefits. 925 So. 2d 57 (Miss. 2006).

(5) In the *Mishna*, a treatise on Jewish law completed in the third century A.D., the text says that if someone slaps another person, "he must pay him two hundred *zuz*." If, however, the offender spits at the other, "and the spittle touched him," or if the offender strips the cloak from the other, "or bare[s] the head of a woman in the street," then "he must pay four hundred *zuz*". The commentator then says, "[t]his is the general principle; it all depends on a person's dignity." Phillip Blackman, 4 MISHNAYATH 66–67, Order Nezikin, Tractate Baba Kamma ch. 8:6 (Judaica Press 1964, 1983). Does this commentary expand your view of the rationales for tort damages?

(6) Do you think that it is better to view injury damages as "rent" or "capital"?

In this connection, consider the following passage from the opinion of Justice Scalia in *Lukhard v. Reed*, 481 U.S. 368, 107 S. Ct. 1807 (1987), holding that it was appropriate for the Virginia Department of Social Services to treat tort awards as income in the determination of eligibility for benefits under the Aid to Families with Dependent Children program:

> Respondent's penultimate argument is that logic requires personal injury awards to be treated as resources rather than income. The argument rests upon the following syllogism: (1) healthy bodies are resources; (2) personal injury awards merely compensate for damage to healthy bodies; and therefore (3) personal injury awards necessarily are resources too.... [T]he minor premise of this syllogism is false.... More importantly, however, so is the major premise. Although there is a sense in which a healthy body can be said to be a resource, it certainly is not one within the meaning of the AFDC statute and regulations, which count only real and personal property (including liquid assets).... Since healthy bodies are worth far more than the statute's $1,000 family resource limit, ... acceptance of respondents' major premise would render every family ineligible for AFDC benefits. The fact that the AFDC statute and its implementing regulations consider only real and personal property in determining families' resources permits (if it does not indeed require) the conclusion that per-

sonal injury awards are compensation for diminution of well-being of a kind not covered by the AFDC statute, except to the extent they compensate for lost wages (to which extent they clearly are gain, …) or for economic expenses caused by the injury (to which extent Virginia permits them to be in large part offset …). Thus, personal injury awards are almost entirely a gain in well-being, as well-being is measured under the AFDC statute, and can reasonably be treated as income even on respondents' definition of the term.

Once this is understood, it is clear that Virginia's policy of treating personal injury awards as income but property damage awards as resources is also reasonable. The former can be viewed as increasing their recipients' pecuniary well-being, and the latter as merely restoring resources to previous levels. The existence of this distinction, coupled with the substantial deference owed to the Secretary's conclusion that Virginia's revised regulations are consistent with HHS's regulations, … leads us to reject respondents' argument that the difference in treatment violates HHS's regulation requiring that "eligibility conditions imposed must not exclude individuals or groups on an arbitrary or unreasonable basis, and must not result in inequitable treatment of individuals of groups.…" 45 CFR § 233.10(a)(1)(1986).

It is of course true that, by considering only real and personal property as the measure of well-being, the AFDC program evaluates need in a way that does not reflect the fullness of life. That portion of a personal injury award which constitutes compensation for loss of earnings will not result in a loss of eligibility, since it merely replaces future income that would otherwise have been earned; but the portion attributable to pain and suffering replaces no other economic income, and will reduce AFDC payments. It can reasonably be urged that a family with monthly pain-and-suffering-award income but with a family member in physical and emotional pain is *not* better off than the family without that additional income but also without that suffering. Physical and emotional well-being, however, is not what the AFDC statute is designed to take into account—as is evident from the fact that there is no argument for increasing AFDC payments above the normal income limit where pain and suffering exists without a tortfeasor who is compensating it. Compensating for the noneconomic inequities of life is a task daunting in its complexity, and the AFDC statute is neither designed nor interpreted unreasonably if it leaves them untouched.

* * *

Are you persuaded by Justice Scalia's reasoning?

J. Michael Veron, *Evaluating the Economic Impact of Personal Injuries*
31 Loyola L. Rev. 825, 837–40 (1986)*

…

The issue is more appropriately viewed from a positive, rather than a negative, perspective. The question is not what the plaintiff cannot do; rather, the question is what

---

* Copyright 1984 J. Michael Veron. Reprinted by permission of the Loyola Law Review.

does the plaintiff do that makes him valuable to an employer? It is that quality which determines the plaintiff's earning capacity. Put another way, the plaintiff's earning capacity is that which enables him to find a job and hold it. Unless that is compromised by the injury, the plaintiff cannot be said to have sustained a loss of earning capacity. Viewed in this light, it seems doubtful that a physician is uniquely qualified (if qualified at all) to answer that question. That question is better answered by the plaintiff's employer, work supervisor, other prospective employers, and labor market analysts.

Even if the plaintiff cannot return to his former employment, the inquiry does not end. Few people have ability so limited that they can only perform one job. Nearly everyone has abilities that qualify him for other earning endeavors. Thus, if the plaintiff cannot return to his former employment, he must consider alternative forms of employment. Even without retaining a vocational expert, it is possible to develop vocational data of this kind.

First, the plaintiff's education and work experience should be examined. What kinds of jobs can he realistically perform in his present condition and with present training? Given his native ability, what kinds of jobs can he be trained to do? How transferable are his skills? Even the most untrained manual laborer with a bad back can work as a security guard, ticket taker, locker room attendant, bartender, process server, or valet, to mention a few. To continue previous examples, the injured pianist can become a music teacher or critic, and the injured neurosurgeon may transfer his talents to research.

The next consideration is the extent to which such moves would affect the individual's post-accident earnings. Obviously, counsel for the plaintiff wants to show that few other jobs are available and that those that are do not pay nearly as well as the plaintiff's former employment. Conversely, defense counsel wants to show a wide variety of available jobs that all pay the same wage the plaintiff earned before the accident. Again, counsel need not retain a vocational expert to develop this information. It is available from trade councils, labor unions, and business associations, as well as from the public library.

The suggestion has ... been made that counsel need not retain a vocational or occupational specialist in order to evaluate a claim of disability. However, this is not to suggest that it is not advisable to do so. To the contrary, a vocational or occupational specialist can offer counsel invaluable insight into a claim of disability—as well as provide effective expert testimony. Vocational or occupational specialists commonly research the physical demands of work in various jobs, the income that can be earned at those jobs, and the availability of employment in those jobs within a particular geographic area. They also are familiar with programs to rehabilitate the earning capacity of injured workers. While vocational experts are becoming a more common feature of personal injury litigation, all too often counsel for both sides are content to allow the question of disability to be decided by medical opinion alone, despite the clear suggestion by the AMA and the American Academy of Orthopaedic Surgeons to look elsewhere for disability ratings.

At any rate, vocational specialists are most helpful in showing whether or not an injury has in fact left the plaintiff worse off economically. The argument can be made that they are better qualified than physicians to determine whether the worker who can no longer straighten his arm completely is really in danger of losing his job, and, if so, whether he can retain his earnings level by doing something else.

If an injured plaintiff really cannot go back to work, what has he lost? As will be seen below, economists usually make several assumptions that warrant scrutiny. First, most economists will commonly assume that the plaintiff would have enjoyed a worklife expectancy identical to the statistical average worklife expectancy of the general American labor force.[24]

Second, they ordinarily will assume that the plaintiff would have enjoyed continued employment for the remainder of his worklife expectancy—or, at worst, no more unemployment than the statistical average of the general American labor force. These and other assumptions will be discussed from an economic standpoint in the next section. However, the two assumptions just described are mentioned here because they involve extra-economic considerations.

Using a statistical average has a certain appeal. An economist can easily defend the average by saying that it is based on the entire labor force and takes into account the best cases, the worst cases, productive and unproductive, sick and healthy workers alike. Of course, this method overlooks the possibility that neither the plaintiff nor his occupation is average.

In evaluating the plaintiff's assumed worklife expectancy, both his prior medical history and the nature of his work must be considered. Did the plaintiff have any pre-existing condition that would have caused an early retirement? This should be explored thoroughly with all medical experts in the case. For example, an orthopaedic examination will frequently show that an injured worker has, *inter alia*, pre-existing arthritis. In a manual laborer, this degenerative condition sooner or later requires either early retirement or a change of employment.

Moreover, some work is by its nature for the young. For example, oilfield work is done by a younger-than-average labor force. There are few sixty-year-old roughnecks, or roustabouts. Thus, while the general labor force might work on the average until the age of sixty-five years or more, oilfield workers move on far sooner to other things, retirement or less dangerous work. Therefore, any assumption that a roughneck's worklife expectancy is that of the average American wage earner is suspect.

Similarly, an assumption of continued employment (or no worse than average employment) based upon a statistically-average American worker can be challenged. Some industries are more volatile than others, and, as a result, workers in those industries experience more frequent unemployment. In fact, it is also characteristic for those industries to experience an unstable worker population as workers come and go. In other words, good times attract workers from other industries wanting to capitalize on the temporary good fortune, while recurrent bad times ultimately discourage workers from careers in certain industries, causing them to seek permanent employment in other, more stable lines of work.

Marital status can be significant as well. Many workers in the offshore oil industry are single. Their lifestyle easily adapts to extended periods of work offshore. However, after these workers marry, many of them look for other work, finding the seven-on and seven-off routine to be less tolerable with a family.

All of these situations suggest that the use of statistical averages by an economist can be challenged....

---

24. The Bureau of Labor Statistics within the Department of Labor is directed by law to "collect, collate, and report at least once each year, or oftener if necessary, full and complete statistics of the conditions of labor." ... These published reports are the primary source used by economists and other experts to calculate the present value of an individual's lost earning capacity.

Martha Chamallas, *The Architecture of Bias: Deep Structures in Tort Law*
146 U. PA. L. REV. 463, 528–29 (1998)*

[Professor Chamallas identifies ways in which the "formal equality on the face of the law of torts bear[s] little connection to gender and race equity as measured by real-world standards." These include]:

Perhaps the most clear-cut example of the operation of the conceptual vicious cycle is the valuation of household services, sometimes called "homemaker" services. For some time, feminists have observed that work done predominantly by women may not be classified as "work." Until quite recently, the law placed no economic value on a homemaker's domestic services, a category which encompasses not only cleaning the house, but also caring for children and other dependents.[255] This dramatic undervaluation of women's work has had consequences not only for distribution of assets upon divorce, when homemakers tried to demonstrate their contributions to the marriage, but also has played a significant role in tort cases for wrongful death and personal injury.[257]

Several of the final reports of gender bias task forces have discussed the continued devaluation of homemaker services and the effects of such devaluation on stay-at-home mothers, employed women, and men. Plaintiffs' attorneys believe that juries harbor negative stereotypes about the value of housework and impose artificial ceilings on the value of a homemaker's life.[258] There is even some evidence that, for comparable injuries, employed women receive higher damage awards for pain and suffering than homemakers, suggesting that negative attitudes towards this kind of work carry over to affect other elements of damages. The devalued status of household services is a form of gender-linked devaluation that reduces awards for employed women and men as well. Working mothers are often awarded paltry sums for their duties as homemakers, and the household tasks that men perform are sometimes invisible, reminiscent of the old common fiction that the wife loses nothing of material value when her husband is injured.

NOTES

(1) Analyze the assumptions that Veron indicates are at issue in the determination of economic damages. When a court calculates loss of earnings, how much consideration should it give to the fact that the plaintiff has lost little in earning capacity if she moves to a new line of work, but has lost much in terms of job satisfaction?

---

* Copyright © 1998 University of Pennsylvania; Martha Chamallas. Reprinted by permission.

255. Most studies regard the following tasks as housework: preparing meals, washing dishes, house cleaning, outdoor tasks, shopping, washing and ironing, paying bills, auto maintenance, driving, and child care.... Substantially more than half of women's working hours are spent on housework, while less than a quarter of men's are so spent....

257. The failure to value women's work in the home is also evidenced by the reluctance of some courts to allow compensation for gratuitous home-based nursing services when they are provided to accident victims by relatives.... It is disproportionately women who provide such services to family members and others....

258. *See, e.g.,* Gail D. Cox, *Juries Place Less Value on Homemakers,* NAT'L L. J., Sept. 14, 1992, at 1, 37 (noting that the valuation of the life of a homemaker is considerably less than it is for women who are employed outside the home, with a ceiling of approximately $450,000).

(2) In the case of the offshore oil worker, what sort of argument should be permitted about his intentions concerning marriage, and the changes in employment that would likely accompany taking that vow? How should one's expectations about his life plan figure into the assessment of damages?

(3) When an employed person is injured, why should her damages depend on her present or expected earnings? The traditional method of calculating tort damages is very anti-egalitarian, isn't it? What is "fair" in this regard? Is it "fair" to impose an equal schedule of damages across similar types of injuries suffered by people with very different economic prospects? Or is it "fair" to impose damages "to each according to his established life style"?

(4) What should be the measure of damages for injuries that keep a family member from performing household services?

(5) Could you formulate a cautionary jury instruction, in a case involving the pain and suffering of a homemaker, that would minimize the chances of bias against non-earners' claims for noneconomic damages?

§ 9.02 Intangibles

FLANNERY v. UNITED STATES

West Virginia Supreme Court of Appeals
297 S.E.2d 433 (1982),
later proceeding, 718 F.2d 108 (4th Cir. 1983),
cert. denied, 467 U.S. 1226 (1984)

MILLER, CHIEF JUSTICE:

In this case from the United States Fourth Circuit Court of Appeals we are asked to determine two certified questions. The first is whether under our State damage law a plaintiff in a personal injury action who has been rendered permanently semi-comatose is entitled to recover for the impairment of his capacity to enjoy life....

This case was initially tried without a jury before the Honorable Charles H. Haden, II, Judge of the United States District Court for the Southern District of West Virginia, who made this summary of the plaintiff's condition in his memorandum opinion and order dated January 22, 1980:

> Flannery was approximately 22 years of age at the time of the accident. He was hospitalized in Cabell-Huntington Hospital from October 28, 1974, through April 12, 1975, and in Appalachian Regional Hospital from that date through April 22, 1975. Subsequent to his hospitalization he has remained in a semi-comatose condition that is not likely to improve. Flannery has a projected life expectancy of thirty years (as measured from 1978), provided he continues to receive good nursing care. Testimony was that he is less likely to live out his full life than a normal healthy person because of his reduced resistance to various diseases and medical conditions, such as pneumonia and urinary tract infections. It is unlikely that Flannery will need sophisticated medical treatment, rather he will require constant nursing and custodial care combined with occasional medical oversight. Flannery's parents are capable of providing custodial

nursing care and have chosen to provide the care that their son needs in their home. They have provided such care since April, 1975, and intend to do so as long as they are able.

Judge Haden awarded the following elements of damages in his memorandum opinion and order: For hospital, medical and nursing expenses incurred prior to the trial, $48,174.80; for future nursing expenses based on a thirty-year life expectancy, $316,984.00; for impairment of earning capacity, including both wages and fringe benefits, $535,855.00; and, for loss of ability to enjoy life, $1,300,000.00, thus, making a total damage award of $2,201,013.80. The court did not award any amount for pain and suffering,[2] nor did it make any award for permanent disability.

I.

The law of damages for personal injuries in this State, as is probably true elsewhere, has evolved from individual cases without a great deal of theoretical cohesion. It basically reflects the rather obvious fact that injuries to the person both physical and mental can occur in an almost infinite variety of patterns.

The basic goal in awarding damages is to fairly and adequately compensate the plaintiff for the injuries and losses sustained. In general we have recognized that compensatory damages for personal injuries are composed of two broad categories. First there are those damages which are termed "liquidated" or "pecuniary" in the sense that they represent some form of expense or economic loss that can be rendered reasonably certain monetarily by a mathematical figure or calculation. These include medical, hospital, nursing, dental, drug and all other similar expenses, both present and future that are incurred in treating, curing and alleviating the plaintiff's physical and mental injuries. Also included in this category are lost wages and lost earning capacity.

The second category consists of intangible damages since they are "unliquidated" in the sense that there is no precise monetary calculation that can be used to determine the amount of the loss. The most obvious of these is pain and suffering. Another element of unliquidated damages arises from the plaintiff's permanent injuries. The term "permanent injury" is used as a threshold condition that must ordinarily be shown in order to recover any future damages[3] surrounding a personal injury as we said in Syllabus Point 9 of *Jordan v. Bero*, W.Va., 210 S.E.2d 618 (1974):

> The permanency or future effect of any injury must be proven with reasonable certainty in order to permit a jury to award an injured party future damages.

---

2. The court's remarks on this point are contained in its memorandum and order of January 22, 1980, p. 9:

It is totally speculative whether or not Mr. Flannery can in fact experience any pain or suffering, or pleasure, of anything whatsoever. Conversely, it is clear to this Court that the Plaintiff has been deprived, wholly, of the capacity to enjoy life. The rule in *Nees v. Julian Goldman Stores, Inc.*, [109 W.Va. 329, 154 S.E. 769 (1930),] stated in the disjunctive and allowing recovery for pain and suffering or loss of the capacity to enjoy life, is tailored to provide for an unfortunate case such as this.

The court further stated in note 5:

The Plaintiff is not sentient and thus, under West Virginia law, pain and suffering are not capable of proof. Under *Nees v. Julian Goldman Stores, Inc.*, however, this very fact establishes Plaintiff's right to recover for his non-sentient condition, for his loss of the ability to enjoy life.

3. The two broad categories of personal injury damages, liquidated and unliquidated, can also be subdivided as to those damages which have presently accrued at the time of the trial and as to those which will necessarily be incurred in the future.

Once a permanent injury is established, then the following elements of future damages can be considered as outlined in Syllabus Point 10 of *Jordan, supra*:

> Future damages are those sums awarded to an injured party for, among other things: (1) Residuals or future effects of an injury which have reduced the capability of an individual to function as a whole man; (2) future pain and suffering; (3) loss or impairment of earning capacity; and (4) future medical expenses.

> . . .

> . . .

What *Jordan* makes clear is that once a permanent injury has been established that in addition to future pecuniary expenses or liquidated damages and losses such as medical, hospital and kindred expenses and loss of future wages and earning capacity, the plaintiff is entitled to additional damages for future pain and suffering and for the permanent effect of the injury itself on "the capability of an individual to function as a whole man." 210 S.E.2d at 634.

We believe that the loss of enjoyment of life is encompassed within and is an element of the permanency of the plaintiff's injury. To state the matter in a slightly different manner, the degree of a permanent injury is measured by ascertaining how the injury has deprived the plaintiff of his customary activities as a whole person. The loss of customary activities constitutes the loss of enjoyment of life.

While the certified question speaks of the loss of capacity to enjoy life by a semi-comatose plaintiff who is unable to sense his loss, this question as argued to us contains two parts. First, whether we recognize the loss of enjoyment of life as a separate element of damages. Second, whether as an incident to such a damage right it must be shown that the plaintiff is conscious of the fact that he has lost any enjoyment of life.

The Court of Appeals, in its decision to certify the question, correctly recognized that our cases in this area were not dispositive. In *Nees v. Julian Goldman Stores, Inc.*, 109 W.Va. 329, 154 S.E. 679 (1930), and *Warth v. Jackson County Court*, 71 W.Va. 184, 76 S.E. 420 (1912), reference was made to the impairment of capacity to enjoy life as a part of the recoverable damages for personal injuries but there was no discussion of how the impairment of the capacity to enjoy life fitted into the overall damage picture.

There are cases where courts have determined that the loss of enjoyment of life in a non-comatose situation is an element of recoverable damages. In these cases the issue is whether the jury can be instructed to consider as a part of the elements of damages the plaintiff's loss of enjoyment of life or whether such factor is already embraced in an existing category such as pain and suffering. In *Mariner v. Marsden*, 610 P.2d 6 (Wyo.1980), the court with no detailed analysis concluded:

> Since loss of enjoyment of life is compensable, the fact finder—in a case in which loss of enjoyment of life is proved—may either make a separate award for loss of enjoyment of life or take into consideration the loss of enjoyment of life in arriving at the total general damages." (Footnote omitted)

In arriving at this conclusion, the Wyoming court in *Mariner v. Marsden, supra* at 12, relied primarily on *Swiler v. Baker's Super Market, Inc.*, 203 Neb. 183, 187, 277 N.W.2d 697, 700 (1979),[6] where the court in discussing the propriety of a statement in a damage

---

6. We note that commentators have not consistently devised or applied a uniform analysis for loss of enjoyment of life damages. . . .

instruction informing the jury it could take into consideration the loss of enjoyment of life experienced by the plaintiff stated:

> "'The argument is that this part of the instruction represents a duplication of the elements of permanent disability and of pain and suffering, and thus the jury was permitted to award double damages for the same loss. There was evidence introduced to support the plaintiff's diminished capacity to enjoy life with respect to activities formerly enjoyed, deprivations of pleasure, and inconvenience.
>
> ....
>
> "'A majority of courts, however, have approved inclusion of loss of enjoyment of life as a consideration that may be instructed upon in a proper case and be considered by the jury.
>
> "'Loss of enjoyment of life may, in a particular case flow from a disability and be simply a part thereof, and where the evidence supports it, may be argued to the jury.'"

(Emphasis omitted)

The cases that recognize the loss of enjoyment of life do not analyze its relationship to the permanency of the plaintiff's injury in any detail. Yet, it is obvious that the loss of enjoyment of life is directly linked to the permanency of the plaintiff's injury and a jury in evaluating the nature and degree of the permanency of the plaintiff's injury will ascertain how such injury has affected his ability to perform and enjoy the ordinary functions of life. This loss of capacity to enjoy life is not a function of pain and suffering in the traditional sense of those words since one can lose his eyesight or a limb and be without physical pain. Yet, it is obvious that such injuries will impair the person's capacity to enjoy life.

Where the element of the loss of enjoyment of life is fitted into the damage picture may be somewhat semantical,[7] but we believe it logically should be a part of evaluating the permanency of the plaintiff's injury. We believe that our definition of a permanent injury which includes "those future effects of an injury which have reduced the capability of an individual to function as a whole man," as set forth in *Jordan, supra* at 643, is the appropriate area for considering the element of the loss of enjoyment of life.

We are not unmindful of the defendant's argument that the law does not permit double recovery for the same damages. We recently spoke to this issue in Syllabus Point 7 of *Harless v. First National Bank in Fairmont*, W.Va., 289 S.E.2d 692 (1982):

> It is generally recognized that there can be only one recovery of damages for one wrong or injury. Double recovery of damages is not permitted; the law does not permit a double satisfaction for a single injury. A plaintiff may not recover damages twice for the same injury simply because he has two legal theories.

Here, however, we have an *element*, a component, of damages that may be considered by a jury in determining the amount of its award. Just as a jury may consider the nature, effect and severity of pain when fixing damages for personal injury, or may consider mental anguish caused by scars and disfigurement, it may consider loss of enjoyment of life....

---

7. At least one court has fitted the loss of enjoyment of life as an element of mental suffering. *E.g., Judd v. Rowley's Cherry Hill Orchards, Inc.*, 611 P.2d 1216, 1221 (Utah 1980) ("Included in mental pain and suffering is the diminished enjoyment of life as well as the humiliation and embarrassment resulting from permanent scars and disability.").

In the present case the trial judge did not award separate amounts for both the permanency of the plaintiff's injuries and the loss of enjoyment of life. If this had been done, there would have been an impermissible duplication of damages. It is obvious from the evidence that the plaintiff was totally and permanently disabled and had by virtue of this fact lost all of life's enjoyment. In this particular case, the $1,300,000 award could be correctly characterized as the amount of the plaintiff's permanent disability resulting from his loss of capacity to enjoy life or as *Jordan* expresses it as his reduced capability "to function as a whole man."[8]

Having determined that the loss of enjoyment of life is an element of a permanent injury award, we consider whether it can be recovered by a semi-comatose plaintiff who because of the severity of his injuries is not aware of his loss of life's enjoyment. We have earlier pointed out that *Jordan* evolved the test that once the medical evidence demonstrates that a plaintiff has a permanent injury then under our law he is permitted to recover future damages such as pain and suffering and medical expenses, but in addition damages for the future effects of the injury which has reduced his capability "to function as a whole man." Thus the permanency of the plaintiff's injury relates to the "whole man" and is cast in terms of an objective standard.

If we put aside the label "loss of enjoyment of life" and look to its underlying function which is to measure the degree of permanent disability to the whole person arising from the injuries inflicted, some of the subjective content of the analysis disappears. Consequently, the plaintiff's lack of knowledge of the extent of his permanent injury is not a factor under *Jordan's* "whole man" test.

We do not believe that the plaintiff's subjective knowledge of the extent of his loss should be controlling. There are obviously many situations, particularly injuries to infants or young children where there experience of life is so minimal that their ability to comprehend the extent of their permanent disability is negligible, and yet these young plaintiffs have not been denied recovery for permanent injuries. A classic illustration is the infant who has been blinded by excessive amounts of oxygen in the incubator.... The same argument, as made in this case, could be advanced in regard to the child's blindness that since he never had any vision or at best only for a limited time span, he would be unaware of what full vision meant and consequently his permanency as reflected by his subjective knowledge of his loss of enjoyment of visual life would be minimal.

The argument that the plaintiff must have an awareness of the extent of his loss as a defense to a permanent injury bears some analogy to the argument that the defendant should not be liable for injuries made more severe because of the plaintiff's preexisting ill health or disability. Thus, the one-eyed person who is blinded in his good eye should only be found half-blind. This principle has been uniformly rejected in the personal injury damage law.... We accordingly hold that a plaintiff in a personal injury action who has been rendered permanently semi-comatose is entitled to recover for the impairment of his capacity to enjoy life as a measure of the permanency of his injuries even though he may not be able to sense his loss of enjoyment of life.

. . . .

---

8. In the present case the trial court was sitting as the factfinder and decided to assign separate amounts for the different categories of damages. Ordinarily, a jury will return a unitary sum for damages in a personal injury action for all compensatory damages and is not required to itemize the individual elements of damages since we look at the entire verdict to determine if it is excessive.

ANALYTICAL FRAMEWORKS FOR ASSESSING TORT DAMAGES

Towards a Jurisprudence of Injury 5-165 to 5-166
(ABA 1984, M. Shapo, Reporter)*

Symptomatic of the difficulties of fixing a philosophical base for tort damages, particularly for personal injuries, is one commentator's assertion that "the damages should not be related to the seriousness of the *injury* inflicted; what they should be geared to is the seriousness of the *loss* incurred."[19] In examining the issues for which this statement provides a point of departure, we review several different analytical structures which may be applied to damages questions.

An English scholar has identified three "approaches" to the subject. One, characterized as "conceptual and objective," treats the plaintiff's life, faculties and capacity for enjoying life as personal assets, each having an objective "value." The second approach is "persons," entailing the premise that "[m]easurement can only be made in terms of human happiness," and requiring assessment in "monetary terms" of "past, present and future loss of pleasure and happiness." Finally, a "functional" approach views damages for nonpecuniary loss as "justified only to the extent that they might effectively be employed to provide the plaintiff with some measure of consolation."[20]

Another writer presents a triad which overlaps the "approaches" just summarized.[21] These categories include, first, the effort to "put the injured person in the same position he would have been in, had he not sustained the wrong";[22] second, a "full compensation" principle for restoration of pecuniary loss, past and future;[23] and third, a "functional compensation" idea, emphasizing "the use to which the money can be put."[24] Still another conceptualization of tort damages contrasts the principle of "fair and reasonable compensation," a "vague and all-embracing formula," with the "pragmatic solution," described frankly as "fixing arbitrary standards of monetary compensation" on the basis of a consensus of court decisions.[25]

NOTES

(1) As it turned out, the West Virginia Supreme Court's labors on the certified question in *Flannery* went for naught. In the Fourth Circuit's decision on the merits of *Flannery*, Judge Haynsworth said that the "capacity to enjoy life" element of the damages award was not allowable under the Federal Tort Claims Act's limitation of liability to compensatory, as distinguished from punitive, damages. He reasoned this way:

> ... It is perfectly clear ... that an award of $1,300,000 for the loss of enjoyment of life cannot provide [Flannery] with any consolation or ease any bur-

---

* Copyright © 1984, The American Bar Association. Reprinted by permission.

19. McGregor, *Compensation Versus Punishment in Damages Awards*, 28 MOD. L. REV. 629, 641 (1965) (emphasis in original).

20. Ogus, *Damages For Lost Amenities: For a Foot, a Feeling or a Function?*, 35 MOD. L. REV. 1, 2–3 (1972).

21. McLachlin, [*What Price Disability: A Perspective on the Law of Damages for Personal Injury*, 59 CAN. BAR REV. 1 (1981)] at 2–12.

22. *Id.* at 2.

23. *Id.* at 4–8.

24. *Id.* at 8–12.

25. Ogus, *supra* note 20, at 4–5.

den resting upon him. The award of the cost of future medical care provides for his maintenance as well as his nursing and professional care. It provides all of the money needed for the plaintiff's care, should he live out his life expectancy. He cannot use the $1,300,000. He cannot spend it upon necessities or pleasures. He cannot experience the pleasure of giving it away. If paid, the money would be invested and the income accumulated until Flannery's death, when it would be distributed to those surviving relatives of his entitled to inherit from him. If it is compensatory in part to any one, it is compensatory to those relatives who will survive him.

Since the award of $1,300,000 can provide Flannery with no direct benefit, the award is punitive and not allowable under the FTCA.

Flannery v. United States, 718 F.2d 108, 111 (4th Cir. 1983).

(2) A view that lines up with the West Virginia court's response to the certified question in *Flannery*, and thus opposes the eventual outcome in the Fourth Circuit's decision in that case, appears in *Rufino v. United States*, 829 F.2d 354, 359–61 (2d Cir. 1987). Construing New York law, the Second Circuit quotes at length, *id.* at 360, from *McDougald v. Garber*, 132 Misc. 2d 457, 460, 504 N.Y.S.2d 383, 386 (Sup. Ct. 1986) ("[p]roof of the loss of enjoyment of life relates not to what is perceived by the injured plaintiff but to the objective total or partial limitations on an individual's activities *imposed by an injury*"), aff'd, 135 A.D.2d 80, 524 N.Y.S.2d 192 (1988), aff'd as modified, 73 N.Y.2d 246, 536 N.E.2d 372, 538 N.Y.S.2d 937 (1989).

(3) What is the most persuasive justification for imposing liability for the sort of loss at issue in *Flannery*? How can a court rationally decide how much is too much in the way of a jury verdict?

(4) What should be the legal test for recovery for pain and suffering in the case of a person with whom one cannot conventionally communicate? One version of a test appears in the opinion of the New York Court of Appeals in its affirmance, with modifications, of the trial court's opinion in *McDonald v. Garber*, quoted in note 2 above. The court of appeals "conclude[d] that cognitive awareness is a prerequisite to recover for loss of enjoyment of life," adopting the trial court's test of "some level of awareness" as "an appropriate standard for all aspects of nonpecuniary loss." 73 N.Y.2d 246, 255, 536 N.E.2d 372, 375, 538 N.Y.S.2d 937, 940 (1989).

A related evidentiary question is how to prove this type of damages. In a case that involved the issue of whether an injury victim could experience conscious pain and suffering, there was testimony from family members that tears would come from the victim's eyes when they would talk to her. The defendant's expert opined that any movements or activity by the victim were "involuntary and automatic neurologic responses." The court concluded that lay opinion evidence was admissible to show consciousness, and could even be used against expert medical testimony. Moreover, the court concluded that the plaintiff did not have to present medical affidavits to defeat a motion for summary judgment. *Cotilletta v. Tepedino*, 151 Misc.2d 660, 573 N.Y.S.2d 396, 398 (Sup. Ct. 1991).

(5) In *McDonald v. Garber, supra*, the New York of Appeals refused to permit separate awards for loss of enjoyment of life and pain and suffering. 73 N.Y.2d at 255–257, 536 N.E.2d at 375–77, 538 N.Y.S.2d at 940–42. The court adhered to an approach that viewed "the plaintiff's inability to enjoy life to its fullest" as "one type of suffering to be factored into a general award for nonpecuniary damages, commonly known as pain and suffering."

D'AMATO v. LONG ISLAND RAILROAD COMPANY
United States District Court, Eastern District of New York
874 F. Supp. 57 (1995)

BARTELS, District Judge.

The defendant the Long Island Railroad Company (the "Railroad") moves this Court under Rule 59(a) of the Federal Rules of Civil Procedure for an order granting the Railroad a new trial on the ground that the damages awarded by the jury were excessive. As an alternative remedy, the Railroad asks for remittitur reducing the jury's award. For the reasons set forth below, defendant's motion is denied.

BACKGROUND

In the early morning hours of March 15, 1991, plaintiff Fred D'Amato, while turning to avoid a spray of sparks from a passing train, tripped and fell over a piece of Railroad equipment which had been left on the side of the tracks in the Hempstead, Long Island Railroad Yard. At the time of his accident, D'Amato, who was employed by the Railroad as an assistant conductor, was in the process of throwing track switches in the Hempstead Yard....

Following the accident, over a two and a half year period, D'Amato missed thirty-six weeks of work and underwent two ambulatory surgeries, one to release a compressed ulnar nerve, the other to relieve D'Amato's carpal tunnel syndrome. Although D'Amato returned to work in his former position, he complains of continued pain and clumsiness in his right hand, as well as pain in his elbow, back, and neck.

... In response to special interrogatories, the jury found that the Railroad was negligent; that its negligence was a proximate cause of D'Amato's injuries; and that D'Amato also was negligent, attributing 15% of the responsibility for the accident to D'Amato's own actions. It further found that D'Amato's injuries were permanent and awarded him damages of $800 for past out-of-pocket expenses; $25,000 for lost earnings; $75,000 for pain and suffering from the time of the accident until the date of the verdict; and $60,000 for future pain and suffering. Plaintiff's damages, $160,800, are reduced by 15% as required by the jury's finding of comparative negligence.

DISCUSSION

On this motion, the Railroad contests the jury's verdict arguing solely that it is grossly excessive and should be set aside.... Although the computation of damages is a fact-finding function within the province of the jury, the court may order a new trial where the jury's verdict is clearly excessive.... An award is excessive when it "'is so high as to shock the judicial conscience and constitute a denial of justice.'" ...

The only amounts the Court considers at issue are those awarded by the jury for past pain and suffering, $75,000, and for future pain and suffering, $60,000....

After evaluating the evidence presented at trial, the Court concludes that the jury's verdict was rationally related to the evidence and reasonable in light of plaintiff's surgeries and the jury's finding of permanency. It is undisputed that, in the two and a half years following his accident, D'Amato underwent two surgeries, one on his elbow, and the other on his wrist. Further, from the time of his accident until the time of trial, he endured repeated examinations, diagnostic tests, and physical therapy sessions. Both D'Amato and his wife testified that, as a result of his injuries and continued pain, D'Amato is not the active and athletic man he once was. He suffers from depression and his everyday activities are restricted. For example, D'Amato no longer easily performs household chores, he does not engage in the outdoor activities he enjoyed before his accident, such as biking and fishing, and he cannot sit for an extended period.

In evaluating the damages awarded in a particular action, courts properly may look to awards in other cases to plaintiffs with similar injuries "'as a point of reference by which to gauge the appropriateness of the award.'" ... The Railroad cites cases in which plaintiffs were awarded lesser amounts for injuries which defendant argues are comparable to those in this case. In order to prevail, however, the Railroad must do more than simply establish that some plaintiffs with similar injuries were awarded smaller verdicts, it must show that the jury's verdict in this case is "clearly outside the maximum limit of a reasonable range." ... Further, the Court bears in mind that "'[t]he power to set aside [a jury's verdict] should be cautiously used because where pain and suffering and permanent injury are involved there can be no exact yardstick and the jury's determination should stand unless it is clearly unreasonable.'" ... The Railroad has not met this burden.

The Court's initial conclusion is supported by a review of cases involving injuries similar to those suffered by D'Amato, confirming that the verdict in this case was well within the range found by other courts to be appropriate. The following cases involving ulnar nerve injuries illustrate parameters drawn by courts. In Paturzo v. Metro-North Commuter R.R., supra, the court ordered a new trial on damages, concluding that a $650,000 verdict was excessive where plaintiff's primary injury was ulnar nerve neuropathy which caused numbness in two fingers and the web of the thumb in the plaintiff's non-dominant hand. In Smith v. Saviolis, 136 A.D.2d 621, 523 N.Y.S.2d 868 (2d Dep't 1988), the court ruled that a jury verdict of $93,500 to a plaintiff who suffered from ulnar sensory nerve entrapment in her wrist resulting from an automobile accident was not excessive as a matter of law.

Two cases involving carpal tunnel syndrome also are instructive. In Schare v. Welsbach Electric Corp., 138 A.D.2d 477, 526 N.Y.S.2d 25 (2d Dep't 1988), the Appellate Division reversed the trial court's order, holding that it inappropriately exercised its discretion in setting aside a jury verdict of $65,000 and entering a judgment of $125,000 based on plaintiff's carpal tunnel syndrome. In Silverstein v. Harmonie Club of the City of New York, 173 A.D.2d 378, 569 N.Y.S.2d 965 (1st Dep't 1991), a $100,000 verdict was held adequate where plaintiff's primary injury was carpal tunnel syndrome.

Finally, illustrative of cases in which courts have evaluated pain and suffering damages to plaintiffs with back injuries are the following cases. In Gumbs v. Pueblo Int'l, Inc., 823 F.2d 768 (3d Cir.1987), where the plaintiff injured her back while shopping, the court held that the verdict reduced by the trial court from $900,000 to $575,000 remained excessive and ordered a new trial on damages or, in the alternative, required plaintiff to accept remittitur in the amount of $235,000. Like D'Amato, Gumbs had difficulty with household chores and was unable to enjoy activities as she had before her accident. However, unlike the plaintiff in this case, Gumbs did not miss even a day of work as a result of her accident. In Williams v. Martin Marietta Alumina, Inc., 817 F.2d 1030 (3d Cir.1987), involving a back injury with limited clinical evidence of injury, the court ordered a new trial on damages, holding that an award of $600,000 was excessive where, of the total award, $317,000 was attributable to damages for pain and suffering. In lieu of facing a new trial, the court determined that plaintiff could choose to accept a reduced damages award for pain and suffering in the amount of $100,000.

The Jury Verdict Research Series reports that verdicts awarded throughout the nation in cases involving ulnar nerve injuries ranged from a low of $1,000 to a maximum award of $4,927,975, with a verdict median of $90,000. Personal Injury Valuation Handbooks ("Valuation Handbooks"), Vol. 3, Release No. 3.12.0, p. 9 (1993). For carpal tunnel syndrome, verdicts ranged from $477 to $324,000, with a verdict median of $30,000. Valuation Handbooks, Vol. 3, Release No. 3.10.0, p. 12 (1993). Finally, for bulging or protruding disc injuries, verdicts from across the country ranged from a low of $283 to a high of $3,000,000, and the median verdict was $46,300. Valuation Handbooks, Vol. 1, Release No. 1.90.0, p. 8 (1994).

Finally, as the Court has concluded that the jury's verdict was not excessive, the Railroad's request for remittitur also is denied....

...

NOTES

(1) Since pain cannot readily be quantified in dollars in conventional exchange transactions, why do we award damages for pain?

Is it possible rationally to construct a formula to quantify pain and suffering in dollars? For legal purposes, is pain and suffering a function of time plus agony in the light of one's personal sensitivity?

(2) Is it somehow repulsive to make D'Amato's injuries into a marketplace item, its true price to be derived from a comparison of legal and quasi-legal sources as if they were newspaper ads that tell consumers the price of products? Is there a more sensitive, but still administratively feasible, way to value his injuries?

(3) If pain and suffering is a market item, how does it differ from orange juice?

(4) Consider the use by plaintiff's lawyers of the "per diem" argument, in which counsel argues, typically with the use of a blackboard or charts, that the jury should assign a dollar value to pain and suffering for particular units of time — "per diem," or even per hour or per second. Many courts do allow this form of argument. See, e.g., *Beagle v. Vasold*, 65 Cal. 2d 166, 53 Cal. Rptr. 129, 417 P.2d 673 (1966). What would be your ruling if a defense attorney moved to prohibit this form of advocacy?

(5) What do you suppose is the intellectual and emotional process that a jury goes through in deciding what price tag to put on someone's pain and suffering?

(6) An argument that pain and suffering damages do not fit with the rationales of tort law appears in Joseph King, Jr., *Pain and Suffering, Noneconomic Damages, and the Goals of Tort Law*, 57 S.M.U. L. Rev. 163 (2004). King contends, for example, that the loss spreading rationale does not justify pain and suffering because loss spreading requires "a rational system by which to value losses." He points out that

> [p]ain and suffering cannot logically be monetized or commodified into noneconomic damages, tends to be influenced by a wide variety of subject-specific and extra-judicial factors, and lacks meaningful criteria for assessment of damages or guidance of juries, all with the inevitable results that such damages are highly variable, unpredictable, and abjectly arbitrary.

Id. at 185. King also argues that the deterrence rationale does not work comfortably with pain and suffering, noting that vicarious liability creates a "disjunction between those who actually pay for tort liability and those who actually engage in the tortious conduct," *id.* at 187. He says that "[e]ven if some message were ordinarily communicated by tort liability, it would emanate from such unpredictable and ill-defined outcomes that it would afford the public no readily discernible guidance," *id.* at 189. King further asserts that corrective justice does not support pain and suffering, in part because of the "incommensurability" of those elements of injury with money. *Id.* at 195.

REPORT OF THE COMMISSION ON
THE EVALUATION OF PAIN

50 Soc. Sec. Bulletin No. 1, 13, 20–23 (Jan. 1987)

. . .

Defining Pain

The Commission recognizes two basic categories of pain, acute and chronic. The distinctions between the two are important for proper assessment of disability and are described in detail below. Acute pain is relatively well understood and is dealt with relatively well by current law. The problem is in the evaluation of individuals with chronic pain and, more specifically, the chronic pain syndrome (CPS).

To ensure uniform understanding, the Commission defined and described pain, and chronic pain states in particular, and agreed to a system of classification for individuals with chronic pain....

Understanding and Defining Pain

The most common conception of the pain process begins with the stimulation of certain specialized nerve endings. The stimulation can be a discrete, localized pin prick or a widespread impact: it may be a "pure pain" event or it may be accompanied by sensations of cold, pressure, etc.; it may occur in the skin or deep within the body.

Whatever the variations of noxious stimulation, the sensation is transmitted from nerve cell to nerve cell via complex and still incompletely understood electrochemical mechanisms, to the spinal cord and ultimately to the brain. The message carried by the nerve cells may be blocked (such as by narcotics), superseded (such as when a pain message is overwhelmed by a higher priority impulse, like fright), or, occasionally, lost or garbled in transition.

When the signal through the neurons reaches a central point (in some instance this occurs in the brain, but other types of pain are received lower in the spinal cord), it is interpreted as a pain message, and an appropriate physical response is triggered. Where the stimulus is a complex one (*e.g.,* involving both pain and fright), the interpretation will be complex as well and the "pain" component of the stimulus might not be recognized as primary.

This model of the pain process, of pain nociception being the brain's interpretation of a complicated message transmitted to it by the nerves in response to an external stimulus, is the generally accepted one, and it works well enough to explain the process when there is a pain stimulus. However, there are a number of conditions involving body damage where there is no pain stimulus at all, and there are others where a pain stimulus occurs without the brain perceiving it. Moreover, a pain stimulus does not always indicate a threat to tissue or body damage, as when a set of muscles receives an unusual amount of use and is "sore" the next day. Thus, even without beginning to consider the so-called "psychological" issues, it is clear that the common model of the pain process has many limitations. For purposes of assessing disability, and especially for shaping the response of the legal system to the problem of pain, some refinements are, therefore, necessary.

First, it is important to differentiate "pain" from "suffering." The greater the pain the more it is believed to cause suffering. However, some pain, like that of childbirth, can be extremely severe and yet be considered rewarding. People may tolerate great pain without reporting suffering particularly if they know that it does not have dire meaning, that it can be relieved, or that it will be short-lived. On the other hand, individuals will report suffering with pain that others might consider minor if the pain is believed to signal dire consequences (such as cancer), if the pain is perceived as never-ending, or if no relief seems possible. In all these situations, individuals perceive pain as a threat to their continued existence—not merely to their lives or their bodies, but to their integrity as persons. That this is the relationship of pain to suffering is strongly suggested by the fact that suffering can be relieved *in the face of continued pain*, by making the source of the pain known, changing its meaning, and demonstrating that it can be controlled and that an end is in sight.

Pain and suffering tend to evoke virtually identical behaviors. As a consequence, both the suffering individual who reports pain and the observer who would evaluate it are faced with trying to differentiate pain behaviors (discussed below) from suffering behaviors. In the case of pain behaviors which are reasonably consistent with significant physical findings, reversal of those behaviors awaits resolution of the underlying medical problem and, very frequently, overcoming the effects of deactivation and overguarding engendered by treatment and the passage of time since onset. In the case of suffering behaviors associated with reports of pain, but in which physical findings are lacking or insufficient to account for the pain alleged, resolution of the problem concerns clarification to the suffering individual that the pain which he or she is experiencing does not inevitably constitute a threat to his or her continued existence. In effect, it is postulated that, in the latter situation, the individual is confounding pain with suffering and does so largely under the mistaken impression that there is no resolution; that their future is threatened indefinitely. "Clarification," however, inevitably involves far more than transmission of information. The long-suffering pain patient has a pervasive repertoire of mental and physical consequences, including the adverse effects of deactivation and overguarding, which, for their reversal, will require systematic and extensive intervention.

This is not to say that suffering is any less intense or less real than pain, merely that it is a broader concept, and that it often confuses the precision of "pain" perception and reporting. Second, the degree of pain caused by a particular stimulus varies enormously from individual to individual.... [C]urrent science offers no objective evidence of the existence or extent of a person's pain. We can observe tissue damage, and under some circumstances we can even measure the nerve impulse arising from stimulation of the pain receptors. We can also observe a person's reactions to the stimuli, but there is no direct external way to interpret that experience as "pain" or to compare objectively one painful experience to the next or one person's pain to another's. What we can objectively observe, and what does serve as the basis for medical and legal inferences, is "pain behaviors."

Pain can also be categorized on the basis of its presumed site of origin and the terms "somatogenic" and "psychogenic" have been used as discussed below.

"Somatogenic" refers to pain generated by tissue damage, prompted by injury or disease. Although most significant physical impairments generate corresponding emotional stress, this category of pain is relatively familiar and straightforward. It can often, however, produce erroneous diagnoses, because the origin of a pain stimulus in a particular part of the body usually, but not always, evidences tissue damage. Professionals and lay persons alike may fail to recognize that "hurt" and "harm" are not the same.

"Psychogenic pain" refers to a specific diagnostic entry in the *Psychiatric Diagnostic and Statistical Manual III* (DSM III). In general this term is difficult to define with disagreement among experts being common. The Commission questioned several expert witnesses about the "psychogenic pain" diagnosis and concluded that individuals with "psychogenic pain" by any commonly accepted definition constitute a very small number. Further, such persons come under the existing mental impairment listing for somatoform disorder used by the Social Security Administration. In contrast, the Commission believes that the mental impairment listing for somatoform disorders does not accurately describe individuals with chronic pain discussed in the following subsection. The Commission held that the medical conditions in groups A and B are not solely psychiatric impairments.

Social conditioning, reenforcing or minimizing pain behaviors and coloring their expression, is a powerful influence. Iatrogenic influences, too, can muddy the neat mind/body distinction, as failed treatment regimens (surgery, drugs, prolonged inactivity) generate their own pains in pursuit of a cure for others.

In the case of chronic pain, the issue can be looked at in another way. It may be useful to distinguish between "having" something (*e.g.*, the body "has" an impairment) and "doing" something (*e.g.*, the individual displays or emits pain behaviors). Pain behaviors have often been interpreted to mean the individual "has" an impairment. And that is often, particularly in acute pain, the case. But it is essential to recognize that those same pain behaviors, however they originate, may now be occurring for other reasons; reasons, for example, reflecting the effects of disuse, the confounding of suffering with pain, or as a consequence of conditioning effects produced by the environment and people around the individual.

The Commission wishes to emphasize the fact that no one can know the pain of another person. Only pain behaviors, not pain itself, are observable to the outsider. Pain behaviors comprise verbal and nonverbal expressions or actions indicating that pain is being experienced. Obvious verbal expressions of pain include moans, gasps, and overt statements or complaints of pain. Facial expressions, guarded movements, limping and the like are also pain behaviors, as is the use of a cane or other assistive device. The alterations in muscle deployment, changes in stance, gait, and body motions are also found when pain is present. Similarly, broader activities, such as frequent reliance upon the health care system (*e.g.*, repeated seeking of medication, surgery, or other therapy) or avoidance of medication, surgery, or other therapy) or avoidance of erstwhile pleasurable events can be understood, in the appropriate context, as pain behaviors.

The special importance of pain behaviors is twofold. First is the fact that pain behaviors are our only way of assessing a person's pain. Because science has developed no laboratory tests for identifying and measuring pain, the only available substitute is careful observation of a wide range of behaviors.

The second factor is that pain behaviors are subject to influence by a variety of factors in addition to pain stimuli, making the assessment of pain particularly complex. It is noteworthy, in particular, that many pain behaviors are least partially under the conscious control of the individual. Individuals vary substantially in their utilization of the repertoire of pain behaviors, and evidence also indicates that there are demonstrable social boundaries giving some groups (defined, for example, by ethnicity, gender, or age) greater "permission" to express their pain in the overt ways of pain behavior. Pain behaviors are also influenced by the effects of the naturally occurring learning process, which automatically accompanies any experience. This becomes a very important issue in considering chronic pain.

The temporal aspect of pain is another obvious basis for classification, and, again, two categories are generally recognized. "Acute" pain is pain of recent onset, most commonly associated with a discrete injury or other trauma. In the absence of residual structural defect or systemic disease, acute pain should subside as the healing process continues—ordinarily less than six months and usually less than one month. Recurring or episodic acute pain is generally associated with identifiable systemic disease, and intermittent bouts of more intense acute pain are punctuated by periods of remission. However, when pain recurs with sufficient frequency over long periods of time, its effects on the individual may be the same as pain that is constantly present for the same duration.

"Chronic" pain is constant or intermittent pain lasting for long periods of time. Six months is a commonly employed duration. Such pain may be associated with a residual structural defect that persists long after the acute episode. An example would be the pain produced by the pressure of an intervertebral disk against a nerve root that remains long after the injury that led to the disk protrusion. Or pain may persist beyond the anticipated healing time of an injury, or beyond the active state of a disease, and be difficult to explain. Indeed, there may be no objective medical evidence of a physical or mental abnormality which could reasonably be expected to generate pain of the nature and intensity experienced, yet alterations of stance, gait, or body mechanisms may clearly signify that pain is present. Unlike acute pain, which may be conceptualized as a warning that something is wrong and is therefore often a useful symptom, chronic pain may become a problem in its own right—a symptom but not necessarily of an underlying impairment.

. . .

One special type of pain that occupied much of the Commission's attention is the condition labeled CPS. CPS is a complex condition which has physical, mental, and social components. Both chronic pain and CPS can be defined in terms of duration and persistence in relation to the extent of demonstrated and observable pathology. Both may or may not have emotional components. However, CPS, as opposed to chronic pain, has the added component of certain recognizable psychological and socioeconomic influences. Some individuals with chronic pain may not be disabled and other persons with the disability due primarily to pain may not have emotional impairments. While there may be some blurring of the boundaries between chronic pain and CPS, the characteristic psychological and sociological behavior patterns inherent in CPS provide a basis for trained clinicians to distinguish between the two conditions and to differentiate the CPS from malingering and from serious emotional disorders.

The typical CPS claimant might be a middle-aged man who, having worked in manual labor all his life, suffers a severe back injury in a fall. He is out of work for a recovery period of 4 months, but the pain persists despite apparent tissue healing. Additional conservation treatment is unproductive, and a more invasive therapeutic regimen of analgesics and surgery proceeds. A year after the originating fall, he is still out of work, still experiencing no abatement of the pain, and well entrenched in a lifestyle of inactivity, pain, and disability.

The stereotypical CPS claimant is not a hypochondriac, a malingerer, or a hysteric. He is not "making up" the pain, not cynically plotting strategies for unwarranted receipt of disability benefits. Instead, his pain is real and very unpleasant, but also very complicated.

The CPS claimant is caught in the web of effects which result from the influence of conditioning or experience. "Illness behaviors" are rewarded and the incentives for recovery are inadequate. There are multiple variations of this theme: for some, the continuation of pain is rewarded by increased concern and solicitousness from spouse and family; for others pain provides a "legitimate" rationale for quitting an unpleasant work environment; for still others, the luxury of concerted medical attention is a powerful lure.

In all these instances, there is a profound but subconscious feedback process in which suffering or pain behaviors occur in large part because the individual's system has come to anticipate that multifarious "good things" happen when he emits pain behaviors, and that relatively "bad things" are in prospect when he recovers. The conditioning is automatic if circumstances are favorable and does not require even the awareness, let alone the intent, of the individual.

Without corrective action, a CPS individual slips ever deeper into a rut over time. The pain never abates, and the status of "pain disabled" provides a certain legitimacy and, sometimes, a steady income. As long as the incentive structure remains unaltered, the prospects for spontaneous recovery are remote.

The Commission believes, however, that CPS is treatable and need not be a permanent condition. While a few individuals will improve spontaneously, others need the assistance of the concerted rehabilitation efforts of trained professionals. Such rehabilitation efforts include those of complex behavior modification training.

. . .

NOTES

(1) What lessons does this Report teach for courts wrestling with questions of how to value noneconomic loss? In pointing out that "no one can know the pain of another person," does the Report imply that it is practically an impossible task to value pain?

(2) Should courts try to distinguish among such categories as "somatogenic pain" and "psychogenic pain" with respect to whether tort damages should be awarded at all?

(3) Should there be money awards for CPS? Compare the Commission's declarations that "[t]he stereotypical CPS claimant is not a hypochondriac, a malingerer, or a hysteric," and is not "'making up' the pain," with its observation that "'[i]llness behaviors' are rewarded" for CPS sufferers. Would the existence of money damages for CPS pain create significant added incentives to suffer further? Would that militate against awarding damages for this condition? But wouldn't that be unjust, given the reality of the pain?

CONSORTI v. ARMSTRONG WORLD INDUSTRIES, INC.

United States Court of Appeals, Second Circuit
72 F.3d 1003 (1995)

LEVAL, Circuit Judge:

Owens-Corning Fiberglas Corporation ("OCF"), a fabricator of asbestos pipe-covering products, appeals from jury verdicts in favor of John Consorti, a pipe insulation worker who developed mesothelioma as the result of exposure to asbestos dust, and his wife Frances for loss of consortium. The trial in the Southern District of New York before Robert W. Sweet, Judge, which consumed 25 trial days, consolidated the claims of four plaintiff couples against numerous manufacturers of asbestos products....

. . .

B. Excessiveness of Award for Pain and Suffering

OCF claims that the award to John Consorti of $12 million for his pain and suffering was excessive and should be set aside. We agree.

1. The Role of Judge and Jury

We note at the start, our finding in no way deprecates the enormous suffering that John Consorti endured. He developed a tumor which gradually enveloped his spine. The tumor pressed against his vocal cords, causing him to lose his voice and choke. It interfered with eating, swallowing, even breathing. His circulatory system was impaired, causing painful and disfiguring swelling of his head and neck. And, as his disease progressed, it became increasingly difficult (later impossible) for him to walk or to care for himself. His pain grew worse as time passed, and was, of course, deepened by the certainty of imminent death. We take it as a given that reasonable people of his age, in good mental and physical health, would not have traded one-quarter of his suffering for a hundred million dollars, much less twelve.

It does not follow that courts should permit a verdict of a hundred million dollars, or twelve million, to stand. While the law seeks by reasonable compensation to make a plaintiff whole, we must recognize that compensation for suffering can be accomplished only in a symbolic and arbitrary fashion. There are at least two serious shortcomings to the endeavor. First, money awards do not make one whole; they do not alleviate pain. Second, there is no rational scale that justifies the award of any particular amount, as opposed to some very different amount, in compensation for a particular quantum of pain.... [2]

We acknowledge furthermore that a judge's training in law gives the judge no greater ability than a jury to determine the dollar amount that appropriately compensates any particular level of suffering.... This recognition can lead judges to abdicate responsibility for review of jury verdicts. As we have no greater knowledge than jurors of the amount of money that suitably compensates for suffering, the question arises why our assessment should take precedence over theirs?

Nonetheless, there are important reasons why courts cannot properly leave it to juries to set the limits of compensation for such injuries. Even where the law is incapable of furnishing a rational answer, it seeks at least to be evenhanded, fair, and predictable. It should be our goal that persons who endure a similar degree of suffering can expect to receive a roughly similar award of compensation, ... and that similarly situated defendants be burdened by similar judgments. If each jury is given unbridled authority to set the level of damages, awards will vary widely and unpredictably. Great discrepancies in awards destroy the fairness of the judicial system, as well as the predictability of litigation. This vigilance must be directed not only against awards that are too high, but

---

2. Juries may be especially inclined to make substantial awards when they believe that the defendant's liability is covered by insurance. While insurance frequently does cover the liability, jurors may neglect to consider the broader effect of their award on insurance premiums....

also against those that are too low. See, e.g., In re Brooklyn Navy Yard Asbestos Litig., 971 F.2d 831, 853–54 (2d Cir.1992) (ordering new trial on issue of pain and suffering where award of $25,000 was so low, given evidence of lengthy and intense suffering, as to shock the conscience). Such goals cannot be achieved unless courts exercise responsibility to keep jury awards within limits....

The unpredictability of jury awards is pernicious not only because it is unfair. Widely varying jury verdicts make it difficult for risk bearers to structure their behavior to efficiently manage risk. While it is an aim of tort law to deter wrongful conduct, see Restatement (Second) of Torts § 901 (1977), at the same time tort law seeks to avoid over-deterrence that would stifle socially valuable enterprise. Where liability costs are relatively predictable, they can be avoided (where it is efficient to do so) or 'built in' to the costs of goods and services.... But errors in valuation may cause over-deterrence — the taking of too many costly precautions, or withdrawal from risky activity altogether. For example, during the liability insurance crisis of the 1980s, many obstetricians reportedly stopped delivering babies, and some manufacturers ceased development or production of certain drugs and goods.... When courts fail to exercise the responsibility to curb excessive verdicts, the effects are uncertainty and an upward spiral. One excessive verdict, permitted to stand, becomes precedent for another still larger one. Unbridled, spiraling, excessive judgments predictably impose huge costs on society.

A failure by courts to impose limits on jury verdicts would cause serious social dislocation. At the first level, unchecked costs attributable to tort liability, and resultant increases in insurance premiums, would inevitably raise the price of goods and services to the public. More serious exaggeration in unchecked jury awards can cause bankruptcies in productive enterprises, with consequent disappearance of jobs, and even bankruptcies among insurers, leaving segments of society unprotected. Finally, in the circumstance represented by asbestos litigation, where it appears virtually certain that the resources of major defendants will eventually be completely consumed by their liabilities, allowing excessive awards to stand in the early stages of the litigation of the many thousands of cases they face will mean that over-compensation of the early plaintiffs will leave insufficient resources for the equally deserving plaintiffs whose cases are heard later.

2. The Award for Consorti's Pain and Suffering

The first step in deciding whether the award of $12 million for John Consorti's pain and suffering is excessive must be to ascertain whether federal or state rules apply. The question has significance in this case because the New York rule, discussed below, is less deferential to the jury's verdict than the federal standard of whether the award was so excessive as to shock the conscience of the court....

...

The question we face is how much money John Consorti may be awarded in damages by reason of his pain and suffering. This is an issue of substantive rights under the laws of New York. If, for example, New York's statutes provided that no compensation was to be awarded for nonpecuniary loss, or scheduled the awardable amounts in the manner of workers' compensation statutes—i.e., $X for injury to an arm, $Y for injury to a leg, $Z maximum for pain and suffering—federal courts ruling in diversity would unquestionably be bound by those substantive rules.... And if a jury's award exceeded those standards, the federal court would be required to reduce the verdict to bring it into compliance with the substantive law of New York. Here, New York law provides that a jury verdict may not exceed that amount which would "deviate[] materially from ... reasonable compensation." N.Y.Civ.Prac.L. & R. §5501(c) (McKinney Supp. 1995). This is the substantive rule provided by New York law. To disregard New York law in this case, in favor of the federal "shocks the conscience" standard, would violate the fundamental constitutional doctrine of Erie....

...

Because the standard of excessiveness is furnished by state law, the best guide for a federal court, if available, would be decisions of the state's courts in comparable cases indicating at what point awards become excessive.... Although a number of pertinent New York State judgments on damages for pain caused by mesothelioma were available, the district court relied instead on McPadden, a recent federal trial court decision.... In McPadden, the district court upheld a jury award of $4.5 million for pain and suffering due to mesothelioma. McPadden et al., 798 F.Supp. at 937–38.

In discussing below the question of excessiveness of the jury's award to [another plaintiff] of $7.5 million for pain and suffering, Judge Sweet converted the $4.5 million McPadden award to a monthly figure of $409,090.91 for McPadden's 11 months of suffering. Multiplication of that figure by [the other plaintiff's] 18 months of suffering produced a figure of $7,363,636.36, which was not substantially lower than the jury's award to Tabolt. Consorti et al., 847 F.Supp. at 1097. Although it was not expressly discussed, the district court presumably used the same conversion of the McPadden award to a monthly amount to justify the jury's $12 million award to Consorti, whose disease the jury predicted to run 32 months from onset to death. Twelve million expressed as a monthly figure over 32 months is $375,000, which is below the $409,090.91 monthly figure Judge Sweet extrapolated from the McPadden judgment.

We disagree with the district court's use of McPadden to justify the jury's award to Consorti for two reasons. First, rigid application of a monthly multiplier for diseases of significantly different durations is an oversimplification, as well as inconsistent with New York precedent. Unquestionably, the duration of suffering is a relevant factor. But it cannot be automatically assumed that suffering which lasts 30 months, from onset of illness to death, should command a verdict three times that of a case where ten months pass from onset to death. In many cases, the degree of average daily suffering will be greater in a case where the disease progresses rapidly. The fact that McPadden's disease progressed three times more rapidly than Consorti's does not necessarily justify an award for Consorti nearly three times the size of McPadden's. Moreover, we believe the court relied excessively on federal district court precedent to justify the jury verdict, giving insufficient regard to a large number of recent New York State court decisions which strongly indicated that the Consorti award was far beyond what New York law permits.

Justice Helen Freedman is the trial judge to whom all New York asbestos litigation has been assigned by administrative order. In the period shortly prior to the Consorti trial, Justice Freedman rendered numerous judgments reducing awards in comparable cases of mesothelioma to levels far below what the jury awarded to Consorti. In Didner v. Keene Corp., Justice Freedman reduced a $3.25 million award to $2.3 million; the plaintiff had suffered 26–27 months of pain and suffering due to mesothelioma.... The court concluded that while Didner's pain and suffering was severe, "courts in this jurisdiction have not countenanced awards of this size for two plus years of pain and suffering." Id.

Four months later, in the consolidated Brooklyn Navy Yard litigation, Justice Freedman reduced fourteen pain and suffering awards in mesothelioma death cases.... The jury awards for pain and suffering from mesothelioma that Justice

Freedman considered ranged from a low of $1 million, for a course of disease that took only three months, to a high of $5 million, in a case of 34 months of suffering. The jury awards thus ranged from 8% to 42% of this jury's award to Consorti. Justice Freedman found all those awards excessive under New York law. Those most comparable in duration to Consorti's were two awards of $5 million in cases where the suffering lasted 34 and 35 months (Cohen and Lopez). Justice Freedman reduced these to $3 million. And as to three awards ranging from $3.2 to $4.25 million, for suffering periods of 26 to 29 months, they were reduced to $2.2 to $2.4 million (Chierico, Savella, and Silver).

While it is difficult, especially without a study of the complete record, to evaluate the pertinence of one judgment for pain and suffering for another, the strong pattern of Justice Freedman's rulings is helpful in evaluating the Consorti awards. In the face of so substantial a pattern of New York judgments communicating that New York courts find excessiveness in such cases at far lower levels, we believe it was error for the district court to conclude that the jury's $12 million award was within the range accepted by New York law.[13] We note furthermore that Justice Freedman employed the "shockingly excessive" standard, while we on appeal must use the standard of CPLR § 5501(c) — "deviates materially from ... reasonable compensation" — a standard less deferential to the jury's appraisal.[14]

Although we recognize that John Consorti's suffering was very great, Justice Freedman's cases also all involved deaths from mesothelioma. It is not suggested to us that the suffering of the plaintiffs she considered was any less horrendous.[15] We recognize that the New York decisions in question were at the trial court level, and thus less compelling as authority than a decision of New York's Court of Appeals. Nonetheless, especially given the uniformity of the large number of decisions, they provide a better indication of New York law than any other authorities cited to us.

Given the consistent pattern, over a considerable number of cases of death by mesothelioma, of reduction of jury verdicts for pain and suffering by New York courts to figures ranging from approximately $1 million to a maximum of $3 million, we conclude an award exceeding $3.5 million would deviate materially from what is deemed reasonable under New York law. Accordingly, we direct entry of a conditional order of a new trial on the issue of damages for pain and suffering, unless plaintiffs accept remittitur to that amount.

---

13. In *McPadden*, the district court observed that in the state court's Brooklyn Navy Yard consolidation, "Justice Freedman allowed several multimillion dollar awards for pain and suffering...." *McPadden et al.*, 798 F.Supp. at 938. Those awards, reducing $5 million verdicts to $3 million, initially served as authority justifying an award of $4.5 million to McPadden, which in turn, converted to a monthly average figure, was used below to justify this award of $12 million.

14. Although we apply the New York "deviates materially" standard, we note that Consorti's award was also so excessive as to "shock the conscience." Hence, we would remit this $12 million award for pain and suffering even if we were to follow federal law, although application of this standard might allow for a slightly higher award than the $3.5 million figure we have allowed.

15. We note that one of the difficulties of remittitur review is the limited data available about the particular cases used for comparison.... But even if we approach the New York precedents on a monthly basis — the way Judge Sweet used the *McPadden* precedent — they offer no better support for this award. Probably in recognition that the course of the disease will involve varying degrees of suffering in different periods, and that a short course is likely to cause greater average daily suffering than one which is slow to develop, Justice Freedman's judgments, stated on a monthly basis, vary roughly inversely to duration. The plaintiffs who died (or were expected to) within a year of the disease's onset received monthly sums of $110,000 to $200,000, while those whose illness lingered from one and a half to three years received between $80,000 and $90,000 per month. This provides no authority for Consorti's monthly figure of $375,000.

...

GERESSY v. DIGITAL EQUIP. CORP.

United States District Court, Eastern District of New York
980 F. Supp. 640 (1997)

WEINSTEIN, Senior District Judge:

[These excerpts come from a lengthy decision on claims by three plaintiffs that they suffered repetitive stress injuries from use of a model of computer keyboard made by the defendant.]

...

Plaintiffs differ. Some are more susceptible to pain than others. Some may be younger, perhaps more deserving in the jury's view, or more vulnerable, or may have led a more difficult life or an easier one. There is an infinite variety of people and reactions to tragedy, further compounding the difficulty of quantifying verdicts.

Even with seemingly objective criteria, such as measurements of the amount of time that a tort victim suffers, different juries produce a seemingly erratic set of verdict data. One scholar in this field, Dean David W. Leebron, attempted to finding a correlation between time suffered and the amount of the award. In his research, he was unable to discover any rationale for jury awards for pain and suffering. Dean Leebron found that "the temporal element of the pain and suffering has no statistically significant effect for durations from half a minute up to one week." David W. Leebron, Final Moments: Damages for Pain and Suffering Prior to Death, 64 N.Y.U.L.Rev. 256, 294 (1989). He concluded, "[t]ort awards ... vary significantly and ... neither the specific facts of the case nor differing views of the functions of the awards can explain such variation." Id. at 259....

Within the same state verdicts vary widely by geographic area....

However inexact, the process for determining the category of award that is a material deviation may be undertaken in three steps. First, identify the normative group—what kinds of cases are sufficiently similar to serve as the referent group for determining what is reasonable? Second, determine what constitutes a deviation from that group. Third, define statistically and intuitively how far a verdict can deviate before that deviation becomes material. After this three step analysis, the court reviews the more traditional examination of economic damages and the statistical analysis for non-economic damages and decides how much leeway should be allowed the fact finders before determining that a jury verdict deviates materially.

a. Identifying the Normative Group for Comparison

... The parties provide experts (subject to the court's power to appoint ... independent experts) who can assist the court in identifying appropriate comparative cases. Such a hearing is by no means ideal. The court does not have the capacity or the time to go through possibly scores of records in order to see what is equivalent. It has to have the information summed up in some convenient way. This is much the same task it undertakes in determining land values from comparable sales (a more developed technique)....

Similar injuries or diagnoses are primary (but not controlling) criteria in choosing sufficiently analogous cases. In evaluating the pain and suffering that results from a tortious event, the court also may consider the causal agent itself and the circumstances surrounding the injury in determining the nature of the anguish for which plaintiff should be compensated. The life changes that follow the tortious event are also of critical importance. If at all possible, cases within the relevant venue should be relied upon because the farther the court moves beyond the place of trial, the more likely it is that community conceptions of reasonableness diverge in various directions.

In determining whether an award is reasonable, it is almost impossible to find cases for comparison where all relevant factors are identical to those in the case under consideration. Rather, the court must review the totality of the circumstances of the proffered sample cases to ascertain whether they can provide a basis for comparison. There are almost no "all fours" cases. As Appendix A [here omitted—Ed.] indicates the decisions on comparability are somewhat arbitrary. The court's evaluation may be supplemented by expert testimony of practitioners and others familiar with state tort cases.

Deviation from the "Normal" Group

Once the court has chosen a group of settlements and verdicts with which to compare the verdict under consideration, there is no simple method for determining whether that verdict is reasonable vis-a-vis those in the normative group. The imprecision inherent in simply making a vague estimate by looking at a comparative group turns the court toward a statistical analysis.

The initial step in considering whether a jury verdict is reasonable as compared to settlements and verdicts in other cases is to determine the variance within the group. "Statisticians use several statistics to measure the amount of variation within a data set." James Brook, A Lawyer's Guide to Probability and Statistics 24 (1990). "[T]he statistic most often seen as a measure of variation within a data set is the standard deviation." Id. at 25....

Even though the entire enterprise is expected to provide only a rough approximation, close to an intelligent and well-informed guess, the court is well advised to rely on sophisticated statistical experts. See generally, e.g., Michael O. Finklestein & Bruce Levin, Statistics for Lawyers 46 (1990); The Evolving Role of Statistical Assessments as Evidence in the Courts 36, 91 (Stephen E. Fienberg ed.1989) (two or three standard deviations, one or two tailed hypotheses).

The discussion which follows is illustrative only. In the instant case the statistical analysis provided by the parties, and largely relied upon in this memorandum, was not satisfactory to the court. Should it actually become necessary to fix the appropriate range of verdicts a full hearing and a more comprehensive statistical analysis will be required....

Defining Material Deviation

The court may use the dollar amount to measure, by standard deviation, how far past settlements or verdicts for pain and suffering have varied from the mean settlement or verdict. "The mean of a set of observations is the value obtained by summing all the observations and dividing by the number of observations." R. Kapadia & G. Anderson, Statistics Explained: Basic Concepts and Methods 68 (1987). Approximately two-thirds of the values under a normal distribution, a symmetrical bell-shaped curve, fall within one standard deviation of the mean, and approximately 95% fall within two standard deviations of the mean. David H. Kaye & David A. Freedman, Reference on Statistics, in Reference Manual on Scientific Evidence 331, 379 (Fed.Jud.Ctr. ed.1994). The data available in the instant case did not generate a symmetrical bell-shaped curve, but for the purposes of this memorandum, it is assumed that classic statistical analysis of such curves is appropriate. Expert statisticians will have to assist the court in dealing with curves that dive off sharply at the lower end, where the limit is zero, while tailing off into what are often very high figures at the upper end.

There are arguments supporting a rule ... of one, two or more standard deviations. Using two standard deviations to define the group of values that constitute reasonable compensation supports the judiciary's efforts to sustain jury verdicts whenever reasonably possible. This approach is consistent with the federal and New York state constitutions that guarantee the right to trial by jury in civil cases. See U.S. Const. amend. VII; N.Y. Const. art. I, § 2. Narrowing the range to figures that fall within one standard deviation, however, speaks to the state policy of controlling jury verdicts. See Legislative Findings and Declarations, Ch. 266, 1986 N.Y. 470 (McKinney). Given the awards in the instant case, and subject to reconsideration on advice of experts, a two standard deviation rule seems appropriate.

...

NOTES

(1) What are the principal social policies at issue in controversies about amounts of damages for intangibles, including pain and suffering?

(2) The court in *Consorti* acknowledges that the legal expertise of judges gives them no advantage, relative to jurors, in determining the appropriate dollar compensation for suffering. Does the legal expertise of the judges in *Consorti* and *Geressy* produce a rational method for review of jury awards for this item?

(3) What advantage does either the *Consorti* or *Geressy* approach have as compared with a "shocks the conscience" standard?

(4) After the Supreme Court vacated the court of appeals decision in *Consorti*, see 518 U.S. 1031 (1996), and the court of appeals subsequently remanded to the district court, see 103 F.3d 2 (2d Cir. 1996), the district court provided a little more balm than did the Second Circuit for the legal suffering of Consorti's survivors, see 9 F. Supp.2d 307 (S.D.N.Y. 1998). The district court recorded, in painful detail, Consorti's last months, a period when tumors pressed against his vocal cords and pain, which could not be relieved by narcotics, made it impossible to walk, sleep or care for himself. It described the toll that the mesothelioma took on the spirit of an previously outgoing individual. Comparing its observations of *Consorti* with other asbestos cases in which it presided, the court decided that $5 million was the "maximum recovery that would not 'deviate materially' from awards in similar situations," and thus required a remitittur of $7 million. *Id.* at 317–20.

(5) Assume that you are the aide to a state legislator, who has concluded that the social costs of valuing pain and suffering through court decisions are unacceptable, and that dollar figures should be assigned to these items as damages through schedules. On assignment from your legislator, how would you go about constructing a schedule that included Consorti's type of injury?

HALEY v. PAN AMERICAN WORLD AIRWAYS

United States Court of Appeals, Fifth Circuit
746 F.2d 311 (1984)

PATRICK E. HIGGINBOTHAM, CIRCUIT JUDGE:

On July 9, 1982, Michael H. Haley, the son of appellees here, was aboard Pan American World Airways Flight 759 when it crashed in Kenner, Louisiana. Haley, along with all 138 passengers and seven crew members, was killed when the Boeing 727 disintegrated upon impact with the ground. After a damages trial, the jury returned a verdict in favor of Michael's parents, Thomas W. Haley and Ann S. Haley, and against Pan American World Airways, Inc. and the United States of America, awarding the Haleys $15,000 for the mental anguish suffered by Michael "prior to the first impact between the plane and the ground,".... The trial court denied defendants' motions for judgment notwithstanding the verdict and for new trial.

Pan Am contends that Louisiana does not allow recovery for pre-impact pain and suffering and that the trial judge abused his discretion in admitting on this issue. The evidence that was introduced, it argues, was insufficient to support the jury's finding that the decedent suffered any such pre-impact fear. Pan Am also challenges as excessive the damages awarded for both pre-impact fear and for loss of love and companionship. We find that Louisiana law permits recovery for a decedent's pre-impact fear and that there was sufficient evidence to support the jury's $15,000 award for this element of damages. We remand, however, with instructions to grant a new trial on the amount of wrongful death damages unless the plaintiffs accept a remittitur to the maximum we consider allowable on the record.

...

We follow the Louisiana law of damages in this diversity suit. Despite the parties' urging, we find no Louisiana court which has squarely confronted the issue of whether the fear a decedent experiences prior to both death *and* physical impact is a legally compensable element of damages. It appears to be undisputed that the Pan Am 727 disintegrated, and Michael died immediately upon impact with the ground.

A broad compensatory principle lies behind Article 2315 of the Louisiana Civil Code.[3] Louisiana, therefore, has long recognized that negligence, which causes fright and serious personal injury, is actionable, *Stewart v. Arkansas Southern Railway Co.*, 112 La. 764, 36 So. 676, 677 (La.1904), and that "fright, fear, or mental anguish while an ordeal is in progress is legally compensable." As Pan Am correctly points out, many of these cases deal with recovery for post-impact mental anguish associated with physical injury. Indeed, article 2315 most commonly compensates for pain and suffering endured by a decedent *after* injury but before death. *See Guidry* [v. Theriot], 377 So.2d [319] at 322 [La. 1979]. Louisiana jurisprudence, however, indicates that fright or mental anguish is a separate element of compensable damages, apart from oft-accompanying physical injury.[5] In *Dawson*,..., for example, the jury compensated the injured plaintiff for the "extreme terror that he would lose his life," experienced "during the ordeal," as well as for the physical symptoms flowing therefrom, experienced afterward. 437 So.2d at 976. Louisiana would, in fact, appear to permit recovery for negligently-induced fright, even in the absence of actual physical injury.[6] *Carroll*, ... 427 So.2d at 25–26; *Butler*, ... 415 So.2d at 252.

While Louisiana courts then, have never expressly allowed recovery for pre-impact apprehension in anticipation of imminent death, they do allow recovery for fear during

---

3. Article 2315 states in part: "Every act whatever of man that causes damage to another obliges him by whose fault it happened to repair it." LA.CIV.CODE ANN. art. 2315 (West Supp. 1984).

5. *See Dawson*, 437 So.2d at 976 (plaintiff compensated for his fear during ordeal); *Kyle*, 357 So.2d at 1391 and 1391 n.3 (element of damages is fear plaintiff experienced at time of accident); *Singleton*, 339 So.2d at 544 (suit brought in tort for "fear of life").

6. *See Stewart*, 36 So. at 677, where the Louisiana Supreme Court expressly rejected the "simple rule that no recovery of any kind can be had for fright occasioned by the negligence of another" and indicated that Louisiana already considered mental distress in itself sufficient to decree damages....

a negligently produced ordeal. We are not prepared to conclude that the Louisiana courts would sever such an "ordeal" into before and after impact components.

This mirrors our reasoning in *Solomon v. Warren*, 540 F.2d 777 (5th Cir. 1976), *cert. denied*, 434 U.S. 801, 98 S.Ct. 28, 54 L.Ed.2d 59 (1977). In *Solomon*, plaintiffs' parents died when, after radioing for aid, their small aircraft crashed into the sea. While there was admittedly no evidence as to the length of time the couple suffered before death or whether they died immediately upon impact, the district court was "'convinced that both of the deceased knew of the impending crash landing at sea, knew of the imminent dangers involved, and are certain to have experienced the most excruciating type of pain and suffering (the knowledge that one is about to die, leaving three cherished children alone).'" *Id*. at 792. In upholding the district court's conclusion that Florida would permit recovery for the decedent's conscious pain and suffering prior to death, we stated

> While in the garden variety of claims under survival statutes, including the Florida Statute—fatal injuries sustained in automobile accidents and the like—the usual sequence is impact followed by pain and suffering, we are unable to discern any reason based on either law or logic for rejecting a claim because in this case as to at least part of the suffering, this sequence was reversed. We will not disallow the claims for this item of damages on that ground.

Id. at 793 (citations omitted).

It would appear then, that Louisiana would recognize a cause of action for pre-impact fear experienced by a decedent in apprehension of impending death.[8] The district court was therefore correct, both in denying Pan Am's motion for judgment notwithstanding the verdict based on the ground the Haleys had failed to state a claim under Louisiana law, and in admitting evidence of pre-impact fear to aid the jury in assessing damages. The cases cited by Pan Am in support of its contention go instead to its stronger sufficiency argument.

Louisiana courts condition a "survival" claimant's recovery on proof of pre-death pain and suffering. *Daniels v. Conn*, 382 So.2d 945 (La.1980). This generally requires affirmative evidence that a decedent was "conscious" after the accident, and did in fact, suffer pain.... [9]

Pan Am argues that the record evidence is insufficient to support the finding that Michael Haley suffered any "conscious" pre-impact fear, as no passenger survived to relate what Michael may have experienced; nor were there any eyewitnesses to testify as to the path of trajectory of the plane prior to its crash. The only evidence offered on this issue was a videotape simulation of the takeoff and crash of Flight 759; a stip-

---

8. At least two other circuits have allowed recovery for a decedent's pre-impact fear in similar airline disasters. *See Shu-Tao Lin v. McDonnell Douglas Corp.*, 742 F.2d 45, 53 (2d Cir.1984) (New York law permits recovery for a decedent's pre-impact fear as there is "no intrinsic or logical barrier to recovery for the fear experienced during a period in which the decedent is uninjured but aware of impending death." *Id*.); *United States v. Furumizo*, 381 F.2d 965 (9th Cir.1967) (affirming district court's award, under Hawaiian law, for the "decedent's pain and suffering during the descent of the Piper plane, its crash to the ground, and the burning of decedent to death," *Furumizo v. United States*, 245 F.Supp. 981, 1015 (D.Hawaii 1965)). *But see In re Air Crash Disaster Near Chicago, Illinois on May 25, 1979*, 507 F.Supp. 21, 23–34 (N.D.Ill. 1980) (no recovery for passenger's alleged fright and terror prior to crash in absence of physical injury causing such distress).

9. This requirement has been relaxed somewhat in recent cases allowing recovery for pain and suffering if there exists some evidence that the decedent was "sensitive to and aware of pain." ...

ulation explaining the known facts culled from the investigation; and the videotaped testimony of both parties' experts. The parties stipulated that the Pan Am plane took off and rose to an altitude of 163 feet before beginning its fatal descent. While the plane rolled to its left, testimony indicated there was not change in gravitational forces. The plane's wing struck a tree fifty-three feet above ground, then the aircraft rolled, impacted and disintegrated some four to six seconds later. Plaintiff's expert, a psychiatrist who had treated survivors of aircraft accidents and was familiar with the physiological effects of stress, explained the five levels of anxiety that culminate in panic. He then rendered his opinion that "most of the people [aboard Flight 759], if not all, would be in an absolute state of pandemonium, panic and extreme state of stress," at least from the time the plane hit the tree, if not from the beginning of its descent and roll, until impact seconds later. Defendant's expert expressed uncertainty as to whether "any of the passengers, in fact realized that they were about to die." He conceded, however, that when the passengers experienced a "violent change in the plane, the last couple of seconds," they "certainly would have been thrown about and *fighting for their lives* and experienced a whole different situation." (Emphasis added).

A number of courts have disallowed recovery in similar situations for lack of evidence the decedent was aware of the danger or in fact suffered any pre-impact terror. In *Shatkin v. McDonnell Douglas Corp.*, 727 F.2d 202 (2d Cir.1984), for example, the Second Circuit reversed a jury award for pre-impact pain and suffering, finding no evidence the decedent-passenger was awake, let alone aware that anything was wrong. *Id.* at 207. The rolling of the plane, the only possible indicia of danger to this particular passenger, was as compatible with normal airline traffic patterns as with imminent disaster. *Id.* at 206–07. In *Shu-Tao Lin v. McDonnell Douglas Corp., supra*, a case arising out of the same air disaster as *Shatkin*, however, the Second Circuit held that the jury had sufficient evidence before it to infer that a passenger sitting on the side of the plane opposite Shatkin, could have seen the left engine break away and experienced pre-impact fear during the thirty seconds between takeoff and crash. *Id.* at 54.

A damages award cannot stand when the only evidence to support it is speculative or purely conjectural.... Nor will we affirm an award for pre-death mental anguish when there is no evidence of its existence.... In reviewing Pan Am's challenge to the sufficiency of the evidence, however, we are bound to consider the evidence and all reasonable inferences therefrom in the light most favorable to the jury verdict.... No one indeed will ever "know" whether Michael Haley was aware of his impending death, or whether he experienced the uncontrollable "panic" of which Dr. Scrignar testified. Eyewitness testimony, however, is not necessary to support an award for conscious pain and suffering....

The evidence at trial was silent as to the exact length of time Michael was aware of his impending death. Perhaps he did not have knowledge that something was wrong at the time the plane began its descent and roll. The inference is more than "reasonable", however, that Michael apprehended his death at least from the time the plane's wing hit the tree. Pan Am's own expert acknowledged that all aboard the plane were "fighting for their lives" at this point. One need not "speculate" that the decedent was aware, for at least four to six seconds, of the impending disaster. The jury could have reasonably inferred therefrom that Michael Haley experienced the mental anguish commonly associated with anticipation of one's own death. We therefore conclude that there was sufficient evidence to support its finding.

II

The jury awarded the Haleys $15,000 for the mental anguish suffered by Michael before the plane's impact.... Pan Am argues that these damages are excessive, and that the district court erred in refusing to grant a new trial or a remittitur. Of course, a jury's assessment of damages is entitled to great deference by a reviewing court and should be disturbed only in those "rare" instances where it "clearly exceeds that amount that any reasonable man could feel the claimant is entitled," ... Unless an award is "so gross or inordinately large as to be contrary to right of reason," ... or so excessive as to suggest "bias, passion, prejudice, corruption, or other improper motive," ... it must be allowed to stand. The fact the trial judge reviewed and approved the verdict in this case makes us even more hesitant to overturn the awarded amount....

Pan Am contends that even if sufficient evidence supports the jury's finding that the decedent suffered pre-impact fear, an award of $15,000 for no more than four to six seconds of such anguish is clearly contrary to reason. In *Solomon v. Warren*, ... however, there was no evidence as to the length of time the couple suffered prior to their death in an airplane crash. Despite the fact that the decedents' pain and suffering may have only been brief, a panel of this court nevertheless affirmed a $10,000 award to each decedent's estate, noting that such recovery was "if anything, on the very low side." 540 F.2d at 793. In *Shu-Tao Lin* ... the Second Circuit affirmed a $10,000 award for a possible thirty seconds of pre-impact fear. 742 F.2d 45 at 53. The Ninth Circuit in *Furumizo* ... affirmed as non-"shocking" a $15,000 award for the decedent's "brief" pain and suffering during the descent and fiery crash of his aircraft. 381 F.2d at 970. In light of these holdings, we cannot say the jury's $15,000 award for Michael Haley's mental anguish in the period prior to the plane's impact, however brief it may have been, was either "shocking" and contrary to "right of reason." We affirm this portion of the award.

. . .

NOTES

(1) In the special case of a few seconds or minutes of pain before death, how can a court justify an award ranging into the thousands of dollars? Would such an award lay the groundwork for impossibly exorbitant awards in cases where the plaintiff faces a long period, perhaps a lifetime, of severe pain? For example, if the $15,000 for Haley's final horror were for one minute of pain, then by multiplication, even an hour of pain would be "worth" $900,000. But no court would allow such an award, and surely no court would allow an award for 365 days times 24 hours times $900,000, not to mention several years' life expectancy as an added multiplier. How do you resolve this logical puzzle?

(2) A point of controversy related to this material is the so-called "golden rule" argument, which one court has characterized as an argument "by which counsel asks the jurors to place themselves in the plaintiff's shoes and to award such damages as they would 'charge' to undergo equivalent pain and suffering." *Beagle v. Vasold*, 65 Cal.2d 166, 182 n.11, 53 Cal. Rptr. 129, 137–38 n.11, 417 P.2d 673, 681–82 n.11 (1966). Courts are very hostile to this argument. Why? Viscerally, it may seem repugnant to allow the jury to consider the notion that one may trade his pain for money. But consider the analogy in the working world of premium pay for dangerous jobs. Is this not persuasive of the legitimacy of the "golden rule" argument as a tool of advocacy?

§9.03 Punitive Damages

The decision below focuses on the awardability of punitive damages in products liability cases. Read it for its discussion of that issue, but primarily for its summary of the verbal standards for the award of punitive damages generally.

WANGEN v. FORD MOTOR COMPANY

Supreme Court of Wisconsin
97 Wis. 2d 260, 294 N.W.2d 437 (1980)

ABRAHAMSON, Justice.

The central question on appeal is whether punitive damages are recoverable in a product liability suit based on negligence or strict liability in tort (sometimes referred to as strict products liability). We conclude that they are recoverable.

I.

This appeal involves two lawsuits which were commenced against Ford Motor Company and others as a result of an automobile accident on July 1, 1975 involving a 1967 Ford Mustang. The cases were consolidated and are before us at the pleading stage; all facts set forth are derived from the pleadings.

The occupants of the 1967 Ford Mustang involved in the accident were Robin DuVall, the driver, Terri Wangen, her sister, Kip Wangen, her brother, and Christopher DuVall, her son. Robin DuVall stopped her 1967 Ford Mustang at an intersection to make a left turn, and a car driven by Patrick J. Hawley ran into the rear end of the Mustang. The DuVall Mustang was pushed into the opposite lane of travel where it collided with a car driven by Thomas J. Curran. The Mustang's fuel tank ruptured, a fire ensued, and all occupants of the Mustang sustained severe injuries. Christopher DuVall and Kip Wangen died as a result of their injuries.

. . .

Plaintiffs in both lawsuits seek compensatory damages from all named defendants and punitive damages from Ford Motor Company.

The claim for compensatory damages against Ford is based on Ford's alleged negligence in the design, manufacture, assembly, sale and distribution of the 1967 Mustang and on Ford's strict liability in tort arising out of the sale of the 1967 Mustang in a defective condition unreasonably dangerous to users....

The allegations in support of recovery of punitive damages from Ford Motor Company are that Ford knew that the fuel tanks on this and other 1967 Mustangs were dangerously defective before and after the manufacture of the car in question; that corrective design changes were made in models manufactured after this particular model but prior to the date of the instant accident; that Ford failed to warn users of the car of the potential danger both after the danger became apparent and after Ford had changed the design to reduce the danger; that Ford failed to recall, repair or modify the defective vehicles after the defect became apparent in order to avoid the expense of those procedures and to prevent potential lost sales caused by adverse publicity; and that Ford's conduct in failing to warn, repair or recall the known defective vehicles constituted intentional, deliberate, reckless, willful, wanton, gross, callous, malicious and fraudulent disregard for the safety of users of Ford's product.

...

We shall turn first to the question of whether punitive damages are recoverable in a product liability action predicated on negligence or strict liability.

...

Ford Motor Company's argument that punitive damages have no place in product liability cases rests on three grounds: (A) Punitive damages have traditionally been awarded in tort actions in which compensatory damages are premised on defendant's commission of an intentional, personal tort, and recovery of punitive damages should not be allowed in product liability suits in which compensatory damages are premised on the defendant's negligence or on strict liability. (B) The claim for punitive damages characterizing Ford's conduct as willful, deliberate, wanton, malicious, and reckless—all elements of gross negligence—is insufficient because the concept of gross negligence has been abolished in Wisconsin. (C) Punitive damages are unnecessary in product liability cases to effect punishment and deterrence, which are the objectives of imposing punitive damages in the traditional tort action, and the elimination of punitive damages in all products liability cases is in the public interest because the recovery of punitive damages produces economically and socially undesirable results.

A.

Ford Motor Company asserts that punitive damages are recoverable only in actions based on intentional, personal torts, and are not recoverable in product liability actions which are grounded in negligence or strict liability. Ford argues that the concept of punitive damages is antithetical to the theories of negligence and strict liability because punitive damages are based on the defendant's intentional conduct. Ford's argument is premised on two assumptions: that intentional conduct is the only conduct justifying punitive damages and that the same facts which justify compensatory damages must be sufficient to justify punitive damages. This court has never adopted this view of punitive damages.

Punitive damages are in the nature of "a demand arising out of a single injurious occurrence," a "theory of relief arising out of the same transaction or occurrence," a "remedy." ...

This court has rested its analysis of punitive damages not on the classification of the underlying tort justifying compensatory damages but on the nature of the wrongdoer's conduct. Although the usual aggravating circumstances required for the recovery of punitive damages are often found as substantive elements of the tort itself, this court has said a claim for punitive damages may be supported by proof of aggravating circumstances beyond those supporting compensatory damages.

Punitive damages rest on allegations which, if proved, demonstrate a particular kind of conduct on the part of the wrongdoer, which has variously been characterized in our cases as malicious conduct or willful or wanton conduct in reckless disregard of rights or interests.

This court has not required proof of an intentional desire to injure, vex or annoy, or proof of malice, in order to sustain an award for punitive damages. "(M)alice or vindictiveness are not the sine qua non of punitive damages." Kink v. Combs, 28 Wis.2d 65, 79, 135 N.W.2d 789, 797 (1965). It is sufficient if the injured party shows a reckless indifference to or disregard of the rights of others on the part of the wrongdoer. "Reckless indifference to the rights of others and conscious action in deliberate disregard of them ... may provide the necessary state of mind to justify punitive damages." 4 Restatement (Second) of Torts sec. 908, comment b, p. 465 (1977). Some commentators speak of the behavior justifying punitive damages as "flagrant indifference to the public safety." ... Prosser, Law of Torts 10 (4th ed. 1971). "A governing principle of these cases in allowing punitive damages has been the presence of 'circumstances of aggravation' in the tortious injury." Mid-Continent Refrigerator Co. v. Straka, 47 Wis.2d 739, 746, 178 N.W.2d 28, 32 (1970). We shall sometimes use the term "outrageous" in this opinion as an abbreviation for the type of conduct which justifies the imposition of punitive damages.

The distinction between the intent necessary to maintain an action for an intentional tort and the frame of mind of the wrongdoer necessary to recover punitive damages was delineated in Meshane v. Second Street Co., 197 Wis. 382, 387, 222 N.W. 320, 322 (1928) as follows:

> "Any exact and precise definition of the technical term in law of the 'malice' that must be shown in order that there may be a basis for punitory damages in addition to compensatory damages for a breach of some duty by a defendant when such is the proper subject of an action in tort is hard to find, and still harder to frame. It is evident, however, from all the authorities that in any particular case, not in and of itself a malicious action, in order that punitory damages may be assessed, something must be shown over and above the mere breach of duty for which compensatory damages can be given; that is, a showing of a bad intent deserving punishment, or something in the nature of special ill will towards the person injured, or a wanton, deliberate disregard of the particular duty then being breached, or that which resembles gross, as distinguished from ordinary, negligence." (Quoted with approval in Mid-Continent Refrigerator Co. v. Straka, 47 Wis.2d 739, 747, 178 N.W.2d 28 (1970).)

In Etzminger v. Ford Motor Co., 47 Wis.2d 751, 757–758, 177 N.W.2d 899, 903 (1970) this court made clear that the award of punitive damages depends on the character of the particular conduct in question, not on the mere fact that the defendant's conduct constituted a tort or a crime:

> "Punitive damages are not allowed for a mere breach of contract ... or for all torts or for crimes but generally for those personal torts, which are malicious, outrageous or a wanton disregard of personal rights which require the added sanction of a punitive damage to deter others from committing acts against human dignity...."

In Anderson v. Continental Ins. Co., 85 Wis.2d 675, 697, 271 N.W.2d 368, 379 (1978), we stated that proof of an intentional tort in an action for compensatory damages does not necessarily mean that an award of punitive damages is appropriate.

> "We do not conclude, however, that the proof of a bad faith cause of action necessarily makes punitive damages appropriate. Punitive damages are awarded to punish a wrongdoer and to serve as a deterrent. Mid-Continent Refrigerator Co. v. Straka, 47 Wis.2d 739, 746, 178 N.W.2d 28 (1970). We pointed out in Mid-Continent that punitive damages are to be awarded 'only where the wrong was inflicted "under circumstances of aggravation, insult or cruelty, with vindictiveness or malice."' (at 747, 178 N.W.2d 28) We also stated therein that there is a distinction between the intent or malice necessary to maintain an action for intentional tort (such as bad faith) and the intent which must be shown to recover punitive damages. For punitive damages to be

awarded in addition to compensatory damages for the tort, there must be a showing of an evil intent deserving of punishment or of something in the nature of special ill-will or wanton disregard of duty or gross or outrageous conduct. In the specific context of the intentional tort of bad faith, exemplary damages are not necessarily appropriate although the plaintiff be entitled to compensatory damages. For punitive damages to be awarded, a defendant must not only intentionally have breached his duty of good faith, but in addition must have been guilty of oppression, fraud, or malice in the special sense defined by Mid-Continent v. Straka."

If there is tortious conduct supporting a claim for compensatory damages, we can find no logical or conceptual difficulty in allowing a claim for punitive damages in a negligence or strict liability action if the plaintiff is able to establish the elements of "outrageous" conduct justifying punitive damages....

This court rejects Ford's argument that as a matter of law, punitive damages cannot be recovered in any product liability case based on strict liability or negligence. We hold that punitive damages are recoverable in a product liability suit if there is proof that the defendant's conduct was "outrageous." Awarding punitive damages in a product liability case is a natural, direct outgrowth of basic common law concepts of tort law and punitive damages....

Having decided that punitive damages are recoverable in a product liability case where there is a showing of malice, vindictiveness, ill-will, or wanton, willful or reckless disregard of plaintiff's rights, we now turn to the plaintiff's complaint to determine if it pleads facts sufficient to support a claim for punitive damages. The plaintiffs' pleading as to their claim for punitive damages are to be construed, as all pleadings are, to do substantial justice to the parties.... The claim should be dismissed as legally insufficient only if it is clear that the plaintiff cannot recover under any condition....

On the basis of the facts pleaded and reasonable inferences therefrom the complaint alleges that Ford knew of the defects in the design of the gas tank and filler neck and in the lack of barrier between the gas tank and passenger compartment in the 1967 Mustang and of the fire hazard associated with the design because of tests run by Ford as early as 1964; that for years before this accident Ford knew that these defects were causing serious burn injuries to occupants of these and similar cars; that years before the accident involved in the instant case Ford knew how to correct these defects in ways that would have prevented the plaintiffs' burns, but Ford intentionally concealed this knowledge from the government and the public; that despite this knowledge Ford deliberately chose not to recall its 1967 Mustangs and not to disclose the defects to the public by the issuance of warnings because Ford wanted to avoid paying the costs of recall and repair and wanted to avoid the accompanying bad publicity; and that Ford's conduct was intentional, reckless, willful, wanton, gross and fraudulent. These facts, if proved by the plaintiff, portray conduct which is willful and wanton and in reckless disregard of the plaintiff's rights. We conclude that the complaint alleges facts sufficient to state a claim for punitive damages in a product liability action predicated on negligence or strict liability.

NOTES

(1) Under *Wangen*, what is the full range of adjectives referring to a plaintiff's conduct that may be used in Wisconsin to support punitive damages in a products liability case? What is the least culpable conduct in this catalog that will justify a punitive award?

(2) Without using any of the adjectives in *Wangen*, how would you summarize the type of conduct that is properly the subject of punitive damages?

(3) What is the purpose of the punitive damages remedy? Is it to furnish certain kinds of incentives? If so, is it intended to influence the conduct of individual defendants or of the general public? Besides the goal of influencing conduct and providing compensation for pecuniary loss and pain and suffering, are there other reasons to change the distribution of wealth between an injurer and an injured party?

Consider this catalog of rationales for punitive damages formulated by Professor Owen: (1) punishment (2) deterrence (3) a "law enforcement" function, that is, the provision of incentives to "private persons to enforce the rules of law by rewarding them for bringing malefactors to justice" (4) a compensatory rationale, under which the law compensates "plaintiffs whose actual damages exceed those for which the law allows recovery and whose recovery in any event has likely been substantially depleted by attorneys' fees." David Owen, *Punitive Damages in Products Liability Litigation*, 74 Mich. L. Rev. 1257 (1976). The Texas Supreme Court adds to this list "an example for the good of the public," and "compensat[ion] for inconvenience." *Hofer v. Lavender*, 679 S.W.2d 470, 474 (Tex. 1984).

(4) Is retribution an appropriate basis for punitive damages? Consider the assertion of a noted English scholar that there is a danger that

> without a sense of retribution we may lose our sense of wrong. Retribution in punishment is an expression of the community's disapproval of crime, and if this retribution is not given recognition then the disapproval may also disappear.

—Goodhart, English Law and the Moral Law 92–93 (1953).

(5) If you believe that punitive damages have a place in tort law, could you assign weighted values to the policy goals served by awards of that kind?

(6) Should a judge tell a jury what the maximum punitive award is that he will allow, instructing them at the same time that they need not award punitive damages at all? If not, what constraints should trial judges place on juries after telling them that they may award punitive damages? Consider, for example, the following instruction in an employment discrimination case:

> Where a plaintiff in a racial discrimination case establishes the elements of malice, or callous reckless indifference ... then a jury is allowed in its discretion to assess punitive damages ... for the purpose of punishment of such defendant, and as a deterrent to others.

Does this instruction provide sufficient guidance to juries? Will it adequately restrain their passions?

(7) Why should civil juries be permitted to impose punitive damages without the defendant being able to invoke the constitutional safeguards that apply to criminal prosecutions?

(8) Would you permit a judge to condition a punitive damages award on the post-injuring event behavior of a defendant—for example, the defendant's undertaking of a positive course of conduct to make sure that injuries of that sort did not occur in the future?

(9) A technical reading of the meaning of the term "punitive damages," a category of award that is prohibited by the Federal Tort Claims Act, appears in *Molzof v. United States*, 502 U.S. 301 (1992). The plaintiff's decedent in *Molzof* suffered irreversible brain

damage, leaving him permanently comatose, because of deprivation of oxygen during surgery in a Veterans Administration hospital. The trial court denied recovery for two items of damages sought by the plaintiff: damages for future medical care that "would duplicate the free medical services already being provided by the veterans' hospital," and a claim for damages for loss of enjoyment of life. The court of appeals affirmed on the ground that awards under either of these headings of damages would be "barred as punitive under the Federal Tort Claims Act." Using a common sense reading of the concept of "punitive," however, the Supreme Court reversed. Basing its decision on "traditional common-law principles," the Court said that the damages sought by the plaintiff were "not punitive damages under the common law or the FTCA because their recoverability does not depend upon any proof that the defendant has engaged in intentional or egregious misconduct and their purpose is not to punish." *Id.* at 312.

(10) For a comprehensive symposium on punitive damages, see 56 So. Cal. L. Rev. 1-203 (1982).

NOTE ON CONSTITUTIONALITY OF PUNITIVE DAMAGES*

The argument over the use of punitive damages has now taken on constitutional dimensions. Initially addressing the issue in *Browning-Ferris Industries of Vermont, Inc. v. Kelco Disposal, Inc.,*[1] the Supreme Court rejected one constitutional attack on punitive awards, but otherwise differing opinions indicated a willingness to consider other arguments on the subject. The case at issue did not involve personal injuries, but rather arose from a dispute between firms over alleged predatory pricing and interference with contractual relations. It involved a punitive award—six million dollars—that was quite large in comparison with the compensatory damages of $51,146.

The Court, speaking through Justice Blackmun, limited its holding to the proposition that the excessive fines clause of the Eighth Amendment "does not apply to awards of punitive damages in cases between private parties."[2] Even on this proposition there was disagreement, focusing on the lessons of a history dating back beyond Magna Carta, between the majority and a separate opinion by Justice O'Connor in which Justice Stevens joined.[3] Justices O'Connor and Stevens did join the majority in agreeing that the award could not be struck down under federal common law.[4]

Although the members of the Court differed on some issues, the entire Court appeared willing to consider later arguments on the applicability of the due process clause of the Fourteenth Amendment to punitive awards. Justice Blackmun said that this "inquiry must await another day,"[5] but two separate opinions specifically manifested a willingness to take up the cudgels on that question. Justices O'Connor and Stevens, besides differing on the historical ground of the excessive fines holding, indicated that they were ready to consider due process attacks on punitive awards.[6] Moreover, Justice Bren-

---

* Adapted in part from Marshall S. Shapo, The Law of Products Liability ¶ 29.10[4][a] (4th ed. 2001 & Supp. 2005).

1. U.S. 257 (1989).
2. *Id.* at 260.
3. *See id.* at 268–73 (opinion of the Court), 287–95 (O'Connor, J., concurring and dissenting).
4. *See id.* at 277–80 (opinion of the Court), 282–83 (O'Connor, J., concurring and dissenting).
5. *Id.* at 277.
6. *Id.* at 283 (O'Connor, J., concurring and dissenting).

nan, in a brief opinion joined by Justice Marshall, expressed concern about the imposition of punitive damages "by juries guided by little more than an admonition to do
what they think is best." Justice Brennan indicated that he "would look longer and
harder at an award of punitive damages" that was based on "skeletal guidance" than on
"one situated within a range of penalties as to which responsible officials had deliber-
ated and then agreed."[7]

Most of the Supreme Court's bouts with punitive damages issues after *Browning-
Ferris*, like that case, have dealt with litigation that did not involve claims for personal
injuries.

The first of these cases, *Pacific Mutual Insurance Company v. Haslip*,[8] was an appeal
from a jury award of punitive damages against a company whose agent misappropriated
health insurance premiums that he had collected, with the result that the plaintiffs' policies lapsed. The award was for "more than 4 times the amount of compensatory damages" and "more than 200 times the out-of-pocket expenses."[9] In upholding the award,
Justice Blackmun's majority opinion emphasized that although the trial court had given
"significant discretion" to the jury, "that discretion was not unlimited." These instructions explained the nature of punitive damages and their function as punishment and
pointed out that it was not compulsory to impose them.[10]

Moreover, the decision below had followed a catalog of criteria set out by the Alabama
Supreme Court, including whether there was "a reasonable relationship between the
punitive damages award and the harm likely to result from the defendant's conduct, as
well as the harm that actually … occurred." Other elements of this catalog included the
"degree of reprehensibility" of the defendant's behavior, the profitability of the wrongful
conduct, the "financial position" of the defendant, and "all the costs of the litigation."
The Court named two mitigating factors—the imposition of criminal sanctions and
"the existence of other civil awards against the defendant for the same conduct."[11]

Since the trial court applied these standards, and the Alabama Supreme Court gave
the case "appropriate review," the Supreme Court affirmed the award. It said that while
the ratio of the punitive award to the other damages was great, it "did not lack objective
criteria."[12]

Subsequently, in *TXO Production Corp. v. Alliance Resources Corp.*,[13] the Court affirmed a ten million dollar award for slander of title that was 526 times the amount of
the $19,000 "actual damages." Despite the "dramatic disparity" in these figures, the
Court could not find the award "'grossly excessive.'" It cited the defendant's "bad faith"
and "the fact that the scheme employed … was part of a larger pattern of fraud, trickery
and deceit," and also mentioned the wealth of the defendant.[14]

The petitioner argued that it had been subjected to a "fundamentally unfair procedure," inter alia, because the trial court had told the jury it could consider "the wealth of
the perpetrator." The Court thought that this argument had not been properly presented to the state supreme court, but it did "note … that in *Haslip* we referred to the

---

7. *Id.* at 281 (Brennan, J., concurring.)
8. 499 U.S. 1 (1991).
9. *Id.* at 23.
10. *Id.* at 19.
11. *Id.* at 21–22.
12. *Id.* at 23–24.
13. 509 U.S. 443 (1993).
14. *Id.* at 462.

'financial position' of the defendant as one factor that could be taken into account in assessing punitive damages."[15]

A later decision—the first of these Supreme Court decisions dealing with a personal injury claim—dealt with a unique set of Oregon procedures, under which there was no judicial review of punitive awards. The Oregon punitive damages statute set out seven specific criteria for the guidance of juries on punitive damage awards. These factors included the likelihood of serious harm, the "profitability of the defendant's misconduct" and its duration, and "[t]he total deterrent effect of other punishment," including other punitive damage awards. The Oregon statute also required "clear and convincing evidence" of the defendant's "wanton disregard" of the safety of others.[16] However, the Supreme Court majority found that the lack of review of the size of punitive awards violated due process. Speaking for the Court, Justice Stevens stressed that "[j]udicial review of the size of punitive damage awards has been a safeguard against excessive verdicts for as long as punitive damages have been awarded."[17] He observed that "[j]ury instructions typically leave the jury with wide discretion in choosing amounts," and argued that "the presentation of evidence of a defendant's net worth creates the potential that juries will use their verdicts to express biases against big businesses, particularly those without strong local presences."[18]

Justice Ginsburg, joined by Chief Justice Rehnquist, dissented. She argued that various limitations in the Oregon law actually "channeled the jury's discretion more tightly ... than in either *Haslip* or *TXO*."[19] As she viewed it, "perhaps most important" among these were the seven criteria in the statute, which she said, together with "precise instructions detailing them," gave jurors in the case at hand "'adequate guidance' in making their award."[20] Because the state required the jury to apply these "objective criteria," Justice Ginsburg said, Oregon's "procedures are perhaps more likely to prompt rational and fair punitive damage decisions than are the *post-hoc* checks" of the kind used in the *Haslip* model.[21]

The Supreme Court then extended its search for limiting principles. Its 1996 decision in the quasi-products liability case of *BMW of North America v. Gore*[22] seized, literally, on the sympathetic vehicle of a $2,000,000 punitive award, reduced on remittitur from $4,000,000, in a case where the jury had found compensatory damages of $4,000. At issue was BMW's repainting of a car that had suffered minor damage during manufacture or transportation without advising the dealer that there had been any repairs to the vehicle. In reversing the punitive award, Justice Stevens said that "[p]erhaps the most important indicium of a punitive damages award is the degree of reprehensibility of the defendant's conduct."[23] He noted, inter alia, that the defendant's conduct had "evinced no indifference to or reckless disregard for the health and safety of others," and that there was no evidence of "deliberate false statements, acts of affirmative misconduct, or concealment of evidence of improper motive, such

---

15. *Id.* at 462–64.
16. See *Honda Motor Co. v. Oberg*, 114 Sup. Ct. 2331, 2345, 2344 (1994) (Ginsburg, J., dissenting).
17. *Id.* at 2335 (majority opinion of Stevens, J.).
18. *Id.* at 2340–41.
19. *Id.* at 2344 (Ginsburg, J., dissenting).
20. *Id.* at 2345.
21. *Id.* at 2347.
22. 116 S. Ct. 1589 (1996).
23. *Id.* at 1599.

as were present in *Haslip* and *TXO*."[24] Moreover, although Justice Stevens noted that the court had not drawn up "a simple mathematical formula" on the ratio of punitive damages to compensatory awards, he described the ratio in this case as "a breathtaking 500 to 1."[25] He also observed that the award was "substantially greater than the statutory fines available in Alabama and elsewhere for similar malfeasance," and said that there appeared to be no "judicial decision in Alabama or elsewhere indicating that application of [BMW's policy on slightly damaged vehicles] might give rise to such severe punishment."[26]

The Court followed *BMW v. Gore* with a 2001 decision that required appellate courts to "apply a *de novo* standard of review" to "district courts' determinations of the constitutionality of punitive damages awards."[27] The Court reversed a court of appeals decision that applied an "abuse of discretion" standard in reviewing a punitive award in a case involving allegations of false advertising and unfair competition. The Court stressed the comparative "institutional" advantages of appellate courts, by contrast with trial courts, in analyzing the difference between punitive awards by juries and "the civil penalties authorized or imposed in comparable cases."[28]

In a 2003 decision that focused in part on the problem of ratios, the Court overturned a $145 million punitive award, rendered in an action against an insurance company for "bad faith" and "fraud" in its handling of an automobile liability claim. One element of the Court's decision in *State Farm Mutual Insurance Co. v. Campbell*[29] arose from the concession by the plaintiffs, the defendant's insureds, that "much of the [defendant's] out-of-state conduct was lawful where it occurred."[30] Describing the plaintiffs' use of the litigation "as a platform to expose, and punish, the perceived deficiencies of State Farm's operations throughout the country,"[31] Justice Kennedy wrote for the majority that juries must be told that they "may not use evidence of out-of-state conduct to punish a defendant for action that was lawful in the jurisdiction where it occurred."[32] More fundamentally, Justice Kennedy declared that the use of such evidence violated due process because it permitted the award of punitive damages "to punish and deter conduct that bore no relation to [the plaintiffs'] harm."[33]

The Court also found constitutional deficiencies under the *Gore* guidepost concerning ratios. Although reiterating that ratios of 4-to-1 mentioned in *Gore* and its predecessor *Haslip* were "not binding," the court said that "[t]hey demonstrate what should be obvious: Single-digit multipliers are more likely to comport with due process, while still achieving the State's goals of deterrence and retribution, than awards with ratios in range of 500 to 1." Specifically with reference to the case before it, the majority said it had "no doubt that there is a presumption against an award that has a 145-to-1 ratio."[34] Also referring to the *Gore* guidepost on comparable penalties, the Court noted that "[t]he most relevant civil sanction under … state law" appeared to be a $10,000 fine for

24. *Id.* at 1599–1601.
25. *Id.* at 1602–03.
26. *Id.* at 1603.
27. *Cooper Indus., Inc. v. Leatherman Tool Group, Inc.*, 532 U.S. 424 (2001).
28. *Id.* at 440.
29. 123 S. Ct. 1513 (2003).
30. *Id.* at 1522.
31. *Id.* at 1521.
32. *Id.* at 1522–1523.
33. *Id.* at 1523.
34. *Id.* at 1524.

fraud, which it described as "an amount dwarfed" by the award at issue.[35] The Court also cited its reference in *Haslip* to an award of more than four times compensatory damages as possibly being "close to the line" of "constitutional impropriety,"[36] as well as its reference to that ratio in *Gore*.[37] The Court in *State Farm* said that "[w]hile these ratios are not binding, they are instructive" and that "[s]ingle-digit multipliers are more likely to comport with due process, while still achieving the State's goals of deterrence and retribution, than awards with ratios in range of 500 to 1."[38]

§ 9.04 Death Cases

[A] Wrongful Death Statutes

STANG v. HERTZ CORP.

New Mexico Supreme Court
81 N.M. 348, 467 P.2d 14 (1970)

TACKETT, JUSTICE. Petitioners seek a review of a decision of the Court of Appeals, which reversed the trial court in a case arising under our Wrongful Death Act, § 22-20-1 through 22-20-3, N.M.S.A., 1953 Comp. The facts … will not be detailed herein, except to state that decedent was a nun, a member of the Sisters of Charity, and had taken the simple but perpetual vow of poverty upon entering the Order. She died some fifteen days after receiving injuries in an automobile accident.

[This excerpt from the opinion deals with the question:] If there is no pecuniary injury to the statutory beneficiaries, may there be recovery for the wrongful death?

. . .

Sections 22-20-1 and 22-20-3, *supra*, of the Wrongful Death Act provide:

(§ 22-20-1)

Whenever the death of a person shall be caused by the wrongful act, neglect or default of another, although such death shall have been caused under such circumstances as amount in law to a felony, and the act, or neglect, or default, is such as would, if death had not ensued, have entitled the party injured to maintain an action and recover *damages* in respect thereof, then, and *in every such case*, the person who or the corporation which, would have been liable, if death had not ensued, shall be liable to an action for damages, notwithstanding the death of the person injured. (Emphasis added.) (§ 22-20-3)

Every such action as mentioned in section 1821 (§ 22-20-1) shall be brought by and in the name or names of the personal representative or representatives of such deceased person, and the jury in every such action may give such damages, compensatory and exemplary, as they shall deem fair and just, taking into consideration the pecuniary injury or injuries resulting from such death to the

---

35. *Id.* at 1526.
36. *Id.* at 1524 (referring to *Haslip*, 499 U.S. at 23–24).
37. *Id.* (referring to *Gore*, 517 U.S. at 581).
38. *Id.*

surviving party or parties entitled to the judgment, or any interest therein, recovered in such action, and also having regard to the mitigating or aggravating
circumstances attending such wrongful act, neglect or default. The proceeds of
any judgment obtained in any such action shall not be liable for any debt of the
deceased: Provided, he or she shall have left a husband, wife, child, father,
mother, brother, sister, or child or children of the deceased child, but shall be
distributed as follows:

> First. [Omitted is a list of priorities to be given particular family relations];
> *if there be none of the kindred hereinbefore named, then the proceeds of such judg-
> ment shall be disposed of in the manner authorized by law for the disposition of
> the personal property of deceased persons.* (Emphasis added.)

> . . . .

The term "personal representative" is used simply to designate the agency, the
trustee, or the person who may prosecute this particular character of statutory action.
Henkel v. Hood, 49 N.M. 45, 156 P.2d 790 (1945). If there be none of the kindred
named in the statute, then the proceeds of such judgment shall be disposed of in the
manner authorized by law for the disposition of the personal property of deceased
persons. Section 22-20-3, *supra*. This statute certainly contemplates that a wrongful
death action shall not fail merely because there is absent pecuniary injury to a statutory beneficiary. *Henkel v. Hood, supra; Hogsett v. Hanna*, 41 N.M. 22, 63 P.2d 540
(1936).

We find in *Henkel v. Hood, supra*, 49 N.M. at 51, 156 P.2d at 794 the following:

> Thus, the personal representative who makes a recovery under the Act, serves
> as a trustee, a "statutory trustee," for discoverable and identifiable beneficiaries
> in the line of named kinship or descent. Nevertheless, by express mandate of
> the Act, he is none the less a trustee for the state and for estate creditors where
> none of the named kin were left, or the line of descent runs out and exhausts
> itself in the fruitless search for an heir. This is rendered clear by the italicized
> language of the statute quoted, *supra*.

Defendant Firestone contends that damages for wrongful death are not recoverable if
there is no pecuniary injury to at least one statutory beneficiary. Defendant Hertz contends that, in the absence of pecuniary injury to a statutory beneficiary, there can be no
recovery of substantial damages. Thus, Hertz at least recognizes the right to sue for
wrongful death, but would limit recovery to only nominal damages. Even though authority may be found in support thereof, we do not agree with those contentions, as
§ 22-20-3, *supra*, clearly permits recovery by other than a statutory beneficiary, and recovery may be had even though there is no pecuniary injury to a statutory beneficiary.
Damages are recoverable by proof of the worth of the life of the decedent, even though
there is no kin to receive the award. *Cerrillos Coal Railroad Company v. Deserant*. . . .

Justice Hudspeth, in a well-reasoned opinion in *Hogsett v. Hanna, supra*, discussed in
detail the statute under consideration here and arrived at the conclusion that a right of
action under the Wrongful Death Act is not dependent or conditioned upon the survival of any kindred. The statute, § 22-20-1, *supra*, allows a cause of action against the
culpable party "in every such case." With this we agree.

The statutes allowing damages for wrongful act or neglect causing death have for
their purpose more than compensation. It is intended by them, also, to promote safety
of life and limb by making negligence that causes death costly to the wrongdoer. . . .

The statute must be considered so that no word and no part thereof is rendered surplusage or superfluous.... To hold that pecuniary injury " ... to the surviving party or parties entitled to the judgment ..." is a prerequisite to a recovery of damages for wrongful death would make superfluous the provision of the statute allowing recovery where there is no surviving kin. Section 22-20-3, *supra*....

Stuart M. Speiser and James E. Rooks, Jr., *Recovery for Wrongful Death* §§ 1.1–1.2 (4th ed. 2005)*

...

The so-called common law "rule" denying a right of recovery for the death of a human killed by the negligence or any other wrongful act of another derives from a dictum of Lord Ellenborough in the case of *Baker v. Bolton*.

In this action at *nisi prius* decided in 1808, plaintiff sued the owners of a stagecoach which had overturned causing the death of his wife. In the declaration it was stated that "plaintiff had wholly lost and been deprived of the comfort, fellowship, and assistance of his said wife, and had from thence hitherto suffered and undergone great grief, vexation, and anguish of mind." Lord Ellenborough instructed the jury to consider only the loss of society and the grief suffered by plaintiff, and that damages were recoverable for these losses only from the time of the accident to the time of death, which was less than a month. He further stated that "in a civil court, the death of a human being could not be complained of as an injury." Lord Ellenborough's off-hand remarks became the basis for the so-called American common law "rule" that there could be no recovery for wrongful death in the absence of statute. Although it was historically dubious and cruelly irrational, his dictum was recited by rote, without any critical examination, by hundreds of decisions in the various courts throughout the length and breadth of the United States. It is still recited in the highest courts of the United States to this day.

...

The explanation for Lord Ellenborough's statement may be found in the early history of the law, where the attitude toward compensation for death was a good deal more humane and practical than it later became, owing to minute distinctions about when an action was or was not permissible.

In the very early days of the Anglo-Saxons, homicide in all forms was regarded as a civil offense, a private wrong. In order to prevent feuds among clannish groups and to encourage peace, what we now call "damages" for the killing of a person were payable to the deceased's relatives. Under medieval Anglo-Saxon law this punitive payment, termed "bot[,]" "wer" or "wergild" ("mans-price" or "man-payment"), was paid by the killer to the kinsmen of the decedent. At first the amount was set by a kind of arbitration, but later an established scale of payments based on the social rank of the decedent was developed.

As the social attitude toward homicide changed so did the legal and, after a transitional period, homicide was no longer viewed merely as a wrong to the decedent's survivors but rather as an offense against the state.

By the time of the Year-books (late 13th Century) the change was complete, and every homicide had become a criminal offense.

Accidental or involuntary homicides were not classed as felonies, nor was the killer subject to capital punishment, but as in the case of most felonies, the property of the defendant was forfeited to the state. Such killings were called homicides *per infortunium*, and, as Lord Hale stated, were not crimes but misfortunes.

There was no private action by the survivors of the injured party at this time partly because the homicide per infortunium involved the forfeiture of the prisoner's goods. The merger doctrine, that a tort is merged into a felony, is probably derived from this situation. As long as the defendant's goods belonged to the Crown, it would be useless to attempt to obtain them. Although the merger doctrine was eventually modified to require merely suspension of the civil action until the felon had been prosecuted under the criminal law, the question was academic because as long as felonious homicide was punishable by execution and forfeiture of property, there was no way to enforce a civil judgment.

. . .

[I]t is clear that the rule in *Baker v. Bolton* was not based on precedent or logic, and certainly not on any concern for the practical needs of a decedent's family. But the fault is not Lord Ellenborough's alone. The fault lies with those judges who have parroted and followed the rule without questioning or closely examining it.

. . .

WITTY v. AMERICAN GENERAL CAPITAL DISTRIBUTORS, INC.
Texas Supreme Court
727 S.W.2d 503 (1987)

ROBERTSON, JUSTICE.

Kimberly Witty sued American General Capital Distributors, Inc. under the Texas Wrongful Death Act, Tex.Civ.Prac. & Rem.Code Ann. § 71.002, 1985 Tex.Sess.Law Serv. 7159 (Vernon) (formerly Tex.Rev.Civ.Stat.Ann. art. 4671); the Survival Statute, Tex.Civ.Prac. & Rem.Code Ann. § 71.021, 1985 Tex.Sess.Law Serv. 7162 (Vernon) (formerly Tex.Rev.Civ.Stat.Ann. art. 5525), alleging damages for the death of her fetus; and alternatively alleging property damage as a result of the destruction of her chattel, the fetus.

The trial court held that Witty's claims were barred as a matter of law because there was no live birth. Summary judgment was granted in favor of American General. The court of appeals held that Witty had a wrongful death cause of action and reversed that part of the trial court judgment holding to the contrary....

Wrongful Death Claim

In 1971, we held that live birth was required for a child to have a cause of action for prenatal injuries. *Yandell v. Delgado*, 471 S.W.2d 569 (Tex.1971). Similarly, where there has been no live birth, the clear, unambiguous language of the Wrongful Death Act precludes recovery for the death of a fetus. The recent codification of the Wrongful Death Act provides recovery for "damages arising from an injury that causes an *individual's* death." Tex.Civ.Prac. & Rem.Code Ann. § 71.002(b) (emphasis added). Prior to the codification, the Act provided recovery of "damages on account of the injuries causing the death of any *person*." Tex.Rev.Civ.Stat.Ann. art. 4671 (Vernon Supp.1941–1985) (emphasis added). The legislature did not intend any substantive change in the Act by substituting the word "individual" for the word "person" in the recodification. Tex.Civ.Prac. & Rem.Code Ann. § 10, 1985 Tex.Sess.Law Serv. 7219 (Vernon). Furthermore, we hold that the legislature did not intend the words "individual" or "person" to be construed to include an unborn fetus.

A wrongful death cause of action is purely a creature of statute. The Texas Wrongful Death Act, similar to those of most states, was patterned after Lord Campbell's Act, The Fatal Accident Act, 9 & 10 Vict., ch. 93 § 1 (1846). *Sanchez v. Schindler*, 651 S.W.2d 249, 251 (Tex.1983). Prior to the passage of Lord Campbell's Act, there was no statutory or common law cause of action for wrongful death.

As we noted in *Sanchez*, "because the difficulties in reducing the refinements of tort law doctrines into statutory form often result in legislation which is either underinclusive or overbroad and which is frequently couched in ambiguous terms which the court must interpret, judicial decision is the best way to develop tort law." *Id.* at 252. Nevertheless, we must determine whether the legislature intended an unborn fetus to be included within our wrongful death statute. And, although our wrongful death statute is remedial in nature and must be liberally construed, we may not rewrite the statute in the guise of construing it.

We find nothing in the legislative history to demonstrate an intent that an unborn fetus be embraced within the scope of the statute. As the dissent so aptly stated in *Presley v. Newport Hospital*, 117 R.I. 177, 365 A.2d 748, 756 (1976) (Kelleher, J., dissenting), such conclusion is "in no way dependent upon whether a fetus is a person in the philosophical, theological, or scientific sense, nor is my belief based upon the Supreme Court's pronouncements in the area of abortion." Despite the fact that "we have made great strides in the field of the sciences and we have read with great respect the writings of learned philosophers and theologians, we [must] remember that such individuals cannot create a right of action at law, for this is the job of the Legislature." *Id.*

In *Yandell* we recognized that until there is a live birth, there is no cause of action for personal injuries to the fetus. Section 71.003, Tex.Civ.Prac. & Rem.Code, provides for application of the Wrongful Death Act, stating that "[t]his subchapter applies only if the individual injured would have been entitled to bring an action for the injury if he had lived." Tex.Civ.Prac. & Rem.Code § 71.003(a), 1985 Tex.Sess.Law Serv. 7160 (Vernon). The fetus has no cause of action for the injury, until subsequent live birth. Under the clear language of the statute, there is no cause of action for death where there would be no cause of action for injuries. Therefore, since there is no cause of action for injuries to a living fetus, there can be no cause of action for death of a fetus.

This court has recognized the fetus as having an existence separate from its mother. *Leal v. C.C. Pitts Sand & Gravel Co.*, 419 S.W.2d 820 (Tex.1967). In *Leal*, this court allowed a cause of action for prenatal injuries where the child was born alive. *Id.* at 822. The common law has recognized the separate existence of a fetus for purposes of inheritance. However, the universal rule, as well as the rule in Texas, is that such ability to take was contingent upon the child's subsequent live birth. *Nelson v. Galveston, H. & S.A. Ry. Co.*, 78 Tex. 621, 14 S.W. 1021 (1890); *see also Justus v. Atchison*, 19 Cal.3d 564, 139 Cal.Rptr. 97, 106, 565 P.2d 122, 131 (1977).

In view of the common law rule that the rights of a fetus were contingent upon live birth, we feel that had there been the legislative intention to create a wrongful death action for an unborn fetus, the legislature would have specifically so stated. The plaintiff has not directed our attention to any evidence of legislative intent to include an unborn fetus within the scope of our Wrongful Death Act, and we have found none.

While it is true that by a ratio of better than two to one, the majority of states have ruled in favor of permitting a wrongful death action on behalf of an unborn fetus, what the cases actually reflect is an honest difference of opinion among the state courts as to the effect to be given similar statutory provisions....

The reasons asserted by other jurisdictions, Kimberly Witty, and the dissent, for allowing the cause of action appear compelling. However, faced with the same arguments and a wrongful death statute similar to ours, the Florida Supreme Court held that, as compelling as the arguments may be, they were not at liberty to rewrite the statute. *Stern v. Miller*, 348 So.2d 303, 307 (Fla.1977). Only the legislature is so empowered. "We are confined to a determination of the legislature's intent." *Id.*

The California Supreme Court found that these same arguments "would be relevant if we were called upon to decide whether California should adopt the proposed cause of action as a matter of judge-made law; they are not persuasive when, as here, the cause of action for wrongful death in this state is a pure creature of statute." *Justus*, 139 Cal.Rptr. at 102, 565 P.2d at 127. The question presented by this case is "not a matter of evolution of the common law, but rather a question of legislative intent." *Egbert v. Wenzl*, 199 Neb. 573, 260 N.W.2d 480, 482 (1977).

We express no opinion with respect to the existence of the fetus as a person in either the philosophical or scientific sense. We hold only that we have found no evidence that the legislature intended to include a fetus within the scope of our wrongful death statute. Therefore, no cause of action may be maintained for the death of a fetus under the wrongful death statute until the right to bring such action is afforded by the legislature.

...

Destruction of Chattel

Witty's remaining contention is that the court of appeals erred in denying her cause of action for recovery of damages resulting from the destruction of her chattel, the fetus. Although we hold that an unborn fetus does not fall within the scope of the Wrongful Death Act or the Survival Statute, we hold as a matter of law, that a fetus is not relegated to the status of chattel....

We reverse that part of the court of appeals' judgment allowing a wrongful death cause of action....

KILGARLIN, J., joined by HILL, C.J. and RAY, J., dissent.

KILGARLIN, JUSTICE.

I unhesitatingly dissent, although I wish—no, fervently yearn—that it were not necessary; for with its opinion, the court has unbelievably resurrected the old common law maxim that it is more profitable for the defendant to kill than to injure. A dead fetus is now worth nothing, but one injured and later born alive may sue. *See* Prosser & Keeton, The Law of Torts, § 127 (5th ed. 1984). One would have assumed that with our belated recognition of a cause of action for prenatal injuries in *Leal v. C.C. Pitts Sand & Gravel Co.*, 419 S.W.2d 820 (Tex.1967), Texas had finally entered the age of enlightenment, albeit tardily, as the penultimate state to adopt the cause. Now, we consign ourselves to the dark ages of tort law and will again merit the dubious distinction of being one of the last states, if ever, to accept a cause of action already recognized in thirty-six jurisdictions: a wrongful death action for the death of a fetus at the hands of a negligent tortfeasor. (I might point out the ratio is actually 4-1/2 to 1, not simply "better than two to one," as the court suggests....)

In reaching its result, the court has not only misstated Texas precedent; it has abdicated our responsibility to interpret statutes — a responsibility we consistently have accepted in the past. *E.g., Yowell v. Piper Aircraft Corp.*, 703 S.W.2d 630 (Tex.1986) (loss of inheritance is a recoverable damage under the Wrongful Death Act); *Sanchez v. Schindler*, 651 S.W.2d 249 (Tex.1983) (damages for wrongful death of a child are not limited to pecuniary loss); *Leal v. C.C. Pitts Sand & Gravel Co.* (wrongful death action can be maintained by statutory beneficiaries of infant for prenatal injuries resulting in death); *Hugo, Schmeltzer & Co. v. Paiz*, 104 Tex. 563, 141 S.W. 518 (1911) (a corporation is a person within the meaning of the Wrongful Death Act); *Nelson v. Galveston, H. & S.A. Ry. Co.*, 78 Tex. 621, 14 S.W. 1021 (1890) (a fetus at the time of its father's death may recover as a Wrongful Death Act beneficiary).

Instead, the court announces a new rule regarding the interpretation of statutes. Apparently, we can no longer interpret a statute unless there is legislative history demonstrating an intent as to who is to be embraced by the statute. I am sure that constitutional scholars will view this pronouncement with sheer amazement. Of course, our new result-oriented position is directly contrary to this court's decisions in past Wrongful Death Act cases. Where did the legislature "demonstrate an intent" that loss of inheritance is a recoverable element of wrongful death damages as this court allowed in *Yowell*? Where did the legislature "demonstrate an intent" that the parents of a deceased child could recover for mental anguish and loss of society and companionship in a wrongful death case as this court mandated in *Sanchez*? Where did the legislature "demonstrate an intent" that prenatal injuries resulting in death were actionable under the Wrongful Death Act as this court determined in *Leal*? Where did the legislature "demonstrate an intent" that under the Wrongful Death Act a corporation is a person as this court decided in *Paiz*? Where did the legislature "demonstrate an intent" that a fetus was a surviving child under the Wrongful Death Act as this court concluded in *Nelson*?

The circularity of the court's rule is further manifested by the failure of the court to point to any evidence that the legislature demonstrated an intent that the words "individual" or "person" do *not* include a fetus. Yet, the court, without any reasoning, discussion or analysis, proclaims its holding that the legislature did not intend an unborn fetus to be an "individual" or "person."

...

The arguments the court uses as further support for its holding, when reduced to raw essential, are: (1) a conclusion, based solely on the premise that because inheritance rights were conditioned on live birth, the universal common law rule was that all rights of a fetus were contingent upon live birth, and (2) no manifestation of legislative intent, for if the legislature had intended fetuses to be covered, it would have said so.

Let us first address the common law, for in arguing that the legislature did not intend fetuses to be covered by the Wrongful Death Act, the court asserts that the common law rule was "the rights of a fetus were contingent upon live birth." From this the court deduces "had there been the legislative intention to create a wrongful death action for an unborn fetus, the legislature would have specifically so stated." ...

It is more than arguable that the common law did not limit rights of fetuses to those born alive. Sir William Blackstone, writing at about the time of the American Revolution "Of the Rights of Persons," said:

> Life ... begins in contemplation of law a[s] soon as an infant is able to stir in the mother's womb. For if a woman is quick with child ... [and] if anyone beat her, whereby the child dieth in her body, and she is delivered of a dead child; this though not murder, was by the antient law homicide or manslaughter.

1 W. Blackstone, Commentaries 129. Blackstone continued:

> An infant *in ventre sa mere*, or in the mother's womb, is supposed in law to be born for many purposes. It is capable of having a legacy, or a surrender of a copyhold estate made to it. It may have a guardian assigned to it; and it is enabled to have an estate limited to it's [sic] use, and to take afterwards by such limitation, as if it were then actually born.

Id. at 130.

It is difficult to fathom how "something" which could be the victim of a homicide or manslaughter is not a person at common law. It likewise defies comprehension how "something" which could be recognized as the object of legal estates or have a guardian could not be a person in the eyes of the common law.[1] The irony of this entire discussion of the common law as it relates to the Wrongful Death Act is that the Texas Supreme Court, almost one hundred years ago, performed a similar exercise. Its conclusion, in *Nelson v. Galveston, H. & S.A. Ry. Co.*, was that under the common law a fetus was sufficiently a person to warrant the fetus being considered a surviving child under the language pertaining to statutory beneficiaries of Texas' Wrongful Death Act. The court would have us believe that *Nelson* stands for the proposition that for purposes of inheritance, the ability of a fetus to take by devise or descent is dependent upon its being born alive. The court would do well to reread *Nelson* to ascertain what it really holds. I might also add that the court, in *Nelson*, did not wander off into the realm of interpreting legislative intent to determine that a fetus was a Wrongful Death Act beneficiary.

. . .

The "live birth" requirement advanced by the court perpetuates an inequity, which the court recognizes, yet dismisses. The illogic of this distinction is amply illustrated by a comparison of *Yandell* and this case. In *Yandell*, the fetus was injured prior to its viability, yet because it was born alive, an action could be maintained for the injuries the child sustained *in utero*. 471 S.W.2d at 570. In our case, the fetus was not born alive, but was fatally injured after viability. Thus, because Mrs. Witty's fetus died before birth, American General, by today's decision, is protected, while the *Yandell* defendant, where the injured infant lived, was exposed to liability. This is clearly inequitable.

Another example of the inequity caused by this distinction is illustrated by the oft-cited Ohio appellate court's hypothetical of the two twins who suffer simultaneous prenatal injuries, and one dies moments prior to birth and the other dies moments after birth. *See Stidam v. Ashmore*, 109 Ohio App. 431, 434, 167 N.E.2d 106, 108

---

1. The court leaves us in a vacuum as how to identify a fetus. We are told it is not a chattel; but, it has an existence separate from its mother; and, it may be philosophically or scientifically a "person," though not legally one.

(1959). Both situations involve nearly identical problems relating to proof of damages and proof of causation; yet, under the rule announced by the court, recovery is allowed for the latter twin, but the live birth requirement would bar recovery for the first twin.

In addition to the obvious inequities, a brief review of the development of the "live birth" requirement shows that it is outdated....

Currently, thirty-five states and the District of Columbia allow wrongful death actions to be brought on behalf of stillborn, viable fetuses. Only eight states do not yet allow this type of recovery. The remaining jurisdictions have not passed on the question.

Furthermore, while problems concerning proof of causation and damages may have been a legitimate concern in 1884, existing medical technology should be able to meet these challenges raised by this cause of action. Neither legal logic nor medical fact supports imposing the live birth requirement in wrongful death suits for prenatal injuries.

"The entire history of the development of tort law shows a continuous tendency to recognize as worthy of legal protection interests which previously were not protected at all." RESTATEMENT (SECOND) OF TORTS § 1 comment e (1965). This case presents us with an opportunity to be consistent with that history by defining "individual" under the Wrongful Death Act to include a fetus. In the absence of *any* legislative intent, it is our constitutional duty to interpret the statute in a manner to prevent inequity. The court has instead chosen to abdicate its role and has announced a rule of law which allows tortfeasors to deprive parents the right to recover for the death of their unborn children. I cannot and will not concur in such a result. I would hold that under our Wrongful Death Act, parents are entitled to assert a cause of action for death of the unborn.

HILL, C.J., and RAY, J., join in this dissenting opinion.

NOTES

(1) Does it seem appropriate that actions for wrongful death should be brought in the name of the personal representative of the deceased person, as provided in the New Mexico statute in *Stang*, rather than that of the statutory beneficiaries?

(2) The *Witty* case raises the question of what the "death of a person" is. For analytical convenience, one may divide the problem into four basic situations:

(a) Injury to a viable fetus who is born alive, suffering consequences of the injury which later prove fatal.

(b) Injury to a viable fetus who is stillborn because of the injury.

(c) Injury to a pre-viable fetus who is born alive, suffering consequences of the injury that are ultimately fatal.

(d) Injury to a pre-viable fetus who is stillborn because of the injury.

It is interesting to consider the difficult frontier in the fourth category, that of the stillborn pre-viable fetus, using as a reference point a case in the third category, that of the pre-viable fetus that survives. Could one persuasively argue that a negligent person should have to compensate for a miscarriage in the first three or four months?

A Pennsylvania decision holds that an eight-week fetus is beyond the limits of a judge-created action, in a case in which the mother was injured in a vehicle accident and had an abortion because of apprehension about possible injuries to the fetus from the crash or from subsequent medical treatment. *Coveleski v. Bubnis*, 535 Pa. 166, 634

A.2d 608 (1993). The court noted that, absent statutory provisions giving a cause of action, no jurisdiction gave recovery for the death of an eight-week fetus not born alive.

But there is legislative provision for such claims. See, e.g, ILL. REV. STAT. ch. 140, § 1180/2.2, which declares that "[t]he state of gestation or development of a human being when an injury is caused, or when an injury takes effect, or at death, shall not foreclose maintenance of any cause of action ... arising from the death of a human being caused by wrongful act, neglect or default." The statute specifies that there is no cause of action against doctors or medical institutions for wrongful death of a fetus caused by a lawful, consented abortion.

(3) Could a cause of action be based on a stillbirth—or a miscarriage—attributable to negligent conduct that caused destructive radiation of the reproductive organs of a parent? Is there a significant distinction between either of these cases and that of the child who is born with serious deformities because of irradiation? Or the case of birth defects attributable to a fertility pill that the mother was taking?

These questions suggest the further inquiry of what basis exists for awarding death damages that are not based on such quantifiable elements as loss of financial support and medical expenses.

(4) A question that goes to the nature of the wrongful death statute is whether a wrongful death action may be brought by the survivors of an injury victim who, while he was alive, recovered a judgment for his injuries. In an Illinois case, a patient who suffered injuries from a drug overdose recovered a substantial judgment against a hospital. After he died, family members sued for wrongful death. The Illinois Supreme Court rejected the action, characterizing the majority rule as that "an action for personal injuries brought during the decedent's lifetime will preclude a subsequent action for wrongful death premised on the same conduct." *Inter alia*, the court rationalized its decision on the grounds that to hold otherwise would "discourage settlements in cases involving serious personal injuries," because "defendants seeking to avoid the burden of successive actions would be reluctant to conclude those claims prior to the injured person's death." *Varelis v. Northwestern Mem'l Hosp.*, 167 Ill.2d 449, 460, 463, 657 N.E.2d 997, 1002, 1004 (1995).

(5) Assuming that the doctrine of interspousal immunity has been eliminated, should a husband be permitted to maintain a wrongful death suit against his wife for the abortion death of a fetus?

(6) In a famous decision, the Supreme Court held that in the first trimester of pregnancy, state criminal laws must leave the abortion decision "to the medical judgment of the pregnant woman's attending physician." Thereafter, until viability, the state may regulate only such details as licensure and qualifications of persons and facilities involved in abortion procedures in a way reasonably related to the preservation and protection of maternal health. *See Roe v. Wade*, 410 U.S. 113 (1973). Could you square this decision with a tort award for pre-viability injuries to a child who is born alive?

The Mississippi Supreme Court abjured the viability/nonviability distinction as "arbitary" in *66 Fed. Credit Union v. Tucker*, 853 So. 2d 104, 114 (Miss. 2003). In a case involving a miscarriage of a fetus that was approximately 19 weeks old, the court used as the standard for the language "any person" in its wrongful death statute the terms of a criminal statute that makes it manslaughter to kill "an unborn quick child," with the definition of "quick child" as "one that has developed so that it moves within the mother's womb." *Id.* at 110, 112, 114. The court said the issue of "whether a child is 'quick' in the womb" would be a question of fact for the jury. An overall rationale for the holding lay in the court's declaration that "[w]hen a family loses a potential member because of tortious conduct of another, it suffers an injury of the same order as when it loses an existing member." *Id.* at 107. How does this language line up with the decision in *Roe v. Wade*?

(7) What is the principal goal the law seeks in valuing damages awarded for death? Should damages depend primarily on the defendant's level of culpability, rather than his luck in colliding with a rich or poor plaintiff?

What is the best social solution to the financial hardships attributable to culpably caused deaths? Would it be better to leave the amelioration of those hardships entirely to the social security system, rather than providing a tort action for them? What about making the sole remedy for such losses a no-fault scheme based on first-party insurance for motoring or other activities?

LOWE v. UNITED STATES

United States District Court, Western District of Arkansas
662 F. Supp. 1089 (1987)

[This case arose out of the explosion of a factory. The excerpts below deal with wrongful death actions by administrators of two people who died as a result of the explosion.]

The term "pecuniary injuries" in a wrongful death action refers to the present value of benefits, including money, goods and services which the deceased would have contributed to the claimed beneficiaries had she lived. *Martin v. United States*, 448 F.Supp. 855 (1977), *affirmed in part and remanded in part*, 586 F.2d 1206 (1978). Various factors are to be considered in reaching a determination of pecuniary injuries, including:

(1) What she customarily contributed in the past and what she might reasonably have been expected to contribute had she lived;

(2) The period during which any beneficiary might reasonably expect to have received contributions from the deceased;

(3) What the deceased earned and what she might reasonably have been expected to earn in the future;

(4) What she spent for customary personal expenses and other deductions;

(5) What instruction, moral training, and supervision of education she might reasonably have given the children had she lived;

(6) Her health;

(7) Her habits of industry, sobriety, and thrift;

(8) Her occupation;

(9) The life expectancy of the deceased and of the spouse; and

(10) The time which will elapse before each child reaches majority.

See: Id. at 876.

The Arkansas Supreme Court has distilled some thirteen factors which are utilized in evaluating awards for mental anguish in wrongful death cases. The factors are:

(1) The duration and intimacy of their relationship and the ties of affection between the decedent and the survivor;

(2) Frequency of association and communication between an adult survivor and an adult decedent;

(3) The attitude of the decedent toward the survivor and of the survivor toward the decedent;

(4) The duration and intensity of the sorrow;

(5) Maturity or immaturity of the survivor;

(6) The violence or suddenness of the death;

(7) Sleeplessness or troubled sleep over an extended period;

(8) Obvious extreme or unusual nervous reaction to the death;

(9) Crying spells over an extended period of time;

(10) Adverse effect on survivor's work or school;

(11) Change of personality of the survivor;

(12) Loss of weight by survivor or other physical symptoms; and

(13) Age and life expectancy of the decedent.

See: *Martin v. Rieger*, 289 Ark. 292, 711 S.W.2d 776 (1986); cited in *Kelley v. Wiggins, Administrator*, 291 Ark. 280, 724 S.W.2d 443 (1987). Of course, such mental anguish must be real and with cause and be more than the normal grief occasioned by the loss of a loved one.... The Court notes from the outset of its consideration of the death cases that a primary factor existing in each case is the suddenness and violent nature of the deaths.

...

KELLY ESTATE

In the *Kelly* case, Willie D. Kelly, the surviving spouse and administrator of the estate of Shirley Kelly, seeks to recover for pecuniary injuries, conscious pain and suffering, mental anguish and "other damages" resulting from her death. Also, claims for mental anguish are made by her four children, her mother, Ruby Jones, a sister, Dorothy Jones, and a brother, Terry Jones. Mrs. Kelly was admitted to Ouachita Hospital in critical condition with third degree burns over 95% of her body. She remained alive in such condition for some 32 hours.

The evidence adduced at trial proves that the funeral expenses totaled $1,505.00. Mrs. Kelly's medical expenses totaled $1,296.00. The government concedes that these sums are correct and appropriate for payment. In regard to lost earning capacity, expert testimony was presented that the total of such damage is $243,726.00. The government concedes that this figure is correct according to regular methods of calculation. She was 29 years old at her death and had an expected work life of 21.5 years. She was earning $2.94 per hour at her death, working 40 hours per week.

As regarding loss of household services, Ronald Murphy testified that Mrs. Kelly would have performed an average of 37.5 hours per week of household services up to the time the youngest of the four children reached age 18. Thereafter, she would have performed an average of 29.5 hours per week of such services. Based upon this data, Dr. Bettinger, plaintiffs' expert witness, calculated that the loss of household services totals $193,827.00. The government concedes that this total is a reasonable amount. Therefore, such sum should be awarded to the estate.

As noted above, Mrs. Kelly survived the explosion and resulting injuries for some 32 hours. During this time she was in and out of consciousness. Also, she was under the influence of various pain medications. Although there is no evidence concerning the precise hours of consciousness/unconsciousness, the Court is of the opinion that a reasonable sum should be awarded for conscious pain and suffering. The testimony supports a finding that she did in fact experience pain and discomfort in her parting hours in the hospital. The nature and severity of the injuries alone support a conclusion that she was not without pain and suffering. Her facial features were burned almost beyond any recognition. Mr. Kelly testified that the nurses administered regular injections of pain medication to ease Shirley's pain. He related outbursts of screams and moans. Under these circumstances the Court concludes that the estate should be awarded $50,000.00 for conscious pain and suffering.

Mr. Kelly claims damages for mental anguish and loss of services and companionship. Mr. Kelly has not remarried since the loss of his wife of almost nine years. They shared a loving husband-wife relationship. He was home at the time of the explosion. He testified that he felt the earth tremble. Soon thereafter, his mother-in-law, Ruby Jones, informed him of the explosion at M-35 and that Shirley had been injured. At that time he was not aware of the severity of the injuries.

He proceeded to the hospital where he was allowed to enter the room in which Shirley was being treated. He testified that she was burned beyond recognition. He testified that she had no hair and that her nose and one ear had been burned off. Her body was covered with glass, cement and brick debris. He stated that he could only remain in her room for twenty minutes. He remained at the hospital throughout her struggle with death.

Following her death, Mr. Kelly suffered severe emptiness resulting from the loss of his wife. This emptiness acutely manifested itself on the special occasions such as Christmas and Mother's Day. His testimony recounted many sleepless nights. On those nights in which sleep did come, his dreams became nightmares. Also, Mr. Kelly testified that he lost some thirty pounds as result of the loss of his wife.

With regard to the claim for mental anguish and loss of marital companionship, services and society by Willie Kelly, the surviving spouse, the Court finds that, in consideration of the factors outlined by the Arkansas Supreme Court, an award of damages in the sum of $100,000.00 is appropriate under the facts of this case.

At the time of the explosion, Mrs. Kelly was survived by four daughters, Sharon Kelly, age seven, Janice Kelly, age five, Diane Kelly, age three, and Sandra Kelly, age 11 months. Sharon Kelly testified that her father picked her up from school the day of the explosion and informed her that her mother was seriously injured. Her father left her with her grandmother, Ruby Jones, where she remained while he returned to the hospital. Although she recalled the incident and the funeral, she had little or no understanding of the nature of her mother's condition. She recalled crying at the funeral but stated that she was not effected seriously by the loss of her mother, other than "missing her." Considering her age and experiences in life at that point, she could not have been expected to react in the same way as a more mature individual would have reacted. Each of the other daughters testified as having no recollection of their mother or the explosion.

Based upon the facts herein, the Court is of the opinion that the daughters did not experience mental anguish for which recovery is warranted. However, each of the daughters have and will continue to suffer the loss of parental guidance which their mother would have provided. Based upon the facts of the case, the Court finds that Sharon Kelly should recover the amount of $75,000.00, Janice Kelly should recover

$80,000.00, Diane Kelly should recover $90,000.00, and Sandra Kelly, who will be deprived of her mother's guidance for virtually her entire life, should recover $100,000.00 for her loss.

Shirley Kelly's mother, Ruby Jones, lived next door to her daughter in the same housing project. Mrs. Jones served her daughter as babysitter while Shirley worked at Celesco. Mrs. Jones and her daughter enjoyed closer than the normal mother/daughter relationship. The close proximity of their respective abodes allowed frequent visits and outings together, in addition to Mrs. Jones' babysitting.

Mrs. Jones was at the hospital soon after Shirley was admitted. She did not initially enter Shirley's room due to her own health. However, she later went into the room. She did not remain there for a substantial period. Mrs. Jones was unable to endure the suffering of her daughter. Mrs. Jones testified that she "just went out" when Shirley died. She related her subsequent medical treatment which was required, including hospitalization. She stated that she lost eighteen pounds thereafter.

Based upon these facts the Court concludes that Ruby Jones has suffered more than the normal grief in the loss of her daughter. Thus, she is entitled to recover for her mental anguish. Upon careful consideration, the Court concludes that an award of $50,000.00 is warranted for such mental anguish.

Since Shirley's death, Mrs. Jones and Shirley's sister, Dorothy Jones, have taken the responsibility for caring for the day-to-day needs of Shirley's four children. Mrs. Jones and Dorothy have sacrificed the past eleven years of their lives for the proper care and training of the children. This is not to imply that Willie Kelly has been less than a father. Willie Kelly provides monetary support for and takes an active part in the lives of his children. However, Ruby Jones and Dorothy Jones have assumed the primary roles of parenthood. Dorothy has never married.

Dorothy was also an employee of Celesco at the time of the explosion. However, she chose not to report to work that fatal day because of the weather conditions. The testimony revealed that because of fiscal needs of the family Shirley was compelled to work. After the explosion and the loss of her sister, Dorothy terminated her employment with Celesco. Her decision was based upon a combination of the memories of her sister, Shirley's painful death and the horror of the facility with its life threatening potential.

Based upon the foregoing the Court finds that Dorothy Jones suffered more than the normal grief associated with the loss of a loved one. Therefore, an award of damages to her for mental anguish is appropriate. The Court concludes that an award of $25,000.00 to Dorothy Jones is warranted.

Shirley Jones was also survived by a brother, Terry Jones. Mr. Jones also lived near Shirley and Willie in the housing project. Mr. Jones was a frequent visitor in the Kelly home and he was in contact with Shirley at least one time per day. Mr. Jones was allowed to see Shirley in the hospital before her death. The sight of her injuries unsettled Mr. Jones. He was unable to return to the hospital thereafter. Mr. Jones testified that he attempted to be strong for the sake of his mother.

Mr. Jones had also been an employee of Celesco prior to the explosion. Like Dorothy Jones, he quit his job at Celesco after the explosion. Thereafter, he enrolled in the Oil Belt Vocational-Technical School in El Dorado. Although portions of his testimony on cross examination could be construed as an admission that he suffered no more than normal grief, the Court is convinced that Mr. Jones suffered that degree of mental and emotional suffering which entitles him to recover for mental anguish under the wrongful death statutes. Therefore, the Court concludes that Terry Jones is entitled to recover the sum of $5,000.00 for his mental anguish.

Therefore, Judgment should be entered for the Estate of Shirley Kelly in the amount of $1,125,427.80.

WALKER ESTATE

Gertie Mitchell, daughter of Eliza Walker and Administratrix in Succession to the Estate of Eliza Walker, deceased, seeks to recover damages from the United States for funeral expenses, lost earnings, mental anguish and lost services.

Mrs. Mitchell was a Registered Nurse employed at Ouachita Hospital at the time of the explosion. However, she was off duty at the time of the explosion. Upon learning of the accident and of her mother's involvement therein, she proceeded to the hospital. Mrs. Mitchell was met by her supervisor who carried her to the room to which her mother's body had been removed. Mrs. Mitchell testified that, except for her mother's unique gold tooth, she would not have been able to identify the body as being that of her mother. Much like the other victims of this explosion, Mrs. Walker had sustained third degree burns to 95% of her body.[6]

The estate incurred a funeral expense of $911.25. There was no medical expense. The estate, by and through Mrs. Mitchell, is entitled to recover that sum.

At the time of her death, Mrs. Walker was 57 years of age. Her life expectancy was 19 years. Her work life expectancy was 5.3 years. Dr. Bettinger testified that her lost earning capacity totaled $38,446.00. The government concedes that this sum is reasonable and accurate.

Mrs. Mitchell seeks to recover for lost services, in the form of babysitting services[7] which her mother would have provided had she survived. Mr. Murphy calculated that

---

6. At trial Mrs. Mitchell attempted to establish that her mother had survived the explosion for some two to two and one-half hours. She based her opinion upon the fact that an X-ray was taken of her mother's skull upon arrival at the hospital. Plaintiff's Exhibit 6 reflects that Mrs. Walker entered Ouachita Hospital at 2:00 p.m. This exhibit reflects that she was pronounced dead at 2:25 p.m. The second page of Exhibit 6, an X-ray examination report, is clearly marked "D.O.A."

The lapse of time between admission and pronouncement is reconciled by consideration of all the surrounding circumstances. There was utter chaos resulting from the explosion. The normally quiet emergency ward at Ouachita Hospital became filled with many burned, lacerated, and broken bodies. The ambulances screamed to and from Celesco in an attempt to save the lives of those imperiled by the horrendous disaster. The urgency of each person's condition required that the doctors and medical staff on duty make instant decisions for the course of emergency care.

In making these decisions, the medical personnel would have been required to assess the condition of the patient initially. In the case of Mrs. Walker, more likely than not it was instantly determined that she was deceased. Upon making such decision the medical staff simply moved to the next victim. Such action was mandated by the circumstances. If other lives were to be saved, time was of the most essence. There was no time for delay. This best explains the time lag between arrival and pronouncement.

Even if she had been alive from a strict medical point of view, the Court finds that there is no evidence that she was conscious at any time from the explosion until her death. The plaintiff must show that there was conscious pain and suffering in order to recover under this element of damages. This burden has not been met. The Court will not infer pain and suffering under the circumstances herein. The evidence and record as a whole strongly supports a finding that Mrs. Mitchell died instantaneously in the explosion. Therefore, no award for conscious pain and suffering is made.

7. The 1976–1980 services claimed are broken down into 24 hours per week for babysitting, 1.5 hour for chauffering, and the remaining 7.5 hours were devoted to cooking, cleaning, dishwashing and washing. The post-1980 services are broken down as 12 hours babysitting, 1.5 hours chauffer-

Mrs. Walker would have provided some 33 hours per week in babysitting services through the year 1980. Thereafter, the number of hours would have been reduced to 21 hours per week for the next five years up to the time Mrs. Mitchell's youngest child reached the age of 18.

The government challenges not the propriety of this type of recovery but, rather, the number of hours claimed. In support of its challenge, the government cites the physical condition of Oscar Walker, who was totally disabled and completely dependent upon his wife. Mr. Walker would have required extra care and comfort in his condition. The additional requirement would have cut significantly into the time claimed for babysitting.

Also, the government contends that, as the children progressed in age, the older children would have assumed more of the duties previously assigned to Mrs. Walker. Finally, the government asserts that the youngest child would not have required a babysitter up to his eighteenth birthday. The Court concludes that the government's challenge on these two bases is well taken and justified under the circumstances.

The Court has reviewed the suggested hours and the objections of the government. From that review, the Court finds that while an award for such lost services is appropriate, a reduction of the hours is warranted. Mrs. Walker had a substantial obligation to her disabled husband in addition to her normal homemaking duties. She worked a full 40 hour week at Celesco, plus time for travel to and from the workplace. Undoubtedly she reserved a small amount of time for her own personal needs, the least of which would be the basic necessities of life. To mount atop of these daily duties the added burden of these claimed babysitting hours would not be a reasonable finding.

Under the circumstances of the case, the Court concludes that a reduction by 50% of the hours, both 1976–1980 and post-1980, is reasonable and necessary. The amount claimed for lost services presented by Dr. Bettinger's testimony is $61,570.00. Reducing that amount by 50%, Mrs. Mitchell, on behalf of the estate, is entitled to recover $30,785.00 for all services lost.

The Court has considered Mrs. Mitchell's claim for mental anguish and concludes that she did suffer more than normal grief with the passing of her mother. She and her mother enjoyed an extremely close mother-daughter relationship. Mrs. Walker was in the Mitchell home often, not only for babysitting, but also for personal purposes. While Mrs. Mitchell and her husband were stationed out of Camden during the course of Mr. Mitchell's military service, Mrs. Walker would take time off from work to go visit her daughter for a week or so at a time. Mrs. Mitchell would return to Camden during periods of time when her husband would be off base on military assignment. They shared many experiences of life together. For her mental anguish, Mrs. Mitchell is entitled to judgment in the sum of $60,000.00.

Concerning the claim of John Nolan, the brother of Mrs. Walker, the Court finds that an award for mental anguish is likewise merited. Mr. Nolan suffered more than the normal grief with the loss of his sister. They engaged in personal visits at least one time each month throughout their adult lives. Although he did not see Mrs. Walker following the accident, he testified that it was his understanding that her remains were collected in a basket at Celesco after the explosion.

---

ing, three hours cooking, two hours cleaning, 1.5 hours dishwashing, and one hour washing. The chauffering, cooking, cleaning, dishwashing, and washing figures remained constant in Mr. Murphy's chart.

Mr. Nolan testified that he suffered through numerous sleepless nights following the death of his sister. He also stated that he required some medical treatment for cardio-vascular difficulties subsequent thereto. He related that his mother had also perished in a fire prior to the Celesco incident. This may or may not have heightened his grief. For his mental anguish, the Court finds that an award of $5,000.00 is reasonable and fair.

Therefore, Judgment shall be entered contemporaneously herewith for Mrs. Gertie Mitchell as Administratrix in Succession of the Estate of Eliza Walker, deceased, in the sum of $135,242.25.

...

HUFF v. WHITE MOTOR CORPORATION
United States Court of Appeals, Seventh Circuit
609 F.2d 286 (1979)

...

TONE, CIRCUIT JUDGE.

...

II.
Excessiveness of Verdict

Because of the possibility that a new trial will not be required, we must rule on defendant's argument that the $700,000 verdict was excessive. The governing legal principles are these: The standard for reviewing the district court's refusal to set aside the verdict on the ground of excessiveness is supplied by federal law even though Indiana law supplies the rule of decision in this diversity case.... The district court's ruling is reviewable only for an abuse of discretion. *Id.* at 1199. *Grunenthal v. Long Island Rail Road*, 393 U.S. 156, 159–160, 89 S.Ct. 331, 21 L.Ed.2d 309 (1968). As stated in *Dagnello v. Long Island Rail Road*, 289 F.2d 797, 806 (2d Cir. 1961), ... we are

> not to decide whether we would have set aside the verdict if we were presiding at trial, but whether the amount is so high that it would be a denial of justice to permit it to stand. We must give the benefit of every doubt to the judgment of the trial court; but surely there must be an upper limit, and whether that has been surpassed is not a question of fact with respect to which reasonable men may differ, but a question of law.

This passage was also quoted, apparently with approval, in the *Grunenthal* case, 393 U.S. at 159, 89 S.Ct. 331, and supplemented by the following footnote:

> The standard has been variously phrased: "Common phrases are such as: 'grossly excessive,' 'inordinate,' 'shocking to the judicial conscience,' 'outrageously excessive,' 'so large as to shock the conscience of the court,' 'monstrous,' and many others." *Dagnello v. Long Island Rail Road Co., supra*, at 802.

393 U.S. at 59 n.4, 89 S.Ct. at 333 n.4.... In applying the *Dagnello* standard, we are required to make a "detailed appraisal of the evidence bearing on damages." *Grunenthal v. Long Island Rail Road*, 393 U.S. at 159, 89 S.Ct. at 333.

Huff was 51 years old when he died and had a life expectancy of 23 years and a work-life expectancy of 14.1 years. His annual earnings were between $9,800 and $9,900. He was also entitled to fringe benefits. Plaintiff's expert economist calculated the present value of Huff's lost earnings at $267,907 and fringe benefits at $60,132; subtracted the present value of the personal maintenance of Huff if he had lived out his life expectancy, $127,935; added the present value of household services over that period (using $3,000 for the first year and increasing the amount 6.84 percent annually); and arrived at a present value of Mrs. Huff's economic loss of $285,600.

The evidence on intangible elements of damages was as follows: The Huffs were high school sweethearts. He was the only man she had ever dated. They had been married for 30 years and had raised four children. The family had moved only once during the marriage. Huff had changed jobs only once. The Huffs loved each other, and she relied on him for advice in making all decisions of consequence.

In her original complaint plaintiff prayed for damages in the amount of $200,000. The complaint as ultimately amended asked for $575,000. In his closing argument, Mrs. Huff's counsel asked the jury to award $285,600 for economic loss, in accordance with the expert economist's calculation, $115,000 for the loss of decedent's counseling and guidance, and $276,000 for the loss of love and affection, for a total of $676,600. The jury awarded $700,000.

Although the economist's estimate that Mrs. Huff's economic loss amounted to $285,600 strikes us as expansive, defendant has not challenged that estimate, concentrating its attack instead on the $414,400 awarded for loss of the decedent's counseling and guidance and love and affection.[15] Nevertheless, defendant points to the disparity between Huff's earnings and the total award, as well as between the economic loss figure and the balance of the award. While at first blush these disparities may seem incongruous, it is apparent upon a moment's reflection that Mrs. Huff's loss of the non-economic intangibles should not be valued lower than a similar loss to one in more fortunate economic circumstances. Disparity between economic loss and other elements of damages is therefore not a basis for challenging the latter.

Defendant points to the cases on the issue of excessiveness of an award for wrongful death listed in 46 A.L.R.3d 680 and 733 (1972) and 47 A.L.R.3d 909 (1973) and provides us with a compendium of 1975–1978 cases on that issue. In none of them was the court even required to rule on an award comparable to the one at bar, and in some of them, all state cases, much lower awards were held to be excessive. Defendant also cites *Palace Bar, Inc. v. Fearnot*, 376 N.E.2d 1159 (Ind.App.1978), in which an award of $93,000 for the wrongful death of a 52-year-old man was held excessive, but, as noted above, we are not to apply state law in deciding this issue. Plaintiff does not cite any case in which a comparable award was ruled upon.

We must acknowledge that we would be more comfortable in deciding the amorphous question before us as we do if other courts had approved comparable awards. Also, we would not have awarded $700,000 if we had been the jury, and we might well have set aside the verdict or ordered a remittitur had we been presiding at the trial. This evaluation by us, however, does not support a reversal. *Dagnello v. Long Island Rail Road*, 289 F.2d at 806. Even though we think the verdict overgenerous, we may not disturb it unless in our judgment it can aptly be described as "grossly excessive" or "monstrous" or with similar pejorative adjectival terms. *Galard v. Johnson*, 504 F.2d at 1199–1200; *Grunenthal v. Long Island Rail Road*, 393 U.S. at 159 n.4, 89 S.Ct. 331. We cannot

---

15. These intangible elements of damages are concededly recoverable under Indiana law.

so describe an award of $414,000 for loss of a husband's love and affection and counsel and guidance in the circumstances presented by this case. Therefore, although we are left with the uncomfortable feeling that the verdict is too high, we think we would be exceeding the limits of our authority if we were to disturb it.

...

NOTES

(1) While a cautious decisionmaker would be wary about trying to judge the quality of personal relationships, that sort of judgment becomes necessary whenever damages rules permit an assessment of affective factors. If those factors are proper elements of damage assessment in wrongful death, would it then be logical to deny a father's claim for "companionship, love and affection" when there was evidence of a severe estrangement between him and a son who died in a negligently caused accident? This is one effect of the decision in *Vulk v. Haley*, 112 Idaho 855, 736 P.2d 1309 (1987), which allowed the testimony of witnesses about statements of the decedent about his relationship with his father. Bolstering the jury's denial of damages to the father was proof that while the boy was in foster care, his father never contacted him and did not provide financial support.

(2) The Arizona Supreme Court has extended recovery for consortium to parents suing for the death of an adult child. The following passage captures several of the court's reasons:

> It is irrelevant that parents are not entitled to the services of their adult children; they continue to enjoy a legitimate and protectible expectation of consortium beyond majority arising from the very bonds of the family relationship. Surely nature recoils from the suggestion that the society, companionship and love which compose filial consortium automatically fade upon emancipation; while common sense and experience teach that the elements of consortium can never be commanded against a child's will at any age. The filial relationship, admittedly intangible, is ill-defined by reference to the ages of the parties and ill-served by arbitrary age distinctions. Some filial relationships will be blessed with mutual caring and love from infancy through death while others will always be bereft of those qualities. Therefore, to suggest as a matter of law that compensable consortium begins at birth and ends at age eighteen is illogical and inconsistent with common sense and experience. Human relationships cannot and should not be so neatly boxed. "The law does not fly in the face of nature, but rather acts in harmony with it." *Harper v. Tipple*, 21 Ariz. 41, 44, 184 P. 1005, 1006 (1919)(citation omitted).

—*Frank v. Superior Court*, 150 Ariz. 228, 722 P.2d 95 (1986).

(3) What are the principal arguments against extending consortium to adult children? Is it persuasive to contend that this extension of liability will produce more litigation and drive up insurance costs?

(4) Consider more generally the strength of the case for awarding consortium for the death of children. Isn't it appropriate to argue that for these purposes, the family should be treated as a unit? Even though survival damages theoretically are different from wrongful death damages, since they go to the administrator of the decedent's estate, why aren't they enough, assuming that the funeral expenses are covered?

[B] Survival Statutes; Contributory Negligence in Death Cases

TEXAS SURVIVAL STATUTE

Tex. Code Ann. (1986)

§ 71.021. Survival of Cause of Action

(a) A cause of action for personal injury to the health, reputation, or person of an injured person does not abate because of the death of the injured person or because of the death of a person liable for the injury.

(b) A personal injury action survives to and in favor of the heirs, legal representatives, and estate of the injured person. The action survives against the liable person and the person's legal representatives.

(c) The suit may be instituted and prosecuted as if the liable person were alive.

PROBLEM

Mr. and Mrs. X have two grown sons, X-1 and X-2. X-1 is married, to Ms. X-1, and X-2 is a bachelor. One day they all go to the funeral of Uncle Y, Mr. X's brother, beloved of the entire family. X-1 is driving. On the way back from the burial, all are seriously injured in an intersection collision between X-1's car and an auto driven by Mr. Z, arguably caused only by Mr. Z's negligence. Mr. X dies in great agony on the way to the hospital. Mrs. X, obviously in terrible pain after the accident, expires in the emergency room. X-2 lingers for a month and then succumbs. X-1 has survived but is permanently disabled, unable to hold a full-time job or to help with household chores. What possible causes of action, under a combination of the Texas "survival" statute set out above and the New Mexico Wrongful Death Act quoted in the *Stang* case, supra § 9.04[A]?

What if X-1 were contributorily negligent?

MITCHELL v. AKERS

Texas Court of Civil Appeals
401 S.W.2d 907 (1966)

DIXON, CHIEF JUSTICE. Appellees Milton Akers and wife Helen Akers filed suit against appellant John T. Mitchell for damages arising out of the drowning of their son, Philip Akers, aged three years and eight months, in appellant's private swimming pool located on appellant's property. Appellees' action was brought as parents in their own behalf pursuant to Art. 4671, Vernon's Ann. Civ. Statutes, and also as sole heirs in behalf of the child's estate pursuant to Art. 5525, V.A.C.S. [the predecessor to Tex. Code Ann. 71.021 above].

The two actions are quite different. Under the common law no recovery of damages was permitted for the death of a person. Such a right was conferred on a surviving husband, wife, child and parents of a deceased by the passage of Art. 4671, *et seq.*, V.A.C.S. It is to be regarded as a new cause of action purely statutory in nature.

On the other hand an action under Art. 5525, *et seq.*, V.A.C.S. is not a new cause of action. The statute provides for the survival of a common law action for damages which was instituted or could have been instituted by a person who sustains injuries later resulting in death. The cause of action may be asserted by the heirs or the administrator of the deceased in behalf of the estate of the deceased....

The contributory negligence of the deceased will defeat recovery under either of the two statutes. But that is a matter which need not concern us here, for the deceased, being a child only three years and eight months of age, as a matter of law cannot be held to have been contributorily negligent....

However, a jury found contributory negligence and proximate cause in answering issues as to whether the mother had failed to keep a proper lookout for the safety of the little boy. These findings are a bar to the recovery by the parents of damages sustained by them as parents as a result of the child's death, which damages they sought under the provisions of Art. 4671, V.A.C.S....

... But does the contributory negligence of the parents also bar a recovery of damages for funeral and burial expenses and for the pain and mental anguish of the deceased when the suit is brought in behalf of the estate of the deceased pursuant to Art. 5525, V.A.C.S. by the parents as the only heirs of the deceased? We have concluded that the question must be answered in favor of the parents as heirs.

An administration of the estate of the child has not been necessary. Appellees are the only heirs of the child. Ordinarily the administrator or the heirs of a person who has sustained injuries resulting in death may recover damages in behalf of the estate of the deceased if the deceased himself could have recovered damages had he survived. Funeral and burial expenses are recoverable by the administrator or heirs in such suit.... So are damages for physical pain and mental anguish endured by deceased preceding his death.

Appellees in answer to appellant's contention point out that the negligence of the parents will not be imputed to a minor child in a suit by the child for injuries sustained by the child. Therefore, reason appellees, the negligence of the parents cannot defeat a recovery of damages by the child's estate in a suit brought after the death of the child by the heirs.

Subsection (d) of Section 41 of the Texas Probate Code, V.A.C.S., contains two provisions which we shall discuss: (1) No conviction shall work corruption of blood or forfeiture except in the case of a beneficiary in a life insurance policy or contract who is convicted and sentenced as a principal or accomplice in willfully bringing about the death of the insured (*see also* Constitution of Texas, Art. 1, Sec. 21, Vernon's Ann.St.); and (2) "nor shall there be any forfeiture by reason of death by casualty."

Early decisions construed the constitutional provision and the statute literally and held that a willful murderer who was an heir of his victim, did not forfeit his right but would inherit his part of the property of the deceased.... However, later decisions hold that without contravening or circumventing the constitutional and statutory provisions a way is provided through equity to compel a murderer to surrender the profits of his crime and thus prevent his unjust enrichment. This result is accomplished by imposing a constructive trust on the murderer's portion of the inheritance in favor of the heirs other than the murderer.... We agree with the statement of Judge Renfro of the Fort Worth Court of Civil Appeals in the Parks case when he said, "Certainly the statutes should not be used as a vehicle to acquire property through parenticide." Such a use would be contrary to public policy.

But we have concluded that the constructive trust doctrine should not be applied in a case coming within the provisions of Subsection (d) of Article 41 of the Probate Code above quoted, which says that there shall be no forfeiture by reason of death by casualty. To hold otherwise would be to say that the Legislature intended in effect to disinherit an unfortunate heir, innocent of intent to kill, whose contributory negligence has been found to be a proximate cause of the death of a person toward whom he occupied the status of an heir.

It is common knowledge that amidst the multitude of hazards which modern living conditions have thrust upon us many accidents occur due to the inadvertent oversight or negligence of father, son, mother, daughter, grandparents, grandchildren or others. We certainly do not view negligence lightly, but it is not to be included in the same category as murder and other intentional acts where moral turpitude revolts us. It would require a miracle man, indeed, to live long in this day and age without having at one time or another committed an act of negligence. And he might well consider himself lucky if his negligence did not result in a fatality.

We know of no Texas case in point, but there are many cases arising in other jurisdictions which are in point. These jurisdictions have statutes similar to our Death Statute and our Survival Statute. The cases hold that a negligent parent, spouse, child, etc. cannot recover under a death statute if his negligence caused or contributed to cause the death; but that he can recover as heir under a survival statute....

... [A]ppellant assails the verdict awarding $5,000 for physical pain and mental anguish suffered by the child. Appellant contends that there is no evidence or there is insufficient evidence to support a finding that the child suffered physical pain and mental anguish between the time he fell into the pool and the time he lost consciousness; and that the award is excessive.

Dr. Gilbert, who arrived on the scene within a few minutes after the child was lifted from the pool, examined the child. It was his opinion that the child died of drowning after struggling for two or three minutes before losing consciousness. During said two or three minutes the child probably endured physical pain and mental anguish. The doctor saw no bruises or marks on the child which might indicate that the child may have fallen against a hard object and become unconscious before becoming immersed in the water. We do not consider that the award of $5,000 is excessive....

NOTES

(1) With which policy goals do the various contributory negligence rules announced in *Mitchell* mesh?

(a) Even assuming a decedent who was at an age at which he could make rational decisions, why should his contributory negligence be a bar to the recovery of survivors, at least under the wrongful death statute?

(b) And why should the mother's contributory negligence bar the wrongful death action by both parents, or at least by the father? To test the wisdom of this rule, ask what result should have obtained if the mother had died after the child's death but before suit, and the father alone had brought the action. Or suppose that both parents had died and a sibling had sued.

(c) On the other hand, does the theory that the survival statute cause of action is the child's make good policy sense in this case? How can it, when the mother, at least, is suing for an injury which occurred under her stewardship? What is the practical effect of *Mitchell*? Does the decision allow an award essentially for harm to a relation—and if this is the case, why should not a parent's contributory negligence bar a suit, at least by that parent?

Does *Mitchell* achieve a desirable level of deterrence?

(2) Do you find analytical distinctions that make a difference between *Mitchell* and the case in which a pregnant woman negligently trips on a defective sidewalk, causing the premature birth of a traumatized child? *See City of Louisville v. Stuckenborg*, 438 S.W.2d 94 (Ky. 1968) (reversing judgment for mother because of her contributory negligence but upholding father's judgment).

Should the parent's sex make a difference in a suit for the death of a child, in which the defendant asserts that a parent should be barred as a wrongful death beneficiary because of the parent's negligence in safeguarding the child? Consider a remark of a prominent nineteenth century jurist about the implications of a standard that would hold women to a lower standard of care than men in negligence cases. Justice Cooley pointed out that a double standard might sometimes require women to meet a higher standard than men—for example, a woman would be required to "be more vigilant and indefatigable in her care of a helpless child." *Hassenyer v. Michigan Cent. RR.*, 48 Mich. 205 (Mich. 1882), discussed in Barbara Welke, *Unreasonable Women: Gender and the Law of Accidental Injury, 1870–1920*, 19 Law & Soc. Inquiry 369, 392–93 (1994).

(3) With respect to the effects of contributory negligence of parents on a suit for a child's death, can you rationally distinguish among the types of damages allowed under the Texas survival statute, as summarized in *Mitchell*?

(4) Under a traditional wrongful death statute, a statutory beneficiary cannot recover for a decedent's pain and suffering. "The philosophy, simply stated, is that an injured person who is dead cannot benefit from an award for his pain and suffering." *Vulk v. Haley*, 112 Idaho 855, 859, 736 P.2d 1309, 1313 (1987).

As a matter of policy, do you favor a statutory scheme that specifies separate recovery for wrongful death and survival actions, as in the Texas statutes involved in *Mitchell v. Akers*? Or would you prefer a statute that allows wrongful death actions with damages that include elements of solace, but does not provide for survival actions for injuries attributable to the conduct that caused the death?

(5) Generally, the barriers to intra-family immunity are falling. Representative is *Surratt v. Thompson*, 212 Va. 191, 183 S.E.2d 20 (1971), holding that in automobile accidents, at least, the interspousal immunity rule is dead. In deciding this case, brought by the administrator of a decedent wife against her husband and the driver of another car, the court stressed that a reason previously given for family immunity—the fear that allowing intra-family suits would destroy domestic harmony—was no longer persuasive because of the "high incidence of insurance covering automobile accidents." This decision parallels another case decided the same day, *Smith v. Kauffman*, 212 Va. 181, 183 S.E.2d 190 (1971), which eliminates parental immunity in actions by children for injuries sustained in motor vehicle accidents. However, the court in that decision noted by quotation of a New Jersey case that it is "ironic that the presence of insurance," having destroyed the "family harmony" rationale for immunity, has "spawned the second rationale, *i.e.*, that of protecting the insurance carriers against fraud and collusion."

To spin out the *Mitchell* problem one yarn further, would you allow a suit by the plaintiff husband Akers against his wife—i.e., against their insurance company—for the contribution of her negligence to the death of their child?

Chapter 10

PROOF

---

§ 10.01 Sufficiency of Evidence

HORNYAK v. POMFRET SCHOOL
United States Court of Appeals, First Circuit
783 F.2d 284 (1986)

COFFIN, CIRCUIT JUDGE.

In this appeal from the granting of a directed verdict for the defendant, we marshal the following facts favorable to the plaintiff. A fifteen year old girl, while on training for position on her school's crew, after one to two and a half hours of rowing, observed and then participated in for the first time an exercise called the "Harvard Step Test". This test required that she, together with several other girls, divided equally on opposite sides, step briskly up and on a sixteen inch high bench, step back to the ground and repeat the process rapidly for two minutes. A photograph in evidence permitted the jury to conclude that the bench was placed on a somewhat uneven surface of a field.

One girl, in a group exercising just prior to plaintiff's group, lost her balance and fell backwards. The sole supervisor was the team's coach, who usually tested the step test bench for stability but had no memory of doing it on the day in question. He did not see the first girl fall and did not see plaintiff fall, since he was mainly looking at a stop watch and counting cadence. No other personnel or even other girls were standing nearby acting as "spotters" to catch or support a falling participant.

Plaintiff herself testified as follows:

Q: And could you tell the court and jury what you noticed while you were doing that test?

A: I felt an unsteadiness as in a feeling—not being solid; vibrations; general wobbling.

Q: And after 30 seconds, then what happened?

A: I fell off the bench.

From these facts, a jury could draw the reasonable inference that the bench was improperly positioned in the first place by the coach, causing an unreasonable risk of harm to a young, inexperienced, and somewhat fatigued group of step test participants. Or it could draw the equally reasonable inference that the supervision given the participants after the tests had begun was unreasonably inadequate. Or both.

As for causation, the fact that there was no direct evidence of the cause of plaintiff's fall does not bar the question of causation from jury consideration. It is of course possible that the vibrations from some five other girls jumping on the bench at the same time may have caused the fall. But, there being no other factors identified, such as ice, snow, wind, or dizziness on the part of plaintiff, it would not be unreasonable for a jury to draw the inference that the cause of plaintiff's fall was the unstable condition of the bench.... [A]s Professor Prosser has written,

> [The plaintiff] need not negative entirely the possibility that the defendant's conduct was not a cause [footnote omitted], and it is enough that he introduces evidence from which reasonable men may conclude that it is more probable that the event was caused by the defendant than that it was not.

William L. Prosser, Handbook of the Law of Torts, 4th ed., p. 242.

We note that appellee has furnished us with no authorities supporting its view on this issue.

Reversed and remanded for a new trial....

NOTES

(1) What were the possible negligences in the coach's conduct?

Why does the court choose to focus only on the positioning of the bench?

Could not "ice, snow, wind, or dizziness," had they existed, have been factors, in at least some circumstances, to support a finding of negligence on the part of the coach?

(2) What was the procedural profile of this case?

Is the determination of whether there was negligence a question of "law" or "fact"?

Under the court's decision, how much leeway is there for the jury to make a "policy" judgment?

(3) What is the evidence from which the jury could have held for the plaintiff on the "causation" issue? Which way do "vibrations" cut?

How do you distinguish between the questions the jury must decide on "negligence" and those on "causation"?

Is this a case about "sufficiency of the evidence"? What do you understand that term to mean?

NOTE ON THE FEDERAL EMPLOYERS' LIABILITY ACT
Towards a Jurisprudence of Injury 10-3 to 10-5
(A.B.A. 1984, M. Shapo, Reporter)*

The Federal Employers' Liability Act, passed in basically its present form in 1908, is a specialized statute imposing liability on railroad employers for personal injuries and death suffered by employees "resulting in whole or in part from the negligence of any of the officers, agents, or employees" of the railroad or because of negligently caused "defect or insufficiency" in equipment.[1] The Act removes contributory negligence as a complete bar to recovery, establishing a comparative negligence standard,[2] and it eliminates the defense of assumption of risk.[3] A separate statute, popularly known as the Jones Act,

---

* Copyright © 1984 The American Bar Association. Reprinted by permission.
1. 45 U.S.C.A. § 51 (1982).
2. *Id.* § 53.
3. *Id.* § 54.

applies the substantive rules of the Federal Employers' Liability Act to deaths and injuries suffered by seamen.[4]

Evidentiary standards. The jurisprudence of the FELA developed rather unexception-
ally until 1943, when expanded views of the test for sufficiency of the evidence began to
appear in the Supreme Court decisions on the statute.[5] Capping this development in
1957, the majority of a divided Court declared in *Rogers v. Missouri Pacific Railroad*[6]
that "the test of a jury case" under the statute was "simply whether the proofs justify
with reason the conclusion that employer negligence played any part, even the slightest,
in producing the injury or death for which damages are sought."[7] Using that standard,
the Court effectively reinstated a jury award for a railroad employee who was injured
when a passing train fanned the flames of vegetation he was burning, causing him to retreat quickly into a culvert from which he slipped and was hurt.

Replying to the argument of Justice Frankfurter that it had improvidently granted
writs of certiorari to review a group of FELA cases including *Rogers*,[8] the majority took
note of the argument that a workers' compensation scheme would be preferable to the
FELA. However, the majority said that the fact that Congress had not enacted such a
law could not "relieve this Court of its obligation to effectuate the present congressional
intention by granting certiorari to correct instances of improper administration of the
Act and to prevent its erosion by narrow and niggardly construction."[9] *Rogers* thus involved a quarrel over concepts of injury law, evidentiary standards and judicial administration. In a separate opinion, Justice Harlan built on Justice Frankfurter's complaint[10]
that Supreme Court review of such cases was comparatively a waste of time. Justice
Harlan said that instead of requiring that verdicts be based on "evidence sufficient to
enable a *reasoning* man to infer both negligence and causation by *reasoning from the evidence*," the Court had created a rule which allowed affirmance of plaintiffs' judgments
on "a scintilla of evidence."[11]

The Court moved the next year to apply its reading of the FELA in *Rogers*—characterizing the statute as "an avowed departure from the rule of the common law"—to situations in which a railroad employee's injury was "caused in whole or in part by the
fault of others performing, under contract, operational activities of his employer."[12]

The Court then turned its interpretation of the statute's evidentiary standards to the
reconciliation of apparently conflicting jury answers to interrogatories. The occasion
was a case[13] in which a railroad worker suffered a terrible infection from the bite of an
insect which allegedly emerged from a stagnant pool along a roadbed. In its answer to
one interrogatory, the jury in this case had said there was no reason for the defendant to
anticipate that the pool "would or might probably result in a mishap or an injury."
However, the Court held that the jury's other findings, including its conclusion that the

---

4. 46 U.S.C.A. § 688 (1976).
5. For a critical review of the liberalized view of a plaintiff's burden in FELA cases, *see* Alder-
man, *What the New Supreme Court Has Done to the Old Law of Negligence*, 18 Law & Contemp.
Probs. 110 (1953).
6. 352 U.S. 500 (1957).
7. *Id.* at 506.
8. *See Ferguson v. Moore-McCormack Lines*, 352 U.S. 521, 524–48 (Frankfurter J., dissenting).
9. *Rogers v. Missouri Pac. R.R.*, 352 U.S. 500, 509 (1957).
10. *See Ferguson*, 352 U.S. at 546–48 (Frankfurter, J., dissenting).
11. *Id.* at 563–64 (Harlan, J., dissenting) (emphasis in original).
12. *Sinkler v. Missouri Pac. R.R.*, 356 U.S. 326, 329–31 (1958).
13. *Gallick v. Baltimore & O. R.R.*, 372 U.S. 108 (1963).

claimant was bitten by an insect, that the pool attracted bugs and was responsible for the bite, and that the defendant knew that the pool attracted bugs, made it "clear that the jury concluded that respondent should have realized the increased likelihood of an insect's biting petitioner while he was working in the vicinity of the pool."[14] Thus, despite Justice Harlan's dissenting view that the Court should not have reviewed the case, which he said "afford[ed] a particularly dramatic example of the inadequacy of ordinary negligence law to meet the social obligations of modern industrial society,"[15] the Court reversed a state court reversal of a plaintiff's judgment.[16] Similarly liberalized views of proof requirements have moved reviewing courts to give special scrutiny to defendants' summary judgments in Jones Act cases.[17]

PROBLEM*

Angel R. Santana, an able-bodied seaman, shipped out on the U.S.N.S. *Cossatot* from Puerto Rico. The *Cossatot*, a T-2 tanker laden with aviation fuel, was bound for Naples, Italy. A leak in one of the tanks necessitated an extended stay in Naples for repairs. Acetylene torches and electric welders were brought aboard. Numerous hoses and cables required to operate the equipment were stretched across the ship. On the day of the accident plaintiff was painting on the main deck to starboard using "red lead" to prevent corrosion. When he finished his shift he went to stow the paint and brush in the bosun's locker located amidship. To do so he had to walk along a certain passageway across which the hoses and cables were laid. Normally, a catwalk spanning the oil pipes on the ship could also be used to gain access to the locker. However, fire hoses placed there during repairs blocked this route. Approximately twenty hoses and cables, each with a diameter of one-half to one inch, lay parallel across plaintiff's path. He testified that they covered an area of about four to six feet and were so placed that he was unable to step between them. He also testified that the hoses and cables, as well as the deck at that spot, were greasy. It was a foggy day and some condensation had formed on the deck and hoses. Plaintiff was wearing industrial work shoes with rubber soles. He had safely negotiated this route on prior occasions, but claimed that this was the first time he had been unable to place his feet directly on the deck. He slipped and fell and sustained back injuries.

Plaintiff's English was limited. An official Spanish interpreter participated. There were no witnesses to the accident. Because a precise account was crucial to the findings of fact and the result, difficulties in communication were magnified. On cross-examination, defendant's counsel sought to clarify the incident:

Q: Assume that, I am assuming that for the purposes of this question, wasn't it possible for you to walk over the hoses, taking certain precautions, especially when you knew that the hoses were there?

A: I took the precautions that I could, but the only thing I could do was to walk over those hoses.

Mr. Ezratty (plaintiff counsel): Excuse me. I believe that the counsel would agree with me that one of the words was *encima*, which means

14. *Id.* at 118–19.
15. *Id.* at 122–23 (Harlan, J., dissenting).
16. *See id.* at 122.
17. *See, e.g., Lies v. Farrell Lines, Inc.*, 641 F.2d 765, 770 (9th Cir. 1981) (Jones Act cases as requiring "a very low evidentiary threshold for submission to a jury").
* Adapted from a federal case.

Mr. Fuste (defense counsel): On. That is what he means.

The Court: Thank you.

Q: What precautions did you take to avoid falling in that area?

A: Well, I tried to jump, I tried to walk carefully on them, but I slipped casually, I slipped and I fell.

Mr. Fuste: Casually he said?

Interpreter: *Por sa safidad.*

Mr. Fuste: What would the translation be for that, *por sa safidad*?

Mr. Ezratty: I don't know.

The Court: Can we agree with the translation?

Mr. Fuste: Mr. Ezratty?

Mr. Ezratty: I am listening.

Mr. Fuste: It means it so happened that I fell, it is an accident thing.

Mr. Ezratty: I will accept that.

The Court: That is the answer the witness said?

Mr. Fuste: Basically.

. . . .

* * *

In an action under the Jones Act, the seamen's equivalent of the FELA, how would you argue Santana's appeal from a directed verdict in favor of the Government?

NOTES

(1) What was Santana's strongest evidence in the Problem case? Compare this set of facts, which arose under the FELA: A railroad posted a crossing watchman to deal with the problem of illegal railway crossings, and provided him with lights that he carried in each hand. On the occasion that was the subject of the suit, the watchman had positioned himself in front of a train that was partly blocking a crossing. A drunk driver, accelerating his car around the train across the unoccupied part of the crossing, ran down the watchman. The district court awarded damages to the watchman against the railroad on the grounds that it was negligent in posting him. What result on appeal?

(2) "The facts are really not at all like fish on the fishmonger's slab. They are like fish swimming about in a vast and sometimes inaccessible ocean; and what the historian catches will depend, partly on chance, but mainly on what part of the ocean he chooses to fish in and what tackle he chooses to use."

—Historian E.H. CARR, WHAT IS HISTORY? 218 (1961 ed.).

§ 10.02 Circumstantial Evidence

PROBLEM

Howard Quam was an engineer on an oil tanker. One evening he went ashore and made two phone calls to his wife, the first at 5:30 and the second at 7:30, during which he told his wife he would be returning to the ship. Quam's body was found the next day in water some distance from the dock where the tanker was moored. His wrist watch and wallet were found in his room on the ship. His widow testified that her husband customarily wore his watch at work. There was evidence that people reached the ship from the pier by walking along a gangway from the pier to a crane barge to which the ship was moored, and then proceeding along a gangplank from the crane barge to the ship. There was general testimony about unsafe conditions on the pier and on the crane barge. Assuming that the ship was responsible for the gangways and the crane barge, could Ms. Quam get to the jury on her claim that the ship was negligent?

BAKER v. CITY OF FESTUS
Missouri Supreme Court
418 S.W.2d 957 (1967)

FINCH, PRESIDING JUDGE. This is an action by a minor child for $25,000 for wrongful death of his mother. At the close of plaintiff's evidence, the trial court sustained a motion for a directed verdict and entered judgment for defendant. Appeal to this court followed.

Plaintiff's allegation of negligence against the City is that on November 4, 1962, his mother, Ruth Baker, "was caused to fall from the bridge and sidewalk thereon along Henry Street where it crosses a ditch near Main Street in said City of Festus due to the negligence of said City in allowing said bridge and sidewalk thereon to become and remain in a dangerous and defective condition, and that as a direct and proximate result of said fall said Ruth Baker, mother of plaintiff herein, was caused to be killed."

Our recital of facts comes entirely from plaintiff's evidence since defendant offered no testimony.

Mrs. Baker left her home at 11:00 a.m. on November 4, 1962, to go to the house of a son, Dale Baker. She was carrying a sack which contained a pie and some tomatoes.

At about 11:45 a.m., two girls came to Dale's home and reported that they thought there was a body in a creek which ran 175 to 200 feet from Dale's house. Mr. Baker was at Dale's house at the time, and he and Dale ran to the creek where they found Mrs. Baker lying face down in the shallow water in the creek. At that point, the creek runs east and west, and Mrs. Baker's body was parallel with the way the creek ran, her head being to the west and her feet to the east.

Henry Street crosses the creek on a concrete bridge or viaduct. Adjacent to the roadway on the east side of the bridge is a sidewalk, and next to the sidewalk is a concrete banister which is about hip high. Photographs show that the concrete banister extended over the creek but that on the north end of the bridge there was an open space six to seven feet wide between the end of the concrete banister and a fence which then ran northwardly adjacent to the sidewalk. At that opening there was a drop of approximately four feet from the sidewalk to the ground immediately below. This open space between the end of the banister and the start of a fence was not over the water where Mrs. Baker was found. It was some ten to twelve feet between the south side of the opening in question and the place where Mrs. Baker was found. At that point the distance from the floor of the bridge to the water in the creek below was approximately seven feet. It is plaintiff's contention that the City was negligent in leaving this opening at the end of the banister and that Mrs. Baker fell through that opening and then rolled down into the creek some ten to twelve feet away.

We have concluded that there was not sufficient evidence from which the jury, without resorting to guesswork, conjecture and speculation, could find that Mrs. Baker's death was proximately caused by negligence of defendant City, assuming, for this purpose, that the City was negligent. Consequently, we limit our consideration to the question of proximate cause.

No one saw Mrs. Baker from the time she left home until her body was found in the creek. No one saw her fall. There was no evidence of any marks on the bridge or sidewalk to show where she fell. Mr. Baker, husband of the deceased, testified that he observed a mark on the ground about four feet out from the edge of the opening at the end of the banister, but there was no evidence as to its size, shape or depth, and no evidence as to whether it was old or new. Dale Baker did not notice this mark at all and did not notice any marks of any kind on the north bank of the creek. There was no testimony of any other marks or any physical evidence that the body of Mrs. Baker rolled a distance of ten or twelve feet from a point opposite the opening in the banister to the point where the body was found. A photograph, Exhibit 6, introduced by plaintiff, shows that the bank of the creek and the ground below the opening had tall grass and weeds growing thereon, but does not exhibit any evidence that these were mashed down or broken by Mrs. Baker's body rolling from opposite the opening to a point in the creek. There simply was no evidence from which it could be said that the mark mentioned by Mr. Baker had any connection with a fall by the deceased.

The same photograph, Exhibit 6, shows a paper sack floating in the water immediately below the concrete banister. It was identified by Mr. Baker as the sack containing the pie and tomatoes with which Mrs. Baker left home that morning. If Mrs. Baker had fallen through the opening ten to twelve feet from the creek, it is unlikely that the paper sack, still apparently intact, would have ended up floating in the water of the creek beneath the banister. On the other hand, if Mrs. Baker fell over the banister into the creek below, it would logically be expected that the sack would have landed in the vicinity where it was found. That banister was not so high that we necessarily must conclude that the deceased could not have fallen over it, perhaps during an epileptic seizure, and landed directly in the creek below. The evidence did show that Mrs. Baker was subject to frequent epileptic seizures.

In determining whether a submissible case is made, we must consider the evidence in the light most favorable to plaintiff and must give the benefit of all favorable inferences that reasonably may be drawn from such evidence, but liability cannot rest upon guesswork, conjecture or speculation beyond inferences reasonably to be drawn from the evidence. *Probst v. Seyer, Mo.,* 353 S.W.2d 798, 91 A.L.R.2d 1252.

Under the facts in this case, we hold that there was not substantial evidence to establish liability without resorting to guesswork, conjecture or speculation. The evidence simply established that deceased was found in the creek, that there was an opening at the end of the banister ten to twelve feet away, and that there was some kind of an unidentified mark on the ground beneath the opening. There was nothing more. Plaintiff also mentions the fact that the evidence disclosed that Mrs. Baker died of a fracture of the cervical spine rather than by drowning, but that merely indicates that she fell and landed on her head, fracturing her spine, and not where she fell. This could have happened if she fell directly into the creek just as well as if she had fallen through the opening in the banister.

The judgment is affirmed.

All of the Judges concur.

NOTES

(1) The decision in *Baker* applies standard language in a conventional way. A similar slant appears in a case in which a 2-1/2-year-old girl sued for injuries from an escalator. The plaintiff offered only testimony of a "slight thump," a whimper by her, and "a little extra movement in the escalator," followed by discovery of a wound on her leg which required 40 sutures. Held, directed verdict in favor of defendant affirmed, on the quoted rationale that only "imagination, speculation, or mere conjecture" could sustain liability; dissent on the grounds that there was enough evidence to apply *res ipsa loquitur*, a doctrine of circumstantial evidence discussed immediately below, § 10.03 infra. *Householder v. Prudential Ins. Co.*, 130 Ill. App. 2d 184, 264 N.E.2d 398 (1970).

(2) Considering critically the decision in *Baker*, why is the plaintiff's theory of the case more "guesswork, conjecture or speculation" than the hypothesis of an epileptic fit? And couldn't one advance at least a third reasonable hypothesis at least as probable as those? On what basis would experts in probability determine the frequency of occurrence of either event hypothesized by the parties? For a rather technical analysis, see Liddle, *Mathematical and Statistical Probability As a Test of Circumstantial Evidence*, 19 Case W. L. Rev. 254 (1968). What level of probability should the law require to support a plaintiff's verdict in a case of this kind?

§ 10.03 Res Ipsa Loquitur

[A] Generally

PROBLEM*

At approximately 7:20 a.m. a substantial portion of a huge brick wall suddenly collapsed, causing extensive damage to adjacent buildings and the death of Bevo Mac Shell, plaintiff's husband and father of the infant plaintiffs. Mr. Shell was the owner and operator of a bar and restaurant located in the most heavily damaged building at 85 Hudson Avenue and sustained fatal injuries in its ensuing collapse.

The wall in question was located on the perimeter of the former Naval Shipyard in Brooklyn, New York. As nearly as can be determined, it was erected between 1805 and 1830 and thus was about 150 years old at the time of its collapse. The wall ran between Hudson Avenue and Evans Street, a distance of some 400 feet. It was 20 to 25 feet in height, four feet wide at the base and tapered to a width of 16 inches at the top. The collapsed portion was a crescent-shaped segment of the top eight feet of the wall's midsection for a distance of approximately 145 feet, directly adjacent to the buildings for which plaintiffs have brought suit.

What is the principal issue?

––––––––––––

––––––––––––

* From the statement of facts in a federal case.

O'CONNOR v. CHANDRIS LINES, INC.

United States District Court, District of Massachusetts
566 F. Supp. 1275 (1983)

...

JULIAN, SENIOR DISTRICT JUDGE.

...

In April 1978, the plaintiff and her husband, Kevin J. O'Connor, purchased from the defendant, through its agent, Olde Harbour Travel of Boston, Massachusetts, passage for an air-sea vacation which included travel by air to Venice, Italy, where they were to join the S.S. Victoria, a sea-going cruise ship, which at all times material to this action was owned and controlled by the defendant. The ship was scheduled to sail from Venice on a fifteen-day Adriatic and Mediterranean cruise including stops and sight-seeing tours at seven cities, countries and islands, including the Holy Land. The cruise was of special significance to Mr. and Mrs. O'Connor because it included visits to holy places in the Holy Land....

They were assigned to Cabin E-57. The cabin was equipped with two bunk beds, one situated on top of the other. From the time the bunks were first used on the night of May 27, until the time of the accident, shortly after midnight on May 30, Mr. O'Connor slept in the upper bunk and the plaintiff slept in the lower. Mr. O'Connor weighed approximately 210 to 215 pounds. They were the only occupants of cabin E-57. Access to the upper bunk was provided by a ladder situated on the side of the bunk opposite the bulkhead to which the bunks were affixed and was so designed that the occupant would simply roll onto the bunk from the ladder. The frames of the bunks were made of wood.

The ship sailed from Venice on May 27, 1978. On May 29, the plaintiff and her husband returned to their cabin at about 11:00 p.m. and retired. Shortly after midnight, May 30, while they were both asleep in their respective bunks, the upper bunk with the husband lying in it suddenly, without warning, broke from the mounting and fell directly on top of the plaintiff as she lay sleeping in her bunk below. The falling bunk struck the plaintiff on the head, chest, arm and leg. The plaintiff was violently awakened by the impact. The husband was trapped in a corner of the cabin by the collapsed bunk and could not free himself to help his wife or reach the telephone to summon help. The plaintiff was able to reach for the phone by her bunk and called for help. The cabin boy arrived, assisted the plaintiff, called the nurse, and extricated the husband from the fallen bunk. The nurse and the cabin boy then administered first aid to the plaintiff and the ship's doctor was summoned....

[A description of the plaintiff's serious cardiovascular injuries is omitted.]

The rule of *res ipsa loquitur* is applicable to this case. The rule is stated in *Jesionowski v. Boston & Maine Railroad Co.*, 329 U.S. 452, 67 S.Ct. 401, 91 L.Ed. 416 (1947) at page 456, 67 S.Ct. at page 403, as follows:

> When a thing which causes injury, without fault of the injured person, is shown to be under the exclusive control of the defendant, and the injury is such, as in the ordinary course of things, does not occur if the one having such control uses proper care, it affords reasonable evidence, in the absence of an explanation, that the injury arose from the defendant's want of care. [cases cited]

In *Johnson v. United States*, 333 U.S. 46, 48, 68 S.Ct. 391, 392, 92 L.Ed. 468 (1948) the Court further clarified the rule:

The rule *res ipsa loquitur* applied in *Jesionowski v. Boston & Maine Railroad Co.* means that the facts of the occurrence warrant the inference of negligence not that they compel such an inference. *Sweeney v. Erving*, 228 U.S. 233, 240 [33 S.Ct. 416, 418, 57 L.Ed. 815].

See also Restatement of the Law, Torts, (Second), § 328D.

At the time of the accident the defendant owned, operated, and was in exclusive control of the sea-going S.S. Victoria. As a carrier of passengers for hire, defendant was under a continuing legal duty to exercise reasonable care for the safety of its passengers. The reasonable care that the defendant was legally required to exercise was the highest degree of care consistent with the safe transportation of its passengers and the practical operation of the undertaking in which it was engaged, in this case a sea-going cruise. The defendant was under a continuing legal duty to provide the cabin passengers, such as the plaintiff and her husband, with sleeping accommodations that were reasonably safe. With specific reference to the bunks in the cabin the defendant was under a continuing legal duty to provide bunks that were soundly constructed and securely held in place, and strong enough with a reasonable margin of safety, to sustain a passenger of the weight of plaintiff's husband. The frames of the bunks were made of wood. There is no evidence of the age of the S.S. Victoria or of the length of time the bunks in Cabin E-57 had been in service, or of the last time prior to the accident they had been surveyed, or inspected or by whom, or of the nature and extent of any such survey or inspection. The only persons in the cabin when the bunk collapsed and fell on the plaintiff were the plaintiff herself and her husband. Both were lying asleep in their respective bunks at the time of the collapse. The sea was calm. No member of the defendant's crew testified at the trial either in person or by deposition concerning the condition of the cabin or of the bunks prior to the accident. I find that no negligent conduct of the plaintiff or her husband was a responsible or contributing cause of the collapse of the bunk. There is no evidence that any conduct on the part of any third person was a cause of the collapse. The collapse of the bunk in the circumstances disclosed by the evidence is something which ordinarily does not occur in the absence of negligence on the part of someone. The evidence does not disclose any other probable explanation for the collapse of the bunk except the negligence of the defendant in permitting the bunk to be or remain in a defective condition. I draw the inference authorized by the rule of *res ipsa loquitur* that the collapse of the upper bunk on the plaintiff and her resulting injuries and consequential damages were in fact caused by the negligence of the defendant.

I find for the plaintiff and assess damages in the amount of $47,197.00 with interest....

LONDONO v. WASHINGTON METROPOLITAN AREA TRANSIT AUTHORITY

United States Court of Appeals, District of Columbia Circuit
766 F.2d 569 (1985)

STARR, CIRCUIT JUDGE.

...

Jessica Londono was approximately two and one-half years old at the time of the incident in question. She was riding on an escalator descending to a WMATA metro rail station in Washington, D.C., in the company of her mother and four other adult relatives, when she suddenly screamed in pain. Upon examination by her mother, Jessica was discovered to have sustained a significant laceration of her right leg. The incident was reported to WMATA personnel, and Jessica received medical treatment.

Plaintiffs brought a diversity action in United States District Court for the District of Columbia, and defendant moved for summary judgment. In opposition to that motion, plaintiffs made clear that they were relying on a theory of *res ipsa loquitur*. The District Court held that plaintiffs had "not established facts sufficient to invoke *res ipsa loquitur*," Memorandum Opinion at 3, and granted summary judgment in favor of WMATA. The plaintiffs' major failing, in the District Court's view, appears to have been an inability to show the specific cause of the accident:

> "First and foremost," plaintiffs have failed to demonstrate a probability that the escalator or part thereof, rather than some other instrumentality, is the cause of the child's injury. The cause of the accident is not known and it simply is not enough to allege that the accident occurred while plaintiffs were descending on an escalator. The nature of the child's injury indicates a possibility that she might have been cut by some protruding object or the like connected to the escalator wall. Not only is this sheer speculation, but inspections done by WMATA and Westinghouse both before and immediately after the accident failed to disclose any such offending instrumentality.... Moreover, the specific vertical direction of the child's laceration points away from an injury caused by an object on the escalator wall, since such an instrumentality would likely produce a diagonal cut.

Memorandum Opinion at 3–4[1]

The court thus relied upon one fact which was, in truth, disputed between the parties, namely the immedia[cy] of a post-incident inspection ... ; the court also relied upon one conclusion for which there appears to have been no evidence, namely, that the direction of the laceration indicated a cause other than the escalator.[2]

Recognizing that causation may be established through circumstantial evidence, the District Court nonetheless opined that the evidence which had been adduced failed to "eliminate[] from consideration a whole host of other possible causes." ... Since plaintiffs' evidence did not make her theory reasonably probable, but merely possible, the court refused to allow a jury to speculate on causation and thus granted summary judgment for the defendant.

...

Since the plaintiffs' case rests on a theory of *res ipsa loquitur*, our analysis naturally must be informed by the elements of that theory as articulated in the local courts of this jurisdiction. As good fortune would have it, the District of Columbia Court of Appeals has spoken quite recently to the elements of *res ipsa loquitur*. As articulated by that court, the conditions required for application of that familiar principle of tort law are as follows:

> (1) the event must be of the kind which ordinarily does not occur in the absence of someone's negligence;

---

1. Westinghouse Electric Corp., the manufacturer of the escalator, was a third party defendant below but is not a party to the appeal.... The Westinghouse submission indicated maintenance or repair work done eight days prior to the incident.

2. A photograph of the wound was submitted with defendant's Memorandum of Points and Authorities of Support of Motion for Summary Judgment, *reprinted in* Appendix at 9. That Memorandum also contained an argument by defense counsel that the direction of the laceration pointed away from its having resulted from a protruding object.

(2) it must be caused by an agency or instrumentality within the exclusive control of the defendant;

(3) it must not have been due to any voluntary action or contribution on the part of the plaintiff. *Bell v. Westinghouse Electric Corp.*, 483 A.2d 324, 329 (D.C.1984) (quoting W. Prosser, Law of Torts § 39, at 214 (4th ed.1971)).

...

We turn ... to the question whether the plaintiffs could adduce sufficient evidence from which a jury would properly be permitted to find the cause of Jessica's laceration. Clearly, if the cause is looked at restrictively as some particular, identified protruding object, there is and will likely be insufficient evidence properly to get to the jury. The post-incident inspection, at whatever time it was done, turned up no such protruding object; in addition, no evidence was forthcoming that any of the adult relatives who accompanied Jessica on the fateful escalator ride observed any such object. However, it is not at all clear that, under District of Columbia law, our view of "cause" should be so restricted to an object or instrument other than the escalator. If, instead, the escalator itself could properly serve in law as the cause of the accident, plaintiffs could satisfy the elements of *res ipsa loquitur* without establishing the *precise* means by which the escalator brought about the injury.

...

[W]e have assumed that the escalator itself, rather than a particular, identified protruding object, may be viewed as the cause of an accident. Second, we have assumed that the fact that an individual is standing on a moving escalator and receives a laceration on the lower part of the leg provides, in itself, some evidence that the laceration was caused by the escalator. Our willingness to make these assumptions under District of Columbia law is guided by the recent District of Columbia Court of Appeals decision to which we have referred and which was rendered after the District Court's ruling in the instant case.

In *Bell v. Westinghouse Electric Corp., supra*, plaintiff had been injured when her foot became caught in a WMATA escalator causing her to fall. Plaintiff testified that, while descending, "she suddenly felt something 'tugging' at her shoe" and that the heel of the shoe broke when she tried to pull free. 483 A.2d at 324. She was also able to offer into evidence the heel of her sandal which showed damage from being grasped by escalator treads. The court held that these facts supported an instruction on *res ipsa loquitur*, stating that "the doctrine of *res ipsa loquitur* applies where 'direct evidence of negligence is lacking, or where there is "little evidence," or where the cause of the injury is left in doubt by the evidence or not clearly shown.'" *Id.* at 329 (quoting *Levy v. D.C. Transit System, Inc.*, 174 A.2d 731, 733 (D.C.1961)).... While the facts of Bell may readily be distinguished from the case at hand, it is clear from the opinion that, under District of Columbia law, *res ipsa loquitur* can apply even where the cause of the accident is in doubt or not clearly demonstrated.

...

... [T]he case cited by the District of Columbia Court of Appeals which is most analogous to the case before us is *Sanone v. J.C. Penney Co.*, 17 Utah2d 46, 404 P.2d 248 (1965). In that case, a two and one-half year old child was descending on an escalator. Halfway down she cried, "Mommy, my foot is caught"; her mother picked the child up and found a deep, severe laceration extending from just below the knee to just above the ankle. *Id.* at 249. The court held that *res ipsa loquitur* applied, even though "[d]ue to the nature of an escalator it was impossible for the plaintiff to know or to show just what caused her injury," *id*. The court echoed and cited [*J.C. Penney Co. v. Livingston*, 271 S.W.2d 906 (Ky. 1954)], stating:

> It is common knowledge that escalators are widely used in public buildings and that thousands of people, including children, use them daily without injury. It is certainly not unreasonable for one to assume that it is safe to use them in the manner and for the purpose for which they were intended. Nor does it depart from reason to draw the inference that if an escalator is so used and an injury occurs there was something wrong in either the construction, maintenance, or operation of the escalator.

Id. at 249–50 (citations omitted).

The single, arguably relevant distinction that may be drawn between *Sanone* and the instant case is that in *Sanone* the child cried out, "Mommy, my foot is caught," while in our case Jessica simply screamed in pain. Whatever a creative torts professor might be able to accomplish with this distinction, we despair of reasonably distinguishing the case on that basis. In the first place, we find it highly difficult to place substantial reliance on differences in the reportive content of the excited utterances of two and one-half year olds who are caught up in the unhappy process of sustaining severe lacerations. In the second place, in *Sanone*, contrary to the child's description of the event, her mother was in fact able to pick her up, leading to the discovery not that the little girl's foot was caught but that her leg had been lacerated. *See id*. at 249.

... [C]ases from other jurisdictions, expressly relied upon by the District of Columbia Court of Appeals in *Bell*, persuade us that under the law of the District of Columbia the cause of Jessica's injury may be identified generally as the escalator rather than a particular, identified protruding object. Moreover, these cases show that the circumstance of being injured while standing on a moving escalator provides evidence that the escalator was the cause of the injury. In sum, we are unable to conclude that the District of Columbia Court of Appeals would have cited those cases in discussing the availability of *res ipsa loquitur* to escalator injuries without having been fully cognizant of their factual settings and reasoning. We, therefore, carry the settings and reasoning of those cases over to the case at hand. We hold, in light of *Bell*, that it is possible for plaintiffs to prove facts sufficient to support a case based on *res ipsa loquitur*. For that reason, the judgment of the District Court is reversed and the case is remanded for further proceedings consistent with this opinion.

It is so ordered.

RESTATEMENT (SECOND) OF TORTS § 328D (1965)[*]

(1) It may be inferred that harm suffered by the plaintiff is caused by negligence of the defendant when:

(a) the event is of a kind which ordinarily does not occur in the absence of negligence;

(b) other responsible causes, including the conduct of the plaintiff and third persons, are sufficiently eliminated by the evidence; and

(c) the indicated negligence is within the scope of the defendant's duty to the plaintiff.

(2) It is the function of the court to determine whether the inference may reasonably be drawn by the jury, or whether it must necessarily be drawn.

(3) It is the function of the jury to determine whether the inference is to be drawn in any case where different conclusions may reasonably be reached.

NOTES

(1) How would you defend the sort of justice that the doctrine of *res ipsa* achieves in *O'Connor*? Is there an alternative way of getting at the truth, or enough truth, to decide the controversy between the O'Connors and the ship line?

(2) Compare with *Londono* the case of *Gilbert v. Korvette, Inc.*, 457 Pa. 602, 327 A.2d 94 (1974), in which the court concluded that there was a *res ipsa* case when a child's foot got caught in an escalator step and was pulled into the comb plate of the conveyance. Would there be any effective defense against *res ipsa* in that case? Is *Londono* a more difficult case? What would be the defendant's strongest argument in *Londono*?

(3) Will the decision in *Londono* likely have desirable effects on the conduct of the Transit Authority?

(4) Consider this recitation of facts in *Scott v. Diamond State Telephone Co.*, 239 A.2d 703 (Del. l968):

> On July 14, 1965, appellant received a telephone call. After the caller had said a few words, a loud explosive noise came through the telephone which knocked appellant off his feet. That noise was followed by a "loud siren noise." Immediately thereafter, appellant had a severe pain in his ear, followed by a continuous ringing in the ear, which still exists.

Affirming a judgment for the defendant telephone company in a bench trial, the Delaware Supreme Court said that the trial judge "undoubtedly realized that, despite modern technical knowledge, some events occur which no one can explain, and felt that this was such an unfortunate occurrence."

Would you have held that way? What distinguishes this sort of case from a case like *O'Connor*? Like *Londono*?

(5) The potential applications of *res ipsa* range across a wide spectrum of activity. Urban readers may be bemused—but plaintiffs are decidedly not amused—by situations where the issue is whether to apply the doctrine to livestock that gets on a highway, causing collisions with vehicles. The situation is a recurring one, and provokes disagreement. The Nebraska court summarizes the conflicting decisions in reversing an appellate court's determination that *res ipsa* does not apply at all to cases of escaped livestock. The case at issue involved a trucker's collision with cattle that had been housed in what the defendant characterized as a "secure, state-of-the-art cattle pen." The court concluded, *inter alia*, that the plaintiff had satisfied the traditional first element of the doctrine "because cattle would not ordinarily escape" from such a pen "in the absence of negligence." *Roberts v. Weber & Sons Co.*, 553 N.W.2d 664, 669 (Neb. 1995).

(6) Explain the applicability, or lack of applicability, of *res ipsa* in the following vehicle cases:

> A. A car goes off the road unexplainedly in wet weather, striking a bystander
>
> > (1) The bystander's suit against the driver
> >
> > (2) The bystander's suit against the manufacturer of the automobile

B. A parked car rolls down a hill and kills a pedestrian, whose estate sues the person who left the car parked.

(7) Which of the following *res ipsa* formulations seems most reasonable?

A. *Res ipsa* evidence is only evidence for the jury, which considers it along with all the other evidence.

B. The defendant must explain the accident or the plaintiff will get a directed verdict (is this different from a rebuttable presumption?).

C. The defendant must shoulder the burden of showing that it was more likely than not that the injury did not result from his negligence. See PROSSER & KEETON, LAW OF TORTS 257–259 (5th ed. 1984); 4 HARPER, JAMES & GRAY, LAW OF TORTS § 19.11 (1986).

(8) Consider the following facts alleged by a visitor to the White Sox baseball park:

Near the end of the game, Higgins went to the men's room located on the right-field side of the upper deck of the stadium.

To return to his seat, Higgins walked down a corridor that ran past a concession stand. A "door" or "window" made of wood and measuring approximately 4 by 6 by 3/4 was attached to the top edge of the stand and was opened when the stand was in use. When opened, the lower edge of the door was swung towards the ceiling and the small end of a hook attached to the ceiling was inserted into the metal eyelet attached to the door.

As Higgins passed the stand, the door fell from its open position and struck his head. There was testimony that, just before the door fell, the crowd in the stadium was screaming and stamping, and that one "could feel the place tremble."

Does *res ipsa* apply?

(9) Should *res ipsa* apply against an airline when an airplane falls into the sea without explanation, and the wreckage yields no clues to the plane's fate?

(10) For a review of *res ipsa* that emphasizes the need for courts "to be sensitive to and explicitly identify and resolve each of the underlying policy issues" raised by the invocation of the doctrine, see Seidelson, *Res Ipsa Loquitur—The Big Umbrella*, 25 DUQ. L. REV. 387 (1987).

DULLARD v. BERKELEY ASSOCIATES COMPANY
United States Court of Appeals, Second Circuit
606 F.2d 890 (1979)

OAKES, CIRCUIT JUDGE:

This is an appeal in a wrongful death diversity action from a judgment of the United States District Court for the Southern District of New York, Kevin T. Duffy, Judge, entered after a jury trial on October 3, 1978, and amended on October 10, 1978. The jury awarded plaintiff $630,000 for the wrongful death of her decedent, a construction foreman struck in the head by a falling "4 X 4" timber.... In a special verdict, the jury fixed the proportionate liability of the parties as follows: 39% with respect to the defendants and third-party plaintiffs[,] The Berkeley Associates Company and its various partners (hereinafter "Berkeley"), the owner and general contractor; 35% with respect to the defendant 400 Concrete Corporation ("400 Concrete"), which had contracted with Berkeley to perform the concrete superstructure work; and 26% with respect to the third-party defendant Castle Concrete Corporation ("Castle"), which had contracted with 400 Concrete to perform the work that 400 Concrete had agreed to perform for Berkeley....

Decedent, a labor foreman employed by Castle, was working on East 53rd Street adjoining the construction site for a high-rise building at the time of his death. Material for the construction was stored at several locations on that street and elsewhere, and appellants used a large crane to lift the material to the upper floors of the building under construction. Decedent was struck and killed by a piece of lumber (4 X 4 X 4) that fell from an undetermined source at least ten stories above ground level. At the time of the accident Castle had stacked wood on the 29th and 31st floors, and there was some testimony that the piece of lumber fell from one of those floors. The appellants had not provided any overhead protection, or more specifically a sidewalk shed, in violation of the New York Labor law, nor did they have any effective system to warn endangered workers of falling objects.

...

Appellants complain that the court erred in giving the jury a *res ipsa loquitur* instruction. All that the court did was to charge the jury that the law "permits but does not require" an inference of negligence against the person having exclusive control of an instrumentality that causes an accident if the accident would not ordinarily have occurred without negligence. This is a simple enough principle of circumstantial evidence and has none of the vice of creating a presumption of negligence that the mere incantation of the Latin phrase so often evokes (although in certain special relationships, *e. g.*, carrier/passenger, it is proper to shift the burden as a matter of policy, *see* W. Prosser, Handbook of the Law of Torts § 40 at 231 (4th ed. 1971)). One would suppose that a timber falling on a person's head from a high building was the quintessential "thing," at least it was in Baron Pollock's mind when he dropped the phrase onto the confused heads of the legal world in the argument in *Byrne v. Boadle*, 2 H. & C. 722, 159 Eng.Rep. 299 (1863) (barrel of flour rolling out of window). After noting that Castle and 400 Concrete each contended that it was not in exclusive control of the instrumentality, the court instructed the jury that this was a question of fact. The court noted that as general contractor and owner, Berkeley was "in control of everything at the job site," and continued that the question then was whether Berkeley had exclusive control of the instrumentality.

Under New York law, these instructions were more than adequate, even overly generous to defendants, for New York permits a "thing to speak for itself" as a matter of inference even when plaintiff has not shown that the instrument was in the defendant's *exclusive* control; the inference may be equally applicable to several persons if "they shared a common duty and there was no indication that any one of them in particular had actually caused the injury." *De Witt Properties, Inc. v. City of New York*, 44 N.Y.2d 417, 427, 406 N.Y.S.2d 16, 21, 377 N.E.2d 461, 466 (1978); *see also* Restatement (Second) of Torts, § 328D, comment g (1965). Here there was evidence (some of which we have already recounted) that Castle, 400 Concrete, and Berkeley "shared a common duty" to keep the workplace safe, and the court was justified in submitting a permissive inference charge to the jury. Although Berkeley complains of the court's language "in control of everything," the court then stated that the jury must find that Berkeley exercised exclusive control over the instrumentality. Reviewing the charge as a whole, we believe that the court fairly stated the law.

...

NOTES

(1) Do you find any more difficulty with the application of *res ipsa* in a case like *Dullard*, with multiple defendants, than in a case like *O'Connor*? Do the difficulties of proof on the part of the plaintiff justify the added problems inherent in the application of *res ipsa* in a multiple defendant case?

Consider the following fact situations with respect to the application of *res ipsa* to one or more of several potential defendants:

(a) The handrail of an airport escalator stops moving and causes a passenger to lose her balance. She pleads *res ipsa* against the port authority, which brings a third-party action against a company that had a maintenance contract to service the escalator.

(b) Two planes collide in mid-air. The court grants a directed verdict for the *plaintiff* against one airline, which fails to offer evidence that explains the collision.

(c) The bottom comes out on a soft drink carton, and a bottle breaks after it falls through the carton to the floor. The plaintiff, injured when a piece of glass cuts her leg, sues the bottler and the retailer.

How can one apply *res ipsa* in any of these cases without violating the requirement that a particular defendant have "exclusive control" of the offensive instrumentality? Does *Restatement* § 328D satisfactorily avoid the problem by eliminating the exclusive control requirement?

[B] In Medical Cases

PROBLEM*

The plaintiff, John Smith, experienced some problems and difficulty with his right arm. In November, 1970, he contacted the defendant, Dr. Jones, an orthopedic surgeon. Dr. Jones diagnosed the problem as the result of a non-union of an old fracture, and advised Mr. Smith that he could perform a compression-plating procedure by which the non-union could be corrected.

After Dr. Jones performed the surgery, Mr. Smith experienced difficulty moving the fingers of his right hand. Signs of infection developed. Five days after the operation, Dr. Jones ordered culture and sensitivity tests. The infection was identified and treated with antibiotics. Following his release from the hospital, Mr. Smith complained of pain, swelling, and a discharge from his arm. Additional tests indicated the presence of different bacteria. Subsequently, a number of additional surgical procedures were performed at the hospital. Mr. Smith's right arm is now paralyzed.

Mr. Smith brought an action against Dr. Jones for malpractice, and the jury returned a verdict of no cause of action.

---

* Adapted from an opinion in a litigated case.

Plaintiffs contend that the case should have been submitted to the jury under the doctrine of *res ipsa loquitur*, arguing that the mere occurrence of the infection in Mr. Smith's arm is sufficient to establish an issue for the jury to consider. Should the plaintiff win a reversal?

JONES v. PORRETTA

Michigan Supreme Court
428 Mich. 132, 405 N.W.2d 863 (1987)

BOYLE, JUSTICE.

We granted leave in these [consolidated] cases to resolve the question whether it is error in a medical malpractice action for the trial court to instruct the jury that a doctor or surgeon is not a guarantor of results. In *Dziurlikowski*, we hold that the instruction given was erroneous, and we reverse the jury's verdict and remand the case for a new trial. We affirm the jury's verdict in *Jones* because we find that the guarantor instruction was balanced by the duty of care instruction and was not erroneously given in the context of the case.

We note that the instructions at issue in these two cases are not identical. In *Jones*, the instruction stated:

> No physician can be required to guarantee results, but the law demands that they [sic] bring and apply to the case at hand that degree of skill and care, knowledge and attention ordinarily possessed and exercised by other orthopedic surgeons in the same specialty under like circumstances.

In *Dziurlikowski*, the instruction was more extensive and included the statement that an adverse result is not, of itself, evidence of negligence:

> The difficulties and uncertainties in the practice of medicine and surgery are such that no one can be required to guarantee results and all the law demands is that the individuals involved bring and apply to the case in hand that degree of skill, care, knowledge and attention ordinarily possessed and exercised by practitioners of the medical profession under like circumstances. The mere fact that an adverse result may occur following surgery is not in itself evidence of negligence.

The differences in these instructions require a distinct analysis in each case. *Jones* raises the issue of the propriety of the "no guarantor of results" language when coupled with amplifying language properly defining in affirmative terms the duty of care of a physician to a patient. The instruction in *Dziurlikowski* combines the "no guarantor" and affirmative duty of care language used in *Jones* with an additional phrase: "The mere fact that an adverse result may occur following surgery is not in itself evidence of negligence." Thus, the issue in *Jones* is simply whether, read as a whole, the instruction correctly described the standard of care in a traditional medical malpractice case. The issue in *Dziurlikowski*, however, is more complex. Due to the nature of this case, we are required to determine whether, in a case where circumstantial evidence of negligence is raised by the proofs, such an instruction, coupled with a statement that an adverse result is not of itself evidence of negligence, interfered with the factfinder's understanding of permissible inferences.

I
Facts

[The court's summary of the facts in *Jones* is omitted.]

In *Dziurlikowski*, the plaintiffs, Ronald and Mary Ann Dziurlikowski, claimed that the defendants, Dr. Thomas Morley, M.D., South Oakland Anesthesia Associates, P.C., Elizabeth Kurcherenko, C.R.N.A., and William Beaumont Hospital had breached the standard of care by failing to follow proper procedures in the giving of anesthetic to the plaintiff husband.

Mr. Dziurlikowski was admitted to William Beaumont Hospital suffering from bleeding ulcers. While in the hospital, he underwent recommended surgery, during which the doctors also found it necessary to remove his gall bladder. This additional complication extended the anticipated length of the surgery from approximately two hours to approximately four hours.

After the surgery, Mr. Dziurlikowski experienced difficulty with movement in his right arm and underwent physical therapy. His condition was diagnosed as a brachial plexus palsy, and at the time of trial he was still unable to use his arm as before.

The plaintiffs claimed that the injury was caused by the anesthesiology team which, they alleged, had failed either to properly position his arm on the operating table or to notice that his arm had been moved during the surgery. The defendants argued that there was no negligence and that brachial plexus palsy was a relatively rare and unfortunate but occasionally unavoidable consequence of extended anesthesia.

… At the close of proofs, the trial court instructed the jury with the appropriate standard jury instructions and then added the disputed instruction on "guarantor of results/adverse result not evidence of negligence." The court additionally instructed, "I charge you that you may not arrive at your verdict by the process of guess, conjecture or speculation."

The jury returned a verdict for the defendants, and the plaintiffs moved for a new trial, claiming that the two additional jury instructions and the ruling with regard to the cross-examination of defendants' expert were erroneous and impermissibly prejudiced the plaintiffs' case. The trial court denied the motion, and the plaintiffs appealed the issues in the Court of Appeals.

The Court of Appeals agreed with the defendants that the second jury instruction on "guess, conjecture or speculation" was not inappropriate, when the instructions were considered in their entirety. It found, however, that the plaintiffs were correct in their contention that the "guarantor" instruction was erroneously given and that the plaintiffs' counsel should have been allowed to impeach defendants' expert by use of the article. The Court of Appeals declined to reverse on the basis of the impeachment ruling, but noted, with regard to the "guarantor" instruction:

> While we are not convinced that the giving of this instruction critically influenced the jury's verdict in this lengthy trial and are therefore reluctant to reverse on this basis, we are bound by the presumptively prejudicial rule of *Javis v. Ypsilanti Bd. of Ed.*, 393 Mich. 689; 227 N.W.2d 543 (1975). 143 Mich.App. 729, 732, 372 N.W.2d 648 (1985).

The defendants appealed the reversal in this Court, and the plaintiffs cross-appealed the remaining two issues.

…

III
Guarantor Instruction in Standard Medical Malpractice Case

We first turn to the guarantor instruction given in *Jones*. We are not convinced that the guarantor instruction in this case was erroneously given. . . .

A physician is not normally held liable in a fault-based system unless it is shown that the conduct violated the standard of professional care. A "no guarantor/bad result" instruction states "well nigh universally recognized principles of medical malpractice law." *Watson v. Hockett*, 107 Wash.2d 158, 163, 727 P.2d 669 (1986). While use of the term "guarantor" is a somewhat formalistic means of advising a jury as to the standard of care in a professional medical malpractice case, it is not a misleading statement when it is followed, as it was in the *Jones* case, with a reiteration of the level of care that a physician owes to a patient. . . .

IV
Guarantor/Bad Result No Evidence of Negligence
Instruction in *Res Ipsa Loquitur* Medical Malpractice Case

We begin our analysis in *Dziurlikowski* by noting first that the plaintiffs and the defendants acknowledge that the case went forward at trial on a theory of *res ipsa loquitur*. Having held in *Jones* that the "no guarantor" instruction was not erroneous, we now consider whether the "no guarantor/bad result no evidence of negligence" instruction was error in this context.

We are well aware of the long-standing debate as to whether this state recognizes the doctrine of *res ipsa loquitur*. The discussion by Justice Smith in his minority opinion in *Indiana Lumbermens Mutual Ins. Co. v. Matthew Stores, Inc.*, 349 Mich. 441, 452–455, 84 N.W.2d 755 (1957) provides an excellent summary of the controversy.

. . .

"Leaving the general problem and looking particularly at the situation in our own jurisdiction, there can be no doubt whatever that as the doctrine of *res ipsa loquitur* is defined by one of the great masters of our law, we do have it

"Holmes, J.

"*Res ipsa loquitur,*—which is merely a short way of saying that, so far as the court can see, the jury from their experience as men of the world may be warranted in thinking that an accident of this particular kind commonly does not happen except in consequence of negligence, and that therefore there is a presumption of fact, in the absence of explanation or other evidence which the jury believe, that it happened in consequence of negligence in this case."

"Morse, J.

"In this case the falling of the roof was in and of itself some evidence that the work of raising it was not being done with the ordinary care and skill. It is true that the mere fact of an injury does not impute negligence on the part of anyone, but, where a thing happens which would not ordinarily have occurred if due care had been used, the fact of such happening raises a presumption of negligence in someone."

"It is too late, in our opinion, to insist that *res ipsa loquitur*, as above defined (and this is a classic definition), does not apply in this State."

. . .

Whether phrased as *res ipsa loquitur* or "circumstantial evidence of negligence," *Mitcham v. Detroit, supra*, 355 Mich. at p. 186, 94 N.W.2d 388, it is clear that such concepts have long been accepted in this jurisdiction. The time has come to say so. We, therefore, acknowledge the Michigan version of *res ipsa loquitur* which entitles a plaintiff to a permissible inference of negligence from circumstantial evidence.

The major purpose of the doctrine of *res ipsa loquitur* is to create at least an inference of negligence when the plaintiff is unable to prove the actual occurrence of a negligent act. According to Prosser & Keeton, Torts (5th ed.), § 39, p. 244, in order to avail themselves of the doctrine, plaintiffs in their cases in chief must meet the following conditions:

(1) the event must be of a kind which ordinarily does not occur in the absence of someone's negligence;[4]

(2) it must be caused by an agency or instrumentality within the exclusive control of the defendant;

(3) it must not have been due to any voluntary action or contribution on the part of the plaintiff.

In *Wilson v. Stilwill,* ..., 411 Mich. at p. 607, 309 N.W.2d 898, this Court noted these conditions, as well as a fourth criterion: "'Evidence of the true explanation of the event must be more readily accessible to the defendant than to the plaintiff.'"

Application of the rule of *res ipsa loquitur* is limited in medical malpractice cases. "It is the general rule, in actions for malpractice, that there is no presumption of negligence from the mere failure of judgment on the part of a doctor in the diagnosis or in the treatment he has prescribed, or from the fact that he has been unsuccessful in effecting a remedy, or has failed to bring about as good a result as someone else might have accomplished, or even from the fact that aggravation follows his treatment." Shain, *Res ipsa loquitur,* 17 S.Cal.L.R. 187, 217 (1944). As a result, and because the jury often cannot rely on its own experience in such cases, expert evidence must usually be presented. "What this means is that ordinarily laymen are not qualified to say that a good doctor would not go wrong, and that expert testimony is indispensable before any negligence can be found." Prosser & Keeton, *supra,* § 39, p. 256.[7]

The rule that a *prima facie res ipsa* medical malpractice case requires more than a showing of bad result is well supported in our cases and in the case law of other states....

In *Zoterell v. Repp,* 187 Mich. 319, 153 N.W. 692 (1915), we discussed the theory of circumstantial evidence of negligence in the malpractice context and concluded there was not competent evidence to raise an issue for the jury. We stated:

The difficulties and uncertainties in the practice of medicine and surgery are such that no practitioner can be required to guarantee results, and all the law demands is that he bring and apply to the case in hand that degree of skill,

---

4. PROSSER & KEETON, § 39, p. 247, note:
     In the unusual case, the basis of past experience, from which the conclusion may be drawn that such events usually do not occur without negligence, is one common to the whole community, upon which the jury are simply permitted to rely.

7. As Prosser & Keeton note: "There are some medical and surgical errors on which any layman is competent to pass judgment and conclude from common experience that such things do not happen if there has been proper skill and care." *Id.* They further note that these would include cases where a surgical instrument is left in the body or where an inappropriate part of the anatomy is removed. *See Sullivan v. Russell,* 417 Mich. 398, 338 N.W.2d 181 (1983).

care, knowledge, and attention ordinarily possessed and exercised by practitioners of the medical profession under like circumstances [citations omitted]; and the bare fact that full recovery does not result, or that a surgical operation is not entirely successful, is not in itself evidence of negligence.

Zoterell, supra, p. 330, 153 N.W. 692.

Fifty years later, in a California case, Justice Roger Traynor expounded on these same concepts:

A physician's duty is to exercise that degree of care and skill ordinarily possessed and exercised by members of his profession under similar circumstances. (*Sinz v. Owens* [1949], 33 Cal. 2d 749, 753 [205 P.2d 3, 8 A.L.R.2d 757].) He does not guarantee a cure. The doctrine of *res ipsa loquitur* cannot properly be invoked to make him an insurer of the recovery of persons he treats. The Latin words cannot obliterate the fact that much of the functioning of the human body remains a mystery to medical science and that risks inherent in a given treatment may occur unexplainably though the treatment is administered skillfully. The occurrence of an injury that is a calculated risk of an approved course of conduct, standing alone, does not permit an inference of negligence.

Such an inference must be based on more than speculation. If it is to be drawn from the happening of an accident, there must be common knowledge or expert testimony that when such an accident occurs, it is more probably than not the result of negligence.

Clark v. Gibbons, 66 Cal.2d 399, 421–422, 58 Cal.Rptr. 125, 426 P.2d 525 (1967).

Thus, in a normal professional negligence case, a bad result, *of itself,* is not evidence of negligence sufficient to raise an issue for the jury. This does not mean that a bad result cannot be presented by plaintiffs as part of their evidence of negligence, but, rather, that, standing alone, it is not adequate to create an issue for the jury. Something more is required, be it the common knowledge that the injury does not ordinarily occur without negligence or expert testimony to that effect.

In a case where there is no expert evidence that "but for" negligence this result does not ordinarily occur, and in which the judge finds that such a determination could not be made by the jury as a matter of common understanding, a prima facie case has not been made, and a directed verdict is appropriate. However, if there is such evidence, even if it is disputed, or if such a determination could be made as a matter of common understanding, the jury is to determine whether plaintiff has proven whether it is more likely than not that defendant's negligence caused plaintiff's injury. The court may grant a motion for a directed verdict only if it is determined that reasonable minds could not differ that this result could ordinarily happen without negligence.

In cases where reasonable minds could differ as to whether this result could ordinarily happen "but for" negligence, the plaintiff is entitled to have the case submitted to the jury, which, acting in its traditional factfinding role, will decide the liability issue. In appropriate cases, the defendant is entitled to have the jury advised in some form that there are "risks inherent in ... treatment," *Clark v. Gibbons, supra,* p. 422, 58 Cal.Rptr. 125, 426 P.2d 525, and that an unfortunate result, standing alone, does not establish a lack of proper care, skill, or diligence. In this case, however, where the proofs have established a res ipsa case for the jury, such a statement as that given is, without additional guidance for the jury, at best, an incomplete instruction on the function of res ipsa loquitur in creating a permissible inference from circumstantial evidence.[10] A *res ipsa* case is a circumstantial evidence case. In a proper *res ipsa loquitur* medical case, a jury is permitted to infer negligence from a result which they conclude would not have been reached unless someone was negligent....

We agree with plaintiffs' observation in *Dziurlikowski* that, when coupled with the instruction that an adverse result is not evidence of negligence, the instruction had the potential to mislead the jury as to a permissible inference which the jury might draw from the plaintiffs' proofs. While it is correct to state that a bad result alone does not raise an inference of negligence, it is also an accurate statement that the bad result did permit the jury to infer negligence if it credited the testimony of plaintiffs' expert witness that such a result did not ordinarily occur in the absence of someone's negligence. The testimony of that witness was such that the trier of fact could have concluded that the defendant was negligent and the jury should have been instructed in some form to enable it to infer negligence if it found that the proofs supported the conclusion that the injury would not have occurred otherwise.... Moreover, such language would be an incorrect statement of law in those classes of medical malpractice cases where common experience indicates that injury does not occur if there is proper skill and care. Where such an instruction is granted, plaintiffs also have a right to have the jury instructed on all of the aspects of a res ipsa case, not just those favorable to the defendant....

Plaintiffs attempted to prove that "but for" negligence, such a complication does not ordinarily occur after surgery.[12] As the basis for this contention was not in the general knowledge of the lay person, plaintiffs were required to, and did, present expert testimony by Dr. Mervin Jeffries to this effect. Although defendants disputed the testimony of plaintiffs' expert, the jury, if it had believed Dr. Jeffries, could have found that "but for" negligence this result would not ordinarily occur. However, while the jury was given the standard circumstantial evidence instruction, SJI2d 3.10,[13] the jury was not instructed on any of these points, and, rather, was told that it could not find that the injury was evidence of negligence. We agree with plaintiffs that this instruction substantially "interfered with the circumstantial inference of negligence which Plaintiffs were entitled to have the jury consider," a material part of this case. Thus, we agree that

---

10. A *balanced* instruction on the effect of an undesirable result in a *res ipsa* case has been found not erroneous in other jurisdictions. *See, e.g., Kennedy v. Gaskell,* 274 Cal.App.2d 244, 250, 78 Cal.Rptr. 753 (1969). In *Gaskell,* the plaintiff suffered a sudden loss of blood pressure after administration of anesthetic and thereafter expired. The court found that the anesthesiologist could have been found negligent under a *res ipsa loquitur* theory and that an instruction was not erroneous which stated:

"A physician is not to be charged with negligence merely because the result is not what was desired. The law recognizes that, in spite of all his skill and learning, there are many factors over which he has no control."

The California courts, however, have also noted the necessity, in the *res ipsa* context, that the instruction be balanced by one which correctly instructs the jury on the inferences which may, but are not required to, be drawn from the evidence.

12. No testimony was presented at trial which indicated that Mr. Dziurlikowski's arm had been moved or hyperextended during surgery, the basis of plaintiffs' theory of negligence. As plaintiffs point out, such evidence was only within the knowledge of defendants. Neither plaintiffs nor their expert witness could know what happened while Mr. Dziurlikowski was under anesthetic.

13. SJI2d 3.10 reads:

It is not necessary that every fact be proven directly by a witness or an exhibit. A fact may be proven indirectly by other facts or circumstances, from which it usually and reasonably follows according to the common experience and observation of mankind. This is called circumstantial evidence, which you are to consider along with other evidence in the case.

plaintiffs have demonstrated that affirmance of the jury's verdict in *Dziurlikowski* would be "inconsistent with substantial justice," and we affirm the decision of the Court of Appeals granting the plaintiffs a new trial.[15]

....

SPIDLE v. STEWARD
Illinois Supreme Court
79 Ill. 2d 1, 37 Ill. Dec. 326, 402 N.E.2d 216 (1980)

CLARK, JUSTICE.

This case concerns the quantum and quality of evidentiary proof necessary to maintain medical malpractice actions based on *res ipsa loquitur* and negligence. In 1972, plaintiff Judith Marie Spidle underwent a supracervical hysterectomy after recurrent attacks of pelvic inflammatory disease. Dr. Lee A. Steward had treated Mrs. Spidle during these attacks and was her surgeon during the operation. Following the operation, she developed vaginal fecal fistula and a drainage sinus at the lower part of the surgical incision, indicating a communication between the vagina, colon and abdominal wall. This caused fecal matter to drain from her incision and from her vagina. Although the abdominal incision was closed relatively soon thereafter, the vaginal fecal fistula persisted for approximately two years before surgically corrected by another doctor. Mrs. Spidle, however, has continued to experience medical difficulties. There was evidence that Dr. Steward's initial surgery caused the fistula....

... At the close of plaintiffs' case, the trial court directed a verdict for Dr. Steward (hereinafter referred to as defendant) on the two complaint counts based upon *res ipsa loquitur* ... The jury found for the defendant on the two counts alleging negligence.

The Fourth District Appellate Court affirmed the trial court, one judge dissenting on the *res ipsa loquitur* issue.

....

Defendant contends that no evidence submitted by plaintiffs was sufficient to support this case going to the jury on the *res ipsa loquitur* counts. Plaintiffs' expert witness, Dr. Thomas Wilson, answered these questions about the probability of negligence:

> Q. Is a hysterectomy, supracervical hysterectomy, removal of the tubes and ovaries, a type of surgery which in ordinary course, is likely to lead and have as one of its results, now, in the ordinary course, mind you, in the ordinary course, likely to lead to and have as one of its results, in the absence of any negligence, the formation of fecal vaginal fistulas?
>
> A. This is a rare and unusual complication of hysterectomies.
>
> Q. It is not one one would normally expect, is it?
>
> A. No.

Defendants argue that the doctor's answer only concerned unusual results, not unusual results ordinarily or most often due to negligence. As such, the defendant contends that, even in a light most favorable to plaintiffs, *res ipsa loquitur* cannot be invoked.

---

15. Where the conditions for *res ipsa loquitur* are met, the doctrine also serves to link the defendants with the negligent act, PROSSER & KEETON, § 39....

While we agree with the defendant and the appellate court that surgeons are not liable merely for unusual, unfortunate results, we think that these answers, combined with other testimony, were sufficient to present a jury question regarding the probability of negligence.

Plaintiffs' counsel asked, in his first question, whether the fistula would, in the absence of negligence, ordinarily result. If the expert had answered that question "no," he would have established directly plaintiffs' initial burden with respect to the probability component of *res ipsa loquitur*. With such an answer, he would have testified, in effect, that supracervical hysterectomies resulting in fistulas more probably than not have negligent antecedents. Such a direct answer ... would be sufficient initially even though it would not have constituted proof that fistulas never happen without negligence. To hold otherwise, to require a plaintiff to conclusively prove negligence, would "obviate the purposes and policy behind shifting the burden of coming forward with the evidence to the defendant" (*Spidle v. Steward* (1979), 68 Ill.App.3d 134, 140, 24 Ill.Dec. 489, 494, 385 N.E.2d 401, 406 (Craven, J., dissenting)). Most courts have agreed with this view and have required plaintiff to show only that the result "ordinarily," not always, had negligent antecedents....

Unfortunately, the expert in this case answered the question indirectly. We cannot conclude with equanimity, from this colloquy alone, whether he meant fistula formation after hysterectomies is usually a result of negligence or whether there is an equal probability that they occur despite the exercise of due care. In this case, however, the expert also testified about the inadvisability of operating on Mrs. Spidle if her pelvic inflammatory disease was in an acute or an acute flare-up stage. The defendant even agreed with the plaintiffs' expert regarding the inadvisability of operating during an acute stage, although denying that Mrs. Spidle was in such a stage. Evidence was introduced, however, that Mrs. Spidle was in an acute stage and that the defendant, after the operation, admitted he "operated a little too soon." In a light most favorable to plaintiffs, a reasonable person could conclude that plaintiffs' expert believed that this fistula, more probably than not, resulted from defendant's negligence. If believed, this is evidence of more than a mere unusual occurrence (*see Hahn v. Illinois Office Equipment Co.* (1976), 42 Ill.App.3d 29, 31, 355 N.E.2d 336), from which the jury could have inferred negligence under *res ipsa loquitur*.

. . . .

The California Supreme Court reached similar conclusions in *Clark v. Gibbons* (1967), 66 Cal.2d 399, 412, 58 Cal.Rptr. 125, 134, 426 P.2d 525, 534. In that case, an expert testified to a low incidence of injuries when due care was used. Other evidence tended to establish specific acts of negligence. The court reasoned that this evidence, combined, presented a jury question under *res ipsa loquitur*. Subsequent cases have struck *res ipsa loquitur* counts where expert testimony of a rare and unusual result was not accompanied by further evidence of negligent acts that could have caused the injury at issue.... When the trial judge in the instant case permitted the ordinary negligence counts to go to the jury, he ruled that a verdict finding the defendant liable could stand. The evidence sufficient to hold defendant liable under negligence specifically does not eliminate the *res ipsa loquitur* doctrine; rather, the foundation for it and the inference of negligence permitted under it were strengthened (Prosser, Torts sec. 40, at 231–32 (4th ed. 1971)), at least to the extent of presenting a jury question.

. . . .

The judgment of the appellate court is affirmed as to its affirmance of the verdict on the negligence counts and reversed as to its affirmance of the dismissal of the *res ipsa lo-*

quitur portions of the complaint. The judgment of the circuit court of Coles County is affirmed as to the negligence counts and reversed as to its dismissal of those portions of plaintiffs' complaint based on *res ipsa loquitur*. The cause is remanded to the circuit court for further proceedings consistent with this opinion.

....

RYAN, JUSTICE, concurring in part and dissenting in part.

Appropriate to my concern about the majority opinion is a statement by Dean Prosser commenting on the doctrine of *res ipsa loquitur*:

> It is a thing of fearful and wonderful complexity and ramifications, and the problems of its application and effect have filled the courts of all our states with a multitude of decisions, baffling and perplexing alike to students, attorneys and judges. Prosser, *Res Ipsa Loquitur in California*, 37 Cal.L.Rev. 183 (1949).

The majority opinion relies on *Clark v. Gibbons* (1967), 66 Cal.2d 399, 58 Cal.Rptr. 125, 426 P.2d 525, in support of its holding that a rare occurrence, plus evidence of specific acts of negligence, are sufficient to submit the case to the jury under a *res ipsa loquitur* instruction. Before demonstrating that the facts of our case are not even sufficient to warrant giving a *res ipsa loquitur* instruction to the jury under the holding of *Clark v. Gibbons*, some general comments about the doctrine are in order.

Before the doctrine applies to a given case, a plaintiff must establish his exercise of due care, that the instrumentality which caused the injury was under the control of the defendant, and that the accident is such as ordinarily does not happen if due care is exercised. (Prosser, Torts sec. 39, at 214 (4th ed. 1971).) The last of these is the essential circumstantial evidence from which the inference of negligence is drawn. The majority, while acknowledging that whether the doctrine applies in the given case is a question of law to be determined by the court, nonetheless holds that the jury should determine whether the elements have been proved from which it may draw inferences of negligence. Although that may be true in a limited area, it is not the general rule.

Essential to the application of the doctrine is the fact that the occurrence is such as in the ordinary course of things would not have happened if due care had been exercised....

There are circumstances that do not fall within the common knowledge of the community. In such cases it is permissible to establish through the use of experts that certain events do not ordinarily occur if due care is exercised. In *Walker v. Rumer* (1978), 72 Ill.2d 495, 21 Ill.Dec. 362, 381 N.E.2d 689, this court held that this essential element in the medical malpractice case can be established by expert testimony and held that the determination must be made *as a matter of law* whether the occurrence is such as in the ordinary course of things would not have happened if the party had exercised due care....

In some States there has developed what is referred to as "conditional" *res ipsa loquitur*, which is applied in cases where the existence of conditions upon which the doctrine depends are disputed, and the applicability of the doctrine thus becomes a question of fact. (2 J. Dooley, Modern Tort Law, sec. 34.66 (1977).) The Law Revision Commission comment to section 646 of the Evidence Code of the State of California (Cal.Evid.Code sec. 646 (Deering 1979 Supp.)) explains that the conditional *res ipsa loquitur* instruction under the Code should be given in cases where the basic facts upon which the doctrine rests are contested.

Clark v. Gibbons, relied on by the majority opinion, fits neither the traditional nor conditional *res ipsa loquitur* pattern. It relies on neither common knowledge nor expert testimony to establish the basic premise that the event is not such as ordinarily occurs in the absence of negligence. It does not rely on the happening of the occurrence alone. The premise from which the inference of negligence may be drawn under the *Clark v. Gibbons* rationale is that proof that when due care is used, an injury *rarely* occurs, accompanied by other evidence of negligence, may be sufficient to warrant an instruction on conditional *res ipsa loquitur....* In that case, however, both Mr. Justice Tobriner and Mr. Chief Justice Traynor wrote concurring opinions which opposed the extension of the *res ipsa loquitur* doctrine. Mr. Justice Tobriner stated:

> To give a *res ipsa* instruction under such circumstances invites a purely speculative leap and entrusts the jury with unreviewable power to impose or withhold liability as it sees fit. (*Clark v. Gibbons* (1967), 66 Cal.2d 399, 415–16, 58 Cal.Rptr. 125, 136–37, 426 P.2d 525, 536–37.)

Mr. Justice Tobriner further observed:

> [T]he rarity of an event may well bear no relationship to negligence. Courts which ignore that fact in formulating the law of *res ipsa loquitur* unjustly penalize physicians and plunge the legal process into an abyss of uncertainty and obfuscation. (*Clark v. Gibbons* (1967), 66 Cal.2d 399, 421, 58 Cal.Rptr. 125, 140, 426 P.2d 525, 540.)

Mr. Chief Justice Traynor, in his concurring opinion, pointed out that the inference of negligence in a *res ipsa loquitur* case must be based on more than speculation. It is drawn from the happening of the accident, and there must be common knowledge or expert testimony that when such an accident occurs, it more probably than not is a result of negligence:

> A showing that such an accident rarely occurs does not justify an inference of negligence without a further showing that when the rare event happens, it is more likely than not caused by negligence. (*Clark v. Gibbons* (1967), 66 Cal.2d 399, 422, 58 Cal.Rptr. 125, 141, 426 P.2d 525, 541.)

Mr. Chief Justice Traynor pointed out that evidence of specific acts of negligence has no relation to *res ipsa loquitur*, which requires the inferences to be drawn from the mere happening of the event. Indicative of the departure of the holding of *Clark v. Gibbons* from the accepted principles of *res ipsa loquitur* is Dean Prosser's comment:

> A badly confused case is *Clark v. Gibbons*, 1967, 66 Cal.2d 399, 58 Cal.Rptr. 125, 426 P.2d 525.... (Prosser, Torts sec. 41, at 243 n. 57 (4th ed. 1971).)

It is also worthy of note that the holding of *Clark v. Gibbons* has had very limited, if any, acceptance outside California, and, as shown by the California cases discussed below, even in that State it has been narrowly applied.

Even assuming the validity of *Clark v. Gibbons*, it is not authority for the giving of a conditional *res ipsa loquitur* instruction under the facts of our case....

... [I]t is clear that *res ipsa loquitur* did not apply. Our case involved complex surgery and was not a commonplace procedure. Also, in our case there is no evidence, by expert testimony, establishing that the event or injury rarely occurs if due care is exercised. The most that Dr. Wilson, plaintiff's expert witness, would say is that "this is a rare and unusual complication." There is no evidence that it is rare and unusual *if due care is used*. The attorney was well aware of what he had to prove. He did not get Dr. Wilson to give the answer that was necessary. The simple fact is that the plaintiff did not prove that which was required. We have no indication as to why the attorney did not pursue the matter further. It may well be that through the use of a discovery deposition he was aware that Dr. Wilson would not say that this occurrence would not ordinarily happen in the absence of negligence, or under the *Clark v. Gibbons* test that it is rare when due care is exercised. In any event, all that is in the record is that it is a rare and unusual complication. This is not enough, under *Clark v. Gibbons*, to authorize the giving of a conditional *res ipsa loquitur* instruction regardless of what other evidence there may be of specific acts of negligence.

As to the specific acts of negligence of the defendant, the evidence of such acts is at the best weak or "sketchy." The evidence must be of a specific act of negligence of a type which could have caused the injury.... The majority opinion relies on the defendant's statement that he "operated a little too soon." Actually, the exact statement, according to the testimony of the plaintiff's husband, was "he said he went in a little too soon." There is no evidence that by operating at the time he did the defendant did not conform to accepted medical standards. Dr. Wilson, plaintiff's expert witness who practiced in obstetrics and gynecology, was questioned by plaintiff's counsel concerning surgery for hysterectomy of a patient who has pelvic inflammatory disease. The witness stated there were acute stages and chronic stages of the disease. An acute stage would be manifested by an elevated white blood cell count to as much as 20,000 to 25,000, and possibly an elevated temperature. If possible, the witness stated, surgery is ordinarily not performed at that time. It is best to treat the patient with antibiotics until the condition is in the chronic or "smoldering" state. Surgery is preferable at that time. The witness stated that normally the white blood cell count is from 5,000 to 10,000. Plaintiff's attorney then asked the witness whether absent an emergency situation a hysterectomy should be performed during a stage when the infection is acute. The doctor responded:

> That is a judgment decision.... The judgment must be made, basically, by the surgeon at the time of the surgical procedure. It is not always possible to tell what's in an abdomen from the outside until one is actually looking inside the abdomen at the time the surgery is done.

On cross-examination, the witness stated that the laboratory at his hospital considers as a normal range of white blood cell count from 5,000 to 10,000, whereas, some laboratories use the outer limits of the normal range of from 5,000 to 11,000 or 12,000. He also stated that the acute stage would be accompanied by a fever and acute pain.

Dr. Steward testified that at the time he performed surgery on plaintiff, she did not have an acute infection. He had been treating her conservatively with antibiotics for the infection since November 1971. The infection would flare up, that is, become acute, and then subside. She had been hospitalized in June 1972 with severe abdominal pain and treated with antibiotics. Her white blood cell count was about 25,000. On July 6, 1972, she was released from the hospital but continued to take antibiotics. On July 31, 1972, he saw the plaintiff. At that time her temperature was normal and he scheduled surgery for August 3, 1972. On August 2 her white blood cell count was taken and it was only 10,900. He stated that in this hospital laboratory the normal limits were considered to be 7,000 to 11,000. He also stated that the normal limits varied, depending upon the techniques that the laboratory uses. He considered her blood count, at that time, to be within normal limits, so he proceeded with the surgery as scheduled.

In light of all this evidence, the alleged statement by the defendant to the plaintiff's husband that he "went in a little too soon" is no evidence that the defendant did not conform to accepted medical procedures. Thus, the plaintiff has failed to prove any of the facets of the *Clark v. Gibbons* test that the occurrence rarely happens if due care is exercised, that the defendant committed a specific act of negligence of a type which could have caused the injury, and that the procedure was commonplace rather than a complex surgery. Under the holding of the California cases previously cited, conditional *res ipsa loquitur* did not apply. The essence of medical malpractice is a violation of the prevailing standard of care. (2 J. Dooley, Modern Tort Law sec. 34.12 (1977).) Even assuming the defendant "went in a little too soon," and that this was the cause of the fistula, this is not proof of a specific act of negligence. Dr. Wilson, the plaintiff's expert, testified that it is a judgment decision which must be made by the surgeon and that it is not always possible to tell what is in an abdomen from the outside. The plaintiff's white blood cell count was within normal range and her temperature was normal. There was no indication that her infection was in an acute stage.

The majority opinion does not refer to another California case which is factually very similar to ours. In *Siverson v. Weber* (1962), 57 Cal.2d 834, 22 Cal.Rptr. 337, 372 P.2d 97, plaintiff brought an action against the defendant doctor, alleging malpractice in the performance of a hysterectomy. Several days after the surgery, plaintiff developed a fistula with complications quite similar to the plaintiff's in our case. The plaintiff testified that the defendant had said to her, "I must have put a suture through the flap of the bladder there which caused the fistula." (57 Cal.2d 834, 837, 22 Cal.Rptr. 337, 338, 372 P.2d 97, 98.) The California Supreme Court held that the doctrine of *res ipsa loquitur* did not apply. The court stated that no witness testified that in the rare cases where fistulas occur they are more probably than not the result of negligence. The court also held that the defendant's statement to the plaintiff that he must have put a suture through the flap of the bladder which caused the fistula cannot properly be regarded as showing probability of negligence. *Clark v. Gibbons* distinguished *Siverson* by noting that in *Siverson* there was no evidence of a negligent act of the type that could have caused the accident, and that none of the witnesses testified that anything was done during the operation which was contrary to good medical practice. These are facts which also distinguish our case from *Clark v. Gibbons*. *Siverson* would therefore appear to be the more appropriate precedent.

It has been noted that plaintiffs rarely lose *res ipsa loquitur* cases at the jury's hands. (James, *Proof of the Breach in Negligence Cases (Including Res Ipsa Loquitur)*, 37 Va.L.Rev. 179, 219 (1951).) ...

... Mr. Justice Tobriner, in his concurrence in *Clark v. Gibbons*, also noted that the holding in that case permitted the jury to speculate and would result in many doctors who had performed no negligent acts being found guilty of malpractice. If such is the possibility under the ordinary *res ipsa loquitur* doctrine, or under the expanded doctrine of *Clark v. Gibbons*, to what greater extent will this be true under the holding of the majority in this case? If, as stated by Professor James, the only serious obstacle to a plaintiff's recovery under *res ipsa loquitur* is getting the case to the jury, then the majority opinion in our case has virtually created a strict liability in malpractice cases under the guise of *res ipsa loquitur*. Now, given only a scintilla of evidence, the jury is permitted to speculate that the basis for drawing the inference of negligence exists.

To impose liability for fault, when in a vast number of cases where liability is imposed there is no fault, seems to me to be intellectually dishonest. It is demeaning to the law, to the legal profession, and to the judicial process because it will appear to the public in general, and to the members of the health care professions in particular, that the legal profession and the courts are playing games with what has come to be a meaningless Latin phrase for the purpose of permitting an injured party to recover on the basis of fault when there is in fact no fault involved.

There is no just reason to stigmatize a doctor and damage his professional reputation when he may have conformed to all accepted professional standards.... In *Siverson v. Weber* the court found that to permit the inferences of negligence under the doctrine of *res ipsa loquitur* solely because an uncommon complication develops would place too great a burden upon the medical profession and might result in an undesirable limitation on the use of operations or new procedures involving an inherent risk of injury even when due care is used. Any system which diverts the doctor's attention from the operating room to the courtroom leaves much to be desired....

If public policy requires that financial responsibility be placed upon the doctor for rare complications on the assumption that in that manner the risk of loss can be better spread to the public at large, I suggest that we be truthful with ourselves and with the public and not continue to attempt to do so through the largely fictitious search for fault.... I suggest that the fault concept be preserved for those who are truly injured through the doctor's malpractice. This will protect the doctor from being unjustly stigmatized; it will relieve him of the heavy burden of balancing medical against legal consequences, and it should enhance the prestige of the legal profession and the courts by demonstrating to the public that the judicial process is in reality and not in name only "seeking after the truth." I seriously invite the legislature of this State to give consideration to this suggestion.

....

NOTES

(1) What should be the procedural effect of *res ipsa* in a medical case? Consider the following formulation in *Clark v. Gibbons*, the California case prominently mentioned in the two decisions excerpted above:

> To avoid the inference *as a matter of law* an individual doctor must go beyond showing that it was unlikely or not probable he was negligent and must establish that he is free from negligence by evidence which cannot be rationally disbelieved. Falling short of such a showing, it remains for the jury to determine whether the inference arising from the doctrine has been rebutted as to any particular doctor.

66 Cal. 2d 399, 411, 426 P.2d 525, 533, 58 Cal. Rptr. 125, 133 (1967).

(2) How do you react to Justice Ryan's comment in *Spidle* about "the largely fictitious search for fault"? Do you think this scathing comment describes what happened in *Spidle*? Would you go so far as to say that the result in *Spidle* is no better than a result achieved by dicing?

Is Justice Ryan's comment an apt description of the general *res ipsa* cases preceding the medical cases in these materials?

(3) Compare with the cases above a case in which a surgical team leaves a piece of gauze, or some other object used during an operation, in the patient's body. Is it a "fiction" to say that that event should give rise to an inference of negligence?

(4) Should *res ispa* apply to the care of a patient who has an emergency appendectomy, from which he emerges with a permanently stiff neck? Assume that the patient, suing the surgeon and the anesthesiologist, testifies that the last thing he remembers is being positioned on the operating table with his neck against a hard rubber protuberance at the top of the table.

(5) Can you define the larger social stakes at issue in *Jones* and in *Spidle*? Will such decisions tend to improve the quality of medical care? Unduly increase the cost of medical care? Make the judicial process more fair to injured patients? More fair to physicians?

How much consideration should a court, faced with such particularized controversies, give to questions like the impact of plaintiffs' judgments on insurance premiums for medical malpractice? Should courts further consider the possible extended consequences of high premiums, including the prospect that they will force some physicians to leave the profession?

(6) What comparative advantages would be achieved by a central focus on "informed consent"? Consider the relative merits of the use of informed consent as the primary determinant of liability in *Jones* and *Spidle*.

(7) What would be the principal difficulties you would expect to encounter in an empirical investigation of the costs and benefits of the *res ipsa* rules applied in *Jones* and *Spidle*? How confident would you be of securing reliable information from physicians about operations they had not undertaken or overcautious conduct in which they had engaged as a result of decisions of this kind?

(8) Would a nonfault insurance system for medical accidents be a desirable solution to the problem posed by these cases? Keeton, *Compensation for Medical Accidents*, 121 U. Pa. L. Rev. 590 (1973), criticizes medical no-fault schemes, emphasizing *inter alia* the difficulties in deciding whether losses have arisen "from mistake or accident occurring during medical treatment," *id*. at 614–615. Keeton points out that difficult causation issues on this point will appear quite often; he contrasts the automobile compensation area, in which it is rather seldom that a question will be raised as to whether loss has arisen out of the maintenance or use of a motor vehicle.

(9) Rather than going the no-fault route, would it be more desirable to deal with the difficulties of proof in cases like *Jones* and *Spidle* by requiring malpractice plaintiffs to go before a screening panel that would make a preliminary determination on the merits of the case? What should be the membership of such a panel? Would the "merits of the case" involve principally "scientific" questions or "legal" issues? Compare the material infra § 17.03.

§ 10.04 Requirement of Expert Testimony

PROBLEM

An attorney for a defendant in a capital case who was convicted for kidnapping and murdering his eight-year-old niece gave the following statement to the jury in the sentencing phase of the case:

* * *

Your Honor, ladies and gentlemen, since ya'll were selected I might add I haven't taken the opportunity to talk to ya'll a lot but I have been honest and in that honesty I haven't tried in any form or fashion to do anything other than see that the facts in this case were presented and they were very ably presented, there's no question about that.

Now, I knew that when I got involved in this case at the beginning they would be. The question in this case is not the facts. Twenty-nine times I said "no questions." Thirty times I said "no objections" to a witness being excused. Each and every one of us knows the young girl died. Like Mr. Foster, I have two young children of my own and believe you me that makes it more difficult for me to stand here in front of you all right now, each and every one of you, than it does for Mr. Foster, I dare say. I don't ask you to appreciate that. I don't ask for that at all. I just want to be straight up and honest about this whole thing and where we are all coming from. Each and every one of you in this jury box know before this case started or had some slight idea, that we were going to be at this point today where we are now and the decision was going to come down to the 12 of you and what you determine to be Mr. Messer's fate.

I dare say, and it has been suggested to me, and I say this in all humble candor, by some both here and in Rome that I ought to argue to this jury to leave him alive is a more cruel punishment because he's got to live with it, so I don't know what to say to you. I really don't. I know that at this particular point there is no question in my mind that verdict this jury spoke in this court room today was the truth. I don't contest that at all. The question is when the judge tells you what the law is in this situation and what is considered to make something aggravating circumstances, what is considered to miti-gate circumstances, he's also going to tell you that in a situation like this you can almost disregard those and leave it up to yourselves, your gut feeling as to what it is you feel speaks the voice of the community.

Now, the community, a great part of the community, has been here in this court room as potential jurors and as members of the audience, and it concerns Polk County. Interestingly enough Judge Winn told me two weeks ago that he didn't think there would be anyone here by the end of the trial that it had been a long time since there had been a trial like this and the last time a good many years ago he could remember that there just wasn't 10 or 15 people by the time the trial got done with, people were just that uninterested. But that's not true in this situation because people have been very in-terested, and very interested right now with what is this community's voice through ya'll going to be.

Unfortunately, I do not agree again with Mr. Foster as to his position that each and every one of you by rendering a verdict that speaks for the death penalty are being brave. In not doing that you're showing people outside of Polk County that you don't know how to deal with people who take the lives of others in Polk County. That's not the issue. Nor is it the bravest thing to do in this situation to vote the death penalty. It would take a heck of a lot more guts to say that there's something in the human being who sits over there, sits over there having to remember what ya'll have just learned about him. There's something that put him on this earth and it's worth leaving on this earth. Ya'll have the power to extinguish him from this earth, a legal right to do that if you so desire. The District Attorney does not have that right. You are but his imple-ment to do that, each one of you, all twelve of you, to the extent that you choose to use that the law allows each and every one of you to do it. That's an awesome respon-sibility and I dare say I would rather be over here than in ya'lls seats, because as a par-ent under these circumstances ... but that's for ya'll to decide. Please however, as the judge will charge you, the decision then as a group, your decision be it give him life or death is your decision, you need not worry about what happens after that decision as to how it's carried out. That makes it a lot easier as far as the decision is concerned in having to live with it but it's still your decision, and if your decision is life that is a de-cision that you have come about to make freely and honestly based upon all that you've heard in the case and there might be some reason to leave this man on the face of the earth then hold onto that decision, if not then let it go, but make it your own decision, each and every one of you, don't make it a decision of your friends and neighbors that you just adopt. I dare say 10 years ago had any of you ever pictured yourselves being in this situation and having to make this decision ten years from then you wouldn't.

Thank you.*

* * *

Could the defendant have sued his lawyer for malpractice on the basis of this statement? Would he have needed the testimony of another lawyer to make his case that his lawyer had been negligent?

SITTS v. UNITED STATES

United States Court of Appeals, Second Circuit
811 F.2d 736 (1987)

KEARSE, CIRCUIT JUDGE:

Plaintiff Kenneth E. Sitts appeals from a final judgment entered in the United States District Court for the Northern District of New York, Howard G. Munson, Chief Judge, summarily dismissing his medical malpractice claim against defendant United States of America, brought under the Federal Tort Claims Act, 28 U.S.C. §§ 1346(b), 2671 *et seq.* (1982), for damages allegedly resulting from a spinal operation he underwent at a Veterans Administration ("VA") Hospital in 1978. The district court granted defendant's motion for summary judgment on the ground that under New York law, which the parties agree is the applicable substantive law, Sitts would be required to introduce at trial expert medical testimony on the issues of negligence and causation and that Sitts had failed to identify any such expert who would testify for him at trial. On appeal, Sitts argues principally that expert testimony was not required in his case because the questions to be decided are within the ordinary experience and knowledge of lay persons and that, in any event, defendant's motion for summary judgment was not adequately supported and revealed the existence of issues of fact to be tried. Finding no merit in these contentions, we affirm.

I. BACKGROUND
A. *The Events*

Most of the pertinent historical facts, relating to spinal surgery undergone by Sitts at a VA Hospital in Syracuse, New York ("Hospital") in 1978, are not in dispute and may be summarized briefly. For some time prior to 1978, Sitts had experienced pain in his lower back and left leg, and had consulted doctors at the Hospital. After bed rest and medication failed to alleviate his symptoms, X-rays and a myelogram were taken and Sitts was diagnosed as having a bulging or herniated disk between the last lumbar vertebra (called "L5" in medical terminology) and the first sacral vertebra (called "S1").

The VA physicians advised a laminectomy to remove the bulging material from the "L5-S1 interspace," and Sitts underwent surgery in November 1978. As performed, however, the surgery removed material from between the first two sacral vertebrae (S1 and S2), and not between L5 and S1. Following the operation, when Sitts' pre-operation symptoms persisted, X-rays and a second myelogram disclosed that the laminec-

---

* From the Appendix to the opinion of Marshall, J., dissenting from denial of certiorari, in *Messer v. Kemp*, 474 U.S. 1088, 1091–93 (1986).

tomy had been performed at the wrong site. In October 1979, Sitts underwent a second operation which resulted in the removal of the bulging material at the L5-S1 interspace.

B. *The Present Lawsuit*

. . . .

Dr. Wayne Eckhart, the orthopedic resident who performed the 1978 operation, testified at his deposition that he had followed the procedure normally used by members of his profession to locate the site of the prescribed laminectomy, *i.e.*, the L5-S1 interspace. As described by Dr. Eckhardt and other orthopedic surgeons whose depositions were taken, the upper end of the human spine normally has five lumbar vertebrae, with adjacent vertebrae separated by cartilage, or disk material, and space; these vertebrae can be manipulated up and down individually in relation to one another in a pistoning-type movement. Below the lumbar vertebrae are the sacral vertebrae; the sacral vertebrae are normally fused together into one bone called the sacrum and cannot be individually pistoned. It is rare that there is movability between the sacral vertebrae—a condition called "lumbarization."

The procedure normally used in locating the operative site for a laminectomy was to make incisions exposing the spine, then to grasp vertebrae and use pistoning motions to find the sacrum, ordinarily the place where no further movement is possible; from that place, the surgeon would simply count vertebrae either up (through the lumbar area) or down (through the sacral area) until he reached the desired level. In the 1978 operation on Sitts, Dr. Eckhardt used this procedure to search for the L5-S1 interspace. Finding bulging and soft disk material between the lowest movable vertebra and the highest immobile vertebra, he concluded that he had located the L5-S1 interspace; he removed that material and concluded the operation.

In fact, the X-rays and myelogram taken after the 1978 operation revealed that Sitts's spine had lumbarization between S1 and S2, and the material removed by Dr. Eckhardt came from that level; the bulging disk material at L5-S1 was not removed until the October 1979 operation.

. . . .

After hearing oral argument, the court granted the United States' motion for summary judgment, rejecting Sitts's contention that simply because the operation was performed at the wrong level of the spine the question of negligence was within the realm of experience of ordinary citizens:

> I do think that this is a case that would need expert medical testimony and, therefore, since the burden is upon the Plaintiff to show that they could make out a prima facie case and they have produced, in my opinion, no evidence whatsoever that the Government was negligent, I am going to grant the motion for summary judgment made by the Government at this time based upon all of the papers that have been filed and the arguments that I have heard today; summary judgment is granted.

. . . .

II. DISCUSSION

. . . .

A. *The Requirement that Expert Medical Testimony Be Presented*

It is well established in New York law that "unless the alleged act of malpractice falls within the competence of a lay jury to evaluate, it is incumbent upon the plaintiff to present expert testimony in support of the allegations to establish a prima facie case of malpractice."

A physician's obligations to his patient are to possess at least the degree of knowledge and skill possessed by the average member of the medical profession in the community in which he practices, to exercise ordinary and reasonable care in the application of that professional knowledge and skill, and to use his best judgment in the application of his knowledge and skill. In order to show that the defendant has not exercised ordinary and reasonable care, the plaintiff ordinarily must show what the accepted standards of practice were and that the defendant deviated from those standards or failed to apply whatever superior knowledge he had for the plaintiff's benefit.... The requirement that the plaintiff introduce expert medical testimony is imposed in part because "without expert assistance a jury will often have no understanding of what constitutes reasonable behavior in a complex and technical profession such as medicine." *Paul v. Boschenstein*, 105 A.D.2d 248, 249, 482 N.Y.S.2d 870, 872 (2d Dep't 1984). The requirement is no less applicable in a case that is tried to the court without a jury....

New York law recognizes the possibility that a deviation from a proper standard of care may be so clear and obvious that it will be within the understanding of the ordinary layman without the need for expert testimony. For example, where a dentist has pulled the wrong tooth, *see Wenger v. Mollin*, 264 N.Y. 656, 191 N.E. 611 (1934), or where an unexplained injury has occurred to a part of the body remote from the site of the surgery, *see Acosta v. City of New York*, 67 Misc.2d, 756, 763, 324 N.Y.S.2d 137, 144–45 (N.Y.Civ.Ct.1971) (dictum), expert testimony is not needed for the establishment of the plaintiff's prima facie case. *See also* W. KEETON, D. DOBBS, R. KEETON & D. OWEN, PROSSER AND KEETON ON THE LAW OF TORTS § 32, at 189 (5th ed. 1984) ("where the surgeon saws off the wrong leg, or there is injury to a part of the body not within the operative field, it is often held that the jury may infer negligence without the aid of any expert") (footnotes omitted). Even where it might initially appear that the matter would be within the trier's ordinary competence, however, as where, for example, the surgeon left a needle inside the patient's body, if the defendant can proffer any evidence to support the view that a proper standard of care was followed, the plaintiff cannot prevail without introducing expert medical testimony....

Further, even where negligence is easily within the layman's realm of knowledge and hence properly provable without expert testimony, expert testimony may be required to prove that the negligence was the proximate cause of the injury complained of, for

> [a]lmost every person who receives the services of a physician is sick or disabled when he first goes to the physician. Thus there lurks the ever present possibility that it was the patient's original affliction rather than the physician's negligence which caused the ultimate damage. (1 Louisell and Williams, Medical Malpractice, par 8.07, p 213.).

Monahan v. Weichert, 82 A.D.2d at 107, 442 N.Y.S.2d at 298. Thus, in *De Falco v. Long Island College Hospital*, 90 Misc.2d 164, 172, 393 N.Y.S.2d 859, 862 (Sup.Ct., Kings Co. 1977), the court held that negligence was adequately proven without expert medical testimony where a soiled bandage had been applied to the plaintiff's eye that had recently undergone surgery, but that expert testimony was needed to establish that the application of the soiled bandage caused the plaintiff's subsequent infection.

In sum, in the view of the New York courts, the medical malpractice case in which no expert medical testimony is required is "rare." ...

Where such evidence is not proffered, the defendant is entitled to judgment as a matter of law, whether by means of a judgment notwithstanding a jury verdict in favor of the plaintiff, ... or dismissal of the case at the close of the plaintiff's evidence, ... or dismissal after an offer of proof where the plaintiff states that no expert medical evidence will be presented, ... or the granting of a motion for summary judgment in opposition to which the plaintiff fails to come forward with such evidence, *see Goodman v. Emergency Hospital*, 96 Misc.2d 1116, 1117–18, 410 N.Y.S.2d 511, 512 (Sup.Ct., Erie Co. 1978).... As the *Goodman* court stated in granting summary judgment, for plaintiff to resist this motion, it is incumbent upon her to produce a statement from an expert which would deny defendants' contention that their treatment was in accord with accepted medical standards in this professional community. This proof is necessary to support her conclusory allegation of a deviation from such standards and that the deviation proximately caused her injuries. Especially so here where the defendants have come forward and presented prima facie proof that plaintiff's claim is without merit.

96 Misc.2d at 1117–18, 410 N.Y.S.2d at 512.

In the present case, we see no error in the district court's ruling that New York's general rule applies and that, especially in light of the deposition testimony of the orthopedic surgeons suggesting that accepted medical practices were followed in the 1978 operation, Sitts would be required to present expert medical testimony at trial to establish a prima facie case of medical malpractice. While it is conceded by defendant that that operation was performed at the "wrong" level of the spine, this does not of itself establish that the operation was negligently performed, for the case does not concern such organs as those that come in pairs, one on each side of the body, or those that are easily visible such as teeth, which anyone would be expected to identify without difficulty. Rather, it is evident from the orthopedists' pretrial description of the standard method of locating the various vertebrae of the spine that that procedure is not visual or simple. It cannot reasonably be thought that either these procedures or the normal anatomical considerations that underlie them are within the common knowledge of ordinary lay persons. Nor could a lay trier of fact reasonably be expected, without expert assistance, to know the degree to which lumbarization at the S1-S2 level is rare, the degree to which Sitts had such lumbarization, and the degree to which lumbarization complicates the surgical procedure, or to know whether preoperative procedures should have revealed such lumbarization to the VA surgeons. Further, given the fact that bulging material was removed from S1-S2 in the 1978 operation and the fact that there was deposition testimony that back patients often are required to undergo spinal surgery more than once, we doubt that a lay person would be equipped to judge, without expert assistance, whether the pain and suffering complained of by Sitts would have been avoided if the 1978 operation had been performed at L5-S1, or whether instead, further surgery would then have been required for the removal of the bulging material at S1-S2.

In sum, this is not, as plaintiff would have it, the rare case in which a prima facie case of medical malpractice may be established without the presentation of expert medical testimony.

[Affirmed.]

NOTES

(1) What would you think would be the behavioral effect of a decision the other way in *Sitts*? Would it be likely to affect the conduct of physicians conducting that sort of operation in the future?

(2) Would you require expert testimony in the following cases?

(a) An obstetrician, whose office records show that a patient's cervix is "very soft, indicative of rapid delivery after onset of labor," tells the patient's husband to take her to the hospital "immediately," during a phone call in which it is communicated that she thinks she is in labor. However, the physician does not get to the hospital until an hour and a half after the call, during which time the patient is negligently treated by an obstetrical resident.

(b) A doctor diagnoses the pregnancy of a 33-year-old married woman as a tumor and orders an operation that causes a miscarriage.

Does it make a difference if the situation is the other way around — a tumor diagnosed as a pregnancy? A Virginia woman claimed this to be the case, alleging that doctors had treated as a pregnancy what turned out to be a 15 1/2 pound malignant tumor. She said that she suspected a tumor because "of a lack of signs of pregnancy and because I did not feel as I did during [an earlier] pregnancy." *'Pregnancy' Case: 3 Physicians Sued*, WASH. POST, c. 1971.

(c) A child suffers brain damage from a fever that goes to 106 degrees on a thermometer that won't go any higher. The child's regular pediatrician is told on the phone about this reading but does not volunteer to meet the parents at the hospital or to make a house call.

(3) Judicial relaxation of the requirement of expert testimony has at least implicitly taken into account what has been called the "conspiracy of silence" — the refusal of physicians to testify against other doctors because of fear of professional or social reprisal. An example of the attitudes underlying the so-called "conspiracy" appears in a letter written by a radiologist to a young colleague in the 1920s, in which he says that he feels "sure that you think too much of your standing in the various societies to even consider appearing against any regular physician in a malpractice suit." Trostler, *Some Lawsuits I Have Met and Some of the Lessons to be Learned from Them*, 25 RADIOLOGY 329, 332–33 (1935) (quoted in *Note, Medical and Dental X-Rays — A Time for Re-Evaluation and State Action*, 43 NOTRE DAME LAWYER 39, 62 (1967)).

It is now somewhat easier to acquire expert testimony in medical cases. Should that incline courts toward a more rigorous interpretation of the expert testimony requirement? Some recent state legislation has required that potential malpractice plaintiffs present a certification from a physician indicating that there is a solid basis for a claim of substandard medical care. Would you vote for such a statutory provision?

(4) How would you react to an unvarying requirement of expert medical testimony in this case: A physician fails to remove a wire that is embedded in a patient's foot. The patient's foot turns blue, and then black, and oozes "some sort of liquid substance." The Tennessee Supreme Court was acid in its judgment that one need not present expert testimony in such a situation:

Even a barefoot boy knows that when his foot is infested by a sticker, splinter, thorn, pin or other foreign object, it must be removed. Most assuredly this lies within the ken of a layman.

Dr. Rogers [the defendant] apparently thought so. He tried to remove it and upon failure merely treated Runnells with antibiotics, resting and soaking, during all of which time the patient grew steadily worse.

The fact that [another doctor subsequently] removed the wire and the patient promptly healed would lead an average layman to conclude that this was the proper practice and failure to do so was a deviation. Medical testimony could hardly have made the case stronger. Moreover, the jury was entitled to give "weight, credit and value" to the Review Board's finding that the patient should have been referred to a consultant. An inevitable corollary is that Dr. Rogers was negligent in practicing beyond his expertise.

—*Runnells v. Rogers*, 596 S.W.2d 87, 90 (Tenn. 1980).

(5) What is the function of the expert testimony requirement in the judicial administration of professional malpractice cases? Is there an underlying premise concerning the cost of professional services? Is there such a premise in the medical cases concerning the allocation of medical resources? Should a court be focusing on cost considerations? Or, rather, on "fairness"? What are the elements of "fairness" in the decision of whether to require expert testimony in such cases?

(6) Where does the border lie between cases involving professional judgment and other cases in which expert testimony ought not to be a rigid requirement? Consider the case in which an "open door" psychiatric ward has a window that can be opened, and a patient opens the window and jumps through it. Is this a case where expert testimony should be required? Is it an adequate characterization to say that the problem is one of marshalling institutional resources to control conduct rather than a "medical" problem? In that respect, is there a meaningful difference between this case and cases involving the placement of chairs at a banquet? See *LaPlante*, supra §4.01. If this problem is denominated a "medical" question, on what basis could one determine whether it falls within the "common knowledge" exception?

(7) How does *res ipsa* relate to the expert testimony requirement? Consider, for example, the question of what the best rule is to apply in a case in which a surgical team leaves a gauze pad in an abdominal incision. What is the most appropriate rule to apply in such a case? Is it *res ipsa*?

§ 10.05 Physical Causation

PROBLEM*

Jill Danton charged Dr. Peter Billings with failing to diagnose properly her motorcycle accident injury. The accident caused a blood clot to form either in her neck or in her skull. Danton contends the clot formed in her neck. If so, and if Billings, to whom she had gone for treatment, had ordered her hospitalized overnight for observation, the clot likely would have been detected early and Danton could have undergone an operation that might have succeeded in removing the clot. Once the clot traveled from the neck to the skull, or if it originated in her skull, as Billings's experts testified, it was inoperable. The clot's presence in her skull caused Danton paralysis and partial blindness.

---

* Adapted from a decision.

Plaintiff's expert, Dr. Woods, testified on *direct* examination:

Q. Are you saying that the injury to the artery occurred not in the skull, but at the base of the neck?

A. No. I am not saying that. I think with the skull fracture—I mean, she undoubtedly had some damage there, but with the Horner's Syndrome, and the subsequent development of this paralysis, rather rapidly, makes me believe, and with my experience this is the more common thing, is that she developed a clot in the region of her internal carotid artery in her neck.

The clot formed gradually, and then finally, if you will excuse the expression, blew off, and went up and blocked the blood supply to the ophthalmic artery of the eye, and of the major portion of the left—of the right side of the brain.

Then on *cross-examination* the following exchange occurred.

Q. Is that your feeling as to the mechanisms or the thing that occurred in Jill Danton's case?

A. Again, I can't tell. She may have had development of a clot in the neck, and I say that because of the development of the Horner Syndrome. The clot then broke loose, and went up, or she may have had a clot which was produced by the local trauma at the siphon.

Q. Are you able to say which of those conditions did occur with a reasonable degree of medical probability?

A. No.

On *redirect* Dr. Woods testified as follows:

Q. Would the arteriograms have been different in your opinion had they been taken fifteen—twenty hours earlier, or ten hours earlier?

A. I believe so, yes.

Q. In what way would they have been different?

A. I believe that they would have shown a developing thrombosis.

* * *

Danton alleged that "Billings's negligence cost her 'a chance' to remedy the injury." Was Dr. Woods's testimony enough to survive a directed verdict?

HOWARD v. MITCHELL

Alabama Supreme Court
492 So. 2d 1018 (1986)

TORBERT, CHIEF JUSTICE.

This is a wrongful death case in which the plaintiff, Betsy Jane Howard, filed suit against the defendants, Dr. Kermit Mitchell, Dr. Joseph Flippen, and Drs. Mitchell and Flippen, a partnership, alleging that negligence on their part proximately caused the death of her child. The defendants filed a motion for summary judgment, alleging that there were no genuine issues of material fact. The trial court granted the motion, and the plaintiff appeals.

In February 1971, the plaintiff first visited the defendants, who are obstetrician/-gynecologists, complaining of spotting and passing blood clots. The defendants learned that the plaintiff had been six to eight weeks pregnant and determined that she had suffered a spontaneous abortion. The plaintiff's blood was typed at that time as having an Rh negative factor. The plaintiff became pregnant again in 1972 and delivered a healthy baby girl in December of that year. The baby's blood was typed at that time as containing the Rh negative factor also. In 1974, the plaintiff again became pregnant and her doctors discovered at this time that she tested positive for an antibody to the Rh positive factor. This pregnancy was spontaneously aborted. The plaintiff became pregnant once again in 1980 and underwent a cesarean section in March 1981. The infant died several days later from a condition known as erythroblastosis fetalis. This condition results from crossing of the mother's antibodies to the Rh positive factor of the fetus through the placenta and into the fetus's bloodstream, where it destroys the fetus's red blood cells. In 1984, after this suit was filed, the plaintiff's child born in 1972 was correctly typed as having the Rh positive factor.

The defendants treated the plaintiff only on the occasion of her first pregnancy in 1971. She alleges that the defendants did not follow the applicable standard of care in their treatment of her. She contends that since her blood was typed as Rh negative and she had just had a spontaneous abortion, the defendants should have treated her with a medicine known as RhoGAM, in order to prevent the formation of the antibodies to the Rh positive factor. She contends that the RhoGAM treatment, had it been given to her by the defendants in 1971, would have prevented the formation of antibodies to the Rh positive factor and thereby prevented the death of her child in 1981.

The issue presented is whether the defendants' summary judgment was proper. In a medical malpractice case, in order to find liability there must be more than a mere possibility that the alleged negligence caused the injury.... There must be some evidence that that negligence probably caused the injury.... This rule, of course, does not eliminate Alabama's "scintilla" rule, for if there is a scintilla of evidence that the negligence complained of probably caused the injury, then a jury question is presented. *Williams, supra; Orange, supra.* After a careful review of the record, we are of the opinion that the plaintiff has not presented a scintilla of evidence that the defendants' failure to give the RhoGAM treatment probably caused the death of her child.

In opposition to the defendants' motion for summary judgment, the plaintiff presented the deposition of her medical expert, Dr. Marvin A. Krane. Through Dr. Krane's deposition testimony, the plaintiff attempted to establish that the defendants had failed to meet the standard of care required of those doctors who treat Rh-negative females following spontaneous abortions. Dr. Krane clearly testified that at the time the plaintiff saw the defendants the accepted medical practice was to give such a person the RhoGAM treatment within 72 hours of the spontaneous abortion, in order to prevent the development of Rh positive antibodies. It is the Rh positive antibodies, allegedly allowed to develop because of the defendants' negligence, which caused the death of the plaintiff's child.

After this testimony, Dr. Krane's deposition then continued on to the crucial point as to when the plaintiff developed the Rh positive antibodies. Dr. Krane testified that there was only a three to five percent chance that the plaintiff could have developed the Rh positive antibodies following the spontaneous abortion for which she was treated by the defendants in 1971. He further testified that there was at least a twenty percent chance that the plaintiff developed the Rh positive antibodies following the birth of her child in 1972. Dr. Krane also testified that there were no tests available now to determine when the plaintiff developed the Rh positive antibodies, and that it was "more likely that it occurred during the full term pregnancy" in 1972. On the plaintiff's re-direct examination of Dr. Krane, he also testified in the following manner:

> If she could have had the RhoGam after the abortion, we could have eliminated—just about eliminated any sensitization [development of the Rh positive antibodies], and then blame the full term pregnancy, but not having had the RhoGam, it's just a matter of conjecture. You have to throw up you're— flip a coin and say which one was it, but you know that most likely you got a better chance to have it after a full term pregnancy than abortion. But which one caused it, I cannot say.

Further, on re-cross examination, Dr. Krane testified to the following:

> [Q:] He was asking you right at the beginning of his redirect about whether or not you could determine when Mrs. Howard became sensitized as between the 1971 abortion or the 1972 full term delivery, and you made the comment that it would just be conjecture, and you would have to, in effect, toss a coin. Is that what you said?
>
> A: That's what I said, sir.
>
> Q: And so it would be just—it wouldn't even be pure conjecture, in the sense that it would lean more and heavily of the full term pregnancy [sic] as you have already said, would it not?
>
> A: I would agree with that, sir.

We believe that the testimony of the plaintiff's medical expert does not present a scintilla of evidence that the defendants' alleged negligence probably caused the death of her child. What was said in *McClinton v. McClinton*, 258 Ala. 542, 544–45, 63 So.2d 594, 597 (1952), is appropriate in this case:

> "Proof which goes no further than to show an injury could have occurred in an alleged way, does not warrant the conclusion that it did so occur, where from the same proof the injury can with equal probability be attributed to some other cause."
>
> But a nice discrimination must be exercised in the application of this principle. As a theory of causation, a conjecture is simply an explanation consistent with known facts or conditions, but not deducible from them as a reasonable inference. *There may be two or more plausible explanations as to how an event happened or what produced it; yet, if the evidence is without selective application to any one of them, they remain conjectures only.* [Emphasis added]

(Quoting *Southern Ry. Co. v. Dickson*, 211 Ala. 481, 486, 100 So. 665, 669 (1924))....

According to the deposition of the plaintiff's own expert, it would admittedly be pure conjecture or speculation as to when the plaintiff developed the Rh positive antibodies. Although there was a three to five percent chance she developed them after the spontaneous abortion, there was more than an "equal probability", specifically, there was a twenty percent chance, that the development could be attributed to another cause, *i.e.*, the full term pregnancy in 1972. In effect, the evidence produced by the plaintiff was without "selective application" to any one theory of causation. Thus, any conclusion that the defendants' alleged negligence led to the development of the Rh positive antibodies would be based on pure speculation or conjecture, which is an improper basis for a jury verdict....

Furthermore, Dr. Krane's deposition testimony indicated that there was only a mere possibility that the alleged negligence of the defendants caused the death of the plaintiff's child. Under the standard set forth in medical malpractice cases, this was not enough to present a jury question. There must be some evidence that the alleged negligence probably caused the injury.... In the absence of any evidence that the defendants' negligence probably caused the death of the plaintiff's child, the trial court properly granted the summary judgment.

...

AFFIRMED.

THOMPSON v. SOUTHERN PACIFIC TRANSPORTATION CO.

United States Court of Appeals, Fifth Circuit
809 F.2d 1167, cert. denied, 108 S. Ct. 76 (1987)

ALVIN B. RUBIN, CIRCUIT JUDGE:

A railroad brakeman worked at various times during a three-year period aboard a train that entered an industrial plant site contaminated by dioxin. After he had been fired by the railroad for being intoxicated on the job, he sued the owner of the contaminated area contending that a disease from which he was suffering, porphyria, had been caused by his exposure to dioxin. The jury returned a verdict in his favor, but, finding that the worker had failed to offer any substantial evidence to support the thesis that his disease was caused by his exposure, we reverse the judgment in his favor and enter judgment for the plant owner.

I.

Christopher Thompson's work as a brakeman for the Southern Pacific Railroad often brought him to Monsanto's Luling, Louisiana plant which was served by the railroad. After he had been employed for three years, he was fired in 1981 for being intoxicated on duty. Soon thereafter, Thompson sued Southern Pacific and Monsanto, alleging that his occupational exposure to hexachlorobenzene or other chemicals at the Luling plant had caused his severe and disabling case of porphyria cutanea tarda. Porphyria cutanea tarda is an illness characterized by chronic skin lesions and abnormal liver function; it may be caused by administration of estrogens, consumption of alcohol, or exposure to certain chemicals. Thompson based his claim against Southern Pacific on the Federal Employers' Liability Act and his claim against Monsanto on Louisiana negligence law.

While discovery was being conducted, Monsanto publicly announced that dioxin had contaminated a small area of the Luling plant site near the Southern Pacific railroad tracks. Monsanto linked the contamination to periods in 1965 and 1967 when the chemical 2,4,5-T, a precursor of dioxin, was loaded and unloaded at the plant. Meanwhile, discovery showed that no hexachlorobenzene had been found at the Luling facility. Thompson then contended that dioxin caused his porphyria.

On the eve of trial, Thompson settled his claim against Southern Pacific for $5,000. After hearing the evidence, the jury rendered a $200,000 verdict against Monsanto. Monsanto moved for a new trial, judgment notwithstanding the verdict, and a remittitur, but the district court judge denied all three motions. Monsanto appeals on the grounds that the verdict was not supported by sufficient evidence....

... Deferring fully to the jury's prerogatives in weighing conflicting evidence and in determining the credibility of witnesses, we find a lack of substantial evidence to support the verdict, for Thompson did not introduce sufficient evidence at trial to establish a link of causation between his alleged exposure to dioxin at Luling and the development of his porphyria.

Thompson called several expert witnesses to support his theory of causation. One, a chemical engineer, described the chemical composition of dioxin and the methods of sampling soil that might be contaminated with dioxin. He further testified that dioxin contaminating the soil can be ingested, inhaled, or absorbed into the body of an individual working nearby. The engineer did not testify, however, about Thompson's degree of exposure to dioxin; he did not know where Thompson worked at Luling or the amount of time Thompson spent at the plant site. In short, his testimony simply indicated that someone working around dioxin-contaminated soil might develop porphyria and described how that possibility could be established without specifically addressing Thompson's exposure. A good deal of his testimony, in fact, focused on reports of dioxin exposure at locations other than Luling. A second expert, a toxicologist, did testify that dioxin caused Thompson's porphyria. He based his opinion on the fact that Thompson worked at a site where dioxin was found and therefore "definitely could have come into contact with it." He did not, however, have any knowledge about the amount or duration of Thompson's exposure. There was, then, an insufficient factual basis for his opinion. On the other hand, Monsanto's toxicology expert testified that, in view of the dioxin measurements made at the site, Thompson would have received an exposure to dioxin less than 2% of the recommended maximum amount for residential areas, an exposure insufficient to cause porphyria. He further testified that Thompson's symptoms were not consistent with dioxin-induced porphyria: in all previous cases of porphyria associated with dioxin exposure, chloracne has accompanied the porphyria, and Thompson has never suffered from chloracne.

The testimony by the physicians called as experts also failed to substantiate the ultimate issue of causation—that dioxin caused Thompson's porphyria. A neurologist, introduced by Thompson, stated that dioxin exposure could cause the kinds of symptoms that Thompson experienced, but did not offer an opinion as to what in fact had caused Thompson to suffer from the disease. While he did not believe it was caused by alcohol, he testified that he had insufficient information about the concentration of dioxin at Luling or the amount of time Thompson worked there to decide whether exposure to dioxin caused the porphyria.

Five other physicians testified, all of whom had treated Thompson for his porphyria, and none believed that dioxin had caused it. One of the doctors was qualified as an expert in the field of internal medicine with specialized training and work in the specific areas of liver diseases and porphyria. He testified that, in his opinion, Thompson's illness was related to his consumption of alcohol and he too thought that Thompson's failure to develop chloracne excluded dioxin as the cause of the porphyria. Two of the other physicians, both specialists in internal medicine, attributed the illness to Thompson's alcohol consumption. The remaining two physicians either were not asked to give an opinion or had no opinion regarding causation.

...

[Reversed.]

BACKES v. VALSPAR CORPORATION
United States Court of Appeals, Seventh Circuit
783 F.2d 77 (1986)

POSNER, CIRCUIT JUDGE.

The district court granted summary judgment for the defendant, Valspar, in this diversity tort suit brought in 1981 by Royal Backes on behalf of his three children, and dismissed the complaint. Backes has appealed. We must decide whether the district judge was right to find that Valspar had carried its burden of proving that there was no genuine issue of material fact. Fed.R.Civ.P. 56(c).

Between 1976 and 1978 the Backes family lived on what was known as the Johnson property, near Rockford, Illinois. During that period one of the children, a 10-year-old girl, developed rheumatoid arthritis. A medical examination revealed lead in her bloodstream. Another child developed an ovarian condition and an abscessed appendix, while the third had learning difficulties. The children's health and mental acuity improved after they moved away. Valspar, a manufacturer of paints, had until 1972 stored wastes on the Tipton property, which adjoins the Johnson property. The wastes contained phenols, lead, mercury, and other materials hazardous to human health....

Dennis Johnson (no relation to the owner of the Johnson property), a chemist formerly employed by the Illinois Environmental Protection Agency, had in 1975, shortly before the Backes moved onto the Johnson property, taken water samples from two wells on the property. Both contained phenols in amounts several times higher than considered safe for human consumption. He told the Johnsons not to drink the water. Other wells, in the vicinity of the Johnson property, were also contaminated. In 1980, after the Backes left, Dennis Johnson found phenolic paint residue on the Johnson property. It had come, he determined, from drums that Valspar had placed on the Tipton property before 1972. He opined in his affidavit in the district court that the two wells on the Johnson property had been contaminated throughout the period in which the Backes had lived there and that the children's medical problems "might or could have been caused by the drinking of the water from the wells in question, which in my opinion continued during 1976 and 1977 to be contaminated with phenolic content and thus hazardous to injestion [sic] by human beings or animals. Such medical problems are consistent with the medical problems demonstrated by the Johnsons. One of the probable causes for that would be the disposing of hazardous wastes, particularly as I have noted the disposal of phenolic content...."

Valspar pointed out that only one of the children, Kathy (the one who had developed arthritis), had been found to have an abnormal level of a mineral, namely lead, in her body. Valspar submitted an affidavit from a chemist which stated that Valspar had used "minute quantities of lead" in the manufacturing process that had produced the wastes stored on the Tipton property. Valspar also pointed out that no doctor had suggested that any of the children's symptoms were related to the water they had drunk and that a lab report of a water sample taken from one of the wells on the Johnson property in 1977 had stated that the sample did not contain unsafe levels of either bacteria or nitrates.

The district judge granted summary judgment on the ground that the plaintiff had not presented competent evidence that Valspar's wastes had caused the children's ailments. The judge discounted Dennis Johnson's affidavit on the ground that Johnson had not been shown to be qualified to testify either about the contents of Valspar's wastes or about the probable causes of the children's illnesses. The judge thought that without the affidavit the evidence of causality was too weak to create a triable issue.

If the record before us were the record of a trial, and the judge had granted a motion by Valspar for a directed verdict, we might well affirm; the evidence of causality is extremely weak, perhaps too weak to persuade a reasonable factfinder that the plaintiff had proved that Valspar was a cause of any of the children's ailments. But at the summary judgment stage the burden of proof is on the moving party, in this case the defendant, to show that the outcome of a trial would be a foregone conclusion because with discovery complete the opposing party has turned up no evidence of an essential element of his case or defense....

If Dennis Johnson was competent to offer opinion evidence, the plaintiff put in enough evidence, though only barely so, to defeat a motion for summary judgment. Johnson's affidavit does not recite his qualifications but does mention that he testified for the Johnsons in their suit in state court against Valspar, a suit in which Valspar won a jury verdict that was upheld on appeal. The fact that Johnson was allowed to testify as an expert witness in a closely related suit is some indication that he is qualified to give expert testimony in this suit. And though the affidavit does not say that Johnson tested the wells in the course of his official duties for the Illinois EPA, the state court's opinion in *Johnson v. Tipton*, 103 Ill.App.3d 291, 293, 59 Ill.Dec. 179, 183, 431 N.E.2d 464, 468 (1982), attached to Backes' reply to the motion for summary judgment, says so. It makes no difference that Dennis Johnson failed to explain the basis for his opinion that the phenols on the Johnson property had come from the drums of Valspar's wastes stored on the Tipton property; for there is other evidence in the record, as yet uncontradicted, that the drums contained phenols.

We also disagree that Dennis Johnson was unqualified to opine on the health effects of water contaminated by phenols. His job was to test wells for the state's environmental protection agency in order to see whether they were contaminated and therefore unsafe to drink, and apparently the job included interpreting the test results, for he thought it his duty to tell the Johnsons to stop drinking the water. This is some evidence (not great) that he has expert knowledge about the health effects of phenol-contaminated water — which is to say "scientific, technical, or other specialized knowledge [that] will assist the trier of fact to understand the evidence or to determine a fact in issue...." Fed.R.Evid. 702. If at trial Valspar challenges Dennis Johnson's qualifications and the judge conducts a voir dire to determine them, it may turn out that Johnson is unqualified, *see, e.g., Gates v. United States*, 707 F.2d 1141, 1144–45 (10th Cir.1983) (*per curiam*), but no *voir dire* has been conducted yet.

The judge suggested that only a doctor can opine on the causes of illness. The law is to the contrary. *See, e.g., Gideon v. Johns-Manville Sales Corp.*, 761 F.2d 1129, 1136 (5th Cir.1985); *Jenkins v. United States*, 307 F.2d 637, 644 (D.C.Cir.1962) (*en banc*). The court in *Jenkins* cited cases where nonphysicians were allowed to testify to the effects of electrical shock on the human body and a toxicologist was allowed to testify about the effect of an acid on the human eye; more recent cases allowing toxicologists to testify about the effects of poisonous substances on human health include *State v. Sugar*, 100 N.J. 214, 242–43, 495 A.2d 90, 105 (1985), and *Nicholas v. City of Alton*, 107 Ill.App.3d 404, 437 N.E.2d 757 (1982). No doubt Dennis Johnson is incompetent to diagnose a case of rheumatoid arthritis; but if as happened here he is shown a medical report in which a child is diagnosed as suffering from rheumatoid arthritis, he may be competent to give an opinion on the cause of that disease. He may, indeed, be more competent to give such an opinion than the doctor who examined the child. The doctor did not know that she had drunk from wells that may have been contaminated. And it is not much use having a doctor examine her now, because she has long since stopped drinking the contaminated water, and the phenols may have been metabolized and have disappeared—after injuring her health. *See* U.S. Environmental Protection Agency, Ambient Water Quality Criteria for Phenol, ... at C-19.

If Dennis Johnson's affidavit were incredible, this would be grounds for deeming him unqualified to give an opinion. But it is not incredible. Although unscientific people (judges and jurors, for example) may give too much weight to mere coincidence, *see e.g.*, Tversky & Kahneman, *Judgment Under Uncertainty: Heuristic and Biases*, in Judgment Under Uncertainty 3 (Kahneman, Slovic & Tversky eds. 1982), the Backes children did experience an unusual concentration of ailments rare in children, while drinking water from wells that may well have been contaminated; and though it may all just be a giant coincidence, Dennis Johnson's affidavit, plausibly, suggests not. Although the wording of the affidavit is rather mealy-mouthed, it attests to a causal relationship with enough definitiveness to resist summary judgment. At trial the depth of Johnson's confidence can be probed.

Decisive weight cannot be given the negative test results in 1977. The report suggests that the water was not even tested for any of the chemicals that allegedly injured the children. As Johnson pointed out in his affidavit, moreover, a single negative reading is not dispositive. The level of contamination may fluctuate; a heavy rain, for example, might dilute the contaminants sufficiently to make the water test normal. Even if the water was pure in 1977, it doesn't follow that it was pure in 1976, when the Backes family moved onto the property and began drinking the water; and their ailments could have stemmed from contamination in the earlier part of their stay.

Besides Dennis Johnson's affidavit, there is the matter of the lead in Kathy's body. Valspar's affidavit states that Valspar used "minute" amounts of lead in the resins whose waste byproducts were stored on the Tipton property. But "minute" is not zero; and the state's environmental protection agency in 1980 and 1981 found excessive amounts of lead in the soil and in the surface water of the Tipton property. Moreover, Valspar would not (as it thinks) get off the liability hook just by showing that some of Kathy's lead poisoning (if that is what she had) was due to lead dumped by other users of the Tipton site. That would just make Valspar a joint rather than sole tortfeasor.

Weak as the record is, it provides some grounding for a belief that the children's symptoms, particularly Kathy's, were due at least in part to wastes dumped by Valspar. Under Illinois law, which the parties concede governs the substantive issues in this diversity suit, Backes cannot prevail without showing a reasonable certainty that Valspar was the cause of his children's ailments, and this is a requirement that the Illinois courts take seriously. *See, e.g., Johnston v. City of Galva*, 316 Ill. 598, 604–05, 147 N.E. 453, 455 (1925); *Illinois Bell Tel. Co. v. Purex Corp.*, 90 Ill.App.3d 690, 698–99, 45 Ill.Dec. 773, 778–79, 413 N.E.2d 106, 111–12 (1980). But a reasonable certainty is not a certainty; it is a probability. We are mindful of the formidable difficulties of proving causation in toxic-waste cases (*see, e.g.*, Rosenberg, *The Causal Connection in Mass Exposure Cases: A "Public Law" Vision of the Tort System*, 97 Harv.L.Rev. 851, 855–59 (1984); Ginsberg & Weiss, *Common Law Liability for Toxic Torts: A Phantom Remedy*, 9 Hofstra L.Rev. 859, 922–23 (1981)); and we are skeptical that Backes can—without mounting a more formidable scientific (including epidemiological, *see* Black & Lilienfeld, *Epidemiologic Proof in Toxic Tort Litigation*, 52 Fordham L.Rev. 732 (1984)) case than he seems prepared to do—persuade a jury that Valspar was a cause of any of the children's illnesses. But we do not think that he can be prevented, on the basis of the record that was before the district court when it granted Valspar's motion for summary judgment, from trying to prove causation. Backes put in enough evidence—the medical reports, his and his wife's depositions, Dennis Johnson's affidavit—to create a genuine issue of fact concerning Valspar's causal responsibility.

REVERSED.

Earon S. Davis, *Ecological Illnesses*
TRIAL, Oct. 1986, at 34–35, 36*

Ecological illnesses (EI) is a term used to describe some of the more subtle but devastating health effects of chemical exposures in the workplace, at home, and outdoors. These illnesses, according to San Francisco immunologist Alan S. Levin, appear to stem from damage to the immune system, from either acute poisoning by toxic chemicals or from chronic, low-level exposures to many substances that ultimately overwhelm the system.

The exact symptoms of EI (also known as environmental hypersensitivity disorder, chemically induced immune system disregulation, total allergy syndrome, maladaptation syndrome, and the twentieth century disease) may vary from person to person, but they generally involve an increasing intolerance to a wide range of chemicals, including ubiquitous substances like formaldehyde, pesticides (either as indoor or outdoor pollutants or as food and water residues), natural gas fumes, perfumes and scents, and solvents. The EI victim may experience a wide range of disabling conditions, from a generalized weakness and joint or muscle pain to mental confusion, depression, and even hypertension, lung disease, heart disease, and neurological disorders.

As the 1979 U.S. Surgeon General Report on Health Promotion and Disease Prevention says, "There is virtually no major chronic disease to which environmental factors do not contribute, directly or indirectly."

A special commission of the Ontario Ministry of Health (Canada) calls ecological illness "environmental hypersensitivity" and describes it as follows:

> Environmental hypersensitivity is a chronic (*i.e.*, continuing for more than three months) multisystem disorder, usually involving symptoms of the central nervous system and at least one other system. Affected persons are frequently intolerant to some foods and they react adversely to some chemicals and to environmental agents, singly or in combination, at levels generally tolerated by the majority. Affected persons have varying degrees of morbidity, from mild discomfort to total disability. Upon physical examination, the patient is normally free from any abnormal objective findings. Although abnormalities of complement and lymphocytes have been recorded, no single laboratory test, including serum IgE, is consistently altered. Improvement is associated with avoidance of suspected agents and symptoms recur with re-exposure.

. . .

The scope of this unusual cluster of illnesses is broad. EI may befall a student moving into a new apartment that has formaldehyde emissions from carpeting and furnishings,

---

* Reprinted with permission of TRIAL (October 1986). Copyright the Association of Trial Lawyers of America.

a high-tech industry worker exposed to hazardous solvents, or a schoolteacher working near a spirit duplicator. A major cause of EI appears to be the pollutants in modern, airtight office buildings.

Indoor pollutants like pesticides, fumes from gas ranges or poorly vented attached garages, detergents, disinfectants, glues and solvents, paints and coatings, defective furnaces, unvented kerosene space heaters, and tobacco smoke play a major role in the development of EI. . . .

Ora Fred Harris, Jr., *Toxic Tort Litigation and the Causation Element: Is There Any Hope of Reconciliation?*
40 Sw. L.J. 909, 938 (1986)*

Another ingenious method of imposing liability for toxic exposure injuries when no proof of legal causation exists is the duration and intensity theory. The fundamental premise of this theory is that to avoid establishing specific causation the plaintiff need only show that the "aggravation of the disease or the exposure was of such duration and intensity that it generally causes the disease in question, even though actual causation or aggravation cannot be established in the claimant's case."[215]

Clearly, this principle, which originated in *Caudle-Hyatt, Inc. v. Mixon,*[216] an asbestos-related workers' compensation case, spurns the possibility of foreclosing a victim of an asbestos-related illness from recovering because of inability to meet the difficult, if not impossible, burden of proving actual causation. Instead, the plaintiff needs to prove only the duration and intensity of the exposure.

Misgivings arise as to the effectiveness of the duration and intensity approach as a palliative to the traditional tort causation rule in the broad spectrum of toxic or hazardous exposure cases. The less demanding duration and intensity test may be palatable in the well-understood area of asbestos-related maladies. Consequently, courts may be more receptive to assuasive devices that circumvent the harsh ramifications of specific causation in these exposure cases, for more is known about the etiology of asbestos-related diseases, and correspondingly less has to be shown with respect to causation to convince a court of the merits of recovery. To the contrary, scientific uncertainty still pervades most other hazardous waste or toxic substance exposure injuries. Thus, in these types of toxic torts, courts may reject a lenient approach like the duration and intensity theory.[219] Even if courts do not totally reject this theory, plaintiffs would have a greater burden of proving duration and intensity of exposure than plaintiffs in asbestos cases.

---

* Originally appearing in Vol. 40, No. 4 of the *Southwestern Law Journal*. Reprinted with permission from the *SMU Law Review*.

215. *Caudle-Hyatt, Inc. v. Mixon*, 220 Va. 495, 260 S.E.2d 193, 196 (1979).

216. *Id.*

219. Scientific uncertainty about the effects of such hazardous substances as dioxin and Agent Orange on human health and the environment prevents analysis under the duration and intensity test of exposures from these substances even though dioxin and Agent Orange have some well-known reputed effects. *In re Agent Orange Prod. Liab. Litig.*, 597 F. Supp. 740, 782 9 (E.D.N.Y.1984); *U.S. v. Vertac Chem. Corp.*, 489 F. Supp. 870, 885 (E.D. Ark. 1980).

NOTES

(1) The plaintiff's attorney in *Howard* was willing to take the case to the Supreme Court of Alabama. What reasoning would he or she have been hoping the court would use to reverse the judgment? Where is the "scintilla" of evidence supporting Howard's case?

Is the Problem on pages 510–11 a stronger case for the plaintiff than *Howard*? Is there enough in the Problem case to overcome the argument that a finding of causation would be only "conjecture"? What do you see as the principal practical difficulty for attorneys in the preparation of medical witnesses in such cases? What is the common sense problem that courts face in trying to decide the "justice" of a case on such a causation issue?

(2) Do the legal issues in the Problem case principally involve "negligence" or "causation"?

(3) In the *Thompson* and *Backes* cases, two distinguished judges reverse trial court findings — Judge Rubin in effect directs a verdict for the defendant and Judge Posner reverses a defendant's summary judgment. Can you effectively distinguish the two cases?

(4) Could a non-chemist lay person have testified about the effects of the water on the Backes children?

Where is the line between testifying as to a "fact" and an "opinion" in such cases?

(5) *Compare* with *Backes* the following passage in a case brought for the consequences of air pollution:

> A contractor testified as to the damage done to the house, carport, etc., and particularly aluminum and metal, including the damage done to the aluminum windows (corroded and pitted) which he had installed only two years previously. Six people (the Pantyas, their son and three neighbors) testified that when there is a northwest wind, they can stand on their porches and see the materials coming out of the Alton Box stack; it forms a cloud over the area in which they live and falls on everything. It was described as specks like tobacco juice, huge black smut-looking things, big as a fingernail, ashes, etc. These particles eat up clothes hanging on the line, make brown spots where they land on buildings, can't be washed off the house or cars because it smears in water and a residue remains; and it causes burning of the eyes. It causes Mr. Pantya's throat to burn, his nose to bleed and his chest becomes congested. One neighbor testified that the cloud settles in the area as if it were a pocket, and she had seen it occur more than 100 times.

Should a jury be able to draw causation inferences from such testimony? What level of inferences were the lay witnesses making, and from what artifacts? What inferences, at what level of physical processes, would a jury have to make to render a plaintiff's verdict?

(6) Can you generalize, in cases like *Backes* and *Thompson*, about the way that the requirements of "proof" relate to "substantive" tort standards — for example the standard for negligence in discharging hazardous wastes or for exposing a worker to toxic chemicals? Is the excerpt from the "Ecological Illnesses" article instructive on this point?

Are you persuaded by the solution mentioned by Harris in his summary of the case of *Caudle-Hyatt v. Mixon*?

How, if at all, should relevant tort standards be affected by the difficulty of proving causation of illnesses that are generally thought to have an environmental basis?

(7) In confronting problems of the kind presented here, can we do more than say that the legal system must constantly make decisions on the basis of provisional knowledge and that for the sake of finality, it is necessary to trust what may turn out to be the worst kinds of guesses?

Consider, in this connection, the following thoughts:

Three centuries ago, when someone put a curse on another person, if the other subsequently exhibited alarming symptoms, perhaps suffering a heart attack and dying, the utterer of the curse might be held to be a witch.

A hundred years ago this would have been considered nonsense, because everyone knew there were no witches.

Today, if the hexed person could show severe emotional distress, and particularly if he could prove that "the witch" knew of his susceptibility to this kind of conduct, he might conceivably have a cause of action in tort.

Observe how we have progressed as our knowledge of psychology has become more sophisticated.

DAUBERT v. MERRELL DOW PHARMACEUTICALS, INC.
Supreme Court of the United States
509 U.S. 579, 113 S. Ct. 2786 (1993)

Justice BLACKMUN delivered the opinion of the Court.

In this case we are called upon to determine the standard for admitting expert scientific testimony in a federal trial.

I

Petitioners Jason Daubert and Eric Schuller are minor children born with serious birth defects. They and their parents sued respondent in California state court, alleging that the birth defects had been caused by the mothers' ingestion of Bendectin, a prescription anti-nausea drug marketed by respondent. Respondent removed the suits to federal court on diversity grounds.

After extensive discovery, respondent moved for summary judgment, contending that Bendectin does not cause birth defects in humans and that petitioners would be unable to come forward with any admissible evidence that it does. In support of its motion, respondent submitted an affidavit of Steven H. Lamm, physician and epidemiologist, who is a well-credentialed expert on the risks from exposure to various chemical substances.[1] Doctor Lamm stated that he had reviewed all the literature on Bendectin and human birth defects—more than 30 published studies involving over 130,000 patients. No study had found Bendectin to be a human teratogen (i.e., a substance capable of causing malformations in fetuses). On the basis of this review, Doctor Lamm concluded that maternal use of Bendectin during the first trimester of pregnancy has not been shown to be a risk factor for human birth defects.

---

1. Doctor Lamm received his master's and doctor of medicine degrees from the University of Southern California. He has served as a consultant in birth-defect epidemiology for the National Center for Health Statistics and has published numerous articles on the magnitude of risk from exposure to various chemical and biological substances. App. 34–44.

Petitioners did not (and do not) contest this characterization of the published record regarding Bendectin. Instead, they responded to respondent's motion with the testimony of eight experts of their own, each of whom also possessed impressive credentials.[2] These experts had concluded that Bendectin can cause birth defects. Their conclusions were based upon "in vitro" (test tube) and "in vivo" (live) animal studies that found a link between Bendectin and malformations; pharmacological studies of the chemical structure of Bendectin that purported to show similarities between the structure of the drug and that of other substances known to cause birth defects; and the "reanalysis" of previously published epidemiological (human statistical) studies.

The District Court granted respondent's motion for summary judgment. The court stated that scientific evidence is admissible only if the principle upon which it is based is "'sufficiently established to have general acceptance in the field to which it belongs.'" 727 F.Supp. 570, 572 (S.D.Cal.1989), quoting United States v. Kilgus, 571 F.2d 508, 510 (CA9 1978). The court concluded that petitioners' evidence did not meet this standard. Given the vast body of epidemiological data concerning Bendectin, the court held, expert opinion which is not based on epidemiological evidence is not admissible to establish causation. 727 F.Supp., at 575. Thus, the animal-cell studies, live-animal studies, and chemical-structure analyses on which petitioners had relied could not raise by themselves a reasonably disputable jury issue regarding causation. Ibid. Petitioners' epidemiological analyses, based as they were on recalculations of data in previously published studies that had found no causal link between the drug and birth defects, were ruled to be inadmissible because they had not been published or subjected to peer review. Ibid.

The United States Court of Appeals for the Ninth Circuit affirmed. 951 F.2d 1128 (1991). Citing Frye v. United States, 54 App. D.C. 46, 47, 293 F. 1013, 1014 (1923), the court stated that expert opinion based on a scientific technique is inadmissible unless the technique is "generally accepted" as reliable in the relevant scientific community. 951 F.2d, at 1129–1130. The court declared that expert opinion based on a methodology that diverges "significantly from the procedures accepted by recognized authorities in the field ... cannot be shown to be 'generally accepted as a reliable technique.'" Id., at 1130, quoting United States v. Solomon, 753 F.2d 1522, 1526 (CA9 1985).

The court emphasized that other Courts of Appeals considering the risks of Bendectin had refused to admit reanalyses of epidemiological studies that had been neither published nor subjected to peer review.... Those courts had found unpublished reanalyses "particularly problematic in light of the massive weight of the original published studies supporting [respondent's] position, all of which had undergone full scrutiny from the scientific community." Id., at 1130. Contending that reanalysis is generally accepted by the scientific community only when it is subjected to verification and scrutiny by others in the field, the Court of Appeals rejected petitioners' reanalyses as "unpublished, not subjected to the normal peer review process and generated solely for use in litigation." Id., at 1131. The court concluded that petitioners' evidence provided

---

2. For example, Shanna Helen Swan, who received a master's degree in biostatics from Columbia University and a doctorate in statistics from the University of California at Berkeley, is chief of the section of the California Department of Health and Services that determines causes of birth defects, and has served as a consultant to the World Health Organization, the Food and Drug Administration, and the National Institutes of Health.... Stewart A. Newman, who received his master's and a doctorate in chemistry from Columbia University and the University of Chicago, respectively, is a professor at New York Medical College and has spent over a decade studying the effect of chemicals on limb development.... The credentials of the others are similarly impressive....

an insufficient foundation to allow admission of expert testimony that Bendectin caused their injuries and, accordingly, that petitioners could not satisfy their burden of proving causation at trial.

We granted certiorari....

II

A

In the 70 years since its formulation in the Frye case, the "general acceptance" test has been the dominant standard for determining the admissibility of novel scientific evidence at trial....

The Frye test has its origin in a short and citation-free 1923 decision concerning the admissibility of evidence derived from a systolic blood pressure deception test, a crude precursor to the polygraph machine. In what has become a famous (perhaps infamous) passage, the then Court of Appeals for the District of Columbia described the device and its operation and declared: "Just when a scientific principle or discovery crosses the line between the experimental and demonstrable stages is difficult to define. Somewhere in this twilight zone the evidential force of the principle must be recognized, and while courts will go a long way in admitting expert testimony deduced from a well-recognized scientific principle or discovery, *the thing from which the deduction is made must be sufficiently established to have gained general acceptance in the particular field in which it belongs.*" 54 App.D.C., at 47, 293 F., at 1014 (emphasis added). Because the deception test had "not yet gained such standing and scientific recognition among physiological and psychological authorities as would justify the courts in admitting expert testimony deduced from the discovery, development, and experiments thus far made," evidence of its results was ruled inadmissible. Ibid.

The merits of the Frye test have been much debated, and scholarship on its proper scope and application is legion. Petitioners' primary attack, however, is not on the content but on the continuing authority of the rule. They contend that the Frye test was superseded by the adoption of the Federal Rules of Evidence. We agree.

...

Here there is a specific Rule that speaks to the contested issue. Rule 702, governing expert testimony, provides: "If scientific, technical, or other specialized knowledge will assist the trier of fact to understand the evidence or to determine a fact in issue, a witness qualified as an expert by knowledge, skill, experience, training, or education, may testify thereto in the form of an opinion or otherwise." Nothing in the text of this Rule establishes "general acceptance" as an absolute prerequisite to admissibility. Nor does respondent present any clear indication that Rule 702 or the Rules as a whole were intended to incorporate a "general acceptance" standard. The drafting history makes no mention of Frye, and a rigid "general acceptance" requirement would be at odds with the "liberal thrust" of the Federal Rules and their "general approach of relaxing the traditional barriers to 'opinion' testimony." Beech Aircraft Corp. v. Rainey, 488 U.S., at 169, 109 S.Ct., at 450 (citing Rules 701 to 705). See also Weinstein, Rule 702 of the Federal Rules of Evidence is Sound; It Should Not Be Amended, 138 F.R.D. 631, 631 (1991) ("The Rules were designed to depend primarily upon lawyer-adversaries and sensible triers of fact to evaluate conflicts"). Given the Rules' permissive backdrop and their inclusion of a specific rule on expert testimony that does not mention "general acceptance," the assertion that the Rules somehow assimilated Frye is unconvincing. Frye made "general acceptance" the exclusive test for admitting expert scientific testimony.

That austere standard, absent from and incompatible with the Federal Rules of Evidence, should not be applied in federal trials.

That the Frye test was displaced by the Rules of Evidence does not mean, however, that the Rules themselves place no limits on the admissibility of purportedly scientific evidence. Nor is the trial judge disabled from screening such evidence. To the contrary, under the Rules the trial judge must ensure that any and all scientific testimony or evidence admitted is not only relevant, but reliable.

... The adjective "scientific" implies a grounding in the methods and procedures of science. Similarly, the word "knowledge" connotes more than subjective 'belief or unsupported speculation. The term "applies to any body of known facts or to any body of ideas inferred from such facts or accepted as truths on good grounds." Webster's Third New International Dictionary 1252 (1986). Of course, it would be unreasonable to conclude that the subject of scientific testimony must be "known" to a certainty; arguably, there are no certainties in science. See, e.g., Brief for Nicolaas Bloembergen et al. as Amici Curiae 9 ("Indeed, scientists do not assert that they know what is immutably 'true' — they are committed to searching for new, temporary theories to explain, as best they can, phenomena"); Brief for American Association for the Advancement of Science and the National Academy of Sciences as Amici Curiae 7–8 ("Science is not an encyclopedic body of knowledge about the universe. Instead, it represents a process for proposing and refining theoretical explanations about the world that are subject to further testing and refinement") (emphasis in original). But, in order to qualify as "scientific knowledge," an inference or assertion must be derived by the scientific method. Proposed testimony must be supported by appropriate validation—i.e., "good grounds," based on what is known. In short, the requirement that an expert's testimony pertain to "scientific knowledge" establishes a standard of evidentiary reliability.[9]

Rule 702 further requires that the evidence or testimony "assist the trier of fact to understand the evidence or to determine a fact in issue." This condition goes primarily to relevance. "Expert testimony which does not relate to any issue in the case is not relevant and, ergo, non-helpful." 3 Weinstein & Berger P 702[02], p. 702–18. See also United States v. Downing, 753 F.2d 1224, 1242 (CA3 1985) ("An additional consideration under Rule 702 — and another aspect of relevancy — is whether expert testimony proffered in the case is sufficiently tied to the facts of the case that it will aid the jury in resolving a factual dispute"). The consideration has been aptly described by Judge Becker as one of "fit." Ibid. "Fit" is not always obvious, and scientific validity for one purpose is not necessarily scientific validity for other, unrelated purposes. See Starrs, Frye v. United States Restructured and Revitalized: A Proposal to Amend Federal Evi-

---

9. We note that scientists typically distinguish between "validity" (does the principle support what it purports to show?) and "reliability" (does application of the principle produce consistent results?). See Black, *A Unified Theory of Scientific Evidence*, 56 Ford.L.Rev. 595, 599 (1988). Although "the difference between accuracy, validity, and reliability may be such that each is distinct from the other by no more than a hen's kick," Starrs, *Frye v. United States Restructured and Revitalized: A Proposal to Amend Federal Evidence Rule 702*, 26 JURIMETRICS J. 249, 256 (1986), our reference here is to evidentiary reliability—that is, trustworthiness. Cf., e.g., Advisory Committee's Notes on Fed.Rule Evid. 602 ("'[T]he rule requiring that a witness who testifies to a fact which can be perceived by the senses must have had an opportunity to observe, and must have actually observed the fact' is a 'most pervasive manifestation' of the common law insistence upon 'the most reliable sources of information'" (citation omitted)); Advisory Committee's Notes on Art. VIII of the Rules of Evidence (hearsay exceptions will be recognized only "under circumstances supposed to furnish guarantees of trustworthiness"). In a case involving scientific evidence, evidentiary reliability will be based upon scientific validity.

dence Rule 702, and 26 Jurimetrics J. 249, 258 (1986). The study of the phases of the
moon, for example, may provide valid scientific "knowledge" about whether a certain
night was dark, and if darkness is a fact in issue, the knowledge will assist the trier of
fact. However (absent creditable grounds supporting such a link), evidence that the
moon was full on a certain night will not assist the trier of fact in determining whether
an individual was unusually likely to have behaved irrationally on that night. Rule 702's
"helpfulness" standard requires a valid scientific connection to the pertinent inquiry as
a precondition to admissibility.

That these requirements are embodied in Rule 702 is not surprising. Unlike an ordinary witness, see Rule 701, an expert is permitted wide latitude to offer opinions, including those that are not based on first- hand knowledge or observation. See Rules 702
and 703. Presumably, this relaxation of the usual requirement of first-hand knowledge—a rule which represents "a 'most pervasive manifestation' of the common law insistence upon 'the most reliable sources of information,'" Advisory Committee's Notes
on Fed.Rule Evid. 602 ... (citation omitted)—is premised on an assumption that the
expert's opinion will have a reliable basis in the knowledge and experience of his discipline.

C

Faced with a proffer of expert scientific testimony, then, the trial judge must determine at the outset, pursuant to Rule 104(a), whether the expert is proposing to testify
to (1) scientific knowledge that (2) will assist the trier of fact to understand or determine a fact in issue. This entails a preliminary assessment of whether the reasoning or
methodology underlying the testimony is scientifically valid and of whether that reasoning or methodology properly can be applied to the facts in issue. We are confident
that federal judges possess the capacity to undertake this review. Many factors will bear
on the inquiry, and we do not presume to set out a definitive checklist or test. But some
general observations are appropriate.

Ordinarily, a key question to be answered in determining whether a theory or technique is scientific knowledge that will assist the trier of fact will be whether it can be
(and has been) tested. "Scientific methodology today is based on generating hypotheses
and testing them to see if they can be falsified; indeed, this methodology is what distinguishes science from other fields of human inquiry." Green, at 645. See also C. Hempel,
Philosophy of Natural Science 49 (1966) ("[T]he statements constituting a scientific explanation must be capable of empirical test"); K. Popper, Conjectures and Refutations:
The Growth of Scientific Knowledge 37 (5th ed. 1989) ("[T]he criterion of the scientific
status of a theory is its falsifiability, or refutability, or testability").

Another pertinent consideration is whether the theory or technique has been subjected to peer review and publication. Publication (which is but one element of peer review) is not a sine qua non of admissibility; it does not necessarily correlate with reliability, see S. Jasanoff, The Fifth Branch: Science Advisors as Policymakers 61–76 (1990),
and in some instances well-grounded but innovative theories will not have been published, see Horrobin, The Philosophical Basis of Peer Review and the Suppression of Innovation, 263 J.Am.Med.Assn. 1438 (1990). Some propositions, moreover, are too particular, too new, or of too limited interest to be published. But submission to the
scrutiny of the scientific community is a component of "good science," in part because it
increases the likelihood that substantive flaws in methodology will be detected. See J.
Ziman, Reliable Knowledge: An Exploration of the Grounds for Belief in Science 130–
133 (1978); Relman and Angell, How Good Is Peer Review?, 321 New Eng.J.Med. 827

(1989). The fact of publication (or lack thereof) in a peer-reviewed journal thus will be a relevant, though not dispositive, consideration in assessing the scientific validity of a particular technique or methodology on which an opinion is premised.

Additionally, in the case of a particular scientific technique, the court ordinarily should consider the known or potential rate of error, see, e.g., United States v. Smith, 869 F.2d 348, 353–354 (CA7 1989) (surveying studies of the error rate of spectrographic voice identification technique), and the existence and maintenance of standards controlling the technique's operation. See United States v. Williams, 583 F.2d 1194, 1198 (CA2 1978) (noting professional organization's standard governing spectrographic analysis)....

Finally, "general acceptance" can yet have a bearing on the inquiry. A "reliability assessment does not require, although it does permit, explicit identification of a relevant scientific community and an express determination of a particular degree of acceptance within that community." United States v. Downing, 753 F.2d, at 1238. See also 3 Weinstein & Berger P 702[03], pp. 702-41 to 702-42. Widespread acceptance can be an important factor in ruling particular evidence admissible, and "a known technique that has been able to attract only minimal support within the community," Downing, supra, at 1238, may properly be viewed with skepticism.

The inquiry envisioned by Rule 702 is, we emphasize, a flexible one. Its overarching subject is the scientific validity—and thus the evidentiary relevance and reliability—of the principles that underlie a proposed submission. The focus, of course, must be solely on principles and methodology, not on the conclusions that they generate.

Throughout, a judge assessing a proffer of expert scientific testimony under Rule 702 should also be mindful of other applicable rules. Rule 703 provides that expert opinions based on otherwise inadmissible hearsay are to be admitted only if the facts or data are "of a type reasonably relied upon by experts in the particular field in forming opinions or inferences upon the subject." Rule 706 allows the court at its discretion to procure the assistance of an expert of its own choosing. Finally, Rule 403 permits the exclusion of relevant evidence "if its probative value is substantially outweighed by the danger of unfair prejudice, confusion of the issues, or misleading the jury...." Judge Weinstein has explained: "Expert evidence can be both powerful and quite misleading because of the difficulty in evaluating it. Because of this risk, the judge in weighing possible prejudice against probative force under Rule 403 of the present rules exercises more control over experts than over lay witnesses." Weinstein, 138 F.R.D., at 632.

III

We conclude by briefly addressing what appear to be two underlying concerns of the parties and amici in this case. Respondent expresses apprehension that abandonment of "general acceptance" as the exclusive requirement for admission will result in a "free-for-all" in which befuddled juries are confounded by absurd and irrational pseudoscientific assertions. In this regard respondent seems to us to be overly pessimistic about the capabilities of the jury, and of the adversary system generally. Vigorous cross-examination, presentation of contrary evidence, and careful instruction on the burden of proof are the traditional and appropriate means of attacking shaky but admissible evidence.... Additionally, in the event the trial court concludes that the scintilla of evidence presented supporting a position is insufficient to allow a reasonable juror to conclude that the position more likely than not is true, the court remains free to direct a judgment, Fed.Rule Civ.Proc. 50(a), and likewise to grant summary judgment, Fed.Rule Civ.Proc. 56.... These conventional devices, rather than wholesale exclusion under an uncompromising "general acceptance" test, are the appropriate safeguards where the basis of scientific testimony meets the standards of Rule 702.

Petitioners and, to a greater extent, their amici exhibit a different concern. They suggest that recognition of a screening role for the judge that allows for the exclusion of "invalid" evidence will sanction a stifling and repressive scientific orthodoxy and will be inimical to the search for truth.... It is true that open debate is an essential part of both legal and scientific analyses. Yet there are important differences between the quest for truth in the courtroom and the quest for truth in the laboratory. Scientific conclusions are subject to perpetual revision. Law, on the other hand, must resolve disputes finally and quickly. The scientific project is advanced by broad and wide-ranging consideration of a multitude of hypotheses, for those that are incorrect will eventually be shown to be so, and that in itself is an advance. Conjectures that are probably wrong are of little use, however, in the project of reaching a quick, final, and binding legal judgment—often of great consequence—about a particular set of events in the past. We recognize that in practice, a gatekeeping role for the judge, no matter how flexible, inevitably on occasion will prevent the jury from learning of authentic insights and innovations. That, nevertheless, is the balance that is struck by Rules of Evidence designed not for the exhaustive search for cosmic understanding but for the particularized resolution of legal disputes.[13]

IV

To summarize: "general acceptance" is not a necessary precondition to the admissibility of scientific evidence under the Federal Rules of Evidence, but the Rules of Evidence—especially Rule 702—do assign to the trial judge the task of ensuring that an expert's testimony both rests on a reliable foundation and is relevant to the task at hand. Pertinent evidence based on scientifically valid principles will satisfy those demands.

The inquiries of the District Court and the Court of Appeals focused almost exclusively on "general acceptance," as gauged by publication and the decisions of other courts. Accordingly, the judgment of the Court of Appeals is vacated and the case is remanded for further proceedings consistent with this opinion.

It is so ordered.

[Omitted is the separate opinion of Chief Justice REHNQUIST, joined by Justice STEVENS.]

NOTE: *DAUBERT* ELABORATED*

The Supreme Court elaborated on *Daubert* in subsequent decisions. One, *General Electric Co. v. Joiner*,[1] dealt with the "abuse of discretion" standard of appellate review. The plaintiff in *Joiner* alleged that his exposure to PCBs from transformers and dielectric fluid made by the defendants had promoted his small cell lung cancer. Although the trial court found there was a genuine issue of material fact as to the plaintiff's exposure

---

13. This is not to say that judicial interpretation, as opposed to adjudicative factfinding, does not share basic characteristics of the scientific endeavor: "The work of a judge is in one sense enduring and in another ephemeral.... In the endless process of testing and retesting, there is a constant rejection of the dross and a constant retention of whatever is pure and sound and fine." B. CARDOZO, THE NATURE OF THE JUDICIAL PROCESS 178, 179 (1921).

* Adapted from MARSHALL S. SHAPO, THE LAW OF PRODUCTS LIABILITY ¶23.04[1][a] (Supp. 2005).

1. 118 S. Ct. 512, *rev'g* 78 F.3d 524 (11th Cir. 1996).

to PCBs, it held inadmissible the testimony of the plaintiff's experts on the ground that they had not shown there was a causal link between exposure to PCBs and small cell lung cancer. The court of appeals reversed on this point, viewing the district court decision as having erred in excluding the testimony of the plaintiff's experts because the court "drew different conclusions from the research than did each of the experts." The appellate court said that the trial court should only "satisfy itself as to the legal reliability of proffered expert testimony, leaving the jury to decide the correctness of competing expert opinions."[2]

The Supreme Court reversed the court of appeals, saying that that court had applied too "stringent" a standard to the district court's ruling, "[f]ailing to give the trial court the deference that is the hallmark of 'abuse of discretion' review." Reviewing the evidence concerning the studies on which the plaintiff's experts had relied, the Court found "it was within the district court's discretion to conclude" that there was insufficient proof of a linkage between PCBs and lung cancer deaths in that body of data. It noted, for example, that animal studies relied on by the plaintiff's experts had involved direct injections of "massive doses of PCBs" into the bodies of infant mice, whereas the plaintiff was "an adult human being whose alleged exposure to PCBs was far less than the exposure in the animal studies." Chief Justice Rehnquist said that "the studies were so dissimilar to the facts presented in [the] litigation that it was not an abuse of discretion for the District Court to have rejected the experts' reliance on them." The Court also noted that the authors of an epidemiological study relied on by the plaintiff's experts had been "unwilling to say that PCB exposure had caused cancer among the workers they examined," and said that therefore this study "did not support the experts' conclusion that [the plaintiff's] exposure to PCBs caused his cancer." With respect to another epidemiological study, the Court pointed out that an increase in lung cancer deaths among workers at a PCB production plant "was not statistically significant" and that the authors of that study "did not suggest a link between the increase in lung cancer deaths and the exposure to PCBs."[3]

Invoking a statement by the Court in *Daubert* that the "focus … must be solely on principles and methodology, not on the conclusions that they generate," the plaintiff argued that "the District Court's disagreement was with the conclusion that the plaintiff's experts drew from the studies" on which they relied. To this argument, Chief Justice Rehnquist responded that "conclusions and methodology are not entirely distinct from one another." Although he noted that "[t]rained experts commonly extrapolate from existing data," he declared that "nothing in either *Daubert* or the Federal Rules of Evidence requires a district court to admit opinion evidence which is connected to existing data only by the ipse dixit of the expert." He added that "[a] court may conclude that there is simply too great an analytical gap between the data and the opinion proffered."[4]

· · ·

The Court followed *Joiner* with a decision emphasizing that the language of Rule 702 "makes no relevant distinction between 'scientific' knowledge and 'technical' or 'other specialized' knowledge." Applying *Daubert* to an offer of the expert testimony of an engineer in a case involving a tire blowout, the Court concluded that it was within the discretion of a trial judge to exclude the expert's testimony. It declared, moreover, that the "evidentiary rationale" of the "gatekeeping" theory of *Daubert* was not "limited to 'sci-

---

2. 78 F.3d at 533.
3. 118 S. Ct. at 517–519.
4. *Id.* at 519.

entific' knowledge." It also said that "it would prove difficult, if not impossible, for judges to administer evidentiary rules under which a gatekeeping obligation depended upon a distinction between 'scientific' knowledge and 'technical' or 'other specialized' knowledge." It pointed out that there was "no clear line that divides the one from the others," and that "[d]isciplines such as engineering rest upon scientific knowledge."[5]

The Court said that the factors mentioned in *Daubert* as possibly bearing on a trial judge's decision to admit or exclude evidence could legitimately be considered in a case involving engineering testimony. It said it could "neither rule out, nor rule in," those factors "for all cases and for all time." It simply concluded that "a trial court should consider the specific factors identified in *Daubert* where they are reasonable measures of the reliability of expert testimony."[6] The Court's application of these views to the engineer's testimony in the tire case drew on the trial court's finding that "'none' of the *Daubert* factors, including that of 'general acceptance' in the relevant expert community, indicated that [the plaintiff's expert's] testimony was reliable," and the trial court's opinion that were "no countervailing factors operating in favor of admissibility." In particular, the Court saw no evidence that other experts used the test used by the plaintiff's experts or that tire experts normally made the kinds of distinctions he made. It also noted that no one had "refer[red] to any articles or papers that validate" the approach of the plaintiff's expert.[7]

NOTES

(1) What advantages does *Daubert* provide to claimants that they did not have under the *Frye* rule?

(2) What parts of *Daubert* will defendants' lawyers be able to exploit in keeping out the testimony of plaintiffs' experts?

(3)* On the remand in *Daubert*, the Ninth Circuit adhered to its former conclusion that the testimony of the plaintiffs' experts was inadmissible. Judge Kozinski emphasized that under *Daubert*, an "expert's bald assurance of validity is not enough" and that "the party presenting the expert must show that the expert's findings are based on sound science," which would "require some objective, independent validation of the expert's methodology."[1] Judge Kozinski found it telling that although "Bendectin litigation has been pending in the courts for over a decade," "[n]one of the plaintiffs' experts has published his work on Bendectin in a scientific journal or solicited formal review by his colleagues." The fact that "no one in the scientific community — except defendant's experts — has deemed these studies worthy of verification, refutation or even comment" indicated to Judge Kozinski that "[i]t's as if there were a tacit understanding within the scientific community that what's going on here is not science at all, but litigation."[2] In that connection, he pointed out that although the plaintiffs' witnesses were "all experts in their respective fields, none claims to have studied the effect of Bendectin on limb reduction defects before being hired to testify in this or related cases."[3] These views ap-

---

5. *Kumho Tire Co. v. Carmichael*, 119 S. Ct. 1167, 1174 (1999).
6. *Id.* at 1175–76.
7. *Id.* at 1178.
   * This note is taken from MARSHALL S. SHAPO, THE LAW OF PRODUCTS LIABILITY ¶ 23.04[1][a] (Supp. 2005).
1. *Daubert v. Merrell Dow Pharmaceuticals, Inc.*, 43 F.3d 1311, 1316 (9th Cir. 1995).
2. *Id.* at 1318.
3. *Id.* at 1317.

peared against the background of Judge Kozinski's observation that "[t]he FDA—an agency not known for its promiscuity in approving drugs—continues to approve Bendectin for use by pregnant women because 'available data do not demonstrate an association between birth defects and Bendectin.'"[4]

(4) Does *Daubert* effectively align the search for "truth" by courts handling litigation with the search for scientific "truth"? Is this desirable?

Consider the declaration of a Texas appellate court, in a Bendectin case, that it would "accept the jury's verdict as true except in very limited circumstances," and its view that the jury verdict is "the bedrock of our jurisprudence, however wrong its conclusion is in the eye of God or objective reality." *Merrell Dow Pharmaceuticals, Inc. v. Havner*, 907 S.W.2d 535, 553 (Tex. Ct. App. 1995). Do you think this is an accurate description of the practical meaning of jury verdicts? Is it one that is congenial to your view of the litigation process? The Texas Supreme Court reversed the appellate court's judgment for the plaintiff, defining the legal problem as one of "balanc[ing] the need to compensate those who have been injured by the wrongful actions of another with the concept deeply embedded in our jurisprudence that a defendant cannot be found liable for any injury unless the preponderance of the evidence supports cause in fact." 953 S.W.2d 706, 718 (Tex. 1997). Among other things, the court said that it did "not hold that publication is a prerequisite for scientific reliability in every case," but it quoted the statement of a precedent that "courts must be 'especially skeptical' of scientific evidence that has not been published or subjected to peer review." *Id.* at 727.

(5) Although *Daubert* originally appeared to be relatively friendly to plaintiffs, a summary of federal opinions between 1980 and 1999 indicated that after the decision, "expert evidence was more regularly contested and more frequently excluded." For example, exclusion of expert testimony rose from 25 percent before *Daubert* to 41 percent five years later, and the percentage of judges who used pre-trial hearings rose from 51 percent in 1991 to 77 percent in 1997. It should be noted that one effect of *Daubert* was to make lawyers more careful about their own witnesses: 48 percent of lawyers surveyed "scrutinized their own experts more carefully." Gary Edmond & David Mercer, Daubert *and the Exclusionary Ethos: The Convergence of Corporate and Judicial Attitudes Towards the Admissibility of Expert Evidence in Tort Litigation*, 26 L. & Pol'y 231, 243–44 (2004) (summarizing studies).

---

4. *Id.* at 1314.

Chapter 11

LIABILITY AND APPORTIONMENT OF DAMAGES AMONG MULTIPLE DEFENDANTS

§ 11.01 Joint Liability and Other Multiple Liabilities

PROBLEM: AN INDIVISIBLE INJURY

In *Summers v. Tice*, 33 Cal. 2d 80, 199 P.2d 1 (1948), the defendants were quail hunters who fired simultaneously. One piece of bird shot hit the plaintiff in the eye and another in the upper lip. The trial court found the defendants jointly liable, the effect of which was that the plaintiff could collect the entire judgment from either, subject to apportionment of the damages by the defendants between themselves. The California Supreme Court affirmed. What would be the proper rationale for this result, if there is one?

PRICE v. HALSTEAD

West Virginia Supreme Court of Appeals
355 S.E.2d 380 (1987)

MILLER, JUSTICE:

. . .

I.

The plaintiffs are the administrator of the estate of Kenneth C. Wall and Mr. Wall's surviving wife, Louise Wall. The complaint alleges that on November 24, 1983, Mr. Wall was driving a pickup truck northbound on U.S. Route 119 near Peytona, West Virginia. His wife and two minor children were passengers in the truck. Stephen E. Garretson was driving in a southerly direction in an automobile owned by his mother, and in which the defendants were passengers. According to the complaint, Mr. Garretson was driving while under the influence of alcohol and marijuana and was traveling at an excessive rate of speed.

The complaint also states that both before and during the trip, Mr. Garretson and his passengers were consuming alcoholic beverages and smoking marijuana. All of the passengers were actively engaged in providing these substances to Mr. Garretson. Mr.

Garretson lost control of his automobile and struck the Wall's vehicle head-on while attempting to pass another southbound vehicle. Mr. Wall was killed and his passengers received serious bodily injuries.

The plaintiffs advanced four theories of recovery against the defendants. First, they alleged that the defendants were engaged in a joint venture, the purpose of which was to "purchas[e] and/or utiliz[e] gas, beer, and marijuana" while joy riding. Second, they alleged the above described activities constituted a joint enterprise. Third, they alleged the defendants were negligent in failing to restrain or remonstrate Mr. Garretson when they knew or should have known he was driving while under the influence of alcohol and drugs. Finally, it is alleged that the defendants, knowing Mr. Garretson was driving while intoxicated, substantially assisted or encouraged his tortious activity by providing him with additional drugs and alcohol.

II.
THEORIES OF JOINT VENTURE AND ENTERPRISE
A.

The plaintiffs attempt to impute liability to the passengers upon alternative theories of joint venture and joint enterprise. While at least one of our older cases apparently used these terms interchangeably, *Horchler v. Van Zandt*, 120 W.Va. 452, 199 S.E. 65 (1938), we take this opportunity to reaffirm our line of cases which serve to distinguish them. A joint venture or, as it is sometimes referred to, a joint adventure, is "an association of two or more persons *to carry out a single business enterprise for profit*, for which purpose they combine their property, money, effects, skill, and knowledge." *Nesbitt v. Flaccus*, 149 W.Va. 65, 73–74, 138 S.E.2d 859, 865 (1964). (Emphasis added).

. . . .

Here, there are no allegations in the complaint which would indicate that the occupants of the car were engaged in any type of business enterprise. Thus, the trial court was correct in dismissing this theory as a matter of law.

B.

A joint enterprise is distinguished from a joint venture by the fact that there is no business motive underlying the parties' efforts in a joint enterprise. This point was made in a rather peripheral fashion in *Stogdon v. Charleston Transit Co.*, 127 W.Va. 286, 292, 32 S.E.2d 276, 279 (1944), where the Court distinguished "between a 'joint adventure' and a 'joint enterprise', the first being for profit and the second not necessarily so." . . .

We have utilized the joint enterprise concept in suits involving automobile accidents where the negligence of the driver is sought to be imputed to the passenger. The most common fact pattern involves a motor vehicle passenger who sues the operator of another vehicle claiming that his negligence was the proximate cause of the accident. This defendant then asserts that the passenger cannot recover because he was engaged in a joint enterprise with the driver of his vehicle, and that his driver's negligence must be imputed to him.

In this case, the plaintiffs seek to hold the passengers directly liable for the negligence of their driver. It is generally recognized that a passenger can be held liable as a defendant for the negligence of his driver if they were engaged in a joint enterprise. This point is tersely stated in 7A Am.Jur.2d *Automobiles and Highway Traffic* § 634 (1980): "It is a general rule that the negligence of a member of a joint enterprise causing injury to a third party is imputable to other members of the enterprise and that all may be held liable for the injury." *See also* 60A C.J.S. *Motor Vehicles* § 444 (1969).

In applying a joint enterprise theory to occupants of a motor vehicle, we have emphasized as the critical element the common right to control the vehicle on the part of
its occupants, as indicated by the single Syllabus of *Stogdon*:

> Where there is no showing of a common right to control the use of an automo-
> bile, an instruction to a jury that it may return a verdict based upon the exis-
> tence of a joint enterprise is erroneous.

This principle was further elaborated upon in Syllabus Point 8 of *Frampton v. Consolidated Bus Lines, Inc.*, 134 W.Va. 815, 62 S.E.2d 126 (1950):

> The relationship of joint enterprise between the owner of an automobile dri-
> ving the same and a guest passenger in the vehicle is not established by the
> mere fact that the driver and passenger were riding together to the same desti-
> nation for a common purpose, where the passenger had no voice in directing
> and controlling the operation of the automobile.

. . .

There has been a rather marked tendency to restrict joint enterprise liability in cases
involving motor vehicle passengers. It is now generally agreed, as we held in *Frampton*,
that something more is required to invoke the doctrine than an agreement to travel to a
particular destination for a common purpose.... Moreover, most courts now reject application of the doctrine of joint enterprise to arrangements to travel together for
merely social or recreational purposes.

From the allegations of the complaint, it appears that the passengers and the driver em-
barked on a common purpose, that of drinking and joy riding. This, however, would not
be the type of endeavor that would give rise to a joint enterprise. Consequently, we find
that the circuit court was correct in rejecting the joint enterprise theory as a matter of law.

. . .

IV.
SUBSTANTIAL ASSISTANCE AND ENCOURAGEMENT

Finally, the plaintiffs rely upon a theory of joint concerted tortious activity as defined in Restatement (Second) of Torts § 876(b) (1966): "For harm resulting to a third
person from the tortious conduct of another, one is subject to liability if he ... (b)
knows that the other's conduct constitutes a breach of duty and gives substantial assistance or encouragement to the other so to conduct himself."[1]

---

1. The remaining portions of Section 876 are:
For harm resulting to a third person from the tortious conduct of another, one is subject to liability
if he

> (a) does a tortious act in concert with the other or pursuant to a common design with
> him, or

. . .

> (c) gives substantial assistance to the other in accomplishing a tortious result and his own
> conduct, separately considered, constitutes a breach of duty to the third person.

In comment d to Section 876 of the RESTATEMENT (SECOND)OF TORTS (1966), these statements are
made relative to Section 876(b):

> Advice or encouragement to act operates as a moral support to a tortfeasor and if the
> act encouraged is known to be tortious it has the same effect upon the liability of the ad-
> viser as participation or physical assistance. If the encouragement or assistance is a sub-
> stantial factor in causing the resulting tort, the one giving it is himself a tortfeasor and is
> responsible for the consequences of the other's act....
> The assistance or participation by the defendant may be so slight that he is not liable
> for the act of the other. In determining this, the nature of the act encouraged, the amount

Specifically, they allege the defendants lent substantial aid and encouragement to Mr. Garretson in his negligent operation of the vehicle. This theory is sometimes termed as aiding and abetting a tort. The basis for imposing liability under an aiding and abetting theory is that if the breach of a duty by the actor was substantially encouraged by the conduct of a third party, then this party may also be found liable. This theory is by no means novel and is expressed in 7A Am.Jur.2d *Automobiles and Highway Traffic* § 635 (1980):

> [A] guest may be held liable for the consequences of the driver's negligent operation of his motor vehicle, where the guest directs or encourages the negligent act, or personally co-operates therein. Ratification of the negligent conduct of the driver by a guest may be equivalent to command, and co-operation may be inferred from acquiescence where there is power to restrain.

In a somewhat related vein, we have held that the employer of a motor vehicle operator could be liable to a third party who was injured when the employee fell asleep and lost control of his automobile. *Robertson v. LeMaster*, 171 W.Va. 607, 301 S.E.2d 563 (1983). The employer's liability in Robertson was not based on *respondeat superior*, but on the fact that he had caused the employee to work twenty-seven hours and when the employee complained that he was exhausted, the employer sent him to his home some fifty miles away. After an extensive review of various legal authorities, we concluded in Syllabus Point 2:

> One who engages in affirmative conduct, and thereafter realizes or should realize that such conduct has created an unreasonable risk of harm to another, is under a duty to exercise reasonable care to prevent the threatened harm.

. . .

In the present case, the facts are even more egregious than in *Robertson* as the passengers are alleged to have directly participated and to have encouraged the driver to continue to drink and smoke marijuana when he was already visibly intoxicated. There can be no question that if the driver was driving under the influence of alcohol or drugs, this would be a violation of our motor vehicle statute. W.Va.Code, 17C-5-2 (1983). We have in the past held on a number of occasions that the violation of a provision of our motor vehicle statutes is *prima facie* evidence of negligence.

. . .

Furthermore, if there is any area of social policy on which there has been virtual unanimity of agreement between courts and legislatures it is the need to stem the tide of injuries and deaths arising from driving under the influence of alcohol and drugs. Courts have increasingly expanded the tort law to hold those who dispense alcoholic beverages liable for injuries inflicted on third parties by those who have consumed too much alcohol.

Several courts have addressed the issue of whether passengers can be liable to a third party when they actively encourage the driver, who is already under the influence of alcohol or drugs, to continue its use and such encouragement leads to an accident. In *Aebischer v. Reidt*, 74 Or.App. 692, 704 P.2d 531, *appeal denied*, 300 Or. 332, 710 P.2d 147 (1985), the court did impose Section 876 liability on a group of automobile passengers. It was alleged in *Aebischer* that the passengers had, at various times throughout the

---

of assistance given by the defendant, his presence or absence at the time of the tort, his relation to the other and his state of mind are all considered.

evening, purchased marijuana and provided it to the driver. It was further alleged that the driver kept grabbing a pipe containing marijuana and that one of the passengers kept refilling it and passing it around to all in the car, including the driver. The Oregon court held that these facts presented a jury question under the aiding and abetting theory and reversed a summary judgment:

> We conclude that a reasonable jury could find from the plaintiff's evidence that defendant provided substantial assistance to Smith's negligent driving by continuing to refill the pipe and passing it to him, or knowing Smith would grab it from him, when he knew or should have known that the marijuana would contribute to Smith's intoxication and further impair his ability to drive. That evidence and the evidence that marijuana can impair driving ability and that Smith was affected by the marijuana was sufficient to present a jury question on Reidt's liability.

74 Or.App. at 696, 704 P.2d at 533.

The defendants cite several cases which they contend stand for an opposite result, but we find them not necessarily contrary....

There is no question that the passengers' involvement in encouraging the driver must be substantial in order to affix Section 876 liability. We would agree with the result in *Olson v. Ische*, 343 N.W.2d 284 (Minn.1984), where the driver and his passenger left a party with each of them carrying a cup of beer. They continued to drink their beer and the accident occurred as they were driving home. There was nothing to suggest that the passenger had substantially encouraged the driver's drinking.

...

What we discern as a proper rule is that a passenger may be found liable for injuries to a third party caused by the intoxication of the driver of the vehicle in which he is riding, if the following conditions are met: (1) the driver was operating his vehicle under the influence of alcohol or drugs which proximately caused the accident resulting in the third party's injuries, and (2) the passenger's conduct substantially encouraged or assisted the driver's alcohol or drug impairment.

In view of the fact that the allegations in the complaint stated that the passengers had substantially contributed to and assisted the driver's continued use of alcohol and drugs while he was already impaired and that the accident was the proximate cause of his impairment, the defendants' motion to dismiss as to the plaintiffs' fourth count should not have been granted. Consequently, the judgment of the circuit court is reversed and this case is remanded.

Affirmed, in part, Reversed, in part, and Remanded.

NOTES

(1) Should there be a difference between the analysis that is applied to the case of a plaintiff who has suffered two wounds after two hunters fired their guns and that used in a case in which the plaintiff suffers two wounds following a volley by four hunters? In the case of the four hunters, should all four be jointly liable? Should joint liability apply to 15 hunters who all fire at the same time, if the plaintiff suffers a single wound?

What should be the result when the victim in a case involving two hunter defendants is killed and the autopsy shows only one wound?

(2) What would be your response to a case in which state officers raided a gambling den, and an unidentified employee of that establishment fired a bullet that hit one of

the officers? If there were 23 gamblers on the premises, could the injured officer successfully join all of them with a complaint alleging that "all of those defendants engaged in said unlawful, common enterprises are jointly and severally liable to the plaintiff for compensatory as well as punitive damages"?

(3) If you consider the result in *Summers* (summarized in the Problem, supra before *Price*) a just one, consider the problem that arises when A, B, and C all fire simultaneously and a single ricocheting shot hits C. Defining "joint liability" to mean that each tortfeasor may be held for the entire injury, would you allow A and B to be held jointly liable?

(4) If you could propose a legislative compensation solution for the problem in *Summers*, what would it be?

(5) The following improbable set of facts is adapted from a state court decision:

> The accident for which the defendant was responsible occurred on August 4, 1961. Later, the plaintiff was involved in three more accidents: on February 11, 1962, November 16, 1962, and January 4, 1965. Most of her injuries in the second, third and fourth accidents involved the same area of her body injured in the first accident.

Should this person be able to recover from the first colliding driver all the damages she sustained in all four accidents, provided that she asserts that the first driver was negligent, and that she was not contributorily at fault in any of the accidents? Assume that the statute of limitations has not run on a suit against the first driver.

(6) Consider the response of the Court of Appeals for the District of Columbia to a case in which the plaintiffs alleged that a lending corporation, brokers for a loan, a settlement attorney, and a man who financed the loan had defrauded them of their home. The jury awarded fraud damages against the various defendants in varying amounts. The damages included a $150,000 figure, including $100,000 compensatory damages, which was assessed against the lending corporation and its president, and an award of $11,600, including $5,100 compensatory damages, which was apportioned among the loan brokers and the financier. The jury specifically found that there was no "joint venture," but the court thought that this finding "by no means resolves the issue of joint and several liability":

> The gravamen of plaintiffs' suit is a single *principal* injury—the loss of their home. District of Columbia law requires that the compensatory damages be awarded jointly and severally against all defendants found liable for contributing to that single *principal* injury....

> Federal appellate courts are statutorily authorized to "modify ... any judgment ... of a court lawfully brought before it for review, and [to] remand the cause and direct the entry of such appropriate judgment as may be just under the circumstances." 28 U.S.C. §2106 (1982).... As local precedent prevents us from awarding the sum total of the compensatory damage awards against all tortfeasors,*[Greet v.] Otis Elevator [Co.]*, 187 A.2d at 898 ("It is a matter of conjecture whether the jury, if properly instructed, would have returned a verdict for the full amount against either defendant."), we are thus left with essentially two options—a new trial, or a modified judgment for less than the sum of the individual awards.

> Recognizing that a new trial, even if restricted to the issue of compensatory damages, would be unduly burdensome on the parties, we prefer in this case to

apply the rule adopted by many other jurisdictions: in actions against joint tortfeasors where the jury has erroneously apportioned damages, without stating an aggregate amount, apportionment of damages should be omitted, and the verdict directed against all defendants for the largest sum found against any defendant.... We accordingly direct the district court to enter a judgment for $100,000 in compensatory damages jointly and severally against all defendants liable to plaintiffs on the fraud claim.

Faison v. Nationwide Mortg. Corp., 839 F.2d 680, 687–88 (D.C. Cir. 1987).

Do you think this is a just solution to the problem described?

(7) Should there be a difference between the basic rule applicable in cases involving a single trauma, for example from an automobile collision or a gunshot, and that applied to cases in which injury is alleged to have arisen from cumulative externalities, as when a downstream landowner sues several factories upstream for pollution? What practical differences are likely to influence decisions in these cases?

(8) Consider the case of a motorist who dies a week after an automobile accident, unaware to the end that he was suffering from terminal lung cancer, which the coroner lists as the cause of death. What would be his representative's chances of success in a suit against the negligent colliding driver, and how would you establish the damages? *Cf. Follett v. Jones*, 252 Ark. 950, 481 S.W.2d 713 (1972).

(9) An interesting set of problems arises when a defendant tries to involve, rather than merely to invoke the help of, the Deity. The problem of ice on the road is illustrative. In a legal malpractice case, a damages issue turned on the value of the plaintiff's claim in an underlying action involving an auto accident. In the accident case, in which a truck had a collision that killed the plaintiff's son after the truck hit a patch of ice, the trial court apportioned damages 40 percent to the truck driver and 60 percent to "Act of God." The appellate court was theologically unpersuaded. It found the central question to be whether the truck driver who skidded on the ice had exercised due care or not. If that driver did behave with due care, the proper characterization of the occurrence was as an unavoidable accident. If she did not, she must be totally responsible. The court quoted a precedent on the point that the cause of skidding on the ice was "inevitably ... a combination of (1) the hazardous condition, and (2) the operation of the motor vehicle." Yet, despite this dual causation, it drew from another precedent the lesson that if the colliding driver in such a situation was negligent, that driver would be "liable for the resulting harm, even though the ice may also have been a cause in fact of the accident." *Sparks v. Craft*, 75 F.3d 257, 263 (6th Cir. 1996).

(10) There has been considerable legislative activity directed to both modification and abolition of the doctrine of joint and several liability. As a member of a state legislature, would you vote to abolish the doctrine or to restrict its application?

SPECIAL NOTE ON INDUSTRYWIDE LIABILITY AND RELATED ISSUES

SHAPO, THE LAW OF PRODUCTS LIABILITY ¶ 12.21[1]–[3] (4th ed. 2001)

Some of the more complex questions concerning joint liability arise from cases in which plaintiffs present themselves as wrestling with the production process of an entire industry. Claimants have pursued diverse strategies with varying results. In some cases, the effort has been to sue virtually the whole industry. In others, the claimant has sighted his artillery on a few dominant firms. In still others, the focus of litigation has been on one firm whose contribution to an injury may be quite uncertain.

One of the most striking extensions of joint liability appears in *Hall v. E.I. DuPont de Nemours & Co.*[533] In this case, Judge Weinstein refused to dismiss an action against several manufacturers of blasting caps and their trade association, who faced a suit by children injured in 18 separate accidents allegedly caused by the devices. Unable to identify the manufacturers of the caps that caused their particular injuries, the plaintiffs alleged that the defendants, "comprising virtually the entire blasting cap industry of the United States," had been negligent in failing to put warnings on individual blasting caps and in not taking other precautions.

Addressing the question of how much joint control of risk was necessary to impose liability, Judge Weinstein emphasized that the plaintiffs were not obliged to show a profit-sharing joint venture. He indicated that it would be sufficient to "prove the existence of an explicit agreement and joint action among the defendants with regard to warnings and other safety features," or to present evidence of "parallel behavior sufficient to support an inference of tacit agreement or cooperation." Moreover, he said it would be possible to infer sufficient joint control because the defendants, "acting independently, adhered to an industry-wide standard or custom with regard to the safety features of blasting caps."

Judge Weinstein also found potential grounds for joint liability in principles of what he characterized as "enterprise liability," a label he applied to the fixing of damages on "the most strategically placed participants in the risk-creating process." Stressing that the particular decision was limited to an industry with relatively few producers, he was not prepared to dismiss the argument that "the entire blasting cap industry and its trade association provide the logical locus at which precautions should be taken and liability imposed." Having set out these premises, Judge Weinstein said, perhaps most extraordinarily, that proof by a preponderance of the evidence that the injury-causing caps had been made by one of the named defendants, even without a showing of which one, would shift the burden of proof on the causation issue to the several defendants.

. . .

… These problems have presented themselves in an especially fascinating fact pattern in the drug area. The focal point is a set of cases arising from attempts to stave off miscarriage through use of the hormone DES, a therapy alleged to have caused unusual vaginal cancers in the very children whose uterine existence doctors sought to preserve by the drug.

. . .

[i] *Rejection of Traditional Doctrine.* A most remarkable decision in this group of cases came from the California Supreme Court. The plaintiffs in *Sindell v. Abbott Laboratories*,[542] representing both themselves and a class, were "DES daughters" who sued several manufacturers among the 200 companies that had made the product; five of these firms were respondents in the appeal. In an opinion by Justice Mosk, the California court rejected several theories proffered by the plaintiff but finally allowed one novel one to stand.

---

533. 345 F. Supp. 353 (E.D. N.Y. 1972).
542. 26 Cal. 3d 588, 607 P.2d 924, 164 Cal. Rptr. 132, *cert. denied*, 449 U.S. 912 (1980).

The first theory was based on *Summers v. Tice*, a classic California decision imposing joint liability on two hunters who negligently shot in the direction of the plaintiff—a judgment reached although there was no way to determine which defendant had fired the shot that caused the injury. The theory of this case had become characterized in the products areas as "alternative liability." The DES defendants in *Sindell* argued that, while in *Summers* there was a 50 percent chance that one of the two defendants was responsible for the plaintiffs' injuries, any one of the two hundred companies that manufactured the DES might have made the exact product that harmed the plaintiff. Thus, the *Sindell* defendants contended that there was "no rational basis" to infer that any of them caused the plaintiffs' injuries and that there was not even a "reasonable possibility" that any of them was reasonable. The court found these arguments "persuasive," saying that "the possibility that any of the five defendants supplied the DES to plaintiff's mother is so remote that it would be unfair to require each defendant to exonerate itself."

Also rejecting the plaintiffs' separate "concert-of-action" theory, the court distinguished precedents including a fowl-hunting case and a drag-racing case. Justice Mosk noted that there was no allegation that each defendant knew that the other defendants' conduct was tortious toward the plaintiff or that they "assisted and encouraged one another" to test the drug inadequately and to provide inadequate warnings.

The court also refused to apply an "enterprise liability" theory based on the blasting cap case discussed above. The court noted that in that case the six manufacturers represented nearly the entire blasting cap industry in the nation, as contrasted with the 200 manufacturers of DES. Moreover, although pointing out that adherence to FDA standards could not "absolve a manufacturer of liability to which it otherwise would be subject," the court declared that, since the "government plays such a pervasive role in formulating the criteria for the testing and marketing of drugs, it would be unfair to impose upon a manufacturer liability for injuries resulting from the use of a drug which it did not supply simply because it followed the standards of the industry."

[ii] *Market Share Theory.* Having rejected these theories, however, the court saved the plaintiff's complaint by formulating a theory based on market shares. Given the allegation that six or seven companies produced 90 percent of the DES marketed, the court said there was "a corresponding likelihood that this comparative handful of producers manufactured the DES which caused plaintiff's injuries, and only a 10 percent likelihood that the offending producer would escape liability." In these circumstances, the court argued that "the injustice of shifting the burden of proof to defendants to demonstrate that they could not have made the substance which injured plaintiff is significantly diminished." The court, although it took note of a commentary suggesting that a plaintiff must show a 75 to 80 percent share of the market to succeed on this theory, held "only that a substantial percentage is required." Under this rule, "[e]ach defendant will be held liable for the proportion of the judgment represented by its share of that market unless it demonstrates that it could not have made the product which caused plaintiff's injuries."

Dissenting, Justice Richardson complained that "'[m]arket share' liability represents a new high water mark in tort law." He conceded the propriety of using market share data for circumstantial proof that a particular defendant probably caused a plaintiff's injuries, but he criticized the majority's use of the evidence as being for "an entirely different purpose, namely, to impose and allocate liability among multiple defendants only one of whom *may* have produced the drug which injured plaintiffs." He found the new theory unjust, moreover, in that it treated claimants using it "far more favorably than ... plaintiffs in routine tort actions." Pointing out that plaintiffs in ordinary tort cases "must take a chance that defendants can be reached and can respond financially," he asked, "On what principle should those plaintiffs who wholly fail to prove any causation, an essential element of the traditional tort cause of action, be rewarded by being offered both a wider selection of potential defendants and a greater opportunity for recovery?" Noting a reference by the majority to the notion that the defendants were "better able to bear the cost" of injuries from defective products, Justice Richardson commented, "A system priding itself on '*equal* justice under law' does not flower when the *liability* as well as the *damage* aspect of a tort action is determined by a defendant's wealth."

...

Sindell is the new flagship of industrywide liability, but it sails along a spectrum of decisions both narrower and broader in their rationalization of plaintiff recovery. The New York Court of Appeals, having originally acquiesced in a "concerted action" theory based on "consciously parallel" conduct by several drug firms,[556] later opted for "a market share theory using a national market."[557] The New York court decided "to apportion liabilities so as to correspond to the over-all culpability of each defendant, measured by the amount of risk of injury each defendant created to the public-at-large." The court said it thought that "use of a national market is a fair method ... of apportioning defendants' liabilities according to their total culpability in marketing DES for use during pregnancy." The court declared that this liability would be "several only, and should not be inflated when all participants in the market are not before the court in a particular case." Although cognizant that this would "prevent some plaintiffs from recovering 100% of their damages," the court observed that it had "eschewed exculpation to prevent the fortuitous avoidance of liability," and said it was "equitably" refusing "to unleash the same forces to increase a defendant's liability beyond its fair share of responsibility."[558]

NOTES

(1) What would be the strongest policy rationale for the *Sindell* decision, summarized above? Could the decision be sustained on the basis that it is likely to produce reasonably fine-tuned deterrence results? Is there a significant danger that such a decision will over-deter the manufacture of useful products?

Is the decision better understood as a Solomonic effort to be "fair"? How can you respond to Justice Richardson's observation that these were plaintiffs who "wholly fail[ed] to prove any causation"?

(2)* Although courts are likely to confine *Sindell* closely to its peculiar facts, the market share approach has been advanced with respect to other disease syndromes associated with products that are more or less generic. The most controversial and potentially the most quantitatively significant application has involved asbestos cases. In their few direct confrontations with attempts to impose industrywide liability for asbestos diseases, the courts have split.

---

556. *Bichler v. Eli Lilly & Co.*, 55 N.Y.2d 571, 584–585, 436 N.E.2d 182, 188, 450 N.Y.S.2d 776, 782 (1982).

557. *Hymowitz v. Eli Lilly & Co.*, 73 N.Y.2d 487, 511, 539 N.E.2d 1069, 1078, 541 N.Y.S.2d 941, 950 (1989).

558. *Id.* at 512–13, 539 N.E.2d at 1078, 541 N.Y.S.2d at 950....

* This note is taken, in large part, from MARSHALL S. SHAPO, THE LAW OF PRODUCTS LIABILITY ¶ 12.21[4], [6] (4th ed. 2001).

On one side, a federal district court predicted that Texas would "adopt some form of *Sindell* liability" in asbestos-related cases.[a] In this litigation, workers exposed to asbestos in various ways filed complaints that sometimes named only one manufacturer and sometimes included as many as 20 asbestos manufacturers. Citing the "inability of the Plaintiff to identify the precise causative agent" as creating the problem of proof central to the *Hall* and *Sindell* cases, the court said that since a landmark Fifth Circuit precedent concerning asbestos, "we have been imposing a kind of *Sindell* liability":

> The proof of causation as related to a particular Defendant's product has been, of necessity, limited to a worker's own testimony and testimony of co-workers who rely on memory with regard to products used over a twenty or thirty year period. Yet, for years, this is all that has been required of plaintiffs.[b]

The court argued further that the "current pro-rata approach to apportionment results in unfairness to the small producer and a windfall to the larger producers," and it concluded that market share liability "cures this inherent defect, and results in apportionment which bears some relationship to causative fault."

By contrast, in denying liability in an asbestos case, another federal district court commented that "in industrywide liability there is no joint venture or enterprise—merely individual, independent acts similarly committed across an industrywide front, one or more of which causes injury. There is only consistency, not a consortium."[c] This court found it "anomalous" that "inadequate industrywide safety standards are considered the cause of the plaintiff's injury, yet manufacturers adhering to the standards may escape liability by proving that their product could not have directly caused the injury." Specifically with reference to the market share theory, the court emphasized that asbestos products are not "fungible commodities." Since products containing asbestos are not "uniformly harmful" because "many products contain different degrees of asbestos," this court opined that a market share theory would not necessarily produce a just correspondence between injuries caused and compensation paid.

On the whole, successful litigation on industrywide liability theories is likely to require either tightly structured industries, as in *Hall v. E.I. DuPont de Nemours & Co.*, or products with identical or closely generic characteristics, as with DES.

§ 11.02 Apportionment of Liability Among Multiple Tortfeasors: Contribution, Indemnity, and Comparative Responsibility

INTRODUCTION

This section deals with judicial apportionment of losses in situations where more than one injurer has been identified. Historically, the basic terminology was that of

---

a. *Hardy v. Johns-Manville Sales Corp.*, 509 F. Supp. 1353, 1359 (E.D. Tex. 1981), *rev'd on other grounds*, 681 F.2d 334 (5th Cir. 1982). In reversing, the court of appeals explicitly indicated that the *Sindell* issue was "not on appeal."

b. *Hardy v. Johns-Manville Sales Corp.*, 509 F. Supp. 1353, 1358 (E.D. Tex. 1981) (referring to *Borel v. Fibreboard Paper Prods. Corp.*, 493 F.2d 1076 (5th Cir., 1973), *cert. denied*, 419 U.S. 869 (1974)).

c. *Starling v. Seaboard Coast Line R.R.*, 533 F. Supp. 183, 189 (S.D. Ga. 1982).

"contribution" and "indemnity." The term "indemnity" means a total transfer of the loss from one party (the indemnitee) to another (the indemnitor). The classic use of the term "contribution" refers to a proportionate division of liability, equally split between or among a number of tortfeasors.

A strong trend in the law has favored apportionment based on relative degrees of responsibility. According to one section of the *Restatement on Apportionment*, "[i]f one defendant and at least one other party or settling tortfeasor may be found by the factfinder to have engaged in tortious conduct that was the legal cause of an indivisible injury, each such party and settling tortfeasor is submitted to the factfinder for assignment of a percentage of comparative responsibility." RESTATEMENT (THIRD) OF TORTS: APPORTIONMENT OF LIABILITY § A19 (2000). Parallel provisions include sections B19, C19, and D19.

PROBLEM

An employee of the Illinois Central was injured when the engineer of a train he was riding braked suddenly to avoid crossing a switch and colliding with a C & O engine. The employee sued both railroads. The Illinois Central settled, but the C & O went to trial, defending against allegations that it was negligent in misaligning or in failing to align the cross-over switch. The C & O cross-claimed against the Illinois Central, asserting that the latter's control tower had failed to alert the train on which the injured employee was riding about the presence of the C & O engine, and had failed to direct the C & O employees working on the Central tracks to close the switch. If the C & O loses in the primary action, should it be able to recover all or part of the judgment from the Illinois Central?

WROBEL v. TRAPANI

Illinois Appellate Court
129 Ill. App. 2d 306, 264 N.E.2d 240 (1970)

ENGLISH, JUSTICE. Third party plaintiff (Trapani) has appealed from a judgment entered by the trial court at the close of all the evidence, upon the motion of third party defendant (Hillesheim) for a directed verdict [in Trapani's suit for indemnification against Hillesheim—Ed.]. This action was initiated by plaintiff, who is not a party to this appeal, on January 4, 1963. Plaintiff was employed by Hillesheim, who was a painting subcontractor of Trapani, the general contractor in charge of construction of a house. Plaintiff's original complaint alleged that the negligence of Trapani was the proximate cause of the injuries he sustained while on the job. An amended complaint in two counts was then filed by plaintiff adding as an additional party defendant Leo Townsend, a carpenter employed by Trapani, who, it was alleged, lowered the upper sash of a window, causing plaintiff to fall from a ladder on the outside of the house. The second count alleged that Trapani wilfully violated the Structural Work Act....

[After filing a third-party action against Hillesheim, Trapani settled with the plaintiff for $45,000; the plaintiff's action against Trapani eventually was dismissed pursuant to stipulation. The case reported here focuses on Trapani's third-party complaint against Hillesheim, which was amended several times.]

. . .

Plaintiff (an employee of Hillesheim) testified that he had placed a ladder against the house and, while standing on it, was sanding and puttying the sill and the sash of a second-floor window. The ladder was adjusted to a 15-foot length and was placed with its base about seven feet from the wall of the house. To the best of his judgment, the bottom of the window was 15 feet above ground level. He stated that while he was working on the outside of the window, Townsend (an employee of Trapani) was working on the inside of the window. During the three or four minutes he was positioned on the ladder prior to the fall, he was applying putty to the upper right-hand corner of the window by using his right hand. He was using his left hand to hold himself in a straight position, by resting it on the top center of the upper sash. He testified that he wasn't sure what rung he was standing on, but his knees were a little lower than the top rung of the ladder. In order to putty the top part of the window, he stepped up one rung, the sash came down about four inches, and he fell backwards off the ladder. He was not in a position to grab hold of any part of the ladder to save himself from falling.

Townsend testified that he was working on the inside of the same window, installing handles on the sash. He had been working there for twenty minutes, during which time he had had a conversation with Wrobel. The sashes on the windows were moved several times during this period. When he had finished work on the lower sash, he pushed it downward. This enabled him to mark the bottom rail of the upper sash to establish a position to insert screws. Then, in order more easily to affix a hardware piece on the bottom rail of the upper sash, he reversed the position of the sashes by raising the lower sash and pushing down on the upper sash so that it came to rest less than half an inch above the window sill, "as far as it would go." He took out his hammer and awl to drive two holes straight down into the rail of the upper sash. He then started to insert the screw "and by pushing down the window went down a half inch."

Right after that, he noticed Wrobel outside with his arms in the air trying to reach for something. It appeared that, just before that, he was reaching with a putty knife in his right hand for the upper righthand corner of the window. Townsend didn't know where Wrobel's left hand was and, prior to the accident, he didn't see his left hand on the sash at any time. He had been standing at about the same height as Townsend on the inside, with their eyes at the same level. After the fall, Townsend rushed downstairs where Wrobel was lying on the ground, Townsend said he was sorry about it, and Wrobel said not to worry because "it isn't your fault."

Townsend noticed that the ladder, which was standing against the house, was not directly underneath the window but was placed with its right rail even with the left side of the window. The top of the ladder reached only to the bottom edge of the window. He testified that the customary place to position the top of a ladder is near the top of the window. Also, it is usual, when working on the right side of a window, to place the ladder on that side. Further, the customary stance for a worker would be one in which his shoulders would be approximately even with the top rung, with the body between the two rails of the ladder.

Trapani, a carpenter of 20 years' experience, and Donald Stewart, a safety engineer, testified that safety standards in connection with the use of ladders indicate that the highest rung on which a person should stand is the fifth from the top. The position of the body should be between the rails. Trapani testified that the bottom of the window was 12' 6" above the ground; and that a ladder fifteen feet long, positioned with its top 12 feet above the ground, would extend 9' 3" from the base of the wall. The expert witness testified that this position would not meet acceptable safety standards.

Trapani seeks to have the judgment of the trial court vacated and judgment entered in his favor based upon two theories of recovery. He contends that, as a matter of law, he is entitled to indemnification from Hillesheim either on the theory of active-passive indemnity or implied contractual indemnity. He also contends, in the alternative, that the judgment should be set aside and the cause remanded for a new trial, because the evidence raised questions of fact under both theories which the jury should have been permitted to decide....

With respect to Trapani's primary contentions urging reversal of the trial court's judgment, we are confronted initially with the applicability of the Structural Work Act to the instant facts. Sections 1 and 9 of the Act provide that certain enumerated persons, including contractors and subcontractors, have a responsibility to erect ladders in a "safe, suitable and proper manner." Ill.Rev.Stat.1961, ch. 48, §§ 60 and 69. Whether a party will be held responsible for any injury occasioned by a wilful violation of the Act or a wilful failure to comply with its provisions, depends upon whether he had charge of the work. *See Kobus v. Formfit Co.*, 56 Ill.App.2d 449, 206 N.E.2d 477. There is no substantial dispute but what both parties to this appeal were in charge of the work. Hillesheim's employee, Wrobel, erected the ladder from which he fell and sustained injuries. Trapani, as general contractor, was in charge of the overall construction and supervised the manner in which the work was being done.

Next, we consider whether there was evidence which, if believed by the trier of fact would establish a wilful violation of the Act or a wilful failure to comply with its provisions on the part of Hillesheim, and we find that it did. Trapani produced evidence to demonstrate that Wrobel (and through his agency, Hillesheim) violated accepted safety standards in the placement of the ladder: the top of the ladder was beneath, instead of above, the window level; he stood on one of the top rungs of the ladder instead of the fifth from the top; the bottom of the ladder was placed too far away from the wall. All of these facts, when viewed in the light of acceptable standards as testified to at trial, indicate that the ladder had been used in a manner sufficiently unsafe to constitute a wilful violation of the Act by the parties in charge of the work. In so holding, we make no adjudication of the third party claim, since Hillesheim also introduced evidence which, if believed, would establish a violation of the Act on the part of Trapani.

Trapani argues that he is entitled to indemnification since his conduct in violation of the Act was merely passive in nature, while that of Hillesheim was active. In litigation under the Structural Work Act, it is well established that the rule forbidding contribution between tort-feasors is not applicable where it is shown that one is an active wrongdoer and the other has but a passive role. *E.g., Rovekamp v. Central Const. Co.*, 45 Ill.App.2d 441, 195 N.E.2d 756. Trapani supports his position through evidence demonstrating that Hillesheim (through Wrobel) placed and used the ladder in an unsafe manner. He argues that his responsibility for the construction project extended merely to general supervision and coordination of the overall project. This, he submits, is sufficient to establish him as the lesser delinquent and Hillesheim as the active delinquent, relying upon *Rovekamp, supra*, where the court stated at page 449, 195 N.E.2d at pages 759–760:

> Although the liability imposed by the Act does not rest upon negligence, there can be degrees of fault among those who, under the Act, are accountable to an injured plaintiff. Who is the more culpable, a party who supervises and coordinates the overall project, or a party who is responsible for the scaffolding and the particular work which produced the injury? Both are in charge of the work, to be sure, but of different phases of the work. Neither can escape liability to

the plaintiff—thus the purpose of the Act is accomplished—but the lesser delinquent, if held accountable by the plaintiff, can transfer its statutory liability to the active delinquent, whose dereliction from duty brought about the plaintiff's injury.

Thus, the question squarely presented for our review is whether the evidence supports Trapani's active-passive theory of the case.... Hillesheim contends that the theory cannot be applied because the act of Townsend, Trapani's employee, was shown to have been a proximate cause of Wrobel's injury. Wrobel testified that he balanced himself while on the ladder by placing his left hand on the top of the window sash, and that Townsend's act of lowering the sash a distance of four inches caused him to fall. Townsend acknowledged that he did lower the sash as he was working on it, but only by a half inch. He also testified that while he did not know where Wrobel's left hand was at the time, he had not seen it resting on the sash prior to the accident.

In our opinion, this conflict in the evidence presented a question of credibility— and, thus, an issue of fact—which could properly have been resolved only by the jury. It relates materially to the factual determination necessary to a correct application of the active-passive rule as a basis for indemnity.

We agree with Trapani that the evidence did not so overwhelmingly favor Hillesheim as to justify the trial court's direction of a verdict for Hillesheim, under the principle of *Pedrick v. Peoria & Eastern R.R. Co.*, 37 Ill.2d 494, 229 N.E.2d 504. We therefore conclude that the judgment must be reversed. We do not, however, agree with Trapani's contention that the evidence was so overwhelming in his favor as to justify reversal with judgment directed against Hillesheim by this court.

. . . .

[Reversed and remanded.]

NOTES

(1) A classic application of the active-passive distinction appears in a colorful but tragic case, *United States v. State of Illinois*, 454 F.2d 297 (7th Cir. 1971). Four injuries, two fatal, occurred when a portion of catwalk on top of a grandstand pulled free from the roof and collapsed during a performance by a Green Beret unit. Suit was brought against the United States under the Federal Tort Claims Act, alleging negligence on the part of the Green Berets. The only proof of negligence by the Green Berets was that they relied upon representations of agents of the state concerning the condition of the grandstand roof and failed to conduct inspections adequate to reveal the way in which the platform was attached to the grandstand. In the federal government's third party action against the state, *held*, Illinois was actively negligent and was liable for indemnity.

(2) An interesting pair of New York cases indicates the reach, and the limits, of indemnity doctrine, in addition to the appeal of apportioning liability according to percentages of relative responsibility. In one of these cases, suit was brought for wrongful death of the plaintiff's husband, caused by a fumigation chemical alleged to have been improperly labeled by the defendant manufacturer. The decedent used the chemical to clean a grain storage bin, under orders from his employer. The manufacturer brought a third party complaint against the employer, contending that the latter had taken insufficient precautions in fumigation. It claimed that the employer had used untrained personnel in the work, failed to follow instructions on the label, and failed to test the premises or to aerate them properly after fumigation. A provision of the workers' com-

pensation statute declared that there could be no recovery in an action brought against the employer by the employee's representative or by "anyone otherwise entitled to recover damages ... on account of such injury or death." The court found that this provision did not bar an action by the manufacturer against the employer for some measure of apportionment of damages. Although that apportionment could include indemnity, the court said generally that the division of damages "should rest on relative responsibility and be determined on the facts," criticizing as "uncertain and largely unpredictable" the "measure of redress that had been allowed by indemnity in favor of a party found negligent against another who played an effective role in causing the damage." *Dole v. Dow Chemical Co.*, 30 N.Y.2d 143, 331 N.Y.S.2d 382, 282 N.E.2d 288, 294, 292, 53 A.L.R.3d 175 (1972).

The court of appeals trimmed the sails of *Dole* in *Rogers v. Dorchester Associates*, 32 N.Y.2d 553, 300 N.E.2d 403 (1973). In that case, the defendants were the owner and management company of an apartment house in which the plaintiff was hurt on an elevator, and the elevator maintenance company. The maintenance company, Otis, had contracted with the management company to "use all reasonable care to maintain the elevator equipment in proper and safe operating condition." The court found circumstantial evidence that it had performed this duty negligently, and then held that it must indemnify the other defendants:

> The very ground of Otis' liability, the exclusive duty to maintain the elevators, for breach of which duty it was cast in judgment, means that the owner and manager had the right, under the maintenance contract, to look to Otis to perform their entire duty to plaintiff. Because by reason of statute (Multiple Dwelling Law, §78), their obligation to plaintiff was nondelegable, they were powerless, as against plaintiff, to avoid liability no matter how extensively they delegated their responsibility to however independent a maintenance contractor. Put another way, the statute had the effect of imputing to them the negligence of any delegate insofar as plaintiff's rights to recover were concerned, but only to that extent.

> On the other hand, as between Otis and the owner or manager, Otis had a contractual obligation to perform its duty of maintenance, for breach of which the owner and manager were held in damages to plaintiff in the first instance. For this breach of duty and the resulting liability of the owner and manager, Otis should be and is liable for the full amount....

> · · ·

> The rule of apportionment in the *Dole* case ... was not intended to and should not be read to vary the substantive duties, as distinguished from the scope of liability for damages and their apportionment, among tort-feasors who are jointly and severally liable whether by virtue of *respondeat superior*, imputed negligence, or concurrent fault. The rule of apportionment applies when two or more tort-feasors have shared, albeit in various degrees, in the responsibility by their conduct or omissions in causing an accident, in violation of the duties they respectively owed to the injured person. (Of course, the rule may be modified by a valid agreement for contractual indemnity.) The *Dole* case, in overruling the use of active-passive terminology for purposes of indemnification in cases involving vicarious liability, imputed negligence, and the like, was largely rejecting a terminology that had caused confusion. The confusion arose because the antonyms seemed to stress the difference between

affirmative and negative conduct instead of weighing the respective degrees of fault, most often treated as primary or secondary. The confusion, however, did not result necessarily in the wrong application of governing principles. On the contrary, the pre-*Dole* cases would, for the most part, categorize nicely under the primary-secondary analysis, the classic analysis and the one common to the rest of the nation....

The rule in the *Dole* case had, primarily, of course, the dramatic effect of allowing comparative apportionment among joint tort-feasors even where their respective degrees of responsibility for the accident were not equal. To this extent the rule in the *Dole* case went beyond merely correcting the peculiar New York development of "active and passive" negligence terminology and doctrine in third-party liability and practice.... It was hardly intended to overturn basic and satisfactory principles of common-law indemnification between vicariously liable tort-feasors and tort-feasors guilty of the acts or omissions causing the harm. In short, the apportionment rule applies to those who in fact share responsibility for causing the accident or harm, and does not extend further to those who are only vicariously liable, as the employer of a negligent employee, the owner of a motor vehicle operated by a negligent driver, or, as here, the owner of a building who contracts with an independent contractor exclusively responsible for maintenance of the building or parts of it.

Professor Phillips supports the "*Dole* rationale of merging the doctrines of contribution and indemnity" in *Contribution and Indemnity in Products Liability*, 42 TENN. L. REV. 85 (1974).

(3)* The movement toward comparative principles has extended to a refusal to grant indemnity to parties whose negligence consists only of their failure to discover and prevent the misconduct of the party against whom indemnity is sought. In a case in which the installer of defective equipment sued the manufacturer, a majority of the Minnesota Supreme Court rejected indemnity and limited "reallocation of loss between joint tortfeasors to contribution based upon relative fault."[a] A dissenter argued that "fundamental fairness and sound economic principles of loss allocation" supported indemnity when the installer's negligence was simply its failure to discover a defect that was not obvious in the process of installation. He noted that the defect had "directly result[ed]" from manufacturer conduct constituting "breaches of contract" and that the case also had presented grounds for recovery under breach of implied warranty and strict liability.[b] Another dissenting justice said that, in such cases, factors like technical expertise and corporate size were important in assessing relative culpability. He expressed doubt that "an intelligible rule or jury instruction could be fashioned which would permit a jury to apply equitable principles necessarily required to justly apportion liability."[c]

(4) Suppose an employee falls because of his own negligence, and that in falling, he hits a bystander. The bystander sues the employer on grounds of *respondeat superior*. At least in theory, should the employer be able to indemnify himself against the employee for a judgment recovered by the bystander?

---

* This note is borrowed from MARSHALL S. SHAPO, THE LAW OF PRODUCTS LIABILITY ¶ 14.08[4][c] (4th ed. 2001).

   a. *Tolbert v. Gerber Indus., Inc.*, 255 N.W.2d 362, 367 (Minn. 1977).

   b. *Id.* at 368 (Kelly, J., dissenting).

   c. *Id.* at 372 (Rogosheske, J., dissenting).

HUNT v. CITY STORES, INC.
Louisiana Supreme Court
387 So. 2d 585 (1980)

WATSON, JUSTICE.

At issue is the propriety of a judgment granting plaintiff an award for personal injuries against the owner of an escalator but dismissing a third party demand by the owner against the manufacturer.

(1) Plaintiff, Jerry Hunt, filed suit individually and as the administrator of the estate of his minor son, David, for damages sustained in an accident on an escalator in a New Orleans department store. Defendants are City Stores, Inc. d/b/a Maison Blanche; its insurer, Travelers Insurance Company; Otis Elevator Company, the manufacturer of the escalator; and its insurer, Commercial Union Assurance Company. Defendants City Stores and Travelers filed a third party demand against Otis for contribution and/or indemnification and against Mrs. Jerry Hunt, David's mother, alleging that her negligence was the sole cause of the accident. The trial court rendered judgment in the amount of $5,184 in favor of plaintiff and against defendants, City Stores and Travelers, and dismissed all demands against Otis and Commercial Union. The Fourth Circuit Court of Appeal, 375 So.2d 1194, affirmed on the ground that *Marquez v. City Stores Co.*, 371 So.2d 810 (La., 1979) controlled that result. Upon application of City Stores and Travelers, a writ of certiorari was granted to review the conclusion that the escalator's defect warranted a judgment against City Stores under LSA-C.C. art. 2317, but not a judgment on the third party demand against the manufacturer under the rationale of *Weber v. Fidelity and Casualty Insurance Co. of N.Y.*, 259 La. 599, 250 So.2d 754 (1971).

On May 27, 1976, twelve year old David Hunt was shopping in the Maison Blanche store at Lake Forest Plaza shopping center in New Orleans. As he rode a descending escalator from the second to the first floor, his right tennis shoe was caught in the space between the moving tread and the escalator's left side panel. Although David was accompanied by his mother and other family members, no one knew exactly why his shoe lodged in the escalator. There was no evidence that the child was misbehaving or that he deliberately wedged his foot in the machine. David testified that he was looking at glittering streamers which hung from the ceiling when the escalator "grabbed" his foot and pulled it into the side opening (Tr. 16). Both knees were injured. The escalator was stopped and David's shoe was cut away to free his foot.

. . . .

While the escalator was beneficial and convenient to Maison Blanche and its customers, the utility of its condition on May 27, 1976, was outweighed by the hazard to small children associated with its use. Although David Hunt only hurt his knees, the injuries to Marquez and Mire [in *Mire v. Otis Elevator Co.*, 357 So.2d 1326 (La. Ct. App. 1978)] were severe enough to warrant partial toe amputations.

This escalator posed a threat to small children in tennis shoes. City Stores was aware of the danger and had a duty to warn of the risk of injury. It failed to do so. The store was at fault in not guarding the public against the risk of harm posed by the escalator.

Although Otis installed and serviced the escalator, its maintenance contract provided:

> It is agreed that we do not assume possession or control of any part of the
> equipment but such remains yours exclusively as the owner. City Stores, Ex-
> hibit # 1, page 3.

Therefore, City Stores d/b/a Maison Blanche was custodian of the defective escalator. It
has not carried the burden of showing any fault by victim Hunt or a third person which
would relieve it of liability. LSA-C.C. art. 2317.

In *Weber v. Fidelity & Casualty Insurance Co. of N.Y.*, ..., a rule of strict liability for
manufacturers of defective products was enunciated. The court stated:

> A manufacturer of a product which involves a risk of injury to the user is liable
> to any person, whether the purchaser or a third person, who without fault on
> his part, sustains an injury caused by a defect in the design, composition, or
> manufacture of the article, if the injury might reasonably have been antici-
> pated. However, the plaintiff claiming injury has the burden of proving that
> the product was defective, *i.e.*, unreasonably dangerous to normal use, and
> that the plaintiff's injuries were caused by reason of the defect.
>
> ....
>
> If the product is proven defective by reason of its hazard to normal use, the
> plaintiff need not prove any particular negligence by the maker in its manufac-
> ture or processing; for the manufacturer is presumed to know of the vices in
> the things he makes, whether or not he has actual knowledge of them.

259 La. 602–603, 250 So.2d 755–756....

Here, the risk of harm was known to Otis but not obvious to the public. Otis engineer David Steel admitted that the industry had experience with the problem of children's tennis shoes getting caught. Roger Harris of Otis, an expert in escalators, testified
that the stores advise Otis of incidents like this. He had "Probably" (Tr. 108) investigated similar cases where children in tennis shoes had gotten their feet caught. He said
that the inconspicuous warning signs which caution against bare feet are the only ones
used by Otis. John Michael Trahan, a former maintenance examiner for Otis, testified
that the small warning signs at the base of the escalator were part of the equipment and
came with the escalator. Despite knowledge of the danger presented to children in tennis shoes, Otis had not warned of that hazard.... Accordingly, the courts below erred in
dismissing the claims against the product manufacturer and its insurer.

. . .

Here ... it was alleged that Otis failed to design and manufacture the escalator in a
reasonably safe manner and failed to warn of the dangers attendant to its use. The escalator was shown to present an unreasonable risk of harm in normal use which could
have been anticipated by the manufacturer. There was no warning of the defect. Otis is
liable for the resulting injury. Therefore, the question presented is whether City Stores
is limited to contribution or if it is entitled to indemnity.

LSA-C.C. art. 2103 provides in pertinent part that: "When two or more debtors are
liable in solido, whether the obligation arises from a contract, a quasi contract, an offense, or a quasi offense, it should be divided between them. As between the solidary
debtors, each is liable only for his virile portion of the obligation." Here both City Stores
and Otis failed to warn the public of a known hazard associated with use of this escalator. Because neither undertook to warn those using the escalator, and both were aware
of the risk, both are equally at fault. While Otis might theoretically manufacture a safer
product, Maison Blanche could purchase a better escalator, switch to stairs or use eleva-

tors. Otis is in a better position to improve the design of the machine than City Stores, but City Stores should not be allowed to keep a defective escalator and pass all liability to the manufacturer. In the absence of some greater fault being shown on the part of either, the obligation is solidary. The loss should be divided. Otherwise, the store owner has no incentive to warn the public, replace the escalator or otherwise prevent future accidents. Otis and its insurer are liable to City Stores and its insurer for contribution of one-half of plaintiff's damages....

Therefore, the courts below erred in dismissing the third party demand of City Stores and its insurer against Otis and its insurer. The judgment of the Court of Appeal is affirmed with respect to the plaintiff's demand against City Stores and Travelers and is amended to award City Stores and Travelers judgment on its third party demand for contribution of one-half the amount awarded to plaintiff against Otis and Commercial Union.

AMENDED AND AS AMENDED AFFIRMED.

[Two dissenting opinions are omitted.]

NOTES

(1) Suppose that someone is injured by a flowerpot that falls from a party wall, one strip of which is owned by one person, and the other jointly owned by two people. If the plaintiff obtains a judgment against all potential defendants, and there are appropriate cross-actions filed, what proportion of the recovery should each have to pay?

(2) Is the result in *Hunt* in accord with the philosophy of your answer to the prior question? What should the law be seeking to accomplish in cases involving apportionment of damages? Is—or ought to be—the key to these cases the promotion of the correct economic incentives to the multiple defendants? Or is the primary goal an "equitable" division of the loss?

(3)* In a trio of 1978 products liability cases,[a] the California Supreme Court took "comparative indemnity" to the point of apportioning liability among tort-feasors who are, respectively, strictly liable and negligent. Particularly interesting was the last case of the three, involving a shopping cart that broke and fell on the plaintiff's foot.[b] The court characterized the jury's verdict as indicating that the liability of the supermarket "rested on both negligence and strict liability principles," with the cart manufacturer's liability being "grounded solely on strict liability principles." The jury fixed the market's comparative fault at 80 percent and the manufacturer's at 20 percent. Reviewing the history of its adoption of "comparative indemnity," the court said that the fundamental vice of the traditional equitable indemnity doctrine—that is, the failure to provide for a fair allocation of liability in cases in which an injury called for "apportionment ... rather than a complete shift of liability"—"was as apparent in cases involving strict product liability as in cases resting solely on negligence principles."

Justice Tobriner, writing for the court, said that with the "advent of ... common law comparative indemnity" it was possible to achieve a "more precise apportionment of li-

---

* This note is adapted from MARSHALL S. SHAPO, THE LAW OF PRODUCTS LIABILITY ¶ 14.08[3] (4th ed. 2001).

a. *American Motorcycle Ass'n v. Superior Court*, 20 Cal.3d 578, 578 P.2d 899, 146 Cal. Rptr. 182 (1978); *Daly v. General Motors Corp.*, 20 Cal.3d 725, 575 P.2d 1162, 144 Cal. Rptr. 380 (1978); *Safeway Stores, Inc. v. Nest-Kart*, 21 Cal.3d 322, 579 P.2d 441, 146 Cal. Rptr. 550 (1978).

b. *Safeway Stores v. Nest-Kart*, 21 Cal.3d 322, 579 P.2d 441, 146 Cal. Rptr. 550 (1978).

ability in circumstances such as the instant case," which he viewed as being one in which the primary fault lay with the market, although the "defectiveness of the shopping cart partially caused the accident." The most desirable method, he said, is to allocate damages "on a comparative fault or a comparative responsibility basis, rather than by fixing an inflexible pro rata apportionment pursuant to the contribution statutes." He declared that the presumed differences between negligence and strict liability are "more theoretical than practical" and contended that to rule otherwise would result in "bizarre, and indeed irrational, consequences." A contrary holding, he argued, would mean that

> a manufacturer who was actually negligent in producing a product would frequently be placed in a better position than a manufacturer who was free from negligence but who happened to produce a defective product, for the negligent manufacturer would be permitted to shift the bulk of liability to more negligent cotortfeasors, while the strictly liable defendant would be denied the benefit of such apportionment.

Concurring, Justice Clark suggested that the legislature should enact a law dividing liability equally among responsible tort-feasors. He asserted that the instant case reflected an "arbitrary" division of responsibility, and that "[b]lind inquiry into relative fault is no better than the flip of a coin." Justice Mosk, dissenting, lamented the "total infusion of negligence theories into the previously independent doctrine of products liability." Referring to a recent precedent that allowed apportionment of responsibility among strictly liable defendants and negligent plaintiffs, he criticized the shopping cart decision as offering manufacturers an additional opportunity to dilute their responsibility by placing in issue the conduct of other defendants.

(4) Is the best solution for apportionment of responsibility to make it completely comparative, according to percentages, doing away with all all-or-nothing categories, such as contributory negligence and indemnity, as well as the rigid fractions of the classic contribution recovery? What are the arguments against such a solution? Is there a stronger argument in favor of comparative apportionment among tort-feasors or in favor of comparative fault between defendants and plaintiffs?

(5) When a defendant has been negligent concerning the risk that a third party will commit an intentional tort on the plaintiff, should that defendant be able to apportion fault to the third party, especially if the third party is not before the court? Consider, for example, the case where the plaintiff sues the operator of a shopping mall on the grounds that it failed to provide adequate security against the risk of criminal attacks, and a criminal who assaulted the plaintiff cannot be found.

§ 11.03   Effect of Settlement on Apportionment

ROLAND v. BERNSTEIN

Court of Appeals of Arizona
828 P.2d 1237 (1991), review denied (Ariz. 1992)

LIVERMORE, Chief Judge.

Plaintiff brought a medical malpractice complaint against Ronald Bernstein, a neurosurgeon, his professional corporation, Desert Neurosurgery, Joseph Marcinkowski, an anesthesiologist, and Tucson General Hospital. Tucson General and Marcinkowski settled the claim for $700,000 each and the case proceeded to trial against Bernstein and his corporation. The jury found plaintiff's damages to be $1,965,000 and the degree of fault to be 47% for Bernstein, 28% for Marcinkowski, and 25% for Tucson General Hospital. The question then arose whether under A.R.S. § 12-2504 the amount Bernstein had to pay should be reduced by the amount of the pre-existing settlements. The trial court held that it should and thus entered a judgment for $565,000 rather than for $923,550 (47% of $1,965,000). This appeal followed. We reverse.

When more than one defendant caused plaintiff's injuries the rule originally was that each such defendant was liable for the whole injury, that recovery against one eliminated the claim against the others, and that no right of contribution existed among defendants. See generally W. Prosser & W. Keeton, Torts §§ 46–52 (5th ed. 1984). Over time the rigor of these rules was relaxed, permitting settlement by one of the defendants without eliminating rights against the others, so long as double recovery did not occur, and contribution among tortfeasors. That result was accomplished in Arizona by passage of the Uniform Contribution Among Tortfeasors Act, A.R.S. § 12-2501 et seq. Section 12-2504, at issue in this case, provides that a settlement with "one of two or more persons liable in tort for the same injury ... does not discharge any of the other tortfeasors from liability for the injury ... but it reduces the claim against the others" by the amount of the settlement. If that section were applicable here the trial judge's ruling would be correct because the $1,400,000 settlement would be deducted from the $1,965,000 verdict to arrive at a $565,000 judgment against Bernstein.

We conclude, however, that § 12-2504 does not apply because it was enacted as part of a statute permitting contribution between defendants liable for the entire amount of damages caused by the concurrent negligence of each of them. It was not designed for this case which was tried under A.R.S. § 12-2506, a more recently enacted statute. Section 12-2506 abolished joint and several liability, limiting recovery against any defendant to that percentage of a plaintiff's total injuries representing that defendant's degree of fault.[1] Because recovery is so limited, contribution can never occur. Section 12-2504, passed as part of a statute regulating contribution, therefore, is not, obviously, applicable to a situation where there is no right to contribution.

This result can be easily squared with the statutory language. Section 12-2504 applies when "two or more persons [are] liable in tort for the same injury." Section 12-2506, on the contrary, provides that "the liability of each defendant for damages is several only and is not joint." In short, each defendant is liable only for the portion of the injury he caused, not the whole injury; no two are liable for the same injury. See Kussman v. City and County of Denver, 706 P.2d 776 (Colo.1985).

In addition, we believe that it would be anomalous to give the benefit of an advantageous settlement, not to the plaintiff who negotiated it, but to the non-settling tortfeasor. Had plaintiff made a disadvantageous settlement, she would have borne that consequence because her recovery against Bernstein would have been limited to $923,550. At a minimum, symmetry requires that if the disadvantage of settlement is hers so ought the advantage be. Beyond that, we see no reason why a non-settling tortfeasor ought to escape the liability that is his by reason of the faulty assessment of probabilities by a settling tortfeasor. Indeed, such a rule might well discourage settlement by the last tortfeasor on the reasoning that his exposure is limited to his degree of fault and even that

---

1. There are exceptions where joint and several liability is retained. They are not applicable here.

might be reduced by reason of pre-existing settlements. These considerations have led most courts considering this question to apply the rule we are adopting....

...

The judgment is reversed and the matter remanded for the entry of a judgment in plaintiff's favor for $923,550....

NOTES

What should the results be in the following cases? Explain your decisions.

(1) Defendant X settles, and Defendant Y goes to trial, sustaining a judgment that is larger than twice the settlement—*i.e.*, more than the number of parties times the amount of the settlement. The jury indicates its belief that Defendant X should "contribute." Defendant Y seeks a credit on the judgment that reflects the settlement. How much should the credit be?

(2) Defendant X settles during trial, unknown to the jury. The jury "exonerates" X, and renders a judgment against Defendant Y for more than twice the settlement. Y seeks a credit on the judgment. How much should it be?

(3) The jury "exonerates" Defendant X, which has settled for $250,000, and then renders a verdict against Defendant Y for an amount slightly in excess of the settlement—$294,000. Y seeks to credit the entire settlement on the judgment. What result?

(4) Defendant X settles, but Defendant Y goes forward to trial. The jury, finding Y completely responsible for the injury, declares that it "exonerates" X of any fault. X seeks a credit against its settlement in the amount of the judgment against Y. Should X receive that credit?

Chapter 12

EXTENDED CAUSATION
AND DUTY

INTRODUCTORY NOTE

In the material that follows throughout this chapter, the defendant generally arguably has fallen below an abstract standard of care, and usually his conduct may be said to be a "but-for" cause of the plaintiff's injury. It is on policy grounds that the defendant in these cases seeks to avoid liability. You should keep your tools of conceptual surgery especially sharp in dealing with this section, for the judicial language is sometimes quite confusing.

§ 12.01 Statutory Violations

READ v. BUCKNER

United States District Court, District of Montana
514 F. Supp. 281 (1981)

OPINION AND ORDER

RUSSELL E. SMITH, DISTRICT JUDGE.

Plaintiff alleges that injuries he sustained while he was riding a motorcycle on U. S. Highway No. 2 were caused by the presence of defendant's goats on the highway. In Count 1 the plaintiff claims that the defendant violated the provisions of MCA § 81-4-201 (1979), which reads:

> It shall be unlawful for any owner or person in control of swine, sheep, or goats to willfully permit the same to run at large.

Damages are claimed under MCA § 81-4-202(1), which reads:

> Any person violating 81-4-201 shall be deemed guilty of a misdemeanor, and upon conviction thereof shall be fined in the sum of $10 for the first offense and in the sum of $20 for each subsequent offense and shall be liable in damage to any party injured thereby, to be recovered in any court having competent jurisdiction.

In Count 2 the plaintiff relies on ordinary negligence.

Defendant contends that MCA §§ 81-4-201 and 202, originally enacted in 1895 ... were enacted for the protection of the property of landowners and that, since there were no motor vehicles in common use at that time, they could not have been enacted for the protection of motorists. With this as a premise, defendant argues that a statute enacted

557

for the protection of one class of people will not afford relief to a class which the Legislature did not intend to protect.[1] However, for the reasons hereafter set forth, as I view the matter, the Act of 1895, as amended in 1945 (Chapter 169, 1945 Laws of Montana), probably resulted from a general modification of the open range law rather than from an intention to protect a specific class of persons.

The special legal status accorded open range livestock cattle and to a lesser extent sheep and horses was a product of the historical development of the open range system in Montana and must be viewed within this historical context. The lands of the plains lying between the Texas panhandle and Canada, and including the plains of the four states comprising the "heartland" Montana, Wyoming, Colorado, and New Mexico were the open range. In the period between 1850 and 1900 the range was truly open.[2] Cattle roamed at large over the plains with a minimum of supervision and care. In the beginning of this era, the range was used for the long drives from the southern plains, which were superior for breeding, to the northern plains, which were superior for grazing.[3] Gradually this use of the range gave way to a different one, a use in which the individual cattlemen grazed their herds around water holes on common land. Little attention was paid to the matter of land titles, and fences were incompatible with this manner of cattle raising. The primary form of control imposed upon an otherwise uncontrolled range, the roundup, was a means of taking inventory, bringing back strays, and determining ownership of cattle.[5]

The open range in the heartland states eventually succumbed to the same pressures which had closed it earlier in the other plains states: homesteaders, fences, railroads, and the extravagance and waste inherent in the system itself. As the nineteenth century closed and cattle raising was shifting from a range to a ranch basis, these pressures brought alterations in the use of the open range. The range boundaries slowly contracted and the herds were smaller.[6] Just as the open range changed, the business practices changed. As the practices changed, the law changed also. Recognizing the need for cooperation, the cattlemen formed the Montana Stockgrowers Association and organized roundup districts. The whole of Chapter 4 of 81 MCA relating to the containment of livestock developed over the years in response to special needs, and the courts developed an exception to the open range law and imposed liability upon owners of livestock whose animals had been intentionally herded or driven onto another's unfenced land.[7]

Despite the fact that the special status afforded by the law to livestock had its origins in the needs of the owners of cattle and lands at a time when there were no automobiles, the Montana Supreme Court in *Bartsch v. Irvine Co.*, 149 Mont. 405, 427 P.2d 302

---

1. *See* 73 Am.Jur.2d Statutes §433 (1974); W. L. PROSSER, Law of TORTS §36 at 192 (4th ed. 1978); *Champlin Refining Co. v. Cooper*, 184 Okl. 153, 86 P.2d 61 (1938). *Accord, Rauh v. Jensen*, 161 Mont. 443, 507 P.2d 520 (1973) (analyzing the problem on the basis of proximate cause).

2. J. SCHLEBECKER, CATTLE RAISING ON THE PLAINS, 1900–1961, p. 1 (1963); M. FRINK, WHEN GRASS WAS KING, p. 117 (1956).

3. J. SCHLEBECKER, CATTLE RAISING ON THE PLAINS, 1900–1961, p. 5 (1963); OPEN RANGE IN OLD MONTANA AND WYOMING, Montana Heritage Series No. 13.

5. R. FLETCHER, FROM GRASS TO FENCES p. 44 (1960); W. P. WEBB, THE GREAT PLAINS, p. 255 (1931); M. Frink, When Grass Was King, p. 11 (1956).

6. M. FRINK, WHEN GRASS WAS KING, pp. 16, 101–09 (1956).

7. *Compare Fant v. Lyman*, 9 Mont. 61, 22 P. 120 (1889), with *Monroe v. Cannon*, 24 Mont. 316, 61 P. 863 (1900). In *Fant* the Supreme Court sustained a verdict where the jury had been instructed that a landowner could not recover if sheep were driven onto his land for pasturage rather than for the purpose of maliciously injuring the land, while in *Monroe* the court sustained an award where the animals were driven onto unfenced lands for pasturage.

(1967), recognized the open range status of a horse on a highway and held that its owner was not responsible where an automobile collided with a horse which had strayed onto a highway. *Bartsch* was followed in *Jenkins v. Valley Garden Ranch, Inc.*, 151 Mont. 463, 443 P.2d 753, 754 (1968). Then in *Sanders v. Mount Haggin Livestock Co.*, 160 Mont. 73, 500 P.2d 397, 400 (1972), the court applied the "willfully driven" exception, initially applied to the pasturage of animals on the open range, to animals on a highway. Thus the special status accorded cattle and horses grazing on the open range has been granted to the same animals on the highway.

It cannot be known but, as has been said, I think it probable that when, by the Act of March 6, 1895, the Legislature removed swine from the special status which permitted them to run at large on the open range, it was probably concerned with the general modification of the open range law rather than with the protection of a specific class of persons.[8] By Chapter 169, 1945 Laws of Montana, the Legislature affirmed its previous action as to swine, and for the first time it denied to goats and sheep the right to run at large. Even if in 1895 the Legislature intended to protect only landowners against damage caused by swine, it is difficult to believe that in 1945 a legislature fully aware of paved roads, automobiles, and accidents did not, by changing the status of sheep and goats, intend that the protection of the law should extend to all who were injured by violations of it. Certainly the language used contains no limitations. In short, I believe that Chapter 169, 1945 Laws of Montana, was a part of the historical process of conforming the open range law to the needs of a modern world.

In my opinion, the complaint states a cause of action under MCA §§ 81-4-201 and 202, and the motion for summary judgment is denied....

RESTATEMENT (SECOND) OF TORTS §§ 286, 288 (1965)*

§ 286. When Standard of Conduct Defined by Legislation or Regulation Will Be Adopted

The court may adopt as the standard of conduct of a reasonable man the requirements of a legislative enactment or an administrative regulation whose purpose is found to be exclusively or in part

(a) to protect a class of persons which includes the one whose interest is invaded, and

(b) to protect the particular interest which is invaded, and

(c) to protect that interest against the kind of harm which has resulted, and

(d) to protect that interest against the particular hazard from which the harm results.

§ 288. When Standard of Conduct Defined by Legislation or Regulation Will Not Be Adopted

The court will not adopt as the standard of conduct of a reasonable man the requirements of a legislative enactment or an administrative regulation whose purpose is found to be exclusively

---

8. The purpose of the Act of March 6, 1895, is not as self-evident as is the purpose of MCA § 81-4-210 prohibiting non-purebred bulls from running at large.

* Copyright © 1965 by The American Law Institute. Reproduced with permission.

(a) to protect the interests of the state or any subdivision of it as such, or

(b) to secure to individuals the enjoyment of rights or privileges to which they are entitled only as members of the public, or

(c) to impose upon the actor the performance of a service which the state or any subdivision of it undertakes to give the public, or

(d) to protect a class of persons other than the one whose interests are invaded, or

(e) to protect another interest than the one invaded, or

(f) to protect against other harm than that which has resulted, or

(g) to protect against any other hazards than that from which the harm has resulted.

William Landes & Richard Posner, *Causation in Tort Law: An Economic Approach*
12 J. LEGAL STUD. 109, 130–131 (1983)**

...

Another class of cases where administrative costs are high, though for a slightly different reason, is where a statute designed for one purpose is invoked for another. *Gorris v. Scott* will illustrate this class of cases.[49] The plaintiff's animals were washed overboard and lost in a storm. The defendant's ship, which was carrying the animals, was not equipped with pens, as required by statute in order to prevent diseases from spreading among the animals. Had the ship been equipped with the pens, the plaintiff's animals would not have been washed overboard in the storm. Nevertheless, the court excused the defendant from liability, on the grounds that the statute did not create a duty to avoid the type of accident that occurred.

At first glance, the decision seems clearly wrong from an economic standpoint. Since the pens were required anyway, the incremental cost of care to prevent the animals from being washed overboard was zero, which had to be less than the expected cost of such an accident. But this reasoning assumes that the cost of the pens really was less than the expected cost of disease which the pens would have prevented, and it may not have been, depending on the motivations behind the statute. To be sure, even if it was not, it is still possible that the cost of the pens was less than the sum of the expected costs of disease and of the animals' being washed overboard by a storm....

But there is a severe practical problem with using this insight as a basis for liability in *Gorris*-type cases. It requires the court to consider a type of accident not before it in the litigation—in *Gorris*, to weigh the costs of the pens against their benefits in disease prevention, though the accident being litigated involved the washing overboard of plaintiff's animals in a storm. The court could, of course, simply have taken for granted that the statute reflected a correct cost-benefit analysis, in which event, as we have seen, the incremental cost of due care to avoid the washing overboard was zero and had to be less than the incremental benefit. This approach is frequently taken in statutory due care cases, under the name of "negligence per se." This is the rule that vi-

---

49. L.R. 9 Ex. 125 (1874).

olation of a statutory standard of care is deemed negligence without opportunity for the defendant to show otherwise through the Hand formula* or some related technique. Even so, or perhaps especially so, violation of the statute might not be negligent for a particular defendant, given his costs of compliance relevant to the benefits of violation. In such a case, adding in effect to the penalties of the statute by making the defendant liable for an unrelated harm could result in overdeterrence. In a case such as this, the court's "causal" analysis serves the purpose, suggested earlier, of refining the legal analysis of negligence. The legal concept sometimes diverges from the economic—notably in the idea of negligence per se based on breach of a statutory duty. The legal concept of cause comes to the rescue in these cases. The combination of negligence and causation analysis equates to the economic concept of negligence and allows the optimal result to be achieved.

Here we pause to answer the objection that our emphasis ... on administrative costs introduces a discordant note into a discussion of causation, for what have the costs of administration to do with the concept of causation? We have two replies. First, where the administrative cost is a cost of determining whether a harm would have been avoided by taking some precaution, the issue in the nervous-injury and freak-accident cases, such cost is just the procedural aspect of a substantive causation inquiry. Second and more interestingly, if we are correct that causation in the law is an inarticulate groping for economically sound solutions rather than an effort at explicating a philosophically coherent concept of causation, it is no surprise that considerations of administrative cost should get smuggled into causal analysis; and of course it has long been recognized in legal discussions of causation that many cases discussed under the rubric of "legal" or "proximate" cause do not involve issues that a philosopher, or indeed any nonlawyer, would describe as causal.

NOTES

(1) Was it "negligence" to violate section 81-4-201 in the fact setting of the *Read* case?

(2) Note that in its footnote 1, the court characterizes a precedent as having dealt with an analogous case in terms of "proximate cause." Does "proximate cause," in that sense, have the same meaning as the "causation analysis" of which Landes and Posner speak? What was the "proximate cause" of the accident in *Read*?

(3) The court in *Read* refers, in its footnote 8, to what it characterizes as the "self-evident" purpose of another statute as being to prohibit "non-purebred bulls from running at large." What would have been the result in a *Read*-type case if the colliding animal had been a non-purebred bull and not a goat?

(4) Give the results in the following cases, in which the plaintiff attempts to use the violation of a statute in support of a personal injury claim, and provide rationalizations for those results:

(a) The defendant, carefully driving an unregistered motor vehicle, unavoidably hits a pedestrian when the car skids on encountering an unexpected slick spot in the road.

(b) The defendant carefully drives on Sunday in violation of a law that prohibits Sunday motoring and unavoidably hits a pedestrian when the car skids on an unexpected slick spot.

---

* The "Learned Hand Test" is quoted supra § 4.03[B].—Ed.

(5) What should be the result in a fireman's suit based on a statute prohibiting the storage of certain flammable material, when the plaintiff is:

(a) Injured while fulfilling the general duties of fighting a fire that started in the prohibited material.

(b) Injured by the flaring up of some of the prohibited material in his face as he is fighting a fire that started from other causes.

PROBLEM

A Coast Guard navigation rule required scows to "carry a white light on each end ... not less than 8 feet above the surface of the water, and ... so placed as to show an unbroken light all around the horizon, and ... of such a character as to be visible on a dark night with a clear atmosphere at a distance of at least 5 miles." Kernan was a seaman on a tug that was towing a scow on the Schuykill River in Philadelphia. The scow carried an open flame kerosene lamp no more than three feet above the water. The lamp ignited highly flammable vapors that lay above extensive oil slicks spread across the river, causing a fire that resulted in Kernan's death. What would be the principal issue in Kernan's negligence suit against the owner of the tug?

KLEIN v. HERLIM REALTY CORP.

New York Supreme Court, Trial Term
184 Misc. 852, 54 N.Y.S.2d 144,
aff'd mem., 269 A.D.2d 934, 58 N.Y.S.2d 344 (1945)

BOTEIN, JUSTICE. The facts in this case, as submitted to me on an agreed statement, are as follows: Defendant owned, managed, and controlled an apartment house in the Borough of the Bronx, reserving to itself control of the hallways and lobbies. At about 5 A. M. on March 23, 1943, a blackout was ordered for the New York area, and plaintiff, a volunteer air raid warden, entered the premises to ascertain why the vestibule or hall lights, which were visible from the outside, had not been extinguished.

Upon entering, plaintiff met two other wardens who had attempted unsuccessfully to arouse the superintendent of the building. Plaintiff searched for a switch controlling the ceiling lights, but found none. He looked for a chair or other article of furniture in the lobby or vestibule and found none. The ceiling in the lobby is approximately nine and one-half feet from the ground, and in order to reach it, the two other wardens interlocked their hands and lifted the plaintiff to a sufficient height to enable him to unscrew the electric light bulbs which were still burning. There were four such bulbs burning in different portions of the lobby, all four of which were visible from the street. Upon extinguishing each of the bulbs the two air raid wardens lowered the plaintiff sufficiently to permit him to step on the ground. When the fourth bulb was unscrewed, the lobby was left in total darkness. As the two wardens were lowering the plaintiff in the same fashion as had been followed previously, and sufficiently low to permit him to step off to the ground, the plaintiff, stepping off in total darkness, missed his step, fell, and sustained a fracture of the left ankle. He sues to recover damages for personal injuries.

At the time in question Section 101, subdivision 2, of the New York State War Emergency Act, provided that "any person who shall violate or disobey any duly promulgated rule, regulation or order concerning (a) the effective screening or extinguishment of all lights, lighting devices and appliances, ... shall be guilty of an infraction."

There was no light switch in the corridor. There were no facilities for screening or shading the lights so as to prevent illumination in the corridor from being visible from the exterior of the building. Apparently the only device for extinguishing the lights centrally was in the control of the superintendent. Plaintiff and his associates were unable to arouse him, with the result that the rules and regulations governing blackouts, as promulgated by the Police Department and the State Director of Civilian Protection, were violated by defendant.

One of plaintiff's duties as an air raid warden was to "direct the enforcement of lighting restrictions so as to insure effectiveness of a blackout" (vid. Rules of Police Department relative to duties of Police and Air Raid Wardens). In its essential aspects, plaintiff's services to the community were not unlike the service of a fireman or patrolman in the performance of duty. Plaintiff was therefore more than a bare licensee on defendant's premises; his relationship bordered on that of an invitee, to whom defendant owed the duty of reasonable care under all the circumstances....

Where a statutory duty is imposed upon one for the direct protection of another, and the latter is injured because this duty is not performed, a cause of action arises in his favor based upon the statute. Where the statute or ordinance is general in character, such as, for example, one defining the degree of care to be exercised in a calling or occupation, failure to use such care is evidence more or less conclusive of negligence, and one injured as a result thereof has a cause of action in negligence. *Di Caprio v. New York Central R. Co.*, 231 N.Y. 94, 97, 131 N.E. 746, 747, 16 A.L.R. 940.

The regulation or statute which defendant in this case violated was not enacted for the direct benefit or protection of air raid wardens, but to promote the defense and safety of our population generally. Consequently, even though defendant did not obey the statute, there is no liability to plaintiff unless plaintiff's injury resulted from defendant's disobedience of the statute. *Di Caprio v. New York Central R. Co., supra....* In other words, plaintiff is not entitled to recover unless it is established that defendant's negligence was the natural and proximate cause of plaintiff's injuries. *Laidlaw v. Sage*, 158 N.Y. 73, 52 N.E. 679, 44 L.R.A. 216....

Plaintiff's injuries were not caused by lack of reasonable care on the part of defendant in the maintenance or operation of his property for the purposes for which it was intended to be used ... ; they were caused by an accident occurring while plaintiff, in implementing a method which to him seemed appropriate under the circumstances, attempted to enforce compliance with the statute.

True, the violation of the statute constitutes negligence, but there is in this case no causal connection between the injury plaintiff received and defendant's disregard of the statutory prohibition or mandate. Here, defendant's negligence merely furnished the condition or occasion upon which the injuries were received, but they did not put in motion the agency by which the injuries were inflicted.

Plaintiff argues that the defendant's violation "set in motion a chain of events which culminated in the accident complained of," and that "the ultimate test is whether this accident would have occurred had the defendant complied with its statutory obligation." In Section 431 of Restatement of the Law of Torts, the rule is stated as follows: "In order to be a legal cause of another's harm, it is not enough that the harm would not have occurred had the actor not been negligent.... The negligence must also be a substantial factor in bringing about the plaintiff's harm. The word 'substantial' is used to denote the fact that the defendant's conduct has such an effect in producing the harm as to lead reasonable men to regard it as a cause, using that word in the popular sense in which there always lurks the idea of responsibility rather than the so-called 'philosophic sense', which includes every one of the great number of events without which any happening would not have occurred. Each of these events is a cause in the so-called 'philosophic sense', yet the effect of many of them is so insignificant that no ordinary mind would think of them as causes."

It is stipulated that, after the last bulb had been extinguished, and after the plaintiff had been lowered by his companions sufficiently to permit him to step to the ground, he missed his step in the darkness and fell, thus sustaining his injuries. Defendant, however, had done nothing to cause or provoke plaintiff to miss his step. A series of new and unexpected causes intervened and brought on the injury, the direct and proximate cause being the fact that plaintiff himself missed his step.

Plaintiff's injury was not the natural and probable consequence of a violation of the statute. It resulted from a cause independent of defendant's negligence in violating the statute. It happened because of an intermedial accident which no one in the position of the defendant could reasonably have anticipated. The dominant feature of foreseeability, which so largely influences the law of negligence, likewise extends to its contributory aspect of proximate cause. *See Babcock v. Fitzpatrick*, 221 App.Div. 638, 225 N.Y.S. 30, and cases cited therein.

I find that defendant's negligence was not the proximate cause of plaintiff's injury and direct judgment in favor of defendant.

NOTES

(1) Explain the meaning of each sentence in the penultimate paragraph in *Klein*.

(2) Is the verbiage in *Klein* essentially a mask for a holding of contributory negligence?

(3) Suppose that in a *Klein* situation, the plaintiff had been injured in the following way: Coming alone into the lobby, he finds a small table from the top of which he can unscrew the lights. He climbs upon the table but one of its legs gives way under his weight, and he falls, injuring his ankle. The superintendent testifies that he had once used the table himself for that purpose when a remote switch was frozen in the "on" position. Should the result be the same as in *Klein*? Would it aid the warden's case if the remote switch had worked erratically for some time before this accident, a fact known to the superintendent, and that it was frozen at the time of the injury? What was the "proximate cause" of the accident in *Read*?[1]

---

1. The authors are grateful to Gill Deford for suggestions on which this question is based.

§ 12.02 Introduction to the Duty Concept

DUNCAN v. RZONCA*

Illinois Appellate Court
133 Ill. App. 3d 184, 478 N.E.2d 603 (1985)

UNVERZAGT, JUSTICE.

The plaintiff, Alan Duncan, a Naperville police officer, appeals the judgment of the circuit court of DuPage County dismissing with prejudice Counts III and IV of his first amended complaint at law for personal injury against defendants Hinsdale Federal Savings and Loan Association (Hinsdale Federal or bank) and Patricia A. Doerr. The court found the counts failed to state a cause of action against these respective defendants. . . .

Plaintiff was injured on May 19, 1983, at approximately 2:17 p.m. in an automobile accident during an emergency response to a robbery alarm from Hinsdale Federal in Naperville. The plaintiff was forced to swerve his squad car in order to avoid a collision when a vehicle, owned by defendant Edward Rzonca and driven by defendant Raymond Rzonca, entered the intersection of Olesen Drive and Chicago Avenue in Naperville. The officer's car struck a telephone pole, and he sustained the injuries and damages claimed in the suit. The alarm, a false one, allegedly was activated by the defendant Doerr's three-year-old son, Charles A. Doerr.

Inter alia, it was alleged that between the period January 10, 1983, to the date in question, May 19, 1983, six alarms, all later discovered to be false, originated from the Hinsdale Federal facility. It was alleged that a false alarm immediately preceding the one in question occurred on May 13, 1983, about 12:37 p.m. and that it also was activated by defendant Doerr's son Charles. In each of the six false alarm instances, certain Naperville police officers, including plaintiff here, responded, assuming that a robbery was in progress at the facility.

Plaintiff's complaint alleged that on the date and at the time in question, May 19, 1983, 2 p.m., Doerr was advised by one of Hinsdale Federal's employees, Carol Crowell, that the last time Doerr was in the bank her son had set off the silent alarm causing the Naperville police to respond. Doerr was requested by Crowell to keep Charles away from the back of her desk where the alarm button, exposed and facing outward from the rear of the desk, was located in the upper right-hand corner of the desk's knee-space. Shortly thereafter, Crowell left Doerr's presence, and another bank employee, Stephen A. Shuman, observed Doerr's son behind Crowell's desk, at or near said alarm button, and directed him to come to the front of the desk. It was alleged the boy had already pushed the button, however, and the alarm was activated. Plaintiff was injured while responding to that false alarm.

. . .

The court granted Hinsdale Federal's motion to dismiss because it found the "two intervening acts, one of the parent-child control or lack thereof, and secondly, the intervening conduct of the plaintiff and the driver defendant in this particular case" made

---

* The late Jim Haddad called this case to the attention of Marshall Shapo.

it "just too far out from foreseeability as well as violating the concept of proximate cause."

The court granted Doerr's motion to dismiss finding that:

> Insofar as the mother and the control is concerned, I think that this is one step closer, but once again on the issue of foreseeability, proximate cause, intervening cause, I don't believe in either instance the plaintiff in this case can make out an action predicated that the negligence, if any, of either of the defendants is a, and I do emphasize the word "a", proximate cause of the injuries, which of course is what it is all about.

Continuing, the court commented:

> There may very well be some contractual duty or contractual liability between the bank and the City of ... Naperville.

> But I don't see that that duty or that responsibility, insofar as multiple activation of a silent alarm, bleeds over and is the kind of duty that is involved insofar as this action is concerned.

...

DUTY

... Hinsdale Federal argues the facts alleged show it owed no duty to plaintiff because his injury occurred while he was off the bank's premises, on his way to the bank, when the accident happened.

...

We ... agree with the plaintiff's argument that the facts alleged ... give rise to a special relationship....

Defendant argues only hindsight could have allowed it to foresee that injury would result from its location of the silent alarm button in the knee space of the customer service desk, or that failure to take physical custody of Charles Doerr or keep him under control would result in injury. It asserts that the test of foreseeability must be met first before policy considerations are weighed, and when the plaintiff has failed to establish the foreseeability of the harm, no duty on the part of the defendant may be said to have arisen.

We agree with plaintiff that the defendant has placed undue emphasis on foreseeability as a "make or break" factor insofar as the court's duty determination is concerned. As plaintiff asserts, "the existence of a legal duty is not dependent on the factor of foreseeability alone, but includes consideration of public policy and social requirements," and that the question of duty is one which is heavily based upon public policy considerations.... The appropriate role of foreseeability was addressed in this court's opinion in *Nelson v. Commonwealth Edison Co.* (1984), 124 Ill.App.3d 655, 80 Ill.Dec. 401, 465 N.E.2d 513. There, this court considered that while the role of the foreseeability factor—especially in the context of duty—was still not entirely clear, "the imposition and scope of a legal duty is dependent not only on the factor of foreseeability (*Cunis v. Brennan* (1974), 56 Ill.2d 372, 375 [, 308 N.E.2d 617]) but involves other considerations, including the magnitude of the risk involved in defendant's conduct, the burden of requiring defendant to guard against that risk, and the consequences of placing that burden upon the defendant...." ... Continuing, the court concluded that:

> While foreseeability is thus a proper matter for a court to consider in making its duty determination, the sounder approach would be to recall that the duty issue is broad in its implication and it is only the jury's negligence deter-

mination which need be strictly confined to the facts of the particular case. [Citations.] In other words, foreseeability is a determinative consideration only where a particular occurrence is so extreme that, as a policy decision, it would be unwise to require defendant to guard against it.

124 Ill.App.3d 655, 663, 80 Ill.Dec. 401, 465 N.E.2d 513.

Accordingly, foreseeability here would be determinative as to the duty issue only if it could be said that the particular occurrence here was so extreme, that as a policy decision, it would be unwise to require the defendant to guard against it.

Contrary to defendant's argument that only "hindsight" could have made the plaintiff's injury foreseeable, judgment of whether the harm was legally foreseeable takes into consideration what was apparent to the defendant at the time of the now complained-of conduct.... Plaintiff's allegations—taken as true for purposes of the motion to dismiss—established that six false alarms were activated at the bank during the period January 10, 1983, to May 19, 1983. The one immediately before the one in question took place six days earlier under virtually identical circumstances and involving the same bank employee, minor child, and the child's mother. The police responded to each alarm assuming that a robbery was in progress, but in each case, it was a false alarm. It may be inferred that the emergency response of the police in each instance created an appreciable risk of harm in that in order to effectively respond to the alarm, the officer or officers would necessarily have to proceed as quickly as possible to the scene. This, in turn, implies traveling by car at high speed through numerous intersections in a relatively densely populated community during daytime hours. Defendant correctly asserts the police have the right to assume other drivers will comply with the applicable traffic regulations and yield to the emergency vehicle. (*Roberts v. Cipfl* (1942), 313 Ill.App. 373, 40 N.E.2d 629.) Nonetheless, there are many situations in which the standard of care exercised must take into account "'that occasional negligence which is one of the ordinary incidents of human life and therefore to be anticipated.'" (Prosser, Torts § 33, at 171 (4th ed. 1971).) Accidents involving emergency vehicles are not so uncommon as to be unforeseeable, and most of them undoubtedly involve some degree of negligent conduct. Prosser also notes that as the gravity of the possible harm increases, the apparent likelihood of its occurrence need be correspondingly less. Prosser, Torts § 31, at 147 (4th ed. 1971).

Hinsdale Federal argues that the recognizable risk of harm, if any, created by its conduct was not an unreasonable risk of harm which would give rise to a duty to guard against it. Defendant notes the risks inherent in police response to an emergency alarm are the same whether the alarm is real or false, and thus the risk of harm to plaintiff was not an unreasonable risk....

. . .

... [P]laintiff points out defendant's negligent conduct resulted in the alarm being sounded falsely, thus actively placing him in a position of risk by necessitating he respond in an emergency—and potentially hazardous—mode to an emergency situation which, in fact, never existed. Plaintiff views the risk thusly created as unreasonable since no valid or excusable reason for the alarm being sounded existed. We note here that plaintiff's complaint not only alleged the defendant failed to prevent the activation of the false alarm, but failed as well either to ascertain whether the alarm had been activated or to notify him that the alarm was false.

In sum, we conclude the risk of harm to the plaintiff by virtue of defendant's conduct was an appreciable one, and was not so unforeseeable as to render it unwise to require the defendant to guard against it.

Other factors to be considered in determining whether the defendant owed a duty to the plaintiff is the magnitude of the defendant's burden in reducing the risk of harm. The burden on the bank would have been minimal, and it could easily have kept inaccessible to the public the rear of the desk where the alarm was located, otherwise relocated the button, or kept a more watchful eye on the boy. The allegations of the complaint which indicate that the bank employee shifted responsibility for keeping the boy away from the alarm to the mother would not relieve the bank of its duty to exercise a reasonable standard of care for the plaintiff's protection, but would go to whether a breach of that duty resulted from the shift of responsibility. (*See* Prosser, Torts § 33, at 176–77 (4th ed. 1971).) Certainly it would not be difficult to determine a location for the alarm button which would be equally as safe from unauthorized inadvertent or intentional activation as it would be accessible for authorized use. The very nature of a silent alarm demands that it be used only to signal the most dire circumstances with the most furtive of movements. Although the reason for the other four of the six false alarms alleged here is not known, it seems apparent that there is either a problem with the alarm system or simply with the location of the button. Logic, if not duty, suggests a change is in order.

Alternatively, the burden of paying particular heed to the whereabouts of a child who was in close proximity to the location of the alarm button for the time it takes the child's adult companion to complete a banking transaction does not seem undue. Actually, the monitoring of children in that area presented no problem until the bank employee seated at the desk got up and left. Moving the button to a location which would be secure from the public at all times and not only when attended by a bank employee, would obviate the need for any monitoring at all. Failing that, the time period involved here is not so long as to create an undue burden on the bank by requiring that it keep children away from the button.

Likewise, the consequences of placing the burden of guarding against the risk of harm on the defendant in this case does not appear to involve extraordinary cost or problems. No doubt a bank charged every day with the safekeeping of the property of its customers can be expected to handle the consequences involved in securing a safe location for a silent emergency alarm button.

In sum, we conclude the allegations of Count III of the plaintiff's complaint were sufficient to raise a duty at law owed to the plaintiff by the defendant Hinsdale Federal.

. . . .

[In considering the case against Ms. Doerr, the court concludes:]

As was true of Hinsdale Federal, the likelihood of injury to the plaintiff was significant and not so "freakish" as to be an unforeseeable consequence of Doerr's failure to conform to a reasonable standard of care. The risk of harm to which the plaintiff was exposed as a result of defendant's negligence was an unreasonable risk of harm which required the defendant to guard against it. A police officer responding to an emergency is subject to risk of harm every day, but society is willing to bear that risk in light of the social need served. The risk becomes socially intolerable and unreasonable when no social need for it exists, particularly when the means of guarding against the risk are eminently available and easily accomplished. Defendant Doerr need only have controlled her three-year-old son for the short time she was in the bank, and then only in that one particular area of the bank. She had actual knowledge of the earlier result of her son's activities, and had the opportunity to prevent a repetition on the day in question.

Doerr additionally argues that the risk which plaintiff was exposed to was the risk normally associated with the function of his employment. Since the concept of duty imposes an obligation to prevent only "unreasonable" risks, she concludes she owed plaintiff no duty, and that her conclusion finds support in the "fireman's rule".

The fireman's rule has been interpreted as imposing a duty of reasonable care on landowners or occupiers to prevent injury to firemen which might result from a cause independent of the fire, but no duty to prevent injury resulting from the fire itself. (*Court v. Grzelinski* (1978), 72 Ill.2d 141, 147–48, 19 Ill.Dec. 617, 379 N.E.2d 281.)

. . .

All parties have acknowledged that police emergency response presents a recognizable risk of harm not only at the scene of the crime, but on the way to the scene of the crime. Clearly more serious injury may result from a collision in which even only one vehicle is traveling at a high speed. Balanced against the probability and gravity of the risk, is the utility of the conduct involved; *i.e.*, speeding to the scene of a crime in order to protect life or property. The risk of collision is reasonable and worthwhile when it is borne in furtherance of that objective; when no need for protection exists, speeding is unjustified and an unreasonable risk.

In sum, we believe Counts III and IV of the plaintiff's amended complaint allege sufficient facts to raise a duty on the part of both Hinsdale Federal and Patricia Doerr.

PROXIMATE CAUSE

Plaintiff asserts the question of proximate cause was one of fact for the jury, and that it was inappropriate for the court to find as a matter of law that the negligence of the defendants was not the proximate cause of his injury.

Merlo v. Public Service Company of Northern Illinois (1942), 381 Ill. 300, 318, 45 N.E.2d 665, establishes that "[w]hat constitutes the proximate cause of an injury in a particular case ... can only be a question of law when the facts are not only undisputed but are also such that there can be no difference in the judgment of reasonable men as to the inferences to be drawn from them."

Defendants urge that such is the case here and, therefore, the court could determine as a matter of law that their alleged negligent conduct did nothing more than furnish a condition, making the injury possible....

We disagree that the inferences to be drawn from the facts alleged here are so undisputed as to permit the court to determine as a matter of law what constituted the proximate cause of the plaintiff's injury here. It is clear that in addition to proximate cause, the question of whether a duty has been breached is also a factual matter for the jury to decide. (*Curtis v. County of Cook* (1983), 98 Ill.2d 158, 163, 74 Ill.Dec. 614, 456 N.E.2d 116.) The question of defendants' negligence becomes a matter of law only where reasonable men of fair understanding agree that defendant was guilty of negligence.... There can be no recovery in tort for negligence unless the defendant has breached a duty owed to plaintiff....

Reasonable men could differ as to the inferences to be drawn from the facts alleged insofar as it may be inferred that the bank's shift of its responsibility for control of the child to the child's mother either did or did not amount to an exercise of due care for plaintiff's benefit. Hinsdale Federal suggests it was not negligent for the reason the child was accompanied by his mother. Further, without more evidence, reasonable men may differ as to whether either defendant's failure to warn the police department about the false alarm or to ascertain whether the button had been pushed constituted a breach of the duty owed plaintiff since the extent of either defendant's knowledge and observation of the boy's activities is not certain.

Under these circumstances, we believe the court erred in determining the issue of proximate cause as a matter of law, and that Counts III and IV should not have been dismissed. *See Gossett v. Burnett* (1968), 251 S.C. 548, 164 S.E.2d 578.

We also find merit in plaintiff's counterargument to defendants' assertions that their alleged negligence was only a condition to, and not a cause of, plaintiff's injury. Noting that the distinction between cause and condition is now almost entirely discredited, Prosser states:

> So far as it has any validity at all, it must refer to the type of case where the forces set in operation by the defendant have come to rest in a position of apparent safety, and some new force intervenes. But even in such cases, it is not the distinction between "cause" and "condition" which is important, but the nature of the risk and the character of the intervening cause.

(Prosser, Torts § 42, at 248 (4th ed. 1971).)

...

The "forces set in operation" here, of course, were the alleged negligent activation of a false alarm. Those forces would "come to rest in a position of apparent safety" only when the risk of harm to the plaintiff created by the defendants' alleged negligence had passed; *i.e.*, when plaintiff arrived safely at the bank. The nature of the risk created by the defendants' alleged negligence was the danger that the responding emergency vehicle would be involved in a collision; when Rzonca's car caused the plaintiff to swerve to avoid that very risk, the so-called condition may be viewed as having done quite as much to bring about the harm to the plaintiff as did the intervening cause, the Rzonca car.

The judgment of the circuit court of DuPage County is reversed, and the cause remanded for further proceedings.

REVERSED AND REMANDED.

...

NOTES

(1) What is the role of "foreseeability" in judging a case like this one? Is it essential to a finding of "duty"? Of "proximate cause"?

(2) What is the relationship between "duty" and "proximate cause" in this case? And how does each concept relate to the question of "negligence"?

(3) If you were writing a jury instruction to substitute for the trial judge's statement supporting his grant of the motion to dismiss (see the block quotes preceding the "duty" section of *Duncan*, supra page 566), how would you phrase it?

(4) How does the court relate the foreseeability argument to "public policy considerations"? What are the social policies principally at issue in this case? How much of the decision is one that could be justified on the basis of economic analysis under a Learned Hand-type rule?

(5) Does a cell phone manufacturer owe a duty of care to a person injured in a car accident resulting from driver distraction? One state court found no duty on the part of Cingular Wireless to a woman injured in a collision with a Cingular customer. The court found "a high degree of foreseeability" lacking and pointed as well to the parties' relationship and to public policy. *Williams v. Cingular Wireless*, 809 N.E.2d 473 (Ind. Ct.

App. 2004). Is that the right outcome if Cingular knows that 450 to 1000 fatalities result annually from cell-phone distraction? See Paul K. Hentzen, Comment, *The Trouble with Telematics: The Uneasy Marriage of Wireless Technology and Automobiles*, 69 UMKC L. Rev. 845 (2001).

BROWN v. CHANNEL FUELING SERVICE, INC.

United States District Court, Eastern District of Louisiana
574 F. Supp. 666 (1983)

ORDER AND REASONS

CHARLES SCHWARTZ, Jr., DISTRICT JUDGE.

This matter is before the Court on the motion of defendant Gremar Compania (Gremar) for summary judgment on the claims asserted against it by plaintiff, Wesley Brown, on the basis that its conduct was not the "legal cause" of plaintiff's injury. Gremar reasons that it owed, and therefore breached, no duty to plaintiff. Both plaintiff and defendant Channel Fueling Service, Inc. (Channel) oppose Gremar's motion for summary judgment on the grounds that Gremar's vessel owed a general duty at large to refrain from negligent acts, and that courts have found causation in situations in which the negligence and injury were far more remote than they are in the present case.

. . .

This action was instituted by plaintiff against his employer, Channel, for personal injuries he allegedly sustained while cleaning oil from the deck of the fuel barge CHANNEL FUELER 10, owned by Channel. Plaintiff later amended his complaint to add Gremar, owner of the M/T APHRODITE B, and Nola Marine, owner of the tug KAREN WAYNE, as defendants. It is undisputed that the M/T APHRODITE B and the KAREN WAYNE collided on September 5, 1981 at 0025 hours at Mile 97 AHP of the Mississippi River. As a result of the collision, heavy crude oil cargo spilled from the fracture of the No. 1 port tank of the APHRODITE B and flowed downriver.

At the time of the collision the barge on which plaintiff was working was approximately six miles downstream from the collision site. The current at the time of the collision was one knot. The oil reached the location of the fuel barge on which plaintiff was working approximately six hours after the collision. For purposes of this motion it was stipulated that oil from the collision had washed onto the deck of the fuel barge CHANNEL FUELER 10 and had congealed into a soft, tar-like substance. As part of his normal duties plaintiff undertook to clean the deck of the barge on September 7, 1981. After completing most of the task, plaintiff lost his footing and fell. Plaintiff thereafter commenced this action, alleging a cause of action against Gremar, among others. Defendant Gremar submits that summary judgment should be granted as a matter of law on the basis that any oil spill that resulted from the APHRODITE B/KAREN WAYNE collision cannot be considered the legal cause of plaintiff's injury.

The determination of whether a defendant is responsible for plaintiff's injury is determined by a "legal cause" analysis. *Spinks v. Chevron Oil Co.*, 507 F.2d 216 (5th Cir.1975). Gremar does not deny that the actions of the colliding vessels in causing oil to spill into the Mississippi River constituted "negligence" to some classes of persons. Gremar does dispute, however, that it is negligent as to the plaintiff, contending that plaintiff's alleged injuries were not proximately or substantially caused by any conduct of this defendant.

For the conduct of defendant to be negligent as to plaintiff, the defendant must owe some duty to the plaintiff which is breached by the negligent conduct of the defendant. *Chavez v. Noble Drilling Corp.*, 567 F.2d 287 (5th Cir.1978). Gremar argues that the mere fact that a person working on a barge six miles downriver may slip and fall while cleaning oil two days after a collision is outside the scope of any duty owed by defendant.

The resolution of the motion before the Court turns on whether a limitation should be placed on defendant's duty. We are of the belief that a limit must be placed as to how far a defendant's responsibility should extend. Although the doctrine that one is only responsible for the foreseeable natural probable consequences of his acts has been subject to great erosion, it has not completely disappeared. Thus, we are of the belief that at some point common sense must take over and dictate as to how far defendant's responsibility should extend. Defendant should not be held responsible for all injuries which occur as a result of the oil spill, no matter how far removed in distance and time. To do so would be to stretch the concept of legal cause too far. " ... somewhere a point will be reached when the courts will agree that the link has become too tenuous—that what is claimed to be consequence is only fortuity." *Petition of Kinsman Transit Company*, 388 F.2d 821, 824–825 (2d Cir.1968). The accident which was allegedly caused by the negligence of defendant is, at best, a fortuitous event for which defendant's conduct was not a legal cause. Plaintiff's accident and resulting injury were too remote from the collision, both in time and space, for plaintiff to recover from Gremar. Phrased in terms of foreseeability, it simply was not foreseeable that oil which spilled into the Mississippi as a result of a collision would splash aboard a barge miles away and cause someone to slip some two days after the collision. Accordingly, the motion of Gremar for summary judgment is granted.

NOTES

(1) Why was the plaintiff's injury "simply ... not foreseeable"? What does "not foreseeable" mean in this context, anyway? Does it refer to the reaction of a neutral person asked to describe all the events that he or she could foresee from an abstract description of a collision involving a vessel carrying oil? Does it refer to what a jury would say was "foreseeable" if the entire case was described to them after such a particular event?

How do you compare the *Brown* court's handling of the "foreseeability" element of the case with the *Duncan* court's treatment of that factor?

(2) Can you describe the way that "distance" and "time" affect the *Brown* court's decision? How would the court have responded if the accident had happened after dawn on September 5th, and just a mile away?

(3) Why does the court say that the defendant's conduct was "not a legal cause" of the plaintiff's injury? Would the fact that an accident is "not foreseeable" always equal a lack of "legal cause"?

§ 12.03 Intervening Criminal Acts

[A] Generally

PROBLEM

A retail gun dealer had his shop in a high crime neighborhood. From the window, passersby could see guns in the shop, which were neither chained nor in cases. The store did not have effective locks or alarm systems. One night after the store closed, a youth broke in and stole a shotgun and shells. He used them to murder another youth, whose father sued the gun dealer. How would you phrase the issues?

ROMERO v. NATIONAL RIFLE ASSOCIATION OF AMERICA, INC.

United States Court of Appeals, District of Columbia Circuit
242 U.S. App. D.C. 55, 749 F.2d 77 (1984)

SCALIA, CIRCUIT JUDGE.

This appeal from a judgment for the defendants in a wrongful death action challenges two rulings of the District Court. The first refused to instruct the jury that a violation of the District of Columbia Firearms Control Regulation Act of 1975, D.C.Code Ann. §§ 6-2301 to -2380 (1981), could constitute negligence per se or evidence of negligence on the part of a defendant whose stolen target pistol was the instrument of the decedent's death. The second granted judgment *non obstante veredicto* ("n.o.v.") to the other defendant, the owner of the building from which the gun was stolen....

I

Appellee National Rifle Association ("NRA") maintains its national headquarters in Washington, D.C., consisting of a main building and an annex. The main building contains offices, a firearms museum, a laboratory, and a firing range used for recreational shooting. The annex contains only clerical offices and is connected to the main building by passageways that are closed and locked after business hours.

Appellee Robert W. Lowe, an NRA employee whose office was in the annex, owned a .22 caliber target pistol and ammunition which he regularly used for recreational shooting at the firing range in the main NRA building. When he left work on November 23, 1979, he left the pistol in his office as he sometimes did, locking it and its ammunition in a closet, and hiding the key to the closet in his desk. That evening, four burglars broke into the annex. In their search of the offices, they found the key to Lowe's closet and stole the gun and ammunition. Four days later, after committing several robberies with the gun, one of the original burglars and an accomplice used it to rob Orlando Gonzalez-Angel. When Gonzalez resisted, the accomplice shot and killed him.

Appellant Mario S. Romero, administrator of the estate of Gonzalez, filed this diversity action in the United States District Court for the District of Columbia against Lowe and the NRA, seeking damages for Gonzalez' death.... At the conclusion of the trial, the judge refused plaintiff's request to instruct the jury that a violation by Lowe of the District of Columbia Firearms Act would constitute either evidence of Lowe's negligence or negligence per se, based on his finding that no violation had occurred.[1] The jury found that Lowe was not liable but that the NRA was. The District Court granted the NRA's subsequent motion for judgment n.o.v. on the grounds that the NRA did not owe any duty of care to Gonzalez and that the NRA's conduct was not the proximate cause of his death.

---

1. The court also refused to permit the jury to consider the plaintiff's strict liability theory and claims for punitive damages. These rulings are not challenged on appeal.

Romero appeals the judgment for Lowe on the ground that the trial court erred in refusing to give the requested instruction. He appeals the judgment for the NRA on the ground that the court erred in setting aside the jury's verdict.

II

We turn first to the directed verdict granted to the defendant NRA. The parties and the District Court have assumed throughout this litigation that the substantive law applicable to this diversity action is that of the District of Columbia. Absent objection, we assume that to be correct.

Under District of Columbia law, three elements are required to render the NRA liable on a negligence theory for damages arising from Gonzalez' death: (1) a duty, owed by the defendant to the plaintiff, to conform to a certain standard of care; (2) a breach of this duty by the defendant; and (3) an injury to the plaintiff proximately caused by the defendant's breach. *See O'Neil v. Bergan*, 452 A.2d 337, 341 (D.C.1982). Consideration of only the first and third is essential to our disposition of this appeal. Here and in the District Court the parties have assumed that both of these elements are questions of fact for the jury, and we accept that proposition without deciding it. Thus, duty of care and proximate causation were only proper issues for the court and only proper grounds for judgment n.o.v. if "the evidence, together with all inferences that can reasonably be drawn therefrom [was] so one-sided that reasonable men could not disagree on the verdict," *Vander Zee v. Karabatsos*, 589 F.2d 723, 726 (D.C.Cir.1978), *cert. denied*, 441 U.S. 962, 99 S.Ct. 2407, 60 L.Ed.2d 1066 (1979).

In the District of Columbia, a defendant can be held liable for damages resulting from intervening acts of third parties "[i]f the danger of an intervening negligent or criminal act should have reasonably been anticipated and protected against...." *St. Paul Fire & Marine Insurance Co. v. James G. Davis Construction Corp.*, 350 A.2d 751, 752 (D.C.1976). However, when the intervening act involves *criminal*, rather than *negligent*, conduct by a third party, the ability to anticipate (or foresee) the intervention with the normally required degree of specificity is not enough. "'The question is not simply whether a criminal event is foreseeable, but whether a *duty* exists to take measures to guard against it ... [, which] is ultimately a question of fairness.'" *Cook v. Safeway Stores*, 354 A.2d 507, 509–10 (D.C.1976) (*quoting Goldberg v. Housing Authority of Newark*, 38 N.J. 578, 583, 186 A.2d 291, 293 (1962)) (emphasis in original). *Cook* held that Safeway was not liable for injuries suffered by a victim of an attempted robbery in one of its stores. The principle of fairness it enunciated was reformulated in a later case, in order to sustain a jury instruction requiring that the particular type of injury be foreseeable. In *Lacy v. District of Columbia*, 424 A.2d 317 (D.C.1980), a District of Columbia schoolgirl who was sexually assaulted by a janitor brought suit for negligence against a schoolteacher, a guidance counselor, the school principal, and the District as employer. The court held that there was no prejudicial error in an instruction requiring the jury to find that *assault*, rather than merely harm in general, was foreseeable before the defendants could be found liable for the janitor's criminal actions.

> [B]ecause of the extraordinary nature of criminal conduct, the law requires that the foreseeability of the risk be more precisely shown. Thus, although normally the "defendant need not have foreseen the precise injury, nor 'should [he] have had notice of the particular method' in which a harm would occur," in order to establish proximate cause, unless the assault was foreseeable, the defendants in this case had no duty to act.

Id. at 323 (*quoting Kendall v. Gore Properties, Inc.*, 236 F.2d 673, 682 (D.C.Cir.1956)) (footnote omitted).[4] The court suggested in dictum that the foreseeability of specifically sexual assault might even be necessary, observing that "it is arguable that the court, by conditioning liability on the foreseeability of 'assaults' rather than the foreseeability of 'sexual assaults,' was more helpful to appellants than the law permits." 424 A.2d at 323–24. *Lacy* described Cook as an application of its specific foreseeability standard, *see id.* at 323, though it seems to us more reasonable to regard *Lacy* as one application of Cook's fairness standard.

Whether expressed in terms of fairness or specific foreseeability, the District of Columbia rule requires that judgment be entered in favor of the NRA. The recent *en banc* decision of the District of Columbia Court of Appeals in *Morgan v. District of Columbia*, 468 A.2d 1306 (D.C.1983), is instructive. Plaintiff was kidnapped by her husband, a District of Columbia police officer, who shot her while being taken into custody. Three months before the incident, she had told the police that her husband had threatened her with a gun, and during the two years before that she had several times reported family arguments and beatings. Plaintiff sued the District and received a favorable jury verdict, which was set aside by judgment n.o.v. The Court of Appeals affirmed the trial judge's ruling on the alternate ground that the police department's actions (or failures to act) "were not, as a matter of law, the proximate cause of [plaintiff's] injuries." 468 A.2d at 1318. The court held that "[a] defendant may not be held liable for harm actually caused where the chain of events leading to the injury appears 'highly extraordinary in retrospect.'" *Id.* at 1318 (*quoting from Lacy v. District of Columbia*, 424 A.2d at 321). The court found the facts of *Morgan* sufficiently extraordinary:

> That Officer Morgan would, three months later, show up on her doorstep and subsequently shoot her while being taken into police custody—after not having done so during the previous two years of marital arguments nor having wrongfully fired his weapon during five years on the force—describes a chain of events that is, in retrospect, highly extraordinary.

468 A.2d at 1318.

The chain of events in this case is equally, if not more, extraordinary and unforeseeable, encompassing Lowe's storage of the weapon, a burglary of the annex, a search of Lowe's desk, discovery of his hidden closet key, a search of the closet, discovery of the gun and ammunition, use of the gun in a robbery, Gonzalez' resistance to the robbery, and the ultimate murder of Gonzalez by someone not a party to the original burglary. Whether or not this sequence of events would be foreseeable under the applicable legal standard if intervening acts of *negligence* were involved, given the intervention of at least four criminal acts, for the NRA "[t]o foresee the convergence of all these events, especially the murder, would constitute an act of prophecy, one based not on reasonable likelihood, but on sheer conjecture." *Romero v. National Rifle Association of America, Inc.*, Civil No. 80-2576, mem. op. at 21 (D.D.C. July 1, 1982) ("mem. op.").

---

4. As this passage indicates, it makes no difference whether we discuss the NRA's liability in terms of duty of care or proximate causation, "since the fundamental analysis appears to remain constant ... whether we speak of an attenuated chain of cause and effect ... or the actor's obligation toward the party he may injure." *Munson v. Otis*, 396 A.2d 994, 996 (D.C.1979) (per curiam). This is merely an acknowledgment that the division of tort analysis into the constituent elements of duty, breach, and causation—or into "negligence" and "causation"—is largely artificial. *See Graham v. M & J Corp.*, 424 A.2d at 107 ("the issue of causation is subsumed in the issue of duty"); W. Prosser, *supra*, § 42 at 245 (when dealing with questions of duty of care and proximate causation, "circumlocution is unavoidable, since all of these questions are, in reality, one and the same").

We are unpersuaded by plaintiff's argument that judgment n.o.v. was improper because the jury should have been allowed to infer constructive knowledge of the overnight presence of guns in the annex from the proximity of the firing range in the main NRA building and the absence of written warnings or instructions to employees to take their weapons home at night. Brief for Appellants at 28–29. Even if correct, the argument goes only to the ability of the NRA to foresee the storage of guns at the annex, not to its ability to foresee the theft of guns, and the other events in the causal chain leading to Gonzalez' murder. On plaintiff's reasoning, the owner of any building, if on actual or constructive notice that some of his employees were using the NRA firing range, would be required to take precautions beyond locking the building and barring the windows or else face liability for criminal acts perpetrated with stolen guns.[5] Indeed, so would any homeowner who possesses a personal firearm. At oral argument, counsel for plaintiff suggested that the latter might be the law, citing as analogous authority *Palmisano v. Ehrig*, 171 N.J.Super. 310, 313–14, 408 A.2d 1083, 1085 (Super.Ct.App.Div.1979), *cert. denied*, 82 N.J. 287, 412 A.2d 793 (1980). But *Palmisano* involved an intervening act of *negligence*, not intervening *criminal* acts, and its holding that "plaintiffs are not required to demonstrate that the precise events could have been foreseen; they are only required to demonstrate that some harm might reasonably be anticipated," 171 N.J.Super. at 313–14, 408 A.2d at 1085, is flatly contrary to the District of Columbia rule governing liability for the criminal acts of third parties.

In short, the NRA was entitled to the benefit of the general rule of nonliability at common law for harm resulting from the criminal acts of third parties. *See Kline v. 1500 Massachusetts Ave. Apartment Corp.*, 439 F.2d 477, 481 (D.C.Cir.1970); *Hall v. Ford Enterprises, Ltd.*, 445 A.2d 610, 611 (D.C.1982). The only District cases departing from that rule involved either a special relationship between the parties to the suit—for example, the relationship of landlord-tenant in *Kline*, which gave the landlord exclusive control over modifications to common facilities such as outside doors and vestibules, and thus foreclosed tenants from taking precautions against crime—or a relationship of control between the defendant and the intervening criminal actor—as, for example, in *Hicks v. United States*, 511 F.2d 407 (D.C.Cir.1975), in which a hospital negligently caused the release of a potentially violent patient. While the District of Columbia Court of Appeals recently declined to "reach the issue of whether liability for the criminal acts of third parties can be imposed on the basis of negligence in the absence of a relationship between the parties," *Hall v. Ford Enterprises, Ltd.*, 445 A.2d at 611, it has indicated that cases involving special relationships are fundamentally different, *id.* at 611 n. 4.... No such factor exists here, and we think the general rule of no liability for the criminal acts of others governs. The District Court properly set aside the judgment against the NRA.

III

We next turn to appellant's attack upon the jury verdict for Lowe. In objecting to the District Court's failure to instruct the jury that Lowe's violation of the D.C. Firearms Act was either per se negligence or at least evidence of negligence, appellant is asking us to posit a legislative purpose of rendering persons liable for the independent criminal acts of others. Such a purpose is of course possible. *See Ross v. Hart-*

---

5. Plaintiff expressly disclaimed any theory based on an agency relationship between Lowe and the NRA.... Hence, it is ownership of the annex, not ownership of the main building with the firing range or the employment relationship between the parties, that is relevant in this case.

man, 139 F.2d 14, 16 (D.C.Cir.1943), *cert. denied*, 321 U.S. 790, 64 S.Ct. 790, 88 L.Ed. 1080 (1944) (truck owner who left keys in ignition in violation of traffic ordinance held liable for damage negligently caused by third party who had stolen the vehicle; "[t]he fact that the intermeddler's conduct was itself a proximate cause of the harm, and was probably criminal, [was] immaterial"). We think, however, that the District of Columbia courts would require such a purpose to appear with a clarity that is not present here.

Lowe's offense, if there was any, consisted of violation of the following provision:

> (a) Except as otherwise provided in this chapter, no person or organization shall within the District receive, possess, have under his control, transfer, offer for sale, sell, give, or deliver any destructive device, and no person or organization shall, within the District possess or have under his or its control any firearm, unless such person or organization is the holder of a valid registration certificate for such firearm.

D.C.Code Ann. § 6-2311(a) (1981). It is not at all apparent that a purpose of this registration requirement is to prevent criminal acts with stolen firearms. The statutory requirements for registration contain many disqualifications bearing upon the registrant's own responsible use of the weapon (*e.g.*, conviction of certain crimes, adjudication as chronic alcoholic, commitment to mental institution, adjudication of negligence in a firearm mishap causing injury, lack of knowledge of the laws of the District pertaining to safe and responsible use of firearms, and even faulty vision, *see id.* at § 6-2313d(a)), but none that appears designed to render the weapons secure against theft. By contrast, the provisions of the Act pertaining to licensed firearms dealers *do* contain requirements that relate to the safeguarding of weapons from theft. *See id.* at § 6-2347(a) ("[n]o licensed dealer shall display any firearm or ammunition in windows visible from a street or sidewalk," and all such devices "shall be kept at all times in a securely locked place affixed to the premises except when being shown to a customer, being repaired, or otherwise being worked on"). The only provision relating to the storage of weapons by owners is § 6-2372, which requires firearms kept at home to be unloaded and disassembled or bound by a trigger lock—which renders them less likely to cause home accidents or acts of violence by family members, but hardly less vulnerable to theft. The legislative history of the Act contains no mention of theft of personal firearms. *See* District of Columbia Council Committee on the Judiciary and Criminal Law, Report to the Council of the District of Columbia of 1976, at 2–6 (Apr. 21, 1976) ("Report"). It sets forth the general purpose of "reduc[ing] the potentiality for gun-related crimes and … deaths," *id.* at 2, but that seems less likely to refer to the prevention of theft than to the "new and stringent [registration] criteria [which] relegate guns … to demonstrably responsible types of persons." *Id.* It points out that very few guns used in crimes and recovered by the police are registered, *id.* at 5—but again, that seems less designed to suggest that registered guns are rarely stolen than to suggest that registered owners are rarely criminals.

…

In sum, neither the nature of the provision in question nor its legislative history clearly indicates a purpose of preventing crimes by gun-thieves. In this respect it differs fundamentally from such enactments as the prohibition against leaving keys in unattended cars, *see Gaither v. Myers*, 404 F.2d 216, 220–21 (D.C.Cir.1968); *Ross v. Hartman*, 139 F.2d at 15–16, the requirement that employment agencies "record the servant's address and … investigate her references," *Janof v. Newsom*, 53 F.2d 149, 150 (D.C.Cir.1931), and the prohibition against a bar owner's serving alcoholic beverages to one who is intoxicated, *see Marusa v. District of Columbia*, 484 F.2d 828, 833 (D.C.Cir.1973), all of which have been held to support liability for the criminal acts of third persons. With such enactments it was clear that the third-party criminal conduct was "the very injury ... which the statute intended to prevent," *Janof v. Newsom*, 53 F.2d at 152. That is not clear here. As discussed in Section II of this opinion, civil liability for the intervening, independent criminal acts of third parties is extraordinary, and District of Columbia courts, in their development of common-law tort rules, have imposed especially stringent requirements to support it.... We think they would similarly require a clear indication of a statutory purpose producing such liability. Since that does not exist here, the trial judge was correct in deeming the Firearms Act irrelevant. His denial of the requested instruction was proper, and the jury verdict for Lowe was rightly sustained.

For the foregoing reasons, the judgments in favor of both defendants must be

Affirmed.

NOTES

(1) Was Judge Scalia careful enough when he said, in note 4 of his opinion, that it made "no difference whether we discuss the NRA's liability in terms of duty of care or proximate causation"?

(2) Is "fairness" or "foreseeability" more of the key to this case?

(3) What is your view about the idea, accepted by Judge Scalia without ruling on the merits of the issue, that both the "duty" question and the "proximate cause" question were for the jury? What is the strongest argument that these issues are better suited to decision by the judge?

BRAUN v. SOLDIER OF FORTUNE MAGAZINE, INC.

United States Court of Appeals, Eleventh Circuit
968 F.2d 1110 (1992)

ANDERSON, CIRCUIT JUDGE:

Soldier of Fortune Magazine, Inc., and its parent, Omega Group, Ltd., (hereinafter collectively referred to as "SOF") appeal a $4,375,000 jury verdict against them in a consolidated tort action brought by Michael and Ian Braun, the sons of a murder victim. The jury found that SOF acted with negligence and malice in publishing a personal service advertisement through which plaintiffs' father's business partner hired an assassin to kill him. We affirm the judgment entered on the jury's verdict.

I. FACTS

In January 1985, Michael Savage submitted a personal service advertisement to SOF. After several conversations between Savage and SOF's advertising manager, Joan Steel, the following advertisement ran in the June 1985 through March 1986 issues of SOF:

> GUN FOR HIRE: 37 year old professional mercenary desires jobs. Vietnam Veteran. Discrete [sic] and very private. Body guard, courier, and other special skills. All jobs considered. Phone (615) 436-9785 (days) or (615) 436-4335 (nights), or write: Rt. 2, Box 682 Village Loop Road, Gatlinburg, TN 37738.

Savage testified that, when he placed the ad, he had no intention of obtaining anything but legitimate jobs. Nonetheless, Savage stated that the overwhelming majority of the 30 to 40 phone calls a week he received in response to his ad sought his participation in criminal activity such as murder, assault, and kidnapping. The ad also generated at least one legitimate job as a bodyguard, which Savage accepted.

In late 1984 or early 1985, Bruce Gastwirth began seeking to murder his business partner, Richard Braun. Gastwirth enlisted the aid of another business associate, John Horton Moore, and together they arranged for at least three attempts on Braun's life, all of which were unsuccessful. Responding to Savage's SOF ad, Gastwirth and Moore contacted him in August 1985 to discuss plans to murder Braun.

On August 26, 1985, Savage, Moore, and another individual, Sean Trevor Doutre, went to Braun's suburban Atlanta home. As Braun and his sixteen year-old son Michael were driving down the driveway, Doutre stepped in front of Braun's car and fired several shots into the car with a MAC 11 automatic pistol. The shots hit Michael in the thigh and wounded Braun as well. Braun managed to roll out of the car, but Doutre walked over to Braun and killed him by firing two more shots into the back of his head as Braun lay on the ground.

. . .

… Appellees contended that, under Georgia law, SOF was liable for their injuries because SOF negligently published a personal service advertisement that created an unreasonable risk of the solicitation and commission of violent criminal activity, including murder. To show that SOF knew of the likelihood that criminal activity would result from placing an ad like Savage's, appellees introduced evidence of newspaper and magazine articles published prior to Braun's murder which described links between SOF personal service ads and a number of criminal convictions including murder, kidnapping, assault, extortion, and attempts thereof. Appellees also presented evidence that, prior to SOF's acceptance of Savage's ad, law enforcement officials had contacted SOF staffers on two separate occasions in connection with investigations of crimes—a solicitation to commit murder in Houston, Texas, and a kidnapping in New Jersey—linked to SOF personal service ads.

In his trial testimony, SOF president Robert K. Brown denied having any knowledge of criminal activity associated with SOF's personal service ads at any time prior to Braun's murder in August 1985.[2] Both Jim Graves, a former managing editor of SOF, and Joan Steel, the advertising manager who accepted Savage's advertisement, similarly testified that they were not aware of other crimes connected with SOF ads prior to running Savage's ad. Steel further testified that she had understood the term "Gun for Hire" in Savage's ad to refer to a "bodyguard or protection service-type thing," rather than to any illegal activity.

At the end of the five day trial, the district court gave the following instructions on negligence to the jury:

> In order to prevail in this case Plaintiffs must prove to your reasonable satisfaction by a preponderance of the evidence that a reasonable reading of the ad-

---

2. Appellees presented evidence that SOF subscribed to a clipping service that culled articles mentioning SOF from hundreds of newspapers and magazines. SOF maintained a multi-volume collection of these articles which was introduced into evidence. These volumes contained none of the articles appellees introduced as evidence that SOF personal service classified ads were linked to criminal activity.

vertisement in this case would have conveyed to a magazine publisher, such as Soldier of Fortune, that this ad presented the clear and present danger of causing serious harm to the public from violent criminal activity. The Plaintiffs must prove that the ad in question contained a clearly identifiable unreasonable risk, that the offer in the ad is one to commit a serious violent crime, including murder.

Now, while Defendants owe a duty of reasonable care to the public, the magazine publisher does not have a duty to investigate every ad it publishes. Defendants owe no duty to the Plaintiffs for publishing an ad if the ad's language on its face would not convey to the reader that it created an unreasonable risk that the advertiser was available to commit such violent crimes as murder.

Now, of course, the tendency to read the advertisement in question in hindsight is hard to avoid, but it must be avoided. The test for you is not how the advertisement in question reads now in light of subsequent events, but rather how the advertisement read to a reasonable publisher at the time of publication. You should view the facts and these instructions with particular care in this case, in view of the First Amendment to the Constitution, which protects the free flow of truthful and legitimate information even when it is of a commercial rather than a political nature.

. . .

The jury returned a verdict in favor of appellees and awarded compensatory damages on the wrongful death claim in the amount of $2,000,000. The jury also awarded appellee Michael Braun $375,000 in compensatory damages and $10,000,000 in punitive damages for his personal injury claim....

... [T]he district court denied SOF's motion for judgment notwithstanding the verdict, but ruled that it would grant SOF's motion for a new trial unless there were an agreement to a remittitur reducing the punitive damages awarded to $2,000,000. Appellees agreed to the remittitur.... SOF appeals.

The district court, sitting in Alabama, properly looked to Georgia law in resolving appellees' negligence claims....

A. Duty Under Georgia Law

. . .

The district court found that publishers like SOF have a duty to the public when they publish an advertisement if "the ad in question contain[s] a clearly identifiable unreasonable risk, that the offer in the ad is one to commit a serious violent crime, including murder." SOF argues that the district court erred in finding that a publisher has a duty "to reject ambiguous advertisements that pose a threat of harm," Brief for Appellants at 24, and contends that a publisher should be held liable for publishing an ad only if the ad explicitly solicits a crime. Since the existence of a duty presents a question of law, we subject the district court's determination to de novo review....

Georgia courts recognize a "general duty one owes to all the world not to subject them to an unreasonable risk of harm." Bradley Center [v. Wessner], 296 S.E.2d [693] at 695. Accordingly, the district court properly found that SOF had a legal duty to refrain from publishing advertisements that subjected the public, including appellees, to a clearly identifiable unreasonable risk of harm from violent criminal activity. To the extent that SOF denies that a publisher owes any duty to the public when it publishes personal service ads, its position is clearly inconsistent with Georgia law. We believe, however, that the crux of SOF's argument is not that it had no duty to the public, but that, as a matter of law, the risk to the public presented when a publisher prints an advertisement is "unreasonable" only if the ad openly solicits criminal activity....

1. Risk-Utility Balancing

To determine whether the risk to others that an individual's actions pose is "unreasonable," Georgia courts generally apply a risk-utility balancing test.... A risk is unreasonable if it is "of such magnitude as to outweigh what the law regards as the utility of the defendant's alleged negligent conduct." Johnson, 143 S.E.2d at 53. Simply put, liability depends upon whether the burden on the defendant of adopting adequate precautions is less than the probability of harm from the defendant's unmodified conduct multiplied by the gravity of the injury that might result from the defendant's unmodified conduct. United States v. Carroll Towing Co., 159 F.2d 169, 173 (2d Cir.1947).

For the reasons stated below, we find that the district court properly struck the risk-utility balance when it instructed that the jury could hold SOF liable for printing Savage's advertisement only if the advertisement on its face would have alerted a reasonably prudent publisher to the clearly identifiable unreasonable risk of harm to the public that the advertisement posed. Our application of Georgia's risk-utility balancing principles persuades us that the duty of care the district court imposed on publishers was an appropriate reconciliation of Georgia's interest in providing compensation to victims of tortious conduct with the First Amendment concern that state law not chill protected speech. Accordingly, we reject SOF's argument that the district court's instructions "place[d] an intolerable burden upon the press." ...

SOF relies heavily on Eimann v. Soldier of Fortune Magazine, Inc., 880 F.2d 830 (5th Cir.1989), ... to support its contention that the district court erred in its application of risk-utility balancing to this case. In Eimann, the son and mother of a murder victim brought a wrongful death action under Texas law against SOF, seeking to hold SOF liable for publishing a personal service ad through which the victim's husband hired an assassin to kill her. The advertisement in question read:

> EX-MARINES—67-69 'Nam Vets, Ex-DI, weapons specialist-jungle warfare, pilot, M.E., high risk assignments, U.S. or overseas. (404) 991-2684.

Id. at 831. The district court instructed the jury that it could find SOF liable if "(1) the relation to illegal activity appears on the ad's face; or (2) 'the advertisement, embroidered by its context, would lead a reasonable publisher of ordinary prudence under the same or similar circumstances to conclude that the advertisement could reasonably be interpreted' as an offer to commit crimes." Id. at 833 (quoting district court instructions). The jury found for plaintiffs and awarded them $1.9 million in compensatory damages and $7.5 million in punitive damages. Id.

The Fifth Circuit reversed the jury's verdict. After applying Texas risk-utility balancing principles similar to Georgia's, the court concluded that "[t]he standard of conduct imposed by the district court against SOF is too high...." Id. at 838. To impose liability whenever the advertised product "could reasonably be interpreted as an offer to engage in illegal activity" would require a publisher to reject all ambiguous ads. Id. at 837. The court stated: "Without a more specific indication of illegal intent than [this] ad or its context provided, we conclude that SOF did not violate the required standard of conduct by publishing an ad that later played a role in criminal activity." Id. at 838.

SOF's reliance on *Eimann* is misplaced. We distinguish *Eimann* from this case based on the instructions to the respective juries.[3] In *Eimann*, the district court violated risk-utility balancing principles when it allowed the jury to impose liability on SOF if a reasonable publisher would conclude "that the advertisement could reasonably be interpreted" as an offer to commit crimes. 880 F.2d at 833 (emphasis added). The Fifth Circuit correctly observed that virtually anything might involve illegal activity, id. at 837, and that applying the district court's standard would mean that a publisher "must reject all [ambiguous] advertisements," id. at 838 (emphasis in original), or risk liability for any "untoward consequences that flow from his decision to publish" them, id.

In this case, the district court stressed in its instructions that the jury could hold SOF liable only if the ad on its face contained a "clearly identifiable unreasonable risk" of harm to the public. We are convinced that the district court's use of phrases like "clear and present danger" and "clearly identifiable unreasonable risk" properly conveyed to the jury that it could not impose liability on SOF if Savage's ad posed only an unclear or insubstantial risk of harm to the public and if SOF would bear a disproportionately heavy burden in avoiding this risk. The jury instructions in *Eimann*, in contrast, did not preclude the jury from imposing liability on the basis of an ambiguous advertisement that presented only an unclear risk of harm to the public.

Furthermore, in *Eimann*, the district court instructed that, even if the face of the ad did not reveal its connection to illegal activity, the jury could hold the publisher liable if a reasonably prudent publisher would discover the connection to crime through investigation of the advertisement's "context." 880 F.2d at 833. It is significant that the district court in this case did not impose such a duty.... The district court here stressed that the jury could find SOF liable only if Savage's ad "on its face" would convey to a reasonable publisher that the ad created a "clearly identifiable unreasonable risk" of harm to the public.

For the foregoing reasons, we conclude that the decision in *Eimann* is distinguishable.

2. First Amendment Limitations

SOF further argues that the district court erred in instructing the jury to apply a negligence standard because the First Amendment forbids imposing liability on publishers for publishing an advertisement unless the ad openly solicits criminal activity....

. . .

Past Supreme Court decisions indicate ... that the negligence standard that the First Amendment permits is a "modified" negligence standard. The Court's decisions suggest that Georgia law may impose tort liability on publishers for injury caused by the advertisements they print only if the ad on its face, without the need to investigate, makes it apparent that there is a substantial danger of harm to the public....

Based upon the foregoing authorities, we conclude that the First Amendment permits a state to impose upon a publisher liability for compensatory damages for negligently publishing a commercial advertisement where the ad on its face, and without

---

3. Appellees also argue that *Eimann* is distinguishable from the present case because the advertisement at issue in *Eimann* was "facially innocuous" and "ambiguous in its message" while Savage's advertisement clearly conveyed that the advertiser was "ready, willing and able" to use his gun to commit crimes.... We agree. The advertisement in *Eimann* merely listed the advertisers' qualifications and indicated a willingness to accept risky assignments in the United States or overseas. Unlike Savage's ad, the ad in *Eimann* did not contain language that would alert a reasonable publisher to the clearly identifiable unreasonable risk that the advertisers were offering criminal services....

the need for investigation, makes it apparent that there is a substantial danger of harm to the public. The absence of a duty requiring publishers to investigate the advertisements they print and the requirement that the substance of the ad itself must warn the publisher of a substantial danger of harm to the public guarantee that the burden placed on publishers will not impermissibly chill protected commercial speech. Cf. [United States v.] Hunter, 459 F.2d [205] at 213 (where law prohibits advertisements that, on their face, communicate discriminatory preference in sale or rental of dwellings, publisher "can easily distinguish between permissible and impermissible advertisements"). Furthermore, these limitations on tort liability ensure that the burden imposed on publishers will have only a minimal impact on their advertising revenue, and, consequently, on their ability to publish non-commercial speech. Cf. id.

We conclude that the instructions fashioned by the district court in this case properly reflect the "modified" negligence standard that the First Amendment permits. The court's instructions modified the ordinary negligence standard to relieve SOF of any duty to investigate the advertisements it prints. In addition, the instructions required that the language of the ad itself contain a clearly identifiable unreasonable risk of harm to the public....

. . .

B. Proximate Cause

SOF's sole remaining claim is that the jury erred in finding that SOF's publication of Savage's ad was the proximate cause of appellees' injuries. SOF argues that the events that intervened between its publication of Savage's ad and the carrying out of the murder plot were entirely unforeseeable and, therefore, that SOF's publication of Savage's ad was too remote in the chain of events leading to appellees' injuries for the jury to hold SOF liable. Since the proximate cause issue does not implicate any constitutional values, we review the jury's factual finding under the traditional standard of deference to the fact finder....

We find that the jury had ample grounds for finding that SOF's publication of Savage's ad was the proximate cause of appellees' injuries. Georgia law recognizes that, "[g]enerally, the intervening criminal act of a third party, without which the injury would not have occurred, will be treated as the proximate cause of the injury, superseding any negligence of the defendant...." Rosinek v. Cox Enterprises, Inc., 166 Ga.App. 699, 305 S.E.2d 393, 394 (1983). If, however, "the criminal act was a reasonably foreseeable consequence of the defendant's conduct, the casual connection between that conduct and the injury is not broken." 305 S.E.2d at 394–95;.... We have already held that the language of Savage's ad should have alerted a reasonably prudent publisher to the clearly identifiable unreasonable risk that Savage was soliciting violent and illegal jobs. It follows that a reasonable jury could conclude that the criminal act that harmed appellees was reasonably foreseeable and, accordingly, that the chain of causation was not broken.

For the foregoing reasons, we AFFIRM the district court's judgment.

AFFIRMED.

ESCHBACH, Senior Circuit Judge, dissenting:

... I differ with the majority's application of the law to the facts of this case. Specifically, in discharging our duty of independent first amendment review of the language of

Savage's ad, ... I remain convinced that the language of the advertisement is ambiguous, rather than patently criminal as the majority believes. And although the majority has carefully culled the legal standards it applies from the jury instructions, I remain concerned over whether the instructions were clear enough that the jury could have done so as well. Because of the confluence of these two concerns—the ambiguity of both the advertisement and the jury instructions—I am not confident that the jury actually found that this advertisement was a clear solicitation for criminal activity. Under these circumstances, I am unable to uphold the crushing third-party liability the jury has imposed on Soldier of Fortune Magazine. I respectfully dissent.

NOTES

(1) What is the heart of SOF's defense against Braun? Is it that SOF did not owe the plaintiff a duty? Is it that the murders broke the causal chain set on foot by the publication of the ad?

(2) What is the economic analysis that the court utilizes in analyzing the duty issue? The court refers to the "risk-utility balancing test" under Georgia law. However, it cites Learned Hand's famous opinion in the *Carroll Towing* case, see supra § 4.03[B], which is actually a "cost/cost" test. Which of these tests seems most relevant to this case?

Is either the risk-utility test or the Learned Hand test appropriately used to determine duty? Or are those tests best reserved for determining the standard of care, with duty depending on other elements of policy?

(3) The defendant presented at least three arguments under the rubric of proximate cause: Intervening cause, unforeseeability, and "remote[ness]." Are these separate concepts? Which is most persuasive?

(4) Suppose the advertising manager of SOF asked you if Savage's ad could be rewritten to avoid liability and still keep Savage as an advertiser. What suggestions would you make?

(5) Can you harmonize *Braun* with *Romero*? Is it contradictory that Lowe won in *Romero*, though his gun was used to kill Gonzalez, while SOF lost in *Braun*, although the murder was committed with the weapon of Savage's associate?

What is the best conceptual explanation of the results in these cases? Is it one cast in terms of "duty"? "Negligence"? "Causation," including "proximate causation"?

(6) At the trial of another suit against *Soldier of Fortune*, a "hit man" testified that "If I had never run an ad in *Soldier of Fortune* I would never have killed anyone." But the publisher of the magazine testified, in the words of a press summary, that "he had no idea what was on the minds of those" who put such ads in the magazine: "I never expected anyone to be so stupid as to advertise in *Soldier of Fortune* their intent to do criminal enterprise." *Killer Tells of Request for His Skills*, N.Y. TIMES, Feb. 21, 1988, at 26. If one takes both these statements as sincere, how would that affect the decision of a case like *Braun*?

(7) Suppose that sheriffs' deputies illegally entrap a person who they have plotted to frame for a series of burglaries. As a result of his unjust conviction on these charges, he winds up in a state reformatory, where he is sexually assaulted by other prisoners. Can he sue the deputies for the physical and emotional consequences of those assaults? What if a consequence of one of the assaults is that he contracts AIDS?*

---

* The authors are indebted to Kevin Osborn for suggesting the latter question.

(8) A variety of possessors of land must now at least give consideration to the possibility of suit based on attacks committed on their property by third parties. See, e.g., Comment, *Landowner Liability for Crimes Committed by Third Parties Against Tenants*, 21 U. RICH. L. REV. 181 (1986).

Much will turn in such cases on the defendant's specific knowledge of the risk of a third-party crime. For example, in the case of a rape committed in a post office, the United States successfully defended when there was no evidence that there had ever "been a crime against the person committed upon the premises of the post office or in its immediate vicinity," and when in the two years before the assault "the only incidents reported at the post office with criminal overtones did not involve actual or threatened injury to invitees." The Eleventh Circuit thought that evidence of similar acts in the square mile in which the post office was located, "undifferentiated with respect to the proximity of such acts to the post office," was "insufficient to support a finding of the foreseeability of plaintiff's tragic injury." *Doe v. United States*, 718 F.2d 1039 (11th Cir. 1983), *rev'g* 533 F. Supp. 245 (S.D. Fla. 1982).

Cf. Tedder v. Raskin, 728 S.W.2d 343 (Tenn. Ct. App. 1987) (no liability against landlord for wound from gunshot that came through wall from neighboring apartment during a struggle with a burglar in the neighboring unit, even granting that the landlord knew that the neighbor was dealing in drugs; "the attempted burglary by a third party was an unusual, unlikely, or remotely possible result (if a result at all) of the drug dealing; and was thus an intervening, superceding cause of the plaintiff's injuries").

[B] Mentally Ill Persons

TARASOFF v. REGENTS OF UNIVERSITY OF CALIFORNIA

California Supreme Court
17 Cal. 3d 425, 551 P.2d 334, 131 Cal. Rptr. 14 (1976)

TOBRINER, JUSTICE.

On October 27, 1969, Prosenjit Poddar killed Tatiana Tarasoff. Plaintiffs, Tatiana's parents, allege that two months earlier Poddar confided his intention to kill Tatiana to Dr. Lawrence Moore, a psychologist employed by the Cowell Memorial Hospital at the University of California at Berkeley. They allege that on Moore's request, the campus police briefly detained Poddar, but released him when he appeared rational. They further claim that Dr. Harvey Powelson, Moore's superior, then directed that no further action be taken to detain Poddar. No one warned plaintiffs of Tatiana's peril.

Concluding that these facts set forth causes of action against neither therapists and policemen involved, nor against the Regents of the University of California as their employer, the superior court sustained defendants' demurrers to plaintiffs' second amended complaints without leave to amend. This appeal ensued.

. . .

We shall explain that defendant therapists cannot escape liability merely because Tatiana herself was not their patient. When a therapist determines, or pursuant to the standards of his profession should determine, that his patient presents a serious danger of violence to another, he incurs an obligation to use reasonable care to protect the intended victim against such danger. The discharge of this duty may require the therapist to take one or more of various steps, depending upon the nature of the case. Thus it may call for him to warn the intended victim or others likely to apprise the victim of the danger, to notify the police, or to take whatever other steps are reasonably necessary under the circumstances.

. . .

Plaintiffs' first cause of action, entitled "Failure to Detain a Dangerous Patient," alleges that on August 20, 1969, Poddar was a voluntary outpatient receiving therapy at Cowell Memorial Hospital. Poddar informed Moore, his therapist, that he was going to kill an unnamed girl, readily identifiable as Tatiana, when she returned home from spending the summer in Brazil. Moore, with the concurrence of Dr. Gold, who had initially examined Poddar, and Dr. Yandell, Assistant to the director of the department of psychiatry, decided that Poddar should be committed for observation in a mental hospital. Moore orally notified Officers Atkinson and Teel of the campus police that he would request commitment. He then sent a letter to Police Chief William Beall requesting the assistance of the police department in securing Poddar's confinement.

Officers Atkinson, Brownrigg, and Halleran took Poddar into custody, but, satisfied that Poddar was rational, released him on his promise to stay away from Tatiana. Powelson, director of the department of psychiatry at Cowell Memorial Hospital, then asked the police to return Moore's letter, directed that all copies of the letter and notes that Moore had taken as therapist be destroyed, and "ordered no action to place Prosenjit Poddar in 72-hour treatment and evaluation facility."

Plaintiffs' second cause of action, entitled "Failure to Warn On a Dangerous Patient," incorporates the allegations of the first cause of action, but adds the assertion that defendants negligently permitted Poddar to be released from police custody without "notifying the parents of Tatiana Tarasoff that their daughter was in grave danger from Prosenjit Poddar." Poddar persuaded Tatiana's brother to share an apartment with him near Tatiana's residence; shortly after her return from Brazil, Poddar went to her residence and killed her.

. . .

Plaintiffs can state a cause of action against defendant therapists for negligent failure to protect Tatiana.

. . . .

Although, ... under the common law, as a general rule, one person owed no duty to control the conduct of another[5] ... nor to warn those endangered by such conduct (Rest.2d Torts, *supra*, §314, com. c.; Prosser, Law of Torts (4th ed. 1971) §56, p. 341), the courts have carved out an exception to this rule in cases in which the defendant

---

5. This rule derives from the common law's distinction between misfeasance and nonfeasance, and its reluctance to impose liability for the latter. (*See* Harper & Kime, *The Duty to Control the Conduct of Another* (1934) 43 Yale L.J. 886, 887.) Morally questionable, the rule owes its survival to "the difficulties of setting any standards of unselfish service to fellow men, and of making any workable rule to cover possible situations where fifty people might fail to rescue ..." (Prosser, Torts (4th ed. 1971) §56, p. 341.) Because of these practical difficulties, the courts have increased the number of instances in which affirmative duties are imposed not by direct rejection of the common law rule, but by expanding the list of special relationships which will justify departure from that rule. (*See Prosser, supra*, §56, at pp. 348–350.)

stands in some special relationship to either the person whose conduct needs to be controlled or in a relationship to the foreseeable victim of that conduct (*see* Rest.2d Torts, *supra*, §§ 315–320). Applying this exception to the present case, we note that a relationship of defendant therapists to either Tatiana or Poddar will suffice to establish a duty of care; as explained in section 315 of the Restatement Second of Torts, a duty of care may arise from either "(a) a special relation ... between the actor and the third person which imposes a duty upon the actor to control the third person's conduct, or (b) a special relation ... between the actor and the other which gives to the other a right of protection."

Although plaintiffs' pleadings assert no special relation between Tatiana and defendant therapists, they establish as between Poddar and defendant therapists the special relation that arises between a patient and his doctor or psychotherapist. Such a relationship may support affirmative duties for the benefit of third persons. Thus, for example, a hospital must exercise reasonable care to control the behavior of a patient which may endanger other persons. A doctor must also warn a patient if the patient's condition or medication renders certain conduct, such as driving a car, dangerous to others.

Although the California decisions that recognize this duty have involved cases in which the defendant stood in a special relationship *both* to the victim and to the person whose conduct created the danger, we do not think that the duty should logically be constricted to such situations....

In their summary of the relevant rulings Fleming and Maximov conclude that the "case law should dispel any notion that to impose on the therapists a duty to take precautions for the safety of persons threatened by a patient, where due care so requires, is in any way opposed to contemporary ground rules on the duty relationship. On the contrary, there now seems to be sufficient authority to support the conclusion that by entering into a doctor-patient relationship the therapist becomes sufficiently involved to assume some responsibility for the safety, not only of the patient himself, but also of any third person whom the doctor knows to be threatened by the patient." (Fleming & Maximov, *The Patient or His Victim: The Therapist's Dilemma* (1974) 62 Cal.L.Rev. 1025, 1030.)

Defendants contend, however, that imposition of a duty to exercise reasonable care to protect third persons is unworkable because therapists cannot accurately predict whether or not a patient will resort to violence. In support of this argument amicus representing the American Psychiatric Association and other professional societies cites numerous articles which indicate that therapists, in the present state of the art, are unable reliably to predict violent acts; their forecasts, amicus claims, tend consistently to overpredict violence, and indeed are more often wrong than right. Since predictions of violence are often erroneous, amicus concludes, the courts should not render rulings that predicate the liability of therapists upon the validity of such predictions.

The role of the psychiatrist, who is indeed a practitioner of medicine, and that of the psychologist who performs an allied function, are like that of the physician who must conform to the standards of the profession and who must often make diagnoses and predictions based upon such evaluations. Thus the judgment of the therapist in diagnosing emotional disorders and in predicting whether a patient presents a serious danger of violence is comparable to the judgment which doctors and professionals must regularly render under accepted rules of responsibility.

We recognize the difficulty that a therapist encounters in attempting to forecast whether a patient presents a serious danger of violence. Obviously we do not require that the therapist, in making that determination, render a perfect performance; the therapist need only exercise "that reasonable degree of skill, knowledge, and care ordinarily possessed and exercised by members of (that professional specialty) under similar circumstances." ... Within the broad range of reasonable practice and treatment in which professional opinion and judgment may differ, the therapist is free to exercise his or her own best judgment without liability; proof, aided by hindsight, that he or she judged wrongly is insufficient to establish negligence.

In the instant case, however, the pleadings do not raise any question as to failure of defendant therapists to predict that Poddar presented a serious danger of violence. On the contrary, the present complaints allege that defendant therapists did in fact predict that Poddar would kill, but were negligent in failing to warn.

Amicus contends, however, that even when a therapist does in fact predict that a patient poses a serious danger of violence to others, the therapist should be absolved of any responsibility for failing to act to protect the potential victim. In our view, however, once a therapist does in fact determine, or under applicable professional standards reasonably should have determined, that a patient poses a serious danger of violence to others, he bears a duty to exercise reasonable care to protect the foreseeable victim of that danger. While the discharge of this duty of due care will necessarily vary with the facts of each case,[11] in each instance the adequacy of the therapist's conduct must be measured against the traditional negligence standard of the rendition of reasonable care under the circumstances. (*Accord Cobbs v. Grant* (1972) 8 Cal.3d 229, 243, 104 Cal.Rptr. 505, 502 p.2d 1.) As explained in Fleming and Maximov, *The Patient or His Victim: The Therapist's Dilemma* (1974) 62 Cal.L.Rev. 1025, 1067: " ... the ultimate question of resolving the tension between the conflicting interests of patient and potential victim is one of social policy, not professional expertise.... In sum, the therapist owes a legal duty not only to his patient, but also to his patient's would-be victim and is subject in both respects to scrutiny by judge and jury."

Contrary to the assertion of amicus, this conclusion is not inconsistent with our recent decision in *People v. Burnick, supra,* 14 Cal.3d 306, 121 Cal.Rptr. 488, 535 P.2d 352. Taking note of the uncertain character of therapeutic prediction, we held in Burnick that a person cannot be committed as a mentally disordered sex offender unless found to be such by proof beyond a reasonable doubt.... The issue in the present context, however, is not whether the patient should be incarcerated, but whether the therapist should take any steps at all to protect the threatened victim; some of the alternatives open to the therapist, such as warning the victim, will not result in the drastic consequences of depriving the patient of his liberty. Weighing the uncertain and conjectural character of the alleged damage done the patient by such a warning against the peril to the victim's life, we conclude that professional inaccuracy in predicting violence cannot negate the therapist's duty to protect the threatened victim.

The risk that unnecessary warnings may be given is a reasonable price to pay for the lives of possible victims that may be saved. We would hesitate to hold that the therapist who is aware that his patient expects to attempt to assassinate the President of the

---

11. Defendant therapists and *amicus* also argue that warnings must be given only in those cases in which the therapist knows the identity of the victim. We recognize that in some cases it would be unreasonable to require the therapist to interrogate his patient to discover the victim's identity, or to conduct an independent investigation. But there may also be cases in which a moment's reflection will reveal the victim's identity. The matter thus is one which depends upon the circumstances of each case, and should not be governed by any hard and fast rule.

United States would not be obligated to warn the authorities because the therapist cannot predict with accuracy that his patient will commit the crime.

Defendants further argue that free and open communication is essential to psychotherapy (*see In re Lifschutz* (1970) 2 Cal.3d 415, 431–434, 85 Cal.Rptr. 829, 467 P.2d 557); that "Unless a patient ... is assured that ... information (revealed by him) can and will be held in utmost confidence, he will be reluctant to make the full disclosure upon which diagnosis and treatment ... depends." (Sen.Com. on Judiciary, comment on Evid.Code, § 1014.) The giving of a warning, defendants contend, constitutes a breach of trust which entails the revelation of confidential communications.

We recognize the public interest in supporting effective treatment of mental illness and in protecting the rights of patients to privacy ... and the consequent public importance of safeguarding the confidential character of psychotherapeutic communication. Against this interest, however, we must weigh the public interest in safety from violent assault. The Legislature has undertaken the difficult task of balancing the countervailing concerns. In evidence Code section 1014, it established a broad rule of privilege to protect confidential Communications between patient and psychotherapist. In Evidence Code section 1024, the Legislature created a specific and limited exception to the psychotherapist-patient privilege: "There is no privilege ... if the psychotherapist has reasonable cause to believe that the patient is in such mental or emotional condition as to be dangerous to himself or to the person or property of another and that disclosure of the communication is necessary to prevent the threatened danger."

We realize that the open and confidential character of psychotherapeutic dialogue encourages patients to express threats of violence, few of which are ever executed. Certainly a therapist should not be encouraged routinely to reveal such threats; such disclosures could seriously disrupt the patient's relationship with his therapist and with the persons threatened. To the contrary, the therapist's obligations to his patient require that he not disclose a confidence unless such disclosure is necessary to avert danger to others, and even then that he do so discreetly, and in a fashion that would preserve the privacy of his patient to the fullest extent compatible with the prevention of the threatened danger....

The revelation of a communication under the above circumstances is not a breach of trust or a violation of professional ethics; as stated in the Principles of Medical Ethics of the American Medical Association (1957), section 9: "A physician may not reveal the confidence entrusted to him in the course of medical attendance ... *unless he is required to do so by law or unless it becomes necessary in order to protect the welfare of the individual or of the community.*" (Emphasis added.) We conclude that the public policy favoring protection of the confidential character of patient-psychotherapist communications must yield to the extent to which disclosure is essential to avert danger to others. The protective privilege ends where the public peril begins.

Our current crowded and computerized society compels the interdependence of its members. In this risk-infested society we can hardly tolerate the further exposure to danger that would result from a concealed knowledge of the therapist that his patient was lethal. If the exercise of reasonable care to protect the threatened victim requires the therapist to warn the endangered party or those who can reasonably be expected to notify him, we see no sufficient societal interest that would protect and justify concealment. The containment of such risks lies in the public interest. For the foregoing reasons, we find that plaintiffs' complaints can be amended to state a cause of action against defendants Moore, Powelson, Gold, and Yandell and against the Regents as their employer, for breach of a duty to exercise reasonable care to protect Tatiana.

....

[Omitted are the concurring and dissenting opinion of Justice Mosk and the dissent of Justice Clark.]

BRADY v. HOPPER
United States Court of Appeals, Tenth Circuit
751 F.2d 329 (1984)

BARRETT, CIRCUIT JUDGE.

The sole question presented on this appeal is whether the federal district court was clearly erroneous in granting the defendant-appellee's, John J. Hopper, Jr., M.D. (Dr. Hopper), motion to dismiss the complaint and cause of action filed by plaintiffs-appellants, James Scott Brady, Timothy John McCarthy and Thomas K. Delahanty (hereinafter for convenience referred to as appellants) for failure to state a claim which would entitle them to relief. The appellants were shot and seriously injured by John W. Hinckley, Jr., during his attempt to assassinate President Reagan in Washington, D.C. on March 30, 1981. For a period from late October 1980, until March 1981, Dr. Hopper, a psychiatrist residing and practicing in Colorado, had treated Hinckley on an out-patient basis.

The district court found/ruled that even assuming that all of the facts and many of the conclusions set forth in appellants' complaint were taken as true, still they would not be sufficient to create a legal duty on the part of Dr. Hopper to protect these appellants from the specific harm done them by Hinckley.

The district court concluded, and we agree, that there are no controlling Colorado decisions on the specific issue involving the duty owed by Dr. Hopper under the circumstances alleged. In a detailed Memorandum Opinion and Order, the district court concluded, as a matter of Colorado law, that there was no duty owed by Dr. Hopper to the appellants absent allegations that, in the forseeability context, Hinckley had conveyed to Dr. Hopper specific threats against specific (namely, the appellants here) victims. *See, Brady v. Hopper*, 570 F.Supp. 1333, 1339 (D.Colo.1983).... The court concluded that the Colorado Supreme Court, if acting in the same case and capacity of the federal district court sitting in this diversity suit, would adopt the rationale announced by the California Supreme Court in the cases of *Tarasoff v. Regents of University of California*, 17 Cal.3d 425, 131 Cal.Rptr. 14, 551 P.2d 334 (1976) and *Thompson v. County of Alameda*, 27 Cal.3d 741, 167 Cal.Rptr. 70, 614 P.2d 728 (1980).

In *Tarasoff*, the Court held that "[w]hen a (psychotherapist, psychiatrist, psychologist or therapist, as used interchangeably) determines, or pursuant to the standards of his profession should determine, that his patient presents a serious danger of violence to another, he incurs an obligation to use reasonable care to protect the intended victim against such danger." 551 P.2d at 340. In *Thompson*, the Court refused to extend the *Tarasoff* obligation imposed upon a third person in a setting where there was no identifiable victim. The Court instead concluded that there was no duty on the part of a third person where the patient had made generalized threats to kill but no specific threats to specifically identifiable victims. 614 P.2d at 735.

In the instant case, the court concluded/found that "[i]n my opinion, the 'specific threats to specific victims' rule states a workable, reasonable, and fair boundary upon the sphere of a therapist's liability to third persons for the acts of their patients." 570 F.Supp. at 1339. The court concluded that absent allegations in a complaint that a psychiatrist is aware of his patient's specific threats to specific victims, there exists no legal duty or obligation on the part of the psychiatrist for harm done by the patient. The court found that " ... [t]he legal obstacle to the maintenance of this suit is that there is no relationship between Dr. Hopper and *plaintiffs* which creates any legal obligation from Dr. Hopper to these plaintiffs." 570 F.Supp. at 1339. This was predicated upon the court's analysis of the Appellants' Complaint, with which we agree, as follows:

> Accepting as true the facts alleged in the complaint and viewing them in a light most favorable to plaintiffs, it is my conclusion that plaintiffs' injuries were not foreseeable; therefore, the plaintiffs fall outside of the scope of defendant's duty. Nowhere in the complaint are there allegations that Hinckley made any threats regarding President Reagan, or indeed that he ever threatened anyone. At most, the complaint states that if Dr. Hopper had interviewed Hinckley more carefully, he would have discovered that Hinckley was obsessed with Jody Foster and the movie "Taxi Driver", that he collected books on Ronald Reagan and political assassination, and that he practiced with guns. According to plaintiffs, if Dr. Hopper had properly performed his professional duties, he would have learned that Hinckley suffered from delusions and severe mental illness, as opposed to being merely maladjusted. Even assuming all of these facts and many of plaintiffs' conclusions to be true, the allegations are still insufficient to create a legal duty on the part of Dr. Hopper to protect these plaintiffs from the specific harm.

570 F.Supp. at 1339.

[The Colorado Supreme Court declined to respond to certified questions on the point.]

We cannot hold that the conclusions of the federal district court, interpreting the applicable law of Colorado under the circumstances of this case, are clearly erroneous.

WE AFFIRM.

Terry Wuester Milne, *"Bless Me Father, for I Am About to Sin ...": Should Clergy Counselors Have a Duty to Protect Third Parties?*
22 Tulsa L.J. 139, 139, 160–161 (1986)*

When a young mother confides in her minister that she abuses her baby while her husband is away, must the minister notify the husband or call a child abuse hotline? When a man who believes his wife is "cheating" calls his priest to tell him that he plans to kill his wife, must the priest take any action? If a member of an unorthodox religion which advocates "free love" among members tells his spiritual counselor that he has contracted AIDS, must the counselor warn other adherents?

...

* Copyright © 1986 by the Tulsa Law Journal. Reprinted by permission of the *Tulsa Law Review*.

... If the clergyperson believes that the benefits of long-term counseling outweigh the short-term crisis, he or she should not be forced to sacrifice the counseling relationship, but should be allowed to determine which situations are appropriate to take "protective action" and which are appropriate to "monitor and counsel further."

It may seem, at first glance, that to allow the clergyperson such discretion runs counter to general concerns of public safety. However, allowing clergypersons to continue to make such determinations according to their experience and their ability will actually serve to better ensure public safety in the majority of cases.

If a duty to "protect" was extended to the clergy, clergy counselors would have to take actions which might contravene their personal determination of what is in the best interests of all concerned. Specifically, when a clergyperson determined that a counselee posed a threat to an identified victim, that clergyperson would be *required* to take some action to "protect" the potential victim. Although *Tarasoff* does not specifically dictate what actions are necessary to fulfill a duty to protect, a clergyperson who either called the police or warned the victim in an appropriate situation, would probably escape liability even if the counselee later committed the threatened act. In this type of situation, although the clergyperson escapes liability, the victim may still have been harmed and the ex-counselee rarely will have been helped. In fact, if the counselee reacts in anger and terminates the counseling relationship, the possibility of future help by the clergyperson is also eliminated.

Thus, although the goal of imposing a "duty to protect" upon clergy is to protect third persons, the effect will frequently be detrimental to the counselee. In addition, no assurance exists that a potential victim, once warned, can do anything to protect himself from harm, even if he does receive some measure of police protection. It takes little imagination to envision the consequences which may result when an already potentially dangerous counselee becomes enraged by a clergyperson's perceived betrayal.

NOTES

(1) If you were arguing the appeal of the *Tarasoff* defendants to a super-court of California appeals, what would be your main theory? Could you plausibly claim that the therapist defendants were not negligent? Or should your main ground of attack be that the defendants had no duty to Tatiana Tarasoff? Where is the line of demarcation between the "negligence" and "duty" issues? Is the case better viewed as one in which the crucial issue is one of "causation"?

(2) How dispositive on the judgment of a later *Tarasoff*-type case should be empirical evidence on the reaction of psychiatrists to the *Tarasoff* decision? Some *Stanford Law Review* members undertook to gather that evidence in Note, *Where the Public Peril Begins: A Survey of Psychotherapists to Determine the Effects of Tarasoff*, 31 STAN. L. REV. 165 (1978). They found, inter alia, that after the decision, therapists "felt increased anxiety when the subject of dangerousness arose during therapy" and speculated that this anxiety might "increase ... overprediction of dangerous behavior," but could not discern "an appreciable change" in the frequency of warnings that therapists gave to "endangered third parties." The researchers also reported that after *Tarasoff*, therapists who gave warnings to anyone—including the families of potential victims and the police—were more likely to warn potential victims themselves. See *id.* at 178–182, 188.

(3) Had Hinckley made a single threat to his psychiatrist to kill the President, would that have established a duty in the psychiatrist to notify the Secret Service?

Must a threat, spoken to a therapist, identify a particular person to establish a duty to that person?

(4) What are the principal conflicting goals that courts must take into account in deciding whether to sustain a demurrer in cases of this sort?

(5) Suppose that a psychiatric patient threatens violence against an identified woman, and later shoots and seriously wounds her. As the shots are fired at the woman, she throws herself over her 8-year-old son, shielding him from the bullets. The child sues the psychiatrist for emotional injuries associated with the trauma of the event. What result?

(6) In a decision issued the day before *Tarasoff*, the California Supreme Court reversed a dismissal and held that an infant plaintiff should have the chance to prove that her injuries ought to have led a reasonably prudent physician to suspect that she was a victim of the battered child syndrome. Posing the question as whether a careful doctor would have confirmed the diagnosis by ordering X-rays and "would have promptly reported his findings to appropriate authorities to prevent a recurrence of the injuries," the California court said the plaintiff should be able to use expert testimony to establish the physician's standard of care. The court rejected the defendant's argument that continued beatings inflicted on the plaintiff by her mother and the mother's common law husband after her release from the hospital were an intervening act that constituted a "superseding cause" defense. Drawing on a precedent for the proposition that "with respect to a determination of the duty ...'foreseeability is a question of fact for the jury,'" the court thought it could not "say categorically that an ordinarily prudent physician who had correctly diagnosed ... battered child syndrome would not have foreseen the likelihood of further serious injuries ... if [the child] were returned directly to the custody of her caretakers." *Landeros v. Flood*, 17 Cal. 3d 399, 412, 551 P.2d 389, 395, 131 Cal. Rptr. 69 (1976), *rev'g* 50 Cal. App. 3d 189, 123 Cal. Rptr. 713 (1975). One must, of course, weigh the inconvenience and cost to physicians of such a decision against its potential deterrent effects, but the problem is not a trivial one. The plaintiff in this particular case was less than a year old when she was brought to the hospital. After her return from the hospital, her mother's common law husband inflicted traumatic blows to one of her eyes and her back, puncture wounds on a leg and across her back, severe bites on her face, and second and third degree burns on a hand.

(7) Can you usefully distinguish the duty to warn third parties of potential violence from a person with a history of mental illness from the more generalized question of whether there should be a cause of action for "negligent release" of that person from a state institution?

(8) The problem of whether to impose liability for a failure to prevent a murderous assault is one that arises in many contexts. A pair of Fifth Circuit cases involving Army personnel, decided one year apart, brackets some of the most interesting issues. First, in *United States v. Shively*, 345 F.2d 294 (5th Cir. 1965), the court refused to impose liability when Army personnel issued a handgun to an off-duty sergeant in civilian clothes who then shot his recently divorced wife and killed himself. The court said that there was "no ordinary reason to anticipate that, possessing such an instrument, a person of mature age, even with known financial and marital problems, will use it to commit a murderous assault upon his former wife." *Id.* at 297.

The court distinguished *Shively* in *Underwood v. United States*, 356 F.2d 92 (5th Cir. 1966), in which it held that the Army was negligent in discharging an airman from a psychiatric clinic and returning him to duty without restriction because there had been no "consideration of an adequate history" of the man's mental illness. The *Underwood* court also found it negligent to issue a .45 pistol without the direction and authority of the airman's supervisor. Besides differences in the applicable laws of the two states in which the incidents had taken place, the court emphasized that "there was no history of mental illness" in *Shively*. Drawing on the factual contrast, the *Underwood* court said that "[w]hat may be reasonably anticipated from 'a person of mature age' and from a person recently hospitalized for mental illness and not yet fully recovered"—a description of the situation of the airman in *Underwood*—"may differ radically." 356 F.2d at 99.

(9) Smythe engaged in "day trading," which has been described as an activity "in which traders place multiple buy and sell orders for securities and hold the positions for a very short period of time, usually less than one day, seeking to profit from the daily fluctuations in stock prices." Smythe lost all his money in day trading conducted through Pinnacle Corp., which like other day traders stressed to its customers the very speculative nature of the activity. After these ruinous losses, Smythe showed up at Pinnacle's offices and went on a shooting rampage during which he killed nine people. Survivors of those victims sued Pinnacle on the basis of what their complaint called Pinnacle's "self-interested and predatory" practices, including the firm's failure to stop Smythe from trading before losing as much money as he lost. The plaintiffs presented experts who testified that this kind of incident was "an accident waiting to happen," referring to three incidents in the past decade involving shooting sprees or death threats by people disappointed over financial losses. Pinnacle moved for summary judgment. What result?

SPECIAL NOTE ON THE PROVISION OF ALCOHOL

The problem of assigning liability for injuries flowing from intoxication has dogged tort law for more than a century. In the classic case, a patron becomes intoxicated at a tavern, or "dram shop," and as a result of the intoxication, causes injury to himself or to a third-person plaintiff. The plaintiff then seeks recovery against the tavern keeper on the theory that the defendant was negligent in serving alcohol to the patron and therefore bears responsibility for the injury. At traditional common law, this liability theory was rejected for failure of causation. The "causal chain" from the tavern keeper's distribution of alcohol to the ultimate injury was broken by the patron's voluntary consumption.

In the latter half of the nineteenth century, temperance became fashionable, and a number of states passed "dram shop acts." These laws superseded the common law approach and imposed liability, usually strict, on sellers of alcohol for damages caused by their intoxicated patrons. But by the mid-twentieth century, after the passage and repeal of Prohibition, temperance ceased to be a social priority, and the common law ruled again.

The rise of the automobile, and hence the automobile accident, sparked a resurgent interest in dram shop liability in the latter half of the twentieth century. Beginning as early as the 1950s, some state courts began to change the common law to recognize a cause of action against alcohol vendors. It was easiest to overcome the causation hurdle when a patron was served alcohol despite apparent intoxication. Arguably, a tavern keeper can foresee that a patron with impaired judgment will continue drinking, will attempt to drive home, and will have an accident. Furthermore, courts could derive a tavern keeper's duty from the responsibilities that come with a state license to sell alcohol.

A number of state legislatures, especially in the 1970s and 1980s, created civil causes of action, some doing so after courts had declined to depart from the traditional common law approach. By contrast, however, some state legislatures passed laws restricting common law claims. Today states employ a variety of approaches to the dram shop problem, some judicial and some statutory, some extending liability and some prohibiting it. It is impossible to articulate a majority rule. Where jurisdictions impose liability, typically they require that the sale of alcohol itself have been illegal, a circumstance that may include sales to apparently intoxicated patrons and sales to minors. In some jurisdictions, illegal sales trigger liability under a theory of negligence per se.

Further complicating the liability picture in this area is the problem of the social host. Unlike the tavern keeper, the social host holds no state license and dispenses alcohol as a courtesy rather than for a profit. Moreover, public policy frowns on an expansion of tort liability that dampens ordinary social interaction. At the same time, driving while intoxicated is no less foreseeable in the case of the social guest than in the case of the tavern patron. States again vary in their approaches to social hosts, though liability for the social host is decidedly less common than for the tavern keeper. Social host liability is more often limited to the illegal provision of alcohol, as when it is given to minors.

§ 12.04 Negligently Inflicted Emotional Distress

[A] Generally

BOYLES v. KERR

Supreme Court of Texas
855 S.W.2d 593 (1993)

PHILLIPS, CHIEF JUSTICE.

...

This is a suit for the negligent infliction of emotional distress. We hold that there is no general duty in Texas not to negligently inflict emotional distress. A claimant may recover mental anguish damages only in connection with defendant's breach of some other legal duty. Because Respondent proceeded below only on the theory of negligent infliction of emotional distress, we reverse the judgment of the court of appeals in her favor.... However, in the interest of justice, we remand for a new trial.

I

On August 10, 1985, Petitioner Dan Boyles, Jr., then seventeen, covertly videotaped nineteen-year-old Respondent Susan Leigh Kerr engaging in sexual intercourse with him. Although not dating steadily, they had known each other a few months and had shared several previous sexual encounters. Kerr testified that she had not had sexual intercourse prior to her relationship with Boyles.

Kerr and Boyles, who were both home in Houston for the summer, had made plans to go out on the night of the incident. Before picking Kerr up, Boyles arranged with a friend, Karl Broesche, to use the Broesche house for sexual intercourse with Kerr. Broesche suggested videotaping the activity, and Boyles agreed. Broesche and two friends, Ray Widner and John Paul Tamborello, hid a camera in a bedroom before Kerr and Boyles arrived. After setting up the camera, the three videotaped themselves making crude comments and jokes about the activity that was to follow. They left with the camera running, and the ensuing activities were recorded.

Boyles took possession of the tape shortly after it was made, and subsequently showed it on three occasions, each time at a private residence. Although he showed the tape to only ten friends, gossip about the incident soon spread among many of Kerr and Boyles' friends in Houston. Soon many students at Kerr's school, Southwest Texas State University, and Boyles' school, the University of Texas at Austin, also became aware of the story. Kerr did not learn of the video until December 1985, long after she and Boyles had stopped seeing each other. After she confronted him, Boyles eventually admitted what he had done and surrendered the tape to Kerr. No copies had been made.

Kerr alleges that she suffered humiliation and severe emotional distress from the videotape and the gossip surrounding it. At social gatherings, friends and even casual acquaintances would approach her and comment about the video, wanting to know "what [she] was going to do" or "why did [she] do it." The tape stigmatized Kerr with the reputation of "porno queen" among some of her friends, and she claimed that the embarrassment and notoriety affected her academic performance. Kerr also claimed that the incident made it difficult for her to relate to men, although she testified to having had subsequent sexually-active relationships. Eventually, she sought psychological counselling.

Kerr sued Boyles, Broesche, Widner and Tamborello, alleging intentional invasion of privacy, negligent invasion of privacy, and negligent (but not intentional) infliction of emotional distress. Before the case was submitted to the jury, however, Kerr dropped all causes of action except for negligent infliction of emotional distress. The jury returned a verdict for Kerr on that claim, assessing $500,000 in actual damages. The jury also found that all defendants were grossly negligent, awarding an additional $500,000 in punitive damages, $350,000 of which was assessed against Boyles. The trial court rendered judgment in accordance with the jury's verdict.

Only Boyles appealed to the court of appeals. That court affirmed the judgment against him, concluding that Kerr established negligent infliction of emotional distress under the facts of this case. The court of appeals also affirmed based on negligent invasion of privacy, even though Kerr abandoned this theory prior to submission of the case to the jury and did not brief or argue it as a basis for affirmance in the court of appeals.

· · ·

Initially, we must determine whether negligent infliction of emotional distress constitutes an independent cause of action in Texas. Kerr claims that we recognized a broad right to recover for negligently inflicted emotional distress in St. Elizabeth Hospital v. Garrard, 730 S.W.2d 649 (Tex.1987). Boyles contends that the Garrard holding is limited to the particular facts of that case.

In Garrard, a hospital negligently disposed of the Garrards' stillborn baby in an unmarked, common grave without the plaintiffs' knowledge or consent. The Garrards sued for negligent infliction of emotional distress, without alleging that they suffered any physical injury. This Court nonetheless concluded that they had stated a cause of action. We determined that "Texas first recognized the tort of negligent infliction of mental anguish in Hill v. Kimball, 76 Tex. 210, 13 S.W. 59 (1890)." 730 S.W.2d at 652. This tort, we said, had been administered under traditional tort concepts, subject only to a refinement on the element of damages: the mental suffering is not compensable unless it manifests itself physically. Id. After determining that the physical manifestation requirement was arbitrary because it "denies court access to persons with valid claims they could prove if permitted to do so," id., we proceeded to abolish it. 730 S.W.2d at 654.

The Court then proceeded, we believe, to create a general duty not to inflict reasonably foreseeable emotional distress. The Court said:

> Clearly, freedom from severe emotional distress is an interest which the law should serve to protect.... Having recognized that an interest merits protection, it is the duty of this court to continually monitor the legal doctrines of this state to insure the public is free from unwarranted restrictions on the right to seek redress for wrongs committed against them.... Thus, we hold that proof of physical injury resulting from mental anguish is no longer an element of the common law action for negligent infliction of mental anguish.

730 S.W.2d at 653–54. Four justices joined in the judgment, but concurred on the grounds that the same result could be reached under the traditional Texas rule allowing emotional distress damages arising from the mishandling of a corpse. Id. at 654. If the Court's holding was, as Boyles contends, limited to the mishandling of corpses, the concurring opinion would not need to have been written, as its rationale would have been incorporated in the majority opinion.

The liability standard under this new tort, however, was never entirely clear. Garrard seemed to indicate that "trivial" emotional distress should not be compensated, 730 S.W.2d at 652, and similarly that the law should protect against "severe" emotional distress. Id. at 653. Rather than articulating any threshold level of severity, however, the Court concluded that "[j]urors are best suited to determine whether and to what extent the defendant's conduct caused compensable mental anguish by referring to their own experience." Id. at 654.

While the holding of Garrard was correct, we conclude that its reasoning was based on an erroneous interpretation of Hill v. Kimball, and is out of step with most American jurisdictions. Therefore, we overrule the language of Garrard to the extent that it recognizes an independent right to recover for negligently inflicted emotional distress. Instead, mental anguish damages should be compensated only in connection with defendant's breach of some other duty imposed by law. This was the basis for recovery prior to Garrard, which expanded the scope of liability based on a misconstruction of Hill v. Kimball.

In Hill, a pregnant woman suffered a miscarriage when she witnessed the defendant severely beating two men in her yard. The woman sued for her physical injuries under negligence, claiming that the emotional trauma of witnessing the beatings produced the miscarriage and that the defendant should have reasonably anticipated the danger to her. The Court found that the plaintiff had stated a cause of action. The basis, however, was the physical injury she had suffered, together with her allegation of foreseeability. The Court reasoned as follows:

> That a physical personal injury may be produced through a strong emotion of the mind there can be no doubt. The fact that it is more difficult to produce such an injury through the operation of the mind than by direct physical means affords no sufficient ground for refusing compensation, in an action at law, when the injury is intentionally or negligently inflicted.... Here, according to the allegations of the petition, the defendant has produced a bodily injury by means of that emotion, and it is for that injury that the recovery is sought. 76 Tex. at 215, 13 S.W. at 59.

The Court considered only whether the plaintiff could recover for her physical injuries, not whether she could otherwise recover for her emotional distress or mental anguish caused by witnessing the beatings. Furthermore, the Court noted that liability would depend on "whether, under the circumstances, and with the lights before him, a reasonably prudent man would have anticipated the danger to her or not." Id. In other words, the defendant was negligent if he should have known that he was imposing an unreasonable risk of physical injury to the plaintiff, not if he merely should have anticipated that the plaintiff would suffer emotional distress.

Hill, therefore, did not recognize a cause of action for negligent infliction of emotional distress. It merely recognized the right to recover for physical injuries under standard negligence principles, notwithstanding that the physical injury is produced indirectly through emotional trauma. Garrard thus did not merely modify Hill, but created an entirely new cause of action.

The dissent vigorously denounces our abolition of the tort created in Garrard, calling it "controlling precedent" that contains a "rather clear pronouncement" of a new tort affirming "the respect for human dignity." 855 S.W.2d at 608, 607, 605 (Doggett, J., dissenting on rehearing). Garrard, however, ill deserves the lofty pedestal to which the dissent has belatedly elevated it. Even today, the justices of this Court cannot agree on the extent of Garrard's reach, see infra at 604 (Gonzalez, J., concurring on motion for rehearing), and we have never embraced its broad holding. Thus, in Freeman v. City of Pasadena, 744 S.W.2d 923 (Tex.1988), we limited the bystander cause of action to those persons meeting the criteria of Dillon v. Legg, 68 Cal.2d 728, 69 Cal.Rptr. 72, 80, 441 P.2d 912, 920 (1968), without even citing Garrard as a potential basis for broader liability. Justice Ray, the author of the Court's opinion in Garrard, while noting in a concurring opinion in Freeman that, because of Garrard, "perhaps the need for a bystander cause of action is now without a basis," 744 S.W.2d at 925, did not explain why the plaintiff in Freeman could not recover under the Garrard tort. Further, the Court held in Reagan v. Vaughn, 804 S.W.2d 463, 466–67 (Tex.1990), that a child could not recover mental anguish damages resulting from a severe injury to a parent, without considering Garrard as a basis for recovery. Even Justice Doggett, who now views Garrard as a landmark in the recovery of emotional distress damages, did not deem it worthy of citation in his vigorous concurring and dissenting in Reagan. In fact, this Court has never upheld a recovery under the Garrard tort.

. . .

Considering our opinions and those of other Texas courts, as well as the law in most American jurisdictions, Garrard could fairly be characterized as an anomaly rather than a landmark. We believe the jurisprudence of our state is better served by overruling Garrard's broad language outright, rather than ignoring it as in Freeman, limiting the case to its facts as in Harmon and Delta, or pretending that the concurring opinion was in fact the rationale of the majority.

By overruling the language of Garrard, we hold only that there is no general duty not to negligently inflict emotional distress. Our decision does not affect a claimant's right to recover mental anguish damages caused by defendant's breach of some other legal duty. See, e.g., Fisher v. Coastal Transp. Co., 149 Tex. 224, 230 S.W.2d 522 (1950) (negligent infliction of direct physical injury); Moore v. Lillebo, 722 S.W.2d 683 (Tex.1986) (wrongful death); Fisher v. Carrousel Motor Hotel, Inc., 424 S.W.2d 627 (Tex.1967) (battery); Stuart v. Western Union Tel. Co., 66 Tex. 580, 18 S.W. 351 (1885) (failure of telegraph company to timely deliver death message); Billings v. Atkinson, 489 S.W.2d 858

(Tex.1973) (invasion of privacy); Leyendecker & Assocs., Inc., v. Wechter, 683 S.W.2d 369 (Tex.1984) (defamation); Pat H. Foley & Co. v. Wyatt, 442 S.W.2d 904 (Tex.Civ.App.— Houston [14th Dist.] 1969, writ ref'd n.r.e.) (negligent handling of corpse).

Also, our holding does not affect the right of bystanders to recover emotional distress damages suffered as a result of witnessing a serious or fatal accident.... The policy concerns that require limiting the emotional distress cause of action in the direct victim case generally do not apply in the bystander case. Before a bystander may recover, he or she must establish that the defendant has negligently inflicted serious or fatal injuries on the primary victim.

. . .

Kerr cannot recover based on the cause of action under which she proceeded. It may well be, however, that she failed to assert and preserve alternative causes of action because of her reliance on our holding in Garrard. We have broad discretion to remand for a new trial in the interest of justice where it appears that a party may have proceeded under the wrong legal theory.... It is even more appropriate where we have also subsequently given formal recognition to a cause of action which might be applicable to the facts of this case. See Twyman, supra (expressly recognizing the tort of intentional infliction of emotional distress). We therefore reverse the judgment of the court of appeals and remand this cause to the trial court for a new trial.

. . .

DOGGETT, Justice, dissenting.

. . .

[F]reedom from severe emotional distress is an interest which the law should serve to protect. St. Elizabeth Hospital v. Garrard, 730 S.W.2d 649, 653 (Tex.1987).

A young woman was found by a jury to have suffered severe emotional distress when her most intimate act was secretly videotaped and displayed to others. To deny her relief, the majority rewrites Texas law and recants the respect for human dignity affirmed by this court in St. Elizabeth Hospital.... [T]he majority now declares that in Texas no legal duty necessary to establish negligence arises from nonconsensual, surreptitious videotaping of a woman engaged in sexual intercourse....

In St. Elizabeth Hospital, we recognized that an emotional loss can be "just as severe and debilitating" as a physical one. 730 S.W.2d at 653. The sexual exploitation of Susan Kerr vividly demonstrates that reality. Dan Boyles, Jr., planned an encounter with Kerr at the home of a friend, Karl Broesche, who suggested videotaping the event. While Boyles was meeting Susan Kerr, two other friends, Ray Widner and John Paul Tamborello, helped Broesche focus a hidden video camera on the bed. After recording themselves making crude jokes and vulgar predictions about the anticipated activities of Boyles and Susan Kerr, the three departed, leaving the camera operating to record the ensuing intercourse without her knowledge or consent.

The recorded tape, shown by Boyles on three occasions to various people, became a topic of conversation, particularly at each of the universities attended by the two. At social gatherings, friends and even casual acquaintances approached Susan Kerr about the video, asking "why [she] did ... it." Stigmatized with the reputation of "porno queen," Susan Kerr alleged severe emotional distress and humiliation from the videotaping, the showing of the tape, and the ensuing notoriety. Eventually, she sought counselling for what a psychologist later diagnosed as "post-traumatic stress disorder." A jury found that Susan Kerr had suffered severe emotional injury as a result of the negligence and gross negligence of the four men.

. . .

With good reason this court has honored the principle that "freedom from severe emotional distress is an interest which the law should serve to protect." St. Elizabeth Hospital, 730 S.W.2d at 654. Reviewing the outmoded rule that denied recovery unless a negligently produced emotional injury manifested itself physically, we concluded that such a restriction "arbitrarily denies court access to persons with valid claims." Id. at 652. We thus held that "proof of physical injury resulting from mental anguish" would no longer be required to establish liability. Id. at 654.

Today, however, the majority denies Susan Kerr the protection promised by the law of Texas, criticizing her for preserving one well-established cause of action while "fail[ing] to assert and preserve alternative causes of action." 855 S.W.2d at 603. Wholly disregarded is Kerr's argument that she brought the only action against the four men who wronged her that she could legally prove. Faulting her choice of alternatives is designed solely to create the illusion that injustice is not the principal product of today's opinion. With no other viable legal remedy available to her, Susan Kerr will, in fact, be left to resolve this "personal dispute[] through normal social means," . . . however that can be arranged.

To deny Susan Kerr the relief of which the jury found she was so deserving, the majority must overrule yet another precedent. In St. Elizabeth Hospital, parents sued for negligent infliction of emotional distress resulting from a hospital's negligent disposal of their stillborn daughter in an unmarked grave. In upholding such an action, we repeatedly referred to the "tort of negligent infliction of mental anguish." . . . We also joined the "established trend in American jurisprudence" by rejecting as "arbitrary" and unreasonable the "physical manifestation requirement." . . .

In overruling our prior decision, the majority diverts Texas from that national trend recognizing the physical manifestation requirement as outmoded. The majority's claim that we have somehow fallen "out of step" with American jurisprudence completely misses the mark. . . . The only question is whether Texas steps forward as in St. Elizabeth Hospital or races backward as the majority insists. Nationally, our prior decision is considered an authority that has provided an example for other states to follow. . . . In the march to justice, Texas should not fear leadership. But rather than leading, today's majority beats a quick retreat. If every such decision of this court is to be erased from the books as being "out of step," Texas is doomed to last place in legal thinking.

And why the rush to retreat? The majority declares with vigor that "judicial resources" would be "strained," . . . with the insignificant, the trivial, with other mere "intimate" affairs of the heart. . . . How can anyone view what happened here as just another "instance of rude, insensitive or distasteful behavior"? . . . When a surreptitiously produced videotape of a woman participating in sexual intercourse makes her the focus of public discussion, how can her injury be dismissed as unworthy of protection? How can the majority's purported difficulty in "'distinguish[ing] severe from nonsevere emotional harm,'" . . . justify denying relief to Susan Kerr for the humiliation and life-long disabling psychological disorder she suffered? How can Boyles' conduct be so callously condoned by the majority's announcement that they and other judges are just too busy to handle such matters? . . .

To give this sudden and unjustifiable reversal of our jurisprudence some degree of respectability the majority employs an analysis apparently drawn from Section 436A of the Restatement (Second) of Torts (1965), a provision that has not changed since we correctly rejected it in St. Elizabeth Hospital. Three decades ago the Restatement approved a physical manifestation limitation based upon the misunderstanding that:

> [E]motional disturbance which is not so severe and serious as to have physical consequences is normally in the realm of the trivial, and so falls within the maxim that the law does not concern itself with trifles.... so temporary, so evanescent, and so relatively harmless and unimportant, that the task of compensating for it would unduly burden the courts and the defendants.... [E]motional disturbance may be too easily feigned, depending, as it must, very largely upon the subjective testimony of the plaintiff; ... recovery for it might open too wide a door for false claimants who have suffered no real harm at all.

Restatement (Second) of Torts § 436A, comment b.

While a claimant can also feign physical injuries, this court does not yet deny all tort litigation on this basis. Instead, we have traditionally relied on the ability of twelve Texas citizens, empaneled as a jury, to distinguish between the fraudulent and the genuine. St. Elizabeth Hospital, 730 S.W.2d at 654. The majority's increasing disdain for mere ordinary Texans making such determinations as jurors is once again apparent today.... To deny a remedy to all because of the meritless actions of a few "arbitrarily den[ies] court access to persons with valid claims" and "do[es] not serve the best interests of the public." St. Elizabeth Hospital, 730 S.W.2d at 652, 654. Certainly the existence of physical symptoms does not affect the authenticity of the emotional injury. A contrary conclusion in effect rewards the weak and punishes the strong, when the injury sustained may be identical:

> Mental suffering is no more difficult to estimate in financial terms, and no less a real injury, than "physical" pain.... [T]he law is not for the protection of the physically sound alone.

W. Page Keeton, Prosser & Keeton on Torts § 54, at 360 (5th ed. 1984) (hereinafter Prosser & Keeton on Torts) (citations omitted). The degree of harm suffered does not change the nature of a wrongful act. If someone's objectionable conduct inflicts severe emotional distress on two victims, only one of whom manifests that distress physically, why should the wrongdoer's fault support recovery for one and not the other?

The unwarranted fear of unwarranted claims has been unequivocally rejected by one leading commentator who appropriately declared that:

> [T]here has long been precedent enough [for emotional injury claims], and no great increase in litigation has been observed.

Prosser & Keeton on Torts § 54, at 360. This comports with the experience of other state courts that have not been overburdened with litigation.... Nor is there the slightest indication that our decision in St. Elizabeth has strained Texas courts by requiring litigation of trivial claims.

Texas need not and does not provide redress for every instance of rude or insensitive behavior that foreseeably results in hurt feelings or embarrassment. St. Elizabeth Hospital, 730 S.W.2d at 653 (extending protection to "severe" emotional injuries). We have sought to balance our desire not to expose parties to litigation over the trivial with our longstanding commitment to assuring redress for serious injuries. See id.; Hill v. Kimball....

Even if it feels compelled to repudiate St. Elizabeth Hospital, to reject totally "an in-dependent cause of action ... for negligently inflicted emotional distress,"[7] ... and to de-clare "there is no general duty in Texas not to negligently inflict emotional distress," ... the majority's refusal to recognize Susan Kerr's claim remains groundless. She should be permitted to recover here in an ordinary negligence action, which initially requires proof of four elements: the existence of a duty, a breach of that duty, a resulting injury, and the foreseeability to a reasonably prudent person that such an injury was a likely re-sult of the breach.... Modifying these standards as they apply to cases involving emo-tional harm would preserve the ability of those suffering severe emotional injury to re-cover damages.

Ordinarily, there are a number of ways to establish a duty, including the undertaking of any conduct that could foreseeably cause an injury. In the context of psychic injuries, foreseeability alone has been viewed by some as insufficient to create an adequate duty. See Marlene F. v. Affiliated Psychiatric Medical Clinic, Inc., 48 Cal.3d 583, 257 Cal.Rptr. 98, 102, 770 P.2d 278, 281 (1989) (foreseeability must be accompanied by a legal duty). Therefore, it is required that a duty be "owed the plaintiff that is assumed by the defen-dant or imposed on the defendant as a matter of law, or that arises out of a relationship between the two." Id. This duty requirement has also been expressed as "some special relationship between the plaintiff and the defendant establishing a higher than usual duty for defendant toward plaintiff." ... Consistent with Texas law, a sufficient duty may arise from a statute or other legal obligation, or may be created when a party "voluntar-ily enters into an affirmative action affecting the interests of another," and the harmful consequences of such conduct are reasonably foreseeable....

To deter litigation over generally inoffensive or otherwise legally acceptable conduct that may produce mental anguish unaccompanied by physical injury, reference could be made to the Restatement of Torts requirement of "extreme and outrageous conduct" of either an intentional or "reckless" nature. Restatement (Second) of Torts §46(1).... The Restatement also requires that the injury be "severe." Restatement (Second) of Torts §46; ... This conforms with our recognition in St. Elizabeth Hospital that there is a right to be free not from all psychic harm, such as that resulting from mere insults, but rather from "severe emotional distress." 730 S.W.2d at 653. This threshold showing of injury establishes a "check on the ... conver[sion of] minor emotional blows into law-suits." ...

In the context of mental anguish, recovery may be had when an actor "should have realized that his conduct involved an unreasonable risk of causing the distress...." Re-statement (Second) of Torts §313(1)(a) ("Emotional Distress Unintended"). The re-quirement of foreseeability in this context has been expressed as conduct that is "likely to produce emotional distress in a person of ordinary sensibilities." ... Inclusion of the reasonably prudent person standard avoids the specter of "compensation for the hurt feelings of the supersensitive plaintiff—the eggshell psyche." ...

Unfortunately, today's writing, unlike St. Elizabeth, fails to examine the relevant legal literature on emotional distress, including that which recommends permitting such an action with reasonable limitations as a part of negligence. If, as the majority in-sists, further restrictions are necessary for negligently produced mental anguish dam-ages absent physical manifestation, these could be imposed without destroying all pro-

7. Although in St. Elizabeth Hospital, we discussed recovery for emotional distress damages as a separate tort, it is more properly viewed as an element of damages in a general negligence action. See *Johnson v. Ruark Obstetrics & Gynecology Assocs.*, 395 S.E.2d at 97.

tection against emotional injury by the following conditions: (1) there must be some legal duty not to cause harm to another beyond that created by foreseeability of injury, such as that arising from a special relationship, a statutory duty, or from the voluntary undertaking of an affirmative action that puts another at risk; (2) that duty must be breached by conduct that is reckless, extreme or outrageous; (3) the resulting psychic harm must be severe; and (4) the likelihood of such an injury must be foreseeable to a reasonably prudent person. These standards would address in a more balanced way the majority's single-minded interest in discouraging unmeritorious suits while maintaining the promised protection of the law to those sustaining severe emotional injuries.

The facts before us satisfy all of these conditions. Although Boyles clearly intended the act of engaging in intimate relations with Susan Kerr which would be videotaped, he did not intend the consequences, in this case the psychic injury suffered. Boyles stressed that he told Kerr that "he was sorry and had not meant to hurt her." Counsel for Boyles conceded at oral argument that "certainly an argument can be made in this case that there was negligence also involved," and that "there is evidence from which" negligence could be argued. By showing and then failing to destroy the tape, he negligently disregarded Kerr's emotional well-being. By Boyle's own admissions, his conduct was negligent; he did not intend to harm Kerr. Further, based on a charge defining "negligence" as "failing to do that which a person of ordinary prudence would have done under the same or similar circumstances," the jury's finding adequately constitutes a determination of foreseeability.

. . .

Peter Bell, *The Bell Tolls: Toward Full Tort Recovery for Psychic Injury*
36 U. FLA. L. REV. 333, 399–408 (1984)*

. . .

The existing restrictive rules are unjust both in their appearance of inconsistency and their real inconsistency. The appearance of inconsistency comes in part from the law's apparent valuation of chattels and other minor interests higher than interests in family relationships. For example, Louisiana allows a plaintiff to recover for emotional distress caused by the loss of a pet cat negligently sent to its death at an animal shelter. Where a mother suffers psychic injury from witnessing a car raised from her dead son's crushed body, however, Louisiana law will not allow recovery from the culpable defendant who caused the death. New York, in its heyday the fount of most tort doctrine, dismisses the psychic injury claims of parents whose children are born with severe birth defects caused by a doctor's negligence. Yet, if the parent's emotional trauma results from receipt of a telegram *mistakenly* telling them that their child had been injured, the New York courts would permit full recovery from the negligent message sender.

These are not isolated examples, but rather represent the mainstream of tort law. Hawaii and California courts have led the country in willingness to entertain tort claims for psychic injury. Yet, the Hawaii Supreme Court recently denied recovery to the estate of a man so emotionally traumatized by his daughter's and grand-daughter's negligently caused deaths that he suffered a fatal heart attack. Paradoxically, the same court upheld recovery to a couple and their three children for emotional distress, val-

---

ued at a total of $1,000, resulting from the death of their nine-year-old dog who suffered heat prostration when negligently kept in a hot van by defendants. The California Supreme Court, which in 1968 opened the courtroom doors to bystander recovery and in 1980 eliminated the ensuing physical injury restriction on psychic injury recovery, shut the door to recovery for a father traumatized by watching the negligent delivery of his stillborn infant. A California appellate court followed their lead in barring a psychic injury suit brought by parents who watched their son die minutes after being electrocuted due to defendant's negligence. The California appellate courts, however, have no difficulty permitting recovery for psychological suffering occasioned by defendant's negligent damaging of the plaintiff's property rather than his child.

These illustrations introduce the discussion of tort law's inconsistent treatment of psychic injury by demonstrating that a significant part of the law runs directly counter to the common intuitive sense of justice.[273] Closer analysis will show that this intuitive sense of injustice is supported by the actual inconsistent treatment of psychic injuries when such injuries become the focus of the court's attention. Actual inconsistency shows up in tort law's unwillingness to provide full recovery for proximately caused physical injuries and the pain and suffering which accompanies them. It also surfaces in the law's differential treatment of particular psychic injuries.

Permitting full recovery for physical injuries while denying it for psychic injuries is inconsistent. The injuries are difficult, if not impossible, to distinguish in essential nature and critical characteristics. The similarity in nature occurs because each contains a substantial component of the other. As more becomes known about the biochemical bases of psychic harm and the psychological roots of physical harm, the indivisibility of the two becomes clearer.[274] Physical injury is experienced through the mind; its significance lies in the reduction of the psychic well-being it causes through pain or inconvenience. Not surprisingly, therefore, the usual grounds for distinguishing the two kinds of injury, susceptibility to fraud, uncertainty of valuation and potential for unlimited liability, do not stand up as legitimate bases for such a distinction.

The most obvious inconsistency in tort law's treatment of physical injury cases involves awards for pain and suffering, which comprise one of the most significant items of recovery in such cases. Recovery for that essentially psychic harm is available to any physically injured plaintiff. There is no requirement that the pain and suffering produce physical consequences for a plaintiff to recover. The courts award pain and suffering

---

273. In order to satisfy the community sense of fairness, apparent inconsistency must be explained both rationally and emotionally. *See, e.g.,* G. Calabresi, [THE COSTS OF ACCIDENTS], at 294. The cost of such explanation in the context of the rules governing psychic injury will be high. Rather than incur those costs, for whatever modest increased sense of fairness might come to pass, society might well simply adopt rules which create the apparent consistency. *See* Calabresi & Melamed, [*Property Rules, Liability Rules, and Inalienability: One View of the Cathedral*, 85 HARV. L. REV. 1089], at 1103–04.

274. For example, several studies emphasize the strong correlation between stress and physical illness. *See* Selzer, *Psychological Stress and Legal Concepts of Disease Causation*, 56 CORNELL L. REV. 951 (1971). All acute psychic injuries involve physical changes in glandular secretions, in the cardiovascular and circulatory systems, and in the gastrointestinal and urinary tracts. *See, e.g.,* Comment, *Mental Distress in Psychological Research*, 21 BAYLOR L. Rev. 520, 525 (1969); Comment, *Negligently Inflicted Mental Distress,* ... [59 GEO. L.J. 1237], at 1259 n.128. Apparently, persons suffering grief reactions, whether normal or abnormal, are much more susceptible to physical diseases, such as colds, allergies and perhaps even cancer. *See* Leibson, *Recovery of Damages for Emotional Distress Caused by Physical Injury to Another*, 15 J. FAM. L. 163, 209 n.103 (1976–77). Recent research at the National Institute of Mental Health and other research centers has disclosed that anxiety has a biochemical basis. N.Y.TIMES, Sept. 7, 1982, at C1, col. 8.

damages even where those damages would not have occurred to a "normal" individual. Where an injury is one which is normally accompanied by pain, the plaintiff need not offer expert testimony to support his claim for pain damages and, in some instances where proof would be particularly difficult, need not offer any proof at all.

In these respects, pain and suffering receives more liberal treatment than psychic injury standing alone.[280] Yet the two are essentially the same. Pain and suffering includes not only physical pain, but also fear, anxiety, worry about future health, embarrassment, humiliation, depression and, in some instances, loss of enjoyment of the normal activities of life. On its face this generally accepted definition suggests that the only significant difference between pain and suffering and psychic injury is the component of physical pain. Extensive research of physical pain the past two decades, however, convincingly indicates there is no such difference. Like psychic injury, pain can be caused by either physical or psychological stimuli.[282] In a clinical setting, persons begin to feel painful stimulation at roughly the same point, but vary widely in the points beyond which they will not permit additional painful stimulation.[283] This variation is chiefly accounted for by psychological factors such as existing emotional tranquility, anxiety levels, learned patterns, cultural conditioning and one's interpretation of the injury's significance.[284] As is the case with much emotional or mental distress, anxiety plays a major part in the perception of pain.[285] For example, studies of patients with frontal lobotomies reveal they rarely complain of severe pain or request medication. The sensory component of pain remains, no pain pathways are severed by a lobotomy, but the suffering and anguish associated with pain has disappeared. The lobotomy has removed only their anxiety. The suffering that accompanies a particular painful stimulus will thus depend in part on the nature of the stimulus, but largely on factors unique to the injured individual: anxiety level, coping abilities, support systems, attitudes and the like.

. . .

The primary reasons advanced for treating pain and suffering differently from purely psychic injury are unconvincing. The first reason is that pain and suffering is

---

280. Courts do not treat pain and suffering differently from the way they treat psychic injury which results from physical injury. In fact, courts usually speak of such resultant psychic injury as part of plaintiff's pain and suffering. In actuality, pain and suffering is really a psychic injury, although courts treat it differently when it does not result from some physical injury.

282. Pain can result from a physical stimulus which activates nerve fibers and sends signals through the nervous system to the brain, which perceives, interprets and responds to the impulses. Melzack & Dennis, *Neurophysiological Foundations of Pain*, in The Psychology of Pain 1 (R. Sternback ed. 1978)[hereinafter cited as Melzack]. Pain can also result from emotional or developmental problems with which one cannot cope adequately. The resulting stress is converted by the subconscious into pain symptoms. Such pain, which may have no organic or physiological origin, is just as real to the individual as physically stimulated pain. Merskey, *Psychiatric Aspects of the Control of Pain* in I Advances in Pain Research and Theory 711, 711–12 (J. Bonica & D. Albe-Fessard eds. 1976); T. Szasz, Pain and Pleasure xxiii–xxiv, 70–71 (2d ed. 1975).

283. In other words, individuals have similar pain thresholds, but markedly different pain tolerances. P. FAIRLEY, THE CONQUEST OF PAIN, ITS NATURE, ANALYSIS AND TREATMENT 58 (1978); M. BOND, PAIN: ITS NATURE ANALYSIS AND TREATMENT 26–27 (1979).

284. A. PETRIE, INDIVIDUALITY IN PAIN AND SUFFERING 1–7 (1967); Weisenberg, *Pain and Pain Control*, 84 PSYCHOLOGICAL BULL. 1008, 1021–23, 1032–35 (1977). Physical factors, such as one's general physical condition may also influence how one experiences pain. *Id.*

285. Anxiety is frequently linked to acute pain. Chronic pain is more often associated with depression, with patients' estimates of the severity of their pain being correlated to their levels of depression. Sternback, *Psychological Factors in Pain*, in I Advances in Pain Research and Therapy 293, 293–94 (J. Bonica & D. Albe-Fessard eds. 1976).

limited to one person per physical injury. With psychic injury, however, many "by-standers" may suffer psychic injury from another's physical injury, thus risking a crushing liability burden not possible with pain and suffering damages. In fact, it seems far more likely that the burden of damages for pain and suffering would be noticeably heavier than damages for bystanders' psychic injuries. Critics also argue that damages for pain and suffering are permitted only because they pay for plaintiff's attorneys fees. Because those fees are already covered, it makes no sense to permit recovery for psychic injuries. Courts have not, however, articulated any concern for payment of plaintiff's attorneys' fees as the rationale underlying compensation for pain and suffering. Moreover, no attempt is made by judge or jury to correlate pain and suffering damages and attorney's fees in any particular case. Such awards continue to be made in England, where a victorious plaintiff can obtain his attorney's fees from the loser. To throw out awards for psychic injury on the ground that attorneys' fees are already provided for by pain and suffering damages would suggest a similar treatment for all intangible injuries, while ignoring the existence of the real injury costs which society wants to reduce.

Although most prominent with respect to pain and suffering, the inconsistent treatment of similar injuries does not end there. Tort law is rife with circumstances in which psychic injury damages are awarded without evidence of ensuing physical injury or where the direct target of the initial harm is someone or something other than the plaintiff. Such recoveries are regularly seen in cases similar to pain and suffering cases, where psychic injuries are parasitic to some other injury done to the plaintiff. Whether the defendant interfered with plaintiff's personal property, real property, or use and enjoyment of his property, courts will permit recovery for plaintiff's psychic injuries which flow from that interference....

This inconsistent recognition of psychic injury as a compensable wrong also occurs in many nonparasitic settings. There is no requirement that a plaintiff whose privacy has been invaded or who has been defamed show some physical manifestation of his injury to recover....

In short, in a pervasive range of cases, tort law allows plaintiffs to recover for psychic injury or its equivalent. This recovery is unaccompanied by any requirement that the plaintiffs clear the major hurdles erected to recovery for purely psychic injury. Absent sound explanation, such inconsistency of treatment speaks as clearly of injustice as the examples at the outset of this section suggest.

....

Richard Pearson, *Liability for Negligently Inflicted Psychic Harm: A Response to Professor Bell*
36 U. Fla. L. Rev. 413, 423–426 (1984)*

...

The basis of Professor Bell's consistency argument is that all intangible harm is similar because it operates on and through the mind. It is therefore inconsistent, for example, to allow recovery for pain and suffering and deny recovery for purely psychic injury.

Such a broad definition of intangible harm, however, is not particularly helpful. In the conventional way we think about such things, as Professor Bell recognizes, there are differences between various forms of intangible harm, such as grief, fright, physical pain, and loss of enjoyment. Two aspirin four times a day may help to relieve back pain, but I doubt it would have helped Mrs. Dillon.** Enough differences exist between the various forms of intangible harm so that a well developed sense of fairness would not necessarily demand the law treat them all alike. Simply because there are differences does not mean that they should necessarily be treated differently. The outcome of the consistency argument should depend on other considerations. I will briefly discuss some of these.

Consistency does not require that the law ignore the circumstances under which the harm was inflicted. Providing a remedy for intentionally inflicted emotional harm, for example, does not necessarily mean a remedy should be provided for negligently inflicted harm. Intentional conduct may generate a greater concern in the law than conduct that is only negligent. The importance of circumstances producing a harm is demonstrated by the law relating to economic loss. Just as all intangible harm can be put into a single category, so can all tangible harm. No matter what form the latter takes, such as impaired capacity to earn, medical expenses, or loss of profits, out-of-pocket economic loss is involved. Yet, circumstances do affect recoverability. Traditionally, purely consequential commercial loss unassociated with personal injury or property damage to the plaintiff is not recoverable. While some recent cases have permitted recovery in narrow circumstances, none have suggested foreseeability as the only test of recovery. Most specifically recognize the need for some other limit on liability. Basic principles of justice do not demand that all general classes of foreseeable harm should be treated the same apart from the circumstances under which harm occurs.

To the extent that consistency in treating all intangible harms the same is desired, there is more than one way to achieve it. Professor Bell points to a number of cases in which plaintiffs have recovered damages for emotional harm as a result of property destruction. I would argue the way to achieve consistency here is to eliminate liability in such cases. The court in *Meyer v. 4-D Insulation Co.* aptly summarized the situation as follows:

> It is entirely common and predictable … that a person will be disturbed and upset when someone negligently breaks the headlight of his or her cherished automobile or causes a softball to crash through a picture window. We do not *yet* live, however, in an "eggshell society" in which every harm to property interests gives rise to a right of action for mental distress.

Professor Bell argues that consistency should be achieved by expanding liability rather than contracting it, but that is not a consistency argument.

My final point about the consistency argument is in a sense political. Whatever similarity there is between psychic harm and physical pain and suffering, I would not urge that as a basis for expanding liability. Many questions have been raised about the appropriateness and magnitude of compensation for physical pain and suffering. Significant inroads into pain and suffering recovery have been made by workers' compensation and no-fault automobile insurance systems. I am not here urging that consistency in the law be achieved by abolishing all recovery for physical pain and suffering, even if that could be accomplished constitutionally. Rather, my point is that emerging attitudes toward

---

** Professor Pearson's reference is to *Dillon v. Legg*, 68 Cal. 2d 728, 69 Cal. Rptr. 72, 441 P. 2d 912 (1968), discussed at length in *Thing v. LaChusa*, infra § 12.04[B]. — Ed.

compensation for intangible harm do not require compensation for all such harm simply because it is provided for some.

...

NOTES

(1) There is a rather well-accepted rule allowing recovery when fright caused by the defendant's fault aggravates a pre-existing physical condition in the plaintiff. See, *e.g.*, *Orlo v. Connecticut Co.*, 128 Conn. 231, 21 A.2d 402 (1941) (aggravation of pre-existing diabetes and arteriosclerosis). Would the rationale underlying the general argument against recovery for psychic harm harmonize with this rule allowing recovery for physical consequences of fright? What is the strongest principled argument for denying recovery for mental or emotional damages without physical impact?

(2) Given the increasing knowledge of the mind and its vulnerabilities, why have a substantial majority of courts continued to deny recovery for NIED? Consider the Florida Supreme Court's response to a case in which a man alleged that a defectively designed accelerator pedal on his Cadillac caused the car to jump forward and fatally strike his mother. The court held "that there is no cause of action for psychological trauma alone when resulting from simple negligence." *Brown v. Cadillac Motor Car Div.*, 468 So. 2d 903 (Fla. 1985). What reasons of policy or fairness militate against recovery on these facts?

(3) Some courts have taken the position that "where the defendant's conduct has been merely negligent, without any element of intent to harm, his fault is not so great that he should be required to make good a purely mental disturbance." *Payton v. Abbott Labs.*, 386 Mass. 540, 552–53, 437 N.E.2d 171, 179 (1982). Is this a rationale, or just a conclusion?

(4) The Fourth Circuit held the line in a pollution case on the requirement of either physical impact or a physical injury. The case arose from a "major discharge" of oil that created a "plume" of oil that extended underground into the plaintiffs' subdivision. However, at the time of suit, there was no showing that the plaintiffs' properties were contaminated by the "plume." Saying that the suit for psychological injury alleged "mere fear of significant health risks," the court denied recovery under nuisance. It said there was no state precedent that allowed a claim "for a private nuisance which is not visible or otherwise capable of physical detection on the plaintiff's property." The court also denied recovery under a negligence theory, emphasizing the alternative requirements of either physical impact or physical injury. *Adams v. Star Enterprise*, 51 F.3d 417, 423 (4th Cir. 1995).

(5) One of the most unusual cases involving chains of psychic consequences is *Sundquist v. Madison Ry.*, 197 Wis. 83, 221 N.W. 392 (1928). In this case, the court allowed recovery in the following situation: The plaintiff was riding in an auto that was hit from the rear by the defendant's street car, an event that produced no physical injury but did cause her to become hysterical. Two months later, in another city, after the approach of a streetcar clanging its bell, the plaintiff again became hysterical, fainted, and subsequently became paralyzed. What considerations should weigh most heavily in the decision of this case?

(6) Although skeptical of establishing a general principle allowing emotional distress damages "without either accompanying physical consequences or an independent underlying tort," the Maine court was inclined to give damages for "serious mental distress" in one circumstance. At issue was the defendant psychotherapist's conduct in a case in which the defendant had been acting as therapist for the plaintiff, who had been

experiencing difficulties in her homosexual relationship with another woman. This therapy continued up to the time that the defendant began developing "some emotional feelings" toward the therapist, with whom she eventually started living. The court thought that psychological harm would be "neither speculative nor easily feigned" in such a case, and emphasized that because patients in psychotherapy are "encouraged to divulge [their] innermost thoughts," they are "extremely vulnerable to mental harm if the therapist fails to adhere to the standards of care recognized by the profession." *Rowe v. Bennett*, 514 A.2d 802, 806–07 (Me. 1986).

SPECIAL NOTE ON THE SNOWMEN OF GRAND CENTRAL TERMINAL

Should someone who has had significant exposure to a carcinogen be able to recover for negligently inflicted emotional distress caused by fear of cancer when he exhibits no symptoms of disease? *Metro-North Commuter R. Co. v. Buckley*, 521 U.S. 424, 1175 S. Ct. 2113 (1997), arose from a suit under the Federal Employers' Liability Act, a statute providing for recovery by railroad workers against negligent employers. Buckley was one of a group of 104 pipefitters who became known as the "Snowmen of Grand Central Terminal" because when they worked in the tunnels under the terminal, they often would be covered with asbestos-laden white powder.[1] Despite the statute's general liberality to claimants, the Supreme Court denied recovery. The Court viewed the central question as "whether the physical contact with insulation dust ... amount[ed] to a 'physical impact'" as it used that term in its decision in *Consolidated Rail Corp. v. Gottshall*, 512 U.S. 532 (1994). Part of the Court's analysis follows:

* * *

... *Gottshall* cited many state cases in support of its adoption of the "zone of danger" test.... [I]n each case where recovery for emotional distress was permitted, the case involved a threatened physical contact that caused, or might have caused, immediate traumatic harm....

Taken together, language and cited precedent indicate that the words "physical impact" do not encompass every form of "physical contact." And, in particular, they do not include a contact that amounts to no more than an exposure—an exposure, such as that before us, to a substance that poses some future risk of disease and which contact causes emotional distress only because the worker learns that he may become ill after a substantial period of time.

... [C]ommon-law precedent does not favor the plaintiff. Common law courts do permit a plaintiff who suffers from a disease to recover for related negligently caused emotional distress, ... and some courts permit a plaintiff who exhibits a physical symptom of exposure to recover, *see, e.g., Herber v. Johns-Manville Corp.*, 785 F.2d 79, 85 (C.A.3 1986); *Mauro v. Owens-Corning Fiberglas Corp.*, 225 N.J.Super. 196, 542 A.2d 16 (App.Div.1988). But with only a few exceptions, common law courts have denied recovery to those who, like Buckley, are disease and symptom free....

---

1. *See High Court to Review FELA Distress Claim by "Snowmen of Grand Central Terminal,"* 24 Prod. Liab. & Safety Rep. 1039–40 (Nov. 8, 1996).

... [T]he general policy reasons to which *Gottshall* referred—in its explanation of why common law courts have restricted recovery for emotional harm to cases falling within rather narrowly defined categories—militate against an expansive definition of "physical impact" here. Those reasons include: (a) special "difficult[y] for judges and juries" in separating valid, important claims from those that are invalid or "trivial," *Gottshall*, 512 U.S., at 557, 114 S.Ct., at 2411; (b) a threat of "unlimited and unpredictable liability," *ibid.*; and (c) the "potential for a flood" of comparatively unimportant, or "trivial," claims, ibid....

...

... [T]he physical contact at issue here—a simple (though extensive) contact with a carcinogenic substance—does not seem to offer much help in separating valid from invalid emotional distress claims. That is because contacts, even extensive contacts, with serious carcinogens are common. See e.g., *Nicholson, Perkel & Selikoff, Occupational Exposure to Asbestos: Population at Risk and Projected Mortality—1980–2030*, 3 AM. J. INDUST. MED. 259 (1982) (estimating that 21 million Americans have been exposed to work-related asbestos); U.S. Dept. of Health and Human Services, 1 Seventh Annual Report on Carcinogens 71 (1994) (3 million workers exposed to benzene, a majority of Americans exposed outside the workplace); Pirkle, et al., *Exposure of the U S Population to Environmental Tobacco Smoke*, 275 JAMA 1233, 1237 (1996) (reporting that 43% of U.S. children lived in a home with at least one smoker, and 37% of adult non-smokers lived in a home with at least one smoker or reported environmental tobacco smoke at work). They may occur without causing serious emotional distress, but sometimes they do cause distress, and reasonably so, for cancer is both an unusually threatening and unusually frightening disease. See Statistical Abstract of United States 94 (1996) (23.5 percent of Americans who died in 1994 died of cancer); American Cancer Society, Cancer Facts & Figures—1997, p. 1 (half of all men and one third of all women will develop cancer). The relevant problem, however, remains one of evaluating a claimed emotional reaction to an increased risk of dying. An external circumstance—exposure—makes some emotional distress more likely. But how can one determine from the external circumstance of exposure whether, or when, a claimed strong emotional reaction to an increased mortality risk (say from 23% to 28%) is reasonable and genuine, rather than overstated—particularly when the relevant statistics themselves are controversial and uncertain (as is usually the case), and particularly since neither those exposed nor judges or juries are experts in statistics? The evaluation problem seems a serious one.

The large number of those exposed and the uncertainties that may surround recovery also suggest what *Gottshall* called the problem of "unlimited and unpredictable liability." Does such liability mean, for example, that the costs associated with a rule of liability would become so great that, given the nature of the harm, it would seem unreasonable to require the public to pay the higher prices that may result? ... The same characteristics further suggest what *Gottshall* called the problem of a "flood" of cases that, if not "trivial," are comparatively less important. In a world of limited resources, would a rule permitting immediate large-scale recoveries for widespread emotional distress caused by fear of future disease diminish the likelihood of recovery by those who later suffer from the disease?....

NOTES

(1) The Court later did create a liability category for one set of FELA claimants exposed to asbestos—workers with established asbestosis. The Court said that "as an element of … asbestosis-related pain and suffering damages," such plaintiffs could recover "mental anguish damages resulting from the fear of developing cancer." The decision stressed, however, that a plaintiff would have "to prove that his alleged fear is genuine and serious." *Norfolk & W. Ry. Co. v. Ayers*, 538 U.S. 135, 141, 157 (2003).

(2) The Court in *Buckley* also denied the plaintiff's claim for the costs of "medical monitoring"—extra checkups that he said he would have to have because of his exposure to asbestos dust—noting that he had no symptoms or manifested disease. The Court considered Buckley's argument that it was "inequitable to place the economic burden of such care on the negligently exposed plaintiff rather than on the negligent defendant." In rejecting "a new full-blown tort law cause of action" for medical monitoring, however, the Court mentioned the "uncertainty among medical professionals about just which tests are most usefully administered and when." It also expressed concern about a potential "flood" of litigation that might ensue from the fact that "tens of millions of individuals may have suffered exposure to substances that might justify some form of substance-related medical monitoring." 117 S. Ct. at 2123. Are you persuaded?

(3) *Buckley* presents one issue among several that have begun to arise in cases dealing with psychological reactions to toxic products with which individuals have come into contact. In one case interpreting Texas law, the Fifth Circuit held that although an asbestos worker could not recover for increased risk of cancer or mesothelioma where he did not show a reasonable medical probability that he would develop either disease, he was entitled to recover for mental anguish that would "reasonably follow" after he was informed by his doctor "that his exposure to defendants' products had heightened his risk of developing these deadly diseases." This was so "even if such distress arises from fear of diseases that are a substantial concern, but not medically probable." *Dartez v. Fibreboard Corp.*, 765 F.2d 456 (5th Cir. 1985).

Shortly thereafter, the same court read Mississippi law to say that an asbestos worker's "fear, which is a present injury, is compensable." *Jackson v. Johns-Manville Sales Corp.*, 781 F.2d 394 (5th Cir.), *cert. denied*, 106 S. Ct. 3339 (1986). Simultaneously, the Third Circuit held that a man exposed to asbestos could be compensated for his "fear of cancer." Like *Dartez*, however, the Third Circuit decision denied recovery for increased risk of cancer because the plaintiff did not show that it was "more likely than not" that he would develop the disease. *Herber v. Johns-Manville Corp.*, 785 F.2d 79 (3d Cir. 1986).

What do you think about the questions of whether there should be liability for (1) fear of disease (2) increased risk of disease (3) medical monitoring? Should it make a difference if X-rays show that there are asbestos particles in the lungs of a plaintiff bringing a claim on any of these bases?

How would it affect your analysis if the plaintiff were the spouse of an asbestos worker who alleged that she feared cancer as a result of exposure to asbestos fibers from her husband's clothing?

(4) One commentator proposes tort recovery for "enhanced risk" on "a proportional basis, but only when a plaintiff can prove that the toxic exposure has more than doubled her risk of contracting disease in the future." Andrew R. Klein, *A Model for Enhanced Risk Recovery in Tort*, 36 WASH. & LEE L. REV. 1173, 1194–95 (1999). "Proportional liability," for these purposes, means "the present value of the risk at the point at which the risk can be identified and given some measurable value[]," with the value

being "equal to the present value of the future losses multiplied by the estimated probability of their occurrence." *Id.* at 1184–85 (quoting Glen O. Robinson, *Probabilistic Causation and Compensation for Tortious Risk*, 14 J. LEGAL STUDIES 779, 786 (1986)).

MOLIEN v. KAISER FOUNDATION HOSPITALS
California Supreme Court
27 Cal. 3d 916, 616 P.2d 813, 167 Cal. Rptr. 831 (1980)

MOSK, JUSTICE.

· · ·

The principal allegations of the first cause of action are as follows: Plaintiff and his wife, Valerie G. Molien, are members of the Kaiser Health Plan. Mrs. Molien went to Kaiser for a routine multiphasic physical examination. There, Dr. Kilbridge, a Kaiser staff physician, negligently examined and tested her, and subsequently advised her she had contracted an infectious type of syphilis. The diagnosis was erroneous, as she did not in fact have the disease. Nevertheless she was required to undergo treatment for syphilis, including the administration of massive and unnecessary doses of penicillin. As a result of defendants' conduct she suffered "injury to her body and shock and injury to her nervous system."

Defendants knew plaintiff husband would learn of the diagnosis, as they instructed Mrs. Molien to so advise him. Thereafter plaintiff was required to undergo blood tests himself in order to ascertain whether he had contracted syphilis and was the source of his wife's purported infection. The tests revealed that he did not have the disease.

As a result of the negligently erroneous diagnosis, plaintiff's wife became upset and suspicious that he had engaged in extramarital sexual activities; tension and hostility arose between the two, "causing a break-up of their marriage and the initiation of dissolution proceedings."

Defendants knew or should have known their diagnosis that plaintiff's wife had syphilis and that he might also have the disease would cause him emotional distress. He has in fact suffered "extreme emotional distress" as a result of the negligent misdiagnosis. Additionally, he has incurred medical expenses for counseling in an effort to save the marriage.

· · ·

The prayer is for damages for mental suffering and loss of consortium, together with medical expenses. The trial court sustained general demurrers to both causes of action, and plaintiff appealed from the ensuing judgment of dismissal.

· · ·

We ... first address plaintiffs' contention that he has stated a cause of action for the negligent infliction of emotional distress. Defendants maintain this issue is governed by *Dillon v. Legg* (1968) 68 Cal.2d 728, 69 Cal.Rptr. 72, 441 P.2d 912; they emphasize that plaintiff was not present when the doctor announced the erroneous diagnosis, but learned of it later from his wife. As we shall explain, however, defendants rely too heavily on *Dillon*: the case is apposite, but not controlling.

A

In *Dillon* a mother sought damages for emotional trauma and physical injury that resulted when she witnessed the negligently inflicted death of her infant daughter. The defendant contended he owed no duty to the mother because she was outside the zone of physical danger at the time of the accident. But the traditional duty approach, we explained, begged the question whether the plaintiff's interests were entitled to legal protection; the finding of a duty was simply "'a shorthand statement of a conclusion, rather than an aid to analysis in itself.'" ... We therefore identified foreseeability of the risk as the critical inquiry: "In order to limit the otherwise potentially infinite liability which would follow every negligent act, the law of torts holds defendant amenable only for injuries to others which to defendant at the time were reasonably foreseeable." ... And the foreseeable risk may entail not only actual physical impact, but emotional injury as well....

. . .

It must be remembered ... that in *Dillon* the plaintiff sought recovery of damages she suffered as a percipient witness to the injury of a third person, and the three guidelines there noted served as a limitation on that particular cause of action.... Here, by contrast, plaintiff was himself a direct victim of the assertedly negligent act. By insisting that the present facts fail to satisfy the first and second of the *Dillon* criteria, defendants urge a rote application of the guidelines to a case factually dissimilar to the bystander scenario. In so doing, they overlook our explicit statement in *Dillon* that an obligation hinging on foreseeability "must necessarily be adjudicated only upon a case-by-case basis.... [N]o immutable rule can establish the extent of that obligation for every circumstance in the future." ...

Hence the significance of Dillon for the present action lies not in its delineation of guidelines fashioned for resolution of the precise issue then before us; rather, we apply its general principle of foreseeability to the facts at hand, much as we have done in other cases presenting complex questions of tort liability. (*See, e.g., Tarasoff v. Regents of University of California* (1976)....

In the case at bar the risk of harm to plaintiff was reasonably foreseeable to defendants. It is easily predictable that an erroneous diagnosis of syphilis and its probable source would produce marital discord and resultant emotional distress to a married patient's spouse; Dr. Kilbridge's advice to Mrs. Molien to have her husband examined for the disease confirms that plaintiff was a foreseeable victim of the negligent diagnosis. Because the disease is normally transmitted only by sexual relations, it is rational to anticipate that both husband and wife would experience anxiety, suspicion, and hostility when confronted with what they had every reason to believe was reliable medical evidence of a particularly noxious infidelity.

We thus agree with plaintiff that the alleged tortious conduct of defendant was directed to him as well as to his wife. Because the risk of harm to him was reasonably foreseeable we hold, in negligence parlance, that under these circumstances defendants owed plaintiff a duty to exercise due care in diagnosing the physical condition of his wife. There remains the question whether plaintiff is barred from recovery by the fact that he suffered no physical injury.

. . .

As early as 1896, this court recognized that mental suffering "constitutes an aggravation of damages when it naturally ensues from the act complained of." (*Sloane v. Southern Cal. Ry. Co.* (1896) 111 Cal. 668, 680, 44 P. 320, 322.) But such suffering alone, we said, would not afford a right of action. (*Ibid.*) We pondered the question whether a nervous disorder suffered by the plaintiff after she was wrongfully put off a train was a physical or a mental injury: "The interdependence of the mind and body is in many respects so close that it is impossible to distinguish their respective influence upon each other. It must be conceded that a nervous shock or paroxysm, or a disturbance of the nervous system, is distinct from mental anguish, and falls within the physiological, rather than the psychological, branch of the human organism. It is a matter of general knowledge that an attack of sudden fright, or an exposure to imminent peril, has produced in individuals a complete change in their nervous system, and rendered one who was physically strong and vigorous weak and timid. Such a result must be regarded as an injury to the body rather than to the mind, even though the mind be at the same time injuriously affected." (*Ibid.*)

The foundation was thus laid, nearly a century ago, for two beliefs that have since been frequently reiterated: first, recovery for emotional distress must be relegated to the status of parasitic damages; and second, mental disturbances can be distinctly classified as either psychological or physical injury. That medical science and particularly the field of mental health have made much progress in the 20th century is manifest; yet, despite some noteworthy exceptions, the principles underlying the decision in *Sloane* still pervade the law of negligence.

...

Plaintiff urges that we recognize the concept of negligent infliction of emotional distress as an independent tort. In this inquiry we first seek to identify the rationale for the Sloane rule. None appears in the opinion, possibly because the court classified the plaintiff's condition, "nervous paroxysm," as a physical injury, and hence had no need to justify a denial of recovery for psychological injury alone. Neither did the *Espinosa* court provide any justification for its rejection of the plaintiff's attempt to "subvert the ancient rule that mental suffering alone will not support an action for damages based upon negligence." (114 Cal.App.2d at p. 234, 249 P.2d at p. 844.) Therefore, we must look elsewhere.

The primary justification for the requirement of physical injury appears to be that it serves as a screening device to minimize a presumed risk of feigned injuries and false claims....

... Although we recognize a need to guard against fraudulent claims, we are not persuaded that the presently existing artificial lines of demarcation are the only appropriate means of attaining this goal. As observed by Presiding Justice Gardner in his concurring opinion in *Allen v. Jones* (1980) 104 Cal.App.3d 207, 216, 163 Cal.Rptr. 445, 451, "In no other area are the vagaries of our law more apparent than in the distinction between mental and emotional distress accompanied by physical manifestation and such discomfort unaccompanied by physical manifestation."

...

[T]he unqualified requirement of physical injury is no longer justifiable. It supposedly serves to satisfy the cynic that the claim of emotional distress is genuine. Yet we perceive two significant difficulties with the scheme. First, the classification is both overinclusive and underinclusive when viewed in the light of its purported purpose of screening false claims. It is overinclusive in permitting recovery for emotional distress when the suffering accompanies or results in any physical injury whatever, no matter how trivial. If physical injury, however slight, provides the ticket for admission to the courthouse, it is difficult for advocates of the "floodgates" premonition to deny that the doors are already wide open: as we observed in *Capelouto v. Kaiser Foundation Hospitals, supra*, 7 Cal.3d at p. 893, 103 Cal.Rptr. at p. 859, 500 P.2d at p. 883, "mental suffering frequently constitutes the principal element of tort damages...." More significantly, the classification is underinclusive because it mechanically denies court access to claims that may well be valid and could be proved if the plaintiffs were permitted to go to trial.

The second defect in the requirement of physical injury is that it encourages extravagant pleading and distorted testimony. Thus it has been urged that the law should provide a remedy for serious invasions of emotional tranquility, "otherwise the tendency would be for the victim to exaggerate symptoms of sick headaches, nausea, insomnia, etc., to make out a technical basis of bodily injury, upon which to predicate a parasitic recovery for the more grievous disturbance, the mental and emotional distress she endured." (Magruder, *Mental and Emotional Disturbance in the Law of Torts* (1936) 49 Harv.L.Rev. 1033, 1059....)

Furthermore, as we observed in *Sloane v. Southern Cal. Ry. Co., supra,* ... the border between physical and emotional injury is not clearly delineated. In 1896 we deemed a "nervous shock or paroxysm" to be distinguishable from mere mental anguish. Today, the notion that physical harm includes "shock to the nervous system" is an accepted aspect of our law of negligence. (*See* BAJI No. 12.71 (6th ed. 1977).) The Restatement, too, attempts to draw the distinction: "The rule (precluding recovery for negligently caused emotional distress alone) applies to all forms of emotional disturbance, including temporary fright, nervous shock, nausea, grief, rage, and humiliation. The fact that these are accompanied by transitory, non-recurring physical phenomena, harmless in themselves, such as dizziness, vomiting, and the like, does not make the actor liable where such phenomena are in themselves inconsequential and do not amount to any substantial bodily harm. On the other hand, long continued nausea or headaches may amount to physical illness, which is bodily harm; and even long continued mental disturbance ... may be classified by the courts as illness, notwithstanding (its) mental character. This becomes a medical or psychiatric problem, rather than one of law." (Rest.2d Torts, § 436A; com. c.)

In our view ... the attempted distinction between physical and psychological injury merely clouds the issue. The essential question is one of proof; whether the plaintiff has suffered a serious and compensable injury should not turn on this artificial and often arbitrary classification scheme.... As Justice Traynor explained in this court's unanimous opinion in *State Rubbish etc. Assn. v. Siliznoff, supra,* 38 Cal.2d at page 338, 240 P.2d 282, the jurors are best situated to determine whether and to what extent the defendant's conduct caused emotional distress, by referring to their own experience. In addition, there will doubtless be circumstances in which the alleged emotional injury is susceptible of objective ascertainment by expert medical testimony.... To repeat: this is a matter of proof to be presented to the trier of fact. The screening of claims on this basis at the pleading stage is a usurpation of the jury's function.

More than half a century ago Roscoe Pound recognized that claims of emotional distress were capable of verification by means more precise than the then-prevailing requirement of physical impact; we think his logic applies equally to the present requirement of physical injury: "In reality (the impact requirement) was a practical rule, growing out of the limitations of trial by jury, the difficulty of proof in cases of injuries manifest subjectively only and the backwardness of our knowledge with respect to the relations of mind and body. In view of the danger of imposition, the courts, on a balance of the interests involved, refused to go beyond cases where there was a voucher for the truth of the plaintiff's claim.... With the rise of modern psychology the basis of this caution in securing an important element of the interest of personality was removed." (Pound, Interpretations of Legal History (1923) pp. 120–121.)

For all these reasons we hold that a cause of action may be stated for the negligent infliction of serious emotional distress. Applying these principles to the case before us, we conclude that the complaint states such a cause of action. The negligent examination of Mrs. Molien and the conduct flowing therefrom are objectively verifiable actions by the defendants that foreseeably elicited serious emotional responses in the plaintiff and hence serve as a measure of the validity of plaintiff's claim for emotional distress. As yet another corroborating factor, we note the universally accepted gravity of a false imputation of syphilis: by statute it constitutes slander per se....

It follows that the trial court erred in sustaining the demurrer to the cause of action for emotional distress.

....

CLARK, JUSTICE, dissenting.

I dissent.

Our court today allows—for the first time—a money award against one who unintentionally disturbs the mental tranquillity of another.

Because such disturbances are commonplace in our complex society, because they cannot be objectively observed or measured, but mainly because it is for the Legislature to create new causes of action and to fix the limits of recovery, this court has until today refused the invitation to open wide the door to damage claims fraught with potential abuse.

· · ·

The fundamental problem is not foreseeing (by unguided hindsight) the consequences of unintentional conduct, but rather realistically limiting liability for those consequences. "It is unthinkable that any one shall be liable to the end of time for all the results that follow in endless sequence from his single act. Causation cannot be the answer; in a very real sense the consequences of an act go forward to eternity, and back to the beginning of the world." (Prosser, *Palsgraf Revisited* (1953) 52 Mich.L.Rev. 1, 24.) In a system compensating injury based on fault, consideration must be given to the "moral blame attached to the defendant's conduct" (*Biakanja v. Irving* (1958) 49 Cal.2d 647, 650, 320 P.2d 16, 19) in fixing liability. When the defendant's act is merely negligent rather than intentional, lesser moral blame attaches, cautioning against extending liability.... Liability should be proportionate to the actor's culpability, having in mind the utility and necessity of the conduct negligently performed. Where, as here, imposition of liability is far disproportionate to the degree of culpability, we do a disservice to the public—who must ultimately bear the cost by sanctioning claims for hurt feelings.[3]

· · ·

---

3. The majority's new cause of action will surely suggest to even the less ingenious a vehicle for avoiding prior limitations on certain causes of actions. For instance, while we have not for some time recognized a cause for alienation of affections—an intentional tort—the net effect of today's judgment is to permit recovery for emotional distress and loss of consortium caused by even the negligent alienation of plaintiff's wife's affections by defendant. And in a case of slander where the plaintiff is unable to establish all conditions to recovery for this intentional tort, cannot he now obtain relief by alleging his mental tranquility was disturbed even negligently—by defendant's utterances?

NOTES

(1) Is there a limiting factor built into the liability rule applied in *Molien*? Does the majority respond adequately, or at all, to Justice Clark's argument about the need to "realistically" limit liability? What is there to keep such liability from going on "to the end of time"?

Is the biggest problem presented in the emotional distress cases one of keeping fraudulent claims to a minimum? Is a greater concern the number of valid claims that would consume judicial resources?

(2) Does the concept of directness of harm help to establish limits? Is there persuasive power in the majority's insistence that by contrast with the *Dillon* plaintiff, Mr. Molien "was himself a direct victim" of the defendant's negligence?

(3) Would you expect *Molien* to have serious negative effects on insurance markets for health care providers? Could this sort of risk be efficiently calculated by those who set insurance premiums?

(4) There is controversy about whether it is a tort for a physician to fail to disclose his HIV-positive status to patients on whom he performs invasive procedures. The Maryland Court of Appeals thought that a duty could be shown, at least during the "legitimate window of mental anxiety" during which patients might reasonably worry about whether the doctor had transmitted the virus to them. In a case involving two women on whom an infected doctor did breast cancer surgery, the court noted that with proper precautions, the risk of transmitting HIV was quite low, but it also pointed to the seriousness of the potential harm. In particular, it cited a provision in the AMA Code of Medical Ethics that said that "[a] physician who knows that he or she is [HIV] seropositive should not engage in any activity that creates a risk of transmission of the disease to others." The court concluded that it could not 'say "as a matter of law that no duty was imposed" on the doctor to warn the patients of his infection or to refrain from surgery. However, noting that then current evidence indicated a 95 percent certainty that HIV will turn up within six months of exposure, if at all, the court said that the plaintiffs could recover for their fear and its physical manifestations only "for the period constituting their reasonable window of anxiety," that is, "the period between which they learned of [the defendant's] illness and received ... HIV negative results," more than a year after their surgeries. *Faya v. Almaraz*, 329 Md. 435, 620 A.2d 327, 333–339 (1993).

In a contrasting decision, involving gynecological examinations by a physician infected with the HIV virus, the Minnesota Supreme Court refused to impose liability without allegations of "actual exposure to HIV." The court reasoned that without such allegations, a plaintiff was "not, as a matter of law, in personal physical danger of contracting HIV, and thus not within a zone of danger for purposes of establishing a claim for negligent infliction of emotional distress." *K.A.C. v. Benson*, 527 N.W.2d 553, 559 (Minn. 1995). In this case, after the defendant physician developed dermatitis on his hands and forearms, he learned that he had tested seropositive for HIV. Following that revelation, the defendant wore two pairs of gloves when caring for patients, in accord with the advice of the state medical board. After receiving that advice from the board, he performed two gynecological exams on the plaintiff. Within a few months of the second exam, the doctor died of AIDS-related complications. There were no findings of HIV seropositivity with respect to any of the more than 300 patients on whom the doctor had performed invasive procedures while wearing gloves. In granting summary judgment to the defendants, the court observed that the named plaintiff's "risk of contracting HIV was no more than a remote possibility." *Id.* at 558.

SPECIAL NOTE ON AN ACTOR'S RESPONSIBILITY FOR RELIGIOUSLY MOTIVATED BEHAVIOR BY ANOTHER

In an interesting case involving a plaintiff's mental state, the 16-year-old plaintiff, an ultraorthodox Jew, was serving as a summer camp counselor. She went with a male counselor to a ski lift that took them to the top of a mountain. On their return trip, the chair lift ceased operation while they were in the chair. Both testified that no one had advised them about the time that the lift would stop carrying passengers. There was evidence that the State of New York, owner of the ski lift, had been negligent in the placement of signs about closing time, in the absence of an attendant, and in leaving an 18-foot gap in a fence area traversed by the lift chairs.

Stranded in the chair, 20 to 25 feet above the ground, the plaintiff "became agitated, panicky and reached a stage of near hysteria." A Jewish law forbade "a woman to stay with a man in a place which is not available to a third person," and there was rabbinical testimony that the plaintiff would have interpreted her situation to fall within this prohibition. The rabbinical expert testified that the plaintiff "might go even to the lengths of jumping to her death to avoid violation" of this rule. With that prohibition in mind, and also faced with spending the night on a mountainside clad only in a cotton skirt, light blouse, and sneakers, the plaintiff "worked her way out of the chair to a position where she was holding onto the bottom of the chair." She remembered only that she next found herself on the ground, bloodied and in pain. She took a tortuous path to a phone, where she summoned aid for her companion.

The trial judge held for the plaintiff, concluding that the state's negligence was the "proximate cause of the injuries." It said that her "freedom from [contributory] negligence is even more evident when we consider her age, judgment, experience, and education," observing that "[t]he State's negligence placed this 16-year-old girl in an untenable position." *Friedman v. State*, 54 Misc. 2d 448, 282 N.Y.S.2d 858 (1967). The appellate division, which affirmed although reducing the plaintiff's damages, said that "negligence ... was clearly established, as was the claimant's freedom from contributory negligence; the latter without reference to the factor of moral compulsion ... upon which factor we do not pass." 31 App. Div. 2d 992, 297 N.Y.S.2d 850 (1969).

NOTES

(1) Wouldn't the result in *Friedman* have been the same if the night had been warm to the point of balminess? Wasn't the state in much the superior position to avoid this loss most cheaply? In its brief, the state conceded that "[d]eath above dishonor is admirable," but asked rhetorically, "Should that subject a property owner to liability simply because it occurs on his premises?" [*Honor on a Ski Lift*, TIME, Jan. 31, 1969, at 40.] How would you respond, as plaintiff's counsel?

(2) If the night had been warm, and Friedman had elected to remain in the chair, should she have been able to recover for emotional distress consequent on the guilt she felt at violating Jewish law? Ought it to make a difference if she had been on the expedition alone, and her distress was related only to being trapped in the chair all night long?

How can courts formulate standards that achieve consistency of results in such cases involving emotional distress?

(3) Courts have taken myriad approaches to the problem of a suicide alleged to have resulted from tortious conduct. At common law, the victim's intentional act is said to break the chain of causation. But section 455 of the *Second Restatement* carves out an exception when negligence induces delirium or insanity in the plaintiff or decedent, who consequently and irrationally fails to control an impulse to injure. Some courts have required an underlying intentional act by the defendant, more than mere negligence. One California court required the sort of "double duty" intent that characterizes intentional infliction of emotional distress, that is, not only that the defendant acted intentionally, but also that the defendant intended to cause harm. *Tate v. Canonica*, 180 Cal. App. 2d 898, 5 Cal. Rptr. 28 (1960). The Wyoming Supreme Court settled on a middle position, requiring underlying intentional and tortious conduct by the defendant. The court permitted a wrongful death claim to proceed against a man who had sexually abused his adult stepdaughter throughout her life, after she died from an overdose of a prescription drug that he had procured at her request. *R.D. v. W.H.*, 875 P.2d 26 (Wyo. 1994).

(4) A clerical employee wrote the words "brain tumor" on a Medicare claim form that came to the home of a woman who had been treated for lung cancer, but who did not, in fact, have a brain tumor. After reading what she took to be a diagnosis on the form, which her husband had left on a table, she became deeply depressed. A day and a half later, she hanged herself. Her husband won a verdict against the medical corporation that had sent the form, and a neurologist employed by the firm. The district court granted judgment n.o.v. on the ground that there was no submissible issue on "proximate causation," but the Eighth Circuit reversed. The appellate court cited expert testimony that the decedent's suicide "resulted from an irresistible impulse — the product of an impulse control disorder caused by her learning of the 'diagnosis' of [a] brain tumor." *Stafford v. Neurological Medicine, Inc.*, 811 F.2d 470 (8th Cir. 1987). Would it be helpful to characterize the central problem in this case as one of "proximate cause"? How would "proximate cause" relate to "causation in fact"? How would it relate to the "negligence issue"?

(5) Suppose that a worker's foreperson harasses the worker unmercifully, knowing of the worker's depressed condition. If the worker commits suicide, should the employer have to pay workers' compensation under statutory language that requires compensation for injury or death "arising in and out of the course of employment"?

[B] The Bystander Problem

THING v. LA CHUSA

California Supreme Court
771 P.2d 814, 257 Cal. Rptr. 865 (1989)

EAGLESON, JUSTICE.

The narrow issue presented by the parties in this case is whether the Court of Appeal correctly held that a mother who did not witness an accident in which an automobile struck and injured her child may recover damages from the negligent driver for the emotional distress she suffered when she arrived at the accident scene. The more important question this issue poses for the court, however, is whether the "guidelines" enunciated by this court in *Dillon v. Legg* (1968) 68 Cal.2d 728, 69 Cal.Rptr. 72, 441 P.2d 912, are adequate, or if they should be refined to create greater certainty in this area of the law.

Although terms of convenience identify the cause of action here as one for negligent infliction of emotional distress (NIED) and the plaintiff as a "bystander" rather than a "direct victim," the common law tort giving rise to plaintiffs' claim is negligence.... It is in that context that we consider the appropriate application of the concept of "duty" in an area that has long divided this court — recognition of the right of persons, whose only injury is emotional distress, to recover damages when that distress is caused by knowledge of the injury to a third person caused by the defendant's negligence. Although we again find ourselves divided, we shall resolve some of the uncertainty over the parameters of the NIED action, uncertainty that has troubled lower courts, litigants, and, of course insurers.

Upon doing so, we shall conclude that the societal benefits of certainty in the law, as well as traditional concepts of tort law, dictate limitation of bystander recovery of damages for emotional distress. In the absence of physical injury or impact to the plaintiff himself, damages for emotional distress should be recoverable only if the plaintiff: (1) is closely related to the injury victim; (2) is present at the scene of the injury-producing event at the time it occurs and is then aware that it is causing injury to the victim and, (3) as a result suffers emotional distress beyond that which would be anticipated in a disinterested witness.

I

On December 8, 1980, John Thing, a minor, was injured when struck by an automobile operated by defendant James V. La Chusa. His mother, plaintiff Maria Thing, was nearby, but neither saw nor heard the accident. She became aware of the injury to her son when told by her daughter that John had been struck by a car. She rushed to the scene where she saw her bloody and unconscious child, whom she believed was dead, lying in the roadway. Maria sued defendants, alleging that she suffered great emotional disturbance, shock, and injury to her nervous system as a result of these events, and that the injury to John and emotional distress she suffered were proximately caused by defendants' negligence.

The trial court granted defendants' motion for summary judgment, ruling that, as a matter of law, Maria could not establish a claim for negligent infliction of emotional distress because she did not contemporaneously and sensorily perceive the accident. Although prior decisions applying the guidelines suggested by this court in *Dillon v. Legg, supra*, 68 Cal.2d 728, 69 Cal.Rptr. 72, 441 P.2d 912, compelled the ruling of the trial court, the Court of Appeal reversed the judgment dismissing Maria's claim after considering the decision of this court in *Ochoa v. Superior Court* (1985) 39 Cal.3d 159, 216 Cal.Rptr. 661, 703 P.2d 1. The Court of Appeal reasoned that while Maria's argument, premised on *Molien v. Kaiser Foundation Hospitals* (1980) 27 Cal.3d 916, 167 Cal.Rptr. 831, 616 P.2d 813, that she was a direct victim of La Chusa's negligence, did not afford a basis for recovery, contemporaneous awareness of a sudden occurence causing injury to her child was not prerequisite to recovery under *Dillon*.

We granted review to consider whether *Ochoa* supports the holding of the Court of Appeal. We here also further define and circumscribe the circumstances in which the right to such recovery exists. To do so it is once again necessary to return to basic principles of tort law.

II
Emotional Distress as a Compensable Item of Damages in Intentional Torts

Although the theory of recovery in issue here is the tort of "negligence," recognition of emotional distress as a distinct item of damage for which recovery may be had even absent physical injury or impact is not limited to negligence actions. Indeed, recovery for intentional conduct that invades the individual's right to peace of mind was recognized long before such recovery was permitted in negligence actions. It is useful, therefore, to place emotional distress as a basis for a negligence action in perspective by briefly reviewing the development of common law recognition of a protectible interest in individual peace of mind—*i.e.*, the right to be free from socially unacceptable conduct that seriously affects another's peace of mind.

The range of mental or emotional injury subsumed within the rubric "emotional distress" and for which damages are presently recoverable "includes fright, nervousness, grief, anxiety, worry, mortification, shock, humiliation and indignity, as well as physical pain." ...

Express or implicit recognition that peace of mind warrants legal protection is found in recovery for emotional distress as an aggravation of damages sought under intentional tort theories. Initially, emotional distress was recognized simply as an item of damages in those actions. With few exceptions, causing mental distress did not itself create a right of action, and where mental distress alone exists the common law rarely permitted recovery of damages. ...

Possibly the first exception to that limitation existed in recovery for assault. ...

Emotional distress is also an accepted item of damage that may be recovered in actions for abuse of process ... ; false imprisonment ... ; libel..., and invasion of privacy. Here, too, recovery has not been limited to circumstances in which the mental distress is an aggravation of a physical injury or impact.

Recognition of emotional distress as a compensable injury when caused by an intentional tort carried with it a judgment that the defendant's conduct was sufficiently outrageous or unacceptable that an award of damages was justified to punish the tortfeasor and deter such conduct by others. This development led in turn to a focus on the nature of the defendant's conduct, rather than on identifying a traditional tort to justify recovery for infliction of emotional distress, and culminated in recognition of the tort now known as intentional infliction of emotional distress.

...

III

...

... [S]hortly before *Dillon*, in *Amaya v. Home Ice, Fuel & Supply Co., supra*, 59 Cal.2d 195, 29 Cal.Rptr. 33, 379 P.2d 512, the court had declined the opportunity to broaden the right to recover for emotional distress. *Amaya*, after confirming that the "impact rule" making a contemporaneous physical impact a prerequisite to recovery for negligently induced fright or shock was not applicable in California, held damages could not be recovered by persons outside the zone of danger created by the defendant's negligence even when that shock was reflected in physiological symptoms. ...

...

The *Amaya* view was short lived, however. Only five years later, the decision was overruled in *Dillon v. Legg*. ...

In *Dillon* itself, the issue was limited. The mother and sister of a deceased infant each sought damages for "great emotional disturbance and shock and injury to her nervous system" which had caused them great mental pain and suffering. Allegedly these injuries were caused by witnessing the defendant's negligently operated vehicle collide with and roll over the infant as she lawfully crossed a street. The mother was not herself endangered by the defendant's conduct. The sister may have been. The trial court had therefore granted the defendant's motion for judgment on the pleadings as to the mother, but had denied it with respect to the sister of the decedent. Faced with the incongruous result demanded by the "zone of danger" rule which denied recovery for emotional distress and consequent physical injury unless the plaintiff himself had been treated with injury, the court overruled *Amaya*.

Reexamining the concept of "duty" as applicable to the *Dillon* facts, the court now rejected the argument that the possibility of fraudulent claims justified denial of recovery, at least insofar as a mother who sees her child killed is concerned, as "no one can seriously question that fear or grief for one's child is as likely to cause physical injury as concern over one's own well-being." (*Dillon v. Legg, supra,* 68 Cal.2d 728, 736, 69 Cal.Rptr. 72, 441 P.2d 912.) The court held instead that the right to recover should be determined by application of "the neutral principles of foreseeability, proximate cause and consequential injury that generally govern tort law." (*Id.* at p. 737, 69 Cal.Rptr. 72, 441 P.2d 912.)

The difficulty in defining the limits on recovery anticipated by the *Amaya* court was rejected as a basis for denying recovery, but the court did recognize that "to limit the otherwise potentially infinite liability which would follow every negigent act, the law of torts holds defendant amenable only for injuries to others which to defendant at the time were reasonably foreseeable." (*Dillon, supra,* 68 Cal.2d at p. 739, 69 Cal.Rptr. 72, 441 P.2d 912.) Thus, while the court indicated that foreseeability of the injury was to be the primary consideration in finding duty, it simultaneously recognized that policy considerations mandated that infinite liability be avoided by restrictions that would somehow narrow the class of potential plaintiffs. But the test limiting liability was itself amorphous.[3]

---

3. Because a general duty exists to avoid causing foreseeable injury to another, the concept of "foreseeability" enters into both the willingness of the court to recognize the existence of a duty, the breach of which permits an action for damages, and into the determination by a trier of fact whether the specific injury in issue was foreseeable. The court explained the distinction in *Ballard v. Uribe* (1986) 41 Cal.3d 564, 573, footnote 6, 224 Cal.Rptr. 664, 715 P.2d 624:

[A] court's task—in determining "duty"—is not to decide whether a *particular* plaintiff's injury was reasonably foreseeable in light of a *particular* defendant's conduct, but rather to evaluate more generally whether the category of negligent conduct at issue is sufficiently likely to result in the kind of harm experienced that liability may appropriately be imposed on the negligent party.

The jury, by contrast, considers "foreseeability" in two more focused, fact-specific settings. First, the jury may consider the likelihood or foreseeability of injury in determining whether, in fact, the particular defendant's conduct was negligent in the first place. Second, foreseeability may be relevant to the jury's determination of whether the defendant's negligence was a proximate or legal cause of the plaintiff's injury.

In the present context, however, we are concerned not with whether an injury is "foreseeable" as a result of the negligent conduct. As the court recognized in *Dillon, supra,* 68 Cal.2d 728, 69 Cal.Rptr. 72, 441 P.2d 912, it is no less "foreseeable" that a person outside the "zone of danger" will suffer emotional distress on observing the injury of a close relative than it is that this person would suffer such distress if he or she were also threatened with injury. Thus, the court's role in deciding whether a "duty" to these persons should be recognized does not depend solely on the "foreseeability" of the emotional distress, but on these policy considerations.

In adopting foreseeability of the injury as the basis of a negligent actor's duty, the *Dillon* court identified the risks that could give rise to that duty as both physical impact and emotional disturbance brought on by the conduct. Having done so, the *Dillon* court conceded: "We cannot now predetermine defendant's obligation in every situation by a fixed category; no immutable rule can establish the extent of the obligation for every circumstance of the future." (68 Cal.2d at p. 740, 69 Cal.Rptr. 72, 441 P.2d 912.) In an effort to give some initial definition to this newly approved expansion of the cause of action for NIED the court enunciated "guidelines" that suggested a limitation on the action to circumstances like those in the case before it.

> We note, first, that we deal here with a case in which plaintiff suffered a shock which resulted in physical injury and we confine our ruling to that case. In determining, in such a case, whether defendant should reasonably foresee the injury to plaintiff [mother], or in other terminology, whether defendant owes plaintiff a duty of due care, the courts will take into account such factors as the following: (1) Whether plaintiff was located near the scene of the accident as contrasted with one who was a distance away from it. (2) Whether the shock resulted from a direct emotional impact upon plaintiff from the sensory and contemporaneous observance of the accident, as contrasted with learning of the accident from others after its occurence. (3) Whether plaintiff and the victim were closely related, as contrasted with an absence of any relationship or the presence of only a distant relationship.

> The evaluation of these factors will indicate the *degree* of the defendant's foreseeability; obviously defendant is more likely to foresee that a mother who observes an accident affecting her child will suffer harm than to foretell that a stranger witness will do so. Similarly, the degree of foreseeability of the third person's injury is far greater in the case of his contemporaneous observance of the accident than that in which he subsequently learns of it. The defendant is more likely to foresee that shock to the nearby, witnessing mother will cause physical harm than to anticipate that someone distant from the accident will suffer more than a temporary emotional reaction. All of these elements, of course, shade into each other; the fixing of the obligation, intimately tied into the facts, depends upon each case.

> In light of these factors the court will determine whether the accident and harm was *reasonably* foreseeable. Such reasonable foreseeability does not turn on whether the particular plaintiff [sic] as an individual would have in actuality foreseen the exact accident and loss; it contemplates that *courts, on a case-to-case basis, analyzing all the circumstances, will decide what the ordinary man under such circumstances should reasonably have foreseen.* The courts thus mark out the areas of liability, excluding the remote and unexpected.

(*Dillon, supra*.... Emphasis added.)

The *Dillon* court anticipated and accepted uncertainty in the short term in application of its holding, but was confident that the boundaries of this NIED action could be drawn in future cases. In sum, as former Justice Potter Stewart once suggested with reference to that undefinable category of materials that are obscene, the *Dillon* court was satisfied that trial and appellate courts would be able to determine the existence of a duty because the court would know it when it saw it. Underscoring the questionable validity of that assumption, however, was the obvious and unaddressed problem that the injured party, the negligent tortfeasor, their insurers, and their attorneys had no means short of suit by which to determine if a duty such as to impose liability for damages would be found in cases other than those that were "on all fours" with *Dillon*. Thus, the only thing that was foreseeable from the *Dillon* decision was the uncertainty that continues to this time as to the parameters of the third-party NIED action.

IV
Post-Dillon Extension

The expectation of the *Dillon* majority that the parameters of the tort would be further defined in future cases has not been fulfilled. Instead, subsequent decisions of the Courts of Appeal and this court, have created more uncertainty. And, just as the "zone of danger" limitation was abandoned in *Dillon* as an arbitrary restriction on recovery, the *Dillon* guidelines have been relaxed on grounds that they, too, created arbitrary limitations on recovery. Little consideration has been given in post-*Dillon* decisions to the importance of avoiding the limitless exposure to liability that the pure foreseeability test of "duty" would create and towards which these decisions have moved.

Several post-*Dillon* decisions of this court are particularly noteworthy in this expansive progression. In the first, *Krouse v. Graham* (1977) 19 Cal.3d 59, 137 Cal.Rptr. 863, 562 P.2d 1022, this court held that the NIED plaintiff need not "visually" perceive the third party injury to satisfy the *Dillon* guideline suggesting that the plaintiff suffer shock from "the sensory and contemporaneous observance of the accident, ..." It was sufficient that the plaintiff knew the position of his wife just outside the automobile in which he was seated that instant before she was struck by defendant's automobile which he had seen and realized was going to strike her. He was, therefore, a "percipient witness to the impact causing [her] injuries." (19 Cal.3d 59, 76, 137 Cal.Rptr. 863, 562 P.2d 1022.)

. . . .

Krouse, supra, 19 Cal,3d 59, 137 Cal.Rptr. 863, 562 P.2d 1022, was followed by *Justus v. Atchison* (1977) 19 Cal.3d 564, 139 Cal.Rptr. 97, 565 P.2d 122, in which the court identified the issue as whether the plaintiff fathers' causes of action for the emotional impact of observing the stillborn birth of their children satisfied the *Dillon* guideline of shock resulting from a direct emotional impact from the sensory and contemporaneous observance of an "accident." The court did not decide this question, ruling instead that the plaintiffs could not recover because neither had learned of the death of the fetus until informed by a doctor. Thus the "disabling shock" occurred only upon being informed by another of the injury. (19 Cal.3d 564, 585, 139 Cal.Rptr. 97, 565 P.2d 122.) By implication, however, it seemed that the injury producing event need not be a sudden occurrence or accident.

However, the court in *Hoyem v. Manhattan Beach City Sch. Dist.* (1978) 22 Cal.3d 508, 523, 150 Cal.Rptr. 1, 585 P.2d 851, reaffirmed the requirement that the shock or emotional distress necessary to a cause of action for NIED under *Dillon* must "result from a 'direct emotional impact' on the plaintiff caused by 'sensory and contemporaneous observance of the accident.'"

. . .

Both the physical harm and accident or sudden occurrence elements were eliminated, however, in *Molien v. Kaiser Foundation Hospitals, supra*, 27 Cal.3d 916, 167 Cal.Rptr. 831, 616 P.2d 813, at least as to those plaintiffs who could claim to be "direct victims" of the defendant's negligence....

In finding the existence of a duty to the husband of the patient, the court reasoned that the risk of harm to the husband was reasonably foreseeable, and that the tortious conduct was directed to him as well as the patient. (*Molien v. Kaiser Foundation Hospitals, supra,* 27 Cal.3d 916, 922, 167 Cal.Rptr. 831, 616 P.2d 813.) The status of the plaintiff mother in *Dillon* was distinguished as she suffered her injury solely as a "percipient witness" to the infliction of injury on another. She was therefore a "bystander" rather than a "direct victim."

The court did not further explain this distinction, or its relevance to whether the plaintiff should be allowed to recover damages for emotional distress. Both decisions had looked to the relationships of the parties to find foreseeability of the injury and thus a "duty to the plaintiff." The basis for finding a duty to the mother in Dillon was the foreseeability of her emotional distress to "the negligent driver who causes the death of a young child [and] may reasonably expect that the mother will not be far distant and will upon witnessing the accident suffer emotional trauma." (*Dillon v. Legg, supra* ...). In *Molien*, "[t]he risk of harm to plaintiff was reasonably foreseeable to defendants. It is easily predictable that an erroneous diagnosis of syphilis and its probable source would produce marital discord and resultant emotional distress to a married patient's spouse; [the physician's] advice to Mrs. Molien to have her husband examined for the disease confirms that plaintiff [husband] was a foreseeable victim of the negligent diagnosis.... [¶] We thus agree with plaintiff that the alleged tortious conduct of defendant was directed to him as well as to his wife. Because the risk of harm to him was reasonably foreseeable we hold ... that under these circumstances defendants owed plaintiff a duty to exercise due care in diagnosing the physical condition of his wife." ...

Molien neither established criteria for characterizing a plaintiff as a "direct" victim, nor explained the justification for permitting "direct" victims to recover when "bystander" plaintiffs could not. The immediate effect of the decision, however, was to permit some persons who had no prior relationship with the defendant that gave rise to a duty, who did not suffer physical injury as a result of emotional distress, who did not observe the negligent conduct, and who had not been at or near the scene of the negligent act to recover for emotional distress on a pure foreseeability-of-the injury basis. The limitations on recovery for emotional distress that had been suggested in the *Dillon* "guidelines" were not applicable to "direct" victims of a defendant's negligence.

The subtleties in the distinction between the right to recover as a "bystander" and as a "direct victim" created what one Court of Appeal has described as an "amorphous nether realm"....

••••

Cases subsequent to *Molien* assumed that the reasoning which led the court to abandon the physical-injury requirement extended to "bystander" NIED actions. Physical manifestation of the serious nature of the mental distress suffered by the plaintiff was no longer an element of the cause of action. (*See Ochoa v. Superior Court, supra,* 39 Cal.3d 159, 216 Cal.Rptr. 661, 703 P.2d 1....)

•••

Ochoa v. Superior Court ... partially explained and limited "direct victim" recovery under *Molien* ... to situations in which the defendant's negligence is "by its very nature directed at" the plaintiff. However, *Ochoa* also indicated that the dimensions of the NIED tort might be expanded further for "bystander" plaintiffs. *Ochoa* confirmed that recovery was permitted even though the injury producing event was not sudden or accidental, and even though its negligent cause was not immediately apparent. The court observed that the factors set forth in *Dillon* had been offered only as guidelines, and suggested that none was essential to recovery for NIED. Foreseeability that the injury would cause emotional distress was the proper inquiry....

The dictum in *Ochoa* was broader than the issue presented in *Ochoa*, however. The plaintiff mother had observed the effects of the defendants' negligent failure to diagnose and properly treat the illness of her teenage son. Her observation of his pain and suffering, and his deteriorating condition, as the defendants failed to either properly care for him or accede to her entreaty that she be permitted to obtain care for him, was the cause of the emotional distress for which she sought to recover. The allegations of the complaint satisfied only two of the *Dillon* factors—she was at the scene of the negligent injury producing conduct and was closely related to the person whose physical injury caused her distress. Defendants' negligence in failing to give proper medical treatment, however, was not a sudden accidental occurrence and thus the second *Dillon* factor was not met: "Whether the shock resulted from a direct emotional impact upon plaintiff from the sensory and contemporaneous observance of the accident, ..."(*Dillon v. Legg, supra*, 68 Cal.2d 728, 740–741, 69 Cal.Rptr. 72, 441 P.2d 912.)

This court, after reviewing several decisions of the Courts of Appeal which had limited recovery for NIED to percipient witnesses of a "sudden occurrence," held that this requirement was an unwarranted restriction on the cause of action authorized in *Dillon*. "Such a restriction arbitrarily limits liability when there is a high degree of foreseeability of shock flows from an abnormal event, and, as such, unduly frustrates the goal of compensation—the very purpose which the cause of action was meant to further." (*Ochoa ... supra....*)

Ochoa also held that the NIED plaintiff need not be aware that the conduct was "tortious." Reasoning that such a requirement leads to anomalous results, the court held that "when there is observation of the defendant's conduct and the child's injury and contemporaneous awareness the defendant's conduct or lack thereof is causing harm to the child, recovery is permitted." (*Ochoa v. Superior Court, supra*, 39 Cal.3d 159, 170, 216 Cal.Rptr. 661, 703 P.2d 1.) Thus, the plaintiff in that case did not have to know that the defendants had negligently misdiagnosed her son. It was enough that she knew that they were refusing or neglecting to give him additional treatment and this was the cause of the additional injury he was suffering.

In sum, however, as to "bystander" NIED actions, *Ochoa* held only that recovery would be permitted if the plaintiff observes both the defendant's conduct and the resultant injury, and is aware at that time that the conduct is causing the injury. The Court of Appeal erred in concluding that *Ochoa ...* held that these NIED plaintiffs need not witness the defendant's conduct.

V

Clarification of Right to Recover for NIED

...

Ochoa ... offers additional guidance, justifying what we acknowledge must be arbitrary lines to similarly limit the class of potential plaintiffs if emotional injury absent physical harm is to continue to be a recoverable item of damages in a negligence action. The impact of personally observing the injury-producing event in most, although concededly not all cases distinguishes the plaintiff's resultant emotional distress from the emotion felt when one learns of the injury or death of a loved one from another, or observes pain and suffering but not the traumatic cause of the injury. Greater certainty and a more reasonable limit on the exposure to liability for negligent conduct is possible by limiting the right to recover for negligently caused emotional distress to plaintiffs who personally and contemporaneously perceive the injury-producing event and its traumatic consequences.

Similar reasoning justifies limiting recovery to persons closely related by blood or marriage since, in common experience, it is more likely that they will suffer a greater degree of emotional distress than a disinterested witness to negligently caused pain and suffering or death. Such limitations are indisputably arbitrary since it is foreseeable that in some cases unrelated persons have a relationship to the victim or are so affected by the traumatic event that they suffer equivalent emotional distress. As we have observed, however, drawing arbitrary lines is unavoidable if we are to limit liability and establish meaningful rules for application by litigants and lower courts.

No policy supports extension of the right to recover for NIED to a larger class of plaintiffs. Emotional distress is an intangible condition experienced by most persons, even absent negligence, at some time during their lives. Close relatives suffer serious, even debilitating, emotional reactions to the injury, death, serious illness, and evident suffering of loved ones. These reactions occur regardless of the cause of the loved one's illness, injury, or death. That relatives will have severe emotional distress in an unavoidable aspect of the "human condition." The emotional distress for which monetary damages may be recovered, however, ought not to be that form of acute emotional distress or the transient emotional reaction to the occasional gruesome or horrible incident to which every person may potentially be exposed in an industrial and sometimes violent society. Regardless of the depth of feeling or the resultant physical or mental illness that results from witnessing violent events, persons unrelated to those injured or killed may not now recover for such emotional upheaval even if negligently caused. Close relatives who witness the accidental injury or death of a loved one and suffer emotional trauma may not recover when the loved one's conduct was the cause of that emotional trauma. The overwhelming majority of "emotional distress" which we endure, therefore, is not compensable.

Unlike an award of damages for intentionally caused emotional distress which is punitive, the award for NIED simply reflects society's belief that a negligent actor bears some responsibility for the effect of his conduct on persons other than those who suffer physical injury. In identifying those persons and the circumstances in which the defendant will be held to redress the injury, it is appropriate to restrict recovery to those persons who will suffer an emotional impact beyond the impact that can be anticipated whenever one learns that a relative is injured, or dies, or the emotion felt by a "disinterested" witness. The class of potential plaintiffs should be limited to those who because of their relationship suffer the greatest emotional distress. When the right to recover is limited in this manner, the liability bears a reasonable relationship to the culpability of the negligent defendant.

The elements which justify and simultaneously limit an award of damages for emotional distress caused by awareness of the negligent infliction of injury to a close relative are those noted in *Ochoa*—the traumatic emotional effect on the plaintiff who contemporaneously observes both the event or conduct that causes serious injury to a close relative and the injury itself. Even if it is "foreseeable" that persons other than closely related percipient witnesses may suffer emotional distress, this fact does not justify the imposition of what threatens to become unlimited liability for emotional distress on a defendant whose conduct is simply negligent. Nor does such abstract "foreseeability" warrant continued reliance on the assumption that the limits of liability will become any clearer if lower courts are permitted to continue approaching the issue on a "case-to-case" basis some 20 years after *Dillon*.

We conclude, therefore, that a plaintiff may recover damages for emotional distress caused by observing the negligently inflicted injury of a third person if, but only if, said plaintiff: (1) is closely related to the injury victim; (2) is present at the scene of the injury producing event at the time it occurs and is then aware that it is causing injury to the victim;[11] and (3) as a result suffers serious emotional distress—a reaction beyond that which would be anticipated in a disinterested witness and which is not an abnormal response to the circumstances. These factors were present in *Ochoa* and each of this court's prior decisions upholding recovery for NIED.

The dictum in *Ochoa* suggesting that the factors noted in the *Dillon* guidelines are not essential in determining whether a plaintiff is a foreseeable victim of defendant's negligence should not be relied on. The merely negligent actor does not owe a duty the law will recognize to make monetary amends to all persons who may have suffered emotional distress on viewing or learning about the injurious consequences of his conduct.... Experience has shown that, contrary to the expectation of the *Dillon* majority, and with apology to Bernard Witkin, there are clear judicial days on which a court can foresee forever and thus determine liability but none on which that foresight alone provides a socially and judicially acceptable limit on recovery of damages for that injury.

VI
Disposition

The undisputed facts establish that plaintiff was not present at the scene of the accident in which her son was injured. She did not observe defendant's conduct and was not aware that her son was being injured. She could not, therefore, establish a right to recover for the emotional distress she suffered when she subsequently learned of the accident and observed its consequences. The order granting summary judgment was proper.

The judgment of the Court of Appeal is reversed.

....

LUCAS, C.J. and PANELLI and ARGUELLES, J.J., concur.

[Omitted is the concurrence of Justice Kaufman, who argued for the reinstatement of the *Amaya* rule, see part III of Justice Eagleson's majority opinion, supra, and said that the plaintiff in *Thing* could not recover because she "was indisputably not within the zone of danger and could not assert a claim for emotional distress as the result of fear for her *own* safety."]

---

11. Once the rhetoric of the dissent has been pierced, it is clear that the dissent, too, recognizes that foreseeability of injury cannot be the sole test of liability, and that the court must ultimately define the limits of liability. While not forthrightly acknowledging the inescapable necessity of limits that will in some cases seem arbitrary, the dissent itself suggests a different, but no less arbitrary, limit—that the plaintiff may recover if he or she witnesses the "immediate" consequences of the third party injury (why stop there? Is that a less arbitrary line?). It is obvious, moreover, that the difficulty in defining the parameters of the line espoused by the dissent has been the cause of further arbitrariness in the irreconcilable rulings of trial courts and the conflicting appellate rulings on cases in which the factual differences offer little or no meaningful distinctions.

The dissent's suggestion that *Rowland v. Christian* (1968) 69 Cal.2d 108, 112–113, 70 Cal.Rptr. 97, 443 P.2d 561, should extend to actions for negligent infliction of emotional distress lacks support in our decisions. Neither *Rowland v. Christian* nor the other cases cited by the dissent (*Tarasoff v. Regents of University of California* (1976) 17 Cal.3d 425, 131 Cal.Rptr. 14, 551 P.2d 334; *J'Aire Corp. v. Gregory* (1979) 24 Cal.3d 799, 157 Cal.Rptr. 407, 598 P.2d 60; *Sun 'n Sand, Inc. v. United California Bank* (1978) 21 Cal.3d 671, 148 Cal.Rptr. 329, 582 P.2d 920; *Weirum v. RKO General Inc.* (1975) 15 Cal.3d 40, 123 Cal.Rptr. 468, 539 P.2d 36) are cases in which damages for negligently inflicted emotional distress were in issue. Recovery for this type of damage, when no other injury is present, has never been subject only to the general principles of foreseeability applied in *Rowland v. Christian* that the dissent would have us adopt here as the basis of liability.

MOSK, JUSTICE, dissenting.

I am in general agreement with the dissent of Justice Broussard. I write separately to point out my other areas of disagreement with the majority opinion.

...

... [T]he majority recite a monotonous inventory of cases with which they find fault. For the past three decades apparently all the courts in tort cases have been out of step except the current majority.

Krouse v. Graham (1977) 19 Cal.3d 59, 137 Cal.Rptr. 863, 562 P.2d 1022, is high on their list as the source of the "roots of the uncertainty reflected by the instant case." Yet the facts in Krouse caused little controversy. Justice Richardson declared for a court unanimous on the point: "the *Dillon* requirement of 'sensory and contemporaneous observance of the accident' does not require a *visual* perception of the impact causing the death or injury. In the matter before us, although [the husband] did not see [his wife] struck by defendant's automobile, he fully perceived the fact that she had been so struck, for he knew her position an instant before the impact, observed defendant's vehicle approach her at a high speed on a collision course, and realized that defendant's car must have struck her. Clearly, under such circumstances [the husband] must be deemed a percipient witness to the impact causing [the wife's] catastrophic injuries." (*Id.* at p. 76, 137 Cal.Rptr. 863, 562 P.2d 1022.)

As Justice Richardson perceptively noted, *Dillon* called for sensory observance of the accident. That means all of the senses, not merely visual perception. The husband in *Krouse* was at the scene, heard the impact, and was himself seriously injured in the accident. How that case can be said to cause the "roots of uncertainty," complained of by the majority, is difficult to comprehend.

...

The next criticism of the majority is directed to *Justus v. Atchinson* (1977), 19 Cal. 3d 564, 139 Cal.Rptr. 97, 565 P.2d 122. Theirs is a strange comment, for in *Justus* the court found no liability. While the plaintiff was in the delivery room, he was shielded from observing the death of the fetus and did not learn the fact until told later by a physician. As we said, "he had been admitted to the theater but the drama was being played on a different stage." (*Id.* at p. 584, 139 Cal.Rptr. 97, 565 P.2d 122.)

...

Some big guns are leveled at *Molien v. Kaiser Foundation Hospitals...*, but they miss the target because of misunderstanding the relevant facts in *Molien*. After giving the wife a physical examination defendant incorrectly and negligently diagnosed her as having syphilis. As a consequence she was directed by the physician to require her husband to undergo physical tests to ascertain if he was the source of her purported infection. Those negligent acts by the physician as to both husband and wife were clearly physical in nature.

Why the majority seem to have some trouble with *Molien* limiting recovery to the "direct victim" of the doctor's negligence is perplexing. To assure that recovery could not be claimed by an indirect victim or a mere casual bystander, the *Molien* court very strictly limited recovery to only a person who was directly and physically affected by the defendant's negligence. In that instance it could be only the wife who was *physically* examined and the husband who was instructed to be *physically* examined. The court made it abundantly clear that "the alleged tortious conduct of defendant was directed to [the husband] as well as to his wife." ... Thus both were direct victims.

That the majority fail to understand *Molien* is underscored by their comment that the parties did not suffer physical injury. The brutal fact is that the defendant committed malpractice in negligently diagnosing the wife in a physical examination as having a serious venereal disease and in directing the husband to undergo a physical examination. I cannot be as casual as the majority in concluding there is no physical aspect to negligent examinations for syphilis. Not physical? Do they believe such examinations are conducted over the telephone?

. . .

The majority next offer lengthy criticism of *Ochoa v. Superior Court.* . . . *Ochoa* understood *Molien* clearly: "In *Molien* defendant's misdiagnosis was, by its very nature directed at both the wife and the husband." . . . However, the *Ochoa* court found in that case "the duty was owed to [the child's mother] as a percipient witness, not as a direct victim of negligence." . . . Such a holding was consistent with *Dillon's* requirements. . . .

. . .

I disagree with the majority opinion not merely for its conclusion—although I concur with Justice Broussard in that respect—but with its wholesale criticism of past opinions of this court and of the Courts of Appeal, some prevailing for three decades. Such callous disregard for the doctrine of stare decisis does not constructively serve the judicial process, nor does it contribute to the guidance of the bench and bar. As Justice Cardozo wrote in The Nature of the Judicial Process (1921) page 34, "Adherence to precedent must . . . be the rule rather than the exception if litigants are to have faith in the even-handed administration of justice in the courts."

BROUSSARD, JUSTICE, dissenting.

I dissent.

"[T]he problem [of negligent infliction of emotional distress] should be solved by the application of the principles of tort, not by the creation of exceptions to them. Legal history shows that artificial islands of exceptions, created from the fear that the legal process will not work, usually do not withstand the waves of reality and, in time, descend into oblivion."

(*Dillon v. Legg* (1968) 68 Cal.2d 728, 747, 69 Cal.Rptr. 72, 441 P.2d 912 [Tobriner, J., admonishing this court not to do what the majority do today].)

The majority grope for a "bright line" rule for negligent infliction of emotional distress actions, only to grasp an admittedly arbitrary line which will deny recovery to victims whose injuries from the negligent acts of others are very real. In so doing, the majority reveal a myopic reading of *Dillon v. Legg, supra,* 68 Cal.2d 728, 69 Cal.Rptr. 72, 441 P.2d 912. They impose a strict requirement that plaintiff be present at the scene of the injury-producing event at the time it occurs and is aware that it is causing injury to the victim. This strict requirement rigidifies what *Dillon* forcefully told us should be a flexible rule, and will lead to arbitrary results. I would follow the mandate of *Dillon* and maintain that foreseeability and duty determine liability, with a view toward a policy favoring reasonable limitations on liability. There is no reason why these general rules of tort law should not apply to negligent infliction of emotional distress actions.

I.

. . .

The majority ignore the fundamental mandate of *Dillon* to consider foreseeability and duty in finding liability. Their only justification for this and a strict rule that will limit liability at the cost of arbitrary results is an amorphous "policy" one. They ironically use the term "amorphous" to describe the concepts of foreseeabiity and duty and state that "[i]n the present context, however, we are concerned *not* with whether an injury is "foreseeable" as a result of the negligent conduct.... [T]he court's role in deciding whether a "duty" to these persons should be recognized *does not depend* solely on the "foreseeability" of the emotional distress, but on these policy considerations." (Maj. opn. at pp. 870–871, fn. 3 of 257 Cal.Rptr., at pp. 819–820, fn. 3 of 771 P.2d, italics added.) "[I]t is clear that foreseeability of the injury alone is *not* a useful "guideline" or a meaningful restriction on the scope of the NIED action.... [¶] [P]olicy considerations justify restrictions on recovery for emotional distress notwithstanding the sometimes *arbitrary result*, and that the court has an obligation to establish those restrictions." (Maj. opn. at p. 878 of 257 Cal.Rptr., at p. 827 of 771 P.2d, italics added.) The majority admit their "policy" reasons are only a balance of "arbitrary lines which deny recovery to some victims whose injury is very real against that of imposing liability out of proportion to culpability for negligent acts," with a view to the "administration of justice of clear guidelines." (*Id.*)

For these reasons, the majority impose the strict requirement that plaintiff be present at the scene of the injury producing event at the time it occurs and is then aware that it is causing injury to the victim. They freely admit to "drawing arbitrary lines" but complain that it is "unavoidable if we are to limit liability and establish meaningful rules for application by litigants and lower courts." (Maj. opn. at p. 879 of 257 Cal.Rptr., at p.828 of 771 P.2d.) Thus what in *Dillon* were guidelines to assist courts in assessing liability become a tripartite test, which includes the above-mentioned strict and arbitrary requirement, and displaces the consideration of foreseeability.

Under the majority's strict requirement, a mother who arrives moments after an accident caused by another's negligence will not be permitted recovery. No matter that the mother would see her six-year-old son immediately after he was electrocuted, lying in a puddle of water in a dying state, gagging and choking in his own vomit, as in *Hathaway v. Superior Court* (1980) 112 Cal.App.3d 728, 169 Cal.Rptr. 435. No matter that the mother would be following her daughters' car "before the dust had settled" to find the mangled bodies of her daughters, who were dead or dying, as in *Parsons v. Superior Court* (1978) 81 Cal.App.3d 506, 509, 146 Cal.Rptr. 495.

The answer to the question of how this court should limit liability does not lie in the majority's rigid application of *Dillon* and the toleration of arbitrary results that will flow therefrom. As the Wyoming Supreme Court suggested, in *Gates v. Richardson* (1986 Wyo.) 719 P.2d 193, the nature of the shock to be compensated requires a realistic approach to the contemporaneous-perception factor: "It is more than the shock one suffers when he learns of the death or injury of a child, sibling or parent over the phone, from a witness, or at the hospital. It is more than bad news. The kind of shock the tort requires is the result of the immediate aftermath of an accident. It may be the crushed body, the bleeding, the cries of pain, and in some cases, the dying words which are really a continuation of the event. The immediate aftermath may be more shocking than the actual impact ..." (*Gates, supra,* at p. 199....) The court there held that a close relative generally should be permitted recovery if she "observed the serious bodily harm or death shortly after its occurrence but without material change in the condition and location of the victim." (*Gates, supra,* 719 P.2d at p. 199....)

The majority's strict requirement does not simply comprise a "bright line" rule that rationally limits liability. It is arbitrary and will lead to unjust results. *Dillon* condemned the "hopeless artificiality" that the majority propounds, and decried the "artificial abstractions which bar recovery contrary to the general rules" of tort law. The requirement is exactly the "mechanical rules of thumb" that *Dillon* explicitly admonished us not to create. We should follow *Dillon* and its progeny and maintain the rational and traditional rule that reasonable foreseeability is the basis for determining liability...."In order to limit the otherwise potentially infinite liability which would follow every negligent act, the law of torts holds defendant amenable only for injuries to others which to defendant at the time were *reasonably foreseeable.*" (*Id....*) As *Dillon* instructed, there is "no good reason why the general rules of tort law, including the concepts of negligence, proximate cause, and foreseeability, long applied to all other types of injury, should not govern the case now before us." ... *Dillon's* test of reasonable foreseeability "facilitates rational risk spreading and correlates liability with the risks that the defendant should expect." ...

II

Of course I share the majority's policy concern that tortfeasors not face *unlimited* liability for their negligent acts. As stated above, the *Dillon* court recognized foreseeability as a general limit on tort liability. The court stated that the purpose of the three guidelines was actually to limit a defendant's liability to "injuries to others which to defendant at the time were reasonably foreseeable." ...

Although I disagree with the majority's method of placing undue and what appears to be almost total reliance on a policy rationale, the Dillon guidelines also attempt to implement public policy in favor of reasonable limitations on liability.... The *Dillon* court did not intend the guidelines to be exclusive ... and it specifically reserved the questions of "whether, in the absence or reduced weight of some of the [three listed] factors, we would conclude that the accident and injury were not reasonably foreseeable and that therefore defendant owed no duty of care to plaintiff." (*Id.* at p. 741, 69 Cal.Rptr. 72, 441 P.2d 912).

To determine whether defendants owed plaintiff a duty of care in this case, I think it is fruitful to reexamine the second *Dillon* guideline in light of *Rowland v. Christian* (1968) 69 Cal.2d 108, 70 Cal.Rptr. 97, 443 P.2d 561, our leading case defining a defendant's duty of care. In *Rowland*, decided just two months after *Dillon*, we held that in the absence of a statutory exception to the legislative mandate that all persons are liable for injuries caused by failure to exercise due care (Civ. Code, § 1714, subd. (a)), "no such exception should be made unless clearly supported by public policy. [Citations.] [¶] A departure from this fundamental principle involves the balancing of a number of considerations; the major ones are the foreseeability of harm to the plaintiff, the degree of certainty that the plaintiff suffered injury, the closeness of the connection between the defendant's conduct, the policy of preventing future harm, the extent of the burden to the defendant and consequences to the community of imposing a duty to exercise care with resulting liability for breach, and the availability, cost, and prevalence of insurance for the risk involved." (*Rowland, supra....*)

While our cases defining a bystander's cause of action for negligent infliction of emotional distress consistently emphasize the first of the *Rowland* factors—foreseeability of harm to plaintiff—discussion of the others has been limited. The second, fourth, and fifth factors may be disposed of quickly: certainty of injury is usually a jury question, particularly since we no longer require physical manifestations of mental distress ... ; moral blame almost always militates in favor of recovery; and the policy of preventing future harm favors the plaintiff, but only slightly since, in most cases, any

Dillon claim is simply added to the primary victim's complaint. The third, sixth and seventh factors, however, merit more discussion.

This court has emphasized the importance of the third *Rowland* factor — nexus between defendant's conduct and the risk of injury — in establishing limitations on recovery. In *J'Aire Corp. v. Gregory* (1979) 24 Cal.3d 799, 808, 157 Cal.Rptr. 407, 598 P.2d 60, we stated that case law "place[s] a limit on recovery by focusing judicial attention on the foreseeability of the injury and the nexus between the defendant's conduct and the plaintiff's injury." There, we limited recovery for the tort of negligent interference with economic advantage "to instances where the *risk of harm* is foreseeable and is *closely connected with the defendant's conduct,* where damages are not wholly speculative and the injury is not part of the plaintiff's ordinary business risk." ...

The sixth and seventh *Rowland* factors — the burden on the defendant and the community, and the cost and availability of insurance — also merit further evaluation. *Amici curiae*[2] contend that recovery in this case would mark an unwarranted expansion of *Dillon,* resulting in a new category of plaintiffs, fewer settlements, higher administrative costs and premiums, delays in payment, increased litigation, and higher awards. *Amici* insist that *Dillon's* second guideline should be applied strictly, as a prerequisite for recovery. Apparently they have convinced the majority since the majority approvingly quote the reasoning in *Borer v. American Airlines, Inc.* (1977) 19 Cal.3d 441, 447, 138 Cal.Rptr. 302, 563 P.2d 858: "We reasoned that we could not ignore the social burden of providing damages ... merely because the money to pay such awards comes initially from the 'negligent' defendant or his insurer. Realistically the burden ... must be borne by the public generally in increased insurance premiums or, otherwise, in the enhanced danger that accrues from the greater number of people who may choose to go without any insurance. We must also take into account the cost of administration of a system to determine and pay [the] awards; ..." (Maj. opn. at p. 878 of 257 Cal.Rptr., at p. 827 of 771 P.2d.)

The authorities upon which *amici* rely do not persuade me that *Dillon* has significantly contributed to any substantial increase in litigation and insurance premiums. Nor do I find any indication that other jurisdictions are retreating from *Dillon.* ... As the *Dillon* court responded to the contention that otherwise meritorious claims should be barred out of fear of increases in number of suits and of fraudulent claims: "'[We] should be sorry to adopt a rule which would bar all such claims on grounds of policy alone, and in order to prevent the possible success of unrighteous or groundless actions. Such a course involves the denial of redress in meritorious cases, and it necessarily implies a certain degree of distrust, which [we] do not share, in the capacity of legal tribunals to get at the truth in this class of claim.'" ...

III

....

The majority charge that, as former Supreme Court Justice Potter Stewart once said about obscenity, the *Dillon* guidelines mistakenly assumed that a court would know "duty" when it saw it. But more appropriate to the majority's opinion and the arbitrary

---

2. Their brief was submitted by the National Association of Independence Insurers, the Association of California Insurance Companies, and the American Insurance Association.

and unjust results it will soon engender is what Potter Stewart said, very simply, upon being appointed to the United States Supreme Court: "Fairness is what justice really is." (*The Young Justice* (Oct. 20, 1958) Time, at p. 24.)

NOTES

(1) How should a court relate foreseeability to duty in a case like *Thing*?

Are foreseeability and "policy" necessarily opposed to each other in the analysis of such cases, or can they be harmonized?

(2) If one wishes to focus on policy considerations in the effort to place sensible limits on liability in bystander-type cases, on which policies should one focus?

    (a) Is control of primary conduct at all relevant in such a case? Are the bystander rules likely to affect the behavior of drivers, or others who engage in activities carrying the risk of injury to third parties and to persons who may witness, or otherwise be affected by, those injuries?

    (b) If "[f]airness is what justice really is," what are the elements of fairness in *Thing*?

(3) Will the decision in *Thing* insure that "like cases will be treated alike" to a significantly greater degree than under the *Dillon* rule? Will whatever gains are achieved in that regard outweigh the losses to "justice" created by the limitations that *Thing* places on *Dillon*? What are the contributions to "justice" of *Dillon* that are foregone by the decision in *Thing*?

(4) One commentator suggests a test for NIED that would broaden recovery for "direct victims," defined as those injured when "the defendant's act or omission adversely affects the victim's sense of personal safety or personal interests," excluding from "personal "interests" the "interest in the well-being of others." Robert J. Rhee, *A Principled Solution for Negligent Infliction of Emotional Distress Claims*, 35 ARIZ. ST. L.J. 805, 854 (2004). For these victims, claims for mental injury "can be evaluated under generally accepted tort principles of duty, proximate cause and damage." *Id.* at 866. By contrast, the author would stringently limit recovery for "collateral victims," that is, people "injured where the defendant's conduct results in death or injury to another, and such death or injury is either witnessed by or communicated to the victim." *Id.* at 855. For this class of victims, there should be recovery "only if the defendant's conduct is reckless or more, and damages should be limited to economic loss." *Id.* at 866. The author's "central thesis" focuses on "a relationship between culpability and the different interests of the plaintiff," and he suggests that his proposal "exposes a defendant to liability only if her conduct is commensurate with the risks imposed on the plaintiff's various interests." *Id.* at 867.

(5) The question of whether duty extends to unmarried cohabitants who witness fatal accidents to partners will doubtless provoke controversy across the country. The year before *Thing*, the California court said no in *Elden v. Sheldon*, 46 Cal. 3d 267, 758 P.2d 582, 586–88 (1988), citing the need for a "bright line" rule to limit liability as well as emphasizing "the state's interest in promoting the marriage relationship." But the New Jersey Supreme Court thought that there was enough of a relationship to support a duty, with respect to an engaged couple who had been cohabiting for more than two years before the accident that killed one of them. The court required, as a prerequisite for recovery, that "[t]he harm precipitating emotional distress must be so severe that it destroys the emotional security derived from a relationship that is deep, enduring, and

intimate." The court thought that people in such a relationship have a "cognizable interest in the continued mutual emotional well-being derived from their relationship." It declared that to allow recovery in the context of such a relationship would not "discourage marriage as a worthwhile and desirable relationship or erode society's commitment to the institution of marriage." *Dunphy v. Gregor*, 136 N.J. 99, 642 A.2d 372, 377–80 (1994).

(6) Argument will also continue about who qualifies as a bystander witness, but it seems clear that one who learns on the telephone of the disappearance of a family member from a medical facility, which allegedly was negligent in observance of nursing standards and the provision of security, cannot claim a duty. In *Ahn v. Kim*, 145 N.J. 423, 678 A.2d 1073 (1996), the plaintiff's deeply depressed husband disappeared from a clinic within six hours of his admission there as a voluntary patient. He was never found, and was declared legally dead five years later. Denying his widow's suit for NIED, the court pointed out that she had not witnessed "either the alleged negligence of the [clinic] staff or the death or disappearance of her husband." It pointed out, moreover, that "[g]enerally, a hospital is not liable to a patient's family members for negligent injury to a patient." 678 A.2d at 1080.

Should medical facilities be liable for emotional consequences to family members who witness the injury or death of a patient resulting from negligence? What would be the principal arguments for allowing, or barring, such a suit?

(7) In a products liability case, a steering column locked on a boat, with the result that the boat circled in the water and struck a water skier, a close friend of the boat owner's daughter. There was evidence that the mutilated victim was treated as a "filial member" of the family and that both the boat owner and her daughter, who was in the boat at the time, suffered overwhelming emotional disturbance as a result of the incident. Could you justify recovery for the boat owner and her daughter, in a principled way?

§ 12.05 Rescuers and Firefighters

DAY v. WAFFLE HOUSE, INC.
Oklahoma Court of Appeals
743 P.2d 1111 (1987)

BAILEY, JUDGE.

This case comes on for review of the Trial Court's grant of Appellee's motion for summary judgment on Appellant's cause of action, which determined the case. Appellant Susan Day (Appellant or Day) and her friend, Freddie Farris, went to Appellee Waffle House restaurant (Appellee or Restaurant) for a meal. Freddie went into the restaurant and ordered his meal, while Appellant went across the street to a convenience store to make a telephone call. While eating, Freddie discovered broken glass in his food, and began spitting out food, broken glass and blood.

At this time, Appellant entered the restaurant, discovered Freddie in distress, and observed a bloody napkin with food and broken glass. She then requested that restaurant employees summon an ambulance. Apparently, the only out-going telephone line was behind locked doors, and, professing their inability to telephone for assistance, the restaurant demanded payment for Freddie's meal. Payment was made, and Appellant placed Freddie in her automobile with the intention to take Freddie to the nearest hospital.

En route to the hospital and as Appellant entered an intersection adjacent to the restaurant on a green light, another automobile collided with Appellant, causing Appellant and Freddie injury. Appellant and Freddie then filed suit against Appellee for their injuries under a negligence theory. On Appellee's motion for summary judgment, Appellant asserted under the uncontroverted facts that Waffle House was negligent as to Freddie as evidenced by the presence of the broken glass in his food, and that Appellee was liable to Appellant for her injuries from the auto accident under the "rescue doctrine". The Trial Court found that Appellee was not negligent as to Appellant, and granted summary judgment for Appellee. From that ruling, Appellant seeks review.

Initially, it is clear under Oklahoma law that an injured person may recover from a food supplier in negligence for injuries sustained by virtue of consumption of tainted or adulterated foods sold by that supplier.... Under a negligence theory, the injured consumer must establish the traditional elements of the existence of a duty to the injured party, a breach of that duty, and damages proximately flowing therefrom....

The law of this state also recognizes that one who rescues or attempts to rescue a person from a dangerous situation and incurs injury by virtue of the rescue or attempt, may recover from the party whose negligence caused the party or another to be in a dangerous situation.... *Merritt v. Okla. Nat. Gas Co.*, 196 Okl. 379, 165 P.2d 342 (1946). Under the "rescue doctrine," negligence as to the victim constitutes negligence as to the rescuer, and there exists an independent duty of care as between the negligent party and the rescuer:

" ... [U]nder the 'rescue doctrine,' efforts to protect the personal safety of another have been held not to supercede the liability for the original negligence which has endangered it. Whether or not the rescuer is to be recognized as 'foreseeable,' it has been recognized since the early case of the crowd rushing to assist the descending balloonist that [a rescuer] is nothing abnormal. 'The risk of rescue if only it be not wanton, is born of the occasion. The emergency begets the man.' THERE IS THUS AN INDEPENDENT DUTY OF CARE OWED TO THE RESCUER HIMSELF, which arises even when the defendant endangers no one's safety but his own." Prosser, Handbook of the Law of Torts, §44, p. 277, (1971 Ed.). (Emphasis added.)

The Honorable Justice Cardozo, on whose statement of the law the Oklahoma Supreme Court relied in *Merritt v. Okla. Nat. Gas. Co., supra*, established the rule thusly:

"Danger invites rescue. The cry of distress is the summons to relief. The law does not ignore these reactions of the mind in tracing conduct to its consequences. It recognizes them as normal. It places their effects within the range of the natural and probable. THE WRONG THAT IMPERILS LIFE IS A WRONG TO THE IMPERILED VICTIM; IT IS A WRONG ALSO TO HIS RESCUER." *Wagner v. International Railway Co.*, 232 N.Y. 176, 133 N.E. 437 (1921), cited in *Merritt v. Okla. Nat. Gas Co., supra*, 165 P.2d 342, 343. (Emphasis added.)

Thus, in actions based on the rescue doctrine under Oklahoma law, an injured party may recover damages for injury sustained in a rescue or attempt from the original tortfeasor if it can be shown that it was the original tortfeasor's negligence that placed the rescued person in peril, and that the rescuer suffered injuries in the rescue or attempt....

Under this law and the uncontroverted facts presented on the motion for summary judgment, we find the trial court erred in granting Appellee judgment. The facts show, although reasonable men might differ, that Appellee arguably breached its duty of reasonable care in serving glass-laced food to Freddie, and that Freddie suffered injuries caused thereby. Appellee owed a commensurate duty to others, such as Appellant, to use ordinary care not to place Appellee's customers in peril, especially since a rescue attempt is a foreseeable consequence of the restaurant's breach of duty.... That Appellant's injuries were sustained in the course of a rescue attempt is undisputed, and an attempt to obtain medical treatment or assistance is such an act as to come within the purview of compensability under the rescue doctrine.... (Plaintiff that was injured as she went for medical assistance may recover under rescue doctrine.) There remained substantial fact questions as to the reasonableness of or negligence in Appellant's and Appellee's respective actions, whether the acts of Appellee were the cause of Appellant's injuries and the application of Oklahoma Law to these facts....

REVERSED AND REMANDED.

. . .

William Landes & Richard Posner, *Causation in Tort Law: An Economic Approach*
12 J. Legal Stud. 109, 132–33 (1983)*

We turn now to ... cases in which, although the probability of the state of the world in which the accident occurred is ex ante slight, administrative costs are also small, and accordingly liability is upheld against proximate-cause arguments by defendants....

The second class of cases in which administrative costs are low are the rescue cases, illustrated by *Wagner v. International Ry. Co.* The plaintiff and his cousin were passengers on the defendant's train. Because of the defendant's negligence, the cousin fell off the train. The plaintiff joined the rescue party and was injured. He was allowed to recover damages from the defendant for the latter's negligence in the injury to his cousin. This is the standard result in these cases, unless the plaintiff himself behaves negligently in carrying out the rescue effort. There can be no argument in these cases that allowing damage recovery will entail additional lawsuits. On the contrary, to the extent that rescue efforts are undertaken—and a rule allowing the rescuer to recover damages for injuries incurred in the course of the rescue attempt encourages such undertakings—the number of accident victims, and hence the number of lawsuits, will be fewer than if recovery is not allowed.

NOTES

(1) The landmark presentation of the rescue doctrine appears in *Wagner v. International Ry. Co.*, 232 N.Y. 176, 133 N.E. 437 (1921), quoted in *Day*. In *Wagner*, the plaintiff and his cousin were passengers on an overcrowded electric railway car. After a "violent lurch" following a turn near a bridge, the cousin was thrown out of the conveyance. The car was stopped, and the plaintiff proceeded back in the darkness to look for his cousin. After finding the cousin's hat, but nothing else, the plaintiff missed his footing and fell beneath the trestle. Justice Cardozo reversed a defendant's verdict that had been

rendered on instructions that the jury could find for the plaintiff only if he had been invited by the conductor to go out on the bridge, and if the conductor had followed with a light. The plaintiff's conduct, Cardozo said, was "reason fitted and proportioned to the time and the event." 232 N.Y. at 182, 133 N.E. at 438.

One of the most poignant opinions to cite *Wagner* is *Sirianni v. Anna*, 55 Misc. 2d 553, 285 N.Y.S.2d 709 (1967), a case in which the plaintiff alleged that the defendants negligently removed her son's kidneys and that her health was substantially impaired by her subsequent donation of one of her kidneys for a transplant. The trial judge in this case was Hamilton Ward, who was the plaintiff's attorney in *Wagner*, but he thought this case distinguishable:

> ... [A]lthough Special Term has fully examined, it has set aside the classical tests of foreseeability and proximate cause, as it holds that the negligence of these defendants came to rest on the body of Carl Sirianni. The premeditated, knowledgeable and purposeful act of this plaintiff in donating one of her kidneys to preserve the life of her son did not extend or reactivate the consummated negligence of these defendants. The conduct of the plaintiff herein is a clearly defined, independent, intervening act with full knowledge of the consequences.

> Special Term has also carefully and fully examined the "rescue doctrine" as set forth in such landmark cases as ... *Wagner v. International Railway Co.*, 232 N.Y. 176, 133 N.E. 437, 19 A.L.R 1 (1921), and the cases cited therein in the brief of Hamilton Ward, the plaintiff Wagner's attorney. In each of these cases, the rescuer acted without knowing his fate. Here, with full knowledge of the consequences of her voluntary action, this plaintiff mercifully surrendered up one of her kidneys and preserved the life of her son. Judge Cardozo, as part of the magnificent language, a trademark of his writings, wrote..., "The risk of rescue, *if only it be not wanton*, is born of the occasion." [Emphasis supplied.] It seems to this Court that Judge Cardozo used the word "wanton" synonymously with the word "wilful", and not in the oft-used sense of reckless disregard. [*See* Ballentine Law Dictionary with Pronounciation, Second Edition.] "The word ordinarily means intentional, as distinguished from accidental or involuntary, ..." Thus, it appears that Judge Cardozo excluded from the rescue doctrine a "wanton" (wilful) act on the part of the rescuer. The act of the plaintiff here is wilful, intentional, voluntary, free from accident and with full knowledge of its consequence.

> Further, in the rescue cases, the rescuer launches to the rescue unmindful of and without knowing his fate. "Danger invites rescue. The cry of distress is the summons to relief." (p. 180, 133 N.E. p. 437). "The emergency begets the man." (p. 180, 133 N.E. p. 438). The rescuer may have considered the nature of his act without contemplating its consequence. This is not the case here. However merciful and natural the act of this mother in preserving the life of her son, Special Term holds that under the circumstances of this case, "the rescue doctrine" has no application.

55 Misc. 2d at 556, 285 N.Y.S.2d at 712.

Was Judge Ward correct about the limitations of attorney Ward's achievement?

(2) Can you summarize concisely the reasons for permitting rescuers to recover against negligent third parties? Is the economic explanation the core of the matter? Or is it any part of the matter at all?

(3) Would you arbitrarily cut off liability at the case of the rescuer of a rescuer, on the grounds that by that time he or she should have known better?

(4) Should the fact that there is time to think and to deliberate be a per se bar to rescuers? Compare with *Sirianni* the following case: An airplane crashes on a mountain because of the negligence of the pilot. Someone who is flying a helicopter in the vicinity hears about the crash on his craft's radio and sees distress signals. He lands to help out, but is injured in the landing, which has to be accomplished in a place that would not be recommended under normal circumstances. Does the *Sirianni* rationale embrace this case?

If you think *Sirianni* can be distinguished from the case just presented, consider the helicopter pilot who flies his craft out to the mountain after hearing on his home radio about the crash, and is likewise injured in landing. Is this case distinguishable from that of the cruising pilot who lands on the spot?

(5) Would you ever give recovery for a physician who was hurt in a rescue attempt? An extraordinary fact situation brought about the litigation in *Carter v. Taylor Diving & Salvage Co.*, 341 F.Supp. 628 (E.D.La. 1972).[a] A deep sea diver, who had been living in a pressurized chamber, was eviscerated when the toilet on which he was sitting was "unaccountably flushed from the outside." The plaintiff was a physician who was an expert in medical diving problems. Forty-six years old, he had cardiac problems himself but had continued to offer his services in cases involving divers offshore. He consented to work on this case, and helped perform an operation in cramped quarters under "great physical and mental strain," saving the diver's life. The incident aggravated the plaintiff's heart condition. However, the court did not think he could recover against the diver's employer, even given the assumption that the employer was negligent and that the diver was contributorily negligent because he left open a valve he should have closed. One recurring theme in the decision is that the plaintiff commanded upwards of $100 an hour for his services.

But cf. *Solgaard v. Guy F. Atkinson Co.*, 6 Cal. 3d 361, 99 Cal. Rptr. 29, 491 P.2d 821 (1971) (recovery allowed for doctor, injured while trying to reach defendant contractor's employees who were trapped by landslide at construction site).

(6) The rescue problem shares a border with the bystander problem. See, *e.g.*, *Lambert v. Parrish*, 492 N.E.2d 289 (Ind. 1986), in which the court summarized the facts this way, *id*. at 290:

> As ... Reverend Lloyd Lambert, sat at his desk at work one February day in 1978, a man burst into his office and told him that the Reverend's wife, Dorothy, had been in a bad automobile accident at the end of the alley behind the office. Rev. Lambert ran from his office, and, as he headed up the alley, slipped on a patch of ice, injuring his back.

The court denied recovery, saying that Rev. Lambert "was not a rescuer," for "[o]nly those who have a close proximity in time and distance to the party requiring assistance are within the class of potential rescuers." Moreover, "a rescuer must in fact attempt to rescue someone," and Rev. Lambert's "only attempt was to reach the scene of the accident." *Id*. at 291.

Assume that Ms. Lambert's injuries turned out to be quite severe. Is it clear that Rev. Lambert would also have been barred on a "bystander" theory if he claimed for a combination of the injuries sustained in falling on the ice and subsequent shock at learning of the extent of his wife's injuries?

---

a. *Aff'd mem.*, 470 F.2d 995 (5th Cir. 1973).

(7) In a rather bizarre Louisiana case, defendant A parked his truck negligently, and defendant B was allegedly negligent in running into it. Defendant B's car caught fire, and the bystander plaintiff started to rescue B and his wife from the vehicle. In the course of the rescue, he discovered a firearm on the floor of B's car and handed it to B. B, delirious and dazed, promptly shot the plaintiff. Can you justify the reversal of judgments for both defendants rendered in *Lynch v. Fisher*, 34 So. 2d 513 (La. Ct. App. 1947), *on rehearing*, 34 So. 2d 513, 519–20 (La. Ct. App. 1948)? Or the combination of results in a later appeal, 41 So. 2d 692 (La. Ct. App. 1949), in which the court affirmed a judgment against A but reversed a judgment against B?

ZANGHI v. NIAGARA FRONTIER TRANSPORTATION COMMISSION

Court of Appeals of New York
85 N.Y.2d 423, 649 N.E.2d 1167, 626 N.Y.S.2d 23 (1995)

TITONE, JUDGE.

In Cooper v. City of New York, 81 N.Y.2d 584, 601 N.Y.S.2d 432, 619 N.E.2d 369, we held that, pursuant to the firefighter rule, police and firefighters may not recover in common-law negligence for line-of-duty injuries resulting from risks associated with the particular dangers inherent in that type of employment. These three appeals require us to determine the scope of this bar to recovery. We conclude that the firefighter rule precludes a police officer or firefighter from recovering in tort when the performance of his or her duties increased the risk of the injury happening, and did not merely furnish the occasion for the injury. Applying that test in each of these cases before us, we hold that all three plaintiffs are barred from recovering on their common-law negligence claims. In Raquet v. Braun, 201 A.D.2d 910, 607 N.Y.S.2d 799, however, we hold that the plaintiff firefighters' statutory claims pursuant to General Municipal Law § 205-a should be reinstated.

. . .

In Zanghi v. Niagara Frontier, 203 A.D.2d 960, 611 N.Y.S.2d 407, plaintiff Police Officer Zanghi, who had been assigned to the Greyhound Bus Terminal during a bus driver strike, was injured when he slipped and fell on a snow-covered metal plate as he was approaching a picketer who was packing snowballs, presumably to throw at departing buses. Plaintiff, and his wife derivatively, sued defendants Niagara Frontier Transportation Commission, Niagara Frontier Transit Authority, the owner of the property,[1] and Greyhound, its tenant, on a negligence theory, alleging specifically that defendants failed to protect him from a "hidden hazard" on the premises—the metal plates rendered slippery by the snow.

In Raquet v. Braun, Volunteer Firefighter Mitchell Spoth died and Volunteer Firefighter Frank Raquet was paralyzed from injuries sustained when the canopy roof on a building addition and a portion of the addition's masonry wall collapsed during a blaze in November 1984. Alleging common-law and statutory negligence claims, the Raquet and Spoth plaintiffs sued defendants Leonard Zane, the owner of the building, and the

---

1. Supreme Court dismissed plaintiff's complaint against Niagara Frontier Transportation Commission on the ground that it was not a party to the lease agreement with Greyhound. The complaint against Niagara Frontier Transit Authority was dismissed as time-barred.

contractors Zane had hired in 1972 to design and construct the addition, including defendants Carol Braun, a professional engineer, J.M. Braun Builders, the contractor who erected the canopy roof, and defendant Benito Olivieri, individually and doing business as Mason Construction, Inc., the mason who constructed the addition's exterior wall. Specifically, plaintiffs alleged that all defendants were negligent because the building was not constructed in compliance with the approved plans and standard procedure. According to plaintiffs, the resulting defects in the structure caused the building to abnormally collapse outward instead of inward, leading to the death and injury of the two firefighters who were positioned on the street. The statutory claims were brought pursuant to General Municipal Law § 205-a [which provides a cause of action to firefighters or their representatives against those whose negligent failure to comply with statutes, ordinances or governmental rules causes injury or death—Ed.], based on all defendants' alleged violations of the State Building Construction Code and the Town of Clarence Code....

In the third case, Ruocco v. New York City Tr. Auth., 204 A.D.2d 76, 611 N.Y.S.2d 513, two police officers, plaintiffs Robert Ruocco and Michael Falcone, were injured when they fell while rushing down a flight of stairs leading into the subway in response to a radio call for assistance from another officer. After they fell, the officers noticed that the stairs were wet and that an employee of the New York City Transit Authority (NYCTA) was standing at the bottom of the stairs with a mop and pail of water. Plaintiffs, and Josephine Falcone derivatively, sued defendant NYCTA in common-law negligence. Specifically, plaintiffs alleged that defendant failed to properly maintain the subway stairway, "which was cracked, worn, uneven, dirty and wet" at the time of the accident, and failed to warn of the danger.

All three sets of defendants moved to dismiss the respective complaints against them on the ground that the common-law negligence action was barred by the "firefighter rule." In each of the cases, the respective trial courts denied the defendants' motions, citing the "separate and apart" exception to the firefighter rule, which would permit a common-law negligence action to go forward if the conduct causing the injury was independent of the conduct for which the officers and firefighters had been summoned. In Raquet, the trial court additionally declined to dismiss the statutory claims....

The rulings on the common-law claims were reversed by the Appellate Division in each case on the ground that the "separate and apart" exception had been rejected by this Court in Cooper v. City of New York, 81 N.Y.2d 584, 601 N.Y.S.2d 432, 619 N.E.2d 369, supra. The uniform conclusion was that all of the common-law negligence claims were barred by the firefighter rule because the injuries were caused by the particular types of risks that the respective police officers and firefighters had assumed as part of their duties. Additionally, in Raquet v. Braun, the Appellate Division dismissed the statutory claims against all defendants, holding that violations of building codes do not give rise to liability pursuant to General Municipal Law § 205-a because they do not "'create hazards additional to those that firefighters already face in their profession.'"....

We affirm the dismissal of the negligence claims in all three cases. We modify in Raquet by reversing and reinstating the statutory claims against defendant Leonard Zane, and otherwise affirm the dismissal of the common-law negligence claims.

. . .

The "firefighter's rule," a product of this State's long-standing common law, precludes firefighters and police officers from recovering damages for injuries caused by "negligence in the very situations that create the occasion for their services".... The rule is applied to bar common-law negligence claims where "the injury sustained is related to the particular dangers which police officers [and firefighters] are expected to assume as part of their duties" (Cooper v. City of New York....

The rationale for applying the firefighter rule has evolved from the initial theory that public safety officers, as licensees entering upon the land, took the property as they found it. With that rationale undermined by Basso v. Miller, 40 N.Y.2d 233, 386 N.Y.S.2d 564, 352 N.E.2d 868, subsequent cases retained the firefighter rule by reliance on the doctrine of assumption of risk—i.e., that persons who accept employment as firefighters or police assume the risks of fire-related or crime-fighting-related injuries, including the risk that property owners and occupants may negligently maintain their premises.... Continued application of the bar is presently grounded on the public policy against awarding damages to firefighters and police for hazards "that create a need for their services" and which they are hired, specially trained and compensated to confront....

In an apparent effort to abate the harsh effects of the firefighter rule, some courts in this State created an exception to the bar of common-law negligence claims where the negligent act causing the injury was "separate and apart" from the act occasioning the need for the officer's services.... As the Appellate Division in each of the cases before us correctly stated, however, that exception was rejected by this Court in Cooper v. City of New York....

In Cooper, this Court explained that the "determinative factor" in applying the firefighter rule's bar is "whether the injury sustained is related to the particular dangers which police officers [and firefighters] are expected to assume as part of their duties".... In these three cases we are essentially asked to define when the requisite "connection" exists between the plaintiff's injury and the special hazards associated with police and fire duties.... We hold that that necessary connection is present where the performance of the police officer's or firefighter's duties increased the risk of the injury happening, and did not merely furnish the occasion for the injury. In other words, where some act taken in furtherance of a specific police or firefighting function exposed the officer to a heightened risk of sustaining the particular injury, he or she may not recover damages for common-law negligence. By contrast, a common-law negligence claim may proceed where an officer is injured in the line of duty merely because he or she happened to be present in a given location, but was not engaged in any specific duty that increased the risk of receiving that injury. For example, if a police officer who is simply walking on foot patrol is injured by a flower pot that fortuitously falls from an apartment window, the officer can recover damages because nothing in the acts undertaken in the performance of police duties placed him or her at increased risk for that accident to happen. On the other hand, if an officer is injured by a suspect who struggles to avoid an arrest, the rule precludes recovery in tort because the officer is specially trained and compensated to confront such dangers.

Applying the pertinent principles to the cases before us, we conclude that the common-law negligence claims in all three cases were properly dismissed. In Zanghi, which involved the police officer who slipped on the snow-covered metal plate, the officer's own trial testimony established that he was focused solely on quickly reaching the picketer who was packing the snowball. Thus, the emergent circumstances exposed plaintiff Zanghi to the risk of injury from slipping on the plate concealed by patches of snow—a risk similar to that faced by the police officers in Cooper, who drove in excess of the speed limit and without regard for the attendant weather and lighting conditions. Accordingly, the risk of slipping while approaching the strikers was one of the particular risks of employment that plaintiff Zanghi was compensated to confront.

Likewise, injury to a firefighter due to the collapse of a burning building is one of the particular risks firefighters are asked to brave by their employment. Without doubt, the performance of the firefighting duties by plaintiffs Spoth and Raquet in Raquet v. Braun increased the risk of being injured by the collapse of the roof and exterior wall.

Also, police officers are commonly called to render assistance to other officers, and may respond in a variety of ways. The primary goal of the officers is to reach the fellow servant quickly and to render assistance; care and caution in the steps taken to reach that location are naturally compromised. The risk that an officer may be injured during the response, due to the loss of footing, a blow out on a tire, or a car collision at an intersection is inherent in police duties. Thus, the officers in Ruocco, who were rushing down stairs to reach a co-worker in need of assistance, were at an increased risk of injury precisely because of the nature of the duty they were performing—responding to a call for backup—and are barred from recovering damages for common-law negligence by the firefighter rule.

[Omitted is a part of the opinion that allows the claims of the Raquet and Spoth plaintiffs under General Municipal Law § 205-a, concerning building code violations that allegedly led to the collapse of the canopy roof and masonry wall.]

... [I]n Zanghi v. Niagara Frontier Transp. Comm., the order of the Appellate Division should be affirmed, with costs; in Raquet v. Braun, the order of the Appellate Division should be modified in accordance with the opinion herein, with costs to appellants as against respondent Leonard Zane, and, as so modified, affirmed, with costs to the other defendants-respondents as against appellants; and, in Ruocco v. New York City Tr. Auth., the order of the Appellate Division should be affirmed, with costs.

...

NOTES

(1) In each of the cases consolidated in *Zanghi*, there were clear allegations of negligence and a close cause-in-fact connection. Had the injuries occurred to bystanders who volunteered to give the aid given by the plaintiffs, there presumably would have been no issue as to the defendant's duty to those volunteers. Indeed, the rescue doctrine would have bolstered the case in favor of the volunteers. Why, then, deny recovery to these plaintiffs? The court refers to the "public policy against awarding damages to firefighters and police for 'hazards that create a need for their services' and which they are hired, specially trained and compensated to confront." Is this a "public policy"?

(2) Which of the following is the best legal category into which to place this court's decision on the common law claims?

   (a) A person whose negligence creates a hazard to which public safety officers must respond owes no duty with respect to injuries the officers sustain while performing their duties.

(b) The defendant's negligence was not the proximate cause of the plaintiff's injury.

(c) The plaintiff's injury was not within the risk created by the defendant's negligence.

(d) The plaintiff assumed the risk of the injury.

(3) Would the *Zanghi* court's decision on the common law claims be at all defensible if there were no governmental compensation scheme for police or firefighters? Keep in mind that when a workers' compensation employee in the private sector is injured, although she is limited to workers' compensation vis-a-vis her employer, she can still recover in tort against any other party whose negligence contributed to her injury. Why should the fortuity of employment as a public safety officer restrict such employees to workers' compensation-type payments?

§ 12.06 The *Palsgraf* Case

PALSGRAF v. LONG ISLAND R. CO.
New York Court of Appeals
248 N.Y. 339, 162 N.E. 99 (1928)

[This was an appeal from the Appellate Division's affirmance, by a 3–2 vote, of a judgment on a jury verdict for the plaintiff.]

CARDOZO, C. J.

Plaintiff was standing on a platform of defendant's railroad after buying a ticket to go to Rockaway Beach. A train stopped at the station, bound for another place. Two men ran forward to catch it. One of the men reached the platform of the car without mishap, though the train was already moving. The other man, carrying a package, jumped aboard the car, but seemed unsteady as if about to fall. A guard on the car, who had held the door open, reached forward to help him in, and another guard on the platform pushed him from behind. In this act, the package was dislodged, and fell upon the rails. It was a package of small size, about fifteen inches long, and was covered by a newspaper. In fact it contained fireworks, but there was nothing in its appearance to give notice of its contents. The fireworks when they fell exploded. The shock of the explosion threw down some scales at the other end of the platform many feet away. The scales struck the plaintiff, causing injuries for which she sues.

The conduct of the defendant's guard, if a wrong in its relation to the holder of the package, was not a wrong in its relation to the plaintiff, standing far away. Relatively to her it was not negligence at all. Nothing in the situation gave notice that the falling package had in it the potency of peril to persons thus removed. Negligence is not actionable unless it involves the invasion of a legally protected interest, the violation of a right. "Proof of negligence in the air, so to speak, will not do." Pollock, Torts (11th Ed.) p. 455; *Martin v. Herzog*, 228 N. Y. 164, 170, 126 N. E. 814...."Negligence is the absence of care, according to the circumstances." Willes, J., in *Vaughan v. Taff Vale Ry. Co.*, 5 H. & N. 679, 688;.... The plaintiff, as she stood upon the platform of the station, might claim to be protected against intentional invasion of her bodily security. Such invasion is not charged. She might claim to be protected against unintentional invasion by conduct involving in the thought of reasonable men an unreasonable hazard that such invasion would ensue. These, from the point of view of the law, were the bounds of her immunity, with perhaps some rare exceptions, survivals for the most part of ancient forms of liability, where conduct is held to be at the peril of the actor.... If no hazard was apparent to the eye of ordinary vigilance, an act innocent and harmless, at least to outward seeming, with reference to her, did not take to itself the quality of a tort because it happened to be a wrong, though apparently not one involving the risk of bodily insecurity, with reference to some one else. "In every instance, before negligence can be predicated of a given act, back of the act must be sought and found a duty to the individual complaining, the observance of which would have averted or avoided the injury." McSherry, C. J., in *West Virginia Central & P. R. Co. v. State*, 96 Md. 652, 666, 54 A. 669, 671 (61 L. R. A. 574)...."The ideas of negligence and duty are strictly correlative." Bowen, L. J., in *Thomas v. Quartermaine*, 18 Q. B. D. 685, 694. The plaintiff sues in her own right for a wrong personal to her, and not as the vicarious beneficiary of a breach of duty to another.

A different conclusion will involve us, and swiftly too, in a maze of contradictions. A guard stumbles over a package which has been left upon a platform. It seems to be a bundle of newspapers. It turns out to be a can of dynamite. To the eye of ordinary vigilance, the bundle is abandoned waste, which may be kicked or trod on with impunity. Is a passenger at the other end of the platform protected by the law against the unsuspected hazard concealed beneath the waste? If not, is the result to be any different, so far as the distant passenger is concerned, when the guard stumbles over a valise which a truckman or a porter has left upon the walk? The passenger far away, if the victim of a wrong at all, has a cause of action, not derivative, but original and primary. His claim to be protected against invasion of his bodily security is neither greater nor less because the act resulting in the invasion is a wrong to another far removed. In this case, the rights that are said to have been violated, the interests said to have been invaded, are not even of the same order. The man was not injured in his person nor even put in danger. The purpose of the act, as well as its effect, was to make his person safe. If there was a wrong to him at all, which may very well be doubted, it was a wrong to a property interest only, the safety of his package. Out of this wrong to property, which threatened injury to nothing else, there has passed, we are told, to the plaintiff by derivation or succession a right of action for the invasion of an interest of another order, the right to bodily security. The diversity of interests emphasizes the futility of the effort to build the plaintiff's right upon the basis of a wrong to someone else. The gain is one of emphasis, for a like result would follow if the interests were the same. Even then, the orbit of the danger as disclosed to the eye of reasonable vigilance would be the orbit of the duty. One who jostles one's neighbor in a crowd does not invade the rights of others standing at the outer fringe when the unintended contact casts a bomb upon the ground. The wrongdoer as to them is the man who carries the bomb, not the one who explodes it without suspicion of the danger. Life will have to be made over, and human nature transformed, before prevision so extravagant can be accepted as the norm of conduct, the customary standard to which behavior must conform.

The argument for the plaintiff is built upon the shifting meanings of such words as "wrong" and "wrongful," and shares their instability. What the plaintiff must show is "a wrong" to herself; *i.e.*, a violation of her own right, and not merely a wrong to some one else, nor conduct "wrongful" because unsocial, but not "a wrong" to anyone. We are told that one who drives at reckless speed through a crowded city street is guilty of a negligent act and therefore of a wrongful one, irrespective of the consequences. Negligent the act is, and wrongful in the sense that it is unsocial, but wrongful and unsocial in relation to other travelers, only because the eye of vigilance perceives the risk of damage. If the same act were to be committed on a speedway or a race course, it would lose its wrongful quality. The risk reasonably to be perceived defines the duty to be obeyed, and risk imports relation; it is risk to another or to others within the range of apprehension. Seavey, *Negligence, Subjective or Objective*, 41 H. L. Rv. 6; *Boronkay v. Robinson & Carpenter*, 247 N. Y. 365, 160 N. E. 400. This does not mean, of course, that one who launches a destructive force is always relieved of liability, if the force, though known to be destructive, pursues an unexpected path. "It was not necessary that the defendant should have had notice of the particular method in which an accident would occur, if the possibility of an accident was clear to the ordinarily prudent eye." *Munsey v. Webb*, 231 U. S. 150, 156, 34 S. Ct. 44, 45 (58 L. Ed. 162).... Some acts, such as shooting are so imminently dangerous to anyone who may come within reach of the missile however unexpectedly, as to impose a duty of prevision not far from that of an insurer. Even today, and much oftener in earlier stages of the law, one acts sometimes at one's peril. Jeremiah Smith, *Tort and Absolute Liability*, 30 H. L. Rv. 328; Street, Foundations of Legal Liability, vol. 1, pp. 77, 78. Under this head, it may be, fall certain cases of what is known as transferred intent, an act willfully dangerous to A resulting by misadventure in injury to B. *Talmage v. Smith*, 101 Mich. 370, 374, 59 N. W. 656, 45 Am. St. Rep. 414. These cases aside, wrong is defined in terms of the natural or probable, at least when unintentional. *Parrot v. Wells-Fargo Co. (The Nitro-Glycerine Case)* 15 Wall. 524, 21 L. Ed. 206. The range of reasonable apprehension is at times a question for the court, and at times, if varying inferences are possible, a question for the jury. Here, by concession, there was nothing in the situation to suggest to the most cautious mind that the parcel wrapped in newspaper would spread wreckage through the station. If the guard had thrown it down knowingly and willfully, he would not have threatened the plaintiff's safety, so far as appearances could warn him. His conduct would not have involved, even then, an unreasonable probability of invasion of her bodily security. Liability can be no greater where the act is inadvertent.

Negligence, like risk, is thus a term of relation. Negligence in the abstract, apart from things related, is surely not a tort, if indeed it is understandable at all. Bowen, L. J., in *Thomas v. Quartermaine*, 18 Q. B. D. 685, 694. Negligence is not a tort unless it results in the commission of a wrong, and the commission of a wrong imports the violation of a right, in this case, we are told, the right to be protected against interference with one's bodily security. But bodily security is protected, not against all forms of interference or aggression, but only against some. One who seeks redress at law does not make out a cause of action by showing without more that there has been damage to his person. If the harm was not willful, he must show that the act as to him had possibilities of danger so many and apparent as to entitle him to be protected against the doing of it though the harm was unintended. Affront to personality is still the keynote of the wrong. Confirmation of this view will be found in the history and development of the action on the case. Negligence as a basis of civil liability was unknown to mediaeval law. 8 Holdsworth, History of English Law, p. 449; Street, Foundations of Legal Liability, vol. 1, pp. 189, 190. For damage to the person, the sole remedy was trespass, and trespass did not lie in the absence of aggression, and that direct and personal. Holdsworth, *op. cit.* p. 453; Street, *op. cit.* vol. 3, pp. 258, 260, vol. 1, pp. 71, 74. Liability for other damage, as where a servant without orders from the master does or omits something to the damage of another, is a plant of later growth. Holdsworth, op. cit. 450, 457; Wigmore, Responsibility for Tortious Acts, vol. 3, Essays in Anglo-American Legal History, 520, 523, 526, 533. When it emerged out of the legal soil, it was thought of as a variant of trespass, an offshoot of the parent stock. This appears in the form of action, which was known as trespass on the case. Holdsworth, *op. cit.* p. 449; *cf.* Scott v. Shepard, 2 Wm. Black. 892; Green, Rationale of Proximate Cause, p. 19. The victim does not sue derivatively, or by right of subrogation, to vindicate an interest invaded in the person of another. Thus to view his cause of action is to ignore the fundamental difference between tort and crime. Holland, Jurisprudence (12th Ed.) p. 328. He sues for breach of a duty owing to himself.

The law of causation, remote or proximate, is thus foreign to the case before us. The question of liability is always anterior to the question of the measure of the consequences that go with liability. If there is no tort to be redressed, there is no occasion to consider what damage might be recovered if there were a finding of a tort. We may assume, without deciding, that negligence, not at large or in the abstract, but in relation to the plaintiff, would entail liability for any and all consequences, however novel or extraordinary. *Bird v. St. Paul Fire & Marine Ins. Co.*, 224 N. Y. 47, 54, 120 N. E. 86, 13 A. L. R. 875; *Ehrgott v. Mayor, etc., of City of New York*, 96 N. Y. 264, 48 Am. Rep. 622; *Smith v. London & S. W. R. Co.*, [1870–1871] L. R. 6 C. P. 14; 1 Beven, Negligence, 106; Street, *op. cit.* vol. 1, p. 90; Green, Rationale of Proximate Cause, pp. 88, 118; *cf. Matter of Polemis*, L. R. 1921, 3 K. B. 560; 44 Law Quarterly Review, 142. There is room for argument that a distinction is to be drawn according to the diversity of interests invaded by the act, as where conduct negligent in that it threatens an insignificant invasion of an interest in property results in an unforeseeable invasion of an interest of another order, as, *e.g.*, one of bodily security. Perhaps other distinctions may be necessary. We do not go into the question now. The consequences to be followed must first be rooted in a wrong.

The judgment of the Appellate Division and that of the Trial Term should be reversed, and the complaint dismissed, with costs in all courts.

ANDREWS, J. (dissenting).

Assisting a passenger to board a train, the defendant's servant negligently knocked a package from his arms. It fell between the platform and the cars. Of its contents the servant knew and could know nothing. A violent explosion followed. The concussion broke some scales standing a considerable distance away. In falling, they injured the plaintiff, an intending passenger.

Upon these facts, may she recover the damages she has suffered in an action brought against the master? The result we shall reach depends upon our theory as to the nature of negligence. Is it a relative concept—the breach of some duty owing to a particular person or to particular persons? Or, where there is an act which unreasonably threatens the safety of others, is the doer liable for all its proximate consequences, even where they result in injury to one who would generally be thought to be outside the radius of danger? This is not a mere dispute as to words. We might not believe that to the average mind the dropping of the bundle would seem to involve the probability of harm to the plaintiff standing many feet away whatever might be the case as to the owner or to one so near as to be likely to be struck by its fall. If, however, we adopt the second hypothesis, we have to inquire only as to the relation between cause and effect. We deal in terms of proximate cause, not of negligence.

Negligence may be defined roughly as an act or omission which unreasonably does or may affect the rights of others, or which unreasonably fails to protect one's self from the dangers resulting from such acts. Here I confine myself to the first branch of the definition. Nor do I comment on the word "unreasonable." For present purposes it sufficiently describes that average of conduct that society requires of its members.

There must be both the act or the omission, and the right. It is the act itself, not the intent of the actor, that is important.... In criminal law both the intent and the result are to be considered. Intent again is material in tort actions, where punitive damages are sought, dependent on actual malice—not on merely reckless conduct. But here neither insanity nor infancy lessens responsibility....

As has been said, except in cases of contributory negligence, there must be rights which are or may be affected. Often though injury has occurred, no rights of him who suffers have been touched. A licensee or trespasser upon my land has no claim to affirmative care on my part that the land be made safe.... Where a railroad is required to fence its tracks against cattle, no man's rights are injured should he wander upon the road because such fence is absent. *Di Caprio v. New York Cent. R. Co.*, 231 N. Y. 94, 131 N. E. 746, 16 A. L. R. 940. An unborn child may not demand immunity from personal harm....

But we are told that "there is no negligence unless there is in the particular case a legal duty to take care, and this duty must be one which is owed to the plaintiff himself and not merely to others." Salmond Torts (6th Ed.) 24. This I think too narrow a conception. Where there is the unreasonable act, and some right that may be affected there is negligence whether damage does or does not result. That is immaterial. Should we drive down Broadway at a reckless speed, we are negligent whether we strike an approaching car or miss it by an inch. The act itself is wrongful. It is a wrong not only to those who happen to be within the radius of danger, but to all who might have been there—a wrong to the public at large. Such is the language of the street. Such the language of the courts when speaking of contributory negligence. Such again and again their language in speaking of the duty of some defendant and discussing proximate cause in cases where such a discussion is wholly irrelevant on any other theory. *Perry v. Rochester Line Co.*, 219 N. Y. 60, 113 N. E. 529, L. R. A. 1917B, 1058. As was said by Mr. Justice Holmes many years ago:

"The measure of the defendant's duty in determining whether a wrong has been committed is one thing, the measure of liability when a wrong has been committed is another." *Spade v. Lynn & B. R. Co.*,....

Due care is a duty imposed on each one of us to protect society from unnecessary danger, not to protect A, B, or C alone.

It may well be that there is no such thing as negligence in the abstract. "Proof of negligence in the air, so to speak, will not do." In an empty world negligence would not exist. It does involve a relationship between man and his fellows, but not merely a relationship between man and those whom he might reasonably expect his act would injure; rather, a relationship between him and those whom he does in fact injure. If his act has a tendency to harm someone, it harms him a mile away as surely as it does those on the scene. We now permit children to recover for the negligent killing of the father. It was never prevented on the theory that no duty was owing to them. A husband may be compensated for the loss of his wife's services. To say that the wrongdoer was negligent as to the husband as well as to the wife is merely an attempt to fit facts to theory. An insurance company paying a fire loss recovers its payment of the negligent incendiary. We speak of subrogation—of suing in the right of the insured. Behind the cloud of words is the fact they hide, that the act, wrongful as to the insured, has also injured the company. Even if it be true that the fault of father, wife, or insured will prevent recovery, it is because we consider the original negligence, not the proximate cause of the injury. Pollock, Torts (12th Ed.) 463.

In the well-known *Polhemis Case*, [1921] 3 K. B. 560, Scrutton, L. J., said that the dropping of a plank was negligent, for it might injure "workman or cargo or ship." Because of either possibility, the owner of the vessel was to be made good for his loss. The act being wrongful, the doer was liable for its proximate results. Criticized and explained as this statement may have been, I think it states the law as it should be and as it is. *Smith v. London & S. W. R. Co. R. R.* (1870–71) L. R. 6 C. P. 14....

The proposition is this: Everyone owes to the world at large the duty of refraining from those acts that may unreasonably threaten the safety of others. Such an act occurs. Not only is he wronged to whom harm might reasonably be expected to result, but he also who is in fact injured, even if he be outside what would generally be thought the danger zone. There needs be duty due the one complaining, but this is not a duty to a particular individual because as to him harm might be expected. Harm to someone being the natural result of the act, not only that one alone, but all those in fact injured may complain. We have never, I think, held otherwise. Indeed in the Di Caprio Case we said that a breach of a general ordinance defining the degree of care to be exercised in one's calling is evidence of negligence as to everyone. We did not limit this statement to those who might be expected to be exposed to danger. Unreasonable risk being taken, its consequences are not confined to those who might probably be hurt.

If this be so, we do not have a plaintiff suing by "derivation or succession." Her action is original and primary. Her claim is for a breach of duty to herself—not that she is subrogated to any right of action of the owner of the parcel or of a passenger standing at the scene of the explosion.

The right to recover damages rests on additional considerations. The plaintiff's rights must be injured, and this injury must be caused by the negligence. We build a dam, but are negligent as to its foundations. Breaking, it injures property down stream. We are not liable if all this happened because of some reason other than the insecure foundation. But, when injuries do result from our unlawful act, we are liable for the consequences. It does not matter that they are unusual, unexpected, unforeseen, and unforeseeable. But there is one limitation. The damages must be so connected with the negligence that the latter may be said to be the proximate cause of the former.

These two words have never been given an inclusive definition. What is a cause in a legal sense, still more what is a proximate cause, depend in each case upon many considerations, as does the existence of negligence itself. Any philosophical doctrine of causation does not help us. A boy throws a stone into a pond. The ripples spread. The water level rises. The history of that pond is altered to all eternity. It will be altered by other causes also. Yet it will be forever the resultant of all causes combined. Each one will have an influence. How great only omniscience can say. You may speak of a chain, or, if you please, a net. An analogy is of little aid. Each cause brings about future events. Without each the future would not be the same. Each is proximate in the sense it is essential. But that is not what we mean by the word. Nor on the other hand do we mean sole cause. There is no such thing.

Should analogy be though helpful, however, I prefer that of a stream. The spring, starting on its journey, is joined by tributary after tributary. The river, reaching the ocean, comes from a hundred sources. No man may say whence any drop of water is derived. Yet for a time distinction may be possible. Into the clear creek, brown swamp water flows from the left. Later, from the right comes water stained by its clay bed. The three may remain for a space, sharply divided. But at last inevitably no trace of separation remains. They are so commingled that all distinction is lost.

As we have said, we cannot trace the effect of an act to the end, if end there is. Again, however, we may trace it part of the way. A murder at Serajevo may be the necessary antecedent to an assassination in London twenty years hence. An overturned lantern may burn all Chicago. We may follow the fire from the shed to the last building. We rightly say the fire started by the lantern caused its destruction.

A cause, but not the proximate cause. What we do mean by the word "proximate" is that, because of convenience, of public policy, of a rough sense of justice, the law arbitrarily declines to trace a series of events beyond a certain point. This is not logic. It is practical politics. Take our rule as to fires. Sparks from my burning haystack set on fire my house and my neighbor's. I may recover from a negligent railroad. He may not. Yet the wrongful act as directly harmed the one as the other. We may regret that the line was drawn just where it was, but drawn somewhere it had to be. We said the act of the railroad was not the proximate cause of our neighbor's fire. Cause it surely was. The words we used were simply indicative of our notions of public policy. Other courts think differently. But somewhere they reach the point where they cannot say the stream comes from any one source.

Take the illustration given in an unpublished manuscript by a distinguished and helpful writer on the law of torts. A chauffeur negligently collides with another car which is filled with dynamite, although he could not know it. An explosion follows. A, walking on the sidewalk nearby, is killed. B, sitting in a window of a building opposite, is cut by flying glass. C, likewise sitting in a window a block away, is similarly injured. And a further illustration: A nursemaid, ten blocks away, startled by the noise, involuntarily drops a baby from her arms to the walk. We are told that C may not recover while A may. As to B it is a question for court or jury. We will all agree that the baby might not. Because, we are again told, the chauffeur had no reason to believe his conduct involved any risk of injuring either C or the baby. As to them he was not negligent.

But the chauffeur, being negligent in risking the collision, his belief that the scope of the harm he might do would be limited is immaterial. His act unreasonably jeopardized the safety of any one who might be affected by it. C's injury and that of the baby were directly traceable to the collision. Without that, the injury would not have happened. C had the right to sit in his office, secure from such dangers. The baby was entitled to use the sidewalk with reasonable safety.

The true theory is, it seems to me, that the injury to C, if in truth he is to be denied recovery, and the injury to the baby, is that their several injuries were not the proximate result of the negligence. And here not what the chauffeur had reason to believe would be the result of his conduct, but what the prudent would foresee, may have a bearing—may have some bearing, for the problem of proximate cause is not to be solved by any one consideration. It is all a question of expediency. There are no fixed rules to govern our judgment. There are simply matters of which we may take account. We have in a somewhat different connection spoken of "the stream of events." We have asked whether that stream was deflected—whether it was forced into new and unexpected channels. *Donnelly v. H. C. & A. I. Piercy Contracting Co.*, 222 N. Y. 210, 118 N. E. 605. This is rather rhetoric than law. There is in truth little to guide us other than common sense.

There are some hints that may help us. The proximate cause, involved as it may be with many other causes, must be, at the least, something without which the event would not happen. The court must ask itself whether there was a natural and continuous sequence between cause and effect. Was the one a substantial factor in producing the other? Was there a direct connection between them, without too many intervening causes? Is the effect of cause on result not too attentuated? Is the cause likely, in the usual judgment of mankind, to produce the result? Or, by the exercise of prudent foresight, could the result be foreseen? Is the result too remote from the cause, and here we consider remoteness in time and space. *Bird v. St. Paul & M. Ins. Co.*, ... where we passed upon the construction of a contract—but something was also said on this subject. Clearly we must so consider, for the greater the distance either in time or space, the more surely do other causes intervene to affect the result. When a lantern is overturned, the firing of a shed is a fairly direct consequence. Many things contribute to the spread of the conflagration—the force of the wind, the direction and width of streets, the character of intervening structures, other factors. We draw an uncertain and wavering line, but draw it we must as best we can.

Once again, it is all a question of fair judgment, always keeping in mind the fact that we endeavor to make a rule in each case that will be practical and in keeping with the general understanding of mankind.

Here another question must be answered. In the case supposed, it is said, and said correctly, that the chauffeur is liable for the direct effect of the explosion, although he had no reason to suppose it would follow a collision. "The fact that the injury occurred in a different manner than that which might have been expected does not prevent the chauffeur's negligence from being in law the cause of the injury." But the natural results of a negligent act—the results which a prudent man would or should foresee—do have a bearing upon the decision as to proximate cause. We have said so repeatedly. What should be foreseen? No human foresight would suggest that a collision itself might injure one a block away. On the contrary, given an explosion, such a possibility might be reasonably expected. I think the direct connection, the foresight of which the courts speak, assumes prevision of the explosion, for the immediate results of which, at least, the chauffeur is responsible.

It may be said this is unjust. Why? In fairness he should make good every injury flowing from his negligence. Not because of tenderness toward him we say he need not answer for all that follows his wrong. We look back to the catastrophe, the fire kindled by the spark, or the explosion. We trace the consequences, not indefinitely, but to a certain point. And to aid us in fixing that point we ask what might ordinarily be expected to follow the fire or the explosion.

This last suggestion is the factor which must determine the case before us. The act upon which defendant's liability rests is knocking an apparently harmless package onto the platform. The act was negligent. For its proximate consequences the defendant is liable. If its contents were broken, to the owner; if it fell upon and crushed a passenger's foot, then to him; if it exploded and injured one in the immediate vicinity, to him also as to A in the illustration. Mrs. Palsgraf was standing some distance away. How far cannot be told from the record—apparently 25 or 30 feet, perhaps less. Except for the explosion, she would not have been injured. We are told by the appellant in his brief, "It cannot be denied that the explosion was the direct cause of the plaintiff's injuries." So it was a substantial factor in producing the result—there was here a natural and continuous sequence—direct connection. The only intervening cause was that, instead of blowing her to the ground, the concussion smashed the weighing machine which in turn fell upon her. There was no remoteness in time, little in space. And surely, given such an explosion as here, it needed no great foresight to predict that the natural result would be to injure one on the platform at no greater distance from its scene than was the plaintiff. Just how no one might be able to predict. Whether by flying fragments, by broken glass, by wreckage of machines or structures no one could say. But injury in some form was most probable.

Under these circumstances I cannot say as a matter of law that the plaintiff's injuries were not the proximate result of the negligence. That is all we have before us. The court refused to so charge. No request was made to submit the matter to the jury as a question of fact, even would that have been proper upon the record before us.

The judgment appealed from should be affirmed, with costs.

POUND, LEHMAN, and KELLOGG, JJ., concur with CARDOZO, C. J.

ANDREWS, J., dissents in opinion in which CRANE and O'BRIEN, JJ., concur.

Judgment reversed, etc.

Ernest Weinrib, *Legal Formalism: On the Immanent Rationality of Law*
97 YALE L.J. 949, 1005–08 (1988)*

. . .

One can ... distinguish two public functions—one political, the other juridical—that formalism ascribes to the positivity of law. The first is the selection of the goal to be embodied in a particular distribution and thereby to be authoritatively inscribed into the schedule of the community's collective purposes.[118] The setting up of a particular distribution is an act of political authority that clothes its determinations with the attributes of positive law. Although the particular distribution must, if it is to actualize an intelligible order, conform to distributive justice, it embodies an extrinsic—and therefore political—purpose. The second function is juridical: to interpret particular transactions and distributions in accordance with the form of justice they instantiate. This function does not depend on a standpoint outside the forms of justice. Rather, it requires courts to specify, in a publicly authoritative way, the meaning of these forms in the context of particular interactions.

A recent case illustrates the distinction between these two functions. In *Lamb v. London Borough of Camden*,[119] the English Court of Appeal was confronted with a problem of proximate cause. The plaintiff homeowner was suing the defendant municipality for the damage resulting from the negligent repair of a sewer pipe. Contractors employed by the defendant had breached a water main and the resulting flood caused the plaintiff's house to subside. Because the house was then unsafe, the plaintiff used it only for storage as it awaited repair. While the house remained vacant squatters moved in. Subsequently, they were evicted, and the plaintiff boarded up the house. Nevertheless squatters moved in again, and this time damaged the house's interior. The question for the court was whether the municipality was liable for the damage done by the second set of squatters.

This case is typical of situations where several causes, including the actions of third parties, intervene between the plaintiff's damage and the tortfeasor's original negligence. Given the number and variety of possible causes, courts have never been able—

---

* Reprinted by permission of The Yale Law Journal Company and William S. Hein Company from *The Yale Law Journal*, Vol. 97, pages 949–1016.

118. This function calls for a political body that is recognized as the locus of collective decision-making, that can evaluate the full range of possible distributions, and that is accountable to the community as a whole for the particular ones that it selects.

119. 2 All E.R. 408 (C.A.) (1981).

and doubtless never will be able — to come up with a definitive verbal formula for resolving these disputes. Confronted with this indeterminacy the members of the court took two different approaches. Lord Denning, declaring it "a question of policy for judges to decide," thought the decisive consideration was that damage to property including damage caused by criminal acts, is usually covered by the owner's insurance, and that the insurers whose business it is to cover the risk should not be allowed by subrogation to pass the cost on to the defendant. Through insurance "the risk of loss is spread throughout the community. It does not fall too heavily on one pair of shoulders alone." He accordingly ruled against liability.

In concurrence with Lord Denning in this result, Lord Justice Watkins made no reference to insurance or to loss-spreading. Instead, he drew attention to what is suggested by "the very features" of the act or event for which damages are claimed. This included such matters as the nature of the event, the time and place of its occurrence, the identity and intentions of the perpetrator, and the responsibility for taking measures to avoid the occurrence. These factors did not produce anything that could be a universal test, but Lord Justice Watkins found that they yielded "the instinctive feeling" that the squatters' damage was too remote for the defendant's liability.

Both Lord Denning and Lord Justice Watkins issued public and authoritative declarations of positive law. There is, however, this difference between them. Lord Denning's approach was essentially political. It first required selecting the particular goal of loss-spreading from among the various goals (including general deterrence, specific deterrence and redistribution to the deepest pocket) that his judgment might promote. It then necessitated electing to effect this goal through the homeowner's property insurance, not through the tortfeasor's liability insurance or through the municipality's self-insurance. Loss-spreading, however, like all external goals, is a matter for distributive justice and cannot be coherently achieved within the relationship of doer and sufferer. Nor is its positing the province of a judge, who is neither in a position to canvass the range of possible collective goals, nor accountable to the community for the particular goal chosen.

Lord Justice Watkins, in contrast, does not attempt to achieve any goal external to the relationship between plaintiff and defendant. His judgment is an exposition of the nature of that relationship through attention to the link between the defendant's wrongdoing and the plaintiff's damage. For him proximate cause is not an occasion for "policy," but is a juridical concept under which the court comprehends the nexus between the litigants by tracing the proximity of the wrongful act to the injurious effect. This concept does not have an existence independent of the interaction to which it is applied, and its features cannot be listed and weighted in a formula that yields a uniquely determinate conclusion. This explains Lord Justice Watkins' reference to intuition. The meaning of proximate cause in this situation is not a result of matching these facts to an independently conclusive formula; it is simply the most plausible construal of the relationship between the parties in light of the factors that are deemed relevant. For these facts, the conclusion constitutes the meaning of the concept they instantiate.

In concentrating on the features of the injurious act rather than on a mediating goal, Lord Justice Watkins treats proximate cause as a concept that bears on the immediate intelligibility of the parties' relationship. Proximate cause so treated is one of the set of concepts through which a delictual interaction is understandable as corrective justice. Because corrective justice is conceived as immanent to the transactions that it regulates, its operation is not intelligible independently of those transactions. The actualization of corrective justice through judicial decisions "is not the subsequent applying to a concrete case of a given universal that we understand first by itself, but it is the actual understanding of the universal itself that the given text constitutes for us." The particular transactions and their intelligibility as corrective justice can be interpreted only from within a public realm of shared social meanings that judicial decision renders legally authoritative. The same process holds for the application to a particular distribution of the components of personhood and equality that are internal to distributive justice. This drawing out of the significance of the forms of justice for particular transactions and distributions is the juridical function of positive law. It is categorically different from the political role of determining the exogenous end that is to be embodied in a distribution.

NOTES

(1) In the famous *Polemis* case, decided just seven years before *Palsgraf*, Lord Justice Scrutton summarized the facts this way:

> The steamship Thrasyvoulos was lost by fire while being discharged by workmen employed by the charterers. Experienced arbitrators, by whose findings of fact we are bound, have decided that the fire was caused by a spark igniting petrol vapour in the hold, the vapour coming from leaks from cargo shipped by the charterers, and that the spark was caused by the Arab workmen employed by the charterers negligently knocking a plank out of a temporary staging erected in the hold, so that the plank fell into the hold, and in its fall by striking something made the spark which ignited the petrol vapour.

In re Polemis, 3 K.B. 560, 575 (1921).

The defendants offered the contention, in Justice Scrutton's characterization, "that the damage is too remote from the negligence, as it could not be reasonably foreseen as a consequence." Justice Scrutton rejected this argument:

> ... I cannot think it useful to say the damage must be the natural and probable result. This suggests that there are results which are natural but not probable, and other results which are probable but not natural. I am not sure what either adjective means in this connection; if they mean the same thing, two need not be used; if they mean different things, the difference between them should be defined.

> . . .

> To determine whether an act is negligent, it is relevant to determine whether any reasonable person would foresee that the act would cause damage; if he would not, the act is not negligent. But if the act would or might probably cause damage, the fact that the damage it in fact causes is not the exact kind of damage one would expect is immaterial, so long as the damage is in fact directly traceable to the negligent act, and not due to the operation of independent causes having no connection with the negligent act, except that they could not avoid its results. Once the act is negligent, the fact that its exact operation was not foreseen is immaterial. This is the distinction laid down by the majority of the Exchequer Chamber in *Smith v. London and South Western Ry. Co.,*.... In the present case it was negligent in discharging cargo to knock down the planks of the temporary staging, for they might easily cause some damage either to workmen, or cargo, or the ship. The fact that they did directly produce an unexpected result, a spark in

an atmosphere of petrol vapour which caused a fire, does not relieve the person who was negligent from the damage which his negligent act directly caused....

Id. at 576–77.

(2) What does Judge Cardozo mean when he says that "negligence, like risk, is ... a term of relation"? How does "negligence," in this sense, relate to "duty"?

(3) In a remarkable series of articles and books over a period of four decades, Leon Green developed a conception of duty that merits the student's attention in considering cases like *Palsgraf.* See, *e.g.*, Green, *The Duty Problem in Negligence Cases*, 28 COLUM. L. REV. 1014 (1928), 29 COLUM. L. REV. 255 (1929).

(4) A draft of the *Restatement (Third)* seeks to compress the problem raised by *Palsgraf,* and more broadly many of the problems addressed in this chapter 12, into a single sentence: "An actor's liability is limited to those physical harms that result from the risks that made the actor's conduct tortious." Restatement (Third) of Torts: Liability for Physical Harm § 29 (Proposed Final Draft, Apr. 6, 2005). The comments and illustrations for this single sentence run to more than 50 pages. See *id.* at 575–633. The drafters comment that "[a]lthough the term 'proximate cause' has been in widespread use in judicial opinions, treatises, casebooks, and scholarship, the term is not generally employed in this Chapter [of which the principal title is "Scope of Liability"] because it is an especially poor one to describe the idea to which it is connected." *Id.* at 574 (Special Note on Proximate Cause).

(5) A separate opinion in an Illinois appellate case employed a "duty" analysis in considering a case in which a 10-year-old girl, struck by a car, sued the owner of a dumpster for parking it at a place where it was known that school children would cross. The plaintiff theorized that the dumpster owner was negligent in placing its chattel in a way that acted "as a barrier and hindrance" to drivers and pedestrians. The majority of the appellate panel, in affirming an order denying a motion to dismiss sought by the dumpster owner, viewed the issue as one of "proximate cause." Judge Jones wrote, in a long concurring opinion:

> The question of whether a duty exists in a particular case and the scope or range of protection thereof is a question of law. The terms "foreseeable" and "proximate cause," however, are properly used with reference to questions of fact. Whether an injury was "foreseeable" is the test used by a jury to determine whether a defendant was guilty of a breach of duty (*see Mieher v. Brown* (1973), 54 Ill.2d 539, 301 N.E.2d 307); whether a defendant's conduct was the "proximate cause" of a plaintiff's injury is the test used by a jury to determine whether there was a causal connection between a defendant's conduct and a plaintiff's injury. Nevertheless, Illinois courts regularly use the terms "foreseeable" and "proximate cause" to decide as a matter of law whether a plaintiff's injury falls within the scope of a duty the defendant owed the plaintiff on the occasion in question. The use of the two terms in this way is unfortunate because it is misleading, tending to obscure the real issue—one of law, not of fact—the court has actually been asked to decide. When a court uses terms that refer to questions of fact to decide a question of law, vagueness, uncertainty, and misunderstanding are a sure consequence. The use of such fact-oriented terms as "proximate cause" and "foreseeability" to determine issues re-

---

* The authors are indebted to Mark Amador for mentioning this case.

lated to the scope of duty obscures the fact that the court is dealing with an issue of law and suggests that the scope of a duty is a question of fact for the jury when it is not. It is simply confusing to use the same terms that are commonly known to relate to questions for the trier of fact in order to determine the question of law of the scope of a duty.

—Jones, J., concurring in *Lemings v. Collinsville Sch. Dist. No. 10*, 118 Ill. App. 3d 363, 454 N.E.2d 1139, 1142 (1983).*

(6) The Illinois Supreme Court merged foreseeability analysis into a more generalized conception of duty in a case in which an automobile passenger was injured in an accident that he attributed to prescription drugs ingested by the driver of his car. The supreme court affirmed a trial court judgment, rendered on a motion to dismiss, that there was no cause of action against the drug manufacturers for failure to warn or against the hospital for prescribing the drug. "[I]t cannot be said," the court concluded, "that [the manufacturers] should have reasonably foreseen that their drugs would be dispensed without warnings by the physicians, that the patient would be discharged from the hospital, drink alcohol, drive a car, lose control of his car, hit a tree, and injure the passenger … on the same day." But the court also said that while "reasonable foreseeability of injury is a key concern in determining whether a duty exists, it is not the only consideration." The court reverted at this point to a basic negligence analysis that would "take into account the likelihood of injury, the magnitude of the burden of guarding against it and the consequences of placing that burden upon the defendant." Specifically with respect to the hospital, the court said that "[h]olding the hospital liable for all harmful acts committed by patients who had been released would be an unreasonable burden on the institution." Justice Simon dissented with respect to the holding that there was no cause of action against the driver's doctors for negligence and against the drug companies for failure to warn. He thought it "foreseeable that the patient could injure himself while driving should he fail to receive the appropriate warnings" from the doctors and that the "injury was a natural consequence of the doctors' failure to issue the warnings." Distinguishing *Palsgraf* in particular, he said that "no extra burden is imposed on a doctor to take precautions or give adequate warnings because the plaintiff's passenger rather than the plaintiff might be injured." *Kirk v. Michael Reese Hosp. & Med. Ctr.*, 117 Ill. 2d 507, 513 N.E.2d 387 (1987), *cert. denied*, 108 S. Ct. 1077 (1988).

Which is your preferred characterization of the problem in the case just described?

(7) Do you think it is more intellectually efficient to discuss issues of this kind in terms of "proximate cause" or "duty"? Does Cardozo's approach in *Palsgraf* fit under either of those classifications, or is it a third category of analysis?

(8) Do you agree with Professor Weinrib about "the juridical function of positive law," and with the contrast he draws between that function and political determinations? Is it illegitimate for judges dealing with tort cases to consider broad policy questions—for example, questions of "distributive justice"?

(9) Landes and Posner offer this economic analysis of *Palsgraf* in *Causation in Tort Law: An Economic Approach*, 12 J. LEGAL STUDIES 109, 128–129 (1983):

> *Palsgraf* was like the nervous-injury cases in involving two distinct states of the world, one far less probable than the other. The probable state of the world, *s* in our formulation, was that the conductor would injure the passenger by helping him to board a moving train. The improbable state, *s'*, was

that if the passenger stumbled he would cause a serious injury to one or more people on the platform. Making the railroad liable for injuries to nonpassengers in this situation would have had no appreciable effect on the railroad's level of care, because the costs of identifying such a state of the world would have exceeded the benefits to the railroad from taking precautions against its occurrence.

Palsgraf involved not only the first element in the nervous-injury cases, a low p(s'), but the third as well, high administrative costs. The causal sequence alleged in the *Palsgraf* case, while possible, was not only improbable but implausible. Maybe the injury to Mrs. Palsgraf occurred as alleged but it is also quite possible that she took the opportunity afforded by her fortuitous proximity to the explosion of the fireworks to seek damages for an unrelated condition. This suspicion is reinforced by the fact that the principal symptom for which she sought damages was a stammer.... Admittedly, however, the facts we emphasize are not stressed—and one, the stammer, is not even mentioned—in the *Palsgraf* opinions, which makes our interpretation of the case highly speculative.

Does this analysis persuade you more than the others discussed above? Is it a misnomer to speak of the problem as one of "causation"?

(10) A different efficiency-oriented perspective appears in an essay by Mark Grady, *Proximate Cause and the Law of Negligence*, 69 Iowa L. Rev. 363 (1984). Grady describes *Palsgraf* as one of the "true reasonable foresight cases," and observes that it "sometimes would cost more to recognize an ancillary risk than the social benefit which would be derived from doing so." See *id*. at 440. Grady identifies "the reasonable foresight doctrine" as only one of "two doctrines of proximate cause," with the other being "the direct-consequences doctrine." He concludes his analysis with these assignments of policy rationales to the two doctrines:

The policy purpose of the direct-consequences doctrine arises in the situation of concurrent efficient causation in which two injurers each has a reasonable opportunity to prevent harm to the victim. In this situation, the direct-consequences doctrine attempts to allocate liability in such a way as to increase the incentive of the last wrongdoer to compensate for the underprecaution mistakes of the original wrongdoer, when doing so will not destroy a more socially valuable incentive of the original wrongdoer to avoid these mistakes in the future. The purpose of the reasonable-foresight doctrine of proximate cause is to avoid the administrative costs of imposing liability for harms that would impose a larger cost on injurers to foresee than the social benefit that would follow from liability.

(11) A still different approach, embodying a critique of both economic theory and corrective justice and favoring a "principle of civil recourse," appears in Benjamin Zipursky, *Rights, Wrongs and Recourse in the Law of Torts*, 51 Vand. L. Rev. 1 (1998). Zipursky surveys a range of commentary, weaving it around cases, with repeated references to *Palsgraf*. He seeks to explain the "substantive standing rule"—a rule requiring a plaintiff to show that the "defendant's conduct was a wrong relative to her"—that is, that "her right was violated." *Id*. at 4. He describes a "principle of civil recourse" that "states that a person ought to be permitted civil recourse against one who has violated her legal rights." *Id*. at 82. Since "torts are relational legal wrongs," see, *e.g., id*. at 60, 87, and because one should not have to suffer a wrong "passively without response," "fair-

ness requires" that the plaintiff should have "recourse against the wrongdoer." *Id.* at 87. By creating "a right of action against the rights-violator," the law provides a way for society to "avoid[] the mayhem and crudeness of vengeful private retribution, but without the unfairness of leaving individuals powerless against invasions of their rights." *Id.* at 85. In a certain sense, "tort law is about getting even." But "[m]ore accurately, it is about not getting even, about what the state gives us in place of getting even." *Id.* at 100.

In a contemporaneous article, Zipursky and John C. P. Goldberg present a "relational concept of duty." *The Moral of McPherson*, 146 U. PA. L. REV. 1733 (1998). They interweave a discussion of *Palsgraf* with their analysis, see *id.* at 1813–24.

(12) Michael Wells suggests that the best test for preventing injustice in cases of the *Palsgraf-Polemis* type is "not to ask whether the injury is itself reasonably foreseeable, but whether it is greater than the reasonably foreseeable harm." *Proximate Cause and the American Law Institute: The False Choice Between the "Direct-Consequences" Test and the "Risk Standard,"* 37 U. RICH. L. REV. 389, 397 (2002). This approach would "fully address[] concerns that unfairness lurks in exposing negligent defendants to surprisingly expansive awards of damages," but would also "advance[] simple justice by permitting innocent victims to recover damages from concededly negligent defendants who cause a foreseeable measure of harm." *Id.* at 423.

---

§ 12.07 "Wrongful Birth" and "Wrongful Life"

GRECO v. UNITED STATES
Supreme Court of Nevada
111 Nev. 405, 893 P.2d 345 (1995)

SPRINGER, JUSTICE.

In this case we certify to the United States District Court for the District of Maryland that a mother has a tort claim in negligent malpractice against professionals who negligently fail to make a timely diagnosis of gross and disabling fetal defects, thereby denying the mother her right to terminate the pregnancy. We further certify that the child born to this mother has no personal cause of action for what is sometimes called "wrongful life."

As Justice Felix Frankfurter observed, "[P]erhaps no field of the law comes closer to the lives of so many families in this country than does the law of negligence...." ... Today it is the Greco family whom the law of negligence touches. The first question before this court is whether Nevada's common law of negligence offers relief to the mother of a child born with severe deformities whose physicians' negligence caused the mother to remain ignorant of the fact that she was carrying a severely deformed fetus. We answer this question in the affirmative. The second question before the

---

2. According to the facts as certified by the United States District Court, Joshua "was born with congenital myelomeningocele (spina bifida). Congenital macro/hydrocephaly, bilateral talipes varus deformity, and Arnold Chiari malformation, type two. Joshua required placement of a ventriculoperitoneal shunt for hydrocephalus. He has paraplegia with no sensation from the hips down and suffers permanent fine and gross motor retardation and mental retardation."

court is whether Sundi Greco's disabled child has any enforceable legal claims arising out of the child's being born with congenital defects. We answer this question in the negative.

In July 1989, appellant, Sundi A. Greco, mother of co-appellant Joshua Greco, ("Joshua") filed suit individually, and on Joshua's behalf, against respondent, the United States of America. Sundi Greco and Joshua alleged that Sundi Greco's doctors at the Nellis Air Force Base in Nevada committed several acts of negligence in connection with Sundi Greco's prenatal care and delivery and that, as a result, both Sundi and Joshua are entitled to recover money damages.[2] The United States moved to dismiss....

On July 20, 1993, the United States District Court for the District of Maryland filed a certification order with this court pursuant to NRAP 5, requesting that this court answer certain questions relating to the negligently caused unwanted birth of a child suffering from birth defects.

The Grecos, mother and child, in this case seek to recover damages from the United States arising out of the negligence of physicians who, they claim, negligently failed to make a timely diagnosis of physical defects and anomalies afflicting the child when it was still in the mother's womb. Sundi Greco asserts that the physicians' negligence denied her the opportunity to terminate her pregnancy and thereby caused damages attendant to the avoidable birth of an unwanted and severely deformed child. On Joshua's behalf, Sundi Greco avers that the physicians' negligence and the resultant denial of Joshua's mother's right to terminate her pregnancy caused Joshua to be born into a grossly abnormal life of pain and deprivation.

These kinds of tort claims have been termed "wrongful birth" when brought by a parent and "wrongful life" when brought on behalf of the child for the harm suffered by being born deformed.

THE CHILD'S CAUSE OF ACTION: "WRONGFUL LIFE"

We decline to recognize any action by a child for defects claimed to have been caused to the child by negligent diagnosis or treatment of the child's mother. The Grecos' argument is conditional and narrowly put, so: if this court does not allow Sundi Greco to recover damages for Joshua's care past the age of majority, it should allow Joshua to recover those damages by recognizing claims for "wrongful life." Implicit in this argument is the assumption that the child would be better off had he never been born. These kinds of judgments are very difficult, if not impossible, to make. Indeed, most courts considering the question have denied this cause of action for precisely this reason. Recognizing this kind of claim on behalf of the child would require us to weigh the harms suffered by virtue of the child's having been born with severe handicaps against "the utter void of nonexistence"; this is a calculation the courts are incapable of performing. Gleitman v. Cosgrove, 49 N.J. 22, 227 A.2d 689, 692 (1967). The New York Court of Appeals framed the problem this way:

> Whether it is better never to have been born at all than to have been born with even gross deficiencies is a mystery more properly to be left to the

---

5. One commentator observes that the term "wrongful life," "was a play on the statutory tort of 'wrongful death'". Alexander M. Capron, *Tort Liability in Genetic Counseling*, 79 Col.L.Rev. 618, 634 n. 62 (1979). The related concepts of wrongful birth and wrongful pregnancy or conception were similarly inspired. *Id.* The commentator concludes that the net effect of these terms has been to "spawn confusion" and distort or impair judicial vision. *Id.*

philosophers and the theologians. Surely the law can assert no competence to resolve the issue, particularly in view of the very nearly uniform high value which the law and mankind has placed on human life, rather than its absence.

Becker v. Schwartz, 46 N.Y.2d 401, 413 N.Y.S.2d 895, 900, 386 N.E.2d 807, 812 (1978). We conclude that Nevada does not recognize a claim by a child for harms the child claims to have suffered by virtue of having been born.

THE MOTHER'S CAUSE OF ACTION

With regard to Sundi Greco's claim against her physician for negligent diagnosis or treatment during pregnancy, we see no reason for compounding or complicating our medical malpractice jurisprudence by according this particular form of professional negligence action some special status apart from presently recognized medical malpractice or by giving it the new name of "wrongful birth."[5] Sundi Greco either does or does not state a claim for medical malpractice; and we conclude that she does.

Medical malpractice, like other forms of negligence, involves a breach of duty which causes injury. To be tortiously liable a physician must have departed from the accepted standard of medical care in a manner that results in injury to a patient.... In the case before us, we must accept as fact that Sundi Greco's physicians negligently failed to perform prenatal medical tests or performed or interpreted those tests in a negligent fashion and that they thereby negligently failed to discover and reveal that Sundi Greco was carrying a severely deformed fetus. As a result of such negligence Sundi Greco claims that she was denied the opportunity to terminate her pregnancy and that this denial resulted in her giving birth to a severely deformed child.

It is difficult to formulate any sound reason for denying recovery to Sundi Greco in the case at hand. Sundi Greco is saying, in effect, to her doctors:

> "If you had done what you were supposed to do, I would have known early in my pregnancy that I was carrying a severely deformed baby. I would have then terminated the pregnancy and would not have had to go through the mental and physical agony of delivering this child, nor would I have had to bear the emotional suffering attendant to the birth and nurture of the child, nor the extraordinary expense necessary to care for a child suffering from such extreme deformity and disability."

The United States advances two reasons for denying Sundi Greco's claim: first, it argues that she has suffered no injury and that, therefore, the damage element of negligent tort liability is not fulfilled; second, the United States argues that even if Sundi Greco has sustained injury and damages, the damages were not caused by her physicians. To support its first argument, the United States points out that in Szekeres v. Robinson, 102 Nev. 93, 715 P.2d 1076 (1986), this court held that the mother of a normal, healthy child could not recover in tort from a physician who negligently performed her sterilization operation because the birth of a normal, healthy child is not a legally cognizable injury.[6] The United States argues that no distinction can be made between a mother who gives birth to a healthy child and a mother who gives birth to a child with severe deformities and that, therefore, Szekeres bars recovery.

---

6. We did observe that the mother might have a contractual remedy against the physician for failure to do what he promised to do—sterilize his patient. *Id.* at 98, 715 P.2d at 1079.

Szekeres can be distinguished from the instant case. Unlike the birth of a normal child, the birth of a severely deformed baby of the kind described here is necessarily an unpleasant and aversive event and the cause of inordinate financial burden that would not attend the birth of a normal child. The child in this case will unavoidably and necessarily require the expenditure of extraordinary medical, therapeutic and custodial care expenses by the family, not to mention the additional reserves of physical, mental and emotional strength that will be required of all concerned. Those who do not wish to undertake the many burdens associated with the birth and continued care of such a child have the legal right, under Roe v. Wade and codified by the voters of this state, to terminate their pregnancies. Roe v. Wade, 410 U.S. 113, 93 S.Ct. 705, 35 L.Ed.2d 147 (1973); NRS 442.250 (codifying by referendum the conditions under which abortion is permitted in this state). Sundi Greco has certainly suffered money damages as a result of her physician's malpractice.

We also reject the United State[s]'s second argument that Sundi Greco's physicians did not cause any of the injuries that Sundi Greco might have suffered. We note that the mother is not claiming that her child's defects were caused by her physicians' negligence; rather, she claims that her physicians' negligence kept her ignorant of those defects and that it was this negligence which caused her to lose her right to choose whether to carry the child to term. The damage Sundi Greco has sustained is indeed causally related to her physicians' malpractice.

Sundi Greco's claim here can be compared to one in which a physician negligently fails to diagnose cancer in a patient. Even though the physician did not cause the cancer, the physician can be held liable for damages resulting from the patient's decreased opportunity to fight the cancer, and for the more extensive pain, suffering and medical treatment the patient must undergo by reason of the negligent diagnosis.... The "chance" lost here, was Sundi Greco's legally protected right to choose whether to abort a severely deformed fetus. If we were to deny Sundi Greco's claim, we would, in effect, be groundlessly excepting one type of medical malpractice from negligence liability. We see no reason to treat this case any differently from any other medical malpractice case. Sundi Greco has stated a prima facie claim of medical malpractice under Nevada law.

DAMAGE ISSUES

The certified question requires us to decide specifically what types of damages the mother may recover if she succeeds in proving her claim. Courts in these cases have struggled with what items of damages are recoverable because, unlike the typical malpractice claim, claims such as Sundi Greco's do not involve a physical injury to the patient's person. We consider each of Sundi Greco's claimed items of damage separately.

Extraordinary Medical and Custodial Expenses

This claim for damages relates to the medical, therapeutic and custodial costs associated with caring for a severely handicapped child. There is nothing exceptional in allowing this item of damage. It is a recognized principle of tort law to "afford compensation for injuries sustained by one person as the result of the conduct of another." W. Page Keeton, et al., Prosser and Keeton on the Law of Torts, § 2 at 6 (5th ed. 1984); see K Mart Corp. v. Ponsock, 103 Nev. 39, 49, 732 P.2d 1364, 1371 (1987) (tort damages serve to make injured party "whole"). Extraordinary care expenses are a foreseeable result of the negligence alleged in this case, and Sundi Greco should be allowed to recover those expenses if she can prove them. This leads us to the question of how to compensate for these kinds of injuries.

Sundi Greco correctly observes that Nevada law requires the parents of a handicapped child to support that child beyond the age of majority if the child cannot support itself.... Nevada recognizes the right of a parent to recover from a tortfeasor any expenses the parent was required to pay because of the injury to his or her minor child.... Accordingly, Sundi Greco claims the right to recover damages for these extraordinary costs for a period equal to Joshua's life expectancy.... We agree with these authorities and conclude that Sundi Greco may recover extraordinary medical and custodial expenses associated with caring for Joshua for whatever period of time it is established that Joshua will be dependent upon her to provide such care.

The United States contends that if this court allows the mother to recover such extraordinary medical and custodial expenses, then it should require the district court to offset any such award by the amount it would cost to raise a non-handicapped child. To do otherwise, argues the United States, would be to grant the mother a windfall....

The offset rule has its origins in two doctrines: the "avoidable consequences rule," which requires plaintiffs to mitigate their damages in tort cases, and the expectancy rule of damages employed in contract cases, which seeks to place the plaintiff in the position he or she would have been in had the contract been performed. Smith, 513 A.2d at 349. We conclude that neither of these doctrines is applicable to the case at bar. To enforce the "avoidable consequences" rule in the instant case would impose unreasonable burdens upon the mother such as, perhaps, putting Joshua up for adoption or otherwise seeking to terminate her parental obligations....

With regard to the expectancy rule, it would unnecessarily complicate and limit recovery for patients in other malpractice cases if we were to begin intruding contract damage principles upon our malpractice jurisprudence. The rule for compensatory damages in negligence cases is clear and workable, and we decline to depart from it.

. . .

Damages for Emotional Distress

Sundi Greco asserts that she is suffering and will continue to suffer tremendous mental and emotional pain as a result of the birth of Joshua. Several jurisdictions allow plaintiffs such as Sundi Greco to recover such damages. In line with these cases, we agree that it is reasonably foreseeable that a mother who is denied her right to abort a severely deformed fetus will suffer emotional distress, not just when the child is delivered, but for the rest of the child's life. Consequently, we conclude that the mother in this case should have the opportunity to prove that she suffered and will continue to suffer emotional distress as a result of the birth of her child.

. . .

SHEARING, J., with whom ROSE, J. joins, concurring in part and dissenting in part.

I agree with the majority that a mother should have a malpractice claim against professionals who negligently fail to make a timely diagnosis of fetal defects. However, I would also allow the impaired child a cause of action, with the measure of damages being the extraordinary expenses attributable to the child's impairment.

In this case, Joshua was born with congenital defects which result in his suffering paraplegia with no sensation from the hips down and permanent fine and gross motor retardation and mental retardation. It is clear that he will require extraordinary care throughout his life.

This case is not a traditional malpractice claim in which a medical professional directly causes a patient to suffer injuries. In order to find any causation from the medical professional's failure to test for abnormalities, one must accept the proposition that if Joshua's mother had been informed of the condition of the fetus, she would have had a therapeutic abortion and Joshua would never have been born.

Courts have had a great deal of difficulty in dealing with the moral implications of compensating parents or a child for that child's birth, when the plaintiffs' claim is essentially that they would all be better off had the child never been born. One reason the issue of compensation is so knotty is that it runs counter to our conception of the preciousness of human life.

This court has held that the birth of a normal healthy child is not "a 'wrong' or the type of injurious consequences for which society should, through its courts, as a matter of public policy, give reparation." ... This court then went on to state "[o]ur decision to disallow tort actions for the birth of a normal child ... simply holds that one cannot recover in tort for such an event because the constituent element of a negligence tort, namely damages, is not present here." Id. at 97–98, 715 P.2d at 1079. The question in this case is whether the birth of a seriously impaired child constitutes "damages" within the contemplation of our tort law.

The majority, along with other courts, rejects the impaired child's cause of action after wrestling with the question of whether damages exist when that determination requires the comparison of the value of an impaired life to the value of no life at all....

However, not all courts have taken the view that these difficulties are so great as to overcome the public policy objectives of tort law—to compensate injured parties and to deter future wrongful conduct. In Turpin v. Sortini, 31 Cal.3d 220, 182 Cal.Rptr. 337, 643 P.2d 954 (1982), the California Supreme Court quoted with approval a lower court opinion which stated:

> "The reality of the 'wrongful life' concept is that such a plaintiff exists and suffers, due to the negligence of others. It is neither necessary nor just to retreat into meditation on the mysteries of life. We need not be concerned with the fact that had defendants not been negligent, the plaintiff might not have come into existence at all. The certainty of genetic impairment is no longer a mystery. In addition, a reverent appreciation of life compels recognition that plaintiff, however impaired she may be, has come into existence as a living person with certain rights."

> ...

> Although it is easy to understand and to endorse these decisions' desire to affirm the worth and sanctity of less-than-perfect life, we question whether these considerations alone provide a sound basis for rejecting the child's tort action. To begin with, it is hard to see how an award of damages to a severely handicapped or suffering child would 'disavow' the value of life or in any way suggest that the child is not entitled to the full measure of legal and nonlegal rights and privileges accorded to all members of society.

Id. 182 Cal.Rptr. at 342, 344–45, 643 P.2d at 958, 961–62 (quoting Curlender v. Bio-Science Laboratories, 106 Cal.App.3d 811, 165 Cal.Rptr. 477, 488 (1980)).

The California Supreme Court went on to hold that both the child and the parents had a cause of action. However, the court rejected the parents' claim for general damages and allowed only the claim for medical expenses and extraordinary expenses for specialized teaching, training and equipment required because of the impairment. Id. 182 Cal.Rptr. at 349, 643 P.2d at 966.

The New Jersey Supreme Court has taken a similar approach, stating in Procanik by Procanik v. Cillo, 97 N.J. 339, 478 A.2d 755 (1984):

> The philosophical problem of finding that such a defective life is worth less than no life at all has perplexed not only Justice Schreiber, but such other distinguished members of this Court.... We need not become preoccupied, however, with these metaphysical considerations. Our decision to allow the recovery of extraordinary medical expenses is not premised on the concept that non-life is preferable to an impaired life, but it is predicated on the needs of the living. We seek only to respond to the call of the living for help in bearing the burden of their affliction.

> Sound reasons exist not to recognize a claim for general damages. Our analysis begins with the unfortunate fact that the infant plaintiff never had a chance of being born as a normal, healthy child. Tragically, his only choice was a life burdened with his handicaps or no life at all. The congenital rubella syndrome that plagues him was not caused by the negligence of the defendant doctors; the only proximate result of their negligence was the child's birth. The crux of the problem is that there is no rational way to measure non-existence or to compare non-existence with the pain and suffering of his impaired existence. Whatever theoretical appeal one might find in recognizing a claim for pain and suffering is outweighed by the essentially irrational and unpredictable nature of that claim. Although damages in a personal injury action need not be calculated with mathematical precision, they require at their base some modicum of rationality.

> Underlying our conclusion is an evaluation of the capability of the judicial system, often proceeding in these cases through trial by jury, to appraise such a claim. Also at work is an appraisal of the role of tort law in compensating injured parties, involving as that role does, not only reason, but also fairness, predictability, and even deterrence of future wrongful acts. In brief, the ultimate decision is a policy choice summoning the most sensitive and careful judgment.

> ...

> We believe that the interests of fairness and justice are better served through more predictably measured damages—the cost of the extraordinary medical expenses necessitated by the infant plaintiff's handicaps. Damages so measured are not subject to the same wild swings as a claim for pain and suffering and will carry a sufficient sting to deter future acts of medical malpractice.

Id. at 763.

The approach of the California and New Jersey courts is sound. These courts refuse to become mired in philosophical discussions of the meaning and value of life, and focus on compensating injured parties and deterring future wrongful conduct.

Our knowledge in the fields of genetics and obstetrics has grown dramatically, with far-reaching consequences for human life. It is clear that responsive treatments and the counseling necessitated by those treatments will develop in accordance with our ever-increasing capability to test and diagnose. It would, therefore, be anomalous for medical practitioners in these fields to be immune from liability for wrongful conduct or for departing from accepted professional standards. Unquestionably the public policy behind tort law supports compensating impaired children and their parents for the special damages resulting from impairment when the negligence of the medical professional results in the birth of the impaired child.

Although this court has stated that the public policy in Nevada is that birth of a normal healthy child is not a legally compensable damage, this court has also recognized that the value of an impaired life is not always greater than the value of non-life. See McKay v. Bergstedt, 106 Nev. 808, 801 P.2d 617 (1990). In addition, the legislature has recognized this fact in setting forth the policy of this state concerning the deprivation of life-sustaining procedures. NRS 449.535-690 ("Withholding or Withdrawal of Life-Sustaining Treatment"). In these statutes, the legislature made clear that a person may choose not to sustain life. The underlying policy recognizes that, in some situations, non-life may be preferable to an impaired life; further, the policy recognizes that each individual has the right to make his or her determination as to the relative value of life and non-life.

. . .

NOTES

(1) Is the fundamental problem in a suit for "wrongful life" one of duty, causation, or damages? Does the root problem differ in suits for "wrongful birth," called by any name?

Why do courts favor "wrongful birth" claims much more than "wrongful life" claims?

(2) What would be the most persuasive philosophical premise of each side in a suit for either tort?

(3) Can a judge avoid being "political" in choosing the premises that guide decision in such a case?

What would be the best approach for a judge who seeks to make a decision based entirely on "legal" grounds—for example, reasoning by analogy to other duty/proximate cause cases? Which set of cases in that category presents the closest analogies?

(4) What role can, or should, economic analysis play in deciding a case in either category? Are these cases subject to the Learned Hand test? A cost-benefit test? A least-cost-avoider test?

(5) A pregnant woman, driving negligently, has a collision that leads to the premature birth of her child, who is hospitalized for more than three weeks with breathing problems arising from the premature birth. The child continues to suffer various kinds of respiratory problems. She sues her mother for these illnesses. What result?

§ 12.08 Economic Loss

MATTINGLY v. SHELDON JACKSON COLLEGE
Alaska Supreme Court
743 P.2d 356 (1987)

MATTHEWS, JUSTICE.

This appeal is from an employer's action against Sheldon Jackson College for alleged willful, reckless, and negligent conduct which resulted in injury to the employer's employees and his business. The employer, George Mattingly, seeks damages for loss of income and profits suffered as a result of the loss of his employees' services, expenses incurred for medical care and hospitalization of his employees, damages for his own emotional distress, and punitive damages. The superior court granted the College's motion for judgment on the pleadings pursuant to Civil Rule 12(c) and 12(b)(6) on the ground that the complaint failed to allege a cause of action, and dismissed the complaint.

We conclude that Mattingly's complaint sets forth sufficient allegations to state a cause of action for negligently caused economic injury to a particularly foreseeable plaintiff. We therefore reverse the superior court's dismissal of Mattingly's complaint and remand for further proceedings on that cause of action. We affirm the superior court's decision as to the remainder of the causes of action which Mattingly asserted.

I. FACTS AND PROCEEDINGS

At the time the cause of action arose, George Mattingly was engaged in a drain cleaning, sewage pumping, and fire protection system enterprise, doing business under the name of Harbor Mechanical and Fire Protection in Sitka and Ketchikan. On April 18, 1983, Sheldon Jackson College contacted Harbor Mechanical to have a drain pipe cleaned on the College campus. Thomas Mattingly, plaintiff's son and an employee of Harbor Mechanical, and two other employees were dispatched to the College to clean the drain pipe.

Three of Sheldon Jackson's employees, also defendants/appellees, excavated and braced a trench to expose the drain pipe so that Mattingly's employees could perform their work. The trench subsequently collapsed on the three Harbor Mechanical employees, completely burying one and partially burying the other two. The three men were taken to the hospital for medical treatment.

Mattingly alleges that his three employees suffered serious physical and psychological injuries. He further alleges that he took time away from his duties as general manager of Harbor Mechanical in Ketchikan to come to Sitka to be by the side of his injured son and employees. He claims that he himself suffered considerable physical and emotional trauma as a consequence of the stress associated with assisting his injured employees and meeting the demands of continuing the business without their help. He further claims that he temporarily lost the services of his son and one employee, that he permanently lost the services of the other employee, and thereby lost business, business reputation and income, and incurred expenses for the medical care and treatment of his employees.

. . . .

II.

. . . .

B. *Cause of Action for Economic Loss Damages Despite Lack of Physical Harm or Injury*

Mattingly argues that the superior court did not consider all possible grounds for the College's liability in negligence before it dismissed his complaint for failure to state a cause of action. Specifically, Mattingly contends that the foreseeable risk of harm to his business should a cave-in occur gave rise to a duty on the part of the College to take reasonable precautions in the excavation and bracing of the trench. Mattingly relies in part on *People Express Airlines, Inc. v. Consolidated Rail Corp.*, 100 N.J. 246, 495 A.2d 107 (1985), in which the New Jersey Supreme Court addressed as a question of first impression whether negligent conduct that interferes with a party's business resulting in purely economic loss without property damage or personal injury is compensable in tort. The court held that economic loss damages are recoverable despite a lack of physical damages or injury if suffered by persons in businesses comprising an identifiable class whom the defendant knows or has reason to know are likely to suffer damages. We are persuaded by the approach of the New Jersey Supreme Court and set forth its analysis in some detail.

In *People Express*, a commercial airline was forced to evacuate its premises and suffered interruption of its business operations as a result of the defendants' negligent acts in allowing a dangerous chemical to escape from a nearby railway car. People Express asserted that it suffered business interruption losses as a result of the evacuation, but there was no property damage or physical injury associated with its economic losses. The court was principally concerned with the fact that People Express suffered no physical harm or property damage.

> The single characteristic that distinguishes parties in negligence suits whose claims for economic losses have been regularly denied by American and English courts from those who have recovered economic losses is, with respect to the successful claimants, the fortuitous occurrence of physical harm or property damage, however slight. It is well-accepted that a defendant who negligently injures a plaintiff or his property may be liable for all proximately caused harm, including economic losses. *See Palsgraf v. Long Island R.R.*, 248 N.Y. 339, 163 N.E. 99 (1928); W. Prosser & W. Keeton, The Law of Torts § 129, at 997 (5th ed. 1984).... Nevertheless, a virtually per se rule barring recovery for economic loss unless the negligent conduct also caused physical harm has evolved throughout this century....

495 A.2d at 109 (citations omitted).

The court examined the reasons for the divergent results for litigants seeking economic losses, such as the necessity to limit damages to reasonably foreseeable consequences of negligent conduct, and the fear of fraudulent claims, mass litigation, and limitless liability or liability out of proportion to the defendant's fault. *Id.* at 110. Although these concerns are valid, the court found that they support only a limitation on, not a denial of, liability.

> The answer to the allegation of unchecked liability is not the judicial obstruction of a fairly grounded claim for redress. Rather, it must be a more sedulous application of traditional concepts of duty and proximate causation to the facts of each case.
>
> ... The physical harm requirement capriciously showers compensation along the path of physical destruction, regardless of the status or circumstances of individual claimants. Purely economic losses are borne by innocent victims, who may not be able to absorb their losses.... In the end, the challenge is to

fashion a rule that limits liability but permits adjudication of meritorious claims.

Id. at 111. As to concerns of fraudulent or baseless claims, another court has stated that "[h]ere, as elsewhere, the answer must be that courts have some expertise in performing their almost daily task of distinguishing the honest from the collusive or fraudulent claim." *Petition of Kinsman Transit Co.*, 388 F.2d 821, 823 (2d Cir.1968). Finally, even in negligence suits involving property damage or physical harm, courts have recognized that a tortfeasor is not necessarily liable for all consequences of his conduct.

> Some limitation is required; that limitation is the rule that a tortfeasor is liable only for that harm that he proximately caused. Proximate or legal cause has traditionally functioned to limit liability for negligent conduct. Duty has also been narrowly defined to limit liability. Compare the majority and dissenting opinions in *Palsgraf v. Long Island R.R., supra*, 248 N.Y. 339, 162 N.E. 99. Thus, we proceed from the premise that principles of duty and proximate cause are instrumental in limiting the amount of litigation and extent of liability in cases in which no physical harm occurs just as they are in cases involving physical injury.

People Express, 495 A.2d at 110.

Moreover, judicial reluctance to allow recovery for purely economic losses is discordant with contemporary tort doctrine.

> The tort process, like the law itself, is a human institution designed to accomplish certain social objectives. One objective is to ensure that innocent victims have avenues of legal redress, absent a contrary, overriding public policy.... This reflects the overarching purpose of tort law: that wronged persons should be compensated for their injuries and that those responsible for the wrong should bear the cost of their tortious conduct.

Id. at 111 (citations omitted).

We agree with the foregoing and therefore hold that

> [A] defendant owes a duty of care to take reasonable measures to avoid the risk of causing economic damages, aside from physical injury [or property damage], to particular plaintiffs or plaintiffs comprising an identifiable class with respect to whom defendant knows or has reason to know are likely to suffer such damages from its conduct. A defendant failing to adhere to this duty of care may be found liable for such economic damages proximately caused by its breach of duty.

Id. at 116. In adopting a rule permitting recovery for purely economic losses, we emphasize the role of foreseeability as it relates both to the duty owed and to proximate cause. "The traditional test of negligence is what a reasonably prudent person would foresee and do in the circumstances; duty is clearly defined by knowledge of the risk of harm or the reasonable apprehension of that risk." *Id.* at 115.

In cases where plaintiffs may successfully recover for purely economic harm, it must be shown that

> the defendants knew or reasonably should have foreseen both that particular plaintiffs or an identifiable class of plaintiffs were at risk and that ascertainable

economic damages would ensue from the conduct. Thus, knowledge or special reason to know of the consequences of the tortious conduct in terms of the persons likely to be victimized and the nature of the damages likely to be suffered will suffice to impose a duty upon the tortfeasor not to interfere with economic well-being of third parties.

Id. Further, the extent of liability and degree of foreseeability stand in direct proportion to one another. The more particular the foreseeability that economic loss will be suffered by the plaintiff as a result of defendant's negligence, the more just it is that liability be imposed and recovery allowed.

> We stress that an identifiable class of plaintiffs is not simply a foreseeable class of plaintiffs. For example, members of the general public, or invitees such as sales and service persons at a particular plaintiff's business premises, or persons travelling on a highway near the scene of a negligently-caused accident … who are delayed in the conduct of their affairs and suffer varied economic losses, are certainly a foreseeable class of plaintiffs. Yet their presence within the area would be fortuitous, and the particular type of economic injury that could be suffered by such persons would be hopelessly unpredictable and not realistically foreseeable. Thus, the class itself would not be sufficiently ascertainable. *An identifiable class of plaintiffs must be particularly foreseeable in terms of the type of persons or entities comprising the class, the certainty or predictability of their presence, the approximate numbers of those in the class, as well as the type of economic expectations disrupted.*

Id. at 116 (emphasis added).

> In this context, those economic losses are recoverable as damages when they are the natural and probable consequence of a defendant's negligence in the sense that they are reasonably to be anticipated in view of defendant's capacity to have foreseen that the particular plaintiff or identifiable class of plaintiffs … is demonstrably within the risk created by defendant's negligence.

Id. at 118.

Turning to the case at bar, we are satisfied that Mattingly has set forth a cause of action and is entitled to have the matter proceed on the issue of negligently caused economic losses, if any. Losses of business income and profit and increases in expenses were pled. Mattingly maintained that the College had a duty to refrain from conduct which would foreseeably interfere with his ability to conduct his business. He is certainly a foreseeable and particularized plaintiff—the trench was dug so that his employees could work in it—who might predictably suffer economic losses if the College negligently caused harm to his business. Mattingly still faces a difficult task in proving his damages, particularly lost profits, to the degree of certainty required in negligence cases. He will also have to demonstrate that he could not have reasonably replaced his injured employees and thereby continued his business.

C. Employer's Right of Action for Loss of Service Against Third Person Tortiously Injuring Employees

1. Negligent Interference with Contract or Business Relations

Apart from his claim for negligently caused economic losses, Mattingly argues that the College's conduct supports a cause of action for negligent interference with his relationships with his employees.

…

Although we have not yet directly addressed the question whether an employer may recover for a third person's negligent injury to an employee, or for negligent interference with the employer's contract with its employees or its prospective economic advantage, several Alaska cases may be read to limit an employer's right of action to intentional interference. In *Long v. Newby*, 488 P.2d 719 (Alaska 1971), we joined the majority of American jurisdictions in recognizing the tort of intentional interference with contractual relations. In *Ellis v. City of Valdez*, 686 P.2d 700 (Alaska 1984), the tort of intentional interference with prospective economic advantage was recognized for the first time in Alaska. We explained that

> the individual's expectation of a fair opportunity to conduct legitimate business affairs free from wrongful intermeddling by others, is also widely protected in American jurisdictions, through the tort of intentional interference with prospective economic advantage. Under this theory, a person who is involved in an economic relationship with another, or who is pursuing reasonable and legitimate prospects of entering such a relationship, is protected from a third person's wrongful conduct *which is intended to disrupt the relationship*.

Id. at 707 (emphasis added). Even assuming that Mattingly's complaint may be liberally construed to make out a claim for interference with his employee relations and prospective economic advantage, nowhere in *Long* or *Ellis* did we hint that negligent interference would support a cause of action.

We now adopt the modern rule that employers may not recover simply for the loss of their employees' services or for loss of profits arising from the negligent injury of their employees by a third person. Of course, a defendant's negligent injury of an employer's employee may be relevant to the employer's cause of action for negligently caused economic losses. Thus, although an employer may not recover under a theory of loss of profits or employee services due to an employee's negligent injury by a third party, the employer might, as in this case, state a cause of action for negligently caused economic loss as discussed in part II.B of this opinion.

...

In re TMI LITIGATION GOVERNMENTAL ENTITIES CLAIMS

United States District Court, Middle District of Pennsylvania
544 F. Supp. 853 (1982)

MEMORANDUM

RAMBO, DISTRICT JUDGE.

The accident at Three Mile Island Reactor No. 2 (TMI) near Harrisburg, Pennsylvania on March 28, 1979 has spawned numerous lawsuits most of which are pending in this court. Ripe for consideration is a motion for summary judgment filed by the defendants, owners of TMI, companies involved with its design and construction and a company which maintained the reactor. The captioned cases were consolidated for pre-trial disposition under the heading "Governmental Entities Claims." Summary judgment will be granted as to all aspects of the cases for the reasons set forth in the following discussion.

The actions seek to recover, on behalf of the Commonwealth of Pennsylvania, two named municipalities, and a class of all other Pennsylvania local municipalities within a radius of 100 miles from Three Mile Island these designated damages:

(1) Overtime and compensatory time and other personnel costs incurred in responding to the nuclear incident;

(2) Operational expenses and emergency purchases incurred in responding to the nuclear incident;

(3) Lost work time as a result of the nuclear incident; and

(4) Other expenses incurred as a result of and/or in response to the nuclear incident.

. . .

Public Expenditures in Performance of Governmental Functions

. . .

Plaintiffs argue that a nuclear power accident is a unique emergency which calls for different rules than those which have developed to deal with an everyday occurrence such as a fire....

. . .

Pennsylvania has passed the Emergency Management Services Code which designates the roles and responsibilities of the Commonwealth and its political subdivisions in the event of an emergency. 35 Pa.C.S.A. § 7101 *et seq.* It is applicable to incidents created by mishaps at a nuclear power facility. 35 Pa.C.S.A. § 7102. The Code is fairly comprehensive, for example it provides for compensation for those who might be injured while engaged in emergency management activities. Yet, it makes no provision for recovery of expenses incurred by the Commonwealth or by any political subdivision in responding to a disaster.

The Commonwealth argued that Pennsylvania and its communities should not have to bear the costs of a nuclear accident alone, rather the costs should be spread nationwide by forcing the liability insurers for nuclear power plants to pay for damages attributable to the plants' operation. In effect the Commonwealth is urging the court to create a nuclear power exception to existing tort law. Disasters come from many industrial sources, and create the need for local governments to respond to emergencies. Hydroelectric dams collapse, tank cars carrying dangerous chemicals derail, fires erupt at oil refineries and hazardous waste dumps emit toxic particles. These potential dangers are a concomitant of a highly industrialized society. Wherever disasters occur local government has traditionally borne the costs. It is not for this court to make the judgment that one industry is more obnoxious or dangerous or less utilitarian than another and force that industry to bear a public expense usually spread through the population by taxation. Such a decision can be made by the legislature after a study of the costs and benefits related to the industry and the desirability of making the industry rather than the public pay for emergency services necessitated by an accident within that particular industry.

Recovery of Economic Losses Absent Injury to Person or Property

All of the causes of action pleaded in the complaints are based on negligence and strict liability. The governmental entities claim damage for their expenditures in the nature of civil defense efforts, and for wages and salaries paid governmental employees. There are no allegations that any of these costs or expenses were incurred in order to protect government property from threatened physical harm, and there are no allegations that any of these costs or expenses were incurred in restoring or repairing government property actually injured in the TMI accident. The losses claimed by these plaintiffs, then, are purely economic losses; they are, in the parlance of the Restatement authors, non-parasitic economic loss. Restatement (Second) of Torts, § 766C, Comment b. Pennsylvania courts have not permitted lawsuits for such losses where plaintiff has suffered no personal injury or property damage. *Muller v. Pennsylvania Gas Co.*, 54 Erie Co. Legal J. 1 (1970) (employee may not recover commissions lost due to a negligently caused fire at his employer's place of business); *Gramby v. Philadelphia Transportation Co.*, 22 Pa.D.&C.2d 366 (C.P.Phila.Co.1960) (manager of a professional boxer injured while a passenger on a bus barred from suit to recover manager's share of the fighter's anticipated purse); *Heyison v. Taylor*, 7 Pa.D.&C.2d 176 (C.P.Allegheny Co.1956) (partners may not sue for damages sustained by partnership because it was deprived of injured partner's services).

Courts have generally precluded recovery in tort for purely economic loss because the conceivable chain of damages has a long reach. As the court stated in *Stevenson v. East Ohio Gas Co.*, 47 Ohio App. 586, 73 N.E.2d 200 (Ohio 1946):

> If one who by his negligence is legally responsible for an explosion or a conflagration should be required to respond in damages not only to those who have sustained personal injuries or physical property damage but also to every one who has suffered an economic loss, by reason of the explosion or conflagration, we might well be appalled by the results that would follow. In the instant case the door would be opened to claims for damages based on delay by all those who may have had contracts with [plaintiff's employer] either to deliver materials to the company or to receive from the company the products manufactured by it. Cases might well occur where a manufacturer would be obliged to close down his factory because of the inability of his supplier due to a fire loss to make prompt deliveries; the power company with a contract to supply a factory with electricity would be deprived of the profit which it would have made if the operation of the factory had not been interrupted by reason of fire damage; a man who had a contract to paint a building may not be able to proceed with his work; a salesman who would have sold the products of the factory may be deprived of his commission; the neighborhood restaurant which relies on the trade of the factory employees may suffer a substantial loss. The claims of workmen for loss of wages who were employed in such a factory and cannot continue to work there because of a fire, represent only a small fraction of the claims which would arise if recovery is allowed in this class of cases.

73 N.E.2d at 203–204.

It may also be in this case that services usually provided by these governmental units either were not performed or were delayed. If the government can recover for its losses, then why not one who lost money due to delay on the Commonwealth's or municipalities' part.

Defendants summarized the policy considerations underlying the rule barring recovery in tort for purely economic losses:

> Thus, while different courts have offered various reasons for denying recovery of economic losses except where parasitic to personal injury or property damage, there appear to be two fundamental concerns which prompt this limitation. One very obvious and often expressed concern is that there is a need to limit potential liability. *See, e.g., Ore-Ida Foods, Inc. v. Indian Head Cattle Co.*, *supra* [290 Or.909], 627 P.2d [469] at 474. A second concern, however, and one which is more often implied than expressed, appears to be a recognition that the tort theories of negligence and strict liability may not have been intended to protect citizens from economic losses unattended by physical injury to persons or property. *See, e.g.*, James, *Limitations on Liability For Economic*

Loss Caused by Negligence: A Pragmatic Appraisal, 25 Vand.L.Rev. 43 (1972). *See also Just's, Inc. v. Arrington Construction Co.,* ... 99 Idaho [462] at 470, 583 P.2d [997] at 1005 ("the common underlying pragmatic consideration is that a contrary rule, which would allow compensation for losses of economic advantage caused by the defendant's negligence, would impose too heavy and unpredictable a burden on the defendant's conduct"); *Stevenson v. East Ohio Gas Co., supra,* 73 N.E.2d at 203–204.

...

Whichever rationale one accepts, the courts have consistently refused to recognize a cause of action in negligence or strict liability for economic injury unattended by physical injury or damage to real or personal property.

...

NOTES

(1) In the Three Mile Island case, in which the district court opinion just above granted summary judgment for the defendants, the Third Circuit vacated the district court decision. The appellate court concluded that the plaintiffs prevailed against the summary judgment motion with their argument that "increased radioactivity and radioactive materials emitted during the nuclear incident permeated the entire area, and ... rendered ... public buildings unsafe for a temporary period of time," and that these events "constituted a physical intrusion" that presented a sufficient showing of "physical harm or injury" to take the case out of the category of "purely economic losses." *Pennsylvania v. General Pub. Utils. Corp.,* 710 P.2d 117 (3d Cir. 1983). But what about the district court's employment of a broad rule opposing recovery for "purely economic loss"? Should there be a blanket rule against liability for the alleged harms summarized following the second paragraph of District Judge Rambo's opinion? If you do not accept such a per se rule, then what limiting factors would you employ to prevent liability from becoming unjustly indeterminate and economically ruinous to the defendant?

(2) Can you square the Alaska court's holdings on the general "economic loss" issue in *Mattingly* with its denial of liability on negligent interference with contract?

(3) Some of the most important case law on the "economic loss" problem has come from oil and chemical spills. Consider a pair of cases:

• In *Union Oil Co. v. Oppen,* 501 F.2d 558 (9th Cir. 1974), the plaintiffs were commercial fishermen who sued for fish kills they attributed to an oil spill in the Santa Barbara channel. Judge Sneed held that the plaintiffs had stated a cause of action, saying, in part, *id.* at 569:

> ... [T]he presence of a duty on the part of the defendants in this case would turn substantially on foreseeability. That being the crucial determinant, the question must be asked whether the defendants could reasonably have foreseen that negligently conducted drilling operations might diminish aquatic life and thus injure the business of commercial fishermen. We believe the answer is yes. The dangers of pollution were and are known even by school children. The defendants understood the risks of their business and should reasonably have foreseen the scope of its responsibilities. To assert that the defendants were unable to foresee that negligent conduct resulting in a substantial oil spill could diminish aquatic life and thus injure the plaintiffs is to suppose a degree of general ignorance of the effects of oil pollution not in accord with good sense.

• In *Louisiana ex rel. Guste v. M/V Testbank*, 752 F.2d 1019 (5th Cir. 1985), *cert. denied sub nom. White v. M/V Testbank*, 477 U.S. 903 (1986), the majority of a sharply divided court denied recovery to a variety of plaintiffs, including marina and boat rental operators and seafood restaurants as well as fishermen who sued for injuries to marine life caused by a large chemical spill. Judge Higginbotham wrote for the court, 752 F.2d at 1029:

> With a disaster inflicting large and reverberating injuries through the economy, as here, we believe the more important economic inquiry is that of relative cost of administration, and in maritime matters administration quickly involves insurance. Those economic losses not recoverable under the present rule for lack of physical damage to a proprietary interest are the subject of first party or loss insurance. The rule change would work a shift to the more costly liability system of third party insurance. For the same reasons that courts have imposed limits on the concept of foreseeability, liability insurance might not be readily obtainable for the types of losses asserted here. As Professor James has noted, "[s]erious practical problems face insurers in handling insurance against potentially wide, open-ended liability. From an insurer's point of view it is not practical to cover, without limit, a liability that may reach catastrophic proportions, or to fix a reasonable premium on a risk that does not lend itself to actuarial measurement." James, [*Limitations on Liability For Economic Loss Caused by Negligence: A Pragmatic Appraisal*, 25 VAND. L. REV. 43 (1972)] at 53. By contrast, first party insurance is feasible for many of the economic losses claimed here. Each businessman who might be affected by a disruption of river traffic or by a halt in fishing activities can protect against that eventuality at a relatively low cost since his own potential losses are finite and readily discernible. Thus, to the extent that economic analysis informs our decision here, we think that it favors retention of the present rule.

(4) One of the weirdest of the economic loss cases is *Petition of Kinsman Transit Co.*, 388 F.2d 821 (2d Cir. 1968), in which Judge Kaufman summarized the facts this way, *id.* at 822:

> [A]s a result of the negligence of the Kinsman Transit Company and the Continental Grain Company the S.S. MacGilvray Shiras broke loose from her moorings and careened stern first down the narrow, S-shaped river channel. She struck the S.S. Michael K. Tewksbury, which in turn broke loose from her moorings and drifted downstream—followed by the Shiras—until she crashed into the Michigan Avenue Bridge. The bridge collapsed and its wreckage, together with the Tewksbury and the Shiras, formed a dam which caused extensive flooding and an ice jam reaching almost 3 miles upstream. As a result of this disaster, transportation on the river was disrupted until approximately March 13, 1959—a period of about 2 months.

Given "all the circumstances," Judge Kaufman concluded, *id.* at 825,

> the connection between the defendants' negligence and the claimants' damages is too tenuous and remote to permit recovery. "The law does not spread its protection so far." Holmes, J., in *Robins Dry Dock, supra*, 275 U.S. at 309, 48 S.Ct. at 135.

> In the final analysis, the circumlocution whether posed in terms of "foreseeability," "duty," "proximate cause," "remoteness," etc. seems unavoidable. As we have previously noted, 338 F.2d at 725, we return to Judge Andrews' frequently quoted statement in *Palsgraf v. Long Island R.R.*, … : "It is all a question of ex-

---

* Adapted.

pediency ... of fair judgment, always keeping in mind the fact that we endeavor to make a rule in each case that will be practical and in keeping with the general understanding of mankind."

Is this a sufficiently analytical response?

(5) Recurrent power crises, occasionally culminating in blackouts, have posed the *Kinsman* question in an exaggerated form. Preliminarily, consider a case of personal injury: In a suit against a power company for failure to keep up with regional energy requirements, could you rationalize recovery for a hospital patient whose condition worsens seriously because of the hospital's need to ration power from emergency generators during a blackout? Are there controlling distinctions between that situation and a suit against a railroad whose train goes off the track because of negligence and runs into a power pole, knocking out the lines which service the hospital?

Now compare a case of a frozen food storage firm that loses everything in a blackout attributable to either of the causes hypothesized for the hospital case just described. Is spoilage of thawed food distinguishable from the worsening of the patient's condition in the hospital case?

(6) At the outer limits of the economic loss cases, and embracing implications of the bystander-relative cases, is a decision by the French Court of Cassation. The court upheld a father's suit for the expenses of a trip from Greece to his son's bedside in Paris after the son had been hit by a toy thrown from the fifth floor of a store. See Catala & Weir, *Delict and Torts: A Study in Parallel*, 39 TUL. L. REV. 701, 740 (1965).

ECONOMIC LOSS IN PRODUCTS LIABILITY

SHAPO, THE LAW OF PRODUCTS LIABILITY (4th ed. 2001)*

¶ 27.02 FOUNDATIONS OF MODERN CONTROVERSY

[1] Santor v. A&M Karagheusian, Inc.

...

The opening shots were fired in 1965 from opposite coasts, and they still reverberate. The first salvo that year came from the New Jersey Supreme Court in *Santor v. A&M Karagheusian, Inc.*,[5] which imposed a strict form of liability against the manufacturer of a carpet afflicted with a line that would not "walk out." The New Jersey court affirmed a plaintiff's judgment on the liability issue, which was rendered on the basis of implied warranty of merchantability.[6] The court suggested that the applicable rule was more appropriately styled strict liability in tort, saying, "It should make no difference that the defect in the product did not or was not likely to cause harm to the purchaser."[7] At various points in its decision, the court discussed several rationales supporting strict forms

---

5. *Santor v. A&M Karagheusian*, 44 N.J. 52, 207 A.2d 305 (1965).

6. The court remanded for a new trial on the issue of damages, saying that the measure of damages "should be the difference between the price paid by plaintiff and the actual market value of the defective carpeting at the time plaintiff knew or should have known that it was defective." *Id.* at 68–69, 207 A.2d at 314.

7. *Id.* at 60, 207 A.2d at 309.

14. *Blagg v. Fred Hunt Co.*, 272 Ark. 185, 189–190, 612 S.W.2d 321, 323–324 (1981)....

*   *Alloway v. General Marine Indus., L.P.*, 149 N.J. 620, 635, 695 A.2d 264, 271 (1997).

of liability, including manufacturer advertising and the circuity of litigation associated with the privity requirement. Its own emphasis was not on "advertising to promote sales" but on the "mere presence of the product on the market," in the context of the asserted fact that the "great mass of the purchasing public has neither adequate knowledge nor sufficient opportunity to determine if articles bought or used are defective." Yet, although advertising was not the court's focal point, the decision had a representational basis: "Existence of the defect means violation of the representation implicit in the presence of the article in the stream of trade that it is suitable for the general purposes for which it is sold and for which such goods are generally appropriate," a representation "found in the law."

. . .

Only a few other decisions have accepted the *Santor* analysis. Applying strict liability in favor of subsequent purchasers of homes, the Arkansas Supreme Court upheld a judgment for economic losses caused by defects. Declaring "that the word 'product' is as applicable to a house as to an automobile," the Arkansas court said that *Santor* "prophetically extended the doctrine" of strict liability.[14]

In 1997, the New Jersey court severely limited *Santor* if not overruled it. Denying tort recovery in a case in which a pleasure boat sank because of a defective seam in the swimming platform, the court said that in the context of the case, "a tort cause of action for economic loss duplicating the one provided by the U.C.C. is superfluous and counterproductive."*

. . .

[2] Seely v. White Motor Co.

[a] Traynor's Majority Opinion

From California came another 1965 decision that embodied what became a clear majority rule. Conscious of the opportunity provided by *Santor* for a more definitive treatment of the then new doctrine of strict products liability, Chief Justice Traynor seized the occasion of a case involving a truck plagued by a violent "galloping" action that made it impossible for the plaintiff to use it as he would have liked in his business. In *Seely v. White Motor Co.*,[15] although accepting express warranty to support the plaintiff's claim for lost profits and the purchase price, Justice Traynor wrote a long dictum opposing the application of the strict liability doctrine to cases of "economic loss." Warranty theory, he suggested, was quite useful in determining obligations in commercial transactions in which parties could bargain effectively about the worth of products for particular purposes. A manufacturer, said Justice Traynor, should not "be held for the level of performance of his products in the consumer's business unless he agrees that the product was designed to meet the consumer's demands." By contrast, manufacturers could "appropriately be held liable for physical injuries caused by defects by requiring [their] goods to match a standard of safety defined in terms of conditions that create unreasonable risks of harm." A resulting conclusion was that parties should be able to agree on allocation of commercial losses where safety was not involved.

---

15. *Seely v. White Motor Co.*, 63 Cal. 2d 9, 403 P.2d 145, 45 Cal. Rptr. 17 (1965).

[b] The Peters Opinion

An important concurring-dissenting opinion by Justice Peters in *Seely* criticized a distinction drawn by Justice Traynor based on the linkage of personal injury to "overwhelming misfortune." Although "'[o]verwhelming misfortunes' *might* occur more often in personal injury cases than in property damage or economic loss cases," Justice Peters wrote, "this is no reason to draw the line between these types of injury when a more sensible line is available." A guideline for this "more sensible" line was whether the plaintiff was an "ordinary consumer," a concept that depended, at least in some measure, on the consumer's "bargaining power." An attendant question was whether the consumer was able "to protect himself from insidious contractual provisions such as disclaimers, foisted upon him by commercial enterprises whose bargaining power he is seldom able to match." An appropriate decision would also consider that this ordinary consumer was "'seldom steeped in the business practice which justifies' the notice requirement" that is part and parcel of traditional commercial law doctrine. Justice Peters thought that the facts of *Seely* were close, but he concluded that the plaintiff was "an ordinary consumer insofar as the purchase ... was concerned, even though he bought the truck for use in his business." He distinguished the plaintiff as "an owner-driver of a single truck he used for hauling and not a fleet-owner who bought trucks regularly in the course of his business."

[c] Traynor's Rebuttal

An answer to Justice Peters' argument appeared in Justice Traynor's recounting of the further history of the truck when it was resold after the plaintiff returned it to the dealer. The experienced trucker who bought it testified that he had no unusual difficulty with it, a point Justice Traynor seized on to suggest that it was "more likely that the truck functioned normally when put to use in [the subsequent purchaser's] business because his use made demands upon it different from those made by plaintiff's use." For Justice Traynor, the unfortunate implications of holding the manufacturer liable without privity for Seely's unbargained commercial loss would have been that the firm would "be liable for business losses of other truckers caused by the failure of its trucks to meet the specific needs of their businesses, even though those needs were communicated only to the dealer."

[d] Majority Rule: Supporting Decisions

The argument generated by the historic confrontation of *Santor* and *Seely* has been refined by decisions during the succeeding decades.... [T]he overwhelming weight of authority supports Traynor's view that economic loss is not recoverable under strict liability.

...

¶ 27.05 "PROPERTY DAMAGE"

A classic distinction in tort law has separated physical injury and "property damage," prime candidates for compensation, from economic loss, a more doubtful applicant. Suits by plaintiffs seeking admission to the liability sanctum of "property damage," as distinguished from "economic loss," have inspired much argument about definitions.

---

147. 476 U.S. 858 (1986).

[7] The Supreme Court's Decision in the *East River* Case

[a] Generally

The Supreme Court rejected distinctions related to the way in which the product itself is injured in *East River S.S. Corp v. Transamerica Delaval Inc.*[147] The Court chose the *Seely* position in this admiralty case, in which defective turbine components allegedly were associated with malfunctions and damage to the turbines themselves. Affirming the Third Circuit's denial of tort recovery, Justice Blackmun emphasized that "[p]roducts liability grew out of a public policy judgment that people need more protection from dangerous products than is afforded by the law of warranty." Justice Blackmun said that "[t]he tort concern with safety is reduced when an injury is only to the product itself," which he asserted "is most naturally understood as a warranty claim." For him, it was not persuasive to draw distinctions based on the manner in which the product is injured. Damages might be "qualitative, occurring through deterioration or internal breakage," or "calamitous." But "either way, since by definition no person or other property is damaged, the resulting loss is purely economic." Damage to the product itself, he said, "means simply that the product has not met the consumer's expectations, or, in other words that the customer has received 'insufficient product value.'"

In this case, in which the turbines involved were part of a group used in four supertankers, Justice Blackmun thought that "[c]ontract law, and the law of warranty in particular, is well suited to commercial controversies ... because the parties may set the terms of their own agreements." He also expressed concern that to permit "recovery for all foreseeable claims for economic loss could make a manufacturer liable for vast sums," adding, "It would be difficult for a manufacturer to take into account the expectations of persons downstream who may encounter its product." ...

An instructive clash of opinions appeared in a Nevada Supreme Court case in which the majority invoked *East River* to deny tort recovery to an insurance company, suing as subrogee for the destruction of an airplane when one of its engines failed. In this suit against the makers of the engine and the craft, the court was willing to concede that the engine "was a defective component part of the ... airplane" and that it thus "arguably destroyed not only itself, but other property as well, i.e., the entire airplane." However, the court reasoned that the original purchaser of the craft "did not purchase an airplane engine and thereafter install the engine on the plane," but bought a "single integrated product consisting of numerous component parts." The court declared that to allow the plaintiff recovery "would be tantamount to extending the manufacturer's warranty," with resultant increases in consumer prices. The court found itself unpersuaded by the fact that the product had crashed "calamitously" and had created an unreasonable risk of physical harm. It drew the line at cases in which there had in fact been personal injury or damage to "other property," saying that in such cases, "the law of strict products liability applies as a prophylactic and a basis for redress." By contrast, the court said that "[w]hen a product 'injures itself' protection derived from the interplay of manufacturer's warranties and insurance supplies a generally adequate basis for consumer redress."[156]

A dissenter emphasized, inter alia, "the possibility of great disparity in size and value between the component part and the whole"; in the case before the court, the plane that

---

156. *National Union Fire Ins. Co. v. Pratt and Whitney Canada Inc.*, 815 P.2d 601, 604–605 (Nev. 1991)....

157. *Id.* at 507 (Rose, J., dissenting).

a. 117 S. Ct. 1783 (1997).

crashed had been worth more than a half million dollars. The dissenter said that the rule applied by the majority "would mean that a plaintiff could recover for the loss of a million dollar airplane so long as the defect which destroyed the plane also caused the plaintiff to stub a toe."[157] ...

The Supreme Court distinguished *East River*, 11 years after issuing that decision, in *Saratoga Fishing Co. v. J.M. Martinac & Co.*,[a] a case involving the addition to a ship of a skiff, a fishing net, and spare parts by the purchaser of the vessel, the equipment having been "resold as part of the ship" when it was "later resold to a subsequent user." The case arose from a fire and flood in the engine room of the vessel that led to its sinking. The Ninth Circuit had denied recovery for the skiff, net, and spare parts, although it allowed recovery for the loss of a tuna catch in the hold which it described as "new property on board ... that belonged to the vessel's owner."

The Supreme Court reversed the Ninth Circuit concerning the added equipment. Justice Breyer's opinion for the majority concluded that the "extra equipment" was "other property" for which recovery could be had in admiralty. He said that to deny recovery "for added equipment simply because of a subsequent sale" would "make[] the scope of a manufacturer's liability turn on what seems, in one important respect, a fortuity, namely whether a defective product causes foreseeable physical harm to the added equipment before or after an Initial User (who added the equipment) resells the product to a Subsequent User." He opined that to reject liability "simply because of some such resale" would decrease the incentives provided by "defective-product tort law ... to encourage the manufacture of safer products." He asked, rhetorically, "why should a series of resales, after replacement and additions of ever more physical items, progressively immunize a manufacturer to an ever greater extent from the liability for foreseeable physical damage that would otherwise fall upon it?"

Justice Breyer's view of the economics of the case premised that "[i]nitial users when they buy typically depend upon, and likely seek warranties that depend upon, a manufacturer's primary business skill, namely the assembly of workable product components into a marketable whole." By contrast, he said that there was "no reason to think that initial users systematically control the manufactured product's quality or ... systematically allocate responsibility for user-added equipment" in ways analogous to the methods by which "manufacturers and component suppliers can allocate through contract potential liability for a manufactured product that does not work."

Responding to the defendants' argument that to impose liability would open too great a field of recovery, Justice Breyer indicated that doctrines like "foreseeability, proximate cause, and the 'economic loss' doctrine" would "limit liability in important ways." The sum of the decision was that "equipment added to a product after the Manufacturer (or distributor selling in the initial distributional chain) has sold the product to an initial User is not part of the product that itself caused physical harm," but rather is "'other property.'"

Justice Scalia dissented. He opined that the court should not have granted certiorari, but rather should have "let the lower federal courts struggle with [the] issue somewhat longer." However, "[r]eluctant[ly]" addressing the merits of the case, he disagreed with the majority. He observed that for a plaintiff that is "a commercial entity," it should "make no difference whether the purchase was made from a '402A seller' or not." He pointed out that "[c]ommercial entities do not typically suffer, at the time they make their purchase, a dis-

---

b. *Sea-Land Serv., Inc. v. General Elec. Co.*, 134 F.3d 149, 153–155 (3d Cir. 1998).

parity in bargaining power that makes it impossible for them to obtain warranty protection on the entire product," and declared that such purchasers were not "unable to insure the product they have purchased, including those portions of it added by upstream owners."

The Third Circuit distinguished *Saratoga Fishing* in a case in which replacement connecting rods failed in maritime diesel engines made by the company that provided the replacement rods. The plaintiff argued that the connecting rods not only damaged themselves, but "damaged other property, i.e., the diesel engine and its casing." The court thought that this distinction was not legally persuasive, characterizing the issue as being "whether replacement parts should be integrated into the engine whole or not." Applying the "integrated product rule," it said that there was "no 'other property'" that would justify recovery on the theory that the loss was property damage. The court said that there was no reason to "deviate" from that rule "simply because the defective component happens to be a replacement part instead of the part originally supplied with the product." It commented that "[s]ince all commercial parties are aware that replacement parts will be necessary, the integrated product should encompass those replacement parts when they are installed in the engine," and noted that the replacement connecting rod was "a component of that engine," having "no use to [the plaintiff] otherwise." The court also observed that the harm for which the plaintiff sought relief, economic loss, was "the exact type of injury that *East River* explains should be the subject of a contract-based warranty suit, not a tort suit."[b]

NOTES

(1) The strength of judicial opposition to strict liability for the economic loss of commercial parties is evident in decisions denying recovery when the claimed loss relates to a serious hazard of personal injury that would exist if the product were put into use. In a case involving a nuclear reactor, the plaintiff alleged that the containment was unable to withstand the forces generated by the steam supply system. But the court, while declaring that it would have "little difficulty" in imposing liability for "ultra-hazardous activity" if a "nuclear catastrophe" occurred, said it would not do so "where the mere prospect of such a catastrophe is alleged." *Cincinnati Gas & Elec. Co. v. General Elec. Co.*, 656 F. Supp. 49, 59 (S.D. Ohio 1986). Does this make sense to you? What is the strongest rationalization for this result?

(2) One sort of case where health-related "economic loss" has drawn decisions favoring claimants is the situation in which a buyer of products containing asbestos incurs

---

   * Adapted from MARSHALL S. SHAPO, THE LAW OF PRODUCTS LIABILITY ¶ 27.05[2][d-1] (4th ed. 2001).

   1. *Transport Corp. of Am., Inc. v. IBM, Inc.*, 30 F.3d 953, 957–958 (8th Cir. 1994). *Accord, Rockford Pharmacy, Inc. v. Digital Simplistics, Inc.*, 53 F.3d 195, 197–199 (1995) (suit alleging "a loss of data installed in [customized] computer system"; plaintiff sought damages for the "original cost of the computer system, including maintenance and replacement expenses"; court of appeals rejected district court's characterization of issue as whether defendant owed "a duty of care that was independent of the parties' contractual relationship"; no recovery under the "economic loss doctrine").

   2. *Apollo Group, Inc. v. Avnet, Inc.*, 58 F.3d 477, 481 (9th Cir. 1995).

   3. *Id.* at 478.

Chapter 13

THE DUTY TO ACT

PROBLEM

A janitor breaks a leg working late Friday night on an upper staircase of a high-rise office building and lies helpless on the landing. An executive who works on the adjoining floor walks by, laden with a full briefcase. He perceives the janitor but ignores his pleas for help. No one works in the building on weekends because there is no heat then, an economy measure that is due to rising energy costs; thus, no one else comes on the scene for three nights and two days. The janitor suffers serious injury from spending the weekend in an unheated building without food or water.

Should the executive have to compensate for this added injury?

McCLURE v. UNITED STATES LINES CO.

United States Court of Appeals, Fourth Circuit
368 F.2d 197 (1966)

HAYNSWORTH, CHIEF JUDGE.

The widow of an American seaman seeks damages because of the death of her husband following a fall into the waters of a French harbor. Her theory is that members of the crew of the American Angler were negligent in the performance of a duty of assistance, arising under French law, when her thoroughly drunken husband was attempting to find his own ship, the Keystone State.

At approximately 11:45 P.M. on March 31, 1961, McClure was attempting to return from authorized shore leave to the Keystone State, which was then moored at the outer mole at the port of La Pallice, France. He alighted from an automobile onto a dock in the inner harbor at La Pallice more than a mile from where the Keystone State was berthed, but at which the American Angler was moored. Although it was realized that McClure was not a member of the crew of the American Angler, several members of her crew undertook to assist him because of his extreme intoxication. The chief engineer brought a chair and seated McClure twenty to twenty-five feet from the edge of the dock. He was given coffee. Twice he was restrained from leaving the area because he was thought to be too intoxicated to travel alone along the waterfront. McClure could not answer questions, but, from his papers, they knew his name and that he was an American seaman.

The master, the chief engineer and the second engineer of the American Angler, with other members of her crew, were among those who observed McClure and provided assistance. Eventually, the master left McClure and returned to the ship. The chief engi-

681

neer then offered to assist McClure in his effort to find his own ship. He told McClure to wait on the dock while he obtained a jacket from aboard ship. At that time, although McClure appeared less intoxicated and seemed to understand what was being said to him, he was still not fit to travel alone. Apparently, no one undertook to watch McClure while the chief engineer went to get his coat. McClure fell into the water about one hundred feet up the pier near the ship's bow. He was promptly hauled from the water by members of the American Angler's company, but attempts to revive him failed.

Under these circumstances, the District Court found no violation of French law and, alternatively, no negligence on the part of the American Angler's crew. The plaintiff has appealed, contending that the finding of ultimate fact was wrong and reversible, and the Court's construction of French law erroneous.

Article 63 of the French Penal Code imposes criminal sanctions upon one "who voluntarily abstains from giving assistance to a person which he could, without risk either to himself or to third persons, give either by his personal action or by securing assistance." Article 1383 of the French Civil Code imposes civil liabilities for injuries caused by an actor's negligence or imprudence. Apparently, upon the theory that a failure to perform obligations imposed by the Good Samaritan statute is an imprudence, French treatises declare that one who fails to perform his duty of assistance is subject to civil liabilities under Articles 1382 and 1383 for the resulting harm as well as to the criminal sanctions of Article 63. Thus, one who sees a drowning man in a canal and who, without risk to himself or anyone else, could easily throw him a life preserver, but does nothing, is liable for civil damages.

Professor von Mehren of Harvard Law School, the expert tendered by the plaintiff to prove the French law, testified that there was no precedent for the imposition of liabilities upon one who did not "voluntarily abstain" from rendering assistance, but whose efforts were ineffectual. Since the men here who were attempting to assist McClure had not "voluntarily abstained" from assisting him within the usual connotation of those words, the District Court concluded there was no violation of the French law. Professor von Mehren had testified, however, that implicit in the interrelation between the two articles from the Civil and Criminal Codes was a duty to act with care in rendering the requisite assistance. If harm, he suggested, results from negligent conduct, the actor is liable for it under French law notwithstanding the fact that he was moved to act by recognition of his duty of assistance. The alternative finding of no negligence was responsive to that interpretation of French law.

The resulting questions tendered directly by the appeal, involving a construction of the standard of care required by the French law of one undertaking to perform his duty of assistance, are difficult and divisive. We need not undertake their answers for we hold that American, not French, law must control the result.

Whatever duty French law may have imposed upon members of the crew of the American Angler in their capacities as individuals, it was not the business of the ship or its owner, the defendant here.

In American jurisdictions, in cases arising under the Jones Act, it is settled that it is not within the scope of his employment for a seaman to aid an intoxicated member of the same crew in returning to their ship. *Re Atlas' Petition*, 7 Cir., 350 F.2d 592.[1]

---

1. A different result was reached where it was customary for dock guards to detain intoxicated seamen and turn them over to a shipmate, and where the shipowner knew of the practice, acquiesced in it, and authorized its men to escort intoxicated crewmen back aboard ship. *See McDonough v. Buckeye S.S Co.*, N.D.Ohio, 103 F.Supp. 473, aff'd, 6 Cir., 200 F.2d 558. There is no suggestion of similar circumstances here.

... An argument was made and rejected in those cases that a seaman who volunteers to assist a drunken shipmate on land acts for the ship, since the ship, otherwise, might be deprived of the services of the drunken seaman after he has become sober. If it is not the business of his ship for a seaman to assist a drunken shipmate back to their ship, he clearly does not act within the scope of his employment in assisting an intoxicated seaman to return to another ship operated by a different shipping line.

Presumptively, the same result would be reached under French law. Article 1384 of the Civil Code provides in translation, "Masters and employers are liable for the damage caused by their servants and employees in the exercise of the functions for which they have been employed." That Article is unelucidated in this record, but it would appear to supply a rule comparable to the scope of employment rules familiar in the courts of the United States. The plaintiff has not shown a more sweeping application of the French Article.

...

We are loath to enter final judgment for the ship, however, for the tacit assumption that the case was governed by French law may have had a significant effect upon the making of the record. Justice seems to require a remand to give the parties an opportunity to produce any additional evidence that may be available which has a material bearing upon the issues as defined within the framework of American law. Our conclusion that, on the present record, American law is the appropriate choice may have a decided effect upon the relevance of evidence thought immaterial under French law. Since, too, the choice of law question was not litigated below, the parties should not be foreclosed from the introduction of additional evidence bearing upon that question in the context of the general rules we have discussed. Our decision that American law controls is based upon the present record and does not foreclose reconsideration in the District Court if additional relevant evidence or considerations are produced.

For those purposes, the judgment is vacated and the case remanded for such further proceedings as may be appropriate not inconsistent with this opinion.

Vacated and remanded.

VERMONT'S "DUTY TO AID THE ENDANGERED ACT"
Vt. Stat. Ann. Title 12, Section 519 (1973)

Section 519. Emergency medical care

(a) A person who knows that another is exposed to grave physical harm shall, to the extent that the same can be rendered without danger or peril to himself or without interference with important duties owed to others, give reasonable assistance to the exposed person unless that assistance or care is being provided by others.

(b) A person who provides reasonable assistance in compliance with subsection (a) of this section shall not be liable in civil damages unless his acts constitute gross negligence or unless he will receive or expects to receive remuneration. Nothing contained in this subsection shall alter existing law with respect to tort liability of a practitioner of the healing arts for acts committed in the ordinary course of his practice.

(c) A person who willfully violates subsection (a) of this section shall be fined not more than $100.00....

Ernest Weinrib, *The Case for a Duty to Rescue*
90 Yale L.J. 247, 291–292 (1980)*

The extent of the duty of beneficence, of course, can still be troubling. It is the inter-determinateness of the duty, the "play-room," that is particularly relevant to this problem. Kant meant by this expression that the form and the amount of the benefaction would vary, depending on the resources of the benefactor, the identity of the recipient, and the recipient's own conception of happiness. The interdeterminateness, however, applies not only to the form of the benefaction but also to the linking of particular benefactors to particular beneficiaries. Why should any particular person be singled out of the whole group of potential benefactors, and why should the benefit be conferred on one rather than another person in need? If a duty "may be *exacted* from a person, as one exacts a debt," it is a debt that leaves unclear the precise terms of discharge as well as the identities of obligor and obligee.

The proper response to this interdeterminacy is not to deny that there is a duty. What is required is to set up social institutions to perform the necessary tasks of coordination and determination. Those institutions would ensure that no person is singled out unfairly either for burdens or for benefits, and that the forms of benefaction correlate both with the resources of those who give and with the needs of those who receive. In fact, all Western democracies undertake to perform this task through programs for social assistance. The institutions they establish, however, are primarily legislative and administrative; precisely because a general duty of beneficence is imperfect, it cannot be judicially enforced. The traditional claim-settling function of courts does not permit the transfer of a resource from one person to another solely because the former has it and the latter needs it. Such judicial action would unfairly prefer one needy person over others[159] and unfairly burden one resourceful person over others. Because the duty of beneficence is general and indeterminate, it does not, in the absence of legislative action that specifies and coordinates, yield judicially enforceable moral claims by individuals against others.

The significant characteristic of the emergency and convenience limitations is that, in combination, they eliminate the "play-room" inherent in the duty of beneficence, thus providing a principled response to Kant and to Epstein and rendering the narrower duty to rescue appropriate for judicial enforcement. An emergency marks a particular person as physically endangered in a way that is not general or routine throughout the society. An imminent peril cannot await assistance from the appropriate social institutions. The provision of aid to an emergency victim does not deplete the social resources committed to the alleviation of more routine threats to physical integrity. Moreover, aid in such circumstances presents no unfairness problems in singling out a particular person to receive the aid. Similarly, emergency aid does not unfairly single out one of a class of routinely advantaged persons; the rescuer just happens to find himself for a short period in a position, which few if any others share, to render a service to some specific person. In addition, when a rescue can be accomplished without a significant

---

* Reprinted by permission of The Yale Law Journal Company and William S. Hein Company from *The Yale Law Journal*, Vol. 90, pages 247–293.

159. The unfairness of preferring the squatters to other homeless persons was adverted to by Lord Justice Megaw in *London Borough of Southwark v. Williams*, [1971] 2 All E.R. 175, 182 (C.A.) (Megaw, L.J.).

disruption of his own projects, the rescuer's freedom to realize his own ends is not abridged by the duty to preserve the physical security of another.[160]

In sum, when there is an emergency that the rescuer can alleviate with no inconvenience to himself, the general duty of beneficence that is suspended over society like a floating charge is temporarily revealed to identify a particular obligor and obligee, and to define obligations that are specific enough for judicial enforcement.

NOTES

(1) *McClure* presents a version of a problem that has fascinated philosophers for a long time, and recently has begun to intrigue lawyers. Any newspaper reader has encountered several episodes that implicitly pose the "duty to act" question. See, e.g., *4 Receive Prison Terms in Barroom Rape*, WASH. POST, Mar. 27, 1984, at A3 (describing sentencing of defendants in a case in which, reportedly, "more than a dozen men raped and beat a woman on [a] bar's pool table while other customers cheered").

(2) Should the law impose liability on a crewman individually in a *McClure* situation:

(a) If he saw McClure staggering off the dock and didn't help him at all?

(b) If he started to help and:

(1) Left to get a coat for himself?

(2) Left to get a coat for McClure?

(3) Left to respond to a report that a seaman on the *American Angler* slipped on the deck and might have broken his leg?

(3) The Illinois Supreme Court drew on the common law rule to deny recovery for the death of a college freshman who, quite intoxicated, lay bloodied in the warming house of the Illinois Central Gulf Railroad for several hours. During that time, employees of the railroad reported this situation and relayed messages about it through railroad channels and indeed to the Chicago police. There was testimony to the effect that the decedent probably would have survived if he had received medical attention earlier. The appellate court had affirmed a judgment on a jury verdict for the plaintiff, after an instruction by the trial judge that the decedent's status as an invitee or a trespasser was irrelevant, because the duty owed to him by the rail line was "the same in either case—to exercise ordinary care for [the decedent's] safety." The supreme court reversed, saying that on retrial the jury would have to decide whether the decedent was "a patron (invitee) or a trespasser." It pointed out that the defendant had not violated the duty it owed to trespassers under state law—that is, "to refrain from willfully and wantonly injuring him," noting that the plaintiff had not brought the case under an exception where the landowner creates a "place of danger."

Beyond that, the court emphasized the "general rule ... that there is no legal duty to rescue an injured stranger." Following the traditional tort law distinction between legal and moral duties, it said, in part:

> The arbitrariness of using an injured trespasser's mere presence on the defendant's premises as justification for imposing a duty to rescue is evident. Em-

---

160. ... Kant writes: "Imperfect duties, accordingly, are only *duties of virtue*. To fulfill them is *merit* (*meritum* = + a); but to transgress them is not so much *guilt* (*demeritum* = – a) as rather mere *lack of* moral *worth* (= 0), unless the agent makes it his principle not to submit to these duties." Is not a person who refuses to rescue another at no cost to himself "making it his principle not to submit to these duties"?

ploying such a rule, a homeowner who finds an injured, drunken stranger lying on his lawn has a legal duty to rescue, but the homeowner who sees his next-door neighbor drowning is under no such legal obligation. In fact, the duty to take action or not to take action would vary as an injured trespasser staggered back and forth across the homeowner's property line. The imposition of a duty to aid would thus turn on a wholly arbitrary circumstance.

Rhodes v. Illinois Cent. G. R.R., 172 Ill. 2d 213, 233–34, 665 N.E.2d 1260, 1270 (1996).

(4) Does Weinrib convince you that "emergency aid does not unfairly single out one of a class of routinely advantaged persons"? What is the compelling reason of policy or philosophy that requires a person to step out of his or her own routine to respond to a threat "that is not general or routine"?

(5) Would you vote for the Vermont statute that is reprinted supra? What is the difference, in terms of your view of how the law should operate, between a legislature making a rule of that sort and a judge applying such a rule in a concrete case, for example, a suit by the rape victim in the case described in Note 1 against a customer of the bar who did not participate in the assault?

At least two other states have passed statutes similar to the Vermont legislation. The Minnesota statute establishes a duty to give "reasonable assistance" "to the extent that the person can do so without danger or peril to self or others." MINN. STAT. ANN. § 604A.01. The language of the Rhode Island statute also is similar. See R.I. GEN. LAWS § 11-56-1.

(6) For an analysis of the problem generally, see M. SHAPO, THE DUTY TO ACT: TORT LAW, POWER AND PUBLIC POLICY 3–73 (1977).

(7) Can D, who sells handguns in a community which does not control the sale of firearms, refuse to sell to C because C has been previously convicted of an offense involving the use of a revolver? Can D refuse to sell a handgun to C because E previously sued D, though unsuccessfully, for D's sale to C of a weapon that C used to shoot E?

(8) In *Bondu v. Gurvich*, 473 So. 2d 1307 (Fla. Dist. Ct. App. 1984), the plaintiff sued a hospital for failure to keep and maintain medical records that would have aided a suit for malpractice. This case, holding that the plaintiff had stated a cause of action, teaches how duties may be found in regulations that embody substantive standards. The court quoted at length from administrative regulations of the state Health and Rehabilitation Services Agency, spelling out in detail the content of medical records that "shall be maintained for every patient admitted for care in the hospital."

(9) There is a spectrum of cases with elements of the "duty to act" problem. At the far end of the spectrum is the case involving the "pure bystander." The spectrum then runs through cases involving various kinds of pre-existing relationships, such as employer and employee. In the category of the employment relationship, consider whether you think that it is appropriate to grant injunctive relief against an employer for failure to segregate smokers from an employee who is susceptible to tobacco smoke.

(10) There are now numerous decisions that impose duties on landlords to protect tenants against the undoubtedly tortious actions of others. Consider whether this duty should extend to a landlord's failure to install speed bumps in a parking lot, in a suit by a child who was struck by a bicycle that sped down a hill leading into the lot.

(11) How far does the duty to act extend to a restaurant customer taken hostage by a robber, who threatens to kill the customer if the cashier does not give up the money in the register? If the cashier refuses to give up the money, does it make a difference

whether the robber carries through on his threat and kills the customer, with a resultant suit for wrongful death, or if the cashier finally turns over the money and the customer sues for terror created by the threat?

(12) A classic example of the kind of special relationship that generates a duty to act is the doctor-patient relationship. Yet the wonders of modern medicine may have created a duty trap. Doctors are supposed to heal, but what are their duties when a dreadfully ill patient wants only to die? The problem is even more sharply focused if the patient, when conscious and rational, has written a "living will" or some other kind of statement that defines the conditions under which she does not wish to have her life prolonged. In a Michigan case, a 38-year-old woman had to be "fed, bathed, diapered, and, at night, tied into bed so she does not push herself over the padded bedrail." Most of the time she "screams, over and over." The woman and her mother and daughter won a $16.5 million verdict against a hospital that kept her on a ventilator after a seizure that put her in this condition. Tamar Lewin, *Ignoring 'Right to Die' Directives, Medical Community is Being Sued*, N.Y. TIMES, June 2, 1996, at A1. This version of the "right to die" problem implicates, as one report summarized it, the view of doctors and hospitals that "saving a life is never against the law." The duty trap arises because in the law's general view of the doctor-patient relationship, the cardinal rule is to save life. On what principles can a court draw in solving this problem in particular cases? Should the existence of an advance directive signed by the patient be dispositive against the doctor's duty to take extraordinary measures to prolong life? Is it a simple battery when doctors insert feeding tubes in defiance of such a directive?

Chapter 14

TORT LAW AND THE ENVIRONMENT

§ 14.01 Private Nuisance

PROBLEM

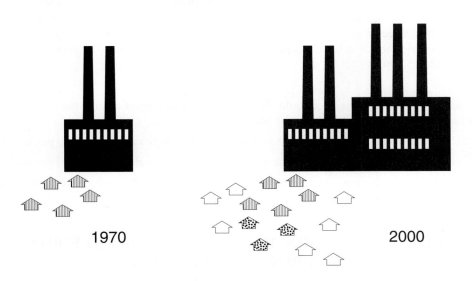

1970   2000

An American Success Story. © Marshall Shapo

The plant cartooned above generates power for a utility whose business has grown substantially over a thirty-year period, along with the general population growth of the community served by the utility. Over that same period, quite a number of families have moved into new, modest homes on the land surrounding the utility. These new-comers joined a community of people (represented by the houses with the vertical lines) who had been residing there when the utility was in its two-small-smokestack phase in the nineteen fifties.

The long-time residents had been suffering from the effects of pollution for many years. After the newcomers had established their residences, the utility built a major, three-smokestack addition to the plant to enable it to keep up with increasing demands for power. After that addition was constructed, many of the newcomers (represented by the houses with sooty dots) began to find that the prevailing winds take polluted air to their little homes as well as to the homes of the old residents. There are now a total of

3,000 homeowners in the area around the utility who are rendered uncomfortable by pollution. No one has tried to quantify the costs of their discomfort, but there have been estimates of property valuations that indicate that the effect of the pollution has been to reduce property values for these 3,000 families by an average of $500 per homestead.

The total value of the factory's production per year is $75,000,000. A lawyer who specializes in environmental litigation estimates that in addition to the reduction in property values caused by the pollution, each homeowner would be able to claim $300 annually in annoyance or inconvenience costs. However, the homeowners could eliminate the discomfort they suffer from the pollution, at least when they are indoors, by completely sealing up their houses at an annualized cost of $100 per home.

The utility now serves 100,000 customers. In order to minimize costs, the utility uses a relatively sooty kind of fuel. Two other types of fuel would reduce pollution but would be more expensive. One of these, which would reduce pollution by about 10 percent, would add five dollars to the bill of each customer per year. Another, which would eliminate the pollution entirely, would add $50 to each customer's bill per year.

Devices are available that would stop all particulate matter that now emerges from the utility's stacks, but a switch to that technology would raise the bills of utility customers by $20 per year. For various reasons, the utility forecasts that to adopt this technology would require it to cut its payroll by 50 employees, who have an average annual salary of $15,000.

* * *

(A) On what legal theories could the homeowners seek relief against the utility, and what remedies, if any, would they be likely to get?

(B) What would be the result if the reduction in property values was $150 per home?

(C) What would be the result if the reduction in property values was $5,000 per home?

(D) What if the homes were very expensive dwellings, and the reduction in property values was $50,000 per home?

COPART INDUSTRIES, INC. v. CONSOLIDATED EDISON COMPANY OF NEW YORK

New York Court of Appeals
41 N.Y.2d 564, 362 N.E.2d 968, 394 N.Y.S.2d 169 (1977)

COOKE, JUSTICE.

"There is perhaps no more impenetrable jungle in the entire law than that which surrounds the word 'nuisance'. It has meant all things to all men" (Prosser, Torts (4th ed.), p. 571). From a point someplace within this oft-noted thicket envisioned by Professor Prosser, this appeal emerges.

Plaintiff leased a portion of the former Brooklyn Navy Yard for a period of five years commencing September 1, 1970. On the demised premises during the ensuing eight or nine months it conducted a storage and new car preparation business, the latter entailing over 50 steps ranging from services such as checking brakes to vehicle cleaning, catering to automobile dealers in the metropolitan area of New York City. Adjacent to the navy yard was defendant's Hudson Avenue plant, engaged in the production of steam and electricity since about 1926. This generating system had five smokestacks and during the time in question its burners were fired with oil having a sulphur content of 1% or less. Prior to 1968, coal had been the fuel employed and the main boiler was equipped with an electrostatic precipitator to remove or control the discharged fly ash. Upon conversion to oil, the precipitator had been deactivated.

Based on allegations that noxious emissions from defendant's nearby stacks caused damage to the exterior of autos stored for its customers such as to require many to be repainted, that reports were received in early 1971 from patrons of paint discoloration and pitting, and that dealers served by plaintiff terminated their business by early May, plaintiff contends that because of said emissions it was caused to cease doing business on May 28, 1971. This action was instituted seeking $1,300,000 for loss of investment and loss of profit, under three causes of action respectively asserting "a deliberate and willful violation of the rights of plaintiff, constituting a nuisance", a "wrongful and unlawful trespass" and violations of "New York City, New York State and federal laws, regulations and guidelines with respect to air pollution." A fourth cause demanded exemplary and punitive damages of $1,000,000 because of defendant's "wrongful and illegal acts."

The case came on for jury trial in 1974. As a result of rulings made at junctures prior to submission for verdict, the third and fourth causes of action were dismissed and the second was merged with the first. After pointing out that plaintiff "framed his case on a branch of the law of wrongdoing called nuisance", the trial court charged nuisance based on negligence and nuisance grounded on an intentional invasion of plaintiff's rights. Negligence was defined and it was pointed out that, although contributory negligence may be a defense where the basis of the nuisance is merely negligent conduct, it would not be where the wrongdoing is founded on the intentional, deliberate misconduct of defendant. Contending that "nuisance is entirely separate and apart from negligence" and that "defendant's intent or negligence is not … an essential element of the cause of action of nuisance", plaintiff excepted to the portions of the charge relating to said subjects.

The jury found in defendant's favor and judgment was entered dismissing the complaint. The Appellate Division, by a divided court, affirmed, (52 A.D.2d 791, 383 N.Y.S.2d 201) the majority stating that …"nuisance is a concept susceptible of more than one meaning", that "(w)hile an absolute nuisance need not contain within its definition a flavoring of negligence, a qualified nuisance may", that "the testimony, especially that of the experts, as developed at trial, showed an inextricable intertwining of negligence with the nuisance claimed, though the complaint did not so frame the issue", that "the proof portrayed the alleged wrong as 'a' nuisance," though dependent upon negligence'", and that, therefore under the circumstances, the instructions to the jury on the issue of negligence were correct. The dissenters, on the other hand, urged that …"(p)utting aside the possibility that there could be liability without fault, and in the absence of proof of negligence by the defendant … a cause of action in nuisance 'does not involve the element of negligence as one of its essential factors'", that the "charge which mingled elements of nuisance and negligence could have been confusing to the jury" and that the "possibility of confusion was compounded by an instruction that the plaintiff, to succeed, was required to prove that the injury to its property was intentionally inflicted." On appeal to this court, plaintiff maintains that the trial court erred in charging (1) that plaintiff was required to prove an intent of the defendant to cause damages, and (2) that plaintiff had a burden of proof as to defendant's negligence and plaintiff's freedom from contributory negligence.

Much of the uncertainty and confusion surrounding the use of the term nuisance, which in itself means no more than harm, injury, inconvenience, or annoyance (*see* Webster's Third New International Dictionary, p. 571; American Heritage Dictionary,

p. 900), arises from a series of historical accidents covering the invasion of different kinds of interests and referring to various kinds of conduct on the part of defendants (Prosser, Torts (4th ed.), pp. 571–572). The word surfaced as early as the twelfth century in the assize of nuisance, which provided redress where the injury was not a disseisin but rather an indirect damage to the land or an interference with its use and enjoyment. Three centuries later the remedy was replaced by the common-law action on the case for nuisance, invoked only for damages upon the invasion of interests in the use and enjoyment of land, as well as of easements and profits. If abatement by judicial process was desired, resort to equity was required. Along with the civil remedy protecting rights in land, there developed a separate principle that an infringement of the right of the crown, or of the general public, was a crime and, in time, this class of offenses was so enlarged as to include any "act not warranted by law, or omission to discharge a legal duty, which inconveniences the public in the exercise of rights common to all Her Majesty's subjects" (Stephen, General View of Criminal Law of England (1890), p. 105). At first, interference with the rights of the public was confined to the criminal realm but in time an individual who suffered special damages from a public nuisance was accorded a right of action....

A private nuisance threatens one person or a relatively few..., an essential feature being an interference with the use or enjoyment of land.... It is actionable by the individual person or persons whose rights have been disturbed (Restatement, Torts, notes preceding §822, p. 217). A public, or as sometimes termed a common, nuisance is an offense against the State and is subject to abatement or prosecution on application of the proper governmental agency.... It consists of conduct or omissions which offend, interfere with or cause damage to the public in the exercise of rights common to all..., in a manner such as to offend public morals, interfere with use by the public of a public place or endanger or injure the property, health, safety or comfort of a considerable number of persons....

As observed by Professor Prosser, public and private nuisances "have almost nothing in common, except that each causes inconvenience to someone, and it would have been fortunate if they had been called from the beginning by different names" (Prosser, Torts [4th ed.], p. 573). Not only does confusion arise from sameness in denomination and from the lack of it in applicability, but also from the fact that, although an individual cannot institute an action for public nuisance as such, he may maintain an action when he suffers special damage from a public nuisance....

This developmental tracing indicates the erroneous concept under which appellant labors. It also points out that nuisance, as a general term, describes the consequences of conduct, the inconvenience to others, rather than the type of conduct involved.... It is a field of tort liability rather than a single type of tortious conduct (Prosser, Torts [4th ed.], p. 573).

Despite early private nuisance cases, which apparently assumed that the defendant was strictly liable, today it is recognized that one is subject to liability for a private nuisance if his conduct is a legal cause of the invasion of the interest in the private use and enjoyment of land and such invasion is (1) intentional and unreasonable, (2) negligent or reckless, or (3) actionable under the rules governing liability for abnormally dangerous conditions or activities (Restatement, Torts 2d [Tent Draft No. 16], §822; Prosser, Torts [4th ed.], p. 574....

In urging that the charge in respect to negligence constituted error, plaintiff's brief opens its discussion with the assertion that "(t)he complaint contained no allegations of negligence and its theory was that of nuisance." This statement is significant in that not only does it miss the fundamental difference between types of conduct which may result in nuisance and the invasion of interests in land, which is the nuisance, but it also over-looks the firmly established principle that negligence is merely one type of conduct which may give rise to a nuisance. A nuisance, either public or private, based on negli-gence and whether characterized as either negligence or nuisance, is but a single wrong (*Morello v. Brookfield Constr. Co.*, 4 N.Y.2d 83, 90, 172 N.Y.S.2d 577, 581, 149 N.E.2d 202, 204), and "whenever a nuisance has its origin in negligence", negligence must be proven and a plaintiff "may not avert the consequences of his (or her) own contributory negligence by affixing to the negligence of the wrongdoer the label of a nuisance". Al-though during trial an issue as to causation developed, whether the deleterious sub-stances reaching the customers' vehicles in plaintiff's custody had their origin at defen-dant's Hudson Avenue property or elsewhere, plaintiff introduced the testimony of different witnesses in support of its contention that defendant operated its plant in a negligent manner. While plaintiff offered expert proof to the effect that it was the gen-eral custom or usage in the power plant industry, during the period in question, to use collectors or precipitators, or both, on oil-fired boilers and also to use magnesium as a fuel oil additive to reduce the formation of acid bearing particulates, defendant submit-ted testimony from similar sources that mechanical and electrostatic precipitators are not commonly utilized on oil-fired burners and that defendant actually was using man-ganese as an additive.

Besides liability for nuisance arising out of negligence and apart from consideration of a nuisance resulting from abnormally dangerous or ultrahazardous conduct or con-ditions, the latter of which obviously is not applicable here (*see* Restatement, Torts 2d, § 822 [Tent Draft No. 16]; ... one may be liable for a private nuisance where the wrong-ful invasion of the use and enjoyment of another's land is intentional and unreasonable. It is distinguished from trespass which involves the invasion of a person's interest in the exclusive possession of land. The elements of such a private nuisance, as charged in ef-fect by the Trial Justice, are: (1) an interference substantial in nature, (2) intentional in origin, (3) unreasonable in character, (4) with a person's property right to use and enjoy land, (5) caused by another's conduct in acting or failure to act (Restatement, Torts, § 822 ...). Thus, plaintiff's exception that "defendant's intent ... is not ... an es-sential element of the cause of action of nuisance" and its criticism of the charge, which was to the effect that as to the private nuisance plaintiff was required to prove that de-fendant's conduct was intentional, are not well taken. "An invasion of another's interest in the use and enjoyment of land is intentional when the actor (a) acts for the purpose of causing it; or (b) knows that it is resulting or is substantially certain to result from his conduct" (Restatement, Torts, § 825 ...).

Negligence and nuisance were explained to the jury at considerable length and its at-tention was explicitly directed to the two categories of nuisance, that based on negligence and that dependent upon intentional conduct. The causes accrued, if at all, prior to the applicable date of the new CPLR article 14-A (CPLR 1411–1413), and the trial court properly charged that contributory negligence may be a defense where the nuisance is based on negligent conduct.... As to nuisance involving a willful or intentional invasion of plaintiff's rights, the jury was instructed that contributory negligence was not a de-fense and, in this respect, plaintiff was not prejudiced and has no right to complain....

Boomer v. Atlantic Cement Co., 26 N.Y.2d 219, 309 N.Y.S.2d 312, 257 N.E.2d 870, ... relied on by plaintiff, does not dictate a contrary result. There, Supreme Court found that defendant maintained a nuisance, same was affirmed by the Appellate Division, and the Court of Appeals concerned itself with the relief to be granted. Although Trial

Term did specifically mention the type of nuisance it found, it is obvious that it was not a nuisance in which the substance of the wrong was negligence since it was held that "the evidence in this case establishes that Atlantic took every available and possible precaution to protect the plaintiffs from dust" (55 Misc.2d, at p. 1024, 287 N.Y.S.2d at p. 113). Rather, it would appear that the nuisance found was based on an intentional and unreasonable invasion, as it was stated that "(t)he discharge of large quantities of dust upon each of the properties and excessive vibration from blasting deprived each party of the reasonable use of his property and thereby prevented his enjoyment of life and liberty therein" (55 Misc.2d, at pp. 1024–1025, 287 N.Y.S.2d at p. 114). Contrary to plaintiff's assertion, Boomer does not negate the necessity of proving negligence in some nuisance actions involving harmful emissions, since negligence is one of the types of conduct on which a nuisance may depend.

Although there are some Judges in the majority who are of the opinion that the charge did not furnish a model of discussion on some subjects, all of that group agree that reversal on the basis of the charge would not be warranted.

The order of the Appellate Division should be affirmed, with costs.

FUCHSBERG, JUDGE (dissenting).

I believe, as did Justices Markewich and Kupferman, who dissented at the Appellate Division, that the charge in this case, by repeatedly presenting an admixture of nuisance and negligence in a manner and to an extent that could have misled the jury, should bring a reversal. All the more is that so because of the Trial Judge's insistent refrain that the injury to the plaintiff's property was required to be intentionally inflicted. Accordingly, I must dissent.

In doing so, I should note that, while in the main I am in agreement with the majority of our court in its discussion of the substantive law of nuisance, I believe the readiness with which it uses the term "negligence" in the context of this action for nuisance is counterproductive to the eradication of the confusion which has so long plagued that subject. Words such as "intent", "negligence" and "absolute liability" refer not to the result of the conduct of a defendant who intrudes unreasonably on the use and enjoyment of another's property, but rather to the method of bringing it about. Too often, as here, it serves to divert from focusing on the basic legal issue.

Nuisance traditionally requires that, after a balancing of the risk-utility considerations, the gravity of harm to a plaintiff be found to outweigh the social usefulness of a defendant's activity (Prosser, Torts [4th ed.], p. 581). For no matter whether an act is intentional or unintentional, there should be no liability unless the social balance of the activity leads to the conclusion that it is unreasonable....

Interestingly, sections 826 and 829A of the Restatement of Torts 2d (Tent Draft Nos. 17, 18) have now given recognition to developments in the law of torts by moving past the traditional rule to favor recovery for nuisance even when a defendant's conduct is not unreasonable. To be exact, section 826 (Tent Draft No. 18, pp. 3–4) reads: "An intentional invasion of another's interest in the use and enjoyment of land is unreasonable under the rule stated in section 822, if (a) the gravity of the harm outweighs the utility of the actor's conduct, or (b) the harm caused by the conduct is substantial and the financial burden of compensating for this and other harms does not render infeasible the continuation of the conduct"....

Indeed, a fair reading of *Boomer v. Atlantic Cement Co....* would indicate that the position articulated by the Restatement's Tentative Draft is consistent with the decision of our court in that case. The plaintiffs in *Boomer* were landowners who were substantially damaged by air pollution caused by the defendant's cement plant. However, since the court found that the adverse economic effects of a permanent injunction which would close the plant would far outweigh the loss plaintiffs would suffer if the nuisance continued, it limited the relief it granted to an award of monetary damages as compensation to the defendants for the "servitude" which had been imposed on their lands.... Taken into account was the fact that an injunction would have put 300 employees out of work and caused forfeiture of a $45,000,000 investment, while plaintiffs' permanent damages were only $185,000 ... and that the burden of compensating for the harm did "not render infeasible the continuation of the conduct" (Restatement, Torts 2d, § 826 [Tent Draft No. 18], pp. 3–4.) ...

On the basis of these principles, it follows that, on reversal the plaintiff in this case should be permitted to sustain its action for damages on proof that the harm is substantial and that the financial burden of compensating for the harm does not render "infeasible" the continuation of the defendant's business activity.

. . .

PAGE COUNTY APPLIANCE CENTER, INC. v. HONEYWELL, INC.
Iowa Supreme Court
347 N.W.2d 171 (1984)

REYNOLDSON, CHIEF JUSTICE.

. . . .

Appliance Center has owned and operated an appliance store in Shenandoah, Iowa, since 1953. In 1975 the store was acquired from his father by John Pearson, who sold televisions, stereos, and a variety of appliances. Before 1980 Pearson had no reception trouble with his display televisions. In early January 1980, however, ITT placed one of its computers with Central Travel Service in Shenandoah as part of a nationwide plan to lease computers to retail travel agents. Central Travel was separated by only one other business from the Appliance Center. This ITT computer was manufactured, installed, and maintained by Honeywell.

Thereafter many of Pearson's customers told him his display television pictures were bad; on two of the three channels available in Shenandoah he had a difficult time "getting a picture that was fit to watch." After unsuccessfully attempting several remedial measures, in late January 1980, he finally traced the interference to the operations of Central Travel's computer. Both defendants concede Pearson's problems were caused by radiation leaking from the Honeywell computer.

Pearson discussed the problem with Kay Crowell, owner of Central Travel. She placed a call to ITT's president in New York. Although he was unavailable, ITT personnel apparently notified Honeywell. ITT's only contact with Pearson was through a telephone call some ten months later. At that time Pearson told ITT's sales representative that Honeywell was working on the problem; he made no effort to follow up on ITT's interest in the problem.

Honeywell indeed was working to correct the situation, and had been since February 1980. Honeywell technicians made repeated trips to make various unsuccessful adjustments to the computer. They found the computer was operating properly; the interference-causing radiation was a design and not a service problem. Pearson then telephoned Armando Benitez, the technicians' supervisor. Pearson testified Benitez told him Honeywell was "way over budget" on the Central Travel computer and that "if you don't like it, you can move."

Nonetheless, in early fall of 1980 Honeywell sent out Phil Brzozoski, one of its engineers from Boston. According to Pearson, when he asked Brzozoski why it had taken him so long to come, the latter replied he would not have been there at all had Pearson not instituted suit; that was the way big business worked. Kay Crowell, admittedly Pearson's friend, testified Brzozoski told her the delay was "good business." Pearson in fact did not bring suit until December 22, 1980, although his counsel sent demand letters to Honeywell and ITT in October 1980. At trial a top Honeywell employee testified it was not company policy to await lawsuits before taking remedial action.

The Honeywell engineers effected a 70 percent improvement in the television reception by certain modifications of the computer in the fall of 1980. Pearson, still dissatisfied, started this action in December. While the suit was pending, Honeywell further modified the computer, finally alleviating Pearson's problems in May 1982.

At trial a Honeywell senior staff engineer admitted the technology to manufacture a non-radiation-emitting computer was available long before it developed this computer, but opined it would have been neither cost nor consumer effective to utilize that technology. He testified Honeywell believed it had corrected Pearson's problems in the fall of 1980.

The Appliance Center's case against Honeywell and ITT finally was submitted to the jury on the theories of nuisance and tortious interference with prospective business relations. It asked for only injunctive relief against Kay Crowell, doing business as Central Travel Service. The latter's motion for summary judgment was sustained. The jury found for the Appliance Center against the remaining defendants on both theories, and further found the Appliance Center should recover $71,000 in compensatory damages and $150,000 in exemplary damages. Following jury trial, Kay Crowell's cross-claim against Honeywell and ITT's cross-claim against Honeywell were submitted to the court. Crowell's cross-claim was dismissed. She did not appeal and is not involved in this proceeding. Trial court awarded ITT full indemnity against Honeywell, in the amount of $221,000, together with attorney fees and costs. Both defendants appeal from the judgment in favor of Appliance Center; Honeywell additionally appeals from the judgment awarding ITT indemnity....

A. ITT argues trial court should have granted its motions for directed verdict because the Appliance Center property was being used for a purpose peculiarly sensitive to computer emissions, and because plaintiff did not prove ITT substantially participated in the creation or maintenance of the alleged nuisance....

Our analysis of ITT's first contention must start with Iowa Code section 657.1, which in relevant part states:

Whatever is ... an obstruction to the free use of property, so as essentially to interfere with the ... enjoyment of ... property, is a nuisance, and a civil action by ordinary proceedings may be brought to enjoin and abate the same and to recover damages sustained on account thereof.

Narrowing our focus, we note the Appliance Center is alleging a "private nuisance," that is, an actionable interference with a person's interest in the private use and enjoyment of his or her property.... It also is apparent that if Central Travel's computer emissions constitute a nuisance it is a "nuisance per accidens, or in fact" — a lawful activity conducted in such a manner as to be a nuisance. *Pauly v. Montgomery,* 209 Iowa 699, 702, 228 N.W. 648, 650 (1930).

Principles governing our consideration of nuisance claims are well established. One's use of property should not unreasonably interfere with or disturb a neighbor's comfortable and reasonable use and enjoyment of his or her estate. A fair test of whether the operation of a lawful trade or industry constitutes a nuisance is the reasonableness of conducting it in the manner, at the place, and under the circumstances shown by the evidence. Each case turns on its own facts and ordinarily the ultimate issue is one of fact, not law.... The existence of a nuisance is not affected by the intention of its creator not to injure anyone.... Priority of occupation and location — "who was there first" — is a circumstance of considerable weight....

When the alleged nuisance is claimed to be offensive to the person, courts apply the standard of "normal persons in a particular locality" to measure the existence of a nuisance.... This normalcy standard also is applied where the use of property is claimed to be affected. "The plaintiff cannot, by devoting his own land to an unusually sensitive use, ... make a nuisance out of conduct of the adjoining defendant which would otherwise be harmless." W. Prosser, *The Law of Torts* § 87, at 579 (4th ed. 1971).

In the case before us, ITT asserts the Appliance Center's display televisions constituted a hypersensitive use of its premises as a matter of law, and equates this situation to cases involving light thrown on outdoor theater screens in which light-throwing defendants have carried the day.... Several of those cases are distinguishable both on facts and by the way the issue was raised.

We cannot equate the rare outdoor theater screen with the ubiquitous television that exists, in various numbers, in almost every home. Clearly, the presence of televisions on any premises is not such an abnormal condition that we can say, as a matter of law, that the owner has engaged in a *peculiarly* sensitive use of the property. This consideration, as well as related considerations of unreasonableness, gravity of harm, utility of conduct, and priority of occupation, are factual determinations that should have been submitted to the jury in this case. We find no trial court error in refusing to direct a verdict on this ground.

....

An action for damages for nuisance need not be predicated on negligence.... Nuisance ordinarily is considered as a condition, and not as an act or failure to act on the part of the responsible party.... A person responsible for a harmful condition found to be a nuisance may be liable even though that person has used the highest possible degree of care to prevent or minimize the effect....

[Omitted, *inter alia,* is a section of the opinion in which the court holds that the defendant should have received a directed verdict on the claim for tortious interference with prospective contractual relations.]

Trial court's instructions required Appliance Center to prove defendants "unreasonably" interfered with the Center's use and enjoyment of its property. Honeywell and ITT objected, in essence, that this permitted the jury to judge "unreasonableness" in a vacuum; that the instructions made no attempt to define the unreasonableness concept. Because reasonableness under our nuisance decisions ordinarily is a question for the jury, ... the court on retrial should provide more guidance for the jury.

In *Bates*, 261 Iowa at 703, 154 N.W.2d at 857, we noted that reasonableness is a function of the manner in which, and the place where, defendant's business is conducted, and the circumstances under which defendant operates. Additional factors, enumerated in *Patz v. Farmegg Products, Inc.*, 196 N.W.2d 557, 561 (Iowa 1972), include priority of location, character of the neighborhood, and the nature of the alleged wrong. The "character and gravity of the resulting injury" is, in fact, "a major factor in determining reasonableness," *Montgomery v. Bremer County Board of Supervisors*, 299 N.W.2d 687, 697 (Iowa 1980). Balanced against the gravity of the wrong is the utility and meritoriousness of the defendant's conduct.... Such relevant factors and others are more succinctly summarized in Restatement (Second) of Torts sections 826, 827 and 828 (1979)....

Both Honeywell and ITT objected because the court did not submit to the jury the issue whether Appliance Center was devoting its premises to an unusually sensitive use.... We hold defendants were entitled to have this question resolved by the jury.

...

[Reversed and Remanded.]

NOTES

(1) A variety of legal theories provide potential vehicles of recovery for the landowner who claims that he has been damaged by a neighbor's activities:

a. *Trespass*, a doctrine that operates when there is a physical entry by a person, or by an object that someone pushes or hurls onto the land. Liability for trespass is absolute, and cannot be avoided by a showing of reasonable care.

b. *Negligence*, the failure to meet the standard of care of reasonable persons in the conduct of that activity.

c. The rule of *Rylands v. Fletcher*, supra § 7.01.

d. "*Nuisance*" cases in which the traditional key phrase is "invasion of another's interest in the private use and enjoyment of land." See RESTATEMENT (SECOND) OF TORTS § 822 (1979). Under this label one finds rather conventional holdings of negligence, as well as other cases that impose liability for action that is intentional and unreasonable. It may be difficult to distinguish the unreasonableness required for nuisance — for example in the case in which the defendant's industrial activities intrude on an otherwise pastoral context — from the unreasonableness of failing to run a factory according to the standard of care expected of reasonable factory owners.

There have been some efforts to classify nuisances into the traditional tripartite division of negligent, intentional, and abnormally dangerous activities, but courts are as likely to view such classification as a matter of convenience based on precedent with little functional significance. Cf., e.g., *Berg v. Reaction Motors Div.*, 37 N.J. 396, 181 A.2d 487, 492 (1962) ("[w]e are here primarily concerned with the underlying considerations of reasonableness, fairness and morality rather than with the formulary labels to be attached to the plaintiffs' causes of action or the legalistic classifications into which they are to be placed"). However, on occasion the characterization of injuries to land can be crucial, as in the case in which there are statutes of limitations for "trespass" or "nuisance."

(2) In one of its most modern garbs, trespass is a foundation for arguments by abortion clinics seeking to keep anti-abortion activists from interfering with patients' efforts to secure abortions. Illustrative is an affirmance of an injunction

granted against anti-abortion campaigners from "trespassing on, blockading, imped-ing or obstructing access or egress from" abortion facilities. *NOW v. Operation Res-cue*, 914 F.2d 582, 584 (4th Cir. 1990) (quoting the district court injunction). The court of appeals said that the activities of the defendants "had crossed the line from persuasion into coercion and operated to deny the exercise of rights protected by law." *Id.* at 585.

(3) An important practical consequence of a finding of trespass is remedial. Some ju-risdictions will "presume[] damages in every case of trespass," a principle that in one case was transferred into a claim for a constitutional violation when police chopped down the door of a medical center with an axe, in pursuit of evidence of Medicaid fraud. Although it denied damages for emotional stress and loss of revenues because it thought there was no proof that the defendants' tortious conduct or constitutional violations had caused those alleged injuries, a federal court awarded $5,000 in "presumed damages," which it labeled a "rough approximation of the harm which plaintiff likely suffered." It character-ized the award as being for a "Fourth Amendment violation analogous to the common law tort of trespass." *Pembaur v. City of Cincinnati*, 745 F. Supp. 446, 457–58 (S.D. Ohio 1990), *aff'd*, 947 F.2d 945 (Table), 1991 WL 216875 (6th Cir. 1991).

(4) The substance of the tentative draft of *Restatement* § 822, paraphrased in the ma-jority opinion in *Copart*, appears in the final *Restatement* under that section number. What difference should the conventional tort culpability categories of intentionality, negligence, and strict liability for abnormally dangerous activities make with respect to either the substantive determination of whether an activity is a nuisance, or the issue of what remedy should be fashioned?

(5) *Copart* is representative of a problem of judicial competence that troubled the New York Court of Appeals in its much discussed decision in *Boomer v. Atlantic Ce-ment Co.*, cited by both opinions in *Copart*. As the majority in *Boomer* put it in deny-ing an injunction, "the judicial establishment is neither equipped in the limited nature of any judgment it can pronounce nor prepared to lay down and implement an effec-tive policy for the elimination of air pollution." 26 N.Y.2d at 223, 309 N.Y.S.2d at 314, 257 N.E.2d at 871. Taking that statement as a good general declaration of the appro-priate range of judicial activity, would you be inclined to say that a judge with a choice to make has an obligation to slant her holding in the direction of "an effective policy for the elimination of air pollution"? Or are judges simply not equipped to make "pol-icy" judgments of that sort?

(6) Courts deciding nuisance cases usually take many factors into account. Consider two elements of decision:

(a) *Priority in time.* Should it ever be dispositive that the complainant was there first, and that the alleged "nuisance" moved in later?

(b) The priority in time issue leads to the broader question of *economic bal-ancing.* On the one hand, it could be argued that a straight priority-in-time rule would stunt development. On the other hand, if one insists that economic efficiency is the only crucial consideration, what does that do to factors like the attachment of residents to their homes, and the sense of community, which are difficult to quantify in economic terms?

(7) To raise the "balancing" question moves us from the substantive standards for nuisance law to the remedy. Read on.

SHOOTOUT OVER A FEEDLOT; A DISAGREEMENT BETWEEN IDAHO APPELLATE COURTS ABOUT WHAT'S IN A NUISANCE

THE APPELLATE COURT DECISION

CARPENTER v. DOUBLE R CATTLE COMPANY

Idaho Court of Appeals
105 Idaho 320, 669 P.2d 643 (1983)

BURNETT, JUDGE.

Dean William Prosser once observed, "There is perhaps no more impenetrable jungle in the entire law than that which surrounds the word 'nuisance.'" W. PROSSER, HANDBOOK OF THE LAW OF TORTS, §86, at 571 (4th ed. 1971). Today we review a case that has thrust us into the jungle of nuisance law. We are asked to define the legal test for determining whether an intended use of property, which incidentally produces adverse effects upon neighboring properties, constitutes a nuisance.

This lawsuit was filed by a group of homeowners who alleged that expansion of a nearby cattle feedlot had created a nuisance. The homeowners claimed that operation of the expanded feedlot had caused noxious odors, air and water pollution, noise and pests in the area. The homeowners sought damages and injunctive relief. The issues of damages and injunctive relief were combined in a single trial, conducted before a jury. Apparently it was contemplated that the jury would perform a fact-finding function in determining whether a nuisance existed and whether the homeowners were entitled to damages, but would perform an advisory function on the question of injunctive relief. The district judge gave the jury a unified set of instructions embracing all of these functions. The jury returned a verdict simply finding that no nuisance existed. The court entered judgment for the feedlot proprietors, denying the homeowners any damages or injunctive relief. This appeal followed. For reasons appearing below, we vacate the judgment and remand the case for a new trial.

The homeowners contend that the jury received improper instructions on criteria for determining the existence of a nuisance. The jury was told to weigh the alleged injury to the homeowners against the "social value" of the feedlot, and to consider "the interests of the community as a whole," in determining whether a nuisance existed....

. . .

II

The concept of nuisance originated in the law of property. At common law, a distinction was maintained between two encroachments upon property rights—interference with possession of land, and interference with the use and enjoyment of land. The first type of encroachment was subject to an "assize of novel disseisin," a remedy for trespass. The latter form of encroachment was subject to an "assize of nuisance," a remedy for a variety of invasions which diminished the owner's enjoyment of his property without dispossessing him of it. Thus, nuisance and trespass have common roots in property law, and occasionally it is difficult to distinguish between them. But where an invasion of property is merely incidental to the use of adjoining property, and does not physically interfere with possession of the property invaded, it generally has been classified as a nuisance rather than as a trespass....

The early concepts of nuisance and trespass shared the common law's reverence for property rights. Invasions of property were deemed wrongful per se, and the parties responsible for such invasions were subject to a form of strict liability. Thus, in the famous case of *Rylands v. Fletcher,* ... an English court held that the owner of a reservoir would be liable to the owner of adjacent property for any injury caused by escaping water. The court stated:

> We think that the true rule of law is, that the person who for his own purposes brings on his lands and collects and keeps there anything likely to do mischief if it escapes, must keep it in at his peril, and, if he does not do so, is prima facie answerable for all the damage which is the natural consequence of its escape. [L.R. 1 Ex. at 279.]

Although a physical intrusion by water might have been viewed as a trespass, rather than as a nuisance, the court noted that the result would have been the same regardless of whether the mischief was caused by "beasts, or water, or filth, or stenches." *Id.* at 280. Thus, the English concept of nuisance was broad, and it carried remedies similar to those available for trespass.

The property-oriented, English concept of a nuisance had its analogue in early American law. In one illustrative case of the nineteenth century, an American court held that title to land gave the owner the right to impregnate the air with odors, dust and smoke, pollute his own water and make noises, provided that he did not substantially interfere with the comfort of others or injure the use or enjoyment of their property. *Pennoyer v. Allen*, 56 Wis. 502, 14 N.W. 609 (1883).

This broad description of nuisance was incorporated into Idaho law. Idaho Code § 52-101, which has antecedents dating to 1881, defines a nuisance as "[a]nything which is injurious to health or morals, or is indecent, or offensive to the senses, or an obstruction to the free use of property, so as to interfere with the comfortable enjoyment of life or property...." The statutory remedies are similarly broad. Idaho Code § 52-111 empowers "any person whose property is injuriously affected, or whose personal enjoyment is lessened by the nuisance [to bring an action] ... and by the judgment the nuisance may be enjoined or abated, as well as damages recovered." Both private and public nuisances in Idaho may be the subjects of such actions brought by affected individuals, and the available remedies are the same in both categories. *See* I.C. §§ 52-102, 107, 111.

However, as the English concept of nuisance was assimilated into American law, it underwent a transformation. It ceased to be solely a creature of property law. As exemplified by the Idaho statutes, nuisance law came to protect life and health, as well as property. A nuisance signified not merely an infringement of property rights, but a wrong against both person and property—a tort.

American tort law in the nineteenth and early twentieth centuries was founded upon the rock of "fault." As the notion of fault burrowed into the concept of nuisance, the strict liability which had attended nuisance in property law began to deteriorate. American courts stressed that liability for nuisance would arise only from "unreasonable" uses of property. In some cases, the courts began to treat nuisance as a form of conduct rather than as a condition affecting the enjoyment of property.... This position later fell into disfavor.

However, American emphasis upon the element of reasonableness persisted. Our courts also underscored the distinction between conditions which are inherently nuisances (nuisances per se) and those conditions which may or may not constitute nuisances, depending upon the surrounding circumstances (nuisances per accidens). Of cases in the latter category, it became customary for the courts to say that whether an invasion of another's enjoyment of property was unreasonable would depend upon all circumstances in the case. These circumstances typically would include the location of the claimed nuisance, the character of the neighborhood, the nature of the offending activity, the frequency of the intrusion, and the effect upon the enjoyment of life, health and property....

Moreover, the American transformation resulted in diminished application of the principle — derived from property law — that where property rights were substantially impaired by a nuisance, the complaining party was entitled to an injunction. This principle, which had complemented the property-based concept of strict liability, entitled a property owner to block an offensive activity on neighboring property, regardless of disparate economic consequences. American courts apparently found this approach ill-suited to the demands of a developing nation.

There evolved two lines of American response to the problem of injunctions. One response was to narrow the scope of cases in which injunctions would be granted, while continuing to recognize an entitlement to damages for injury to property rights. Thus, in *Clifton Iron Co. v. Dye*, 87 Ala. 468, 6 So. 192 (1889), the Alabama Supreme Court held that a mining company would not be enjoined from washing its ores simply because the operation polluted a stream below. The court held that the aggrieved parties' recourse was in damages. Similarly, in *New York City v. Pine*, 185 U.S. 93, 22 S.Ct. 592, 46 L.Ed. 820 (1902), the United States Supreme Court held that two farmers would not be entitled to an absolute injunction against construction of a dam designed to enhance the water supply of the city, even though it adversely affected their properties. However, the Supreme Court held that a conditional injunction would issue unless the farmers were compensated in damages....

Ultimately, the approach exemplified by these cases developed into the "comparative injury" doctrine. Under this doctrine, the comparative benefits and hardships of discontinuing one activity for the protection of another would be weighed in determining whether injunctive relief or damages represented the more appropriate remedy for a nuisance. The Idaho Supreme Court adopted the comparative injury doctrine in *Koseris v. J.R. Simplot Co.*, 82 Idaho 263, 352 P.2d 235 (1960). As explained later in this opinion, our Supreme Court in *Koseris* acknowledged the right to recover damages for the invasion of one's property, even where the comparative injury doctrine might bar injunctive relief.

The second line of American response to the injunction problem was to narrow the scope of cases in which nuisances were found to exist. This was achieved by incorporating the social value — the "utility" — of the offending activity into the litany of circumstances to be weighed in determining whether a particular use of property was "unreasonable." Thus, the utility of an offending activity militated not merely against the issuance of an injunction, but also against a determination that the offending activity was a nuisance at all. This second line of response found expression in the general ("black letter") principles set forth by the RESTATEMENT OF TORTS (1932) (herein cited as the First Restatement). Section 826 of the First Restatement declared that an invasion of another's enjoyment of property would be deemed unreasonable, and therefore a nuisance, unless the utility of the actor's conduct outweighed the gravity of the harm.

The Idaho Supreme Court never explicitly adopted the First Restatement. However, in *McNichols v. J.R. Simplot Co., supra*, the Court may have intimated a similar approach. In that case, emissions from a large phosphate plant were alleged to have adversely affected a small neighboring business. Both damages and injunctive relief were sought. As noted earlier in this opinion, the Supreme Court in *McNichols* found certain jury instructions to be incomplete; and the Court reversed a judgment for the phosphate plant. However, the Court also mentioned, without disapproval, other instructions stating that existence of a nuisance should be determined in light of "all circumstances," and outlining the factors to be weighed. These factors included "inconsequentialness of the relative size of importance of the respective businesses (relative benefit or loss is a pertinent factor)...." ... This ambiguous language later was deemed to support a pattern jury instruction stating that "the interests of the community as a whole" should be considered in determining whether a nuisance exists. *See* Idaho Jury Instructions (IDJI) 491 (1st ed. 1974 & 2d ed. 1982).

Thus, when confronted with a choice between the two American lines of response to the problem of injunctions in nuisance cases, Idaho appeared to choose both. *Koseris* adopted the "comparative injury" doctrine, restricting the cases qualifying for injunctions without narrowing the scope of nuisance cases in which an aggrieved party was entitled to be compensated in damages. However, *McNichols* and IDJI 491 allowed the offending activity's value to the community to be considered in determining whether any nuisance existed at all.

Idaho's uncertain direction reflected a national confusion which led Dean Prosser to deliver his characterization of nuisance law as a "jungle." Indeed, Dean Prosser's treatise on torts, in its 1964 edition, reflected the ambivalence of the time. Prosser expounded the black letter test of the First Restatement, balancing the gravity of harm against the utility of the offending activity, for determining existence of a nuisance. However, he further noted that "[i]n an action for damages, the relative hardship upon the plaintiff and the defendant is not material, once the nuisance is found to exist." W. PROSSER, HANDBOOK OF THE LAW OF TORTS 621 (3d ed. 1964). In the 1971 edition of his treatise, Prosser further observed that in a case where the balancing test would preclude an injunction, nevertheless, "the defendant's conduct may be found to be so unreasonable that he should pay for the harm...." W. PROSSER, HANDBOOK OF THE LAW OF TORTS 604 (4th ed. 1971).

Dissatisfaction with the First Restatement also was expressed by the courts. In *Boomer v. Atlantic Cement Co.*, 26 N.Y.2d 219, 309 N.Y.S.2d 312, 257 N.E.2d 870 (1970), the New York Court of Appeals held that parties adversely affected by dust from a cement plant would be entitled to recover damages for the harm, although the value of the cement plant to the community was so great that its operation would not be enjoined. The Oregon Supreme Court also refused to follow the First Restatement's test for determining existence of a nuisance. In *Furrer v. Talent Irr. Dist.*, 258 Or. 494, 466 P.2d 605 (1970), the Court rejected the contention:

> that in every case the jury has the power to exonerate the defendant from liability because it feels that the social value of the defendant's conduct outweighs the harm which the defendant has visited upon the plaintiff.... [I]f the plaintiff's land is harmed by the conduct of the defendant, the latter cannot escape compensating the plaintiff for the harm simply by showing that the defendant's use had a greater social value than the plaintiff's. [466 P.2d at 613.]

> ...

... [I]t was clear by 1970 that the First Restatement's black letter test for existence of a nuisance had ceased to be—if, indeed, it ever was—an adequate expression of case law. The days were drawing to a close when an economic activity could escape all liability under nuisance law for harm caused to its neighbors, simply because a large measure of social utility was ascribed to it.

III

The seeds of reform had been sown. They took root in fertile soil when the American Law Institute (ALI), which had begun to write a new restatement of the law of torts, turned its attention to the subject of nuisances in 1970.

[Omitted is a historical review of the development of the Restatement drafts.]

B. *The Second Restatement*

Ultimately, the provisions of Tentative Draft No. 18 were approved and incorporated into the private nuisance sections of chapter 40, RESTATEMENT (SECOND) OF TORTS (1977) (herein cited as the Second Restatement). The Second Restatement, like its predecessor, divides such nuisances into two groups: (a) "intentional and unreasonable" invasions of another's interest in the use and enjoyment of property, and (b) invasions which are "unintentional" but otherwise actionable under general tort principles. Second Restatement at § 822.

The first category is broader than the term "intentional" at first glance might suggest. Section 825 of the Second Restatement explains that an invasion is "intentional" if the actor knows that the invasion is resulting, or is substantially certain to result, from his activity. Thus, the purpose of an activity, such as a feedlot, may not be to invade its neighbors' interests in the use and enjoyment of their property; but the invasion is "intentional" within the meaning of the Second Restatement if the proprietors of the activity know that such an invasion is resulting — or is substantially certain to result — from the intended operation of their business. We focus upon "intentional" invasion, in this sense, because it is the type of nuisance alleged to exist in the present case.

The Second Restatement treats such an "intentional" invasion as a nuisance if it is "unreasonable." Section 826 of the Second Restatement now provides two sets of criteria for determining whether this type of nuisance exists:

> An intentional invasion of another's interest in the use and enjoyment of land is unreasonable if
>
> (a) the gravity of the harm outweighs the utility of the actor's conduct, or
>
> (b) the harm caused by the conduct is serious and the financial burden of compensating for this and similar harm to others would not make the continuation of the conduct not feasible.

The present version of § 826, unlike its counterpart in the First Restatement, recognizes that liability for damages caused by a nuisance may exist regardless of whether the utility of the offending activity exceeds the gravity of the harm it has created. This fundamental proposition now permeates the entire Second Restatement. The commentary to § 822, which distinguishes between "intentional" and "unintentional" invasions, and which serves as the gateway for all succeeding sections, emphasizes that the test for existence of a nuisance no longer depends solely upon the balance between the gravity of harm and utility of the conduct. Comment d to § 822 states that, for the purpose of determining liability for damages, an invasion may be regarded as unreasonable even though the utility of the conduct is great and the amount of harm is relatively small. Comment g to the same section reemphasizes that damages are appropriate where the harm from the invasion is greater than a party should be required to bear, "at least without compensation."

The distinction between damages and injunctive relief is carried over in the commentary to § 826. Comment e recognizes that the utility of an activity may be greatly reduced if it does not compensate those whom it harms. Comment f stresses that an intentional invasion, for which damages may be sought, is unreasonable where the harm can be compensated even if the gravity of the harm does not outweigh the utility of the conduct.

C. *Evaluation of The Second Restatement*

The Second Restatement clearly has rejected the notion that if an activity's utility exceeds the harm it creates, the activity is not a nuisance and therefore is free from all liability in damages or for injunctive relief. *See Pendergrast v. Aiken*, 293 N.C. 201, 236 S.E.2d 787 (1977) (adopting Tentative Draft 18 of the Second Restatement). It discards those earlier authorities which had responded to the problem of disparate economic consequences of injunctions by narrowing the concept of nuisance. Thus, the Second Restatement today is inconsistent with the Idaho Supreme Court's decision in *McNichols, supra*, insofar as that decision is said to support IDJI 491. As noted earlier, this pattern instruction would require a jury to consider "the interest of the community as a whole" in determining whether a nuisance exists. IDJI 491 enunciates a single test for existence of a nuisance—regardless of whether damages or an injunction are sought—and obliquely incorporates the utility of the offending activity into the unified test. The pattern instruction perpetuates a discredited line of authority rejected by the Second Restatement.

In contrast, the Idaho Supreme Court's decision in *Koseris, supra*, is entirely consistent with—and in some respects might be said to have presaged—the Second Restatement. In that case, a plaintiff sought injunctive relief, but claimed no damages, from fumes emitted by the same phosphate plant involved in *McNichols*. The phosphate plant offered to prove, among other things, that its facility was important to the economies and tax bases of certain counties in southeastern Idaho. The trial court disallowed the proof. On appeal our Supreme Court said:

> We are constrained to hold that the trial court erred in sustaining objections to those offers of proof, since they were relevant as bearing upon the issue whether respondents, in seeking *injunctive relief*, were pursuing the proper remedy; nevertheless, on the theory of *damages* which respondents had waived, the ruling was correct. [82 Idaho at 270, 352 P.2d at 239. Emphasis added.]

Both the Second Restatement and *Koseris* recognize that utility of the activity alleged to be a nuisance is a proper factor to consider in the context of injunctive relief; but that damages may be awarded regardless of utility. Evidence of utility does not constitute a defense against recovery of damages where the harm is serious and compensation is feasible. Were the law otherwise, a large enterprise, important to the local economy, would have a lesser duty to compensate its neighbors for invasion of their rights than would a smaller business deemed less essential to the community. In our view, this is not, and should not be, the law in Idaho.

Koseris and the Second Restatement also share a recognition of the fundamental difference between making an activity compensate those whom it harms, and forcing the activity to discontinue or to modify its operations. The damage question goes to a person's basic right in tort law to recover for harm inflicted by another. The injunction question is broader; it brings into play the interest of other persons who may benefit from the activity. Comparative benefits and hardships must be weighed in determining whether injunctive relief is appropriate. Thus, the Second Restatement is consistent with the "comparative injury" standard adopted in *Koseris*. *See also Hansen v. Indep. School Dist. No. 1*, 61 Idaho 109, 98 P.2d 959 (1939).

We believe that *Koseris* and the Second Restatement furnish better guidance than IDJI 491 for the future path of nuisance law in Idaho. The law of nuisance profoundly affects the quality of life enjoyed by all Idahoans. It should be broad in coverage, as our statutes provide, and fair in its application. It should not contain blind spots for large or important enterprises.

However, our view is not based simply upon general notions of fairness; it is also grounded in economics. The Second Restatement deals effectively with the problem of "externalities" identified in the ALI proceedings. Where an enterprise externalizes some burdens upon its neighbors, without compensation, our market system does not reflect the true cost of products or services provided by that enterprise. Externalities distort the price signals essential to the proper functioning of the market.

This problem affects two fundamental objectives of the economic system. The first objective, commonly called "efficiency" in economic theory, is to promote the greatest aggregate surplus of benefits over the costs of economic activity. The second objective, usually termed "equity" or "distributive justice," is to allocate these benefits and costs in accordance with prevailing societal values. The market system best serves the goal of efficiency when prices reflect true costs; and the goal of distributive justice is best achieved when benefits are explicitly identified to the correlative costs.

Although the problem of externalities affects both goals of efficiency and distributive justice, these objectives are conceptually different and may imply different solutions to a given problem. In theory, if there were no societal goal other than efficiency, and if there were no impediments to exchanges of property or property rights, individuals pursuing their economic self-interests might reach the most efficient allocation of costs and benefits by means of exchange, without direction by the courts. *See* Coase, *The Problem of Social Cost*, 3 J.L. & ECON. 1 (1960). However, the real world is not free from impediments to exchanges, and our economic system operates within the constraints of a society which is also concerned with distributive justice. Thus, the courts often are the battlegrounds upon which campaigns for efficiency and distributive justice are waged.

Our historical survey of nuisance law, in Part II of this opinion, has reflected the differing emphasis upon efficiency and distributive justice. As noted, the English system of property law placed a preeminent value upon property rights. It was thus primarily concerned with distributive justice in accord with those rights. For that reason the English system favored the injunction as a remedy for a nuisance, regardless of disparate economic consequences. However, when the concept of nuisance was incorporated into American law, it encountered a different value system. Respect for property rights came to be tempered by the tort-related concept of fault, and the demands of a developing nation placed greater emphasis upon the economic objective of efficiency relative to the objective of distributive justice. The injunction fell into disfavor. The reaction against the injunction, as embodied in the First Restatement, so narrowed the concept of nuisance itself that it rendered the courts impotent to deal with externalities generated by enterprises of great utility. This reaction was excessive; neither efficiency nor distributive justice has been well served.

In order to address the problem of externalities, the remedies of damages and injunctive relief must be carefully chosen to accommodate the often competing goals of efficiency and distributive justice.... *Koseris* and the Second Restatement recognize the complementary functions of injunctions and damages. Section 826(a) of the Second Restatement allows both injunctions and damages to be employed where the harm created by an economic activity exceeds its utility. Section 826(b) allows the more limited remedy of damages alone to be employed where it would not be appropriate to enjoin the activity but the activity is imposing harm upon its neighbors so substantial that they cannot reasonably be expected to bear it without compensation.

We follow *Koseris* and adopt § 826 of the Second Restatement. To the extent that IDJI 491 is inconsistent with our decision today, we urge that it be modified. In any event, IDJI 491 is merely recommendatory in nature; it is not mandatory....

...

The element of feasibility illustrates the interrelationship between § 826(a) and § 826(b). If a plaintiff suffers serious harm from an intentional invasion of the use and enjoyment of his property, he is entitled to injunctive relief or damages—or a mix of these remedies—if the trier of fact determines that the gravity of the harm exceeds the utility of the defendant's conduct. If the harm does not outweigh the utility, but remains serious, the plaintiff's remedy is limited to damages—subject, however, to the further limitation that if the nature of the activity (not the particular enterprise conducting it) is such that payment of compensation in damages would cause the activity to be discontinued, then the damage award will be viewed as having the same impact as an injunction. In those circumstances, full compensation will not be awarded unless the gravity of the harm has been found to exceed the utility of the defendant's conduct.

IV

We now resume our focus upon the instant case. The feeding of large congregations of animals within the confined area of a feedlot may create problems that affect the use and enjoyment of neighboring properties.... In general, feedlots are subject to the same principles of nuisance law which apply to other economic activities.... General nuisance instructions were given to the jury in this case.

The actual instructions need not be set forth at length. In summary, the district court instructed the jury on the concept of an "intentional" invasion, within the meaning discussed earlier in this opinion. The court then informed the jury that a nuisance characterized by such an invasion could be found to exist only if the invasion were found to be unreasonable, and that "gravity of any harm" and "utility of defendants' conduct" should be weighed as factors in determining unreasonableness. The court also instructed the jury to take into account such factors as "the interests of the community as a whole," the "general public good," and the "social value" of the defendants' conduct. In short, the district judge gave the jury a set of instructions which did not conform precisely to, but were consistent with, the First Restatement and IDJI 491. The court took no account of *Koseris*, nor of the dual criteria for determining the existence of a nuisance under § 826 of the Second Restatement. The jury was given no instruction on damage liability comparable to § 826(b) of the Second Restatement. We conclude that the jury was improperly instructed, in light of our adoption today of the Second Restatement's criteria for determining existence of a nuisance.

...

... The case must be remanded for a new trial to determine whether a nuisance exists under the full criteria set forth in § 826 of the Second Restatement.

...

THE SUPREME COURT DECISION

CARPENTER v. DOUBLE R CATTLE COMPANY

Idaho Supreme Court
108 Idaho 602, 701 P.2d 222 (1985)

BAKES, JUSTICE.

Plaintiffs appealed a district court judgment based upon a court and jury finding that defendant's feedlot did not constitute a nuisance. The Court of Appeals, 105 Idaho 320, 669 P.2d 643, reversed and remanded for a new trial. On petition for review, we vacate the decision of the Court of Appeals and affirm the judgment of the district court.

. . .

The Law of Nuisance

The Court of Appeals adopted subsection (b) of Section 826 of the Restatement Second, that a defendant can be held liable for a nuisance regardless of the utility of the conduct if the harm is "serious" and the payment of damages is "feasible" without jeopardizing the continuance of the conduct. We disagree that this is the law in Idaho.

At the outset, it is important to again note that appellants neither requested such an instruction nor assigned as error the failure of the trial court to give an instruction consistent with the new rule stated above. In fact, the appellants initially argued both at trial and on appeal that the Second Restatement should not apply and objected to giving any instructions based on the Restatement. It is therefore not surprising that the trial court did not give an instruction on the new rule in Section 826(b), Restatement (Second). Further, the instructions given were consistent with both the First Restatement and Section 826(a) of the Second Restatement, and also our decisions in *McNichols v. J.R. Simplot Co.*, 74 Idaho 321, 262 P.2d 1012 (1953) (action for damages and injunction), and *Koseris v. J.R. Simplot Co.*, 82 Idaho 263, 352 P.2d 235 (1960) (action for injunction only).

The Court of Appeals, without being requested by appellant, adopted the new subsection (b) of Section 826 of the Second Restatement partially because of language in *Koseris* which reads:

> We are constrained to hold that the trial court erred in sustaining objections to those offers of proof [evidence of utility of conduct], since they were relevant as bearing upon the issue whether respondents, in seeking injunctive relief, were pursuing the proper remedy; nevertheless, on the theory of damages which respondents had waived, the ruling was correct. 82 Idaho at 270, 352 P.2d at 239.

The last phrase of the quote, relied on by the Court of Appeals, is clearly *dictum*, since the question of utility of conduct in a nuisance action for damages was not at issue in *Koseris*. It is very doubtful that this Court's dictum in *Koseris* was intended to make such a substantial change in the nuisance law. When the isolated statement of *dictum* was made in 1960, there was no persuasive authority for such a proposition. Indeed, no citation of authority was given. The ... cases from other jurisdictions which the Court of Appeals relied on for authority did not exist until 1970.... The Second Restatement, which proposed the change in the law by adding subsection (b) to Section 826, was also not in existence until 1970. Therefore, we greatly discount this Court's dictum in the

1960 *Koseris* opinion as authority for such a substantial change in the nuisance law. The case of *McNichols v. J.R. Simplot Co.*, 74 Idaho 321, 262 P.2d 1012 (1953) should be viewed as the law in Idaho that in a nuisance action seeking damages the interests of the community, which would include the utility of the conduct, should be considered in the determination of the existence of a nuisance. The trial court's instructions in the present case were entirely consistent with *McNichols*. A plethora of other modern cases are in accord. *E.g., Nissan Motor Corp. v. Maryland Shipbuilding & Drydock Co.*, 544 F.Supp. 1104 (D.Md.1982) (utility of defendant's conduct is factor to be considered in determining existence of nuisance in damages action); *Little Joseph Realty, Inc. v. Town of Babylon*, 41 N.Y.2d 738, 395 N.Y.S.2d 428, 363 N.E.2d 1163 (N.Y.Ct.App.1977) (indicating that New York still adheres to balancing of risk and utility, requiring that harm to plaintiff must outweigh social usefulness of defendant's activity); *Pendergrast v. Aiken*, 293 N.C. 201, 236 S.E.2d 787 (1977) (balancing of harm versus utility retained, despite change of section 826 Restatement (Second) of Torts); *Pate v. City of Martin*, 614 S.W.2d 46 (Tenn.1981) (determination of existence of nuisance in action for damages and injunction cannot be determined by exact rules, but depends on circumstances of each case, including locality and character of surroundings, as well as utility and social value of defendant's conduct).

The State of Idaho is sparsely populated and its economy depends largely upon the benefits of agriculture, lumber, mining and industrial development. To eliminate the utility of conduct and other factors listed by the trial court from the criteria to be considered in determining whether a nuisance exists, as the appellant has argued throughout this appeal, would place an unreasonable burden upon these industries. We see no policy reasons which should compel this Court to accept appellant's argument and depart from our present law. Accordingly, the judgment of the district court is affirmed and the Court of Appeals decision is set aside.

Costs to respondents. No attorney fees.

DONALDSON, C.J., and SHEPARD, J., concur.

BISTLINE, JUSTICE, dissenting.

. . .

The majority today continues to adhere to ideas on the law of nuisance that should have gone out with the use of buffalo chips as fuel. We have before us today homeowners complaining of a nearby feedlot—not a small operation, but rather a feedlot which accommodates 9,000 cattle. The homeowners advanced the theory that after the expansion of the feedlot in 1977, the odor, manure, dust, insect infestation and increased concentration of birds which accompanied all of the foregoing, constituted a nuisance. If the odoriferous quagmire created by 9,000 head of cattle is not a nuisance, it is difficult for me to imagine what is. However, the real question for us today is the legal basis on which a finding of nuisance can be made.

. . .

The majority's rule today overlooks the option of compensating those who suffer a nuisance because the interests of the community outweigh the interests of those afflicted by the nuisance. This unsophisticated balancing overlooks the possibility that it is not necessary that one interest be ignored when the community interest is strong. We should not be adopting a rule of preference which suggests that if the community interest is preferred any other interest must be disregarded. Instead, § 826(b) accommodates adverse interests by contemplating continuation of the facility which creates the nuisance while compensating those who suffer the direct impact of the nuisance — in the instant case the homeowners who live in the vicinity of the feedlot.

The majority's rule today suggests that part of the cost of industry, agriculture or development must be borne by those unfortunate few who have the fortuitous luck to live in the immediate vicinity of a nuisance producing facility. Frankly, I think this naive economic view is ridiculous in both its simplicity and its outdated view of modern economic society. The "cost" of a product includes not only the amount it takes to produce such a product but also includes the external costs: the damage done to the environment through pollution of air or water is an example of an external cost. In the instant case, the nuisance suffered by the homeowners should be considered an external cost of operating a feedlot and producing beef for public consumption. I do not believe that a few should be required to pay this extra cost of doing business by going uncompensated for a nuisance of this sort. If a feedlot wants to continue, I say fine, providing compensation is paid for the serious invasion (the odors, flies, dust, etc.) of the homeowner's interest. My only qualification is that the financial burden of compensating for this harm should not be such as to force the feedlot (or any other industry) out of business. The true cost can then be shifted to the consumer who rightfully should pay for the *entire* cost of producing the product he desires to obtain.

The majority today blithely suggests that because the State of Idaho is sparsely populated and because our economy is largely dependent on agriculture, lumber, mining and industrial development, we should forego compensating those who suffer a serious invasion. If humans are such a rare item in this state, maybe there is all the more reason to protect them from the discharge of industry. At a minimum, we should compensate those who suffer a nuisance at the hands of industry and agriculture. What the majority overlooks is that the cost of development should not be absorbed by few, but rather should be spread out and paid by all. I am not convinced that agriculture or industry will be put out of business by requiring compensation for the nuisance they generate. Let us look at the case before us. The owners of the feedlot will not find themselves looking for new jobs if they are required to compensate the homeowners for the stench and dust and flies attendant with 9,000 head of cattle. Rather, meat prices at the grocery store will undoubtedly go up. But, in my view it is far better that the cost of the nuisance be carried by the consumer of a product than by the unfortunate homeowners currently suffering under adverse conditions. Some compensation should be paid the homeowners for suffering the burden from which we all benefit.

The decision of the Court of Appeals is an outstanding example of a judicial opinion which comes from a truly exhaustive and analytical review. *See* 105 Idaho 320, 669 P.2d 643 (1983). I see no need to reiterate the authority cited therein. The Court of Appeals clarified the standard for determining the existence of a nuisance. Because the jury instructions were inconsistent with this Idaho law, the Court of Appeals properly vacated the lower court judgment.

. . .

[The brief opinion of Justice Huntley, concurring with Justice Bistline's dissent, is omitted.]

Mitchell Polinsky, *Resolving Nuisance Disputes: The Simple Economics of Injunctive and Damage Remedies*
32 STAN. L. REV. 1075, 1110–1112 (1980)*

... The present discussion deals only with the situation of one injurer and one victim and concentrates on the set of assumptions that seems most realistic—strategic behavior, costly redistribution, and understated damages.

The first argument against injunctive remedies was that they allowed the plaintiff to "extort" the defendant, that is, to obtain compensation possible far in excess of the plaintiff's actual damages. But in the framework of this article, "excess" compensation simply means that the plaintiff is sharing the gains from trade with the defendant. Neither party is "entitled" to these gains in the first place; rather, the desirability of those transfers depends on the distributional goal society wishes to promote. If the distributional goal strongly favors the plaintiff and if redistribution by other means is costly, then excess compensation may be desirable.

Even if the distributional effects of extortion are undesirable, turning from injunctive remedies to damages does not necessarily avoid them. If the court has imperfect information and is likely to understate the plaintiff's damages, then the defendant can "extort" the plaintiff in two ways. First, since the defendant's output will initially exceed the efficient output when damages are understated, the plaintiff will have an incentive to bribe the defendant to reduce output. But the defendant can hold out for more than his lost profits, thereby extorting the plaintiff. Moreover, the defendant can threaten to increase output beyond his profit maximizing output, thereby extorting the plaintiff in a different way. Thus, the extortion argument against the injunctive remedy may be misguided even on its own terms if one accepts the realistic assumption that the court underestimates the plaintiff's damages.

The second argument for damage remedies concerned the efficiency consequences of unsuccessful extortion. According to this argument, strategic behavior under the injunctive remedy might lead to the enforcement of the injunction when enforcement was inefficient. Given strategic behavior, this criticism is valid whenever the entitlement point does not coincide with the efficient outcome. However, the same type of criticism applies at least as forcefully to the damage remedy when, as frequently happens, courts underestimate the plaintiff's damages. As noted in the previous paragraph, when damages are understated, the defendant can employ strategic behavior to extort the plaintiff in two ways: He can reject the plaintiff's "bribe" to reduce output, or he can carry out threats to increase output. Either way, the efficiency loss from strategic behavior under the damage remedy could be larger than the efficiency loss under the injunctive remedy.

The third argument favoring damage remedies was that they are distributionally more flexible—the liability schedule apparently can be precisely adjusted to allow overcompensation ("bonus payments") or undercompensation to achieve desired distributional results. In contrast, it was noted, the distributional outcome under the injunctive remedy is uncertain because of strategic behavior. However, damage remedies are potentially superior in pursuing distributional goals only when the courts have perfect information about the plaintiff's actual damages. Even then, the distributional flexibility

---

of damage remedies is quite limited. It was shown that liability schedules that overcompensate the plaintiff are subject to the same kinds of strategic behavior problems that arise under the injunctive remedy. Moreover, no advantage accrues to using a liability schedule that undercompensates the plaintiff. And when, as can realistically be assumed, courts understate damages, the distributional advantages of the damage remedy may disappear altogether.

...

This article should not be viewed as constructing a case for the use of injunctive remedies. Rather, its goal has been to examine systematically whether the arguments favoring damage remedies are logically coherent. They are not. Under none of the assumptions examined are damage remedies unambiguously favored, except, possibly, when there are many victims. And under the most realistic set of assumptions—strategic behavior, costly redistribution, and understated damages—the argument could easily go either way.

Though neither remedy can be established conclusively as superior in the abstract, the better remedy in practice may be clear depending on the circumstances. Suppose, for example, that efficiency is of paramount concern. If it seems that the parties would act strategically, and the court knows the victim's damages but not the injurer's benefits, the damage remedy is clearly superior. Inadequate information about the injurer's benefits would prevent the court from accurately setting the entitlement at the efficient point, so that the injunctive remedy will fail because of strategic behavior. However, by assigning an absolute entitlement to the victim and using a damage remedy with liability equal to actual damages, the efficient outcome can be guaranteed.

On the other hand, if the court lacks information about both damages and benefits, then an argument can be made for the injunctive remedy. The argument is especially strong if the efficiency loss from too little activity by the injurer is small relative to the loss from excessive activity. Under the injunctive remedy, the court could give an absolute entitlement to the victim and know that, at worst, the parties will remain at the entitlement point because of bargaining failure. Under the damage remedy, however, the court's lack of information may well result in a liability schedule which leads the injurer to engage in too much activity, especially if the injurer carries out extortion threats. This could easily result in a much larger efficiency loss.

Bringing distributional issues back into consideration may simplify the choice of remedy. For example, if the distributional goal does not strongly favor one party and the court knows the victim's damages and the injurer's benefits, then the damage remedy with liability equal to actual damages is preferable. It can reach the efficient outcome and simultaneously redistribute income to the desired extent. However, if the distributional goal strongly favors one party and efficiency is less important, an injunctive remedy may be better.

While the arguments developed in this article cannot provide a unique answer—indeed, that is the point of the article— they may help clarify the goals in resolving nuisance disputes and, given the goals, the principles relevant to choosing the better remedy.

NOTES

(1) How can courts choose "neutrally" whether to order an injunction, or to construct a remedy that effectively forces residents to accept a cash offer for their property from an entrepreneur who conducts risky activities? Journalistic accounts of local con-

troversies capture some of the social and economic texture of the problem. One article, for example, reports a controversy in the small Texas panhandle community of Phillips over an offer by the Phillips Petroleum Company, whose refinery tanks posed serious risks of explosion, to provide new lots for homes in the neighboring town of Borger, and to aid in defraying the cost of moving. One resident said he would accept the offer, although it was not nearly enough to cover the cost of moving. He said he did not "see what's to be gained by a lawsuit," observing that with the changes that had taken place in the town, there was little left except memories. A more recalcitrant homeowner, who had returned to Phillips after moving to Borger, said that her children had "never fit in" in Borger and complained, "If they take this town, we can never tell the kids this is where we're from." *Oil Company Town, Facing Eviction, Digs in for Legal Battle*, N.Y. Times, Feb. 23, 1986, at 22.

(2) Consider the case where homeowners confronted with a pollution hazard can avoid danger to health by locking themselves into houses sealed up with a special sealant provided by the polluter. How can a court quantify the cost to the homeowners of shutting themselves up like that?

A much-cited article by Professor Michelman refers to "demoralization costs." See *Property, Utility and Fairness: Comments on the Ethical Foundations of "Just Compensation" Law*, 80 Harv. L. Rev. 1165, 1214 (1967). Is this a concept that would be useful in dealing with problems where landowners suing for claimed nuisances are not producing saleable goods or services on their own land?

(3) In another notable article, Calabresi and Melamed stress that "distributional effects should be carefully evaluated in making the choice for or against inalienability." They observe that

> the citizens of a town may be granted an entitlement to be free of water pollution caused by the waste discharges of a chemical factory; and the entitlement might be made inalienable on the grounds that the town's citizens really would be better off in the long run to have access to clean beaches. But the entitlement might also be made inalienable to assure the maintenance of a beautiful resort area for the very wealthy, at the same time putting the town's citizens out of work.

Property Rules, Liability Rules, and Inalienability: One View of the Cathedral, 85 Harv. L. Rev. 1089, 1124 (1972). The authors cite a magazine article that describes, in their characterization, a controversy over a proposal to build a chemical factory that would pollute beaches in an economically depressed community. The article notes that the controversy arrayed resort developers and environmental groups, opposing the factory, against representatives of unemployed town residents who supported it. *Id.* at 1124 n.66, citing Frady, *the View from Hilton Head*, Harper's, May 1970, at 103–112.

(4) A 2002 symposium in the *Washburn Law Journal* includes several interesting articles on the comparative advantages and disadvantages of tort in the environmental context and regulation. See, e.g., Keith N. Hylton, *When Should We Prefer Tort Law to Environmental Regulation?*, 41 Washburn L.J. 515, arguing that the flexibility of tort law makes it a useful tool, in part because regulatory officials are "vulnerable to bribery from third parties or from the class of offenders they are supposed to monitor," *id.* at 520, and because of the superior ability of private law to bring private information to the surface, see *id.* at 524–27. Moreover, he finds nuisance law to be "both capable and a preferable method of enforcing local emission standards." See *id.* at 531. Indeed, it

may even be useful with respect to "global emission standards," for example, by allowing a community to challenge the emission levels of regulated firms if "the global standards were set too low" "because of the political influence of producers" or industries. See *id.* at 533. Cf. Peter Cane, *Using Tort Law to Enforce Environmental Regulations?*, 41 WASHBURN L.J. 427, concluding that "[t]he justification for tort law in the regulatory state must rest on its role as a mechanism for imposing obligations of repair on the basis of ideas of personal responsibility" and that "the case for tort law cannot rest on its regulatory potential." *Id.* at 466. Compare also Christopher Schroeder's observation that there are three "distinctive features of environmental regulation that tort law does not share": "A regulatory regime sets the desired level of environmental quality through public processes, its structure and mode of operation stress the prevention of harm before it occurs, and the levels of environmental quality our existing regulatory structure targets as its goals differ from the levels that would emerge from a weighing of the competing private costs and benefits through the tort system." *Lost in the Translation: What Environmental Regulation Does That Tort Cannot Duplicate*, 41 WASHBURN L.J. 583, 605.

(5) For a wide-ranging review of history, jurisprudence, and economic theory, see George P. Smith II, *Nuisance Law: The Morphogenesis of an Historical Revisionist Theory of Contemporary Economic Jurisprudence*, 74 NEB. L. REV. 658 (1995). Smith views the doctrine *sic utere tuo ut alienum non laedas* — "use your own property in such a manner as not to injure that of another" — as "form[ing] the base of the pyramid of real property interests," with private nuisance being its "apex," *id.* at 698. He views the obligation of courts as "to make decisions that are consistent with basic tenets of economic efficiency since this presents the core of a reasonable judicial decision." *Id.* at 740.

§ 14.02 Public Nuisance

PROBLEM

In his book, *Supership*, Noel Mostert writes about a Norwegian tanker named the Polycomander which ran aground on the Spanish coast in May 1970, carrying "a full cargo of crude oil." The wreck caused a spill of about sixteen thousand tons of the oil, which caught fire on the ocean, causing "a fire storm." Mostert writes that the heat from this conflagration generated "hurricane force winds" that "whirled aloft a huge amount of oil, spraying it into a fine mist" and swept it up "to high altitudes." The mist then "condensed into drops," ultimately causing "a black rain" that fell on the coast. Some of this ghastly precipitation caused "extensive" damage "to homes, gardens, and crops" in and around the villages of Panjon and Bayona, and "cattle died of eating oil-covered grass."[1]

If this incident had taken place on a United States coastline, under what theories could a cattle owner have sued the tanker owner for the death of livestock?

---

1. NOEL MOSTERT, SUPERSHIP 43–44 (Knopf 1974).

HAMPTON v. NORTH CAROLINA PULP CO.*

United States District Court, Eastern District of North Carolina

49 F. Supp. 625 (1943)

MEEKINS, DISTRICT JUDGE.

This is a civil action at law brought by the plaintiff against the defendant in which the plaintiff seeks to recover from the defendant damages in the sum of $30,000 for the alleged wrongful diversion and destruction of fish in the navigable waters of the Roanoke River near Plymouth, North Carolina. A motion to dismiss the cause for failure of the complaint "to state a claim upon which relief can be granted" was heard by me at Raleigh in Term and thereafter briefs were filed in due course.

Well, Fish is the subject of this story. From the fifth day of the Creation down through the centuries, some of which lie behind us like a hideous dream, fish have been a substantial factor in the affairs of men. After giving man dominion over all the Earth, God gave him dominion over the fish in particular, naming them first in order, reserving unto Himself only one certain fruit tree in the midst of the Garden, and Satan smeared that—the wretch! Whatever else we may think of the Devil, as a business man he is working success. He sat in the original game, not with one fruit tree, but with the cash capital of one snake, and now he has half the world grabbed and a diamond hitch on the other half.

Great hunters lived before Nimrod, who was a mighty one before the Lord, and great fishermen before Izaak Walton, whose followers are as numberless as the sands of the sea—not counting the leaves of the forest, as if anybody ever did, or could, except the quondam Literary Digest, which polled itself to death in the late Summer and middle Fall of 1936.

The most notable group of fishermen of all time was that headed by Peter, the impulsive Apostle, and his followers Thomas, Nathaniel, the sons of Zebedee, and two other Disciples, seven fishermen in all—a working majority of The Twelve.

Considered solely as a food product, fish have unlimited possibilities—quantitative and qualitative. We are told that a few little fishes and seven loaves, five loaves and two fishes, according to St. Luke, were more than sufficient to feed a hungry multitude of four thousand men, together with the women and children present, and of the fragments there were seven baskets full of fish. Quantitative.

Professor Agassiz, the eminent Harvard scientist said: "Fish is a good brain food." One wrote to know "in what quantities should it be taken?" The great scientist wrote back: "In your case, a whale a day for thirty days." Qualitative.

. . .

As it is the biggest fish that always breaks the hook or bites the line in two, so, here, the huge sum of thirty thousand dollars is asked as compensation for fish that were never caught. I can remember when that sum would buy a lot of fish. I have seen six-pound

---

* The authors are grateful to Alex Bell, a former student and faculty colleague of Marshall Shapo, for calling this case to his attention.

roe shad retail for five cents apiece and cured herrings sell for two dollars a thousand— one hundred and twenty pounds of shad for one dollar and five herrings for one cent.

And this large sum is now asked for whose Fish? Certainly not the plaintiff's, because he never owned them. I repeat the question, whose Fish? The answer is plain: they belonged to the Public.

...

The plaintiff, in substance, alleges that he is now, and has been since 1911, the owner and in possession of those two certain tracts of land, situate on opposite sides of the Roanoke River, and known respectively as the "Kitty Hawk" and "Slade" Fisheries; that the properties are ideally located for the business of fishing, and have for a number of years, during the fishing season, been operated for that purpose by the plaintiff and his ancestors in title, expensive equipment having been placed and maintained thereon for the proper and profitable conduct of such business; that, from time immemorial, great quantities of fish of the kinds specified have been accustomed, during the Spring of each year, to make their way from the Ocean through Albermarle Sound, and thence into the fresh-water spawning grounds in the upper reaches of the Roanoke River; and that, by reason of this annual migration of fish, plaintiff's fishing business, and his "Kitty Hawk" and "Slade" Fisheries, have been "principally and particularly valuable."

It is alleged that the defendant is the owner of a boundary on the Roanoke River situate below the plaintiff's property which the fish, entering the river in their annual migration to the spawning grounds, are compelled to pass before reaching that portion of the river running between the plaintiff's properties; that, during the period referred to in the complaint, the defendant has maintained upon the boundary a plant for the manufacture of sulphate pulp, bleached and unbleached; that, in the course of the manufacturing operation, during the three years immediately preceding the institution of this action, the defendant has from day to day discharged into the waters of the Roanoke River, opposite its plant, a large volume of poisonous and deleterious waste and matter injurious to the fish then in passage to the spawning grounds, with the result that the annual migration of the fish upstream has been interrupted or diverted and large quantities of them have been destroyed; and that, as a natural consequence thereof, the plaintiff's business, and the usufruct of his property, during each of the three years have greatly diminished—all to the plaintiff's great and lasting damage in the sum of $30,000.00.

Measured by these allegations, it is not open to question that the acts of the defendant were palpably wrongful. They were, indeed, in violation of various criminal statutes of the State, designed to conserve the public good. If, then, upon indictment, the acts charged were admitted or established, no Court could hesitate to pronounce the defendant guilty of the creation and maintenance of a public nuisance and impose the maximum penalties of the statutes as are therein provided. But the right of the plaintiff to recover damages for this alleged wrong presents a far different question. In a case of pure tort, the wrongdoer is responsible for all the damages directly caused by his misconduct, and for all indirect and consequential damages, resulting naturally and probably from the wrongful acts, which are susceptible to ascertainment with a reasonable degree of certainty. Damages which are not the natural and probable result of the act complained of, but which are contingent or merely possible, or based upon a conjectural probability of future loss, and so beyond the scope of reasonable determination, are too remote and are not recoverable.... It is well settled that in actions by private individuals, based upon the creation or maintenance of a public nuisance, there can be no recovery, even of nominal damages, upon the mere establishment of the wrongful act. In such cases it is essential to the plaintiff's cause of action that he show an appreciable injury....

At the outset, therefore, I am confronted with the inquiry as to whether, in his allegations of injury and damage, the plaintiff has brought himself within the requirements of these rules. In other words, are the damages alleged by the plaintiff the natural and probable consequences of defendant's wrongful act, capable of ascertainment with reasonable certainty, or are they merely contingent or possible consequences based upon a conjectural apprehension of events?

If it be assumed that a portion of the fish diverted or destroyed would otherwise have been caught by the plaintiff, the question still remains as to the proportion and kinds of these oviparous denizens of the silent deep which would have made their way into plaintiff's seines or nets. The answer to this question is more than difficult; it is obviously impossible with any reasonable degree of certainty. The plaintiff, doubtless, would be able to show his catch during preceding seasons. But experience joins with common sense in teaching that the result in one season affords no criterion of the result in others. The truth is that nothing in the field of industry is more uncertain or variable than the business of fishing, or the profits to be derived therefrom in any given period. Success [or] failure depends upon such a variety and diversity of contingencies—the eccentricities of climate, unanticipated seasonal changes, the clarity and temperature of inland streams, the whims and vagaries of sun and wind and tide, as is illustrated by what happened on the Sea of Tiberias in obedience to the command: "Cast the net on the other side of the ship." Through the operation of these natural forces millions of shad and herring, which may have spawned in one season in the upper Roanoke River, may spawn the next in some other freshwater stream far removed from the menace of plaintiff's reticulated snares. By reason thereof, many a promising and hopeful season has ended in disaster, and the business of fishing, in any given stream during any given period, has been reduced to an unpredictable gamble.

As previously stated, in actions in tort, the damages recoverable, whether direct or consequential, must flow naturally and reasonably from the wrongful act alleged. I am of the opinion that the attempt to so estimate and segregate the damages in this case would involve a misty maze of conjecture and speculation as unprofitable as calculating the mechanical value of a cubic mile of pea-soup fog off the Grand Banks of Newfoundland.

While these considerations seem to point unerringly to the solution of the question considered, I am not disposed to rest my decision upon this weakness in the plaintiff's case. For there is, I think, an even more patent and fundamental defect. It is uniformly held in North Carolina, and generally elsewhere, that, in order for a private citizen to sustain an action predicated upon a public nuisance, he must establish an injury, which is not only appreciable, but special and peculiar to himself, differing not only in degree, but in kind from that common to the public.... And, while the Courts of North Carolina have been alert in such cases to administer relief where an injury peculiar to the complainant has been shown, they have been equally zealous and alert in denying relief, where the injury alleged, upon studious consideration, has been held to be merely of the kind suffered by all citizens alike. Particularly is this true where the nuisance considered was initially of a public nature, and did not become so merely by reason of an aggregation of private injuries so widespread or so long continued as to constitute a public menace. The rule is that no private individual may have relief in law or equity from the actual or threatened consequences of a public nuisance; the exception relates only to those who are able to show an appreciable injury peculiar to themselves.

This case falls, I think, within the rule and not within the exception. The plaintiff alleges no invasion of his soil, no obstruction of his right of ingress or egress, no interference with the movement or installation of his nets, seines or other fishing equipment, no dissemination of noxious odors or disease-bearing insects destructive of health or comfort, no corruption of the surrounding atmosphere or of his private wells or springs, nor other injury of a kind recognized as warranting a recovery in an action based upon a public nuisance....

True, it is alleged that defendant's wrongful acts constitute a trespass, as well as a nuisance, and that the usufruct of plaintiff's business and property has been seriously impaired — "usufruct" being used, manifestly, in the sense of profit. But the first of these allegations is obviously a conclusion of the pleader, while the latter must of necessity be referred to defendant's wrongful diversion or destruction of the fish. Otherwise no casual connection is discernible between the wrongdoing alleged and the consequences experienced, and the complaint is fatally defective.... Stated concisely, the alleged injury consists in the diminution of annual revenues from the plaintiff's business and property; the alleged wrong in defendant's diversion or destruction of fish in the Roanoke River, through the daily discharge into that stream of poisonous and deleterious matter.

The complaint is fatally defective for the reason that the plaintiff did not own either the River or the fish therein. Both, upon the allegations and implications of the complaint, belonged to the State. It is true that the plaintiff had the right to fish in the River, and to appropriate to his own use the fish so taken therefrom. But the plaintiff had not reclaimed the fish in question. Moreover, his right of fishery was neither several nor exclusive. Nor was it incidental to his riparian ownership, but a right held in common with the public.... To illustrate: A trapper operating muskrat traps in the Great Dismal Swamp may maintain an action for damage to or destruction of his traps by reason of fire wrongfully set out by another. But it can hardly be said that the trapper could maintain a claim for diminution of profits by reason of the actual destruction or the necessitated change of range of the rats. He has no right of property in any rat until he reclaims it by reducing it to actual possession. Here, the plaintiff does not seek damage for injury to and loss of his traps, that is to say, injury to and loss of his nets, seines, boats, lands, buildings and other necessary equipment, and for the obvious reason that the wrong he complains of, by the very nature of it, could not produce such injury or loss. The plaintiff seeks only to recover for diminution of his profits by reason of the alleged wrongful diversion and destruction of fish in which he had no right of property, and precisely for the same reason that the trapper had none in the rats. It seems to me the analogy is perfect.

If, therefore, the plaintiff has sustained an injury, then so has every citizen of the State. If the plaintiff may maintain this action, every citizen of the State may maintain a like action for the same wrong.

Careful consideration of the briefs and authorities cited, supplemented by independent research, constrains the conclusion that the plaintiff may not recover for an injury to property in which he had no vestige of special interest. Having failed to bring himself within the terms of the exception, he is bound by the rule.

...

[Dismissed.]

RESTATEMENT (SECOND) OF TORTS § 821B (1977)*

§ 821B. Public Nuisance

(1) A public nuisance is an unreasonable interference with a right common to the general public.

(2) Circumstances that may sustain a holding that an interference with a public right is unreasonable include the following:

(a) Whether the conduct involves a significant interference with the public health, the public safety, the public peace, the public comfort or the public convenience, or

(b) whether the conduct is proscribed by a statute, ordinance or administrative regulation, or

(c) whether the conduct is of a continuing nature or has produced a permanent or long-lasting effect, and, as the actor knows or has reason to know, has a significant effect upon the public right.

...

Comment:

...

d. Criminal character. It has been stated with some frequency that a public nuisance is always a criminal offense. This statement is susceptible to two interpretations. The first is that in order to be treated as a public nuisance, conduct must have been already proscribed by the state as criminal. This is too restrictive. The second is that any conduct that is found to be a public nuisance is for that reason a criminal offense, either at common law or under statute. While this has been true in most of the cases in which the statement has appeared and is still so in many states, it affords little assistance in determining what conduct amounts to a public nuisance. It no longer has significance in states where the general crime of public nuisance has ceased to exist. In any event, there is clear recognition that a defendant need not be subject to criminal responsibility. Thus a municipal corporation, which cannot be prosecuted for a crime, may still be liable in tort for the creation or maintenance of a public nuisance if the conduct is such that a private individual would be liable. In addition, other remedies such as the recovery of damages in tort by one who has suffered particular damages (*see* § 821C) or abatement of the nuisance or injunction may lie in favor of the state or even a private individual who suffers particular harm.

e. Unreasonable interference. The common law criminal offense of public nuisance involved an interference with a right common to the general public. Little more than this in the way of a standard for determining what kinds of interferences constitute the crime of public nuisance was to be found in the cases. But as the tort action came into the picture, the use of the single word "nuisance" to describe both the public and the private nuisance, led to the application in public nuisance cases, both criminal and civil, of an analysis substantially similar to that employed for the tort action for private nuisance.... Thus, by analogy to the rules stated in § 822, the defendant is held liable for a public nuisance if his interference with the public right was intentional or was unintentional and otherwise actionable under the principles controlling liability for negligent or reckless conduct or for abnormally dangerous activities. Liability was not normally

---

imposed for a pure accident that did not fall into one of the three traditional categories or tort liability. In each of these categories, some aspect of the concept of unreasonableness is to be found. If the interference with the public right is intentional, it must also be unreasonable. (*See* §822, and §§826–831), involving the weighing of the gravity of the harm against the utility of the conduct). If the interference was unintentional, the principles governing negligent or reckless conduct, or abnormally dangerous activities all embody in some degree the concept of unreasonableness....

...

Subsection (2) has listed three sets of circumstances for determining whether an interference with a public right is unreasonable. They are listed in the disjunctive; any one may warrant a holding of unreasonableness. They also do not purport to be exclusive. Some courts have shown a tendency, for example, to treat significant interferences with recognized aesthetic values or established principles of conservation of natural resources as amounting to a public nuisance. The language of Subsection (2) is not intended to set restrictions against developments of this nature....

...

g. Interference with public right. Conduct does not become a public nuisance merely because it interferes with the use and enjoyment of land by large number of persons. There must be some interference with a public right. A public right is one common to all members of the general public. It is collective in nature and not like the individual right that everyone has not to be assaulted or defamed or defrauded or negligently injured. Thus the pollution of a stream that merely deprives fifty or a hundred lower riparian owners of the use of the water for purposes connected with their land does not for that reason alone become a public nuisance. If, however, the pollution prevents the use of a public bathing beach or kills the fish in a navigable stream and so deprives all members of the community of the right to fish, it becomes a public nuisance.

It should be noted that in some states there are statutes defining a public nuisance to include interference with "any considerable number of persons;" and under these statutes no public right as such need be involved.

It is not, however, necessary that the entire community be affected by a public nuisance, so long as the nuisance will interfere with those who come in contact with it in the exercise of a public right or it otherwise affects the interests of the community at large. The obstruction of a public highway is a public nuisance, although no one is travelling upon the highway or wishes to travel on it at the time. In many cases the interests of the entire community may be affected by a danger to even one individual. Thus the threat of communication of smallpox to a single person may be enough to constitute a public nuisance because of the possibility of an epidemic; and a fire hazard to one adjoining landowner may be a public nuisance because of the danger of a conflagration. In any case in which a private nuisance affects a large number of persons in their use and enjoyment of land it will normally be accomplished by some interference with the rights of the public as well. Thus the spread of smoke, dust or fumes over a considerable area filled with private residence may interfere also with the use of the public streets or affect the health of so many persons as to involve the interests of the public at large.

h. Relation to private nuisance. Unlike a private nuisance, a public nuisance does not necessarily involve interference with use and enjoyment of land. A public nuisance as such does not afford a basis for recovery of damages in tort unless there is particular harm to the plaintiff, as stated in §821C. When the particular harm consists of interference with the use and enjoyment of land, the public nuisance may also be a private nuisance, as when a bawdy house that interferes with the public morals and constitutes a crime also interferes with the use and enjoyment of land next door. In this case the landowner may recover either on the basis of the particular harm to him resulting from the public nuisance or on the basis of the private nuisance.

i. Action for damages distinguished from one for injunction. There are numerous differences between an action for tort damages and an action for an injunction or abatement, and precedents for the two are by no means interchangeable. In determining whether to award damages, the court's task is to decide whether it is unreasonable to engage in the conduct without paying for the harm done. Although a general activity may have great utility it may still be unreasonable to inflict the harm without compensating for it. In an action for injunction the question is whether the activity itself is so unreasonable it must be stopped. It may be reasonable to continue an important activity if payment is made for the harm it is causing, but unreasonable to continue it without paying.

On the other hand an award of damages is retroactive, applying to past conduct, while an injunction applies only to the future. In addition, for damages to be awarded significant harm must have been actually incurred, while for an injunction harm need only be threatened and need not actually have been sustained at all. (*See* § 821F, Comment b). To maintain a damage action for a public nuisance, one must have suffered damage different in kind from that suffered by the general public; this is not necessarily true in a suit for abatement or injunction. (*See* § 821C).

...

NOTES

(1) What would you think was the principal rationale, at common law, for requiring that conduct be criminal to constitute a public nuisance?

(2) What is the reason for the persistence of the requirement, articulated in the district judge's opinion in *Hampton* on the basis of the old common law and reemphasized in *Restatement* comment i, that a private litigant seeking damages must prove harm "different in kind from that suffered by the general public"?

Faced with a very persistent Mr. Hampton, who brought a state court action as well, the North Carolina Supreme Court held that it was an error to sustain a demurrer to his complaint. *Hampton v. North Carolina Pulp Co.*, 223 N.C. 535, 27 S.E.2d 538 (1943). The court commented that "[t]he insistence with which we are urged to draw an equation before the law between all injuries sustained from the postulated common right—of the nature and character pointed out—which must in their nature be trivial, strongly suggests an imbalance somewhere in the doctrinal theory or its attempted application." *Id.* at 546, 27 S.E.2d at 545. Focusing more specifically on cases like Hampton's, the court declared:

> That a man engaged in commercial fishing, wherever prosecuted—having an established trade or business necessary to the public and profitable to himself—may have that industry wiped out and his business utterly destroyed by a series of acts not only wrongful in themselves, but in violation of criminal law, and in such circumstances be denied access to the courts because his injury is no different in kind and degree from that of an angler of the Isaac Walton type, or a denizen of the Great Smoky Mountains who had never heard of the Roanoke River or the fish that disport themselves therein, or even a person in the common fishery as yet untouched by the nuisance, is a position which the court would hesitate to take.

Id.

Further confronting the economic theory implicit in the common law rule as the district court had applied it in Hampton's case, the state court observed:

> No useful distinction can be made out of the circumstance that these rights are usually asserted by the owners of several and exclusive fisheries. The necessity is precisely the same; that is, that the fish come in to the nets. We are sure that the convenient access which plaintiff had from his riparian property to the run of the fish is an advantage of which he cannot be lawfully deprived by the alleged nuisance. It is true that he might obtain access to the fish by going to more distant points where the nuisance had not yet affected the fish, if there were such places, but "if a man's time and money are worth anything," he has received a substantial damage in being driven to this necessity.

Id. at 548, 27 S.E.2d at 546.

Whether amused or not by the district court's performance, the Fourth Circuit felt itself bound by the state court decision and reversed in the federal proceeding, 139 F.2d 840 (4th Cir. 1944).

(3) Professor Osborne Reynolds criticizes the limitations of traditional public nuisance doctrine in *Public Nuisance: A Crime in Tort Law*, 31 Okla. L. Rev. 318 (1978). Specifically attacking the "special injury" requirement, he calls it a "rather arbitrary limitation," proposing that it would be "more logical" to have a rule which simply made plaintiffs show "injury in fact": "Arguably, if a person is entitled to enjoyment of a right, or if he personally suffers an injury, his right to relief should not depend, and ordinarily does not, on his showing that his harm is quite different from that suffered by others." *Id.* at 337.

(4) What policy goals are most prominent in the background of "public nuisance" law?

(5) The fact that large numbers of people come on a property does not make it public nuisance territory if the property is privately owned. In a case involving serious injuries to a spectator at a Yale-Harvard football game, occurring when a goalpost was pulled down at the end of the game, the court emphasized that "[t]he Yale Bowl is not alleged to be public property" and that spectators must have tickets to be admitted. The court thought that in the absence of a statute to the contrary, "it would be improper to eliminate the public nuisance requirement that the public must have an unfettered right to go upon the property." *Cimino v. Yale Univ.*, 638 F. Supp. 952, 953–55 (D. Conn. 1986).

RESTATEMENT (SECOND) OF TORTS § 821C (1977)*

§ 821C. Who Can Recover for Public Nuisance

(1) In order to recover damages in an individual action for public nuisance, one must have suffered harm of a kind different from that suffered by other members of the public exercising the right common to the general public that was the subject of interference.

(2) In order to maintain a proceeding to enjoin to abate a public nuisance, one must

(a) have the right to recover damages, as indicated in Subsection (1), or

(b) have authority as a public official or public agency to represent the state or a political subdivision in the matter, or

---

(c) have standing to sue as a representative of the general public, as a citizen in a citizen's action or as a member of a class in a class action.

Comment:

. . .

b. Difference in kind and degree. The private individual can recover in tort for a public nuisance only if he has suffered harm of a different kind from that suffered by other persons exercising the same public right. It is not enough that he has suffered the same kind of harm or interference but to a greater extent or degree....

. . .

e. Private nuisance. When the nuisance, in addition to interfering with the public right, also interferes with the use and enjoyment of the plaintiff's land, it is a private nuisance as well as a public one. In this case the harm suffered by the plaintiff is of a different kind and he can maintain an action not only on the basis of the private nuisance itself, but also, if he chooses to do so, on the basis of the particular harm from the public nuisance....

. . .

h. Pecuniary loss. Pecuniary loss to the plaintiff resulting from the public nuisance is normally a different kind of harm from that suffered by the general public. A contractor who loses the benefits of a particular contract or is put to an additional expense in performing it because of the obstruction of a public highway preventing him from transporting materials to the place of performance, can recover for the public nuisance. The same is true when it can be shown with reasonable certainty that an established business has lost profits, as when the obstruction of the highway prevents a common carrier from operating buses over it or access to the plaintiff's place of business is made so inconvenient that customers do not come to it. If, however, the pecuniary loss is common to an entire community and the plaintiff suffers it only in a greater degree than others, it is not a different kind of harm and the plaintiff cannot recover for the invasion of the public right.

. . .

Comment on Subsection (2):

j. Action to enjoin or abate. A public official who is authorized to represent the state or an appropriate subdivision in an action to abate or enjoin a public nuisance may of course maintain the action. An administrative agency may also be given this authority, whether it promulgated the administrative regulations it is seeking to enforce or not.

So also a person who has suffered damages that are different from those suffered by other members of the public and who is thus able to bring an action in tort for his damage is able to seek an injunction against the public nuisance. It has been the traditional rule that if a member of the public has not suffered damages different in kind and cannot maintain a tort action for damages, he also has no standing to maintain an action for an injunction. The reasons for this rule in the damage action are that it is to prevent the bringing of a multiplicity of actions by many members of the public and the bringing of actions for trivial injury. These reasons are much less applicable to a suit to enjoin the public nuisance and there are indications of a possible change. Statutes allowing citizens' actions or authorizing an individual to represent the public, and extensive general developments regarding class actions and standing to sue are all pertinent....

NOTES

(1) Suppose that a utility employing nuclear power has an accident that poses a risk of a meltdown of the radioactive core of the power plant. In order to minimize that risk, the utility begins to vent radioactive gas into the air around the plant. Should residents in nearby homes be able to get any legal relief, either by preventing the venting of the gas, or by securing financial compensation? In this connection, ask yourself the following questions:

(a) How do you apply the substantive standard for determining whether there is a "public nuisance"?

(b) Should residents be able to get an injunction against the venting?

(c) Who can bring an action?

(d) Apart from securing injunctive relief, which parties, if any, could sue for damages, for example in connection with mental distress consequent on apprehensions of cancer risks associated with the venting?

(2) A non-profit neighborhood improvement group sued a service organization providing free daily meals to indigent persons. Some of these persons, as they walked to and from the service center, apparently trespassed in yards and unoccupied homes, "sometimes urinating, defecating, drinking and littering," and there were many arrests for that behavior. Should the service organization be enjoined for public nuisance despite the otherwise lawful and charitable orientation of its activity?

(3) Consider a passage from a decision in the much-publicized case that formed the basis for the book and movie *A Civil Action*. In that case, Massachusetts residents attributed several injuries, including leukemia in children, to the presence of toxic chemicals in groundwater:

> Defendants argue that plaintiffs, as private persons, have no standing to bring an action based on the public nuisance of a restriction on use of Woburn's groundwater. The general rule is that the private injury sustained where a common right is impaired is "merged in the common nuisance and injury to all citizens, and the right is to be vindicated [through suit by a public official]." ... But when a plaintiff has sustained "special or peculiar damage", he or she may maintain an individual action.... Injuries to a person's health are by their nature "special and peculiar" and cannot properly be said to be common or public.... As plaintiffs allege that they have suffered a variety of illnesses as a result of exposure to the contaminated water, they have standing to maintain this nuisance action.
>
> However, plaintiffs may only seek to obtain damages for their special injuries.... If a nuisance is found, plaintiffs are entitled to recover (1) the loss in rental value of their property, if any, (2) compensation for physical injuries, and (3) upon a showing of independent personal injury, damages for emotional distress.

Anderson v. W.R. Grace & Co., 628 F. Supp. 1219, 1233 (D. Mass. 1986).

Can you distinguish the question of "standing" from the "substantive law" standard for public nuisance with respect to the requirement that a plaintiff "suffer harm of a different kind from that suffered by other persons exercising the same public right"? Is the remedy issue further distinguishable with respect to that requirement?

(4) What are the major concerns that courts must consider in deciding the question of whether a plaintiff has standing to sue for a public nuisance? How much of the prob-

lem is one of controlling costs, both the expenses of litigation for potential defendants and administrative costs for the courts? How much weight would you give to the argument of plaintiffs that they should be given free rein on the theory that they are serving as "private attorneys general," whose willingness to undertake litigation relieves the public fisc of the expenses of bringing a suit?

(5) Who, if anyone, should be able to bring suit to prevent a factory from discharging smoke on a heavily traveled strip of interstate highway?

(6) Organizations with environmental concerns have employed nuisance-like suits under federal legislation to stop discharges of pollutants into the environment. Illustrative is litigation under the Clean Water Act, which requires companies to file public reports on discharges of pollutants into public sewage systems. Because evidence of discharges above the legal limits may effectively constitute an admission of culpability, a lawyer for the Natural Resources Defense Council was quoted as saying, "It's like shooting fish in a barrel, and we've shot a lot of fish." James Thornton, quoted in "*Citizen Suits*" *Become a Popular Weapon In the Fight Against Industrial Polluters*, WALL ST. J., Apr. 17, 1987.

Chapter 15

MEDIA AND COMMUNICATION TORTS

§ 15.01 Defamation

[A] Generally

INTRODUCTION TO DEFAMATION

A childhood expression is that "sticks and stones may break my bones but names will never hurt me." But adults—and even children—know better. Words or pictures can lacerate like fists. The law of defamation recognizes, at least, that the harmful effects of certain statements about others may seriously tarnish their reputations. This branch of the law is quite complicated. Here are the simplest parts of the defamation skeleton:

(1) Defamation deals with injuries to reputation. *Restatement (Second) of Torts* § 559 (1977) defines a communication as "defamatory" if "it tends so to harm the reputation of another as to lower him in the estimation of the community or to deter third persons from associating or dealing with him."

(2) A defamation must be published—*i.e.*, communicated—to a person other than the person defamed. RESTATEMENT (SECOND) § 577 & cmt. b. Most litigation on allegedly defamatory material deals with statements printed or broadcast by mass media, but a casual statement by one person to another about a third person is sufficient for publication.

The most modern issues in this category concern the nature of publication in the age of cyberspace. The Internet has generated, among other issues, the question of who a "publisher" is. Section 320 of the Communications Decency Act says that "[n]o provider or user of an interactive computer service shall be treated as the publisher or speaker of any information provided by another information content provider." This decision effectively overruled a New York trial court decision that said that a computer network could be considered a publisher of allegedly libelous statements posted by an unidentified user of one of the defendant's bulletin boards.[1] There has been criticism of the statute on the ground that it protects "cyberspace intermediaries" that "have some ability to prevent or at least stem serious online defamation injury."[2]

(3) Sometimes there are important legal consequences that turn on the question of whether defamatory material is libel or slander. While "[i]t is impossible to define and

---

1. *Stratton Oakmont, Inc. v. Prodigy Servs. Co.*, 1995 WL 3323710 (N.Y. Sup. Ct. 1995).
2. Susan Freiwald, *Comparative Institutional Analysis in Cyberspace: The Case of Intermediary Liability for Defamation*, 14 HARV. J.L. & TECHNOL. 569, 585, 636–37 (2001).

difficult to describe with precision" these two categories, see RESTATEMENT (SECOND) § 568 cmt. b, the rough classification scheme is this: Libel is "[t]he publication of defamatory matter by written or printed words," see *id.* cmt. d, whereas slander is spoken words. Conceptually, radio and television present a borderline case, but the Restatement settles the question by calling broadcast defamation libel. *Id.* § 568A.

Now things get more complicated. The following materials track these questions:

• Is the material sued upon defamatory? This issue presents a number of problems related to technical standards for both slander and libel. First, there is the requirement that slander plaintiffs must classify the alleged defamation in particular categories in order to avoid having to prove "special damages." This is explained in the Note on Slander Per Se and Special Damages, infra subpart [2]. Second, there is a rule that has required libel plaintiffs to prove "special damages" when suing on a publication that was not "defamatory on its face," that is, a publication concerning which one must show extrinsic facts in order to demonstrate the defamatory meaning. (See *Menefee v. Codman,* infra subpart [3].)

• Did the communication sufficiently refer to the plaintiff? (See *Loeb v. Globe Newspaper Co.,* infra subpart [1].)

• Was the communication one of "fact" or "opinion"? The *Restatement (Second)* says that "[a] defamatory communication may consist of a statement of fact," § 565, or of "a statement in the form of an opinion," but a statement of the latter kind "is actionable only if it implies the allegation of undisclosed defamatory facts as the basis for the opinion," § 566. (The material infra § 15.01[C] explores the fact/opinion distinction.)

• Was the defendant "privileged" to make the communication?

Some of the privileges against defamation actions are absolute, such as those connected with judicial proceedings, an arena in which the privilege exists not only for judges, but for witnesses and jurors. There is also absolute immunity for defamations uttered in the course of legislative proceedings, and for officials of government agencies in certain circumstances, see infra § 18.03.

There are also a number of qualified privileges. Some depend on the defendant's interest, some depend on the interest of the listener or reader, and some involve a common interest in the publisher and the person to whom the defamation is published. An example of a common interest is a case in which the publisher and the recipient are both members of the same business firm, and the defamatory material concerns a person who is applying to that company for a job. Generally, a qualified privilege of this kind must be exercised "in a reasonable manner and for a proper purpose." As to the grounds of belief, many courts require that the defendant have "probable cause" for believing the statement to be true; others require only "good faith." See W. PROSSER & W.P. KEETON ON TORTS 832–35 (5th ed. 1984).

One qualified privilege, on which much important recent litigation has centered, applies unless the plaintiff shows that the defendant acted with malice, that is, at least recklessly of the truth. This is the privilege spelled out in *New York Times v. Sullivan,* 376 U.S. 254, 84 S. Ct. 710, 11 L. Ed. 2d 686 (1964), with respect to defamations of public officials relating to their official conduct, and then elaborated in the *Butts-Walker* cases, 388 U.S. 130, 87 S. Ct. 1975, 18 L. Ed. 2d 1094 (1967), as to public figures.

The material infra § 15.01[B] deals with the refinements introduced into the law of defamation by the Supreme Court's decision in *Gertz v. Robert Welch,* published in 1975, and later precedents. That body of law deals with constitutional privileges, standards of liability and damages rules.

[1] Identification of the Plaintiff
LOEB v. GLOBE NEWSPAPER CO.
United States District Court, District of Massachusetts
489 F. Supp. 481 (1980)

ZOBEL, DISTRICT JUDGE.

Plaintiffs in these cases are the publisher (Loeb v. Globe Newspaper Co., ...), editors (Bucknam v. Globe Newspaper Co....), and other employees (Adams, et al. v. Globe Newspaper Co....) of the Manchester (New Hampshire) Union Leader, a daily newspaper. They claim that the Boston Globe, another daily newspaper, "maligned" and "defamed" them in its editorials and in a syndicated column. The cases are before the court on defendant's motions for summary judgment....

In the winter of 1972, the Manchester Union Leader received nationwide attention for its coverage of the New Hampshire Presidential Primary. During the course of the primary, the publisher of the newspaper engaged in a celebrated exchange with one candidate, and, as appears from the exhibits, the newspaper was dominated by colorful reporting and commentary on the primary, in the course of which the Union Leader itself became a popular topic of media commentary. The newspaper was the subject of at least three pieces in the Boston Globe, and those publications gave rise to the instant claims.

Plaintiffs in Bucknam and Adams, respectively Union Leader editors and staff members, complain of the same statements, both made in an "Opposite the Editorial Page" column in the March 7, 1972 issue of the Boston Globe: that the Union Leader is "probably the worst newspaper in America", and that the publisher of the Union Leader "runs a newspaper by paranoids for paranoids." In Loeb, the publisher of the Union Leader relies on the same statements as well as six others. Loeb includes four excerpts from a March 7, 1972 editorial: that he had been fined three million dollars in a prior legal action, that he "edits his paper like a 19th Century yellow journal", that his views are "venomous" and that his newspaper is a "daily drip of venom". In addition, he complains of a Globe cartoon of March 1, 1972 ... in which he is depicted with a cuckoo springing from his forehead. He also complains of a statement in a March 9, 1972 editorial that he "never backed a presidential winner." In each of the three claims, plaintiffs argue that the publications were false and derogatory and that professional and social harms resulted from publication.

...

These actions are brought by three Union Leader editors (Bucknam) and twenty-four other employees (Adams), among them office boys, reporters and assistant editors, who claim that two excerpts of a 1972 Globe editorial set out above are false and derogatory statements which libel them.

In support of its motions for summary judgment, defendant argues that the claims are barred as a matter of law because the excerpts in question are not sufficiently specific in their reference to plaintiffs to support tort liability. Defendant is correct.

A "guiding principle" in group libel law was not long ago enunciated by the Court of Appeals for the First Circuit thus: "Defamation of a large group gives rise to no civil action on the part of an individual member of the group unless he can show special application of the defamatory matter to himself," Arcand v. Evening Call Pub. Co., 567 F.2d

1163, 1164 (1st Cir. 1977), citing, inter alia, Restatement, Torts, Second, § 564A, Comment a; Neiman-Marcus v. Lait, 13 F.R.D. 311 (S.D.N.Y.1952).

In Adams, the twenty-four plaintiffs represent a small group of employees from the total 325 individuals employed by the Union Leader in March 1972. They state without explanation that "the libel was directed at the editorial management and staff", of which they profess to be members, but beyond that assertion venture no support for a claim of the "special application of the defamatory matter to (themselves)," Arcand v. Evening Call Pub. Co., 567 F.2d at 1164. See also Restatement, Torts (Second) § 564A(b) (plaintiff must show that "the circumstances of publication reasonably give rise to the conclusion that there is particular reference to ... (him)"). In Arcand v. Evening Call Pub. Co., supra, the Court supported the predisposition against group libel with the holding of Neiman-Marcus v. Lait, supra, a case very similar on its facts to Adams and Bucknam. In Neiman-Marcus, the Court observed that the "complaint that a group of 382 saleswomen had been generally called prostitutes was dismissed because (the) group was too large to infer defamation of a member thereof", 567 F.2d at 1164. There is little to distinguish Neiman-Marcus from this case except, possibly, that the insufficiently particular reference to "saleswomen" in Neiman-Marcus was far more specific than either of the general characterizations of the Union Leader. The publication in question does not reasonably give rise to the conclusion that there is "special application", Arcand v. Evening Call Pub. Co., supra, at 1164 or "particular reference", Restatement, Torts, Second, § 564A(b) to these twenty-four office boys, reporters and assistant editors, or to any of them. No tort liability can therefore be held to lie, and with respect to their claim, defendant's motion for summary judgment is allowed.

In Bucknam, three of the Union Leader's eight editors at the time of the alleged libel asserted claims identical to those set forth in Adams. The claims differ, presumably, because these plaintiffs are editors, and it may be argued as an alternative argument to that made in Adams that the Bucknam plaintiffs would be likelier targets of a general criticism of the newspaper by virtue of their greater authority. Nevertheless, neither pleadings nor affidavits suggest that the Globe text provides a reasonable basis to focus on these three men, and as to these three editors no "special application" or "particular reference" can be reasonably inferred from the general commentary published in the Globe.

Arcand v. Evening Call Pub. Co., supra, defines a "second principle" of group libel, that a cause of action may lie "if a defamatory statement applies to all members of a small group". 567 F.2d at 1164. However, a claim cannot come within this second principle merely by denominating a small subset of a large group of plaintiffs, unless the small group so defined reasonably appears to have been identified by the text. Because no "special application" or "particular reference" to this group of three plaintiffs can be inferred from the Globe text, there can be no claim of defamation of "all members of a small group", Arcand v. Evening Call Pub. Co., 567 F.2d at 1164. Plaintiffs in Bucknam are under the same duty as those in Adams to establish tort liability by supporting "special application" or "particular reference" with respect to the individuals denominated as plaintiffs. Because there is no support for such a claim, and because no particular reference to these plaintiffs can be reasonably inferred from the text, the claim in Bucknam, like that in Adams, is insufficient to give rise to tort liability. Defendant's motion for summary judgment in Bucknam is accordingly allowed.

...

NOTES

(1) Why were the claims of the three editors in the *Bucknam* branch of the case insufficient as a matter of law? Should not a jury have been able to decide whether there was sufficient reference to them?

(2) Perhaps the most obvious case for a defendant on the identification issue is *Michigan United Conservation Clubs v. CBS News*, 485 F. Supp. 893 (W.D. Mich. 1980), which arose from a show called "The Guns of Autumn," a "graphic portrayal of men hunting and killing game animals." The plaintiffs alleged that the defendants had set out to "discredit, malign, downgrade, ridicule and vilify the American sport hunter and especially the more than one million sport hunters within the State of Michigan," who four named plaintiffs sought to represent. Held, with respect to the branch of the suit on behalf of the million hunters, "the defamation of a group this large can have no personal application to individual members."

(3) *Neiman-Marcus v. Lait*, 13 F.R.D. 311 (S.D.N.Y. 1952) is, through modern eyes, the epitome of political incorrectness, but it is also a textbook case on the identification issue. The basis for the case was a book titled *U.S.A. Confidential*, which among other things discussed sexual practices in Dallas around 1950. The holdings occupy a spectrum of law:

> (a) "Some Neiman models are call girls—the top babes in town." The plaintiffs in this group were nine individual models who were the "entire group of models" when the book was published. On this count, the defendant did not even move to dismiss. *Id.* at 316 n.1.

> (b) Regarding the Neiman men's store, "most of the sales staff are fairies." Fifteen salesmen of a total of 25 in the men's store sued. Employing the standards of the day as to what constituted defamation, the court concluded that there was sufficient identification here, saying that "[a]n imputation of gross immorality to some of a small group casts suspicion upon all, where no attempt is made to exclude the innocent." The court added that if the defendants' failure to move to dismiss the claim concerning the models was "a concession of a valid cause of action," it was "difficult to perceive a legalistic distinction between the statements that 'some Neiman models are call girls' and 'most of the sales staff are fairies.'" *Id.* at 315–316 & n.1.

> (c) The authors also wrote, "[t]he salesgirls are good, too—pretty, and often much cheaper [than the models]—twenty bucks on the average." As noted in *Loeb*, given that there were 382 saleswomen, the *Neiman-Marcus* court concluded that there was no identification: "[n]o reasonable man would take the writers seriously and conclude from the publication a reference to any individual saleswoman." *Id.* at 316.

(4) A magazine published an article on teenagers' sexual conduct with the thesis "that contemporary teenagers 'are both sexually advanced ... and sexually daring.'" A large photograph with the article, covering most of two pages, showed five people at a prom, three of whom were smoking and one drinking from a plastic cup. The fifth student was the plaintiff, "looking in the direction of the camera with an apparently friendly expression." She wore "a black sleeveless dress and [was] neither drinking nor smoking." Beneath the photograph and the headlines and first parts of the text of the article was a "disclaimer" in small italic type that said that "[t]he individuals pictured are unrelated to the people or events described in this story" and said that "[t]he names of the teenagers interviewed for the story have been changed." What result, on the plaintiff's defamation claim?

[2] The Slander Rules

PROBLEM*

Plaintiff suffers from a congenital defect that has resulted in the shortening of his left leg. In June 1983, he began driving and performing promotion work for defendant Celebrity Limousine Services, Inc., which is owned by defendants Richard Dickes and John K. Eshleman. Plaintiff was to be paid $200 per week plus fifteen percent of the gross receipts Celebrity secured from plaintiff's efforts.

In July, 1983, the production company for the play Private Lives retained Celebrity to provide limousine services while the play was running in Philadelphia. Plaintiff was assigned to meet certain members of the company, including Richard Burton and Brook Williams, at 30th Street train station and drive them to the Palace Hotel. Two days later, on July 19, 1983, plaintiff drove Williams and Sally Burton, Burton's wife, to a supermarket, where he helped his passengers carry packages to the car. Later that same day, plaintiff drove Burton, Mrs. Burton, and Williams to other stores and returned them to the hotel.

Plaintiff alleges that on July 20, 1983, Dickes told him that he would be reassigned from the Burton job, but would continue to drive for the rest of the production company. He further alleges that Williams asked Celebrity to remove plaintiff as the driver for the Burton job because the party was embarrassed to have a person who walked with a limp carrying packages for them. According to plaintiff, Burton said that he, his wife, and Williams did not feel comfortable riding with a handicapped driver, and then requested that Dickes not allow the media to know of his dissatisfaction with plaintiff....

Plaintiff ... alleges that Burton and Williams published statements that were slanderous per se and made with the intent to humiliate plaintiff and cause him emotional distress.

* * *

Putting aside technical questions of what is "slanderous per se," should the plaintiff be able to recover money from Burton and Williams for their statements about him?

NOTE ON SLANDER PER SE AND SPECIAL DAMAGES

The traditional analysis of slander includes four categories known as "slander per se." Historically, it was necessary for a claim of slander to fit into one of these categories for it to be actionable without proof of "special damages," i.e., specific pecuniary loss. The magic categories include the imputation of unchastity to a woman and the imputation that the plaintiff committed a crime. The other "per se" classifications are the imputation of a loathsome disease, and the utterance of a statement that tends to injure one in his business, trade, profession or office. The importance of fitting a plaintiff's claim into a "per se" category may be illustrated by noting that emotional distress alone will not be characterized as "special damages." See, e.g., W. PROSSER & W.P. KEETON ON TORTS 794 (5th ed. 1984). Thus, even an extraordinary insult that in fact wounds the plaintiff deeply would not survive a directed verdict motion if it does not classify as slander per se, and if the claimant is unable to show pecuniary loss he will not be able to recover.

"Special damages," in the particular context of defamatory remarks, means "a particular loss, of a material nature, supported by specific evidence." 2 FOWLER HARPER,

---

* Taken from a judicial opinion.

FLEMING JAMES, & OSCAR GRAY, LAW OF TORTS § 5.14 (1986). General damage to reputation, unsupported by concrete evidence of probable injury like loss of business receipts attributable to the defamation, will not make a case where the law requires a showing of "special damages."

NOTES

(1) A California court ruled that words not slanderous "on their face" may nonetheless be slanderous per se in light of extrinsic circumstances. The occasion was a case with unusual facts involving a dispute between neighboring business owners. While the plaintiff, a car dealer, was appearing in a live television advertisement, the defendant angrily strode into the picture saying, "You son of a bitch." The court acknowledged that the words "[l]iterally ... imply a miracle of nature," and did not charge a crime, nor lack of chastity. Still, "after giving the matter considerable thought," the court decided that the words could have been understood under the circumstances to signify the plaintiff's untrustworthiness as a merchant. *White v. Valenta*, 44 Cal. Rptr. 241 (Cal. Ct. App. 1964).

(2) Suppose that A falsely asserts that B authorized the signing of a letter that would have illegally released the funds of C from a commodities account, the effect of which would have been that B was embezzling money from C, who was trusting B with his investments. Suppose further that the letter did not accomplish its allegedly larcenous purpose but that A's remark about B caused C to fire him as his investment adviser. Was A's remark about B slander per se?

(3) The language, "You're not so smart. Your wife is an ex-whore from Butte, Montana," attracts the slander per se label in *Hollman v. Brady*, 233 F.2d 877 (9th Cir. 1956). The plaintiff alleged that these words caused her husband to doubt her when he became intoxicated and to abuse her verbally.

(4) Should the oral assertion that someone is a "member of the Mafia" be actionable without a showing of special damages?

(5) The court mixed common sense psychology with slander law in *Stanley v. Taylor*, 4 Ill. App. 3d 98, 278 N.E.2d 824, *cert. denied*, 409 U.S. 983 (1972). In that case the defendant, a school teacher angered by what she considered her principal's lack of courage in decision-making, told him "[y]ou are just like that old Lee Harvey Oswald that shot and killed President Kennedy, and that old Jack Ruby who shot and killed him in Dallas." She later repeated similar references at least twice, and the jury found that these utterances were worth $75,775 to the plaintiff. However, the appellate court reversed. It held that the words were not actionable per se under the circumstances, noting that the outburst was "spontaneous and made directly to plaintiff and was obviously more thoughtless than anything else, and a considered evil intention to defame is not easily imputed therefrom." The circumstances would have made it "apparent to the observer that what was said was nothing more than an irrational argumentative characterization not worthy of serious consideration."

[3] The Basic Libel Rules

PROBLEM

The following passage appears in a decision on a suit by Robert Guccione, the publisher of *Penthouse* magazine.

In the "Bits & Pieces" section of its November 1983 issue, *Hustler* printed a half-page article by Flynt that commented on Guccione's practice of being photographed, fully clothed, with naked *Penthouse* models. The article, entitled "What a Ham!" and labeled "Editorial opinion," was accompanied by a photo from the September 1983 issue of *Penthouse*, depicting a clothed Guccione with his arm around an unclothed model sitting on his knee. The article included the following sentence: "Considering he is married and also has a live-in girlfriend, Kathy Keeton ... we wonder if he would let either of them pose nude with a man" (elipsis in original). Guccione contends primarily that the quoted language falsely accuses him of committing adultery in 1983, when the article appeared. He also suggests that it falsely implies that he was then living with his wife and girlfriend simultaneously. It is undisputed that Robert and Muriel Guccione married in 1956, separated in 1964, and divorced in 1979; Guccione has not remarried. It is also undisputed that Guccione has cohabited with Kathy Keeton since 1966.

What will be the issues of libel law?

MENEFEE v. CODMAN

California District Court of Appeal
155 Cal. App. 2d 396, 317 P.2d 1032 (1957)

VAN DYKE, PRESIDING JUSTICE.

This is an appeal from a money judgment on one count of respondent's complaint and from an order granting a new trial on the remaining two counts as to which the jury had returned defense verdicts. The action was for libel.

Respondent is a resident of Fair Oaks community, near Sacramento. Since 1948 her husband has published a weekly newspaper for which respondent wrote a column dealing with shopping news and her personal thoughts and observations. The Menefees had four young children. In addition to her household duties and her work on the newspaper, respondent also taught psychology part time at Sacramento State College. She participated actively in community affairs and bore an excellent reputation as housewife, mother, church attendant, teacher and writer.

Appellant is a long-time resident of Fair Oaks community. She is descended from a pioneer family, is a member of the Daughters of the American Revolution, owns property in excess of $100,000, and has long interested herself in community affairs, in which she generally takes strong partisan positions and concerning which she has a penchant for public utterances, both verbal and in the form of long letters to the editors of newspapers. She sometimes publishes and circulates tracts of her own. She is an influential member of her community.

Count I of the complaint herein charged that appellant wrote and published of respondent the following:

Seems strange that such an obscure little person as "plain Audrey" should assume such a responsibility. ("How one small head ..." ... Some of us here think that plain Audrey ... should have been named 'Narcissus'. Hunt up your psychology textbooks for that one— ...)

Will plain Audrey's "Operation Europe" or "Mission to Europe" include other activities besides Telling the World how to become popular in a small town (or is Audrey really qualified to advise them?) and how to run a rural newspaper?

The second count averred that appellant wrote and published of respondent the following:

Plain Audrey's Trip to Europe still is causing a lot of local yokel comment whenever mentioned. We see a late movie advertised—could that have been the real reason Plain Audrey went to Europe? The movie is titled "Under the Paris Sky"—at the Guild Theatre, 35th and Broadway. The gal on the advertisement looks as though she wore a dirndl. When we come across Plain Audrey's column on Paris, where she tells about her trip to the water front, then we'll know. Meanwhile Plain Audrey's water front "coverage" will intrigue us. But what we all want to know is, *who* covered Audrey while Audrey covered the water front? Surely Audrey didn't slip along uncovered—no, she told us she wore a dirndl and an old blouse. Oh, well, we were just reminded of that old game about who took care of the caretaker's daughter. We just changed the wording.

By the third count, respondent alleged that appellant wrote and published of and concerning her, the following:

The San Juan Record's Associate Editor, no less! reported on her recent trip to Europe that she wore an old blouse and dirndl (was it? or slacks?) along the Paris waterfront. We presume she was "covering the waterfront"? We feel sorry indeed that she didn't have proper clothes for this assignment, and we venture to suggest that the Editor, Boss, Dear Selden or what-you-prefer open a charge account at I. Magnin's (that is, if his credit rates that good), and then his hard-working lille wife won't have to slink along the waterfront in an outdated dirndl (if that's what she wore?).

Sample Magnin advertising leaflet attached—it says, "A fulfillment of your most luxurious dreams"—and these dreams go as high as $69.95 for a "permanently pleated" gown. Time O'Day indicated in advertisement.

It was alleged that there was attached to said writing, and addressed and mailed therewith, an advertisement for nightgowns and negligees. The advertisement contained pictures of ladies in various and sundry types and designs of nightgowns, negligees or other bedroom attire.

Alleging in each count that she had been an instructor and during a part of the years of 1951 and 1952 had been engaged in the occupation and profession of Associate Professor on a part-time basis at the Sacramento State College, that she had for several years been engaged in the occupation of Women's Editor and Associate Editor of a newspaper of general circulation, to-wit, the San Juan Record, that at all times she possessed and enjoyed a good name and reputation and a wide following of readers in Sacramento County, respondent asserted that as a natural and proximate result of the alleged publications she had been greatly injured and prejudiced in her reputation, in her calling, occupation and profession as an instructor, editor and columnist, and had lost, and would continue to lose, gains and profits which otherwise would have accrued to her in her said calling, occupation and profession to her damage in the sum of $15,000. Respondent further alleged in each count that by reason of the publications she had been caused to suffer grievous mental suffering and humiliation to her damage in the further sum of $15,000, and that the publications had been made maliciously with the intent to injure her; wherefore she demanded exemplary and punitive damages.

Appellant demurred generally to the pleading, contending that the alleged defamatory publications were each not libelous per se or libelous on the face; that only general damages, as opposed to special damages, were pleaded and, therefore, that no cause of action was stated. The demurrers were overruled. Throughout the trial this contention of appellant was asserted by her and it here constitutes one of the major issues on appeal.

In 1944, there was published in the Southern California Law Review, Volume 17, Page 347, an article by Professor Charles E. Carpenter, the first paragraph of which reads as follows:

> The well established historical distinction between libel and slander is already, by reason of its artificial, illogical and unsound character, sufficiently confusing. But the existing confusion has been increased by the wholly unwarranted doctrine of "libel per se," which has recently arisen in California and several other States. This doctrine is to the effect that, if the publication is defamatory on its face—that is if extrinsic circumstances are not necessary to reveal its defamatory character—it is "libelous per se" and an action may be maintained without alleging or proving special damages. If the defamatory character of the publication is not obvious on its face but is hidden and requires inquiry into extrinsic circumstances to make it so, then it is not actionable unless special damages are alleged and proved. A peculiarity of the situation is that the parents of this odd creature—the courts—do not realize, despite the labor pains of its birth, that they have brought forth a child. This article is written for the benefit of lawyers and courts of the States that have produced the new offspring, so that they may see that it is a new creature, and that it is ugly and illegitimate and ought promptly to be strangled.

As though fearful that the attack of Professor Carpenter and other law writers upon the misbegotten infant's right to live might result in judicial filicide, the Legislature in 1945 legitimated the child by enacting Chapter 1489 of the statutes of that year. Therein it declared that a libel which is defamatory without the necessity of explanatory matter, such as inducement, innuendo, or other extrinsic fact, is said to be a libel on its face; that defamatory language not libelous on its face is not actionable unless the plaintiff alleges and proves that he has suffered special damage as a proximate result thereof; that special damage consists of all damages which plaintiff alleges and proves that he has suffered in respect to his property, business, trade, profession or occupation, including such amounts of money as the plaintiff alleges and proves he has expended as a result of the alleged libel, and no other. Respondent contends that the defamatory words pleaded in each count are libelous per se and further contends that if this be not true then she has sufficiently pleaded and proved special damages as that term is statutorily defined. If she is right in her first contention, then we do not reach the second, for if a publication is libelous on its face then all damages—general, special or exemplary—properly pleaded under applicable rules of pleading may be recovered according to the proof.

The sting of the charge in Count I of the complaint is found in the matter we have quoted: "Seems strange that such an obscure little person as 'plain Audrey' should assume such a responsibility. ('How one small head'... Some of us here think that plain Audrey ... should have been named 'Narcissus'. Hunt up your psychology textbooks for that one.)" The Greek myth centering around Narcissus and his affair with Echo is commonly known and understood. While to state that a person ought to have been named, that is that a person resembled, Narcissus could scarcely be called complimentary, it would not, however, be a statement libelous on its face. But a different connotation entirely is brought in by the direction: "Hunt up your psychology textbooks for that one", for it was shown that from the myth of Narcissus there has stemmed a term commonly used in psychology to classify, with respect to adults, a definite pathology called narcissism or narcism. When appellant instructed her readers to hunt up their psychology textbooks to discover what she meant by saying respondent ought to have been named Narcissus, she made it plain that she was not referring to anything innocent in nature. Even the dictionary uses the term "narcissism" as meaning, psychologically speaking, "Erotic feeling aroused by one's own body and personality, regarded by Freud as a normal state in sexual development; pathologically, fixation at, or regression to this stage." There was definite proof as to what appellant's readers would have found had they obeyed her admonition. A qualified witness, a professor of psychology from Boston University, testified that the word "Narcissus" has a special meaning to a psychologist in the field of abnormal psychology; that it refers to abnormal self-love; that is to a form of self-love in which a person falls in love with himself as a man might fall in love with a woman; that it is an abnormal psychological characteristic or trait; that there are degrees of this trait as of any trait; that the term would not be used to refer to normal behavior; that it would only be used to refer to psychopathic or abnormal behavior; that the degrees would extend all the way from a person who did not engage in any overt sexual practices related to himself to a person who also engaged in masturbation and other forms of abnormal sexual behavior to a very excessive extent and to the exclusion of sexual relations with members of the opposite sex; that one suffering from narcissism would find it impossible to have normal sexual relations with a member of the opposite sex; that while it is not common for psychologists to refer to a person suffering from narcissism as a Narcissus he could be so called and there would be no mistaking what was meant; that the terms defined had no other meaning in psychology textbooks except the abnormal condition above described, and that every textbook on abnormal psychology described narcissism as did all textbooks on general psychology which contained a section on abnormal psychology. By directing her readers to texts on psychology, appellant plainly indicated that she was not dealing with the innocuous Greek myth, but with something they would find related to that myth in psychology textbooks. It cannot be properly argued with respect to the pleading in Count I that there is any ambiguity in the publication by reason of which an innocent and non-libelous meaning could fairly be ascribed thereto. To ascribe to any individual the sexual deviation described in psychology textbooks as constituting narcissism, whatever the degree of such deviation, is to expose that person to hatred, contempt, ridicule, obloquy, and to cause him to be shunned or avoided. And certainly such a publication has a tendency to injure him in his occupation. Particularly is this true when spoken of a teacher or a writer. We hold that the publication stated in Count I of respondent's complaint was libelous on its face and, therefore, did not require the pleading of explanatory matters such as inducement, innuendo, or other extrinsic fact. Of course, the fact that such matters were pleaded is immaterial here for if matter libelous on its face be shown, a pleading of explanatory matter may be disregarded as surplusage.…

By the second allegedly libelous publication appellant told her readers: "Plain Audrey's Trip to Europe still is causing a lot of local yokel comment whenever mentioned. We see a late movie advertised — could that have been the real reason Plain Audrey went to Europe? The movie is titled 'Under the Paris Sky' — at the Guild Theatre, 35th and Broadway. The gal on the advertisement looks as though she wore a dirndl. When we come across Plain Audrey's column on Paris, where she tells about her trip to the waterfront, then we'll know. Meanwhile Plain Audrey's waterfront 'coverage' will intrigue us. But what we all want to know is, *who* covered Audrey

while Audrey covered the water front? Surely Audrey didn't slip along uncovered —
no, she told us she wore a dirndl and an old blouse. Oh, well, we were just reminded
of that old game about who took care of the caretaker's daughter. We just changed
the wording."

Appellant argues that the foregoing publication was not libelous on its face because
from the whole publication it is apparent that what is said is fairly susceptible of an innocent and non-defamatory meaning....

Respondent asserts that in this publication the sting of the charge is in the question,
"*who* covered Audrey while Audrey covered the waterfront?", insisting that the words
are used in the sexual sense and pointing to the dictionary definition appearing in Webster's New International Dictionary wherein the verb "cover" is defined *inter alia* as "to
copulate with (a female); to serve; as, a horse covers a mare." Respondent points to testimony that gossiping groups discussing this letter considered that appellant was accusing respondent of street-walking in Paris to cover the expenses of her European trip.
Appellant cites the numerous definitions of the word "cover" to be found in dictionaries
and insists that the words she used are to be construed according to innocent meanings.
Her own testimony was that by the word "cover" she meant "watched by government
agents" lest respondent engage in subversive activities of the communist variety. The
question then in construing the pleading is whether or not the publication as pleaded is
libelous on its face. If the words used are reasonably susceptible of non-defamatory
construction, then Count II does not state a cause of action unless it includes, as respondent contends it does, a proper pleading of special damage within the terms of the
statute. It is difficult to ascribe an innocent meaning to this publication. The use of the
verb "cover" as meaning copulation is as indicated by the dictionary definition generally
connected with the breeding of animals; it might be described as a barnyard colloquial-
ism but appellant asserted that plain Audrey's trip to Europe was causing a lot of local
yokel comment whenever mentioned and city folk often refer to the farm population as
"local yokels". Then comes the reference to the movie and the attached advertisement
which shows a woman scantily clad in what appears to be a negligee, a brassiere, and little else. The title of the movie is given in the advertisement as "Under the Paris Sky."
The foregoing preface is followed by the words "Meanwhile Plain Audrey's waterfront
'coverage' will intrigue us. But what we all want to know is, *who* covered Audrey while
Audrey covered the waterfront?" The implication is plain that somebody covered Audrey while she was on the waterfront, and the query is who was it that did so. "Surely",
appellant continued, "Audrey didn't slip along uncovered," all of which appellant asserted reminded her "of that old game about who took care of the caretaker's daughter."
Is all of this reasonably susceptible of an innocent construction? Isn't it plain that appellant is here seeking to expose respondent to ridicule, if no worse? We think the only reasonable construction of the whole publication is that upon its face it does expose respondent to ridicule. That much we think is certain even if it can be reasonably argued
that the publication does not charge respondent with prostitution. But if the publication did expose respondent to ridicule, and such we think is its fair meaning, then it
was libelous, and it was unnecessary, in stating a cause of action, to plead explanatory
circumstances and special damage.

The third count presents little difficulty. The libelous matter reads: "The San Juan
Record's Associate Editor, no less! reported on her recent trip to Europe that she wore
an old blouse and dirndl (was it? or slacks?) along the Paris waterfront. We presume she
was covering the waterfront"? We feel sorry indeed that she didn't have proper clothes
for this assignment, and we venture to suggest that the Editor, Boss, Dear Selden or

what-you-prefer open a charge account at I. Magnin's (that is, if his credit rates that good), and then his hard-working lille wife won't have to slink along the waterfront in an outdated dirndl (if that's what she wore?) Sample Magnin advertising leaflet attached—it says, 'A fulfillment of your most luxurious dreams'—and these dreams go as high as $69.95 for a 'permanently pleated' gown." Attached to the writing and published with it as a part thereof was an advertisement for nightgowns and negligees. Here the reasonable construction of the entire publication is that respondent wore an old blouse along the Paris waterfront and that she was thus unsuitably clad; that her husband should not have condemned her to slink along the waterfront in such clothing and should have furnished her with proper clothes for her trip along the waterfront, that is, with expensive nightgowns and negligees. Fairly construed, the publication, taken as a whole, exposed respondent to contempt, ridicule, obloquy and avoidance. It also had a clear tendency to injure her in her occupation as teacher and writer. It was libelous on its face.

Although appellant contends that respondent failed to prove a cause of action, it is apparent that the contention is concerned with the necessity of pleading and proving special damages, which contentions we have already treated. It could not be claimed that the evidence was insufficient to support the verdict of the jury as to Count I, nor insufficient to have supported verdicts on Counts II and III had the jury ruled in favor of respondent on those counts, for it was substantially shown that there was much talk and comment among people living in the Fair Oaks community after the various libelous publications were made, the comment ranging all the way from ridicule to assertions that appellant was charging respondent with sexual misbehavior of a gross nature. There was testimony also that respondent did suffer general damage as defined by Civil Code Section 48a, Subdivision 4, that is, loss of reputation, shame, mortification, and hurt feelings. There was substantial support also for the jury's finding as to Count I that appellant had been motivated by express malice in her writings concerning respondent. In short, the record fully supports the jury's finding that as to Count I respondent had been generally damaged in the sum of $100 and that she was entitled to exemplary damages in the sum of $5,000. The jury found in appellant's favor on Counts II and III, but had their verdicts been otherwise reasonable awards of general and exemplary damages would have been supported.

· · ·

The court instructed the jury that:

> ... [O]ne cannot justify his conduct in assailing the reputation of another by saying that he acted merely in jest unless it is perfectly manifest from the language employed that it can in no respect be regarded as an attack upon the person to whom it relates. Nor is the publication of a statement reflecting on the plaintiff rendered any the less libelous by the fact that the defendant circulated the statement merely to amuse her readers.

In her testimony the appellant had taken the stand that she, in what she said, was merely "poking fun" at the respondent; that she was jesting and was not dealing seriously with the subject matter of her statements. The instruction was proper under the circumstances and in view of appellant's testimony....

· · ·

The judgment and the order appealed from are affirmed.

· · ·

LOOKING AT LIBEL AND ITS CONSEQUENCES
Trial, Sept. 1986, at 96–97*

About 180 lawyers, libel litigants, scholars, economists, and journalists met in New York City in mid-June to exchange views on why people sue for libel, the cost of libel suits, and effects of libel suits on the media. The conference on The Cost of Libel: Economic and Policy Implications was jointly sponsored by the Gannett Center for Media Studies and Columbia University.

Discussed during the one-day session—

• Contrary to popular belief, money is rarely the point in libel suits. Plaintiffs feel they clear their reputations simply by suing—not solely by winning their suits—according to a survey by Randall Bezanson, Gilbert Cranberg, and John Soloski of the University of Iowa.

The Iowa Libel Research Project also found that plaintiffs frequently would not have sued if their complaints had been treated with more understanding and seriousness.

Underscoring this finding was former Mobil Oil president William Tavoulareas, the plaintiff in *Tavoulareas v. Washington Post Co.*, 763 F.2d 1472 (D.C. Cir. 1985). Tavoulareas said that his initial aim after denying a 1979 *Washington Post* story about alleged business improprieties was simply to gain a retraction. "They absolutely wouldn't retract, even when I showed them evidence contradicting their story," he said....

The press believes that money is no object in defending professional integrity; media will often spend large sums in protracted litigation rather than settle. This suggests that libel law is out of step with what plaintiffs and defendants really ask of it.

• Fear of libel suits has a restraining influence on media instincts to cover controversial issues, but not uniformly. Stephen Renas, Charles Hartmann, and James Walker of Wright State University, Dayton, Ohio, surveyed 206 editors, asking them: If the standard of proof in libel were changed from actual malice to negligence and strict liability, what would be the effect on their newsrooms?

Newspapers depending on street sales would be less shy of controversy than subscription papers.

Papers with competitors would be less deterred from controversial reporting than those publishing alone in their communities.

Surprisingly, those papers that had been sued in the past 15 years, but had not paid damages, would be more worried about eased liability standards than those that had actually paid damages.

Neither newspaper size nor possession of libel insurance significantly affected responses.

---

* Reprinted with permission of TRIAL (September 1986). Copyright the Association of Trial Lawyers of America.

NOTES

(1) Can you rationalize, on policy grounds, the rule that a libel must not require proof of extrinsic circumstances in order to support general damages?

(2) If the material sued on in *Menefee* was properly described as "libel per se" under the then existing state of California law, what is the most persuasive general argument that you could make against imposing liability on the defendant?

(3) Just a couple of years after *Menefee*, the California Supreme Court disapproved the appellate court's dictum that libel plaintiffs must prove special damages when the defendant's words may be construed in a nondefamatory way. The case was one in which, as the court characterized it, "the sting of the alleged libel is that ... a communist-line paper ... endorsed and recommended plaintiff for election [to a city council] and that therefore he was a communist sympathizer or fellow traveler." In specifically disapproving the "possible-innocent-meaning rule," the supreme court said that when it could "be reasonably inferred from the language used that defendant intended to charge plaintiff with communist sympathies and that many readers so interpreted the article," and when a defendant's demurrer effectively admitted that intent, "it ill befits defendant to contend that it should escape liability on the ground that owing to a possible innocent meaning some of its readers did not draw the defamatory inference it intended that they should." *MacLeod v. Tribune Pub. Co.*, 52 Cal. 2d 536, 343 P.2d 36, 44 (1959).

(4) The following statements were the grounds for a counterclaim by a county highway superintendent against a civil engineer who sued him for dismissal from employment:

(a) The counterclaiming plaintiff "doesn't have the guts to fire."

(b) He "wouldn't make a pimple on an engineer's ass."

(c) He was a "liar," a "gutless bastard" and a "black son of a bitch."

Which of these statements, if any, would support a defamation action?

(5) Is the accusation that a high school athlete is a "quitter" grounds for a libel suit? A press story reported that one of five Phoenix-area students labeled with that word in a yearbook caption had settled a libel claim for $4,500. *Student Wins Claim Over Label in Yearbook*, WASH. POST, Jan. 20, 1987, at A9.

(6) A police officer sued a sergeant for calling him "a little fruit" during roll call, and telling one of his colleagues, "you're riding with the fruit tonight." Would this language state a cause of action?

What about a present-day repetition of the language in *Nieman-Marcus v. Lait*, summarized in note 3 after *Loeb*, supra?

(7) Finally, consider Groucho Marx's declaration in "Duck Soup": "Remember you're fighting for this woman's honor, which is more than she ever did." Could the subject of the statement successfully sue its maker?

[B] Constitutional Defamation Law

DEFAMATION AND THE CONSTITUTION

Since 1964, the Supreme Court has transformed American libel law, placing various publishers of defamatory material under a partial umbrella of constitutional protection. This process began with the case of *New York Times Co. v. Sullivan*, 376 U.S. 254 (1964), in which the court formulated a privilege for those who defamed public officials in ways related to the performance of their official duties. Officials could succeed against such defendants only if they could show that the publication was done with "actual malice," which was defined to mean either knowledge of the falsity of the publication or "reckless disregard of whether it was false or not." Presently, the centerpiece of the Supreme Court's defamation jurisprudence is the case of *Gertz v. Robert Welch, Inc.* The excerpts below from that case, which has been severely edited, are designed to present relevant judicial history preceding *Gertz*, and a summary of the rules of law announced in that decision.

GERTZ v. ROBERT WELCH, INC.
United States Supreme Court
418 U.S. 323, 94 S. Ct. 2997, 41 L. Ed. 2d 789 (1974)

MR. JUSTICE POWELL delivered the opinion of the Court.

This Court has struggled for nearly a decade to define the proper accommodation between the law of defamation and the freedoms of speech and press protected by the First Amendment. With this decision we return to that effort. We granted certiorari to reconsider the extent of a publisher's constitutional privilege against liability for defamation of a private citizen....

I

In 1968 a Chicago policeman named Nuccio shot and killed a youth named Nelson. The state authorities prosecuted Nuccio for the homicide and ultimately obtained a conviction for murder in the second degree. The Nelson family retained petitioner Elmer Gertz, a reputable attorney, to represent them in civil litigation against Nuccio.

Respondent publishes American Opinion, a monthly outlet for the views of the John Birch Society. Early in the 1960's the magazine began to warn of a nationwide conspiracy to discredit local law enforcement agencies and create in their stead a national police force capable of supporting a Communist dictatorship. As part of the continuing effort to alert the public to this assumed danger, the managing editor of American Opinion commissioned an article on the murder trial of Officer Nuccio. For this purpose he engaged a regular contributor to the magazine. In March 1969 respondent published the resulting article under the title "FRAME-UP: Richard Nuccio And The War On Police." The article purports to demonstrate that the testimony against Nuccio at his criminal trial was false and that his prosecution was part of the Communist campaign against the police.

In his capacity as counsel for the Nelson family in the civil litigation, petitioner attended the coroner's inquest into the boy's death and initiated actions for damages, but he neither discussed Officer Nuccio with the press nor played any part in the criminal proceeding. Notwithstanding petitioner's remote connection with the prosecution of Nuccio, respondent's magazine portrayed him as an architect of the "frame-up." According to the article, the police file on petitioner took "a big, Irish cop to lift." The article stated that petitioner had been an official of the "Marxist League for Industrial Democracy, originally known as the Intercollegiate Socialist Society, which has advocated the violent seizure of our government." It labeled Gertz a "Leninist" and a "Communist-fronter." It also stated that Gertz had been an officer of the National Lawyers

Guild, described as a Communist organization that "probably did more than any other outfit to plan the Communist attack on the Chicago police during the 1968 Democratic Convention."

These statements contained serious inaccuracies. The implication that petitioner had a criminal record was false. Petitioner had been a member and officer of the National Lawyers Guild some 15 years earlier, but there was no evidence that he or that organization had taken any part in planning the 1968 demonstrations in Chicago. There was also no basis for the charge that petitioner was a "Leninist" or a "Communist-fronter." And he had never been a member of the "Marxist League for Industrial Democracy" or the "Intercollegiate Socialist Society."

The managing editor of American Opinion made no effort to verify or substantiate the charges against petitioner. Instead, he appended an editorial introduction stating that the author had "conducted extensive research into the Richard Nuccio Case." And he included in the article a photograph of petitioner and wrote the caption that appeared under it: "Elmer Gertz of Red Guild harrasses Nuccio." Respondent placed the issue of American Opinion containing the article on sale at newsstands throughout the country and distributed reprints of the article on the streets of Chicago.

Petitioner filed a diversity action for libel in the United States District Court for the Northern District of Illinois. He claimed that the falsehoods published by respondent injured his reputation as a lawyer and a citizen. Before filing an answer, respondent moved to dismiss the complaint for failure to state a claim upon which relief could be granted, apparently on the ground that petitioner failed to allege special damages. But the court ruled that statements contained in the article constituted libel *per se* under Illinois law and that consequently petitioner need not plead special damages. 306 F.Supp. 310 [N.D.Ill.1969].

After answering the complaint, respondent filed a pretrial motion for summary judgment, claiming a constitutional privilege against liability for defamation. It asserted that petitioner was a public official or a public figure and that the article concerned an issue of public interest and concern. For these reasons, respondent argued, it was entitled to invoke the privilege enunciated in *New York Times Co. v. Sullivan*, 376 U.S. 254, 84 S.Ct. 710, 11 L.Ed.2d 686 (1964). Under this rule respondent would escape liability unless petitioner could prove publication of defamatory falsehood "with 'actual malice'—that is, with knowledge that it was false or with reckless disregard of whether it was false or not." ... Respondent claimed that petitioner could not make such a showing and submitted a supporting affidavit by the magazine's managing editor. The editor denied any knowledge of the falsity of the statements concerning petitioner and stated that he had relied on the author's reputation and on his prior experience with the accuracy and authenticity of the author's contributions to American Opinion.

The District Court denied respondent's motion for summary judgment in a memorandum opinion.... The court did not dispute respondent's claim to the protection of the *New York Times* standard. Rather, it concluded that petitioner might overcome the constitutional privilege by making a factual showing sufficient to prove publication of defamatory falsehood in reckless disregard of the truth. During the course of the trial, however, it became clear that the trial court had not accepted all of respondent's asserted grounds for applying the *New York Times* rule to this case. It thought that respondent's claim to the protection of the constitutional privilege depended on the contention that petitioner was either a public official under the *New York Times* decision or a public figure under *Curtis Publishing Co. v. Butts*, 388 U.S. 130, 87 S.Ct. 1975, 18

L.Ed.2d 1094 (1967), apparently discounting the argument that a privilege would arise from the presence of a public issue. After all the evidence had been presented but before submission of the case to the jury, the court ruled in effect that petitioner was neither a public official nor a public figure. It added that, if he were, the resulting application of the *New York Times* standard would require a directed verdict for respondent. Because some statements in the article constituted libel *per se* under Illinois law, the court submitted the case to the jury under instructions that withdrew from its consideration all issues save the measure of damages. The jury awarded $50,000 to petitioner.

Following the jury verdict and on further reflection, the District Court concluded that the *New York Times* standard should govern this case even though petitioner was not a public official or public figure. It accepted respondent's contention that that privilege protected discussion of any public issue without regard to the status of a person defamed therein. Accordingly, the court entered judgment for respondent notwithstanding the jury's verdict. This conclusion anticipated the reasoning of a plurality of this Court in *Rosenbloom v. Metromedia, Inc.,* 403 U.S. 29, 91 S.Ct. 1811, 29 L.Ed.2d 296 (1971).

Petitioner appealed to contest the applicability of the *New York Times* standard to this case. Although the Court of Appeals for the Seventh Circuit doubted the correctness of the District Court's determination that petitioner was not a public figure, it did not overturn that finding. It agreed with the District Court that respondent could assert the constitutional privilege because the article concerned a matter of public interest, citing this Court's intervening decision in *Rosenbloom v. Metromedia, Inc., supra.* The Court of Appeals read *Rosenbloom* to require application of the *New York Times* standard to any publication or broadcast about an issue of significant public interest, without regard to the position, fame, or anonymity of the person defamed, and it concluded that respondent's statements concerned such an issue. After reviewing the record, the Court of Appeals endorsed the District Court's conclusion that petitioner had failed to show by clear and convincing evidence that respondent had acted with "actual malice" as defined by New York Times. There was no evidence that the managing editor of American Opinion knew of the falsity of the accusations made in the article. In fact, he knew nothing about petitioner except what he learned from the article. The court correctly noted that mere proof of failure to investigate, without more, cannot establish reckless disregard for the truth. Rather, the publisher must act with a "high degree of awareness of ... probable falsity." *St. Amant v. Thompson,* 390 U.S. 727, 731, 88 S.Ct. 1323, 1325, 20 L.Ed.2d 262 (1968).... The evidence in this case did not reveal that respondent had cause for such an awareness. The Court of Appeals therefore affirmed.... For the reasons stated below, we reverse.

II

The principal issue in this case is whether a newspaper or broadcaster that publishes defamatory falsehoods about an individual who is neither a public official nor a public figure may claim a constitutional privilege against liability for the injury inflicted by those statements. The Court considered this question on the rather different set of facts presented in *Rosenbloom v. Metromedia, Inc.,* 403 U.S. 29, 91 S.Ct. 1811, 29 L.Ed.2d 296 (1971). Rosenbloom, a distributor of nudist magazines, was arrested for selling allegedly obscene material while making a delivery to a retail dealer. The police obtained a warrant and seized his entire inventory of 3,000 books and magazines. He sought and obtained an injunction prohibiting further police interference with his business. He then sued a local radio station for failing to note in two of its newscasts that the 3,000 items seized were only "reportedly" or "allegedly" obscene and for broadcasting references to "the smut literature racket" and to "girlie-book peddlers" in its coverage of the court proceeding for injunctive relief. He obtained a judgment against the radio station, but the Court of Appeals for the Third Circuit held the *New York Times* privilege applicable to the broadcast and reversed. 415 F.2d 892 (1969).

This Court affirmed the decision below, but no majority could agree on a controlling rationale. The eight Justices who participated in *Rosenbloom* announced their views in five separate opinions, none of which commanded more than three votes. The several statements not only reveal disagreement about the appropriate result in that case, they also reflect divergent traditions of thought about the general problem of reconciling the law of defamation with the First Amendment. One approach has been to extend the *New York Times* test to an expanding variety of situations. Another has been to vary the level of constitutional privilege for defamatory falsehood with the status of the person defamed. And a third view would grant to the press and broadcast media absolute immunity from liability for defamation. To place our holding in the proper context, we preface our discussion of this case with a review of the several *Rosenbloom* opinions and their antecedents.

In affirming the trial court's judgment in the instant case, the Court of Appeals relied on Mr. Justice Brennan's conclusion for the *Rosenbloom* plurality that "all discussion and communication involving matters of public or general concern," 403 U.S., at 44, 91 S.Ct., at 1820, warrant the protection from liability for defamation accorded by the rule originally enunciated in *New York Times Co. v. Sullivan*, ... [In *New York Times*], [t]his Court concluded that a "rule compelling the critic of official conduct to guarantee the truth of all his factual assertions" would deter protected speech, ... and announced the constitutional privilege designed to counter that effect:

> The constitutional guarantees require, we think, a federal rule that prohibits a public official from recovering damages for a defamatory falsehood relating to his official conduct unless he proves that the statement was made with "actual malice" — that is, with knowledge that it was false or with reckless disregard of whether it was false or not....

Three years after *New York Times*, a majority of the Court agreed to extend the constitutional privilege to defamatory criticism of "public figures." This extension was announced in *Curtis Publishing Co. v. Butts* and its companion, *Associated Press v. Walker*, 388 U.S. 130, 162, 87 S.Ct. 1975, 1995, 18 L.Ed.2d 1094 (1967). The first case involved the Saturday Evening Post's charge that Coach Wally Butts of the University of Georgia had conspired with Coach "Bear" Bryant of the University of Alabama to fix a football game between their respective schools. *Walker* involved an erroneous Associated Press account of former Major General Edwin Walker's participation in a University of Mississippi campus riot. Because Butts was paid by a private alumni association and Walker had resigned from the Army, neither could be classified as a "public official" under *New York Times*. Although Mr. Justice Harlan announced the result in both cases, a majority of the Court agreed with Mr. Chief Justice Warren's conclusion that the *New York Times* test should apply to criticism of "public figures" as well as "public officials."[7] The Court

---

7. Professor Kalven once introduced a discussion of these cases with the apt heading, "You Can't Tell the Players without a Score Card." Kalven, *The Reasonable Man and the First Amendment: Hill, Butts, and Walker*, 1967 SUP. CT. REV. 267, 275. Only three other Justices joined Mr. Justice Harlan's analysis of the issues involved. In his concurring opinion, Mr. Chief Justice Warren stated the principle for which these cases stand — that the *New York Times* test reaches both public figures and public officials. Mr. Justice Brennan and Mr. Justice White agreed with the Chief Justice on that question. Mr. Justice Black and Mr. Justice Douglas reiterated their view that publishers should have an absolute immunity from liability for defamation, but they acquiesced in the Chief Justice's rea-

extended the constitutional privilege announced in that case to protect defamatory criticism of nonpublic persons who "are nevertheless intimately involved in the resolution of important public questions or, by reason of their fame, shape events in areas of concern to society at large." *Id.* at 164 (Warren, C.J., concurring in result), 87 S.Ct., at 1996.

In his opinion for the plurality in *Rosenbloom v. Metromedia, Inc.,* ... Mr. Justice Brennan took the *New York Times* privilege one step further. He concluded that its protection should extend to defamatory falsehoods relating to private persons if the statements concerned matters of general or public interest. He abjured the suggested distinction between public officials and public figures on the one hand and private individuals on the other. He focused instead on society's interest in learning about certain issues: "If a matter is a subject of public or general interest, it cannot suddenly become less so merely because a private individual is involved, or because in some sense the individual did not 'voluntarily' choose to become involved." *Id.,* at 43, 91 S.Ct., at 1819. Thus, under the plurality opinion, a private citizen involuntarily associated with a matter of general interest has no recourse for injury to his reputation unless he can satisfy the demanding requirements of the *New York Times* test.

Two members of the Court concurred in the result in *Rosenbloom* but departed from the reasoning of the plurality. Mr. Justice Black restated his view, long shared by Mr. Justice Douglas, that the First Amendment cloaks the news media with an absolute and indefeasible immunity from liability for defamation. *Id.,* at 57, 91 S.Ct., at 1826.

...

III

We begin with the common ground. Under the First Amendment there is no such thing as a false idea. However pernicious an opinion may seem, we depend for its correction not on the conscience of judges and juries but on the competition of other ideas. But there is no constitutional value in false statements of fact. Neither the intentional lie nor the careless error materially advances society's interest in "uninhibited, robust, and wide-open" debate on public issues. *New York Times Co. v. Sullivan,* 376 U.S., at 270, 84 S.Ct., at 721. They belong to that category of utterances which "are no essential part of any exposition of ideas, and are of such slight social value as a step to truth that any benefit that may be derived from them is clearly outweighed by the social interest in order and morality." *Chaplinsky v. New Hampshire,* ... (1942).

Although the erroneous statement of fact is not worthy of constitutional protection, it is nevertheless inevitable in free debate.... And punishment of error runs the risk of inducing a cautious and restrictive exercise of the constitutionally guaranteed freedoms of speech and press....

The need to avoid self-censorship by the news media is, however, not the only societal value at issue. If it were, this Court would have embraced long ago the view that publishers and broadcasters enjoy an unconditional and indefeasible immunity from liability for defamation.... Yet absolute protection for the communications media requires a total sacrifice of the competing value served by the law of defamation.

The legitimate state interest underlying the law of libel is the compensation of individuals for the harm inflicted on them by defamatory falsehoods....

---

soning in order to enable a majority of the Justices to agree on the question of the appropriate constitutional privilege for defamation of public figures.

Some tension necessarily exists between the need for a vigorous and uninhibited press and the legitimate interest in redressing wrongful injury. As Mr. Justice Harlan stated, "some antithesis between freedom of speech and press and libel actions persists, for libel remains premised on the content of speech and limits the freedom of the publisher to express certain sentiments, at least without guaranteeing legal proof of their substantial accuracy." *Curtis Publishing Co. v. Butts.* . . .

. . .

. . . [We] conclude that the States should retain substantial latitude in their efforts to enforce a legal remedy for defamatory falsehood injurious to the reputation of a private individual. The extension of the *New York Times* test proposed by the *Rosenbloom* plurality would abridge this legitimate state interest to a degree that we find unacceptable. And it would occasion the additional difficulty of forcing state and federal judges to decide on an ad hoc basis which publications address issues of "general or public interest" and which do not — to determine, in the words of Mr. Justice Marshall, "what information is relevant to self-government." *Rosenbloom v. Metromedia, Inc.,* 403 U.S., at 79, 91 S.Ct., at 1837. We doubt the wisdom of committing this task to the conscience of judges. Nor does the Constitution require us to draw so thin a line between the drastic alternatives of the *New York Times* privilege and the common law of strict liability for defamatory error. The "public or general interest" test for determining the applicability of the *New York Times* standard to private defamation actions inadequately serves both of the competing values at stake. On the one hand, a private individual whose reputation is injured by defamatory falsehood that does concern an issue of public or general interest has no recourse unless he can meet the rigorous requirements of *New York Times.* This is true despite the factors that distinguish the state interest in compensating private individuals from the analogous interest involved in the context of public persons. On the other hand, a publisher or broadcaster of a defamatory error which a court deems unrelated to an issue of public or general interest may be held liable in damages even if it took every reasonable precaution to ensure the accuracy of its assertions. And liability may far exceed compensation for any actual injury to the plaintiff, for the jury may be permitted to presume damages without proof of loss and even to award punitive damages.

We hold that, so long as they do not impose liability without fault, the States may define for themselves the appropriate standard of liability for a publisher or broadcaster of defamatory falsehood injurious to a private individual.[10] This approach provides a more equitable boundary between the competing concerns involved here. It recognizes the strength of the legitimate state interest in compensating private individuals for wrongful injury to reputation, yet shields the press and broadcast media from the rigors of strict liability for defamation. . . .

---

10. Our caveat against strict liability is the prime target of Mr. Justice WHITE'S dissent. He would hold that a publisher or broadcaster may be required to prove the truth of a defamatory statement concerning a private individual and, failing such proof, that the publisher or broadcaster may be held liable for defamation even though he took every conceivable precaution to ensure the accuracy of the offending statement prior to its dissemination. In Mr. Justice WHITE's view, one who publishes a statement that later turns out to be inaccurate can never be "without fault" in any meaningful sense, for "[i]t is he who circulated a falsehood *that he was not required to publish*". . . .

. . . In light of the progressive extension of the knowing-or-reckless-falsity requirement . . . one might have viewed today's decision allowing recovery under any standard save strict liability as a more generous accommodation of the state interest in comprehensive reputational injury to private individuals than the law presently affords.

IV

Our accommodation of the competing values at stake in defamation suits by private individuals allows the States to impose liability on the publisher or broadcaster of defamatory falsehood on a less demanding showing than that required by *New York Times.* This conclusion is not based on a belief that the considerations which prompted the adoption of the *New York Times* privilege for defamation of public officials and its extension to public figures are wholly inapplicable to the context of private individuals. Rather, we endorse this approach in recognition of the strong and legitimate state interest in compensating private individuals for injury to reputation. But this countervailing state interest extends no further than compensation for actual injury. For the reasons stated below, we hold that the States may not permit recovery of presumed or punitive damages, at least when liability is not based on a showing of knowledge of falsity or reckless disregard for the truth.

The common law of defamation is an oddity of tort law, for it allows recovery of purportedly compensatory damages without evidence of actual loss. Under the traditional rules pertaining to actions for libel, the existence of injury is presumed from the fact of publication. Juries may award substantial sums as compensation for supposed damage to reputation without any proof that such harm actually occurred. The largely uncontrolled discretion of juries to award damages where there is no loss unnecessarily compounds the potential of any system of liability for defamatory falsehood to inhibit the vigorous exercise of First Amendment freedoms. Additionally, the doctrine of presumed damages invites juries to punish unpopular opinion rather than to compensate individuals for injury sustained by the publication of a false fact. More to the point, the States have no substantial interest in securing for plaintiffs such as this petitioner gratuitous awards of money damages far in excess of any actual injury.

We would not, of course, invalidate state law simply because we doubt its wisdom, but here we are attempting to reconcile state law with a competing interest grounded in the constitutional command of the First Amendment. It is therefore appropriate to require that state remedies for defamatory falsehood reach no farther than is necessary to protect the legitimate interest involved. It is necessary to restrict defamation plaintiffs who do not prove knowledge of falsity or reckless disregard for the truth to compensation for actual injury. We need not define "actual injury," as trial courts have wide experience in framing appropriate jury instructions in tort actions. Suffice it to say that actual injury is not limited to out-of-pocket loss. Indeed, the more customary types of actual harm inflicted by defamatory falsehood include impairment of reputation and standing in the community, personal humiliation, and mental anguish and suffering. Of course, juries must be limited by appropriate instructions, and all awards must be supported by competent evidence concerning the injury, although there need be no evidence which assigns an actual dollar value to the injury.

We also find no justification for allowing awards of punitive damages against publishers and broadcasters held liable under state-defined standards of liability for defamation. In most jurisdictions jury discretion over the amounts awarded is limited only by the gentle rule that they not be excessive. Consequently, juries assess punitive damages in wholly unpredictable amounts bearing no necessary relation to the actual harm caused. And they remain free to use their discretion selectively to punish expressions of unpopular views. Like the doctrine of presumed damages, jury discretion to award punitive damages unnecessarily exacerbates the danger of media self-censorship, but, unlike the former rule, punitive damages are wholly irrelevant to the state interest that justifies a negligence standard for private defamation actions. They are not compensation for injury. Instead, they are private fines levied by civil juries to punish reprehensible conduct and to deter its future occurrence. In short, the private defamation plaintiff who establishes liability under a less demanding standard than that stated by *New York Times* may recover only such damages as are sufficient to compensate him for actual injury.

V

Notwithstanding our refusal to extend the *New York Times* privilege to defamation of private individuals, respondent contends that we should affirm the judgment below on the ground that petitioner is either a public official or a public figure. There is little basis for the former assertion....

Respondent's characterization of petitioner as a public figure raises a different question.

...

In this context it is plain that petitioner was not a public figure. He played a minimal role at the coroner's inquest, and his participation related solely to his representation of a private client. He took no part in the criminal prosecution of Officer Nuccio. Moreover, he never discussed either the criminal or civil litigation with the press and was never quoted as having done so. He plainly did not thrust himself into the vortex of this public issue, nor did he engage the public's attention in an attempt to influence its outcome. We are persuaded that the trial court did not err in refusing to characterize petitioner as a public figure for the purpose of this litigation.

We therefore conclude that the New York Times standard is inapplicable to this case and that the trial court erred in entering judgment for respondent. Because the jury was allowed to impose liability without fault and was permitted to presume damages without proof of injury, a new trial is necessary. We reverse and remand for further proceedings in accord with this opinion.

...

[The concurrence of Justice Blackmun is omitted, as are the dissents of Chief Justice Burger and Justice Douglas. A brief excerpt only is given from the dissent of Justice Brennan, and Justice White's dissent has been substantially edited.]

MR. JUSTICE BRENNAN, dissenting.

...

The Court does not discount altogether the danger that jurors will punish for the expression of unpopular opinions. This probability accounts for the Court's limitation that "the States may not permit recovery of presumed or punitive damages, at least when liability is not based on a showing of knowledge of falsity or reckless disregard for the truth." ... But plainly a jury's latitude to impose liability for want of due care poses a far greater threat of suppressing unpopular views than does a possible recovery of presumed or punitive damages. Moreover, the Court's broad-ranging examples of "actual injury," including impairment of reputation and standing in the community, as well as personal humiliation, and mental anguish and suffering, inevitably allow a jury bent on punishing expression of unpopular views a formidable weapon for doing so. Finally, even a limitation of recovery to "actual injury"—however much it reduces the size or frequency of recoveries—will not provide the necessary elbowroom for First Amendment expression.

...

MR. JUSTICE WHITE, dissenting.

For some 200 years—from the very founding of the Nation—the law of defamation and right of the ordinary citizen to recover for false publication injurious to his reputation have been almost exclusively the business of state courts and legislatures. Under typical state defamation law, the defamed private citizen had to prove only a false publication that would subject him to hatred, contempt, or ridicule. Given such publication, general damage to reputation was presumed, while punitive damages required proof of additional facts. The law governing the defamation of private citizens remained untouched by the First Amendment because until relatively recently, the consistent view of the Court was that libelous words constitute a class of speech wholly unprotected by the First Amendment, subject only to limited exceptions carved out since 1964.

But now, using that Amendment as the chosen instrument, the Court, in a few printed pages, has federalized major aspects of libel law by declaring unconstitutional in important respects the prevailing defamation law in all or most of the 50 States. That result is accomplished by requiring the plaintiff in each and every defamation action to prove not only the defendant's culpability beyond his act of publishing defamatory material but also actual damage to reputation resulting from the publication. Moreover, punitive damages may not be recovered by showing malice in the traditional sense of ill will; knowing falsehood or reckless disregard of the truth will not [sic][now?—Ed.] be required.

. . .

The Court proceeds as though it were writing on tabula rasa and suggests that it must mediate between two unacceptable choices—on the one hand, the rigors of the *New York Times* rule which the Court thinks would give insufficient recognition to the interest of the private plaintiff, and, on the other hand, the prospect of imposing "liability without fault" on the press and others who are charged with defamatory utterances. Totally ignoring history and settled First Amendment law, the Court purports to arrive at an "equitable compromise," rejecting both what it considers faultless liability and *New York Times* malice, but insisting on some intermediate degree of fault. Of course, the Court necessarily discards the contrary judgment arrived at in the 50 States that the reputation interest of the private citizen is deserving of considerably more protection.

The Court evinces a deep-seated antipathy to "liability without fault." But this catch-phrase has no talismanic significance and is almost meaningless in this context where the Court appears to be addressing those libels and slanders that are defamatory on their face and where the publisher is no doubt aware from the nature of the material that it would be inherently damaging to reputation. He publishes notwithstanding, knowing that he will inflict injury. With this knowledge, he must intend to inflict that injury, his excuse being that he is privileged to do so—that he has published the truth. But as it turns out, what he has circulated to the public is a very damaging falsehood. Is he nevertheless "faultless"? Perhaps it can be said that the mistake about his defense was made in good faith, but the fact remains that it is he who launched the publication knowing that it could ruin a reputation.

In these circumstances, the law has heretofore put the risk of falsehood on the publisher where the victim is a private citizen and no grounds of special privilege are invoked. The Court would now shift this risk to the victim, even though he has done nothing to invite the calumny, is wholly innocent of fault, and is helpless to avoid his injury. I doubt that jurisprudential resistance to liability without fault is sufficient ground for employing the First Amendment to revolutionize the law of libel, and in my view, that body of legal rules poses no realistic threat to the press and its service to the public. The press today is vigorous and robust. To me, it is quite incredible to suggest that threats of libel suits from private citizens are causing the press to refrain from publishing the truth. I know of no hard facts to support that proposition, and the Court furnishes none.

The communications industry has increasingly become concentrated in a few powerful hands operating very lucrative businesses reaching across the Nation and into almost every home. Neither the industry as a whole nor its individual components are easily intimidated, and we are fortunate that they are not. Requiring them to pay for the occasional damage they do to private reputation will play no substantial part in their future performance or their existence.

In any event, if the Court's principal concern is to protect the communications industry from large libel judgments, it would appear that its new requirements with respect to general and punitive damages would be ample protection. Why it also feels compelled to escalate the threshold standard of liability I cannot fathom, particularly when this will eliminate in many instances the plaintiff's possibility of securing a judicial determination that the damaging publication was indeed false, whether or not he is entitled to recover money damages. Under the Court's new rules, the plaintiff must prove not only the defamatory statement but also some degree of fault accompanying it. The publication may be wholly false and the wrong to him unjustified, but his case will nevertheless be dismissed for failure to prove negligence or other fault on the part of the publisher. I find it unacceptable to distribute the risk in this manner and force the wholly innocent victim to bear the injury; for, as between the two, the defamer is the only culpable party. It is he who circulated a falsehood that he was not required to publish.

It is difficult for me to understand why the ordinary citizen should himself carry the risk of damage and suffer the injury in order to vindicate First Amendment values by protecting the press and others from liability for circulating false information. This is particularly true because such statements serve no purpose whatsoever in furthering the public interest or the search for truth but, on the contrary, may frustrate that search and at the same time inflict great injury on the defenseless individual. The owners of the press and the stockholders of the communications enterprises can much better bear the burden. And if they cannot, the public at large should somehow pay for what is essentially a public benefit derived at private expense.

. . .

Not content with escalating the threshold requirements of establishing liability, the Court abolishes the ordinary damages rule, undisturbed by *New York Times* and later cases, that, as to libels or slanders defamatory on their face, injury to reputation is presumed and general damages may be awarded along with whatever special damages may be sought. Apparently because the Court feels that in some unspecified and unknown number of cases, plaintiffs recover where they have suffered no injury or recover more than they deserve, it dismisses this rule as an "oddity of tort law." The Court thereby refuses in any case to accept the fact of wide dissemination of a per se libel as prima facie proof of injury sufficient to survive a motion to dismiss at the close of plaintiff's case.

I have said before, but it bears repeating, that even if the plaintiff should recover no monetary damages, he should be able to prevail and have a judgment that the publication is false. But beyond that, courts and legislatures literally for centuries have thought that in the generality of cases, libeled plaintiffs will be seriously shortchanged if they must prove the extent of the injury to their reputations. Even where libels or slanders are not on their face defamatory and special damage must be shown, when that showing is made, general damages for reputation injury are recoverable without specific proof.[38]

The Court is clearly right when at one point it states that "the law of defamation is rooted in our experience that the truth rarely catches up with a lie."* ... But it ignores what that experience teaches, viz., that damage to reputation is recurringly difficult to prove and that requiring actual proof would repeatedly destroy and chance for adequate compensation. Eminent authority has warned that

> it is clear that proof of actual damage will be impossible in a great many cases where, from the character of the defamatory words and the circumstances of publication, it is all but certain that serious harm has resulted in fact.

W. Prosser, Law of Torts § 112, p. 765 (4th ed. 1971).

The Court fears uncontrolled awards of damages by juries, but that not only denigrates the good sense of most jurors—it fails to consider the role of trial and appellate courts in limiting excessive jury verdicts where no reasonable relationship exists between the amount awarded and the injury sustained. Available information tends to confirm that American courts have ably discharged this responsibility.

The new rule with respect to general damages appears to apply to all libels or slanders, whether defamatory on their face or not, except, I gather, when the plaintiff proves intentional falsehood or reckless disregard. Although the impact of the publication on the victim is the same, in such circumstances the injury to reputation may apparently be presumed in accordance with the traditional rule. Why a defamatory statement is more apt to cause injury if the lie is intentional than when it is only negligent, I fail to understand. I suggest that judges and juries who must live by these rules will find them equally incomprehensible.

...

With a flourish of the pen, the Court also discards the prevailing rule in libel and slander actions that punitive damages may be awarded on the classic grounds of common-law malice, that is, "'(a)ctual malice' in the sense of ill will or fraud or reckless indifference to consequences." In its stead, the Court requires defamation plaintiffs to show intentional falsehood or reckless disregard for the truth or falsity of the publication.... I see no constitutional difference between publishing with reckless disregard for the truth, where punitive damages will be permitted, and negligent publication where they will not be allowed. It is difficult to understand what is constitutionally wrong with assessing punitive damages to deter a publisher from departing from those standards of

---

38. Having held that the defamation plaintiff is limited to recovering for "actual injury," the Court hastens to add:

"Suffice it to say that actual injury is not limited to out-of-pocket loss. Indeed, the more customary types of actual harm inflicted by defamatory falsehood include impairment of reputation and standing in the community, personal humiliation, and mental anguish and suffering." ... It should be pointed out that under the prevailing law, where the defamation is not actionable *per se* and proof of "special damage" is required, a showing of actual injury to reputation is insufficient; but if pecuniary loss is shown, general reputation damages are recoverable. The Court changes the latter, but not the former, rule. Also under present law, pain and suffering, although shown, do not warrant damages in any defamation action unless the plaintiff is otherwise entitled to at least nominal damages. By imposing a more difficult standard of liability and requiring proof of actual damage to reputation, recovery for pain and suffering, though real, becomes a much more remote possibility.

* This statement appears in note 9 of the Court's opinion, 418 U.S. at 344, omitted in this edition of the case.—Ed.

care ordinarily followed in the publishing industry, particularly if common-law malice is also shown.

· · ·

I fail to see how the quality or quantity of public debate will be promoted by further emasculation of state libel laws for the benefit of the news media.[41] If anything, this trend may provoke a new and radical imbalance in the communications process. It is not at all inconceivable that virtually unrestrained defamatory remarks about private citizens will discourage them from speaking out and concerning themselves with social problems. This would turn the First Amendment on its head....

· · ·

While some risk of exposure "is a concomitant of life in a civilized community," *Time, Inc. v. Hill*, ... the private citizen does not bargain for defamatory falsehoods....

· · ·

... Whether or not the course followed by the majority is wise, and I have indicated my doubts that it is, our constitutional scheme compels a proper respect for the role of the States in acquitting their duty to obey the Constitution. Finding no evidence that they have shirked this responsibility, particularly when the law of defamation is even now in transition, I would await some demonstration of the diminution of freedom of expression before acting.

· · ·

NOTES

(1) Is Justice Powell's solution in *Gertz* sufficiently responsive to the reality of modern mass media?

(2) Consider each of the following factors with respect to the effects of defamatory communication:

(a) The possibility of effective reply.

(b) Behavioral data on the proposition that the truth never catches up with a libel.

(c) The frequency of publication of the offending medium.

(d) The nature of the medium—e.g., print as compared with video broadcast, radio broadcast, or the Internet.

(e) The possibility of having a reply in the same "spot."

---

41. *Cf.* Pedrick, [49 CORNELL L.Q.] at 601–602:

"A great many forces in our society operate to determine the extent to which men are free in fact to express their ideas. Whether there is a privilege for good faith defamatory misstatements on matters of public concern or whether there is strict liability for such statements may not greatly affect the course of public discussion. How different has life been in those states which heretofore followed the majority rule imposing strict liability for misstatements of fact defaming public figures from life in the minority states where the good faith privilege held sway?"

See also T. EMERSON, THE SYSTEM OF FREEDOM OF EXPRESSION 519 (1970) ... : "[O]n the whole the role of libel law in the system of freedom of expression has been relatively minor and essentially erratic."

How much should each of these factors weigh in the determination of the appropriate culpability standards and rules concerning the privilege to defame individuals in the following categories:

(a) Public officials?

(b) Persons without official posts who are consistently involved in public affairs of the kind that are the subject of the defamatory communication?

(c) Private citizens whose professional role propels them into particular events with news value?

(d) Private citizens who are brought quite involuntarily into the public spotlight by fortuitous events?

(e) Private citizens who are defamed in matters relating only to their private lives?

(3) *Gertz* was only an intermediate point in a continuing chronicle, which could well occupy a casebook by itself. Here is a thumbnail sketch of some of the descendants of *Gertz* and *New York Times*:

(a) *Time, Inc. v. Firestone*, 424 U.S. 448, 96 S. Ct. 958 (1976): The fact that divorce proceedings involving an heir to a fortune and his wife were a "cause celebre" did not make the wife a "public figure," even though she "may have held a few press conferences during the divorce proceedings in an attempt to satisfy inquiring reporters."

(b) *Wolston v. Reader's Digest Ass'n*, 443 U.S. 157, 99 S. Ct. 2701 (1979): A "mere citation for contempt" arising from a failure to respond to a grand jury subpoena related to an espionage investigation did not render a man a "public figure" for purposes of a book on Soviet espionage.

(c) *Dun & Bradstreet, Inc. v. Greenmoss Builders, Inc.*, 472 U.S. 749, 105 S. Ct. 2939 (1985): Where the defendant communicated to five confidential subscribers a credit report that grossly misrepresented a contractor's assets and liabilities, a plurality said that in cases of "speech involving no matters of public concern," a claimant could recover both presumed and punitive damages even in the absence of "actual malice." 472 U.S. at 761.

(4) The Court in *Sullivan* and *Gertz* wrote at length on the constitutional dimensions of the fault requirement in defamation, but in neither case did the Court say much about falsity. At common law, defamatory statements were presumptively false. The logic ran that a plaintiff's reputation should be regarded as good, so a statement that impugns that reputation must be false. Truth was available as an affirmative defense, but as with any ordinary affirmative defense, the defendant bore the burden of proof. *Sullivan* and *Gertz* changed that norm by placing the burden of proving actual malice—a standard that implicitly requires proof of falsity—on public figures and public officials. But may states in cases of private-figure plaintiffs still burden defendants to prove that an assertion is true? In a case involving allegations of a private-figure plaintiff's links to organized crime, a 5–4 majority of the Supreme Court answered no, at least when the matter is of public concern and the defendant is a newspaper. Justices Brennan and Blackmun would have rejected any distinction between media and non-media defendants. *Philadelphia Newspapers, Inc. v. Hepps*, 475 U.S. 767, 106 S. Ct. 1558 (1986).

(5) Beginning journalism students learn that one does not put material in quotations marks unless the speaker said them. Is deliberately altering a speaker's words a per se instance of *New York Times* malice? In *Masson v. New Yorker Magazine, Inc.*, 501 U.S. 496

(1991), the Supreme Court said it is not, "unless the alteration results in a material change in the meaning conveyed by the statement." However, pointing out that "quotations may be a devastating instrument for conveying false meaning," the Court said that "if the alterations of [the plaintiff's] words gave a different meaning to the statements, bearing upon their defamatory character, then the device of quotations might well be critical in finding the words actionable."

Masson arose from material, first published in *The New Yorker*, in which the author Janet Malcolm quoted the psychoanalyst Jeffrey Masson, who had been appointed projects director of the Sigmund Freud Archives, as saying that he was "like an intellectual gigolo" and that he would have made the house containing the archives "a place of sex, women, fun." The author had tape recorded some conversations with the plaintiff, but these remarks did not appear in the tapes, and although she had typed up notes containing the alleged quotes, she said she had discarded her handwritten originals. Two jury verdicts—one inconclusive and a later one in favor of the defendants—followed the Supreme Court decision. In a remarkable ending subsequent to the second jury trial, the author's 2-year-old granddaughter apparently pulled out a thin notebook from a bookcase. The notebook had some of Malcolm's missing notes, including the quotations she had been unable to document in the original. *Anthony Lewis, Stranger than Fiction*, N.Y. TIMES, Aug. 25, 1996, at A15.

(6) Assuming that the personal injury from false words can be as severe in its way as harms done by motor vehicles, but given that a broad latitude for the press is of crucial importance to our political institutions, would the ideal solution to the problem of media defamation be federally subsidized defamation insurance?

[C] "Opinion"

HENDERSON v. TIMES MIRROR COMPANY

United States District Court, District of Colorado
669 F. Supp. 356 (1987)

CARRIGAN, DISTRICT JUDGE.

This is the case of the mouse that roared invective. One of the defendants, Darrel "Mouse" Davis, in a statement to newspaper reporters, called the plaintiff a "sleaze-bag agent" who "slimed up from the bayou." ... Plaintiff, J. Harrison Henderson III, is an agent for professional football players. By this lawsuit, Henderson takes exception to Davis' comments and seeks damages....

... Henderson alleges that in January 1985 the Denver Gold professional football team wanted to hire, and negotiated directly with, a quarterback named Raphel Cherry. During the course of the negotiations, Cherry hired the plaintiff as his agent to assist in negotiations. After the plaintiff commenced representing Cherry, negotiations with the Gold collapsed. Thereafter "Mouse" Davis, as head coach of the Gold, told news reporters that the Gold had offered Cherry more than $100,000 before Henderson became his agent and upped the asking price to $200,000, thus terminating the negotiations. Davis admittedly referred to the plaintiff as a "sleazebag" who kind of "slimed up from the bayou"....

While it can be agreed generally that the terms "sleazebag" and "slime" do not rank as descriptive words one would prefer to have in letters of recommendation, their meanings in the context of Davis' comments is so imprecise that they cannot be considered as asserting facts. While it may not be a compliment to be called a "sleaze-bag agent," or "sleaze-bag journalist," or "sleaze-bag coach," or whatever kind of sleaze-bag one may happen to be, the mere absence of complimentary affect does not render a statement defamatory.

Nor does the mere description of one's means of locomotion as "sliming" rise to the legal status of slander; for the term is too slippery to be a fact one can grasp and hold up to the lamp of truth in order to test whether the defense of truth applies. . . .

Here, the context is a recruiting dispute in the rough and rowdy world of professional football. . . .

Certainly, the sports world is an environment where the kind of "robust" debate endorsed by the Supreme Court in *New York Times, Inc. v. Sullivan*, . . . has flourished. Even the once fastidious etiquette of Wimbledon has succumbed to the more gross and tawdry vernacular formerly more characteristic of hockey rinks and football stadia. The world of Damon Runyon was not portrayed in the idiom of the church supper.

Moreover, our Anglo-American linguistic heritage has long recognized vigorous and colorful insult as an art form, albeit not always creative. As noted by the court in *Raible v. Newsweek, Inc.*, 341 F.Supp. 804, 808–09 (W.D.Pa.1972), "Americans have been hurling epithets at each other for generations. . . . Certainly such name calling . . . does not always give rise to an action for libel." In 1800, Charles Lamb wrote to Samuel Coleridge: "For God's sake (I never was more serious) don't make me ridiculous any more by terming me gentlehearted in print . . . substitute drunken dog, ragged head, seldshaven, odd-eyed, stuttering, or any other epithet which truly and properly belongs to the gentleman in question." *Letter to Samuel Taylor Coleridge* (August 1800). W.S. Gilbert once declared that "[n]o one can have a higher opinion of him than I have — and I think he is a dirty little beast." And that indomitable master of the language, Winston Churchill, upon bumping into a woman in the street who declaimed, "Sir, you are drunk," replied, "Madam, you are ugly, and the difference between you and me is that in the morning I shall be sober; but you will still be ugly!"

Unfortunately, such creativity in the art of abusive epithet has all but disappeared. It is all too rare today to hear the clear, clean ring of a really original insult. We have become in our opprobrium, as in other areas of life, conformists copying from the deluge of daily drivel from television or from the only occasionally more original print media.

Historically, an insultee had several options for seeking redress in circumstances such as those here presented. For example, he could have challenged the insultor to a duel. Or, following the lead of literature, one in the plaintiff's position might have trapped "Mouse" Davis in a wine cellar. *See* E.A. Poe, *The Cask of Amontillado*, at 1 (1846) ("[t]he thousand injuries of Fortunato I had borne as best I could, but when he ventured upon insult I vowed revenge"). However, I am bound by the literature of law, and those precedents oblige me to conclude that Davis' utterances, however unfair or inappropriate, were mere opinion rather than assertions of fact and, therefore, the plaintiff's claims for defamation must be dismissed. . . .

NOTE

Are the remarks sued upon in *Henderson* just good clean fun? What is the best statement of a general principle that tells a court how to draw the line between opinionated insults and factual defamations?

PROBLEM

Consider the following translation of a restaurant review, which appeared in a French language "Guide to New York":

Mr. Chow
324 E. 54th Street
(between 1st and 2nd Avenues)
(751-9030)
Every Day until 11:45

Still another Chinese restaurant, but this one is the latest darling of fashionable society.... While his London restaurant enjoys an honorable reputation (although it is clearly overrated) the branch which the clever Mr. Chow has just opened in New York is simply astounding from a culinary point of view. In a pinch, you might not care that you have to wait ten minutes to obtain chopsticks instead of forks, that it is impossible to have the basic condiments (soy sauce, hot sauce, etc.) on the table, that the principal concern of the waiters (Italians) is to sell you expensive alcoholic drinks, but the last straw is that the dishes on the menu (very short) have only the slightest relationship to the essential spirit of Chinese cuisine. With their heavy and greasy dough, the dumplings, on our visit, resembled bad Italian ravioli, the steamed meatballs had a disturbingly gamy taste, the sweet and sour pork contained more dough (badly cooked) than meat, and the green peppers which accompanied it remained still frozen on the plate. The chicken with chili was rubbery and the rice, soaking, for some reason, in oil, totally insipid. Had we been specially punished for being so pretentious as to drink only tea? Apparently not, for the drinkers of alcohol seemed as badly off as we. At a near-by table, the Peking lacquered duck (although ordered in advance) was made up of only one dish (instead of three traditional ones), composed of pancakes the size of a saucer and the thickness of a finger. At another table, the egg-rolls had the gauge of andouillette sausages, and the dough the thickness of large tagliatelle. No matter, since the wine kept flowing. We do not know where Mr. Chow recruits his cooks, but he would do well to send them for instruction somewhere in Chinatown. There, at least, they still know the traditions....

As attorney for an infuriated Mr. Chow, which phrases or sentences would you focus on for a defamation suit? What would be your expectations of success?

OLLMAN v. EVANS

United States Court of Appeals, District of Columbia Circuit, En Banc
242 U.S. App. D.C. 301, 750 F.2d 970, cert. denied, 471 U.S. 1127 (1985)

STARR, CIRCUIT JUDGE.

This defamation action arises out of the publication of a syndicated column by Rowland Evans and Robert Novak in May 1978. The question before us is whether the allegedly defamatory statements set forth in the column are constitutionally protected expressions of opinion or, as appellant contends, actionable assertions of fact. We conclude, as did the District Court, that the challenged statements are entitled to absolute First Amendment protection as expressions of opinion.

I

Rowland Evans and Robert Novak are nationally syndicated columnists whose columns appear regularly in newspapers across the country. According to the complaint in this case, which was filed by plaintiff Bertell Ollman on February 15, 1979, an Evans and Novak column appeared on or about May 4, 1978 in *The Washington Post* and other newspapers across the Nation.... Attached to the complaint as Exhibit A was a photocopy of the column, styled "The Marxist Professor's Intentions," as it appeared in *The Washington Post* on May 4, 1978....

The plaintiff, Bertell Ollman, is a professor of political science at New York University. The complaint averred that Mr. Ollman "is widely esteemed among his colleagues and enjoys the highest possible reputation as a scholar of integrity and a teacher." ... In March 1978, Mr. Ollman was nominated by a departmental search committee to head the Department of Government and Politics at the University of Maryland. The committee's recommendation "was duly approved by the Provost of the University and the Chancellor of the College Park campus." ...

With this professional move from Washington Square to College Park, Maryland thus in the offing, the Evans and Novak article appeared. Since the years of litigation that have followed revolve entirely around this single column, we will begin by describing its contents in some detail. In our description, we will highlight the specific portions that Mr. Ollman assails as false and defamatory. The column begins as follows:

> What is in danger of becoming a frivolous public debate over the appointment of a Marxist to head the University of Maryland's department of politics and government has so far ignored this unspoken concern within the academic community: the avowed desire of many political activists to use higher education for indoctrination.

The column immediately goes on to state that:

> [t]he proposal to name Bertell Ollman, Professor at New York University, as department head has generated wrong-headed debate. Politicians who jumped in to oppose Ollman simply for his Marxist philosophy have received a justifiable going-over from defenders of academic freedom in the press and the university. Academic Prince Valiants seem arrayed against McCarythite [sic] know-nothings.

With these opening two paragraphs as lead-in, the authors then pose what they deemed the pivotal issue in the debate: "But neither side approaches the crucial question: not Ollman's beliefs, but his intentions. *His candid writings avow his desire to use the classroom as an instrument for preparing what he calls 'the revolution.'* Whether this is a form of indoctrination that could transform the real function of a university and transcend limits of academic freedom is a concern to academicians who are neither McCarthyite nor know-nothing." (Emphasis added).

The columnists thus, in the first three paragraphs, articulated a view of what should be the central question in what they viewed as a fruitless debate. The authors then go on in the next paragraph to state: "To protect academic freedom, that question should be posed not by politicians but by professors. But professors throughout the country troubled by the nomination, clearly a minority, dare not say a word in today's campus climate."

With this observation, the authors turn in the following six paragraphs to a discussion of Mr. Ollman and his writings. Evans and Novak state that "[w]hile Ollman is described in news accounts as a 'respected Marxist scholar,' *he is widely viewed in his profession as a political activist.* Amid the increasingly popular Marxist movement in university life, he is distinct from philosophical Marxists. *Rather, he is an outspoken proponent of 'political Marxism.'* " (Emphasis added).

The authors next relate Mr. Ollman's two unsuccessful efforts to win election to membership on the council of the American Political Science Association. In these elections, the column states (and appellant does not dispute) that Professor Ollman ran as a candidate of the Caucus for a New Political Science and finished last out of sixteen candidates each time. "Whether or not that represents a professional judgment by his colleagues, as some critics contend, the verdict clearly rejected his campaign pledge: 'If elected ... I shall use every means at my disposal to promote the study of Marxism and Marxist approaches to politics throughout the profession.'"

Evans and Novak then direct the four ensuing paragraphs of the column to a summary of an article by Mr. Ollman, entitled "On Teaching Marxism and Building the Movement" in the Winter 1978 issue of *New Political Science*. In this article, Mr. Ollman claims that most students conclude his political science course with a " 'Marxist outlook.' " The authors go on:

> Ollman concedes that will be seen "as an admission that the purpose of my course is to convert students to socialism."
>
> That bothers him not at all because "a correct understanding of Marxism (as indeed of any body of scientific truths) leads automatically to its acceptance." ... The "classroom" is a place where the students' bourgeois ideology is being dismantled. "Our prior task" before the revolution, he writes, "is to make more revolutionaries."

Moving to a brief discussion of Mr. Ollman's principal work, *Alienation: Marx's Conception of Man in Capitalist Society*, the authors described the work as "a ponderous tome in adoration of the master (Marxism 'is like a magnificiently rich tapestry'). Published in 1971, it does not abandon hope for the revolution forecast by Karl Marx in 1848." This brings the columnists to the last statement specifically identified in the complaint as defamatory:

> *Such pamphleteering is hooted at by one political scientist in a major eastern university, whose scholarship and reputation as a liberal are well known.* "Ollman has no status within the profession, but is a pure and simple activist," he said. Would he say that publicly? "No chance of it. Our academic culture does not permit the raising of such questions." (Emphasis added).

Evans and Novak then bring the column to a close, indicating in the penultimate paragraph that " '[s]uch questions' would include these: What is the true measurement of Ollman's scholarship? Does he intend to use the classroom for indoctrination? Will he indeed be followed by other Marxist professors? Could the department in time be closed to non-Marxists, following the tendency at several English universities?"

In the column's final paragraph, the authors return to their opening theme that "such questions" as set forth in the previous paragraph should not be raised by politicians, even if, as the anonymous political scientist claimed, they cannot be raised within the Academy. They conclude the column by calling upon academics to address these questions:

> Here are the makings of a crisis that, to protect its integrity and true academic freedom, academia itself must resolve.

. . .

The District Court granted Evans and Novak's motion for summary judgment, concluding that the column simply reflected the columnists' opinion and their "interpretation of [Mr. Ollman's] writings." Memorandum Opinion at 5. Thus, the District Court held that the opinion was absolutely protected by the First Amendment. This appeal followed.

II

A

This case presents us with the delicate and sensitive task of accommodating the First Amendment's protection of free expression of ideas with the common law's protection of an individual's interest in reputation. It is a truism that the free flow of ideas and opinions is integral to our democratic system of government. Thomas Jefferson well expressed this principle in his First Inaugural Address, when the Nation's memory was fresh with the passage of the notorious Alien and Sedition Acts:

> If there be any among us who would wish to dissolve this Union or to change its republican form, let them stand undisturbed as monuments of the safety with which error of opinion may be tolerated where reason is left free to combat it.

At the same time, an individual's interest in his or her reputation is of the highest order. Its protection is an eloquent expression of the respect historically afforded the dignity of the individual in Anglo-American legal culture. A defamatory statement may destroy an individual's livelihood, wreck his standing in the community, and seriously impair his sense of dignity and self-esteem.

The judiciary's task in accommodating these competing interests is by no means new: at common law, the fair comment doctrine bestowed qualified immunity from libel actions as to certain types of opinions in order that writers could express freely their views about subjects of public interest. However, since *Gertz v. Robert Welch, Inc.*, 418 U.S. 323, 94 S.Ct. 2997, 41 L.Ed.2d 789 (1974), the nature of this accommodation has fundamentally changed. In *Gertz*, the Supreme Court in *dicta* seemed to provide absolute immunity from defamation actions for all opinions and to discern the basis for this immunity in the First Amendment. The Court began its analysis of the case by stating:

> Under the First Amendment there is no such thing as a false idea. However pernicious an opinion may seem, we depend for its correction not on the conscience of judges and juries but on the competition of other ideas. But there is no constitutional value in false statements of fact. Neither the intentional lie nor the careless error materially advances society's interest in "uninhibited, robust, and wide-open debate on the public issues."

By this statement, *Gertz* elevated to constitutional principle the distinction between fact and opinion, which at common law had formed the basis of the doctrine of fair comment. *Gertz's* implicit command thus imposes upon both state and federal courts the duty as a matter of constitutional adjudication to distinguish facts from opinions in order to provide opinions with the requisite, absolute First Amendment protection. At the same time, however, the Supreme Court provided little guidance in *Gertz* itself as to the manner in which the distinction between fact and opinion is to be discerned. That, as we shall see, is by no means as easy a question as might appear at first blush.

Indeed, *Gertz* did not focus on this distinction at all. Rather, assuming without lengthy discussion that the statements in that case could be construed as statements of fact, the Court held that the plaintiff, who was a private rather than public figure, could prove that the statements at issue there were libelous upon demonstrating that they were negligently made. The distinction in our law between public and private figures, however, does not directly bear on the distinction between fact and opinion. Expressions of opinion are protected whether the subject of the comment is a private or public figure.... In a word, *Gertz's* reasoning immunizes an opinion, not because the opinion is asserted about a public figure, but because there is no such thing as a "false" opinion.

. . .

It is a fitting illustration of the complexity of language and communication that many statements from which actions for defamation arise do not clearly fit into either category. These statements pose more subtle problems and are the stuff of which litigation is made. The principal difficulty arises from statements that on first analysis seem to be based upon perceptions of events, but are not themselves simply a record of those perceptions. Such statements may imply in some contexts the existence of facts not disclosed by the author.[14] An example of such a statement, set forth in the *Restatement (Second) of Torts*, is: "Mr. Jones is an alcoholic."[15] These statements obviously can be as damaging to reputation as statements which on their face describe particular historical events.

The degree to which such kinds of statements have real factual content can, of course, vary greatly. We believe, in consequence, that courts should analyze the totality of the circumstances in which the statements are made to decide whether they merit the absolute First Amendment protection enjoyed by opinion. To evaluate the totality of the circumstances of an allegedly defamatory statement, we will consider four factors in assessing whether the average reader would view the statement as fact or, conversely, opinion. While necessarily imperfect, these factors will, we are persuaded, assist in discerning as systematically as possible what constitutes an assertion of fact and what is, in contrast, an expression of opinion.

First, we will analyze the common usage or meaning of the specific language of the challenged statement itself. Our analysis of the specific language under scrutiny will be aimed at determining whether the statement has a precise core of meaning for which a consensus of understanding exists or, conversely, whether the statement is indefinite and ambiguous.... Readers are, in our judgment, considerably less likely to infer facts from an indefinite or ambiguous statement than one with a commonly understood meaning. Second, we will consider the statement's verifiability—is the statement capable of being objectively characterized as true or false? ... Insofar as a statement lacks a plausible method of verification, a reasonable reader will not believe that the statement has specific factual content.... And, in the setting of litigation, the trier of fact obliged in a defamation action to assess the truth of an unverifiable statement will have considerable difficulty returning a verdict based upon anything but speculation. Third, moving from the challenged language itself, we will consider the full context of

---

14. One commentator labels such statements "deductive opinions." *See* Keeton, *Defamation and Freedom of the Press*, 54 Tex.L.Rev. 1221, 1250–51 (1976) (contrasting evaluative opinions expressing a value judgment and deductive opinions purporting to convey information). Restatement (Second) of Torts § 566 also attempts to categorize opinions which imply factual allegations....

15. Restatement (Second) of Torts § 566, example 3. "A writes to B about his neighbor C: 'I think he must be an alcoholic.'"

the statement—the entire article or column, for example—inasmuch as other, unchallenged language surrounding the allegedly defamatory statement will influence the average reader's readiness to infer that a particular statement has factual content.... Finally, we will consider the broader context or setting in which the statement appears. Different types of writing have, as we shall more fully see, widely varying social conventions which signal to the reader the likelihood of a statement's being either fact or opinion.

...

III

Now we turn to the case at hand to apply the foregoing analysis. As we have seen, Mr. Ollman alleges various instances of defamation in the Evans and Novak column. Before analyzing each such instance, we will first examine the context (the third and fourth factors in our approach) in which the alleged defamations arise. We will then assess the manner in which this context would influence the average reader in interpreting the alleged defamations as an assertion of fact or an expression of opinion.

From the earliest days of the Republic, individuals have published and circulated short, frequently sharp and biting writings on issues of social and political interest. From the pamphleteers urging revolution to abolitionists condemning the evils of slavery, American authors have sought through pamphlets and tracts both to stimulate debate and to persuade. Today among the inheritors of this lively tradition are the columnists and opinion writers whose works appear on the editorial and Op-Ed pages of the Nation's newspapers. The column at issue here is plainly part and parcel of this tradition of social and political criticism.

The reasonable reader who peruses an Evans and Novak column on the editorial or Op-Ed page is fully aware that the statements found there are not "hard" news like those printed on the front page or elsewhere in the news sections of the newspaper. Readers expect that columnists will make strong statements, sometimes phrased in a polemical manner that would hardly be considered balanced or fair elsewhere in the newspaper. *National Rifle Association v. Dayton Newspaper, Inc., supra,* 555 F.Supp. at 1309. That proposition is inherent in the very notion of an "Op-Ed page." Because of obvious space limitations, it is also manifest that columnists or commentators will express themselves in condensed fashion without providing what might be considered the full picture. Columnists are, after all, writing a column, not a full-length scholarly article or a book. This broad understanding of the traditional function of a column like Evans and Novak will therefore predispose the average reader to regard what is found there to be opinion.

A reader of this particular Evans and Novak column would also have been influenced by the column's express purpose. The columnists laid squarely before the reader their interest in ending what they deemed a "frivolous" debate among politicians over whether Mr. Ollman's political beliefs should bar him from becoming head of the Department of Government and Politics at the University of Maryland. Instead, the authors plainly intimated in the column's lead paragraph that they wanted to spark a more appropriate debate within academia over whether Mr. Ollman's purpose in teaching was to indoctrinate his students. Later in the column, they openly questioned the measure or method of Professor Ollman's scholarship. Evans and Novak made it clear that they were not purporting to set forth definitive conclusions, but instead meant to ventilate what in their view constituted the central questions raised by Mr. Ollman's prospective appointment. In the penultimate paragraph of the column, as we have already seen, the authors expressly posed the following "questions:"

What is the true measurement of Ollman's scholarship? Does he intend to use the classroom for indoctrination? Will he indeed be followed by other Marxist professors? Could the department in time become closed to non-Marxists, following the tendency at several English universities?

Prominently displayed in the Evans and Novak column, therefore, is interrogatory or cautionary language that militates in favor of treating statements as opinion.

A

Having reviewed the context of the challenged statements, we turn next to the alleged defamation that, in our view, is most clearly opinion, namely that "[Ollman] is an outspoken proponent of political Marxism." This kind of characterization is much akin to the characterization, "fascist," found absolutely protected in *Buckley v. Littell, supra.* This is unmistakably a "loosely definable, variously interpretable statement[] of opinion ... made inextricably in the contest of political, social or philosophical debate...." 539 F.2d at 895. It is obviously unverifiable. Since Mr. Ollman concedes that he is a Marxist, *see* Letter of B. Ollman to the Editors of *The Washington Post* (May 8, 1978), R. 3, the trier of fact in assessing the statement would have the dubious task of trying to distinguish "political Marxism" from "non-political Marxism," whatever that may be.

Nor is the statement that "[Mr. Ollman] is widely viewed in his profession as a political activist" a representation or assertion of fact. "Political activist" is a term, like "political Marxism," that is hopelessly imprecise and indefinite. It is difficult to imagine, much less construct, a means of deciding the quantum of political activity justifying the label "activist." While Mr. Ollman argues that this assertion is defamatory since it *implies* that he has no reputation as a scholar, we are rather skeptical of the strength of that implication, particularly in the context of this column. It does not appear the least bit evident that "scholarship" and "political activism" are generally understood to be incompatible. Moreover, Evans and Novak set out facts which signalled to the reader that this statement represents a characterization arising from the columnists' view of the facts. In the paragraph immediately following this statement, the column indicated that Mr. Ollman on no less than two occasions finished dead last among all candidates for election to the governing Council of the American Political Science Association, when he ran on the platform: "If elected ... I shall use every means at my disposal to promote the study of Marxism and Marxist approaches to politics throughout the profession." A reasonable reader would conclude that the authors' judgment that Mr. Ollman was "widely viewed as a political activist" was a characterization based upon the latter's unsuccessful electoral endeavors within his profession.

B

Next we turn to Mr. Ollman's complaints about the column's quotations from and remarks about his writings, and specifically his article, "On Teaching Marxism and Building the Movement."[34] We note in this respect that even before the appearance of the constitutionally based opinion privilege in Gertz, commentary on another's writing was considered a privileged occasion at common law and therefore received the benefit of the fair comment doctrine. When a critic is commenting about a book, the reader is

---

34. POLITICAL SCIENCE, Winter 1978 at 5. R. 3. The column also commented upon Professor Ollman's book, ALIENATION: MARX'S CONCEPTION OF MAN IN A CAPITALIST SOCIETY (1971), calling the volume "ponderous" and dismissing it as "pamphleteering." These comments are obviously paradigms of opinion: Evans and Novak are merely making clear their dislike of the book's style and substance.

on notice that the critic is engaging in interpretation, an inherently subjective enterprise, and therefore realizes that others, including the author, may utterly disagree with the critic's interpretation.[36] The average reader further understands that because of limitations of space, not to mention those limitations imposed by the patience of the prospective audience, the critic as a practical matter will be able to support his opinion only by rather truncated quotations from the book or work under scrutiny. The reader is thus predisposed to view what the critic writes as opinion. In this context, courts have rightly been wary of finding statements to be defamatory, unless the statements misquote the author, put words into the author's mouth or otherwise clearly go beyond the realm of interpretation.

Evans' and Novak's statements about Mr. Ollman's article clearly do not fall into the category of misquotation or misrepresentation. First, the plaintiff complains of the following statement: "Ollman concedes that [the fact that most students have a 'Marxist outlook' after taking his course] 'will be seen as an admission that the purpose of my course is to convert students to socialism.'" Tellingly, however, the quoted words are accurately reproduced from Mr. Ollman's article. *See* "On Teaching Marxism and Building the Movement" at 5. To be sure, the quotation has not been printed in its complete context.[37] But that is neither here nor there; the quotation of remarks without the complete context in which the remarks appeared is entirely commonplace when summarizing a written work in a brief space. We are fully aware that this practice can be highly irritating when the context does not seem fully and fairly stated. The balm for the irritation, however, cannot be a libel suit, unless triers of fact are to sit in editorial judgment.[38]

Professor Ollman also objects to the column's posing the question, prompted in Evans' and Novak's view by Mr. Ollman's article, of whether he intended to use the classroom for indoctrination. As we noted previously, the column in no wise affirmatively stated that Mr. Ollman was indoctrinating his students. Moreover, indoctrination is not, at least as used here in the setting of academia, a word with a well-defined meaning. To paraphrase Justice Harlan in another context, *see Cohen v. California*, 403 U.S. 15, 25, 91 S.Ct. 1780, 1788, 29 L.Ed.2d 284 (1971), what is indoctrination to one per-

---

36. Indeed, Mr. Ollman seems to accept the proposition that several interpretations of his writing are possible. *See Letter of B. Ollman to the Editors of THE WASHINGTON POST (May 8, 1978)* (suggesting that "the real test of what a teacher does in class is not what he says about what he does (for that allows various interpretations) but what he actually does in class"). R. 3.

37. After the words which are quoted in the Evans' and Novak's columns, Professor Ollman's article continues:

> I can only answer that in my view—a view which denies the fact/value distinction—a correct understanding of Marxism (as indeed of any body of scientific truths) leads automatically to its acceptance. I hasten to add that this is not reflected in my grading practices: non-Marxist students (*i.e.*, students who do not yet understand Marxism) do at least as well as the rest of the class given by bourgeois professors. [*sic*] Furthermore, I do not consider that I introduce more "politics" into my course than do other social science professors, or that I am more interested than they are in convincing students of the correctness of my interpretations.

38. We note that in this case Mr. Ollman took advantage of another recourse. The Washington Post published Mr. Ollman's letter to set his statements in his article in a fuller context. *See* Letter of B. Ollman to the Editors of The Washington Post (May 8, 1978). R. 3.

Of course, at some point the deletion or omission of proper context can be so egregious as to amount to misquotation. Omitting a negative word from a sentence with the result that that sentence has a meaning opposite to that which the author intended is a rather clear cut example of a misquotation.

son is merely the vigorous exposition of ideas to another. We therefore conclude that the column's statements concerning "indoctrination" constitute protected opinion.

Mr. Ollman also complains of the statement: "His candid writings avow his desire to use the classroom as an instrument for preparing what he calls the 'revolution.'" This statement, unlike the column's remarks about indoctrination, is stated without any interrogatory language to allow the reader to discount it as opinion. However, it is clear from the context that the statement represents Evans' and Novak's interpretation of Mr. Ollman's writing. And, like the charge of indoctrination, this statement does not have a well-defined meaning or admit of a method of proof or disproof. What to one person is a patently improper use of the classroom for political purposes may represent to another no more than the imparting of ideas, in the faith that ideas have consequences.

C

Finally, we turn to the most troublesome statement in the column.* In the third-to-last paragraph, an anonymous political science professor is quoted as saying: "Ollman has no status within the profession but is a pure and simple activist." The District Court interpreted this remark as a statement that Mr. Ollman "lack[ed] a reputation in his field as scholar." ...

Certainly a scholar's academic reputation among his peers is crucial to his or her career. Like the peripatetic philosophers of ancient Greece, modern scholars depend upon their reputation to enable them to pursue their chosen calling. We also acknowledge that at least one pre-*Gertz* case has held that the common-law privilege of fair comment does not extend protection to remarks which disparage one's status among one's peers. *See Cepeda v. Cowles Magazines and Broadcasting, Inc.*, 328 F.2d 869 (9th Cir.1964) (holding that, inter alia, remarks that a baseball player had "doghouse status" with the San Francisco Giants' hierarchy was not protected by fair comment).

We are of the view, however, that under the constitutionally based opinion privilege announced in *Gertz*, this quotation, under the circumstances before us, is protected. A confluence of factors leads us to this conclusion. First, as we have stated, inasmuch as the column appears on the Op-Ed page, the average reader will be influenced by the general understanding of the functions of such columns and read the remark to be opinion.[41] The identical quotation in a newspaper article purporting to publish facts or in an academic publication which purported to rate status within a given discipline would, of course, be quite another matter. But here we deal with statements by well-known, nationally syndicated columnists on the Op-Ed page of a newspaper, the well-recognized home of opinion and comment. In addition, the thrust of the column, taken as a whole, is to raise questions about Mr. Ollman's scholarship and intentions, not to state conclusively from Evans' and Novak's first-hand knowledge that Professor Ollman is not a scholar or that his colleagues do not regard him as such.

---

* The analysis in this portion of the opinion is concurred in only by Circuit Judges Tamm and Wilkey and Senior Circuit Judge MacKinnon.

41. Consistent with the point that an Op-Ed piece is in itself a signal to the reader that what is being read is opinion, the Supreme Court has very recently had occasion to remind us that the expression of editorial opinion "lies at the heart of First Amendment protection." *FCC v. League of Women Voters,* — U.S. — , 104 S.Ct. 3106, 3118, 82 L.Ed.2d 278 (1984). Speaking for the Court, Justice Brennan emphasized the editorial's crucial role in "arousing" citizens to reflect on the important issues of the day and stated that "[p]reserving the free expression of editorial opinion ... is part and parcel of 'our profound national commitment ... that debate on public issues should be uninhibited, robust, and wide-open.'" *Id.* (quoting *New York Times v. Sullivan*, 376 U.S. 254, 270, 84 S.Ct. 710, 721, 11 L.Ed.2d 666 (1964)).

Moreover, the anonymous professor's unflattering comment appears only after the columnists expressly state that Mr. Ollman is a professor at New York University, a highly respected academic institution, a fact which provides objective evidence of Mr. Ollman's "status." So too, the controversy itself was occasioned by Professor Ollman's nomination by the departmental search committee as chairman of an academic department at the University of Maryland, a fact stated in the column's opening paragraph which also plainly suggested to the average reader that Professor Ollman did in fact enjoy some considerable status in academia. Finally in this regard, the column expressly states that Professor Ollman's imminent ascension to the departmental chairmanship at Maryland was troubling only to a clear minority of academics. Thus, the charge of "no status" in this context would plainly appear to the average reader to be "rhetorical hyperbole" within the meaning of *Greenbelt*, and which in turn would lead the reader to treat the statement as one of opinion.[42]

We note especially in this respect that the anonymous academician quoted in the column goes on to say that he would not repeat his charge publicly, stating that: "[o]ur academic culture does not permit the raising of such questions." Thus, while Mr. Ollman's critic is asserting a proposition about Mr. Ollman, he is simultaneously implying

---

42. While generally agreeing with the methodological approach employed here, the dissent goes to some considerable length to argue that the statement is verifiable, such as by conducting a poll of all members of the American Political Science Association. That, however, is most assuredly an extraordinarily burdensome and utterly impracticable procedure in a field as huge and disparate as political science. Indeed, the fact that the anonymous statement did not purport to be linked to any such poll or other systematic inquiry into Mr. Ollman's reputation in the political science community suggests that the statement was an expression of opinion, not of fact. But at all events, the end result of any such poll is cloudy, as Judge Bork maintains and the dissent commendably admits. Indeed, the dissent suggests a rather limited office for this sort of inquiry, arguing that a poll or expert testimony "could surely establish that Ollman enjoys *some* reputation as an academic scholar...." Dissent at 4 (emphasis in original).

If that is what a poll could show, there is no need either to sacrifice First Amendment values or go to all the expense and trouble of canvassing the views of thousands of political scientists from Maine to California. Indeed, the irony of the dissent's approach is that the Evans and Novak column made it crystal clear to the reasonable reader that Ollman does enjoy "some reputation" in the political science community. As we have already seen, the article states at the very outset that Mr. Ollman is a professor at a distinguished university and has been recommended by a Faculty Search Committee to chair the department of a large and well-known state university. It is, of course, those passing on Ollman's credentials to step into a prestigious post at a major university who would have a pressing and important need to examine his professionalism and scholarship, as opposed to the armchair opinion of a solitary anonymous professor responding off the cuff to a columnist's inquiry. Those clearly stated indicia of professional success and standing overwhelmingly suggest to the reasonable reader that the statement is one of rhetorical hyperbole. *See also* concurring opinion of Bork, J., at 33–37.

The dissent refuses to accept the real-world, common-sense conclusion that the statement was, in context, rhetorical hyperbole, concluding that the article "could as well be understood to portray Ollman's prominence *as due solely to his vociferousness....*" Dissent at 5 (emphasis added). Surely this contention is itself utterly hyberbolic. An understanding derived from the article, fairly read as a whole, that Mr. Ollman is a mere vociferous organ of political Marxism and nothing more is at the least, entirely fanciful. In light of the well-known peer review process by which academic appointment and tenure decisions are made, the reasonable reader would most reasonably conclude that Ollman, whatever his politics, enjoyed a goodly measure of repute among scholars highly familiar with his work. It suspends belief to suggest that New York University and the University of Maryland have taken or proposed to take into the community of scholarship one whose reputation was grounded solely upon his vociferousness. The reasonable reader would, to the contrary, regard the anonymous professor's statement as an extravagant way of saying that he thought Mr. Ollman's work was without merit and that his assessment was not unique.

that, in the contemporary academic environment, no evidence can publicly be adduced to support it. Whether right or wrong, this admission by the anonymous political scientist would clearly tend to make the reader treat this proposition as opinion.

But most fundamentally, we are reminded that in the accommodation of the conflicting concerns reflected in the First Amendment and the law of defamation, the deep-seated constitutional values embodied in the Bill of Rights require that we not engage, without bearing clearly in mind the context before us, in a Talmudic parsing of a single sentence or two, as if we were occupied with a philosophical enterprise or linguistic analysis. Ours is a practical task, with elemental constitutional values of freedom looming large as we go about our work. And in that undertaking, we are reminded by *Gertz* itself of our duty "to assure to the freedoms of speech and press that 'breathing space' essential to their fruitful exercise." *Gertz, supra*, 418 U.S. at 342, 94 S.Ct. at 3008. For the contraction of liberty's "breathing space" can only mean inhibition of the scope of public discussion on matters of general interest and concern. The provision of breathing space counsels strongly against straining to squeeze factual content from a single sentence in a column that is otherwise clearly opinion. As the Ninth Circuit so succinctly put it, "[t]he court must consider all the words used, not merely a particular phrase or sentence." *Information Control Corp. v. Genesis One Computer Corp.*, ... 611 F.2d at 784.

IV

The judgment of the District Court is therefore

Affirmed.

. . .

BORK, CIRCUIT JUDGE, with whom WILKEY and GINSBURG, CIRCUIT JUDGES, and MACKINNON, SENIOR CIRCUIT JUDGE, join, concurring:

While I concur in the judgment of the court and in much of Judge Starr's scholarly exposition, I write separately because I do not think he has adequately demonstrated that all of the allegedly libelous statements at issue here can be immunized as expressions of opinion. The dissents, on the other hand, while acknowledging the importance of additional factors, seem actually premised on the idea that the law makes a clear distinction between opinions, which are not actionable as libel, and facts, which are. In my view, the law as enunciated by the Supreme Court imposes no such sharp dichotomy. Some lower courts have assumed, as do some members of this court, not only that this opinion vs. fact formula is controlling but that it is governed, at least primarily, by grammatical analysis. I think that incorrect. Any such rigid doctrinal framework is inadequate to resolve the sometimes contradictory claims of the libel laws and the freedom of the press.

This case illustrates that point. It arouses concern that a freshening stream of libel actions, which often seem as much designed to punish writers and publications as to recover damages for real injuries, may threaten the public and constitutional interest in free, and frequently rough, discussion. Those who step into areas of public dispute, who choose the pleasures and distractions of controversy, must be willing to bear criticism, disparagement, and even wounding assessments. Perhaps it would be better if disputation were conducted in measured phrases and calibrated assessments, and with strict avoidance of the ad hominem; better, that is, if the opinion and editorial pages of the public press were modeled on The Federalist Papers. But that is not the world in which we live, ever have lived, or are ever likely to know, and the law of the first amendment must not try to make public dispute safe and comfortable for all the participants.

That would only stifle the debate. In our world, the kind of commentary that the columnists Rowland Evans and Robert Novak have engaged in here is the coin in which controversialists are commonly paid.

...

...

II

There are several factors that convince me Ollman cannot maintain this action. These considerations are of the type that the Supreme Court and other courts have deemed important: the danger to first amendment freedoms and the functional meaning of the challenged statement as shown by its context and its qualities as recognizable rhetorical hyperbole. The factors here are: Ollman, by his own actions, entered a political arena in which heated discourse was to be expected and must be protected; the "fact" proposed to be tried is in truth wholly unsuitable for trial, which further imperils free discussion; the statement is not of the kind that would usually be accepted as one of hard fact and appeared in a context that further indicated it was rhetorical hyperbole.

A

Plaintiff Ollman, as will be shown, placed himself in the political arena and became the subject of heated political debate. That fact has significance in two ways. The first, and more conventional, point is that the existence of a political controversy is part of the total context that gives meaning to statements made about Ollman. When we read charges and countercharges about a person in the midst of such controversy we read them as hyperbolic, as part of the combat, and not as factual allegations whose truth we may assume. It will be seen, as the events are recounted, how true that is in Ollman's case.

My second point is less conventional, though by no means ruled out by case law as a next step in the evolution of doctrine in this troubling field. It is this: in order to protect a vigorous marketplace in political ideas and contentions, we ought to accept the proposition that those who place themselves in a political arena must accept a degree of derogation that others need not. Because this would represent a further development of the law I have argued it more fully than the first point. But it is not necessary to accept this proposition in order to accept the first point, that political controversy is part of the context that tends to show that some apparently factual assertions should be treated as rhetorical hyperbole and hence as opinions.

...

A hot public controversy erupted the day after Ollman's nomination for the chairmanship of the department was disclosed. Among the participants in the dispute, which was extensively covered by the news media, were the Republican Acting Governor of Maryland, two members of the university's board of regents, a state senator, a member of the Prince George's County council, the associate general secretary of the American Association of University Professors, the Washington Post columnist Richard Cohen, and the three Democratic candidates for governor. Ollman's nomination thus became an issue in the 1978 Maryland gubernatorial race. The debate about his nomination and politics received nationwide press coverage.

In the midst of this controversy, Ollman announced that he had begun to market a new board game called "Class Struggle," which he said he had been working on for seven years. He said, "This game will give our people [a] view of how our society works, and for whom." Players representing workers moved a little hammer around the board; those representing capitalists moved a little top hat. Players moved to the final confrontation—revolution. "'Not a violent overthrow,' Ollman emphasized, 'but a structural change.'" The Washington Post, Apr. 28, 1978. The Evans and Novak column appeared on May 4.

The president of the university rejected Ollman's appointment, and The Washington Post, in an editorial generally critical of the decision, said: "A teacher's politics may be his own business, but it becomes a legitimate criterion by which to judge his appointment when it calls into question his classroom intentions. In recent weeks, Mr. Ollman's public statements have not made his case more appealing. To many, his remarks have suggested that he is in fact more interested in polemics than in political science." The Washington Post, July 23, 1978, at C 6, col. 1.

The important point about all of this is that Ollman was not simply a scholar who was suddenly singled out by the press or by Evans and Novak. Whatever the merits of his scholarship, he was also a political man who publicly tried to forward his political goals. He had entered the political arena before he put himself forward for the department chairmanship. That candidacy merely widened the area within which he was known and raised for debate a topic of legitimate political concern, a debate which his further actions fueled. That being so, he must accept the banging and jostling of political debate, in ways that a private person need not, in order to keep the political arena free and vital.

· · ·

The concept of the public, political arena that I have employed has at least some of the same functional characteristics as the concept of a person who is a public figure for limited purposes. That similarity may prompt the objection that the public figure concept applies only to distinguish between negligence and actual malice for purposes of liability. That is, of course, an accurate statement of current doctrine, but I know of no case holding that the concept may not be put to the use proposed, to assist in deciding how much public bumping a person must accept as a risk of the controversies he chooses to engage in.

· · ·

[Omitted are several separate opinions, including a concurrence and partial dissents.]

WALD, CIRCUIT JUDGE, with whom CIRCUIT JUDGES EDWARDS and SCALIA join, dissenting in part.

I basically agree with the plurality's outline of the appropriate strategy for identifying absolutely privileged opinion and its judgment that most of the statements made by Evans and Novak about the plaintiff are non-actionable statements of opinion. However, in my mind the columnists' statement that "Ollman has no status within the profession, but is a pure and simple activist" is an assertion of fact for which its authors can be made to answer, consistent with the requirements of the first amendment, in a suit for libel.

In many areas of the law, the factual nature of statements about reputation is recognized and indeed taken for granted. Lay witnesses are generally allowed to testify as to someone's reputation in the community for veracity or violence, for example, although they cannot give their personal opinion as to those matters.... Expert witnesses are often asked in the course of their testimony whether other authors, scholars or practitioners are generally regarded as authorities in the field, and their own qualifications may be established or attacked on the basis of professional reputation. . . .

Similarly, as the plurality concedes, the law of libel has long recognized the basically factual nature of attacks on reputation. I do not dispute the plurality's assertion that the first amendment often demands modifications of the common law of libel so as to limit the chilling effect of potential civil liability on an "uninhibited, robust, and wide-open debate on public issues." . . . In particular, the first amendment demands that we evaluate the allegedly libelous statement in the context in which it appeared to determine whether it can claim the constitutional privilege for statements of opinion. Yet I find that a fair application of both the plurality's test and the approach suggested by Judge Bork in his concurrence indicates that the statement before us is more a statement of fact than of opinion.

The plurality would ask four questions about the particular statement at issue: (1) do the words have a "precise core of meaning"; (2) is the statement verifiable; (3) how do the immediate context — in this case the article — and (4) the broader context affect the likelihood that the statement will be read as an assertion of fact? Although Judge Bork calls for a more flexible, ad hoc balancing approach to the fact-opinion distinction, his analysis of this case strikes me as conceptually indistinguishable from the plurality's approach. I fully agree that the distinction between fact and opinion is rarely self-evident or exact and that we should not attempt to impose any mechanical set of categories on the complexities of libel litigation. Although the task may not always be an easy one, however, we are surely obliged to articulate some set of principles to guide the district court in determining which types of statements can give rise to a libel action.

Indeed, despite the plea for a case-by-case consideration of the "totality of circumstances," Judge Bork apparently recognizes precisely this obligation. After purporting to engage in an open-textured balancing of first amendment values, Judge Bork relies on three factors of his own in order to immunize libel defendants from suit. He reasons that (1) Ollman should be expected to endure the challenged statement because he placed himself in a public, political debate, (2) the factual nature of the "no status" statement is inherently unsuitable for jury determination, and (3) the functional meaning and general context of the statement indicate its rhetorical purpose. The first of these factors represents an unprecedented extension into the fact-opinion doctrine of the distinction between public and private officials for the purposes of defamation suits. The second two considerations merely restate the plurality's test. The challenged statement is surely capable of adjudication if it admits of a stable core of meaning and if Ollman's professional reputation is in fact verifiable. Similarly, the functional meaning or practical impact of the "no status" assertion can only be determined in light of the factual and social context surrounding the appellees' column.

In any event, I believe that the challenged statement is properly characterized as a factual assertion rather than a rhetorical hyperbole under either the majority's or Judge Bork's approach. The statement that Ollman has no status within his profession undoubtedly admits of a sufficiently ascertainable and stable core of meaning: a decisive plurality of his fellow political scientists do not regard him as a good scholar. That one might find a wide diversity of views among political scientists about Ollman's work and about what constitutes scholarly excellence in no way undermines the commonly understood meaning of a statement like this about reputation. The statement says to the ordinary reader that, however each individual scholar evaluates excellence, there is an overwhelming consensus that Ollman does not have it.

Furthermore, Ollman's scholarly reputation is adequately verifiable. One could, for instance, devise a poll of American Political Science Association members as to their opinion, on a scale of one to ten, of the scholarly value of Ollman's work. Testimony of prominent political scientists or other measures of reputation would also serve to verify or refute the statement about Ollman's reputation without sending the jury into a sea of speculation.

... Whatever their limits as truth finding devices, expert testimony or a poll could surely establish whether Ollman enjoys some reputation as an *academic scholar* as opposed to a mere activist—whether that scholarly reputation is supported by consensus or sharp disagreement among his colleagues. Given appropriate instruction by the trial judge, a jury is as well equipped to determine whether an individual has or has not established professional reputation in this context as it is in a host of others. Although I share Judge Bork's concern that juries may, in some defamation cases, tend to underemphasize the limits imposed by the first amendment, I cannot subscribe to his astonishing view that "[t]he *only* solution to the problem libel actions pose would appear to be close judicial scrutiny to ensure that cases about the types of speech and writing essential to a vigorous first amendment *do not reach the jury.*" *Id.* at p. 997 (emphasis added). Instead, I believe that any such problems should be remedied through careful supervision by the trial judge and vigorous appellate review, not through stripping the jury of its historic function merely because qualities such as "professional reputation" are difficult to adjudicate.

The plurality cites the statement that "[o]ur academic culture does not permit the raising of such questions" as a concession of non-verifiability by Evans and Novak and their source that should warn the reader not to accept the foregoing statement about reputation as one of fact. Op. of Starr, J., at p. 991. But to me—and I believe to the ordinary reader as well—the liberal professor's refusal to be cited publicly means simply that Ollman's writings are not *openly* attacked in the academic community as mere polemics. Moreover, the majority's implication that Ollman has no verifiable reputation—that there is no way of evaluating the conglomeration of his colleagues' opinions, public or private, of his work—is belied by the characterization of the political scientist quoted as one "whose scholarship and reputation as a liberal are well known," as well as by the complex procedures for hiring, evaluation and tenure decisions set up by academic institutions throughout the nation. As judges we are familiar as well with how prominently academic reputation and stature figures in judicial nominations, evaluations and confirmation proceedings.

The plurality readily concedes that a statement about one's professional reputation, even the very statement before us, might be deemed a factual assertion in a different context. Yet the majority concludes that the facts, noted in the article, that Ollman was at the time a professor at New York University and was the top candidate for the position of chairman of the political science department at the University of Maryland would undermine a reader's belief in the factual accuracy of the statement. *See* Op. of Starr, J., at p. 990 & n. 42. But as I read the article, these "facts" could as well be understood as an assertion that Ollman's prominence is due solely to vociferousness and is entirely out of proportion to his poor reputation as a scholar among his peers. Indeed, the article as a whole, while it purports merely to raise questions about Ollman's qualifications, promotes itself as a call to sanity and objectivity and away from mere polemics. Thus, the immediate context in which this statement was made does little to warn a reader to regard with skepticism what might otherwise appear to be an assertion of fact.

...

HARRY T. EDWARDS, CIRCUIT JUDGE, concurring in part and dissenting in part.

For the most part, I thoroughly agree with and I am happy to concur in Judge Starr's thoughtful and well-reasoned opinion. Unfortunately, I cannot fully subscribe to the result reached.

After agonizing over this case, I have finally concluded that it is untenable even to suggest that the statement "*Ollman has no status within the profession, but is a pure and simple activist*" is an absolutely privileged "opinion." Indeed, as a former member of the academic community, I am somewhat taken aback by the notion that one's reputation within the profession (which is *easily* verifiable) may be so freely and glibly libelled. I can find no meaningful case authority to convince me that the First Amendment is designed to condone such loose muckraking.

Had Evans and Novak said that, *in their view*, Ollman "appeared to be a person without real status within the profession," this might be a different case. But they went much further and cited another "well known" scholar to support a verifiable claim that Ollman *in fact* had "no status within the profession." I agree with Judge Wald that "the statement says to the ordinary reader [and to the sophisticated reader as well] that, however each individual scholar evaluates excellence, there is an overwhelming consensus that Ollman does not have it." This is not a privileged opinion.

Having reached this conclusion, I concur in part in Judge Starr's opinion and concur in full in Judge Wald's and Judge Scalia's partial dissents.

SCALIA, CIRCUIT JUDGE, with whom CIRCUIT JUDGES WALD and HARRY T. EDWARDS, join, dissenting in part.

More plaintiffs should bear in mind that it is a normal human reaction, after painstakingly examining and rejecting thirty invalid and almost absurd contentions, to reject the thirty-first contention as well, and make a clean sweep of the matter. I have no other explanation for the majority's affirmance of summary judgment dismissing what seems to me a classic and cooly crafted libel, Evans and Novak's disparagement of Ollman's professional reputation. Judge Wald's opinion has fully responded to the straightforward contention of the majority opinion that this disparagement should be regarded as a mere nonactionable statement of opinion. I write separately to survey in somewhat greater detail the concurrence's more scenic route to what turns out to be the same destination.

It seems to me that the concurrence embarks upon an exercise of, as it puts it, constitutional "evolution," with very little reason and with very uncertain effect upon the species. Existing doctrine provides ample protection against the entire list of horribles supposedly confronting the defenseless modern publicist:

—The need to give special scope to political rhetoric is already met by recognition that hyperbole is an expected form of expression in that context. If Evans and Novak had chosen to call Ollman a traitor to our nation, fair enough. No reasonable person would believe, in that context, that they really meant a violation of 18 U.S.C. §2381 (1982).... The concurrence correctly claims the defense of this doctrine for the "no status" assertion. Surely it did not mean that Ollman had no status—only that his regard in the profession was not *high*. But to say, as the concurrence does, that hyperbole excuses not merely the exaggeration but *the fact sought to be vividly conveyed by the exaggeration* is to mistake a freedom to enliven discourse for a freedom to destroy reputation. The libel that "Smith is an incompetent carpenter" is not converted into harmless and nonactionable word-play by merely embellishing it into the statement that "Smith is the worst carpenter this side of the Mississippi."

—The expectation that one who enters the "public, political arena," Bork op. at 1004, must be prepared to take a certain amount of "public bumping," *id.*, is already fulsomely assured by the *New York Times Co. v. Sullivan*, 376 U.S. 254, 84 S.Ct. 710, 11 L.Ed.2d 686 (1964), requirement of actual malice in the defamation of public figures....

...

... I distrust the more general risk of judicial subjectivity presented by the concurrence's creative approach to first amendment jurisprudence. It is an approach which embraces "a continuing evolution of doctrine," *id.* at 995,* not merely as a consequence of thoughtful perception that old cases were decided wrongly at the time they were rendered (*see, e.g., Brown v. Board of Education*, 347 U.S. 483, 74 S.Ct. 686, 98 L.Ed. 873 (1954)); and not even in response to a demonstrable, authoritatively expressed development of public values (*see, e.g., Roberts v. Louisiana*, 428 U.S. 325, 336 (1976) (plurality opinion)); but rather in reaction to judicially perceived "modern problems," Bork op. at 995, which require "evolution of the law in accordance with the deepest rationale of the first amendment," *id.* at 998. It seems to me that the identification of "modern problems" to be remedied is quintessentially legislative rather than judicial business—largely because it is such a subjective judgment; and that the remedies are to be sought through democratic change rather than through judicial pronouncement that the Constitution now prohibits what it did not prohibit before. The concurrence perceives a "modern problem" consisting of "a freshening stream of libel actions, which ... may threaten the public and constitutional interest in free, and frequently rough, discussion," *id.* at 993, and of claims for damages that are "quite capable of silencing political commentators forever," *id.* at 995. Perhaps that perception is correct, though it is hard to square with the explosion of communications in general, and political commentary in particular, in this "Media Age." But then again, perhaps those are right who discern a distressing tendency for our political commentary to descend from discussion of public issues to destruction of private reputations; who believe that, by putting some brake upon that tendency, defamation liability under existing standards not only does not impair but fosters the type of discussion the first amendment is most concerned to protect; and who view high libel judgments as no more than an accurate reflection of the vastly expanded damage that can be caused by media that are capable of holding individuals up to public obloquy from coast to coast and that reap financial rewards commensurate with that power. I do not know the answers to these questions, but I do know that it is frightening to think that the existence or nonexistence of a *constitutional* rule (the willfully false disparagement of professional reputation in the context of political commentary cannot be actionable) is to depend upon our ongoing personal assessments of such sociological factors. And not only is our cloistered capacity to identify "modern problems" suspect, but our ability to provide condign solutions through the rude means of constitutional prohibition is nonexistent. What a strange notion that the problem of excessive libel awards should be solved by permitting, in political debate, intentional destruction of reputation—rather than by placing a legislative limit upon the amount of libel recovery. It has not often been thought, by the way, that the press is among the least effective of legislative lobbyists.

---

* These remarks of Judge Bork, and some other remarks that Judge Scalia later quotes, are omitted in the editing of Judge Bork's opinion above. — Ed.

...

For the foregoing reasons, I join Judge Wald's dissent on the professional status point.

NOTES

(1) What seems to you to be the heart of the issue in *Ollman*?

Had Ollman prevailed in his suit, what would you expect to be the effect on the behavior of columnists and editors? What part of that effect would constitute a social loss, and what part would represent a social gain?

How much of the concern over liability in such a case, buried in the arguments about First Amendment values, lies in the belief that significant numbers of responsible publishers would face ruin if the decision went the other way? How much lies in fear about the uncertainty that would afflict insurers trying to set premiums for defamation insurance for publications that could be construed as statements of either "fact" or "opinion"?

(2) The Supreme Court's principal decision on the "fact/opinion" distinction is *Milkovich v. Lorain Journal Co.*, 497 U.S. 1 (1990). The case arose from language in a newspaper column that allegedly libeled a high school wrestling coach with respect to his testimony at a judicial hearing concerning an altercation at a wrestling meet where several people were injured. The phrase "the big lie" and the word "lie" appeared in headlines over the column, which also included the columnist's statement that the lesson that would be learned from the hearing by people who attended the wrestling meet was, "If you get in a jam, lie your way out." The columnist also said that anyone who was at the meet "knows in his heart that [the plaintiff coach and a school superintendent, who also testified at the hearing] lied at the hearing after each having given his solemn oath to tell the truth."

The majority, in an opinion by Chief Justice Rehnquist, concluded that a jury could have found the column to have contained defamatory assertions about a "fact" rather than an "opinion." The Chief Justice said that "[e]ven if [a] speaker states the facts upon which he bases his opinion, if those facts are either incorrect or incomplete, or if his assessment of them is erroneous, the statement may still imply a false assertion of a fact." He declared that "simply couching such statements in terms of opinion does not dispel these implications," saying that "the statement, 'In my opinion Jones is a liar,' can cause as much damage to reputation as the statement, 'Jones is a liar.'" By contrast, he said that it "would not be actionable" to say, "In my opinion Mayor Jones shows his abysmal ignorance by accepting the teachings of Marx and Lenin." *Id*. at 18–20.

Is the Chief Justice's interpretation of this group of hypotheticals persuasive?

(3) A state law decision on a labor controversy involved the word "scab," a traditional term of union opprobrium. The state case is *Steinhilber v. Alphonse*, 68 N.Y.2d 283, 501 N.E.2d 550, 508 N.Y.S.2d 901 (1986). The material sued upon was a recorded message on a union telephone ("It is with amazement I report to you, the good membership of this union that Louise "the scab" Steinhilber has been named secretary of the week by a local radio station … She lacks only three things to get ahead, talent, ambition, and initiative"), and a banner displayed during picketing activity ("#1 SCAB LOUISE STEINHILBER SUCKS"). In affirming a dismissal, the court of appeals took as a given that "[p]laintiff concededly was a 'scab' during [a] strike," and concluded:

To be sure, in another context, a flat statement that a person lacks talent or ambition or initiative might be viewed as a factual assertion, if considered under the first and second *Ollman* factors.... But, "even apparent statements of fact may assume the character of statements of opinion, and thus be privileged, when made in public debate, heated labor dispute, or other circumstances in which an 'audience may anticipate [the use] of epithets, fiery rhetoric or hyperbole'" (*Information Control Corp. v. Genesis One Computer Corp.*, 611 F.2d 781, 784 [9th Cir.].... Here, the inescapable conclusion from the verbal context of the entire message and all of the circumstances under which it was delivered is that the statement would be understood by the ordinary listener for what it is: a tasteless effort to lampoon plaintiff for her activities as a "scab", conduct which to the union was an unpardonable transgression.

—501 N.E.2d at 556.

Do you agree with this analysis? What do you see as the major weight in the social balance that overcomes the hurt to Steinhilber?

(4) Substitute an "m" for the "b" at the end of "scab" and do you have a defamatory term? The Colorado Supreme Court said that it depends on whether, in context, the statement in which the word is used "contains or implies a verifiable assertion of fact or can reasonably be understood as stating an actual fact." The context was a two part news feature concerning a "living will" kit that included a living will form, a medical directive form and other documents related to the implementation of living wills. One of the broadcasts included a commentary by a medical ethicist who said of the packet, "I think it's a scam." Although the court noted that the term scam is defined in the dictionary as "a fraudulent or deceptive act or operation," it thought that as the ethicist used it, it was "nothing more than a subjective judgment regarding the value of the ... packet, expressed in imaginative and hyperbolic terms."

The court took a similar view of the ethicist's assertion concerning purchasers of the $29.95 packet that "what they get back is they've been taken—is what it amounts to—totally taken." The court pointed out that the broadcast had juxtaposed "the disclosed facts that living will forms were available at little or no cost from local hospitals and libraries, that many medical ethicists were of the opinion that this form was all that was needed to implement a valid living will, and that [the plaintiff] charged $29.95 for its product." The court noted that the broadcast had begun by asking whether the packet was "worth it," and that "[t]he implication is that it is not." This implication, the court said, was "not a verifiable fact": "The worth of a given service or product is an inherently subjective measure which turns on myriad considerations and necessarily subjective economic, aesthetic, and personal judgments"—for example, the convenience of having various documents in the packet that might aid in implementing a living will. *NBC Subsidiary (KCNC-TV), Inc. v. The Living Will Center*, 879 P.2d 6, 11–14 (Colo. 1994).

(5) One of the most colorful presentations of the qualified privilege of fair comment and criticism appeared in a 1901 case, *Cherry v. Des Moines Leader*, 114 Iowa 298, 86 N.W. 323, in which a writer for the Odebolt Chronicle gave this description of a stage performance by the Cherry Sisters:

"Effie is an old jade of 50 summers, Jessie a frisky filly of 40, and Addie, the flower of the family, a capering monstrosity of 35. Their long skinny arms, equipped with talons at the extremities, swung mechanically, and anon waived frantically at the suffering audience. The mouths of their rancid features opened like caverns, and sounds like the wailings of damned souls issued therefrom. They pranced around the stage with a motion that suggested a cross between the *danse du ventre* and fox trot,—strange creatures with painted faces and hideous mien. Effie is spavined, Addie is stringhalt, and Jessie, the only one who showed her stockings, has legs with calves as classic in their outlines as the curves of a broom handle."

In affirming a directed verdict for the defendants, the court disagreed with the plaintiffs' argument that the question of malice, apparently in the sense of spite or ill will, should have been put to the jury:

> The evidence should raise a probability of malice, and be more consistent with its existence than its absence. When the occasion is privileged the presumption arises that the publication was bona fide and without malice, and it is incumbent on plaintiff to overcome this presumption. If, from defendant's point of view, strong words seemed to be justified, he is not to be held liable, unless the court can say that what he published was to some extent, at least, inconsistent with the theory of good faith. These rules are well settled, and need no citation of authorities in their support. One who goes upon the stage to exhibit himself to the public, or who gives any kind of a performance to which the public is invited, may be freely criticized. He may be held up to ridicule, and entire freedom of expression is guaranteed dramatic critics, provided they are not actuated by malice or evil purpose in what they write. Fitting strictures, sarcasm, or ridicule, even, may be used, if based on facts, without liability, in the absence of malice or wicked purpose. The comments, however, must be based on truth, or on what in good faith and upon probable cause is believed to be true, and the matter must be pertinent to the conduct that is made the subject of criticism.

> ...

> If there ever was a case justifying ridicule and sarcasm,—aye, even gross exaggeration,—it is the one now before us. According to the record, the performance given by the plaintiff and the company of which she was a member was not only childish, but ridiculous in the extreme. A dramatic critic should be allowed considerable license in such a case. The public should be informed as to the character of the entertainment, and, in the absence of proof of actual malice, the publication should be held privileged.

(6) A famous literary lawsuit involved two noted writers. Mary McCarthy, appearing on the Dick Cavett Show on public television, said that Lillian Hellman was "tremendously overrated, a bad writer, and a dishonest writer." To Cavett's inquiry, "What is dishonest about her?," McCarthy replied, "Everything. But I said once in some interview that every word she writes is a lie, including 'and' and 'the.'" McCarthy defended against Hellman's libel action, in part, with the argument that her remark was a statement of opinion. Would you grant her summary judgment?

(7) Statistics for the first decade of the 21st century indicated that media defendants had become steadily more successful in defamation actions. From 2000 to 2005, their rate of winning cases increased to 53.8 percent from 36.3 percent in the 1980s and 40.2 percent in the 1990s. According to a report of the Media Law Resource Center, there were just 14 trials in 2005 on "libel, privacy and other related claims based on the gathering and publication of information," and the media defendants won half of those trials. This total of 14—the recent annual average—was down from an annual average of 27 trials in the 1980s. The president of the organization Media/Professional commented

that the media was "getting smarter in terms of deciding what cases to take to trial and what cases to settle." However, other observers stressed that the cost of defending trials was "about 80% of the expenses for media insurers," and that "the cost of defending claims is going up." Moreover, although the pricing of media insurance was "extremely stable," media insurers said that an emerging concern for them was rising numbers of claims for infringement of intellectual property. See Gloria Gonzalez, *Media winning more libel cases*, Bus. Ins., Mar. 27, 2006, at 3 & 20.

§ 15.02 Privacy and Publicity Rights

PROBLEM

News reports quoted Marion G. (Pat) Robertson, a candidate for the 1988 Republican presidential nomination, as saying that it was "outrageous" and "reprehensible" to publish the fact that his first child was conceived out of wedlock and that he then had misrepresented his wedding date to "protect his family." Robertson said that "to intrude into a man's family life and to try and hurt a person's wife and children is outrageous."[a]

What are the chances that Robertson would win a tort suit against a newspaper that published factual stories on these points?

TIME, INC. v. HILL
United States Supreme Court
385 U.S. 374, 87 S. Ct. 534, 17 L. Ed. 2d 456 (1967)

Harold R. Medina, Jr., New York City, for appellant.

Richard M. Nixon, New York City, for appellee.

MR. JUSTICE BRENNAN delivered the opinion of the Court.

The question in this case is whether appellant, publisher of *Life Magazine*, was denied constitutional protections of speech and press by the application by the New York courts of §§ 50–51 of the New York Civil Rights Law, McKinney's Consol. Laws, c. 6[1] to

----

a. *Robertson Assails "Outrageous" Reports*, Wash. Post, Oct. 9, 1987, at A1.

1. The ... text of the New York Civil Rights Law §§ 50–51 is as follows:

§ 50. *Right of privacy*

A person, firm or corporation that uses for advertising purposes, or for the purposes of trade, the name, portrait or picture of any living person without having first obtained the written consent of such person, or if a minor of his or her parent or guardian, is guilty of a misdemeanor.

§ 51. *Action for injunction and for damages*

Any person whose name, portrait or picture is used within this state for advertising purposes or for the purposes of trade without the written consent first obtained as above provided may maintain an equitable action in the supreme court of this state against the person, firm or corporation so using his name, portrait or picture, to prevent and restrain the use thereof; and may also sue and recover damages for any injuries sustained by reason of such use and if the defendant shall have knowingly used such person's name, portrait or picture in such manner as is forbidden or declared to be unlawful by the last section, the jury, in its discretion, may award exemplary damages....

award appellee damages on allegations that LIFE falsely reported that a new play portrayed an experience suffered by appellee and his family.

The article appeared in LIFE in February, 1955. It was entitled "True Crime Inspires Tense Play," with the subtitle, "The ordeal of a family trapped by convicts gives Broadway a new thriller, 'The Desperate Hours.'" The text of the article reads as follows:

> Three years ago Americans all over the country read about the desperate ordeal of the James Hill family, who were held prisoners in their home outside Philadelphia by three escaped convicts. Later they read about it in Joseph Hayes's novel, *The Desperate Hours*, inspired by the family's experience. Now they can see the story re-enacted in Hayes's Broadway play based on the book, and next year will see it in his movie, which has been filmed but is being held up until the play has a chance to pay off.
>
> The play, directed by Robert Montgomery and expertly acted, is a heart-stopping account of how a family rose to heroism in a crisis. LIFE photographed the play during its Philadelphia tryout, transported some of the actors to the actual house where the Hills were besieged. On the next page scenes from the play are re-enacted on the site of the crime.

The pictures on the ensuing two pages included an enactment of the son being "roughed up" by one of the convicts, entitled "brutish convict," a picture of the daughter biting the hand of a convict to make him drop a gun, entitled "daring daughter," and one of the father throwing his gun through the door after a "brave try" to save his family is foiled.

The James Hill referred to in the article is the appellee. He and his wife and five children involuntarily became the subjects of a front-page news story after being held hostage by three escaped convicts in their suburban, Whitemarsh, Pennsylvania, home for 19 hours on September 11–12, 1952. The family was released unharmed. In an interview with newsmen after the convicts departed, appellee stressed that the convicts had treated the family courteously, had not molested them, and had not been at all violent. The convicts were thereafter apprehended in a widely publicized encounter with the police which resulted in the killing of two of the convicts. Shortly thereafter the family moved to Connecticut. The appellee discouraged all efforts to keep them in the public spotlight through magazine articles or appearances on television.

In the spring of 1953, Joseph Hayes' novel, *The Desperate Hours*, was published. The story depicted the experience of a family of four held hostage by three escaped convicts in the family's suburban home. But, unlike Hill's experience, the family of the story suffer violence at the hands of the convicts; the father and son are beaten and the daughter subjected to a verbal sexual insult.

The book was made into a play, also entitled *The Desperate Hours*, and it is LIFE's article about the play which is the subject of appellee's action. The complaint sought damages under §§ 50–51 on allegations that the LIFE article was intended, to, and did, give the impression that the play mirrored the Hill family's experience, which, to the knowledge of defendant " ... was false and untrue." Appellant's defense was that the article was "a subject of legitimate news interest," "a subject of general interest and of value and concern to the public" at the time of publication, and that it was "published in good faith without any malice whatsoever...." A motion to dismiss the complaint for substantially these reasons was made at the close of the case and was denied by the trial judge on the ground that the proofs presented a jury question as to the truth of the article.

The jury awarded appellee $50,000 compensatory and $25,000 punitive damages. On appeal the Appellate Division of the Supreme Court ordered a new trial as to damages but sustained the jury verdict of liability. The court said as to liability:

> Although the play was fictionalized, LIFE's article portrayed it as a reenactment of the Hills' experience. It is an inescapable conclusion that this was done to advertise and attract further attention to the play, and to increase present and future magazine circulation as well. It is evident that the article cannot be characterized as a mere dissemination of news, nor even an effort to supply legitimate newsworthy information in which the public had, or might have a proper interest.

18 A.D.2d 485, 489, 240 N.Y.S.2d 286, 290. At the new trial on damages, a jury was waived and the court awarded $30,000 compensatory damages without punitive damages.

The New York Court of Appeals affirmed the Appellate Division "on the majority and concurring opinions at the Appellate Division," two judges dissenting....

[Omitted is a discussion of applicable state case law.]

... We hold that the constitutional protections for speech and press preclude the application of the New York statute to redress false reports of matters of public interest in the absence of proof that the defendant published the report with knowledge of its falsity or in reckless disregard of the truth.

The guarantees for speech and press are not the preserve of political expression or comment upon public affairs, essential as those are to healthy government. One need only pick up any newspaper or magazine to comprehend the vast range of published matter which exposes persons to public view, both private citizens and public officials. Exposure of the self to others in varying degrees is a concomitant of life in a civilized community. The risk of this exposure is an essential incident of life in a society which places a primary value on freedom of speech and of press.... We have no doubt that the subject of the LIFE article, the opening of a new play linked to an actual incident, is a matter of public interest. "The line between the informing and the entertaining is too elusive for the protection of ... [freedom of the press]." *Winters v. People of State of New York*, 333 U.S. 507, 510, 68 S.Ct. 665, 667, 92 L.Ed. 840. Erroneous statement is no less inevitable in such a case than in the case of comment upon public affairs, and in both, if innocent or merely negligent, " ... it must be protected if the freedoms of expression are to have the 'breathing space' that they 'need ... to survive'...." *New York Times Co. v. Sullivan*,.... We create a grave risk of serious impairment of the indispensable service of a free press in a free society if we saddle the press with the impossible burden of verifying to a certainty the facts associated in news articles with a person's name, picture or portrait, particularly as related to nondefamatory matter. Even negligence would be a most elusive standard, especially when the content of the speech itself affords no warning of prospective harm to another through falsity. A negligence test would place on the press the intolerable burden of guessing how a jury might assess the reasonableness of steps taken by it to verify the accuracy of every reference to a name, picture or portrait.

In this context, sanctions against either innocent or negligent misstatement would present a grave hazard of discouraging the press from exercising the constitutional guarantees. Those guarantees are not for the benefit of the press so much as for the benefit of all of us. A broadly defined freedom of the press assures the maintenance of our political system and an open society. Fear of large verdicts in damage suits for innocent or merely negligent misstatement, even fear of the expense involved in their defense, must inevitably cause publishers to "steer ... wider of the unlawful zone," *New York Times Co. v. Sullivan*....

But the constitutional guarantees can tolerate sanctions against *calculated* falsehood without significant impairment of their essential function. We held in *New York Times* that calculated falsehood enjoyed no immunity in the case of alleged defamation of a public official concerning his official conduct. Similarly, calculated falsehood should enjoy no immunity in the situation here presented us....

We find applicable here the standard of knowing or reckless falsehood, not through blind application of *New York Times Co. v. Sullivan*, relating solely to libel actions by public officials, but only upon consideration of the factors which arise in the particular context of the application of the New York statute in cases involving private individuals. This is neither a libel action by a private individual nor a statutory action by a public official. Therefore, although the First Amendment principles pronounced in *New York Times* guide our conclusion, we reach that conclusion only by applying these principles in this discrete context. It therefore serves no purpose to distinguish the facts here from those in *New York Times*. Were this a libel action, the distinction which has been suggested between the relative opportunities of the public official and the private individual to rebut defamatory charges might be germane. And the additional state interest in the protection of the individual against damage to his reputation would be involved.... Moreover, a different test might be required in a statutory action by a public official, as opposed to a libel action by a public official or a statutory action by a private individual. Different considerations might arise concerning the degree of "waiver" of the protection the State might afford. But the question whether the same standard should be applicable both to persons voluntarily and involuntarily thrust into the public limelight is not here before us.

II

Turning to the facts of the present case, the proofs reasonably would support either a jury finding of innocent or merely negligent misstatement by LIFE, or a finding that LIFE portrayed the play as a reenactment of the Hill family's experience reckless of the truth or with actual knowledge that the portrayal was false. The relevant testimony is as follows:

Joseph Hayes, author of the book, also wrote the play. The story theme was inspired by the desire to write about "true crime" and for years before writing the book, he collected newspaper clippings of stories of hostage incidents. His story was not shaped by any single incident, but by several, including incidents which occurred in California, New York, and Detroit. He said that he did not consciously portray any member of the Hill family, or the Hill family's experience, although admitting that "in a very direct way" the Hill experience "triggered" the writing of the book and the play.

The LIFE article was prepared at the direction and under the supervision of its entertainment editor, Prideaux. He learned of the production of the play from a news story. The play's director, Robert Montgomery, later suggested to him that its interesting stage setting would make the play a worthwhile subject for an article in LIFE. At about the same time, Prideaux ran into a friend of author Hayes, a free-lance photographer, who told Prideaux in casual conversation that the play had a "substantial connection with a true-life incident of a family being held by escaped convicts near Philadelphia." As the play was trying out in Philadelphia, Prideaux decided to contact the author. Hayes confirmed that an incident somewhat similar to the play had occurred in Philadelphia, and agreed with Prideaux to find out whether the former Hill residence would be available for the shooting of pictures for a LIFE article. Prideaux then met with Hayes in Philadelphia where he saw the play and drove with Hayes to the former Hill residence to test its suitability for a picture story. Neither then nor thereafter did Prideaux question Hayes about the extent to which the play was based on the Hill incident. "A specific question of that nature was never asked, but a discussion of the play itself, what the play was about, in the light of my own knowledge of what the true incident was about, confirmed in my mind beyond any doubt that there was a relationship, and Mr. Hayes' presence at this whole negotiation was tacit proof of that."

Prideaux sent photographers to the Hill residence for location photographs of scenes of the play enacted in the home, and proceeded to construct the text of the article. In his "story file" were several news clippings about the Hill incident which revealed its nonviolent character, and a New York Times article by Hayes in which he stated that the play "was based on various news stories," mentioning incidents in New York, California, Detroit and Philadelphia.

Prideaux's first draft made no mention of the Hill name except for the caption of one of the photographs. The text related that a true story of a suburban Philadelphia family had "sparked off" Hayes to write the novel, that the play was a "somewhat fictionalized" account of the family's heroism in time of crisis. Prideaux's research assistant, whose task it was to check the draft for accuracy, put a question mark over the words "somewhat fictionalized." Prideaux testified that the question mark "must have been" brought to his attention, although he did not recollect having seen it. The draft was also brought before the copy editor, who, in the presence of Prideaux, made several changes in emphasis and substance. The first sentence was changed to focus on the Hill incident, using the family's name; the novel was said to have been "inspired" by that incident, and the play was referred to as a "re-enactment." The words "somewhat fictionalized" were deleted.

Prideaux labeled as "emphatically untrue" defense counsel's suggestion during redirect examination that from the beginning he knew that the play had no relationship to the Hill incident apart from being a hostage incident. Prideaux admitted that he knew the play was "between a little bit and moderately fictionalized," but stated that he thought beyond doubt that the important quality, the "heart and soul" of the play, was the Hill incident.

The jury might reasonably conclude from this evidence — particularly that the New York Times article was in the story file, that the copy editor deleted "somewhat fictionalized" after the research assistant questioned its accuracy, and that Prideaux admitted that he knew the play was "between a little bit and moderately fictionalized" — that LIFE knew the falsity of, or was reckless of the truth in, stating in the article that "the story reenacted" the Hill family's experience. On the other hand, the jury might reasonably predicate a finding of innocent or only negligent misstatement on the testimony that a statement was made to Prideaux by the free-lance photographer that linked the play to an incident in Philadelphia, that the author Hayes cooperated in arranging for the availability of the former Hill home, and that Prideaux thought beyond doubt that the "heart and soul" of the play was the Hill incident.[11]

III

We do not think, however, that the instructions confined the jury to a verdict of liability based on a finding that the statements in the article were made with knowledge of their falsity or in reckless disregard of the truth. The jury was instructed that liability

---

11. Where either result finds reasonable support in the record it is for the jury, not for this Court, to determine whether there was knowing or reckless falsehood....

could not be found under §§ 50–51 "merely because of some incidental mistake of fact, or some incidental incorrect statement," and that a verdict of liability could rest only on findings that (1) LIFE published the article, "not to disseminate news, but was using plaintiffs' names, in connection with a fictionalized episode as to plaintiffs' relationship to *The Desperate Hours*"; the Court variously restated this "fictionalization" requirement in terms such as whether appellant "altered or changed the true facts concerning plaintiffs' relationship to *The Desperate Hours*, so that the article, as published, constituted substantially fiction or a fictionalized version...," whether the article constituted "fiction," or was "fictionalized"; and that (2) the article was published to advertise the play or "for trade purposes." This latter purpose was variously defined as one "to amuse, thrill, astonish or move the reading public so as to increase the circulation of the magazine or for some other material benefit," "to increase circulation or enhance the standing of the magazine with its readers," and "for the publisher's profits through increased circulation, induced by exploitation of the plaintiffs."

The court also instructed the jury that an award of punitive damages was justified if the jury found that the appellant falsely connected appellee to the play "knowingly or through failure to make a reasonable investigation," adding "You do not need to find that there was any actual ill will or personal malice toward the plaintiffs if you find a reckless or wanton disregard of the plaintiffs' rights."

Appellee argues that the instructions to determine whether LIFE "altered or changed" the true facts, and whether, apart from incidental errors, the article was a "substantial fiction" or a "fictionalized version" were tantamount to instructions that the jury must find that LIFE knowingly falsified the facts. We do not think that the instructions bear that interpretation, particularly in light of the marked contrast in the instructions on compensatory and punitive damages. The element of "knowingly" is mentioned only in the instruction that punitive damages must be supported by a finding that LIFE falsely connected the Hill family with the play "knowingly or through failure to make a reasonable investigation." Moreover, even as to punitive damages, the instruction that such damages were justified on the basis of "failure to make a reasonable investigation" is an instruction that proof of negligent misstatement is enough, and we have rejected the test of negligent misstatement as inadequate. Next, the trial judge plainly did not regard his instructions as limiting the jury to a verdict of liability based on a finding of knowing or reckless falsity, he denied appellant's motion to dismiss after the close of the evidence because he perceived that it was for the jury to find "whether the LIFE article was true or whether an inference could be obtained from reading it that it was not true." This implies a view that "fictionalization" was synonymous with "falsity" without regard to knowledge or even negligence, except for the purpose of an award of punitive damages....

The requirement that the jury also find that the article was published "for trade purposes," as defined in the charge, cannot save the charge from constitutional infirmity. "That books, newspapers, and magazines are published and sold for profit does not prevent them from being a form of expression whose liberty is safeguarded by the First Amendment." *Joseph Burstyn, Inc. v. Wilson*, 343 U.S. 495, 501–502, 72 S.Ct. 777, 780, 96 L.Ed. 1098....

· · ·

The judgment of the Court of Appeals is set aside and the case is remanded for further proceedings not inconsistent with this opinion.

It is so ordered.

[Omitted are the concurring opinions of Justices Black and Douglas and Justice Harlan's separate opinion, concurring and dissenting.]

MR. JUSTICE FORTAS, with whom THE CHIEF JUSTICE and MR. JUSTICE CLARK join, dissenting.

... The Court today does not repeat the ringing words of so many of its members on so many occasions in exaltation of the right of privacy. Instead, it reverses a decision under the New York "Right of Privacy" statute because of the "failure of the trial judge to instruct the jury that a verdict of liability could be predicated only on a finding of knowing or reckless falsity in the publication of the LIFE article." In my opinion, the jury instructions, although they were not a textbook model, satisfied this standard.

In the first place, the Court does not adequately deal with the fact that the jury returned a verdict for exemplary or punitive damages, under special instructions dealing with them, as well as for compensatory damages. As to exemplary damages, the jury was specifically instructed that these might be awarded "only" if the jury found from the evidence that the defendant "falsely connected plaintiffs with *The Desperate Hours*, and that this was done knowingly or through failure to make a reasonable investigation." The jury was then informed that "You do not need to find that there was any actual ill will or personal malice toward the plaintiffs *if you find a reckless or wanton disregard of the plaintiffs' rights*." (Emphasis supplied.) The jury awarded appellee $50,000 compensatory and $25,000 punitive damages. The judgment was reversed solely on the quantum of damages, the Appellate Division sustaining the finding of liability for both compensatory and exemplary damages. The Appellate Division's conclusion was that the award of damages was excessive, and it criticized the admission of certain evidence as improperly tending to cause the jury to return inflated damages. In subsequent proceedings before the trial court on assessment of damages, a jury was waived by stipulation of the parties, the case proceeded to reassessment of damages and the judge fixed the amount of damages at $30,000, compensatory only. Judgment thereupon was affirmed by the Court of Appeals. It is this judgment that is before us—namely, jury findings of liability based on instructions covering both exemplary and compensatory damages, and an award stated to be for compensatory damages alone.

The Court refers only to that part of the instructions as to exemplary damages which speaks in terms of the "failure to make a reasonable investigation," and condemns it as permitting a verdict based solely on "negligent misstatement." I respectfully submit that the instruction cannot fairly be so read. The instruction requires the jury to find both that (1) defendant "falsely connected" plaintiffs with the play, and (2) did so knowingly or through failure to make a reasonable investigation. This is certainly a charge satisfying the Court's requirement that "a verdict of liability could be predicated only on a finding of knowing or reckless falsity in the publication of the LIFE article." An error in the course of investigation might be mere negligent misstatement. Failure to make a reasonable investigation is something else. The standard of a "reasonable investigation" is certainly a minimum yardstick by which to measure the liability of publishers. It is certainly not incompatible with the full flavor of the First Amendment and disregard of this standard in the circumstances is recklessness. It might well be that what constitutes an adequate basis for a jury finding of failure to make a reasonable investigation would differ, for example, in the case of a daily newspaper as compared with a feature magazine. But here no such problem arises. The truth was in a folder on the desk of the author of the story. It was deliberately disregarded by his editor. Lead time on the story was three months.

In addition, however, even if appellee had to rely only upon the instructions to the jury on compensatory damages, I do not agree that we should set aside the jury verdict and reverse the New York Court of Appeals. Such drastic action—the reversal of a jury verdict by this remote Court—is justified by the Court on the ground that the standard of liability on which the jury was instructed contravenes the Fifth Amendment. But a jury instruction is not abracadabra. It is not a magical incantation, the slightest deviation from which will break the spell. Only its poorer examples are formalistic codes recited by a trial judge to please appellate masters. At its best, it is simple, rugged communication from a trial judge to a jury of ordinary people, entitled to be appraised in terms of its net effect. Instructions are to be viewed in this commonsense perspective, and not through the remote and distorting knothole of a distant appellate fence. Read in this perspective, the core of the instructions here on compensatory damages—even if we disregard the fact that the jury found liability under the more exacting instructions relating to exemplary damages—was sufficient to meet the majority's test. The gravamen of the court's charge, repeated *three times* in virtually the same words, was the following:

> It is for you to determine whether, in publishing the article, the defendant Time, Incorporated *altered* or *changed* the true facts concerning plaintiffs' relationship to *The Desperate Hours*, so that the article, as published, constituted substantially a fiction or *fictionalized version* for trade purposes.... (Emphasis supplied.)

The jury was also instructed that "Before the plaintiffs can be entitled to a verdict ... you must find that the statements concerning the plaintiffs in the article *constituted fiction*, as compared with news, or matters which were newsworthy." (Emphasis supplied.) With all respect, I submit that this is close enough to this Court's insistence upon "knowing or reckless falsity" as to render a reversal arbitrary and unjustified. If the defendant *altered* or *changed* the true facts so that the article as published was a *fictionalized* version, this, in my judgment, was a knowing or reckless falsity. "Alteration" or "change" denotes a positive act—not a negligent or inadvertent happening. "Fictionalization" and "fiction" to the ordinary mind mean so departing from fact and reality as to be *deliberately* divorced from the fact—not merely in detail but in general and pervasive impact. The English language is not so esoteric as to permit serious consequences to turn upon a supposed difference between the instructions to the jury and this Court's formulation. Nor is the First Amendment in such delicate health that it requires or permits this kind of surgery, the net effect of which is not only an individual injustice, but an encouragement to recklessness and careless readiness to ride roughshod over the interests of others.

...

NOTES

(1) What analytical similarities are there between the problem of culpability in *Time Inc. v. Hill* and that in a conventional negligence case like *LaPlante*, supra § 4.01[A]? Why shouldn't this case be resolved like any negligence action, perhaps subject to a ceiling or prohibition on the award of punitive damages?

(2) What is the difference between the tort that Hill sought to establish and "defamation"? Is the principal injury in *Hill* one to "reputation" or "personality"? Or is it practically useful to make that distinction?

If *Hill* is not a "libel action," as Justice Brennan is at pains to point out, why should the court apply to it the same standards that are used in libel actions? Does Brennan persuasively rationalize his application of the "actual malice" test?

(3) The Supreme Court affirmed a plaintiff's jury verdict in a "false light" privacy case, while reading a lecture on the meaning of malice to the court of appeals in *Cantrell v. Forest City Publishing Co.*, 419 U.S. 245 (1974). The case involved a Sunday magazine feature about the impact on a family of the loss of its husband and father in a bridge collapse. The writer made numerous, knowingly false statements about the family's attitudes and the living conditions in their home. The nature of these misrepresentations, which were alleged to subject the plaintiffs to shame and humiliation, perhaps distinguishes the case factually from that of the Hills, whom the *Life* story arguably presented in a light more heroic than the historical facts warranted. The trial court allowed a compensatory award but struck a demand for punitive damages, on the basis that there was no evidence that the story was presented "maliciously within the legal definition of that term." The court of appeals read this conclusion as meaning there was no "actual malice" under the *Times-Hill* standard, and thus held that there should have been directed verdicts for all defendants. The Supreme Court found erroneous this reading of the trial court's legal rulings. Justice Stewart distinguished the "common-law 'malice'" necessary to support a punitive damage award—which he found it clear was what the trial judge had thought lacking in the plaintiffs' proof—from *Times-Hill* "actual malice." He thus thought it quite consistent to justify a compensatory award while at the same time denying punitive damages.

(4) Does Justice Brennan in *Hill* give sufficient consideration to the entrepreneurial aspects of journalism, specifically to the fact that stories like that of the Hills sell magazines? It may be pointed out in this connection that the New York Civil Rights statute involved in *Hill* represented a response to a case in which the New York Court of Appeals denied recovery in a common law action for direct commercial appropriation of a personal likeness. This was *Roberson v. Rochester Folding Box Co.*, 171 N.Y. 538, 64 N.E. 442 (1902), in which the defendant flour miller circulated 25,000 lithographic prints of the plaintiff's likeness as advertisements bearing the words "Flour of the Family." Although the statute has served as the basis for many lawsuits based on direct use of one's name or picture for advertising purposes, it has also evolved into a vehicle for actions for disclosing private facts, see the Note immediately following on the publication of truthful material, as well as for the "fictionalization" claim in *Time, Inc. v. Hill*. At least with respect to the application of the New York statute to publications that invade the private lives of persons who have not voluntarily sought the spotlight, is it not relevant that mass media employ commercial advertising techniques to create images for themselves as vehicles for entertainment? Given this image-making, why should constitutional doctrine provide a test for professional misconduct that is more liberal for journalists than for practitioners in other lines of work?

SPECIAL NOTE ON THE PUBLICATION
OF TRUTHFUL MATERIAL

Would you ever allow an action against a news medium for the publication of truthful material, if the facts were of a kind that an individual had taken measures to conceal, and had no bearing on the political process in the conventional use of that term? What if the publication concerned events that had happened twenty years or more before, and the plaintiff had since built a new life?

Two classic cases on the publication of truth are *Melvin v. Reid*, 112 Cal. App. 285, 297 P. 91 (1931), and *Sidis v. F-R Pub. Corp.*, 113 F.2d 806 (2d Cir.), *cert. denied*, 311

U.S. 711 (1940). In *Melvin*, the court imposed liability in favor of a woman, then living quietly as a housewife, against the makers of a motion picture who used her correct name in portraying unsavory events in which she had played a role twenty years previously. In *Sidis*, the court denied recovery to a man who had been a child math prodigy, suffered several nervous breakdowns, and became something of a recluse. Sidis had clearly shunned publicity—although he evidently did consent to be interviewed for the mercilessly accurate portrait that was the subject of the suit. What public and private interests must be balanced in these situations? Are the cases distinguishable? Would they be if Sidis had not consented to be interviewed, and the story about him had been derived entirely from interviews with his friends and neighbors?

The plaintiff in a more recent case, the student body president at a California community college, who had undergone gender corrective surgery, recovered for a paper's publication of that fact after events in the wake of her allegations that college administrators had misused student funds. The newspaper's columnist put it this way: "More Education Stuff: The students at the College of Alameda will be surprised to learn their student body president, Toni Diaz, is no lady, but is in fact a man whose real name is Antonio." No information had reached the public about Diaz's sex-change operation during her election campaign for the student presidency. *Diaz v. Oakland Tribune, Inc.*, 139 Cal. App. 3d 118, 188 Cal. Rptr. 762 (1983).

What would be the strongest argument the newspaper could make against requiring it to pay the total of $250,000 compensatory damages and $525,000 punitive damages awarded to the plaintiff?

Another case involving publication of truthful material inspired disagreement between Louisiana courts. At issue was a feature called "Page from Our Past," which reproduced front pages from old editions of the defendant newspaper. One such reproduction contained an article referring to 25-year-old criminal convictions of brothers who, after serving penitentiary time and being pardoned, had "married, raised families, and ... been law-abiding citizens to this day." The state appellate court, in arguing for the imposition of liability, declared that to deny recovery "would mean that regardless of the passage of time and a complete rehabilitation, persons once convicted or accused of crimes must be subject to constant anxiety that the matter may resurface at the whim of a newspaper publisher or a television newscast director." *Roshto v. Hebert*, 413 So.2d 927, 933 (La. Ct. App. 1982). But Justice Lemmon, writing for the Louisiana Supreme Court in a decision that reversed the appellate court's judgment for the plaintiffs, commented that "[t]he particular form of invasion of privacy in this case is complicated by the implication of federal constitutional guarantees under the First Amendment." Acknowledging that reproduction of the article was "arguably insensitive or careless," he wrote that "the passage of a considerable length of time after the pertinent event does not of itself convert a public matter into a private one." In denying recovery, he concluded that "more than insensitivity or simple carelessness is required for the imposition of liability ... when the publication is truthful, accurate and non-malicious." *Rushto v. Hebert*, 439 So.2d 428, 431–32 (La. 1983).

NOTES

(1) The specialized problem of the privacy of rape victims has received the attention of the Supreme Court. In *Cox Broadcasting Corp. v. Cohn*, 420 U.S. 469 (1975), the court reversed a judgment in favor of the father of a rape victim who sued on the basis of a state statute that made it a misdemeanor to publish or broadcast the name or iden-

tity of rape victims. Justice White's opinion emphasized the fact that the defendant had published information that was on the public record.

In its later decision in *Florida Star v. B.J.F.*, 491 U.S. 524 (1989), the Court applied the First Amendment to bar a suit against a newspaper that published the name of a victim of sexual assault by an unknown assailant. The newspaper got the plaintiff's name from a report that the sheriff's department placed in its press room, to which it did not restrict access. Justice Marshall wrote for the Court that "where the government has made certain information publicly available, it is highly anomalous to sanction persons other than the source of its release." *Id.* at 535.

(2) Suppose that a state law requires the sealing of records of the names of the natural parents of adopted children. Should disclosure of a natural parent's name, discovered by means other than sealed court files, be actionable for "invasion of privacy"?

(3) An interesting modern challenge to privacy law appears in the practice of "outing," the unconsented revelation of a person's sexual orientation. Those who engage in "outing" rationalize that, with particular reference to "outed" persons in the entertainment field, the practice attacks homophobia and "provid[es] role models." Note, *Celebrity Privacy Rights and Free Speech: Recalibrating Tort Remedies and "Outed" Celebrities*, 32 Harv. Civ. R.-Civ. Lib. L. Rev. 449, 458 (1997) [hereafter, *Harvard Note*]. Legal problems arise for plaintiffs who sue for harms resulting from outing under the "public disclosure" tort and also under theories of defamation, false light, and intentional infliction of emotional distress. For analysis of these theories, see *Harvard Note*, supra, and Kathleen Guzman, *About Outing: Public Discourse, Private Lives*, 73 Wash. U. L.Q. 1531 (1995) [hereafter, Guzman]. Among the problems with respect to defamation actions is the difficulty, in the case of many persons, of characterizing homosexuality. As noted by Guzman, supra, at 1571, "[m]any people who engage or have engaged in homosexual activity would not self-define as 'homosexual.'" Another problem is that "courts have considered a statement defamatory only if it prejudices an individual in the eyes of a number of 'right-minded' people." *Harvard Note*, supra, at 471.

Should courts permit tort damages for outing? With respect to the private facts tort, Guzman argues that "the revelation of information that is integral to self-definition or that could endanger the person about which it is revealed should be actionable." Guzman, supra, at 1590. Another commentator proposes that, under the private facts tort, courts should "locate the offensiveness in the fact, not the substance, of the revelation of a private fact." She suggests that "[p]ublicity of any fact that an individual has sought to keep private is highly offensive to a reasonable person's sensibilities; that the fact is sexual orientation is relevant only insofar as it indicates that revelation of this private fact may expose the individual to illegitimate harm." *Harvard Note*, supra, at 483.

Do these arguments overcome the interest of the "outer" in trying to combat homophobia? Do they outweigh the public's "right to know"?

(4) Would you allow a suit for the unconsented publication of the following kinds of photos?

> (a) A picture of a couple who are in fact happily married, engaged in a serious and animated discussion on a park bench, used without reference to their names as an illustration for a story on broken marriages, along with a caption that indicates that the picture exemplifies a marital quarrel.

(b) A picture of an elderly sidewalk vendor, taken from an angle that accentuates pathetic aspects of his face, used on the cover of a magazine which features a story on economic problems of the aged.

(c) A picture of lovemaking by the couple described in (a), taken with a telescopic lens through the bedroom window of their rural home.

DOUGLASS v. HUSTLER MAGAZINE, INC.
United States Court of Appeals, Seventh Circuit
769 F.2d 1128 (1985), cert. denied, 475 U.S. 1094 (1986)

POSNER, CIRCUIT JUDGE.

Robyn Douglass, the actress and model, obtained $600,000 in damages in this diversity suit against the corporation that publishes *Hustler* magazine, for invasion of her right of privacy. 607 F.Supp. 816. *Hustler* (as we shall call the magazine and its publisher interchangeably) has appealed, raising questions of tort law, freedom of the press, and trial procedure; Douglass has cross-appealed, complaining about the judge's action in reducing the punitive damages awarded by the jury.

Robyn Douglass moved to Chicago in 1974 and began a career as an actress and model. That year she posed nude together with another woman for the freelance photographer Augustin Gregory, a codefendant with *Hustler* in the district court. The photographs were intended for a forthcoming feature in *Playboy* magazine, the "Ripped-Off" pictorial. Gregory testified that he required all his photographic models to sign releases allowing him to do with the photographs whatever he wanted. Robyn Douglass testified (and the jury was entitled to believe) that all she signed was a release authorizing *Playboy* to publish or otherwise use the photographs "for any lawful purpose whatsoever, without restrictions." The release does not refer to sale as such; but in granting rights not only to *Playboy* but to its "assigns and licensees," Douglass in effect gave *Playboy* carte blanche to dispose of the photos in any lawful way it wanted. Some of the photographs were published in *Playboy* in March 1975 as planned. Gregory had in 1974 also taken nude photographs of Douglass for a "Water and Sex" pictorial, also intended for *Playboy*; and there is a similar conflict over the release.

Douglass's career throve in the following years. She appeared eight times nude in *Playboy* but also made television commercials for Chicago advertising agencies and appeared in television dramas and in movies—notably "Breaking Away," where she had a starring role. Meanwhile in 1980 Gregory had become the photography editor of *Hustler*. This move was not unconnected with his earlier photographing of Douglass. The magazine wanted to publish nude photos of celebrities and in negotiations over becoming *Hustler's* photography editor Gregory had shown management some of his photographs of Douglass. After he was hired, management asked Gregory for releases authorizing publication of these photographs. He testified that he couldn't find the releases at first but that eventually he submitted to Hustler two releases signed by Douglass, one for the photo session for the "Ripped-Off" pictorial, the other for the "Water and Sex" pictorial. At trial *Hustler* was able to produce only photostats of the releases allegedly signed by Douglass. The parties stipulated that, if called as a witness, a handwriting expert would testify that Douglass's signature had been forged on one of the releases and that the photostat of the other was too poor to allow the authenticity of the signature on it to be determined.

Douglass heard that there was to be a photo feature on her in the January 1981 issue of Hustler (an acquaintance had seen an announcement of it in a previous issue). She complained to the magazine that it had no authority to publish any photos of her. It responded with photostatic copies of the alleged releases, which within two or three days she denounced to Hustler as forgeries. The issue containing the feature had already been printed and distributed to retailers; and though it had not yet appeared on newsstands or been mailed to subscribers, *Hustler* made no effort to recall the issue, and it was widely sold. The feature, entitled "Robyn Douglass Nude," contained nude photographs from the two photo sessions for *Playboy* and stills (not nude) from two of her movies. The magazine paid Gregory a fee, over and above his regular salary, for the photographs he had supplied.

This suit charges that Gregory and *Hustler* invaded Douglass's right to privacy under the common law of Illinois by publishing "Robyn Douglass Nude." The feature, she charged, invaded her right of privacy in two ways: it cast her in a "false light," and it appropriated valuable commercial rights that belong to her. At trial she presented evidence that the publication of the feature had caused her emotional distress, and had killed her career of making commercials in Chicago because advertisers thought she had voluntarily appeared in what they considered an extremely vulgar magazine. An economist testified that the present value of her lost earnings was $716,565 at the time of trial (1983).

The judge gave the jury a verdict form with a blank beside each defendant's name for the amount of compensatory damages if the jury found either defendant liable, and a separate blank beside each name for punitive damages. The jury found both defendants liable and awarded the plaintiff $500,000 in compensatory damages against each defendant and $1,500,000 in punitive damages against *Hustler*. The judge remitted all but $100,000 of the punitive damages and Douglass accepted the remittitur. The award of compensatory damages against Gregory was not executed because on the eve of trial he had made an agreement with Douglass that if he testified truthfully, and consistently with his deposition, she would not execute any judgment against him. Hence the real judgment was only $600,000. Gregory has not filed an appearance in this court.

Hustler argues that the facts, even when viewed favorably to the plaintiff, do not make out a cause of action under the Illinois common law of privacy, so that the judgment should be reversed with directions to dismiss the complaint; or that if they do, still the complaint must be dismissed because the plaintiff failed to prove "actual malice" by clear and convincing evidence, as required by the Constitution. Alternatively it argues that a new trial should be ordered because of errors in the instructions to the jury, and other trial errors.

First of all, *Hustler* denies that Illinois even recognizes the "false light" tort. Illinois' substantive law governs this suit, apart from the defendants' First Amendment defense; and no Illinois court has ever found liability for such a tort, and one case states "that in Illinois actions for invasions of privacy are limited to use of an individual's name or likeness for commercial purposes." *Kelly v. Franco*, 72 Ill.App.3d 642, 646, 28 Ill.Dec. 855, 858–59, 391 N.E.2d 54, 57–58 (1979). But the statement was dictum....

Like every other division of the tort law of privacy, the "false light" tort (on which see the compendious summary in the Second Restatement of Torts § 652E, at pp. 394–400 (1977)) can be criticized, especially for overlapping with the tort of defamation.... Why should a plaintiff be able to circumvent the technical limitations with which the tort of defamation is hedged about by calling his suit one for placing him in a false light? Several answers are possible, however:

1. Some of those limitations seem not to reflect considered policy, but instead to be fossil remnants of the tort's prehistory in the discredited practices of Star Chamber and the discredited concept of seditious libel. *See, e.g.*, Prosser and Keeton on the Law of Torts § 111, at pp. 771–72 (5th ed. 1984). If they are gotten around by allowing a plaintiff to plead invasion of privacy, there is no great loss.

2. The principal limitations concern the requirement of proving special damages in some cases.... Since Robyn Douglass proved special damages (*i.e.*, a pecuniary loss), these limitations would not have impeded her even if she had brought this suit as one for defamation. As for the other limitations in the law of defamation, *Hustler* has not shown how any of them, either, would have posed an embarrassment for Douglass on the facts of this case. And if she had sued for defamation she would not have had to prove (though it was not difficult to prove) that the offending materials had been widely publicized, an element of invasion of privacy that has no counterpart in the law of defamation.

3. Part of Douglass's claim is that *Hustler* insinuated that she is a lesbian; and such a claim could of course be the basis for an action for defamation. But the rest of her claim fits more comfortably into the category of offensive rather than defamatory publicity. The difference is illustrated by *Time, Inc. v. Hill*, 385 U.S. 374, 87 S.Ct. 534, 17 L.Ed.2d 456 (1967). *Life* magazine had presented as true a fictionalized account of the ordeal of a family held hostage by escaped convicts. The members of the family were shown being subjected to various indignities that had not actually occurred. The article did not defame the family members in the sense of accusing them of immoral, improper, or other bad conduct, and yet many people would be upset to think that the whole world thought them victims of such mistreatment. The false-light tort, to the extent distinct from the tort of defamation (but there is indeed considerable overlap), rests on an awareness that people who are made to seem pathetic or ridiculous may be shunned, and not just people who are thought to be dishonest or incompetent or immoral. We grant, though, that the distinction is blurred by the fact that a false statement that a woman was raped is actionable as defamation, *see, e.g., Youssoupoff v. Metro-Goldwyn-Mayer Pictures, Ltd.*, 50 Times L.Rep. 581, 584 (C.A.1934), though in such a case the plaintiff is represented to be a victim of wrongdoing rather than a wrongdoer herself.

At all events, the criticisms of the false-light tort have to our knowledge persuaded the courts of only one state that recognizes a tort of invasion of privacy to withhold recognition of this subtype of the tort—North Carolina, in [Renwick v. News & Observer Publishing Co., 310 N.C. 312, 312 S.E.2d 405 (1984)].... Almost all signs point to Illinois' recognizing it when a suitable case arises. A more difficult question is whether the facts of this case make out a false-light tort. We must decide in what light *Hustler* may be said to have cast Robyn Douglass, and (by comparison with her activities as a *Playboy* model) in what if any sense the light could have been found to be a false one. To answer these questions we shall have to enter imaginatively into a world that is not the natural habitat of judges—the world of nude modeling and (as they are called in the trade) "provocative" magazines.

The feature "Robyn Douglass Nude" in the January 1981 issue of *Hustler* occupies three full pages about a third of the way from the end of the magazine. The first page is dominated by a picture of Douglass, shown from the front, rain-splattered, wearing only an open raincoat. This is one of the photos that had been taken for the "Water and Sex" pictorial. Her mouth is open and her eyes closed. The text on the page reads:

> She played Katherine, the Midwestern coed in the film *Breaking Away*, and Jamie, the shapely newspaper reporter in the TV series *Galactica 1980* (below). But in HUSTLER seductive young actress Robyn Douglass plays herself. In these never-before-published photos this hot new star strips away her screen image to reveal the flesh of a real woman. An accomplished stage performer and TV-commercial model (Orbit gum, Gatorade and United Airlines), Robyn has been trained to use her body as a tool of her trade. These photos show just how well she's learned to use that tool.

The "below" reference is to an innocuous still photo from the television series.

The second page of the feature is given over to four more photographs of Douglass, two from "Water and Sex" and two from the "Ripped-Off" pictorial. (To be precise, these and the other nude photos in "Robyn Douglass Nude" were photos that had been taken for the two *Playboy* pictorials but, apparently, had not actually been published.) The photographs from "Water and Sex" again show Douglass from the front with the raincoat playing out behind her. In one picture her mouth is open while in the other she seems to be looking abstractedly at herself. In the two photos from "Ripped-Off," Douglass, now wearing a slip rather than a raincoat, appears to be engaged in erotic play with the other woman in the pictorial.

The last page of the feature has the following text beneath a picture of Douglass, fully clothed, on a motorcycle:

> When asked to audition for the role of Katherine in *Breaking Away* (above), Robyn sought out the character's most emotional scene to read for director Peter Yates. "You only have a short time to prepare; so I went through the script to try to find the climactic moments for Katherine." From the looks of Robyn (who's blond in the photos of her and a female friend), she's never had difficulty finding climactic moments.

The rest of the page is given over to two photographs from the "Ripped-Off" pictorial. The underwear visible in the other two photographs from this session has indeed been ripped off; the two women are naked. Douglass is straddling the other woman and the two appear to be engaged in sexual activity.

Douglass argues that the *Hustler* feature casts her in a false light in two respects. First, it insinuates that she is a lesbian, which (all agree) she is not. Second, it insinuates that she is the kind of person willing to be shown naked in *Hustler*. Nothing in the feature itself suggests that the nude photographs of her are appearing without her permission and against her will, and readers might well assume that she had cooperated in the preparation of the feature in order to stimulate interest in her films. Moreover, she had been described in a previous issue of *Hustler* as a forthcoming "*Hustler* celebrity-exclusive," and in another issue *Hustler's* chairman, Larry Flynt, had announced in an editorial column that he does not publish photographs of women without their consent. It is (or so a jury could find) as if *Hustler* had said, "Robyn Douglass is proud to pose nude for *Hustler* magazine." To complete this part of her argument Douglass asserts that voluntary association with *Hustler* as a nude model is degrading.

We would not ourselves think that *Hustler* was seriously insinuating—or that its readership would think—that Robyn Douglass is a lesbian. *Hustler* is a magazine for men. Few men are interested in lesbians. The purpose of showing two women in apparent sexual embrace is to display the charms of two women. Moreover, the photos obviously are posed rather than candid shots; they show what the photographer wanted the women to do, not necessarily what the women wanted to do. Nevertheless we cannot say that a reasonable jury seeing the pictures and reading the accompanying text with its references to "climactic moments" and "female friend" could not infer that Douglass was being represented to be a lesbian.

The question whether she was also being depicted in a degrading association with *Hustler* invites attention to the difference between libel and false light. It would have been difficult for Douglass to state this claim as one for libel. For what exactly is the imputation of saying (or here, implying) of a person that she agreed to have pictures of herself appear in a vulgar and offensive magazine? That she is immoral? This would be too strong a characterization in today's moral climate. That she lacks good taste? This would not be defamatory.... The point is, rather, that to be shown nude in such a setting before millions of people — the readers of the magazine — is degrading in much the same way that to be shown beaten up by criminals is degrading (although not libelous, despite the analogy to being reported to have been raped), though of course if Douglass consented to appear nude in this setting she is responsible for her own debasement and can get no judicial redress.

That the setting is indeed a degrading one requires only a glance through the issue of *Hustler* in which "Robyn Douglass Nude" was published to confirm. The cover shows a naked woman straddling and embracing a giant peppermint stick. The titles of several articles in the issue are printed on the cover, next to the picture, including along with some titles that are not related to sex "New Discovery: How to Give Women Vaginal Orgasms." This is directly below "Nude Celebrity: Robyn Douglass, Star of *Galactica* and *Breaking Away*." The inside cover is a full page of advertisements for pornographic video cassettes. On page 5 there is the "publisher's [Larry Flynt's] statement" — a call to tax the churches. This sounds another theme of *Hustler*: "irreverence," which has the practical meaning in *Hustler* of hostility to or contempt for racial, ethnic, and religious minorities. Then there is a "World News Roundup" — the news is all concerned with sex — and a page of coarse advice to readers who have sexual problems. Between these two features is a full-page advertisement entitled "Get Any Girl *Within 5 Minutes* or YOU PAY NOTHING!" with subtitles such as "Turn Women Into Putty." The issue contains many similar sexual advertisements, some with obscene pictures and text. The reader arrives next at a regular monthly feature, "Asshole of the Month," in which a man's head — in this issue the head of a professor at the Harvard Law School, who in January 1981 was in charge of the criminal division of the Justice Department — is shown protruding from the rear of a donkey. The next few pages consist of vulgar photographs, some from pornographic movies, plus jokes and cartoons many of which are racially offensive; all are offensive in one way or another. In one cartoon, a doctor in an abortion clinic is feeding a fetus to a rat in an alley. Then there is an illustrated feature on pornographic movies, followed by four book reviews (two of erotic works) and "How to Achieve Vaginal Orgasms." The magazine sobers up a little with a symposium on gun control, punctuated however by tasteless cartoons such as one in which a black child says to Santa Claus, "I'd like a new little brother for Christmas. We could use the extra welfare check!" The symposium is followed by a nude pictorial, by more tasteless cartoons, and by a mock advertisement for a "Starving Cambodian Baby Doll."

We shall leave off here, on page 51 of a 136-page issue, having sufficiently indicated the character of the magazine. To be depicted as *voluntarily* associated with such a sheet (the Harvard law professor's association is not represented as voluntary) is unquestionably degrading to a normal person, especially if the depiction is erotic (the depiction of the professor is not); for although the magazine is offensive on several planes, the sexual is the one most emphasized....

Hustler argues that publication of "Robyn Douglass Nude" could not be degrading to one who had posed nude for *Playboy*. This fact distinguishes the case from the two cases that give the most support to Douglass's false-light claim: *Wood v. Hustler Magazine, Inc.*, 736 F.2d 1084 (5th Cir.1984), where the plaintiff was not a model or actress and her nude photo (taken by her husband) had not been published previously and had not been intended to be published; and *Braun v. Flynt*, 726 F.2d 245 (5th Cir.1984), where the photo of the plaintiff that was published on the same page with offensive matter in another "provocative" magazine published by Flynt (Chic) was not a nude photo; the plaintiff was wearing a bathing suit. *See id.* at 247–48. (It should be apparent by now that this little niche of the law of privacy is dominated by Larry Flynt's publications.)

To evaluate *Hustler's* contention required the jury to compare the two magazines. We shall use for comparison the issue of *Playboy* in which the "Ripped-Off" pictorial appeared, though the jury had other issues of *Playboy* to peruse as well. The cover shows a young woman with partially naked buttocks and thighs but otherwise clothed. The only (other) suggestion of sex on the cover is the words "Ripped Off! A Torrid Nine-Page Pictorial," which by its position on the cover appears to be a reference to the cover girl. The inside cover is a conventional advertisement for Scotch whisky. Besides advertisements (none sexual), the issue contains fiction, a column of sexual advice (more refined than its *Hustler* counterpart), book reviews (only one of a book on sex), and articles. None of the stories or articles is obscene, though one story is erotic (a "Ribald Classic") and there are many bawdy cartoons and jokes (but not vicious ones, like many of those in *Hustler*) and four nude pictorials. In one of the pictorials a woman is doing exercises and being massaged; some of the frames contain an erotic suggestion of a mild sort. Two of the other pictorials show nude women in various poses but there is no suggestion that they are engaged in erotic activity. The last nude pictorial is "Ripped-Off," which turns out to consist of photographs of nude women (some in erotic poses) by different photographers. Two of the photographs are by Gregory, and one of them is of Robyn Douglass, though she is not identified by name. Although she is shown removing the slip of the other woman, as in the *Hustler* pictures, the text beneath the picture weakens any inference of lesbianism: "How long since you've seen a girl—let alone two—in lingerie like this? 'I pick very feminine, almost outdated slips for the girls to wear in this scene,' says photographer Gregory. 'To me, that made it more of a fantasy, more of a turn-on.'" Among other pictures in "Ripped-Off," one could be taken to be an (obviously simulated) photograph of sexual intercourse.

Although many people find *Playboy*, with its emphasis on sex and nudity, offensive, the differences between it and *Hustler* are palpable. *Playboy*, like *Hustler*, contains nude pictorials, but the erotic theme is generally muted, though there are occasional photographs that an earlier generation would have considered definitely obscene. And unlike *Hustler*, *Playboy* does not carry sexual advertisements, does not ridicule racial or religious groups, and avoids repulsive photographs—though most of the jokes and cartoons have sex as their theme, and not all are in good taste. We cannot say that it would be irrational for a jury to find that in the highly permissive moral and cultural climate prevailing in late twentieth-century America, posing nude for *Playboy* is consistent with respectability for a model and actress but that posing nude in *Hustler* is not (not yet, anyway), so that to portray Robyn Douglass as voluntarily posing nude for *Hustler* could be thought to place her in a false light even though she had voluntarily posed nude for *Playboy*. Apart from the evidence of the magazines themselves, Douglass presented evidence that advertising agencies in Chicago were afraid of their clients' reactions if she appeared in commercials after her appearance in *Hustler*, but cared nothing about her appearing nude in *Playboy*. And of course the issue for us is not whether the jury was right but whether a reasonable jury could have found a false-light tort on the facts of this case.

However, since Douglass gave a general release to *Playboy*, it can be argued that she consented to have her photographs appear in any lawful setting; and there is no contention that "Robyn Douglass Nude," or the issue of *Hustler* in which it appeared, could lawfully have been suppressed on obscenity or other grounds. The jury could find, however, that only Douglass or *Playboy* could give consent to the publication of the photographs and that neither had done so. True, by giving *Playboy* a general release Douglass took a risk that her nude photographs would end up in an offensive setting that would damage her career as a model for television commercials, and it might seem that someone who takes such a risk cannot have a high regard for her privacy. But the risk she took and the risk that materialized were not the same. She took what may have seemed a trivial risk that *Playboy* would resell her photographs to a competitor, not the risk that the competitor would steal them. *Playboy* has an interest, on which Douglass could reasonably rely in executing a release to *Playboy*, in not degrading its models and in maintaining exclusive rights to its photos of them. The woman in the *Wood* case assumed the risk that her husband would sell *Hustler* the nude photograph that he took of her, but this did not deprive her of the right to sue for invasion of privacy when *Hustler* published the photograph having gotten it from someone who had broken into her house and stolen it.

We conclude that Robyn Douglass has a cause of action against *Hustler* for portraying her in a false light. Further, we think the jury did not exceed the bounds of reason in finding that *Hustler* also violated her rights under the commercial-appropriation branch of the right of privacy — what is sometimes called the "right of publicity," which *Hustler* concedes is a part of the common law of Illinois. This is the right to prevent others from using one's name or picture for commercial purposes without consent. Although originally the forbidden use was putting one's name or picture into an advertisement, it is apparent from *Zacchini v. Scripps-Howard Broadcasting Co.*, 433 U.S. 562, 97 S.Ct. 2849, 53 L.Ed.2d 965 (1977), that the right can extend to publication in the nonadvertising portions of a magazine or broadcast. This extension is closely related to copyright.... Zacchini had perfected a "human cannonball" act that lasted about 15 seconds. A television station broadcast the whole act as part of a news program. The station argued that the act was newsworthy; in copyright terms this would make the broadcasting of it a "fair use." *Hustler* makes a similar argument here — Robyn Douglass is newsworthy and "Robyn Douglass Nude" was fair comment on her career. But the station could have done a story on Zacchini without showing his entire act; and showing the whole act was likely to shrink the paying audience for it — people could see it on television for nothing. Thus there was an invasion of Zacchini's rights, analogous to copyright, under state tort law. Similarly, Robyn Douglass or her agents must have control over the dissemination of her nude photographs if their value is to be maximized. *Hustler* can run a story on her and use any photographs that are in the public domain or that it can buy but it cannot use photographs made by others for commercial purposes and (temporarily) withheld from public distribution....

The unauthorized publication did impair the commercial exploitation of Douglass's talents, though probably not as much as she asserts and mainly because of where they were published. But an important aspect of the "right of publicity" is being able to control the place as well as time and number of one's public appearances; for example, no celebrity sells his name or likeness for advertising purposes to all comers. In any event, Douglass was not paid by *Hustler* for the right to publish nude photos of her.

Of course the issue in *Zacchini* was not whether the common law created a right of action against the television station—let alone the common law of Illinois (the case came from Ohio)—but whether the Constitution barred such a right of action if it existed in state law. There are no Illinois cases like *Zacchini*. But forced to guess, we guess that Illinois would recognize a "right of publicity" on the facts of *Zacchini* and the analogous facts of the present case. Indeed, this may be an easier case than *Zacchini*, where the performance had been in public, though in a different medium. This case approaches very closely to a violation of common law copyright, as in the theft and unauthorized publication of an author's manuscript. Of course Douglass would have no claim if Gregory had gotten a general release from her. But by executing only a limited release, she retained a right in the photos he took of her that, if not quite a property right, is nevertheless given legal protection under the (misleading) rubric of privacy.

[Omitted is the court's discussion of several other issues, including some matters on which it bases a reversal. The passage below deals with the plaintiff's argument that she did not have to prove actual malice because she was not a "public figure":]

But a successful actress and model who has appeared nude many times in *Playboy* magazine cannot be called a "private person"; she is a public figure in a literal sense. The lifting of the burden of proving actual malice in defamation cases from the shoulders of plaintiffs who are not public figures reflects two things: the fact that people who do not thrust themselves into the public eye have on average a greater sense of privacy than those who do; and the difficulty that obscure people have, compared to celebrities, in commanding the media's attention to efforts to rebut innuendoes about them (whether defamatory, or merely offensive in a false-light sense). *See Gertz v. Welch*, 418 U.S. 323, 344–45, 94 S.Ct. 2997, 3009, 41 L.Ed.2d 789 (1974). But not only is Robyn Douglass no shrinking violet; she is a budding celebrity eager to be seen in the nude by millions of people—she *had* been seen in the nude by millions of people, the readers of *Playboy*, before *Hustler* got hold of her photographs. She is not like the plaintiff in *Braun v. Flynt, supra*, who did not become a public figure merely because her job in a local amusement park included feeding "Ralph, the Diving Pig" from a bottle of milk while treading water.

As an original matter one might want to confine the class of public figures to government officials and other politicians; freedom of political speech, and in particular freedom to criticize government officials and aspirants to public office, was the original concern of the First Amendment. But it is too late in the day to make such a distinction, at least at this judicial level. Art, even of the questionable sort represented by erotic photographs in "provocative" magazines—even of the artless sort represented by "topless" dancing—today enjoys extensive protection in the name of the First Amendment.... And so with news about art and entertainment. Entertainers can therefore be public figures for purposes of a publisher's or a broadcaster's First Amendment defense to a charge of false-light invasion of privacy. *See, e.g., Lerman v. Flynt Distributing Co.*, 745 F.2d 123, 136–38 (2d Cir.1984).... Robyn Douglass clearly is one.

· · ·

NOTES

(1) Is it more persuasive to characterize Douglass's case as one of "appropriation," "false light," or "fictionalization"? Does the key to the actionability of her claim lie in the

fact that she has a property right in photos of herself, in an independent concept of reputation, or in yet distinguishable notions of personal dignity?

(2) What are the principal legal distinctions and similarities between *Hill* and *Douglass*? Should the same legal standard be applied to the determination of liability in both cases?

(3) Does Judge Posner make artistic judgments in *Douglass*? If courts are to be open to claims involving the kinds of interests that are involved in a case like *Douglass*, is there any way to avoid making judgments of that kind?

(4) Hannah Holland became a regional celebrity through her work as a TV news anchor in a Midwestern state. While vacationing in Florida, she participated in a "wet t-shirt" contest in a nightclub, during which she disrobed entirely. The defendants put pictures of her in videos and on websites, describing her as the "naked anchor woman." She resigned her news job under pressure. Does she have a tort claim? On what theory?

(5) Compare, with *Douglass*, *Sheets v. Salt Lake County*, 45 F.3d 1383 (10th Cir. 1995). The plaintiff, widower of a woman killed by a bomb, voluntarily turned over her diary to a city detective. Another detective testified that he told the plaintiff that the diary would remain confidential. However, a county investigator to whom the diary was distributed shared photocopied excerpts with an author who wrote a book about the bomb murders of the plaintiff's wife and another person, which included direct quotes from the diary. In affirming a judgment for the plaintiff, the court noted that facts about him revealed in the diary were "not particularly controversial or embarrassing," but stressed that "information need not be embarrassing to be personal" and said that whether the information was "sufficiently personal to be protected" was for the jury. The defendants argued that the plaintiff "could not have expected" confidentiality, given the number of investigators who had access to the diary. But the court emphasized that "[t]o turn a diary over to a limited group for what one perceives to be a limited and proper purpose is quite different than inviting publication of the material."

(6) *Restatement (Second)* § 652D says:

> One who gives publicity to a matter concerning the private life of another is subject to liability to the other for invasion of his privacy, if the matter publicized is of a kind that
>
> (a) would be highly offensive to a reasonable person, and
>
> (b) is not of legitimate concern to the public.

Would this provision support a privacy suit against a physician who writes a confidential letter to a judge considering a child custody case, detailing the doctor's judgments of the mental state of one of the contesting parents, who had been diagnosed as suicidal?

(7) Section 652D has been used to justify a verdict against a plastic surgeon who employed "before" and "after" slide photographs of a patient on a television program in connection with a department store promotion, as well as at a presentation at the store itself. The District of Columbia Court of Appeals thought that a jury could have decided that this publicity was "highly offensive to a reasonable person." The court found "persuasive" a distinction urged by the plaintiff "between the private fact of her reconstructive surgery and the fact that plastic surgery is a matter of legitimate public interest." *Vassiliades v. Garfinckel's*, 492 A.2d 580, 588–89 (D.C. 1985).

(8) The "privacy" tort has taken on some doctrinal complexity in cases of the sort discussed here. Students should consider alternative routes to a cause of action. For example, in the case described in note 5, involving a letter concerning a party to a custody dispute, the plaintiff claimed under three theories: "[u]nreasonable intrusion upon ... seclusion," "unreasonable publicity of her private life" under *Restatement (Second)* § 652D, and an independent state law theory of "implied right to privacy ... without regard to Restatement principles."

A still different avenue to recovery exists in cases in which the person publicizing the allegedly confidential information is a member of a profession that holds itself out as keeping confidences. See, e.g., *Vassiliades*, supra note 7, in which the court holds that "breach of a physician-patient relationship is an actionable tort." 492 A.2d at 592. Cf. *Horne v. Patton*, 291 Ala. 701, 287 So. 2d 824 (1973) (overturning demurrers on an implied contract theory as well as an invasion of privacy count).

WHITE v. SAMSUNG ELECTRONICS AMERICA, INC.: *THE PANEL DECISION*
United States Court of Appeals, Ninth Circuit
971 F.2d 1395 (1992)

GOODWIN, Senior Circuit Judge.

This case involves a promotional "fame and fortune" dispute. In running a particular advertisement without Vanna White's permission, defendants Samsung Electronics America, Inc. (Samsung) and David Deutsch Associates, Inc. (Deutsch) attempted to capitalize on White's fame to enhance their fortune. White sued, alleging infringement of various intellectual property rights, but the district court granted summary judgment in favor of the defendants. We affirm in part, reverse in part, and remand.

Plaintiff Vanna White is the hostess of "Wheel of Fortune," one of the most popular game shows in television history. An estimated forty million people watch the program daily. Capitalizing on the fame which her participation in the show has bestowed on her, White markets her identity to various advertisers.

The dispute in this case arose out of a series of advertisements prepared for Samsung by Deutsch. The series ran in at least half a dozen publications with widespread, and in some cases national, circulation. Each of the advertisements in the series followed the same theme. Each depicted a current item from popular culture and a Samsung electronic product. Each was set in the twenty-first century and conveyed the message that the Samsung product would still be in use by that time. By hypothesizing outrageous future outcomes for the cultural items, the ads created humorous effects....

The advertisement which prompted the current dispute was for Samsung video-cassette recorders (VCRs). The ad depicted a robot, dressed in a wig, gown, and jewelry which Deutsch consciously selected to resemble White's hair and dress. The robot was posed next to a game board which is instantly recognizable as the Wheel of Fortune game show set, in a stance for which White is famous. The caption of the ad read: "Longest-running game show. 2012 A.D." Defendants referred to the ad as the "Vanna White" ad. Unlike the other celebrities used in the campaign, White neither consented to the ads nor was she paid.

Following the circulation of the robot ad, White sued Samsung and Deutsch in federal district court under: (1) California Civil Code § 3344; (2) the California common law right of publicity.... The district court granted summary judgment against White on each of her claims. White now appeals....

White first argues that the district court erred in rejecting her claim under section 3344. Section 3344(a) provides, in pertinent part, that "[a]ny person who knowingly uses another's name, voice, signature, photograph, or likeness, in any manner, ... for purposes of advertising or selling, ... without such person's prior consent ... shall be liable for any damages sustained by the person or persons injured as a result thereof."

White argues that the Samsung advertisement used her "likeness" in contravention of section 3344. In Midler v. Ford Motor Co., 849 F.2d 460 (9th Cir.1988), this court rejected Bette Midler's section 3344 claim concerning a Ford television commercial in which a Midler "sound-alike" sang a song which Midler had made famous. In rejecting Midler's claim, this court noted that "[t]he defendants did not use Midler's name or anything else whose use is prohibited by the statute. The voice they used was [another person's], not hers. The term 'likeness' refers to a visual image not a vocal imitation." Id. at 463.

In this case, Samsung and Deutsch used a robot with mechanical features, and not, for example, a manikin molded to White's precise features. Without deciding for all purposes when a caricature or impressionistic resemblance might become a "likeness," we agree with the district court that the robot at issue here was not White's "likeness" within the meaning of section 3344. Accordingly, we affirm the court's dismissal of White's section 3344 claim.

White next argues that the district court erred in granting summary judgment to defendants on White's common law right of publicity claim. In Eastwood v. Superior Court, 149 Cal.App.3d 409, 198 Cal.Rptr. 342 (1983), the California court of appeal stated that the common law right of publicity cause of action "may be pleaded by alleging (1) the defendant's use of the plaintiff's identity; (2) the appropriation of plaintiff's name or likeness to defendant's advantage, commercially or otherwise; (3) lack of consent; and (4) resulting injury." ... The district court dismissed White's claim for failure to satisfy Eastwood's second prong, reasoning that defendants had not appropriated White's "name or likeness" with their robot ad. We agree that the robot ad did not make use of White's name or likeness. However, the common law right of publicity is not so confined.

The Eastwood court did not hold that the right of publicity cause of action could be pleaded only by alleging an appropriation of name or likeness. Eastwood involved an unauthorized use of photographs of Clint Eastwood and of his name. Accordingly, the Eastwood court had no occasion to consider the extent beyond the use of name or likeness to which the right of publicity reaches. That court held only that the right of publicity cause of action "may be" pleaded by alleging, inter alia, appropriation of name or likeness, not that the action may be pleaded only in those terms.

The "name or likeness" formulation referred to in Eastwood originated not as an element of the right of publicity cause of action, but as a description of the types of cases in which the cause of action had been recognized. The source of this formulation is Prosser, Privacy, 48 Cal.L.Rev. 383, 401–07 (1960), one of the earliest and most enduring articulations of the common law right of publicity cause of action. In looking at the case law to that point, Prosser recognized that right of publicity cases involved one of two basic factual scenarios: name appropriation, and picture or other likeness appropriation....

Even though Prosser focused on appropriations of name or likeness in discussing the right of publicity, he noted that "[i]t is not impossible that there might be appropriation of the plaintiff's identity, as by impersonation, without the use of either his name or his likeness, and that this would be an invasion of his right of privacy." ... At the time Prosser wrote, he noted however, that "[n]o such case appears to have arisen." Id.

Since Prosser's early formulation, the case law has borne out his insight that the right of publicity is not limited to the appropriation of name or likeness. In Motschenbacher v. R.J. Reynolds Tobacco Co., 498 F.2d 821 (9th Cir.1974), the defendant had used a photograph of the plaintiff's race car in a television commercial. Although the plaintiff appeared driving the car in the photograph, his features were not visible. Even though the defendant had not appropriated the plaintiff's name or likeness, this court held that plaintiff's California right of publicity claim should reach the jury.

In Midler, this court held that, even though the defendants had not used Midler's name or likeness, Midler had stated a claim for violation of her California common law right of publicity because "the defendants ... for their own profit in selling their product did appropriate part of her identity" by using a Midler sound-alike. Id. at 463–64.

In Carson v. Here's Johnny Portable Toilets, Inc., 698 F.2d 831 (6th Cir.1983), the defendant had marketed portable toilets under the brand name "Here's Johnny"—Johnny Carson's signature "Tonight Show" introduction—without Carson's permission. The district court had dismissed Carson's Michigan common law right of publicity claim because the defendants had not used Carson's "name or likeness." Id. at 835. In reversing the district court, the sixth circuit found "the district court's conception of the right of publicity ... too narrow" and held that the right was implicated because the defendant had appropriated Carson's identity by using, inter alia, the phrase "Here's Johnny." Id. at 835–37.

These cases teach not only that the common law right of publicity reaches means of appropriation other than name or likeness, but that the specific means of appropriation are relevant only for determining whether the defendant has in fact appropriated the plaintiff's identity. The right of publicity does not require that appropriations of identity be accomplished through particular means to be actionable. It is noteworthy that the Midler and Carson defendants not only avoided using the plaintiff's name or likeness, but they also avoided appropriating the celebrity's voice, signature, and photograph. The photograph in Motschenbacher did include the plaintiff, but because the plaintiff was not visible the driver could have been an actor or dummy and the analysis in the case would have been the same.

Although the defendants in these cases avoided the most obvious means of appropriating the plaintiffs' identities, each of their actions directly implicated the commercial interests which the right of publicity is designed to protect. As the Carson court explained:

> [t]he right of publicity has developed to protect the commt ofal interest of celebrities in their identities. The theory of the right is that a celebrity's identity can be valuable in the promotion of products, and the celebrity has an interest that may be protected from the unauthorized commercial exploitation of that identity.... If the celebrity's identity is commercially exploited, there has been an invasion of his right whether or not his "name or likeness" is used.

Carson, 698 F.2d at 835. It is not important how the defendant has appropriated the plaintiff's identity, but whether the defendant has done so. Motschenbacher, Midler, and Carson teach the impossibility of treating the right of publicity as guarding only against a laundry list of specific means of appropriating identity. A rule which says that the right of publicity can be infringed only through the use of nine different methods of appropriating identity merely challenges the clever advertising strategist to come up with the tenth.

Indeed, if we treated the means of appropriation as dispositive in our analysis of the right of publicity, we would not only weaken the right but effectively eviscerate it. The right would fail to protect those plaintiffs most in need of its protection. Advertisers use celebrities to promote their products. The more popular the celebrity, the greater the number of people who recognize her, and the greater the visibility for the product. The identities of the most popular celebrities are not only the most attractive for advertisers, but also the easiest to evoke without resorting to obvious means such as name, likeness, or voice.

Consider a hypothetical advertisement which depicts a mechanical robot with male features, an African-American complexion, and a bald head. The robot is wearing black hightop Air Jordan basketball sneakers, and a red basketball uniform with black trim, baggy shorts, and the number 23 (though not revealing "Bulls" or "Jordan" lettering). The ad depicts the robot dunking a basketball one-handed, stiff-armed, legs extended like open scissors, and tongue hanging out. Now envision that this ad is run on television during professional basketball games. Considered individually, the robot's physical attributes, its dress, and its stance tell us little. Taken together, they lead to the only conclusion that any sports viewer who has registered a discernible pulse in the past five years would reach: the ad is about Michael Jordan.

Viewed separately, the individual aspects of the advertisement in the present case say little. Viewed together, they leave little doubt about the celebrity the ad is meant to depict. The female-shaped robot is wearing a long gown, blond wig, and large jewelry. Vanna White dresses exactly like this at times, but so do many other women. The robot is in the process of turning a block letter on a game-board. Vanna White dresses like this while turning letters on a game-board but perhaps similarly attired Scrabble-playing women do this as well. The robot is standing on what looks to be the Wheel of Fortune game show set. Vanna White dresses like this, turns letters, and does this on the Wheel of Fortune game show. She is the only one. Indeed, defendants themselves referred to their ad as the "Vanna White" ad. We are not surprised.

Television and other media create marketable celebrity identity value. Considerable energy and ingenuity are expended by those who have achieved celebrity value to exploit it for profit. The law protects the celebrity's sole right to exploit this value whether the celebrity has achieved her fame out of rare ability, dumb luck, or a combination thereof. We decline Samsung and Deutch's invitation to permit the evisceration of the common law right of publicity through means as facile as those in this case. Because White has alleged facts showing that Samsung and Deutsch had appropriated her identity, the district court erred by rejecting, on summary judgment, White's common law right of publicity claim.

. . .

In defense, defendants cite a number of cases for the proposition that their robot ad constituted protected speech. The only cases they cite which are even remotely relevant to this case are Hustler Magazine v. Falwell, 485 U.S. 46, 108 S.Ct. 876, 99 L.Ed.2d 41

(1988) and L.L. Bean, Inc. v. Drake Publishers, Inc., 811 F.2d 26 (1st Cir.1987). Those cases involved parodies of advertisements run for the purpose of poking fun at Jerry Falwell and L.L. Bean, respectively. This case involves a true advertisement run for the purpose of selling Samsung VCRs. The ad's spoof of Vanna White and Wheel of Fortune is subservient and only tangentially related to the ad's primary message: "buy Samsung VCRs." Defendants' parody arguments are better addressed to non-commercial parodies. The difference between a "parody" and a "knock-off" is the difference between fun and profit.

. . .

In remanding this case, we hold only that White has pleaded claims which can go to the jury for its decision.

AFFIRMED IN PART, REVERSED IN PART, and REMANDED.

WHITE v. SAMSUNG ELECTRONICS AMERICA, INC.: *ON PETITION FOR REHEARING*
United States Court of Appeals, Ninth Circuit
989 F.2d 1512 (1993)

. . .

The full court has been advised of the suggestion for rehearing en banc. An active judge requested a vote on whether to rehear the matter en banc. The matter failed to receive a majority of the votes of the nonrecused active judges in favor of en banc consideration. . . .

The petition for rehearing is DENIED and the suggestion for rehearing en banc is REJECTED.

KOZINSKI, Circuit Judge, with whom Circuit Judges O'SCANNLAIN and KLEINFELD join, dissenting from the order rejecting the suggestion for rehearing en banc.

I

Saddam Hussein wants to keep advertisers from using his picture in unflattering contexts.[1] Clint Eastwood doesn't want tabloids to write about him. Rudolf Valentino's heirs want to control his film biography. The Girl Scouts don't want their image soiled by association with certain activities.[4] George Lucas wants to keep Strategic Defense Initiative fans from calling it "Star Wars." Pepsico doesn't want singers to use the word "Pepsi" in their songs. . . . And scads of copyright holders see purple when their creations are made fun of.

Something very dangerous is going on here. Private property, including intellectual property, is essential to our way of life. It provides an incentive for investment and innovation; it stimulates the flourishing of our culture; it protects the moral entitlements of people to the fruits of their labors. But reducing too much to private property can be bad medicine. Private land, for instance, is far more useful if separated from other pri-

---

1. SEE EBEN SHAPIRO, *Rising Caution on Using Celebrity Images*, N.Y. Times, Nov. 4, 1992, at D20 (Iraqi diplomat objects on right of publicity grounds to ad containing Hussein's picture and caption "History has shown what happens when one source controls all the information").

4. *Girl Scouts v. Personality Posters Mfg.*, 304 F.Supp. 1228 (S.D.N.Y.1969) (poster of a pregnant girl in a Girl Scout uniform with the caption "Be Prepared").

vate land by public streets, roads and highways. Public parks, utility rights-of-way and sewers reduce the amount of land in private hands, but vastly enhance the value of the property that remains.

So too it is with intellectual property. Overprotecting intellectual property is as harmful as underprotecting it. Creativity is impossible without a rich public domain. Nothing today, likely nothing since we tamed fire, is genuinely new: Culture, like science and technology, grows by accretion, each new creator building on the works of those who came before. Overprotection stifles the very creative forces it's supposed to nurture.

The panel's opinion is a classic case of overprotection. Concerned about what it sees as a wrong done to Vanna White, the panel majority erects a property right of remarkable and dangerous breadth: Under the majority's opinion, it's now a tort for advertisers to remind the public of a celebrity. Not to use a celebrity's name, voice, signature or likeness; not to imply the celebrity endorses a product; but simply to evoke the celebrity's image in the public's mind. This Orwellian notion withdraws far more from the public domain than prudence and common sense allow. It conflicts with the Copyright Act and the Copyright Clause. It raises serious First Amendment problems. It's bad law, and it deserves a long, hard second look.

. . .

The ad that spawned this litigation starred a robot dressed in a wig, gown and jewelry reminiscent of Vanna White's hair and dress; the robot was posed next to a Wheel-of-Fortune-like game board. See Appendix. The caption read "Longest-running game show. 2012 A.D." The gag here, I take it, was that Samsung would still be around when White had been replaced by a robot.

Perhaps failing to see the humor, White sued, alleging Samsung infringed her right of publicity by "appropriating" her "identity." . . .

The majority isn't, in fact, preventing the "evisceration" of Vanna White's existing rights; it's creating a new and much broader property right, a right unknown in California law. It's replacing the existing balance between the interests of the celebrity and those of the public by a different balance, one substantially more favorable to the celebrity. Instead of having an exclusive right in her name, likeness, signature or voice, every famous person now has an exclusive right to anything that reminds the viewer of her. After all, that's all Samsung did: It used an inanimate object to remind people of White, to "evoke [her identity]." 971 F.2d at 1399.

Consider how sweeping this new right is. What is it about the ad that makes people think of White? It's not the robot's wig, clothes or jewelry; there must be ten million blond women (many of them quasi-famous) who wear dresses and jewelry like White's. It's that the robot is posed near the "Wheel of Fortune" game board. Remove the game board from the ad, and no one would think of Vanna White. . . . But once you include the game board, anybody standing beside it—a brunette woman, a man wearing women's clothes, a monkey in a wig and gown—would evoke White's image, precisely the way the robot did. It's the "Wheel of Fortune" set, not the robot's face or dress or jewelry that evokes White's image. The panel is giving White an exclusive right not in what she looks like or who she is, but in what she does for a living.

This is entirely the wrong place to strike the balance. Intellectual property rights aren't free: They're imposed at the expense of future creators and of the public at large. Where would we be if Charles Lindbergh had an exclusive right in the concept of a heroic solo aviator? If Arthur Conan Doyle had gotten a copyright in the idea of the detective story, or Albert Einstein had patented the theory of relativity? If every author and celebrity had been given the right to keep people from mocking them or their work? Surely this would have made the world poorer, not richer, culturally as well as economically.

This is why intellectual property law is full of careful balances between what's set aside for the owner and what's left in the public domain for the rest of us: The relatively short life of patents; the longer, but finite, life of copyrights; copyright's idea-expression dichotomy; the fair use doctrine; the prohibition on copyrighting facts; the compulsory license of television broadcasts and musical compositions; federal preemption of overbroad state intellectual property laws; the nominative use doctrine in trademark law; the right to make soundalike recordings.[20] All of these diminish an intellectual property owner's rights. All let the public use something created by someone else. But all are necessary to maintain a free environment in which creative genius can flourish.

The intellectual property right created by the panel here has none of these essential limitations: No fair use exception; no right to parody; no idea-expression dichotomy. It impoverishes the public domain, to the detriment of future creators and the public at large. Instead of well-defined, limited characteristics such as name, likeness or voice, advertisers will now have to cope with vague claims of "appropriation of identity," claims often made by people with a wholly exaggerated sense of their own fame and significance.... Future Vanna Whites might not get the chance to create their personae, because their employers may fear some celebrity will claim the persona is too similar to her own. The public will be robbed of parodies of celebrities, and our culture will be deprived of the valuable safety valve that parody and mockery create.

Moreover, consider the moral dimension, about which the panel majority seems to have gotten so exercised. Saying Samsung "appropriated" something of White's begs the question: Should White have the exclusive right to something as broad and amorphous as her "identity"? Samsung's ad didn't simply copy White's schtick—like all parody, it created something new. True, Samsung did it to make money, but White does whatever she does to make money, too; the majority talks of "the difference between fun and profit," 971 F.2d at 1401, but in the entertainment industry fun is profit. Why is Vanna White's right to exclusive for-profit use of her persona—a persona that might not even be her own creation, but that of a writer, director or producer—superior to Samsung's right to profit by creating its own inventions? Why should she have such absolute rights to control the conduct of others, unlimited by the idea-expression dichotomy or by the fair use doctrine?

... [I]t may seem unfair that much of the fruit of a creator's labor may be used by others without compensation. But this is not some unforeseen byproduct of our intellectual property system; it is the system's very essence. Intellectual property law assures authors the right to their original expression, but encourages others to build freely on the ideas that underlie it. This result is neither unfair nor unfortunate: It is the means by which intellectual property law advances the progress of science and art. We give authors certain exclusive rights, but in exchange we get a richer public domain. The majority ignores this wise teaching, and all of us are the poorer for it.

---

20. See 35 U.S.C. § 154 (duration of patent); 17 U.S.C. §§ 302–305 (duration of copyright); 17 U.S.C. § 102(b) (idea-expression dichotomy); 17 U.S.C. § 107 (fair use); *Feist Pubs., Inc. v. Rural Tel. Serv. Co.*, 499 U.S. 340,—, 111 S.Ct. 1282, 1288, 113 L.Ed.2d 358 (1991) (no copyrighting facts)....

...

Finally, I can't see how giving White the power to keep others from evoking her image in the public's mind can be squared with the First Amendment. Where does White get this right to control our thoughts? The majority's creation goes way beyond the protection given a trademark or a copyrighted work, or a person's name or likeness. All those things control one particular way of expressing an idea, one way of referring to an object or a person. But not allowing any means of reminding people of someone? That's a speech restriction unparalleled in First Amendment law.

...

For better or worse, we are the Court of Appeals for the Hollywood Circuit. Millions of people toil in the shadow of the law we make, and much of their livelihood is made possible by the existence of intellectual property rights. But much of their livelihood — and much of the vibrancy of our culture — also depends on the existence of other intangible rights: The right to draw ideas from a rich and varied public domain, and the right to mock, for profit as well as fun, the cultural icons of our time.

NOTES

(1) *White* is not about "privacy" at all, is it? What is the best characterization of the "right" at issue in this case? Appropriation of a property right? Violation of a "right of publicity"?

(2) What is the core of Samsung's alleged offense? Is it something like the tort of conversion — something like stealing? Under that type of theory, what allegedly was being converted?

(3) Has Samsung interfered with White's relationship with her viewing public?

(4) Is there a theory on which White could sue if she found the ad personally offensive rather than an appropriation of something that belonged to her? What if she alleged that she suffered severe emotional distress from the appearance of the ad?

(5) Is there a way to measure the adverse economic effects of this decision on creativity? Is Judge Kozinski's dissenting view largely a matter of faith, rather than proof?

(6) Following Vanna White came the very large footprints of the basketball immortal Kareem Abdul-Jabbar. He sued General Motors for an advertisement that associated the birth name under which he played in college — Lew Alcindor — with a GM car. Abdul-Jabbar had not used the name "Lew Alcindor" for commercial purposes for many years. GM did not get his consent, and did not pay him, for the use of "Lew Alcindor" in the commercial. However, it convinced the district court that the great center had "abandoned the name Lew Alcindor and ... abandoned the right to protect that name." The Ninth Circuit reversed on claims under common law privacy and the California right of publicity statute at issue in *White*, as well as the Lanham Act. It opined that the California "statute's reference to 'name or likeness' is not limited to present or current use," and it concluded that "[t]o the extent GMC's use of the plaintiff's birth name attracted television viewers' attention, GMC gained a commercial advantage." Inter alia, it viewed the question of "[w]hether or not Lew Alcindor 'equals' Kareem Abdul-Jabbar in the sense that ... the glamorously dressed robot equalled Vanna White ... is a question for the jury." *Abdul-Jabbar v. General Motors Corp.*, 75 F.3d 1391, 1400 (9th Cir. 1996).

Chapter 16

INTERFERENCE WITH ECONOMIC AND OTHER RELATIONS

§ 16.01 Torts Involving Contracts and Refusals to Deal — Generally

PROBLEM

A dentist had a medical malpractice insurance policy with M Company for twenty-seven years. The company cancelled the policy, without explanation, just after the dentist testified in a malpractice suit, under subpoena, against another dentist insured by the same company. On what grounds might the dentist whose insurance was cancelled have sued the insurer, and with what chances of success?

RESTATEMENT (SECOND) OF TORTS §§ 766, 767 (1979)*

§ 766. Intentional Interference with Performance of Contract by Third Person

One who intentionally and improperly interferes with the performance of a contract (except a contract to marry) between another and a third person by inducing or otherwise causing the third person not to perform the contract, is subject to liability to the other for the pecuniary loss resulting to the other from the failure of the third person to perform the contract.

§ 767. Factors in Determining Whether Interference is Improper

In determining whether an actor's conduct in intentionally interfering with a contract or a prospective contractual relation of another is improper or not, consideration is given to the following factors:

(a) the nature of the actor's conduct,

(b) the actor's motive,

(c) the interests of the other with which the actor's conduct interferes,

(d) the interests sought to be advanced by the actor,

(e) the social interests in protecting the freedom of action of the actor and the contractual interests of the other,

---

(f) the proximity or remoteness of the actor's conduct to the interference and

(g) the relations between the parties.

Comment:

. . .

b. Privilege to interfere, or interference not improper. Unlike other intentional torts such as intentional injury to person or property, or defamation, this branch of tort law has not developed a crystallized set of definite rules as to the existence or non-existence of a privilege to act.... Because of this fact, this Section is expressed in terms of whether the interference is improper or not, rather than in terms of whether there was a specific privilege to act in the manner specified. The issue in each case is whether the interference is improper or not under the circumstances; whether, upon a consideration of the relative significance of the factors involved, the conduct should be permitted without liability, despite its effect of harm to another. The decision therefore depends upon a judgment and choice of values in each situation. This Section states the important factors to be weighed against each other and balanced in arriving at a judgment; but it does not exhaust the list of possible factors....

PINO v. PROTECTION MARITIME INSURANCE COMPANY

United States Court of Appeals, First Circuit
599 F.2d 10, cert. denied, 444 U.S. 900 (1979)

LEVIN H. CAMPBELL, CIRCUIT JUDGE.

This admiralty case involves allegations that the defendant maritime insurance companies, owned and operated by Ernest Enos, were "blacklisting" plaintiff-appellees (a group of seamen working, at one time or another, out of Gloucester, Massachusetts) by demanding higher insurance premiums from the owners of vessels on which they worked. The plaintiffs claimed, *inter alia*, that the higher premiums were unjustified and that the defendants had tortiously interfered with their employment rights. Their suit was alleged to be within the admiralty jurisdiction of the federal courts, and both injunctive relief and damages were sought.

The case was tried to a judge sitting in admiralty in the district of Massachusetts. The court found that defendants insured 70% to 75% of the Gloucester fishing fleet at regular annual premiums of, in 1971, $650 to $800 per crewman. These rates were comparable to those of defendants' competitors. The court also found, however, that defendants required the owners of vessels to send them a "settlement sheet" containing the name and address of every member of the crew after all fishing trips completed by vessels they insured. These sheets were reviewed by Enos in part to learn whether any seamen who allegedly created a "special risk of loss" had been aboard. When such seamen were identified, the vessels owners were told that they would have to pay higher premiums sometimes as much as an additional $6,500 to cover these men. As a result, the named seamen encountered great difficulty finding employment. The court also found that the practice of requiring settlement sheets began after defendants, as a result of prior litigation, were enjoined from using an exclusionary endorsement system, under which specific seamen were excluded from coverage under insurance policies.[3] It

---

3. That system, which also interfered with the named seamen's ability to find employment, had been found to have been adopted with malice and to be beyond the scope of defendants' legitimate

held that eight of the fourteen plaintiffs had been designated high-risk seamen under the added premium system not for legitimate risk-related reasons, but because they had filed personal injury claims against the defendant insurance companies and had prosecuted their claims to judgment, instead of settling them to Enos' satisfaction.

The court adopted the Restatement (First) of Torts § 766 (1939), as a rule of decision. It found that defendants' economic pressure exerted on the boat owners was "a purposeful inducement and cause … to disrupt or abort the relationships of employment at will existing between the fishermen and the boat owners," and held that, "defendants' intentional tortious interference with plaintiffs' employment relationships was not privileged." *See* Restatement (First) of Torts §§ 767, 769 (1939).

The court awarded interim injunctive relief pending a hearing on the issue of damages. That injunction enjoined defendants from:

> 1. charging any additional premium to the owner of any commercial fishing vessel because he has signed on as a crewmember any one or more of (the eight prevailing plaintiffs); and

> 2. demanding as a condition for the issuance, maintenance, or continuation of any insurance policy that the owner of the fishing vessels make available to any of the three defendants … a settlement sheet which contains the names of any crewmember.

It is from this judgment and temporary injunction that defendants appeal. *See* 28 U.S.C. § 1292(a)(1).

Defendants challenge the admiralty jurisdiction of the court and argue that, even if the court did have jurisdiction, it was not empowered to grant injunctive relief. Alternatively, they argue that the injunction exceeds the scope of the court's authority that it is punitive, overbroad, harsh and disproportionate to the tortious conduct on which it is based. In respect to the finding of liability, they argue that the court erred in finding that their acts were not privileged business conduct and in relying on certain evidence.

· · ·

Application of Substantive Law: The district court adopted the Restatement (First) of Torts § 766 (1939) as "a recognized national standard from which to fashion a controlling principle of substantive federal maritime law." That section provides in pertinent part:

> [O]ne who, without a privilege to do so, induces or otherwise purposely causes a third person not to

> > (a) perform a contract with another, or

> > (b) enter into or continue a business relationship with another is liable to the other for the harm caused thereby.

This standard has been applied in similar cases by the Massachusetts state courts. *E.g., Pino v. Trans-Atlantic Marine, Inc.*, 358 Mass. 498, 265 N.E.2d 583, 587 (1970). We find no error.

Defendants argue that because plaintiffs did not work under long-term employment contracts, any refusal to hire was not a breach of contract within § 766(a), but rather fell within § 766(b). *See* Restatement (First) of Torts § 766, Comment c. A finding of a violation of § 766(b) requires that the alleged tortfeasor have acted with the purpose of de-

---

business privilege. *See Pino v. Trans-Atlantic Marine, Inc.*, 358 Mass. 498, 265 N.E.2d 583, 586–87 (1970)....

terring one from dealing with another, Restatement (First) of Torts § 766, Comment d, and here, defendants assert, their only purpose was the legitimate one of covering their insurance risks. The court, however, found that this was not so — that,

> eight of the fourteen plaintiffs were designated as added-premium seamen not for legitimate risk-related reasons but because of their inability to amicably settle insurance claims to Enos' satisfaction, and because of their retention of counsel, filing of personal injury actions, and prosecution of those claims to judgment, as they had every right to do.

The court further found that defendants knew that the exorbitant added premiums would cause ship owners to discharge plaintiffs and would discourage plaintiffs from seeking legal representation and making work-related injury insurance claims. These findings, which are not clearly erroneous, sustain the finding of purposeful conduct. *See* Restatement (First) of Torts § 766, Comment d....

By the same token, the court did not err in finding that defendants had exceeded the limits of legitimate business privilege. *See* Restatement (First) of Torts §§ 767, 769, 771. The burden of proving otherwise was on defendants ... and they did not do so. There is no privilege to deter people from exercising their legal rights by penalizing those who do. The sections defining business privileges all contain provisions indicating that defendants' conduct, as found by the court, would not be within their scope: there are no "social interests" in protecting defendants' conduct, § 767(e), and §§ 769 and 771 do not apply if the actor employs improper means, §§ 769(a), 771(c).

...

Defendants' primary objection [on the scope of the remedy — Ed.] is that the injunction prohibits them from raising the premiums for any of the eight prevailing plaintiffs for any reason. They argue that this interferes with their lawful business activity, and that the injunction should merely prohibit the imposition of an unjustified additional premium. Defendants also object to the prohibition against their requiring settlement sheets for vessels they insure. They argue that this aspect of the injunction interferes with their collection of information regularly and properly used in assessing premiums, and that it prevents them from obtaining information as to all seamen, not merely the eight prevailing plaintiffs.

We note, initially, that the injunction entered is a temporary one, effective pending disposition on the issue of damages and subject at all times to modification, if the district court is persuaded of a change in circumstances. The court found that none of Enos' legitimate underwriting criteria justified Enos' additional premium as to the eight prevailing plaintiffs at the time of its decision. Given these facts, the court did not abuse its discretion in ordering defendants not to raise plaintiffs' premiums. An insurance company is entitled, of course, to raise its premiums where legitimate considerations dictate. But the testimony elicited from Enos revealed that, in setting premiums, he relied on few, if any, objective criteria or statistical guidelines. The court found that Enos, whom it described as "evasive," set premiums largely on a subjective, ad hoc basis.[8]

---

8. The district court found:

"[Enos] conceded that he has never consulted with any outside person, expert or otherwise, on loss experience, premium-setting, or any other technical aspect of the insurance business. He further conceded that, in fact, the amount of the added premium boils down to a subjective judgment on his part, which he claims makes the premium commensurate with the risk assumed by the insurance company in 'allowing' that man to be a member of an insured crew. Counsel stipulated that the rate of premium is free of any state or federal regulation.... After considerable evasion, Enos also

Given the difficulty the court would have faced in policing an order allowing Enos to set only "legitimate" additional premiums in the face of his elusive rate-setting practices, and the indication that the higher premiums were being misused to deter seamen from exercising their rights, it was within its discretion to temporarily enjoin Enos from charging any additional premiums as to the eight plaintiffs.

We are less confident that the injunction against requiring settlement sheets from insured boat owners is appropriate. The interests of the prevailing plaintiffs would seem to have been fully protected by the injunction against raising their premiums; as this was not a class action, it is not clear that the injunction as to the settlement sheets was required. The court did find that the practice of requiring settlement sheets was adopted after the exclusionary endorsement system was enjoined by the federal district court in *Protection Maritime Insurance Co. v. Foley*, No. 70-1116-G (D.Mass.1971), and that the list was used,

> with an eye toward learning the earnings of the crew, the whereabouts of the crew and vessel, and, *most notably, the presence of any crew members who created, in [Enos'] sole judgment*, a special risk of loss.

(Emphasis added.) The court also found that these sheets were obtained after voyages were completed, that defendants "had no way of knowing who might be a crew member on an insured vessel prior to any given trip," and that defendants knew the consequences of their practices for plaintiffs' employment prospects. It did not state, however, that the collection of the information on the settlement sheets had no legitimate function, or that requiring the settlement sheets was largely a way of pressuring boat owners into not hiring "blacklisted" fishermen. Given these facts and, in addition, the finding that Enos had some legitimate basis for requiring additional premiums for those plaintiffs whose claims were dismissed, we conclude that this aspect of the injunction is too broad. As the court may not have articulated fully its reasons for adopting this aspect of its order, however, we remand with instructions to vacate unless the court, after making suitable findings of fact, concludes that this aspect of the order is necessary to protect the rights of the eight prevailing plaintiffs.

The judgment of liability is affirmed, as is the order temporarily enjoining defendants from assessing higher premiums as to the prevailing plaintiffs. The order enjoining the use of settlement sheets is remanded for reconsideration in light of this opinion.

So ordered.

NOTES

(1) Why shouldn't problems of insurer-insured relationships like that in *Pino* be left to the market? If Pino was a better risk than the defendant's premiums reflected, shouldn't a competitor come in to insure him more cheaply?

(2) John Pino, the named plaintiff in the federal case excerpted above, fought with Enos and his companies for more than a decade. He also had litigated in the state courts on the theory that Enos had excluded him from insurance coverage because he sued for injuries that occurred on board ship when a knife slipped as he was opening a lobster at mealtime. Pino alleged that the table on which he was cutting the lobster had contributed to his injury, because "the fittings which held the table in a rigid position were

---

admitted that 24 or 25 fishermen, out of a total insured work force of at least 200 men, were subject to an added premium."

'faulty'"; Enos argued that the claim was "baseless." In the same year that the defendant denied coverage for him, Pino alleged, the defendant had also "excluded from insurance coverage seven or eight other Gloucester fishermen who had made claims for personal injuries." The Massachusetts Supreme Judicial Court affirmed a damage award and an injunction, saying that "[e]ven though the plaintiff's 'contract of employment' may be terminable at the will of either party, the plaintiff is still entitled to appropriate remedies to prevent the defendants from unlawfully interfering with his employment." *Pino v. Trans-Atlantic Marine, Inc.*, 358 Mass. 498, 265 N.E.2d 583 (1970).

On remand of the decision reprinted in the text above, the district court awarded some lost earnings, $1,000 to each plaintiff for humiliation and emotional distress, and $9,000 a piece in punitive damages—the latter item taking into account "[d]efendants' blatant disregard for and circumvention of ... earlier ... decisions" by federal and state courts. *Pino v. Protection Maritime Ins. Co.*, 454 F. Supp. 277 (D. Mass. 1980).

(3) How much protection should someone like Pino get against retaliation for what an insurer considers frivolous litigation? Consider, for example, the case of a seaman injured while driving along the shore on Sunday. Asserting that he was on a busman's holiday to study fishing techniques, he makes a claim for compensation, arguing that he was within the scope of his employment. Could an insurer defend against an "interference" suit by arguing that this claim was "baseless" and therefore reason to exclude coverage?

(4) Compare with *Pino* the issues presented by another case involving an insurance defendant, *Crisci v. Security Ins. Co. of New Haven*, 66 Cal. 2d 425, 58 Cal. Rptr. 13, 426 P.2d 173 (1967). In this case, Mrs. Crisci, the owner of an apartment building, had a $10,000 general liability policy with Security. A tenant in the apartment sued for serious physical injuries and a psychosis that she attributed to an accident that occurred when a tread in a staircase gave way. Despite a profile of psychiatric testimony on which the defense would be successful only if the jury "believe[d] all of the defendant's psychiatric evidence and none of the plaintiff's," Security rejected a $9,000 settlement demand, even though Crisci offered to pay $2,500 of the settlement. The case against Crisci went to a jury, which awarded the tenant $100,000. The result was to make Crisci indigent, with serious physical and emotional consequences. Crisci then sued her insurer, and won a verdict that included $91,000, apparently representing her economic losses, and $25,000 for mental suffering. The court considered a variety of legal standards, including a test that would require the plaintiff to show that the insurer acted in bad faith and a test imposing liability whenever an insurer's rejection of a settlement is followed by a verdict in excess of policy limits. The court affirmed Crisci's verdict on the basis of an intermediate rule, one that required an insurer to give the interests of the insured at least as much consideration as it gives to its own interests.

(5) The so-called "bad faith" tort has emerged in a majority of jurisdictions as a weapon in suits against first-party insurers. Professor Henderson, summarizing the case law, has noted that a handful of jurisdictions have gone beyond "bad faith" to allow tort suits against one's own insurer for gross negligence, even for negligence, and in one jurisdiction perhaps on a non-fault basis. Roger C. Henderson, *The Tort of Bad Faith in First-Party Insurance Transactions After Two Decades*, 37 Ariz. L. Rev. 1153, 1158–60 (1995). The types of behavior for which suit has been allowed are numerous:

> The classic fact situation giving rise to a claim of bad faith in first-party insurance transactions involves the refusal of an insurer to pay the policy benefits. Although this ... still remains the paradigm case today, courts have extended the duty of good faith and fair dealing to other situations. Some of these situa-

tions are closely related to an outright refusal to pay, for example where an insurer unduly delays payment. Other decisions extending the duty are much further removed from the duty to pay policy benefits and may be more debatable in several respects.

· · ·

Somewhat like the admonition that "justice delayed is justice denied," the failure of an insurer to timely process and pay policy benefits, even though the benefits are eventually paid, may constitute an act of bad faith by an insurer. There is no doubt that an insurer needs a certain amount of time to investigate and process claims, but once it becomes clear that the benefits are due, delaying payment is as good as not paying at all.

In addition to outright refusals or delays in paying benefits, there seems to be no limit to the ways in which an insurer may be held to violate an insured's right to good faith and fair dealing in the claims process. Courts have recognized that an insurer is subject to liability for attempting to deceive an insured, misinterpreting records or policy provisions for the purpose of defeating coverage, using undue threats to force an insured to agree to an unfair settlement, falsely accusing an insured of wrongdoing, exploiting an insured's vulnerable position, making oppressive demands not required under the policy, conditioning payment of an undisputed portion of a claim on settlement of a disputed portion, unfairly imposing a premium increase in retaliation for filing a claim, destroying evidence that would support the insured's claim for benefits, relying on evidence that would be inadmissible at trial, wrongfully refusing to defend its insured against a liability claim by a third party, and refusing to pay a third-party tort claimant who has obtained a final judgment against its insured.

(6) The simple fact that one person knows that his conduct is substantially certain to cause another to breach his contract with a third party is insufficient, without more, to establish an interference tort. Illustrative is a case in which A agreed to purchase medical diagnostic equipment from B for use in a facility that A had contracted to establish for C, a medical partnership. C breached its agreement with A, well aware that A, stuck with diagnostic equipment usable only by C, would breach with B. After an initial suit by A against B for restitution of A's down payment on the equipment, B brought a third-party action against C for tortious interference with B's contract with A. Noting that the section 767 factors for determination of whether there has been a tortious interference include motive, the Seventh Circuit dismissed a third-party interference claim. It said that state law would "require[] more than the knowledge that one's conduct is substantially certain to result in one party breaking its contract with another." *R.E. Davis Chem. Corp. v. Diasonics, Inc.*, 826 F.2d 678 (7th Cir. 1987).

(7) Judge Posner elaborates on the idea that the "interference" tort is "really a branch of the law of unfair competition" in situations "where no breach of contract results from the interference" in *Frandsen v. Jensen-Sundquist Agency, Inc.*, 802 F.2d 941 (7th Cir. 1986). This case involved a suit by a minority shareholder in a holding company (Company A), of which the principal asset was the majority of stock in a bank, against a large holding company (Company B) that acquired Company A over the plaintiff's protest. The originally proposed deal would have involved what amounted to an acquisition by Company B of Company A for cash, followed by a merger of Company A's bank into a bank subsidiary of Company B. Subsequent maneuvering, following the plaintiff's refusal to go along with this deal, concluded with an agreement by Company

A to sell the shares in its bank to Company B and then liquidate. In rejecting the suit, Judge Posner commented:

> For First Wisconsin [Company B] to want to acquire First Bank of Grantsburg from Jensen-Sundquist [Company A] and to make suggestions for how the sale could be carried out in a way that would violate nobody's legal rights would not violate the norms of fair competition; it would exemplify them.

802 F.2d at 948.

(8) Is there something about torts involving the conduct of economic affairs that requires more precise standards than other torts?

(9) In the nineteen fifties, movie studios refused to hire certain people to write screenplays because of alleged Communist affiliations or leanings. Can you visualize a cause of action for such conduct?

(10) A complicated set of legal issues appeared in a much publicized federal litigation in which the plaintiff was the actress Vanessa Redgrave. She sued the Boston Symphony Orchestra for canceling a series of concerts in which she was to narrate *Oedipus Rex*. The orchestra cancelled the series after threats that the performances would be disrupted by subscribers angered by Redgrave's support for the P.L.O. and her critical views of Israel. In response to certified questions from the First Circuit, the Massachusetts Supreme Judicial Court declared that acquiescence to third party pressure would not provide a defense to the orchestra against a claim under the state civil rights act. In the same response, however, several justices of the state court indicated their belief that the Orchestra had a complete defense to the state civil rights act claim based on its right, secured by the state constitution, to make artistic judgments. *Redgrave v. Boston Symphony Orchestra*, 399 Mass. 93, 502 N.E.2d 1375 (1987). The state court's opinions on the latter point convinced the First Circuit, which was inclined to avoid a decision on federal constitutional issues, that state law protected the Orchestra from liability under the Massachusetts civil rights statute. See *Redgrave v. Boston Symphony Orchestra*, 855 F.2d 888 (1st Cir. 1988). The federal court did uphold Redgrave's separate breach of contract claim for consequential damages, although it reduced a $100,000 jury award on that count to $12,000.

(11) Law students may find it easy to picture why the Law School Admissions Test provokes some serious controversies about occasions when the Educational Testing Service cancels a test taker's test scores, and reports the cancellation to law schools to which the test taker has applied. In a First Circuit case, ETS investigated a 300-point differential between the plaintiff's third taking of the test and her scores on the first and second tests. A handwriting expert concluded that the answer sheets and registration form for the third test had not been written by the same person who had written the answer sheets on the first two tests. The plaintiff sued ETS for cancelling her score on the third test. She invoked, among other theories, wrongful interference with an "advantageous contractual relationship" with the University of California Law School. That institution had admitted the plaintiff after the report of the third test score, but had revoked her acceptance after ETS's cancellation of that score; it later accepted her provisionally. ETS successfully resisted the suit, with its defense on warranty and contract counts resting on its "reasonableness and good faith" in securing the services of three different handwriting experts, its giving the test taker a right to be heard with counsel, and its provision of an option to retake the third examination without charge. The court further reasoned that it must reject the interference claim because "[s]ince ETS acted in good faith, its actions can hardly be characterized as "without justification." *Johnson v. Educ. Testing Serv.*, 754 F.2d 20 (1st Cir.), *cert. denied*, 472 U.S. 1029 (1985).

FREEMAN & MILLS v. BELCHER OIL COMPANY

Supreme Court of California
11 Cal. 4th 85, 900 P.2d 669, 44 Cal. Rptr. 2d 420 (1995)

LUCAS, CHIEF JUSTICE.

We granted review in this case to resolve some of the widespread confusion that has arisen regarding the application of our opinion in Seaman's Direct Buying Service, Inc. v. Standard Oil Co. (1984) 36 Cal.3d 752, 206 Cal.Rptr. 354, 686 P.2d 1158 (Seaman's). We held in that case that a tort cause of action might lie "when, in addition to breaching the contract, [defendant] seeks to shield itself from liability by denying, in bad faith and without probable cause, that the contract exists." ...

In the present case, the Court of Appeal reversed judgment for plaintiff and remanded the case for a limited retrial, but also suggested that "it is time for the Supreme Court to reexamine the tort of 'bad faith denial of contract.'" ...

In light of certain developments occurring subsequent to Seaman's that call into question its continued validity, we find it appropriate to reexamine that decision.... As will appear, we have concluded that the Seaman's court incorrectly recognized a tort cause of action based on the defendant's bad faith denial of the existence of a contract between the parties....

I. Facts

We first review the underlying facts, taken largely from the Court of Appeal opinion herein. In June 1987, defendant Belcher Oil Company retained the law firm of Morgan, Lewis & Bockius (Morgan) to defend it in a Florida lawsuit. Pursuant to a letter of understanding signed by Belcher Oil's general counsel (William Dunker) and a Morgan partner (Donald Smaltz), Belcher Oil was to pay for costs incurred on its behalf, including fees for accountants. In February 1988, after first obtaining Dunker's express authorization, Smaltz hired plaintiff, the accounting firm of Freeman & Mills, Incorporated, to provide a financial analysis and litigation support for Belcher Oil in the Florida lawsuit.

In March, an engagement letter was signed by both Morgan and Freeman & Mills. At about this time, William Dunker left Belcher Oil and was replaced by Neil Bowman. In April 1988, Bowman became dissatisfied with Morgan's efforts and the lawyers were discharged. Bowman asked Morgan for a summary of the work performed by Freeman & Mills and, at the same time, directed Smaltz to have Freeman & Mills stop their work for Belcher Oil. Smaltz did as he was asked. Freeman & Mills's final statement was for $70,042.50 in fees, plus $7,495.63 for costs, a total of $77,538.13.

Freeman & Mills billed Morgan, but no payment was forthcoming. Freeman & Mills then billed Belcher Oil directly and, for about a year, sent monthly statements and regularly called Bowman about the bill, but no payment was forthcoming. In August 1989, Smaltz finally told Freeman & Mills that Belcher Oil refused to pay their bill. Freeman & Mills then wrote to Bowman asking that the matter be resolved. In September 1989, Bowman responded, complaining that Belcher Oil had not been consulted about the extent of Freeman & Mills's services and suggesting Freeman & Mills should look to Morgan for payment of whatever amounts were claimed due.

Ultimately, Freeman & Mills filed this action against Belcher Oil, alleging (in its second amended complaint) causes of action for breach of contract, "bad faith denial of

0

contract," and quantum meruit. Belcher Oil answered and the case was presented to a jury in a bifurcated trial, with punitive damages reserved for the second phase. According to the evidence presented during the first phase, the amount owed to Freeman & Mills (as indicated on their statements) was $77,538.13.

The jury returned its first phase verdict. On Freeman & Mills's breach of contract claim, the jury found that Belcher Oil had authorized Morgan to retain Freeman & Mills on Belcher Oil's behalf, that Freeman & Mills had performed its obligations under the contract, that Belcher Oil had breached the contract, and that the amount of damages suffered by Freeman & Mills was $25,000. The jury also answered affirmatively the questions about whether Belcher Oil had denied the existence of the contract and had acted with oppression, fraud, or malice. Thereafter, the jury returned its verdict awarding $477,538.13 in punitive damages and judgment was entered consistent with the jury's verdicts.

In three post-trial motions, Freeman & Mills asked for orders (1) "correcting" the jury's verdicts and the court's judgment to reflect compensatory damages of $77,538.13 and punitive damages of $425,000 (on the ground that the jury's questions showed this was its true intent); (2) awarding attorney fees as sanctions for the litigation tactics of Belcher Oil's attorneys; and (3) awarding prejudgment interest on the compensatory damage award. Over Belcher Oil's opposition, all three motions were granted—but with some changes in the course of correcting the judgment—by giving Freeman & Mills $131,614.93 in compensatory damages (the $25,000 actually awarded by the jury, plus the $77,538.13 included in the punitive damage award, plus $29,076.80 for prejudgment interest), and $400,000 (not $425,000 as requested) in punitive damages.

Belcher Oil appealed from the "corrected" judgment. Freeman & Mills cross-appealed from a mid-trial order denying its request to amend its complaint to add a cause of action for fraud, an issue not presently before us. The Court of Appeal majority, finding no "special relationship" between the parties to justify a tort theory of recovery under Seaman's, reversed the judgment and remanded the case to the trial court for a retrial limited to the issue of damages under plaintiff's breach of contract cause of action. (The Court of Appeal dissenting justice would have sustained the tort cause of action and remanded for retrial of the damage issue as to both causes of action.) As will appear, we affirm the judgment of the Court of Appeal, concluding that a tort recovery is unavailable in this case.

II. The Seaman's Decision

The tort of bad faith "denial of contract" was established in a per curiam opinion in Seaman's, supra.... These were the facts before the court in that case: In 1971, Seaman's Direct Buying Service, a small marine fueling station in Eureka, wanted to expand its operation by developing a marine fuel dealership in conjunction with a new marina under development by the City of Eureka. When Seaman's approached the city about a long-term lease of a large parcel of land in the marina, the city required Seaman's to obtain a binding commitment from an oil supplier. To that end, Seaman's negotiated with several companies and, by 1972, reached a tentative agreement with Standard Oil Company of California.

Both Seaman's and Standard Oil signed a letter of intent setting forth the basic terms of their arrangement, but that letter was subject to government approval of the contract, continued approval of Seaman's credit status, and future agreement on specific arrangements. Seaman's showed the letter to the city and, shortly thereafter, signed a 40-year lease with the city....

Shortly thereafter, an oil shortage dramatically reduced the available supplies of oil and, in November 1973, Standard Oil told Seaman's that new federal regulations requiring allocation of petroleum products to those that had been customers since 1972 precluded its execution of a new dealership agreement. In response, Seaman's obtained an exemption from the appropriate federal agency. Standard Oil appealed and persuaded the agency to reverse the order, but Seaman's eventually had the exemption reinstated contingent on a court determination that a valid contract existed between the parties....

Seaman's then asked Standard Oil to stipulate to the existence of a contract, stating that a refusal would force it to discontinue operations. Standard Oil's representative refused the request, telling Seaman's, "See you in court." Seaman's business collapsed and it sued Standard Oil for damages on four theories—breach of contract, fraud, breach of the implied covenant of good faith and fair dealing, and interference with Seaman's contractual relationship with the city....

The case was tried to a jury, which returned its verdicts in favor of Seaman's on all theories except fraud, awarding compensatory and punitive damages. Standard Oil appealed.... We considered "whether, and under what circumstances, a breach of the implied covenant of good faith and fair dealing in a commercial contract may give rise to an action in tort." ... For purposes of completeness, we quote from Seaman's at some length:

"It is well settled that, in California, the law implies in every contract a covenant of good faith and fair dealing. [Citations.] Broadly stated, that covenant requires that neither party do anything which will deprive the other of the benefits of the agreement. [Citation.] [¶] California courts have recognized the existence of this covenant, and enforced it, in cases involving a wide variety of contracts.... [¶] In the seminal cases of Comunale v. Traders & General Ins. Co. [(1958)] 50 Cal.2d 654, 328 P.2d 198, and Crisci v. Security Ins. Co. [(1967)] 66 Cal.2d 425, 58 Cal.Rptr. 13, 426 P.2d 173, this court held that a breach of the covenant of good faith and fair dealing by an insurance carrier may give rise to a cause of action in tort as well as in contract. [Citation.]

"While the proposition that the law implies a covenant of good faith and fair dealing in all contracts is well established, the proposition advanced by Seaman's—that breach of the covenant always gives rise to an action in tort—is not so clear. In holding that a tort action is available for breach of the covenant in an insurance contract, we have emphasized the 'special relationship' between insurer and insured, characterized by elements of public interest, adhesion, and fiduciary responsibility. [Citation.] No doubt there are other relationships with similar characteristics and deserving of similar legal treatment.

"When we move from such special relationships to consideration of the tort remedy in the context of the ordinary commercial contract, we move into largely uncharted and potentially dangerous waters. Here, parties of roughly equal bargaining power are free to shape the contours of their agreement and to include provisions for attorney fees and liquidated damages in the event of breach. They may not be permitted to disclaim the covenant of good faith but they are free, within reasonable limits at least, to agree upon the standards by which application of the covenant is to be measured. In such contracts, it may be difficult to distinguish between breach of the covenant and breach of contract, and there is the risk that interjecting tort remedies will intrude upon the expectations of the parties. This is not to say that tort remedies have no place in such a commercial context, but that it is wise to proceed with caution in determining their scope and application.

"For the purposes of this case it is unnecessary to decide the broad question which Seaman's poses. Indeed, it is not even necessary to predicate liability on a breach of the implied covenant. It is sufficient to recognize that *a party to a contract may incur tort remedies when, in addition to breaching the contract, it seeks to shield itself from liability by denying, in bad faith and without probable cause, that the contract exists.* (Italics added.)

"It has been held that a party to a contract may be subject to tort liability, including punitive damages, if he coerces the other party to pay more than is due under the contract terms through the threat of a lawsuit, made '"without probable cause and with no belief in the existence of the cause of action."' [Citation.] There is little difference, in principle, between a contracting party obtaining excess payment in such manner, and a contracting party seeking to avoid all liability on a meritorious contract claim by adopting a 'stonewall' position ('see you in court') without probable cause and with no belief in the existence of a defense. Such conduct goes beyond the mere breach of contract. It offends accepted notions of business ethics. [Citation.] Acceptance of tort remedies in such a situation is not likely to intrude upon the bargaining relationship or upset reasonable expectations of the contracting parties." ...

Seaman's concluded that, because a good faith denial of the existence of a binding contract is not a tort..., the trial court's failure to instruct the jury on the requirement of bad faith was error ... and that error was prejudicial....

...

... [M]uch confusion and conflict has arisen regarding the scope and application of our Seaman's holding. For example, does the Seaman's tort derive from breach of the implied covenant or from some other independent tort duty? ... Does the Seaman's tort extend to a bad faith denial of liability under a contract, as well as denial of its existence? ... Is a "special relationship" between the contracting parties a prerequisite to a Seaman's action? ...

... [I]n Harris [v. Atlantic Richfield], 14 Cal.App.4th 70, 17 Cal.Rptr.2d 649, the Court of Appeal denied a tort recovery for bad faith contract breach in violation of public policy. The court elaborated on the applicable policy considerations as follows: "The traditional goal of contract remedies is compensation of the promisee for the loss resulting from the breach, not compulsion of the promisor to perform his promises. Therefore, 'willful' breaches have not been distinguished from other breaches. [Citation.] The restrictions on contract remedies serve purposes not found in tort law. They protect the parties' freedom to bargain over special risks and they promote contract formation by limiting liability to the value of the promise. This encourages efficient breaches, resulting in increased production of goods and services at lower cost to society. [Citation.] Because of these overriding policy considerations, the California Supreme Court has proceeded with caution in carving out exceptions to the traditional contract remedy restrictions. [Citations.]" ...

The Harris court set forth as reasons for denying tort recovery in contract breach cases (1) the different objectives underlying the remedies for tort and contract breach, (2) the importance of predictability in assuring commercial stability in contractual dealings, (3) the potential for converting every contract breach into a tort, with accompanying punitive damage recovery, and (4) the preference for legislative action in affording appropriate remedies. (Harris....)

As we shall see ... the foregoing policy considerations fully support our decision to overrule Seaman's rather than attempt to clarify its uncertain boundaries. (We observe that plaintiff has asked us to take judicial notice of certain records purportedly showing there were only a few jury verdicts involving Seaman's claims during the period from

1981 to 1994. Because jury verdicts are an inconclusive indicia of excessive litigation, and because defendant has raised some doubts regarding the accuracy and completeness of the submitted materials, the application for judicial notice is denied.)

C. Criticism by Courts of Other Jurisdictions

We decided Seaman's in 1984. Since then, courts of other jurisdictions have either criticized or declined to follow our Seaman's analysis....

Ninth Circuit Judge Kozinski expressed his candid criticism of Seaman's in a concurring opinion in Oki America, Inc. v. Microtech Intern., Inc. (9th Cir.1989) 872 F.2d 312, 314–317 (Oki America). Among other criticism, Judge Kozinski found the Seaman's holding unduly imprecise and confusing. As he stated, "It is impossible to draw a principled distinction between a tortious denial of a contract's existence and a permissible denial of liability under the terms of the contract. The test ... seems to be whether the conduct 'offends accepted notions of business ethics.' [Citation.] This gives judges license to rely on their gut feelings in distinguishing between a squabble and a tort. As a result, both the commercial world and the courts are needlessly burdened...."

...

Judge Kozinski also mentioned the substantial costs associated with Seaman's litigation, and the resulting interference with contractual relationships. "Perhaps most troubling, the willingness of courts to subordinate voluntary contractual arrangements to their own sense of public policy and proper business decorum deprives individuals of an important measure of freedom. The right to enter into contracts—to adjust one's legal relationships by mutual agreement [] is too easily smothered by government officers eager to tell us what's best for us." ... Judge Kozinski concluded by observing that "Seaman's is a prime candidate for reconsideration." ...

...

D. Scholarly Criticism

Scholarly commentary on Seaman's also has been generally critical of our Seaman's holding and underlying analysis. (See, e.g., Ashley, Bad Faith Actions; Liability and Damages (1994) § 11.08, at p. 28 [the Seaman's court, in creating a new tort of "stonewalling" based on "inapposite" authority, "can only be described as out of balance," having "lost touch with the traditions of contract law"]; Putz & Klippen, Commercial Bad Faith: Attorney Fees—Not Tort Liability—is the Remedy for "Stonewalling" (1987) 21 U.S.F.L.Rev. 419, 459 (hereafter Putz & Klippen) [finding "no rational way" to distinguish denial of contract existence from other denials of liability]; Sebert, Punitive and Nonpecuniary Damages in Actions Based Upon Contract: Toward Achieving the Objective of Full Compensation (1986) 33 U.C.L.A.L.Rev. 1565, 1640–1641 (hereafter Sebert) stating that Seaman's is an "unhappy compromise" that is "both troubling and likely to be mischievous" by creating a "meaningless distinction" between denial of contract existence and other breaches]; Snyderman, What's So Good About Good Faith? The Good Faith Performance Obligation in Commercial Lending (1988) 55 U.Chi.L.Rev. 1335, 1363 (hereafter Snyderman) [stating that Seaman's "represents a potentially disastrous expansion of the bad faith tort into the commercial realm"]; ... Comment, Tort Remedies for Breach of Contract: The Expansion of Tortious Breach of the Implied Covenant of Good Faith and Fair Dealing into the Commercial Realm (1986) 86 Colum.L.Rev. 377, 401 (hereafter Columbia Comment) [finding "no principled distinction" between denial of a contract's existence, and denial that certain parts or terms exist, and concluding that Seaman's ultimate result "will be to expose commercial parties to tort-level damages whenever a party refuses to perform under the contract"]....

Additionally, several of these commentaries emphasize the extreme difficulty courts experience in distinguishing between tortious denial of a contract's existence and permissible denial of liability under the terms of the contract.... Further confusion concerns the quantum of proof required to establish a denial of the existence of the contract....

The foregoing commentaries raise a wide variety of additional criticisms that support reconsideration of the Seaman's decision, including widespread confusion among judges and juries in applying its holding, inappropriately excessive damage awards, overcrowded court dockets and speculative litigation, delay and complication of ordinary contract breach claims, deterrence of contract formation, and restraint on zealous advocacy....

...

As set forth above, the critics stress, among other factors favoring Seaman's abrogation, the confusion and uncertainty accompanying the decision, the need for stability and predictability in commercial affairs, the potential for excessive tort damages, and the preference for legislative rather than judicial action in this area.

Even if we were unimpressed by the nearly unanimous criticism leveled at Seaman's, on reconsideration the analytical defects in the opinion have become apparent. It seems anomalous to characterize as "tortious" the bad faith denial of the existence of a contract, while treating as "contractual" the bad faith denial of liability or responsibility under an acknowledged contract. In both cases, the breaching party has acted in bad faith and, accordingly, has presumably committed acts offensive to "accepted notions of business ethics." (Seaman's, supra, 36 Cal.3d at p. 770, 206 Cal.Rptr. 354, 686 P.2d 1158.) Yet to include bad faith denials of liability within Seaman's scope could potentially convert every contract breach into a tort. Nor would limiting Seaman's tort to incidents involving "stonewalling" adequately narrow its potential scope. Such conduct by the breaching party, essentially telling the promisee, "See you in court," could incidentally accompany every breach of contract.

For all the foregoing reasons, we conclude that Seaman's should be overruled. We emphasize that nothing in this opinion should be read as affecting the existing precedent governing enforcement of the implied covenant in insurance cases. Further, nothing we say here would prevent the Legislature from creating additional civil remedies for noninsurance contract breach, including such measures as providing litigation costs and attorney fees in certain aggravated cases, or assessing increased compensatory damages covering lost profits and other losses attributable to the breach, as well as restoration of the Seaman's holding if the Legislature deems that course appropriate....

VII. Conclusion

The judgment of the Court of Appeal, reversing the trial court's judgment in plaintiff's favor and remanding the case for a retrial limited to the issue of damages under plaintiff's breach of contract cause of action, and for judgment in favor of defendant on plaintiff's bad faith denial of contract cause of action, is affirmed.

...

MOSK, JUSTICE, concurring and dissenting.

I concur in the judgment. I disagree, however, with the majority's conclusion that Seaman's Direct Buying Service, Inc. v. Standard Oil Co. (1984) 36 Cal.3d 752, 206

Cal.Rptr. 354, 686 P.2d 1158 (Seaman's) was wrongly decided. Although in retrospect I believe its holding was too broad, our task, both for the sake of sound public policy and stare decisis, is to clarify rather than repudiate that holding.

... I agree that the bad faith denial of the existence of a contract or contractual liability, alone, cannot give rise to tort liability. I agree as well with the tautological proposition that a breach of contract is made tortious only when some "independent duty arising from tort law" is violated.

In my view, however, this "independent duty arising from tort law" can originate from torts other than those traditionally recognized at common law. There are some types of intentionally tortious behavior unique to the contractual setting that do not fit into conventional tort categories. Allowing for the possibility of tort causes of action outside conventional categories is consistent with the malleable and continuously evolving nature of the tort law. "'The law of torts is anything but static, and the limits of its development are never set. When it becomes clear that the plaintiff's interests are entitled to legal protection against the conduct of the defendant, the mere fact that the claim is novel will not of itself operate as a bar to the remedy.'" (Soldano v. O'Daniels (1983) 141 Cal.App.3d 443, 454–455, 190 Cal.Rptr. 310, quoting Prosser on Torts (4th ed. 1971) pp. 3–4.)

Seaman's should be viewed within the context of this common law tradition of innovation. When Seaman's is understood in light of its facts, it stands for the proposition, in my view, that a contract action may also sound in tort when the breach of contract is intentional and in bad faith, and is aggravated by certain particularly egregious forms of intentionally injurious activity. Because, as will be explained, there is no such tortious activity in the present case, I concur in the majority's disposition.

I will discuss below the various circumstances under which courts have found or may find a breach of contract to be tortious — circumstances broader than may be suggested by the majority's holding. As I will explain, a tortious breach of contract outside the insurance context may be found when (1) the breach is accompanied by a traditional common law tort, such as fraud or conversion; (2) the means used to breach the contract are tortious, involving deceit or undue coercion or; (3) one party intentionally breaches the contract intending or knowing that such a breach will cause severe, unmitigatable harm in the form of mental anguish, personal hardship, or substantial consequential damages. I will then explain why in my view Seaman's was correctly decided. Finally, I will explain why Seaman's is distinguishable from the present case.

I.

The notion that a breach of contract might be tortious causes conceptual difficulty because of the fundamental difference between the objectives of contract and tort law. "''[Whereas] [c]ontract actions are created to protect the interest in having promises performed," "[t]ort actions are created to protect the interest in freedom from various kinds of harm. The duties of conduct which give rise to them are imposed by law, and are based primarily on social policy, not necessarily based upon the will or intention of the parties....'''"....

This difference in purpose has its greatest practical significance in the differing types of damages available under the two bodies of law. "Contract damages are generally limited to those within the contemplation of the parties when the contract was entered into or at least reasonably foreseeable by them at that time; consequential damages beyond the expectations of the parties are not recoverable." (Applied Equipment Corp., supra, 7 Cal.4th at p. 515, 28 Cal.Rptr.2d 475, 869 P.2d 454.) Damages for emotional distress and mental suffering, as well as punitive damages, are also generally not recoverable...."This limitation on available damages serves to encourage contractual relations and commercial activity by enabling parties to estimate in advance the financial risks of their enterprise." ..."In contrast, tort damages are awarded to compensate the victim for injury suffered. [Citation.] 'For the breach of an obligation not arising from contract, the measure of damages ... is the amount which will compensate for all the detriment proximately caused thereby, whether it could have been anticipated or not.' ..." Both emotional distress damages and punitive damages are, under the proper circumstances, available to the tort victim.

Tort and contract law also differ in the moral significance that each places on intentional injury. Whereas an intentional tort is seen as reprehensible—the deliberate or reckless harming of another—the intentional breach of contract has come to be viewed as a morally neutral act, as exemplified in Justice Holmes's remark that "[t]he duty to keep a contract at common law means a prediction that you must pay damages if you do not keep it—and nothing else." (Holmes, The Path of the Law (1897) 10 Harv.L.Rev. 457, 462.) This amoral view is supported by the economic insight that an intentional breach of contract may create a net benefit to society. The efficient breach of contract occurs when the gain to the breaching party exceeds the loss to the party suffering the breach, allowing the movement of resources to their more optimal use. (See Posner, Economic Analysis of Law (1986) 107–108.) Contract law must be careful "not to exceed compensatory damages if it doesn't want to deter efficient breaches." (Id. at p. 108.)

But while the purposes behind contract and tort law are distinct, the boundary line between the two areas of the law is neither clear nor fixed. As Justice Holmes also observed, "the distinction between tort and breaches of contract, and especially between the remedies for the two, is not found ready made." (Holmes, The Common Law (1881) 13.) Courts have long permitted a party to a contract to seek tort remedies if behavior constituting a contract breach also violates some recognized tort duty. The courts "have extended the tort liability for misfeasance to virtually every type of contract where defective performance may injure the promisee. An attorney or an abstractor examining a title, a physician treating a patient, a surveyor, an agent collecting a note or lending money or settling a claim, or a liability insurer defending a suit, all have been held liable in tort for their negligence.... The principle which seems to have emerged from the decisions in the United States is that there will be liability in tort for misperformance of a contract whenever there would be liability for gratuitous performance without the contract—which is to say, whenever such misperformance involves a foreseeable, unreasonable risk of harm to the interests of the plaintiff." (Prosser & Keeton on Torts (5th ed. 1984) Tort and Contract, pp. 660–661, fns. omitted.) Stated another way, "'[c]onduct which merely is a breach of contract is not a tort, but the contract may establish a relationship demanding the exercise of proper care and acts and omissions in performance may give rise to tort liability.'"

. . .

Nor are the rules that determine whether the action will sound in tort or contract, or both, clear-cut. When the breach of contract also involves physical injury to the promisee, or the destruction of tangible property, as opposed to damage to purely economic interests, then the action will generally sound in tort. Thus, a manufacturer that sells defective automobiles may be liable to an automobile dealer in contract for delivery of nonconforming goods, but will be liable in tort if one of the nonconforming automobiles leads to an accident resulting in physical injury. But society also imposes tort duties to protect purely economic interests between contracting parties—such as the duty of care imposed on accountants for malpractice (see Lindner v. Barlow, Davis & Wood (1962) 210 Cal.App.2d 660, 665, 27 Cal.Rptr. 101), or on banks for wrongfully dishonoring checks (see Weaver v. Bank of America (1953) 59 Cal.2d 428, 431, 30 Cal.Rptr. 4, 380 P.2d 644) — as well as the recognition of intentional torts such as promissory fraud. The complete failure to perform a contractual obligation generally sounds in contract, but once a contractual obligation has begun, a failure to perform which injures the promisee may sometimes sound in tort. (Prosser & Keeton on Torts, supra, pp. 661–662.) Perhaps the most reliable manner to differentiate between actions that are purely contract breaches and those that are also tort violations is the following abstract rule: courts will generally enforce the breach of a contractual promise through contract law, except when the actions that constitute the breach violate a social policy that merits the imposition of tort remedies.

It is also true that public policy does not always favor a limitation on damages for intentional breaches of contract. The notion that society gains from an efficient breach must be qualified by the recognition that many intentional breaches are not efficient.... As Judge Posner explained in Patton [v. Mid-Continent Systems], 841 F.2d at page 751: "Not all breaches of contract are involuntary or otherwise efficient. Some are opportunistic; the promisor wants the benefit of the bargain without bearing the agreed-upon costs, and exploits the inadequacies of purely compensatory remedies (the major inadequacies being that pre-and post-judgment interest rates are frequently below market levels when the risk of nonpayment is taken into account and that the winning party cannot recover ... attorney's fees)." Commentators have also pointed to other "inadequacies of purely compensatory remedies" that encourage inefficient breaches (i.e. breaches that result in greater losses to the promisee than gains for the promisor): the lack of emotional distress damages, even when such damages are the probable result of the breach, and the restriction of consequential damages to those in the contemplation of the parties at the time the contract was formed....

In addition to fully compensating contract plaintiffs and discouraging inefficient breaches, the imposition of tort remedies for certain intentional breaches of contract serves to punish and deter business practices that constitute distinct social wrongs independent of the breach. For example, we permit the plaintiff to recover exemplary damages in cases in which the breached contract was induced through promissory fraud, even though the plaintiff has incurred the same loss whether the contract was fraudulently induced or not.... Our determination to allow the plaintiff to sue for fraud and to potentially recover exemplary damages is not justified by the plaintiff's greater loss, but by the fact that the breach of a fraudulently induced contract is a significantly greater wrong, from society's standpoint, than an ordinary breach. "We are aware of the danger of grafting tort liability on what ordinarily should be a breach of contract action.... However, no public policy is served by permitting a party who never intended to fulfill his obligations to fraudulently induce another to enter into an agreement." (Las Palmas Associates v. Las Palmas Center Associates (1991) 235 Cal.App.3d 1220, 1238, 1 Cal.Rptr.2d 301.)

As the above illustrate, the rationale for limiting actions for intentional breaches of contract to contract remedies — that such limitation promotes commercial stability and predictability and hence advances commerce — is not invariably a compelling one. Breaches accompanied by deception or infliction of intentional harm may be so disruptive of commerce and so reprehensible in themselves that the value of deterring such actions through the tort system outweighs the marginal loss in the predictability of damages that may result. But in imposing tort duties to deter intentionally harmful acts among contracting parties, courts must be cautious not to fashion remedies which overdeter the illegitimate and as a result chill legitimate activities. (See Posner, Economic Analysis of Law, supra, at p. 108.) Thus, courts should be careful to apply tort remedies only when the conduct in question is so clear in its deviation from socially useful business practices that the effect of enforcing such tort duties will be, as in the case of fraud, to aid rather than discourage commerce.

As observed above, not all tortious breaches of contract arise from conventional torts. Numerous courts have recognized types of intentionally tortious activity that occur exclusively or distinctively within the context of a contractual relationship. The most familiar type of tortious breach of contract in this state is that of the insurer, whose unreasonable failure to settle or resolve a claim has been held to violate the covenant of good faith and fair dealing. (Egan v. Mutual of Omaha Insurance Co., supra, 24 Cal.3d 809, 169 Cal.Rptr. 691, 620 P.2d 141.) Tort liability is imposed primarily because of the distinctive characteristics of the insurance contract: the fiduciary nature of the relationship, the fact that the insurer offers a type of quasi-public service that provides financial security and peace of mind, and the fact that the insurance contract is generally one of adhesion. (Id. at pp. 820–821, 169 Cal.Rptr. 691, 620 P.2d 141.) In these cases, the special relationship between insurer and insured supports the elevation of the covenant of good faith and fair dealing, a covenant implied by law in every contract and generally used as an aid to contract interpretation (Foley [v. Interactive Data Corp.], 47 Cal.3d at p. 684, 254 Cal.Rptr. 211, 765 P.2d 373), into a tort duty.

Because the good faith covenant is so broad and all-pervasive, this court and others have been reluctant to expand recognition of the action for tortious breach of the covenant beyond the insurance context. (See Foley, supra, 47 Cal.3d at p. 692, 254 Cal.Rptr. 211, 765 P.2d 373 [no special relationship in the employment context].... Unfortunately, the preoccupation of California courts with limiting the potentially enormous scope of this tort has diverted attention away from the useful task of identifying specific practices employed by contracting parties that merit the imposition of tort remedies. Other jurisdictions not so preoccupied have made greater progress in developing a common law of tortious breach of contract. While the cases are not easily amenable to classification, they appear to fit into two broad categories.

The first category focuses on tortious means used by one contracting party to coerce or deceive another party into foregoing its contractual rights. For example, in Advanced Medical v. Arden Medical Systems (3d Cir.1992) 955 F.2d 188, Advanced Medical, Inc. (Advanced), a distributor of medical products, entered into an agreement with a manufacturer of a high-technology blood analysis device, whereby the former was designated as the latter's exclusive distributor for the mid-Atlantic region. The manufacturing company was eventually acquired by Johnson & Johnson, which disapproved of the exclusive distributorship. Instead of merely breaching the agreement, Johnson & Johnson used a variety of questionable tactics to "drive Advanced out of the contract," including marketing competing products not made available to Advanced, and withholding its support services. (Id. at pp. 190–191.) The court, applying Pennsylvania law, held that in addition to a breach of contract, there was sufficient evidence to submit the question of punitive damages to a jury on a theory of Johnson & Johnson's "tortious interference" with its own contract. (Id. at pp. 201–202.) (See also Adam's v. Crater Well Drilling, Inc. (1976) 276 Or. 789, 556 P.2d 679, 681 [punitive damages justified when contracting party uses threat of prosecution to obtain more than is owed under the contract]; John A. Henry & Co., Ltd. v. T.G. & Y Stores & Co. (10th Cir.1991) 941 F.2d 1068, 1072–1073 [punitive damages allowed under Oklahoma law when commercial tenant attempts to compel landlord to release it from its lease by fabricating defects in the landlord's maintenance and sending letters complaining of such defects to the landlord's lender, thereby disparaging the former's reputation]; Jones v. Abriani (1976) 169 Ind.App. 556, 350 N.E.2d 635, 649 [punitive damages upheld when defendant mobile home salesman threatened to forfeit plaintiffs' down payment if plaintiffs did not accept delivery of a home with numerous defects and then reneged on promise to repair these defects].) One commentator provides another example of this kind of tortious breach derived from a case that was originally a companion to Seaman's: a major motion picture studio threatens to blacklist an actor appearing in one of its productions if he does not forfeit his contractual right to a prominent billing. (Ashley, Bad Faith Actions (1994) § 11.04, p. 6.)

The use of tortious means to breach a contract can also entail the use of deception by one of the contracting parties for the purpose of causing the other party to forego its contractual rights. In Motley, Green & Co. v. Detroit Steel & Spring Co. (C.C.S.D. N.Y. 1908) 161 F. 389, for example, the plaintiff was an exclusive sales agent within a given territory for the defendant, an automobile parts company. The defendant allegedly made a sham sale to another company for the sole purpose of extricating itself from the contract with the plaintiff. The court concluded that it was tortious for the defendant, in addition to breaching the contract, "to invite a third party to unite with him and aid him in breaking the contract in such a way as possibly to escape liability in an action for nonperformance." (Id. at p. 397.) The court compared the case to one cited in a tort treatise of a plaintiff who was an "'actor, ... engaged to perform in the character of Hamlet, ... and that the defendants and others maliciously conspired together to prevent the plaintiff from so performing, and from exercising his profession in the theater, and in pursuance of the conspiracy hired and procured divers persons to go to the theater and hoot the plaintiff, and the persons so hired, did.... '" (Ibid....)

A second type of tortious intentional breach has been found when the consequences of the breach are especially injurious to the party suffering the breach, and the breaching party intentionally or knowingly inflicts such injury. Cases of this type have generally occurred outside the commercial context, involving manifestly unequal contracting parties and contracts concerning matters of vital personal significance, in which great mental anguish or personal hardship are the probable result of the breach. In these cases, courts have permitted substantial awards of emotional distress damages and/or punitive damages, both as a means of providing extra sanctions for a defendant engaging in intentionally injurious activities against vulnerable parties, and as a way of fully compensating plaintiffs for types of injury that are neither readily amendable to mitigation nor generally recoverable as contract damages. For example, in K-Mart Corp. v. Ponsock (Nev.1987) 103 Nev. 39, 732 P.2d 1364, 1370, disapproved on other grounds by Ingersoll-Rand Co. v. McClendon (1990) 498 U.S. 133, 137, 111 S.Ct. 478, 482, 112 L.Ed.2d 474, the Nevada Supreme Court allowed a $50,000 award of punitive damages to stand when an employer discharged a long-term employee on a fabricated charge for the purpose of defeating the latter's contractual entitlement to retirement benefits. (See also Ainsworth v. Franklin County Cheese Corp. (1991) 156 Vt. 325, 592 A.2d 871, 871, 874–875 [punitive damages permitted when a defendant/employer discharged on pretext of good cause the plaintiff/employee in order to extricate itself from the obligation to pay severance benefits].)

In other cases of this type, an intentional breach of a warranty of habitability by a landlord or building contractor has given rise to substantial emotional distress or punitive damages awards. For example, Missouri courts recognize that a wrongful eviction will sound in tort as well as contract. (Ladeas v. Carter (Mo.Ct.App.1992) 845 S.W.2d 45, 52; see also Emden v. Vitz (1948) 88 Cal.App.2d 313, 318–319, 198 P.2d 696 [wrongful eviction accompanied by verbal abuse sounds in tort]; Hilder v. St. Peter (1984) 144 Vt. 150, 478 A.2d 202, 210 [punitive damages permitted against a landlord who, "after receiving notice of a defect, fails to repair the facility that is essential to the health and safety of his or her tenant"]; B & M Homes, Inc. v. Hogan (Ala.1979) 376 So.2d 667, 671–672 [substantial emotional distress damages award against contractor who refused to repair construction defects leading to great personal discomfort]; Ducote v. Arnold (La.Ct.App.1982) 416 So.2d 180, 183–185 [damages for mental anguish permitted for breach of home remodeling contract].) The New Mexico Supreme Court, in Romero v. Mervyn's (1989) 109 N.M. 249, 784 P.2d 992, 999–1001, citing Seaman's with approval, upheld a punitive damage award against a department store, which had entered into an oral agreement to pay the medical expenses of a customer accidentally injured on its premises, and then reneged on its agreement.

The principle that certain contractual interests of vulnerable parties deserve greater protection than ordinary contract damages would otherwise provide has led our Legislature to authorize special sanctions for various types of intentional breaches. For example, one who is the victim of an intentional breach of warranty of consumer goods may recover twice the amount of actual damages (Civ.Code, § 1794, subd. (c)) and treble damages may be awarded to a retail seller who is injured by "willful or repeated" warranty violations (id.,§ 1794.1, subd. (a)). Labor Code section 206 provides for treble damages for the willful failure to pay wages after the Labor Commissioner determines the wages are owing. But the fact that the Legislature has acted in some instances to afford these special protections does not mean that it has preempted the courts from exercising their traditional role of fashioning appropriate tort remedies for various kinds of intentionally injurious conduct.

In sum, the above cited cases show that an intentional breach of contract may be found to be tortious when the breaching party exhibits an extreme disregard for the contractual rights of the other party, either knowingly harming the vital interests of a promisee so as to create substantial mental distress or personal hardship, or else employing coercion or dishonesty to cause the promisee to forego its contractual rights. These cases illustrate the recognition by a number of jurisdictions that an intentional breach of contract outside the insurance context, and not accompanied by any conventional tortious behavior such as promissory fraud, may nonetheless be deemed tortious when accompanied by these kinds of aggravating circumstances.

With this in mind, I next reconsider the Seaman's case.

II.

…

Seaman's was correct, in my view, in refusing to rely on the general breach of the covenant of good faith and fair dealing as a justification for imposing tort remedies, and instead seeking to identify specific practices used by Standard that violated "accepted notions of business ethics." Seaman's wisely recognized that courts do not have to choose between the wholesale transformation of a breach of the implied good faith covenant into a tort and the complete refusal to recognize a cause of action for tortious breach of contract. In retrospect, however, Seaman's holding appears to be both overly broad and overly narrow. It was overly narrow because, as numerous authorities cited by the majority point out, there is no logical reason to distinguish between the tort of "bad faith denial of the existence of a contract" and "bad faith denial of liability under a contract." The former is but a subspecies of the latter. Both forms of bad faith are equally reprehensible on the defendant's part and equally injurious to plaintiff.

Seaman's was overly broad because, for a number of reasons, it appears to have been unwise to impose tort liability for all breaches that involve bad faith denial of a contract or liability under the contract. Although the bad faith denial of contractual liability may be ethically inexcusable, we should hesitate to categorically impose tort liability on such activity for fear it may overly deter legitimate activities that we wish to permit or encourage....

Seaman's was nonetheless correctly decided, in my view, on narrower grounds than bad faith denial of the contract's existence. As discussed above, a number of cases allow tort damages for an intentional breach which the breaching party knows will probably result in significant emotional distress or personal hardship. In the commercial sphere, we do not as a rule permit such recovery for personal distress—the frustrations that attend breached contracts, unreliable suppliers, and the like are part of the realities of commerce. Society expects the business enterprise to go to the marketplace to seek substitutes to mitigate its losses, and to seek contract damages for those losses that cannot be mitigated. But there are some commercial cases in which the harm intentionally inflicted on an enterprise cannot be mitigated, and in which ordinary contract damages are insufficient compensation. Seaman's is such a case. In Seaman's, because of the unusual combination of market forces and government regulation set in motion by the 1973 oil embargo, Standard's conduct had a significance beyond the ordinary breach: its practical effect was to shut Seaman's out of the oil market entirely, forcing it out of business. In other words, Standard intentionally breached its contract with Seaman's with the knowledge that the breach would result in Seaman's demise. Having thus breached its contract with blithe disregard for the severe and, under these rare circumstances, unmitigatable injury it caused Seaman's, Standard was justly subject to tort damages.

In sum, I would permit an action for tortious breach of contract in a commercial setting when a party intentionally breaches a contractual obligation with neither probable cause nor belief that the obligation does not exist, and when the party intends or knows that the breach will result in severe consequential damages to the other party that are not readily subject to mitigation, and such harm in fact occurs. This rule is a variant of the more general rule of tort law that, as Holmes said, "the intentional infliction of temporal damage is a cause of action, which, as a matter of substantive law, ... requires a justification if the defendant is to escape." (Aikens v. Wisconsin (1904) 195 U.S. 194, 204, 25 S.Ct. 3, 5, 49 L.Ed. 154.) A breach should not be considered tortious if the court determines that it was justified by avoidance of some substantial, unforeseen cost on the part of the breaching party, even if such cost does not excuse that party's nonperformance. (See Corbin on Contracts (1994 Supp.) § 654E, p. 109.) Nor should a tortious breach under these circumstances be recognized if it is clear that the party suffering the harm voluntarily accepted that risk under the contract. But the intentional or knowing infliction of severe consequential damages on a business enterprise through the unjustified, bad faith breach of a contract is reprehensible and costly both for the party suffering the breach and for society as a whole, and is therefore appropriately sanctioned through the tort system.

III.

The present case, on the other hand, is essentially a billing dispute between two commercial entities. Belcher Oil Company claimed, apparently in bad faith and without probable cause, that it had no contractual agreement with Freeman & Mills. That is, Belcher Oil not only intentionally breached its contract, but then asserted a bad faith defense to its liability. As explained above, the solution which the Legislature has devised for this kind of transgression is the awarding of the other party's attorney fees, and this is precisely what occurred — Freeman & Mills was awarded $212,891 in attorney fees pursuant to Code of Civil Procedure sections 128.5 and 2033, subdivision (c). To permit the award of punitive damages in addition to this sum would upset the legislative balance established in the litigation sanctions statutes and make tortious actions — intentional breach of contract and the assertion of a bad faith defense — which we have consistently held not to be tortious.

On this basis, I concur in the majority's disposition in favor of Belcher Oil on the bad faith denial of contract cause of action.

NOTES

(1) What are the principal differences between tort law and contract that are relevant to cases like *Freeman & Mills*? What are the principal objectives of the two bodies of law? What sorts of damages are associated with each, and to what policy bases of each body of law do those damages respond?

(2) What are the most significant objections to making a case like *Freeman & Mills* a tort case, with respect to the effects of such a decision on business activity? If contract law seeks to foster predictability and stability, does tort law have a destabilizing effect? Could not tort law contribute to the long-run stabilization of markets, by assuring people that severe consequences will follow seriously dysfunctional, even morally reprehensible, behavior by contracting parties?

Would giving a tort cause of action to parties like Freeman and Mills put an undue strain on the ability of courts to render rational judgments?

(3) If one's initial premise is that people should be able autonomously to construct bargains that appear to be in their individual best interests, then when — if ever — should contract law place "moral significance," to use Justice Mosk's phrase, on "intentional injury" by a contracting party?

(4) If a court decided that it was appropriate to recognize a cause of action for bad faith denial of the existence of a contract, how should it construct the elements of that cause of action in order to prevent a situation in which every breach of contract becomes a tort?

§ 16.02 Discharge of Employees

SULLIVAN v. MASSACHUSETTS MUTUAL LIFE INSURANCE
United States District Court, District of Connecticut
802 F. Supp. 716 (1992)

JOSE A. CABRANES, CHIEF JUDGE.

This case takes us to the outer limits of the erosion of the doctrine of employment at will under Massachusetts law created by the enforcement of putative oral contracts and employer liability for discharges said to be contrary to public policy. Plaintiff John D. Sullivan ("Sullivan") sues his former employer, Massachusetts Mutual Life Insurance Company ("Mass. Mutual") and its wholly-owned subsidiary, Massachusetts Mutual Corporate Investors, Inc. ("Corporate Investors"), alleging that he was fired because he "blew the whistle" on suspected securities law violations at Mass. Mutual and that he was fired in breach of an oral contract providing that he would be dismissed only for good cause. Pending before the court is Defendants' Motion for Summary Judgment....

The Complaint (filed Aug. 9, 1988) ("Complaint") initially made out three claims for relief. Plaintiff's first claim alleges that he was terminated by defendants in breach of contract. The second claim alleges that plaintiff was discharged in violation of public policy....

The facts relevant to defendants' motion for summary judgment are these. Plaintiff was hired by Mass. Mutual as an assistant securities analyst in February, 1985, at a salary of $28,500. Plaintiff was apparently in the early stages of his career in business....

By his own account, plaintiff's difficulties began when in April 1986 he was apprised by defendants' in-house counsel, Attorney Wallace Rodger ("Rodger"), that defendants' employees were in possession of material inside information of Cardis Corporation, a company in which defendants held stock that they were planning to sell. On the order of Rodger, defendants decided not to sell stock in Cardis, even though defendants later determined that they did not in fact possess material non-public information. This decision was made in plaintiff's absence before plaintiff learned of the situation, but afterwards Rodger expressed concern to plaintiff that a securities law violation might have occurred had sales in Cardis not been suspended.

Plaintiff states that Rodger also told plaintiff that Richard Morrison, an officer senior to plaintiff in plaintiff's division, might possess material inside information regarding World ACCO Corporation ("ACCO"). Defendants had begun selling ACCO stock in early April 1986. On April 29, 1986, Rodger and plaintiff met with Morrison to discuss possible inside information defendants possessed concerning ACCO, and afterwards suspended trading in ACCO. Defendants contend that there is no evidence, however, that insider trading actually occurred.

Plaintiff alleges that, subsequent to these events, which coincided roughly in time with several well-publicized Wall Street insider-trading scandals, he became concerned that he would be subject to liability for possible insider trading violations in his job at Mass. Mutual. Plaintiff asserts that he expressed these concerns repeatedly to his superiors at Mass. Mutual, and proposed that defendants insulate trading operations from other divisions of Mass. Mutual to prevent possible insider trading....

[The court summarizes evidence of both parties concerning plaintiff's allegations about his concerns with insider trading by the defendant. This evidence includes the fact that the plaintiff failed the Level 3 Chartered Financial Analyst examination and that his knowledge of the securities laws was confined to his preparation for that examination and "reading the newspapers." It also includes the plaintiff's assertion that a corporate official told him that he "should not be concerned with defendants' compliance with the securities laws," that "'everyone in the industry engaged in some insider trading,' and that the activities of the persons implicated by plaintiff's concerns were valuable to defendants."]

Plaintiff was discharged by Mass. Mutual on August 25, 1986. Plaintiff contends that he was fired because he "discovered, disclosed, and complained of" insider trading violations or what plaintiff calls "near violations." Defendants contend that plaintiff was fired because of unsatisfactory work performance and point to various supervisors' complaints about the quality of plaintiff's work unrelated to any allegations of insider trading.

· · ·

At oral argument, plaintiff conceded that, contrary to earlier assertions, ... he is not prepared to prove that defendants ever violated the securities laws.... Rather, plaintiff asserted that he reasonably believed that defendants had violated the securities laws and that he was discharged for having expressed concern over such possible violations.... Although plaintiff did not raise the issue at oral argument, he presumably continues to press his claim that he was discharged in part for proposing an improved system to ensure defendants' compliance with the securities' laws. (Indeed, this claim may be encompassed by plaintiff's contention that he was discharged on account of his "concerns" over insider trading.)

... Both defendants move for summary judgment on plaintiff's claims for breach of contract and wrongful discharge.

The parties agree that, at least for the purposes of this motion, all of plaintiff's claims are governed by the law of Massachusetts.

· · ·

Partial summary judgment is ... proper for defendants on plaintiff's first claim, which alleges a breach of contract....

· · ·

Whether plaintiff may recover on his second contractual theory turns on whether he was discharged in violation of public policy. The Massachusetts courts have held that a discharge in violation of public policy amounts to a breach of the implied covenant of good faith and fair dealing inherent in the contract of employment....

Plaintiff alleges that he was fired because he discovered, disclosed, and complained of defendants' violations of state and federal law and governing ethical codes with respect to the insider trading of securities. Plaintiff argues in particular that he was discharged because he complained about violations and "near violations" of the securities laws and ethical codes by defendants and proposed to defendants that procedures be improved to prevent future insider trading violations. Plaintiff's claims are multifaceted, and require extensive discussion of this evolving area of the law.

The Massachusetts Supreme Judicial Court has articulated the grounds of employer liability for discharging an employee in violation of public policy recognized thus far under Massachusetts law. These are: (1) firing an employee because the employee asserted a legally guaranteed right; (2) firing an employee because the employee did what the law requires; (3) firing an employee because the employee refused to do what the law forbids; or (4) firing an employee for cooperating with an ongoing criminal investigation by the authorities.... However, the Supreme Judicial Court also has recognized the evolving nature of public policy discharge liability. See Mello v. Stop & Shop Cos., 402 Mass. 555, 524 N.E.2d 105, 106 (1988) ("Our cases have not attempted in general terms to identify those principles of public policy that are sufficiently important and clearly defined to warrant recovery by an at will employee who is discharged for engaging in, or refusing to engage in, particular conduct"). In Mello, the Supreme Judicial Court assumed that discharging an employee for "whistleblowing" violates public policy, and upheld a judgment for the employer notwithstanding a plaintiff's jury verdict on the narrow ground that the evidence did not support a finding that the plaintiff was discharged for complaining about illegal activity, as opposed to activity in violation of the employer's internal policies.... In view of the expansive and evolving nature of liability for discharge against public policy under Massachusetts law, and the widespread recognition of liability for discharging "whistleblowers" in other jurisdictions, I conclude that plaintiff may state a claim upon which relief can be granted if he was fired because he "blew the whistle" on illegal practices at Mass. Mutual and Corporate Investors.

Defendants argue that the federal and state securities laws plaintiff contends he reasonably believed to have been violated were not intended to benefit plaintiff, and that therefore public policy does not support his claim for relief. This argument lacks merit. The purpose of public policy discharge liability is to promote obedience to the law regardless of whether the plaintiff is himself a victim of the disclosed illegal activity. By encouraging employees to "blow the whistle" on illegal activity and adding a disincentive for employers to violate the law, the theory of liability, it is said, advances public policy as expressed in statutes and regulations.

Defendants also contend that whistleblowing is protected only when the alleged violations of law concern the public health or safety. This argument lacks a basis in both policy and precedent. While many whistleblowing cases do concern health and safety, the cases themselves do not purport to state such a limitation. Indeed, there are reported cases in which employees discharged for disclosing violations of law unrelated to health or safety have been held to state a claim. See, e.g., Appeal of Bio Energy Corp., 607 A.2d 606 (N.H.1992) (violation of wage regulations); Schriner v. Meginnis Ford Company, 228 Neb. 85, 421 N.W.2d 755 (1992) (odometer tamperage); Harless v. First National Bank in Fairmont, 162 W.Va. 116, 246 S.E.2d 270 (1978) (violation of consumer lending protection statutes); but see Fowler v. Great Amer. Ins. Cos., 653 F.Supp. 692, 697 (N.D.Ill.1987) (holding in the alternative that Illinois insurance code did not establish sufficiently important public policy to protect employee from discharge). Indeed, statutory protection for whistleblowers makes no distinction between laws related to health or safety and laws advancing other goals. See, e.g., N.H.Rev.Stat.Ann. § 275-E:2; Cal.Labor Code § 1102.5(b); 26 Me.Rev.Stat.Ann. § 833(1)(A). The limitation that defendants propose would, in fact, be contrary to one of the central purposes of the liability for discharge contrary to public policy, which is to promote public policy as expressed by law. It is noteworthy that in Mello, supra, the Supreme Judicial Court assumed that a discharge in retaliation for reporting fraud—in that case, fraud unrelated to health or safety—would give rise to employer liability for a discharge contrary to public policy.

Defendants also emphasize that plaintiff did not himself discover any securities law violations. Rather, plaintiff merely "tagged along" when Attorney Rodger had expressed some concern over possible violations. This argument does not defeat liability. While perhaps it is more heroic to be both an investigator and a whistleblower, the policies of the theory of liability are equally advanced by protecting those who learn of wrongdoing from others rather than discovering it firsthand.

Defendants' principal arguments have been that no violations of law in fact occurred (a point now effectively conceded by plaintiff); that plaintiff never reported any supposed violations to the authorities during his tenure at Mass. Mutual; and that plaintiff never even told anyone at Mass. Mutual or Corporate Investors that he would report suspected violations to the authorities. Plaintiff responds to these arguments by asserting that he may make out a claim if he was fired for expressing his reasonable belief that violations had occurred. Although the parties did not brief the issue, at oral argument plaintiff drew the court's attention to the Mello case discussed above. In Mello, the court remarked in dicta that we assume that an at will employee who "blew the whistle" within his company on wrongdoing is entitled to protection (even though before discharge he did not complain to public authorities). We shall further assume that whistleblowing based on a reasonable, good faith (but erroneous) belief that the employer is violating the law should be protected in particular circumstances.

Although these rules were both stated as dicta in Mello, I am persuaded that the Massachusetts Supreme Judicial Court would apply both if the questions were presented to it today. With respect to the contention that plaintiff's merely internal complaints were inadequate, I note that in Noriss v. Lumbermen's Mutual Casualty, 881 F.2d 1144, 1153 (1st Cir.1989), the Court of Appeals for the First Circuit, applying Massachusetts law, held that an employer could be liable for the discharge of an employee because of his purely internal complaints of violations of Nuclear Regulatory Commission regulations. This rule makes sense. A rule that would permit the employer to fire a whistleblower with impunity before the employee contacted the authorities would encourage employers promptly to discharge employees who bring complaints to their attention, and would give employees with complaints an incentive to bypass management and go directly to the authorities. This would deprive management of the opportunity to correct oversights straightaway, solve the problem by disciplining errant employees, or clear up a misunderstanding on the part of a whistleblower. The likely result of a contrary rule would be needless public investigations of matters best addressed internally in the first instance. Employers benefit from a system in which the employee reports suspected violations to the employer first; the employee should not, in any event, be penalized for bestowing that benefit on the employer. See Appeal of Bio Energy Corp., 607 A.2d at 608–09 (despite language of New Hampshire Whistleblower's Protection Act requiring employee to report suspected violation to the authorities, the employee is protected from discharge once he makes an internal complaint). I conclude that plaintiff's failure to contact the authorities concerning the alleged violations while he worked at Mass. Mutual does not by itself defeat his claim.

As noted earlier, plaintiff concedes that he cannot prove that any actual violations of the securities laws took place during his tenure at Mass. Mutual, but relies upon the Mello decision, which assumed that an employee may recover if he is discharged for reporting merely suspected violations, where the belief is reasonable and in good faith. Such a rule is by no means unusual.... It may be argued that an employee should be required to prove the existence of an actual violation of law, since it is the public policy of the law alleged to have violated that is supposedly advanced by holding the employer liable for discharging a whistleblower. Arguably the goal of promoting obedience to law is not served when there has, in fact, been no legal violation. On the other hand, a standard of reasonable belief encourages a whistleblower to come forward, rather than remain silent out of fear that he might be wrong. Particularly in light of the Mello decision, I am persuaded that, if presented with the question, the Massachusetts Supreme Judicial Court would hold that the absence of a provable violation would not bar plaintiff's claim.

An issue lurking within the reasonable belief standard is whether plaintiff may make reasonable mistakes as to the law as well as reasonable mistakes as to the facts. In other words, is plaintiff protected by a form of "reverse qualified immunity"? I believe that the Massachusetts Supreme Court would hold that plaintiff may make reasonable mistakes as to the law, since the policy concerns of encouraging whistleblowing are similar if not identical to those with respect to mistakes of fact. Many areas of the law are evolving and unclear. Since Massachusetts law appears to favor encouraging whistleblowing, it would seem anomalous, for example, for a whistleblower to lose the protection of the law if he reported the violation of a law later held to contravene the Interstate Commerce Clause, or the violation of an agency regulation later held to exceed statutory authority. Cf. Melchi, 597 F.Supp. at 583 (employee made out prima facie case of public policy discharge without presenting evidence that falsification of nuclear power plant records is illegal) (Michigan law). On the other hand, reasonableness as to mistakes of law would have to be considered in view of the plaintiff's expertise. In this case, a jury could very well conclude that, in view of plaintiff's extremely limited knowledge of securities law, he could not make any reasonable conclusions at all with respect to possible legal violations.

It may be argued with substantial force that the Massachusetts law governing liability for discharges against public policy has significant disadvantages. The focus on the reasonableness of a whistleblower's beliefs requires courts to decide extremely fact-intensive disputes rife with credibility and state-of-mind issues that are frequently not amenable to summary judgment and thus inevitably require a trial. Jury decisions will tend to be random, inviting litigation and discouraging settlement. In effect, a "reasonable belief" standard permits employees to bring suit if they ever voiced any concern about any possible legal violation, in the hope that, two, three, or even seven years after the fact, a jury will find that the voiced concern was the cause of the discharge. Possible violations of law are, of course, pervasive in our highly regulated system of industry and commerce. The possibility of retributive lawsuits by employees discharged for legitimate reasons cannot be discounted.

Given the increased threat of litigation over discharge decisions, employers will naturally seek to screen out potential litigants in the hiring process. Screening costs add an obvious, additional burden to the economy. Less obvious, but perhaps no less real, is the potential effect on hiring patterns. Inasmuch as increased litigation increases the cost of firing employees, employers will tend to hire those employees who may appear to present the least risks of discharge—that is, who appear to present the least risks with respect to ability to do the job and cooperate with fellow workers. Such a pattern may well work to the disadvantage of new entrants to the job market, such as racial or ethnic minorities lacking established credentials but who present potential, if uncertain, possibilities of excellence. Ethnic and cultural diversity, with their arguably attendant potential for employee tension and consequent employee discharge, may tend to lose favor in the workplace.

It is true that liability for discharges against public policy may deter employers from discharging employees who have brought to light violations of law, and will therefore increase the likelihood of "whistleblowing." However, there is a strong likelihood that the law will result in over-deterrence. Employers may be forced to retain malcontents who might, if discharged, sue on the grounds that they were fired because they voiced concerns about compliance with some law. In this case, as in others, voiced concerns in fact may amount to a possible libel of one's supervisors or fellow employees. Tensions in such circumstances will naturally rise. Requiring an employer to retain an employee who causes tension necessarily diminishes efficiency in the workplace, and therefore diminishes productivity in the economy as a whole. It is not at all clear that easing an individual plaintiff's burden in proving a discharge against public policy advances the general interest or welfare of workers as a group.

Lastly, the institutional role of the courts must be considered. While some states have statutes that protect whistleblowers, in Massachusetts and Connecticut the employees' whistleblowing rights are now largely the product of evolving common law. It is a substantial extension of the judicial role to determine or develop rules of general application regarding the discharge of employees. See generally Adler v. American Standard Corp., 830 F.2d 1303, 1306–07 (4th Cir.1987) (courts should be reluctant to expand liability for discharge contrary to public policy, since public policy is unclear and should be left to the legislature). Fact-intensive scrutiny of employment decisions represents a substantial judicial inquiry into the management of enterprises of all types. It is highly doubtful that Connecticut, for example, would adopt the apparent Massachusetts rule excusing a discharged employee from having to prove that an actual violation of law occurred.

...

Several of plaintiff's alleged bases of recovery ... however, are not viable even under a "reasonable belief" standard. Plaintiff may not recover on a theory that he was discharged for proposing an improved system whereby defendants would comply with the securities laws. The Massachusetts Supreme Judicial Court has held that a discharge based on proposals related to the employer's purely internal policies does not support public policy discharge liability. Smith-Pfeffer, 533 N.E.2d at 1371–72; see also Mello, 524 N.E.2d at 107 & n. 3 (discharge for complaints of violations of company policy not protected).

Furthermore, plaintiff has no claim for allegations that he was fired because he expressed concerns about "near violations." Public policy is concerned with preventing actual violations, and in protecting employees who are discharged for acting upon their reasonable, good faith belief that a violation of law has occurred or will occur.

Plaintiff has asserted that he expressed concern over violations of ethical codes for persons in the securities industry. Massachusetts law is clear that to give rise to liability the discharge must come from a violation of "clearly established public policy." Hobson v. McLean Hospital Corp., 402 Mass. 413, 522 N.E.2d 975, 977 (1988). Ethical codes in the securities industry are promulgated by private groups, do not have the force of law, and therefore do not establish public policy.

...

V.

Plaintiff has conceded that he cannot prove that defendants violated the securities laws, and presumably the jury should be so instructed. The only issues that remain are whether plaintiff was discharged because he reasonably believed in good faith that the defendants had committed violations of law, and whether he was discharged because he complained of the suspected violations.

A.

Many facts in this case would point to a conclusion that any belief on the part of plaintiff that there had been legal violations was not reasonable. Plaintiff had little training in the area of insider trading; indeed, his duties consisted primarily of ministerial calculations, and he failed the short Chartered Financial Analyst course in which the insider trading subject matter had been presented. Plaintiff's apparent reliance on newspaper articles would on its face appear to be a grossly inadequate education in the complex area of securities law.... However, in light of the allegation in plaintiff's affidavit to the effect that his superior told him "everyone in the industry" engaged in insider trading and that he should drop his concerns due to the profitability of the activities of the persons whom plaintiff allegedly suspected of insider trading..., I am not prepared on the record to date to conclude that no reasonable juror could find that plaintiff reasonably believed in the circumstances that actual violations of federal or state law had occurred.

B.

As to whether plaintiff was fired because of his alleged whistleblowing, several facts would support the inference that he was not fired for this reason. During his tenure at Mass. Mutual, plaintiff never threatened to report any violations to the authorities, and when he did so, it was initially in an anonymous letter to the SEC at least a month after he had been fired. And ... defendants have adduced several examples of management's dissatisfaction with plaintiff's work quite apart from the issue of insider trading. Defendants have also noted that the persons who decided to terminate plaintiff were not those whom plaintiff had suspected of insider trading. A jury could infer that the allegations of insider trading were merely revenge for plaintiff's discharge. On the other hand, plaintiff has averred in a sworn statement that one of his supervisors told him that if he persisted in expressing his concerns over insider trading, he would be "out the door." ... I cannot conclude on the basis of the record to date that no reasonable jury could find that plaintiff was discharged because he "blew the whistle" on the suspected violations of law.

...

NOTES

(1) Unless there are contractual standards governing the circumstances under which an employee may be dismissed, why shouldn't an employer simply be able to get rid of an unruly employee? Even if one granted an exception for situations in which the employee "blows the whistle" on conduct that threatens the physical safety of others, why should employee rights extend to whistleblowing for securities violations? Should any violation of a consumer protection statute be enough?

(2) An underlying premise of defendants in discharge cases is that, in a free market, an employer is the best judge of its own economic interests, and therefore of the societal welfare that is served by its enterprise. What is the principal counterargument in favor of employees?

(3) Many states require that the public policy that serves as a basis for wrongful discharge actions should be embodied in a statute. See Edward T. Ellis, *Tort-Based Theories of Wrongful Discharge*, C947 ALI-ABA 381 (1994). Would you limit the tort to that kind of case?

(4) If you were drafting a statute to protect whistleblowers against summary dismissal, what requirements would you put in the law for plaintiffs to meet?

The Sarbanes-Oxley Act, a comprehensive attack on various kinds of corporate abuses, includes a whistleblower provision, 18 U.S.C. § 1514A. This provision enables employees of publicly traded companies to sue for compensatory damages for retaliatory actions by employers if the employees "provide information, cause information to be provided, or otherwise assist in an investigation regarding any conduct which the employee reasonably believes constitutes a violation of" various sections of the securities laws or SEC regulations, "or any provision of Federal law related to fraud against shareholders." One of the most difficult issues, as *Sullivan* suggests, is whether an employee "reasonably believes" that the company's activities violate the law. Robert Vaughn analyzes this concept in detail in *America's First Comprehensive Statute Protecting Corporate Whistleblowers*, 57 ADMIN. L. REV. 1, 16–21 (2005), concluding that "[r]easonable belief is a flexible standard that considers the experience and background of the employees and the context in which they act," *id.* at 104. Just one example of the difficult issues that may arise under the statute is the question of whether the information the whistleblower brings forward is "material." Vaughn notes that "[t]he standard of materiality applicable to proxy statements, mergers and most SEC disclosure requirements emphasizes whether there is 'a substantial likelihood that a reasonable shareholder would consider it important.'" As he explains it, "[t]his standard must be applied to a reasonable investor considering the 'total mix' of information available." He says that "[i]n regard to contingent and speculative information, materiality depends upon a balancing of the probability that an event will occur with the likely magnitude of the event in relation to a company's overall activities." *Id.* at 38–39.

(5) If you were writing a passage in an employers' manual concerning liability for wrongful discharge, how would you describe *Sullivan* and what sort of advice would you give about its lessons for prudent employer practice concerning employees whose presence has become irritating?

Chapter 17

COMPENSATION SYSTEMS AND OTHER ALTERNATIVES TO TORT LAW

§ 17.01 Automobile Accidents

PREFATORY NOTE

Over a good part of the twentieth century, many challenges were mounted to the notion that fault should be the principal basis on which compensation is awarded for personal injuries. An important response to those challenges occurred early in the century, when American legislatures adopted workers' compensation statutes, which provided recovery without a showing of fault for job-related injuries. Another feature of the American system of payments for injuries is the more comprehensive, federal statutory system of social security payments for those who are able to show disability, not necessarily work connected, that prevents them from engaging in gainful employment.

The section below surveys efforts to structure a "no-fault" solution to the quantitatively enormous, functionally defined problem of the automobile accident. Later sections deal with broader attempts to compensate victims of accidents in general, as well as other schemes with social welfare approaches.

Many studies and proposals have focused on the automobile accident as an urgent problem in compensation reform and one that may be effectively handled by separate legislative treatment. A Columbia University committee made an important proposal of this kind in 1932. The Canadian province of Saskatchewan enacted an automobile compensation plan in 1946. Many other models have since been offered. A landmark proposal is that of Robert Keeton and Jeffrey O'Connell in their book *Basic Protection for the Traffic Victim*, published in 1965.[1]

Over a period of years centering in the 1970's, several states enacted a variety of automobile plans, and the National Conference of Commissioners on Uniform State Laws approved the Uniform Motor Vehicle Accident Reparations Act (UMVARA) and recommended that all the states adopt it.[2]

---

1. Chapter 4 of the Keeton-O'Connell book summarizes the models that had been constructed to that date.

2. A summary by one of the co-draftsmen, based on the comments to the UMVARA proposal, appears in Henderson, *The Uniform Motor Vehicle Accident Reparations Act*, 44 Miss. L.J. 107 (1973).

The materials below, which are highly selective, are designed to bring out basic issues in the automobile compensation controversy. The first excerpt is from an article by Keeton three years after the appearance of the comprehensive Keeton-O'Connell plan.

After that are presented summaries of and excerpts from a number of alternative schemes, together with arguments focused both on specific features of plans and on the general question of whether to have a special plan for automobiles. One should read this material asking whether reform is needed, inquiring as to what alternatives are available, and finally trying to construct an ideal solution.

In this effort, it is important both to keep in mind the fundamental tort doctrines that have been studied in this course, and to define one's policy goals. In particular, it will be useful to be clear about one's assumptions about the effects of law on conduct. It also would aid analysis to articulate the relative importance you attach to the achievement of a fair distribution of accident losses as compared with the goal of influencing how people conduct themselves on the roads.

[A] Is There a Need for Change?

Robert E. Keeton, *Basic Protection and the Future of Negligence Law*
3 U. Rich. L. Rev. 1 (1968)*

. . .

What objectives should a good set of laws for compensating traffic victims serve?

First, it should be aimed not simplistically at compensating but more sensitively at compensating fairly. That is, it should determine both entitlement to compensation and liability for compensation on principles that are fair and just. There are differences about implementation no doubt, but surely a consensus on this objective.

Second, a good set of laws should offer reasonable assurance of financial responsibility for paying the compensation determined to be legally owing. Up through the nineteenth century the common law did very little about this. Today, in contrast, every state legislature has enacted some form of financial responsibility legislation. Thus it appears we now have a consensus on this objective, too.

Third, a good set of laws for compensating traffic victims ought to distribute losses to some extent rather than imposing catastrophic burdens on individuals, whether victims or defendants. Perhaps a few will dissent here, but the history of state legislation encouraging the purchase of liability insurance, and sometimes even compelling it, is not to be explained solely as a movement for assuring financial responsibility. That objective could have been served by bonds or policies under which the bondsman or insurer, having paid a victim, was always entitled to recover in turn from the tortfeasor. Instead liability insurance pays on behalf of the tortfeasor. In short, liability insurance distributes losses. Its prevalence manifests a consensus for a system of distribution and against a system involving crushing individual burdens, whether upon victims or upon tortfeasors.

Fourth, a good set of laws ought not only to *distribute* but also, in the process, to *allocate fairly* the cost of compensating for injuries in traffic accidents. This objective is, in a sense, a corollary of the first objective of compensating fairly. It is simply a somewhat more specific development of that point. Here, too, there may be differences about implementation, but surely not about the objective.

Fifth, a good set of laws ought to operate with reasonable efficiency, minimizing waste.

Sixth, a good set of laws ought to minimize inducements to exaggeration and fraud.

Seventh — and I place this so late in the catalogue of objectives because there is more dissent about it, not because it occupies this place in my own order of priorities, in which rather it comes alongside providing fair and just compensation — a good set of laws ought to provide its payments promptly to meet the resulting economic burdens as they occur and to provide medical and other rehabilitative services as soon as they are needed.

How well does the common law of negligence serve these seven objectives?

Measured against the first objective, the present system fails even to do well in compensating, much less in compensating fairly. It pays nothing to some deserving traffic victims and too little to others. It underpays especially the most severely injured persons, if it pays them at all. Moreover, among these are the most deserving of all traffic victims. In contrast, as field studies in state after state demonstrate, it overpays victims with minor injuries.

The present system also distributes unfairly the burden of costs resulting from accidental losses. We can predict the number of accidents and the toll of losses that will occur on roads of the quality we choose to provide, crowded with cars in the numbers we choose to operate, in the hands of drivers we choose to license. It is not alone carelessness of individual operators that produces these accidents. In the phrase of Professor Calabresi, we have made a "decision for accidents" of this order of magnitude by choosing not to spend more for safer roads and not to give up the many advantages we gain from using so many vehicles and licensing drivers so freely. In reality, then, part of the cause of the accident toll is the set of community choices about roads and vehicles and drivers. The law, too, should attribute part of the accident toll to these choices. That is, it should place part of the burden on the whole group who benefit from these choices, and it should distribute the burden, to the extent it is feasible to do so, in proportion to the benefits derived from motoring of this degree of intensity. In this sense, motoring should pay its way in our society. Moreover, insurance is a mechanism through which it is quite feasible to distribute this burden widely and fairly. Under the present system, in contrast, motoring and motorists generally escape a large part of accident costs. It is imposed instead on the unlucky persons who are the victims of uncompensated loss.

Second, the present system falls well short of the objective of assuring financial responsibility for payment of the benefits it declares to be due. Countrywide, it is a fair estimate even today that somewhere between ten and fifteen percent of the cars on our highways are uninsured for coverage that would pay victims injured by their operation. Moreover, the persons operating these cars tend to be the less responsible drivers, causing a disproportionate percentage of injuries. It is true that through uninsured motorist coverage and like devices the percentage of wholly uncompensated injuries is sharply reduced. But provisions of this kind are almost always subject to low limits, besides being very unfair in that they make the wrong people bear the burden of losses even within the limits.

Third, the present system falls even further short of the objective of distributing loss to avoid catastrophic burdens on individuals. Financial irresponsibility itself accounts in part for this failure because it leaves legally deserving victims of severe injury uncompensated and thus under crushing economic burdens. In addition, the present system leaves many other victims uncompensated because of its harsh rules for determining who are the legally deserving victims—its rules, for example, against allowing any compensation to the cases of unavoidable accident and contributory fault. Who among us can defend as a work of justice the denial of compensation to the pedestrian who is struck on the sidewalk by a car out of control as the result of a so-called unavoidable accident, occurring when an apparently healthy driver suffers an unpredictable heart attack?

The last illustration is one of many that mark the present system as a failure under the fourth objective also—the objective of allocating fairly the costs of injuries sustained in traffic accidents. Moreover, the proposition that motoring should pay its way is relevant to this as well as to the first objective of compensating fairly. Not until much greater recognition is given to this proposition will the unfair allocation of the burden of accident losses be corrected.

Fifth, the present system is wasteful, requiring an annual fortune in tax dollars to support the trial of claims of traffic victims, and requiring too that motorists maintain a form of insurance so inefficient that it delivers net benefits of less than forty-five cents for each dollar of premiums paid in.

[In a later article, Keeton presented the following breakdown based on the American Insurance Association Cost Study in 1968:

General Overhead		33 cents
Claims Administration		
Defense Side	13 cents	
Claimants' Side	10 cents	
Total Claims Administration Cost		23 cents
Total Overhead		56 cents
Net Amount Paid to Victims Above Losses (in theory for pain and suffering)		21.5 cents
Paid to Compensate for Losses Also Compensated from Other Sources (including income tax saving)		8 cents
Paid to Compensate for Losses Not Compensated from Other Sources		14.5 cents
Net Paid to Victims Altogether		44 cents
		100 cents[a]]

a. From Keeton, *The Case for No-Fault Insurance*, 44 Miss. L. Rev. 1, 5 (1973).

Sixth, the present system has built-in inducements to exaggeration and even outright fraud that add both to its unfairness and to its wasteful costs. It lends itself on the one hand to an appalling percentage of shoot-the-moon, go-for-broke claims and on the other hand to bargaining on distress in defense. As the Governor of the Commonwealth of Massachusetts put it, describing the claims side of this picture in a message to the legislature in 1966, "too many motorists view our present insurance system as a treasure trove to be exploited whenever one is 'fortunate' enough to be involved in an accident." The effects of the other side of this dismal picture — the hard-bargaining defense the system inherently encourages — is summarized in the report of Professor Conard and his colleagues at Michigan, telling us that "the man who has a severe injury is likely to settle for it quickly only if he settles for a relatively small amount."

This last point is perhaps the most severe manifestation of the failure of the present system to meet the seventh objective — prompt payments. Payments are delayed, however, not only in these severe cases but also in cases of less severe injury. Indeed, any system of compensation that depends typically on one lump-sum settlement of each claim will commonly make its payments too late, even when it is operating at its best and the delay is only weeks or months. At its worst, with delays of years, it cruelly aggravates the hardships inevitably produced by injury because the payments are delayed so long that they cannot serve the important needs they are designed in theory to serve.

...

NOTES

(1) What are the primary failings of the present legal process as it relates to the consequences of automobile accidents? Do any of these problems seem susceptible to highly specific solutions, rather than comprehensive reform of the applicable tort law?

(2) What do you consider to be the primary goals of the law that covers the auto accident problem? Do you think that any of the principal goals are in conflict with each other? For example, if the law were to provide compensation for virtually all auto accident victims, would you think that would negatively affect its ability to achieve deterrence goals?

(3) Consider the following summary of statistics on the disposition of automobile claims:

> Settlement is overwhelmingly the rule for the most numerous category of injury claims, that involving automobile injuries. This is clear from a Department of Transportation study of bodily injury liability and uninsured motorist claims. The DOT research indicates that while 46 per cent of claimants retained an attorney and one-third of those persons filed suit, only ten per cent of those filing suit went to trial, and more than one half of that number settled during trial. The outcome of this process of winnowing is that "less than 1% of all claimants went all the way to a verdict," and that "one-fourth of these claimants received less than the insurer had offered."

Towards a Jurisprudence of Injury 7-21 to 7-22 (ABA 1984, M. Shapo Rptr.) (citing 1 DEPARTMENT OF TRANSPORTATION, AUTOMOBILE PERSONAL INJURY CLAIMS 121 (1970)).

How does this data affect your judgment of whether there is a need for a significant change in the traditional tort law as it relates to auto accidents?

(4) How far can you generalize from the problems you have identified in the law relating to auto accidents to the problems you see in tort law generally? What are the special characteristics of auto accidents that would seem to call for legislative solutions? Are the problems inherent in automobile tort law and tort law in general similar enough that the solution should embrace the entire tort system?

[B] Compensation Plans

HOW TRADITIONAL AND NO-FAULT SYSTEMS WORK

Stephen J. Carroll & James S. Kakalik with David Adamson,
No-Fault Automobile Insurance: A Policy Perspective,
R-4019/1-ICJ, Santa Monica, CA: RAND, 1991, pp. 4–7*

THE TRADITIONAL SYSTEM

In the traditional fault-based system, injured people can seek compensation for all their losses from the driver who caused the accident. These losses include economic and noneconomic loss. However, a driver's responsibility is limited to the extent he or she was at fault.

In the traditional system, consumers can purchase three kinds of injury insurance coverage. Drivers can buy **Bodily Injury (BI)** insurance to pay compensation they owe someone they injured. Drivers can also buy **Uninsured Motorist (UM)** insurance to cover themselves for any compensation due them that they cannot obtain from an uninsured motorist. Finally, drivers may buy a form of no-fault insurance called **Medical Payments (MedPay)**, which covers their own medical costs, typically to low policy limits.

A Typical Injury Case

How does this system work in practice? Suppose you are injured in a car crash in a state that uses the traditional system (a "tort" state). The bill for your medical expenses comes to $701. You also lose $265 in wages because you missed work. (These losses were typical for people injured in auto accidents in the mid-1980s; half of them had smaller economic loss, half greater.)

You typically submit a liability claim to the other driver's BI insurer or, if he did not have BI insurance and you had purchased UM coverage, to your own insurer. You seek compensation for both your economic loss ($966) and your noneconomic loss.

After you negotiate with the other driver's insurer, you usually settle. The settlement amount depends on a variety of factors, such as your share of responsibility for the accident, your injuries, how they affected your everyday activities, and whether you hired an attorney. Our data show that the liability compensation provided someone with about $1,000 in economic losses ranged from nothing to over $25,000. However, let us say you end up with $3000 — $966 for your economic loss and $2,034 for your noneconomic loss. (Our data indicate that people with about $1,000 in economic loss who received liability compensation had average compensation that was just over three times their economic loss.) If you hire a lawyer to help you pursue your claim, you will probably receive more than the average, but you will pay some of whatever you receive (typically about one-third) in lawyer fees.

You also submit your medical bills to your own insurer for reimbursement under your MedPay coverage. There is little to negotiate about: MedPay covers your medical costs regardless of who is at fault, and the amount of your bill is clear. So long as costs are below the policy limit, typically in the $1,000 to $5,000 range, you receive the full

---

* Reprinted by permission.

amount, $701. In sum, you collect $3,701 ($3,000 from liability insurance, either the other driver's BI or your own UM, and $701 from MedPay.)

Incidentally, your employer-provided health-care insurance may have covered most of your medical bills, and your sick pay may have covered the time you had to take off work. But those payments generally do not enter into the determination of what either the other driver's insurance company, or your own, owe to you.

Of course, there is no guarantee that your claim will come out this way. If you had not purchased MedPay auto insurance, you would only get your liability compensation, $3,000. If the other driver was uninsured and if you did not have UM coverage, or if you were totally at fault for the accident, you would get no liability compensation. Your compensation would be limited to your $701 MedPay payment for your medical bills, if you had MedPay coverage. Finally, if you cannot collect liability compensation and do not have MedPay, you get nothing at all from auto insurance.

A More Serious Injury Case

What if the accident is more serious and you are severely injured? The procedure is pretty much the same as above: You submit the same kinds of claims—a liability claim against the other driver's BI insurance or your own UM policy and, if you have MedPay coverage, a claim against it as well. Your compensation depends on your injuries, your economic and noneconomic losses, and your share of fault for the accident. However, an additional factor comes into play: policy limits. The compensation you get from the other driver's BI insurance, or your own UM insurance, and from your MedPay coverage may be capped by policy limits.

Suppose, for example, your medical costs total $50,000, you lose another $50,000 in wages due to time off work, and you incur substantial pain and suffering. Even if the other driver has BI insurance, your compensation will be limited by the amount of coverage provided by his or her BI policy. Odds are that the other driver's policy carries a per-person limit of $50,000 or less. (Over half of all drivers who had BI coverage had a per-person limit of $50,000 or less in 1986.)

If the other driver is uninsured and you have UM, you can collect up to the limit of your own UM policy. Odds are that your UM compensation will be $25,000 or less. (Over half the drivers who had UM coverage had a per-person limit of $25,000 or less in 1986.) You can also collect your MedPay benefits up to its policy limit, say $5,000. (Eighty-six percent of the drivers who had MedPay coverage had a per-person limit of $5,000 or less.)

In sum, you sustain $100,000 in economic loss and substantial noneconomic loss, but your compensation will probably be no greater than $55,000, if the other driver is insured.[2] If the other driver is not insured and you have UM, you receive $30,000; if you are entirely at fault, you receive $5,000. Here, too, if you hire a lawyer to help you pursue your claim, you will pay some of whatever you receive (typically about one-third) in lawyer fees.

NO-FAULT SYSTEMS

No-fault systems differ from the traditional system in two ways:

    1. No-fault processes serious injury cases differently from less serious injury cases. Seriously injured people can pursue liability claims for all their eco-

---

2. In principle, you could seek compensation from the other driver's personal assets. However, as a practical matter this rarely happens.

nomic and noneconomic losses; less seriously injured people can seek compensation only for economic losses. The dividing line between serious and less serious injuries is drawn in terms of a threshold. There are two types of threshold:

- **A verbal threshold** distinguishes claims in terms of a description of the injury (for example, "dismemberment" or "significant and permanent loss of an important bodily function").

- **A dollar threshold** specifies a dollar amount that medical costs must exceed before an injured person can pursue a liability claim.

2. No-fault also provides enhanced insurance against one's own economic losses. Known as **Personal Injury Protection (PIP)**, this insurance covers economic losses up to the policy limit, without regard to fault. PIP pays only economic losses (such as medical expenses and lost wages), not noneconomic losses.

The Typical Injury Case in a No-Fault System

How does a no-fault system work in practice? Let us look back at the case discussed above and assume that the state no-fault plan has a verbal threshold and provides for a $15,000 PIP benefit level. You had $966 in economic loss ($701 in medical costs and $265 in lost wages). Suppose your injuries are not serious enough to get you over the threshold. Your PIP insurance will compensate you for your medical costs. PIP will also compensate you for 72 percent of your lost wages.[3] If you have PIP insurance, you recover $892 from your own insurer, enough to fully compensate you for your economic loss, taking tax effects into account. Of course, if you do not have PIP, you get nothing. (Although all current no-fault states mandate the purchase of PIP coverage, some people go uninsured.)

If your injuries are sufficiently serious to get you over the threshold, you can pursue a liability claim against the other driver. (About 18 percent of the people with approximately $1,000 in economic losses have injuries that will get them over a verbal threshold.) Once past the threshold, the liability system's rules and procedures apply; you will obtain the same liability compensation for noneconomic loss as under the traditional system, and you will obtain compensation for any economic loss that exceeds what PIP will compensate. If your liability compensation for noneconomic loss is $2,034, you will collect that from the other driver's BI insurer (or your own UM policy). You will also collect $74 in liability compensation for your economic loss that exceeds the PIP compensation due you. If you have PIP coverage, you will recover the $892 from your PIP policy.

The More Serious Injury Case Under No-Fault

What happens to you in the other cases—$50,000 in medical costs and $50,000 in lost wages? Much the same as what happened to you under the traditional system. However, you first collect from your own PIP policy up to the limit—$15,000 in this case. You then claim against the other driver's insurer for your uncompensated economic loss and your noneconomic losses and collect up to the maximum of the other

---

3. Because your PIP compensation is not subject to income taxes, you are "made whole" if you are compensated for your lost after-tax wages. Rather than engage in complicated calculations, no-fault plans generally provide compensation for a specified portion of before-tax lost wages. The portion varies from state to state, averaging 72 percent over all current no-fault states.

driver's liability coverage, say $50,000. Your compensation is $65,000. You still do not fully recover your economic losses, let alone any compensation for your noneconomic losses, but you get somewhat more than you would have under the traditional system, because you collect PIP rather than MedPay. PIP pays lost wages as well as medical bills and generally has higher policy limits.

TYPES OF NO-FAULT STATUTES

Towards a Jurisprudence of Injury 11–13
(ABA 1984, M. Shapo Rptr.)*

One group of these laws, which generally have been labeled as "modified no-fault," eliminates the tort action for relatively nonserious injuries.... Among these "modified no-fault" states, one or two have been called "pure" no-fault jurisdictions because of their provision of relatively high benefits and their placement of very restrictive limits on tort actions. The other principal category of first-party auto compensation laws is that of the so-called "add-on" statutes. One text describes these laws as "provid[ing] only for expanded medical payments and disability income coverage on the traditional automobile [liability] insurance policy," without "any limitations on the right for the injured victim to sue for damages."

NOTES

(1) How do the policies that appear to underlie the various statutory models described above compare with the policies that support the tort law that would apply to auto accidents in the absence of a statute? Compare how (a) a modified no-fault statute, with relatively low thresholds for suit, and (b) a no-fault statute that barred tort actions for all but the most serious injuries, would serve the goals of (1) deterrence, (2) compensation, (3) loss-spreading, and (4) treating like cases alike.

(2) Consider the traditional elements of a negligence case: duty, negligence, causation and damages. When a compensation statute eliminates most tort claims while providing relatively high payments, what social benefits would the statute sacrifice with respect to the policies served by each of these elements? What benefits would the statute confer?

(3) Consider the following catalog of issues concerning automobile compensation plans. If you believe there should be a legislative change in the tort law applicable to auto accidents, which issues seem most important to you? Or, if you do not think there should be a comprehensive legislative compensation scheme, which of these questions do you find most relevant to whatever need you are willing to concede has been demonstrated?

• If benefits are guaranteed without a lawsuit, should this be done on a third-party or first-party basis? If it is done on a third-party basis, should parties be excluded who clearly could not recover under the common law fault system? If there are no such exclusions, how should the payment to such parties be financed?

• Under a first-party plan, should there be any exclusions based on specified kinds of conduct?

• Should there be an option to choose basic first-party protection for personal injuries or to have liability insurance?

• Under a first-party plan, should the personal injury action be retained above certain dollar figures for provable pecuniary losses? If so, what should the minimum be? Should there be a separate threshold figure for pain and suffering?

• Indeed, should pain and suffering damages be allowed at all under a comprehensive first-party protection plan? Specifically, how would you handle the problem of disfigurement in a case in which the quantifiable economic damages are low?

• What ceilings, in dollars or percentages, should be imposed on claims for income loss?

• Should loss of earning power be allowed as an element of recovery? Specifically, how would your plan respond to the problem of disabling injuries caused to a young person who appears at the time of the injuries to have a bright economic future, but who has not secured accident insurance that measures up to his or her prospects?

• What voluntary possibilities should there be for added coverage with respect to personal injury?

• What choices should be available for property damage coverage?

• Should a compensation plan be tied to criminal and civil penalties for specified kinds of driving conduct?

• Should a tax on vehicles, gauged to collision safety factors, be used as a primary or supplementary basis for a compensation fund?

• Should compensation payments be conditioned on efforts at rehabilitation?

• Should other accident insurance, or other "collateral sources," be subtracted from compensation payments made by first- or third-party insurers, or by a government fund?

[C] Effects of Plans

PROBLEM

A and B are drivers involved in an intersection collision. B is injured, and can prove the following damages: Medical costs, $2,500; four weeks of lost wages, at $1,000 per week; pain and suffering, $1,000.

Assume that the jurisdiction in which the accident took place has a "no-fault" statute, which does not permit tort suits unless the plaintiff can prove injuries above a $5,000 threshold for pain and suffering and a $10,000 threshold for economic damages, including wage losses and medical bills. The standard attorney's fee in this sort of case is one-third of any settlement or judgment.

(a) Compare the dollar outcomes under a traditional tort regime and the hypothesized "no-fault" statute.

(b) What if B were contributorily negligent, in a state where contributory fault was a complete bar to recovery?

(c) What if A had injuries identical to B's, both parties were equally negligent and the jurisdiction had a pure comparative negligence rule?

OVERVIEW

Towards a Jurisprudence of Injury 11-13 to 11-17
(ABA 1984, M. Shapo Reporter)*

General reduction of litigation. Data on the effects of these plans is voluminous, and it sends a spectrum of signals for the formulation of legal policy. A Department of Transportation study published in 1977 analyzed statistics on the operation of "no-fault" systems in states with a variety of plans. The economic effects of "no-fault" varied according to particular features of these laws. While the study referred to the difficulty of rendering "any firm conclusions" because of the "paucity of data," it found that the statistics "strongly suggest[ed] that these systems are at least to some extent realizing the administrative cost savings theoretically inherent in such a shift."[6] The impact of no-fault on litigation was generally rather considerable although it varied from state to state.[7] The study concluded that there was a consistent "decline in the level of motor ve-hicle tort litigation" after the introduction of no-fault plans and that "no-fault played a major role in these States in reducing tort actions."[8]

Premium levels. Changes in insurance premium levels have varied according to the type of no-fault statute. In Michigan, with its relatively "pure" no-fault plan, data col-lected over five years showed an 11 per cent decrease in total bodily injury premiums. During the same period, there were increases between about 13 and 18 per cent in those premium levels in states with "modified" no-fault plans, whether their benefits were rel-atively high or low. In states with "add-on" no-fault plans, bodily injury premiums rose considerably, by 49.5 per cent in the five-year period.[9]

. . .

Consumer assessments of no-fault. The data on how citizens react to no-fault plans are not entirely clear in their message. Professor Widiss, a long-time student of the auto compensation problem, reported that a "substantial majority" of survey respondents who made claims under the Massachusetts legislation were "at least moderately pleased with the way in which their claims had been processed." Although about one-third of the re-spondents were "'fairly dissatisfied' or 'very dissatisfied' with either the amount received or the way in which their claims had been handled, or with both," he concluded that in general the "positive attitudes" toward the Massachusetts plan were "most encouraging."

Arguably more ambiguous results appeared in a study conducted by the Michigan Insurance Bureau, dealing with the state legislation most generous in its no-fault bene-fits and most restrictive in its limitations on the tort action. Responding to questions concerning specific features usually associated with no-fault plans, the Michigan study's respondents indicated very positive attitudes towards no-fault, but only 17 per cent said Michigan no-fault was a "good system," while 55 per cent called it a "poor system." No-fault advocates were quick to point out, however, that "almost two-thirds of those giv-ing a 'poor' rating identified the reasons for that rating as being due to problems that

---

* Copyright © 1984 The American Bar Association. Reprinted by permission.

6. U.S. Dept. Transp., Pub. No. 6100.2, State No-Fault Automobile Insurance Experience 1971–1977, at 45–46 (1977) [hereafter, "DOT study"].

7. *Compare, e.g., id.,* at 47 (Massachusetts statistics showing much lower levels of lawsuits) *with id.* at 51–52 (Florida statistics somewhat lower than previous levels in that state).

8. *Id.* at 57.

9. *See, e.g.,* O'Connell and Beck, [1979 Ins. L.J.], at 133–35 (summarizing results from Note, *No-Fault Automobile Insurance: An Evaluative Survey,* 30 Rutgers L. Rev. 909 (1977)).

plague the entire automobile insurance system and are not directly related to fault versus no-fault systems," for example the cost and availability of insurance and the industry's rating and pricing practices. Moreover, another 38 per cent of those who rated the Michigan system "poor" indicated that their dissatisfaction related to matters of property damage, rather than personal injury.[13]

Effects on accidents. One confronts a mixed bag of data concerning the efforts of no-fault laws on accidents. The Department of Transportation study of 16 states found "no discernible jump in accident frequency" following the implementation of no-fault statutes.[14] However, noting that one of the "important sought for benefits of no-fault reform has been to create or reinforce incentives to car buyers or manufacturers to, respectively, purchase or make safe vehicles or effective safety equipment," the DOT study concluded that "no-fault plans have not, at least so far, fulfilled their promise in terms of encouraging 'accident cost avoidance.'"[15]

CONCLUSIONS OF A DEPARTMENT OF TRANSPORTATION STUDY

DEPARTMENT OF TRANSPORTATION, STATE NO-FAULT AUTOMOBILE INSURANCE
EXPERIENCE 1971–1977, at 75–79 (1977)

No Fault Insurance and Selected "Problems" of the Automobile Accident Reparations System

Unlimited Medical Benefits: Three States, Michigan, New Jersey and Pennsylvania, provide unlimited medical benefits as a feature of their no-fault plans. While clearly a most valuable benefit for victims, this provision has apparently caused problems for insurers. One problem relates to the very large contingent loss reserves that insurers must set aside in the cases of very seriously and permanently injured victims. With an "unlimited exposure" and a loss that may take years, even decades, to develop, it becomes extremely difficult for insurance actuaries to set their reserves with confidence. Then, too, while the catastrophically injured victim is, in a statistical sense, very rare, some companies merely by chance may be disproportionately impacted by an unusually large number of such claims.... In assessing the various ramifications of the "unlimited medical benefits" problem, however, it is important to keep the overall cost implication in proportion. The Michigan Insurance Department has cited a NAII study to the effect that the total cost of medical claims exceeding $25,000 in Michigan is $8 per car per year.[2]

...

Tort Threshold: The principal cost saving device common to all no-fault plans is a restriction limiting certain losses that can be recovered in tort. Most plans have adopted a "dollar threshold", *e.g.*, a victim can sue for intangible damages (*e.g.*, "pain and suffering") only if his medical costs exceed some predetermined "threshold", say $500. An-

13. O'Connell and Beck, *supra* note 9, at 142–43.
14. DOT Study, *supra* note 6, at 60.
15. *Id.* at 63.
2. Insurance Bureau, Michigan Department of Commerce, *No-Fault Insurance After Three Years: A Report to the Governor*, October, 1976, p. 7.

other type is known as the "verbal" threshold, *i.e.*, a victim can sue for intangible damages only, for example, in the case of death, serious permanent disfigurements, or total disability for a fixed period of time.

The "dollar" threshold has, in some States at least, become a significant source of difficulty. As noted earlier, inflation has tended to erode its effectiveness as a cost saver. Many observers believe that the thresholds were originally set too low and that their cost saving potential was, from the beginning, seriously overestimated. Others believe that the fixed dollar thresholds have actually become "targets" for victims and their lawyers to "shoot at," thereby encouraging unneeded or marginal treatment in order to raise medical costs beyond the threshold.

The development of the "verbal" threshold was, at least in part, an effort to overcome the problems of the fixed dollar threshold and many States with the latter are now considering changing. There may still prove to be some problems in the interpretation of "verbal" thresholds, although at this juncture, they seem to be working reasonably well.

Fraud: Fraud has proved to be a serious problem in some localities, *e.g.*, Miami and environs, and has been alleged to be so in other selected areas. It does not seem to be a general problem, however, and its connection to no-fault (except in the context, cited previously, of building up medical costs to pass the threshold) is tenuous.

. . .

Insurance availability: . . . There is an aspect of no-fault insurance plans that does relate directly to the problems of insurance availability, *i.e.*, the compulsory nature of the motorist's participation in the system. Prior to the introduction of no-fault, only three States—New York, Massachusetts and North Carolina—made auto insurance compulsory although every State, in varying degrees, imposed through its financial responsibility law some kind of pressure on drivers to carry liability coverage. No-fault, because of its compulsory nature, greatly increases that pressure on motorists who might otherwise not buy insurance. Among this category of motorist are many who find it difficult to obtain voluntary insurance coverage in the standard market and are thereby, forced into the higher cost non-standard market or assigned risk program.

In the final analysis, however, insurance availability is a function of the competitive environment which along with rate adequacy and the insurance classification are factors which are equally applicable to both fault and no-fault systems.

Summary of Findings Regarding No-Fault Benefits and Costs

. . .

Adequacy of No-Fault Benefits: All known evidence indicates that State no-fault plans, in varying degrees provide more adequate and equitable benefits than the tort liability system.

— There has been a major increase in the percentage of paid claimants, such as those injured in single vehicle accidents, who would not have been compensated under the tort system.

— A high degree of satisfaction with the amount of benefits provided was found among victims who were paid in Massachusetts.

— In States with unlimited first party medical benefits for accident victims, such as Michigan, New Jersey and Pennsylvania, unprecedented levels of compensation are being provided to grievously injured accident victims. Based on required insurance limits in tort states and previous data for tort recovery for seriously injured victims it is reasonable to conclude that seriously injured victims at least in these three states have a better chance of recovering their economic loss under the no-fault system.

—Available evidence suggests that the number of tort bodily injury lawsuits has fallen with the introduction of personal injury protection coverage.

—Given the universality of coverage under the various no-fault plans, it can be reasonably assumed that a far greater proportion of victims are now being compensated at some level for their economic losses than under insured tort liability.

Timeliness of No-Fault Benefits: The goal of providing more prompt payment of economic loss appears to be achieved under the no-fault system.

—In Massachusetts 63.3 percent of no-fault claimants received their first payment within 90 days.

—Eighty-four percent of the accident victims in a recent Massachusetts survey expressed satisfaction with the timeliness of their payments.

Coordination of No-Fault Benefits: The effective coordination of benefits from various compensation systems affects the potential for savings in all such systems.

—While data on coordination of no-fault benefits with other insurance coverages are sparse, significant premium savings appear to be available where benefit coordination is possible.

—In Massachusetts, at least, accident victims who are compensated for their economic losses do not seem to be pursuing duplicate recoveries to the degree which might have been expected.

The Administration Cost Efficiency of No-Fault: The decline in the number of first-party, no-fault claims reflects a clear shift from inefficient third-party benefits towards more efficient first-party benefits. Although the quantitative evidence is meager, being reflected chiefly in the relative reduction in claims personnel, this would appear to indicate that cost efficiency has improved with no-fault.

Impact on the Court System: Available evidence indicates that the burden on the courts and the legal system is being reduced.

—Massachusetts, Florida, New Jersey and Michigan consistently show a decline in motor vehicle tort litigation after the introduction of no-fault.

—The reduction in the incidence of tort litigation seems to be especially true for the less seriously injured victims.

Rehabilitation of Accident Victims: While no conclusive data on rehabilitation under no-fault plans exists, the observed improvement in timeliness and adequacy of payments clearly provides positive incentives for rehabilitation.

. . .

ECONOMIC EFFECTS OF NO-FAULT

Stephen J. Carroll & James S. Kakalik with David Adamson, No-Fault
Automobile Insurance: A Policy Perspective,
R-4019/1-ICJ, Santa Monica, CA: RAND, 1991, pp. 9–15*

GENERAL CONCLUSIONS

No-fault can yield substantial savings over the traditional system. No-fault can also increase costs over the traditional system. It all depends on the particular plan's provisions.

No-fault plans reduce transaction costs, regardless of their specific provisions. Those plans that ban claims for noneconomic loss reduce transaction costs by about 80 percent; those that allow seriously injured people to pursue liability claims for noneconomic loss reduce transaction costs by about 20 to 40 percent. Since transaction costs constitute about one-third of total costs, the net reductions from the latter plans equal approximately 10 percent of the total costs of injury compensation.

No-fault plans match compensation more closely with economic loss by increasing the fraction of economic loss that is compensated and by reducing the amount of compensation paid people in excess of their economic loss. As a result, injured people with smaller losses tend to recover amounts approximating their medical costs and lost wages, while more seriously injured people whose compensation is capped by policy limits recover a larger share of their economic loss, because they can collect both enhanced PIP benefits and liability compensation.

No-fault plans generally speed up compensation. Injured people begin receiving payments on average about two months sooner under no-fault than under the traditional system.

EFFECTS OF AN ILLUSTRATIVE NO-FAULT PLAN

To demonstrate no-fault's effects, let us examine an illustrative no-fault plan—one with a verbal threshold and a $15,000 PIP policy limit. Our full report analyzes 21 different alternative plans in detail....

How Much Does It Cost to Compensate for Auto Injuries?

In the mid-1980s, the compensation provided to people injured in auto accidents in tort states, including people who received no auto-insurance compensation at all, averaged $4,681 in 1989 dollars. Insurers' transaction costs—legal fees and claim-processing costs—averaged $793 per injured person. Overall, the total injury coverage costs of the traditional system averaged $5,474 per injured person, as shown in Table 1.

Using our models, we estimate that these same people, with the same injuries and losses, would receive an average of $3,764 in compensation, and insurers' transaction costs would average $528, under the illustrative plan. Compared to the traditional system, the illustrative no-fault plan reduces the total amount spent on compensating injured people by 22 percent.

---

* Reprinted by permission.

TABLE 1
Effects on Total Injury Coverage Costs[a]

	Traditional System ($)	No-Fault Alternative[b] ($)
Gross compensation	4,681	3,764
Insurers' Transaction costs	793	528
Total injury coverage costs	5,474	4,292
Effect on total injury coverage costs	−22%	

a. Average per injured person; all dollar amounts have been adjusted for inflation and are expressed in 1989 dollars.
b. Verbal threshold, $15,000 PIP benefit level

How Much of That Total Amount Is Spent on Transaction Costs, and How Much Do Injured People Take Home?

Out of the $5,474 spent per injured person in tort states, claimants take home an average of $3,645, or 67 percent, in compensation.[1] The remaining $1,829 is spent on the insurers' transaction costs ($793 or 14 percent) and on the claimants' transaction costs ($1,036 or 19 percent). (See Fig. 1.)

The illustrative no-fault plan reduces the transaction costs about 39 percent (equaling a 13-percent savings in total injury coverage costs). By eliminating compensation for non-economic losses to people below the threshold, the plan also reduces the overall average amount claimants take home, from $3,645 to $3,182 (equaling a 9-percent savings in total injury coverage costs).

How Does That Compensation Compare to Economic Loss?

Under the traditional system, injured people with relatively low levels of economic loss—less than $5,000—receive compensation that averages two to three times their economic loss. Injured people with much higher economic losses—$25,000 to $100,000, for example—receive compensation equal to just over half their economic loss, on average.

Under the illustrative no-fault plan, less serious injury cases tend to recover amounts closer to their economic losses.... People with less than $5,000 in economic loss receive compensation that averages less than 1.5 times their economic loss. Cases involving more serious injury (economic losses of $25,000 to $100,000) get back a higher proportion of those losses—about two-thirds.

No-fault substantially reduces the proportion of claimants who receive compensation for noneconomic loss and substantially increases the proportion of claimants who are fully compensated for their economic loss. Under the traditional system, 62 percent of the injured people receive compensation that exceeds their economic loss. In contrast, the illustrative no-fault plan provides more than full compensation for economic loss to less than 25 percent of the injured. Under the traditional system, 27 percent of people who suffer some economic loss obtain less than full compensation for that loss from auto insurance. Under the illustrative no-fault plan, only 16 percent of these people get less than full compensation for their economic loss....

---

1. Net or "take home" compensation is total compensation less the injured person's legal fees and related processing expenses.

Fig. 1. Effects on Claimants' Net Compensation and Transaction Costs

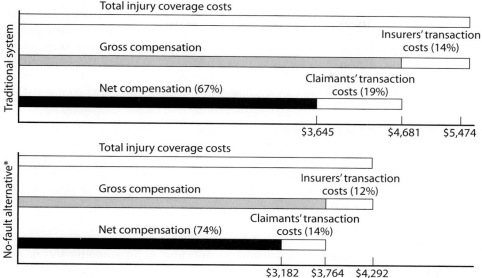

* Verbal threshold, $15,000 PIP benefit level

How Long Does it Take to Get Paid?

No-fault plans speed up compensation from auto insurance to injured people by an average of two months. Under no-fault, the vast majority of the people injured in auto accidents receive some compensation from PIP insurance soon after the accident.... In the traditional system, MedPay auto insurance provides rapid compensation to some people. However, many others lack MedPay coverage and have to wait for compensation from BI or UM liability insurance, typically a much longer process. Some of these people, of course, collect sooner from non-auto-insurance sources, such as private health insurance or sick-leave pay.

The no-fault plan examined here reduces the average time required for payouts to begin from 181 days to 116 (about a two-month reduction) after the accident.[2]

EFFECTS OF DIFFERENT NO-FAULT PLAN PROVISIONS

Dozens of no-fault plans can be developed by combining various thresholds and PIP benefit levels. These variations can substantially influence the effects each plan will have....

The Threshold

The threshold determines which cases go into the liability system and which are compensated only by PIP. The more stringent the threshold, the greater the reduction in injury coverage costs. At a $50,000 PIP benefit level, for example, a $5,000 threshold reduces injury coverage costs by 6 percent, from $5,474 per injured person in the tradi-

---

2. Our data do not indicate when the claimant provided sufficient information on his or her losses to allow claim processing to begin. We can only indicate the effect of no-fault plans on the time between the accident and when the claimant received compensation.

tional system to $5,150 in the no-fault plan. A verbal threshold reduces those costs by 12 percent, and an absolute ban reduces them by 52 percent.

Thresholds reduce costs by reducing both the amount paid out in compensation for noneconomic loss and transaction costs. By reducing the number of injured people whose injuries and losses allow them to cross the threshold, higher thresholds reduce the total paid in compensation for noneconomic loss. For example, at a $50,000 PIP benefit level, a $5,000 threshold cuts the amount spent on compensation in excess of economic loss by 27 percent, and an absolute-ban threshold eliminates compensation for noneconomic loss.

If fewer people have access to the liability system, there will be fewer disputes about who caused the accident and how much noneconomic loss claimants had. Fewer disputes, in turn, mean lower transaction costs. A $5,000 threshold reduces transaction costs by 29 percent (from $1,829 per injured person in the traditional system to $1,298 in the no-fault plan) when combined with a $50,000 PIP benefit level. An absolute-ban alternative reduces transaction costs by 83 percent.

The PIP Benefit Level

The PIP benefit level determines how much compensation for economic loss people receive under no-fault. At any given threshold, a higher PIP benefit level increases costs by increasing compensation for economic loss. For example, combining a verbal threshold with a $15,000 PIP benefit level reduces injury coverage costs by 22 percent. Using the same threshold but raising the PIP benefit level to $50,000 reduces savings to 12 percent. And if the PIP benefit level is very generous—$250,000—costs will actually increase by 5 percent over the traditional system.

Effects of Other Provisions

Although the two indispensable components of no-fault are the threshold and the benefit level, other provisions may also be added, such as deductibles or offsets against private health insurance. What effect would a PIP deductible and a private health-insurance offset have? Table 3 [here omitted—Ed.] shows how these provisions affect total costs under [an] illustrative no-fault plan ($15,000 PIP benefit level, verbal threshold)....

A $500 PIP deductible reduces total costs slightly (from 22 percent savings to 25 percent) and reduces total compensation either to zero, for those whose economic loss is less than $500, or by the amount of the deductible. Because a deductible eliminates payouts for economic losses below the deductible, injured people recover a smaller fraction of their economic losses, and a greater fraction of injured people receive nothing.

Mandating that injured people collect medical costs first from their private health insurers rather than their auto insurers reduces spending on auto-insurance compensation dramatically. For example, the 22-percent savings in the illustrative no-fault plan would jump to 33-percent savings with a private health-insurance offset. Health-insurance offsetting would also decrease compensation to injured people from auto-insurance sources. To the extent that the offset eliminates "double dipping" (that is, claimants collecting from both health and auto insurance for the same losses), this provision accomplishes real savings. Otherwise, the offset simply shifts costs from auto to health insurance.

. . .

EFFECTS OF NO-FAULT ON ACCIDENTS

Don Dewees, David Duff & Michael Trebilcock,
Exploring the Domain of Accident Law 22–26 (1996)*

The introduction of no-fault automobile insurance schemes in the 1970s in Quebec, New Zealand, and a number of Australian and American states has given researchers an opportunity to investigate the impact of the tort system in deterring automobile accidents. Nevertheless, despite numerous studies during the past decade, no strong consensus has emerged with respect to the significance of this deterrence effect....

Empirical Studies

If the tort system plays an appreciable role in deterring automobile accidents, jurisdictions that adopt no-fault schemes should, other things equal, have noticeably higher automobile accident rates than those in which the common law is untouched. Furthermore, since "threshold" schemes preclude more tort actions than "add-on" jurisdictions and since "comprehensive" plans eliminate more suits than "threshold" jurisdictions, one would expect auto accident rates to be positively correlated with the degree to which these schemes preclude tort claims. In fact, the empirical evidence is far from conclusive.

United States. Two U.S. studies purport to demonstrate precisely the result predicted by deterrence theories of the tort system. Medoff and Magaddino estimated the impact of no-fault automobile legislation on the "liability loss rate" by regression analysis on cross-sectional data for all U.S. states during the year 1977. Working with more comprehensive data from all states and Washington D.C. during the period 1967–75, Landes measured the effect of different legislative thresholds on the incidence of fatal accidents.

Despite differences in data sets, dependent variables, and structural equations, the conclusions of both studies are highly complementary. Medoff and Magaddino derive a direct relationship between the loss rate and the scope of each state's no-fault coverage. Estimating coefficients on dummy variables representing different aggregations of these no-fault schemes—from add-on and threshold jurisdictions together ("compulsory" no-fault), to threshold jurisdictions alone ("mandatory" no-fault), to a subcategory of the most significant threshold jurisdictions ("pure" no-fault)—the authors report increased loss rates over tort jurisdictions of 7.4% in "pure" no-fault states, 6.3% in "mandatory" no-fault states, and 4.0% in "compulsory" no-fault states. Depending on the stringency of the state's laws, these additional losses represent costs of between $13.8 and $51 million.

Landes's conclusions are even more striking. Estimating coefficients on three measures of the stringency of no-fault laws, she reports a positive correlation between the stringency of each "legal variable" and the numbers of fatal accidents. States with "relatively modest restrictions on tort suits" are estimated to have experienced between 2% and 5% more fatal accidents as a result of adopting no-fault, while states with "more restrictive" laws experienced as many as 10% to 15% more fatal accidents. In sum, she concludes, the states that adopted no-fault between 1971 and 1975 experienced a total of between 376 and 1,009 additional automobile fatalities during the years the laws were in effect.

Although these studies suggest that the tort system may play an important role in de-terring automobile accidents, they are vulnerable to several criticisms. With respect to the Medoff and Magaddino study, questions can be raised regarding both the large number of independent variables relative to the limited sample size of 1977 data and the choice of the "liability loss rate" as the dependent variable. In particular, since this dependent variable involves four components (average claim cost, average premium per vehicle, number of accidents, and number of insured vehicles), its increase could just as easily signify a rise in average claim cost, a fall in average premiums per vehicle, or a drop in the number of insured vehicles, as it could reflect an increase in the number of accidents. While the authors reject the prospect of a rise in average claim costs, the evi-dence on which they base this conclusion is limited. Nor do they address the very real possibility that average premiums per vehicle may have fallen as a result of the enact-ment of no-fault automobile legislation—a particularly significant omission given that this is one of the avowed objectives of no-fault automobile insurance. As a result, little weight can be attached to the study.

The Landes study is also open to criticism. On a basic conceptual level, critics have questioned her use of fatal accidents as a dependent variable. As O'Connell and Lev-more point out, because all tort thresholds examined by Landes are exceeded in the case of any accident causing death, it is difficult to understand why no-fault jurisdictions would experience any increase in such accidents. Further, as Zador and Lund explain, since most threshold states abolished tort law only for relatively minor injuries, leaving major injuries and property damage to the tort system, and since injury claims without associated property damage are extremely rare, the extent to which at-fault drivers are penalized by increased insurance premiums was largely unaffected by no-fault laws. Thus, a substantial reduction of liability-induced precautions (to the extent that they exist) seems implausible....

... [E]ven assuming the validity of her statistical work, there is no empirical basis for Landes's conclusion that the effects she derives stem from reductions in driver care as opposed to increased driving stimulated by lower insurance costs or by changes in the premium structure accompanying the introduction of no-fault in U.S. states.

In addition to these criticisms, the results of the Medoff and Magaddino and the Landes studies have been challenged by more recent empirical work. A 1985 report by the U.S. Department of Transportation concluded bluntly that "no-fault insurance laws do not lead to more accidents." However, the lack of scientific rigor upon which the as-sessment was based makes it even more unreliable than the contrary findings just con-sidered. Nevertheless, the same conclusion has also been reached in two recent econo-metric studies. In one attempt to replicate Landes's study with data covering the period 1967–80, the coefficients of all legal variables were insignificantly different from zero. Similarly, Kochanowski and Young found no significant relationship between no-fault automobile legislation and the rate of fatal accidents. On the other hand, a more recent study by Sloan and others concludes that no-fault plans that exclude 25% of all tort claims increase auto fatalities by 18%. Thus, the empirical results are sharply contested.

New Zealand and Australia. Two studies have analyzed the impact of no-fault legisla-tion in New Zealand and Australia. In the first, reviewing raw data on driving activity and accident rates in New Zealand before and after the introduction of no-fault acci-dent compensation in 1972, Brown found "no significant increase in motoring activity" and "no noticeable increase in additional rates" as a result of the legislation. In the sec-ond, comparing fatal accidents in New Zealand and all Australia states and territories during the years 1970–81, McEwin reports that while add-on no-fault legislation had no effect on traffic fatalities, comprehensive no-fault schemes were responsible for a 16% annual increase in automobile fatalities per capita. As a result, he concludes, "the right to sue for personal injury loss is an important factor in promoting road safety."

Although the more rigorous character of the latter study makes it the better choice between the two, even it is not without ambiguities. McEwin admits that "the problems involved in modeling road accidents" suggest that little weight should be placed on the size of the impact derived. More important, as with the Landes study, it is impossible to attribute any effect to the abolition of tort actions per se, as opposed to the flat-rate premium structure and substantial cost externalization that accompanied the change from fault to no-fault....

Quebec. Two studies have examined the effect on the rate of motor vehicle accidents in Quebec of the no-fault scheme introduced there in 1978. In Gaudry's study, looking only at the first 12 months of the new regime, legal reform was associated with a 26.9% increase in all automobile accidents, a 26.3% increase in accidents involving material damages above a specified amount (despite the fact that this amount increased from $200 to $250), a 31.8% increase in accidents with at least one injury (no deaths), and a 7.0% increase in automobile fatalities. While the larger figures probably contain a substantial reporting bias, the reported impact on the number of fatal accidents is free from any such defect.

Perhaps surprisingly, Gaudry attributes the effects that he does derive not to the no-fault scheme itself, but instead partly to more stringent enforcement of compulsory insurance after 1978, leading previously uninsured drivers to drive with less care, and partly to the adoption of a flat-rate premium structure that substantially reduced the cost of driving to high-risk drivers. While emphasizing the difficulty of distinguishing among different components of the 1978 reform, he concludes that "previous moral hazard experience with compulsory automobile insurance and the very strong evidence of adverse selection caused by the subsidization of high risk drivers suggest that the contribution of no-fault, as such, to the reduction of driver care and deterrence was very small. Thus, it is the insurance regime, rather than the liability regime, that is central to Gaudry's conclusions.

Despite strikingly similar empirical findings, Devlin attributes increases in automobile fatalities directly to the abolition of civil suits for negligent driving. Estimating an increase of about 4.7% in fatal accidents as a result of the flat-rate premium structure, and an increase of 9.6% in fatal accidents, accidents involving bodily injury and property damage only (representing total monetary losses of about $260 million per year) attributed to a reduction in average driving care, Devlin concludes that "irrespective of how the first-party insurance is priced" no-fault compensation reduces average driving care and increases the incidence of automobile accidents. For two reasons, this conclusion should be cautiously received. First, by emphasizing a strong inverse relationship between driving care and no-fault compensation, Devlin downplays the deterrent effect of the injury itself; since monetary compensation can never perfectly alleviate noneconomic losses from injuries (and since no-fault typically limits recovery for pain and suffering), Devlin's focus on the marginal impact of eligibility for monetary compensation seems inflated. Second, by minimizing the significance of first-party insurance pricing, Devlin ignores the important role of the insurance regime in shaping driver care and activity levels. In fact, while her model controls for total kilometers driven and for the proportion of young male drivers among the total driving population, it fails to account for the elimination of experience-rating under the Quebec scheme. As a result, any attempt to attribute lower average driving care to the abolition of tort liability, as opposed to changes in the structure of insurance premiums, is inherently problematic.

...

———

Frank Sloan, Bridget Reilly & Christoph Schenzler, *Effects of Tort Liability and Insurance on Heavy Drinking and Drinking and Driving*

38 J. L. & Econ. 49 (1995)*

...

One of the most egregious forms of reckless driving behavior is driving under the influence of alcoholic beverages (DUI). The probability of crash involvement rises dramatically with the percentage of blood-alcohol concentration. Half or more of all motor vehicle fatalities have been attributed to alcohol use. The emphasis of public policy against reckless driving in general and drunk driving in particular has been on criminal rather than on civil sanctions. The trend toward mandatory criminal sanctions reflects a belief that sanctions are more effective if punishment is certain.

Using self-reported data on patterns of alcohol use among individuals, this study investigates the role that tort liability and third- and first-party insurance play in binge drinking and in driving under the influence of alcohol. Effects of alcohol prices and criminal sanctions on binge drinking and driving under the influence of alcohol are also analyzed.

Our theoretical analysis predicted that variables associated with a "taste for drinking" should lead to more binge drinking, and raising price and curbing availability of alcoholic beverages should reduce binge drinking. Insurance, tort, and criminal penalties that make careless drivers pay more for careless behavior should decrease the number of binge-drinking episodes.

...

As predicted by the model, higher alcohol prices and curbing availability by imposing minimum-drinking-age laws reduced the amount of binge drinking, but only the result for price is statistically significant. The Tobit coefficient implies that a 10 percent increase in the price of alcoholic beverages would decrease the expected number of binge episodes per month by 0.09 on average. The minimum drinking age tended to keep more youths from binging at all; for youths who had at least one episode, those covered by such a statute also tended to binge less.

Judging from the coefficients and levels of statistical significance, it is apparent that efforts to penalize careless behavior deter binge drinking. Requiring that drivers purchase minimum amounts of automobile liability insurance lowered the frequency of binge drinking, mainly through the effect of such statutes on decreasing the probability of binge drinking at all during the month before the survey. Requiring liability insurance reduced the number of binge episodes per month by 0.09 on average, the same as increasing price by 10 percent. This effect is for the omitted reference group, states in which the surcharge for a DUI was among the five lowest in the United States. In the five states with the highest surcharges for a DUI, mandating automobile insurance coverage reduced the number of binging episodes in the past month by 0.21 on average. In the remaining states, the Tobit results predict a decrease of 0.18 episodes.

———

. . .

Where no-fault laws barred victims from suing, the number of binge episodes increased. However, the effect implied by the Tobit coefficient on the no-fault variable, which is statistically significant at the 10 percent level, is virtually zero. Imposing dramshop liability did not influence binge drinking in any of the regressions.

The results imply that switching from contributory to pure comparative or modified comparative negligence increased binge drinking. The Tobit coefficients, both statistically significant at the 1 percent level, imply very similar marginal effects. Compared to states with contributory negligence, the number of binge-drinking episodes per month was 0.28 higher in states with pure and with modified comparative negligence. To the extent that the negligence rule makes a difference, one would expect switching to pure comparative negligence to have had a greater effect.

. . .

Outcome studies of traffic fatalities measure the failure to take care indirectly. By contrast, in this study, the dependent variables for binge drinking and driving conditional on binge drinking are direct measures of behavior. Although the measures used in this analysis could be subject to underreporting, given the many plausible relationships, may respondents must have reported their behavior fairly accurately. In fact, if there is underreporting, it is noteworthy that a rather high percentage of adults (14 percent) reported that they consumed five or more alcoholic beverages on one occasion, and of these individuals, 19 percent reported driving after having, in their opinion, too much to drink.

Two major findings emerge from the empirical analysis. First, deterrence of drinking and driving is achieved by curbing behavior that leads to DUIs, namely, binge drinking. Once individuals engage in binge drinking, it appears that many policies designed to be deterrents have little influence. This finding is supported by Kenkel's empirical analysis of binge drinking and driving using data from a supplement to the 1985 Health Interview Survey. Second, in our research, tort liability rules — contributory rather than comparative negligence, the traditional negligence rule rather than no-fault, and compulsory liability insurance coupled with experience-rating of premiums — are more effective in reducing binge drinking than are criminal sanctions. Our empirical evidence on the effect of experience rating on binge drinking is consistent with empirical evidence from other lines of insurance that shows that basing premiums on experience influences insureds' behavior in socially desirable ways.

Dramshop laws show no effects on the measures used in this analysis. In other work, Chaloupka and coauthors and we found that such laws reduced both motor vehicle and other types of alcohol-related deaths. One possibility is that dramshop laws simply displace binge drinkers from commercial establishments to other locations. But if this were so, one would expect reductions in driving per binge episode, which was not observed.

Of the deterrents considered, other than tort liability and insurance, increasing alcohol prices and implementing minimum-drinking-age laws appear to be most effective. While some of the regressions imply that mandatory minimum fines deter DUIs and the number of binge-drinking episodes, responses to the length of mandatory jail terms are the strongest. But, taken as a group, the results on criminal sanctions, especially on jail terms, are too inconsistent to merit much confidence.

Finally, the model's implications are partly supported. Most important, we found evidence that penalizing harmful behavior did reduce the rate of binge drinking, which the model predicts. But we found the penalties overall have no effect on driving following binge episodes, while the model predicted that higher penalties should increase the care level per binge episode. Raising the price of bingeing, either the money price or availability through the minimum drinking age, decreased the amount of bingeing, as expected, but it also reduced the frequency of driving after bingeing, which was not predicted by the model. Possibly a low price leads to drinking habits that in turn change risk preferences, a complication beyond the scope of our static model and available data.

NOTES

(1) Which data concerning no-fault seem most significant to you? The statistics on how much of the premium dollar actually winds up in the pocket of claimants? The statistics on the behavioral effects of no-fault? The reactions of ordinary citizens to the implementation of no-fault plans?

(2) Given the statistics, what do you regard as the most important social problems that must be solved with respect to the effects of automobile accidents? Should policymakers be concentrating on the problem of overcompensation for small losses? Undercompensation for large losses? Deterrence of drunk driving? What ought to be their basic stance with respect to noneconomic loss, particularly pain and suffering?

(3) What do the statistics presented in this section persuade you is the most rational position for a legislator confronting choices among the following sorts of no-fault models:

(a) A $2,000-threshold plan with a complete preservation of tort remedies beyond that.

(b) A $50,000-threshold plan with unlimited compensation for wage losses and a requirement of deductibility for all collateral sources—that is, payments made by others than the tortfeasor as reimbursement for injury costs, for example, payments from medical or hospitalization insurance.

(c) A first-party insurance plan that completely replaces the tort action, limiting wage loss recovery under that plan to $2,500 per month but with the possibility of purchasing supplemental insurance for wage losses.

(4) How does the data presented here relate to "justice"? What are the principal components of "justice"? The ability to sue for a violation of "rights"? The ability to collect on the basis of "fault"? The right to compensation for injury? Promptness of disposition of claims?

[D] Summary: Alternatives to Tort for Vehicle Injuries

This section seeks to stimulate an overall consideration of the general issue of whether state legislatures, or Congress, should opt for a legislative solution to the claims of auto accident victims. The section begins with brief summaries of a few alternatives to traditional no-fault plans for automobile injuries. It includes a variety of analyses and commentaries concerning a broad spectrum of approaches to the problem. Taken together, the materials should help you determine how you would vote on the broad question of whether to adopt automobile compensation legislation of some kind. They are designed to push you to define your goals and premises concerning this kind of legislation.

A "CONSUMER CHOICE" PLAN
Jeffrey O'Connell, *et al., The Comparative Costs of Allowing Consumer Choice of Auto Insurance in All Fifty States*
55 Md. L. Rev. 160, 163–64 (1996)*

... [O]ne possible answer ... is a reform that replaces no-fault laws, burdened as they are not only with payments made without regard to fault for economic losses up to the limits purchased, but also with expensive—and arguably even subsidized—claims for noneconomic loss. This new reform could give motorists the option of foregoing claims for noneconomic loss, without forcing them to do so. It would also provide for automatic payment for economic loss at a fixed level. Under this reform, in no-fault or add-on states, motorists are given the option of purchasing PIP coverage at the state's compulsory insurance level currently required for tort liability for personal injury (PI). For example, if a state requires a minimum of $20,000 of PI tort liability, one could meet that requirement by buying $20,000 of PIP. (But just as one can buy more than the minimum PI coverage, one could also buy higher PIP limits.) Persons electing such PIP coverage could never sue nor be sued for noneconomic loss if involved in accidents with any other motorist, PIP insured or not. Such PIP motorists would only be allowed to claim in tort against other motorists, whether covered by PIP or otherwise, for economic loss in excess of their PIP coverage. If an injury was caused by a tortfeasor's alcohol or drug abuse, however, there would be no restriction on the right to sue in tort. As to accidents between PIP insureds and those electing to stay in the tort system, tort insureds would make a claim against their own insurer for both economic and noneconomic loss (under coverage termed "tort maintenance coverage"), just as they do today under uninsured motorist coverage. Tort claims for economic loss in excess of an insured's own tort maintenance coverage would be allowed against PIP insureds. In accidents between two tort liability insureds, the current common-law tort system allowing claims for economic and noneconomic loss would apply without change.

Further details of the proposal are as follows: PIP coverage would be in excess of all collateral sources, and payable periodically. When claims for economic loss in excess of either PIP or tort maintenance coverages are pursued, a reasonable attorney's fee in addition to economic loss would be recoverable. For the purposes of the cost study..., we assume no change would be made in the law applicable to property damage. In other words, liability coverage for property damage claims would still be required.

...

A PLURALISTIC SOLUTION
Alfred Conard, *The Economic Treatment of Automobile Injuries*
63 Mich. L. Rev. 279, 326 (1964)*

Recent empirical research makes possible new and fresh approaches to the problem of economic reparation for automobile injuries. As a lawyer who has been engaged in some of the research and who has given some thought to its implications, I present the following as some of my personal conclusions:

1. The way ahead is not through a single plan for automobile injuries; it is through keeping alive the plurality of existing programs—from social security to tort damages—with some extensions, additions, and correlations.

2. One urgent need that should be filled immediately is the adoption of a program that would provide rehabilitation, from surgery to vocational training, for every automobile injury victim, regardless of the circumstances of his injury.

3. A second urgent need is an extension of subsistence through the social security system to automobile injury victims and dependents of victims who are not now "fully covered" because they have not spent enough time in "covered employment."

4. A third desideratum—although less urgent than the preceding ones—is a program of basic income maintenance for wage-earners; this would not apply to non-wage-earners.

5. Tort actions would continue, but damage rules should be revised to deduct from recoverable damages the amounts that injury victims have recovered or can recover from health insurance, rehabilitation programs, social security, and disability insurance.

6. Measures should be taken to enhance the personal responsibility of tort-feasors. Suggested for consideration are exclusion of punitive damages and psychic damages from insurance coverage; denial of unconditional bankruptcy discharges for personal injury judgments; permitting insurance companies to set up safety incentive rates without regard to "actuarial justification."

7. Incentives to make and accept reasonable settlement offers should be increased by assessing the opponents' full costs of litigation on the party who rejects a reasonable settlement offer.

8. The classic "automobile injury compensation plan" and the more recent compulsory liability insurance laws are decidedly inferior to other practicable treatments of the reparation problem.

Alma Cohen & Rajeev Dehejia, *The Effect of Automobile Insurance and Accident Liability Laws on Traffic Fatalities*
47 J. L. & Econ. 357, 357–60, 382, 385 (2004)

I. INTRODUCTION

This paper examines how economic incentives and liability regulation influence driver behavior and, in turn, traffic fatalities. We use the introduction of compulsory insurance and no-fault liability regulation to examine the moral hazard effects of automobile insurance, compulsory insurance laws, and no-fault liability laws. We analyze a panel of 50 U.S. states and the District of Columbia for 1970–98, a period in which many states adopted compulsory insurance regulations and/or no-fault laws. Using compulsory insurance as an instrument for the proportion of uninsured motorists, we find that automobile insurance has significant moral hazard costs, namely, reducing precautions and increasing traffic fatalities. We also find that limiting motor vehicle liability through no-fault liability laws leads to an increase in traffic fatalities. Overall our results indicate that, whatever benefits flow from increasing the incidence of automobile insurance and from moves to a no-fault system, there are also significant moral hazard costs to doing so.

Traffic accidents have very large costs that merit substantial attention by economists. These accidents claim over 40,000 lives each year in the United States, roughly the same as the number of Americans killed during the Vietnam War. Americans spend roughly $100 billion each year on automobile insurance premia, and they bear over $250 billion in uninsured accident costs each year. The incidence of motor vehicle crashes and traffic fatalities is likely to be influenced significantly by choices made by drivers (including whether to use seat belts or air bags, how carefully to drive, whether to drink alcohol, and how much to drive). Accordingly, economists have long been interested in how these choices are influenced by agents" economic incentives and by various legal rules and policy measures.

Beginning in 1970, most U.S. states adopted compulsory automobile insurance requirements. Over the same period, 16 states adopted no-fault automobile insurance. The impact of these policy shifts on traffic fatalities is of interest for two reasons. First, identifying this effect—which we shall see is significant—is necessary for assessing the social desirability of these policies. Second, these changes in automobile insurance regulations provide a large-scale natural experiment through which we can examine the moral hazard effects of automobile insurance and the incentive effects of liability exposure. In this sense, the changes in laws that we examine offer an interesting window on a larger set of phenomena.

Specifically, we investigate two related issues. First, we examine whether having automobile insurance (empirically, we examine the proportion of uninsured motorists) has a moral hazard effect on traffic fatalities. As a theoretical matter, insurance does have the moral hazard cost of reducing the policyholder's incentives to take precautions against the insured loss. This is also theoretically the case for the particular type of insurance that we examine, namely, insurance for automobile accidents. However, the question is whether the reduction in precautions against automobile accidents produced by automobile insurance—which theory predicts—is empirically significant. For example, it might be that drivers" concern for their own safety and health provides sufficient incentives for them to take precautions (to the extent that taking precautions is affected at all by incentives) and that the presence of insurance makes little difference on the margin. Although there has been much interest in the incidence of automobile insurance and uninsured motorists, whether automobile insurance leads to moral hazard costs is an open question that has not been addressed by existing research.

Our strategy for examining this issue is to look at the consequences of a natural experiment: the adoption of compulsory insurance regulations in some states governed by tort law. Because this change produces a reduction in the number of uninsured motorists not attributable to other confounding factors, we are able to test the consequences of a reduction in the number of uninsured motorists on traffic fatalities. Although some work on compulsory insurance has been done, none of these papers makes the connection between such regulations and traffic fatalities. Richard Derrig and coauthors, who do connect the two, find insignificant effects on fatalities rates. Our results indicate that a reduction in the incidence of uninsured motorists produces an increase in traffic fatalities.

The second issue we examine is the effect on traffic fatalities of the reduction in liability brought about by no-fault laws. Early work by M. Elisabeth Landes suggested that by reducing incentives to drive carefully, such laws have led to an increase in traffic fatalities in the United States. Subsequent results have been mixed: Paul Zador and Adrian Lund found the opposite effect; S. Paul Kochanowski and Madelyn Young and Derrig and coauthors found no significant effect; and J. David Cummins, Richard Phillips, and

Mary Weiss recently found a significant positive effect of no-fault liability laws on traffic fatalities. However, all states that adopted no-fault limitations on liability also adopted compulsory insurance requirements at the same time, and these earlier studies did not attempt to separate the effects of the two elements of the legislation. Thus, they did not isolate the effect of limitations on liability as distinct from the effects of the accompanying adoption of compulsory insurance requirements. We consider the two elements of legislation simultaneously and in this way are able to identify the effect of no-fault limitations on liability separately from the effect of compulsory insurance requirements. We find that no-fault limitations on liability do increase fatalities. Specifically, we estimate that the effect of such limitations is to increase fatalities by about 10 percent.

* * *

[The authors discuss data, here omitted, on "the effect of no-fault regulation on fatalities.":] ... [W]e see that the direct effect is positive and significant. Thus, ... the effect of reduced liability dominates the effect of reduced insurance. The magnitude of the effect is on the order of 10 percent. This corresponds to 5,160–6,450 lives in the United States depending on the year.... [W]e reestimate the effect in a 4-year window of the passage of no-fault legislation. Since the sample size is greatly reduced, it is not surprising that the effect is no longer statistically significant. However, the sign of the effect remains positive, although the magnitude is smaller.... [W]e estimate the effect on fatalities per vehicle-mile traveled and find a positive and significant effect. The magnitude of this effect is on the order of 7 percent of fatalities per vehicle-mile.... [W]e observe that the threshold effect for fatalities is also positive and statistically significant.... [W]e demonstrate the robustness of our estimate to additional controls. Overall, these results provide strong evidence of the incentive effects of no-fault regulation. In [a prior section] we observed that although drivers who are uninsured might in principle drive more carefully under a no-fault system, insured drivers experience a reduction in their exposure to liability and would accordingly drive less carefully. Given the relative proportions of these two groups, it is natural that the latter effect dominates for fatalities.

While the effect of no-fault legislation on traffic fatalities is important, we wish to stress ... that it is not the sole consideration in assessing such a system. No-fault systems have benefits in terms of reducing administrative costs, and these benefits might make it worthwhile even if it increases traffic fatalities. Whether this would be the case, of course, would depend on the magnitude of the effect, if any, on traffic fatalities.

[The authors also note that the "clearly beneficial" effects of no-fault insurance are that it "reduces the risk-bearing costs of drivers and leads to compensation of some victims who otherwise would receive less or no compensation."]

Walter J. Blum & Harry Kalven, Jr., *Public Law Perspectives on a Private Law Problem*
31 U. CHI. L. REV. 641, 719–723 (1964)*

...

We of course find attractive the two main objectives of plans: to compensate all victims and to provide medical and emergency expense payments promptly. Nor can there

---

be any argument but that the common law fails to achieve either of these. It does not achieve the first because it intends as a matter of policy to leave some victims uncompensated; and it cannot as a matter of practice achieve the second inasmuch as it limits liability to fault and hence subjects that issue to controversy.

In analyzing plans it quickly becomes apparent that the old common law issue of liability translates into a question of costs. Changing the form of the question does not cause the underlying issue to evaporate. Any plan requires coverage of additional victims in order to achieve its twin objectives. Additional coverage of victims means additional cost. The central policy problem, in weighing the merits of plans, is: How is this additional cost to be defrayed?

The solution most frequently suggested is to put the cost on motorists, and thus to pose the issue of strict liability versus negligence. We have been unable to find a satisfactory justification for imposing the additional cost on motorists. Once the fault criterion has been laid aside, we see no basis in common sense for charging them. We are unimpressed with arguments based on the perception of an irreversible historical trend. And we derive no support for charging motorists from economic analysis of the superior risk bearing formula.

But this is by no means the end of the argument.

[After describing and criticizing two ways to finance the cost of additional coverage, and discussing a blend of these two methods, the authors find "the main challenge" in another alternative:]

[T]he last approach is not to shift losses directly but to put the burden on all victims as a class—a class which is coextensive with the entire population. The image is of compulsory accident insurance for everyone; but in reality so wide a scheme of accident insurance would require use of the taxing mechanism to collect premiums, producing what can be viewed as an extension of social security.

The greatest strength of this approach is that it frames the problem candidly and coherently. From the very beginning the proponents of plans have insisted that the auto accident be viewed as an instance of human misfortune calling for a welfare remedy. When the situation is looked at in this manner, it immediately becomes apparent that the problem is bigger than that which the proponents started out to solve. The welfare universe is not limited to victims of auto accidents but includes victims of all other kinds of human misfortune. We can think of no ground for singling out the misfortune of auto accidents for special welfare treatment.

The social security perspective also has the merit of bringing to the surface the profound question of why the state should do anything about human misfortunes. We infer that those who urge the state to intervene have mixed motives. To some extent they favor sumptuary legislation in behalf of prudence. They are willing to restrict the power of the individual to choose because they distrust every man's capacity to make prudent judgments about privately carrying accident insurance. But more important, they are concerned over the financial ability of people to absorb misfortune. They see that by no means is everyone prosperous enough to buy adequate insurance against misfortune. The attraction of financing protection through the tax mechanism is that the necessary funds can be collected on some progressive tax basis, so that the richer will pay the costs for the poorer. Intervention by the state thus is sought in order to mitigate the evils of poverty. We are tempted to hazard the grand generalization that at the root of most of our major social issues lies the concern with what is thought to be poverty. The automobile compensation plan is no exception.

While social security provides a candid and coherent approach to the problem of the accident victim, it leaves unanswered the common law's main question of justice. In addressing itself to the problem of the needy auto accident victim, the social security approach tells us that his claim to help from society should be on a par with the claims of others who suffer from misfortune. But it cannot tell us why losses caused by negligent motorists should not be shifted to these drivers. The common law's solution was to make negligent motorists poorer in order to compensate victims in full for their losses. The question is whether this is any less just because the needs of victims are provided for by society.

We would argue that, in theory, the case for shifting the loss to a faulty driver rather than leaving it with the victim or as a charge on society is not thereby impaired. Theory would thus call for drawing a distinction between responding immediately to the victim's needs and deciding at leisure under the fault principle who ultimately should bear the cost. Once the dust had settled on all payments, no one would have been compelled to pay taxes or premiums on insurance to cover losses caused him by the fault of another.

We may, however, be in an area where there is a wide gulf between the theoretical and the practical. The effort to be this pure in allocating costs according to fault presents formidable difficulties quite apart from any controversy about the appropriateness of fault as a criterion of liability. To implement the suggested principle fully, the welfare fund would have to be allowed to recover over against the negligent actors. This complication raises two awful prospects: We can anticipate that motorists would then carry liability insurance against the threat of subrogation by the welfare fund, and the crucial equity would lie in adjustments between the insurance carriers and the welfare fund. And logic would seem to require that the welfare fund also be obligated to sue contributorily negligent victims. The specter of these two results might well induce us to accept the social security approach without a negligence rider.

A middle ground has been suggested. The social security approach could be used to underwrite relief for those in need without allowing any recovery over by the welfare fund. Victims of faulty drivers, however, would be left with their common law actions intact, subject only to deduction for welfare payments which they have received from the fund. Under such an arrangement, losses below a certain level would be borne by the public generally and would be allocated wholly without regard to fault, while losses above that level would be allocated according to the fault principle — some remaining on victims and some shifted to drivers as the principle dictated. This result is in effect the Saskatchewan plan. For those who have a wholesale lack of enthusiasm for the fault principle, retaining it in this context might well appear as a foolish luxury.

So much for the perplexities of either marrying or divorcing social security and fault.

The old common law issue of justice apart, the social security approach to the problem of auto accident victims has some distinctive disadvantages of its own. If economic considerations have a bearing on accident causing behavior, this approach would seem to run the greatest risk of lessening deterrence. Neither drivers nor pedestrians would perceive any relationship between their taxes and their conduct in respect to automobiles. The approach also has the disadvantage of supplanting the private insurance industry in a major sector of its activities, and replacing it with taxation and government administration of welfare benefits. Such a development would add to the power of government and weaken what now is an important private pool of power. Finally, the approach calls for one more — and perhaps an irreversible — reduction in the area of individual autonomy.

It is not comfortable for us to end by repeating all the well-aired objections to social security. We are aware that we are a long way from home. And it is no accident that we have travelled so far from the tort world from which we began. Private law cannot borrow goals from public law fields without accepting the obligation to make a proper public law analysis. In the case of automobile compensation plans, such an analysis shows that the special problem cannot be solved adequately without solving a larger problem. This much, at least, we have learned from this venture in applying public law perspectives to an important private law problem.

CONCLUSIONS OF THE A.B.A. SPECIAL COMMITTEE ON THE TORT LIABILITY SYSTEM

Towards a Jurisprudence of Injury 11-17 to 11-20
(A.B.A. 1984, M. Shapo Rptr.)*

Conclusion. The accumulating data on statutes dealing with compensation of automobile victims sound an uncertain trumpet. Perhaps the better metaphor is that of a disorganized, cacophonous orchestra. The firmest conclusions we can draw are that certain kinds of no-fault plans achieve significant reductions in systematic costs, that no-fault laws have varying effects on citizen perceptions of justice, and that the evidence is in conflict on whether they have a deleterious impact on accident rates.

The years since 1965, when Robert Keeton and Jeffrey O'Connell rationalized a modified no-fault plan at book length, have witnessed a continuing flow of scholarly ideas in the area of traffic accidents. O'Connell, having proposed the extension of the no-fault principle throughout accident law,[20] has refined that position to suggest an elective no-fault system under which insurers would provide coverage for specified economic losses, even in the absence of a viable tort claim. For certainty of recovery, insureds would trade "an absolute pre-accident assignment of any tort claims ... against third parties in relation to any disability coming within the terms of the policy."

O'Connell's development of these proposals through the nineteen seventies appears to have responded to the stalling of the legislative movement for no-fault. Richard Epstein, arguing for strict liability as, on balance, the preferred solution to the auto accident problem,[23] noted in 1980 that in the last half of the seventies, there had "been no new enactment of a state no-fault system.[24] O'Connell's separate practical compromise within the framework of tort law was to suggest a discarding of the defenses of contributory and comparative fault, with the costs thus generated being absorbed by abolition of the collateral source rule.[25] By comparison, Saul Levmore was willing to permit judicial determinations of fault, but proposed to eliminate most trial time spent on the

---

20. *See, e.g.*, O'Connell, *Expanding No-Fault Beyond Auto Insurance: Some Proposals*, 59 Va. L. Rev. 749 (1973).

23. See Epstein, *Automobile No-Fault Plans: A Second Look at First Principles*, 13 Creighton L. Rev. 769 (1980).

24. *Id.* at 770.

25. *See* O'Connell, *A Proposal to Abolish Contributory and Comparative Fault, with Compensatory Savings by Also Abolishing the Collateral Source Rule*, 1979 U. Ill. L.F. 591.

damages issue. His vehicle was a "self-assessment" system under which tort damages would be based on first-party insurance coverage of the plaintiff.[26]

Having considered an array of available data and of scholarly argument that surrounds the subject, we reach several conclusions for legal policy. We do find significant cause for anxiety about the possible counter-deterrent effect of no-fault statutes. However, on balance we are inclined to think that the adoption of low-threshold no-fault laws is justifiable as saving systematic costs and speeding basic levels of compensation to accident victims.[27] We note that in practice, with the increased development of loss insurance features in personal automobile policies, the insurance industry is effectively achieving a no-fault effect at the lower economic end of the accident spectrum. We observe also that the rise in various collateral benefits, a development which has been noted for more than a quarter century,[28] has provided significant amelioration of the lot of automobile injury victims.

At the same time, we emphasize that legislatures choosing modified no-fault plans can allow providers of first-party insurance the option of subrogating themselves to their policyholders' rights against culpable parties or their liability insurers. That opportunity has significant potential for the achievement of both greater equity and more efficient loss distribution. We suggest, indeed, that the opening of this avenue to no-fault insurers would assure that social savings achieved by no-fault would not accrue to faulty injurers.[29]

While we judge the choice of low-threshold "modified no-fault" plans to be a reasonable one, if not one compelled by the data and considerations of justice, we seriously question the "add-on" type of automobile compensation statute. We think the data on premium increases under add-on plans confirm what intuition suggests: these laws are wasteful. One may expect them to fall of their own weight, thus confirming the value of decentralized experimentation.

We do stress, however, the importance of preserving the tort remedy as injuries become more severe. There is some statistical evidence that tort law has significant deterrent effects on auto accidents. Moreover, while the evidence is not clear how citizens compare the justice of tort and no-fault systems, we think it reasonable to assume that the tort system provides an important psychological outlet for seriously injured victims who would be dissatisfied with "no-fault" benefits and desirous of an impartial hearing of their substantive case. In that connection, we emphasize that the background of tort law may provide an assumed intellectual foundation of personal rights which many survey respondents do not articulate.

While recommending the retention of a substantial part of the tort action for vehicle accidents, we have recognized the increase in collateral benefits typically paid to traffic victims. We note, however, that many collateral benefits, especially those tied to em-

---

26. *See* Levmore, *Self-Assessed Valuation Systems for Tort and Other Law*, 68 VA. L. Rev., *e.g.*, at 811–13, 835–37 (1982).

27. While acceptable political solutions are not necessarily a test of legal wisdom, it is interesting to note that in the first decade of no-fault experience, only one state which adopted such a scheme—Nevada—completely repealed its plan. *See* Epstein, *supra* note 23, at 770.

28. *See, e.g.,* CONARD, THE ECONOMIC TREATMENT OF AUTOMOBILE INJURIES, IN DOLLARS, DELAY AND THE AUTOMOBILE VICTIM 422–25 (Walter E. Meyer Research Inst. of Law 1968).

29. *Cf.* Keeton & O'Connell, *Alternative Paths Towards Nonfault Automobile Insurance*, 71 COLUM. L. Rev. 241, 256–60 (1971) (proposing pooling mechanism to guarantee that "not only will cost savings resulting from the surrender of a Basic Protection [first-party] policyholder's negligence claims go to his own company rather than the other driver's company, but also that his company will pass along to him, in the form of reduced premium charges, a fair share of all such cost savings.").

ployment, will fluctuate with economic conditions. To excise tort remedies from the law, if that is done on the basis of assumptions that collateral payments will always exist at current or higher levels, might create serious injustices on a large scale.

We add some observations concerning relationships among the traditional tort system, modified no-fault schemes, and the practical side of law practice. The removal of very small claims from courts should reduce the use of lawyers simply as clerks for claims processing.[32] At the same time, we perceive benefits in the preservation of the tort action for more serious accidents. The economic value of those cases will continue to attract attorneys. The incentives associated with such cases, which frequently feature challenging legal problems, will tend to inspire the sort of high quality professional work which serves the reasoned development of the law as well as the interests of clients.

Alfred Conard, *Macrojustice:*
A Systematic Approach to Conflict Resolution
5 GA. L. REV. 415, 421–22, 428 (1971)*

[Conard presents a "macrojural" mode of analysis with three characteristics: (1) It "distinguishes sharply" between "the things we wish people would do" and "what actually happens." (2) It is quantitative, requiring the collection of large amounts of data. (3) It is "concerned not so much with the effects of a system on any single case as with its effect on the aggregate of cases."]

[In the excerpt below, he deals with the implications of this analysis in the automobile compensation area.]

If we think of automobile injury compensation in the traditional microjural way, we probably think of an innocent injury victim suing a guilty driver and recovering a monetary judgment which the guilty driver is obliged to pay. However, once we looked at it comprehensively, we discovered a much broader and more varied picture. In the first place, we discovered that of all the compensation received by serious injury victims, only one third comes from tort claims. The other two thirds comes from various no-fault programs, such as health insurance, life insurance, collision insurance, sick leave, and social security. Of the one third which does come from tort claims, not over three percent is paid by guilty drivers.[14] The other ninety-seven percent is paid by insurance premiums collected from millions of automobile owners, many of whom are guilty of nothing at all.

We also made separate studies of the inputs and outputs of some of the principal systems through which injury victims may obtain compensation. We found that the tort system delivers about forty-four dollars of compensation for every one hundred dollars

---

32. In jurisdictions which have not adopted no-fault, the development of a corps of paralegal personnel offers an alternative for the processing of small claims. It would also be possible to develop specialized small claims tribunals for vehicle accidents, allowing people to represent themselves in relatively informal court settings without funneling cases onto a relatively expensive legal track.

14. ... The figures indicate that about one and one quarter percent of the total compensation is paid by about three percent of the defendants from their own pockets.

invested in it by taxpayers and premium payers. The workmen's compensation system renders about sixty dollars per one hundred dollars of input; the life insurance system delivers about eighty dollars per one hundred dollars contributed; the group health insurance system produces about ninety dollars for every one hundred dollars invested; and the social security system metes out about ninety-seven dollars for every one hundred dollars of taxes paid in.[15]

The sum of these observations is that the idea of a guilty driver paying an innocent injury victim — the idea around which the negligence trial is built — is only a very, very tiny part of contemporary reality. It is like Lassie averting a train wreck by awakening the railroad telegrapher. It may happen, but not often enough to suggest that dog-raising is a good way of promoting railroad safety.

Discoveries like this help us to think much more intelligently about how we might go about changing the laws to achieve more desirable effects. Suppose, for instance, that we want to make it easier for injured persons to get their doctor bills paid. On the one hand, we might change the tort liability system by adopting a rule of comparative negligence. This would probably increase the amount of doctor bills recovered, but it would do so at a cost of two hundred and twenty-five dollars for every one hundred dollars gained for injury victims. An alternative would be to require individuals to carry group health insurance which might be expected to increase the payment of medical bills at a cost of only one hundred and eleven dollars for every one hundred dollars of medical bills paid.

In going from a fault system to a no-fault system, we would have to consider the possibility of losing the deterrent effect created by the risk that a negligent driver will have to pay expenses from his own pocket. Our study tells us that only three out of one hundred drivers ever suffer this fate because the rest are covered by insurance or are judgment-proof.

[After discussing other applications of his analysis with respect to crime and imprisonment, and replying to various objections to this approach, Conard concludes:]

Since the days of Jeremy Bentham, we have generally agreed that the law should seek the greatest good for the greatest number. However, until now we have known very little about what the law actually accomplishes for either great or small numbers. We have known even less about what price in harm we pay for each gain in good. Today, I believe we are moving toward the discovery of how much good is done to how many persons by the processes which we call justice. If we can learn where the greatest good for the greatest number lies, we will have created something which deserves the name of "macrojustice."

NOTES

(1) What appear to be the different premises of the various authors represented above about the role of civil litigation as a means of resolving disputes about injuries caused by automobile accidents?

(2) Does the tort system provide, on the whole, a "fair" method of compensating for vehicle accidents?

If you represented an organization comprised of low-income persons, which approach to the auto compensation problem would you favor?

---

15. ... A more recent study indicates a ratio of forty-eight percent instead of forty-four percent for the tort system. Dep't of Transp., Report on Motor Vehicle Crash Losses and Their Compensation in the United States 51 (1971).

(3) Do you think the tort system is "just" as it applies to auto accidents generally? What do *you* mean by "justice" for these purposes? Does that concept necessarily include a notion of individualized determinations of "fault"?

Is it possible to achieve "macrojustice," in the sense that Conard coins the word in the excerpt just above, through individualized trials of "fault"?

Do you think that the concept of "fault" is likely to be a meaningful one in the process of settling and litigating automobile tort claims? Would the fact that the tort rule bars all contributory negligence claimants, or that it is a comparative fault rule, influence your answer to this question?

(4) Given that litigation of the sort represented by suits over auto injuries does impose significant costs on society and on many litigants, what are the social benefits conferred by litigation?

(5) Consider whether it would be an improvement on the typical auto compensation plan to have a broader scheme that tied traffic law enforcement and vehicle design to a compensation fund. A particularly interesting presentation of such an idea appears in Bernard Carl's Note, *A Social Insurance Scheme for Automobile Accident Compensation*, 57 VA. L. REV. 409 (1971). Carl's complex plan includes a federal rating system for autos calibrated on their propensity to cause accident losses, federal licensing of drivers, and a "general motor vehicle compensation fund" that is derived from taxes on vehicles and drivers. The scheme would fully replace the tort system, Department of Transportation "caseworkers" would serve both investigative and insurance-adjusting functions, and all data collected on accidents would go into a federal data bank.

Would you support such a scheme over the tort system? Would you vote for it instead of a conventional "no-fault" statute?

§ 17.02 Workers' Compensation

[A] The Concept of Accidental Injury

JOHANNESEN v. NEW YORK CITY DEPARTMENT OF HOUSING PRESERVATION AND DEVELOPMENT
Court of Appeals of New York
84 N.Y.2d 129, 638 N.E.2d 981, 615 N.Y.S.2d 336 (1994)

BELLACOSA, JUDGE.

The determinative issue on this municipal, self-insurer, employer's appeal is whether claimant's bronchial asthma, aggravated by exposure to excessive amounts of secondhand cigarette smoke in a confined work environment, constitutes an accidental injury compensable under the Workers' Compensation Law. The Workers' Compensation Board found an accidental injury and the Appellate Division affirmed.... Because the decision accords with established precedents and is supported by substantial evidence, we affirm.

I.

The facts are essentially uncontroverted. Claimant, Veronica Johannesen, was an office assistant for the City of New York when, in 1981, she was assigned to work at the City's Department of Housing Preservation and Development. The office in which claimant worked consisted of one large room for approximately 50 employees, at least half of whom smoked cigarettes. The room was crammed with desks and file cabinets, so that the employees worked in close proximity to one another. The windows were kept closed because of smoke from the kitchen of a restaurant located below the office. Also, the office ventilation system did not function properly. A co-employee, who worked on the same office floor as claimant, confirmed claimant's factual allegations.

By 1983, claimant began wheezing and coughing at work. Her breathing worsened and, in January 1985, she was diagnosed as suffering from bronchial asthma aggravated by exposure to the tobacco smoke and dust in the workplace. Her treating physician recommended that she work only in a smoke-free environment. Claimant's transfer requests, however, were repeatedly denied.

In 1985, claimant sought workers' compensation benefits based on her asthmatic episodes of wheezing, coughing and spitting. Prior to the administrative hearing, in January 1986, claimant experienced two sudden and traumatic asthmatic attacks at work. On both occasions she was rushed to a hospital for emergency medical treatment and assistance for her breathing difficulty.

...

II.

The Workers' Compensation Law was enacted for socioeconomic remediation purposes "as a means of protecting work[ers] and their dependents from want in case of injury" on the job.... An employee is entitled to receive compensation on a "no-fault" basis for all injuries "arising out of and in the course of the employment" (Workers' Compensation Law § 10 [1]; see also, § 2 [7]; § 21.... Under Workers' Compensation Law § 2 (7), "injury" and "personal injury" means only "accidental injuries arising out of and in the course of employment and such disease or infection as may naturally and unavoidably result therefrom". To effectuate the statutory objectives, Workers' Compensation Law § 21 (1) creates a presumption that injuries "arising out of and in the course of" employment are compensable under section 10 (1) as "accidents".... Moreover, given the remedial nature of the Workers' Compensation Law, the Court has construed the statute and given the Board, as "trier[] of the facts", a very wide latitude in determining whether a disabling condition is an accident.... In particular, the Court has noted also that an accidental injury must be gauged by the "common-sense viewpoint of the average [person]"....

On this appeal, the causal relationship between claimant's inhalation of the second-hand tobacco smoke and the aggravation of her bronchial asthma is not disputed. Thus, the sole focus of this Court's law question inquiry is whether claimant sustained an accidental injury within the meaning of the Workers' Compensation Law....

... [T]he appellant employer argues that routine exposure to tobacco smoke in the work environment did not constitute an "accidental injury" in the early 1980s, though it acknowledges that it does today. Second, the Department asserts that the average person would not view claimant's bronchial asthma as an "accidental injury" because the asthma condition is solely an allergic or other type of sensitivity reaction to an everyday environmental condition and did not occur in an unexpected or unusual circumstance. Lastly, appellant asserts that even if the circumstances are deemed an "accident," the evidence is legally insufficient as to the "time-definiteness" component affixed under Matter of Middleton v Coxsackie Correctional Facility, ... 341 N.E.2d 527....

Matter of Mack v. County of Rockland ... 525 N.E.2d 744 ... does not aid or support appellant's cause. That case is an "occupational disease" case and this one is an "accidental injury" case. A different analysis applies here.

In Mack, the claimant, a psychiatric social worker, suffered an aggravation of a pre-existing eye disorder as a result of exposure to cigarette smoking in a poorly ventilated workplace. The Court affirmed an order of the Appellate Division which dismissed the claim that she suffered an "occupational disease" within the meaning of the Workers' Compensation Law.... The Court held that because the claimant's injury was caused solely by the "environmental condition[] of her work place, not by any distinctive feature of the occupation of a psychiatric social worker", the claimant could not maintain a claim based on occupational disease.... The focus of an "occupational disease" claim is on the nature of the work ... not the nature of the workplace environment. Accordingly, denial of a claim in the occupational disease category is not definitive for an accidental injury in the workplace category....

The term of art, accidental injury, lacks a statutory definition and, thus, requires a distinctive analysis and tracking of pertinent precedents. An accidental injury need not result suddenly or from the immediate application of some external force but may accrue gradually over a reasonably definite period of time.... There, a correction officer contracted tuberculosis through exposure, over a period of three or four months for two or three hours a day, to an infected, coughing inmate. In holding that the claimant's tuberculosis was an accidental injury, the Court in Middleton relied on Matter of Pessel v. Macy & Co., 40 A.D.2d 746, affd 33 N.Y.2d 721, 349 N.Y.S.2d 995, 304 N.E.2d 565, where we held that a claimant's exposure to repeated bursts of cold air over a period of three months, which activated an underlying arthritic condition, was an accidental injury.... Gradual injury was also recognized as a compensable disability accident in Matter of Michelfelder v. Van Alstyne, 217 App. Div. 810, 217 N.Y.S. 923, affd. 245 N.Y. 569, where a garage mechanic, while in the course of his employment, routinely inhaled carbon monoxide gas from which he developed bronchitis....

In the present case, claimant's bronchial condition progressively worsened from 1981 to 1986. The injury may have been gradual, but the record substantiates that her working environment was highly dangerous for her and aggravated her asthma. Professor Larson has noted that "most jurisdictions have at some time awarded compensation for conditions that have developed, not instantaneously, but gradually over periods ranging from a few hours to several decades, culminating in disability from ... asthma" (1B Larson, Work[ers'] Compensation Law § 39.10, at 7-384 [1993]).

Appellant, citing Matter of Lerner v. Rump Bros., 241 N.Y. 153, 156, 149 N.E. 334, interjects, however, that the absence of a "catastrophic or extraordinary" event disqualifies these events from the accidental injury category. While exposure to cigarette smoke in our society and in workplaces may have been and still is relatively endemic, the facts surrounding this claimant's exposure, even from Middleton's "common sense" viewpoint of the average person, demonstrate an exacerbative and excessive quality. Claimant was required to work in an unventilated office and forced to share the polluted atmosphere with numerous smokers, who were all around her. She was allowed no alternative but to inhale the dense, dangerous and debilitative smoke-filled air. Graphically, she suffered two bronchial breakdowns at work requiring emergency medical attention. Claimant worked in an office where the tools of her trade are papers, pens, files, computers and telephones. Cigarette smoke is surely not a natural by-product of the Department of Housing Preservation and Development's activities and her employment role. Thus, unlike Lerner, this risk was not a commonly understood, ordinary incident to the environmental workplace. Just as the Court rejected the employer's contention in Matter of Gardner v New York Med. Coll., 280 App. Div. 844, 113 N.Y.S.2d 394, affd. 305 N.Y. 583, 111 N.E.2d 644, that a sneeze could not be an "accident" because people normally sneeze, we reject this employer's assertion that exposure to tobacco smoke was not an accident essentially because many people still smoke. The seriously adverse environmental conditions to which claimant was subjected as part of her job and workplace reasonably qualify as an unusual hazard, not the "natural[] and unavoidabl[e]" result of employment (Workers' Compensation Law § 2 [7]).

We are also satisfied that the severe bronchial aggravation, reflected among other facets of this case, by two on-the-job asthma episodes, requiring immediate emergency medical attention, met the time-definite component of the accidental injury rule.... We perceive no legally cognizable distinction between this claimant's "attack" following years of exposure to excessive levels of secondhand cigarette smoke in her workplace and the now quintessential cardiac collapse cases ensuing from extended periods of strain for which awards are customarily upheld....

Claimant's predisposition with an asthma condition does not change the analysis or result. It is well settled that where causally related injuries from a claimant's employment precipitate, aggravate or accelerate a preexisting infirmity or disease, the resulting disability is compensable....

. . .

Finally, in a policy-based argument, appellant suggests that recovery here will open floodgates and make every allergic reaction, common cold or ordinary ailment compensable. This argument is often advanced when precedent and analysis are unpersuasive.... The holding in this case does not change existing criteria and legal principles for determining whether a work-related and work-site injury is accidental. Claimants are still required to make showings of unusual environmental conditions or events assignable to something extraordinary that caused an accidental injury. This claimant did so to the satisfaction of the Board and each court that has reviewed the matter.... The award should be upheld.

. . .

NOTES

(1) How would you define an "injury" for the general purposes of the workers' compensation law?

(2) What are the characteristics of an "accidental injury" under the New York workers' compensation law?

(3) If half the people in an office smoke, why are physiological reactions to cigarette smoke not "a commonly understood, ordinary incident" of that workplace?

(4) What goals of workers' compensation are advanced by this decision?

(5) If one assumes that the smoke in the office where Johannesen worked caused no overt adverse effects to the two dozen other nonsmokers who worked there, why is the cost of her asthmatic episodes properly assessed to the City?

(6) If there are two people working together in one office, is it a tort for one to smoke if the other indicates that the second-hand smoke will cause her severe asthma? What type of tort action would have the best chance of succeeding?

Could Johannesen have brought a tort action against all the smokers in her office as a class?

PEORIA COUNTY BELWOOD NURSING HOME v. INDUSTRIAL COMMISSION
Illinois Supreme Court
115 Ill. 2d 524, 505 N.E.2d 1026, 106 Ill. Dec. 235 (1987)

CHIEF JUSTICE CLARK delivered the opinion of the court.

The claimant, Wanda Cagle, filed a claim for compensation under the Workers' Compensation Act (Ill.Rev.Stat.1983, ch. 48, par. 138.1 *et seq.*) (the Act) on August 24, 1979, alleging that she developed carpal tunnel syndrome as a result of her employment in the laundry room of her employer, Peoria County Belwood Nursing Home (Belwood). Both the arbitrator and, on review, the Industrial Commission found that the claimant had sustained an accidental injury as a result of repeated trauma to her wrist in her operation of two large washing machines in the laundry room of the nursing home....

The issue raised in this appeal is whether an injury sustained as a result of work-related repetitive trauma is compensable under the Workers' Compensation Act without a finding that the injury occurred as a result of one specific incident traceable to a definite time, place and cause.

In the case at bar, the claimant worked for respondent for 12 years, the last six years in the laundry room. The duties of her employment required her to carry bags of laundry weighing between 25 and 50 pounds. After sorting the laundry in these bags, she would load two 200-pound-capacity washing machines by operating a spring-loaded door into each of three compartments. Each day the claimant loaded the machines six times.

Although claimant initially alleged that her injury occurred on October 5, 1976, the arbitrator amended the claimant's application to reflect the date of injury as October 4, 1976, a date when claimant testified she experienced symptoms at work. On October 5, 1976, claimant consulted Dr. John McLean, a neurologist, regarding her symptoms of pain, numbness, and tingling. She continued to work until August 23, 1977, when she underwent outpatient surgery for carpal tunnel syndrome—"a complex of symptoms resulting from compression of the median nerve in the carpal tunnel with pain and burning or tingling parathesias in the fingers and hand, sometimes extending to the elbow." Dorland's Illustrated Medical Dictionary 1289 (26th ed. 1981).

The arbitrator awarded benefits for temporary total disability and for 25% permanent total disability. The Industrial Commission affirmed that award, and the circuit court confirmed the Commission's decision. The appellate court affirmed the circuit court judgment.

... The first issue is whether the Industrial Commission's finding that the claimant sustained an "accidental injury" is contrary to the manifest weight of the evidence....

The more narrow issue presented in this appeal is what is meant by the term "accidental injury" within the meaning of the Act.

In the instant case, the claimant was found to have presented sufficient medical evidence to establish that her injury was work related. We do not believe that finding is against the manifest weight of the evidence. However, whether the claimant's injury is "accidental" is the crux of this case. We believe that the purpose behind the Workers'

Compensation Act is best served by allowing compensation in a case like the instant one where an injury has been shown to be caused by the performance of the claimant's job and has developed gradually over a period of time, without requiring complete dysfunction. In order to achieve this result we believe the case of *International Harvester Co. v. Industrial Com.* (1973), 56 Ill.2d 84, 305 N.E.2d 529, and that line of cases following *International Harvester*, should be interpreted so as to include a case like the instant one. We do not believe that in so doing we are partaking in judicial legislation; rather we are engaging in necessary and proper judicial statutory interpretation so as to implement the purpose of the Workers' Compensation Act.

The Workers' Compensation Act was intended to provide financial protection for injured workers regardless of a showing of negligence or contributory negligence, while precluding the employee from common law tort remedies.... To that end, it has been consistently held that the Act should be liberally construed to accomplish its purpose and objects....

Requiring complete collapse in a case like the instant one would not be beneficial to the employee or the employer because it might force employees needing the protection of the Act to push their bodies to a precise moment of collapse. Simply because an employee's work-related injury is gradual, rather than sudden and completely disabling, should not preclude protection and benefits. The Act was intended to compensate workers who have been injured as a result of their employment. To deny an employee benefits for a work-related injury that is not the result of a sudden mishap or completely disabling penalizes an employee who faithfully performs job duties despite bodily discomfort and damage.

As the appellate court correctly stated, an employee who alleges injury based on repetitive trauma must still meet the same standard of proof as other claimants alleging an accidental injury. There must be a showing that the injury is work related and not the result of a normal degenerative aging process.

The claimant in the instant case testified that she experienced pain and tingling in her left arm while working her regular shift on October 4, 1976. She informed Dr. McLean on October 5, 1976, that she had extreme difficulty gripping the washer doors on October 4, due to the pain she was experiencing. The medical testimony the claimant presented was uncontroverted. Therefore, we now hold that the Industrial Commission's finding that the claimant suffered an accidental injury under the Act is not against the manifest weight of the evidence.

...

[Judgment affirmed.]

[The concurrence of JUSTICE MORAN is omitted.]

NOTES

(1) Consider the Illinois court's effort to deal with the real-life implications of the *Peoria County* case. How can a judge go about deciding whether the social benefits from "playing hurt" outweigh the social costs of continuing to work despite serious but not disabling pain? Does the statute give meaningful guidance on that question?

(2) The lawyer for the claimant in the *Peoria County* case asserted that the decision would force employers to "look at the assembly line." Saying that "[b]efore, they looked ... at productivity and production," he declared that the decision would make employers look at "what workers do '50 times an hour, eight hours a day, 52 weeks a

year, for 20 years.'"—Morton Goldfine, quoted in *Workers' comp case worries business*, CHICAGO DAILY L. BULL., Apr. 25, 1987, at 6. The president of the Illinois Manufacturers' Association countered that the decision would contribute to the state's loss of employment—"three times the rate of the national average [and the] erosion goes on." A lawyer's newspaper reported that this official said that workers' compensation claims were the "second most serious problem for Illinois manufacturers, surpassed only by the high cost and unavailability of liability insurance."—Arthur R. Gottschalk, quoted and paraphrased in *id*. The same year, the National Council on Compensation Insurance estimated that workers' compensation insurers had lost $1.4 billion in 1986. The organization reportedly attributed the losses to a combination of factors, including inadequate premium rates, declining interest rates, and both inflation of health care costs and reductions in the scope of Medicare coverage. *Workers' Compensation Losses Reach $1.4 Billion According to NCCI Analysis*, RISK MGMT., Aug. 1987, at 60.

[B] Some Background on Workers' Compensation

[1] *History and Premises*

Towards a Jurisprudence of Injury 10-45 to 10-47
(ABA 1984, M. Shapo Rptr.)*

For a hundred years and more, the case of workplace injuries has presented a vexing problem of legal policy. Over the last half of the nineteenth century, the development of three common law defenses for employers was a principal factor in the low incidence of compensation for injured workers. The first expression of the "fellow-servant" exception to the general rule of the vicarious liability of employers occurred in a case involving injuries to a butcher's employee when an overloaded van broke down. However, as the leading treatise writer on workers' compensation has said, "it became clear that the real implications of the decision involved not butcher-boys and chambermaids, but trainmen, miners, factory workers."[1] The contemporaneous evolution of the doctrines of assumption of risk and contributory negligence contributed to a situation in which approximately four-fifths of all injured workers went uncompensated. In a valuable study of nineteenth century tort law, Professor Gary Schwartz comments that in his target states, New Hampshire and California, "the law's treatment of workers' injuries was singularly complex, ungenerous, and troubling."

Historical highlights. The seed for the workers' compensation idea appeared in 1884 in Germany, where Bismarkian legislation provided money awards for workplace injuries on the basis of job relatedness rather than negligence. English legislation in 1897 specifically established the theory of workmen's compensation. Responding to political pressure which built up from the beginning of the century, eleven American states had adopted workers' compensation laws by 1911, and by 1915, compensation statutes covered 41.2 per cent of all employees in this country. In 1980, every state had a workers' compensation program, and the array of federal compensation statutes included the Black Lung legislation as well as three federal workers' compensation plans. Workers'

---

* Copyright © 1984 The American Bar Association. Reprinted by permission.
1. A. Larson, The Law of Workmen's Compensation § 4.30 at 25–26 (1978).

compensation covered 88 per cent of the employed labor force, and benefits paid in 1980 totaled $13.4 billion.

Purposes. Workers' compensation has several purposes. One, well recognized in the case law, is to "spread the loss more evenly throughout industry." Workers' compensation also has been rationalized on the basis that occupational injuries are an expense of production; as Lloyd George put it with characteristic pungency, "[t]he cost of the product should bear the blood of the working man." Political arguments for workers' compensation legislation emphasized the idea that government may intervene when a significant fraction of the population carries "burdens beyond their bearing." An oft-stated explanation is that workers' compensation is a "social compromise" which balances the interests of the employer, the employee and the general public. The basic politics of this compromise involves a trade by the employee of his or her common law right of action for the certainty of a nonfault recovery, albeit a relatively small one.

Financing. The principal three methods of financing workers' compensation are through private insurance, insurance purchased through governmental agencies set up for that purpose, and self-insurance. Under the various financing mechanisms, workers' compensation benefits have come to include cash payments for disability or death, medical benefits, and the provision of rehabilitation services.

Nature of benefits. The question of what the nature of workers' compensation benefits is provides the crux of "the most far-reaching controversy" in the area. Arthur Larson describes this dispute as centering on the "current movement to restore the centrality of the wage-loss principle," which he views as the historic basis of workers' compensation law. He contrasts the "schedule" principle, under which permanent partial benefits are awarded for impairment of function in addition to other payments, arguing that that approach creates excessive costs in both insurance rates and litigation time.

---

[2] Basic Data

William J. Nelson, Jr., *Workers' Compensation: Coverage, Benefits, and Costs, 1985*

51 Soc. Sec. Bulletin No. 1, at 4 (Jan. 1988)

...

The Federal Act of 1908 was the first effective workers' compensation law in the United States. It provided limited benefits for certain Federal employees engaged in hazardous work. By 1911, workers' compensation legislation had been enacted in 10 States; by 1921, all but 6 States had established such programs. Today, 50 State workers' compensation programs and 3 Federal programs cover workers in the District of Columbia, Federal Government employees, and longshore and harbor workers.

The Black Lung program, generally considered a specialized workers' compensation program, was established in 1970 to provide monthly cash benefits to totally disabled coal miners and their survivors. Medical benefits are also payable to an individual diagnosed as having pneumoconiosis (black lung disease) and for the treatment of conditions resulting from the disease. The benefit program is jointly administered by the Social Security Administration and the Department of Labor. Benefits are financed from general revenue funds and from monies acquired through an excise tax on mined coal tonnage.

The State programs generally are administered by industrial commissions or special units within State departments of labor, and the Federal programs are administered by the U.S. Department of Labor (except in the District of Columbia, which administers its own program). Although all programs are based on the principle of compensation without regard to fault, the enactment of a different law in each jurisdiction and repeated subsequent amendments to that law results in many variations among the State programs.

In the framework of their compensation systems, one difference among the States is in the method of ensuring that compensation will be paid. Employers provide benefits through three mechanisms: private or commercial insurance, publicly operated insurance, and self-insurance (used primarily by large employers who are able to provide proof of their financial ability to carry their own risk).

In all but six States, employers may buy commercial insurance to provide the required protection for workers. In four of these States—Nevada, Ohio, Washington, and West Virginia—employers either must insure with exclusive State insurance funds or must self-insure. In North Dakota and Wyoming, employers must insure only through an exclusive State fund.

Both the amount of benefits paid to workers and the cost of the program to employers rose substantially from 1984 to 1985. Workers' compensation benefits totaled $22.5 billion in 1985, an increase of 14.1 percent from the amount paid in the previous year and the largest increase in 6 years. Program costs, including acquisition expenses, profits, and administrative costs, totaled $29.3 billion, a 16.7 percent increase from the 1984 total.

Coverage

In 1985, about 84.3 million workers were protected under workers' compensation laws—about 2.4 million more workers than had been covered in 1984. This increase of almost 3 percent followed an increase of 5 percent from 1983 to 1984. The number of workers covered during the past 10 years generally has followed changes in the total employment figures during the period. The proportion of covered workers to all wage and salary workers was 87 percent in 1985, approximately the same as it had been in each year since 1973.

Workers most likely to be exempted from coverage include domestics, agricultural workers, and casual laborers. Coverage is also incomplete among workers in small firms (3–5 employees), nonprofit institutions, and State and local governments, with the extent of coverage varying from State to State....

Types of Payments

About two-thirds ($15.1 billion) of the workers' compensation payments in 1985 were in the form of compensation—money payments—and the remaining one-third ($7.4 billion) was for medical care provided to disabled workers.... Compensation to disabled workers totaled $13.4 billion and survivors of workers who died from work-related causes received $1.7 billion.

Disability insurance payments have increased by nearly 62 percent since 1980; survivor payments were up only half that rate—31 percent—in the same period. Payments for medical and hospital care rose 86 percent in the same 5-year period.

The distribution of benefits between the Black Lung program and the regular workers' compensation programs (all except black lung) was markedly different. Cash compensation paid to disabled workers and survivors accounted for roughly 65 percent of all payments made under regular programs, compared with 95 percent under the Black Lung program.

...

[C] Injuries Arising "Out Of" Employment

UNITED PARCEL SERVICE OF AMERICA v. FETTERMAN
Virginia Supreme Court
230 Va. 257, 336 S.E.2d 892 (1985)

PER CURIAM.

The question presented in this workers' compensation case is whether the claimant, a parcel delivery service employee, sustained an accidental injury arising out of the employment when he strained his back while bending over to tie his shoe.

Randall F. Fetterman sustained a lumbosacral strain on March 19, 1984, during the course of his employment as a driver for United Parcel Service of America. The claimant's duties included loading, unloading, and delivering packages weighing an average of 35 pounds.

On the day in question, the claimant was unloading packages from his truck. He was reaching across the rear of the truck and pulling parcels to place them on a hand cart when he noticed that his right shoe was untied. He raised his foot to the back of the truck, bent over to tie the shoe, and felt acute pain in his lower back.

At the hearing level, a deputy commissioner denied the claim for compensation. She decided that the injury did not meet the requirement of arising out of the employment because it could not fairly be traced to the employment as a contributing proximate cause and it did not follow as a natural incident of the work. The hearing commissioner concluded that the claimant's conduct in bending over to tie his shoe was not a risk of the employment but, rather, was merely coincidental with the employment.

Upon review, the full Commission unanimously decided the claim was compensable. The Commission disagreed with the deputy's reasoning and opined that "the work environment certainly had something to do with the manner in which the employee went about tying his shoe and this was no doubt necessary for him to continue his work." On appeal, the employer and its insurance carrier contend the Commission erred. We agree.

An accident arises out of the employment when there is a causal connection between the claimant's injury and the conditions under which the employer requires the work to be performed.... Under this test, an injury arises "out of" the employment when it has followed as a natural incident of the work and has been a result of the exposure occasioned by the nature of the employment. Excluded is an injury which comes from a hazard to which the employee would have been equally exposed apart from the employment. The causative danger must be peculiar to the work, incidental to the character of the business, and not independent of the master-servant relationship. The event must appear to have had its origin in a risk connected with the employment, and to have flowed from that source as a rational consequence....

Applying these principles to the present case, we hold this injury did not arise out of the claimant's employment. Under these circumstances, the act of bending over to tie the shoe was unrelated to any hazard common to the workplace. In other words, nothing in the work environment contributed to the injury. Every person who wears laced shoes must occasionally perform the act of retying the laces. The situation of a loose shoelace confronting the claimant was wholly independent of the master-servant relationship.

For these reasons, the award appealed from will be reversed and the application will be dismissed.

Reversed and dismissed.

OLSTEN OF RICHMOND v. LEFTWICH

Virginia Supreme Court
230 Va. 317, 336 S.E.2d 893 (1985)

POFF, JUSTICE.

This is an employer's appeal from the Industrial Commission's order awarding an employee workers' compensation benefits for disability resulting from an accident during the course of employment. The principal question posed is whether the accident arose out of the employment.

In June 1982, Shirley W. Leftwich suffered a cervical and lumbar sprain in an automobile accident. In September, she returned to work at Olsten of Richmond where she was employed as a customer representative. On a weekend in January 1983, Olsten moved its offices to a new location. Mrs. Leftwich reported for work on Monday, January 17, expecting to resume her regular duties. Although she was dressed as usual in high-heel shoes, Olsten directed her to work with other employees in moving and unpacking the boxes and storing the contents on shelves in a closet.

After working at her new task for more than an hour, Mrs. Leftwich suffered a sudden, severe pain in her back. Unable to straighten to a standing position, she was placed on a stretcher and transported by rescue squad to a hospital where she remained for five weeks under the care of Dr. John A. Ayers, II, a specialist in orthopedic surgery.

Dr. Ayers diagnosed her injury as severe lumbar sprain. In a report dated March 4, 1983, he stated, "It is my impression that the injury of January 17, 1983 was an exacerbation of her previous injury of June 10, 1982 from which she was still having minor residuals." Based on an examination conducted later, Dr. Herman Nachman, another orthopedist, opined that Mrs. Leftwich's condition "was not the result of the injury received in the June 10, 1982 [accident] but rather ... the incident that occurred at work on January 17, 1983."

Danna Kinard, Olsten's branch manager and Mrs. Leftwich's supervisor, was standing beside Mrs. Leftwich when the January accident occurred. Kinard testified that Mrs. Leftwich "had high heels on and she bent over ... and picked up the side of the box and got it off the floor". As she "was beginning to pull it up ... she screamed with pain ... broke out in a sweat ... and she dropped the box."

A deputy commissioner denied the claimant's application for benefits. Upon review, the full Commission found that Mrs. Leftwich's disability was caused by "an exacerbation of a prior injury", reversed the deputy's decision, and entered an award in favor of the claimant.

On appeal, Olsten and its insurer, Travelers Insurance Company, contend that there was no evidence to show that the injury arose out of the employment. We disagree. The work in progress was work specially assigned by the employer. Mrs. Leftwich suffered an "injury by accident". Code § 65.1-7. That injury, which we have defined as an "obvious sudden mechanical or structural change in the body", *Virginia Electric, Etc., Co. v. Quann*, 197 Va. 9, 12, 87 S.E.2d 624, 626 (1955), occurred while she was engaged in a new work assignment involving physical exertion to which she was unaccustomed.

"In Virginia we have adopted the 'actual risk test,' which requires only that the employment expose the workman to the particular danger from which he was injured, notwithstanding the exposure of the public generally to like risks." *Lucas v. Lucas*, 212 Va. 561, 563, 186 S.E.2d 63, 64 (1972) (citation omitted). The testimony of the employer's district manager shows that the January accident occurred while Mrs. Leftwich was exposed to a particular danger. Medical reports submitted by two specialists confirm that Mrs. Leftwich's disability was caused by the accident resulting from that danger. It is immaterial whether her work incapacity was related solely to the injury sustained in the January accident. "When an injury sustained in an industrial accident accelerates or aggravates a pre-existing condition, ... disability resulting therefrom is compensable under the Workers' Compensation Act." *Ohio Valley Construction Co. v. Jackson*, 230 Va. 56,—, 334 S.E.2d 554, 555 (1985)....

We hold, therefore, that the evidence supports a finding that the claimant's disability was causally related to an accident which arose out of the claimant's employment. *Cf. United Parcel Service of America v. Fetterman*, 230 Va.—, 336 S.E.2d 892 (1985)....

[Omitted is a discussion of the claimant's testimony about the incident.]

Affirmed.

NOTES

(1) What was the Virginia legislature's purpose in using the words "out of ... employment" in its workers' compensation statute? How would that purpose be disserved if the court had allowed Fetterman to collect benefits under the statute?

(2) Compare the results that the Virginia court achieved in *Leftwich* with those reached by the Illinois court in the *Peoria County* case, supra § 17.02[A]. What are the difficulties of social accounting that these cases pose? Do either of these decisions tend to convert the workers' compensation statute into general social legislation?

(3) Is the problem in these cases better described as one of whether there was "an accident," or an issue of "causal connection," or something else?

DARCO TRANSPORTATION v. DULEN
Supreme Court of Oklahoma
922 P.2d 591 (1996)

OPALA, JUSTICE.

The answers to two questions are dispositive of whether Dulen's ... injuries are compensable under Oklahoma's workers' compensation regime. The pertinent queries are: (1)

Had the claimant abandoned his employment when he was injured? and (2) Is the risk of being struck by a train at a railroad crossing purely personal or does it have a causal connection with, so as to arise out of, Dulen's employment with Darco Transportation … ? We answer the first question in the negative and the latter in the affirmative.

I

THE ANATOMY OF LITIGATION

Dulen was injured when a tractor-trailer rig, which he was driving, entered a railroad crossing and was struck by an oncoming train. Dulen and Polly Freeman … his co-driver, were hired by Darco to transport goods cross-country. On the night of September 7, 1993 Dulen stopped his rig behind another truck (also a Darco rig) when the signal arms at a railroad crossing lowered. The arms malfunctioned and came up before the train had reached the intersection. The first Darco truck proceeded across the tracks and Dulen followed. While the first truck avoided being hit, the claimant's rig was rammed by the train. The record discloses that the protective arms did not relower until Dulen's semi was on the tracks.

Freeman died as a result of the accident and Dulen was severely hurt. At the scene of the collision a female traffic investigator (with the local police department) noticed that Freeman, who was clad only in a T-shirt, sustained physical injuries primarily to the right side of her body. She observed that Dulen's pants were unbuttoned, unzipped and resting mid-hip when he was readied for transportation to the hospital. Her report also reflects that the passenger door on Dulen's rig was intact but the driver-side windshield and door were knocked out.

Apart from the investigating officer's report and testimony, there was other evidence about Dulen and Freeman's attire on the night of the accident. It shows that on occasion male truck drivers, when on long hauls, do unbutton their pants for comfort's sake. There was also testimony that the claimant's rig was equipped with a sleeping facility and that Freeman, when travelling, slept only in a T-shirt.[2]

After Dulen was admitted to the hospital, the investigator approached him there for information to complete a supplemental accident report. The officer questioned the claimant—then in apparent shock and suffering from lacerations and fractures of the face, jaw and body—about how the accident had happened. She noted in her report that Dulen said, "I was fucking her and now, oh, my God, I have killed her." According to the officer, Dulen told her that, when the accident occurred, Freeman was sitting in his lap facing him.

In later testimony Dulen explained that—by his earlier statement at the hospital— he meant that he had been living in an intimate relationship with Freeman for five months before the accident and felt responsible for her death because she was driving with him. He denied telling the officer that Freeman, when killed, was sitting in his lap and that they were having sex. Other evidence before the trial tribunal reveals that there was not enough room between the steering wheel and the seat for two people (of Dulen and Freeman's size) physically to fill that space together.

The trial judge found the claimant's injuries (1) occurred in the course of and arose out of his employment and (2) resulted directly from the railroad-crossing arms' malfunction. Dulen appealed to secure temporary total disability. After reviewing the record, a three-judge panel modified the trial tribunal's order by awarding

---

2. The accident occurred shortly after midnight.…

temporary total disability and setting a counsel fee. The employer appealed; the Court of Appeals sustained the three-judge panel's order. Employer's certiorari quest followed.

II
THE STANDARD OF REVIEW

When examining the compensation tribunal's factual resolutions, this court applies the any-competent-evidence standard.... It is only in the absence of competent evidence that a trial tribunal's decision may be viewed as erroneous as a matter of law and hence subject to appellate vacation.

III

...

Oklahoma's jurisprudence has long recognized that a compensable work-related injury must both (1) occur in the course of[12] and (2) arise out of[13] the worker's employment. 85 O.S.1991 § 3(7).[15] These two distinct elements are not to be understood as synonymous.

...

We must be mindful that in this case we are applying workers' compensation law.[17] The concept of a worker's contributory fault, which the compensation statute discarded, must not — under the guise of appellate re-examination of the evidence — be resurrected obliquely as a defense against the employer's liability.

The Workers' Compensation Court was faced with the task of determining if Dulen, when injured, was performing work in furtherance of his master's business — i.e., whether he was then "in the course of employment." More precisely stated, if the trial tribunal tended to believe that Dulen and Freeman were having sex at the critical time, the question to be decided was whether the claimant's conduct is to be deemed horseplay — a complete departure from or abandonment of his employment. The issue so formed, which is one of fact, concerns itself solely with the "course of employment" bounds — not with the risk incident to employment, i.e., the "arising out of" element.[19]

---

12. The term "in the course of employment" relates to the time, place or circumstances under which the injury is sustained....

13. The term "arise out of employment" contemplates the causal connection between the injury and the risks incident to employment....

15. The pertinent terms of 85 O.S.1991 § 3(7) make compensable " ... only accidental injuries arising out of and in the course of employment.... *Provided, only injuries having as their source a risk not purely personal but one that is reasonably connected with the conditions of employment shall be deemed to arise out of the employment.*" [Emphasis added.]

17. Oklahoma first enacted workers' compensation law in 1915.... The act abolished the employee's common-law negligence action against the master and its corollary defenses of contributory negligence and assumption of the risk.... Modern workers' compensation statutes remove the element of fault as a baseline requirement for ascribing liability for work-connected injuries and replace it with the concept of strict responsibility....

19. For an elucidation of what the phrase "in the course of employment" covers, see supra note 7. See also 1A A. LARSON, THE LAW OF WORKMEN'S COMPENSATION §§ 23 et seq. (1995), where in discussing horseplay he observed: "Much of the difficulty in the current controversy over horseplay cases is the result of confusing the 'course of employment' and 'arising out of employment' issues, with a general but mistaken tendency to assume the latter is the principal issue. Whenever the basic controversy stems from the nature of a course of conduct deliberately undertaken by the claimant, there is primarily a question of course of conduct. Whenever the controversy stems from the nature of a source of injury to the claimant, there is primarily a question of 'arising out of the employment.'" *Id.* at § 23.61.

Assuming as a fact that—when the collision occurred—Dulen was having sex while also driving the rig, the trial judge could still find that this servant's acts constituted no more than a careless, negligent or forbidden genre of performance but did not amount to pure frolic which, under the circumstances, was tantamount to total abandonment of the master's business. On this record, such a finding would not be legally or factually incorrect. Both the terms of 85 O.S.1991 § 12 and Oklahoma's jurisprudence bar contributory negligence as a defense against the claim. The text of 85 O.S.1991 § 11[22] clearly provides that an injury is compensable "without regard to fault" on the worker's part. The record contains ample evidence reasonably supporting the notion that claimant's injury was work-related,[23] i.e., occurred while he was en route to his assigned destination.[24] Above all, uncontroverted is the stubborn fact that Dulen, when injured, occupied his assigned work station—the driver's seat behind the steering wheel of Darco's truck[25] The record offers no proof that Dulen had deviated from or abandoned his master's mission (transporting goods to San Francisco).[26]

The law's outer framework—unchanged since the very inception of this court's compensation jurisprudence—strongly militates in this case against withholding compensation benefits for misconduct that plainly falls short of workstation abandonment—regardless of how morally reprehensible the worker's on-the-job carelessness might have been.

. . .

The record, which reflects several witnesses' testimony that the railroad-crossing equipment malfunctioned, is devoid of any proof that the protective arms were in good working order. The trial tribunal found the equipment's failure was the direct cause of the claimant's injuries. Its finding rests on competent evidence. At the time of Dulen's injuries, he was employed as a Darco truck driver with an assigned task—that of transporting goods to the West Coast. This required his presence on the highways. A causal connection between the act in which Dulen was engaged, when injured, and his job description is clear. Because the perils of this servant's travel for his master are co-extensive with the risks of employment, Dulen's injuries undeniably arose out of his work.

IV

SUMMARY

When conflicting inferences may be drawn from undisputed facts, the controversy presents a fact question. There is competent evidence to support the trial tribunal's decision that Dulen's injuries were caused by the railroad-crossing equipment's malfunction. Two insuperable hurdles absolutely militate against overturning the trial tri-

---

22. The pertinent terms of 85 O.S.1991 § 11 are: "Every employer ... shall pay ... for the disability or death of his employee resulting from an accidental personal injury sustained by the employee arising out of and in the course of his employment, *without regard to fault as a cause of such injury*...." [Emphasis added.]

23. An employee's activity is "work related" if the employer's purposes are being advanced, either directly or indirectly....

24. Darco's operations manager (Chester Cooper) testified that, at the time of the accident, the claimant was properly en route to his assigned destination.

25. There is not a scintilla of evidence that during the critical time in question Dulen was ever away from his assigned work station.

26. Oklahoma's jurisprudence does not allow compensation for injuries to a servant who deviated from an assigned destination on a personal errand.... The record offers cogent proof that the claimant's work task created the necessity for travel and that he was following an accepted path to reach his assigned destination.

bunal's findings and exonerating the employer as a matter of law. Assuming Dulen
and Freeman, at the critical temporal point, were engaged in sexual intercourse, (1)
there is undisputed proof that, when the collision occurred, Dulen remained at the
steering wheel and hence cannot be deemed to have then "abandoned" his assigned
work station and (2) there is competent evidence to support the trial judge's finding
which ascribes the accident's cause, not to copulation-related inattention, but to defective railroad-crossing warning equipment. A disposition that would deny Dulen's
claim, as the dissent appears to champion, could result only from this court's original
and legally unauthorized change in the trial tribunal's finding which would declare
Dulen guilty of contributory fault—a defense which is explicitly withheld by the provisions of 85 O.S.1991 § 11 from the master's arsenal of weapons. On certiorari previously granted,

THE OPINION OF THE COURT OF APPEALS IS VACATED AND THE ORDER
OF THE THREE-JUDGE PANEL SUSTAINED.

ALMA WILSON, C.J., and LAVENDER, SIMMS and HARGRAVE, JJ., concur.

...

WATT, J., with whom KAUGER, V.C.J., HODGES and SUMMERS, JJ. join, dissenting.

Today's opinion sustains an award of workers' compensation benefits to a claimant
for injuries sustained while engaging in sexual intercourse. I cannot accede to the majority's decision. It is my opinion that the claimant's activities at the time of his accident
constituted a form of "horseplay" not covered by the Workers' Compensation Act. By
engaging in sexual intercourse, the claimant transformed his otherwise legitimate work-
related conduct into conduct that did not "aris[e] out of ... his employment".... Accordingly, I believe that the trial court erred as a matter of law in awarding claimant
workers' compensation benefits.

Additional facts not mentioned by the majority include the following. On the night
of the accident, claimant and his co-driver/girlfriend, Polly Freeman, were driving
through California in a convoy with another company truck. When the other truck
went the wrong way at an intersection, claimant pulled his rig to the side of the road
and waited several minutes for the other truck to rejoin him. The record does not reveal
the activities of claimant and his girlfriend during that time period. When the other
truck returned to the correct course, claimant pulled in behind and followed. The accident occurred minutes later at a railroad crossing in the town of Shaftner, California.

When claimant's rig was struck by the train, Freeman was thrown from the cab and
fatally crushed by claimant's truck. Claimant suffered the injuries for which he now
seeks workers' compensation benefits. The investigating officer, Shaftner Police Officer
Mary Beechie, testified that she discovered claimant just minutes after the accident
standing outside his truck with his pants unzipped and pushed down to "about mid-
hip." The officer testified that Freeman was clad only in a T-shirt. All of the physical evidence indicated that Freeman was sitting on claimant's lap facing him at the time of
impact and that Freeman was thrown from the driver's side of the cab during the collision. As stated by the majority, the passenger-side door of the rig was completely intact
and the driver-side door and windshield were knocked out. Other evidence established
that strands of Freeman's hair were found on the top of the driver's side door frame and
that Freeman suffered lacerations only on the right side of her body.

Moreover, claimant admitted that he and Freeman were having sexual intercourse at
the time of the accident....

I assign no credibility to claimant's reflective, self-serving trial testimony in which he recanted his earlier statements regarding sexual intercourse.

...

Even if we were required to apply the "any-competent-evidence" standard in reviewing the issue here, I do not believe that this Court is obliged to mechanically apply any test which would compel us to affirm an unjust, irrational or absurd lower court decision....

An injury is considered to have been received "in the course of the employment" when it was sustained while the worker was doing the duty which he was employed to perform.... It is readily apparent in this case that claimant's injuries arose in the course of his employment. He was driving a company truck on a routine route and transporting goods for his employer at his employer's behest. At the time of the accident claimant was, in fact, engaged in doing the duties which he was employed to perform. However, as the foregoing precedent makes clear, that fact alone does not necessarily mean that claimant's injuries arose out of his employment.

An injury is considered to have "arisen out of the employment" only if (1) there is a causal connection between the conditions under which the work was required to be performed and the resulting injury, and (2) the injury resulted from a risk reasonably incident to the employment.... A compensable injury "need not have been foreseen or expected, but after the event it must appear to have had its origin in a risk connected with the employment, and have flowed from that source as a rational consequence." ...

Inherent in any job that requires travel is the risk that an employee will become involved in an accident. Injuries sustained by an employee during such mishaps are generally compensable, even when the accident is caused by the employee's own negligence or carelessness.... Further, where a worker is injured during a prank or horseplay in which the worker did not actively participate, the injury is deemed to have arisen out of the employment so as to be compensable. J.C. Hamilton Co. v. Bickel.... See also Willis v. State Indus. Comm'n, 78 Okla. 216, 190 P. 92, 94 (1920) (worker who is a victim of another's prank should not be denied compensation). Whether claimant was negligent or careless at the time of his accident is not an issue in this proceeding. Nor is this Court faced with a situation where claimant was injured during horseplay in which he did not actively participate. This case presents a situation where claimant was injured while actively participating in sexual intercourse, which I deem to be the legal equivalent of "horseplay," "fooling," "frolic," "skylarking" or "play" indulged in for an employee's own amusement. By his own admission the night of the accident, self-serving trial testimony notwithstanding, claimant was engaged in a frolic of his own at the time of the accident.

In Terry Motor Co. v. Mixon, 350 P.2d 953, 955 (Okla.1960), we held that "an injury sustained as the result of play indulged in by an employee for his own amusement does not arise out of the employment, and any disability resulting therefrom is not compensable." Terry cited with approval 99 C.J.S. § 225, which states: Under what is apparently the majority view, an injury to an employee as a result of sportive acts of coemployees, horseplay, or skylarking is not compensable as not arising out of the employment where the injured employee was a participant, initiator, or instigator....

Sustaining an injury while engaged in sexual intercourse is not the type of risk reasonably incident to driving a semi tractor-trailer rig. Claimant's employer neither condoned such acts nor could it have derived any benefit therefrom. Claimant's willing participation in such non-work-related activities were independent of and completely disconnected from the performance of any duties of his job as a truck driver. As such, his injuries did not "arise out of his employment" within the meaning of the Act and are not compensable.

...

NOTES

(1) What was the Oklahoma legislature's purpose in using the words "in the course of … employment" in its workers' compensation statute? Was that purpose, on balance, served or disserved by the decision in Dulen's case?

(2) Counsel for Dulen accused the dissent of "bad reasoning." He told a reporter that Dulen clearly would have received compensation if he had sustained his injuries "by running a red light after spilling coffee on himself or while reaching down to insert a tape into a cassette deck." Dave Lenckus, *Comp ruling tests limits of 'horseplay,'* BUSINESS INSURANCE, Apr. 15, 1996, at 1. Are those analogies persuasive? Which opinion did have the better reasoning?

(3) Dulen's lawyer explained that his case was "largely … founded on his claim that the Santa Fe railroad … was responsible for the collision." Lenckus, supra note 2, at 32. The lawyer said that he was "unsure" about how the "typical offset of third-party recoveries and workers comp benefits" would "work out." He pointed out "that workers comp insurers usually pay … benefits first and then subrogate against third parties." *Id.* Consider the court's summary of the facts, including the malfunctioning of the signal arms at the crossing. Taking a policy view of the case, unconstrained by statute and precedent, how would you apportion the burden of Dulen's injuries among Darco, the railroad and Dulen?

(4) Was, or was not, Dulen doing his job at the time of the accident?

[D] Stress

KELLY'S CASE

Massachusetts Supreme Judicial Court
394 Mass. 684, 477 N.E.2d 582 (1985)

O'CONNOR, JUSTICE.

In this workers' compensation case, we hold that an employee who has an emotional breakdown as a result of being told that she will be laid off from one department and transferred to another one, has suffered a personal injury "arising out of and in the course of … employment" within the meaning of G.L. c.152, §26.

This is the insurer's appeal from a judgment entered in the Superior Court, and affirmed by the Appeals Court, 17 Mass. App. 727, 462 N.E.2d 348 (1984), awarding compensation under G.L. c. 152 to Helen J. Kelly, the employee....

… Kelly was employed by Raytheon Corporation for twenty-two years prior to August, 1977. At the time of the events giving rise to this case, she worked as an associate training specialist and was responsible for running Raytheon's training center. She was happily married, had two grown children, and got along well with her supervisor.

On Friday, August 19, 1977, Kelly's supervisor called her aside and told her that the company was cutting back in her department and that she would be laid off. Kelly began to cry, was unable to compose herself, and went home early. She remained upset over the weekend. When she returned to work on Monday, August 22, she was told that she could transfer to the cable department and work there as a foreperson. Kelly was not pleased to work in the cable department, and on that same day she became depressed, developed chest pains, and was taken to a hospital where she was put on medication.

Kelly remained out of work for six weeks. She returned to work in the cable department on October 5, 1977, but on October 14 she again developed chest pains and was taken to the hospital. Thereafter, she underwent psychiatric treatment for depression, she lost weight, and she experienced difficulty in sleeping. Based on the testimony of her psychiatrist, the single member found that Kelly "has been totally disabled from August 22, 1977 to date" and that "her depression was caused by her hearing that she was to be laid off from one department and transferred to another." The single member concluded, however, that Kelly had not suffered an injury arising out of and in the course of her employment and therefore was not entitled to compensation. The reviewing board agreed. That conclusion is not to be reversed unless a different conclusion is required as a matter of law.... We believe that the law does require a different conclusion.

The findings of the single member clearly establish that Kelly suffered a "personal injury" within the meaning of the act. We have held in several cases that emotional disability, if caused by employment, is a compensable personal injury under G.L. c. 152. *Simmons v. Merchants Mut. Inc. Co.*, 394 Mass. 1007, 476 N.E.2d 221 (1985). *Foley v. Polaroid Corp.*, 381 Mass. 545, 550, 413 N.E.2d 711 (1980). *Albanese's Case*, 378 Mass. 14, 17, 389 N.E.2d 83 (1979). *Fitzgibbons's Case*, 374 Mass. 633, 637–638, 373 N.E.2d 1174 (1978). In none of those cases did we suggest that entitlement to workers' compensation for emotional disability requires proof of facts in addition to those required when the disability is only physical, and we discern no basis in G.L. c. 152 for such a requirement. Nor can it properly be contested that Kelly's injury was caused by hearing that she would lose her position as a training specialist. Regardless of whether Kelly's experience is viewed as a forced transfer from one position to another or as a layoff, the single member has determined with finality that Kelly's disability is attributable to that event. The only new question presented by this case, then, is whether disability that results from an employee's learning that she will be laid off from one department and assigned to another may be said to arise out of and in the course of employment, as is required for entitlement to workers' compensation under G.L. c. 152.

A disability arises out of and in the course of employment if it is "attributable to the 'nature, conditions, obligations or incidents of the employment; in other words, [to] employment looked at in any of its aspects.'" *Zerofski's Case*, 385 Mass. 590, 592, 433 N.E.2d 869 (1982), quoting *Caswell's Case*, 305 Mass. 500, 502, 26 N.E.2d 328 (1940). Thus, the question is whether the event that caused Kelly's disability was an incident of employment "in any of its aspects." We have no doubt that that event was such an incident, particularly in view of the long-standing principle that the workers' compensation statute should be construed, whenever possible, in favor of the employee so as "to promote the accomplishment of its beneficent design." ... Kelly, then, is within the class of persons the Legislature sought to protect by G.L. c. 152.

We reject any contention that Kelly is not entitled to workers' compensation unless her emotional disability resulted from an unusual and objectively stressful or traumatic event. "Our decisions place injuries attributable to specific events at work within the business risks covered by the act, even when employment does not expose employees to an unusual risk greater than that experienced by the general public. *Caswell's Case*, 305 Mass. 500, 502 [26 N.E.2d 328] (1940) (injury at work during hurricane)....” *Zerofski's Case, supra*, 385 Mass. at 595 n. 2, 433 N.E.2d 869. Furthermore, it is settled law that an employer takes his employee “as is,” that is, with whatever peculiar vulnerabilities to injury the employee may have, and that “an identifiable incident or strain need not be unusual or severe to support compensation if the particular employee succumbs to it. *See, e.g., McManus's Case*, 328 Mass. 171 [102 N.E.2d 401] (1951) (bending over caused hernia).” ...

Nothing in *Simmons v. Merchants Mut. Ins. Co., supra*, or *Foley v. Polaroid Corp., supra*, is at variance with the above stated principles. Although the work-related events in those cases were unusually stressful, we attached no significance to the unusualness of the stress in arriving at our holdings. The unusualness of the stress in each case simply served to identify specific work-related events as causes of the employees' emotional disabilities. In the instant case, despite the absence of an unusual, objectively stressful, event, the single member's finding has nevertheless established that a specific work-related event caused the employee's emotional disability. Nothing more is needed to satisfy G.L. c. 152.

Cases involving injuries due to gradual deterioration, or bodily wear and tear, are inapposite. When disability results, not from a single work-related event or series of events, but from gradual deterioration, a causal relationship between employment and the disability can only be established by showing that the employment exposed the employee to “an identifiable condition [of the employment] that is not common and necessary to all or a great many occupations.” *Zerofski's Case, supra* at 595, 433 N.E.2d 869. *Compare Zerofski's Case, supra* at 596, 433 N.E.2d 869 (“Prolonged standing and walking are simply too common among necessary human activities to constitute identifiable conditions of employment”), with *Madden's Case*, 222 Mass. 487, 496, 111 N.E. 379 (1916) (“When a pre-existing heart disease of the employee is accelerated to the point of disablement by the exertion and strain of the employment, not due to the character of the disease acting alone or progressing as it would in any rational work,” the injury is compensable under the act). However, when an injury is attributable to a specific work-related event, as here, or a series of such events, rather than to gradual wear and tear, the employee need not show that the employment exposed him or her to an unusual risk greater than that experienced by the general public. “To be compensable, the harm must arise *either* from a specific incident or series of incidents at work, *or* from an identifiable condition that is not common and necessary to all or a great many occupations” (emphasis added). *Zerofski's Case, supra*, 385 Mass. at 594–595, 433 N.E.2d 869.

· · ·

... We recognize that layoffs and job transfers are frequent events, and that emotional injuries are more prone to fabrication and less susceptible to substantiation than are physical injuries. Nevertheless, it is within the Legislature's prerogative to determine, as a matter of public policy, whether one of the costs of doing business in this Commonwealth shall be the compensation of those few employees who do suffer emotional disability as a result of being laid off or transferred, and it is also the Legislature's prerogative to say whether determination of the existence of such a disability is appropriately left to the expertise of the industrial Accident Board. We construe G.L. c. 152, § 26, as providing that an employee who suffers emotional disability as a result of layoff or transfer is entitled to workers' compensation, and as vesting in the Industrial Accident Board the responsibility to make the relevant factual determination. Because the single member found that Kelly suffered such a disability, we affirm the judgment of the Superior Court.

So ordered.

HENNESSEY, CHIEF JUSTICE (dissenting, with whom WILKINS and LYNCH, JJ., join).

Today the court has held that an employee is entitled to workers' compensation for an emotional injury caused by news of her economically-motivated work transfer. By reversing the board's finding that Kelly did not suffer a work-related injury within the meaning of G.L. c. 152, § 26, the court has expanded the scope of our workers' compensation law far beyond what the Legislature ever intended. As a result, the critical distinction between workers' compensation and unemployment insurance is disappearing. Accordingly, I dissent.

. . . .

Where employees have received compensation for mental or emotional disorders caused by nonphysical work-related trauma, we have previously relied on findings by the board that the injury resulted from a "single traumatic event ... a stress greater than the ordinary stresses of everyday work," *Fitzgibbons's Case*, 374 Mass. 633, 638, 373 N.E.2d 1174 (1978), or a series of "specific, stressful work-related incidents." *Albanese's Case*, 378 Mass. 14, 18 n. 4, 389 N.E.2d 83 (1979). *See Foley v. Polaroid Corp.*, 381 Mass. 545, 550, 413 N.E.2d 711 (1981). We have said that what is critical in determining causation is not the subjective feelings of the employee but the objective event "triggering the ... feelings." *Fitzgibbons's Case, supra*, 374 Mass. at 639, 373 N.E.2d 1174.

In this case, the testimony before the single member indicated that the employee suffered disabling depression when faced with the loss of a satisfying job and a transfer to a less desirable assignment. There was no evidence that the layoff was motivated by other than economic reasons or that the information was given to the employee in a particularly stressful manner. Nor did the board accept evidence that the employee's treatment in her new assignment aggravated her emotional condition.

Thus, in the circumstances of this case, the single member and the review board were fully warranted in concluding that the event triggering the employee's depression—the termination of her position and her transfer within the company—did not constitute the type of "mentally traumatic [event]" which would be sufficient to identify employment as the cause of her disability. *Fitzgibbons's Case, supra* at 638, 373 N.E.2d 1174. Rather the type of decision made here is "common and necessary to ... a great many occupations," *Zerofski's Case, supra*, 385 Mass. at 595, 433 N.E.2d 869, and while such decisions may understandably cause stress among some affected employees it is no "greater than the ordinary stresses of everyday work," and is therefore noncompensable. *Fitzgibbons's Case, supra.*

When compared to the events causing the employees' mental injuries in the *Fitzgibbons, Albanese,* and *Foley* cases, it becomes apparent that we are not presented with a similarly *identifiable stressful work-related incident here. In Fitzgibbons's Case, supra*, the employee suffered an emotional breakdown and subsequently committed suicide after learning that a subordinate had died while performing an assigned duty. In *Albanese's Case, supra*, the claimant was a "working foreman," caught between the conflicting demands of labor and management, who became incapacitated after a series of workplace confrontations in which management attempted to undermine his authority. In *Foley v. Polaroid Corp., supra*, the employee's emotional injury resulted from his employer's conduct in response to charges of rape and assault brought against the employee by a coworker. The employer carried out a private investigation of the complaint resulting in the filing of criminal charges, compelled the employee to take a leave of absence pending trial, discouraged other employees from testifying on his behalf, and subsequently transferred the employee, after he was acquitted of the charges, to a new work location where he received no assignments.

In all three prior cases the events causing the employees' injuries were unusually stressful by any objective criteria. Here, however, the employee's depression was precipitated by notice of an ordinary employment decision. The extraordinary nature of her emotional response reflected her admitted apprehension over the prospect of unemployment. In these circumstances, "[a]pprehension over the prospect of losing one's job does not arise 'out of the nature, conditions, obligations or incidents of the employment.'... Rather it is a state of mind which arises from the common necessity of working for a living. Social legislation designed to relieve the consequences of losing one's job is found elsewhere." *Korsun's Case*, 354 Mass. 124, 128, 235 N.E.2d 124 (1968).

The court's opinion incorrectly states that we have never before suggested that a stricter standard of proof is required under G.L. c. 152, § 26, for establishing the causal nexus between employment and emotional injury. In fact, we have never before allowed compensation for emotional injuries without proof that the injuries resulted from particularly stressful work-related incidents.... We have emphasized ... the nature of the objective event which triggered the emotional reaction of the employee to determine whether an emotional injury is sufficiently work-related, and this is the reasoning which has been followed by several other jurisdictions. *See Seitz v. L & R Indus.*, 437 A.2d 1345 (R.I.1981) (psychic injury due to routine transfer to new work location was not compensable); *School Dist. No. 1, Village of Brown Deer v. Department of Indus., Labor & Human Relations*, 62 Wis.2d 370, 215 N.W.2d 373 (1974) (teacher's depression on learning student council recommended her dismissal was not compensable)....

In our previous cases we have required a showing of one or more specific stressful, traumatic events as the cause of the emotional injury. By departing from those limits, the court has opened workers' compensation to distressed claimants who have simply experienced economically inevitable terminations and transfers. I think the court has departed from the legislative intent, and I also think that this judicial venture will invite claims in such numbers as to have a substantial economic impact upon employers.

NOTES

(1) In *Carter v. General Motors Corp.*, 361 Mich. 577, 106 N.W.2d 105 (1960), the majority of a sharply divided court upheld a workers' compensation award on facts that it summarized this way:

> Plaintiff had worked as a machine operator for defendant, General Motors Corporation, with intermittent layoffs, since 1953. On October 8, 1956 he was recalled to work after a 5-month layoff and worked for 4 days on a "brace job" and then was transferred on October 12th to a "hub job". This operation required him to take a hub assembly (consisting of a case and cover) from a nearby fellow employee's table to his own workbench, remove burrs with a file and grind out holes in the assembly with a drill, and place the assembly on a conveyor belt. Plaintiff was unable to keep up with the pace of the job unless he took 2 assemblies at a time to his workbench, and he feared another layoff should he prove unable satisfactorily to do the work. He was instructed repeatedly by his foreman not to take 2 assemblies at a time because the assembly parts became mixed up on the conveyor belt when he did so. However, plaintiff continued having trouble "getting on to the job" as it was supposed to be

performed. Thus, when he took only 1 hub assembly at a time, he fell behind; when he fell behind, he took 2 assemblies; but, when he took 2 assemblies, he got the assemblies mixed up and was berated by the foreman.

We are told that the dilemma in which plaintiff found himself resulted on October 24, 1956 in an emotional collapse variously described as paranoid schizophrenia and schizophrenic reaction residual type. He was subsequently hospitalized for a period of 1 month, during which time he received shock therapy.

What would have been the best arguments that both parties could have made on this question?

(2) *Carter*, supra, generated some extraordinary offshoots. In a particularly remarkable incident, an unhappy auto worker having an "acute psychotic break with reality" shot to death three foremen. He then himself sued for workers' compensation. He argued, according to a press report, that "working conditions and racial bigotry at the plant aggravated a pre-existing but non-disabling tendency toward schizophrenia and paranoia." A state workers' compensation referee held that he was entitled to compensation. News item, WALL ST. J., Mar. 7, 1973, at 1.

The incident also produced grave consequences in a foreman who witnessed the shooting. He developed serious emotional problems and suffered two heart attacks and a stroke. A report of his widow's suit for compensation characterized her as claiming that her husband was literally "scared to death." *Foreman was scared to death, widow charges*, undated Chicago newspaper clipping, c. Feb. 26, 1980.

(3) Stress-related claims for workers' compensation have come from high up the employment ladder. See, e.g., *Lockwood v. Indep. Sch. Dist. No. 877*, 312 N.W.2d 924 (Minn. 1981), in which a high school principal developed serious psychological problems as his duties and job pressures increased with the growth of his school. He identified, in particular, "(1) problems with a new curriculum director; (2) increased student disciplinary problems; (3) the addition of a computer system; and (4) an increase in the size of the faculty." The results were that he fell behind in his work, experienced problems in sleeping and an inability to control his temper. A majority of the Minnesota court denied recovery, declaring that "[r]eallocating the costs resulting from stress-related disability between health insurance and workers' compensation insurance is a major policy determination." *Id.* at 927.

(4) Whatever one's views about the validity of workers' compensation claims for emotional disturbances, stress in the workplace is a significant element of health problems and injury among employees. The National Institute for Occupational Safety and Health has said that "[p]sychological disorders are one of the 10 leading work-related diseases and injuries," identifying such problems as anxiety, irritability, substance abuse, sleep difficulties and headaches. *Mental Disorders from Job Stress Costly to U.S. Workforce, CDC Says*, 16 O.S.H. REP. 499 (BNA 1986). NIOSH has also said that 60 to 80 per cent of all industrial accidents are related to stress, and there are reports that the proportion of claims for stress or mental disorders has risen as compared with workers' compensation claims. Cain, *Job stress cases mounting: Experts*, BUSINESS INSURANCE, Mar. 2, 1987, at 1.

The press story just cited quotes the director of governmental relations for the National Federation of Independent Business as saying that "[w]orkers' compensation was designed to deal with physical injuries, not psychological ones." — Gary Jenkins, quoted in Cain, supra, at 28. Do you agree with this statement as a general proposition?

[E] Relationship of Workers' Compensation and Tort

PROBLEM

A state workers' compensation statute, after reciting the dangers of industrial employment and declaring that "[t]he remedy of the worker has been uncertain, slow and inadequate," said:

> The state, therefore, declares that all phases of the [industrial] premises are withdrawn from private controversy, and sure and certain relief for workers, injured in their work, and their families and dependents is hereby provided regardless of questions of fault and to the exclusion of every other remedy, proceeding or compensation....

A warehouseman developed chronic foot pain to a point that he could not do heavy duty work, and his doctor advised his firm that he should receive light duty work. The company would not allow the worker to return to work unless he could "work full capacity." After his physician refused to give a full medical release, the company terminated his employment. The worker then sued on a theory of "handicap discrimination" under the state's anti-discrimination statute. The trial court dismissed the action. In support of the dismissal against the employee's appeal, the employer argued that the "exclusion" of other remedies in the workers' compensation statute barred the claim. What result?

NOTES

(1) Why did the American legislatures that adopted workers' compensation statutes make the remedy exclusive, as a general matter?

(2) Some state workers' compensation laws make an exception to the exclusivity provision when the employer has committed an "intentional wrong." A New Jersey decision has drawn a particularly interesting distinction in denying one count while validating another brought under this language. The occasion was a claim for asbestos-caused disease. On the first count, the court adopted the "substantial certainty" language in the definition of "intent" in *Restatement (Second) of Torts* § 8A to bar an action based on the employer's knowledge of "even the strong probability of a risk" that asbestos might cause illness. Even though the defendants' conduct "clearly amounts to deliberately taking risks with employees' health," the court said, their knowledge of the risk would "come up short of the 'substantial certainty' needed to find an intentional wrong resulting in avoidance of the exclusive-remedy bar of the compensation statute."

By contrast, the court thought the plaintiffs had a "valid cause of action for aggravation of their initial occupational diseases" because of allegations that the defendants, in order to keep the plaintiffs from leaving their employment, had "fraudulently concealed from plaintiffs the fact that they were suffering from asbestos-related diseases." The court thought there was a legally significant "difference between, on the one hand, tolerating in the workplace conditions that will result in a certain number of injuries or illnesses, and, on the other, actively misleading the employees who have already fallen victim to those risks of the workplace." *Millison v. E.I. du Pont de Nemours & Co.*, 101 N.J. 161, 501 A.2d 505 (1985).

(3) "Intentional wrong"-type exceptions in some compensation statutes may breed some knotty questions of statutory interpretation. A very specific elaboration of such language appears in the West Virginia statute that defines "deliberate intention" to include a requirement

That such specific unsafe working condition was a violation of a state or federal safety statute, rule or regulation, whether cited or not, or of a commonly accepted and well-known safety standard within the industry or business of such employer, which statute, rule, regulation or standard was specifically applicable to the particular work and working condition involved....

W. VA. CODE § 23-4-2(c)(2)(ii)(C) (1985 Repl. Vol.).

This sort of provision can generate some rather technical arguments. Consider, for example, a case in which a chemical worker ascribed chemically induced illness to his employer's violation of procedures described in internal safety data sheets. He contended that the disjunctive "or" in the clause "or of a commonly accepted and well-known safety standard within the industry *or* business of such employer" would apply, as the court characterized his argument, to a "violation of a discrete safety rule promulgated by a 'single business.'" In rejecting this argument, the court viewed the statute as "protect[ing] against flagrant violations of national and state safety statutes, rules, and regulations," but thought "[i]t would be rare that a 'commonly accepted and well-known' safety standard could be established by showing that it exists in only one facility." Without evidence that there was a similar standard "recognized by a business or industrial entity conducting the same or similar activities as the defendant," the court thought "there seldom will be a jury question" under the statutory exception. *Handley v. Union Carbide Corp.*, 804 F.2d 265 (4th Cir. 1986).

[F] Workers' Compensation in Operation: A Complex Picture

Towards a Jurisprudence of Injury 10-47 to 10-52
(ABA 1984, M. Shapo Rptr.)*

...

The [National] Commission [on State Workmen's Compensation Laws] specifically considered the tort remedy as an alternative to workers' compensation, but concluded that it would be "distinctly inferior." It found that "the issue of negligence is particularly elusive in the work setting," entailing expensive legal determinations and uncertain outcomes, with an added complication presented by overcrowded court dockets. A major problem associated with a tort solution, the Commission argued, would be that "[s]ome workers eventually would receive damage awards in excess of workmen's compensation benefits, but others would receive no protection."[15]

On the other end of the compensation spectrum, the Commission was unconvinced that the transfer of disability claims to social insurance programs would yield administrative efficiencies, and suggested that to extend national health care to cover all work-related impairments would cause adverse effects on employees in general. Although the Commission expressed the hope that the Occupational Safety and Health Act would

---

* Copyright © 1984 The American Bar Association. Reprinted by permission.
15. [Report of the National Commission on State Workmen's Compensation Laws] 119–20 (1972).

have beneficial protective effects, it noted that workers' compensation "has the virtue that the linkage of benefits paid to insurance costs should automatically provide a strong incentive for safety."[16]

...

Relationship to tort. A significant related area of litigation involves products liability claims in tort, typically brought by injured workers against manufacturers whose goods are means of production. This kind of lawsuit poses special conceptual problems, for a suit by an employee against a manufacturer, either in negligence or under strict liability, may well incite the manufacturer to seek contribution or indemnity from the employer for the latter's alleged negligence. The legal difficulty inheres in the argument that the workers' compensation employer should not be responsible to anyone for negligence because the firm has made a deal with the employee for a nonfault system of liability.[25]

Uncertainty about effects. Paralleling the criticisms of workers' compensation for being either too costly or too stingy are concerns that not enough is known about the effects of that system. One area of substantial uncertainty is the effect of workers' compensation on employee conduct. A recent study concludes that even if one believes that workers systematically underestimate job hazards, "we still do not know whether imposing workers' compensation reduces that underestimate, leaves it unchanged, or increases it."[26]

At the same time, efforts to determine the effects of workers' compensation on employer incentives yield many complexities. One researcher has found that states which meet the National Commission's recommended benefit floor of two-thirds of average weekly wages have higher rates of accident frequency and lower rates of accident severity than states which fall below the standard.

Contemporaneously another group of investigators, analyzing self-insured firms, found that while it is "generally true" that increases in compensation benefits will inspire larger investments in safety, there are several situations in which benefits increases are "likely to reduce or have no effect" on such outlays. Those circumstances include periods of rapid inflation in the price of safety investments, payment of significant premiums for hazardous work, and the use of engineering controls rather than personal protective equipment "in hazardous industries where the demand for labor is very responsive to changing labor costs (*e.g.*, firms that face significant foreign competition.)"[28] ... [T]hese investigators suggest that in the last described situation, the preference of the Occupational Safety and Health Administration for engineering controls over personal protective equipment means that "OSHA and the WC system work at cross-purposes."

With respect to the funds that in fact find their way into the pockets of injured workers, research has indicated a gap in knowledge concerning the appropriate replacement rate for earnings analogous to the deficiency in information about worker incentives. Moreover, students of the subject emphasize that a determination of how much reimbursement actually occurs for losses "cannot resolve policy questions about the socially optimal degree of earnings replacement that should be achieved through workers' compensation benefits."[31] Other analysts, comparing workers' compensation with the tort

---

16. *Id.* at 120–21.

25. A brief summary of authorities appears in L. Darling-Hammond & T. Kniesner, The Law and Economics of Workers' Compensation 48–49 (Rand R-2716-ICJ 1980).

26. *Id.* at 59.

28. R. Victor, L. Cohen & C. Phelps, *Workers' Compensation and Workplace Safety* 50 (Rand R-2918-ICJ 1982).

31. *See* L. Darling-Hammond & T. Kniesner, *supra* note 25, at 62–65.

system, have derived the "remarkable observation" that "one cannot conclude, on the basis of data generally cited to demonstrate the superiority of workers' compensation over negligence, that workers' compensation has effected an improvement in terms of the wage loss compensation and deterrence objectives over the evolving negligence system it replaced."[32]

...

[G] The Frontiers of Compensation Law

AMERICAN MUT. INS. CO. v. JONES
United States Court of Appeals, District of Columbia Circuit
138 U.S. App. D.C. 269, 426 F.2d 1263 (1970)

BAZELON, CHIEF JUDGE.

Appellants, an employer and his insurance carrier, seek to reverse an order of the District Court which found, notwithstanding a contrary determination by a Deputy Commissioner of the Department of Labor, that appellee was entitled to benefits for permanent total disability[1] under the Longshoremen's and Harbor Workers' Act. Three questions are presented by the record. First, whether the Deputy Commissioner's finding that appellee was not permanently totally disabled was supported by sufficient evidence to make a contrary conclusion by the District Court improper. Second, whether appellee is barred from receiving compensation for total disability because the Act provides a scheduled award for his injury. Third, whether appellee's limited intelligence constitutes a "previous disability" within the meaning of § 8(f) of the Act, so that compensation for permanent total disability should be paid not by the employer but rather by the Special Fund created by § 44 of the Act.[4]

I.

Appellee is a 63-year-old man of limited intelligence[5] whose only past work has been as a laborer. In 1951, he twice fractured his right arm while working for appellant Rose Brothers as a roofer's helper. Because of these injuries, he lost the use of his right hand for all but the lightest work. He can lift less than seven pounds with the hand, and can barely use it to hold a pencil to write.

---

32. Ashford & Johnson, *Negligence vs. No-Fault Liability: An Analysis of the Workers' Compensation Example*, 12 SETON HALL L. REV. 725, 766 (1982). *See also* Phillips, *The Relationship Between the Tort System and Workers' Compensation — The True Cost, In Conference on Workers' Compensation and Workplace Liability* 99 (final edited proceedings, National Legal Center for the Public Interest 1981). Noting *inter alia* an estimate that workers' compensation premiums comprised less than half the dollar figure of total work accident costs, Professor Phillips suggests that "[t]he safety incentive of tort liability should operate to reduce these losses significantly, thereby ultimately resulting in cost savings."

1. From 1951, the date of the injury, through 1957, the employer and carrier paid appellee a total of $11,000 in compensation, the maximum allowable for permanent partial disability under the law in force at the time of the accident....

4. 33 U.S.C. § 944 (1964)....

5. A clinical psychologist, Dr. Horlick, testified that appellee's rating on the Wechsler-Bellvue Intelligence Scale was 69.

At the hearing before the Deputy Commissioner, a physician, Dr. Wenger, characterized appellee's injury as a "35 to 45 percent" disability of the hand. He stated that appellee could "probably function well in a suitable employment." Dr. Horlick, a clinical psychologist, testified that because of appellee's limited intelligence, he could not be trained for jobs that "would require a minimum of ability," and that he would be a "liability in any employment." A counsellor with the United States Employment Service testified that appellee had registered with them in 1958 and that, as of the time of the hearing in 1963, they had been unable to find him employment. Nevertheless, apparently basing his conclusion upon Dr. Wenger's testimony alone, the Deputy Commissioner concluded "that the claimant's disability ... was and is confined solely to the right upper extremity."

By its own terms, this finding indicates that the Deputy Commissioner misapprehended the controlling law. The Act makes clear that "disability" is an economic and not a medical concept.[7] "The degree of disability in any case cannot be measured by physical condition alone, but there must be taken into consideration the injured man's age, his industrial history, and the availability of that type of work which he can do." Even a relatively minor injury must lead to a finding of total disability if it prevents the employee from engaging in the only type of gainful employment for which he is qualified.[9]

Here, the evidence of economic disability is overwhelming. Even if the burden is on the claimant to show the unavailability of other employment, appellee's unsuccessful search for work over a period of years, and the testimony of Dr. Horlick, are sufficient to meet that burden. Appellants cannot sustain the Deputy Commissioner's finding on the basis of Dr. Wenger's conclusion that appellee could "probably" perform "suitable employment." There must be some showing that such 'suitable employment' is actually available.

II.

Appellants suggest that, since § 8(c) of the Act provides a specific award for loss of a hand, such an injury can never be the basis for an award of compensation for total disability. The suggestion is without merit. As § 8(a) makes clear, in certain enumerated cases permanent total disability shall be conclusively presumed, and "in *all* other cases permanent total disability shall be determined in accordance with the facts." Where, as here, the facts show permanent total disability, claimants are not limited to the scheduled awards.

III.

Testimony at the hearing before the Deputy Commissioner indicated that appellee's injury would not have resulted in permanent total disability had his intelligence not been substantially below normal. This raises the question whether appellee's mental deficiency should be considered a "previous disability" so as to bring into play the provisions of § 8(f)(1) of the Act:

> If an employee receives an injury which of itself would only cause permanent partial disability but which, combined with a previous disability, does in fact cause permanent total disability, the employer shall provide compensation

---

7. 33 U.S.C. § 902(10) (1964) provides: "'Disability' means incapacity because of injury to earn the wages which the employee was receiving at the time of injury in the same or any other employment."

9. Conversely, a continuing injury that does not result in any loss of wage-earning capacity cannot be the foundation for a finding of disability. *Owens v. Traynor*, 274 F.Supp. 770 (D.Md.1966).

only for the disability caused by the subsequent injury; *Provided, however,* that in addition to compensation for such permanent partial disability, and after cessation of the payments for the prescribed period of weeks, the employee shall be paid the remainder of the compensation that would be due for permanent total disability. Such compensation shall be paid out of the special fund established in [33 U.S.C. § 944 (1964]).

Not without some hesitation, we conclude that § 8(f)(1) should not apply in the circumstances of this case.

Section 8(f)(1), sometimes referred to as the "second injury provision," was included in the Act as a protection to both employers and employees. "It protects that employer who has hired, say, a one-eyed worker who goes and loses his other eye and becomes a total disability. The employer without this sort of thing would have to pay total permanent disability compensation. Then, on the other hand, this also protects the worker with one eye from being denied employment on account of his being an extra risk."[17]

Neither the language nor the purpose of the Act would seem to support any distinction between physical and mental disability for the purpose of § 8(f)(1).[18] Likewise, it is immaterial whether the disability is the result of a previous work-connected injury, an injury not connected with employment, a congenital defect, or perhaps even a disability resulting from social and economic causes.[21] Nevertheless, § 8(f)(1) does not apply to every case of permanent total disability in which a present injury is not the sole cause of the disability.[22] It was not intended to provide a windfall to employers, nor to actively encourage employment of the handicapped. Its purpose was simply to remove that aspect of discrimination against the disabled which would otherwise be encouraged by the very statute intended to protect them.

Any such discrimination, however, must rest upon knowledge of the characteristic upon which the discrimination is to be based. In consequence, courts have distinguished between "manifest"[24] and "latent"[25] conditions for purposes of apportioning claims between employers and special funds such as the present one. Although some jurisdictions make the question turn upon the employer's actual knowledge of the employee's condition, such a test has obvious practical difficulties in application. Practice under the Longshoremen's Act has followed the more general rule, and sought to define

---

17. Testimony of John B. Andrews, Secretary of the American Association for Labor Legislation, in Hearings on S. 3170 Before the House Committee on the Judiciary, 69th Cong. 1st Sess. 208 (1926), cited in *Lawson v. Suwannee S. S. Co.*, 336 U.S. 198, 202, 69 S.Ct. 503, 93 L.Ed. 611 (1949).

18. Similarly, compensation is regularly awarded for disability when the only injury received is a psychological one....

21. *Cf. Lawson v. Suwannee S. S. Co., supra* note 19, at 204, 69 S.Ct. at 506: "A distinction between a worker previously injured in industry and one handicapped by a cause outside of industry has no logical foundation if we accept the premise that the purpose of the fund is that of aid to the handicapped."

22. *Cf.* § 8(a) of the Act, 33 U.S.C. § 908 (a) (1964), which provides that certain enumerated injuries shall be conclusively presumed to result in permanent total disability, and that "[i]n all other cases permanent total disability shall be determined in accordance with the facts." It has never been suggested that § 8(f)(1) was intended to be coextensive with all cases of permanent total disability found under the quoted portion of § 8(a).

24. *E.g. Subsequent Injuries Fund v. Industrial Accident Comm'n*, 53 Cal.2d 392, 1 Cal.Rptr. 833, 348 P.2d 193 (1960) (preexisting schizophrenia found manifest)....

25. *E.g. Boyd-Campbell Co. v. Shea*, 254 F.Supp. 483 (S.D.Tex.1966) (congenital anomalies of spine); *United States Fidelity & Guaranty Co. v. O'Keffe*, 240 F.Supp. 813 (S.D.Fla. 1962) (inadequate underlying personality).

certain classes of disability as "manifest" or "latent" without regard to the employer's actual knowledge of the employee's condition.

Clearly, some degrees of mental retardation are so severe that they cannot fairly be characterized as other than "manifest."[29] The question is whether appellee's disability was of such degree during the time of his employment. On the present record, we cannot say that it was. As of 1963, his intelligence quotient on the Wechsler-Bellvue scale was measured as 69; according to any of the standard nomenclatures, this would place him at the borderline of mental retardation. But even aside from all the problems regarding the accuracy of such tests, the degree of mental retardation cannot be adequately gauged by intelligence quotient alone. Its true measure is the extent to which, *because of* inadequately developed intelligence, an individual's ability to learn and to adapt to his environment is impaired. We need not here decide where the line should be drawn. It is sufficient for present purposes that nothing in the record gives any indication that appellee, up to the time of his injuries, showed a sufficient degree of social maladaption due to limited intelligence that his disability could be fairly classed as "manifest."

We are constrained to add a final word. It may well be true that the Congress which passed the Longshoremen's and Harbor Workers' Compensation Act in 1927 had no real expectation that mental disabilities would ever become significant in its operation. But by using general language in the statute, Congress indicated an intention not to fix compensable injuries forever into the molds that could be cast by the medical and behavioral sciences forty years ago. Perhaps to a greater extent than any similar group in our society, the mentally retarded are underemployed in terms of their capacity for useful and productive work. We are aware of no information that would indicate to what, if any, extent this underemployment is due to the discrimination sought to be avoided by §8(f)(1) of the Act, rather than to prejudice, fear, or discomfort. Furthermore, if mental deficiency is to play a significant part in the administration of the special fund, it seems likely that Congress, after a careful investigation, could do a better job than the Labor Department and the courts in drawing a line between "manifest" and "latent" mental retardation. Finally, our dissenting brother suggests that the Act represents a social choice different from that which we see in it. We express no opinion whatsoever on the social and political merits of the many available options. We do suggest, however, that an examination of the Act in light of the vast developments in the social and behavioral sciences since 1926—an examination that can be carried out in depth only by the Congress—would certainly be worthwhile.

Affirmed.

WILBUR K. MILLER, SENIOR CIRCUIT JUDGE (dissenting).

On September 6, 1951, Willie B. Jones fell when a wheel barrow he was pushing overturned. He suffered an injury to his right wrist and hand. For temporary total disability and permanent partial disability, the employer and insurance carrier paid compensation in the total sum of $11,000, the limit of the Act. The last payment was made September 17, 1957.

On September 5, 1958, Jones filed a claim against his employer for additional benefits. He alleged that due to his physical impairment caused by the injury and other factors, including his limited skills and lack of education, he had been unable to obtain employment and so had had no earnings since September 17, 1957. He alleged that,

---

29. For example, adults with an I.Q. under 20 will almost invariably need complete care and constant supervision if they are to survive. Department of Health, Education & Welfare, *Mental Retardation, in Health, Education and Welfare Indicators*, June 1962, at vi.

therefore, as a result of the injury of September 6, 1951, he had suffered permanent total disability.

The Deputy Commissioner found there was no medical or other evidence that Jones had any disabling condition causally related to the injury of September 6, 1951, except that for which he had been fully compensated. He therefore rejected appellant's claim for additional compensation.

Jones sought review in the District Court and obtained summary judgment directing the Deputy Commissioner to award him compensation benefits for permanent total disability. Consequently the latter ordered the employer and insurance carrier to pay $19,355 for the period from September 18, 1957, to April 23, 1968, and thereafter to pay at the rate of $35.00 per week. They were also ordered to pay the reasonable cost of medical treatment and care required in the future. On appeal, my colleagues affirm. They do so on the theory that disability is an economic, not a medical, concept, and that the evidence of economic disability is "overwhelming." That may be, but there must also be some proof of causation; it is lacking here. I think the record as a whole supports the Deputy Commissioner's findings and his denial of the claim for additional compensation. That being true, the courts have no right to substitute their judgment for his.

Jones is barely above a moron in intelligence. He had several diseases and on February 6, 1961, sustained a fracture of his right shoulder in a fall on ice. The evidence showed that he is addicted to alcohol, has a police record, and made very little effort to get work. At the time of the hearing in the District Court he was receiving public assistance and had been receiving it for some time. I think he should continue to be a public charge. The cost of maintaining this unfortunate should be spread out among all the people, *i.e.*, it should be borne by the government. It is wrong, in the circumstances here, to impose that cost upon only two members of the public—the employer and the insurance carrier, who have already discharged their legal liability.

I would reverse.

NOTES

(1) Did Jones have a "previous disability"? What was it?

(2) Are there tort analogies that might usefully be applied to the *Jones* case?

How would you argue against the dissent's contention that the claimant did not prove causation? What was the "proximate cause" of the disability, in the sense that Judge Andrews used that term in *Palsgraf*?

(3) In theory, what incentives would *Jones* create with respect to the hiring practices of employers? In practice, what effect is it likely to have on actual conduct—and on resource allocation—given the kind of employment involved in the case?

WHETRO v. AWKERMAN

Michigan Supreme Court
383 Mich. 235, 174 N.W.2d 783 (1970)

T. G. KAVANAGH, JUSTICE. These cases were consolidated....

They turn on the same question, for the damages for which workmen's compensation was awarded in each case were caused by the Palm Sunday 1965 tornadoes which devastated parts of Southern Michigan.

Carl Whetro was injured when the tornado destroyed the residence wherein he was working for his employer and seeks reimbursement for his medical expenses. Henry E. Emery was killed when the motel in which he was staying while on a business trip for his employer was destroyed by the tornado, and his widow seeks compensation for his death.

In each case the hearing referee found that the employee's injury arose out of and in the course of his employment. The award was affirmed by the appeal board in each case and by the Court of Appeals in the *Whetro* case.

The defendant-appellants in both cases base their defense on the assertion that tornadoes are "acts of God" or acts of nature and injuries which are caused by them do not arise "out of" the employment and hence are not compensable under the Workmen's Compensation Act.

For this reason they maintain that the cases were erroneously decided as a matter of law and the awards should be set aside.

The appellants in each case maintain that the injury did not arise "out of" the employment because that phrase as it is used in the act refers to a causal connection between the event which put in motion the forces which caused the injury and the work itself or the conditions under which it is required to be performed.

Employment as a caretaker-gardener or salesman, they argue, does not include tornadoes as incidents or conditions of the work, and the path of injury is determined by the tornado, not the employment.

Appellants cite a series of Michigan decisions involving injury by lightning; *Klawinski v. Lake Shore & Michigan Southern R. Co.* (1915), ... ; *Thier v. Widdifield* (1920), ... ; *Nelson v. Country Club of Detroit* (1951), ... ; *Kroon v. Kalamazoo County Road Commission* (1954), in which compensation was denied and assert that a tornado is like lightning in that it acts capriciously, leaving its victims and the untouched side by side. The decisions in all of these "lightning cases" denied compensation on the ground that the injury did not arise "out of" the employment because the employment did not expose the workman to any increased risk or to a more hazardous situation than faced by others in the area.

The Court of Appeals was able to distinguish between a tornado and a bolt of lightning as a causative force of injury and base its decision affirming the award for Carl Whetro on the reasoning of the Massachusetts supreme court in *Caswell's Case* (1940), 305 Mass. 500, 26 N.E.2d 328, wherein recovery was allowed for injuries received when a brick wall of the employer's factory was blown down on workmen during a hurricane. This "contact with the premises" met the requirement that the injury arise "out of" the employment in the mind of the Court of Appeals.

We are unable to accept the distinction drawn between a tornado and bolt of lightning when viewed as the cause of an injury. As we see it, a tornado, no less than a bolt of lightning or an earthquake or flood is an "act of God" and if the phrase "out of" the employment in the Workmen's Compensation Act necessarily entails the motion of proximate causality, no injury received because of an "act of God" should be compensable.

But we are satisfied that it is no longer necessary to establish a relationship of proximate causality between employment and an injury in order to establish compensability. Accordingly we no longer regard an "act of God" whether it be a tornado, lightning, earthquake, or flood as a defense to a claim for a work connected injury. Such a defense retains too much of the idea that an employer should not pay compensation unless he is somehow at fault. This concept from the law of tort is inconsistent with the law of workmen's compensation.

The purpose of the compensation act as set forth in its title, is to promote the welfare of the people of Michigan relating to the liability of employers for injuries or death sustained by their employees. The legislative policy is to provide financial and medical benefits to the victims of work connected injuries in an efficient, dignified and certain form. The act allocates the burden of such payments to the most appropriate source of payment, the consumer of the product.

Fault has nothing to do with whether or not compensation is payable. The economic impact on an injured workman and his family is the same whether the injury was caused by the employer's fault or otherwise.

We hold that the law in Michigan today no longer requires the establishment of a proximately causal connection between the employment and the injury to entitle a claimant to compensation. The cases which have allowed recovery for street risks, increased risks, and on the premises accidents were made without consideration of the proximate causal connection between the nature of the employment and the injury. They have brought the law in Michigan to the point where it can be said today that if the employment is the occasion of the injury, even though not the proximate cause, compensation should be paid.

Such a development of the Michigan law is paralleled by the development of the law in England and Massachusetts—the two jurisdictions which served as Michigan's model in the original legislative drafting and judicial construction of the Workmen's Compensation Act.

The early Michigan case of *Hopkins v. Michigan Sugar Co.* (1915) ... imported the "causality" concept into the requirement that the injury must arise "out of" the employment. The court drew this interpretation from the English case of *Fitzgerald v. Clark & Son* (1908), 2 KB 796, and the *McNicol's Case* (1913), 215 Mass. 497, 102 N.E. 697, L.R.A. 1916A, 306. Both of these jurisdictions have since adopted the doctrine of positional risk. *See Powell v. Great Western Railway Co.* (1940), 1 All Eng.Rep. 87, and *Baran's Case* (1957), 336 Mass. 342, 145 N.E.2d 726.

The Massachusetts court said in *Baran's Case*, p. 344, 145 N.E.2d p. 727: "We think that they [recent cases] disclose the development of a consistent course which is a departure from the earlier view expressed, for example in [McNicol's Case].... The injury 'need not arise out of the nature of the employment.... The question is whether his employment brought him in contact with the risk that in fact caused his death.'"

The English court, in *Powell, supra*, held that if the work required the employee to be at the place of injury the accident arose "out of" his employment.

Accordingly, we hold that the employment of Carl Whetro and Henry E. Emery in each case was the occasion of the injury which they suffered and therefore the injuries arose "out of" and in the course of their employment.

The award in each case is affirmed.

For the reasons set forth therein, in keeping with the policy observed in *Bricker v. Green* (1946) ... and *Parker v. Port Huron Hospital* (1960) ... the rule of law announced herein will apply to the instant case and all claims for compensation arising after March 12, 1970 the date of the filing of this opinion.

T. M. KAVANAGH and ADAMS, JJ., concurred with T. G. KAVANAGH, J....

BRENNAN, CHIEF JUSTICE.

The function of the workmen's compensation act is to place the financial burden of industrial injuries upon the industries themselves, and spread that cost ultimately among the consumers.

This humane legislation was developed because the industrialization of our civilization had left in its wake a trail of broken bodies.

Employers were absolved from general liability for negligence, in exchange for the imposition of more certain liability under the act.

But it is a mistake to say that employers were absolved from fault. Liability is the basis of legal remedy. Fault is the basis of moral responsibility.

The workmen's compensation law is society's expression of the moral responsibility of employers and consumers to the workmen whose health and whose lives are sacrificed to industrial and commercial progress and production.

Fault is not the same thing as proximate cause. The compensation law does not use the word *cause*. Rather, it expresses the concept of employer and consumer responsibility in the phrase "arising out of and in the course of" the employment.

The terms "arising out of" and "in the course of" are not redundant. They mean two different things. An adulterous cobbler shot at his last by his jealous wife may be "in the course of" his employment. But the injury does not "arise out of" his job. On what basis of moral responsibility should his injuries be paid for by his employer? By what logic would society decree that his disability should add a farthing to the price of shoes?

The workmen's compensation law is not a utopian attempt to put a price tag on all human suffering and incorporate it into the cost of living.

Lightning, flood, tornados and estranged wives will always be with us, in this vale of tears. They were the occasion of human injury when our forebears were tilling the soil with sharp sticks. They are not a byproduct of the industrial revolution, nor are they in any sense the moral responsibility of those who profit by or enjoy the fruits of, our modern industrialized society.

I would reverse without apology for the precedents.

DETHMERS and KELLY, JJ., concurred with BRENNAN, C.J.

BLACK, JUSTICE. These cases present another "out of and in the course of" question, arising under perdurable section 1 of part II of the workmen's compensation law.... Had the question not been previously decided, I would be ready to support the applied reasoning of Justice T. G. Kavanagh.... The question however has been settled by a series of unanimous decisions of this Court; the quoted statutory phrase meanwhile remaining as it was when the Court undertook first to examine it.

On that first occasion the Court ruled without dissent (*Klawinski v. Lake Shore & Michigan Southern R. Co.*, ...) that the death of an employee engaged "in the course of," the death having been caused *directly* by a bolt of lightning striking from above during "a violent wind and rain storm," did not arise "out of" his employment. The reasoning of the Court was based upon a memorandum opinion of the industrial commission of Wisconsin wherein this question was posed, "Did the injury grow out of the employment and did the industry cause the injury?", with answer as follows ... :

> We are of the opinion that this language refers to industrial accidents; those caused by the industry and chargeable to the industry, and does not apply to injuries resulting from those forces of nature described in the common law as acts of God, such forces as are wholly uncontrolled by men.[1]

1. This reasoning is quite unsound. Our statute has never, whether by words employed or record left by the 1912 drafting committee, exacted of a claimant that he show "the industry caused the injury." He need only show "out of and in the course of."

For *Klawinski's Case* these controlling facts were stipulated:

Mr. Klawinski was a section hand, working for the defendant railroad. The section gang of which Mr. Klawinski was a member had been working at the time on defendant's right of way when the storm came up. Upon order of the foreman and assistant foreman, most of the gang including Mr. Klawinski took shelter in a nearby barn. While they were in the barn, the storm meanwhile raging, Mr. Klawinski was killed by a bolt of lightning.

Klawinski was followed by *Nelson v. Country Club of Detroit* (1951) ... and again by *Kroon v. Kalamazoo County Road Commission* (1954).... Both opinions were unanimous. The 3 cases stand for a settled judicial view and a uniformly continuant application of that view over a long period of years. The precise essence thereof is that, no matter the fact of a workman being engaged in the course of his employment at the time, an otherwise compensable injury then and there sustained by him does not arise, "out of" his employment, if the immediately causal force of that injury is what all 3 cases refer to as an act of God.

I am unable to distinguish the 3 cited cases from that which is before us. Nor is any member of the Court. All agree that the lightning bolt which struck the barn and killed Mr. Klawinski came from above, out of that "violent wind and rain storm" to which the respondent industrial board referred in its findings of fact (pp. 644, 645, 152 N.W. 213).[2] The legal result would have been the same, under *Klawinski*, had that "violent wind and rain storm" blown the barn down upon Mr. Klawinski with fatal effect....

... I do not believe that *Klawinski, Nelson* and *Kroon* were settled right. It seems to me that if it is shown that a workman is engaged in the course of his employment when he is stricken violently from on High, whether by windstorm, hurricane, tornado, typhoon, cloudburst resulting in a flash flood, or say an earthquake, then whatever disabling or fatal injury is sustained by him has arisen out of his employment as well as in the course thereof.

The very fact that the workman is engaged in the course of his employment, literally doing the work assigned to him by the employer in the place or under the circumstances designated by such employer, is sufficient to establish that he was stricken "out of" that employment.

[JUSTICE BLACK concludes that he will vote with the opinion of JUSTICE T.G. KAVANAGH, but stresses that he would prefer a "declaration of overrulement of *Klawinski, Nelson,* and *Kroon*, effective for application to like claims for workmen's compensation arising after this date...."]

NOTES

(1) What does Justice T.G. Kavanagh mean in *Whetro* when he says it is "no longer necessary to establish a relationship of proximate causality"? What "causal connection" requirement is left?

Could Whetro's case be effectively distinguished from Emery's?

(2) What does Chief Justice Brennan mean by "fault" in his *Whetro* opinion?

(3) What defense, if any, does Justice T.G. Kavanagh leave for employers whose employees die while physically on the job? Would he allow compensation for the

---

2. I agree fully with Justice T. G. Kavanagh when he says "We are unable to accept the distinction drawn between a tornado and bolt of lightning when viewed as the cause of (his) injury." That is the very reason why I find myself bound to follow the *Klawinski, Nelson* and *Kroon* cases.

death of a candy company employee caused by eating peanut butter from a jar that was sitting on a shelf, into which rat poison had been placed? Cf. *Roos v. Loft, Inc.*, 247 A.D. 842, 286 N.Y.S. 360 (1936). What about a fatal heart attack suffered by an employee who was eating lunch, when there was no indication at all of strain during his morning's work?

If one accepts the result achieved by Justice T.G. Kavanagh's opinion in Emery's case, is there any reason one should oppose legislative proposals for 24-hour accident compensation for employees, funded by assessments on employers?

(4) What was the problem of jurisprudence that troubled Justice Black in *Whetro*? Is prospective overruling the most desirable solution in this kind of case? What about overruling that is prospective with the exception that recovery is granted for claimant in the case in which the court changes the law? Should it make a difference as to what judicial technique is used in overruling decisions that the case is a tort suit or an action under a statutory compensation scheme?

SOME CONCLUDING QUESTIONS

(1) On balance, does workers' compensation appear to be the best solution for the problem to which it is directed? Would it be better to move workers' compensation more in the direction of the tort system, or more towards a broad social insurance solution? Do any of the cases that you have read in this section weigh significantly in your answer to these questions? Remember that as the main body of workers' compensation cases go, these decisions present relatively unusual legal problems.

(2) How would you rank, in terms of priorities, the goals the law should have in dealing with the problem of workplace injuries?

§ 17.03 Medical Maloccurrences

INJURY IN THE HOSPITAL: STATISTICS ON INJURIES IN THE COURSE OF MEDICAL CARE

Hospitals can be unsafe places. This has been the lesson of a number of studies of injuries occurring in the course of medical care. A much cited document has been the Harvard Medical Practice Study, which reviewed 31,000 randomly chosen hospital records in New York State in 1984.[1]

The investigators in the Harvard study concluded that the "statewide incidence rate of adverse events" in the course of hospital care was 3.7 out of every 100 hospital admissions, with "the rate of adverse events due to negligence" being 1.0 percent. They thus found that "[t]he percentage of adverse events due to negligence was 27.6 percent." The raw statistics indicated that "of the 2,671,863 patients discharged from acute care hospitals in New York State in 1984, there were 98,609 adverse events and 27,179 adverse events due to negligence."[2]

---

1. Troyen Brennan, et al., Incidence of Adverse Events and Negligence in Hospitalized Patients, 324 N. Eng. J. Med. 370 (1991).
2. *Id.* at 371.

Review of these files indicated that in that year, negligence had been the cause of "6895 deaths and 877 cases of permanent and total disability." The investigators opined that "[u]nder the tort system, all of these could have led to successful litigation." Cautioning that they "could not measure all negligent acts, and made no attempt to, but measured only those that led to injury," the investigators observed that "[m]edical records are probably a poor source of information on negligence that does not cause injury" and pointed out that their data "reflect not the amount of negligence, but only its consequences."[3]

These statistics largely replicated past data, and have been dramatically augmented by a later, heavily publicized study. The Harvard researchers noted that up to that time the "only other large-scale effort to estimate the incidence of iatrogenic injury"—that is, injury in the course of medical care—was a study by the California Medical Association. That study found an overall rate of 4.6 percent of "potentially compensable events," a category analogous to the "adverse events" classification in the Harvard study, with a negligence rate of 0.8 percent.[4]

In late 1999, the Institute of Medicine, a part of the National Academy of Sciences, released a study that, as summarized in a press report, "suggest[ed] that medical errors kill 44,000 to 98,000 people a year."[5] A press summary observed that although "these numbers were previously known in the world of health care," the prestige of the academy had contributed to a "galvanizing effect," producing calls for action to revamp the health care system.[6]

ISSUES CONCERNING "REFORM": OVERVIEW

Towards a Jurisprudence of Injury 11-25 to 11-38
(A.B.A. 1984, M. Shapo Rptr.)*

. . .

In a way unparalleled in many areas of endeavor which generate tort actions, this branch of the law features a poignant connection between the nature of the defendant's activity and the character of the plaintiff's injury: the typical allegation is that in attempting to heal, the physician has created further health problems. This linkage has a counterpart in the concerns which have been voiced about the direction of medical malpractice law. In responding to the burdens caused by individual injuries, it is asserted, the law has produced costs of its own which may prove detrimental to the overall welfare of those who need medical care.

. . .

Legislative changes. The "malpractice problem," both real and perceived, led many state legislatures, principally in the nineteen seventies, to adopt several kinds of rules which change the common law in ways designed to reduce liability costs. These efforts at reform have spanned substance and practice, as well as limits on the personal liability

---

3. *Id.* at 373.

4. *Id.*

5. Robert Pear, *Group Asking U.S. for New Vigilance in Patient Safety*, N.Y. TIMES, Nov. 30, 1999, at 1 & jump.

6. Peter T. Kilborn, *Ambitious Effort to Cut Mistakes in U.S. Hospitals*, N.Y. TIMES, Dec. 26, 1999, at 1, 14.

* Copyright © 1984 The American Bar Association. Reprinted by permission.

of physicians and other providers of health care. Some laws have sought to decrease the quantum of damages by eliminating the "ad damnum" clause, in which the plaintiff's attorney names a dollar amount for the claim. One other specific effort to hold down damage figures has been the enactment of provisions reducing tort awards by the amount of collateral sources received by plaintiffs.

Several medical malpractice statutes have dealt with substantive rules of law. One group of statutes has sought to clarify the rules of "informed consent," for example by "creating a presumption in favor of a written consent which meets specified statutory criteria." A related kind of rule requires patients claiming guarantees of cure to prove them by a written document. Other provisions bearing on the substantive law have modified or eliminated the doctrine of *res ipsa loquitur* in medical cases.

Many of these laws have made statutes of limitations more favorable to physicians, for example by restricting rules which permit patients to plead that they did not discover malpractice for a time after it occurred. Other states have adopted specific, relatively short statutes of limitations for malpractice cases.

Some legislatures have restricted the amounts payable for contingent fees, limiting attorneys to flat rates of compensation diminishing in proportion to the amount of recovery. Florida has enacted a statute requiring the unsuccessful party in a malpractice case to pay a reasonable attorney's fee to the winner.

Responding to allegations of systematic inefficiency, many states have passed laws to change the process of resolving medical malpractice claims. These statutes have included provisions for both voluntary and compulsory screening panels, and some permit the parties to choose arbitration.

. . .

Alternative approaches compared.... After analyzing the malpractice question in particular..., we suggest that in our blemished world, the tort system remains the best legal foundation for dealing with medical maloccurrences. Some of our reasons appear on consideration of widely varying alternative solutions. On the one hand, as Schwartz and Komesar argue, Professor Epstein's "contractarian" approach[34] to medical malpractice "neglects the basic problem" that "the consumer of medical services, more than the consumer of most goods and services, lacks the information and sophistication needed for bargaining."[35] On the other hand, referring to the contrasting alternative of "no-fault," Schwartz and Komesar point out that "[i]t is not clear how great the real savings" under such a system would be. Indeed, they contend, a no-fault regime might encourage the practice of "defensive medicine" — often taxed to the tort system — "because the physician would be liable for any bad outcome and would thus gain maximum protection from highly redundant safeguards."[36]

Benefits of tort system. After considering both knowns and unknowns of the law of medical malpractice, we believe the tort approach provides a significant, and necessary, deterrent against incompetent and careless rendition of medical services. It also confers intangible benefits, for example in citizen perceptions of the justice of imposing liability on those culpably responsible for injuries. If the tort system offers these benefits imper-

---

34. *See, e.g.,* Epstein, *Medical Malpractice: The Case for Contract,* 1876 A.B. Found. Research J. 87.

35. W. Schwartz & N. Komesar, [Doctors, Damages and Deterrence: An Economic View of Medical Malpractice (Rand, R2340-NIH/RC 1978)], at 18.

36. *Id.* at 19.

fectly, we find no evidence that alternative general approaches would be superior either in producing cost-effective medical care or in generating just results.

The experimentation of state legislatures with discrete modifications of the common law of medical malpractice impresses us as a more sensible approach than efforts to achieve comprehensive solutions. Like citizens at large, some of us would quarrel with particular enacted changes, but we believe the process of state experimentation is consonant with the values of decentralized decision making which we commend in this Report.

Dollar limitations: A case in point. We do counsel caution about the adoption of even particularized legislative solutions to questions basically amenable to common law judging. Illustrative of the reasons for our wariness are provisions limiting dollar recoveries in malpractice cases. We are cognizant of the cost pressures that have driven legislatures to enact this kind of limitation. Yet many large awards for medical malpractice represent costs that historically have been judged as being rationally convertible into dollars. Schwartz and Komesar have pointed out that in cases of catastrophic medical injury, "the effect on life style is enormous, and a jury properly assesses the loss as a real injury that can only be compensated monetarily."[37]

We do not mean to suggest that it is beyond the power of legislatures, or representative of unwise legislative judgment, to set such ceilings in order to achieve urgent social goals, such as reducing the overall cost of health care. We emphasize, however, the need to consider the effects of medical carelessness as true costs of the system, and the efficacy of tort litigation in controlling those costs. If statutory dollar maximums reflect an implicit premise that malpractice awards are particularly openhanded and that they carry unwarranted assumptions of medical affluence, the facts deserve to be confronted. If health care costs are in fact closely tied to affluence, including the affluence of health care providers, tort law may provide rational control indeed.

. . .

Troyen A. Brennan & Donald A. Berwick, *New Rules: Regulation, Markets, and the Quality of American Health Care* 188–94, 196–97 (1996)*

... [C]laims rates and premiums leveled off in the late 1970s and early 1980s. But tort reform does not necessarily promote better-quality care; just the opposite may be true. Insofar as these reforms reduced claims rates, they also reduced the deterrent effect associated with malpractice litigation, in theory thereby increasing the number of medical injuries due to substandard care.

Some might argue that to the extent that it reduces the anger and emotional suffering that characterize physician attitudes toward medical malpractice, tort reform may induce the profession to undertake more thoroughgoing quality improvement efforts. However, there is no empirical basis for this suggestion, and even the conceptual argument does not seem strong. Of course, there is also little empirical evidence of a deterrent effect associated with tort litigation. The theory of deterrence would have it that increased malpractice claims create economic incentives that in turn lead to reduced rates of medical injury. Most of the evidence on this issue derives from the Harvard Medical

---

37. *Id.* at 11.
* Reprinted by permission of Troyen A. Brennan & Donald A. Berwick.

Practice Study. Though some publications from that study, including some coauthored by Troyen Brennan, have suggested that there may be a deterrent effect, in the final analysis, there is no statistically significant evidence of deterrence. Therefore the entire role of malpractice in the regulation of the quality of care must be assessed.

In any case, claims rates again began to rise in the mid-1980s. This led to greater proliferation of the tort reforms discussed above, as many more states enacted mandatory collateral source offsets, screening panels, mandatory periodic payment, and changes in attorney fees. More states also began simply to cap awards.... In 1975, the California legislature had put a cap of $250,000 on noneconomic damages, a provision that was subsequently found to be constitutional. During the same year, Indiana limited recovery for any injury or death of a patient to $500,000. These efforts to limit or cap total awards were little emulated until the crisis of the mid-1980s; between 1985 and 1987, another twenty-one states adopted such caps.

Once in place in almost fifty states, various packages of tort reform had significant effect. Epidemiological studies have demonstrated that changes in liability rules are associated with deflation in claims rates and premiums. At an aggregate level, claims rates across the country showed significant deflation, with overall claims per one hundred physicians per year decreasing from a high of nearly seventeen in 1987 to a low of eleven in 1991.

The success of tort reform has been the dominant story in malpractice litigation over the past twenty years. It continues unabated in the mid-1990s....

The commitment to tort reform, both at the state and at the federal level, is difficult to understand in light of the available empirical evidence on medical injury and malpractice litigation. Research studies suggest that medical injuries are very common, leading to extraordinary levels of disability and even death. However, only one in seven of negligent medical injuries gives rise to a medical malpractice claim. Hence one can hardly make a case that there is overclaiming by injured patients. Though research reveals that many claims are brought in cases in which there is no negligence or injury, other evidence suggests that the medical malpractice system does a relatively good job of distinguishing meritorious and nonmeritorious claims. With most of the enormous costs of injury now borne by health insurers and disability insurers, one could imagine that the country's reaction might be to increase malpractice litigation rather than restrict it.

But this conundrum simply emphasizes the fundamentally peculiar role that malpractice litigation plays in health care. Physicians are so emotionally devastated when they are sued that professional organizations tend to make reduction of malpractice litigation a primary policy goal. The suffering described by physicians, both in their responses to specific questions and in the language they use to describe the system of malpractice litigation, is far out of proportion to any financial repercussions of a suit. The greater part of academic legal analysis of tort law focuses on financial incentives, but in malpractice cases, the emotional impact appears to be even greater.

In fact, most physicians do not understand malpractice litigation as part of the overall system of quality improvement or as a remedy for social concerns about prevalence of medical injuries. Instead, they continue to approach medical injury, and the much less frequent malpractice claim, as a random event, a "bolt of lightning." In most cases, risk management, or coping with claims after an injury has occurred, is distinguished both organizationally and conceptually from any efforts at quality assurance or quality improvement. Malpractice has been carefully fenced off from rational quality assurance that physicians or hospitals might undertake. That is why quality improvement and malpractice litigation, even in the academic literature, are so rarely mentioned in the same breath....

Under traditional medical malpractice law, the physician was the sole target of liability. Doctrines of the fellow servant and of charitable immunity made it difficult to sue nurses and hospitals. These points of law, however, eventually fell into desuetude. More important, the tort doctrines of *apparent* and *ostensible authority*, subsets of the more generic concept of *agency liability*, slowly made their way into malpractice litigation. In most of tort law, employers are liable for the negligence of their employees. As most physicians are independent contractors with hospitals, agency liability is not applicable. However, in cases of negligence by physicians who bear a closer relationship to the hospital—for instance, physicians employed in emergency departments or as radiologists, anesthesiologists, or pathologists—it is possible, through an apparent or ostensible authority doctrine, to hold the hospital liable.

In holding a hospital liable, one begins to treat malpractice not as the individual moral fault of a particular physician but as a systemic issue to be addressed by the organization. Once the move is made from individual liability to organizational liability, the potential for use of modern methods of quality improvement is open. Presumably, for instance, a hospital would be able to evaluate its risk for medical injuries, an analysis that is radically different from an individual physician's inquiries into aspects of isolated cases. Tort litigation can be transformed into rational regulatory incentives when the frame of reference is deficiencies in repetitive processes of care. The shift is from individual instances to analysis of the system as a whole.

* * *

The fact that the common law has tarried at the doorstep of hospital responsibility for medical injuries has not chilled the interest of some academic observers in full-blown *enterprise liability* in medical care. Enterprise liability would involve making hospitals or other institutions assume all the liability for medical malpractice....

* * *

NOTES

(1) What are the principal benefits that the present law of medical malpractice provides to society? What costs does the present system inflict, and on whom?

(2) To which evils are the following sorts of reforms addressed, and how well do you think the particular reforms would correct the problems at which they are targeted?

    (a) A reduction of tort awards by the amount of collateral sources received, including payments from medical and hospitalization insurers, as well as from other payors than the defendant.

    (b) Dollar caps on the total amount of damages.

    (c) Dollar caps on pain and suffering awards.

    (d) Limitations on the doctrine of informed consent.

    (e) Elimination or modification of the application of the doctrine of *res ipsa loquitur* in medical cases.

(3) Another avenue of attack on medical liability law has been legislation to limit attorneys' fees. Would you vote for a statutory limitation on lawyers' fees in medical mal-

practice cases? Why should legislatures constrain fee arrangements for plaintiffs' lawyers in medical malpractice cases any more than they should for plaintiffs' lawyers in suits for attorney malpractice? Suits for products injuries? Litigation over commercial contracts?

(4) Speaking generally, does it seem more desirable to focus financial responsibility for medical maloccurrences on individual providers, or on health care institutions?

(5) Again speaking generally, should the principal basis for awarding compensation for medical injuries continue to be fault, or should American jurisdictions adopt a no-fault solution? Read on.

A Proposed Alternative to the Civil Justice System for Resolving Medical Liability Disputes: A Fault-Based, Administrative System

ii–vii (Specialty Society Medical Liability Project,
American Medical Association, 1988)*

Because the existing judicial system is not entirely fair either to patients or physicians and is not an effective or efficient method of medical liability dispute resolution, it is reasonable to consider whether an alternative could be developed which would be fairer and more efficient. However, the system of trial by jury has strong historical roots in this country and there are significant constitutional and political limitations on the range of alternatives to the civil justice system that can be implemented even on a limited basis. In particular, there must be a meaningful *quid pro quo* provided to patients in order to justify withdrawing their claims from the jury system as there is in no-fault automobile and workers compensation systems.

The Medical Liability Project does not suggest a general rejection of the tort system, nor does it advocate the abandonment of traditional tort reform. However, the Project has concluded that a persuasive case can be made for employing on an experimental basis an administrative alternative to the tort system for resolving medical liability disputes....

The Claims Resolution Function

The administrative system for adjudicating medical liability can be divided into three parts: (1) the pre-hearing and initial hearing stage; (2) the final decision of the Board; and (3) judicial review. The proposed system would provide a significant benefit to patients by making available to any patient who has a claim of reasonable merit an experienced attorney from the Medical Board's general counsel's office who will litigate the claim on behalf of the patient free of charge.

Under proposed pre-hearing procedures, claims reviewers from the Medical Board will quickly evaluate claims and dismiss those without merit. For claims with merit, the claims reviewers will submit the matter to an expert in the same field as the health care provider. The expert will review the claim and make a judgment as to whether it has merit. The claims reviewer also will assist the patient in evaluating the claim and any settlement offers.

If the claim is not settled, it will be assigned to one of the Medical Board's hearing examiners. In order to encourage reasonable and timely settlements, blind settlement offers by the parties will be required prior to a hearing. A party would be subject to sanctions if the outcome of the case is not an improvement over a settlement offer that the party has rejected. The hearing examiner also will oversee expedited discovery and ensure that the parties have valid expert evidence available to support their case. At the hearing itself, the examiner will have broad authority to conduct the proceedings, including authority to call an independent expert to provide assistance in deciding the case. The hearing examiner will be required to render a written decision within 90 days of the hearing. In that decision, the hearing examiner will determine whether the health care provider is liable for the claimant's injury and, if so, will determine the size of the damage award.

The hearing examiner's decision will be subject to review by the Medical Board. The Board will have discretion to award fees and costs incurred in an appeal if the appeal presented no substantial question. The Medical Board will hear these cases as an appellate body in panels of three members. The Medical Board will make a full independent determination whether the health care provider's conduct was inadequate and caused the claimant's injury. Appeal from the Medical Board's decision will be to the intermediate appellate court of the state, where the review will be limited to whether the Board acted contrary to statute or the Board's own rules.

. . .

In addition to acting as an adjudicator of medical liability claims, the Medical Board also will develop rules and substantive guidelines to complement the statutory standards....

The Performance Monitoring Function

1. In conjunction with its expanded authority to handle medical liability claims, the Board's performance monitoring function will be strengthened. Specifically, all settlements and awards based on medical liability will be reported to the Board's investigative branch. This does not mean that every or even many liability determinations will lead to disciplinary actions. What it means is that every liability determination will give rise to an initial screening of the physician's practices as reported to the Medical Board. The primary purpose of this endeavor, as with all performance monitoring, will be education and rehabilitation....

2. In conjunction with the proposals for monitoring physician performance by the Medical Board, our proposal calls for enactment of three categories of changes designed to further strengthen physician credentialing. First, reporting requirements will be increased by requiring hospitals and other health care institutions to conduct periodic physician performance reviews (a modified version of those required by the Joint Commission on the Accreditation of Healthcare Organizations) and to report to the Medical Board any conclusions that a physician's performance has been substandard. Insurers will be required to report cancellations and failures to renew for reasons that are not class based. All physicians will be required to report instances of suspected incompetence, impairment, or drug or alcohol dependence to the hospital credentials committee or other credentialing entity. In order to facilitate physician reporting, the state will provide immunity to physicians who report suspected problems in good faith. All of these reporting requirements are designed to increase substantially the amount of information available on physician performance.

Second, this information must be maintained in a form that is accessible to those who conduct professional review activities under the proposed system. To facilitate this process, the Medical Board will create and maintain a clearinghouse (or utilize the one established pursuant to the Health Care Quality Improvement Act of 1986) for reports from insurers, reports from hospitals and other entities and disciplinary actions taken by other states....

Finally, the Project calls for the furtherance of quality assurance/risk protection goals by requiring all physicians to complete a number of continuing medical education "credit hours" per year....

In addition to the settlements and awards that are automatically reported, performance complaints—from hospitals, physicians, the public or employees of the Medical Board—will be sent to a claims reviewer at the Board for investigation. As with claims of medical liability, the claims reviewer will evaluate these complaints and, if appropriate, make a recommendation to the Board's general counsel's office to pursue complaints that appear meritorious. A member of the general counsel's office will then make a decision whether to initiate a disciplinary charge. Once a disciplinary charge is initiated, a member of the general counsel's office will prosecute the charge before a hearing examiner who, after an appropriate due process proceeding, will make a decision as to what, if any, action is appropriate. The examiner's action is subject to review by the Board, which is required to provide notice of any disciplinary action to credentialing entities, insurers and other state Medical Boards.

The Structure of the Board

In order to perform the complex and sensitive functions outlined above, the existing Medical Boards will be restructured or a new agency will be created. Membership on the Board will have to become full time, probably for a five year term. Members will be selected by the governor—from a list of nominees selected by a nominating committee—and approved by the legislature. The Project recommends a seven-person Board, of which at least two but no more than three members are physicians. It is also crucial that the Medical Board members be widely recognized as experienced and neutral, and that they be committed to attempting a bold new approach to the problems of medical negligence. To ensure the Board's quality, all of its employees, from claims reviewers to hearing examiners, must be selected and retained on the basis of their ability and commitment to resolving claims efficiently and fairly.

...

The Legal Elements of Medical Liability

...

The rules governing standard of care based on custom and locality would be abolished in favor of a standard that focuses on whether the challenged actions fall within a range of reasonableness, to be determined by reference to the standards of a prudent and competent practitioner in the same or similar circumstances. The hearing examiner would be required to consider a variety of factors in determining the range of reasonableness, including the expertise of and means available to the health care provider, the state of medical knowledge, the availability of facilities and access to transportation and communication facilities. With respect to proof of liability, the statute also would set standards for evidentiary matters such as the qualifications of experts, the use of manufacturer's instructions on drugs and medical devices and the use of medical literature.

A significant modification in the causation standard is also proposed. Traditionally, recovery has been denied unless the physician was at least 50% responsible for the patient's loss. The causation standard would be modified to allow recovery if the physician's negligence was a "contributing factor" in causing the injury. Damages under this standard would be apportioned according to the physician's degree of fault.

The informed consent doctrine would be codified under the current "minority" rule which requires that the adequacy of the disclosure should be measured from the perspective of the reasonable patient. The privilege to withhold information (for therapeutic reasons) and standards for determining individual responsibility for disclosure also would be included in the statutory "informed consent" doctrine.

In the area of damages, non-economic damages (and punitive damages) would be capped at an amount that is tied to a percentage of the average annual wage in the state. Special damages would be awarded under a series of guidelines designed to ensure that those damages represent a realistic "replacement cost." ...

The rule of joint and several liability would be abolished so that defendants would be liable for damages only in proportion to their actual liability. In addition, any award of future damages, where the present value of such damages exceeds $250,000, would be made in accordance with a periodic payment schedule. Finally, damages generally would be reduced by collateral source payments.

NOTES

(1) What are the best arguments for and against the A.M.A.'s proposed administrative system for medical cases?

Dr. Sidney Wolfe, director of Public Citizen Health Research Group, called the plan "reckless and dangerous for patients." Wolfe declared that the scheme would "greatly reduce the amount of money" that injury claimants could recover, and concluded, "It's unimaginable how this would be a benefit to any patient at all." Schmidt, *AMA Proposal Would Limit Malpractice Awards*, WASH. POST, Jan. 14, 1988, at A23. Putting aside the question of whether the AMA plan would violate the constitutional right to jury trial, do you perceive it as providing a net benefit to society?

(2) Research has shown that a majority of injured patients are never compensated. A summary of the difficulties in the medical liability system identified, among other things, "random claiming behavior, unpredictable jury verdicts, and different (often conflicting) incentives among participants." Tort reform that simply limits recovery conserves costs, but does little to expand the pool of compensated victims. At the same time, however, a no-fault system with reduced administrative costs does not save money when the volume of potential claimants is fully realized—unless the amount of compensation is simultaneously reduced. Reform under these conditions has been described as charting "a course between the Scylla of undue access constraint and the Charybdis of system expense." David Studdert, *et al.*, *Can the United States Afford a "No-Fault" System of Compensation for Medical Injury?*, 60 LAW & CONTEMP. PROBS. 1, 2–3, 17–18 (Spring 1997).

Studdert and his colleagues, examining data from Utah and Colorado, showed that a no-fault system based on a Swedish system could compensate injury more efficaciously than the existing negligence system. The Swedish model compensates injury that "could have been avoided"—a standard more relaxed than negligence, but more stringent than all-inclusive liability. Compensating "all Swedish events" in Utah would cost $90.9 million, more than the state medical malpractice system cost of $25–30 million and more than malpractice insurance premiums of $55–60 million. However, if one omitted from calculations the first four weeks of disability, capped pain and suffering at $100,000, excluded household production, and discounted wage replacement to sixty-six percent, that would reduce the Utah costs to a more modest $54.9 million. Moreover, the reformed system would compensate 1465 patients, considerably more than the 210 to 240 successful claimants under the existing system. *Id.* at 28, 31–32.

Consider the proposals just summarized as well as any other terms you might suggest. What terms do you find more or less reasonable? More or less objectionable? Consider in particular the use of deductibles; threshold periods; disability thresholds; minimum periods of hospitalization; awards for pain and suffering; compensation discounts; and whether or not to compensate for household production losses.

(3) The Virginia and Florida no-fault medical plans, which are limited to "newborns with severe neurological impairments," are administered by those states' workers' compensation commissions. Two researchers report on a survey of these plans:

> ... [Obstetricians' malpractice] [p]remiums in Florida and Virginia decreased after no-fault, both absolutely and relative to the national average, which showed smaller declines in this quiescent period following the last medical malpractice crisis in the mid-1980s. The cut in annual liability premiums was substantially larger than the annual assessment for BIF [the Virginia Birth Injury Fund—Ed.] or NICA [Florida's Neurological Injury Compensation Association—Ed.]....
>
> By directly affecting a small number of cases of relatively high severity and high volatility, a much larger objective of insurance market stability was achieved. Further, both programs operated successfully, collecting premiums and resolving claims with non-tort process. This achievement should not be minimized, in light of the assertions by no-fault detractors who doubted the technical feasibility of defining compensable events in advance then paying them without high levels of disputation.
>
> ...
>
> As a liability insurance reform, the reforms have created substantial tort protection and lowered premiums for almost all obstetricians in the two states. However, they have in the process delivered very little new compensatory no-fault coverage to patients because so few claims have been filed or compensated, far fewer than anticipated, although above comparable tort rates of earlier years. Low no-fault claiming rates appear to result from poor information among patients and even lawyers, little outreach by programs, hostility among knowledgeable claimant attorneys, and the apparent ease of making tort claims in court, despite the statutes' intended exclusive no-fault administrative programs.
>
> ...

—Randall R. Bovbjerg & Frank A. Sloan, *No-Fault for Medical Injury: Theory and Evidence*, 67 U. CINC. L. REV. 53, 99–100, 102 (1998).

(4) How do you think that patients and physicians in the United States would respond to a medical no-fault system?

(5) Would you provide a tort option to a medical no-fault system? How would you structure the choice that claimants must make between the two?

§ 17.04 Social Insurance Solutions: An Introduction

Like a rainbow, the social insurance solution to personal injuries shines brightly for some commentators who decry the costs of litigation and the numbers of injury victims who go undercompensated or who receive no compensation at all.

The excerpt below poses the question of whether the best solution to this aspect of the injury problem would be to supplant the tort system entirely with legislation that fully defines the basic terms and conditions of compensation for personal injury. The first thoroughgoing solution of that sort adopted in the democratic world is the New Zealand Accident Compensation Act. As you read the material, ask whether the New Zealand solution would transplant well to the United States. If you think not, can you sketch a home-grown product that would serve American needs more effectively, while doing away with the tort system?

Richard Miller, *An Analysis and Critique of the 1992 Changes to New Zealand's Accident Compensation Scheme*
52 MD. L. REV. 1070 (1993)*

Because of alleged deficiencies in the tort system as a means of dealing with personal injury accidents in the United States, there continues to be great interest in New Zealand's no-fault accident compensation scheme as a possible alternative.

The New Zealand scheme, first adopted in 1972, provided benefits — without requiring any proof of fault — to persons suffering "injury by accident."[3] These benefits included medical and rehabilitative expenses, compensation for eighty percent of lost earnings as long as disability continued, and lump-sum payments of up to $27,000(N.Z.) for non-economic losses, as well as other necessary expenses. The most significant feature of the scheme, however, was that where it provided "cover" — where a person suffered "injury by accident" — the right to bring a civil action in tort for damages was abolished.

The New Zealand scheme has been described by W.F. Birch, New Zealand's Minister of Labour, as "one of the world's most advanced schemes for compensating the victims of accidents...." But the current New Zealand government, a National rather than a Labour government, has imposed what Minister Birch characterizes as "the most radical reforms to the accident compensation scheme since it first provided cover in 1974." Most of these reforms took effect when the Accident Rehabilitation and Compensation Act of 1992 went into force on July 1, 1992.[8]

It is the purpose of this paper to describe the more significant changes made by the National government to New Zealand's accident compensation scheme and to analyze their likely effects.

---

  3. Accident Compensation Act, 1982, No. 181, 1982 N.Z. Stat. 1552 [hereinafter 1982 Act] (consolidating and amending the 1972 Accident Compensation Act and its amendments).
  8. Accident Rehabilitation and Compensation Insurance Act 1992, No. 13 [hereinafter 1992 Act].

First, however, it is important to note the clearly identifiable change in the underlying philosophy of the accident compensation scheme. Justice Owen Woodhouse, who may rightly be called the Father of the New Zealand accident compensation scheme, identified the basic principle of the original program as community or collective — as opposed to individual — responsibility. In his view, the scheme reflected a concept of social insurance; it was not a private insurance scheme.

By contrast, the present government considers the new Act to be a scheme of accident insurance, including premiums to be paid by individuals who will benefit under the program. This important philosophical change is reflected in the title of the new Act, the Accident Rehabilitation and Compensation Insurance Act of 1992, and in the new name of the former Accident Compensation Corporation, the governmental body that operates the scheme: the Accident Rehabilitation and Compensation Insurance Corporation. It is also reflected in another change of language: Charges against those who must pay for the scheme, formally referred to as "levies," are now explicitly called "premiums."[13]

I. The Right to Bring a Common-Law Action

As in the prior law, the most important feature of the new Act is that civil tort actions for compensatory damages for covered personal injuries are abolished. Importantly, however, as under the 1982 Act, a victim is not precluded from bringing a civil tort action for damages with respect to injuries not covered by the scheme;[15] therefore, a rule or court decision of no coverage opens the door to a possible claim for damages under the common law of torts.

II. Coverage

The prior Act covered "personal injury by accident," which was defined to include: "the physical and mental consequences of any such injury or of the accident"; "medical, surgical, dental, or first aid misadventure," otherwise undefined; "incapacity resulting from an occupational disease or industrial deafness," as more specifically defined; and "actual bodily harm (including pregnancy and mental or nervous shock)" arising from acts or omissions that fit the description of certain sexual crimes.

An important difference in the new Act is the apparent exclusion of cover for mental distress not associated with physical injury to the person seeking cover.[22] This exclusion may result in denial of cover of injuries from intentional or negligent infliction of emotional distress.

Perhaps the most radical change to coverage is the extent to which the Act now seeks to define coverage for harm caused by the acts or omissions of health care professionals. While the former Act merely stated that personal injury by accident included "medical, surgical, dental, or first aid misadventure," without further definition, the new Act includes a definition of medical misadventure spanning nearly two pages.[24] The result is

---

13. See 1992 Act, supra note 8, § 134. Section 134 reads, "Levies paid or payable under the Accident Compensation Act 1982 shall be deemed to be premiums paid or payable for the purposes of this Act."

15. Civil actions at law to recover punitive or exemplary damages for outrageous conduct are still permitted.

22. The new Act states that "[f]or the purposes of this Act, 'personal injury' means the death of, or physical injuries to, a person, and any mental injury suffered by that person which is an outcome of those physical injuries to that person...." 1992 Act, supra note 8, § 4(1)....

24. The Act states:

    (1) For the purposes of this Act, —

    "Medical error" means the failure of a registered health professional to observe a standard of care and skill reasonably to be expected in the circumstances. It is not medical

that in cases in which claimants seek compensation for "medical misadventure," proceedings are likely to turn into actions to prove medical negligence or malpractice.

III. Benefits

A. Retention of Earnings-Related Compensation

Under the new Act, there have been significant changes in benefits. Nonetheless, it should be noted that earnings-related compensation, measured as eighty percent of lost earnings, remains in place. Further, as in the former Act, the employer pays for the first week of benefits if the injury is a work injury, and the Accident Corporation pays for all earners' injuries, on or off the job, after the first week. The maximum amount payable as compensation for loss of earnings is $1,179(N.Z.)—about $650(U.S.)—per week.[30]

B. Elimination of Lump Sums for Non-Economic Losses

Perhaps the most important and controversial change—from the viewpoint of employees and labor unions—is the elimination of lump-sum payments for non-economic losses. The 1982 Act allowed lump-sum payments of up to $17,000 for permanent loss or impairment of bodily function, and lump-sum payments of up to $10,000 for loss "of amenities or capacity for enjoying life, including loss from disfigurement; and ... pain and suffering, including nervous shock and neurosis." Together, these items

---

error solely because desired results are not achieved or because subsequent events show that different decisions might have produced better results:

"Medical misadventure" means personal injury resulting from medical error or medical mishap:

"Medical mishap" means an adverse consequence of treatment by a registered health professional, properly given, if—

    (a) The likelihood of the adverse consequence of the treatment occurring is rare; and

    (b) The adverse consequence of the treatment is severe.

(2) For the purposes of the definition of the term "medical mishap", the likelihood that treatment of the kind that occurred would have the adverse consequence shall be rare only if the probability is that the adverse consequence would not occur in more than 1 percent of cases where that treatment is given.

(3) Where the likelihood that an injury would occur is in the ordinary course rare, but is not rare having regard to the circumstances of the particular person, it shall not be medical mishap if the greater risk to the particular person injured—

    (a) Was known to that person; or

    (b) In the case of a person who does not have legal capacity, was known to that person's parent, legal guardian, or welfare guardian, as the case may be,

—prior to the treatment.

...

(5) Medical misadventure does not include personal injury arising from abnormal reaction of a patient or later complication arising from treatment procedures unless medical misadventure occurred at the time of the procedure.

(6) A failure to obtain informed consent to treatment from the person on whom the treatment is performed or that person's parent, legal guardian, or welfare guardian, as the case may be, is medical misadventure only if the registered health professional acted negligently in failing to obtain informed consent.

(7) Medical misadventure does not include a failure to diagnose correctly the medical condition of any person or a failure to provide treatment unless that failure is negligent.

(8) Medical misadventure does not include any personal injury resulting from the carrying out of any drug trial or clinical trial where the injured person has agreed in writing to participate in the trial.

...

30. This maximum is subject to annual adjustments to reflect "movements in average weekly earnings." ...

constituted a significant part of the cost of the accident compensation scheme. The elimination of these non-economic losses moves the scheme away from its historical roots as a substitute for the civil tort action.

C. Provision of an Independence Allowance

In place of lump sums for non-economic losses, the new Act provides for an "independence allowance" based upon the degree of the claimant's disability, commencing not earlier than thirteen weeks after the injury for which it is paid. The allowance is $40 per week, paid quarterly, for a person with 100 percent disability, to be scaled downward, in accordance with regulations to be promulgated, for those with lesser disability. No allowance is paid to those with less than ten percent disability. Under this provision, the degree of a person's disability must be reassessed at intervals of not more than five years.

The purpose of the independence allowance, in the language of Minister of Labour Birch, is "to enable those injured to meet the additional costs arising from a permanent disability during the remainder of their li[ves]." The relatively small amount provided is designed "to cover miscellaneous expenses associated with disability." The payment is to be adjusted annually to reflect changes in the Consumer Price Index. It cannot be converted to a lump sum.

In addition to the independence allowance, additional expenses and costs for care — for purchase or modification of motor vehicles, modifying a residence, household help, childcare, and for wheelchairs and other necessary equipment or appliances — will be covered, as in the prior Act, as part of the rehabilitation of the accident victim.

D. Re-evaluation of the Permanence of Incapacity

An important change, at least from the perspectives of both moral hazard and rehabilitation, is the elimination of the provision in the former Act that prohibited reduction of the earnings-related compensation of a person determined to be permanently incapacitated. This provision was designed to encourage permanently disabled workers to seek rehabilitation, though it may have led some workers to feign permanent incapacity. Section 51 of the new Act requires periodic reassessments at intervals of not less than six months for individuals assessed at having a capacity for work of less than eighty-five percent, unless the Accident Corporation "is satisfied that no purpose would be served by a further assessment...."

E. Earnings-Related Compensation Not Allowed as a Substitute for Unemployment Compensation

Even more significant is a provision in the new law that prevents the accident compensation scheme from being used, at least after the first twelve months following the incapacity, as unemployment compensation. By virtue of section 59(2) of the former Act, claimants who were able to return to work, though not necessarily in their previous occupations, would continue to receive earnings-related compensation if there was no "appropriate" work available. In view of the serious recession in New Zealand, this provision evidently became very expensive: Minister Birch estimated that it was costing $40 million annually in recent years. Under the new Act, there is a grace period of twelve months after the incapacity has started, but if at that time the worker is determined to have a capacity for work of eighty-five percent or more, eligibility for earnings-related compensation ceases, irrespective of whether suitable employment opportunities are available.

F. Loss of Earning Capacity of Non-Earners

A feature of the prior Act that had been criticized was the treatment of non-earners who became accident victims. Children under 16 or in school or apprenticeship programs who were injured were allowed minimal earnings-related compensation based in part on lost earning capacity. But homemakers—including those who had taken time off from their profession or outside occupation to raise a family—and other non-earners were not entitled to earnings-related compensation based on their lost earning capacity. The new Act purports to deal with that problem by allowing certain persons to pay premiums to purchase the right to receive compensation for lost earning capacity in the event of an accident.[53]

G. Medical and Health Benefits

One of the problems complained of under the prior Act was that accident victims had access to expensive and often preferred private hospitals and other private medical and surgical services not available under the public health system to victims of illness. This created an incentive for doctors and patients to classify illnesses as accidents. Another problem was that patients who were charged little or nothing for their health care had little motivation or incentive to keep costs low.

Recognizing these problems, the New Zealand government has evidently inaugurated "user part charges" for publicly funded health care and required, or intends to promulgate regulations to require, accident victims to "pay user charges for pharmaceuticals, laboratory diagnostic tests and some public hospital services on the same basis as the sick," and also to require them to "pay the same targeted user charges for general practitioner visits as the sick." With regard to private hospitals and other health care providers, the Government evidently intends to increase beneficiaries' charges by reducing the maximum that the Accident Corporation can pay.

IV. Funding and Deterrence

Apart from the change of label for philosophical purposes from "levies" to "premiums," there are some significant changes wrought by the new Act both in the way that the scheme will be funded and in the way that premiums will be allocated and adjusted to internalize costs to those who cause accidents.

A. The Former Act

Under the former Act, levies on employers covered both work- and nonwork-related accidents of earners, levies on motor vehicle owners covered motor vehicle accidents, and general taxes covered accidents to non-earners. Levies on employers varied according to the past accident-cost-experience of the industrial group into which each em-

---

53. 1992 Act, supra note 8, §45. The new provision, however, seems inadequate to the task: First, it only applies to those who are or have been earners, id. §45(1), who have had 12 months of continuous employment, id. §45(2)(a), and who make the election while still employed or within a month after ceasing to be employed, id. §45(2)(b). Second, the amount to be treated as earnings must be specified, id. §45(5), and that amount may be "the weekly earnings of the person calculated under this Act as if the incapacity of the person commenced more than 5 weeks before the date of the election" or a lesser amount. Id. §45(6). Third, compensation is payable under this provision for a maximum of 5 years from the date of the incapacity, irrespective of how long the incapacity actually continues. Id. §45(8). And fourth, the amount of the premiums charged is to be determined "with the objective of there being sufficient in any year to meet the full costs of the compensation payable under this section in that year and future years for any claims made under this section in respect of personal injury suffered in that year and the costs of administration of this section in that year." Id. §45(10). A less generous provision can hardly be imagined. Certainly it offers little to compensate an injured homemaker who earned professional competence by virtue of her education but who was either working at an entry-level position when she elected to purchase the protection or, under the highly restrictive requirements of this section, could not purchase the protection at all.

ployer fell; levies on motor vehicle owners varied according to the class of vehicle. While there was authority under the former Act to engage in experience rating by awarding bonuses and assessing penalties to individual employers, this authority was not being exercised. Statutory authority to impose levies on motor vehicle drivers and to impose penalties for poor driving records was also never exercised.

B. The New Act

1. Work Injuries.—Under the new Act, employers pay premiums, again adjusted by industry class, into an employer account that covers only work injuries and certain industrial diseases, not including work-related motor vehicle injuries.[67]

2. Earners' Nonwork Injuries.—One of the most controversial features of the 1992 Act is the removal from employers of the obligation to fund employees' nonwork injuries, and the imposition on employees of the obligation to pay for insurance against such injuries.

The initial premium for non-earners is 70 cents per $100 of earnings. The new Act requires employers to withhold premiums from employees' wages and pay them into the Earners' Account.

3. Non-earners' Injuries.—Apart from a new section that permits some non-earners to pay premiums for protection against loss of earning capacity, benefits for non-earners who are injured other than in motor vehicle accidents will continue to be funded by general tax revenues.

4. Motor Vehicle Accident Injuries.—The costs of motor vehicle accidents will continue to be borne—at least in part—by motor vehicle owners, through premiums to be paid in conjunction with the annual registration and licensing of vehicles. There is, however, an interesting innovation: in order "to assist with public health costs of injuries arising from motor vehicle accidents," the government increased the tax on "motor spirit" by two cents per liter and is obligated to pay this amount to the Accident Corporation annually for the benefit of the Motor Vehicle Account. The avowed purpose of this charge is to "alert individual drivers to the real costs of accidents, especially public health costs."

5. Medical Misadventure Injuries.—In the former Act, health professionals were treated no differently from other self-employed persons, occupations, or businesses: their levies were based upon their industry class, which, in turn, was charged in accordance with the injury experience of persons working in that industry. In short, premiums were not based on the accidental harm the professional caused to patients, but on the injury experience of the professional and the professional's employees with regard to their own accidental injuries. In consequence, levies to health professionals—who are in a relatively nondangerous profession—tended to be relatively low.

The 1992 Act, however, creates a new account known as the Medical Misadventure Account. Its purpose is to finance benefits required to be paid under the new Act to vic-

---

67. Id. §§ 100, 101. A unique feature of the new Act with regard to employees' work injuries is that an employer may apply for the status of "exempt employer." Id. §§ 105–07. If the status is granted by the Accident Rehabilitation and Compensation Insurance Corporation, the exempt employer becomes, in effect, a self-insurer with regard to its employees' work injuries for a 12-month period following each such injury. Id. § 106(1). One year following the injury, the Accident Corporation assumes the obligation with respect to that employee. Id. § 106(2). The reward to an employer for becoming an exempt employer is to have its premium reduced to reflect the cost saving to the Accident Corporation. Id. § 106(3). The status of exempt employer may only be granted for one year at a time. Id. § 105(1), (2).

tims of what may be deemed medical malpractice. Premiums are to be set by classes of certified health professionals as established by regulations. Classes may include different fields of specialization, as well as different categories of health professionals. Funds to pay benefits to victims of medical misadventure are to be derived from " any premiums that may be payable by registered health professionals of the same class as the registered health professional responsible for the medical misadventure."

The upshot is that, for the first time since the advent of its accident compensation scheme, New Zealand has created a system of economic accountability to third persons — where one class of injury-causers will be charged for the costs of injuries not just to that class's employees but to other persons whom that class has injured.

6. Experience Rating and Internalizing Costs. — The new Act provides for "experience rating," which may result in "no-claims bonuses, increased premiums, or claim thresholds." Experience rating is applicable to all those from whom premiums are to be collected — employers (including self-employeds), motor vehicle owners, earners, and persons liable to pay medical misadventure premiums.[87]

With regard to premiums on employers, the New Zealand government apparently felt that experience rating would overcome the "problems of broad industry classifications" and regarded "[t]he introduction of experience rating [to be] an essential part of the change in emphasis towards an insurance scheme funded by premiums."

Apart from the fairness that might be associated with experience rating, however, there is some indication that the Government was also concerned with deterrence of accidents. Thus, for example, with regard to the assessment of a motor vehicle fuel tax, Minister Birch stated:

> While impacting on all road users, this premium is expected to have a particular impact on young drivers, especially 16- to 24-year old males. This group has a particularly high accident rate and therefore has a disproportionate effect on public health costs. They often drive vehicles owned by others, such as their parents, and this additional premium will impact on them directly when they purchase petrol.

V. Critique

...

It does appear that the scheme, although outlined in a single statute, now embodies five distinctive schemes of compensation:

First, as just described, a modest welfare scheme for injured non-earners.

Second, a fairly classical workers' compensation scheme covering accidents and industrial diseases arising out of and in the course of employment and funded almost entirely by employers....

Viewed in isolation as a separate system, ... there is nothing very exceptional about the provisions for compensation to earners for work injuries.

Third, the provisions dealing with compensation and premiums for earners' non-work injuries constitute a first-party accident insurance scheme. This scheme differs

---

87. ... While the language providing for experience rating of earners, self-employeds, motor vehicle owners, and health professionals appears to be discretionary — using the word "may" — the section dealing with experience rating of individual employers "on the basis of the actual costs of work injuries that occur in the employment of that employer" seems to be mandatory — using the word "shall." ...

from private schemes in that (1) it is mandated by the Government; (2) the coverage is relatively comprehensive, including disability income, health and other benefits, rather than just lump sums or just disability income; and (3) a government corporation stands in for the private insurers who might otherwise offer such insurance.

Fourth, the scheme with regard to motor vehicle accidents constitutes a total no-fault motor vehicle accident program. Presumably, it too will be fully funded—including public health costs—by user charges, that is, the premiums to be paid by owners and the fuel tax to be paid by drivers and owners who purchase the fuel.

Fifth, the new provisions dealing with medical misadventure seem to establish a quasi-medical-malpractice action. Under the former Act it was necessary for the claimant to establish "medical, surgical, dental, or first aid misadventure," which was not otherwise defined in the Act. As Margaret Vennell described, there has been considerable difficulty in determining what kind of acts, omissions, or other medically related misfortunes constitute medical misadventure. While judges have increasingly deemed proof of medical error amounting to a breach of the appropriate standard of care to be relevant to the question of medical misadventure in both omission-to-act and other cases, such proof was not relevant in every case. It also remained at least theoretically possible to define medical misadventure in all cases in a way that focused on the accidental nature of the injury to the victim rather than on the fault of the medical professional.

Under the new Act, however, a fault requirement has been expressly inserted into the framework of the accident compensation system. With the exception of those who claim "medical mishap," which, as restrictively defined in the Act, is likely to constitute a small minority of claims, all other medical misadventure claimants, to prevail, must establish "medical error," which essentially requires proof of negligence—that is, malpractice.

...

... One is tempted to characterize the new medical misadventure scheme as an unnatural union of fault and no-fault, grossly unfair to many victims of medical error.

There is, however, a potentially positive aspect to the new Act: the attempt to reassert accountability through experience rating. It has been my view that the former Act significantly undermined deterrence of accidents by externalizing accident costs and by eliminating from public consciousness the concept of negligence or fault with regard to personal injuries. Under the 1992 Act, experience rating is mandatory for work injuries and may be inaugurated for all other categories where premiums are required. This change reflects an intent to internalize the costs of accidents, and that intent is praiseworthy. Unfortunately, there may be insurmountable difficulties in attempting fairly to "experience rate" individual New Zealand employers, and even greater problems may arise with regard to the experience rating of individual earners. On the other hand, as is the case with motorists in the United States, premiums might profitably be increased for those motor vehicle owners whose vehicles have been involved in the violation of traffic laws.

With regard to medical misadventure, to the extent that findings of negligence are now required for recovery in cases of medical misadventure, experience rating of health professionals may be fairly imposed. Such increased premiums could serve to deter health-provider negligence. It is unfortunate, however, that the nature of the new system ... will discourage medical misadventure claims, even justified ones. Increases in premiums ... are not likely to come close to matching the actual costs of medical error.

...

VI. Conclusions

A. Fairness

The New Zealand accident compensation scheme continues to exhibit serious unfairness to non-earners. Neither the new independence allowance nor the election to purchase benefits for loss of earning capacity seem adequately to compensate non-earners who lose significant future earning capacity by reason of accident. This unfairness, as is often the case, will adversely affect women who are raising children or working at low-paying jobs, or both, at the time they suffer their accidental harm. There is also serious unfairness to claimants seeking compensation for medical error....

There is other evidence of unfairness: before the original scheme was adopted, employers were not only liable for workers' compensation but were also subject to tort actions brought by their employees and most importantly, to personal injury actions, such as products liability actions, brought by non-employees. A significant trade-off was encompassed in the original scheme. In exchange for immunity from tort actions brought by workers and others, employers would cover their workers for nonwork-related as well as work-related accidents. Further, accident victims gave up their common-law right to recover for pain and suffering, in exchange for the availability of lump-sum payments, although limited in amount. Under the new Act, however, the employee has been deprived of both the lump-sum payment and the employer's payment to cover nonwork accidents. These benefits have been replaced only by an insignificant independence allowance of up to $40(N.Z.) per week. On the other hand, employers remain exempt from both worker lawsuits and personal injury actions brought by others.

To state the dilemma more starkly, while benefits paid by employers have been significantly reduced, employers remain immune from product liability and other tort actions arising out of personal injuries to third persons. In effect, the costs of accidents negligently caused by manufacturing companies, agricultural producers, service companies, landlords, nonhealth professionals and other employers, are being subsidized both by accident victims and by workers who now pay individual premiums. This subsidy is in addition to the subsidy already provided to New Zealand employers by their immunity from personal injury tort liability. From a global perspective, New Zealand producers who participate in international markets will further increase their competitive advantage against firms from nations that allow liability claims by injured persons.

...

C. Accident Policy

From a policy perspective, ... applying political labels is not nearly as significant as the extent to which the new scheme serves or disserves important values. In the case of an accident compensation scheme, well-being is clearly the primary value. Well-being may be served in two ways: (1) by compensating accident victims and (2) by preventing and deterring accidents.

1. Compensation.—With regard to earnings-related compensation—that is, income replacement for earners—the new Act seems to provide compensation in about as adequate and timely a fashion as that provided in the prior Act. For most earners, benefits should continue to prove very adequate in replacing lost earnings, even without lump-sum payments for non-economic loss. The plight of injured non-earners—who have lost the right to receive lump-sums for non-economic losses—seems on the whole worse than under the prior Act, notwithstanding the availability of a meager in-

dependence allowance and limited optional insurance. The well-being of most victims of medical misadventure is likely to diminish significantly compared with their situation under the prior Act: those claiming medical error may find themselves embroiled in a contentious, if not adversarial, process subject to several appeals, which may delay their recovery or result in a denial of compensation altogether if fault cannot be proven. Few will qualify to recover under the highly restricted claim of medical mishap....

2. Deterrence.—The intention to internalize accident costs is commendable. Notwithstanding doubts about the effectiveness of experience rating as a deterrent and its fairness to small firms and individuals, the possibility that a poor accident record can lead to higher premiums could reintroduce a greater consciousness of the need for safety and accident prevention into the national psyche—a consciousness that in my opinion has diminished since the advent of the accident compensation scheme. Because of those doubts, however, it remains to be seen whether and to what extent experience rating will actually be carried out.

Although the changes to medical misadventure are likely to undermine the comprehensiveness of the accident compensation scheme, they are, ironically, likely to strengthen considerably deterrence and injury prevention in the case of health care professionals, at least for the near term. Once it is learned that findings of medical error are to be reported to professional disciplinary bodies and that determinations of medical error can result in payment of higher premiums, health care professionals can be expected to react by undertaking greater care in the provision of health services. Indeed, it would not be a surprise to hear complaints that physicians are beginning to practice "defensive medicine" in order to avoid claims of medical error. On the other hand, once the weaknesses and ineffectiveness of the scheme—from the point of view of a claimant alleging medical misadventure—become understood, the deterrent effect is likely to decline.

Notwithstanding the confusion of principles and the weakness of deterrence, it is likely that, as to most of its features, the New Zealand scheme as amended will become even more attractive as a substitute for the tort system than the former Act. First, workers' compensation schemes are already in place in most developed nations. Second, the worker-financed nonwork-accident insurance scheme with employer withholding of premiums seems a relatively painless way to finance compensation for such injuries. Third, the total no-fault motor vehicle injury scheme financed by owner premiums and taxes on motor fuel may not appear too radical a departure in jurisdictions that are familiar with partial motor vehicle no-fault schemes. When one adds to this mix the perceived, if illusory, savings achieved by eliminating all personal liability and liability insurance for personal injury, the adoption of the new scheme, including even the limited but "free" benefits for non-earners, may appear very attractive to all but personal injury lawyers and those, like this commentator, who are concerned about deterrence of accidents and efficiency. Adoption of such a system outside of New Zealand to replace an ongoing tort system without provision for a tort liability back-up would in my opinion be most unfortunate....

· · ·

NOTES

(1) Consider whether the New Zealand legislation would achieve an appropriate balance of just and efficient results for the persons involved in the following occurrences:

Drivers A and B collide in the city of Euphoria, attributable to A's speeding and B's making an illegal turn. A, a Euphoria resident, is driving his own flower delivery truck and B is a tense, overworked businessman from the nearby metropolis of Zenith, who is driving his own car through Euphoria to a convention in a resort city 400 miles away. B's pregnant wife, C, working equally hard as a computer specialist, is a passenger. She hopes that she will be able to persuade B to use some of the convention time for much-needed vacation. The collision breaks both B's legs, and the shock of the accident causes him to have a heart attack. The accident occurs in a high-crime neighborhood, and a thief takes advantage of the ensuing confusion to steal C's jewels. She resists, and in the struggle the thief strikes C in the abdomen. This blow causes trauma to the child she is carrying, who is born with diminished mental and physical capacities as a result.

(2) Do you see any reasons for segregating the following categories from each other, or from an otherwise general scheme?

    (a) Motoring injuries

    (b) Occupational accidents

    (c) Injuries inflicted during the commission of a crime

(3) Why should there be a separate plan for incapacity due to accident, as contrasted with illness? Should it make a difference, in fashioning compensation schemes for illness, that a disease is congenital, occupational, or contagious?

(4) Should contributory fault ever be a bar to recovery under a social insurance-type plan? What about drunk driving? Injuries sustained at industrial employment while a worker claimant is under the influence of illegal drugs?

(5) Should comprehensive legislation for accident compensation include relief for earthquake victims? In this regard, consider which class of persons would be in the best position to avoid the risk of damage to a structure built in an earthquake zone: (a) Builder-sellers, who have relatively easy access to seismic maps (b) Buyers, who know that they are purchasing homes in earthquake territory (c) Local governments, whose building codes do not emphasize earthquake protection. How much does a change in any of these factual assumptions change the profile of the socially desirable legislative scheme? Cf. Comment, *Earthquake Damage: Need for a Viable Cause of Action*, 1972 LAW & SOC. ORDER 450.

(6) Could defamation be classified as an "accident" for purposes of a comprehensive compensation plan?

(7) What is the relative importance of the following factors in determining the optimal social response to injuries?

    (a) An identifiable cause

    (b) Fault

    (c) The victim's need

(8) What would be the most useful framework for a basic law school course on the law connected with injuries?

- Tort and compensation law
- The legal system's response to risk and loss through injury
- The social system's response to misfortune

(9) On reconsideration, why should we separate accidents from misfortunes generally? Or does a pluralistic approach seem to you to capture the genius of American democracy?

(10) What relation should a general accident plan bear to the laws applicable to governmental liability for personal injury? See Chapter 18 for material on suits against government and officers.

§ 17.05 Assessing Data and Policy Concerning the Tort Liability System

Don Dewees, David Duff & Michael Trebilcock, *Exploring the Domain of Accident Law* 412–13, 432–34, 437–38 (1996)*

The conclusions and implications that we have drawn from our empirical research are summarized in the following principal points.... :

1. The tort system performs so poorly in compensating most victims of personal injury that we should abandon tort as a means of pursuing this compensation objective, turning instead to other instruments.

2. The tort system performs unevenly in deterring the causes of personal injuries, so its scope should be restricted to situations where its effect seems likely to justify its high costs.

3. The regulatory system has achieved varying success in reducing personal injuries; its performance can be improved by reducing its use in areas in which it is ineffective, by expanding its use where it more effective, and by improving its design.

4. Compensation systems can create substantial deterrent incentives through risk-rating of premiums and through the design of benefits to reduce moral hazard problems.

5. Wherever feasible, accident costs should be internalized to classes of activities and to individual actors through the design of appropriate insurance arrangements, rather than through the tort system.

6. Compensation of most victims in the motor vehicle and medical malpractice fields would best be achieved through no-fault insurance which incorporates as essential features: risk-rating of premiums, the elimination of nonpecuniary damages, deductibles for short-term pecuniary loss, compensation for medical and rehabilitation costs, and reasonably complete wage-loss replacement. This implies separate systems separately funded, each with features similar to existing workers' compensation schemes. Tort liability would be retained only for the few cases in which intentional, reckless, or grossly negligent infliction of serious injury could be proven.

7. Workers' compensation should be retained for workplace injuries, with more attention to risk-rating of premiums, but product liability suits for workplace-related injuries should be prohibited.

8. Product liability should be governed by negligence doctrines, not strict liability, and should not be available for workplace cases covered by workers' compensation.

Table 7-1. Compensation for Injury, Illness, and Fatality in
the Principal Loss-Shifting Systems

Loss-Shifting System	Amount ($ billions)	Percentage
A. Fault-based		
Tort	50	9.0
B. Cause-based		
Workers Compensation	30	5.4
No-fault auto insurance	2	0.4
Black Lung Benefits Program	2	0.3
Veterans' benefits	21	3.8
C. Loss-based		
Private first-party insurance		
Health	185	33.0
Life	24	4.4
Disability	6	1.1
Social (public) Insurance		
Health: Medicaid & Medicare	159	29.0
Other federal and state	40	7.2
Disability: SSD, SSI	35	6.3
State short-term disability	2	0.4
Total:	556	100

SOURCE: Kenneth S. Abraham and Lance Liebman (1993), "Private Insurance, Social Insurance,
and Tort Reform: Toward a New Vision of Compensation for Illness and Injury," 93 *Colum. L. Rev.*
75 at 78–80, 82, 83.

9. Environmental injuries should continue to be controlled primarily through government regulation, with tort playing a residual role in situations where causation can readily be proven.

10. Many personal injuries occur in situations outside both the tort system and the compensation schemes that we recommend here, and these victims are often currently undercompensated for medical costs, lost income, and costs of rehabilitation, especially in the case of permanent total or partial disability. These accidents are quite diverse, and we have no recommendations regarding deterrence. The compensation problem might best be attacked by a comprehensive medical insurance system like that in Canada and by more comprehensive long-term wage-loss disability coverage.

. . .

... Privately held health insurance, life insurance, and sick leave and disability insurance account for about 38% of loss payments in the United States (table 7-1). Social or public loss insurance includes Medicare and Medicaid; other federal and state health insurance plans; two federal programs providing compensation, at Social Security rates, to those who are permanently and totally disabled—Social Security Disability (SSD) and Supplement Security Income (SSI); and a few state-run short-term disability programs. Together they account for about 43% of loss payments. Table 7-1 summarizes the relative contributions of various sources of compensation for injury and illness in the United States in the late 1980s.

Three general points can be made about the existing mixed system of compensation. First, the tort system contributes a small fraction of total compensation for economic losses from injuries.... Second, the plethora of compensatory systems leads to coordination problems, giving rise to both over- and undercompensation. Third, there are still very significant and systematic gaps in compensation coverage for injury and illness. For example, about 18% of the U.S. population hold no private insurance for medical costs (about 35 million people), while others are significantly underinsured. Nevertheless, a recent Rand study estimates that 84% of the costs of basic health care with respect to injuries from accidents in the United States were borne by some source other than the injured individual, and Medicare raises this figure to 93% for the elderly.

Much more serious gaps exist with respect to income loss arising from nonoccupationally induced disability. The Rand survey of injured individuals found that about one-quarter of injuries occurred while people were engaged in home activities, another quarter while people were on the job or on their way to and from work, and about 30% while people were engaged in leisure activities. Focusing on the location, rather than the activity, about one-third of accidents occurred in private residences, one-quarter on streets and highways, and about 8% on industrial or construction sites. Focusing on the cause, 40% were caused by slips and falls, 30% by products, and 20% by motor vehicles. Over all types of accidents, individuals bear about 38% of the pecuniary cost directly in out-of-pocket payments or in reduced earnings. While those experiencing short-term work loss recover about 66% of their pre-tax income loss, those permanently unable to work, or restricted significantly in their work, recover only about 20% of their pre-tax income loss. The compensation gaps are likely to be substantially more severe with respect to illness-related disabilities. This has led to criticisms of workers' compensation schemes as reflecting an "industrial preference" and of broader accident compensation schemes, such as the New Zealand Accident Compensation Plan, as reflecting an "accident preference." It has also led to proposals for general compensation schemes for victims of accidents and disabilities. However such schemes must confront the possibility that illness-related disabilities may be 10 times as numerous as injury-related disabilities.

. . .

Our recommendations represent a relatively simple set of revisions to tort law that would drastically reduce the scope of tort litigation in the United States and would greatly improve compensation for two types of pecuniary losses: medical costs and lost income arising from disability. Replacing tort with no-fault auto insurance would eliminate perhaps one-third to one-half of personal injury tort litigation in the United States. Replacing medical malpractice litigation with a no-fault system would greatly reduce the relatively small number of these suits. In the product liability area, our proposed ban on product liability suits arising from workplace injuries would eliminate 40% of product liability claims, and the replacement of strict liability with negligence would likely raise the reduction in product liability suits above 50%. If product liability cases represent about 10% of all tort litigation, then our product liability proposals would eliminate perhaps 5% of all tort claims. The overall effect of our proposals would thus reduce personal injury tort litigation in the United States by up to one-half, a far more dramatic change than any sought or achieved in the "tort reforms" of the 1980s.

We propose that this radical restriction of the scope of tort law be accompanied by two residual compensation schemes that would better compensate injury victims not covered by our three no-fault schemes than does the tort system and at a far lower administrative cost. First, we recommend a system of universal health insurance so that all personal injury victims need not bear directly the cost of their medical care. While this represents a radical proposal for the United States, it represents established policy in all other industrialized countries. Second, we recommend that long-term disability insurance substantially replace lost income arising from injuries and illness not covered by our three no-fault schemes. These two proposals will provide much broader and more effective compensation for pecuniary losses than does the tort system at a fraction of the administrative cost.

. . .

NOTE

If you could be a supreme legislator for the United States, would you choose to adopt a comprehensive compensation statute for injuries in all kinds of activities? Or would you opt to keep the present system of injury compensation in substantially its present form? Explain your position.

SPECIAL NOTE ON THE SEPTEMBER 11TH VICTIM COMPENSATION FUND

The attacks of September 11, 2001, led to a highly specialized compensation system, fully funded by Congress.[1] The statute provided compensation to the relatives of persons who died as a result of planes crashing into the World Trade Center Towers and the Pentagon, and the crash of a hijacked plane in a Pennsylvania field, and also to persons who "suffered physical harm" from the crashes. The legislation offered an unusual, if not unique, alternative to claimants. They could elect to take an award from the Victim Compensation Fund (VCF) or to bring tort actions against entities whose acts or omissions were alleged to have contributed to the happening of the attacks or their consequences. However, if people claimed against the Fund, they "waive[d] the right to file a civil action ... for damages sustained as a result of" the attacks. These are some of the details of the statute and of the Rules promulgated by the Department of Justice for its administration by a Special Master:

No-fault. The statute specifies that "the Special Master shall not consider negligence or any other theory of liability," and he "may not include amounts for punitive damages in any compensation paid."

Economic loss. The Rules, as explicated by the Special Master, included numerical tables that assessed the economic loss of survivors principally on the basis of the earnings of decedents.

Noneconomic loss. Congress defined "noneconomic loss" broadly to include not only pain and suffering and "loss of society and companionship" and "loss of consortium" but also "loss of enjoyment of life" and "hedonic damages." The Rules created a presumption of $250,000 for the noneconomic loss of each decedent and "an additional $100,000 for the spouse and each dependent" of a decedent.

Minimum awards. The Rules specified minimum awards, before deductions for collateral sources, of $500,000 when a decedent had a spouse or dependent and $300,000 when a decedent had no spouse or dependents.

Collateral sources. The statute required the Special Master to deduct from awards "the amount of the collateral source compensation the claimant has received or is entitled to

---

1. Pub. L. No. 107-42 (Sept. 22, 2001), *codified at* 49 U.S.C.A. § 49101.

receive," and included in the definition of collateral sources "life insurance, pension funds, death benefit programs, and payments by Federal, State, or local governments related to" the attacks.

Treatment of the airlines. A separate title in the statute provided for $5 billions in compensation to the airlines for losses attributable to the attacks. Although those who did not claim under the Fund could sue the airlines in tort, and could even claim punitive damages, the liability of the carriers for any damages could not exceed the limits of their liability insurance coverage.

Ultimately, the Fund paid out more than $7 billion to more than 5,500 persons.[2] According to a Rand Corporation report, payments for death claims ranged "from $250,000 to $7.1 million, with a mean of $2.08 million and a median of $1.68 million," and awards for personal injury ranged from $500 to $8.6 million.[3] It was estimated that overall benefits paid out to people and businesses from various sources, including charities, totaled more than $38 billion.

NOTES

(1) What do you think Congress' principal purposes were in passing this legislation? Was it wise to pass a compensation statute for this particular purpose?

(2) Was it a sensible solution to allow claimants to choose between the alternatives of awards from the Fund and suing private defendants?

(3) How do the provisions of the statute that created the VCF compare with other statutory schemes that provide compensation for personal injuries?

(4) If claimants decided not to claim against the Fund, they could have sued such parties as the airlines and the airport security companies—for failure to provide sufficient security; the maker of the hijacked airplanes—for failure to sufficiently protect cockpits against invasion by hijackers; and the owners and operators of the World Trade Center—for failure to construct or maintain buildings in a way that would minimize deaths and injuries from such attacks. How do the provisions summarized above compare with the tort law that would be applicable to such defendants?

(5) Before deductions for collateral sources, the Special Master's compensation tables would have provided $613,714 to the family of a married victim who died at 35 with two dependent children, if the victim earned $10,000 per year. But if the decedent earned $225,000 per year, the payment would be $3,805,087. Can you justify this disparity?

(6) Should Congress fashion a statute that would provide compensation to victims of terrorism in the future? If you think so, what should be the principal provisions of that legislation?

(7) For a discussion of these issues in the context of injury compensation generally, see MARSHALL S. SHAPO, COMPENSATION FOR VICTIMS OF TERRORISM (Oceana/Oxford 2005).

---

2. See KENNETH FEINBERG, WHAT IS LIFE WORTH? XI (Public Affairs 2005).
3. LLOYD DIXON & RACHEL KAGANOFF STERN, COMPENSATION FOR LOSSES FROM THE 9/11 ATTACKS 25 (Rand Inst. for Civil Justice 2004).

Chapter 18

THE FINAL BATTLEMENTS: LIABILITY OF GOVERNMENTS AND OFFICIALS

§ 18.01 The Federal Tort Claims Act

THE FEDERAL TORT CLAIMS ACT
28 U.S.C.A.

§ 1346 (1993). *United States as defendant*

...

(b) ... [T]he district courts ... shall have exclusive jurisdiction of civil actions on claims against the United States, for money damages ... for injury or loss of property, or personal injury or death caused by the negligent or wrongful act or omission of any employee of the Government while acting within the scope of his office or employment, under circumstances where the United States, if a private person, would be liable to the claimant in accordance with the law of the place where the act or omission occurred.

§ 2674 (1994). *Liability of United States*

The United States shall be liable, respecting the provisions of this title relating to tort claims, in the same manner and to the same extent as a private individual under like circumstances, but shall not be liable for interest prior to judgment or for punitive damages.

If, however, in any case wherein death was caused, the law of the place where the act or omission complained of occurred provides, or has been construed to provide, for damages only punitive in nature, the United States shall be liable for actual or compensatory damages....

§ 2680 (1994). *Exceptions*

The provisions of this chapter and section 1346(b) of this title shall not apply to—

(a) Any claim based upon an act or omission of an employee of the Government, exercising due care, in the execution of a statute or regulation, whether or not such statute or regulation be valid, or based upon the exercise or performance or the failure to exercise or perform a discretionary function or duty on the part of a federal agency or an employee of the Government, whether or not the discretion involved be abused.

(b) Any claim arising out of the loss, miscarriage, or negligent transmission of letters or postal matter....

(f) Any claim for damages caused by the imposition or establishment of a quarantine by the United States....

(h) Any claim arising out of assault, battery, false imprisonment, false arrest, malicious prosecution, abuse of process, libel, slander, misrepresentation, deceit, or interference with contract rights: *Provided*, That, with regard to acts or omissions of investigative or law enforcement officers of the United States Government, the provisions of this chapter and section 1346(b) of this title shall apply to any claim arising, on or after the date of the enactment of this proviso, out of assault, battery, false imprisonment, false arrest, abuse of process, or malicious prosecution. For the purpose of this subsection, 'investigative or law enforcement officer' means any officer of the United States who is empowered by law to execute searches, to seize evidence, or to make arrests for violations of Federal law.

(i) Any claim for damages caused by the fiscal operations of the Treasury or by the regulation of the monetary system.

(j) Any claim arising out of the combatant activities of the military or naval forces, or the Coast Guard, during time of war.

DALEHITE v. UNITED STATES

United States Supreme Court
346 U.S. 15, 73 S. Ct. 956, 97 L. Ed. 1427 (1953)

MR. JUSTICE REED delivered the opinion of the Court.

[This case arose from the Texas City Disaster, an explosion of fertilizer produced by the Government for emergency relief abroad. Dalehite was a test case, brought to represent over 300 personal and property claims for a total of $200 million. The District Court rendered judgment on the verdict for the plaintiffs, but the Court of Appeals reversed. The excerpts below begin midway in the opinion of Justice Reed.]

III. That the cabinet-level decision to institute the fertilizer export program was a discretionary act is not seriously disputed. Nor do we think that there is any doubt that the need for further experimentation with FGAN [Fertilizer Grade Ammonium Nitrate—Ed.] to determine the possibility of its explosion, under conditions likely to be encountered in shipping, and its combustibility was a matter to be determined by the discretion of those in charge of the production. Obviously, having manufactured and shipped the commodity FGAN for more than three years without even minor accidents, the need for further experimentation was a matter of discretion. Reported instances of heating or bag damage were investigated and experiments, to the extent deemed necessary, were carried on. In dealing with ammonium nitrate in any form, the industry, and of course Ordnance, was well aware that care must be taken. The best indication of the care necessary came from experience in FGAN production. The TVA had produced FGAN since 1943, and their experience ... was not only available to Ordnance but was used by them to the most minute detail. It is, we think, just such matters of governmental duties that were excepted from the Act.

We turn, therefore, to the specific acts of negligence charged in the manufacture. Each was in accordance with, and done under, specifications and directions as to how the FGAN was produced at the plants. The basic "Plan" was drafted by the office of the Field Director of Ammunitions Plants in June, 1946, prior to beginning production. It was drawn up in the light of prior experience by private enterprise and the TVA. In fact it was, as we have pointed out, based on the latter agency's engineering techniques, and specifically adopted the TVA process description and specifications. This Plan was distributed to the various plants at the inception of the program.

Besides its general condemnation of the manufacture of FGAN, the District Court cited four specific acts of negligence in manufacture. Each of these acts looked upon as negligence was directed by this Plan. Applicable excerpts follow. Bagging temperature was fixed.[36] The type of bagging[37] and the labeling thereof[38] were also established. The PRP coating, too, was included in the specifications.[39] The acts found to have been negligence were thus performed under the direction of a plan developed at a high level under a direct delegation of plan-making authority from the apex of the Executive Department. The establishment of this Plan, delegated to the Field Director's Office, ... clearly required the exercise of expert judgment.

This is to be seen, for instance, in the matter of the coating. The PRP was added in order to insure against water absorption. At stake was no mere matter of taste; ammonium nitrate when wet cakes and is difficult to spread on fields as a fertilizer. So the considerations that dictated the decisions were crucial ones, involving the feasibility of the program itself, balanced against present knowledge of the effect of such a coating and the general custom of similar private industries.

And, assuming that high bagging temperatures in fact obtained as the District Court found, the decision to bag at the temperature fixed was also within the exception. Maximum bagging temperatures were first established under the TVA specifications. That they were the product of an exercise of judgment, requiring consideration of a vast spectrum of factors, including some which touched directly the feasibility of the fertilizer export program, is clear. For instance, it appears several times in the record that the question of bagging temperatures was discussed by the Army plant officials, among others. In January, 1947, the Bureau of Explosives of the Association of American Railroads wrote to Ordnance concerning a box-car fire of FGAN. The letter suggested a reduction of bagging temperatures. The Field Director of Ammunition Plants consulted the commanding officers on the matter. Those of two of the plants which manufactured the Texas City FGAN replied that loading was effected at about 200_F. Both, however, recommended that reduced temperatures would be inadvisable. It would be possible to keep the product in graining kettles for a longer period or to install cooling equipment. But both methods would result in greatly increased production costs and/or greatly re-

---

36. "Water shall be turned off and discharging of kettle commenced when temperature reaches 200_F."

The relevance of the bagging temperature apparently stemmed from certain testimony that large masses of FGAN, if maintained at temperatures of around 300_ F. might spontaneously ignite under certain conditions of mass and confinement. The Government proffered extensive evidence, however, that the FGAN shipped to Texas City did not leave the plants at nearly that temperature, and of course there is no evidence as to the the temperature at which it was loaded on the ships.

37. "*Packaging.* — Ammonium nitrate for fertilizer shall be packed 100 lbs. per bag. Moisture proof paper or burlap bags, as described below, shall be used. (Specifications as to size may have to be altered to meet the manufacturer's requirement)." Then follow detailed specifications.

38. Marking: Fertilizer (Ammonium Nitrate) 32.5% Nitrogen.

Notice of contents appeared on the bill of lading, so far as important, as follows: 1,000 Bags, Fertilizing Compounds (manufactured fertilizer) NOIBN, dry in paper bags.

39. "The PRP mixture is composed of one part Paraffin, three parts rosin, and one part petrolatum, thoroughly mixed and melted. This provides a coating which repels moisture and holds the clay in place around each granule."

duced production. This kind of decision is not one which the courts, under the Act, are empowered to cite as "negligence"; especially is this so in the light of the contemporary knowledge of the characteristics of FGAN.[40]

As well, serious judgment was involved in the specification of the bag labels and bills of lading. The importance of this rests on the fact that it is the latest point in time and geography when the Government did anything directly related to the fire, for after bagging the FGAN was of course physically in the hands of various non-governmental agents. So, since there was serious room for speculation that the most direct operative fact causing the immediate fire on the *Grandcamp* arose from errors that the French Council, longshoremen or ship staff committed, it was and is important for the petitioners to emphasize the seriousness of the alleged labeling mistake.

This, too, though, falls within the exception for acts of discretion. The Plan had been prepared in this regard by the Transportation Officer of the Director's Office. His decision in the matter was dictated by the ICC regulations. These did not provide for a specific classification for the material other than as fertilizer. Labeling it as anything but "oxidizing material" was not required—indeed was probably forbidden—and even this requirement was waived for bags of less than 200 pounds. To the extent, then, that the Army had a choice in the matter, its decision not to seek to list its FGAN in any other fashion was within the exception. The immunity of a decision as to labeling, in fact, is quite clearly shown by the fact that the ICC's regulations, for instance, could not be attacked by claimants under the Act by virtue of the first phrase of § 2680(a).

In short, the alleged "negligence" does not subject the Government to liability. The decisions held culpable were all responsibly made at a planning rather than operational level and involved considerations more or less important to the practicability of the Government's fertilizer program.

"There must be knowledge of a danger, not merely possible, but probable", *MacPherson v. Buick Motor Co.*, 217 N.Y. 382, 389, 111 N.E. 1050, 1053, L.R.A. 1916F, 696. Here, nothing so startling was adduced. The entirety of the evidence compels the view that FGAN was a material that former experience showed could be handled safely in the manner it was handled here. Even now no one has suggested that the ignition of FGAN was anything but a complex result of the interacting factors of mass, heat, pressure and composition.

IV. The findings of negligence on the part of the Coast Guard in failing to supervise the storage of the FGAN, and in fighting the fire after it started, were rejected by a majority of the Court of Appeals.... We do not enter into an examination of these factual findings. We prefer, again, to rest our decision on the Act.

The District Court's holding that the Coast Guard and other agencies were negligent in failing to prevent the fire by regulating storage or loading of the fertilizer in some dif-

---

40. Captain Hirsch, commanding one of the three plants which manufactured the Texas City FGAN, wrote to the Field Director's Office requesting "that your office stipulate a maximum temperature at which the fertilizer may be loaded in order to eliminate" bag deterioration through heat. In reply, the Office stated that it "has had discussions concerning a loading temperature lower than 200 F. for ammonium nitrate fertilizer, but it is felt that this is a matter of process control and not properly an item to be incorporated into specifications." Hirsch interpreted this as meaning that "this facility should not take any active interest in the condition that the ammonium nitrate fertilizer reaches its destination." In reply from the Field Director's Office, this was labeled a "distortion of our statement concerning the bagging temperature as a matter of process control into indifference to any aspect of acceptability or suitability." The specifications were left unchanged as to bags or bagging temperatures.

ferent fashion is like his specific citations of negligence discussed above. They are classi-
cally within the exception. "The power to adopt regulations or by-laws ... for the
preservation of the public health, or to pass ordinances prescribing and regulating the
duties of policemen and firemen ... are generally regarded as discretionary, because, in
their nature, they are legislative." *Weightman v. Corporation of Washington*, 1 Black 39,
49, 17 L.Ed. 52. The courts have traditionally refused to question the judgments on
which they are based....

As to the alleged failure in fighting the fire, we think this too without the Act. The
Act did not create new causes of action where none existed before.

> ... the liability assumed by the Government here is that created by "all the cir-
> cumstances," not that which a few of the circumstances might create. We find
> no parallel liability before, and we think no new one has been created by, this
> Act. Its effect is to waive immunity from recognized causes of action and was
> not to visit the Government with novel and unprecedented liabilities. *Feres v.
> United States*, 340 U.S. 135, 142, 71 S.Ct. 153, 157, 95 L.Ed. 152.

It did not change the normal rule that an alleged failure or carelessness of public
firemen does not create private actionable rights. Our analysis of the question is determined by what was said in the *Feres* case. *See* 28 U.S.C. §§ 1346 and 2674, 28
U.S.C.A. §§ 1346, 2674. The Act, as was there stated, limited United States liability to
"the same manner and to the same extent as a private individual under like circumstances".... Here, as there, there is no analogous liability; in fact, if anything is doc-
trinally sanctified in the law of torts it is the immunity of communities and other
public bodies for injuries due to fighting fire. This case, then, is much stronger than
Feres. We pointed out only one state decision which denied government liability for
injuries incident to service to one in the state militia. That cities, by maintaining fire-
fighting organizations, assume no liability for personal injuries resulting from their
lapses is much more securely entrenched. The Act, since it relates to claims to which
there is no analogy in general tort law, did not adopt a different rule. *See Steitz v. City
of Beacon*, 295 N.Y. 51, 64 N.E.2d 704, 163 A.L.R. 342. To impose liability for the alleged nonfeasance of the Coast Guard would be like holding the United States liable
in tort for failure to impose a quarantine for, let us say, an outbreak of foot-and-
mouth disease.

V. Though the findings of specific and general negligence do not support a judgment
of government liability, there is yet to be disposed of some slight residue of theory of
absolute liability without fault. This is reflected both in the District Court's finding that
the FGAN constituted a nuisance, and in the contention of petitioner here. We agree
with the six judges of the Court of Appeals, 197 F.2d 771, 776, 781, 786, that the Act
does not extend to such situations, though of course well known in tort law generally. It
is to be invoked only on a "negligent or wrongful act or omission" of an employee. Absolute liability, of course, arises irrespective of how the tortfeasor conducts himself; it is
imposed automatically when any damages are sustained as a result of the decision to engage in the dangerous activity. The degree of care used in performing the activity is irrelevant to the application of that doctrine. But the statute requires a negligent act. So it
is our judgment that liability does not arise by virtue either of United States ownership
of an "inherently dangerous commodity" or property, or of engaging in an "extra hazardous" activity. *United States v. Hull*, 1 Cir., 195 F.2d 64, 67.

Petitioners rely on the word "wrongful" though as showing that something in addition to negligence is covered. This argument, as we have pointed out, does not override

the fact that the Act does require some brand of misfeasance or nonfeasance, and so could not extend to liability without fault; in addition, the legislative history of the word indicates clearly that it was not added to the jurisdictional grant with any overtones of the absolute liability theory. Rather, Committee discussion indicates that it had a much narrower inspiration: "trespasses" which might not be considered strictly negligent. Hearings before a Subcommittee of the Senate Committee on the Judiciary on S. 2690, 76th Cong., 3d Sess., 43–44. Had an absolute liability theory been intended to have been injected into the Act, much more suitable models could have been found, *e.g.*, the Suits in Admiralty Act, 41 Stat. 525, 46 U.S.C. §§ 742–743, 46 U.S.C.A. §§ 742, 743, in regard to maintenance and cure....

Affirmed.

MR. JUSTICE DOUGLAS and MR. JUSTICE CLARK took no part in the consideration or decision of this case.

Appendix.

The District Court's analysis of the specific aspects of the manufacture was foreshadowed by his theory of the foreseeability of the risk which he set out early in the findings. His first finding of fact contained these words: "This record discloses blunders, mistakes, and acts of negligence, both of omission and commission, on the part of Defendant, its agents, servants, and employees, in deciding to begin the manufacture of this inherently dangerous Fertilizer." It was his conclusion that, through early experiments, the United States had "learned many facts, but did not pursue such investigation far enough to learn all the facts.... What facts it did learn, however, were sufficient to give Defendant knowledge and to put Defendant on notice, and if not, then upon inquiry that would if pursued, have led to knowledge and notice that such Fertilizer which it decided to and began to manufacture was an inherently dangerous and hazardous material, a dangerous explosive, and a fire hazard. Such facts learned by Defendant pointed to and showed that such Fertilizer should not be manufactured, in that it was, under certain conditions and circumstances, most dangerous to everyone handling it in any way and to the public. Yet Defendant's servants, agents and employees, in whose hands Defendant had left the matter, negligently went forward in the manufacture, handling, distribution, shipping, etc. of such Fertilizer...."

"After the manufacture and/or the shipping, distribution, and handling of Fertilizer had begun, there were experiments, events and incidents of which Defendant knew, or of which Defendant could have known by the use of the diligence of a reasonably prudent person, showing such Fertilizer to be very dangerous, both from the standpoint of fire and explosion. With this knowledge, Defendant should have ceased the manufacture and sale of such Fertilizer, or should have taken steps to insure the safety of persons manufacturing and handling such Fertilizer and the public...."

"Defendant in manufacturing such Fertilizer, and particularly the Fertilizer on the Grandcamp and High Flyer, did so by a Formula made and evolved by Defendant or under its direction. It used as a coating of such Fertilizer, a substance or substances which rendered same highly susceptible to fire or explosion. There were various types of coating, but the coating finally used made the Fertilizer a very dangerous explosive and fire hazard. More than any other one thing, I think this coating made this commodity one of the most dangerous of explosives...."

" ... Such Fertilizer was by Defendant, or under its direction, placed or sacked in bags made from paper or other substances which were easily ignited by contact with fire or by spontaneous combustion or spontaneous ignition of the Fertilizer. Such bags also become torn and ragged in shipping and particles of the bags became mixed with the Fertilizer and rendered same more dangerous and more susceptible to fire and explosion."

" ... Such Fertilizer was placed and packed in bags at high degrees of temperature, which temperature rendered the Fertilizer more susceptible to fire and explosion. Such Fertilizer was so packed that it did not get cool, but continued at high temperature while being shipped. This was particularly true of the Fertilizer which exploded on the Steamships Grandcamp and High Flyer. Same was packed in sacks at a high degree of temperature, which temperature continued with only slight reduction, if any, when the Fertilizer was shipped across the nation to Texas City and there loaded onto such Steamships."

"Defendant was negligent in the manner in which it marked and labelled such sacks of Fertilizer, including the Fertilizer on the Grandcamp and High Flyer, in that same was not labelled and marked as a dangerous explosive and fire hazard as required by the Rules and Regulations of the Interstate Commerce Commission...."

" ... It was the duty of Defendant, well knowing as it did the dangerous nature and character of such Fertilizer which Defendant shipped or caused to be shipped to Texas City, to notify and advise all the carriers handling same, including the Steamships Grandcamp and High Flyer, and to notify and advise the City and State Officers at Texas City, of the dangerous nature and character of such Fertilizer, to the end that such carriers and their employees and such officers could, it possible, protect themselves and the public against the danger of fires from and explosions of such Fertilizer."

The District Court concluded:

"Clearly such Fertilizer ought never to have been manufactured. From the beginning on down, it was a dangerous commodity and a dangerous nuisance."

MR. JUSTICE JACKSON, joined by MR. JUSTICE BLACK and MR. JUSTICE FRANKFURTER, dissenting.

All day, April 15, 1947, longshoremen loaded bags of ammonium nitrate fertilizer aboard the S.S. *Grandcamp*, docked at Texas City, Texas. Shortly after 8 a.m. next morning, when work resumed, smoke was seen coming from the No. 4 hold and it was discovered that fire had broken out in the fertilizer. The ship's master ordered the hatch covered and battened down and steam was introduced into the hold. Local fire-fighting apparatus soon arrived, but the combined efforts to extinguish the fire were unavailing. Less than an hour after smoke was first seen, 880 tons of fertilizer in the No. 4 hold exploded and, in turn, detonated the fertilizer stored in the No. 2 hold. Fire spread to the dock area of Texas City and to the S.S. *High Flyer*, berthed at an adjoining pier and carrying a cargo of sulphur and ammonium nitrate fertilizer. Further efforts to extinguish or even contain the fire failed and, about 11 p.m., tugs unsuccessfully attempted to tow the *High Flyer* out to sea. Shortly after one o'clock on the morning of April 17, the sulphur and fertilizer aboard the *High Flyer* exploded, demolishing both that ship and the S. S. *Wilson B. Keene*, lying alongside. More than 560 persons perished in this holocaust, and some 3,000 were injured. The entire dock area of a thriving port was leveled and property damage ran into millions of dollars.

This was a man-made disaster; it was in no sense an "act of God." The fertilizer had been manufactured in Government-owned plants at the Government's order and to its specifications. It was being shipped at its direction as part of its program of foreign aid. The disaster was caused by forces set in motion by the Government, completely controlled or controllable by it. Its causative factors were far beyond the knowledge or control of the victims; they were not only incapable of contributing to it, but could not even take shelter or flight from it.

... [T]he Government here urges that (1) a private person would not be liable in these circumstances, and (2) even if a private person were liable, the Government is saved from liability by the statute's exception of discretionary acts.

This is one of those cases that a judge is likely to leave by the same door through which he enters. As we have been told by a master of our craft, "*Some* theory of liability, some philosophy of the end to be served by tightening or enlarging the circle of rights and remedies, is at the root of any decision in novel situations when analogies are equivocal and precedents are silent."[3] So, we begin by avowing a conception of the function of legal liability in cases such as this quite obviously at variance with the approach of the Court.

Congress has defined the tort liability of the Government as analogous to that of a private person. Traditionally, one function of civil liability for negligence is to supply a sanction to enforce the degree of care suitable to the conditions of contemporary society and appropriate to the circumstances of the case. The civil damage action, prosecuted and adjusted by private initiative, neither burdening our overworked criminal processes nor confined by the limits of criminal liability, is one of the law's most effective inducements to the watchfulness and prudence necessary to avoid calamity from hazardous operations in the midst of an unshielded populace.

Until recently, the influence of the Federal Government has been exerted in the field of tort law to tighten liability and liberalize remedies.[4] Congress has even imposed criminal liability without regard to knowledge of danger or intent where potentially dangerous articles are introduced into interstate commerce. But, when the Government is brought into court as a tort defendant, the very proper zeal of its lawyers to win their case and the less commendable zeal of officials involved to conceal or minimize their carelessness militate against this trend. The Government, as a defendant, can exert an unctuous persuasiveness because it can clothe official carelessness with a public interest. Hence, one of the unanticipated consequences of the Tort Claims Act has been to throw the weight of government influence on the side of lax standards of care in the negligence cases which it defends.

It is our fear that the Court's adoption of the Government's view in this case may inaugurate an unfortunate trend toward relaxation of private as well as official responsibility in making, vending or transporting inherently dangerous products. For we are not considering here every-day commodities of commerce or products of nature but a complex compound not only proven by the event to be highly dangerous, but known from the beginning to lie somewhere within the range of the dangerous. Ammonium nitrate, as the Court points out, had been "long used as a component in explosives." This grade of it was manufactured under an explosives patent, in plants formerly used

---

3. CARDOZO, THE GROWTH OF THE LAW, p. 102. (Emphasis his own.)

4. *See, e.g.*, the Federal Employers' Liability Act, ... which abolished the defense of assumption of risk and changed contributory negligence from a complete bar to recovery to a factor which mitigated damages; the Jones Act, ... which gave a cause of action against their employers to seamen, under the substantive rules of the F.E.L.A.; the Federal Employees Compensation Act of 1916, ... in which the Government set up a compensation system for its own employees; the Longshoremen's and Harbor Workers' Compensation Act, ... which sets up a system of workmen's compensation for the described employees and imposes liability without fault on their employers. In cases arising under the last-named Act, the Government is a party to judicial review of any award, representing the interests of the claimant....

for the manufacture of ordnance, under general supervision of the Army's Chief of Ordnance, and under the local direction of the Army's Field Director of Ammunition Plants. Advice on detailed operations was sought from such experienced commercial producers of high explosives as the du Ponts and the Atlas and the Hercules powder concerns. There is not the slightest basis for any official belief that this was an innocuous product.

Because of reliance on the reservation of governmental immunity for acts of discretion, the Court avoids direct pronouncement on the duty owing by the Government under these circumstances but does sound overtones and undertones with which we disagree. We who would hold the Government liable here cannot avoid consideration of the basic criteria by which courts determine liability in the conditions of modern life. This is a day of synthetic living, when to an ever-increasing extent our population is dependent upon mass producers for its food and drink, its cures and complexions, its apparel and gadgets. These no longer are natural or simple products but complex ones whose composition and qualities are often secret. Such a dependent society must exact greater care than in more simple days and must require from manufacturers or producers increased integrity and caution as the only protection of its safety and well-being. Purchasers cannot try out drugs to determine whether they kill or cure. Consumers cannot test the youngster's cowboy suit or the wife's sweater to see if they are apt to burst into fatal flames. Carriers, by land or by sea, cannot experiment with the combustibility of goods in transit. Where experiment or research is necessary to determine the presence or the degree of danger, the product must not be tried out on the public, nor must the public be expected to possess the facilities or the technical knowledge to learn for itself of inherent but latent dangers. The claim that a hazard was not foreseen is not available to one who did not use foresight appropriate to his enterprise.

Forward-looking courts, slowly but steadily, have been adapting the law of negligence to these conditions.[6] The law which by statute determines the Government's liability is that of the place where the negligent act or omission occurred. This fertilizer was manufactured in Iowa and Nebraska, thence shipped to Texas. Speculation as to where the negligence occurred is unnecessary, since each of these jurisdictions recognizes the general proposition that a manufacturer is liable for defects in his product which could have been avoided by the exercise of due care. Where there are no specific state decisions on the point, federal judges may turn to the general doctrines of accepted tort law, whence state judges derive their governing principles in novel cases. We believe that whatever the source to which we look for the law of this case, if the source is as modern as the case itself, it supports the exaction of a higher degree of care than possibly can be found to have been exercised here.

We believe it is the better view that whoever puts into circulation in commerce a product that is known or even suspected of being potentially inflammable or explosive is under an obligation to know his own product and to ascertain what forces he is turn-

---

6. Judge Lummus, for the Supreme Judicial Court of Massachusetts, articulated this development in *Carter v. Yardley Co., Ltd.*, 319 Mass. 92, 64 N.E.2d 693, 164 A.L.R. 559. That opinion contains what is perhaps a more decisive statement of the trend than does the earlier landmark opinion of Judge Cardozo for the New York Court of Appeals, *MacPherson v. Buick Motor Co.*, 217 N.Y. 382, 111 N.E. 1050, L.R.A. 1916F, 696. [Justice Jackson here cites a number of cases as "examples from complex manufactured products which come before appellate tribunals in the present day."] Recovery was not had in all of these cases, but all of them have emphasized that the manufacturer owes some duty of care to certain classes of people who might be injured by defects in his product.

ing loose. If, as often will be the case, a dangerous product is also a useful one, he is under a strict duty to follow each step of its distribution with warning of its dangers and with information and directions to keep those dangers at a minimum.

It is obvious that the Court's only choice is to hold the Government's liability to be nothing or to be very heavy, indeed. But the magnitude of the potential liability is due to the enormity of the disaster and the multitude of its victims. The size of the catastrophe does not excuse liability but, on its face, eloquently pleads that it could not have resulted from any prudently operated Government project, and that injury so sudden and sweeping should not lie where it has fallen. It should at least raise immediate doubts whether this is one of those "discretionary" operations Congress sought to immunize from liability. With this statement of our general approach to the liability issue, we turn to its application to this case.

. . .

The Government's attack on the purely factual determination by the trial judge seems to us utterly unconvincing. Reputable experts testified to their opinion that the fire could have been caused by spontaneous combustion. The Government's contention that it was probably caused by someone smoking about the hold brought forth sharp conflict in the testimony. There was no error in adopting one of two permissible inferences as to the fire's origin. And, in view of the absence of any warning that FGAN was inflammable or explosive, we would think smoking by longshoremen about the job would not be an abnormal phenomenon.

The evidence showed that this type of fertilizer had been manufactured for about four years at the time of the explosion in Texas City. Petitioner's experts testified to their belief that at least a segment of informed scientific opinion at the time regarded ammonium nitrate as potentially dangerous, especially when combined with carbonaceous material as it was in this fertilizer. One witness had been hired by the War Production Board to conduct tests into explosion and fire hazards of this product. The Board terminated these tests at an intermediate stage, against the recommendation of the laboratory and in the face of the suggestion that further research might point up suspected but unverified dangers. In addition, there was a considerable history over a period of years of unexplained fires and explosions involving such ammonium nitrate. The zeal and skill of government counsel to distinguish each of these fires on its facts appears to exceed that of some of the experts on whose testimony they rely. The Government endeavored to impeach the opinions of petitioner's experts, introduced experts of its own, and sought to show that private persons who manufactured similar fertilizer took no more precautions than did the Government.

In this situation, even the simplest government official could anticipate likelihood of close packing in large masses during sea shipment, with aggravation of any attendant dangers. Where the risk involved is an explosion of a cargo-carrying train or ship, perhaps in a congested rail yard or at a dock, the producer is not entitled as a matter of law to treat industry practice as a conclusive guide to due care. Otherwise, one free disaster would be permitted as to each new product before the sanction of civil liability was thrown on the side of high standards of safety.

It is unnecessary that each of the many findings of negligence by the trial judge survive the "clearly erroneous" test of appellate review. Without passing on the rest of his findings, we find that those as to the duty of further inquiry and negligence in shipment and failure to warn are sufficient to support the judgment. We construe these latter findings not as meaning that each omission in the process of bagging, shipping, and failure to warn, if standing alone, would have imposed liability on the Government, but rather that due care is not consistent with this seriatim resolution of every conflict between safety and expediency in favor of the latter. This Court certainly would hold a private corporation liable in this situation, and the statute imposes the same liability upon the Government unless it can bring itself within the Act's exception, to which we now turn.

The Government insists that each act or omission upon which the charge of negligence is predicated—the decisions as to discontinuing the investigation of hazards, bagging at high temperature, use of paperbagging material, absence of labeling and warning— involved a conscious weighing of expediency against caution and were therefore within the immunity for discretionary acts provided by the Tort Claims Act. It further argues, by way of showing that by such a construction the reservation would not completely swallow the waiver of immunity, that such discretionary decisions are to be distinguished from those made by a truck driver as to the speed at which he will travel so as to keep the latter within the realm of liability.

We do not predicate liability on any decision taken at "Cabinet level" or on any other high-altitude thinking. Of course, it is not a tort for government to govern, and the decision to aid foreign agriculture by making and delivering fertilizer is no actionable wrong. Nor do we find any indication that in these deliberations that any decision was made to take a calculated risk of doing what was done, in the way it was done, on the chance that what did happen might not happen. Therefore, we are not deterred by fear that governmental liability in this case would make the discretion of executives and administrators timid and restrained. However, if decisions are being made at Cabinet levels as to the temperature of bagging explosive fertilizers, whether paper is suitable for bagging hot fertilizer, and how the bags should be labeled, perhaps an increased sense of caution and responsibility even at that height would be wholesome. The common sense of this matter is that a policy adopted in the exercise of an immune discretion was carried out carelessly by those in charge of detail. We cannot agree that all the way down the line there is immunity for every balancing of care against cost, of safety against production, of warning against silence.

. . .

The Government ... relies on the body of law developed in the field of municipal liability for torts which deal with discretionary, as opposed to ministerial, acts. Whatever the substantiality of this dichotomy, the cases which have interpreted it are in hopeless confusion; some have used "discretionary" and "ministerial" interchangeably with "proprietary" and "governmental," while others have rather uncritically borrowed the same terminology from the law of mandamus. But even cases cited by the Government hold that, although the municipality may not be held for its decision to undertake a project, it is liable for negligent execution or upkeep.

We think that the statutory language, the reliable legislative history, and the common-sense basis of the rule regarding municipalities, all point to a useful and proper distinction preserved by the statute other than that urged by the Government. When an official exerts governmental authority in a manner which legally binds one or many, he is acting in a way in which no private person could. Such activities do and are designed to affect, often deleteriously, the affairs of individuals, but courts have long recognized the public policy that such official shall be controlled solely by the statutory or administrative mandate and not by the added threat of private damage suits. For example, the Attorney General will not be liable for false arrest in circumstances where a private person performing the same act would be liable,[15] and such cases could be multiplied.[16] The official's act might inflict just as great an injury and might be just as wrong as that of the private person, but the official is not answerable. The exception clause of the Tort Claims Act protects the public treasury where the common law would protect the purse of the acting public official.

But many acts of government officials deal only with the housekeeping side of federal activities. The Government, as landowner, as manufacturer, as shipper, as warehouseman, as shipowner and operator, is carrying on activities indistinguishable from those performed by private persons. In this area, there is no good reason to stretch the legislative text to immunize the Government or its officers from responsibility for their acts, if done without appropriate care for the safety of others. Many official decisions even in this area may involve a nice balancing of various considerations, but this is the same kind of balancing which citizens do at their peril and we think it is not within the exception of the statute.

The Government's negligence here was not in policy decisions of a regulatory or governmental nature, but involved actions akin to those of a private manufacturer, contractor, or shipper. Reading the discretionary exception as we do, in a way both workable and faithful to legislative intent, we would hold that the Government was liable under these circumstances. Surely a statute so long debated was meant to embrace more than traffic accidents. If not, the ancient and discredited doctrine that "The King can do no wrong" has not been uprooted; it has merely been amended to read, "The King can do only little wrongs."

NOTES

(1) Compare the following two cases with respect to possibilities of recovery under the Federal Tort Claims Act:

(a) An employee of the Army Corps of Engineers, which operates the floodgates at Sault Ste. Marie on Lake Superior, makes a mistake in measuring the amount of water that goes through the gates, with the result that there is serious flooding on the plaintiff's property.

(b) An official of the Army Corps of Engineers makes a decision to let more water through the floodgates, in order to maintain the lake level of Lake Superior within a range specified in an international agreement, with the result that the plaintiff's property is flooded.

(2) Does the failure to properly maintain a traffic light on federal property fit within the FTCA discretionary function?

(3) Suppose that a school child sues the Government for alleged negligence in failing to assign teachers in an army base school to hall duty in a way that minimizes student violence. Is that a viable FTCA case? Cf. the *Butler* decision, supra § 4.05.

(4) Consider a suit for injuries allegedly caused by a decision of an employee of a state highway department concerning the alignment of a road. Would that claim be barred, per se, under a state statute with a discretionary function exception that was identical to the one in the FTCA?

---

15. *Gregoire v. Biddle*, 2 Cir., 177 F.2d 579.
16. *Spalding v. Vilas*, ... (Postmaster General).... The overwhelming weight of authority in the states is to the same effect....

(5) Consider these facts, drawn from a federal case: An armed hijacker took over a plane carrying two passengers and ordered it to land for refueling. Ten minutes after the landing, the co-pilot emerged from the plane, apparently to negotiate for fuel, and an associate of the hijacker also left the craft and was taken into custody. About five minutes later, the FBI agent in charge at the scene ordered two other agents to block the plane's path with their car, and then ordered them to shoot out the tires. After they did so, they heard shots from inside the airplane. The agent in charge then ordered one of his associates to shoot out an engine of the plane. After that, moaning was heard from inside the plane and it was discovered that the hijacker had killed his hostages and fatally wounded himself. An FBI handbook, as well as inter-office memoranda in the agent's office, placed considerable emphasis on hostage safety and pilot cooperation in hijacking situations. Sued by survivors of the gunman's victims, the Government offered the discretionary function defense. What would be the likely outcome of the case?

(6) Assume that an Army general orders the shipment of a nerve gas by train over a route that is clearly more dangerous than another route from the point of view of risk to adjoining residents, but significantly better than the other route from a military perspective. If a tank car overturns, and residents of the surrounding area are injured by the escape of the gas, what legal issues will arise?

(7) Why does the Tort Claims Act permit only damages, and not injunctive relief?

(8) Assume that a United States military adviser dies in the line of duty, on an assignment on which his services are committed to the aid of the armed forces of another country, with the purpose of containing a revolutionary movement. If the United States has not declared war on the other country, could the adviser's family sue the Government, alleging negligence in assigning him to this duty?

(9) Is the true ground of decision in *Dalehite* one of "discretion" or "no negligence"? Should the degree of danger or the amount of knowledge possessed by government officials figure into the question of whether a decision is "discretionary"?

(10) Assuming there was negligence in *Dalehite*, how can one justify the result reached by the majority, in light of the imposition of negligence liability on such defendants as the Radisson Hotel in *LaPlante*, supra § 4.01?

PROBLEM

"Everybody talks about the weather, but nobody does anything about it." On a November Friday, two lobstering vessels set out from Hyannis, Massachusetts, for the fishing grounds on the southeastern edge of Georges Bank. Before they left port, the lobstermen, as they usually did, listened to the marine weather predictions of the National Weather Service. This forecast, at 11 a.m., predicted good weather for the next day. Later broadcasts, at 5 p.m. and 11 p.m., repeated the prediction. At about the time the lobstermen arrived at the fishing grounds on Saturday, the 5 a.m. marine report included a gale warning, with predictions of northwest winds of 30 to 40 knots, diminishing by night, and seas six to twelve feet, subsiding at night. Even by that time, however, the weather was heavier than predicted; winds ran to 70 knots and seas were 30 to 40 feet high. It was the kind of storm known as a "bomb," because of its "sudden and explosive development." Several men on the vessels were lost.

There was evidence that the Weather Service could have made accurate predictions but for the malfunctioning of a weather-reporting buoy on Georges Bank. After the buoy was damaged, apparently by a passing ship, repairs had left the device in a condition in which its wind speed and direction data were erratic. One replacement buoy went adrift, and could not be put back into service until January. Another replacement buoy went adrift and was lost. The Government did not attempt repairs to the original, malfunctioning buoy.

What will the Government's defense be in a suit for the deaths of the lobstermen? Will the defense be successful?

NOTES

(1) Between 1951 and 1962, the federal government detonated more than 100 atomic bombs above ground at a test site in Nevada. In subsequently monitoring downwind communities for radiation effects, the government "deviated from optimum practices based on the best available scientific knowledge," at least in part "to avoid arousing public concern." Many residents in the area of fallout suffered from and died of cancer. But in *Allen v. United States*, 816 F.2d 1417 (1988), the Tenth Circuit rejected more than a thousand FTCA claims. Though the 1946 Atomic Energy Act directed the Atomic Energy Commission "to make arrangement ... for ... the protection of health during research and production activities," there was no showing that "test site personnel ignored or failed to implement specific procedures mandated by the AEC for monitoring and informing the public." The court ruled that the Atomic Energy Commission, as well as designated safety officers, had acted within their "discretionary" duties under the statute. Reluctantly concurring, Judge McKay lamented, "[T]he rule that 'the king can do no wrong' still prevails at the federal level in all but the most trivial of matters.... [T]he FTCA ... is largely a false promise in all but 'fender benders' and perhaps some cases involving medical malpractice by government doctors."

A landmark case mentioned in the *Allen* opinions is *Indian Towing Co. v. United States*, 350 U.S. 61 (1955). The suit in *Indian Towing* was for negligent maintenance and inspection of a lighthouse light. The Government argued that under the clause of the FTCA that imposes liability "in the same manner and to the same extent as a private individual under like circumstances," it could not be sued for "activities which private persons do not perform" — that is, "for negligent performance of 'uniquely governmental functions.'" In his opinion for the court in that case, referring to the "under like circumstances" language of the Tort Claims Act, Justice Frankfurter called state court efforts to develop the "governmental"-"non-governmental" distinction an "awkward and contradictory" attempt "to escape from the basic historical doctrine of sovereign immunity." *Id.* at 65. Frankfurter declared that "[t]he Federal Tort Claims Act cuts the ground from under that doctrine," saying that the legislation was "not self-defeating by covertly embedding the casuistries of municipal liability for torts." *Id.* He said that "it is hard to think of any governmental activity on the 'operational level,' our present concern, which is 'uniquely governmental,' in the sense that its kind has not at one time or another been, or could not conceivably be, privately performed." *Id.* at 68. Frankfurter concluded that "[t]he broad and just purpose which the statute was designed to effect was to compensate the victims of negligence in the conduct of governmental activities in circumstances like unto those in which a private person would be liable and not to leave just treatment to the caprice and legislative burden of individual private laws." *Id.* at 68–69.

(2) In decisions reaching back to the nineteenth century, courts provided an escape hatch for plaintiffs confronting governmental immunity by making a distinction between "proprietary" and "governmental" functions. The theory was that immunity did

not protect governments from suits for injuries resulting from the sorts of activities in which governments act like private entrepreneurs rather than performing the kind of function that only governments can perform. Illustratively, the Alabama court once granted recovery for the death of a convict killed by police while working on the street — presumably a proprietary function — but dismissed the case of a convict shot by a prison guard while he was trying to flee a road gang, since presumably the guard was acting in performance of a "governmental" duty. See Shapo, *Municipal Liability for Police Torts: An Analysis of a Strand of American Legal History*, 17 U. MIAMI L. REV. 475, 478–79, 485 & nn. 64–65 (1963).

(3) The Supreme Court turned back an attack on the *Dalehite* majority's denial of "absolute liability" for "extra hazardous activities" in a case where military overflights caused sonic booms, producing property damage. *Laird v. Nelms*, 406 U.S. 797 (1972). Justice Rehnquist, writing for the majority, concluded that the plaintiffs had not shown a "negligent or wrongful act" under the statute. He also rejected what he viewed as an attempt at "dressing up the substance of strict liability for ultra-hazardous activities in the garments of common-law trespass." Justice Stewart's dissent emphasized the change of direction from *Dalehite* represented by *Indian Towing*, supra note 1, and also the anomaly that private persons would be liable for blasting.

Do you agree with Justice Rehnquist's conclusion, given the Act's requirement that plaintiffs show a "negligent or wrongful act or omission"? If you do, would you support an amendment to the Act that would allow suits for sonic boom damage and other harm non-negligently caused by similarly high-risk activity? How would you write the amendment?

(4) The Supreme Court has refused to allow FTCA recovery for injuries to servicemen caused by the negligence of government employees "where the injuries arise out of or are in the course of activity incident to service." In the absence of an express legislative resolution of the issue, the Court would not infer that Congress had "created a new cause of action dependent on local law for service-connected injuries or death due to negligence"; the Court noted that "the relationship of military personnel to the Government has been governed exclusively by federal law." *Feres v. United States*, 340 U.S. 135 (1950).

(5) A case involving a vaccine-caused injury that made its way to the Supreme Court resulted in a unanimous decision for the claimant, on allegations that employees of the Bureau of Biologics had "knowingly approved the release of a lot" of the vaccine "that did not comply with safety standards." *Berkovitz by Berkovitz v. United States*, 108 S. Ct. 1954, 1964 (1988). On the "scanty" record before it, the Court chose not to decide the issue of "whether agency officials appropriately exercise policy judgment in determining that a vaccine product complies with the relevant safety standards," *id.* at 1963. However, speaking through Justice Marshall, the Court made clear that the discretionary function exception did not apply "if the Bureau's policy did not allow the official who took the challenged action to release a noncomplying lot on the basis of policy considerations." *Id.* at 1964.

(6) Although the maintenance of surfaces, either roads for driving or floors for walking, might appear to involve choices of the sort that do not involve policymaking, the Government has been at least partially successful in defending such cases. Consider, for example:

• *Williams v. United States*, 50 F.3d 299 (4th Cir. 1995), a slip and fall case in which the plaintiff was injured in the lobby of a building leased by the Government, which had a comprehensive maintenance contract with a private firm. The plaintiff alleged that the Government was negligent in letting water accumulate on the floor on a day of "torrential" rains and not warning of the condition. The court concluded that "[t]he decision to hire an independent contractor to render services for the United States is precisely the type of decision that the exception is designed to shield from liability because it involves exercising judgment based on considerations of policy." It said that in making that decision, the Government "had to weigh concerns of expense, administration, payment, access to the Premises, and a veritable plethora of factors." *Id.* at 310. *Inter alia*, it pointed to the "detailed, comprehensive nature" of the Government's contract with the contractor and "the burdens allocated under the contract to [the contractor] to ensure well maintained Premises."

• *Cope v. Scott*, 45 F.3d 445 (D.C. Cir. 1995), which split its holdings on allegations concerning the danger of a road surface in Rock Creek Park in the District of Columbia. On the one hand, the court applied the discretionary function exception to what it characterized as road conditions that "could have been prevented only by reducing ... traffic load, initially paving ... with a different surface, resurfacing [a] curve entirely, or at least milling the curve to create grooves in the surface." This, the court said, would "require balancing factors" such as the road's "overall purpose, the allocation of funds among significant project demands, the safety of drivers and other park visitors, and the inconvenience of repairs as compared to the risk of safety hazards." *Id.* at 451. But the court vacated a dismissal concerning an allegation of failure to post warning signs; it said that "the discretion regarding where and what type of signs to post is not the kind of discretion protected by the discretionary function exception." *Id.*

(7) An FTCA decision drew on two overlapping concepts of duty under state law in a case involving the infectious disease brucellosis, which afflicted cattle leased to the plaintiffs after a sale to Ag Assets, a leasing agent, by the Bookouts, the original owners of the animals. A Government veterinarian, who examined a group of 47 animals on the Bookout farm during the same month in which the plaintiffs made their leasing deal, discovered brucellosis in three of those cattle. He had those three animals slaughtered and quarantined the other 44, but he did not investigate whether those cattle had had contact with other cattle on the Bookout farm. Following the sale to Ag Assets by the Bookouts, a group of 52 cattle were delivered to the plaintiffs, a private veterinarian having certified all of the Bookouts' cattle to be free of brucellosis. When the disease subsequently appeared in the herd to which the plaintiffs had added the leased cattle, they were forced to destroy the entire herd. After settling with the Bookouts, the plaintiffs sued the Government, claiming that its veterinarian was negligent in failing to investigate the Bookouts' cattle sufficiently, failing to quarantine the entire herd, and failing to warn prospective customers.

In denying recovery, the court invoked the idea that state statutes on animal health and brucellosis "impose[d] a duty on government officials to the public as a whole rather than to a particular individual." Thus establishing that the plaintiffs must show a "special duty or relationship" in order to recover, the court could find none. Its analysis in this regard drew on general tort concepts of duty. Considering the plaintiffs' argument that the government "veterinarian should have known that they would have been foreseeable victims," the court commented that this sort of duty issue had been "likened to an inquiry into proximate cause." It said that there was no evidence to indicate that the government veterinarian "had knowledge, or should have known, that [the original owners of the cattle] would later ship some of their cattle to [the plaintiffs]." It further pointed out that although the plaintiffs might have relied on assurances by the original owners, the leasing agent, or the health certificates, "they had no reason to know of, or to rely on, [the federal veterinarian's] quarantining" only the group of cattle that he did quarantine on the farm of the original owners. *Stratmeyer v. United States*, 67 F.3d 1340, 1347–48 (7th Cir. 1995).

(8) What is the principal purpose of the discretionary function exception of the Tort Claims Act? To protect regulatory activity from litigation? To assure a wide range of choice for policy-making? To insure that litigation will not undercut the implementation of policy where to do so would affect the feasibility of that policy?

§ 18.02 Governmental "Duty to Act"

PROBLEM*

Josephine and Frank Sorichetti were married in 1949, and had three children, the youngest being Dina, who was born in 1969. It appears that Frank drank excessively and that the couple's relationship was quite stormy. Frank became violent and abusive when under the influence of alcohol. In January 1975, Josephine obtained an order of protection in Family Court following a particularly violent incident in which her husband had threatened her and punched her in the chest so forcefully as to send her "flying across the room." The order recited that Frank was "forbidden to assault, menace, harass, endanger, threaten or act in a disorderly manner toward" Josephine. By June 1975, Frank's drinking and abusiveness had intensified. Consequently, Josephine moved out of their residence and took her own apartment. Upon her return in early July to obtain her personal belongings, Frank attacked her with a butcher knife, cutting her hand, which required suturing, and threatened to kill her and the children. The police were summoned from the 43rd precinct, but Frank had fled by the time they arrived. A second order of protection was issued by Family Court and a complaint filed in Criminal Court by Josephine. Frank was arrested by detectives from the 43rd precinct, but Josephine subsequently dropped both the Family Court and criminal charges based on Frank's promise to reform.

Frank's drinking and violent behavior continued, however, and in September 1975, Josephine served divorce papers on him. Frank became enraged and proceeded to destroy the contents of their apartment. He broke every piece of furniture, cut up clothes belonging to his wife and Dina, threw the food out of the refrigerator and bent every knife and fork. The police from the 43rd precinct were summoned, but they refused to arrest Frank because "he lived there."

Family Court entered a third order of protection that also ordered Frank Sorichetti to stay away from Josephine's home. During the ensuing months, Frank continued to harass his wife and daughter, following them in the mornings as they walked to Dina's school and threatening that they "were Sorichettis" and were going to "die Sorichettis," and that he was going to "bury them." Josephine reported these incidents to the 43rd precinct. Additionally, Frank created disturbances at Josephine's place of employment on a number of occasions with the result that she was discharged. On October 9, 1975, Frank was arrested by officers of the 43rd precinct for driving while intoxicated.

---

* Adapted from a decision.

On November 6, 1975, Josephine and Frank appeared in Family Court where the order of protection was made final for one year. Included in the order was a provision granting Frank visitation privileges with his daughter each weekend from 10:00 a.m. Saturday until 6:00 p.m. Sunday. It was agreed that Dina would be picked up and dropped off at the 43rd precinct. As required by the Family Court Act, the order also recited that: "[T]he presentation of this Certificate to any Peace Officer shall constitute authority for said Peace Officer to take into custody the person charged with violating the terms of such Order of Protection and bring said person before this Court and otherwise, so far as lies within his power, to aid the Petitioner in securing the protection such Order was intended to afford."

On the following weekend, Josephine delivered Dina to her husband in front of the 43rd precinct at the appointed time. As he walked away with the child, Frank turned to Josephine and shouted, "You, I'm going to kill you." Pointing to his daughter, he said, "You see Dina; you better do the sign of the cross before this weekend is up." He then made the sign of the cross on himself. Josephine understood her husband's statements and actions to be a death threat, and she immediately entered the police station and reported the incident to the officer at the desk. She showed him the order of protection and reported that her husband had just threatened her and her child. She requested that the officer "pick up Dina and arrest Frank." She also reported the past history of violence inflicted by Frank. The officer told Josephine that because her husband had not "hurt her bodily—did not touch her" there was nothing the police could do. Josephine then returned home.

At 5:30 p.m. the following day, Sunday, Josephine returned to the station house. She was distraught, agitated and crying. She approached the officer at the front desk and demanded that the police pick up Dina and arrest her husband who was then living with his sister some five minutes from the precinct. She showed the officer the order of protection and related the threats made the previous morning as well as the prior incidents and Frank's history of drinking and abusive behavior. The officer testified that he told Josephine that if "he didn't drop her off in a reasonable time, we would send a radio car out."

The officer referred Josephine to Lieutenant Leon Granello, to whom she detailed the prior events. He dismissed the protective order as "only a piece of paper" that "means nothing" and told Josephine to wait outside until 6:00. At 6:00 p.m., Josephine returned to the Lieutenant who told her, "why don't you wait a few minutes ... Maybe he took her to a movie. He'll be back. Don't worry about it." Josephine made several similar requests, but each time was told "to just wait. We'll just wait." In the meantime, at about 5:20 or 5:30, Officer John Hobbie arrived at the station house. He recognized Josephine, who by then was hysterical, from prior incidents involving the Sorichettis. Specifically, just a few months previously, on June 28, 1975, Hobbie had intervened in an altercation in which Frank, while intoxicated and being abusive, had tried to pull Dina away from a babysitter, cursing and saying, "if I don't have her, the mother shouldn't have her." Hobbie had taken Frank, Dina, and the babysitter to the 43rd precinct, where a decision was made not to let Frank have the child. Frank had started cursing and became loud and abusive. He calmed down somewhat when threatened with removal from the station house, and left when told that the police were holding the child until her mother arrived. In a second incident on October 9, 1975, Officer Hobbie transferred Frank to a hospital for detoxification following Frank's arrest by officers of the 43rd precinct for driving while intoxicated.

After speaking with Josephine on November 9, 1975, Officer Hobbie informed Lieutenant Granello of his prior experiences with Frank. He told the Lieutenant that Sorichetti was a "very violent man" and that Dina was "petrified" of him. Officer Hobbie recommended that a patrol car be sent to Sorichetti's home. Lieutenant Granello rejected this suggestion, contending initially that no patrol cars were available and later that "not enough time ha[d] gone by."

At 6:30, Lieutenant Granello suggested that Josephine call home to see if Dina had been dropped off there. She did so and was informed that the child was not there. She continued to plead that the officer take immediate action. The Lieutenant again told Josephine, "Let's just wait." At 7:00, the Lieutenant told Josephine to leave her phone number and to go home, and that he would call her if Sorichetti showed up. She did as suggested.

At about the same time, Frank Sorichetti's sister entered her apartment and found him passed out on the floor with an empty whiskey bottle and pill bottle nearby. The woman also found Dina, who was severely injured. Between 6:55 and 7:00 p.m., Sorichetti had attacked the infant repeatedly with a fork, a knife and a screwdriver and had attempted to saw off her leg. Police from the 43rd precinct, responding to a 911 call, arrived within five minutes and rushed the child, who was in a coma, to the hospital. The infant plaintiff was hospitalized for 40 days and remains permanently disabled. Frank Sorichetti was convicted of attempted murder and is currently serving a prison sentence.

Dina Sorichetti sued the municipality for its police officers' lack of response to her mother's pleas. What result?

DE LONG v. COUNTY OF ERIE

New York Court of Appeals
60 N.Y.2d 296, 457 N.E.2d 717, 469 N.Y.S.2d 611 (1983)

WACHTLER, JUDGE.

In this suit for damages brought by the family and estate of a woman killed by a burglar, a jury found the City of Buffalo and the County of Erie liable for negligent processing of and response to the victim's call for emergency assistance made on the special 911 number established and serviced by the defendants. The Appellate Division ... affirmed the judgment with two Judges dissenting and the defendants have appealed.

Two primary issues are presented on the appeal. First, whether by creating the special service, accepting the call for emergency assistance and assuring the caller that help was on the way, the municipal agencies may be said to have established a special relationship with and duty to her, sufficient to hold them liable for negligently directing the police patrol cars to the wrong locality and taking no further action when the responding officers reported no such address as that given....

In October, 1976 the decedent, Amalia De Long, resided with her husband and three small children in Kenmore, a village adjacent to the City of Buffalo. Her home at 319 Victoria Boulevard was located approximately 1,300 feet from the Kenmore Police Department. One of her neighbors was a captain in that department.

On the morning of October 25 she telephoned for emergency police assistance by dialing 911. At 9:29 her call was answered by a complaint writer employed by Erie County to respond to such requests. The call, lasting approximately 14 seconds, was recorded in its entirety as follows:

> Caller: "Police?"
>
> Complaint Writer: "911."
>
> Caller: "Police, please come, 319 Victoria right away."
>
> Complaint Writer: "What's wrong?"
>
> . . .
>
> Caller: "I heard a burglar; I saw his face in the back; he was trying to break in the house; please come right away."
>
> Complaint Writer: "Okay, right away."
>
> Caller: "Okay."

The complaint writer erroneously reported the address as 219 Victoria, and mistakenly assumed that the call had originated in Buffalo because he knew there was a Victoria Avenue in the city. Accordingly, after stamping the complaint card "flash" to indicate its high priority, he placed it on a conveyor belt which ran through a glass partition to the radio dispatcher for the Buffalo Police Department. At 9:30 the dispatcher broadcast a report of a burglary in progress to patrol cars in the vicinity of Victoria Avenue in the city. Three minutes later the officers who had responded to the call informed the dispatcher that there was no such address and that the highest number on Victoria was 195. At 9:34 the dispatcher "cleared the call", in effect telling the officers at the scene to disregard it. The dispatcher himself took no further action on the call.

At approximately 9:42 Mrs. De Long was seen running from her house, unclothed and bleeding profusely. She collapsed on the sidewalk in front of her home. A neighbor called the Kenmore Police and within a minute a police car responded—a few minutes later paramedics arrived. However by 9:53 she displayed no vital signs. An autopsy revealed that she had been stabbed several times and had died from loss of blood.

After filing a notice of claim against the city and the county, the decedent's husband commenced an action seeking damages for wrongful death and conscious pain and suffering.

At the trial it was shown that prior to 1975 the City of Buffalo had adopted the 911 number as the one to call for emergency services, including police and fire protection. At that time a person dialing the number within the city would immediately be connected with the Buffalo Police Department where a complaint writer would take the information and give it to a radio dispatcher who in turn would contact the appropriate patrol cars or other emergency vehicles. The complaint writers, originally police officers and later mostly civilians, together with the dispatchers were trained and supervised by a lieutenant or acting lieutenant from the Buffalo Police Department. In March of 1975 Erie County formed a new agency known as Central Police Services which took over the complaint writing function from the city and extended the 911 services to several communities beyond the city limits, including the Village of Kenmore. Thus in 1975 and 1976 the telephone directory for Erie County listed 911 as the emergency number for the "local police".

Under the system adopted by the county, however, a 911 call made within the City of Buffalo or the extended area would not automatically connect the caller with the police department servicing the caller's area. Instead the call would go to the Center for Emergency Services which, pursuant to an agreement with the city, was located in the old 911 room in the Buffalo Police Department headquarters. The stated purpose of the center was to "accept telephone requests for emergency services for all Public Safety Agencies within the service area of the Center, and relay, transfer, or forward such requests to the Public Safety Agency concerned, without requiring the caller to re-dial another telephone number." At this center the county employed its own complaint writers many of whom, including the one who answered the call in this case, had held the same position with the city. In accordance with the agreement the city was required to provide training, supervision and assistance to the complaint writers for a year or more and was still doing so in October, 1976. A Buffalo police lieutenant or acting lieutenant remained in the room to coordinate the activities of the complaint writers and Buffalo police dispatchers and to furnish assistance of a supervisory nature when necessary.

Most of the procedures previously followed by the city were adopted by the county and incorporated in the "Manual for 911 Services". The major additional requirement imposed by the county was that the complaint writers obtain information concerning the location or municipality involved so that the complaint could be forwarded to the police department or other emergency service responsible for that area. This was the subject of additional training for those complaint writers who had previously been employed by the city. They were further instructed to determine the origin of the call at the outset because calls from the city were necessarily processed differently from those originating elsewhere. In the case of city calls the complaint card was placed on a conveyor belt which ran to the Buffalo police dispatcher's office in the room next to the center. For the noncity calls, buttons were installed at the complaint writer's desk which permitted him to immediately transfer the call to the appropriate agency and monitor it to insure that the connection had been made and that the call had been properly routed.

There was also a standard operating procedure for cases in which officers responding to the scene of a priority complaint reported "no such address". In that event the dispatcher was required to notify the lieutenant in charge or the complaint writer. They in turn would either replay the recording of the call to check the information or consult one of the street directories or "duplicate street" listings available at the center to determine whether the address provided could be located in another community.

The transcript of the recording and the testimony of various witnesses connected with the center showed that the complaint writer had failed to comply with the applicable regulations in several respects. He had neglected to obtain (1) the caller's name, (2) the complete street address which would have indicated Victoria Boulevard and not Victoria Avenue as he assumed and (3) the name of the locality or municipality where the call originated. He also neglected to verify the information by repeating it.

In addition, the police dispatcher completely neglected to initiate the follow-up procedures. He had not notified the lieutenant in charge or the complaint writer that the investigating officers could find no such address. He had simply disregarded the call because he assumed it was a "fake".

On the issue of damages for wrongful death the plaintiff called an economist who, over the defendants' objection, testified concerning the value of a housewife's services.

The jury returned a verdict for the plaintiff awarding $200,000 for conscious pain and suffering and $600,000 for wrongful death. Each of the defendants was found 50% responsible for the loss.

The Appellate Division affirmed. Two Justices dissented solely on the ground that a new trial should be granted with respect to the amount of damages recoverable for the wrongful death.

On this appeal the defendants initially contend, as they did in the courts below, that the complaint should be dismissed in its entirety because they owed no special duty to protect the decedent from an attack by a third party. The argument is based on the familiar rule that a municipality cannot be held liable for negligence in the performance of a governmental function, including police and fire protection, unless a special relationship existed between the municipality and the injured party (*see, e.g., ... Riss v. City of New York*, 22 N.Y.2d 579, 293 N.Y.S.2d 897, 240 N.E.2d 860; *Motyka v. City of Amsterdam*, 15 N.Y.2d 134, 256 N.Y.S.2d 595, 204 N.E.2d 635; *Schuster v. City of New York*, 5 N.Y.2d 75, 180 N.Y.S.2d 265, 154 N.E.2d 534; *Steitz v. City of Beacon*, 295 N.Y. 51, 64 N.E.2d 704).

This, of course, is not a case in which there was no contact between the victim and the municipality prior to her death. The plaintiff is not seeking to hold the defendants liable as insurers for failing to protect a member of the general public from a criminal act of which they were not aware but should have anticipated and prevented.... He is not urging that there should be a police officer on every corner or at every place where a crime is likely to occur (*cf. Steitz v. City of Beacon, supra*). Nor is this a case in which the police refused a plea for assistance (*e.g., Riss v. City of New York, supra*; ... or failed to offer assistance when confronted with a situation arguably requiring police intervention....) In those instances it has been urged with some force that the proper allocation of public resources and available police services is a matter for the executive and legislative branches to decide (*Riss v. City of New York, supra*).

In this case the decision had been made by the municipalities to provide a special emergency service which was intended and proclaimed to be more efficient than normal police services. Those seeking emergency assistance were advised not to attempt to call the general number for the local police, which ironically might have avoided the tragedy encountered in this case, but were encouraged to dial the 911 number to obtain a quicker response. In addition, and most significantly, the victim's plea for assistance was not refused. Indeed she was affirmatively assured that help would be there "right away". Considering the fact that she was merely a block and a half from the local police station, and was not yet at the mercy of the intruder, it cannot be said as a matter of law that this assurance played no part in her decision to remain in her home and not seek other assistance. Unfortunately, it only increased the risk to her life.

Under similar circumstances it has been held that a special relationship was created so as to require the municipality to exercise ordinary care in the performance of a duty it has voluntarily assumed. Thus a city may be held liable for neglecting to provide crossing guards for school children when it has voluntarily undertaken the task which the children's parents could justifiably expect to be regularly and properly performed.... Similarly a municipality which has affirmatively certified a building as safe may be held liable to the owners for injury caused by known, blatant and dangerous violations.... The basic principle, as Judge Cardozo observed, is this: "If conduct has gone forward to such a stage that inaction would commonly result, not negatively merely in withholding a benefit, but positively or actively in working an injury, there exists a relation out of which arises a duty to go forward" (*Moch Co. v. Rensselaer Water Co.*, 247 N.Y. 160, 167, 159 N.E. 896)....

Whether a special duty has been breached is generally a question for the jury to decide.... But it should be emphasized that whether the municipality has acted reasonably depends upon the circumstances of the particular case. When an emergency service is involved it must be recognized that the circumstances are often quite demanding and that some mistakes will occur, even when the service is well organized and conscientiously administered. Allowance must be made for this and although any error, however slight, may have dire consequences it will not always justify an award for damages. In this case, however, there was ample basis for the jury to conclude that neither defendant exercised ordinary care in the handling of the call and that they should share responsibility for the foreseeable consequences. We have therefore concluded that there is no basis for reversing and dismissing the complaint against either defendant.

···

NOTES

(1) Consider the following statement of facts:

> Yolanda Davidson was stabbed four times by Jack Blackmun while in a public laundromat. On three earlier occasions women had been stabbed at the same or nearby laundromats. The evening before Yolanda's stabbing, two police officers had the laundromat under surveillance when another stabbing occurred; the police chased the suspect but failed to catch him. The next evening the officers had the laundromat under surveillance for the purpose of preventing assaults and apprehending the felon. The officers were aware of Yolanda's presence in the laundromat throughout the surveillance. After about an hour of surveillance, they saw a man on the premises who closely resembled the attacker of the previous evening and, while watching him for 15 minutes, identified him as the likely perpetrator of that assault. As the officers watched, the suspect entered and left the laundromat "several times." The officers did not warn Yolanda. Eventually she was stabbed.

Would you sustain a demurrer?

(2) In *Riss v. City of New York*, 22 N.Y.2d 579, 240 N.E.2d 860, 293 N.Y.S.2d 897 (1968), mentioned in *De Long*, the court denied recovery to a woman who was maimed by assailants hired by her ex-fiancee, after she had made repeated calls to the police reporting threats against her by that individual. One detective told Ms. Riss, in the characterization of Judge Keating's dissenting opinion, "that she would have to be hurt before the police could do anything for her."

Writing for the majority in rejecting the plaintiff's claim, Judge Breitel said that it was not for courts, "in the absence of legislation, to carve out an area of tort liability for police protection to members of the public." In arguing against the denial of liability, Judge Keating, a former United States Senator, said that "[a]lthough in modern times the compensatory nature of tort law has generally been the one most emphasized, one of its most important functions has been and is its normative aspect. It sets forth standards of conduct which ought to be followed." What value judgments are implicit in this statement?

(3) Consider an alternative argument of Judge Keating in his dissent in *Riss*: that the imposition of liability might induce "officials" to improve police protection. Doesn't the general level of police protection established by municipal officials simply represent a rough-and-ready decision by the people? Why isn't this, ultimately, a decision for the

political arm, without judicial intervention? Would it be a good answer to say that not even the government—and "the people"—can be above "the law"?

(4) A Washington appellate case presents two interesting issues concerning the liability of the Spokane Humane Society for an attack by a pit bull on a five-year-old boy. The Humane Society had a contract with the city to "supply all animal control services," including the impounding of dogs running at large. The plaintiffs sued the Society because it had not impounded the animal that attacked the child, despite numerous complaints that this dog and another pit bull were roaming unleashed. The first issue was whether the Society, which was incorporated as a private, nonprofit corporation, was a "public or governmental entity," and thus entitled to the general protection of the public duty doctrine. On this point, the court held for the defendant, emphasizing that the city had "contractually delegated to the Society the authority to enforce the animal regulations of its ordinance." This did not prove an insuperable barrier to the plaintiffs, however, since the court also held that there was a genuine issue of material fact concerning the "special relationship exception" in light of numerous complaints to the Society, extending over a five-month period, about pit bulls running loose in the plaintiffs' neighborhood. *Champagne v. Spokane Humane Soc'y*, 47 Wash. App. 887, 737 P.2d 1279 (1987), *rev. denied*, 108 Wash. 2d 1035, 1987 WL 503434.

(5) An interesting group of cases concerns the duty of governmental agencies to perform inspections, for example, workplace inspections. Plaintiffs' claims are likely to collide with the discretionary function exception of the Federal Tort Claims Act, see supra § 18.01. In one case, an en banc First Circuit rejected a claim by a worker who suffered "grievous" injuries when her hair was pulled into a machine, and who alleged that an inspector for the Occupational Safety and Health Administration (OSHA) should have documented the problem that caused the accident. *Irving v. United States*, 162 F.3d 154 (1st Cir. 1998), *cert. denied*, 120 S. Ct. 47 (1999). Although sympathetic at the human level, the court could not find a remedy, given the discretionary function exception:

> ... [T]he discretion granted to OSHA inspectors is deeply rooted in policy considerations. The OSH Act's purpose is to provide for a satisfactory standard of safety, not to guarantee absolute safety.... A corollary to this observation is that OSHA may legitimately devote its limited enforcement resources to monitoring workplaces and working conditions that pose the most serious threats to worker health and safety. OSHA has done so in part, for example, by adopting inspection priorities and an administrative plan to govern programmed general inspections....

> The function of an OSHA compliance officer is an integral part of OSHA's enforcement policies. When conducting inspections under the auspices of an administrative plan, OSHA compliance officers are expected to study the layout of the facility they are about to investigate, to review its health and safety records, and to interview employer and employee representatives during the inspection about working conditions. One might expect that as a result of such study, OSHA inspectors will make daily judgments about what risks and safety issues most urgently require their attention. At bottom, OSHA inspectors must visit numerous workplaces, all of which present different challenges and issues, and they simply cannot be expected to inspect every item in every plant. The day-to-day decisions made by compliance officers thus further OSHA's enforcement policy of ensuring adequate safety in workplaces with a view toward efficient and effective use of limited enforcement resources, and are thus grounded in policy....

We are not persuaded by the plaintiff's contention that all inspections ought to be painstakingly comprehensive because individual companies rely on OSHA inspections to improve their health and safety conditions. The OSH Act, in no uncertain terms, places primary responsibility for workplace safety on employers, not on the federal government. . . .

Even if the decision may seem wrong in retrospect, or if its implementation is negligent, such decisionmaking by its nature typically requires a balancing of interests (e.g., how to deploy scarce government resources in the accomplishment of worthwhile—but expensive—public needs).

—*Id.* at 168–69.

In an analogous decision, the Tenth Circuit rejected a claim for negligence on the part of the Mine Safety and Health Administration (MSHA), whose inspector had assisted a mine official with the installation of a lighting package on a mining machine and then indicated where to connect the add-on lights to the power supply. The mining company's engineer apparently misconstrued the instructions and this led to a power connection that resulted in an explosion that killed 15 miners. In rejecting claims by the miners' families against the Government for MSHA's alleged provision of "negligent technical assistance" to the mining company, the court "conclude[d] that MSHA owes no duty of care to mine operators in its provision of technical assistance." The court expressed its bias against "plac[ing] the burden of guarding against injury on the agency," citing "Congress's clear intention that operators remain primarily responsible for mine safety" as a "particularly important consideration" under state law. *Ayala v. United States*, 49 F.3d 607, 611–12 (10th Cir. 1995).

(6) What duty, if any, does a governmental agency owe to the public with respect to monitoring its own mass production procedures for safety regulation? The Louisiana Supreme Court refused to grant immunity to the state Department of Public Safety, which had presented a "no duty" defense in a case involving the automatic relicensing of a driver who the agency knew to be subject to seizures. At the time of the relicensing, the driver "was regularly experiencing seizures" that could not be controlled by medication. The court rejected what it viewed as an attempt to base immunity on "the public duty doctrine." Saying that knowledge of the disorder presented a "red flag," the court said that the licensing agency had a duty "to adopt reasonable procedures to prevent issuance or automatic renewal of the license of a driver whose known physical condition poses a present danger or probable future danger to the motoring public." *Fowler v. Roberts*, 556 So. 2d 1, 7 (1989). Given the number of drivers who are licensed and the number of vehicle accidents that occur, does this decision open the door too wide to tort claims against licensing agencies?

ESTATE OF SINTHASOMPHONE v. CITY OF MILWAUKEE
United States District Court, Eastern District of Wisconsin
838 F. Supp. 1320 (1993)

TERENCE T. EVANS, Chief Judge.

I open this decision by repeating what I said in a decision issued in this case (and three other consolidated cases) a year and a half ago, on March 5, 1992, 785 F.Supp. 1343. In that decision, I wrote: "I'm on 25th and State, and there is this young man. He's buck naked. He has been beaten up . . . He is really hurt . . . He needs some help."

With these words, a caller asked a Milwaukee emergency 911 operator to send help to a person in need of assistance. When the call was made, on May 27, 1990, the name Jeffrey Dahmer was largely unknown. Today, everyone knows the story of the 31-year-old chocolate-factory worker, a killing machine who committed the most appalling string of homicides in this city's history. Dahmer's misdeeds have been widely chronicled. Dahmer, who is white, has confessed to killing 17 young men between the ages of 14 and 28. Eleven of the victims were black, and most were lured into Dahmer's web with promises of, among other things, a sexual experience. The case is incredibly gruesome and bizarre; the dismembered bodies of many of the victims—hearts in the freezer, heads in the fridge—were preserved in Dahmer's small near-westside apartment. The leftovers were deposited in a barrel of acid, conveniently stationed in the kitchen. Dahmer pled guilty to 15 of his 16 Milwaukee County homicides. The 15 murders were committed between January of 1988 and July of 1991. Last month, a jury rejected Dahmer's insanity plea. Today he is a guest of the state of Wisconsin, having been sentenced to life imprisonment without the possibility of parole. Dahmer's recent well-publicized state court trial dealt with a narrow issue; his mental state at the time of the murders. These four federal civil cases raise broader issues, issues that concern the community at large. The issues here concern the conduct of several police officers, policies and attitudes of the police department toward minorities and gays, and the rights of some of the victims of Dahmer's madness. This decision will address some of the issues presented in the cases.

The telephone call for help on May 27 was made from a phone booth just a half a block away from Dahmer's apartment. The subject of the call was Konerak Sinthasomphone, a 14-year-old Laotian boy. Later that evening, after the police had responded to the call and determined that nothing was amiss, Dahmer killed Sinthasomphone. He went on to kill others.... After the arrest, Dahmer confessed to 17 murders. The estate of Konerak Sinthasomphone and his family have filed a lawsuit claiming that the police officers and the City of Milwaukee violated their constitutional rights.... The defendants include Joseph Gabrish, John Balcerzak, and Richard Porubcan, the three Milwaukee police officers who responded to the May 27 call, and the City of Milwaukee itself. The defendants have moved to dismiss the cases....

[In] ... my March 5, 1992, decision, [the] Sinthasomphone case survived the rule 12 motion to dismiss.

So what remains in this case are the claims of Sinthasomphone[1] against Officers Gabrish, Balcerzak, and Porubcan and the claim against the City of Milwaukee. The claim against the city alleges a violation of the equal protection clause of the 14th amendment to the United States Constitution. Against the three officers, Sinthasomphone alleges a violation of the equal protection clause and, in the major allegation in the case, violations of substantive provisions of the due process clause of the 14th amendment. The three officers have now moved for summary judgment dismissing the due process claim against them. In their motion, the officers argue that they have a qualified immunity from suit. This decision will address the officers' motion for summary judgment.

To properly address the motion for summary judgment I must again return to the facts, most of which are undisputed. Jeffrey Dahmer met Konerak Sinthasomphone at the Grand Avenue Mall in Milwaukee on the afternoon of May 26, 1991. Sinthasom-

---

1. I refer to the claims of the estate of Konerak Sinthasomphone and the claims of the parents collectively as the claims of "Sinthasomphone."

phone was 14 years old, 5' 3" tall, and weighed 110 pounds. He was Laotian and spoke English as well as Laotian. Dahmer offered to pay Sinthasomphone to go home with him so Dahmer could take nude or semi-nude pictures of him. The two proceeded to Dahmer's apartment at 924 North 25th Street in Milwaukee, where Dahmer did, in fact, take pictures of Sinthasomphone. Dahmer offered Sinthasomphone a drink, which was laced with Halcion. Sinthasomphone fell into a deep sleep, during which Dahmer, according to his deposition testimony, drilled a small hole in Sinthasomphone's head. He then poured diluted hydrochloric acid into the hole. Dahmer claims that he did this sort of thing in an attempt to induce a "zombie-like state" which would allow him to control his victims, including Sinthasomphone.

During the early morning hours of May 27, while Sinthasomphone was drugged, Dahmer left his apartment to buy beer. While he was gone, Sinthasomphone somehow managed to leave the apartment and find his way to the street, where he was seen by, among others, young women named Sandra Smith and Nicole Childress.

At 25th and State, Smith saw a person she describes as a Chinese boy, running naked from State Street toward an alley next to her mother's apartment at 936 North 25th Street. The boy fell to the ground. Smith thought he was 11 or 12 years old; he had, she says, scrapes on his knees, buttocks, and right shoulder and what appeared to be blood running down his inner thigh from his buttocks. Smith asked Childress to call the police.

While Childress was telephoning, a white male, who turned out to be Dahmer, approached Smith and told her he was Sinthasomphone's friend. He said that Sinthasomphone had a habit of getting drunk on weekends. Smith suspected that Dahmer had caused some of Sinthasomphone's injuries. Dahmer began to lead Sinthasomphone away, with Sinthasomphone trying to break free.

Before they got far, police officers Gabrish and Balcerzak arrived. They were responding to the following dispatch:

> 36, you got a man down. Caller states there's a man badly beaten and is wearing no clothes, lying in the street. 2-5 and State. Anonymous female caller. Ambulance sent.

The officers began to assess the situation. It appeared to Gabrish that Dahmer was assisting Sinthasomphone in walking. The officers say there was no sign that Sinthasomphone was trying to break away from Dahmer.

Balcerzak stayed with Dahmer while Gabrish questioned Sinthasomphone. Sinthasomphone did not answer questions. Dahmer, who unknown to the officers was obviously trying to avoid detection, was calm, courteous, and helpful; he responded politely. He gave Balcerzak his name, date of birth, and employment identification. He told Balcerzak that Sinthasomphone was a house guest who drank too much. He said Sinthasomphone's name was John Mung and that he was 18 or 19 or 19 or 20. Balcerzak repeated questions in an attempt to determine Dahmer's truthfulness; his answers remained consistent.

A few minutes after Balcerzak and Gabrish arrived, another squad came to the scene. Officers Richard Porubcan, also a defendant here, and Pete Mozejewski were providing "informal backup" to Balcerzak and Gabrish.

The officers decided to take Sinthasomphone and Dahmer back to Dahmer's apartment. Either because Sinthasomphone stumbled or because he was resisting, Gabrish and Porubcan physically escorted him. They entered the rear of the apartment building and went to Dahmer's apartment. Once inside Dahmer's apartment, the officers saw no signs of any assault, struggle, or conflict. The officers found Sinthasomphone's clothing and saw colored, almost nude photographs of Sinthasomphone posing in a fashion which led them to conclude that Dahmer and Sinthasomphone had a consensual gay relationship....

The officers, thinking they had verified that Sinthasomphone belonged with Dahmer, left Sinthasomphone in the apartment. Dahmer killed Sinthasomphone some 30 minutes later.

Other facts which are not included in the parties' formal proposed findings of fact but which shed light on the situation are that the fire department ambulance arrived at the scene before the police. One of the rescue personnel thought Sinthasomphone needed treatment, but the ambulance crew was sent away by the police. When the police arrived, Sandra Smith says that she tried to give them information that Dahmer had called Sinthasomphone by different names and that Sinthasomphone was trying to escape from Dahmer. Rather than listening to her, an officer threatened her with arrest, and she left the scene. She went to the home of her mother, Glenda Cleveland. Ms. Cleveland called the police department later to inquire about the incident, and during her call she emphasized that the naked person taken from the scene was just a boy, not an adult.

The issue on the currently pending motion for summary judgment is whether, on these facts, the police officers are entitled to a qualified immunity from suit. In recent years, the doctrine of qualified immunity has expanded the protection it offers to police officers and other public officials. Today, the law is such that the existence of a qualified immunity from suit is almost the norm.... Police officers are immune from suit unless their conduct violates a clearly established right of which a reasonable person would have known....

The possible application of these principles to the present issue was foreshadowed in my decision of March 5, 1992. I implied that the claim based on a violation of the equal protection clause, if proven, would violate clearly established law: "the cases uniformly emphasize that if police action—or even police inaction is a product of intentional discrimination, it violates the equal protection clause." At 1350. Recognizing this principle, the officers have not asked for a qualified immunity from the equal protection claim.

The claim of a substantive due process violation is more difficult to resolve....

The three police officers in this case are entitled to qualified immunity unless their conduct violated Konerak Sinthasomphone's clearly established constitutional rights. A first step in the analysis is a determination of what his constitutional rights were....

The analysis begins with DeShaney v. Winnebago County Dept. of Social Services, 489 U.S. 189, 109 S.Ct. 998, 103 L.Ed.2d 249 (1989). In that case, the United States Supreme Court emphasized that the purpose of the Constitution "was to protect the people from the State, not to ensure that the State protected them from each other." Id. at 196, 109 S.Ct. at 1003. Joshua DeShaney, who was 5 years old, was beaten and rendered profoundly retarded by his father, with whom he lived. Social workers and other local officials had received complaints that the father was abusing the boy, but they did not remove him from his father's custody. After he was beaten for the last time, Joshua and his mother brought a case in this court, pursuant to 42 U.S.C. § 1983, alleging that Joshua's substantive due process right to liberty was abridged when the officials failed to intervene to protect him from his father. The United States Supreme Court ultimately held that the State's failure to protect an individual against private violence does not constitute a violation of the due process clause.

The Court also rejected the contention that the state officials had entered into a "special relationship" with Joshua because the officials knew he faced a special danger from his father, proclaimed their intention to protect him, and thus had a duty to do so in a reasonably competent fashion. A special relationship exists, the Court said, when "the State takes a person into its custody and holds him there against his will ...", most often in a prison or mental hospital, not under circumstances like those present in DeShaney.

Similarly, in Archie v. City of Racine, 847 F.2d 1211 (7th Cir.1988), the court of appeals for this circuit upheld my dismissal of claims that a Racine Fire Department dispatcher had failed to send a rescue vehicle to a woman who later died. In Ellsworth v. City of Racine, 774 F.2d 182 (7th Cir.1985), cert. denied, 475 U.S. 1047, 106 S.Ct. 1265, 89 L.Ed.2d 574, the court of appeals upheld the dismissal of a claim that the Racine Police Department, after agreeing to provide protection to the wife of an undercover narcotics officer, failed to protect her from a beating by a masked assailant....

A few cases reach a contrary result in situations in which there is little room to misunderstand what the results of one's actions or inaction will be. In White v. Rochford, 592 F.2d 381 (7th Cir.1979), a pre-DeShaney case, the court of appeals for this circuit determined that Chicago police violated the Constitution when they left three children, unattended, in a car on the Chicago Skyway after arresting the adult who had been driving the car in which the children were riding. After exposure to the cold, the children left the car, crossed eight lanes of freeway traffic, and wandered around on the roadway at night searching for a telephone.

In Ross v. United States, 910 F.2d 1422 (7th Cir.1990), a 12-year-old boy slipped into the water of Lake Michigan. A friend summoned help, and within 10 minutes two lifeguards, two fire fighters, one police officer, and two civilians, who were scuba-diving nearby, responded. However, before any rescue attempt could begin, a Lake County deputy sheriff arrived in a marine patrol boat. He insisted on enforcing an agreement between the city of Waukegan, Illinois, and Lake County, Illinois, which required the county to provide all police services on Lake Michigan. Pursuant to that agreement, the sheriff had promulgated a policy that directed all members of the sheriff's department to prevent any civilian from attempting to rescue a drowning person and contemplated that only divers from the city of Waukegan Fire Department could perform rescues. The deputy ordered all rescue attempts to stop. When the civilian scuba divers offered to attempt a rescue at their own risk, the deputy threatened to arrest them. Twenty minutes later, 30 minutes after the first would-be rescuers had arrived, the officially authorized divers pulled the boy from the water. He later died. The court found that the complaint stated a claim against both Lake County and the individual deputy.

I concluded in my March 5, 1992, decision that "having dissected these cases, the Sinthasomphone plaintiffs have not merely alleged that the police officers failed to protect Konerak Sinthasomphone from Jeffrey Dahmer." At 1349. Rather, the plaintiffs framed their complaint in terms of the positive actions of the police. The comment on this point, of course, was limited to the nature of the defense motion under consideration at the time. That motion was a rule 12 motion to dismiss based on the facial inadequacy of the complaint. The present matter involves a fully developed rule 56 motion for summary judgment.

In my decision of March 5, 1992, I said that "the DeShaney doctrine is not without some small cracks in its surface; hairline, perhaps, but cracks nonetheless." ... In this case, I am not convinced that Sinthasomphone was "in custody" or in a "special relationship" with the three police officers. Not every person the police usher from one place to another is in custody or a special relationship with them. . . .

In the March 5 decision I stated that the "line between DeShaney and Ross (the most favorable Seventh Circuit case supporting the plaintiffs' claims) may not be entirely clear, but it is discernable." At 1348. I spoke of courts "threading" their way through the maze. There very well may be a way to reconcile all of these cases and others which remain unmentioned, but it is not an easy task.

Recognizing that the issue is difficult almost compels the conclusion that the officers are entitled to a qualified immunity from suit. We must remember that the claims in this case are for violations of the United States Constitution, which primarily protects citizens from state action. If the police officers were the ones who killed Sinthasomphone, they would be liable. However, that is not what happened here. The dastardly acts were committed, we must remember, not by the officers but by Dahmer, a maniac of the first order.

Now, one might not necessarily disagree with those who say that the officers did not do good police work: One could conclude that they did not listen to the witnesses; that they did not investigate as thoroughly as they should have; that they foolishly believed that Jeffrey Dahmer was telling them the truth; that they were callous; and that they were rude to Glenda Cleveland. But the issue in this case is not whether they were good or bad cops in general or during the evening of May 27, 1990. The issue instead is whether, under clearly established constitution doctrine, the officers were required to know that leaving Sinthasomphone with Dahmer would have dire consequences.

The best way to determine when a substantive due process right is clearly established—a legal issue—is to concentrate on the facts. . . . The relevant facts are those possessed by the officers at the time of the incident, not those which emerge after the situation turns out to be as wrought with horror as occurred here, or in DeShaney. In hindsight, of course, Sinthasomphone should not have been left with Dahmer. But one must look at what the police officers knew at the time. And what they knew and how they acted must be viewed in the real world of busy and stressful police work in urban America in the twilight of the 20th Century. Even assuming that the officers failed to do adequate police work, the situation was not sufficiently clear to allow the conclusion that they had to know the inevitable horror which would follow their actions. No one could have clearly known or suspected that Dahmer was a monster who killed and cannibalized his victims. The possibility that the man who willingly took the police to his apartment on May 27 would turn out to be a man whose name today is legendary in the annals of serial killers in America was at best a billion-to-one shot. The police were not, constitutionally, required to know or appreciate that the billion-to-one shot would come up on top.

· · ·

The danger in Ross was undeniably evident: anyone has to know the inevitable result of leaving someone under water for 30 minutes. On the other hand, one does not inevitably know that getting a naked person off the streets, taking him to an apartment where his clothes and near-naked pictures of him are present, and leaving him there with a person who convincingly presents himself as a friend will result in death and dismemberment.

In terms of the information available to the officers, this case is much more like DeShaney than Ross. If, in the face of all the information the state actors had, Joshua DeShaney enjoyed no constitutional right to protection, I cannot conclude that it is clearly established that Sinthasomphone had such a right. The officers are entitled to a qualified immunity. Summary judgment dismissing the due process claim against them is GRANTED. Only the claims alleging a denial of equal protection remain.

NOTES

(1) What is the difference between the applicability of the equal protection and due process clauses to the officers in *Sinthasomphone*?

(2) Why didn't the intervention of the officers in *Sinthasomphone*, which culminated in taking the youth and Dahmer back to Dahmer's apartment, independently create a substantive due process right that overcame the officers' qualified immunity?

(3) Considering the general justice of the case, unconstrained by its statutory and constitutional framework, how do you think the financial consequences of the death of Konerak Sinthasomphone should be allocated, if at all, between the police officers and the city of Milwaukee?

(4) In a later opinion in the case, the court, *inter alia*, denied the City's motion to dismiss against a background including the assertion by the U.S. Commission on Civil Rights that the Milwaukee Police Department had for "two decades 'manifested a police culture unsympathetic, and even antagonistic, in its dealings with minority communities of the City.'" The court concluded that a jury should resolve the question of whether the individual officers had "acted in a discriminatory fashion." *Estate of Sinthasomphone v. City of Milwaukee*, 878 F. Supp. 147, 151 (E.D. Wis. 1995).

(5) *DeShaney v. Department of Social Services*, 489 U.S. 189 (1989), summarized in *Sinthasomphone*, is the fountainhead of the case law. Chief Justice Rehnquist's majority opinion, which rejected the claim of a horribly beaten young boy for failure of social service personnel to take him away from his abusive father, concluded with an emphasis on federalism:

> The people of Wisconsin may well prefer a system of liability which would place on the State and its officials the responsibility for failure to act in situations such as the present one. They may create such a system, if they do not have it already, by changing the tort law of the State in accordance with the regular lawmaking process. But they should not have it thrust upon them by this Court's expansion of the Due Process Clause of the Fourteenth Amendment.

489 U.S. at 203.

A social worker involved in the *DeShaney* case said that her reaction to the news of the child's final injuries was, "I just knew the phone would ring some day and Joshua would be dead." 489 U.S. at 209 (Blackmun, J., dissenting) (quoting 812 F.2d 298, 300 (7th Cir. 1987)). Given that testimony, is there such a difference between acts and failures to act that there should be liability for police beatings, but no liability for this failure to prevent a clearly known risk?

(6) What is the most persuasive defensive concept in a case like that of *Sinthasomophone* or that of *DeShaney*?:

- Discretionary function
- No special duty
- In the case of officers, qualified immunity

(7) One may compare with *Sinthasomphone* and *DeShaney* a Wisconsin state case in which police allegedly did not fulfill a promise to arrest a man who had threatened a

woman with whom he had a two-year relationship. The promise allegedly was targeted to a time and place where the man would be. A few days after the promise went unful-filled, the man killed the woman. The Wisconsin Supreme Court rejected the claim, saying that "law enforcement officials must retain the discretion to determine, at all times, how best to carry out their responsibilities." With reference to the profile presented by the case, the court explained:

> Complaints of sexual assault and threats are, unfortunately, not rare in inter-spousal and boyfriend-girlfriend relationships. Nevertheless, as tragic and hor-rifying as these crimes are, the situations do not always lead to an immediately dangerous escalation of violence to the point of homicide....
>
> We look to our police departments to enforce our laws and to maintain order in what is becoming an increasingly dangerous society. Routinely, police face critical situations, many of which have the potential for violence. On a typical day, any given law enforcement officer may be arresting and question-ing suspects, interviewing and counseling victims, talking to witnesses, rescu-ing children, and investigating criminal activity. In the course of their work, police must often try to console and reassure people who are distraught and fearful. Faced with escalating violence, they must continuously use their dis-cretion to set priorities and decide how best to handle specific incidents. Police officers must be free to perform their responsibilities, using their experience, training, and good judgment, without also fearing that they or their employer could be held liable for damages from their allegedly negligent discretionary decisions.

—*Barillari v. City of Milwaukee*, 194 Wis. 2d 247, 261–62, 533 N.W.2d 759, 764–65 (1995).

Judge Abrahamson, dissenting, said that "an officer's promise to appear or send other officers to appear at an agreed time and place to arrest an assailant whose appear-ance at that place and time has been prearranged is of a different nature than ... more general promises to protect and arrest." She thought that the plaintiffs should get to the jury on "whether the more specific promise was made," whether the failure to fulfill the promise was negligent, and "whether any negligence was a substantial factor in causing the harm." 194 Wis. 2d at 264, 533 N.W.2d at 765–66.

(8) What is the principal policy argument that you would advance as an attorney for an officer or government in cases of this sort? An argument based on the concern that a decision for the plaintiff would create a disincentive to provide public services? An ar-gument based on a principled opposition to judicial incursion into the legislative province by reallocation of governmental resources? What counterarguments would you anticipate that plaintiffs would make?

PROBLEM

Consider this description of "disorders which occurred in the City of Miami in August, 1968, while the Republican National Convention was being held on Miami Beach":

> A rally featuring civil rights speakers was scheduled in Miami for the afternoon and evening of August 7th. Merchants bordering the rally area requested in-creased police protection as they were fearful of possible results of the assembly. Subsequently, numerous city police officers were stationed in the vicinity. As

the evening wore on, these officers were removed by direct order of the Mayor. This removal was confirmed by an order issued by the Sheriff of the County.

Thereafter, certain participants in the rally lost restraint and turned to plundering neighboring stores. By the time police control was re-established, damage in excess of $100,000.00 had been sustained by the merchants....

The merchants sued the city and certain officials, alleging that "removal of the officers was a careless and negligent act" because the defendants "knew, or should have known," that there would be damage to the plaintiffs' interests. What would have been the principal arguments for both parties, and what result?

SPECIAL NOTE ON OFFICIALS' IMMUNITIES AND LIABILITIES

Certain public officials, including judges, prosecutors, members of Congress and their aides, and constitutional officers in the executive branch, enjoy immunity from money damages in tort liability predicated on their conduct when discharging public functions. The Supreme Court had occasion to discuss this immunity—part common law, part constitutional law—in 1997, in an interlocutory appeal from *Jones v. Clinton*, 990 F. Supp. 657 (E.D. Ark. 1998), discussed in Chapter 1, which involved allegations of sexual harassment against President Clinton for alleged advances on Paula Jones when Mr. Clinton was governor of Arkansas.

The Court in *Clinton v. Jones* denied immunity. It would have been difficult to construe then-Governor Clinton's alleged conduct as in any way "official," and the Court explained that official immunity must be defined functionally. Even the "absolute" immunity of a judge "does not extend to actions performed in a purely administrative capacity." Thus the encounter alleged by Paula Jones fell outside the scope of any official function. The Court further declined President Clinton's request for a stay for the remainder of his term—"temporary immunity" as the court of appeals characterized it. Despite concerns about separation of powers, the Court decided that the case could proceed, as long as the District Court remained sensitive to the President's official obligations.

While rejecting Mr. Clinton's request for "temporary immunity," the Court articulated the general rationale for granting absolute immunity. It quoted a precedent on the idea that officials such as prosecutors and judges "represent the interest of society as a whole." Thus society is best served by affording them "the maximum ability to deal fearlessly and impartially with the public at large." Immunity "forestall[s] an atmosphere of intimidation that would conflict with their resolve to perform their designated functions in principled fashion." *Clinton v. Jones*, 520 U.S. 681, 693, 117 S. Ct. 1636, 137 L. Ed. 2d 945 (1997) (quoting *Ferri v. Ackerman*, 444 U.S. 193, 202–04 (1979)).

In one precedent the Court mentioned, former President Nixon was sued over the firing of an Air Force employee allegedly "by means of a trumped-up reduction in force, knowing that such a discharge was contrary to the civil service laws." The Supreme Court granted immunity in that case. Presidential immunity is necessarily broad, extending to the "outer perimeter" of official duties, the Court reasoned, "[b]ecause of the singular importance of the Presiden[cy.]" "Cognizance of ... personal vulnerability frequently could distract a President from his public duties." *Nixon v. Fitzgerald*, 457 U.S. 731, 102 S. Ct. 2690, 73 L. Ed. 2d 349 (1982). It should be noted, however, that the Court had required President Nixon, while in office, to comply with a subpoena in connection with the Watergate investigation. The Court rejected an "absolute, unqualified

Presidential privilege of immunity from judicial process under all circumstances." *United States v. Nixon*, 418 U.S. 683, 94 S. Ct. 3090, 41 L. Ed. 2d 1039 (1974).

NOTES

(1) Why should government officials be entitled to any sort of immunity? Consider, in this regard, the declaration of Chief Justice Marshall in *Marbury v. Madison*, 1 Cranch 137, 163 (1803): "[T]he very essence of civil liberty certainly consists of the right of every individual to claim the protection of the laws, whenever he receives an injury."

(2) A much quoted sentence on absolute immunity for officials appears in a decision by Learned Hand providing absolute immunity to the Attorney General of the United States and other officials, in a suit by a man interned for several years during World War II. Judge Hand summarized the rationale for immunity as that "it is impossible to know whether the claim is well founded until the case has been tried, and ... to submit all officials, the innocent as well as the guilty, to the burden of a trial and to the inevitable danger of its outcome, would dampen the ardor of all but the most resolute." *Gregoire v. Biddle*, 177 F.2d 579, 581 (2d Cir. 1949).

(3) Should the rank or status of an official make a difference in what kind of immunity he or she receives—that is, absolute immunity or qualified immunity, the latter basically defined as requiring that the defendant have acted in good faith in taking the action at issue? In a companion case to *Nixon v. Fitzgerald*, the Supreme Court granted qualified immunity, although it refused to grant absolute immunity, to senior aides to President Nixon who allegedly participated in the conspiracy to violate Fitzgerald's constitutional and statutory rights. *Harlow v. Fitzgerald*, 457 U.S. 800 (1982). Can you distinguish, in this regard, a Cabinet officer acting in an administrative role, a Cabinet officer acting in a quasi-judicial role, a presidential aide, and a police officer?

Should the kind of tort, or quasi-tort, make a difference? Are there meaningful distinctions with respect to immunity defenses between a wrongful discharge and a brutal beating? Is there a meaningful distinction between federal and state officials?

(4) What similarities and differences are there between the kind of immunity for which Clinton contended, and which Nixon was granted, and the immunity granted for "discretionary function[s]" in the Federal Tort Claims Act?

(5) One of the few categories of officials who have absolute immunity is judges. Why should this be? In *Stump v. Sparkman*, 435 U.S. 349 (1978), an Indiana state judge successfully invoked absolute immunity against charges that he had facilitated a sterilization operation on an unknowing minor. Why should not a judge have to show, at the least, that there was no clearly established law on the subject or that he did not, in bad faith, ignore the probable illegality of approving the sterilization petition?

(6) As one might expect from a situation in which a vigorous citizenry is presented with expanded opportunities to sue officials, there has been a rich and fascinating development of case law on the subject of official immunity.

Consider how you would react to the following cases involving high government officials:

(a) An attorney general authorizes a warrantless wiretap, on grounds of national security, on the phone of a person who is a member of an antiwar group suspected of making plans to blow up heating tunnels linking federal buildings. At the time, with some support from the lower courts, the Justice Department believes these taps to be constitutional. However, two federal district court decisions, rendered just after the attorney general authorizes the tap on the plaintiff's phone, bar the use of warrantless wiretaps in cases involving alleged domestic threats to national security. A year later, the Supreme Court affirms one of these decisions, concluding that the attorney general does not have the power to order such taps. *Mitchell v. Forsyth*, 472 U.S. 511 (1985) (dictum that absolute immunity would not apply, but attorney general should get summary judgment on the basis of qualified immunity because the question of legality "was open at the time he acted").

(b) The National Security Adviser orders a wiretap on the home telephone of a National Security Council staff member, seeking to trace the source of a leak of classified information on American bombing of Cambodia. *Halperin v. Kissinger*, 807 F.2d 180 (D.C. Cir. 1986), rejected absolute immunity: "If performance of a national security *function* does not entitle the Attorney General to absolute immunity, then the fact that the National Security Adviser's '*entire* function is defined by the interrelated concepts of national security and foreign policy'... can hardly justify the conferral of absolute immunity upon that office as such." *Id.* at 194. Because of the immediate national security concerns surrounding the bombing, the court held that it was appropriate to grant summary judgment to the defendant concerning the initiation of the wiretap. However, the continuation of the tap for more than a year with "no product bearing upon national security concerns" presented a jury question, for it was "impossible to find that no reasonable jury could conclude that continuation of the wiretap after May 1970 was objectively unreasonable." *Id.* at 191.

(7) Members of Congress have an express Constitutional immunity for defamatory remarks made in Congress, for the "Speech or Debate" clause in Article One, Section 6, declares, "for any Speech or Debate in either House, they shall not be questioned in any other Place." This protection does not, however, extend to newsletters and press releases issued by members of Congress. Senator William Proxmire found that out when he presented his "Golden Fleece of the Month" award to a researcher who conducted a study that Proxmire characterized as "determin[ing] why monkeys clench their jaws." Reversing a summary judgment for the senator in the researcher's suit for defamation, the Supreme Court said that though press releases were valuable tools for members of Congress to use in "tell[ing] the public about their activities," they were "not a part of the legislative function or the deliberations that make up the legislative process." *Hutchinson v. Proxmire*, 443 U.S. 111, 133 (1979).

----

§ 18.03 The "Constitutional Tort"

MONROE v. PAPE
United States Supreme Court
365 U.S. 167 (1961)

MR. JUSTICE DOUGLAS delivered the opinion of the Court.

This case presents important questions concerning the construction of R.S. § 1979, 42 U.S.C. § 1983, 42 U.S.C.A. § 1983, which reads as follows:

Every person who, under color of any statute, ordinance, regulation, custom or usage, of any State or Territory, subjects, or causes to be subjected, any citizen of the United States or other person within the jurisdiction thereof to the deprivation of any rights, privileges, or immunities secured by the Constitution and laws, shall be liable to the party injured in an action at law, suit in equity, or other proper proceeding for redress.

The complaint alleges that 13 Chicago police officers broke into petitioners' home in the early morning, routed them from bed, made them stand naked in the living room, and ransacked every room, emptying drawers and ripping mattress covers. It further alleges that Mr. Monroe was then taken to the police station and detained on "open" charges for 10 hours, while he was interrogated about a two-day-old murder, that he was not taken before a magistrate, though one was accessible, that he was not permitted to call his family or attorney, that he was subsequently released without criminal charges being preferred against him. It is alleged that the officers had no search warrant and no arrest warrant and that they acted "under color of the statutes, ordinances, regulations, customs and usages" of Illinois and of the City of Chicago. Federal jurisdiction was asserted under R.S. § 1979, which we have set out above, and 28 U.S.C. § 1343, 28 U.S.C.A. § 1343[1]....

The City of Chicago moved to dismiss the complaint on the ground that it is not liable under the Civil Rights Acts nor for acts committed in performance of its governmental functions. All defendants moved to dismiss, alleging that the complaint alleged no cause of action under those Acts or under the Federal Constitution. The District Court dismissed the complaint. The Court of Appeals affirmed.... The case is here on a writ of certiorari which we granted because of a seeming conflict of that ruling with our prior cases....

I.

Petitioners claim that the invasion of their home and the subsequent search without a warrant and the arrest and detention of Mr. Monroe without a warrant and without arraignment constituted a deprivation of their "rights, privileges, or immunities secured by the Constitution" within the meaning of R.S. § 1979. It has been said that when 18 U.S.C. § 241, 18 U.S.C.A. § 241, made criminal a conspiracy "to injure, oppress, threaten, or intimidate any citizen in the free exercise or enjoyment of any right or privilege secured to him by the Constitution," it embraced only rights that an individual has by reason of his relation to the central government, not to state governments. *United States v. Williams*, 341 U.S. 70, 71 S.Ct. 581, 95 L.Ed. 758.... But the history of the section of the Civil Rights Act presently involved does not permit such a narrow interpretation.

Section 1979 came onto the books as § 1 of the Ku Klux Act of April 20, 1871....

[Much of Justice Douglas' summary of legislative history is omitted.]

The debates were long and extensive. It is abundantly clear that one reason the legislation was passed was to afford a federal right in federal courts because, by reason of

---

1. This section provides in material part:

   The district courts shall have original jurisdiction of any civil action authorized by law to be commenced by any person:

   · · ·

   (3) To redress the deprivation, under color of any State law, statute, ordinance, regulation, custom or usage, of any right, privilege or immunity secured by the Constitution of the United States or by any Act of Congress providing for equal rights of citizens or of all persons within the jurisdiction of the United States.

prejudice, passion, neglect, intolerance or otherwise, state laws might not be enforced and the claims of citizens to the enjoyment of rights, privileges, and immunities guaranteed by the Fourteenth Amendment might be denied by the state agencies.

...

... Opponents of the Act, however, did not fail to note that by virtue of § 1 federal courts would sit in judgment on the misdeeds of state officers. Proponents of the Act, on the other hand, were aware of the extension of federal power contemplated by every section of the Act. They found justification, however, for this extension in considerations such as those advanced by Mr. Hoar:

> The question is not whether a majority of the people in a majority of the States are likely to be attached to and able to secure their own liberties. The question is not whether the majority of the people in every State are not likely to desire to secure their own rights. It is, whether a majority of the people in every State are sure to be so attached to the principles of civil freedom and civil justice as to be as much desirous of preserving the liberties of others as their own, as to insure that under no temptation of party spirit, under no political excitement, under no jealousy of race or caste, will the majority either in numbers or strength in any State seek to deprive the remainder of the population of their civil rights.

Although the legislation was enacted because of the conditions that existed in the South at that time, it is cast in general language and is as applicable to Illinois as it is to the States whose names were mentioned over and again in the debates. It is no answer that the State has a law which if enforced would give relief. The federal remedy is supplementary to the state remedy, and the latter need not be first sought and refused before the federal one is invoked. Hence the fact that Illinois by its constitution and laws outlaws unreasonable searches and seizures is no barrier to the present suit in the federal court.

We had before us in *United States v. Classic*, ... § 20 of the Criminal Code, 18 U.S.C. § 242, 18 U.S.C.A. § 242, which provides a criminal punishment for anyone who "under color of any law, statute, ordinance, regulation, or custom" subjects any inhabitant of a State to the deprivation of "any rights, privileges, or immunities secured or protected by the Constitution or laws of the United States." Section 242 first came into the law as § 2 of the Civil Rights Act, Act of April 9, 1866, 14 Stat. 27. After passage of the Fourteenth Amendment, this provision was re-enacted and amended by §§ 17, 18, Act of May 31, 1870, 16 Stat. 140, 144. The right involved in the *Classic* case was the right of voters in a primary to have their votes counted. The laws of Louisiana required the defendants "to count the ballots, to record the result of the count, and to certify the result of the election." *United States v. Classic*, ... 313 U.S. 325–326, 61 S.Ct. 1043. But according to the indictment they did not perform their duty. In an opinion written by Mr. Justice (later Chief Justice) Stone, in which Mr. Justice Roberts, Mr. Justice Reed, and Mr. Justice Frankfurter joined, the Court ruled, "Misuse of power, possessed by virtue of state law and made possible only because the wrongdoer is clothed with the authority of state law, is action taken 'under color of' state law." ... There was a dissenting opinion; but the ruling as to the meaning of "under color of" state law was not questioned.

That view of the meaning of the words "under color of" state law, 18 U.S.C. § 242, 18 U.S.C.A. § 242, was reaffirmed in *Screws v. United States*, ... 325 U.S. 108–113, 65 S.Ct. 1038–1041. The acts there complained of were committed by state officers in performance of their duties, viz., making an arrest effective....

We adhered to that view in *Williams v. United States, supra,* 341 U.S. 99, 71 S.Ct. 578.

Mr. Shellabarger, reporting out the bill which became the Ku Klux Act, said of the provision with which we now deal:

> The model for it will be found in the second section of the act of April 9, 1866, known as the "civil rights act." ... This section of this bill, on the same state of facts, not only provides a civil remedy for persons whose former condition may have been that of slaves, but also to all people where, under color of State law, they or any of them may be deprived of rights....

Thus, it is beyond doubt that this phrase should be accorded the same construction in both statutes—in § 1979 and in 18 U.S.C. § 242, 18 U.S.C.A. § 242.

Since the *Screws* and *Williams* decisions, Congress has had several pieces of civil rights legislation before it. In 1956 one bill reached the floor of the House. This measure had at least one provision in it penalizing actions taken "under color of law or otherwise." A vigorous minority report was filed attacking, *inter alia,* the words "or otherwise." But not a word of criticism of the phrase "under color of" state law as previously construed by the Court is to be found in that report.

[Justice Douglas summarizes two other pieces of recent legislation to which minority reports were filed, and says that as to neither was there criticism of the Court's construction of the "under color of" language.]

If the results of our construction of "under color of" law were as horrendous as now claimed, if they were as disruptive of our federal scheme as now urged, if they were such an unwarranted invasion of States' rights as pretended, surely the voice of the opposition would have been heard in those Committee reports. Their silence and the new uses to which "under color of" law have recently been given reinforce our conclusion that our prior decisions were correct on this matter of construction.

We conclude that the meaning given "under color of" law in the *Classic* case and in the *Screws* and *Williams* cases was the correct one; and we adhere to it.

In the *Screws* case we dealt with a statute that imposed criminal penalties for acts "wilfully" done. We construed that word in its setting to mean the doing of an act with "a specific intent to deprive a person of a federal right." 325 U.S. at page 103, 65 S.Ct. at page 1036. We do not think that gloss should be placed on § 1979 which we have here. The word "wilfully" does not appear in § 1979. Moreover, § 1979 provides a civil remedy, while in the *Screws* case we dealt with a criminal law challenged on the ground of vagueness. Section 1979 should be read against the background of tort liability that makes a man responsible for the natural consequences of his actions....

[Omitted is a passage in which Justice Douglas holds that "Congress did not undertake to bring municipal corporations within the ambit of § 1979," and thus affirms the dismissal as to the city of Chicago.]

Reversed.

[Justice Harlan's concurring opinion is omitted.]

MR. JUSTICE FRANKFURTER, dissenting....

Abstractly stated, this case concerns a matter of statutory construction. So stated, the problem before the Court is denuded of illuminating concreteness and thereby of its far-reaching significance for our federal system. Again abstractly stated, this matter of statutory construction is one upon which the Court has already passed. But it has done so under circumstances and in settings that negative those considerations of social policy upon which the doctrine of *stare decisis*, calling for the controlling application of prior statutory construction, rests.

... The complaint alleges that on October 29, 1958, at 5:45 a.m., thirteen Chicago police officers, led by Deputy Chief of Detectives Pape, broke through two doors of the Monroe apartment, woke the Monroe couple with flashlights, and forced them at gunpoint to leave their bed and stand naked in the center of the living room; that the officers roused the six Monroe children and herded them into the living room; that Detective Pape struck Mr. Monroe several times with his flashlight, calling him "nigger" and "black boy"; that another officer pushed Mrs. Monroe; that other officers hit and kicked several of the children and pushed them to the floor; that the police ransacked every room, throwing clothing from closets to the floor, dumping drawers, ripping mattress covers; that Mr. Monroe was then taken to the police station and detained on "open" charges for ten hours, during which time he was interrogated about a murder and exhibited in lineups; that he was not brought before a magistrate, although numerous magistrate's courts were accessible; that he was not advised of his procedural rights; that he was not permitted to call his family or an attorney; that he was subsequently released without criminal charges having been filed against him. It is also alleged that the actions of the officers throughout were without authority of a search warrant or an arrest warrant; that those actions constituted arbitrary and unreasonable conduct; that the officers were employees of the City of Chicago, which furnished each of them with a badge and an identification card designating him as a member of the Police Department; that the officers were agents of the city, acting in the course of their employment and engaged in the performance of their duties; and that it is the custom of the Department to arrest and confine individuals for prolonged periods on "open" charges for interrogation, with the purpose of inducing incriminating statements, exhibiting its prisoners for identification, holding them *incommunicado* while police officers investigate their activities, and punishing them by imprisonment without judicial trial. On the basis of these allegations various members of the Monroe family seek damages against the individual police officers and against the City of Chicago....

[Omitted, *inter alia*, is Justice Frankfurter's summary of legislative history and of the few cases decided under the statute before *Monroe*.]

The unwisdom of extending federal criminal jurisdiction into areas of conduct conventionally punished by state penal law is perhaps more obvious than that of extending federal civil jurisdiction into the traditional realm of state tort law. But the latter, too, presents its problems of policy appropriately left to Congress. Suppose that a state legislature or the highest court of a State should determine that within its territorial limits no damages should be recovered in tort for pain and suffering, or for mental anguish, or that no punitive damages should be recoverable. Since the federal courts went out of the business of making "general law," *Erie R. Co. v. Tompkins*, ... such decisions of local policy have admittedly been the exclusive province of state lawmakers. Should the civil liability for police conduct which can claim no authority under local law, which is actionable as common-law assault or trespass in the local courts, comport different rules? Should an unlawful intrusion by a policeman in Chicago entail different consequences than an unlawful intrusion by a hoodlum? These are matters of policy in its strictly legislative sense, not for determination by this Court. And if it be, as it is, a matter for congressional choice, the legislative evidence is overwhelming that § 1979 is not expressive of that choice. Indeed, its precise limitation to acts "under color" of state statute, ordinance or other authority appears on its face designed to leave all questions of the nature and extent of liability of individuals to the laws of the several States except when a State seeks to shield those individuals under the special barrier of state authority. To extend Civil Rights Act liability beyond that point is to interfere in areas of state policymaking where Congress has not determined to interfere.

Nor will such interference be negligible. One argument urged in *Screws* in favor of the result which that case reached was the announced policy of self-restraint of the Department of Justice in the prosecution of cases under 18 U.S.C. § 242, 18 U.S.C.A. § 242.... Experience indicates that private litigants cannot be expected to show the same consideration for the autonomy of local administration which the Department purportedly shows.[68]

Relevant also are the effects upon the institution of federal constitutional adjudication of sustaining under § 1979 damage actions for relief against conduct allegedly violative of federal constitutional rights, but plainly violative of state law. Permitting such actions necessitates the immediate decision of federal constitutional issues despite the admitted availability of state-law remedies which would avoid those issues. This would make inroads, throughout a large area, upon the principle of federal judicial self-limitation which has become a significant instrument in the efficient functioning of the national judiciary. *See Railroad Commission of Texas v. Pullman Co.*, 312 U.S. 496, 61 S.Ct. 643, 85 L.Ed. 971, and cases following. Self-limitation is not a matter of technical nicety, nor judicial timidity. It reflects the recognition that to no small degree the effectiveness of the legal order depends upon the infrequency with which it solves its problems by resorting to determinations of ultimate power. Especially is this true where the circumstances under which those ultimate determinations must be made are not conducive to the most mature deliberation and decision. If § 1979 is made a vehicle of constitutional litigation in cases where state officers have acted lawlessly at state law, difficult questions of the federal constitutionality of certain official practices—lawful perhaps in some States, unlawful in others—may be litigated between private parties without the participation of responsible state authorities which is obviously desirable to protect legitimate state interests, but also to better guide adjudication by competent record-making and argument.

Of course, these last considerations would be irrelevant to our duty if Congress had demonstrably meant to reach by § 1979 activities like those of respondents in this case. But where it appears that Congress plainly did not have that understanding, respect for principles which this Court has long regarded as critical to the most effective functioning of our federalism should avoid extension of a statute beyond its manifest area of operation into applications which invite conflict with the administration of local policies. Such an extension makes the extreme limits of federal constitutional power a law to regulate the quotidian business of every traffic policeman, every registrar of elections, every city inspector or investigator, every clerk in every municipal licensing bureau in this country. The text of the statute, reinforced by its history, precludes such a reading.

In concluding that police intrusion in violation of state law is not a wrong remediable under R.S. § 1979, the pressures which urge an opposite result are duly felt. The dif-

---

68. In the last twenty years the lower federal courts have encountered a volume of litigation seeking Civil Rights Act redress for a variety of wrongs ranging from arbitrary refusal by housing department officials to issue architect's certificates, *Burt v. City of New York*, 2 Cir., 156 F.2d 791, to allegedly malicious charges made by a state grand jury. *Lyons v. Baker*, 5 Cir., 180 F.2d 893.... Most courts have refused to convert what would otherwise be ordinary state-law claims for false imprisonment or malicious prosecution or assault and battery into civil rights cases on the basis of conclusory allegations of constitutional violation....

ficulties which confront private citizens who seek to vindicate in traditional common-law actions their state-created rights against lawless invasion of their privacy by local policemen are obvious, and obvious is the need for more effective modes of redress. The answer to these urgings must be regard for our federal system which presupposes a wide range of regional autonomy in the kinds of protection local residents receive. If various common-law concepts make it possible for a policeman—but no more possible for a policeman than for any individual hoodlum intruder—to escape without liability when he has vandalized a home, that is an evil. But, surely, its remedy devolves, in the first instance, on the States. Of course, if the States afford less protection against the police, as police, than against the hoodlum—if under authority of state "statute, ordinance, regulation, custom, or usage" the police are specially shielded—§ 1979 provides a remedy which dismissal of petitioners' complaint in the present case does not impair. Otherwise, the protection of the people from local delinquencies and shortcomings depends, as in general it must, upon the active consciences of state executives, legislators and judges.[71] Federal intervention, which must at best be limited to securing those minimal guarantees afforded by the evolving concepts of due process and equal protection, may in the long run do the individual a disservice by deflecting responsibility from the state lawmakers, who hold the power of providing a far more comprehensive scope of protection. Local society, also, may well be the loser, by relaxing its sense of responsibility and, indeed, perhaps resenting what may appear to it to be outside interference where local authority is ample and more appropriate to supply needed remedies.

This is not to say that there may not exist today, as in 1871, needs which call for congressional legislation to protect the civil rights of individuals in the States. Strong contemporary assertions of these needs have been expressed. *Report of the President's Committee on Civil Rights, To Secure These Rights* (1947); Chafee, *Safeguarding Fundamental Human Rights: The Tasks of States and Nation*, 27 Geo.Wash.L.Rev. 519 (1959). But both the insistence of the needs and the delicacy of the issues involved in finding appropriate means for their satisfaction demonstrate that their demand is for legislative, not judicial, response. We cannot expect to create an effective means of protection for human liberties by torturing an 1871 statute to meet the problems of 1960.

Of an enactment like the Civil Rights Act, dealing with the safeguarding and promotion of individual freedom, it is especially relevant to be mindful that, since it is projected into the future, it is ambulatory in its scope, the statute properly absorbing the expanding reach of its purpose to the extent that the words with which that purpose is conveyed fairly bear such expansion. But this admissible expansion of meaning through the judicial process does not entirely unbind the courts and license their exercise of what is qualitatively a different thing, namely, the formulation of policy through legislation.... It is not a work for courts to melt and recast this statute. "Under color" of law meant by authority of law in the nineteenth century. No judicial sympathy, however strong, for needs now felt can give the phrase—a phrase which occurs in a statute, not in a constitution—any different meaning in the twentieth....

This meaning, no doubt, poses difficulties for the case-by-case application of § 1979. Manifestly the applicability of the section in an action for damages cannot be made to turn upon the actual availability or unavailability of a state-law remedy for each individual plaintiff's situation. Prosecution to adverse judgment of a state-court damage claim cannot be made prerequisite to § 1979 relief. In the first place, such a requirement

---

71. The common law seems still to retain sufficient flexibility to fashion adequate remedies for lawless intrusions....

would effectively nullify § 1979 as a vehicle for recovering damages.[72] In the second place, the conclusion that police activity which violates state law is not "under color" of state law does not turn upon the existence of a state tort remedy. Rather, it recognizes the freedom of the States to fashion their own laws of torts in their own way under no threat of federal intervention save where state law makes determinative of a plaintiff's rights the particular circumstance that defendants are acting by state authority. Section 1979 was not designed to cure and level all the possible imperfections of local common-law doctrines, but to provide for the case of the defendant who can claim that some particular dispensation of state authority immunizes him from the ordinary processes of the law.

It follows that federal courts in actions at law under § 1979 would have to determine whether defendants' conduct is in violation of, or under color of, state law often with little guidance from earlier state decisions. Such a determination will sometimes be difficult, of course. But Federal District Courts sitting in diversity cases are often called upon to determine as intricate and uncertain questions of local law as whether official authority would cloak a given practice of the police from liability in a state-court suit. Certain fixed points of reference will be available. If a plaintiff can show that defendant is acting pursuant to the specific terms of a state statute or of a municipal ordinance, § 1979 will apply. If he can show that defendant's conduct is within the range of executive discretion in the enforcement of a state statute, or municipal ordinance, § 1979 will apply. *See Hague v. C.I.O.*, 307 U.S. 496, 59 S.Ct. 954, 83 L.Ed. 1423. Beyond these cases will lie the admittedly more difficult ones in which he seeks to show some "'custom or usage' which has become common law."[73]

...

[Justice Frankfurter, noting in conclusion that the complaint alleges that it was the "custom or usage" of the Chicago Police Department to arrest and jail persons for "long periods of time on 'open' charges," says that the complaint "suffices to raise the narrow issue of whether the detention *incommunicado*, considered alone, violates due process."]

NOTE ON THE DEVELOPMENT OF SECTION 1983 THROUGH THE SEVENTIES

Towards a Jurisprudence of Injury 10-10 to 10-19
(A.B.A. 1984, M. Shapo Rptr.)*†

The effects of *Monroe* have been tremendous. The federal courts have applied the *Monroe* interpretation of section 1983 as a vehicle, if not the exclusive vehicle, for the

---

72. This is so not only because of the practical impediment to Civil Rights Act relief which would be posed by a two-suit requirement, but because the efficient process of judicial administration might well require that a plaintiff present his federal constitutional contention to the state courts along with his state-law contentions, that he there assert the federal unconstitutionality of maintaining the defense of state authorization to a state-law tort action.... Of course, once that federal contention is properly presented to the state courts, plaintiff has open for review here an adverse state-court judgment; but if plaintiff were successful in this Court, the effect of our disposition would be to return plaintiff to the state courts for a state-law measure of relief.

73. The quotation is from Senator Thurman in the legislative debates on the Ku Klux Act — Ed.

* With adapting material.

† Copyright © 1984 The American Bar Association. Reprinted by permission.

reapportionment of state legislatures and the desegregation of public schools. They have used the statute to block the arbitrary actions of state social service departments on welfare benefits, and to set limits on refusal of other sorts of governmental largesse, for example, even denials of liquor licenses.

Although *Monroe* held that section 1983 did not apply to municipal corporations, the Supreme Court revised that position in 1978 in the *Monell* case,[5] declaring that a local government might be liable when execution of a "policy or custom, whether made by its lawmakers or by those whose edicts or acts may fairly be said to represent official policy, inflicts ... injury."[6] Building on that case, in which female employees of a city agency attacked a policy requiring them to take unpaid pregnancy leaves before leaves were medically required, the Court proceeded to reject an effort to bestow a qualified immunity on municipalities whose officers act in good faith.[7] The Court has also held that the term "laws" in section 1983 applies generally to federal statutes, rather than only to civil rights or equal protection legislation.[8]

Limitations on the right. In developing the section 1983 cause of action, the Supreme Court was bold in its fashioning and elaboration of a remedy which was virtually nonexistent twenty-five years ago, even though it rested on a statute now more than a century old. However, the Court also has been careful to set certain boundaries on section 1983 claims. Illustrative of these limits, in an area in which the "constitutional tort" moves close to the line of ordinary tort law, is a case in which the Court refused to apply the statute to a claim that a police department's circulation of the plaintiff's mug shot as an "active shoplifter" placed a "stigma" on his reputation.[9] Justice Rehnquist, writing for the Court, said in effect that the action was simply one for defamation.[10] Declaring that the plaintiff's "interest in reputation is simply one of a number which the State may protect against injury by virtue of its tort law," Justice Rehnquist concluded that the interest in reputation asserted by the plaintiff was "neither 'liberty' nor 'property' guaranteed against state deprivation without due process of law."[11]

In the track of the mug shot decision, another limitation on the section 1983 cause of action appeared in a case in which a state prisoner sued prison officials for losing hobby materials which he had ordered by mail.[12] Writing for the Court in its denial of recovery, Justice Rehnquist emphasized both that the deprivation of property "did not occur as a result of some established state procedure," and that there was no "contention that it was practicable for the State to provide a predeprivation hearing."[13] Perhaps the sharpest point in the decision concerning the relation of section 1983 jurisprudence to state tort law was Justice Rehnquist's notation that "[t]he State provides a remedy to persons who believe they have suffered a tortious loss at the hands of the State," citing a state tort claims procedure for prisoners' claims.[14]

---

5. *Monell v. Department of Social Services*, 436 U.S. 658 (1978).
6. *Id.* at 694.
7. *Owen v. City of Independence*, 445 U.S. 622, 638, 651–52 (1980) ("[t]he knowledge that a municipality will be liable for all of its injurious conduct, whether committed in good faith or not, should create an incentive for officials who may harbor doubts about the lawfulness of their intended actions to err on the side of protecting citizens' constitutional rights").
8. *Maine v. Thiboutot*, 448 U.S. 1, 4–5 (1980).
9. *Paul v. Davis*, 424 U.S. 693 (1976).
10. *See id.* at 697–98.
11. *Id.* at 712.
12. *Parratt v. Taylor*, 451 U.S. 527 (1981).
13. *Id.* at 543.
14. *Id.*

Immunities. A rich area of controversy under this remarkable statute has involved issues of official immunity. One of the most important decisions following *Monroe*, *Scheuer v. Rhodes*,[15] involved claims by survivors of youths who died in the gunfire on the campus of Kent State University in May of 1970. The defendants included the Governor of Ohio, senior officers of the Ohio National Guard, and the president of the University. The plaintiffs' theory was that the defendants had "intentionally, recklessly, willfully and wantonly" caused an unnecessary deployment of the National Guard on the campus and ordered Guard members to perform illegal actions which resulted in the deaths. In an opinion by Chief Justice Burger, the court unanimously rejected the argument that the immunity of these officials was absolute. It defined:

> ... in varying scope, a qualified immunity ... available to officers of the executive branch of Government, the variation being dependent upon the scope of discretion and responsibilities of the office and all the circumstances as they reasonably appeared at the time of the action on which liability is sought to be based. It is the existence of reasonable grounds for the belief formed at the time and in light of all the circumstances, coupled with good-faith belief, that affords a basis for qualified immunity of executive officers for acts performed in the course of official conduct.

Following the Kent State case, the Court undertook to delineate the immunities of various officials, including the absolute immunity of some. For example, dealing with a judicial order of a sterilization operation on a 15-year-old girl who was not told of the true nature of the surgery, the Court held the judge absolutely immune from a section 1983 suit. In that case, *Stump v. Sparkman*,[16] the Court rejected the contention that the action was "so unfair" and "so totally devoid of judicial concern" for the plaintiff's interest that it was not a judicial act.[17] The vitality of the absolute immunity defense has been reaffirmed not only for judges, but for a variety of persons connected with the judicial process, including prosecuting attorneys[18] and witnesses.[19] With liability thus delimited, however, the Court has refused to immunize private persons who conspire to persuade an admittedly immune judge to exercise his jurisdiction in a corrupt manner.[20]

Broad issues and practical consequences. For section 1983 jurisprudence, it is a momentous question whether the "relevant duty is a statutory duty (undoubtedly well punctuated by constitutional values)" but "not a constitutional one,"[31] or whether the Constitution has "immediate concrete meaning" and provides, "within the four corners of the instrument, sufficient policy guidance to define its legal consequences."[32] However that broad issue comes to be resolved, it is clear that there are many tort fibers interwoven into section 1983 doctrine. Even in a decision putting aside the question of negligence liability under the statute, the Supreme Court made reference to tort principles as standards for decision.[33] Moreover, in one of its decisions refusing immunity to municipalities under section 1983, the Court declared that "[d]octrines of tort law have

---

15. *Scheuer v. Rhodes*, 416 U.S. 232, 247–48 (1974).
16. 435 U.S. 349 (1978).
17. *Id.* at 363.
18. *Imbler v. Pachtman*, 424 U.S. 409 (1976).
19. *Briscoe v. LaHue*, 103 S. Ct. 1108 (1983).
20. *Dennis v. Sparks*, 449 U.S. 24 (1980).
31. Cox, *Constitutional Duty and Section 1983: A Response*, 15 VALP. U. L. REV. 453, 495 (1981).
32. *See id.* at 492–93.
33. *See Procunier v. Navarette*, 434 U.S. 555, 566 (1978).

changed significantly over the past century, and our notions of governmental responsibility should properly reflect that evolution."[34]

NOTES

As is evident in the text Note above, *Monroe* is a case of enormous reach, presenting questions that sweep across much of this course, as well as issues that go to the core of constitutional rights. This material is presented here primarily to make you think anew about the relationship of tort and compensation doctrine to public policy. The questions below are only suggestive of the breadth of the problems that have arisen in the wake of *Monroe*.

(1) What does Justice Douglas mean by "the background of tort liability that makes a man responsible for the natural consequences of his actions"? Does this suggest that police officers or other officials should be liable under section 1983 for "negligence," as well as "intentional torts"?

In this regard, should one be able to predicate section 1983 liability on a technically illegal but not brutal search and seizure that would bar the use at a criminal trial of evidence thereby obtained? On police misjudgment of how far one legally may go in restraining potential violence in a political demonstration?

(2) Compare the form of liability that has arisen under section 1983 with the liabilities that have become part of the traditional torts landscape. Consider, for example, the question of whether damages caused by non-negligent use of explosives by state employees, in the course of constructing a state building, would be compensable under section 1983.

(3) Now compare the development of section 1983 law with the body of law that has arisen under the Federal Tort Claims Act:

   (a) Could one sue under section 1983 for the explosion of fertilizer that was manufactured and bagged under orders of state officials in the same way as the fertilizer in *Dalehite*, supra § 18.01?

   (b) Consider the summary of the Kent State case in the historical Note above, and the quotation of the qualified immunity standard from Chief Justice Burger's opinion. What significant similarities or distinctions do you see between that formulation and the Supreme Court's interpretation of the Federal Tort Claims Act in *Dalehite*?

How closely does the court's formula in the Kent State case mesh with analogous traditional "tort" doctrine?

(4) Frank Pape, the named defendant in *Monroe v. Pape*, died in 2000 at age 91. An obituary said that he "won, indeed often seemed to strive for, a reputation as the toughest cop in Chicago." It characterized a biography of Pape as "likening the restraining effect" of the *Monroe* decision "to the *Miranda* decision." N.Y. TIMES, Mar. 12, 2000, at 49.

SPECIAL NOTE ON THE *BIVENS* REMEDY

The Supreme Court presented *Monroe* with a robust sibling in 1971 in *Bivens v. Six Unknown Named Agents of Federal Bureau of Narcotics*, 403 U.S. 388. This was a case in-

---

34. *Owen v. City of Independence*, 445 U.S. at 657.

volving an allegedly unreasonable arrest and search. Basing its decision directly on the Constitution, the Court said that the plaintiffs could recover money damages for violations of the Fourth Amendment by federal agents under color of their authority, rejecting the argument that the plaintiffs could get such redress only by a tort action in the state courts. *Bivens* thus provides an action for violations of constitutional rights against federal officers that parallels the *Monroe* remedy against state officials.

After *Bivens*, Congress removed from the Tort Claims Act the exclusions it originally had made in that legislation for assault, battery, false imprisonment, false arrest, abuse of process and malicious prosecution, with respect to "acts or omissions of investigative or law enforcement officers of the United States Government." Pub. L. No. 93-253 (1974); see 28 U.S.C.A. § 2680(h), supra § 18.01, at 934.

SPECIAL NOTE ON THE CONTINUING DEVELOPMENT OF SECTION 1983

The interpretation of section 1983 has generated continuing battles among the Justices of the Supreme Court. Some of the most interesting recent cases, like many of the earlier ones, pose questions about the linkages between the construction of the Ku Klux Act and tort doctrine. In studying this history, you should be asking yourself where "tort" and section 1983 law are exactly parallel, and what explanations there are for any divergences.

(1) One group of decisions has touched rather directly on tort-like questions of duty and culpability.

(a) One case involved a suit against state officials based on a murder by a parolee five months after his release. In one part of the decision, the Court, although not formally deciding whether the parole board had a "duty" to avoid the harm, said that in the particular circumstances, the death of the plaintiff's decedent was "too remote a consequence of the parole officers' action to hold them responsible under the federal civil rights law."[1]

(b) The Court manifested great reluctance to apply section 1983 to negligent conduct. Initially it temporized, saying that nothing in the language of the statute or its legislative history limited it "solely to intentional deprivations of constitutional rights."[2] However, while continuing to insist in a later decision that section 1983 "contains no state-of-mind requirement independent of that necessary to state a violation of the underlying constitutional right,"[3] the Court flatly declared that "the Due Process clause is simply not implicated by a negligent act of an official causing unintended loss of or injury to life, liberty, or property."[4] Without "rul[ing] out the possibility that there are other constitutional provisions that would be violated by mere lack of due care,"[5] the Court declared that "lack of due care suggests no more than a failure to measure up to the conduct of a reasonable person." This provided the basis for its declaration that "[t]o hold that injury caused by such conduct is a deprivation within the meaning of the Fourteenth Amendment would trivialize the centuries-old principles of due process of law."[6]

---

1. *Martinez v. California*, 444 U.S. 277, 285 (1980).
2. *Parratt v. Taylor*, 451 U.S. 527, 534 (1981).
3. *Daniels v. Williams*, 474 U.S. 327, 329–30 (1986).
4. *Id.* at 328.
5. *Id.* at 334.
6. *Id.* at 332.

(c) A few weeks later, a 5–4 majority denied recovery to a convict who was trying to move elderly prisoners out of a potential tear gas zone during a prison riot, and was shot by a prison officer who was participating in an assault to free another officer who had been taken hostage. Writing for the Court, Justice O'Connor said that the guard's "failure to make special provision for [the plaintiff] may have been unfortunate, but is hardly behavior from which a wanton willingness to inflict unjustified suffering" might be inferred. The guard's "oversight," therefore, did "not rise to the level of an Eighth Amendment violation" under that amendment's "cruel and unusual punishment" language. *Whitley v. Albers*, 475 U.S. 312, 325 (1986).

(d) In a case involving alleged improprieties in the management of a residency program at a state hospital, the question was the "appropriate Fourth Amendment standard" applicable to a search of the office of the physician who had primary responsibility for training psychiatric residents. Justice O'Connor's opinion for the majority said "that public employer intrusions on the constitutionally protected privacy interests of government employees for non-investigatory, work-related purposes, as well as for investigations of work-related misconduct, should be judged by the standard of reasonableness under all the circumstances." *O'Connor v. Ortega*, 480 U.S. 709, 725–26 (1987). Speaking for four dissenters, Justice Blackmun argued that in the absence of a "special need," the Court should not dispense with the traditional Fourth Amendment requirements of warrant and probable cause. *Id.* at 732.

(2) Damages issues have also been controversial:

(a) In a prisoner's suit for failure to protect him against foreseeable assaults by other prisoners, the Court held that a jury could assess punitive damages "when the defendant's conduct is shown to be motivated by evil motive or intent, or when it involves reckless or callous indifference to the federally protected rights of others." This threshold, wrote Justice Brennan, applied "even when the underlying standard of liability for compensatory damages is one of recklessness." *Smith v. Wade*, 461 U.S. 30, 56 (1983).

(b) In a case involving the wrongful suspension of a teacher, Justice Powell held that "damages based on the abstract 'value' or 'importance' of constitutional rights are not a permissible element of compensatory damages" in section 1983 cases. *Memphis Community School Dist. v. Stachura*, 477 U.S. 299, 310 (1986).

(3) There has been considerable struggle over the ambit of liability for local governmental units permitted by the *Monell* decision, see page 975:

(a) In one case, a county prosecutor ordered deputy sheriffs to "go in and get" two people inside a medical clinic because they could presumably provide evidence on welfare fraud. In executing the order, the deputies chopped down a door with an ax, and searched the clinic. Interpreting *Monell*'s allowance of suits against local governmental units for "official policy" decisions, Justice Brennan's opinion for the Court declared that the prosecutor's order constituted action "as the final decisionmaker for the county," and thus held that the clinic owner stated a claim under section 1983. *Pembaur v. City of Cincinnati*, 475 U.S. 469, 485 (1986).

(b) In another section 1983 case, involving a suit against a municipality, a policeman fatally shot a man outside a bar. Justice Rehnquist wrote that it was error to provide instructions that "allowed the jury to infer a thoroughly nebulous 'policy' of 'inadequate training' on the part of the municipal corporation from [a] single incident," and that "sanctioned the inference that the 'policy' was the cause of the incident." This approach, he said, "provides a means for circumventing *Monell*'s limitations altogether." The standard of proof for plaintiffs who sought to employ "a single incident of unconstitutional activity" to support a claim under *Monell* required proof that the incident "was caused by an existing, unconstitutional municipal policy, which policy can be attributed to a municipal policymaker." *City of Oklahoma City v. Tuttle*, 471 U.S. 808, 823–24 (1985).

(c) The Court continued to demonstrate division and wariness concerning the issue of whether suits based on "negligence" qualify for section 1983 protection. A per curiam majority dismissed as improvidently granted a writ that called up a case which closely focused the question of whether a city could be liable for inadequate training of police officers. Justice O'Connor spoke for four dissenters. Citing *Monell*, she wrote that "the 'inadequacy' of police training may serve as the basis for 1983 liability only where the failure to train amounts to a reckless disregard for or deliberate indifference to the rights of persons within the city's domain." *City of Springfield v. Kibbe*, 480 U.S. 257, 268–69 (1987).

(4) Although it is clear that tort and the "constitutional tort" developed by *Monroe* and its progeny are hardly identical, they appear to be concentric in concept. In a 1999 case, the opinion of the Court declared that "there can be no doubt that claims brought pursuant to § 1983 sound in tort," adding that "[j]ust as common-law tort actions provide redress for interference with protected personal or property interests, § 1983 provided relief for invasion of rights protected under federal law." *City of Monterey v. Del Monte Dunes at Monterey, Ltd.*, 526 U.S. 687, 119 S. Ct. 1624, 1638 (1999). The Court's opinion incorporated Justice Scalia's remarks elaborating this point in a separate opinion, in which he wrote that "[t]here is no doubt that the cause of action created by § 1983 is, and was always regarded as, a tort claim." 119 S. Ct. at 1647 (Scalia, J., concurring in part and concurring in the judgment).

NOTES

(1) Why would Mr. Justice Frankfurter, the passionate advocate of social justice who defended Sacco and Vanzetti, and who served as an architect of the New Deal, oppose the Court's expansive interpretation of the Ku Klux Act in *Monroe*?

(2) In light of the turbulent history of this nation since *Monroe*, and given what you have learned about the Court's subsequent interpretations of section 1983, would you be inclined to say that the *Monroe* decision has promoted or diminished respect for the law?

(3) What appear now to be the benefits, and the hazards, of the approach the Court took to its judicial role in *Monroe*?

(4) Do *Monroe* and its descendants seek to interpret and enforce social morality? What lessons does the body of "constitutional tort" law teach about the role of courts in that endeavor? Are they different lessons from those that you have learned about traditional tort law?

Table of Cases

Index

P

PALSGRAF CASE, 644–651

PHYSICIANS AND SURGEONS (See MEDICAL MALPRACTICE, MEDICAL MALOCCURRENCES)

POLICE OFFICERS (See LAW ENFORCEMENT OFFICERS)

POLLUTION (See ENVIRONMENTAL HARM)

PRIMA FACIE TORT, 71–78

PRIVACY (See INVASION OF PRIVACY)

PRIVILEGES, INTENTIONAL TORTS
Generally, 81–111

PRODUCTS LIABILITY
Generally, 320–385
Cigarettes, 354–364
Comparative fault and contributory negligence, 378–385
Defects
Generally, 326–373
Consumer expectations test, 370–372
Design defects (See subhead: Design defects)
Manufacturing defects, 326, 369
Restatement (Second) of torts §402A, 321, 322
Restatement (Third) of Torts: Products Liability §§ 1, 2, 368–369
Risk/utility test, 369
Defenses
Assumption of risk, 379, 383
Comparative fault and contributory negligence, 381–385
Misuse of product, 380–384
Design defects
Generally, 330–373
Consumer expectations, 370–372
Manifestly unreasonable design, 330
Motor vehicles and crashworthiness, 330–338
Reasonable alternative design, availability of, 368–369
Drugs and vaccines, 338–353
Economic loss, 902–908

Joint liability and multiple liabilities, 539–543
Market share theory, 541–543
Punitive damages, 573–578
Rationale for strict products liability, 322–325
Restatement (Second) of Torts § 402A, 321–322
Restatement (Third) of Torts: Products Liability §§ 1, 2, 368–369
Theories of liability summarized, 326
Tobacco products, 354–364
Unavoidably unsafe products (comment k to section 402A), 338–353
Used products, sellers of, 496, 499
Warnings, generally, 373–377

PROOF (See EVIDENCE)

PROPERTY, DEFENSE OF, 86–94

PROXIMATE CAUSE (See also DUTY AND PROXIMATE CAUSE)
Economic approach and causal analysis, 560–561
"Legal cause," 571–572
Medical malpractice action, lack of informed consent, 222–223
Palsgraf dissent, 647–651
Statutory violations, 560–564

PSYCHOLOGISTS, PSYCHIATRISTS OR PSYCHOTHERAPISTS
Third parties, duty to protect or warn, 582–594

PUBLIC OFFICIALS, LIABILITY OF (See GOVERNMENT LIABILITY)

PUNITIVE DAMAGES
Generally, 441–446
Constitutionality of, 446–450

R

RAPE
Date rape, consent issues in tort claims based on, 117
Privacy of victims, invasion of, 786–787

RECKLESSNESS
Degrees of culpability, 196–197